D1032315

LAW AND JURISPRUDENCE IN AMERICAN HISTORY

CASES AND MATERIALS

Eighth Edition

■ ■ ■

By

Stephen B. Presser
Raoul Berger Professor of Legal History
Northwestern University School of Law,
Professor of Business Law, Kellogg School of Management
Northwestern University

Jamil S. Zainaldin
President, Georgia Humanities Council
Adjunct Faculty, Department of History, Emory University

AMERICAN CASEBOOK SERIES®

WEST®

Mat #41207619

610 Opperman Drive
St. Paul, MN 55123
1–800–313–9378

Printed in the United States of America

ISBN: 978–0–314–27857–9

To ArLynn, to Ingrid,
and to our colleagues and students.

PREFACE TO THE EIGHTH EDITION

There were two principal aims of this casebook when it first appeared 32 years ago. The first aim, recognizing the sad fact that most undergraduates and law students in America are woefully uninformed about general U.S. history, was for us to try to give them a basic outline, including the English background of the common law, the struggle between the Hamiltonian Federalists and the Jeffersonian Republicans in the Early Republic, the commercial expansion of the country in the beginning of the Nineteenth Century, the Civil War, the Gilded Age, the Progressive Era, the New Deal, the Warren Court Era, and the current struggle between the advocates of a living constitution and the proponents of original understanding. The course begins with the battle between Sir Edward Coke and James I over the question whether the common law should limit the King's prerogative and ends (more or less) with the impeachment of Bill Clinton, *Bush v. Gore*, and a brief peek at *NFIB v. Sebelius*, where the questions are whether the President is above the law and whether the Supreme Court is above politics. We have tried to craft a book that can be used either in undergraduate or law school courses, but, as a second special aim for the law students, we made an attempt to suggest that the basic doctrines studied in the first year of law school (contracts, torts, property, business organizations) have common themes and are linked as reflections of political, economic, social, intellectual, and cultural developments in American society.

For both undergraduates and law students, we also sought to demonstrate that the law is a means of articulating and enforcing the primary values of American society, including, in particular, restraining arbitrary power, implementing popular sovereignty, promoting economic advancement, and maintaining a separation of public and private spheres. We recognize that these four primary values are in tension, and together they contribute to a sort of schizophrenic quality in American legal institutions. This last insight also makes the book useful for teaching to foreign LLM students, particularly those from civil law countries. We stress the common law approach to legal matters, and we seek to illuminate the unique characteristics of the American common law system, which is often difficult for those trained in the civil law to fathom. Our aim for them is to suggest the greater role U.S. law and legal institutions play in the articulation of social values in America than is the case in civil law countries, as well as exploring the greater opportunity that courts have for formulating policy in our polity. Thus, we seek to make clearer why it is that in civil law countries judges are regarded essentially as bureaucratic functionaries, but in our common law country judges are inevitably recognized as creative actors with discretion to accommodate the law to changing social circumstances. Hence our occasional emphasis on judicial biography.

This casebook was strongly influenced by Presser's work with Morton Horwitz at Harvard and Zainaldin's study with Stanley Katz at Chicago. We were taught by these two titans that ideology had an important influence on law, and that law both responded to and shaped the social situation of Americans. The two of us are products of the sixties and seventies when revolution was in the air, and when idealism reigned on the campus. There is a tension in our book because one of us is a Burkean conservative, and the other is a mainstream liberal, but what we strived for in the casebook was a teaching tool that could be wielded by anyone subscribing to any political, social, economic, or ideological view. As one early reviewer of our casebook, William Nelson, noted, we were also rather profoundly influenced by Critical Legal Studies, and its understanding that politics played an important if not the most important role in the formation of American law. We also understood (and still understand) that similar themes are to be found in the development of public and private law, and that profound Constitutional change (for example that which was manifest in the early years of the republic, in the Civil War, and in the New Deal) is followed by sweeping changes in private law (the formative era of American common law in the early nineteenth century, the laissez-faire doctrines of the late nineteenth and early twentieth centuries, and the redistributive private law doctrines of the late twentieth and early twenty-first centuries).

As already indicated, we pay a great amount of attention to important judges, including Sir Edward Coke, John Marshall, Samuel Chase, Oliver Wendell Holmes, Jr., Earl Warren, Skelly Wright, Sandra Day O'Connor, Anthony Kennedy, and Antonin Scalia, but we have also tried to suggest that the law is also formed and influenced by executives, such as Alexander Hamilton, Thomas Jefferson, Abraham Lincoln and Franklin Roosevelt and by lawyer-activists and lawyer-scholars such as Andrew Hamilton, Robert Rantoul, David Dudley Field, Herbert Wechsler, Alexander Bickel, Arthur Allen Leff, and Cass Sunstein. Accordingly we have our students read not only great cases (e.g. *Dartmouth College*, *Schechter Poultry*, *Jones & Laughlin*, *Planned Parenthood v. Casey*, *Lee v. Weisman*, *Williams v. Walker-Thomas*, *Bush v. Gore*), but also law review articles (Wechsler's "Neutral Principles," Llewellyn's "Some Realism about Realism," Leff's "Some Realism about Nominalism" etc.) and some key documents (for example, the Declaration of Independence, The Pennsylvania Constitution of 1776, the Massachusetts Constitution of 1780, The Federal Constitution, and The Seneca Falls Resolutions, and the articles of Impeachment brought against Samuel Chase and the report of the special prosecutor in the impeachment proceedings against William Jefferson Clinton).

Early editions of the casebook were somewhat traditional in outlook, emphasizing the evolution of public and private law doctrines, but subsequent revisions have tried to come to grips with controversial issues involving gender, race, liberty, privacy, and redistribution. The last Chapter of the casebook, for example, called "The Battle for the Soul of the Legal Academy," is an exploration of law and economics, critical legal studies, law and literature and feminism, and how these academic meta-theories may have contributed to Constitutional developments involving race, religion, and abortion, to mention just the most salient topics. The casebook, then, seeks to limn not only doctrinal and constitutional change, but also the issues that have dominated legal education, and to illuminate some of the struggles in legal practice and in the courts.

Accordingly, since the second edition we have called the casebook "Law and Jurisprudence in American History" to emphasize that the course is not just about the development of doctrine, but is also about the manner in which Americans have disagreed on the nature of law itself. The materials tell the story of a movement from the traditional English way of thinking about law as a reflection of a divinely-ordained order to the modern American Holmesian notion of law as what is currently regarded as convenient. While much of the course addresses transformations in American law and jurisprudence, there is still an effort to suggest that ways of thinking about the law, and legal doctrines, characteristically endure, so that even today, one can find traces of natural law thinking, and one can find echoes of the laissez-faire doctrines that dominated in the late nineteenth and early twentieth century jurisprudence. Less explicitly, but still emphatically, we try to present law as a discipline with a strong moral dimension, and there is within this book what Paul Carrington called a "romantic" element of the law, the fond belief that there is such a thing as the rule of law, and that even though Thrasymachus may not have gotten it completely wrong, there is still, in American law and jurisprudence, the ability to restrain the lash of power in the interest of the whole society.

This eighth edition eliminates the previous seven prefaces, and adds to the seventh edition additional materials on the Constitution and Slavery, a long note on *NFIB v. Sebelius* (the ACA or "Obamacare" decision), and references to many new monographs on legal and constitutional history which will be found in expanded notes and comments on many topics. We have also sought to correct some of the inevitable minor glitches which creep into a text after several decades. We are grateful to all of our colleagues who made suggestions for changes, and, in particular to Bret Boyce, a professor at the University of Detroit Mercy School of Law (and a former student of Presser's) who very graciously combed virtually the entire text for errors and omissions. Presser's three law school research assistants, Cheryl Friedman, Kelly Hamren-Anderson, and Andrew Hess, also reviewed the manuscript, and performed many other helpful tasks to bring this edition to publication. We remain grateful to a succession of wonderful editors and officials at West, including, in particular, Louis Higgins, Bonnie Karlan, and Roxanne Birkel, and, for this edition, Greg Olson.

As is true for most of our fellows who toil in the vineyards of American Legal History, it is our belief that American law and American society are inseparably intertwined. Tocqueville got it right when he claimed that sooner or later every important American political issue ends up in the courts. The strengths and weaknesses, the nobility and shame, the high aspirations and the immediacy of self-interested actors work their way through our national history equally as through law. We make, actually, grander claims for this book and for our discipline. Accordingly, it should come as no surprise that here and there in this book we sprinkle our commentary with citations to the ancients of Greece and Rome—deep thinkers whose illumination of the human condition is never out of date. Our work is based on a confidence in our American Constitutional system, one that seeks justice for the whole society even as it promotes the rights of individuals. In American history, as it was with the ancients, this is never quite done with the purity of ideas and consistency of thought that some might wish for. True to Plato's allegory of the cave and St. Paul's articulation of the thought that we see but "through a glass, darkly," we think the record of history is one of grasping at thoughts and ideas, of imperfectly achieved goals and aspirations. Perfection and perfect consistency cannot be attained on this orb, and this is as it must be. For us Americans, in particular, when we cease changing, we cease living. Our law is for our lives, but it is also part of a conversation stretching back thousands of years and across many civilizations. This humbling and yet ennobling aspect of American jurisprudence is what we seek to impart to the users of this text.

STEPHEN B. PRESSER

JAMIL S. ZAINALDIN

Chicago, Illinois
Atlanta, Georgia
December 2012

SUMMARY OF CONTENTS

TABLE OF CONTENTS

TABLE OF CASES

The principal cases are in bold type.

TABLE OF AUTHORITIES

Other Authorities

Aynes, Richard L., *Bradwell v. Illinois*: Chief Justice Chase's Dissent and the Sphere of Women's Work, 59 La.L.Rev. 521 (1999)---------------- 758

Aynes, Richard L., Constricting the Law of Freedom: Justice Miller, The Fourteenth Amendment, and the *Slaughter-House* Cases, 70 Chicago–Kent L.Rev. 627 (1994)------------- 646

Aynes, Richard L., On Misreading John Bingham and the Fourteenth Amendment, 103 Yale L.J. 57 (1993) -- 646

Ayres, Ian and Gertner, Robert, Filling Gaps in Incomplete Contracts: An Economic Theory of Default Rules, 99 Yale L.J. 87 (1989)----------------------------------1085

Baade, Hans W., Original Intent in Historical Perspective: Some Critical Glosses, 69 Tex.L.Rev. 1001 (1991)----------------------------------- 176

Babcock, Barbara Allen, Clara Shortridge Foltz: Constitution–Maker, 66 Ind.L.J. (1991) --------- 759

Babcock, Barbara Allen, Clara Shortridge Foltz: First Woman, 30 Ariz.L.Rev. 673 (1988)-------------- 759

Babcock, Barbara Allen, Reconstructing the Person: The Case of Clara Shortridge Foltz, in Revealing Lives: Autobiography, Biography, and Gender 131 (Susan Groag Bell & Marilyn Yalom eds., 1990)------------------------------------ 759

Bailyn, Bernard, comments, in 1 Pamphlets of the American Revolution 411–13 (1965) ----------- 81

Bailyn, Bernard, ed., 1 Pamphlets of the American Revolution 487 (1965) -- 118

Bailyn, Bernard, The Debate on the Constitution (2 vols., 1993) ------- 168

Bailyn, Bernard, The Ideological Origins of the American Revolution (1967)------------------------43, 539, 540

Bailyn, Bernard, The Ordeal of Thomas Hutchinson 70–107-------- 98

Bailyn, Bernard, The Ordeal of Thomas Hutchinson 70–107 (1974) -- 43

Bailyn, Bernard, The Origins of American Politics (1965)------------ 43

Baker, John H., An Introduction to English Legal History (2002) ------ 10

Baker, John H., An Introduction to English Legal History 456–59 (3d ed. 1990)------------------------------ 375

Baker, John H., The Common Law Tradition: Lawyers, Books, and the Law (2003)--------------------------------5

Baker, John H., The Legal Profession and the Common Law. Historical Essays (1986) --------------------- 5, 302

Baker, Kara, Is Justice For Sale in Ohio? An Examination of Ohio Judicial Elections and Suggestions for Reform Focusing on the 2000 Race for the Ohio Supreme Court, 35 Akron L.Rev. 159 (2001)------- 450

Balkin, Jack M. and Levinson, Sanford, Legal Historicism and Legal Academics: The Role of Law Professors in the Wake of *Bush v. Gore*, 90 Geo. L.J. 173 (2001)----1383

Balkin, Jack M. and Levinson, Sanford, Understanding the Constitutional Revolution, 87 Va. L. Rev. 1045, 1067 (2001) -----------1385

Balkin, Jack M., Bush v. Gore and the Boundary Between Law and Politics, 110 Yale L.J. 1407, 1427 (2001)------------------------ 1381, 1382

Balkin, Jack M., ed., What *Brown v. Board of Education* Should Have Said (2001)--------------------------1043

Balkin, Jack M., The Use that the Future Makes of the Past: John Marshall's Greatness and Its Lessons for Today's Supreme Court Justices, 43 Wm and Mary L. Rev. 1321 (2002) --------------------------- 398

Bannister, Robert C., Social Darwinism: Science and Myth in Anglo–American Social Thought, 1988------------------------------------- 780

Barnett, Randy E., The Original Meaning of the Commerce Clause, 68 U.Chi.L.Rev. 101 (2001) ------- 993

Baron, Jane B., Resistance to Stories, 67 S.Cal.L.Rev. 255 (1994)-------1252

Baron, Jane B., The Many Promises of Storytelling in Law, 23 Rutgers L.J. 79 (1991)------------------------------1252

Barry, Kathleen, Susan B. Anthony: A Biography of a Singular Feminist (1988)-----------------------------688, 768

Bartlett, Irving H., John C. Calhoun: A Biography (New York, 1993) -- 532

Bartlett, Katherine T., Feminist Legal Scholarship: A History through the Lens of the California Law Review, 100 Cal. L. Rev. 381 (2012) ------1284

Basch, Norma, In the Eyes of the Law: Women, Marriage, and Property in Nineteenth Century New York 168 (1982)-----------------------------695, 742

Beard, Charles, Economic Interpretation of the Constitution of the United States (1913) ---------- 539

Beccaria, Cesare, On Crimes and Punishments and Other Writings, translated by Richard Davies, edited by Richard Bellamy (Cambridge Texts in the History of Political Thought, 1995) ---------------------- 150

Becker, Carl, The Declaration of Independence (1922)---------------- 121

Boorstin, Daniel, The Mysterious Science of the Law iii (Peter Smith, ed. 1973) ---- 347
Boorstin, Daniel, The Mysterious Science of the Law: An Essay on Blackstone's Commentaries (1941) ---- 329
Bork, Robert, The Tempting of America: The Political Seduction of the Law (1990) ---- 176, 1059
Bowen, Catherine Drinker, The Lion and the Throne 291–306 (1956) ---- 10
Bowman, Cynthia Grant and Schneider, Elizabeth M., Feminist Legal Theory, Feminist Law–Making, and the Legal Profession, 67 Fordham L.Rev. 249 (1998) ---- 1287
Bowman, Cynthia Grant, Bibliographical Essay: Women and the Legal Profession, 7 J.of Gender, Social Policy & the Law 149 (1998–1999) ---- 759
Bowman, Cynthia Grant, Street Harassment and the Informal Ghettoization of Women, 106 Harv.L.Rev. 517 (1993) ---- 1314
Boyd, S., ed., The Whiskey Rebellion: Past and Present Perspectives (1985) ---- 196
Boyer, Allen D., ed., Law Liberty and Parliament: Selected Essays on the Writings of Sir Edward Coke (2004) ---- 10
Boyer, Allen D., Sir Edward Coke and the Elizabethan Age (2003) ---- 5, 10
Boyer, Paul, Urban Masses and Moral Order in America, 1820–1920 (1978) ---- 421
Boyle, The Politics of Reason: Critical Legal Theory and Local Social Thought, 133 U.Pa.L.Rev. 685 (1985) ---- 1208
Breyer, Stephen, Madison Lecture: Our Democratic Constitution, 77 N.Y.U.L.Rev. 245 (2002) ---- 1335
Bridwell, R. and Whitten, R., The Constitution and the Common Law (1977) ---- 435
Bridwell, R. Randall, Theme v. Reality in American Legal History, 53 Ind.L.J. 450, 473 ---- **430**
Brinig, Margaret F. and Allen, Douglas W., These Boots are Made for Walking: Why Most Divorce Filers are Women, 2 Am. L. & Econ. Rev. 126 (2000) ---- 720
Brinkley, Alan, Polsby, Nelson W., and Sullivan, Kathleen M., New Federalist Papers: Essays in Defense of the Constitution (1997) ---- 179
Brinkley, Alan, The End of Reform: New Deal Liberalism in Recession and War, 1995 ---- 937
Brisbin, Richard A., Justice Antonin Scalia & the Conservative Revival (1997) ---- 1335
Broder, David S., A Party Split, The Washington Post, August 7, 1996 ---- 737
Brophy, Alfred L., A Revolution which Seeks to Abolish Law, Must End Necessarily in Despotism: Louisa McCord and Antebellum Southern Legal Thought, 5 Cardozo Women's L.J. 33 (1998) ---- 571
Brophy, Alfred L., Humanity, Utility and Logic in Southern Legal Thought: Harriet Beecher Stowe's Vision in *Dred: A Tale of the Great Dismal Swamp*, 78 Boston U.L.Rev. 113 (1998) ---- 503
Brophy, Alfred L., Let Us Go Back and Stand upon the Constitution: Federal–State Relations in *Scott v.* Sandford, 90 Col. L.Rev. 192 (1990) ---- 571
Brophy, Alfred L., Over and Above . . . There Broods a Portentous Shadow,—the Shadow of *Law*,: Harriett Beecher Stowe's Critique of Slave Law in *Uncle Tom's Cabin*, 12 J. Law & Religion 457 (1996) ---- 503
Brophy, Alfred L., The Rule of Law in Antebellum College Literary Addresses: The Case of William Greene, 31 Cumb.L.Rev. 231 (2001) ---- 571
Brown, Gillian, Domestic Individualism: Imagining Self in Nineteenth–Century America, 1990 ---- 780
Brown, John R., Tribute: Admiralty Judges: Flotsam on the Sea of Maritime Law?, 25 Hous.J.Int.L. 257 (2003) ---- 186
Bruchey, Stuart, Enterprise: The Dynamic Economy of a Free People, 1990 ---- 780
Bruchey, Stuart, The Roots of American Economic Growth 1607–1861 (1965) ---- 333
Buckley, F.H. and Ribstein, Larry E., Calling a Truce in the Marriage Wars, 2001 U. Ill.L.Rev. 561 ---- 719
Buckley, F.H., ed., The Fall and Rise of Freedom of Contract (1999) ---- 1075
Buckley, William F. Jr., ed., American Conservative Thought in the Twentieth Century, 1970 ---- 938
Burns, Robert P., A Theory of the Trial 9 (1999) ---- 66
Butler, Jon, Becoming America: The Revolution before 1776 (2000) ---- 329
Calhoun, Charles W., ed., The Gilded Age: Essays on the Origins of Modern America, 1996 ---- 780

Zelden, Charles L., Bush v. Gore: Exposing the Hidden Crisis in American Democracy (Abridged and updated edition, 2010) ------------ 1382
Zimmermann, Joan G., The Jurisprudence of Equality: The Women's Minimum Wage, the First Equal Rights Amendment, and *Adkins v. Children's Hospital,* 1905–1923, The Journal of American History 188 (June, 1991) ---------- 981
Zuckerman, Michael, Peaceable Kingdoms: New England Towns in the Eighteenth Century, 1983 --- 330
Zuckert, Michael P., The Natural Rights Republic: Studies in the Foundation of the American Political Tradition (1996)---------- 121
Zunz, Olivier, Making America Corporate, 1870–1920 (1990) ---- 909
Zunz, Olivier, Making America Corporate, 1870–1920, 1990------ 782

LAW AND JURISPRUDENCE IN AMERICAN HISTORY

CASES AND MATERIALS

Eighth Edition

PROLOGUE

THE ENGLISH HERITAGE

■ ■ ■

INTRODUCTION: The Development of Legal Institutions and Common Law to the Time of Sir Edward Coke

Many of the dynamics of modern law, society, and political institutions are evident in the first 400 years following the Norman conquest of England in 1066. The Romans invaded England in 43 A.D. By 300 A.D., we can speak of Britannia, as the Romans named it, as "Romanized." With Italy and Rome threatened by the invasions of the Goths and Vandals, in 407 A.D. Constantine III called Britain's military legions home. Without Roman protection, the Britons were soon overwhelmed by invading bands of Angles and Saxons from Germany, and later Vikings and Danes. These new occupiers set up their own kingdoms, though in time the Danes and English emerged as the dominant elements. (The word "law" is derived from Danish.) Edward "the Confessor" (1042–66), an Englishman, was the first to unite the country under a single ruler, though his hold was tenuous. The Christian Church was by now an established institution, through the influence of the Romans and the later efforts of missionaries. Its clergy were among the few who were literate. Customs, laws or "dooms" of particular kings, "oaths," and grants of land ("bocs," which is the origin of the word "book" because it contained the written record of land grants) made up the legal infrastructure of this essentially primitive society.

In Anglo–Saxon England, most village conflicts were settled informally among warring clans, and the king's law was more a guide than a mandate. Still, what was later to become English criminal law originated in this Anglo–Saxon era with the concept of a superior right of the king to impose his own brand of law on anyone violating his "peace," which extended to his habitations and eventually to markets and roads.

No less important is the Anglo–Saxon concept of "right" which was an extension of the sphere of the King's Peace. A right was understood as the space to which the King's Peace extended, and this space, which might include a physical or geographic area, also could include persons. The Anglo–Saxon term "folc riht" embodied this notion of a personal right.

Edward the Confessor's death in 1066 left an already unstable country vulnerable. That same year Duke William II of Normandy crossed the channel and defeated Harold, Edward's successor, and his Anglo–Saxons at the Battle of Hastings. William the Conqueror, as he became known, embarked on an ambitious resettlement of the English lands by Norman nobles, and he imposed a new regime of central administration. The Anglo–Saxon shires (or counties, supervised by the shire-reeve, or "sheriff") were kept intact, as were local units of the shire, known as "hundreds." These ancient administrative forms each had local courts run by laymen, and continued to be useful. The inspired contribution of the Normans was to create, in steps, a bureaucracy on top of these local customary institutions that in time established the king and his courts as the basis of a new law "common" to the realm. This administrative structure carved out royal jurisdiction for felonies, certain civil disputes, and taxation; introduced a process in writing, known as royal "writs", for initiating action; and formed centralized royal "courts" to adjudicate civil complaints and criminal actions. The name "court" was taken from the noun describing the royal household that included advisors and administrators. The Normans also introduced juries, a Norman practice, and "justiciars" or judges to whom the king delegated his authority as his representative in the courts.

French, the language of the Norman king and his barons, also became the language of the royal courts. "Law French" was an amalgamation of Anglo–French that gave us words such as *plaintiff, defendant*, and *brief.* Latin, the language of the church and the educated, found its way into law through the writ system; writs were issued on parchment in Latin, and bore a royal seal. The writ initiated civil action in a royal court by asserting a right or complaining of a wrong. Among the better known writs are *habeas corpus, mandamus,* and *certiorari.* Until 1731 Latin was the language of record in common law courts.

The *Magna Carta* (1215) or Great Charter grew from the disgruntlement of Norman barons who believed their customary rights were being abused by King John. These abuses included arbitrary arrests and imprisonment, the imposition of fines, and other grievances. At Runnymede Meadow, on the banks of the Thames River, nobles extracted from John his written approval of a list of specific rights. The Great Charter was something of a housekeeping document, the sorting out of rights that were presumed to exist and in need of affirmation. The real importance of this document comes from the meaning later attributed to it. For the first time, it set forth a concept of a supreme law that no person was above, not even a king.

The Great Charter also contained phrases and concepts later generations on both sides of the Atlantic would reinterpret in light of contemporary events, such as "No scuttage [taxation] or aid shall be imposed in our kingdom except by the common council of the kingdom. . . " Chapter 39 of the Charter reads: "No free man shall be taken or imprisoned or disposed, or outlawed, or banished, or in any way destroyed, nor will we go upon him, nor send upon him, except by the legal judgment of his peers or by the law of the land." While the Charter was revised, reissued, and confirmed many times, Chapter 39 clearly points to what we now know as due process of law, and to law as a potential bulwark against arbitrary power—an extraordinary and early contribution to constitutionalism.

In 1397–1399 the enlargement of the great Westminster Hall was completed. Here the royal central courts finally came to rest, assuming the trappings of a permanent and authoritative judicial system. They included the Court of Common Pleas (civil and appellate jurisdiction), the Court of Kings Bench (criminal and appellate jurisdiction), and the Court of Exchequer (jurisdiction over taxation, finances, and accounting involving the king). The existence of circuit courts, or "assizes," in the countryside allowed the central courts to stay put and to function primarily as courts of appeal. It was from this early royal adjudicatory system that the main elements of the future Anglo–American legal system sprung: the development of substantive common law; a highly formalized process for initiating, hearing and trying cases; a class of professionals who represented clients before these courts; a system of record keeping, and a judicial establishment known for its competence and expertise. The Normans and Angevins (the Normans' French successors to the crown) introduced system, process, and rules, backed by the royal authority and the emergence of a professional class prepared to encourage allegiance to law.

The distinction between common law and legislation in post-Conquest England was murky. The courts were formed by officials from the King's household. These included his political advisors (the *Curia Regis*) and the *justiciars*, his personal representatives. Similarly, legislation was the product of the king in his council and tended to take on the character of *ad hoc* lawmaking and adjudication in response to complaints, a process not unlike judging. In any event, this lawmaking was seen as a complement to rather than a departure from custom and common law. The authority of the king to participate in lawmaking was unquestioned, though his presence in the legal process being carried out in his courts came to be more a fiction than a fact, creating the opportunity for the tension between the King and his judges which you will soon observe.

Not until after the reign of King Edward III (1327–1377) did Parliament begin to form as a distinctive body composed of Lords and Commons, each of whose consent (with the king's) was eventually necessary for the enactment of laws. During the later Tudor period, and especially during the reign of Henry VIII (1491–1547), legislation took on the form of a distinct departmental activity based on careful drafting of bills, Parliamentary debate, and policy making. As Parliament evolved into a formal institution with specific powers, it eventually began to assert a self-conscious power to change law, including common law, or to enact new law, its only limit being its capacity to bind a future Parliament, although this development was not completed until well into the Seventeenth Century. At the same time that the "High Court of Parliament" as it was then called, began to evolve into an institution to make rather than interpret the law, adjudication was evolving as the task of a distinct non-legislative department—a judiciary—though there is little doubt that judges enjoyed latitude in interpreting the language of legislation. The precise nature and authority of the legislative and judicial jurisdictions, however, were based on custom and practice. The possibility for conflicting interpretations of authority and law was always present among king, Parliament, and the courts; the tricky part was how to determine the rules to play by when fundamental questions of authority and jurisdiction were involved, as occurred in the reign of King James I.

Medieval law (1066 to approximately 1500) was complex, entwined in "feudal" custom and practice. Under feudalism, the social system of the Normans, the king owned the land and granted rights to others, his "tenants," to its use. In return they made payment, rendered services, or may have owed other obligations. A tier of rights might descend from king and through nobles, to farmers, to craftsmen, and finally to the lowest order who were "serfs," usually the Anglo–Saxons in Norman England. For all practical purposes, a serf lacked any rights at all. In theory, only the king owned lands outright. Feudalism was not a Norman invention; it was a pattern of rule and service common in Europe at the time of the Conquest, and one that the Normans brought with them. The expectations that formed around feudal rights of tenure and obligations were evident in the complex law (to modern eyes) that took form through disputes in courts. Long after feudalism receded as a social system, its vestiges could still be found in English law.

Norman land law, because it was rooted in a variety of tenures, called upon conceptual powers that arrayed minute detail with overarching ideas. Not surprisingly, a final Norman contribution to Anglo–American legal history was the treatise writer, the unofficial clarifier who drew law together by explaining the significance of leading cases. The first great treatise writer in English history was known as "Bracton," (c. 1210–1268). The man (or men) who wrote Bracton's work was probably a judge, and Bracton's treatise on *The Laws and Customs of England* was not only a guide for the judges who followed: it was the first work to present early Norman law as a "system" (the common law) that contained basic "rules" discovered through logical analysis of precedent. Using both Canon and Roman law for comparison, Bracton was the first to use concepts and theories to explain an unwritten law. To use F.W. Maitland's words, he was the "crown and flower of English jurisprudence." He gave intellectual credibility to English common law—and to the profession of lawyers. More about Bracton soon.

The importance of the relationship between the crown and the church cannot be overestimated as a matter of English history, and had far-reaching effects in law. The relationship was often problematic, as the murder of Archbishop Thomas á Becket at the instigation of King Henry II showed (1170). Difficulties could flare up around any number of areas, from jurisdiction, to the ownership of church lands, to the binding force of papal decrees. Because the common law developed apart from Canon law with its Roman law roots, Church and common law courts at times clashed in politically tinged contests of the kind that you will soon see occupying James I and Sir Edward Coke. These clashes were not only about the authority to decide cases, but also involved fundamental differences in legal procedure and the sources of law, and pitted emerging desires for English nationalism against the continental Roman heritage.

Centralized kingship, the rise of central courts, the emergence of a class of learned legal professionals, the formation of a common law that encompassed substance and process, a distinction between precedent-based adjudication and legislation, the idea of a supreme law, and the presence of an intellectual and conceptual approach to law are among the elements of the new legal system the early Norman and Angevin kings and their successors called into being. The elements exerted a profound shaping influence not only on the constitutional development of English law spanning almost 900 years, but on the English colonies of the seventeenth and eighteenth centuries who viewed themselves as beneficiaries of the rights and privileges of the English constitutional system.

Note: Early English legal history is normally divided chronologically by kingships. The reign of French Norman kings includes the Normans, Angevins, and Plantagenets (1066–1485). The Tudors of Welsh origin succeeded to the throne in 1485 and ruled through 1603. In 1603 King James VI of Scotland, a Stuart, acceded to the throne as King James I of England. The Stuart line ended with Queen Anne (1714).

Further Reading:

J.H. Baker, *The Legal Profession and the Common Law. Historical Essays*, 1986

J.H. Baker, *The Common Law Tradition: Lawyers, Books, and the Law,* 2003

Allen D. Boyer, *Sir Edward Coke and the Elizabethan Age*, 2003

John Hudson, *The Formation of the English Common Law: Law and Society in England from the Norman Conquest to Magna Carta,* 1996

Frederick Pollock and Frederic W. Maitland, *The History of English Law*, 1898

S.F.C. Milsom, *Historical Foundations of the Common Law*, 1981

Theodore F. T. Plucknett, *A Concise History of the Common Law*, 1956

A. THE KING AND THE CHIEF JUSTICE: JAMES I AND SIR EDWARD COKE

The Common Law, the Civil Law Tradition, the Church, and the King

There are two great strands of legal thought in the West. One is the Anglo–American "Common Law" tradition originating with the England of the Middle Ages. The other is the Civil Law tradition originating in Continental Europe. Through the historical processes of colonization, innovation, and adoption, the two systems have become the dominant traditions in the world today.

The "civilian" tradition has its origins in classical Roman law. In the sixth century, Roman Emperor Justinian promulgated a new summary and update of the law in the *Corpus Juris Civilis.* During the Middle Ages, approximately 500 to 1450, legal scholars developed and spread Roman law through the Byzantine Empire. The defining characteristic of the civilian tradition is the written law, or code, founded on broad principles and doctrines. Legislative in nature, Civil Law was interpreted and applied by courts on the basis of deduction from first principles. Because the Roman-based legal tradition is founded on scholarship and official statements of what the law is, it is sometimes referred to as "the learned laws." The legislator is the most powerful actor in this tradition. For civilians, the lawyer and judge function more as trained technicians of law, for their task is not to discover the law, or even interpret it, but to apply it.

In contrast, the developing English common law was founded on local customs, traditions, and precedent. Its method of proceeding was the case, and its manner of proceeding was adversarial, with each party represented by attorneys. The rules of the common law were derived from prior cases, and therefore are "unwritten" (to distinguish them from officially-promulgated and drafted legislation). Moving from the specifics of the case to general principles, the common law mode of reasoning was inductive. The centrality of tradition, custom, the law case, the attorney, the judge, and the inductive method of reasoning is what most distinguishes common law from Roman law. The judge and the lawyer are the most important actors in this tradition, and their job is to "discover" the law.

The "learned laws" exerted an impact in England through the Church's Latin culture and Canon law, which borrowed from classical Roman law. Though the Romans introduced Christianity in the British Isles, it was Augustine's mission in Canterbury around the time of 600 that is dated as the English Church's beginning. The Synod of Whitby in 664 consolidated the Church in the medieval era, insuring that the Roman branch of Christianity prevailed over the Celtic branch. William the

Conqueror, a Christian, strengthened the Church and among his first acts was the appointment of Norman prelates with close ties to the Holy See. William also created a system of courts through which the bishops' spiritual authority was exercised. These courts were called "ecclesiastical" because they pertained to matters of the Church, the Greek word for which is *ekklesia.* They were made distinct from the "temporal" or regular courts at the levels of the county shire and local hundreds, and also from the king's court (*Curia Regis*).

Jurisdiction of the ecclesiastical courts was based on the law of the Church, or Canon law. The influence of the Church ranged widely in English society, and so therefore did its law. The Church exercised jurisdiction over marriage, other familial issues, inheritance of personal property, sexual offenses, and breaches of faith. Church law was administered by bishops' chancellors. Appeals lay to the archbishop and ultimately to papal delegates or to the Papal Curia in Rome. Because church law was administered by clergy learned in Canon law, the jurisprudence of the English Church developed separately from common law. At times, Church law seemed to be a rival system to common law because it was continental in origin and not beholden to English traditions or customs.

Conflicts between the Church and the crown in early English history were inevitable, and they tended to flare around issues of taxation and revenues (the king controlled most of the Church's land), the appointment of bishops, and discipline by the Church of royal officials and representatives. As we will see in the dispute between Coke and James I, there was also the question of what was, or was not, temporal or spiritual. Much of this conflict was worked out not through contests between pope and king, but through private litigation. By means of the "writ of prohibition," a judge who believed the common law's jurisdiction was being sidestepped could pluck a case out of the ecclesiastical court.

The relationship between Church and Crown changed fundamentally in 1534, when Parliament enacted the Supremacy Act and officially broke all ties with the Church in Rome. Henry VIII originally instigated what became the English Reformation because the Pope denied his request for an annulment of his marriage to Catherine of Aragon, which would have freed him to marry Anne Boleyn. Even if Henry had not forced the issue, the Reformation probably would have occurred in England at some point, for its appeal was present before Henry wed Anne. On the continent, the Protestant Reformation was begun by Martin Luther when he nailed his Ninety–Five Theses to the door of the Wittenberg Church in 1517.

While Henry disapproved of the study of Canon law at Oxford and Cambridge, he did create the Regius Chair of Civil Law at Cambridge. Also during his reign the Society of Doctors of Civil Law was founded. The judges and advocates in the ecclesiastical courts, which were continued under the Reformed English Church, were doctors of Civil Law, and this body of scholars furnished the legal and clerical professionals for other courts outside the common law. On the continent and in England during the Renaissance, there was a revival of interest in classical Roman literature and law, as well as classical Greek philosophy. There were some English royal advisors who favored a "reception" of the Civil law as a replacement for the common law, seeing the continental system as more rational, consistent, and based on time-proven principles. Civil law was also well suited to a system of centralized administration and control, making it an ideal tool for European monarchial absolutism.

The English Reformation led to a number of royal administrative developments that shifted more power to the crown. One was the creation of the Ecclesiastical Court of High Commission by the king, which replaced the pope in criminal matters and became the legal mechanism for enforcing conformity to the new Church of England. As we will see, this court used the oath *ex officio* to force a person to testify against himself in opposition of the common law privilege against self-incrimination. Another encroachment on common law was the Court of Chancery. The Court of Chancery grew out of petitions to the king for special justice because the civil complainant, for one reason or another, could not gain satisfaction through the royal central courts. Initially created from the king's court in the late fourteenth century, Chancery, because it was not a common law court, was bound by less formality of procedure and was not hindered by precedent or rules. By 1460 its jurisdiction (and business) enlarged, making it as important as the common law courts. The Court of Chancery dispensed "justice" in accordance with the dictates of "conscience." This was an Aristotelian concept popular during the Renaissance that held great appeal, and when operating in unison with common law, offered an important corrective to England's relatively rigid legal system.

Under the Tudors, however, and especially Henry VIII, Chancery showed a certain disdain for common law as it adopted an aggressive stance in relation to the central courts. Tudor Chancellors tended to be Church men who served the king; their background was in Canon and Civil law and they were inclined toward continental systems and the idea of centralized power. As we will see, the widening gulf between courts of common law and equity reached a highpoint during the reign of the Stuart King James I, with the face off between the king, Coke, and behind the scenes, Lord Ellesmere, who served as James's Chancellor (1596–1617).

Courts like Chancery that grew from the king's council took the name of "conciliar" or "prerogative" courts because they were created by means of the king's prerogative to satisfy claims of justice made to him personally. The Court of Star Chamber, taking its name from the gilded stars on the roof of the chamber it met in, was one such court founded in 1487; it functioned as the king's tool for the prosecution of crimes and offences that could not be tried at common law or could not be entrusted to a jury. These were usually cases of a political nature, and included offenses like riot, libel, forgery, perjury, and conspiracies. Because Star Chamber acted outside of the common law, it enjoyed streamlined procedures that made action speedy. The Attorney General prosecuted cases, and trials were by affidavit and interrogation rather than by jury. Torture, or its threat, was the usual tool for obtaining confessions, and punishments included fines, imprisonment, the pillory, branding, and cutting off of ears—but not death. Star chamber rulings could not be appealed.

For a portion of its history, like the Court of Chancery, Star Chamber was accepted as a supplement to common law courts, and it may well have corrected deficiencies in the central royal courts that frustrated notions of justice and fairness. The potential for abuse of executive power was always present, however, and under Henry VIII, traditionally regarded as one of the most absolute and ruthless of English kings, Star Chamber became a useful tool for persecuting dissidents and non-conformists. Under the Scots Stuarts, who never enjoyed the popularity of the Welsh Tudor monarchs Henry and Elizabeth, the Star Chamber prerogatives began to chafe, especially when, Charles I, the son of James, used it in place of convening Parliament. Eventually Parliament abolished Star Chamber as one of the reforms of the English Revolution.

In all, the centralization of authority under Henry VIII and the Tudors, and his elevation as the head of the Reformed Church of England was an extraordinary augmentation of royal power. The common law, with its origin in custom and archaic feudal traditions, was certainly open to criticism. Its procedures had become dilatory, and its use of Law French highly archaic. The common law was also the exclusive domain of a learned profession, lawyers and judges, jealous of their position as the sole interpreters and transmitters of an unwritten law. To legal scholars trained in Canon and Roman law, the common law was a throwback to a more primitive time.

Yet, as you will soon note, it was this law, according to Coke, that was and ought to be supreme in the land because it was source of English liberties and rights, protector of both ruler and ruled, as he put it. Henry's (and later the Stuarts') reach for power was part of a modern European trend toward centralizing national authority and lawmaking. The existence of Chancery and Star Chamber, and the prerogative courts that borrowed their procedure from Civil law, offered an impressive set of legal tools that any modern monarch would want to have. They also became symbols in a power struggle between Parliament and the king that would lead to the violent events of the English Civil War and the interregnum of 1640–1660, but not be finally settled until the "Glorious Revolution" of 1688. For colonial Americans, the significance of these events was not fully felt until almost a century later. Then, the Americans rediscovered the political theory and argumentation of the radical Whigs who had struck at monarchial power in the name of English liberty, and employed these arguments against the British. As the colonials moved toward Revolution, the target was Parliament instead of the king, and the goal was creation of a republic, instead of the constitutional monarchy England had become. This gets a bit ahead of our story, though.

Further Reading:

J.H. Baker, *An Introduction to English Legal History*, 2002

Harold J. Berman, *Law and Revolution: The Formation of the Western Legal Tradition,* 1983

Allen D. Boyer, *Sir Edward Coke and the Elizabethan Age*, 2003

Allen D. Boyer, ed., *Law Liberty and Parliament: Selected Essays on the Writings of Sir Edward Coke*, 2004

Sir Edward Coke, *Selected Writings*, (3 vols. Steve Sheppard, ed., 2004)

R.H. Helmholz, *Canon Law and the Law of England*, 1987

Michael H. Hoeflich, *Roman and Civil Law and the Development of Anglo–American Jurisprudence,* 1997

Karl N. Llewellyn, *The Common Law Tradition: Deciding Appeals*, 1960

Peter Stein, *Roman Law in European History*, 1999

James Stoner, *Common Law and Liberal Theory: Coke, Hobbes and the Origins of American Constitutionalism*, 1992

Stephen D. White, *Sir Edward Coke and the "Grievances of the Commonwealth," 1621–1628,* 1979

CATHERINE DRINKER BOWEN, THE LION AND THE THRONE*

291–306 (1956).

* * *

* * * Attorney General Coke, sharp driving tool of crown authority, put on the robes of judgeship and became to all appearances the champion of another cause. "There is a maxim," he told the Lower House: "*The common law hath admeasured the King's prerogative.* It is not I, Edward Coke, that speaks it but the records that speak it." "The King," he advised James, "cannot take any cause out of any of his courts and give judgment upon it himself." "No person," he wrote in the *Second Institute,* "ought in any ecclesiastical court to be examined upon the cogitation of his heart or what he thinketh."

Such pronouncements, had they come from England's Attorney General, would have been near to treason. As Elizabeth's servant moreover, Coke could hardly have shaped the words; his mind was turned another way. But spoken by Chief Justice Coke, the words were to come as natural evolvement, behind them the long affirmation of Coke's years as scholar, judge and Commons man. * * *

* * *

Coke's change of direction was logical: Stuart England was not Tudor England; a man could with honesty uphold Elizabeth's prerogative and cry down James's. Not only had Elizabeth her country's welfare at heart, with skill and strength to sustain it, but the situation around her had been different. Tudor England suffered under continual threat from the Continental Catholic powers. "War-and-no-war," Ralegh had called it in 1593, begging for fighting ships against the Spaniard. To a growing nation, unity is above all essential, a strong central government, discipline throughout the realm. A succession of armadas, then as now, can blow away the very breath of civil liberties. Elizabeth, like her father before her, was careful not to let such questions come to full public issue; when they reared their heads, * * * she put the talker in the Tower. Her Commons were too inexperienced for effective protest, her judges of common law had not yet seen the need for independent action.

James came to the throne, and for a brief year or two the issue and the antagonists seemed to remain the same; in the Gunpowder trials it was Rome, Spain, a foreign enemy that Coke, Attorney General, continued to fight. Yet by the year 1607, James had revealed himself to those with eyes to see. This good-natured prince, fond of theological disputation and the deer hunt, desired to rule England as he had ruled Scotland, above the state and above the law. Parliaments were a trial laid on recurrently, like God's plagues on Pharaoh. There were kings, James wrote blandly, "before any Parliaments were holden, or laws made" * * *. Squarely behind James stood Lord Chancellor Ellesmere, served by Masters in Chancery, Clerks in Chancery and a battery of civilians learned in Roman law. At Ellesmere's side Archbishop Bancroft exercised the wide legal powers of the Anglican Established Church. "*Rex est lex loquens,*" said Ellesmere. "The King is the law speaking." "It is clear by the word of God in the Scripture," said Bancroft, "that judges are but delegates under the King." "The twelve Judges of the realm," said Francis Bacon, "are as the twelve lions under Solomon's Throne. They must be lions, but yet lions under the throne, being circumspect that they do not check or oppose any points of sovereignty." Edward Coke did not agree. "The King is under God and the law!" he said.

The pronouncements clashed * * *. Each voice represented a theory of government. * * * Ellesmere and Coke as chief antagonists were well matched, superficially similar. Both men despised disorder, remaining convinced that England should be ruled by "the better sort," which meant gentlemen with a substantial yearly income from land and manor. Both were strikingly handsome. If spectators came to Chancery for a sight of the old lord presiding whitehaired in his robes (Ellesmere was sixty-seven), Coke had an added attraction, the dramatic quality of the unexpected. To the end of his official life no one knew what Coke might say or do; the quality of outrageousness remained.

Coke's first point of attack was * * * Archbishop Bancroft's disciplinary body, the Ecclesiastical High Commission. This was a group of men, led by Bishops and Privy Councilors, who in 1559 had been authorized by Act of Parliament to keep order within the Established Church, discipline the clergy and punish such lay offenses as were included in the ecclesiastical jurisdiction * * *. Toward the end of Elizabeth's reign, however, the Commission began to extend its powers; already in the 1590's there had been murmurs against it, mostly from Puritans and Nonconformists. Since James's accession the Commission had grown larger; it numbered nearly eighty and called itself a court—the *Court of High Commission*—encroaching, Coke noted with concern, on common-law jurisdiction.

Against this encroachment there was but one recourse. If cases already on trial by the High Commission could be proven to be lay cases rather than ecclesiastical, trial might be summarily stopped by a writ of prohibition.* The distinction between "lay" and "ecclesiastical" was not, however, easy to come at, the Church authority being wide and reaching far beyond theological or clerical matters. Since time immemorial * * * the Church had regulated family affairs. Marriage and divorce, baptism, burial and the making of wills were under ecclesiastical jurisdiction. Church courts were empowered to punish perjury, defamation, drunkenness, breaches of faith, mistreatment of wives by husbands, incontinence and crimes of sexual behavior not covered by the common law. * * *

Elizabeth, as head of the Established Church, quite naturally upheld this ecclesiastical jurisdiction, exercised once by Rome and transferred to Episcopal Canterbury only by long and bitter struggle. To Coke as to Elizabeth the transfer meant national independence, an English Church authority rather than a Roman one. Why should they not uphold it? When, in the House of Commons, James Morrice in 1593 opposed the High Commission and the oath ex officio which governed its procedure, Speaker Coke did not defend him.

But times and rulers change. Elizabeth had never called herself "a little God to rule over men," nor said, as James did: "General laws, made

---

* A "Writ of Prohibition" was an order from Coke's court of "Common Pleas" or from the "Court of King's Bench" ("common law" courts) to a "prerogative" or "ecclesiastical" court forbidding either of the latter courts from hearing a matter in which the common law courts had exclusive jurisdiction.

publicly in Parliament, may by the King's authority be suspended upon causes known only to him." Above the horizon a cloud loomed; Coke saw it darken England's sky. Archbishop Bancroft presented complaints * * * in the form of twenty-five elaborate articles of grievances against the common-law courts. * * * In 1607 a new law dictionary appeared in London, entitled The Interpreter, dedicated to Bancroft, much read and talked of. Under the word "king" was to be found the following: "He is above the law by his absolute power; he may alter or suspend any particular law that seemeth hurtful to the publick estate. Thus much in short because I have heard some to be of opinion that the laws be above the King." Dr. Cowell, the author, served as Professor of Civil Law at Oxford * * *.

* * *

During these months, when Coke and Parliament together challenged Archbishop Bancroft, there ran in the courts a notorious suit * * *. Fuller's Case, it was called, after the barrister who defended it. Nicholas Fuller, a Parliament man (member for London) had been much employed by Puritans in their troubles with the ecclesiastical discipline.* Voluble, active, indiscreet, Fuller was given to protesting subsidy bills in Parliament and saying unkind things about the Scots. * * * At the moment he had in tow no less than twenty Puritan clients, most of whom were trying to escape fines for nonconformity. Two of these—Lad, a Norfolkman, and Mansell, a preacher—had been imprisoned for contempt because at their trial before the High Commission they refused the oath ex officio. Fuller, in defense of his clients * * * insulted the bishops in open court. High Commission procedure, said he, was "popish, under jurisdiction not of Christ but anti-Christ"; the oath ex officio led "to the damnation of their souls that take it"; he had heard said that bishops embezzled the fines of poor nonconformist preachers instead of paying them properly into Exchequer.

Fuller, upon this, found himself in custody for contempt. * * * The two clients were forgotten; to this day, no one knows what became of Lad and Mansell. But for nearly nineteen months, Fuller's Case rocked back and forth between King's Bench and High Commission—directed largely by Fuller himself from the White Tavern in Southwark, where Archbishop Bancroft had locked him in. King's Bench defended its prohibition on grounds that a barrister's conduct in court was a lay matter, to be tried at

* The English "Puritans" were Protestants who opposed many "Popish" practices of the Established Church of England and of the ecclesiastical courts. In particular they protested the use of the oath *ex officio,* a proceeding whereby the ecclesiastical courts could question a person on his or her beliefs and impose punishment if these beliefs did not accord with orthodoxy. The resistance to the oath *ex officio* became an important foundation for the Anglo–American constitutional principle against self-incrimination. See generally, John H. Langbein, "The Historical Origins of the Privilege Against Self–Incrimination at Common Law," 92 Mich.L.Rev. 1047, 1073—1074 (1994), and Eben Moglen, "Taking the Fifth: Reconsidering the Origins of the Constitutional Privilege Against Self–Incrimination," 92 Mich.L.Rev. 1086 (1994) and sources there cited.

common law. Archbishop Bancroft declared otherwise. In the end * * * Fuller was convicted, fined two hundred pounds and put in Fleet Prison. The charge was slander, schism, heresy, impious error, and the holding of pernicious opinions.

* * * [F]or the common law it was a notable defeat * * *. Putting Fuller in jail only heightened popular feeling and emphasized the point at issue: Was the High Commission a court of record, with power to imprison and to fine? Bancroft, Ellesmere and James said *Yes;* the common law said *No.* London visitors wrote home to their counties about Nicholas Fuller and his case, Parliament discussed it. The Lower House took Fuller's side. King James showed agitation. By Elizabeth's Act of Supremacy (1559) James was monarch over Church as well as state; who impugned ecclesiastical authority impugned the sovereign. "I pray you," he wrote to Sir Robert Cecil, "forget not Fuller's matter. I prophecy unto you that when so ever the ecclesiastical dignity together with the King's government thereof shall be turned into contempt and vanish in this kingdom, the kings hereof shall not longer prosper in their government and the monarchy shall fall to ruin."

Dr. Cowell had been right; it was high time for an authoritative definition of the word "king." Lord Chancellor Ellesmere was ready to add a definition of his own. * * * During Fuller's troubles a magnificent forum presented itself. Calvin's Case came to court in a blaze of fame and dignity. It was a test case to determine if a man born in Scotland after James's accession could call himself an English subject and inherit English lands—in a sense, James's own suit, brought largely at his instigation. Parliament had defeated the royal plan of union with Scotland; James hoped to salvage at least the rights of citizenship for his onetime countrymen. Fourteen judges, drawn from all three courts, tried Calvin's Case in Exchequer Chamber; each judge, during several days of trial, gave an oral opinion before a crowded courtroom. Ellesmere spoke last; the gist of his oration centered upon neither Calvin nor Scotland. It was a heavy salvo directed at loose talkers who during the past months had expressed themselves too vividly concerning the oath *ex officio,* bishops in general and the royal prerogative in particular. Certain new-risen philosophers, said Ellesmere scornfully, looked upon the common law as above the monarch, even daring to declare that "kings have no more power than the people from whom they take their temporal jurisdiction!" Such persons called upon the law of nature, asking "if kings or people did first make laws?" Near treason! said Ellesmere warmly. "The monarch is the law. *Rex est lex loquens,* the king is the law speaking."

In his place nearby, Coke must have heard it with gloom and revulsion. "Our constitution," Ellesmere went on indignantly, "is to be obeyed and reverenced," not bandied by persons walking in Paul's aisle or sitting in ordinaries "drowned with drink, blown away with a whiff of tobacco!"

Such "busy questionists" cited Plato and Aristotle on the framing of states and commonwealths. In Ellesmere's opinion, Plato and Aristotle were men "lacking knowledge of God, born in popular states, mislikers of monarchies" and no more fit to give laws "than Sir Thomas More's *Utopia* and such pamphlets as we have at every mart."

* * * [T]he Lord Chancellor, without referring openly to the court of Common Pleas, had employed the oratorical trick of classifying thoughtful, purposeful men all in one lump with popular demagogues—and, by the use of More's name, with "popery" too. Ellesmere added a three-column definition of the English common law that must have well-nigh curdled Coke's blood. Pronouncing the word *moreover* like an ejaculation, he fired a parting shot: "Moreover! Had Calvin's Case proven difficult, his Majesty himself should have decided it—the most religious, learned and judicious king that ever this kingdom or island had!"

Such a statement, made officially in an English courtroom—and by the Lord Chancellor himself—was a slap in the face of Edward Coke and all who held his ideas on government. "It is not customary," the great Chief Justice Fortescue once had said, "for the kings of England to sit in court or pronounce judgment themselves." Every English lawyer knew it, a maxim bred in the bone. Against it the Chief Justice of Common Pleas had but one official recourse: to withdraw suits from prerogative courts whenever and however he could, narrow down the Roman law jurisdiction and starve it to bones. By siege or by assault, Coke's weapons were slight. Mere legal quibbles, some called them—prohibitions, for instance. Yet giants still were vulnerable if pebbles could be found.

During the year following Fuller's imprisonment and Ellesmere's oration, prohibitions flowed out from Common Pleas under Coke's seal. Fuller's friends meanwhile distributed pamphlets, designed to get him out of jail, eloquent with Fuller's previous courtroom arguments, many of which were clever and some of which were sound. Coke, defending his own position, even borrowed certain of the phrases—unless, indeed, Coke had inspired it in the first place. * * *

Archbishop Bancroft watched the prohibitions roll from Common Pleas in term time and was alarmed. He appealed to James, advised him of the danger. Let his Majesty summon Coke and his brethren, tell them they overstepped.

* * *

The Privy Council met customarily on Sunday morning at Whitehall Palace. * * * On Sunday, November 6, 1608, common-law judges and ecclesiastics were summoned to Whitehall. The two sides, said James, might give their reasons and cite authorities; he would act as arbitrator to decide if the disputed prohibitions were valid. It was a role James fancied, being quick at disputation; next to running down a deer he loved to track the argument to its undefended lair. Actually, decision on this Sunday morning would hang not upon individual suits prohibited but on a final interpretation of Elizabeth's original patent authorizing the Court of High Commission—several long skins of parchment, to Bancroft perfectly explicit and clear. Coke thought differently. Could the patent be proven faulty, High Commission was ruined. Bancroft was prepared to defend it, Coke to destroy it.

Yet as the meeting progressed, no valid arguments were produced. Opponents stood sullen, merely denying each other's statements. James, impatient, demanded if the patent were too long a document—the judges too busy to read it?—and adjourned the meeting until the following Sunday, when "he hoped both sides would be better prepared." * * * But Coke, before the churchmen could reach the door, burst out with a long, disagreeable speech, repeating, among other insults, Nicholas Fuller's charge that commissioners had embezzled their fines. Archbishop Bancroft retorted indignantly. James interrupted, warned the two, "Take heed of heat in this business!" adding that he intended to make note of those who disregarded his wishes.

Next Sunday, Bishops and Judges reconvened. James sat in his chair, the disputants remained standing before him. Sir Julius Caesar, a Doctor of Roman Law, took notes. * * * Coke, as spokesman for the judges, this time was well prepared. ("Questions short," wrote Caesar; "deliberations long, conclusions pithy.") Ecclesiastical courts, said Coke, had undoubted authority to proceed, so long as no temporal matters were involved. But let a temporal issue enter the case, and it must be transferred to the common-law courts—even in causes of clearly ecclesiastical nature. Drawing on statutes of Edward II, III, VI, Coke acknowledged that civil lawyers construed these statutes otherwise. * * *

The King broke in. Common-law judges, he said, were like papists who quoted Scripture and then put upon it their own interpretation, to be received unquestioned. Just so, "judges allege statutes, reserving the exposition thereof to themselves." At this point some one, probably Bancroft, brought up the touchy matter of James's own powers. Coke's *Report* gives the statement unidentified:

> "In cases where there is not express authority in law, the King may himself decide it in his royal person; the Judges are but delegates of the King, and the King may take what causes he shall please from the determination of the Judges and may determine them himself. And the Archbishop said: that this was clear in divinity, that such authority belongs to the King by the Word of God in the Scripture. To which it was answered by me: that the King in his own person cannot adjudge any case, either criminal—as treason, felony, & c., or betwixt party and party; but this ought to be determined and adjudged in some court of justice, according to the Law and Custom

of England. * * * And it was greatly marvelled [Coke adds in comment] that the Archbishop durst inform the King that such absolute power and authority, as is aforesaid, belonged to the King by the Word of God."

The sovereign, Coke told James, might sit in Star Chamber, "and this appears in our books." But only to consult with the judges, not *in judicio.*

(In Star Chamber was a chair of state, emblazoned with the royal arms. For thirty years Coke had seen it empty; Elizabeth never claimed her right to sit. There were powers a wise sovereign did not put to public test.) "And it appears by Act of Parliament," Coke went on, addressing the King, "that neither by the Great Seal nor by the Little Seal, justice shall be delayed; *ergo,* the King cannot take any cause out of any courts and give judgment upon it himself. * * * "

Here the record becomes confused and it is difficult—as always in Coke's *Reports*—to separate what was said at the moment from what may have been added later. It is unlikely that James would have endured without interruption so long and violent a speech. From Sir Julius Caesar and various newsletters, it appears that at some point James broke in, told Coke he "spoke foolishly." Himself, the King, as supreme head of justice, would defend to the death his prerogative of calling judges before him to decide disputes of jurisdiction. Moreover, he would "ever protect the common law."

"The common law," Coke interjected, "protecteth the King."

"A traitorous speech!" James shouted. "The King protecteth the law, and not the law the King! The King maketh judges and bishops. If the judges interpret the laws themselves and suffer none else to interpret, they may easily make, of the laws, shipmen's hose!"

At this point James shook his fist and Sir Julius Caesar, after one brief sentence, stopped taking notes. Coke's *Report* picks up the story. "Then the King said that he thought the Law was founded upon Reason, and that he and others had Reason as well as the Judges. To which it was answered by me, that true it was that God had endowed his Majesty with excellent science and great endowments of Nature. But his Majesty was not learned in the Laws of his Realm of England; and Causes which concern the Life, or Inheritance, or Goods, or Fortunes of his Subjects are not to be decided by natural Reason but by the artificial Reason and Judgment of Law, which requires long Study and Experience before that a man can attain to the cognizance of it; and that the Law was the golden Metwand and Measure to try Causes of the Subjects, which protected his Majesty in safety and Peace: With which the King was greatly offended, and said that then he should be under the Law, which was treason to affirm (as he said). To which I said, that Bracton saith, *Quod Rex non debet esse sub homine, sed sub Deo et Lege*—that the King should not be under man, but under God and the Laws."

SIR RAFE BOSWELL TO DR. MILBORNE

" * * * the Lord Coke humbly prayed the king to have respect to the Common Lawes of his land & c. He prayed his Majesty to consider that the Ecclesiastical Jurisdiction was forren. After which his Majesty fell into that high indignation as the like was never knowne in him, looking and speaking fiercely with bended fist, offering to strike him, & c. Which the Lo. Cooke perceaving fell flatt on all fower; humbly beseeching his Majestie to take compassion on him and to pardon him if he thought zeale had gone beyond his dutie and allegiance. His Majestie not herewith contented, continued his indignation. Whereuppon the Lo. Treasurer [Robert Cecil] the Lo. Cooke's unckle by marriage, kneeled down before his Majestie and prayed him to be favourable. To whom his Majestie replied saying, What hast thou to doe to intreate for him? He answered, In regard he hath married my neerest kinswoman, & c."

* * * [I]t was a tremendous scene: a king's fist raised against a judge, the small pale hunchback throwing himself between. "My little great Lord," they called Cecil now; he carried more power and more care than any man in England, and after his father's example he remained faithful to his friends.

Very likely, Coke did fall on his face. It was that or a cell in the Tower. The Chief Justice of Common Pleas knelt, and rose, and went out into November city streets. King James, having disposed of these vexing questions, as it seemed in one brief forenoon, turned his face again to Royston where the red deer ran.

Next morning a new prohibition, under Coke's seal, went out to High Commission from the Court of Common Pleas.

NOTES AND QUESTIONS

1. Few figures in Anglo–American legal history are as imposing as Sir Edward Coke. At one time or another he held practically every position of political and legal importance: High Steward of Cambridge University (1575), Solicitor–General (1592), Speaker of the House of Commons (1593), Attorney–General (1594), and Chief Justice of both the Court of Common Pleas (1606) and King's Bench (1613). Early in Coke's career he began to publish his thirteen-volume series of Reports which interspersed descriptions of cases with Coke's own analysis. Later in his life he turned to a more extensive investigation of law, publishing the four-volume Institutes of the Laws of England; commentaries on the English law relating to real property (First Institute, Coke on Littleton (1628)), statutes of Parliament (Second Institute (1642)), Criminal Law (Third Institute (1644)), and the jurisdiction and history of the various English courts (Fourth Institute (1644)). Until well into the

nineteenth century these works of Edward Coke were still frequently cited as authoritative in American courtrooms.

2. Probably as important as Coke's writing, however, was his prolonged struggle with James I and James's officers over the limits of the King's prerogative, with which this excerpt is primarily concerned. How could James I maintain that he was not subject to English Law? Note that Ellesmere, in defending the King's prerogative, seems to make a special effort to impeach Plato and Aristotle's teachings. What does this have to do with the issue at hand? Why does Ellesmere think that Plato and Aristotle are suspect because they lived in "popular states?"

3. You will remember that when Coke was explicating "the statutes of Edward II, III, VI" to demonstrate that Ecclesiastical courts had no authority in cases involving temporal matters, Coke conceded that "civil lawyers construed these statutes otherwise * * *; " immediately thereafter James broke in and stated that Common law judges "were like papists who quoted Scripture and then put upon it their own interpretation * * *. " James stated also that "judges allege statutes, reserving the exposition thereof to themselves." What point was James trying to make? How could anyone suggest that the interpretation of statutes was not best done by judges? Does James's later suggestion that "If the judges interpret the laws themselves and suffer none else to interpret, they may easily make, of the laws, shipmen's hose!" have any bearing on this? On the other hand, what did Coke mean when he told James I that legal cases "are not to be decided by natural Reason but by the artificial Reason and Judgement of Law * * * which requires long Study and Experience before that a man can attain to the cognizance of it * * *. "? Exactly what was the nature of Coke's jurisprudence? Is it anything like ours? James I fears runaway interpretation by judges. Was that fear justified? Is it in our own time? For an argument that the essence of "Constitutionalism" both for England and for us is in "[t]he belief that the language of the law means something, and that its meaning is intended to bind down those who would interpret it," and that Law Dictionaries (note that one is involved in the dispute between James I and Coke) can help, see Gary L. McDowell, "The Politics of Meaning: Law Dictionaries and the Liberal Tradition of Interpretation," 44 Am. J. Leg. Hist. 257, 283 (2000). For further reflection on Coke's approach to law see, e.g., Michael W. McConnell, "Tradition and Constitutionalism Before the Constitution," 1998 U.Ill.L.Rev. 173, John V. Orth, "Did Sir Edward Coke Mean What He Said," 16 Const. Comm. 33 (1999), and Richard J. Ross, "The Memorial Culture of Early Modern English Lawyers: Memory as Keyword, Shelter and Identity," 10 Yale J. L. & Hum. 229 (1998).

4. James appears to have won this round with Coke, at least if Coke's falling on the floor can be regarded as capitulation. Why did Coke capitulate? Or did he? You will have noted that Coke did not immediately cease issuing prohibitions. After some years of judicial contests between Coke and the prerogative courts, however, Coke was first "kicked upstairs" from the Court of Common Pleas to the Court of King's Bench (where he could do less damage), and was eventually dismissed from the bench completely. Coke was tempo-

rarily restored to the King's good graces, and was even made a Privy Councilor by James. Still later, however, Coke began once again to oppose the Royal Prerogative, as a member of the English Parliament, where he clashed with both James and James's son and successor, Charles I. For the full story see, in addition to the book by Catherine Drinker Bowen from which this excerpt has been taken, Stephen D. White, Sir Edward Coke and the "Grievances of the Commonwealth" 1621–1628 (1979), and on the conflict between the Chancellors and Coke, see Catherine Drinker Bowen, The Temper of a Man: Francis Bacon 133–74 (1963). For an excellent and accessible study of Coke's theories and their importance to American Constitutionalism, see David N. Mayer, "The English Radical Whig Origins of American Constitutionalism," 70 Wash.U.L.Q. 131 (1992). For the sources of Coke's conception of the English common law, see the provocative collection of essays edited by Ellis Sandoz, The Roots of Liberty: Magna Carta, Ancient Constitution, and the Anglo American Tradition of Rule of Law (1992). You have probably discerned that both Coke and James, at some level, agree that the source of law is not man, but God. The belief that there is some "law of nature" or of "nature's God," is a powerful one in both English and American jurisprudence, which will come up from time to time in the course. Coke's feelings on this issue were shared and developed by many great common lawyers, including in particular Sir William Blackstone (whom we will meet later) and Edmund Burke. For an introduction to natural law thinking, particularly as demonstrated by Burke, and its relevance to the current debate over "human rights," see, e.g., Bruce P. Frohnen, "Multicultural Rights? Natural Law and the Reconciliation of Universal Norms With Particular Cultures," 52 Cath. U. L. Rev. 39 (2002). For Coke's application of Natural Law in *Calvin's Case*, see Polly J. Price, Natural Law and Birthright Citizenship in *Calvin's Case*, 9 Yale J.L. & Hum. 73 (1997). For Coke's continuing influence on American law, see, e.g., James R. Stoner, Jr., Common Law and Liberal Theory: Coke, Hobbes, and the Origins of American Constitutionalism (1992).

5. In 1649 Charles I was beheaded following a dispute with Parliament during the English Civil Wars of 1642–1660. What do you suppose this dispute between the Stuart Kings and Parliament had to do with the debate you have just read between Coke and James I? During the period between the end of Charles's reign and the restoration of the monarchy, in the person of Charles's son, Charles II, in 1660, England was governed by the military, led initially by the famous Puritan, Oliver Cromwell, self-styled Lord Protector. Following the death of Cromwell, the Puritan dictatorship proved too much for the English, and the monarchy's re-establishment was greeted with much enthusiasm and introduced a period of political quiescence. This serenity came to an end during the reign of Charles II's brother, James II, to whom we now turn.

B. THE TRIAL OF THE SEVEN BISHOPS

LADY TREVELYAN, ED., II THE WORKS OF LORD MACAULAY*

39–41, 145–147, 150–152, 153–156, 157–160, 164–167, 168–178, 182–184 (1866).

[These excerpts begin with a discussion of the First Declaration of Indulgence, issued by James II, a Catholic, on April 4, 1687].

In this Declaration the King avowed that it was his earnest wish to see his people members of that Church to which he himself belonged. But, since that could not be, he announced his intention to protect them in the free exercise of their religion. * * * He had long been convinced, he said, that conscience was not to be forced, that persecution was unfavourable to population and to trade, and that it never attained the ends which persecutors had in view. He repeated his promise, already often repeated and often violated, that he would protect the Established Church in the enjoyment of her legal rights. He then proceeded to annul, by his own sole authority, a long series of statutes. He suspended all penal laws against all classes of Nonconformists. He authorised both Roman Catholics and Protestant Dissenters to perform their worship publicly. He forbade his subjects, on pain of his highest displeasure, to molest any religious assembly. He also abrogated all those Acts which imposed any religious test as a qualification for any civil or military office.

That the Declaration of Indulgence was unconstitutional is a point on which both the great English parties have always been entirely agreed. Every person capable of reasoning on a political question must perceive that a monarch who is competent to issue such a Declaration is nothing less than an absolute monarch. Nor is it possible to urge in defence of this act of James those pleas by which many arbitrary acts of the Stuarts have been vindicated or excused. It cannot be said that he mistook the bounds of his prerogative because they had not been accurately ascertained. For the truth is that he trespassed with a recent landmark full in his view. Fifteen years before that time, a Declaration of Indulgence had been put forth by his brother. * * * That Declaration, when compared with the Declaration of James, might be called modest and cautious. The Declaration of Charles dispensed only with penal laws. The Declaration of James dispensed also with all religious tests. The Declaration of Charles permitted the Roman Catholics to celebrate their worship in private dwellings only. Under the Declaration of James they might build and decorate temples, and even walk in procession along Fleet Street with crosses, images, and censers. Yet the Declaration of Charles had been pronounced illegal in the most formal manner. The Commons had resolved that the King had no

* These excerpts are taken from the masterwork of Thomas Babington Macaulay, 1st Baron Macaulay, The History of England from the Accession of James the Second (5 vols. 1849–61). As you will see, the work can hardly be called objective, but many have believed it profound.

power to dispense with statutes in matters ecclesiastical. Charles had ordered the obnoxious instrument to be cancelled in his presence, had torn off the seal with his own hand, and had, both by message under his sign manual, and with his own lips from his throne in full Parliament, distinctly promised the two Houses that the step which had given so much offence should never be drawn into precedent.

* * *

On the twenty-seventh of April 1688, the King put forth a second Declaration of Indulgence. In this paper he recited at length the Declaration of the preceding April. His past life, he said, ought to have convinced his people that he was not a person who could easily be induced to depart from any resolution which he had formed. * * * He announced that he meant to hold a Parliament in November at the latest; and he exhorted his subjects to choose representatives who would assist him in the great work which he had undertaken.

On the fourth of May, * * * he made an Order in Council that his Declaration of the preceding week should be read, on two successive Sundays, at the time of divine service, by the officiating ministers of all the churches and chapels of the kingdom. In London and in the suburbs the reading was to take place on the twentieth and twenty-seventh of May, in other parts of England on the third and tenth of June. The Bishops were directed to distribute copies of the Declaration through their respective dioceses.

When it is considered that the clergy of the Established Church, with scarcely an exception, regarded the Indulgence as a violation of the laws of the realm, as a breach of the plighted faith of the King, and as a fatal blow levelled at the interest and dignity of their own profession, it will scarcely admit of doubt that the Order in Council was intended to be felt by them as a cruel affront. It was popularly believed that Petre* had avowed this intention in a coarse metaphor borrowed from the rhetoric of the East. He would, he said, make them eat dirt, the vilest and most loathsome of all dirt. But tyrannical and malignant as the mandate was, would the Anglican priesthood refuse to obey? The King's temper was arbitrary and severe. The proceedings of the Ecclesiastical Commission were as summary as those of a court martial. Whoever ventured to resist might in a week be ejected from his parsonage, deprived of his whole income, pronounced incapable of holding any other spiritual preferment, and left to beg from door to door. * * * It might also well be apprehended that, if the clergy refused to read the Declaration, the Protestant Dissenters would misinterpret the refusal, would despair of obtaining any toleration from the members of the Church of England, and would throw their whole weight into the scale of the Court.

* Father Edward Petre, a Jesuit extremist, had been James's confidential adviser since 1678.

The clergy therefore hesitated. * * *

* * *

On the eighteenth a meeting of prelates and of other eminent divines was held at Lambeth. * * * After long deliberation, a petition embodying the general sense was written by the Archbishop with his own hand. It was not drawn up with much felicity of style. Indeed, the cumbrous and inelegant structure of the sentences brought on Sancroft** some raillery * * * But in substance nothing could be more skilfully framed than this memorable document. All disloyalty, all intolerance, was earnestly disclaimed. The King was assured that the Church still was, as she had ever been, faithful to the throne. He was assured also that the Bishops would, in proper place and time, as Lords of Parliament and members of the Upper House of Convocation, show that they by no means wanted tenderness for the conscientious scruples of Dissenters. But Parliament had, both in the late and in the present reign, pronounced that the sovereign was not constitutionally competent to dispense with statutes in matters ecclesiastical. The Declaration was therefore illegal; and the petitioners could not, in prudence, honour, or conscience, be parties to the solemn publishing of an illegal Declaration in the house of God * * *.

This paper was signed by the Archbishop and by six of his suffragans, Lloyd of Saint Asaph, Turner of Ely, Lake of Chichester, Ken of Bath and Wells, White of Peterborough, and Trelawney of Bristol. * * *

It was now late on Friday evening; and on Sunday morning the Declaration was to be read in the churches of London. It was necessary to put the paper into the King's hands without delay. The six Bishops crossed the river to Whitehall. The Archbishop, who had long been forbidden the Court, did not accompany them. * * * James directed that the Bishops should be admitted. He had heard from his tool Cartwright that they were disposed to obey the royal mandate, but that they wished for some little modifications in form, and that they meant to present a humble request to that effect. His Majesty was therefore in very good humour. When they knelt before him, he graciously told them to rise * * *. James read the petition: he folded it up; and his countenance grew dark. "This," he said, "is a great surprise to me. I did not expect this from your Church, especially from some of you. This is a standard of rebellion." The Bishops broke out into passionate professions of loyalty: but the King, as usual, repeated the same words over and over. "I tell you, this is a standard of rebellion." "Rebellion!" cried Trelawney, falling on his knees. "For God's sake, sir, do not say so hard a thing of us. No Trelawney can be a rebel. Remember that my family has fought for the crown. Remember how I served Your Majesty when Monmouth was in the West." "We put down

** William Sancroft, Archbishop of Canterbury, and thus leading prelate of the Established Church (Anglican Protestants).

the last rebellion," said Lake: "we shall not raise another." "We rebel!" exclaimed Turner; "we are ready to die at your Majesty's feet." "Sir," said Ken, in a more manly tone, "I hope that you will grant to us that liberty of conscience which you grant to all mankind." Still James went on. "This is rebellion. This is a standard of rebellion. Did ever a good Churchman question the dispensing power before? Have not some of you preached for it and written for it? It is a standard of rebellion. I will have my Declaration published." "We have two duties to perform," answered Ken, "our duty to God, and our duty to Your Majesty. We honour you: but we fear God." "Have I deserved this?" said the King, more and more angry: "I who have been such a friend to your Church? I did not expect this from some of you. I will be obeyed. My Declaration shall be published. You are trumpeters of sedition. What do you do here? Go to your dioceses; and see that I am obeyed. I will keep this paper. I will not part with it. I will remember you that have signed it." "God's will be done," said Ken. "God has given me the dispensing power," said the King, "and I will maintain it." * * * The Bishops respectfully retired. That very evening the document which they had put into the hands of the King appeared word for word in print, was laid on the tables of all the coffeehouses, and was cried about the streets. * * * How the petition got abroad is still a mystery. Sancroft declared that he had taken every precaution against publication, and that he knew of no copy except that which he had himself written, and which James had taken * * *. The veracity of the Archbishop is beyond all suspicion. But it is by no means improbable that some of the divines who assisted in framing the petition may have remembered so short a composition accurately, and may have sent it to the press. The prevailing opinion, however, was that some person about the King had been indiscreet or treacherous.

In the City and Liberties of London were about a hundred parish churches. In only four of these was the Order in Council obeyed. * * * Even in the chapel of Saint James's Palace the officiating minister had the courage to disobey the order. The Westminster boys long remembered what took place that day in the Abbey. Sprat, Bishop of Rochester, officiated there as Dean. As soon as he began to read the Declaration, murmurs and the noise of people crowding out of the choir drowned his voice. He trembled so violently that men saw the paper shake in his hand. Long before he had finished, the place was deserted by all but those whose situation made it necessary for them to remain.

Never had the Church been so dear to the nation as on the afternoon of that day. The spirit of dissent seemed to be extinct. Baxter from his pulpit pronounced an eulogium on the Bishops and parochial clergy. The Dutch minister, a few hours later, wrote to inform the States General that the Anglican priesthood had risen in the estimation of the public to an incredible degree. The universal cry of the Nonconformists, he said, was that they would rather continue to lie under the penal statutes than separate their cause from that of the prelates.

Another week of anxiety and agitation passed away. Sunday came again. Again the churches of the capital were thronged by hundreds of thousands. The Declaration was read nowhere except at the very few places where it had been read the week before. The minister who had officiated at the chapel in Saint James's Palace had been turned out of his situation: a more obsequious divine appeared with the paper in his hand: but his agitation was so great that he could not articulate. In truth the feeling of the whole nation had now become such as none but the very best and noblest, or the very worst and basest, of mankind could without much discomposure encounter.

Even the King stood aghast for a moment at the violence of the tempest which he had raised. What step was he next to take? * * * The prelates who had signed the petition might be cited before the Ecclesiastical Commission and deprived of their sees. But to this course strong objections were urged in Council. It had been announced that the Houses would be convoked before the end of the year. The Lords would assuredly treat the sentence of deprivation as a nullity, would insist that Sancroft and his fellow petitioners should be summoned to Parliament, and would refuse to acknowledge a new Archbishop of Canterbury or a new Bishop of Bath and Wells. * * * If therefore it were thought necessary to punish the Bishops, the punishment ought to be inflicted according to the known course of English law. * * * It was accordingly resolved that the Archbishop and the six other petitioners should be brought before the Court of King's Bench on a charge of seditious libel. That they would be convicted it was scarcely possible to doubt. The Judges and their officers were tools of the Court. * * * The refractory prelates would probably be condemned to ruinous fines and to long imprisonment, and would be glad to ransom themselves by serving, both in and out of Parliament, the designs of the Sovereign.

On the evening of the eighth of June the seven prelates, furnished by the ablest lawyers in England with full advice, repaired to the palace, and were called into the Council chamber. Their petition was lying on the table. The Chancellor took the paper up, showed it to the Archbishop, and said, "Is this the paper which your Grace wrote, and which the six Bishops present delivered to His Majesty?" Sancroft looked at the paper, turned to the King, and spoke thus: "Sir, I stand here a culprit. I never was so before. * * * Since I am so unhappy as to be in this situation, Your Majesty will not be offended if I avail myself of my lawful right to decline saying anything which may criminate me." "This is mere chicanery," said the King. "I hope that Your Grace will not do so ill a thing as to deny your own hand." * * * "Sir," said the Archbishop, "I am not bound to accuse myself. Nevertheless, if Your Majesty positively commands me to answer,

I will do so in the confidence that a just and generous prince will not suffer what I say in obedience to his orders to be brought in evidence against me." "You must not capitulate with your Sovereign," said the Chancellor. "No," said the King; "I will not give any such command. If you choose to deny your own hands, I have nothing more to say to you."

The Bishops were repeatedly sent out into the antechamber, and repeatedly called back into the Council room. At length James positively commanded them to answer the question. He did not expressly engage that their confession should not be used against them. But they, not unnaturally, supposed that, after what had passed, such an engagement was implied in his command. Sancroft acknowledged his handwriting; and his brethren followed his example. * * * The Chancellor then told them that a criminal information would be exhibited against them in the Court of King's Bench, and called upon them to enter into recognisances. They refused. They were peers of Parliament, they said. They were advised by the best lawyers in Westminster Hall that no peer could be required to enter into a recognisance in a case of libel; and they should not think themselves justified in relinquishing the privilege of their order. The King was so absurd as to think himself personally affronted because they chose, on a legal question, to be guided by legal advice. "You believe every body," he said, "rather than me." He was indeed mortified and alarmed. For he had gone so far that, if they persisted, he had no choice left but to send them to prison; and, though he by no means foresaw all the consequences of such a step, he foresaw probably enough to disturb him. They were resolute. A warrant was therefore made out directing the Lieutenant of the Tower to keep them in safe custody, and a barge was manned to convey them down the river.

* * * When the Seven came forth under a guard, the emotions of the people broke through all restraint. Thousands fell on their knees and prayed aloud for the men who had, with the Christian courage of Ridley and Latimer, confronted a tyrant inflamed by all the bigotry of Mary. Many dashed into the stream, and, up to their waists in ooze and water, cried to the holy fathers to bless them. * * * The very sentinels who were posted at the Traitors' Gate reverently asked for a blessing from the martyrs whom they were to guard. Sir Edward Hales was Lieutenant of the Tower. He was little inclined to treat his prisoners with kindness. For he was an apostate from that Church for which they suffered; and he held several lucrative posts by virtue of that dispensing power against which they had protested. He learned with indignation that his soldiers were drinking the health of the Bishops. He ordered his officers to see that it was done no more. But the officers came back with a report that the thing could not be prevented, and that no other health was drunk in the garrison. * * * All day the coaches and liveries of the first nobles of England were seen round the prison gates. * * *

* * *

The Bishops edified all who approached them by the firmness and cheerfulness with which they endured confinement, by the modesty and meekness with which they received the applauses and blessings of the whole nation, and by the loyal attachment which they professed for the persecutor who sought their destruction. They remained only a week in custody. On Friday, the fifteenth of June, the first day of term, they were brought before the King's Bench. An immense throng awaited their coming. From the landing place to the Court of Requests they passed through a lane of spectators who blessed and applauded them. "Friends," said the prisoners as they passed, "honour the King; and remember us in your prayers." These humble and pious expressions moved the hearers even to tears. When at length the procession had made its way through the crowd into the presence of the Judges, the Attorney General exhibited the information which he had been commanded to prepare, and moved that the defendants might be ordered to plead. The counsel on the other side objected that the Bishops had been unlawfully committed, and were therefore not regularly before the Court. The question whether a peer could be required to enter into recognisances on a charge of libel was argued at great length, and decided by a majority of the Judges in favour of the crown. The prisoners then pleaded Not Guilty. That day fortnight, the twenty-ninth of June, was fixed for their trial. In the meantime they were allowed to be at large on their own recognisances. * * *

The Bishops were now permitted to depart to their own homes. The common people, who did not understand the nature of the legal proceedings which had taken place in the King's Bench, and who saw that their favourites had been brought to Westminster Hall in custody and were suffered to go away in freedom, imagined that the good cause was prospering. Loud acclamations were raised. The steeples of the churches sent forth joyous peals. * * *

Such was the concourse, and such the agitation, that the Dutch Ambassador was surprised to see the day close without an insurrection. The King had been anxious and irritable. In order that he might be ready to suppress any disturbance, he had passed the morning in reviewing several battalions of infantry in Hyde Park. It is, however, by no means certain that his troops would have stood by him if he had needed their services. * * * There were * * * many bonfires that evening in the City. Two Roman Catholics, who were so indiscreet as to beat some boys for joining in these rejoicings, were seized by the mob, stripped naked, and ignominiously branded.

Sir Edward Hales now came to demand fees from those who had lately been his prisoners. They refused to pay anything for a detention which they regarded as illegal to an officer whose commission was, on their principles, a nullity. The Lieutenant hinted very intelligibly that, if they came into his hands again, they should be put into heavy irons and should lie on bare stones. "We are under our King's displeasure," was the answer; "and most deeply do we feel it: but a fellow subject who threatens us does but lose his breath." * * *

Before the day of trial the agitation had spread to the farthest corners of the island. From Scotland the Bishops received letters assuring them of the sympathy of the Presbyterians of that country, so long and so bitterly hostile to prelacy. The people of Cornwall, a fierce, bold, and athletic race, among whom there was a stronger provincial feeling than in any other part of the realm, were greatly moved by the danger to Trelawney, whom they reverenced less as a ruler of the Church than as the head of an honourable house, and the heir through twenty descents of ancestors who had been of great note before the Normans had set foot on English ground. All over the country the peasants chanted a ballad* of which the burden is still remembered:

And shall Trelawney die, and shall Trelawney die?

Then thirty thousand Cornish boys will know the reason why.

The miners from their caverns reechoed the song with a variation:

Then twenty thousand under ground will know the reason why.

The rustics in many parts of the country loudly expressed a strange hope which had never ceased to live in their hearts. Their Protestant Duke, their beloved Monmouth, would suddenly appear, would lead them to victory, and would tread down the King and the Jesuits under his feet.

The ministers were appalled. * * * But the King's resolution was fixed. "I will go on," he said. "I have been only too indulgent. Indulgence ruined my father."

* * *

[THE DAY OF THE TRIAL ARRIVED]

On the twenty-ninth of June, Westminster Hall, Old and New Palace Yard, and all the neighbouring streets to a great distance were thronged with people. Such an auditory had never before and has never since been assembled in the Court of King's Bench. Thirty-five temporal peers of the realm were counted in the crowd.

All the four Judges of the Court were on the bench. Wright, who presided, had been raised to his high place over the heads of many abler and more learned men solely on account of his unscrupulous servility.

* There is some doubt about the authenticity of this ballad. Macaulay's source for this "was given to inventing Cornish traditions and fictitious historical documents." Sir Charles Firth, A Commentary on Macaulay's History of England 103–104 (1938).

Allibone was a Papist, and owed his situation to that dispensing power, the legality of which was now in question. Holloway had hitherto been a serviceable tool of the government. Even Powell, whose character for honesty stood high, had borne a part in some proceedings which it is impossible to defend. * * *

The counsel were by no means fairly matched. The government had required from its law officers services so odious and disgraceful that all the ablest jurists and advocates of the Tory party had, one after another, refused to comply, and had been dismissed from their employments. Sir Thomas Powis, the Attorney General, was scarcely of the third rank in his profession. Sir William Williams, the Solicitor General, had great abilities and dauntless courage: but he wanted discretion; he loved wrangling; he had no command over his temper; and he was hated and despised by all political parties. * * *

On the other side were arrayed almost all the eminent forensic talents of the age. Sawyer and Finch, who, at the time of the accession of James, had been Attorney and Solicitor General, and who, during the persecution of the Whigs in the late reign, had served the crown with but too much vehemence and success, were of counsel for the defendants. With them were joined two persons * * * reputed the two best lawyers that could be found in the Inns of Court; Pemberton, who had, in the time of Charles the Second, been Chief Justice of the King's Bench, who had been removed from his high place on account of his humanity and moderation, and who had resumed his practice at the bar; and Pollexfen, who had long been at the head of the Western circuit, and who * * * was known to be at heart a Whig, if not a republican. Sir Creswell Levinz was also there, a man of great knowledge and experience, but of singularly timid nature. He had been removed from the bench some years before, because he was afraid to serve the purposes of the government. He was now afraid to appear as the advocate of the Bishops, and had at first refused to receive their retainer: but it had been intimidated to him by the whole body of attorneys who employed him that, if he declined this brief, he should never have another.

* * *

The junior counsel for the Bishops was a young barrister named John Somers. He had no advantages of birth or fortune; nor had he yet had any opportunity of distinguishing himself before the eyes of the public: but his genius, his industry, his great and various accomplishments, were well known to a small circle of friends; and in spite of his Whig opinions, his pertinent and lucid mode of arguing and the constant propriety of his demeanour had already secured to him the ear of the Court of King's Bench. * * *

The jury was sworn. It consisted of persons of highly respectable station. The foreman was Sir Roger Langley, a baronet of old and honourable family. With him were joined a knight and ten esquires, several of whom are known to have been men of large possessions. There were some Nonconformists in the number: for the Bishops had wisely resolved not to show any distrust of the Protestant Dissenters. One name excited considerable alarm, that of Michael Arnold. He was brewer to the palace; and it was apprehended that the government counted on his voice. The story goes that he complained bitterly of the position in which he found himself. "Whatever I do," he said, "I am sure to be half ruined. If I say Not Guilty, I shall brew no more for the King; and if I say Guilty, I shall brew no more for anybody else."

* * *

The information charged the Bishops with having written or published, in the county of Middlesex, a false, malicious, and seditious libel. The Attorney and Solicitor first tried to prove the writing. For this purpose several persons were called to speak to the hands of the Bishops. But the witnesses were so unwilling that hardly a single plain answer could be extracted from any of them. Pemberton, Pollexfen, and Levinz contended that there was no evidence to go to the jury. Two of the Judges, Holloway and Powell, declared themselves of the same opinion; and the hopes of the spectators rose high. All at once the crown lawyers announced their intention to take another line. Powis, with shame and reluctance which he could not dissemble, put into the witness box Blathwayt, a Clerk of Privy Council, who had been present when the King interrogated the Bishops. Blathwayt swore that he had heard them own their signatures. His testimony was decisive. "Why," said Judge Holloway to the Attorney, "when you had such evidence, did you not produce it at first, without all this waste of time?" It soon appeared why the counsel for the crown had been unwilling, without absolute necessity, to resort to this mode of proof. Pemberton stopped Blathwayt, subjected him to a searching cross examination, and insisted upon having all that had passed between the King and the defendants fully related. "That is a pretty thing indeed," cried Williams. "Do you think," said Powis, "that you are at liberty to ask our witnesses any impertinent question that comes into your heads?" The advocates of the Bishops were not men to be so put down. "He is sworn," said Pollexfen, "to tell the truth and the whole truth; and an answer we must and will have." The witness shuffled, equivocated, pretended to misunderstand the questions, implored the protection of the Court. But he was in hands from which it was not easy to escape. At length the Attorney again interposed. "If," he said, "you persist in asking such a question, tell us, at least, what use you mean to make of it." Pemberton, who, through the whole trial, did his duty manfully and ably, replied without hesitation: "My Lords * * * I will deal plainly with the

Court. If the Bishops owned this paper under a promise from His Majesty that their confession should not be used against them, I hope that no unfair advantage will be taken of them." "You put on His Majesty what I dare hardly name," said Williams. "Since you will be so pressing, I demand, for the King, that the question may be recorded." "What do you mean, Mr. Solicitor?" said Sawyer, interposing. "I know what I mean," said the apostate: "I desire that the question may be recorded in court." "Record what you will. I am not afraid of you, Mr. Solicitor," said Pemberton. Then came a loud and fierce altercation, which Wright could with difficulty quiet. In other circumstances, he would probably have ordered the question to be recorded, and Pemberton to be committed. But on this great day the unjust judge was overawed. He often cast a side glance towards the thick rows of Earls and Barons by whom he was watched, and before whom, in the next Parliament, he might stand at the bar. He looked, a bystander said, as if all the peers present had halters in their pockets. At length Blathwayt was forced to give a full account of what had passed. It appeared that the King had entered into no express covenant with the Bishops. But it appeared also that the Bishops might not unreasonably think that there was an implied engagement. Indeed, from the unwillingness of the crown lawyers to put the Clerk of the Council into the witness box, and from the vehemence with which they objected to Pemberton's cross examination, it is plain that they were themselves of this opinion.

However, the handwriting was now proved. * * *

The crown lawyers then * * * undertook to prove that the Bishops had published a libel in the county of Middlesex. The difficulties were great. The delivery of the petition to the King was undoubtedly, in the eye of the law, a publication. But how was this delivery to be proved? No person had been present at the audience in the royal closet except the King and the defendants. The King could not well be sworn. It was therefore only by the admissions of the defendants that the fact of publication could be established. Blathwayt was again examined, but in vain. He well remembered, he said, that the Bishops owned their hands; but he did not remember that they owned the paper which lay on the table of the Privy Council to be the same paper which they had delivered to the King, or that they were even interrogated on that point. * * * As witness after witness answered in the negative, roars of laughter and shouts of triumph, which the Judges did not even attempt to silence, shook the hall.

It seemed that at length this hard fight had been won. The case for the crown was closed. Had the counsel for the Bishops remained silent, an acquittal was certain; for nothing which the most corrupt and shameless Judge could venture to call legal evidence of publication had been given. The Chief Justice was beginning to charge the jury, and would undoubtedly have directed them to acquit the defendants; but Finch, too anxious to be perfectly discreet, interfered, and begged to be heard. "If you will be heard," said Wright, "you shall be heard; but you do not understand your own interests." The other counsel for the defence made Finch sit down, and begged the Chief Justice to proceed. He was about to do so, when a messenger came to the Solicitor General with news that Lord Sunderland could prove the publication, and would come down to the court immediately. Wright maliciously told the counsel for the defence that they had only themselves to thank for the turn which things had taken. The countenances of the great multitude fell. Finch was, during some hours, the most unpopular man in the country. Why could he not sit still as his betters, Sawyer, Pemberton, and Pollexfen, had done? His love of meddling, his ambition to make a fine speech, had ruined everything.

Meanwhile the Lord President was brought in a sedan chair through the hall. Not a hat moved as he passed; and many voices cried out "Popish dog." He came into court pale and trembling, with eyes fixed on the ground, and gave his evidence in a faltering voice. He swore that the Bishops had informed him of their intention to present a petition to the King, and that they had been admitted into the royal closet for that purpose. This circumstance, coupled with the circumstance that, after they left the closet, there was in the King's hands a petition signed by them, was such proof as might reasonably satisfy a jury of the fact of the publication.

Publication in Middlesex was then proved. But was the paper thus published a false, malicious, and seditious libel? Hitherto the matter in dispute had been whether a fact which everybody well knew to be true could be proved according to technical rules of evidence; but now the contest became one of deeper interest. It was necessary to enquire into the limits of prerogative and liberty, into the right of the King to dispense with statutes, into the right of the subject to petition for the redress of grievances. During three hours the counsel for the petitioners argued with great force in defence of the fundamental principles of the constitution, and proved from the Journals of the House of Commons that the Bishops had affirmed no more than the truth when they represented to the King that the dispensing power which he claimed had been repeatedly declared illegal by Parliament. Somers rose last. He spoke little more than five minutes: but every word was full of weighty matter; and when he sat down his reputation as an orator and a constitutional lawyer was established. He went through the expressions which were used in the information to describe the offence imputed to the Bishops, and showed that every word, whether adjective or substantive, was altogether inappropriate. The offence imputed was a false, a malicious, a seditious libel. False the paper was not; for every fact which it set forth had been shown from the journals of Parliament to be true. Malicious the paper was not; for the defendants had not sought an occasion of strife, but had been placed by the government in such a situation that they must either oppose themselves to the royal will, or violate the most sacred obligations of conscience and honour. Seditious the paper was not; for it had not been scattered by the writers among the rabble, but delivered privately into the hands of the King alone; and a libel it was not, but a decent petition such as, by the laws of England, nay by the laws of imperial Rome, by the laws of all civilised states, a subject who thinks himself aggrieved may with propriety present to the sovereign.

The Attorney replied shortly and feebly. The Solicitor spoke at great length and with great acrimony, and was often interrupted by the clamours and hisses of the audience. He went so far as to lay it down that no subject or body of subjects, except the Houses of Parliament, had a right to petition the King. The galleries were furious; and the Chief Justice himself stood aghast at the effrontery of this venal turncoat.

At length Wright proceeded to sum up the evidence. His language showed that the awe in which he stood of the government was tempered by the awe with which the audience, so numerous, so splendid, and so strongly excited, had impressed him. He said that he would give no opinion on the question of the dispensing power; that it was not necessary for him to do so; that he could not agree with much of the Solicitor's speech; that it was the right of the subject to petition; but that the particular petition before the Court was improperly worded, and was, in the contemplation of law, a libel. Allibone was of the same mind * * *. Holloway evaded the question of the dispensing power, but said that the petition seemed to him to be such as subjects who think themselves aggrieved are entitled to present, and therefore no libel. Powell took a bolder course. He avowed that, in his judgment, the Declaration of Indulgence was a nullity, and that the dispensing power, as lately exercised, was utterly inconsistent with all law. If these encroachments of prerogative were allowed, there was an end of Parliaments. The whole legislative authority would be in the King. "That issue, gentlemen," he said, "I leave to God and to your consciences."

It was dark before the jury retired to consider of their verdict. The night was a night of intense anxiety. * * *

The solicitor for the Bishops sate up all night with a body of servants on the stairs leading to the room where the jury was consulting. It was absolutely necessary to watch the officers who watched the doors; for those officers were supposed to be in the interest of the crown, and might, if not carefully observed, have furnished a courtly juryman with food, which would have enabled him to starve out the other eleven. Strict guard was therefore kept. Not even a candle to light a pipe was permitted to enter. Some basins of water for washing were suffered to pass at about four in the morning. The jurymen, raging with thirst, soon lapped up the whole. * * * Voices, high in altercation, were repeatedly heard within the room: but nothing certain was known.

At first nine were for acquitting and three for convicting. Two of the minority soon gave way: but Arnold was obstinate. Thomas Austin, a country gentleman of great estate, who had paid close attention to the evidence and speeches, and had taken full notes, wished to argue the question. Arnold declined. He was not used, he doggedly said, to reasoning and debating. His conscience was not satisfied; and he should not acquit the Bishops. "If you come to that," said Austin, "look at me. I am the largest and strongest of the twelve; and before I find such a petition as this a libel, here I will stay till I am no bigger than a tobacco pipe." It was six in the morning before Arnold yielded. It was soon known that the jury were agreed: but what the verdict would be was still a secret.

At ten the Court again met. The crowd was greater than ever. The jury appeared in the box; and there was a breathless stillness.

Sir Samuel Astry spoke. "Do you find the defendants, or any of them, guilty of the misdemeanour whereof they are impeached, or not guilty?" Sir Roger Langley answered, "Not Guilty." As the words were uttered, Halifax sprang up and waved his hat. At that signal, benches and galleries raised a shout. In a moment ten thousand persons, who crowded the great hall, replied with a still louder shout, which made the old oaken roof crack; and in another moment the innumerable throng without set up a third huzza, which was heard at Temple Bar. The boats which covered the Thames gave an answering cheer. A peal of gunpowder was heard on the water, and another, and another; and so in a few moments, the glad tidings went flying past the Savoy and the Friars to London Bridge, and to the forest of masts below. As the news spread, streets and squares, market places and coffeehouses, broke forth into acclamations. Yet were the acclamations less strange than the weeping. For the feelings of men had been wound up to such a point that at length the stern English nature, so little used to outward signs of emotion, gave way, and thousands sobbed aloud for very joy. * * *

* * *

The prosecution of the Bishops is an event which stands by itself in our history. It was the first and the last occasion on which two feelings of tremendous potency, two feelings which have generally been opposed to each other, and either of which, when strongly excited, has sufficed to convulse the state, were united in perfect harmony. Those feelings were love of the Church and love of freedom. * * * In 1688 the cause of the hierarchy was for a moment that of the popular party. More than nine thousand clergymen, with the Primate and his most respectable suffragans at their head, offered themselves to endure bonds and the spoiling of their goods for the great fundamental principle of our free constitution. The effect was a coalition which included the most zealous Cavaliers, the most zealous Republicans, and all the intermediate sections of the community. * * * Those classes of society which are most deeply interested in the preservation of order, which in troubled times are generally most ready to strengthen the hands of government, and which have a natural antipathy to agitators, followed, without scruple, the guidance of a venerable man, the first peer of the Parliament, the first minister of the Church, a Tory in politics, a saint in manners, whom tyranny had in his own despite turned into a demagogue. Many, on the other hand, who had always abhorred episcopacy, as a relic of Popery, and as an instrument of arbitrary power, now asked on bended knees the blessing of a prelate who was ready to wear fetters and to lay his aged limbs on bare stones rather than betray the interests of the Protestant religion and set the prerogative above the laws. With love of the Church and with love of freedom was mingled, at this great crisis, a third feeling which is among the most honourable peculiarities of our national character. An individual oppressed by power, even when destitute of all claim to public respect and gratitude, generally finds strong sympathy among us. * * * It is probable, therefore, that, even if no great political or religious interest had been staked on the event of the proceeding against the Bishops, England would not have seen, without strong emotions of pity and anger, old men of stainless virtue pursued by the vengeance of a harsh and inexorable prince who owed to their fidelity the crown which he wore.

Actuated by these sentiments our ancestors arrayed themselves against the government in one huge and compact mass. All ranks, all parties, all Protestant sects, made up that vast phalanx. * * * The Archbishop soon after his acquittal put forth a pastoral letter which is one of the most remarkable compositions of that age. He had, from his youth up, been at war with the Nonconformists, and had repeatedly assailed them with unjust and unchristian asperity. * * * But now his heart was melted and opened. He solemnly enjoined the Bishops and clergy to have a very tender regard to their brethren the Protestant Dissenters, to visit them often, to entertain them hospitably, to discourse with them civilly, to persuade them, if it might be, to conform to the Church, but, if that were found impossible, to join them heartily and affectionately in exertions for the blessed cause of the Reformation.

Many pious persons in subsequent years remembered that time with bitter regret. They described it as a short glimpse of a golden age between two iron ages. Such lamentation, though natural, was not reasonable. The coalition of 1688 was produced, and could be produced, only by tyranny which approached to insanity, and by danger which threatened at once all the great institutions of the country. If there has never since been similar union, the reason is that there has never since been similar misgovernment. It must be remembered that, though concord is in itself better than discord, discord may indicate a better state of things than is indicated by concord. Calamity and peril often force men to combine. Prosperity and security often encourage them to separate.

NOTES AND QUESTIONS

1. James's Declarations of Indulgence, which appear to be based on the proposition that there ought to be religious liberty for English subjects should have been popular measures, shouldn't they? Why were they not? In answering this question ask yourself, "What is the connection between the trial of the Seven Bishops and the controversy between Sir Edward Coke and James I?"

2. James II seems honestly to have believed that he had the power and the right to suspend operation of some statutes passed by Parliament (the "dispensing power"). Was this a novel idea? Would his grandfather, James I, have agreed? Why did the Seven Bishops disagree? When James II's brother, Charles II, had tried to exercise this power, as you read in the beginning of this excerpt, Charles II was persuaded to back down. Why did he forbear exercise of the dispensing power when James II did not? Does it help to know that James II regarded the word "republican" as an epithet? See J.P. Kenyon, The Stuarts 147 (1958). What, exactly, is a "republican," as the term was used in this excerpt from Macaulay? For that matter, what's a "Whig?" What's a "Tory?" Is the case of the Seven Bishops really about republicans, whigs, and tories? It is possible, of course, that James II did not perceive the issue of the dispensing power as a political one at all, but acted simply as a result of his adherence to the Catholic faith. He was reported to have said, for example, that "his principle aim" was "the advancement of the Catholic religion." Kenyon, supra, at 155. Still, does it seem to you that the Catholic–Protestant controversy in England is a sufficient explanation for the affair of the Seven Bishops? Note that the author of this excerpt, Lord Macaulay, frequently stresses that the Bishops were members of one of the Houses of Parliament, the House of Lords. Note also that when the Bishops were incarcerated in the Tower of London "[a]ll day the coaches and liveries of the first nobles of England were seen round the prison gates * * *." Why?

3. If Macaulay's account is accurate, the Trial of the Seven Bishops excited not only the nobles, but also the common people. Why do you suppose Macaulay finds it necessary to tell us that if King James II had put the Bishop of Cornwall, Trelawney, to death "Then thirty thousand Cornish boys" and "twenty thousand under ground" "will know the reason why?" Why would the "rustics in many parts of the country" expect at this time the resurrection of the Duke of Monmouth? Is Macaulay's account trustworthy? For a somewhat dryer-eyed version of James II's struggles to preserve Stuart principles of Royal supremacy, see J.R. Jones, Country and Court: England 1658–1714 234–255 (1978).

4. The procedures before and during the actual trial are worth some comment. Why did the Seven Bishops believe that they should be set free without posting bond? Note that this demand was not acquiesced in. We learn from this excerpt that it was the usual practice for prisoners held at the tower to pay the costs of their detention, even where, as here, they were released pending trial. Does this practice make sense to you?

5. Why was it that only "third-rank" lawyers could be induced to prosecute the Bishops, and how was it that the Bishops were able to recruit the best legal talent in England for their defense? You have seen that one of the Bishops' lawyers, the experienced but timid Sir Creswell Levinz, was even blackmailed into serving as defense counsel "by the whole body of attorneys who employed him," who told him that, "if he declined this brief, he should never have another." Why was this threat by "attorneys" that Creswell would never have another "brief" an effective one?

6. We will study seditious libel in a variety of contexts. For our purposes now, we can assume that the prosecution in a case of seditious libel must prove two elements—(1) publication, and (2) seditiousness. You will have seen that in the attempt to prove publication it was necessary for the Crown to prove that the document in question was actually written by the Bishops. The King had extracted this admission from them when he interrogated them in the Privy Council chambers. Why was the prosecution so hesitant to produce this particular bit of evidence? When the evidence was introduced, and it resulted in defense counsel Pemberton's accusing the King of breaking his promise to the Bishops, Macaulay suggests that Pemberton could have been immediately imprisoned by the Chief Judge, Wright. On what basis? Why did Wright decline to commit Pemberton after this affront to the King? How could Wright be "overawed" when he saw "the thick Rows of Earls and Barons by whom he was watched"?

7. On the basis of this excerpt, what do you take to be the test for "seditiousness?" Note that Macaulay says that to determine this question "It was necessary to enquire into the limits of prerogative and liberty, into the right of the King to dispense with statutes, into the right of the subject to petition for the redress of grievances." Did everyone involved agree that it was necessary to reach these "Constitutional" issues?

8. When one of the prosecutors argued that "no subject or body of subjects, except the Houses of Parliament, had a right to petition the King," writes Macaulay, "The galleries were furious * * * the Chief Justice himself stood aghast at the effrontery of this venal turncoat." Was the prosecutor's position really so ridiculous? Consider these comments from the actual charge to the jury of Allybone, J., commenting on whether the Bishop's petition "shall be in the construction of law a libel in itself, or a thing of great innocence.":

> * * * [N]o man can take upon him to write against the actual exercise of the government, unless he have leave from the government, but he makes a libel, be what he writes true or false; for if once we come to impeach the government by way of argument, it is the argument that makes it the government or not the government.
>
> * * * [N]o private man can take upon him to write concerning the government at all; for what has any private man to do with the government if his interest be not stirred or shaken? It is the business of the government to manage matters relating to the government. It is the

> business of subjects to mind only their own properties and interests. * * * If the government does come to shake my particular interest, the law is open for me, and I may redress myself by law. And when I intrude myself into other men's business that does not concern my particular interest, I am a libeller.
>
> * * * I do agree that every man may petition the government or the king in a matter that relates to his own private interest, but to meddle with a matter that relates to the government, I do not think my lords the bishops had any power more than any others. When the Houses of Lords and Commons are in being it is a proper way of applying to the king. * * * if every private man shall come and interpose his advice, I think there can never be an end to advising the government. * * *

12 Howell's State Trials 183, 427–28 (1688). Powell, J., disagreed with the interpretation of the law offered by Allybone. Powell maintained that unless a petition to the King was accompanied by "threats of the people's being discontented," it would not amount to seditious libel. Allybone replied that "every libel against the government carries in it sedition, and all the other epithets that are in the information." Id., at 429. What is Allybone's great concern about "popular petitions?" Would Allybone share Macaulay's belief about the relative *benefits* of discord?

9. What does the outcome of this trial suggest as to the connection between the crime of seditious libel and the rights and powers of King, parliament, and people? The notion that there is such a connection was clearly rejected by some of the Judges in the trial of the Seven Bishops, but do you think the jury agreed with these judges? Does it surprise you to learn that before the jury reached a verdict they were not permitted to eat, drink, or use candles? In the next reading, the trial of John Peter Zenger, we will further explore the early role of the jury, the nature of the law of seditious libel, and the implications for executive power.

10. Very soon after the trial of the Seven Bishops a coalition of English nobles invited the Protestant William, King of the Netherlands, to come to England. In the "Glorious Revolution" of 1688, William forced James II to flee England for France, and in 1689 William and his wife Mary (daughter of James II) became King and Queen of England. They were granted their crowns by the House of Lords and the House of Commons, which should tell you what implications about Parliamentary supremacy can be drawn from the events of 1688–89.

James's excesses in the Trial of the Seven Bishops went far toward provoking those who finally replaced him. In American law, however, the importance of the trial of the Seven Bishops has more to do with the jury's supposed defense of English liberties than it does with the power politics of Crown and Nobles, as you will see not only in the Zenger trial, but in the trial of Gideon Henfield, infra. The terms of the settlement of the crown on William and Mary, which altered the "constitution" of England, were written into the Bill of Rights of 1689, enacted in Parliament, and appeared in the Act of Settlement of 1701.

On the radical importance of the Bill of Rights of 1689, see Lois G. Schwoerer, "The Bill of Rights: Epitome of the Revolution of 1688–89," in Three British Revolutions: 1641, 1688, 1776, at 224 (J.G.A. Pocock, ed.1980), and on Locke and his importance to the Glorious Revolution of 1688, see Ms. Schwoerer's, "Locke, Lockean Ideas, and the Glorious Revolution," 51 Journal of the History of Ideas 531 (1990).

So ended the battle between Coke and James at the beginning of the century, and between divine right of Kings and Parliamentary Sovereignty during the Civil War. Perhaps the greatest legacy of the seventeenth century to Americans, however, was not so much in the eventual outcome of the struggle—Parliamentary Sovereignty—as in the means of its accomplishment: the "people" had taken into their own hands the right and power to set up a new form of government in accordance with a theory of the state.

CHAPTER 1

THE EMERGENCE OF THE THEORY OF THE POPULAR WILL AS THE BASIS OF LAW IN THE AMERICAN COLONIES: LEGAL AND CONSTITUTIONAL PERSPECTIVES ON THE AMERICAN REVOLUTION

■ ■ ■

A. INTRODUCTION

In less than a century, the North American colonies evolved from distant outposts into smaller-scaled replicas of English society, enjoying a high degree of political independence, each possessing a unique landed and commercial economy. By the middle of the eighteenth century, some of the colonies were beginning to rival the mother country in volume of trade and in population. In fact, after London, the largest urban concentrations of Englishmen were in the New World.

The colonies remained cognizant of their English commercial and political heritage. In places like New York, originally a Dutch settlement, the colonists themselves could be merciless cultural imperialists. As much as they could, they patterned their executive, legislative and judicial branches of government after those of the English; colonial lawyers purchased English law books and pleading manuals and cited English precedent in their courts. Colonials read English newspapers, followed London gossip and politics, and, when they could, journeyed to London itself to view the seat of learning and culture of their Empire. There was also considerable movement back and forth among top-level imperial personnel. Royal governors and their advisors generally resided in America for short periods of time, using colonial office as a stepping stone for some higher or more lucrative position in England. Deeper, more personal bonds between colony and mother country formed out of common language, culture, and kinship.

Ironically, their practical success in mimicking English society produced great stress for Americans. Colonials were acutely aware of the subtle differences that remained. They never quite replicated English government, nor were they permitted to. There were hedges, accretions of power peculiar to local circumstances, and legal peculiarities because of the particular necessities and customs of settlements. Together, these anomalies made colonial political life factious, unstable, and highly introspective. The royal governor of the colony was not quite a king, true to the English model, for his opponents could appeal over his head to the English Parliament or the administrative agency for the colonies, the "Board of Trade." The colonial assemblies were not quite like Parliament, since their enactments were subject to stringent review and possible rejection by the King and his ministers in London. The colonial councils, modeled on the English House of Lords, lacked real dignity and legitimacy in the absence of a titled American nobility. Finally, colonial law was not quite like that of the English, since everyone recognized the futility of applying *in toto* a common law, with its hoary medieval origins, to a society as diverse and derivative as America. As America lacked a traditional social structure and hierarchy of institutions based on legal privilege, the rulers were never far removed from the people. Self-rule became a way of life long before it became an article of belief. Nevertheless, the fiction of imperial societal identity persevered as long as colonials thought of themselves as Englishmen. And, as long as they thought of themselves primarily as participants in an English empire, they were bound to think of their political peculiarities in negative terms, as imperfect fragments needing repair or restructuring to bring them more in accord with the English originals.

The movement toward American independence could not begin until a new vision of American society recognized political validity in the historically determined colonial systems of government. When Americans began to view their "imperfections" as beneficial, and when the eighteenth-century English polity, instead of being idealized, came to be perceived as a corruption of some ancient constitutional order, then the logic of distant rule began to recede. This realization that classic English liberty remained pristine *only* in America was slow in coming. The feeling was encouraged by American observation of the newly-acquired sovereignty of the eighteenth century English Parliament, and by the perception of arbitrary rule by key ministers that Parliamentary absolutism eventually encouraged. The ultimate stimulus leading to a break was Parliament's dogged resolve in the 1760's to reestablish its mercantilist hold over the colonial economy. The most notorious of Parliamentary measures was the 1765 Stamp Tax. It was repealed within the year, but was soon followed by other taxing measures. These led to a vigorous debate among colonials over the province of English Parliamentary sovereignty in the New World. This pamphlet literature spawned a self-examination that grew into a wondrous self-discovery. The eventual severance from England from this point on became nearly inevitable.

The American Revolution was unlike any other; some have wondered if it was a revolution at all. The patriotic tracts of the 1760's and 1770's often read like debates over fine points of supposedly ancient law. Some have become classics of constitutional thought in the West. Official colonial resistance to Parliamentary enactments frequently took the form of colonial legislative "resolves." The Declaration of Independence itself issued from a "Congress duly convened," presented grievances in brief-like fashion, and appealed to a higher "law" than the dictates of the English Parliament or King. The new American "states" immediately set about constructing new governments based on written constitutions, and these documents were promoted as embodiments of the fundamental law that gave rise to the Declaration of Independence and was thought to have been reflected in the Magna Carta, the opinions and treatises of Sir Edward Coke, and the English Bill of Rights of 1689. Everywhere, it would seem, the language of the lawyer was evident, and this language, quoting ancient precedent, was used to support revolutionary acts.

It was in the sulphurous mix of law and politics of the 1760's and 1770's in America that a new ideology was born. The materials in this chapter are offered as glimpses into the process at work. True to the evolution of a Revolutionary frame of mind, they are set against the shifting background of individual personalities and local politics. Both factors, we believe, help explain the halting nature of development, the uncertain groping toward new modes of thought within an inherited framework of ideas.

Those interested in pursuing these themes might begin with the discussion of the evolution of American politics in Bernard Bailyn's now classic The Origins of American Politics (1965) and follow developments through his The Ideological Origins of the American Revolution (1967) and The Ordeal of Thomas Hutchinson (1974). Provocative insights into the nexus between colonial politics and law are to be found in Stanley N. Katz, The Politics of Law in Colonial America: Controversies Over Chancery Courts and Equity Law in the Eighteenth Century, 5 Perspectives in American History 257 (1971) (reprinted in hardcover as D. Fleming and B. Bailyn, eds., Law in American History (1971)) and Professor Katz's introduction and annotation of the trial of John Peter Zenger, A Brief Narrative of the Case and Trial of John Peter Zenger, by James Alexander (S.N. Katz, ed., 1963). Also useful for colonial legal history are the essays and the bibliographical introduction in David H. Flaherty, ed., Essays in the History of Early American Law (1969). Constitutional issues in the early state and federal governments are explored in Gordon S. Wood, The Creation of the American Republic 1776–1787 (1969), and Forrest McDonald, Novus Ordo Seclorum: The Intellectual Origins of the Constitution (1985) and legal issues are treated in Lawrence Friedman, A History of American Law 27–90 (1973), Morton Horwitz, The Transformation of American Law 1780–1860 1–30 (1977) and William Nelson, The Americanization of the Common Law: The Impact of Legal Change on Massachusetts Society, 1760–1830 1–64 (1975). The concept of "Republicanism" has emerged in the last few years as a useful tool in unlocking the political, legal, and constitutional problems of the eighteenth and nineteenth centuries. For works that employ a "Republican" analysis, see, e.g., the works cited and discussed in Morton Horwitz, Republicanism and Liberalism in American Constitutional Thought, 29 Wm. & Mary L.Rev. 57 (1987), and James T. Kloppenberg, The Virtues of Liberalism: Christianity, Republicanism, and Ethics in Early American Political Discourse, 74 J.Am.Hist. 9 (1987). Finally, and of importance throughout the readings in this casebook, cameos of English and American legal history are offered in the definitions of many terms in a good Law Dictionary such as Black's Law Dictionary (9th ed. 2009). No fledgling legal historian should be without one.

B. THE TRIAL OF JOHN PETER ZENGER FOR SEDITIOUS LIBEL

JAMES ALEXANDER, A BRIEF NARRATIVE OF THE CASE AND TRIAL OF JOHN PETER ZENGER, PRINTER OF THE NEW YORK WEEKLY JOURNAL* (1735)

S. Katz, ed., A Brief Narrative of the Case and Trial of John Peter Zenger Printer of the New York Weekly Journal by James Alexander 58–70, 71–77, 78–79, 81–83, 84–85, 87–88, 91–92, 95–96, 99–101 (1963).

[John Peter Zenger was a printer in the colony of New York in the early Eighteenth Century. By 1735 he had printed many items in his New York Weekly Journal which were critical of the Royal Governor of New York, William Cosby. These pieces were not written by Zenger, but were produced by political opponents of Cosby, one of whom was a man named James Alexander, an important New York lawyer. Zenger was prosecuted for the publication of these articles, pursuant to the legal doctrine of seditious libel, the same doctrine that was involved in the *Seven Bishops'* case. What follows are excerpts from what purports to be a report of Zenger's trial. Though it is supposedly written in the first person by Zenger, the document was actually produced by James Alexander, the anti-Cosby lawyer.

While the Zenger trial grew out of what was essentially a narrow provincial power struggle for the spoils of office, as one important study of the case suggests, it was nevertheless, "clearly the most significant political trial of the prerevolutionary period—perhaps of the entire colonial era." Paul Finkelman, "Politics, the Press, and the Law: The Trial of John Peter Zenger," in Michael R. Belknap, ed. American Political Trials 25, 26 (Revised, Expanded Edition, 1994). As you read the account of the trial, see if you can discern why it became of such great importance, and why this report of the case, reprinted many times, became " 'the most famous publication issued in America' before the revolution." Id., at 39.

This trial involves a number of complex matters, not all of which will be readily intelligible to you. As you read through the excerpts from the trial you should be looking principally for three things. First, the debate over the legal definition of the crime of seditious libel; second, the differing conceptions of the appropriate roles for judge and jury; and third, the ideas expressed about the proper participation in governance of the colony by governor and people and how this differed from the situation in England. "Mr. Attorney" is the Attorney General of the colony of New York, the prosecutor in the trial. "Mr. Hamilton" is one of Zenger's lawyers, an outside counsel brought in from Philadelphia following the disbarment of Zenger's original attorneys by "Mr. Chief Justice." The narrative begins with Mr. Attorney explaining and reading the "Information," the document which sets forth Zenger's offense, to the Judge and jury.]

[1. ZENGER'S ALLEGED CRIME]

Mr. Attorney. May it please Your Honors, and you, gentlemen of the jury; the information now before the Court, and to which the Defendant Zenger has pleaded not guilty, is an information for printing and publishing a false, scandalous and seditious libel, in which His Excellency the Governor of this Province, who is the King's immediate representative here, is greatly and unjustly scandalized as a person that has no regard to law nor justice; with much more, as will appear upon reading the information. This of libeling is what has always been discouraged as a thing that tends to create differences among men, ill blood among the people, and oftentimes great bloodshed between the party libeling and the party libeled. There can be no doubt but you gentlemen of the jury will have the same ill opinion of such practices as the judges have always shown upon such occasions: But I shall say no more at this time until you hear the information, which is as follows:

* * *

> * * * John Peter Zenger, late of the City of New York, printer (being a seditious person and a frequent printer and publisher of false news and seditious libels, and wickedly and maliciously devising the government of our said lord the King of this His Majesty's Province of New York under the administration of His Excellency William Cosby, Esq.; Captain General and Governor-in-Chief of the said Province, to traduce, scandalize and vilify, and His Excellency the said Governor and the ministers and officers of our said lord the King, of and for the

said Province to bring into suspicion and the ill opinion of the subjects of our said lord the King residing within the said Province) the twenty-eighth day of January * * * at the City of New York, *did falsely, seditiously and scandalously* print and publish * * * a certain *false, malicious, seditious, scandalous* libel, entitled *The New York Weekly Journal* * * * in which libel * * * among other things therein contained are these words:

> *Your appearance in print at last* gives a pleasure to many, though most wish you had come fairly into the open field, and not appeared behind *retrenchments* made of the supposed laws against libeling and of what other men have said and done before; these *retrenchments,* gentlemen, may soon be shown to you and all men to be weak, and to have neither law nor reason for their foundation, so cannot long stand you in stead: Therefore, you had much better as yet leave them, and come to what *the people of this City and Province* (the City and Province of New York meaning) think are the points in question (*to wit*) *They* (the people of the City and Province of New York meaning) *think as matters now stand that their* LIBERTIES *and* PROPERTIES *are precarious, and that* SLAVERY *is like to be entailed on them and their posterity if some past things be not amended, and this they collect from many past proceedings.* (Meaning many of the past proceedings of His Excellency the said Governor, and of the ministers and officers of our said lord the King, of and for the said Province.)

[The information then quoted a second article, also said to be a "false, malicious, seditious, and scandalous" libel:]

> *One of our neighbors* (one of the inhabitants of New Jersey meaning) *being in company, observing the strangers* (some of the inhabitants of New York meaning) *full of complaints, endeavored to persuade them to remove into Jersey; to which it was replied, that would be leaping out of the frying pan into the fire, for, says he, we both are under the same Governor* (His Excellency the said Governor meaning) *and your Assembly have shown with a witness what is to be expected from them; one that was then moving to Pennsylvania,* (meaning one that was then removing from New York with intent to reside at Pennsylvania) *to which place it is reported several considerable men are removing* (from New York meaning) *expressed, in terms very moving, much concern for the circumstances of New York* (the bad circumstances of the Province and people of New York meaning) *seemed to think them very much owing to the influence that some men* (whom he called tools) *had in the administration* (meaning the administration of government of the said Province of New York) *said he was now going from them, and was not to be hurt by any measures they should take, but could not help having some concern for the wel-*

fare of his countrymen, and should be glad to hear that the Assembly (meaning the General Assembly of the Province of New York) *would exert themselves as became them, by showing that they have the interest of their country more at heart than the gratification of any private view of any of their members, or being at all affected by the smiles or frowns of a governor* (His Excellency the said Governor meaning), *both which ought equally to be despised when the interest of their country is at stake. You, says he, complain of the lawyers, but I think the law itself is at an end;* WE (the people of the Province of New York meaning) SEE MEN'S DEEDS DESTROYED, JUDGES ARBITRARILY DISPLACED, NEW COURTS ERECTED WITHOUT CONSENT OF THE LEGISLATURE (within the Province of New York meaning) BY WHICH, IT SEEMS TO ME, TRIALS BY JURIES ARE TAKEN AWAY WHEN A GOVERNOR PLEASES (His Excellency the said Governor meaning), MEN OF KNOWN ESTATES DENIED THEIR VOTES CONTRARY TO THE RECEIVED PRACTICE, THE BEST EXPOSITOR OF ANY LAW: *Who is then in that Province* (meaning the Province of New York) *that call* (can call meaning) *anything his own, or enjoy any liberty* (liberty meaning) *longer than those in the administration* (meaning the administration of government of the said Province of New York) *will condescend to let them do it, for which reason I have left it* (the Province of New York meaning), *as I believe more will.* [The information concluded by charging that the publication of these articles by Zenger was:]

To the great disturbance of the peace of the said Province of New York, to the great scandal of our said lord the King, of His Excellency the said Governor, and of all others concerned in the administration of the government of the said Province, and against the peace of our sovereign lord the King his crown and dignity, etc. * * *

R. Bradley, Attorney General

To this information the Defendant has pleaded *not guilty,* and we are ready to prove it.

[2. THE LEGAL ARGUMENTS BEGIN]

Mr. Hamilton. May it please Your Honor; I am concerned in this cause on the part of Mr. Zenger the Defendant. The information against my client was sent me a few days before I left home, with some instructions to let me know how far I might rely upon the truth of those parts of the papers set forth in the information and which are said to be libelous. * * * I cannot think it proper for me (without doing violence to my own principles) to deny the publication of a complaint which I think is the right of every free-born subject to make when the matters so published can be supported with truth; and therefore I'll save Mr. Attorney the trouble of examining his witnesses to that point; and I do (for my client) confess that he both printed and published the two newspapers set forth in the information, and I hope in so doing he has committed no crime.

* * *

> [Here my journeyman and two sons (with several others subpoenaed by Mr. Attorney, to give evidence against me) were discharged, and there was silence in the Court for some time.]

Mr. Chief Justice. Well Mr. Attorney, will you proceed?

Mr. Attorney. Indeed sir, as Mr. Hamilton has confessed the printing and publishing these libels, I think the jury must find a verdict for the King; for supposing they were true, the law says that they are not the less libelous for that; nay indeed the law says their being true is an aggravation of the crime.

Mr. Hamilton. Not so neither, Mr. Attorney, there are two words to that bargain. I hope it is not our bare printing and publishing a paper that will make it a libel: You will have something more to do before you make my client a libeler; for the words themselves must be libelous, that is, *false, scandalous, and seditious* or else we are not guilty.

> [* * * Mr. Attorney [then] * * * observed upon the excellency as well as the use of government, and the great regard and reverence which had been constantly paid to it, both under the law and the gospel. That by government we were protected in our lives, religion and properties; and that for these reasons great care had always been taken to prevent everything that might tend to scandalize magistrates and others concerned in the administration of the government, especially the supreme magistrate. And that there were many instances of very severe judgments, and of punishments inflicted upon such, as had attempted to bring the government into contempt; by publishing false and scurrilous libels against it, or by speaking evil and scandalous words of men in authority; to the great disturbance of the public peace. And to support this, he cited 5 Coke 121 * * *, Wood's Instit. 430, 2 Lilly 168, I Hawkins 73.11.6. From these books he insisted that a libel was a malicious defamation of any person, expressed either in printing or writing, signs or pictures, to asperse the reputation of one that is alive or the memory of one that is dead; if he is a private man, the libeler deserves a severe punishment, but if it is against a magistrate or other public person, it is a greater offense; for this concerns not only the breach of the peace, but the scandal of the government; for what greater scandal of government can there be than to have corrupt or wicked magistrates to be appointed by the King to govern his subjects under him? And a greater imputation to the state cannot be than to suffer such corrupt men to sit in the sacred seat of justice, or to have any meddling in or concerning the administration of justice; And from the same books Mr. Attorney insist-

ed that * * * whether the libel is true or false, or if the party against whom it is made is of good or evil fame, it is nevertheless a libel: For in a settled state of government the party aggrieved ought to complain for every injury done him in the ordinary course of the law. He said it was likewise evident that libeling was an offense against the law of God. Act. XXIII. 5. Then said Paul, I wist not brethren, that he was the High Priest: For it is written, thou shalt not speak evil of the ruler of the People. 2 Pet. X. II. Despise government, presumptuous are they, self-willed, they are not afraid to speak evil of dignitaries, etc. He then insisted that it was clear, both by the law of God and man, that it was a very great offense to speak evil of or to revile those in authority over us; and that Mr. Zenger had offended in a most notorious and gross manner in scandalizing His Excellency our Governor, who is the King's immediate representative and the supreme magistrate of this Province: For can there be anything more scandalous said of a Governor than what is published in those papers?

* * * If this was not a libel, he said, he did not know what was one. Such persons as will take those liberties with governors and magistrates he thought ought to suffer for stirring up sedition and discontent among the people. And concluded by saying that the government had been very much traduced and exposed by Mr. Zenger before he was taken notice of; that at last it was the opinion of the Governor and Council that he ought not to be suffered to go on to disturb the peace of the government by publishing such libels * * *.]

* * *

[3. HAMILTON ON THE RIGHTS OF SUBJECTS AND THE DIFFERENCES IN LAW IN ENGLAND AND AMERICA]

Mr. Hamilton. May it please Your Honor; I agree with Mr. Attorney, that government is a sacred thing, but I differ very widely from him when he would insinuate that the just complaints of a number of men who suffer under a bad administration is libeling that administration. * * *

* * *

I was in hopes, as that terrible Court, where those dreadful judgments were given and that law established which Mr. Attorney has produced for authorities to support this cause, was long ago laid aside as the most dangerous court to the liberties of the people of England that ever was known in that kingdom; that Mr. Attorney knowing this would not have attempted to set up a Star Chamber here, nor to make their judgments a precedent to us: For it is well known that what would have been judged treason in those days for a man to speak, I think, has since not only been practiced as lawful, but the contrary doctrine has been held to be law.

* * *

Is it not surprising to see a subject, upon his receiving a commission from the King to be a governor of a colony in America, immediately imagining himself to be vested with all the prerogatives belonging to the sacred person of his Prince? And which is yet more astonishing, to see that a people can be so wild as to allow of and acknowledge those prerogatives and exemptions, even to their own destruction? Is it so hard a matter to distinguish between the majesty of our Sovereign and the power of a governor of the plantations? Is not this making very free with our Prince, to apply that regard, obedience and allegiance to a subject which is due only to our Sovereign? And yet in all the cases which Mr. Attorney has cited to show the duty and obedience we owe to the supreme magistrate, it is the King that is there meant and understood, though Mr. Attorney is pleased to urge them as authorities to prove the heinousness of Mr. Zenger's offense against the Governor of New York. * * * Let us not (while we are pretending to pay a great regard to our Prince and his peace) make bold to transfer that allegiance to a subject which we owe to our King only. What strange doctrine is it to press everything for law here which is so in England? I believe we should not think it a favor, at present at least, to establish this practice. In England so great a regard and reverence is had to the judges, that if any man strikes another in Westminster Hall while the judges are sitting, he shall lose his right hand and forfeit his land and goods for so doing. And though the judges here claim all the powers and authorities within this government that a Court of King's Bench has in England, yet I believe Mr. Attorney will scarcely say that such a punishment could be legally inflicted on a man for committing such an offense in the presence of the judges sitting in any court within the Province of New York. The reason is obvious; a quarrel or riot in New York cannot possibly be attended with those dangerous consequences that it might in Westminster Hall; nor (I hope) will it be alleged that any misbehavior to a governor in the plantations will, or ought to be, judged of or punished as a like undutifulness would be to our Sovereign. From all which, I hope Mr. Attorney will not think it proper to apply his law cases (to support the cause of his Governor) which have only been judged where the King's safety or honor was concerned. It will not be denied but that a freeholder in the Province of New York has as good a right to the sole and separate use of his lands as a freeholder in England, who has a right to bring an action of trespass against his neighbor for suffering his horse or cow to come and feed upon his land, or eat his corn, whether enclosed or not enclosed; and yet I believe it would be looked upon as a strange attempt for one man here to bring an action against another, whose cattle and horses feed upon his grounds not enclosed, or indeed for eating and treading down his corn, if that were not enclosed. Numberless are the instances of this kind that might be given, to show that what is good law at one time and in one place is not so at another time and in another place; so that I think the law seems to expect that in these parts of the world men should take care, by a good fence, to preserve their property from the injury of unruly beasts. And perhaps there may be as good reason why men should take the same care to make an honest and upright conduct a fence and security against the injury of unruly tongues.

Mr. Attorney. I don't know what the gentleman means, by comparing cases of freeholders in England with freeholders here. What has this case to do with actions of trespass, or men's fencing their ground? The case before the Court is whether Mr. Zenger is guilty of libeling His Excellency the Governor of New York, and indeed the whole administration of the government. Mr. Hamilton has confessed the printing and publishing, and I think nothing is plainer than that the words in the information are *scandalous, and tend to sedition, and to disquiet the minds of the people of this Province.* And if such papers are not libels, I think it may be said there can be no such thing as a libel.

Mr. Hamilton. May it please Your Honor; I cannot agree with Mr. Attorney: For though I freely acknowledge that there are such things as libels, yet I must insist at the same time that what my client is charged with is not a libel; and I observed just now that Mr. Attorney in defining a libel made use of the words *scandalous, seditious, and tend to disquiet the people;* but (whether with design or not I will not say) he omitted the word *false.*

Mr. Attorney. I think I did not omit the word *false:* But it has been said already that it may be a libel notwithstanding it may be true.

Mr. Hamilton. In this I must still differ with Mr. Attorney; for I depend upon it, we are to be tried upon this information now before the Court and jury, and to which we have pleaded *not guilty,* and by it we are charged with printing and publishing *a certain false, malicious, seditious and scandalous libel.* This word *false* must have some meaning, or else how came it there? * * * But to show that it is the principal thing which, in my opinion, makes a libel, I put the case, if the information had been for printing and publishing a certain *true* libel, would that be the same thing? Or could Mr. Attorney support such an information by any precedent in the English law? No, the falsehood makes the scandal, and both make the libel. And to show the Court that I am in good earnest and to save the Court's time and Mr. Attorney's trouble, I will agree that if he can prove the facts charged upon us to be *false,* I'll own them to be *scandalous, seditious* and *a libel.* So the work seems now to be pretty much shortened, and Mr. Attorney has now only to prove the words *false* in order to make us guilty.

Mr. Attorney. We have nothing to prove; you have confessed the printing and publishing; but if it was necessary (as I insist it is not) how can we prove a negative? But I hope some regard will be had to the authorities that have been produced, and that supposing all the words to be true, yet that will not help them, that Chief Justice Holt in his charge to the jury in the case of Tutchin made no distinction whether Tutchin's papers were *true* or *false;* and as Chief Justice Holt has made no distinction in that case, so none ought to be made here; nor can it be shown in all that case there was any question made about their being *false* or *true.*

* * *

[4. HAMILTON ARGUES TO THE COURT THAT TRUTH IS A DEFENSE]

Mr. Chief Justice. You cannot be admitted, Mr. Hamilton, to give the truth of a libel in evidence. A libel is not to be justified; for it is nevertheless a libel that it is *true.*

Mr. Hamilton. I am sorry the Court has so soon resolved upon that piece of law; I expected first to have been heard to that point. I have not in all my reading met with an authority that says we cannot be admitted to give the truth in evidence upon an information for a libel.

* * *

Mr. Chief Justice. I pray show that you can give the truth of a libel in evidence.

Mr. Hamilton. I am ready, both from what I understand to be the authorities in the case, and from the reason of the thing, to show that we may lawfully do so. But here I beg leave to observe that informations for libels is a child if not born, yet nursed up and brought to full maturity, in the Court of Star Chamber.

Mr. Chief Justice. Mr. Hamilton you'll find yourself mistaken; for in *Coke's Institutes* you'll find informations for libels long before the Court of Star Chamber.

* * *

Mr. Hamilton. I know it is said *that truth makes a libel the more provoking, and therefore the offense is the greater, and consequently the judgment should be the heavier.* Well, suppose it were so, and let us agree for once *that truth is a greater sin than falsehood:* Yet as the offenses are not equal, and as the punishment is arbitrary, *that is,* according as the judges in their discretion shall direct to be inflicted; is it not absolutely necessary that they should know whether the libel is *true* or *false,* that they may by that means be able to proportion the punishment? For would it not be a sad case if the judges, for want of a due information, should chance to give as severe a judgment against a man for writing or publishing a lie as for writing or publishing a truth? And yet this (with submission), as monstrous and ridiculous as it may seem to be, is the natural consequence of Mr. Attorney's doctrine *that truth makes a worse libel than falsehood,* and must follow from his not proving our papers to be *false,* or not suffering us to prove them to be *true.* But this is only reasoning upon the case, and I will now proceed to show what in my opinion will be sufficient to induce the Court to allow us to prove the truth of the words which in the information are called libelous. * * * [A]greeable to this it was urged by Sir Robert Sawyer in the trial of the seven bishops, *that the falsity, the malice, and sedition of the writing were all facts to be proved.* But here it may be said Sir Robert was one of the bishops' counsel, and his argument is not to be allowed for law: But I offer it only to show that we are not the first who have insisted that to make a writing a libel, it must be *false.* And if the argument of a counsel must have no weight, I hope there will be more regard shown to the opinion of a judge, and therefore I mention the words of Justice Powell in the same trial, where he says (of the petition of the bishops, which was called a libel, and upon which they were prosecuted by information) that *to make it a libel, it must be false and malicious and tend to sedition;* and declared, *as he saw no falsehood or malice in it, he was of opinion that it was no libel.* Now I should think this opinion alone, in the case of the King, and in a case which that King had so much at heart and which to this day has never been contradicted, might be a sufficient authority to entitle us to the liberty of proving the *truth* of the papers which in the information are called *false, malicious, seditious* and *scandalous.* If it be objected *that the opinions of the other three judges were against him,* I answer that the censures the judgments of these men have undergone, and the approbation Justice Powell's opinion, his judgment and conduct upon that trial has met with, and the honor he gained to himself for daring to speak truth at such a time, upon such an occasion, and in the reign of such a King, is more than sufficient in my humble opinion, to warrant our insisting on his judgment as a full authority to our purpose * * *. And in the case of Tutchin, which seems to be Mr. Attorney's chief authority, that case is against him; for he was upon his trial put upon showing the truth of his papers, but did not; at least the prisoner was asked by the King's counsel whether he would say they were *true*? And as he never pretended that they were true, the Chief Justice was not to say so. But the point will still be clearer on our side from Fuller's case, *for falsely and wickedly causing to be printed a false and scandalous libel, in which (amongst other things) were contained these words,* "Mr. Jones has also made oath that he paid ×5000 more by the late King's order to several persons in places of trust, that they might complete my ruin, and invalidate me forever. Nor is this all; for the same Mr. Jones will prove by undeniable witness and demonstration that he has distributed more than ×180,000 in eight years last past by the French King's order to persons in public trust in this kingdom." Here you see is a scandalous and infamous charge against the late King; here is a charge no less than high treason against the *men in public trust* for receiving money of the French King, then in actual war with the Crown of Great Britain; and yet the Court were far from bearing him down with that Star Chamber doctrine, *to wit, that it was no matter whether what he said was true or false;* no, on the contrary, Lord Chief Justice Holt asks Fuller, "Can you make it appear they are true? Have you any witnesses? You might have had subpoenas for your witnesses against this day. If you take upon you to write such things as you are charged with, it lies upon you to prove them true, at your peril. If you have any witnesses, I will hear them. How came you to write those books which are not true? If you have any witnesses, produce them. If you can offer any matter to prove what you have wrote, let us hear it." Thus said and thus did that great man Lord Chief Justice Holt upon a trial of the like kind with ours, and the rule laid down by him in this case is *that he who will take upon him to write things, it lies upon him to prove them at his peril.* Now, sir, we have acknowledged the printing and publishing of those papers set forth in the information, and (with the leave of the Court) agreeable to the rule laid down by Chief Justice Holt, we are ready to prove them to be true, at our peril.

Mr. Chief Justice. Let me see the book.

[Here the Court had the case under consideration a considerable time, and everyone was silent.]

Mr. Chief Justice. Mr. Attorney, you have heard what Mr. Hamilton has said, and the cases he has cited, for having his witnesses examined to prove the truth of the several facts contained in the papers set forth in the information, what do you say to it?

Mr. Attorney. The law in my opinion is very clear; they cannot be admitted to justify a libel; for, by the authorities I have already read to the Court, it is not the less a libel because it is true. I think I need not trouble the Court with reading the cases over again; the thing seems to be very plain, and I submit it to the Court.

Mr. Chief Justice. Mr. Hamilton, the Court is of opinion, you ought not to be permitted to prove the facts in the papers: These are the words of the book, "It is far from being a justification of a libel, that the contents thereof are true, or that the person upon whom it is made had a bad reputation, since the greater appearance there is of truth in any malicious invective, so much the more provoking it is."*

Mr. Hamilton. These are Star Chamber cases, and I was in hopes that practice had been dead with the Court.

Mr. Chief Justice. Mr. Hamilton, the Court have delivered their opinion, and we expect you will use us with good manners; you are not to be permitted to argue against the opinion of the Court.

---

* Mr. Chief Justice was here reading from `1 William Hawkins, A Treatise of the Pleas of the Crown 194 (1716–1721).

Mr. Hamilton. With submission, I have seen the practice in very great courts, and never heard it deemed unmannerly to—

Mr. Chief Justice. After the Court have declared their opinion, it is not good manners to insist upon a point in which you are overruled.

Mr. Hamilton. I will say no more at this time; the Court I see is against us in this point; and that I hope I may be allowed to say.

Mr. Chief Justice. Use the Court with good manners, and you shall be allowed all the liberty you can reasonably desire.

[5. HAMILTON TURNS TO THE JURY. WHAT IS A LIBEL?]

Mr. Hamilton. I thank Your Honor. Then, gentlemen of the jury, it is to you we must now appeal for witnesses to the truth of the facts we have offered and are denied the liberty to prove * * * And were you to find a verdict against my client, you must take upon you to say the papers referred to in the information, and which we acknowledge we printed and published, are *false, scandalous and seditious;* but of this I can have no apprehension. You are citizens of New York; you are really what the law supposes you to be, *honest and lawful men;* and, according to my brief, the facts which we offer to prove were not committed in a corner; they are notoriously known to be true; and therefore in your justice lies our safety. And as we are denied the liberty of giving evidence to prove the truth of what we have published, I will beg leave to lay it down as a standing rule in such cases, *that the suppressing of evidence ought always to be taken for the strongest evidence;* and I hope it will have that weight with you. But since we are not admitted to examine our witnesses, I will endeavor to shorten the dispute with Mr. Attorney, and to that end I desire he would favor us with some standard definition of a libel, by which it may be certainly known whether a writing be a libel, yea or not.

Mr. Attorney. The books, I think, have given a very full definition of a libel; they say *it is in a strict sense taken for a malicious defamation, expressed either in printing or writing, and tending either to blacken the memory of one who is dead, or the reputation of one who is alive, and to expose him to public hatred, contempt, or ridicule.* § 2. *But it is said that in a larger sense the notion of a libel may be applied to any defamation whatsoever, expressed either by signs or pictures, as by fixing up a gallows against a man's door, or by painting him in a shameful and ignominious manner.* § 3. *And since the chief cause for which the law so severely punishes all offenses of this nature is the direct tendency of them to a breach of public peace by provoking the parties injured, their friends and families, to acts of revenge, which it would be impossible to restrain by the severest laws, were there no redress from public justice for injuries of this kind, which of all others are most sensibly felt; and since the plain meaning of such scandal as is expressed by signs or pictures is as obvious to common sense, and as easily understood by every common capacity, and altogether *as provoking as that which is expressed by writing or printing, why should it not be equally criminal?* § 4. *And from the same ground it seemeth also clearly to follow that such scandal as is expressed in a scoffing and ironical manner makes a writing as properly a libel, as that which is expressed in direct terms; as where a writing * * * pretending to recommend to one the characters of several great men for his imitation, instead of taking notice of what they are generally esteemed famous for, pitched on such qualities only which their enemies charge them with the want of, as by proposing such a one to be imitated for his courage who is known to be a great statesman but no soldier, and another to be imitated for his learning who is known to be a great general but no scholar, etc., which kind of writing is as well understood to mean only to upbraid the parties with the want of these qualities as if it had directly and expressly done so**[*]

Mr. Hamilton. Ay, Mr. Attorney; but what certain standard rule have the books laid down, by which we can certainly know whether the words or the signs are malicious? Whether they are defamatory? Whether they tend to the breach of the peace, and are a sufficient ground to provoke a man, his family, or friends to acts of revenge, especially those of the ironical sort of words? And what rule have you to know when I write ironically? I think it would be hard, when I say *such a man is a very worthy honest gentleman, and of fine understanding,* that therefore I meant *he was a knave or a fool.*

* * *

Mr. Chief Justice. Mr. Hamilton, do you think it so hard to know words are ironical, or spoke in a scoffing manner?

Mr. Hamilton. I own it may be known; but I insist, the only rule to know is, as I do or can *understand* them; I have no other rule to go by, but as I *understand* them.

Mr. Chief Justice. That is certain. All words are libelous or not, as they are *understood.* Those who are to judge of the words must judge whether they *are scandalous* or *ironical, tend to the breach of peace,* or are *seditious:* There can be no doubt of it.

Mr. Hamilton. I thank Your Honor; I am glad to find the Court of this opinion. Then it follows that those twelve men must *understand* the words in the information to be *scandalous,* that is to say *false;* for I think it is not pretended they are of the *ironical* sort; and when they understand the words to be so, they will say we are guilty of publishing a *false libel,* and not otherwise.

Mr. Chief Justice. No, Mr. Hamilton; the jury may find that Zenger printed and published those papers, and leave it to the Court to judge whether they are libelous; you know this is very common; it is in the na-

[*] Also taken from Hawkins, supra.

ture of a special verdict, where the jury leave the matter of law to the Court.

Mr. Hamilton. I know, may it please Your Honor, the jury may do so; but I do likewise know they may do otherwise. I know they have the right beyond all dispute to determine both the law and the fact, and where they do not doubt of the law, they ought to do so. This of leaving it to the judgment of the Court *whether the words are libelous or not* in effect renders juries useless (to say no worse) in many cases; but this I shall have occasion to speak to by and by; and I will with the Court's leave proceed to examine the inconveniences that must inevitably arise from the doctrines Mr. Attorney has laid down; and I observe, in support of this prosecution, he has frequently repeated the words taken from the case of *Libel. Famosis* in 5. Co. This is indeed the leading case, and to which almost all the other cases upon the subject of libels do refer; and I must insist upon saying that according as this case seems to be understood by the Court and Mr. Attorney, it is not law at this day: For though I own it to be base and unworthy to scandalize any man, yet I think it is even villainous to scandalize a person of public character, and I will go so far into Mr. Attorney's doctrine as to agree that if the faults, mistakes, nay even the vices of such a person be private and personal, and don't affect the peace of the public, or the liberty or property of our neighbor, it is unmanly and unmannerly to expose them either by word or writing. But when a ruler of a people brings his personal failings, but much more his vices, into his administration, and the people find themselves affected by them, either in their liberties or properties, that will alter the case mightily, and all the high things that are said in favor of rulers, and of dignities, and upon the side of power, will not be able to stop people's mouths when they feel themselves oppressed, I mean in a free government. * * *.

* * *

[6. HAMILTON RETURNS TO THE THEME OF THE POLITICAL RIGHTS OF THE SUBJECT]

Mr. Hamilton. * * * I pray, what redress is to be expected for an honest man who makes his complaint against a governor to an Assembly who may properly enough be said to be made by the same governor against whom the complaint is made? The thing answers itself. No, it is natural, it is a privilege, I will go farther, it is right which all freemen claim, and are entitled to complain when they are hurt; they have a right publicly to remonstrate the abuses of power in the strongest terms, to put their neighbors upon their guard against the craft or open violence of men in authority, and to assert with courage the sense they have of the blessings of liberty, the value they put upon it, and their resolution at all hazards to preserve it as one of the greatest blessings heaven can bestow. * * * We know His Majesty's gracious intentions to his subjects; he desires no more than that his people in the plantations should be kept up to their duty and allegiance to the Crown of Great Britain, that peace may be preserved amongst them, and justice impartially administered; that we may be governed so as to render us useful to our Mother Country, by encouraging us to make and raise such commodities as may be useful to Great Britain. But will any one say that all or any of these good ends are to be effected by a governor's setting his people together by the ears, and by the assistance of one part of the people to plague and plunder the other? * * * when a governor departs from the duty enjoined him by his Sovereign, and acts as if he was less accountable than the Royal Hand that gave him all that power and honor which he is possessed of; this sets people upon examining and enquiring into the power, authority and duty of such a magistrate, and to compare those with his conduct, and just as far as they find he exceeds the bounds of his authority, or falls short in doing impartial justice to the people under his administration, so far they very often, in return, come short in their duty to such a governor. * * * For men who are not endued with wisdom and virtue can only be kept in bounds by the law; and by how much the further they think themselves out of the reach of the law, by so much the more wicked and cruel men are. I wish there were no instances of the kind at this day. And wherever this happens to be the case of a governor, unhappy are the people under his administration, and in the end he will find himself so too; for the people will neither love him nor support him. I make no doubt but there are those here who are zealously concerned for the success of this prosecution, and yet I hope they are not many, and even some of those I am persuaded (when they consider what lengths such prosecutions may be carried, and how deeply the liberties of the people may be affected by such means) will not all abide by their present sentiments. * * * There are others that are under stronger obligations, and those are such as are in some sort engaged in support of a governor's cause by their own or their relations' dependence on his favor for some post or preferment; such men have what is commonly called duty and gratitude to influence their inclinations, and oblige them to go his lengths. I know men's interests are very near to them, and they will do much rather than forgo the favor of a governor and a livelihood at the same time; but I can with very just grounds hope, even from those men, whom I will suppose to be men of honor and conscience too, that when they see the liberty of their country is in danger, either by their concurrence, or even by their silence, they will like Englishmen, and like themselves, freely make a sacrifice of any preferment of favor rather than be accessory to destroying the liberties of their country and entailing slavery upon their posterity.

* * *

* * * I think it will be agreed that ever since the time of the Star Chamber, where the most arbitrary and destructive judgments and opin-

ions were given that ever an Englishmen heard of, at least in his own country: I say prosecutions for libels since the time of that arbitrary Court, and until the Glorious Revolution, have generally been set on foot at the instance of the Crown or its ministers; and it is no small reproach to the law that these prosecutions were too often and too much countenanced by the judges, who held their places at pleasure (a disagreeable tenure to any officer, but a dangerous one in the case of a judge). To say more to this point may not be proper. And yet I cannot think it unwarrantable to show the unhappy influence that a sovereign has sometimes had, not only upon judges, but even upon Parliaments themselves.

It has already been shown how the judges differed in their opinions about the nature of a libel in the case of the seven bishops. There you see three judges of one opinion, that is, of a wrong opinion in the judgment of the best men in England, and one judge of a right opinion. How unhappy might it have been for all of us at this day if that jury had understood the words in that information as the Court did? Or if they had left it to the Court to judge whether the petition of the bishops was or was not a libel? No they took upon them, to their immortal honor! to determine both *law* and *fact,* and to *understand* the petition of the bishops *to be no libel, that is, to contain no falsehood nor sedition,* and therefore found them *not guilty.*

* * *

[7. HAMILTON REITERATES THE TASK OF THE JURY. CLOSING STATEMENTS]

Mr. Hamilton. * * * I must insist that where matter of law is complicated with matter of fact, the jury have a right to determine both. As for instance; upon indictment for murder, the jury may, and almost constantly do, take upon them to judge whether the evidence will amount to murder or manslaughter, and find accordingly; and I must say I cannot see why in our case the jury have not at least as good a right to say whether our newspapers are a libel or not libel as another jury has to say whether killing of a man is murder or manslaughter. The right of the jury to find such a verdict as they in their conscience do think is agreeable to their evidence is supported by the authority of Bushel's case, in Vaughan's Reports, pag. 135, beyond any doubt. * * * The reason given in the same book is *because the judge (as judge) cannot know what the evidence is which the jury have,* that is, *he can only know the evidence given in court; but the evidence which the jury have may be of their own knowledge, as they are returned of the neighborhood. They may also know from their own knowledge that what is sworn in court is not true; and they may know the witnesses to be stigmatized, to which the Court may be strangers.* But what is to my purpose is that suppose that the Court did really know all the evidence which the jury know, yet in that case it is agreed *that the judge and jury may differ in the result of their evidence as well as two* *judges may,* which often happens. And in pag. 148, the judge subjoins the reason why it is no crime for a jury to differ in opinion from the Court, where he says *that a man cannot see with another's eye, nor hear by another's ear; no more can a man conclude or infer the thing by another's understanding or reasoning.* From all which (I insist) it is very plain *that the jury are by law at liberty (without any affront to the judgment of the Court) to find both the law and the fact in our case* * * *.

* * *

* * * I sincerely believe that were some persons to go through the streets of New York nowadays, and read a part of the Bible, if it was not known to be such, Mr. Attorney, with the help of his *innuendoes,* would easily turn it into a libel. As for instance, *Is.* IX. 16, *The leaders of the people cause them to err, and they that are led by them are destroyed.* But should Mr. Attorney go about to make this libel, he would read it thus; *The leaders of the people* [*innuendo,* the Governor and Council of New York] *cause them* [*innuendo,* the people of this Province] *to err, and they* [the people of this Province meaning] *that are led by them* [the Governor and Council meaning] *are destroyed* [*innuendo,* are deceived into the loss of their liberty] which is the worst kind of destruction. * * * Then if Mr. Attorney is at liberty to come into court, and file an information in the King's name without leave, who is secure whom he is pleased to prosecute as a libeler? And as the Crown law is contended for in bad times, there is no remedy for the greatest oppression of this sort, even though the party prosecuted is acquitted with honor. And give me leave to say as great men as any in Britain have boldly asserted that the mode of prosecuting by information (when a Grand Jury will not find *billa vera*) is a national grievance, and greatly inconsistent with that freedom which the subjects of England enjoy in most other cases. * * *

Gentlemen; the danger is great in proportion to the mischief that may happen through our too great credulity. A proper confidence in a court is commendable; but as the verdict (whatever it is) will be yours, you ought to refer no part of your duty to the discretion of other persons. If you should be of opinion that there is no falsehood in Mr. Zenger's papers, you will, nay (pardon me for the expression) you ought to say so; because you don't know whether others (I mean the Court) may be of that opinion. It is your right to do so, and there is much depending upon your resolution as well as upon your integrity.

* * *

* * * [T]he question before the Court and you gentlemen of the jury is not of small nor private concern, it is not the cause of a poor printer, nor of New York alone, which you are now trying: No! It may in its consequence affect every freeman that lives under a British government on the

main of America. It is the best cause. It is the cause of liberty; and I make no doubt but your upright conduct this day will not only entitle you to the love and esteem of your fellow citizens; but every man who prefers freedom to a life of slavery will bless and honor you as men who have baffled the attempt of tyranny; and by an impartial and uncorrupt verdict, have laid a noble foundation for securing to ourselves, our posterity, and our neighbors that to which nature and the laws of our country have given us a right—the liberty—both of exposing and opposing arbitrary power (in these parts of the world, at least) by speaking and writing truth.

> [Here Mr. Attorney observed that Mr. Hamilton had gone very much out of the way, and had made himself and the people very merry: But that he had been citing cases not at all to the purpose; * * * All that the jury had to consider of was Mr. Zenger's printing and publishing two scandalous libels, which very highly reflected on His Excellency and the principal men concerned in the administration of this government, which is confessed. That is, the printing and publishing of the *Journals* set forth in the information is confessed. And concluded that as Mr. Hamilton had confessed the printing and there could be no doubt but they were scandalous papers * * * therefore he made no doubt but the jury would find the Defendant guilty, and would refer to the Court for their direction.]

Mr. Chief Justice. Gentlemen of the jury. The great pains Mr. Hamilton has taken to show how little regard juries are to pay to the opinion of the judges, and his insisting so much upon the conduct of some judges in trials of this kind, is done no doubt with a design that you should take but very little notice of what I might say upon this occasion. I shall therefore only observe to you that as the facts or words in the information are confessed: The only thing that can come in question before you is whether the words as set forth in the information make a libel. And that is a matter of law, no doubt, and which you may leave to the Court. But I shall trouble you no further with anything more of my own, but read to you the words of a learned and upright judge* in a case of the like nature.

> To say that corrupt officers are appointed to administer affairs is certainly a reflection on the government. If people should not be called to account for possessing the people with an ill opinion of the government, no government can subsist, for it is very necessary for all governments that the people should have a good opinion of it. And nothing can be worse to any government than to endeavor to procure animosities; as to the management of it, this has been always looked upon as a crime, and no government can be safe without it be punished.

---

* The Chief Judge reads from the opinion of Chief Judge Holt in Tutchin's Case, Rex v. Tutchin, 14 Howell's State Trials 1095, 1128 (1704).

Now you are to consider whether these words I have read to you, do not tend to beget an ill opinion of the administration of the government? To tell us, that those that are employed know nothing of the matter, and those that do know are not employed. Men are not adapted to offices, but offices to men, out of a particular regard to their interest, and not to their fitness for the places; this is the purport of these papers.

Mr. Hamilton. I humbly beg Your Honor's pardon: I am very much misapprehended, if you suppose what I said was so designed.

Sir, you know; I made an apology for the freedom I found myself under a necessity of using upon this occasion. I said there was nothing personal designed; it arose from the nature of our defense.

The jury withdrew and in a small time returned and being asked by the Clerk whether they were agreed of their verdict, and whether John Peter Zenger was guilty of printing and publishing the libels in the information mentioned? They answered by Thomas Hunt, their foreman, *Not Guilty,* upon which there were three huzzas in the hall which was crowded with people and the next day I was discharged from my imprisonment.

NOTES AND QUESTIONS

1. What exactly did Zenger publish? He seems to have suggested that Governor Cosby was taking steps that would plunge the colony into "slavery." How could that have been taken seriously? Why did Governor Cosby and his followers think that it was so terrible for Zenger to report gossip that people were leaving the colony? On the other hand, could the real irritation have been caused by Zenger's charges that the "law" was at an end in the colony, that judges were unfairly dismissed, and that trials by jury had been infringed? In this connection, is it important that, as was the case in the trial of the Seven Bishops, the proceeding was started against Zenger by an "Information?" The alternative to proceeding by information in a criminal matter is the securing of an indictment from a grand jury. Cosby tried and failed to obtain indictments against Zenger from grand juries.

The trial of Zenger was primarily the result of a struggle between opposing wealthy and powerful factions in the colony of New York. When Governor William Cosby arrived in 1732 he began a course of action by which he failed to steer between these contending groups of prominent New Yorkers. He soon collided with Lewis Morris, a New York and New Jersey politician who was then chief justice of the New York supreme court. In 1734, after Morris's court refused to cooperate in helping Cosby to recover some remuneration he claimed to be owed by another colonial official, Governor Cosby replaced Morris with James Delancey, "Mr. Chief Justice" at the trial. Morris and his supporters then launched a vigorous campaign to discredit Cosby. First, Morris ran successfully as an Assembly candidate from Westchester County, overcoming efforts by a pro-Cosby sheriff to fix the election against him. Second, the Morrisite faction, which included James Alexander, Zenger's original lawyer, gained control of the New York city council. Finally, the Morrisites established Zenger's New York Weekly Journal in order to print materials critical of Cosby. James Alexander wrote most of the articles, while Zenger, a German immigrant, handled the printing.

Before Zenger's trial Lewis Morris had gone to London himself to plead for Cosby's removal and for his own reinstatement as Chief Justice. Morris argued, among other things, that Cosby had accepted an illegal gift of one thousand pounds, that he had upset certain land titles, that he had wrongly taken part in legislative proceedings, and that he had failed to summon some members of the colony's upper house, the Council (the Morrisite members). The verdict in the Zenger trial was an important political victory for the Morrisites, who were able to use the trial in order to paint themselves as popular champions struggling against the arbitrary rule of Cosby and his supporters. Still, Cosby maintained a tight control over the New York Assembly, and Cosby managed to convince royal officials in London of his propriety and his competence. Cosby soon died, however, and was replaced by George Clarke, a respected member of the Council, and a more astute politician than Cosby. Clarke managed to appease the rival New York factions by distributing political and financial rewards in generous quantities to prominent members of both what had been the Cosbyite and Morrisite factions. Lewis Morris was soon made governor of New Jersey, where he eventually found himself in grave difficulties with a "popular" faction. The broad ideas expressed in the Zenger trial on freedom of speech critical of government as essential to liberty do not seem to have been as important to the Morrisites once they regained power, and, as we will soon see, the doctrine of seditious libel in America was very much alive even after American independence *and* the First Amendment to the Federal Constitution of 1787.

For a discussion of the lack of immediate practical impact of the Zenger case, and for a discussion of early American notions about freedom of the press in general, see Leonard Levy's Emergence of a Free Press (1985).

For an excellent and full account of the background of the Zenger trial and the legal issues involved see S. Katz, ed. A Brief Narrative of the Case and Trial of John Peter Zenger, Printer of the New York Weekly Journal 1–35 (1963). As indicated earlier, an astute treatment is Paul Finkelman, "Politics, the Press, and the Law: The Trial of John Peter Zenger," in Michael Belknap, ed., American Political Trials 25–44 (Revised Expanded Edition, 1994). See also, for a brilliant meditation on whether Zenger's attorney's efforts were really in the service of sensible law and politics, Eben Moglen, "Considering Zenger: Partisan Politics and the Legal Profession in Provincial New York," 94 Colum.L.Rev. 1495 (1994). Whatever the immediate impact on American politics and law of the Zenger trial, however, these issues are still well worth our examination, as they were never far from the surface of American affairs in the late eighteenth and early nineteenth centuries.

2. You will have noticed that almost at the very beginning of the case Hamilton admits for the record that Zenger published the newspaper articles in question, and that consequently, many witnesses were discharged. Following this admission by Hamilton there was "silence for some time" in the court. Why? Apparently "Mr. Attorney" thought that this admission by Hamilton was tantamount to a guilty plea. How could he think this? Is an explanation suggested by Mr. Attorney's position that it was worse to publish a "true libel" than a false one? Why would a "true libel" be worse? Can you relate this theory to the fears expressed by Judge Allybone about "discord" in the trial of the Seven Bishops? Does it help make sense of Mr. Attorney's argument to know that the Bible is quoted by him on the point that governments are sanctified because of their protection of life, religion, and property, and that the Bible actually states that it is wrong to criticize governors?

3. Contrast Hamilton's views on the sanctity of government with those of Mr. Attorney. In particular, note that Hamilton is at great pains to point out that a colonial governor is quite a different man from a King. Note, however, that Hamilton is not above criticizing Kings either. It seems important to his argument for him to criticize the "Star Chamber," the court which decided some of the English seditious libel cases. Hamilton attempts to disparage this case law by disparaging the court of Star Chamber. By the end of the sixteenth century the Star Chamber, whose origins as a court were somewhat obscure, had become "a separate court which exercise[d] 'the high and preeminent power' reserved to the King's Council 'in causes that might in example or consequence concern the state of the commonwealth.' " See generally 1 W. Holdsworth, A History of English Law 495–508 (paperback ed., 1969). Star Chamber was one of the "prerogative courts." Particularly under the Tudors, it was "bound to look into matters which might concern the safety of the state [and] it was not strictly bound by the straight rules of the common law in dealing with such matters." In addition to its work in punishing criminal libels, the Star Chamber court heard cases of conspiracy, riots, and "above all" it was used by the Tudor Kings to suppress religious dissidents, or "recusants." Holdsworth, supra, at 504. The court was able to act more effectively and swiftly than the common law courts; it had the power to examine witnesses on its own, and "where occasion required, it habitually employed torture." Id., at 505. The court of Star Chamber was formally abolished in 1641, a period when the English Parliament had begun to flex its muscles, to restrict the Royal prerogatives, and to set in motion the events that would lead to Revolution and Regicide. See, e.g., L. Smith, This Realm of England 1399–1688, 224–227 (3d ed., 1976). In light of this history, can you see some connection between the episode involving Coke and James I, the trial of the Seven Bishops, and Hamilton's argument at Zenger's trial? Note that Hamilton refers several times to the trial of the Seven Bishops and the public approbation of Judge Powell's opinion and the verdict in that case.

4. Even if Mr. Attorney's views on the English law of seditious libel were correct, Hamilton would not be willing to concede that the law was the same in America, would he? For example, he points out that in America the law would not order the cutting off of the right hand and the forfeiture of

goods of a man who struck another in the presence of sitting judges, though English law might theoretically require it. Hamilton also argues that the law of trespass would be different in America, since in America no one would have the right to bring an action for trespass when his neighbor's animals fed on his unenclosed land or ate his unenclosed corn, although such an action would lie for damage to enclosed or unenclosed land in England. Mr. Attorney replies to all of this by saying, "I don't know what the gentleman means, by comparing cases of freeholders in England with freeholders here." He suggests that this has nothing to do with the case at hand. Do you see the connection?

5. The comparison of English and American law comes before Hamilton launches into his argument to the court that evidence of the "truth" of a seditious libel should be admitted. Hamilton wants, in fact, to get the court to rule that truth is a defense to the crime of seditious libel. He demonstrates that the information was for publishing a "false, malicious, seditious, and scandalous" libel, and that in one case, that of John de Northampton, the falsity of what the defendant published was emphasized in his trial. Furthermore, Hamilton argues that one of the counsel in the Seven Bishops' trial, and one of the judges in that case, Powell, both maintained that falsity was an element of the crime. Hamilton stated that when one considered the approbation that Powell's opinion had met with since the trial "and the honor he gained to himself for daring to speak truth at such a time, upon such an occasion, and in the reign of such a King, [it] is more than sufficient * * * to warrant our insisting on his judgment as a full authority to our purpose * * *." Do you agree? Does approbation and honor make good law?

6. As well as citing authorities, Hamilton argues from "the reason of the thing." This is his argument that it is appropriate to admit evidence of the truth of the libel, even if true libels are *worse* than false ones, so that the appropriate punishment can be meted out. In other words, if the libels are in fact true, Hamilton is implicitly suggesting, this evidence should be admitted into court so Zenger can be more severely punished. Do you think that Hamilton intends this argument seriously? To whom in the courtroom is Hamilton speaking? Hamilton, "the most famous and skillful attorney in the colonies," reportedly "argued the case without fee, as a proper hero ought to do." Finkelman, supra, at 35, 26. Are you, however, impressed with the strictly legal quality of Hamilton's arguments? After examining the arguments that Hamilton makes in this case, and knowing that he was imported especially for the case from Philadelphia, do you understand what is meant by the term "Philadelphia lawyer?"

7. Assume that Hamilton wanted evidence of truth to be admitted for other purposes than punishing Zenger more severely. Note that the court rules that truth is *not* a defense, and further, that no evidence of truth may be introduced. The court makes this ruling after reading a contemporary law book, Hawkins, *Pleas of the Crown*. It is quite clear that the English law at the time of the Zenger trial was as stated in Hawkins. In light of this, how do you account for the fact that Hamilton is permitted to argue to the jury, fol-

lowing this ruling, that they can *presume* the truth of what Zenger published? Could it be that Hamilton is actually better off *not* being permitted to offer evidence of the truth of what Zenger published?

8. The jury finds Zenger "not guilty." Is this verdict in accordance with the instructions of the judge? Do you discern any differences between the manner in which the Zenger jury operated and your understanding of the way juries function today? The Zenger trial suggests the possibility of manipulating the jury in a manner that frustrates law enforcement, a perennial problem in American law. Jury trials are much less frequently used in civil law countries than they are in ours, and there is constant pressure for the elimination of jury trials in civil, if not criminal matters. Nevertheless, for an argument that "the democratized jury trial is 'one of the greatest achievements of our public culture'," see Robert P. Burns, A Theory of the Trial 9 (1999). Burns's book has been hailed as "unquestionably the best translation of the trial experience into academic language I've ever read," by political scientist Lief Carter, "Book Review," 12 The Law and Politics Book Review 102 (2002), and is the subject of a symposium in Volume 28, number 2, Spring 2003 issue of Law and Social Inquiry. For further reflection on the question of "jury nullification" and/or the Zenger trial, see, e.g., John Clark, "The Social Psychology of Jury Nullification," 24 Law & Psychol. Rev. 39 (2000), Matthew P. Harrington, "The Law–Finding Function of the American Jury," 1999 Wis. L. Rev. 377 (1999), Stanton D. Krauss, "An Inquiry Into the Right of Criminal Juries to Determine the Law in Colonial America," 89 J. Crim. Law & Criminology 111 (1998), David A. Pepper, "Nullifying History: Modern–Day Misuse of the Right to Decide the Law," 50 Case W. Res.L.Rev. 599 (2000), Simon Stern, Note, "Between Local Knowledge and National Politics: Debating Rationales for Jury Nullification After *Bushell's Case*," 111 Yale L. J. 1815 (2002).

9. Though Hamilton implicitly criticizes Tudor and Stuart absolutism, Hamilton is careful in his arguments not to cast aspersions on the current English monarch. This attitude did not prevail forever, as shown in the dispute in Virginia over what has come to be called the "Parsons' cause."

NOTE ON THE PARSONS' CAUSE

During the colonial period in Virginia the Church of England, as an established church, was publicly supported. Pursuant to legislation in colonial Virginia, ministers were to be paid, principally in tobacco, on an annual basis. Because the price of tobacco varied, so did the real wages of the clergy. In 1755 the first colony-wide attempt was made to provide for payments to the clergy in *currency* instead of tobacco. This statute "superceded" a 1748 Act on the same subject and provided for payment in currency at a rate slightly below the market value of the formerly-required tobacco payments.

At this time the activities of the colonial legislatures were circumscribed by the "Instructions" to the "Royal Governors," the Chief Executives of the colonies. These Instructions were written directions given by the King to his appointed governors, and, because they set certain limits on what the Governors and Colonial Legislatures could do, they were primitive analogues of our modern State and Federal Constitutions. See generally L. Labaree, Royal Instructions to British Colonial Governors (2 vols., 1935). The King also had the power of "Disallowance," the right to set aside any law passed by the assembly of one of the colonies. When the King formally approved of an Act, it was said to be "confirmed." In deciding whether to confirm or to disallow an Act, the King was advised by various officials, including the Privy Council and a special committee for the colonies, the "Board of Trade."

The 1755 Act probably violated two Royal Instructions. First, the Act was only to be in force for ten months, while the Instructions barred laws enacted for periods of less than two years. Second, the Instructions prohibited acts repealing former laws unless they were accompanied by clauses suspending them until the Crown's officers could decide whether or not they should be allowed. There was no suspending clause in the 1755 Act, and arguably it repealed the former act setting salaries, since the monetary equivalents were slightly below the market value of tobacco.

The Virginia clergy, since they correctly perceived that payments according to the 1755 statute would mean a reduction in their salaries, sought to avoid the effects of that law both by appeal to the King and by seeking redress in the colonial courts. Since the 1755 Act probably violated Royal instructions, the argument for royal disallowance was a very persuasive one. To allow the Act to stand would have been derogatory to the Royal prerogative, not only because of the Royal instructions, but also because the 1748 Act had been "confirmed" by the King. The Parsons argued to the King's ministers on the Board of Trade that to allow the 1755 act to "supercede" the 1748 Act which had received the King's approval would be to suggest that the colonial legislature was superior to the King. Agents for the colonial legislature in London argued that the failure of the tobacco crop had made the 1755 Act (and a 1758 Act in the same terms as the 1755 Act) necessary, and that since the duty to pay in tobacco would have been so onerous, the "clergy, as such, from Principles of Christianity ought to be first to acquiesce" in it. The Board of Trade, however, was convinced of the danger of allowing infringements on the Royal prerogative, and recommended that the King disallow the 1755 and 1758 Acts. In addition, the Board of Trade, on behalf of the King, strongly enjoined the Virginia governor from acquiescing in acts which were contrary to the King's instructions. Neither the King nor his agents, however, would go so far as to declare that the 1755 and 1758 Acts, having been disallowed, were void *ab initio,* and that the colonial courts should treat them as if they never existed. Had they so acquiesced in the wishes of the Parsons, the declaration of nullity *ab initio* would have allowed the Parsons to sue for the wages in tobacco they would otherwise have collected. Still, since there was also no declaration that the acts were valid until disallowed, it remained the task of the Virginia courts to declare whether the salaries could be paid in currency until the Acts were disallowed.

In one case, that of Clergyman Alexander White, the Virginia court ruled that the 1758 Act could be treated as valid until the disallowance, and while the governor might be subject to royal censure for violation of his instructions, this had no effect on the interim validity of colonial legislation. Through a technical error in the record, the court also prevented an appeal to the Courts in London. One case, that of John Camm, did make it on appeal to the King in Council, sitting, in effect, as a Supreme Court for the colonies. The ruling of the King in Council affirmed the Virginia court's holding against Camm, and the notes taken by the council's clerk suggest that the King in Council supported the argument that the Acts were not void *ab initio,* but remained in force until disallowed. For an account of these cases, and a discussion of the English constitutional implications, see Joseph Henry Smith, Appeals to the Privy Council from the American Plantations 607–626 (1950), on which the foregoing account has been based. Smith's recital of the circumstances of these cases strongly suggests that more was going on than the neutral application of constitutional or legal principles. Consider Smith's report on suits brought by parsons while Camm's appeal to the King in Council was pending:

> * * * The conduct of these suits was apparently handicapped by the reluctance of able counsel to plead the clerical cause and by the prejudicial conduct of [Virginia officials.] Cleric Thomas Warrington brought suit in the Elizabeth City County Court, but upon a special verdict the court as a matter of law adjudged the 1758 act valid. Plaintiff appealed to the General Court with some hopes of success, but the appellate court refused to hear any further causes until Camm's appeal was determined. The most publicized cause was that commenced by James Maury, preceptor of Thomas Jefferson and rector of Fredericksville parish, in the Hanover County Court in 1763. In this cause the court adjudged the 1758 act to be "no law," sustaining a demurrer that the act, not having received the royal assent, did not have the force of law and that it had been declared null and void by the King in Council. But a jury summoned on a writ of inquiry to settle the damages brought in only one penny for the plaintiff. Although the evidence was uncontradicted that the tobacco commuted at 16/8 per hundred pounds had a market value of 50 shillings per hundred, the jury was swayed to this determination by the irrelevant rhetoric of young Patrick Henry. This budding demagogue sought to show that the act of 1758 had every characteristic of a good law, that it was a law of general utility, and that it could not, consistently with an alleged original compact between the King and people, be annulled by the King. From this it was inferred that the King, by disallowing acts of a salutary nature, from being the father of his people, degenerated into a tyrant and forfeited all rights to the obedience of his subjects. Further strictures followed upon the unbecoming conduct of the clergy in the cause and their proper place in the societal structure. Counsel for Maury in vain urged that as the verdict was contrary to the weight of the evidence, the jury ought to be sent out again. The verdict was accepted by the bench; motions to have recorded the evidence of the plaintiff as to the quantum of damages and for a new trial were denied. * * *

Joseph H. Smith, Appeals to the Privy Council from the American Plantations 620–621 (1950). Copyright © 1950, by Columbia University Press, reprinted with the permission of the publisher and the author.

QUESTIONS

1. Do Patrick Henry's statements sound to you like the same deference toward the King that Hamilton professed in *Zenger?* Indeed, when clergyman Camm's suit was in the Virginia General Court, the highest court in the colony, after a lot of skirmishing in the pleadings, the defendants argued that "unless acts passed by the governor and legislature, although unjust and contrary to gubernatorial instructions and former confirmed acts, might stand as law, the people in Virginia were not free." Does this have anything to do with Henry's arguments?

2. Why does Professor Smith call Patrick Henry's comments on behalf of the defendants in Maury's case "irrelevant"? Henry argued that the 1758 Act "could not, consistently with an alleged original compact between the King and the people, be annulled by the King." What about the eventual verdict in Maury's case, said by Smith to have been produced by Henry? Why was the verdict, for the *plaintiffs,* the clergymen, a verdict of one penny, said to be "contrary to the weight of the evidence"? Why was Henry's argument that of a "budding demagogue"?

3. Why do you suppose the King in Council were unwilling to declare the 1755 and 1758 Acts void *ab initio?* Camm's final appeal to the King in Council was not decided until 1766. Note that shortly before this episode, in 1763, the French and Indian War was concluded. Could this be relevant? We turn next to the events of the 1760's and 1770's that might have concerned the King in Council, and that laid the foundation for the American Revolution.

4. Our treatment of the colonial period in American history is truncated by the need to produce a one-volume casebook, but there is a powerful case to be made that most, if not all, of the legal institutions of American legal history had their beginnings in the English colonies in the seventeenth and early eighteenth centuries. For some introductory materials to law in the colonial period, see, e.g., Jack P. Greene, ed., The Nature of Colony Constitutions: Two Pamphlets on the Wilkes Fund Controversy in South Carolina by Sir Edgerton Leigh and Arthur Lee (1970), Peter Charles Hoffer, Law and People in Colonial America (1992), and W. Keith Kavanaugh, ed., Foundations of Colonial America: A Documentary History, 3 vols. (1973), and Donald S. Lutz, ed., Colonial Origins of the American Constitution: A Documentary History (1998).

C. THE WRITS OF ASSISTANCE CASE

Paxton's case (1761), more popularly known as the "writs of assistance" case, may have been the most important legal event leading up to the American Revolution. John Adams said of the case, sixty years later,

"Then and there the child Independence was born." While other events of this era may have had more immediate political impact (for example the Stamp Act crisis of 1765), it is difficult to overestimate the importance of the legal and ideological thought that grew out of Paxton's case.

The "writ of assistance" took its name from the powers vested in the bearer, who could command the assistance of any local public official in making entry and seizure. Contraband goods discovered in the search were then placed in the custody of the Vice–Admiralty court sitting in Boston, where proceedings for condemnation and forfeiture were begun. Since Vice–Admiralty court typically sat without a jury and relied mainly on the testimony of customs officials and their informants, it was fairly easy for the government to produce a result favorable to its interests. Attorney–General Trowbridge drafted a "general" writ of assistance for the colony of Massachusetts in 1755. Customs officials had to apply to court for the writ, but from 1755 until 1760 the Chief Justice of the province, cooperating with the Attorney–General, routinely issued the general writ to customs officials allowing them to search houses and vessels for illegally imported merchandise.

In January 1760 the London Magazine published an article highly critical of "general" writs of assistance. The practice in English law, according to the anonymous author, was to countenance only "special" writs; writs issued on a one-time basis. This may have caused Chief Justice Sewall of the Massachusetts Superior Court to doubt the legality of the colony's general writ. Sewall died in September of 1760. Shortly thereafter James Paxton and others applied for the writ, but the Massachusetts court postponed acting in light of Sewall's "late doubt" and because of the vacancy on the court. In November, Thomas Hutchinson, then Lieutenant Governor of Massachusetts, was appointed to the vacancy. The new Chief Justice was widely known to be a friend of the general writ of assistance; he may even have had a hand in drafting the 1755 version. Paxton's application for the writ was to be heard in February of 1761. Hutchinson probably expected the hearing to be simply a conference before the bench involving no more than two or three attorneys.

A considerable public interest began to build, however. Paxton was growing notorious in the colony for his alleged racketeering in the customs business. He was currently a defendant in another government case, accusing him of embezzlement. The Boston Gazette labelled Paxton a "rat gnawing at the innards" of the city's life. The Gazette also portrayed the current Governor and Chief Justice Hutchinson as Paxton's patrons. The newspaper also reprinted the London Magazine article which questioned the legal basis of general writs. A group of prominent merchants petitioned the court to be heard on the question. The Massachusetts Surveyor–General of the Customs then entered the case and requested "to be heard on the same subject: And that writs of Assistance may be granted to himself and his officers as usual." The brilliant and fiery James Otis, Jr. then resigned his post as Advocate–General, which position would have required him to represent the Customs Office, and agreed to argue against the writ on behalf of Boston and of the petitioning merchants. The government then invited Jeremiah Gridley to argue its position in support of the general writs. Gridley was eminent in the colonial bar, and a whig in temperament and sympathy. He was a good friend and law teacher of both James Otis, Jr. and of John Adams. What had begun as a routine investigation was thus escalating into a great confrontation between Boston's merchants and the Royal provincial government.

Like the Zenger case, the writs case must also be understood in terms of local politics. An economic and political confrontation had been brewing in the colony for some years. Because of lax enforcement of the British customs laws, Boston smuggling was a common and respectable business in the eighteenth century. The entire molasses trade, essential to the New England economy, was built upon massive customs evasions. Royal customs officials at dockside often participated in evasions by extracting token customs for the sake of appearances in London, and many of these officials grew rich as a result. In the late 1750's, however, England needed money to finance the Seven Years War and sought it through customs revenue, pursuant to good mercantilist strategy. With the 1755 writ at their disposal, Boston officials began serious smuggling prosecutions. The Vice–Admiralty court cooperated, issuing judgments with uncommon speed and regularity. Especially galling to Bostonians was the fact that the admiralty judges, the customs officers, and customs informants were permitted a large share in forfeited booty. Nor were Bostonians unaware of the stinging inequities of their situation. Few judges in other colonies would grant the general writ of assistance. Neighboring Rhode Island, Boston's chief mercantile competitor, flouted the law with impunity. Rhode Island's Vice–Admiralty court uncharacteristically sat with a jury. Judgments against merchants were rare. Boston's economic woes worsened as the result of a disastrous fire in 1759. By 1760 a depression seemed to be settling over the city. In terms of total tonnage of trade, Boston slipped behind New York and Philadelphia.

Aggravating matters further was the instability of the current Massachusetts government. The years under Governor Shirley's administration, 1741–1757, had been politically harmonious because of his skill in dispensing patronage. Shirley was replaced by Thomas Pownall in 1757, and then Francis Bernard replaced Pownall in 1760. This rapid turnover upset fragile political alliances, and set off a wild run on patronage and position. This political in-fighting infiltrated virtually every level of government, including the administration of justice.

The Hutchinson–Otis controversy, an important sidelight of the writs case, illustrates these precarious politics. James Otis, *Sr.* actively lobbied for the Chief Justiceship after Sewall's death. Otis, Sr. had apparently understood that Lieutenant Governor Hutchinson, whose political star was on the rise, would lend his support. Besides, former Governor Pownall had promised Otis, Sr. a seat on the bench when one became available. One can thus understand Otis's anger and sense of betrayal when Governor Bernard appointed Hutchinson. Supporters of Otis and opponents of Bernard noted that the writs case was pending, Hutchinson's support of royal policy was well known, and that the Governor received one-third of all contraband confiscated in Massachusetts. Hutchinson retained his seat on the Council, a body usually allied with the Governor against the lower house. Otis, Sr., meanwhile, was the Speaker of the House. Both Otis, Sr. and Hutchinson were capable of using their authority in personal and partisan ways. It should be noted, finally, that in October and November James Otis, Jr. had represented his father in negotiating for Hutchinson's support for Otis, Sr.'s judicial ambitions, but resigned his government job immediately after his father's defeat. In such ways could personal animosity flare up into local political conflagration.

As you read the case and materials below, search for points of comparison and contrast with *Zenger*. Why was this case, more so even than *Zenger,* so important to colonial radicals? In what ways are the two cases similar? Review the earlier discussion of Sir Edward Coke and his conflict with the King, for he will figure prominently in the argument of Otis. Pay strict attention to the politicking in the arguments of counsel on both sides, and in particular to the elliptical movement from the political to the legal to the ideological in Otis's presentation.

1. THE FEBRUARY HEARING

Our chief source for what occurred in Hutchinson's courtroom at the first hearing of the case is John Adams. Adams sat in the gallery and took notes. Later, he expanded these notes into what he called an "Abstract." Portions of this Abstract appear below. Crucial to an understanding of the arguments at the hearing is a knowledge of the legislation involved (three English statutes and one Massachusetts statute). For this reason we have included a short explanation of the legislation.

II L. KINVIN WROTH AND HILLER B. ZOBEL, EDS., LEGAL PAPERS OF JOHN ADAMS*

107–113 (1965).

* * * The term "writ of assistance" had originally been applied to process in favor of a particular litigant in the Exchequer or in Chancery, enabling him to obtain the sheriff's help in collecting a debt or gaining pos-

session of property to which he was entitled. The writs sought by the Crown officials in Boston in 1761, however, were general standing warrants, good from the date of issue until six months after the death of the issuing sovereign, which permitted the holder to enter any house by day, with a constable or other officer, and there search for smuggled goods without special application to a court.

The earliest relevant statute, an Act of Parliament passed in 1660, authorized the issuance "to any person or persons" of a warrant to enter any house to search for specific goods, upon oath made of their illegal entry before "the lord treasurer, or any of the barons of the Exchequer, or chief magistrate of the port or place where the offense shall be committed, or the place next adjoining thereto."** Both the language and the legislative history of this enactment make reasonably clear that its purpose was to authorize a special search warrant of limited extent, under control of a higher authority. The statute central to the controversy was the Act of 1662, which, in setting up a comprehensive scheme of customs administration for the British Isles, first used "writ of assistance" to describe a customs search warrant. The act provided that "any person or persons, authorized by writ of assistance under the seal of his majesty's court of exchequer," might enter any premises in the day time, with a constable or other officer, using force if necessary, and there seize any contraband goods found.*** It has been argued on the basis of the language and legislative history of this and other contemporary acts, that the Act of 1662 was intended to incorporate no more than the special warrant embodied in the Act of 1660. The language of the two statutes is open to the contrary construction, however, and, since the parliamentary debates contain no affirmative statement on the precise point in question, contrary inferences may also be drawn from the legislative history. The actual intent of Parliament in the Act of 1662 thus cannot be determined.

Whatever the legislative intent, a course of practice under the statute soon developed which was a surer guide to construction in the courts than ambiguous language and incomplete history. There are some indications that in the years after 1662 searches were carried out under special warrant, probably as a result of an attempt to follow the former practice under the Act of 1660. Apparently, however, the view prevailed that the Act of 1662 had created a new process, limited neither by the earlier statute nor by practice under the ancient equitable writ. There is no reported decision on the point prior to the argument at Boston in 1761, but before 1685 a form of the writ granting unlimited powers of general search seems to have been in use in the Exchequer. Other evidence indicates that from some time in the first half of the 18th century, the writ was established as a general standing warrant issued by the Exchequer on the

** 12 Car. 2, c. 19 § I. (1660).

*** 13 & 14 Car. 2, c. 11 ¶ 5(2) (1662).

application of the Commissioners of Customs, to be held by the principal customs officers for use by them or their subordinates as the occasion demanded. Abuses of the instrument were probably avoided by virtue of the fact that ordinarily the principal officers required the same showing of information and probable cause that a justice would have required for the issue of a special search warrant. Furthermore, even with probable cause, the officer who searched and found nothing was liable in damages for the trespass.

The use of the writ in the colonies depended upon a third statute, the Act of 1696, by which colonial customs control was generally strengthened and reorganized, and colonial customs officials were given the powers of their English counterparts, whatever those might be.* In Massachusetts, both before and after the passage of this act, the powers of search granted to customs officers by statute and inherent in their commissions were exercised, but there is little affirmative evidence that general warrants were issued in support of these powers. According to Thomas Hutchinson, however, Governor Shirley, in office from 1741 until 1757, issued what were apparently general warrants to the customs officers. When Hutchinson himself pointed out the illegality of this practice, the Governor directed "the officers to apply for warrants from the superior court; and from that time, writs issued, not exactly in the form, but of the nature of writs of assistance issued from the court of exchequer in England."

This development brought a fourth act into play—a Province law of 1699 which conveyed to the Superior Court the powers of the Exchequer.**

JOHN ADAMS, "ABSTRACT" OF THE ARGUMENT IN THE WRITS OF ASSISTANCE CASE

The speeches of Mr. Gridley and Mr. Thacher appear in Quincy's Reports of Cases Argued and Adjudged in the Superior Court of Judicature of the Province of Massachusetts Bay, Between 1761 and 1772 479–82 (1865), Otis's remarks appear in the Massachusetts Spy for April 29, 1773, p. 3, cols. 1–3. Boston Superior Court February 1761.

* * *

Mr. Gridley. I appear on the behalf of Mr. Cockle*** and others, who pray "that * * * they cannot fully exercise their Offices in such a manner as his Majesty's Service and their Laws in such cases require, unless your Honors who are vested with the power of a Court of Exchequer for this Province will please to grant them Writs of Assistance * * *."

---

* 7 & 8 Will. 3, c. 22 § 6(2) (1696).

** 11 Will. 3, c. 3, 1 A & R 370 (1699).

*** James Cockle was Collector of Customs at Salem from 1760 to 1764. Cockle had applied for the Writ at about the same time Paxton did, although Paxton may have been the first to apply.

May it please your Honors, it is certain it has been the practice of the Court of Exchequer in England, and of this Court in this Province, to grant Writs of Assistance to Custom House Officers. Such Writs are mentioned in several Acts of Parliament, in several Books of Reports; and in a Book called the Modern Practice of the Court of Exchequer, We have a Precedent, a form of a Writ, called a Writ of Assistance for Custom House Officers, [which was issued in 1755] * * * to Mr. Paxton under the Seal of this Court, and tested by the late Chief Justice Sewall * * *.

The first Question therefore for your Honors to determine is, whether this practice of the Court of Exchequer in England * * * is legal or illegal. And the second is, whether the practice of the Exchequer (admitting it to be legal) can warrant this Court in the same practice.

In answer to the first, I cannot indeed find the Original of this Writ of Assistance. It may be of very ancient, to which I am inclined, or it may be of modern date. This however is certain, that the Stat. of the 14th. Car. 2nd.* has established this Writ almost in the words of the Writ itself. "And it shall be lawful to and for any person or persons *authorized by Writ of Assistance under the seal of his Majesty's Court of Exchequer* to take a Constable, Headborough, or other public Officer, inhabiting near unto the place, and in the day time to enter and go into any house, Shop, Cellar, Warehouse, room, or any other place, and in case of Resistance, to break open doors, Chests, Trunks and other Package, and there to seize any kind of Goods or Merchandize whatever prohibited, and to put the same into his Majesty's Warehouse in the Port where Seisure is made."

By this act and that of 12 Car.2nd.** all the powers in the Writ of Assistance mentioned are given * * *. Now the Books in which we should expect to find these Writs, and all that relates to them are Books of Precedents, and Reports in the Exchequer, which are extremely scarce in this Country; we have one, and but one that treats of Exchequer matters, and that is called the "Modern practice of the Court of Exchequer," and in this Book we find one Writ of Assistance * * *. Books of Reports have commonly the Sanction of all the Judges, but books of Precedents never have more than that of the Chief Justice. Now this Book has the Imprimatur of Wright, who was Chief Justice of the King's Bench, and it was wrote by Brown, whom I esteem the best Collector of Precedents; I have Two Volumes of them by him, which I esteem the best except Rastall and Coke. But we have a further proof of the legality of these Writs, and of the settled practice at home of allowing them; because by the Stat. 6th Anne which continues all Processes and Writs after the Demise of the Crown, *Writs of Assistance are continued among the Rest.****

---

* The 1662 Act, 13 & 14 Car. 2, c. 11 § 5(2).

** The 1660 Act, 12 Car. 2, c. 19 § I.

*** Since the courts were thought to derive their power of granting writs from the individual King, when the King died the new King had to continue, or reaffirm this power.

It being clear therefore that the Court of Exchequer at home has a power by Law of granting these Writs, I think there can be but little doubt, whether this Court as a Court of Exchequer for this Province has this power. By the Statute of the 7th. & 8th. W. 3d.,* it is enacted "that all the Officers for collecting and managing his Majesty's Revenue, and inspecting the Plantation Trade in any of the said Plantations, shall have the same powers & c. as are provided for the Officers of the Revenue in England; also to enter Houses, or Warehouses, to search for and seize any such Goods, and that the like Assistance shall be given to the said Officers as is the Custom in England."

Now what is the Assistance which the Officers of the Revenue are to have here, which is like that they have in England? Writs of Assistance under the Seal of his Majesty's Court of Exchequer at home will not run here. They must therefore be under the Seal of this Court. For by the law of this Province 2 W.3d. Ch. 3** "there shall be a Superior Court & c. over the whole Province & c. who shall have cognizance of all pleas & c. and generally of all other matters, as fully and [amply] to all intents and purposes as the Courts of King's Bench, Common Pleas and Exchequer within his Majesty's Kingdom of England have or ought to have."

It is true the common privileges of Englishmen are taken away in this Case, but even their privileges are not so in cases of Crime and fine. 'Tis the necessity of the Case and the benefit of the Revenue that justifies this Writ. Is not the Revenue the sole support of Fleets and Armies abroad, and Ministers at home? without which the Nation could neither be preserved from the Invasions of her foes, nor the Tumults of her own Subjects. Is not this I say infinitely more important, than the imprisonment of Thieves, or even Murderers? yet in these Cases 'tis agreed Houses may be broke open.

In fine the power now under consideration is the same with that given by the Law of this Province to Treasurers towards Collectors, and to them towards the subject. A Collector may when he pleases distrain my goods and Chattels, and in want of them arrest my person, and throw me instantly into Gaol. What! shall my property be wrested from me!—shall my Liberty be destroyed by a Collector, for a debt, unadjudged, without the common Indulgence and Lenity of the Law? So it is established, and the necessity of having public taxes effectually and speedily collected is of infinitely greater moment to the whole, than the Liberty of any Individual.

*Thacher.**** In obedience to the Order of this Court I have searched * * * but have not found any such Writ as this Petition prays. * * * I have found Two Writs which bear the Title of Brev. Assistentice, but these are

* The 1696 Act, 7 & 8 Will. 3, c. 22 § 6.

** The 1699 Act, 11 Will. 3, c. 3, 1 A & R 370.

*** Oxenbridge Thacher was asked by the court to argue. He appears to be allied with Otis.

only to give possession of Houses & c. in cases of Injunctions and Sequestration in Chancery. By the Act of Parliament any private Person as well as Custom House Officer may take a Sheriff or Constable and go into any Shop & c. and seize & c. (here Mr. Thacher quoted an Authority * * * which intended to shew that Writs of Assistance were only temporary things).

The most material question is whether the practice of the Exchequer is good ground for this Court. * * *

In England all Informations of uncustomed or prohibited Goods are in the Exchequer, so that the Custom House Officers are the Officers of that Court under the Eye and Direction of the Barons* and so accountable for any wanton exercise of power.

The Writ now prayed for is not returnable. If the Seizures were so, before your Honors, and this Court should enquire into them you'd often find a wanton exercise of power. At home they seize at their peril, even with probable Cause.

[*Otis:*]

I * * * appear not only in obedience to your order, but also in behalf of the inhabitants of this town, * * * and out of regard to the liberties of the subject. And I take this opportunity to declare, that whether under a fee or not, (for in such a cause as this I despise a fee) I will to my dying day oppose, with all the powers and faculties God has given me, all such instruments of slavery on the one hand, and villainy on the other, as this writ of assistance is. It appears to me (may it please your honours) the worst instrument of arbitrary power, the most destructive of English liberty, and the fundamental principles of the constitution, that ever was found in an English law-book. * * *

I shall not think much of my pains in this cause as I engaged in it from principle. I was sollicited to engage on the other side. I was sollicited to argue this cause as Advocate–General, and because I would not, I have been charged with a desertion of my office; to this charge I can give a very sufficient answer, I renounced that office, and I argue this cause from the same principle; and I argue it with the greater pleasure as it is in favour of British liberty, at a time, when we hear the greatest monarch upon earth declaring from his throne, that he glories in the name of Briton, and that the privileges of his people are dearer to him than the most valuable prerogatives of his crown.** And as it is in opposition to a kind of power, the exercise of which in former periods of English history, cost one King of

* The Exchequer judges were called "Barons."

** George III in his accession speech on November 18, 1760, had stated that "The civil and religious rights of my loving subjects are equally dear to me with the most valuable prerogatives of my crown: and, as the surest foundation of the whole, and the best means to draw down the divine favour on my reign, it is my fixed purpose to countenance and encourage the practice of true religion and virtue." Boston News–Letter, January 15, 1761, at 1 cols. 2–4.

England his head and another his throne. I have taken more pains in this cause, than I ever will take again: Although my engaging in this * * * has raised much resentment; but I think I can sincerely declare, that I cheerfully submit myself to every odious name for conscience sake; and from my soul I despise all those whose guilt, malice or folly has made my foes. * * * The only principles of public conduct that are worthy a gentleman, or a man are, to sacrifice estate, ease, health and applause, and even life itself to the sacred calls of his country. * * * I will proceed to the subject of the writ. * * * I will admit, that writs of one kind, may be legal, that is, special writs, directed to special officers, and to search certain houses, & c. especially set forth in the writ, may be granted by the Court of Exchequer at home, upon oath made before the Lord Treasurer by the person, who asks, that he suspects such goods to be concealed in THOSE VERY PLACES HE DESIRES TO SEARCH. The Act of 14th Car. II. [1662] which Mr. Gridley mentions proves this. And in this light the writ appears like a warrant from a justice of peace to search for stolen goods. Your Honours will find in the old book, concerning the office of a justice of peace, precedents of general warrants to search suspected houses. But in more modern books you will find only special warrants to search such and such houses specially named, in which the complainant has before sworn he suspects his goods are concealed; and you will find it adjudged that special warrants only are legal. In the same manner I rely on it, that the writ prayed for in this petition being general is illegal. It is a power that places the liberty of every man in the hands of every petty officer. * * *

In the first place the writ [that is sought by the customs officials in this case] is UNIVERSAL, being directed "to all and singular justices, sheriffs, constables and all other officers and subjects, & c." So that in short it is directed to every subject in the king's dominions; every one with this writ may be a tyrant: If this commission is legal, a tyrant may, in a legal manner also, controul, imprison or murder any one within the realm.

In the next place, IT IS PERPETUAL; there's no return, a man is accountable to no person for his doings, every man may reign secure in his petty tyranny, and spread terror and desolation around him, until the trump of the arch angel shall excite different emotions in his soul.

In the third place, a person with this writ, IN THE DAY TIME may enter all houses, shops, & c. AT WILL, and command all to assist.

Fourth, by this not only deputies, & c. but even THEIR MENIAL SERVANTS ARE ALLOWED TO LORD IT OVER US—What is this but to have the curse of Canaan with a witness on us, to be the servant of servants, the most despicable of God's creation. Now one of the most essential branches of English liberty, is the freedom of one's house. A man's house is his castle; and while he is quiet, he is as well guarded as a prince in his castle. This writ, if it should be declared legal, would totally annihilate this privilege. * * * This wanton exercise of this power is no chimerical suggestion of a heated Brain—I will mention some facts. Mr. Pew had one of these writs, and when Mr. Ware succeeded him, he endorsed this writ over to Mr. Ware, so that THESE WRITS ARE NEGOTIABLE from one officer to another,* and so your Honours have no opportunity of judging the persons to whom this vast power is delegated. Another instance is this.—Mr. Justice Wally had called this same Mr. Ware before him by a constable, to answer for a breach of the Sabbath day acts, or that of profane swearing. As soon as he had done, Mr. Ware asked him if he had done, he replied, yes. Well then, says he, I will shew you a little of my power—I command you to permit me to search your house for unaccustomed goods; and went on to search his house from the garret to the cellar, and then served the constable in the same manner. But to shew another absurdity in this writ, if it should be established, I insist upon it EVERY PERSON by 14th of Car. II. HAS THIS POWER as well as Custom-house officers; the words are, "it shall be lawful for any person or persons authorized, & c." What a scene does this open! Every man prompted by revenge, ill humour or wantonness to inspect the inside of his neighbour's house, may get a writ of assistance; others will ask it from self defence; one arbitrary exertion will provoke another, until society will be involved in tumult and in blood. Again these writs ARE NOT RETURNED. Writs in their nature are temporary things; when the purposes for which they are issued are answered, they exist no more; but these monsters in the law live forever, no one can be called to account. Thus reason and the constitution are both against this writ. Let us see what authority there is for it. No more than one instance can be found of it in all our law books, and that was in the zenith of arbitrary power, viz. In the reign of [Charles II] when Star-chamber powers were pushed in extremity by some ignorant clerk of the Exchequer. But had this writ been in any book whatever it would have been illegal. ALL PRECEDENTS ARE UNDER THE CONTROUL OF THE PRINCIPLES OF THE LAW. Lord Talbot says, it is better to observe these than any precedents though in the House of Lords, the last resort of the subject. No Acts of Parliament can establish such a writ; Though it should be made in the very words of the petition it would be void, "AN ACT AGAINST THE CONSTITUTION IS VOID." * * * But these prove no more than what I before observed, that *special* writs may be granted *on oath* and *probable suspicion*. The Act of 7th and 8th of William III. that the officers of the plantations shall have the same powers, & c. is confined to this sense, that an officer should show probable grounds, should take his oath on it, should do this before a magistrate, and that such magistrate, if he thinks proper should issue a special warrant to a constable to search the places. * * *

* The Editors of Adams's legal papers could find no documentation to support these charges of Otis's. * * * II Wroth and Zobel, supra, note 144.

It is the business of this court to demolish this monster of oppression, and to tear into rags this remnant of Star Chamber tyranny.—* * ***

* * *

NOTES AND QUESTIONS

1. You will remember that the Otis family and Thomas Hutchinson collided over the appointment to the Superior Court. Did this influence Otis's conduct in this hearing? What, exactly, were Otis Sr.'s feelings toward Hutchinson? The old conflict erupted again in 1765 with acrimonious charges and countercharges appearing in the Massachusetts Gazette. Otis Jr. charged that in 1760 Hutchinson had violated an "agreement" to support his father, which was contained in a letter. Here is Hutchinson's own recollection, written in 1765:

> The next day after the death of the late Chief Justice several gentlemen spake to me and told me they hoped the Governor would nominate me for his successor. It was some surprize to me, and I answered them in no other way than by thanking them for their favourable opinion of me, and expressing a diffidence of my own abilities. I was not determined in my own mind that it would be adviseable for me to undertake so great a trust; nor did I know the Governor's mind concerning it. Before the Chief Justice was buried Mr. OTIS came to [me] with a letter from his father desiring me, whom he had always looked upon as his friend, to use my interest with the Governor that he might be one of the Justices of the Superior Court. While I was reading the letter Mr. OTIS said to me, that he had heard one proposed for the place of Chief Justice, and if I had any thoughts of it, neither he nor his father had a word more to say, no person in the Province would be more agreeable to them; but if I had not, he thought his father had a better pretence to a place in the Court than anybody else, having been longer at the bar than any other gentlemen and having had the promise of the place in former administrations, to which facts I was knowing. I told Mr. OTIS the proposal to me was new and what I had not time to consider of, and expressed my doubts of my abilities to give the Country satisfaction. I said many civil things of his father, as I had done before and have since, and of the friendship there had been between us; but I must deny that I gave him any reason to suppose that I was determined to refuse the place; or that I promised to use my interests with the Governor that his father should be appointed.
>
> A few days after I received it I was informed by Gentlemen of undoubted veracity, that Mr. OTIS the Son had declared that neither he nor his father would give up their pretensions to the Lieutenant Governor nor any other person, that he uttered many revengeful threats; particularly, that he would do all the mischief he could to the Government, and would set

* This last sentence does not appear in the account in the Massachusetts Spy, but is to be found in the "Joseph Hawley Common Place Book," a manuscript copy of Adams's "Abstract." See generally II Wroth & Zobel, supra, at 134 n., 149 n.

> the Province in a flame, & c. if his father should not be appointed (the town was full of the talk of it) and I soon after had reason to suspect that these threats were carrying into execution. * * *

Quoted in M.H. Smith, The Writs of Assistance Case 216–217 (1978). When Hutchinson says that Otis had carried into execution his threat to "set the province aflame," what do you suppose he meant? Were Otis's arguments directed exclusively at the court?

2. Since Jeremiah Gridley was thought to be a friend of colonial liberty and a champion of Massachusetts causes, his willingness to argue the government's case must have raised a few eyebrows. Yet there may be something more in Gridley's decision. M.H. Smith, in his seminal The Writs of Assistance Case (1978), suggests that Gridley *and* Otis met privately with John Adams after the hearing to fill in Adams's Notes, thus giving birth to the remarkably complete "Abstract" in April, 1761. Id., at 285–287. Smith also believes that Gridley may have intentionally weakened the government's case. Id. at 282–285. Consider Gridley's interpretation of the 1660 and 1662 legislation, and Otis's point-by-point rebuttal. What would have been the effect of Gridley's talk of "necessity," and of his citation of Wright, C.J.? Where have you encountered Wright, C.J. before? If Gridley intentionally sabotaged the Government's case, and if Gridley helped Adams and Otis complete the account of the February hearing, what meaning, then, would Adams's Abstract have had?

3. Do you believe, with Otis, that the writs of assistance were the "worst instrument of arbitrary power, the most destructive of English liberty, and the fundamental principles of the constitution, that ever was found in an English lawbook?" Why does he think this? Incidentally, Otis suggests that the reign of Charles II was the "zenith of arbitrary power." Does that make sense? Is Otis's essentially rambling argument any more or less "relevant" than Hamilton's in the *Zenger* case or Henry's in the *Parsons' cause?* For a more clear-eyed discussion of what the term "liberty" really meant to eighteenth-century American lawyers see John Phillip Reid, The Concept of Liberty in the Age of the American Revolution (1988).

4. By now you should be able to grasp why Adams saw the "birth of the child Independence" at this dispute. Otis seems to have used Coke as a sort of midwife to give birth to the "child Independence." The question which then needs to be answered is whether Otis's use of Coke was motivated by something other than an objective reading and a neutral application of legal precedent.

Consider Bernard Bailyn's comments, in 1 Pamphlets of the American Revolution 411–13 (1965).* His discussion of Otis carries the analysis beyond

---

Otis's speech which you have just read, and shows on what authority Otis relied:

> * * * The ultimate problem, Otis said, was not so much the writs as the laws of Parliament controlling the American economy that made such writs necessary. These navigation laws and the writs issued to enforce them invaded the invaluable "privilege of house" by which every subject of English laws was rendered "as secure in his house as a prince in his castle." Both navigation laws and writs of assistance, therefore, violate "the fundamental principles of law"; both, therefore, run against the constitution, and they are, consequently, void. For "an act against the constitution is void: an act against natural equity is void: and * * * the executive courts must pass such acts into disuse," the common law having the power to control an act of Parliament.
>
> It was a doctrine familiar to English law; and to substantiate it Otis cited Coke's celebrated judgment in *Bonham's Case* (1610) that "it appears in our books that in many cases the common law will control acts of Parliament, and sometimes adjudge them to be utterly void: for when an act of Parliament is against common right or reason, or repugnant, or impossible to be performed, the common law will control it, and adjudge such act to be void"—to which Otis would add for further support the dicta of other seventeenth-century justices endorsing Coke's words * * * [But Otis may not have accurately presented Coke's views, because] Coke had not meant that positive, statute laws were restricted to areas defined by a higher law binding on Parliament and that they could be nullified—declared to be legally nonexistent—by the judges as custodians of the higher law when they exceeded these bounds. Nor had Coke conceived of his dictum as going beyond private law considerations into the realm of constitutional construction. Coke had meant only that the basis of statute law, like that of common law, was reason and justice, and that when laws created unreasonable or manifestly unjust or self-contradictory situations—situations wherein law violated the principles of law—it was the duty of the courts, not to annihilate the statutory provisions, but, as Coke's successor Hobart put it, "to mold them to the truest and best use." Coke's concern had been the traditional one of interpreting statutes strictly when reason and justice required it, adjusting, that is, in the lower courts inequities and impracticalities created by decrees of the highest court, Parliament.
>
> It was upon the judicial nature of Parliament, and its presumed devotion to the same principles of justice and reason that animated all courts of law that Coke's doctrine ultimately rested. And it was, consequently, the great historic shift in the understanding of Parliament's role that took place in the mid and later seventeenth century that gave a new meaning to Coke's doctrine, and that created for James Otis, a century later, the central intellectual problem of his life. In the course of the searing controversies of the English Civil War—controversies that de-

stroyed the foundations of public order and touched off a series of penetrating discussions of public authority—Coke's assumption that Parliament was animated by the same sense of justice and reason as other courts, and that its pronouncements were susceptible to equitable interpretation by judges, fell away before a conception of Parliament as the monopolist of absolute sovereign power, the creator, not the discoverer, of law, unbound by any rulings but its own. In the Glorious Revolution, which secured the absolute supremacy of Parliament over all other agencies of government, Coke's presumptions in *Bonham's Case* were, in effect, abandoned, and the location of an absolute and arbitrary legislative authority fixed firmly and indisputably in Parliament.—In effect abandoned: but not in law; for Coke's words, reinforced by later, more expansive pronouncements, remained on the books, to the bewilderment of those who would apply them to an absolute, unchallengable legislative sovereign distinct from courts of law. * * * By 1761, when Otis introduced the doctrine of *Bonham's Case* into the discussion of Anglo–American relations, the dominant understanding of English jurists and scholars—an understanding which colonial resistance would only confirm—was classically phrased by Blackstone, who admitted that the rule was familiar in law that acts of Parliament contrary to reason are void; "but if the Parliament will positively enact a thing to be done which is unreasonable, I know of no power that can control it." So too Lord Camden, who opposed the Stamp Act on the ground that "there are some things" a sovereign body cannot rightfully do, in the end concluded that once Parliament did declare its will against right "he did not think himself, nor any man else, at liberty to call it any more in question."

* * *

5. It is the "legalism" of colonial resistance, implicit in Otis's use of precedent and authority—indeed in the expression of discontent within the framework of a law case—which makes it difficult to label the Revolutionary movement as "radical" or "conservative." The question of whether the American Revolution was legal, or "constitutional" has been increasingly attracting the attention of scholars. For a fine review of some of this literature see Stephen A. Conrad, The Constitutionalism of "the Common-law Mind," 13 Law & Social Inquiry 619 (1988). The most ambitious effort to prove the "constitutionality" of the Revolution is John Phillip Reid's Magisterial three volume Constitutional History of the American Revolution (Vol. I, The Authority of Rights, 1986; Vol. II, The Authority to Tax, 1987; Vol. III, The Authority to Legislate, 1991).

As Bailyn notes, the emergence of a sovereign Parliament in the eighteenth century is an incident of the modernization of the state with a strong executive authority. The supremacy of the English common law as originally articulated by Coke would appear to be medieval in character, relying as it does on static and immutable principles of "right reason" and "justice." Were the American Revolutionaries some kind of political "throwbacks"?

6. Hutchinson suspended judgment following the arguments in February. It is likely that the court leaned in favor of Otis, and against the writs. It also appears that Hutchinson wanted to know more about the practice in England. He asked William Bollan, the colony's agent in London, to submit a memorandum on the English practice. Bollan's memorandum reached Hutchinson in August. Bollan stated that the Chief Justice had asked him whether writs of assistance were issued by the exchequer only in cases where there was "special information" and only where particular houses and particular goods sought were specified. What happened next, as Bollan later recalled, appears below:

* * *

> Mr. Bollan sent [the Chief Justice] a copy of the writ of assistance, taken out of the court of exchequer, which writ is directed to the officers of the admiralty, justices of peace, mayors, sheriffs, constables, & all other his Majestys officers, ministers, & subjects in England, requiring them to permit the commissrs. of the customs, & their officers by night or day to enter on board any vessel to search & c & in the daytime to enter the vaults, cellars, warehouses, shops, & other places where any goods & c lye conceal'd, or are suspected to lye conceal'd, for which the customs are not paid, to inspect & search for the said goods & c and to do all things which according to the laws in that behalf shou'd be done, and commanding them to be aiding & assisting to the said commissrs. & their officers in the execution of the premises. On the copy sent this endorsement was made, NB. These writs upon any application of the commissrs. of the customs to the proper officer of the court of exchequer are made out of course by him, without any affidavit, or order of the court.

* * *

Quoted in M.H. Smith, supra, at 541. Some time after the receipt of this copy of the English writ, the Massachusetts Superior Court hearing was reconvened.

2. THE NOVEMBER, 1761 HEARING

PAXTON'S CASE OF THE WRIT OF ASSISTANCE

Samuel M. Quincy, ed., Reports of Cases Argued and Adjudged in the Superior Court of the Province of Massachusetts Bay Between 1761 and 1762 by Josiah Quincy, Junior 51–57 (1865).

[We begin with Thacher's speech against the legality of the writs.]

Mr. Thacher first read the Acts of 14 Car. 2 [(1662)] and 7 & 8 of Wm. & Mary [1696], upon which the Request for this Writ is founded.

Though this Act of Parliament has existed 60 Years, yet it was never applied for, nor ever granted, till 1756; which is a great Argument against granting it; not that an Act of Parliament can be antiquated, but Non-user is a great Presumption that the Law will not bear it; this is the Reasoning of Littleton and Coke. * * * Moreover, when an Act of Parliament is not express, but even doubtfull, and then has been neglected and not executed, in such a Case the Presumption is more violent.

Ch. Justice. The Custom House Officers have frequently applied to the Governour for this Writ, and have had it granted them by him, and therefore, though he had no Power to grant it, yet that removes the Argument of Non-user.

Mr. Thacher. If this Court have a Right to grant this Writ, it must be either *ex debita Justitia* or discretionary. If *ex debita Justitia,* it cannot in any Case be refused; which from the Act itself and its Consequences, he argued, could not be intended. It can't be discretionary; for it can't be in the Power of any Judge at discretion to determine that I shall have my House broken open or not. As says Just. Holt, "There can be no discretionary Power whether a Man shall be hanged or no." * * *

He moved further that such a Writ is granted and must issue from the Exchequer Court, and no other can grant it; 4 Inst. 103; and that no other officers but such as constitute that Court can grant it. 2 Inst. 551. That this Court is not such a one, * * * This Court has in the most solemn Manner disclaimed the Authority of the Exchequer; this they did in the Case of McNeal of Ireland & McNeal of Boston. * * * This they cannot do in Part; if the Province Law gives them any, it gives them all the Power of the Exchequer Court; nor can they chuse and refuse to act at Pleasure. But supposing this Court has the Power of the Exchequer, yet there are many Circumstances which render that Court in this Case an improper Precedent; for there the Officers are sworn in that Court, and are accountable to it, are obliged there to pass their Accounts weekly; which is not the Case here. In that Court, there Cases are tried, and there finally; which is another Diversity. Besides, the Officers of the Customs are their Officers, and under their Check, and that so much, that for Misbehaviour they may punish with corporal punishment. * * * 7 & 8 W. & M. does not give the authority.

* * *

Mr. Otis. * * * Let a Warrant come from whence it will improperly, it is to be refused, and the higher the Power granting it, the more dangerous. The Exchequer itself was thought a Hardship in the first Constitution. [Otis here cited precedents from the time of Charles I, when the Privy Council authorized customs officers to break into houses, and he refers to practices in Massachusetts prior to 1755, when customs officers, simply by virtue of their commissions, engaged in similar breaking and entering. Is this relevant?]

It is worthy Consideration whether this Writ was constitutional even in England; and I think it plainly appears it was not; much less here, since it was not there invented till after our Constitution and Settlement. Such a Writ is generally illegal. Hawkins, B. 2, ch. 1, Of Crim.Jur., Viner, Tit. Commission, A., 1 Inst. 464 29M.*

Mr. Auchmuty. [arguing on behalf of the government.] * * * From the Words of the Law, this Court may have the Power of the Exchequer. Now the Exchequer always had that Power; the Court cannot regard Consequences, but must follow Law. * * *

Mr. Gridley. This is properly a Writ of Assist*ants,* not Assistance; not to give the Officers a greater Power, but as a Check upon them. For by this they cannot enter into any House, without the Presence of the Sheriff or civil Officer, who will always be supposed to have an Eye over and be a Check upon them. Quoting History is not speaking like a Lawyer. If it is Law in England, it is Law here; it is extended to this Country by Act of Parliament. * * * By Act of Parliament they are entitled to like Assistants, if the court cannot grant them it; and how can the Court grant them like Assistance, if they cannot grant this Writ. Pity it would be, they should have like Right, and not like Remedy; the Law abhors Right without Remedy. But the General Court [the Massachusetts Legislature, in the 1699 provincial Act] has given this Court Authority to grant it, and so has every other Plantation Court given their Superior Court.

The Justices were unanimously of Opinion that the Writ might be granted * * *.

3. BOSTON GAZETTE, 4 JAN. 1762

[Though appearing unsigned, this broadside was probably written by Otis.]

SINCE the advancement of so great a lawyer as the Hon. Mr. H–TCH–NS–N to the *first* J-st-s seat, it would be deem'd the highest impertinence for any one to express the least surprize, that the Superior Court of this province, should after *solemn hearing,* adjudge themselves authoriz'd to grant *such* a writ, as the WRIT OF ASSISTANCE; or even to doubt, whether *by law,* they have power so to do: I hope however, I may say without offence * * * that I heartily wish it never may [be used.]

* The authorities here referred to include the statements that "If commission issues to take J.S. and his goods, without indictment, or suit of the party, or other process, this is not good; for it is against the law." and "The surest construction of a statute is by the rule and reason of the common law." Otis probably is also here referring to Chapter 29 (originally Chapter 39) of Magna Carta, which provided (freely translated) that "No free man shall be taken, imprisoned * * * except by the law of the land."

* * * I do therefore *from principle* declare against an illicit trade; I would have it *totally* suppress'd, with this proviso only, *that* it may have the same fate in the other governments; otherwise all the world will judge it unequitable: it is because we only are severely dealt with, that we complain of unreasonable treatment * * *.

But it is not trade only that will be affected by this new severity: every householder in this province, will necessarily become *less secure* than he was before this writ had any existence among us; for by it, a *custom house officer* or ANY OTHER PERSON *has a power given him, with the assistance of a peace officer,* to ENTER FORCEABLY *into a* DWELLING HOUSE, *and rifle every part of it where he shall* PLEASE *to suspect uncustomed goods are lodgd*! * * * Will any one then under *such* circumstance, ever again boast of *british* honor or *british* privilege?—I expect that some *little leering* tool of power will tell us, that the publick is now amus'd with *mere chimeras* of an overheated brain; but I desire that men of understanding, and morals, would only recollect an instance of this sort; when a late comptroller of this port, by virtue of his *writ of assistance,* FORCEABLY enter'd into and rummag'd the house of a *magistrate* of this town; and what render'd the insolence intollerable, was, that he did not pretend a suspicion of contraband goods as a reason for his conduct, but it was only because the honest magistrate had a day before taken the liberty to execute a good and wholesome law of this province against the comptroller.—

IT is granted that upon *some occasions,* even a *brittish* freeholder's house may be forceably opened; but * * * it ought never to be done, and it never is done, but in cases of the most urgent necessity and importance; and this necessity and importance always is, and always ought to be determin'd by *adequate* and *proper* judges: Shall so tender a point as this is, be left to the discretion of ANY person, to whomsoever this writ may be given! shall the *jealousies* and *mere imaginations* of a custom house officer, * * * be accounted a sufficient reason for his breaking into a freeman's house! * * * what, if it should appear, that there was no just grounds of suspicion; what reparation will he make? is it enough to say, that damages may be recover'd against him in the law? * * * Is not this vexation *itself* to a man of a well disposed mind? and besides, may we not be insolently treated by our *petty tyrants* in *some* ways, for which the law prescribes no redress? and if this should be the case, what man will hereafter think his rights and privileges worth contending for, or even worth *enjoying.*

* * *

BUT admitting *there is such* a practice at home, and that it is not disputed, even at this time, when there is so warm a sense of liberty there; it may nevertheless be an Infringement upon the constitution: and let it be observed, there may be at some times a necessity of conceeding to measures there, which bear hard upon liberty; which measures ought not to be drawn into precedent here, because there is not, nor can be such necessity for them here; and to take such measures, without any necessity at all, would be as violent an infraction on our liberties, as if there was no pretence at all to law or precedent. It is idle then, to tell us we ought to be content under the same restrictions which they are under at home * * * when it is tolerated then only *thro' necessity,* and there is no necessity for it here. In *England* something may be said for granting these writs, tho' I am far from saying that anything can justify it. In *England* the revenue and the support of government, in some measure, depend upon the customs; but is this the case here? are any remittances made from the officers here? has the king's revenue, or the revenue of the province ever received the addition of a farthing, from all the collections, and all the seizures that have been made and forfeited, excepting what has been remitted by the late worthy collector Mr. *B-r-ns?*—I assert nothing: but if no benefit accrues to the publick, either here or at home, from all the monies that are receiv'd *for the use of the publick.* Is not this PECULATION? and what reason can there be, that *a free people* should be expos'd to all the insult and abuse, to the risque and even the *fatal consequences,* which may arise from the execution of a writ of assistance, ONLY TO PUT FORTUNES INTO PRIVATE POCKETS.

I desire it may be further consider'd, that the custom house officers at home, are under certain *checks* and *restrictions,* which they cannot be under here; * * * In *England* the exchequer has the power of controuling them in *every respect;* * * * and they do in fact account to it for money receiv'd, and for their BEHAVIOR, once every week—so that the people there have a short and easy method of redress, in case of injury receiv'd from them: but is it so here? Do the officers of the customs here account with the Superior Court, or lodge monies received into the hands of that court; or are they as officers under any sort of check from it?—Will they *concede* to such powers in the Superior Court? or does this court, notwithstanding *these* are powers *belonging* to the exchequer—notwithstanding *it is said to be vested with* ALL THE POWERS *belonging to the exchequer*—and, further, notwithstanding *this very writ of assistance* is to be granted AS a power belonging to the exchequer, will the Superior Court itself, assume the power of calling these officers to account, and punish them for misbehavior? * * * Have we not seen already, ONE of those officers, and he an *inferior* one too, REFUSING to account to *any power* in the province, for monies receiv'd by him *by virtue of his office,* belonging to the province, and which we are assured by the JOINT DECLARATION of the three branches of the legislature is UNJUSTLY as well as *illegally* detain'd by him? Does not every one then see that a writ of assistance in the hands of a custom house officer here, is in reallity a *greater* power & more to be dreaded, than it is in England? *greater* because UNCONTROUL'D—

and can a community be safe with an uncontroul'd power lodg'd in the hands of *such* officers, some of whom have given abundant proofs of the danger there is in trusting them with ANY?

NOTES AND QUESTIONS

1. Thacher's February and November arguments are largely concerned with the scope of powers that ought to be exercised by the Superior Court, and over what matters it ought to exercise jurisdiction. Why is it such a matter of concern to Thacher that the Massachusetts Superior Court of Judicature be limited to common-law jurisdiction? Why are the writs of assistance potentially more dangerous in the colonies, assuming that England and the colonies use the same form of writ? When Gridley intones that "Law and not History" should be used to resolve the case, what accusation is he levelling? Are not "law and history" the same things?

2. In the "anonymous" editorial, Otis contends that colonials should not be bound by legal practices in England which "bear hard upon liberty." He does admit, though, that sometimes it is necessary to limit liberty in pursuit of some higher policy. Why? According to Otis, is there a "higher policy" to recommend the general writ of assistance? How does he interpret the application of the writ in Massachusetts? Why might he still be inclined to view the writ as a provocation toward "bloody tumults?" What do you suppose Otis would believe a colony can do, if the English have mistaken the law? Does he imply that the *people* have a role?

3. Who was correct on the legality of the writs? The confusion about the actual state of the law in the writs case was evident as well in the Zenger case, but here it seems more profound. Consider the course of conduct and the views on the law of Writs of Assistance after 1761, discussed in the following reading. See if you can understand how law cases in the colonies became a means of resistance to England.

4. ENFORCING THE WRITS AFTER 1761: THE MALCOM–SHEAFFE EPISODE

While the writ of assistance was declared legal by the Massachusetts Superior Court, enforcing the writ was another matter. A successful search required the cooperation of an "assistant" to the customs officer, and, in a sense, the cooperation of the suspected smuggler. Does the following description of an encounter between a customs officer and a Boston merchant indicate that the cooperation of "the people" was also necessary? By this date, 1767, "the people" of Boston were an important political force. They rioted in 1765 when royal stamp officials attempted to enforce the infamous "Stamp Act."* Hutchinson's house was then burned to

* The Stamp Act, 26 Statutes at Large 179 (1765), was the first direct tax levied by Parliament upon America. It was designed to raise £60,000 annually, and the revenues were to help provide for British military forces in America. Special "stamps" showing prepayment of tax were to be affixed to virtually all papers. The Act required "stamps" on all legal documents, printed

the ground with "special savagery," in the words of Governor Bernard, probably in "payment" not only for perceived sympathies for the Stamp Act, but also for Hutchinson's position in the writs case. Though most colonial judges in the 1760s refused to grant the writ, Hutchinson did not take this "popular" course. Much pressure was thus brought to bear on the Massachusetts court by the people of Boston.

As resistance moved out of the courtroom and into the street, so did the habit of thinking in legal terms. It was after 1765 that the Writs case began to grow in importance—when Parliament's exercise of sovereign power to tax American colonists seemed to confirm Otis's prediction of "bloody tumults." Recall Otis's statement of America's dilemma: were the colonists bound to follow England's law, right or wrong? And if English law was wrong, what was the appropriate response? As you read the next excerpt, ask yourself if any of the participants in the episode acted "unlawfully."

M.H. SMITH, THE WRITS OF ASSISTANCE CASE**

443–453 (1978).

* * * [T]he sequence of events seems to have started with information given to the Boston custom house * * * that illegally imported wines and spirits had been taken to the house of Captain Daniel Malcom, a former seafarer and now a small-time merchant, in the early hours of 23 September 1766. They belonged to "one Simenton of Casco Bay," with whom Malcom and his partner William Mackay were known to have had dealing. Benjamin Hallowell, comptroller of customs, and William Sheaffe, deputy collector, laid plans to search Malcom's house the following morning, 24 September. They determined to use a writ of assistance in Hallowell's possession, and presumably it was in relation to this that they wrote to Stephen Greenleaf, sheriff of Suffolk County, asking him to meet with them at 8 A.M. However, Greenleaf was out of town; and a deputy sheriff, Benjamin Cudworth, * * * was enlisted instead. Two custom house understrappers attended in addition.

The party arriving at Malcom's dwelling, he admitted them, and allowed Hallowell and Sheaffe to look round the outbuildings and kitchen, and into a cellar. But when they asked to inspect a partitioned-off area of the cellar Malcom told them that this was in the tenancy of Mackay, and that he himself did not have the key. Sheaffe thereupon went off and asked for the key from Mackay, who protested that "it was very extraor-

---

matter, and playing cards. Penalties for non-payment could be imposed by vice-admiralty courts as well as the common law courts. Resistance to the act was unprecedented, and it was repealed in 1766. See generally Edmund S. & Helen M. Morgan, The Stamp Act Crisis: Prologue to Revolution (Rev. ed. 1962).

dinary Proceedings to search private Dwelling Houses," and instead accompanied Sheaffe back to Malcom's house. Outside he saw Deputy Sheriff Cudworth and the supporting customs men who had been posted there. * * * Mackay commented on this scene to Malcom: it was, he said, "beset by the whole Possey of the Custom House Officers and Mr. Cudworth the Deputy Sheriff." Malcom, who seems to have been fairly amiable up to now, reacted with an appropriate display of spirit. Or perhaps it was because the possibility of a forcible break-in was beginning to emerge. Hallowell and Sheaffe having, * * * "insisted upon having the said Cellar Door opened * * * Malcom solemly swore that it should not be & if any Man attempted it he would blow his Brains out." * * *

At this, Malcom put on a sword, took up a brace of pistols, and repeated his intention (as he himself put it) that "the first Man that would break upon my House without having Legal Authority for the same, I would kill him on the Spot." An attempt to persuade him of the customs officers' "Legal Authority" availed nothing. * * * It was a convincing show (although Malcom afterward claimed that the pistols were not loaded). * * * "Mr. Hallowell called me aside," William Mackay testified, "and begged I would advice Malcom to open the Doors and if there was anything there * * * he would endeavour to make it as easy as possible and that for Peace sake he would give up his Part [his share in the seizure] and Mr. Sheaffe would do the same * * *." * * *

After "near two Hours" expostulating with Malcom, and "the Deputy Sheriff Benjamin Cudworth not being willing to enter the said Cellar by Force," Hallowell and Sheaffe * * * went off to report the morning's frustrations * * *. [A]t the custom house they met up with Sheriff Stephen Greenleaf, now returned to Boston. The discomfited pair told Greenleaf of the Malcom fracas, and Hallowell showed him the writ of assistance "and desired him to go with him & the said Collector to aid and assist them in making proper Search * * *." * * *

It may be a sign that Greenleaf was still unconvinced about the writ of assistance that when he met with Hallowell and Sheaffe after lunch they presented him with not only the writ but with a warrant they had procured from Justice Foster Hutchinson (a brother of Lieutenant Governor and Chief Justice Thomas Hutchinson, and himself a reliable establishmentarian). This warrant, * * * had been issued upon Hallowell and Sheaffe swearing to having received information of an illegal importation concealed in Malcom's house; it ordered "the Civil Officers * * * to be aiding & assisting" Hallowell and Sheaffe "to Enter the House & Cellar of * * * Daniel Malcom." * * *

However, the warrant proved as useless as the writ * * *. This time Malcom had shuttered his windows and locked his doors; and not only were the search party thus barred from the house itself, a fastened gate kept them out of the curtilage as well. While Malcom sat indoors with

Mackay and a few other cronies the invaders fretted in the street outside, where the demeanor of bystanders was not such as to encourage heroic assault on the invested dwelling.

The possibility of public commotion had not gone unanticipated. [At a meeting of the Governor's Council called about this matter, where Sheriff Greenleaf was asked to assist the Customs officers] there had been talk of the sheriff raising the *posse comitatus,* an ancient institution of the common law whereby the "force of the county," consisting of practically all able-bodied men in the neighborhood, might be called out to quell tumultuous disorder. It was talk that accorded with the position taken by most of the councilors: the sheriff had powers enough of his own, and "any Aid from his Excellency and the Board does not appear, at present, to be needful." This was * * * the hesitation of councilors, whose concern for the government interest stopped well short of foolhardiness, to associate themselves with so unpopular a cause as customs search: under the stimulus of the Stamp Act experience the previous year a powerful patriot spirit was both in the air and on the streets. * * *

According to Sheriff Greenleaf and the customs men, the total failure that befell their afternoon expedition was explained and excused by the ugly rhubarbing of a hostile street mob whose numbers would be augmented in the event of an actual forcing of Malcom's house, by a ringing of the bell of the Old North meeting house. * * * The attitude of the onlookers/mobsters toward a call to assist was true to the local tradition of colorable legality: not so much outright refusal as insistence * * * that the name of the informer on Malcom first be made known and sworn to. Raising the *posse comitatus,* reported Sheriff Greenleaf rather needlessly, would have been "not only in vain, but highly imprudent." Time passed, darkness came on, and Greenleaf and the customs men called it a day: "The Warrant would not justify a forcible Entrance into any Dwelling House after sun set." The invaders thus routed, Malcom sent out some buckets of wine to his well-wishers in the street.

The sheriff and the customs men went straight to Governor Bernard to tell of the failure of their mission to search Malcom's house. They had been "obliged to quit it," they said, "having been assured that an Attempt to force it would cost some of them their Lives." Bernard had them return the following morning, to repeat their story before the Council. What he purposed—to gather attested descriptions of the Malcom affair that would remind Westminster yet again of Boston's incorrigible turbulence—naturally met with resistance from councilors of patriot sympathy. He was allowed to have his way, but apparently at the price of postponing actual despatch of the incriminating depositions. In the time thus gained a town meeting was convened, which set up a committee whose first task was to obtain copies of the tale as told by Sheriff Greenleaf and the custom house. This done, a batch of counterdepositions—orchestrated, probably, by James Otis—was collected, also for transmission to England.

Malcom himself disputed much that Hallowell and Sheaffe had said, he protested innocence of anything smuggled being under his roof, denied having seen (presumably in the afternoon, when he was barricaded indoors) "any Writ of Assistance nor any other Power or Authority whatsoever to break open my House," and asserted an intention to thwart or pursue the invaders only "in Law as far as Justice would go." * * * Benjamin Goodwin spoke of the bystanders he saw outside [Malcom's house]: "People that was passing by about their Business seeing the Officers in the Street askt what the Matter was and stood and talk't 5 or 6 or so, and I never saw People that was going to a Funeral behave more solemn and concern'd than they did. * * * "Other deponents testified to their being about fifty onlookers, all well-behaved. * * * As for a reported plan to ring the bell of the Old North, Paul Revere swore he had heard nothing of it * * *.

* * *

Counterdepositions playing down the Malcom incident were still being collected when Governor Bernard dispatched the originals, together with his own story, to the Earl of Shelburne and the Board of Trade on 10 October. But John Temple, surveyor general of customs, got in still earlier. Temple's report to the customs commissioners in London, * * * was dated 1 October. His turn of speed may have had something to do with an implacable hatred [of] Governor Bernard. Though the foot-dragging decision to leave Sheriff Greenleaf to his own resources in the afternoon expedition was less the governor's fault than the Council's, it would have been Bernard whom the authorities in London identified [as lacking firmness.] * * * It was all rather hard on Bernard. Not only was he belabored in the Boston press for letting on about the Malcom incident to the government in England: the man who got in first with the story, and whose own fealty to the crown interest was to become more and more ambiguous, was blaming him for the incident ever having happened.

The customs commissioners' reaction to the Temple report was not specially galvanic. * * * [T]he writ of assistance element had been overtaken by the Opinion of Attorney General De Grey on the question * * *. Writing to the Treasury on 31 October 1766, the commissioners had simply accepted De Grey's view that writ of assistance search had no lawful place in America and made the obvious recommendation, that it was "expedient to have the interposition of Parliament for granting the proper power to the Officers of the Revenue in America * * * ": in other words, the situation following from the De Grey Opinion needed to be put right by legislation. [The English customs commissioners forwarded a report on the incident to the English Treasury, and stated,] "In the Case now laid before Your Lordships, it is stated that the Officers had a Writ of Assistants legally granted. The Writ of Assistants directed by the Act of the 14th of King Charles 2nd is to be under the Seal of the Court of Exchequer, but the Court of Exchequer do not issue their Writs into the Plantations." * * *

The Treasury made no overt move until 14 January 1767. By this time Governor Bernard's collection of depositions had arrived in England; and the Board of Trade, no doubt aware that the Treasury already had papers on the same subject and glad enough of a reason to drop this hot potato * * * passed the entire batch over. Stimulated, perhaps, by Board of Trade agitation over the general law and order aspect, the Treasury took a bolder line than that recommended by the customs commissioners. * * * The crown's legal advisers must be asked to think again. Causing all the Malcom papers to be sent to the attorney general and solicitor general, the Treasury made no bones about "the violent resistance made by * * * [Malcom] * * * and others to the Execution of a legal Writ commanding Aid and Assistance to be given to the Officers of his Majesty's Customs * * * ", and squarely demanded "what proceedings may be fit to be carried on against the sd. Daniel Malcom for his Offences mentioned in the said Affidavits."

But there was no budging De Grey and his colleague. On February 6 De Grey and the Solicitor general again stated that

> no Civil Action or Criminal Prosecution can be brought against any of the Parties complained of, for obstructing the Officers of the Customs in the execution of their office, inasmuch as the Writ of Assistance by virtue of which they entered the House and Cellar was not in this case a legal Authority.

[the Treasury] * * * On 14 February tried again * * * :

> It has occurred to their Lordships that an Act of Assembly of the province of Massachsets Bay had passed & been confirmed by the King in the 11th year of Wm. the 3d. intitled an Act for establishing a Superior Court of Judicature within that province by which Act Jurisdiction and cognizance is given to that Superior Court of all matters as fully and amply to all Intents and purposes whatsoever as the Courts of King's Bench Common Pleas & Exchqr. within his Majestys Kingdom of England have or ought to have and it also appearing to my Lords upon a search made by their order amongst the papers and Documents of the Plantation Office that Writts of Assistance have been by constant usage since the period of passing that Act issued out of the Superior Court at Boston as a Court of Exchequer. My Lords direct me to desire you forthwith to lay this matter before Mr. Attorney and Mr. Sollr. Genl, together with the case and their opinion for their reconsideration whether as this Act of Assembly duly passed into a Law of the province is made supplementary to and in

> aid of the Act of the 7 & 8 of King William [the Act of Frauds, 1696], and as in fact & by constant usage the superior Court of the Province has exercised the Jurisdiction as a Court of Exchequer of Granting Writts of Assistance such Writt of Assistance do not give a legal Authority to the Officers of the Customs to search & c. * * *

Standards of historical research and reporting were none too high here: the Superior Court of Massachusetts, far from having issued writs of assistance from when it was first set up, took to the practice only in 1755; besides, any records of issuances were likelier to be with the customs commissioners than in the Plantation Office. * * *

* * * [T]here is no record of the law officers having replied * * *. Of course, for a working department, even the mighty Treasury, to bandy points of law with the law officers of the crown was to court a snub. All the same, it was not necessarily a case of the law officers merely standing on their dignity. A sense of the practical probabilities could have come into it. Aside altogether from the point of law, the factual evidence was by no means unanimous in the custom house's favor. The law officers could not ignore the sheaf of pro-Malcom testimony gathered by the Boston town meeting, and the strong likelihood that a local jury would prefer it and acquit Malcom in triumph.

* * *

And so in 1767 the British government decided to do what the customs commissioners had been recommending since the previous fall. The chancellor of the exchequer, Charles Townshend, included in his legislation for a new American import duty revenue a clause designed to establish writ of assistance search in all the colonies * * * :

> And whereas by an Act of Parliament made in the thirteenth and fourteenth Year of the Reign of King Charles the Second, intituled, An Act for preventing Frauds, and regulating Abuses, in his Majesty's Customs, and several other Acts now in Force, it is lawful for any Officer of his Majesty's Customs authorised by Writ of Assistances under the Seal of his Majesty's Court of Exchequer, to take a Constable, Headborough, or other Publick Officer inhabiting near unto the place, and in the Day-time to enter and go into any House, Shop, Cellar, Warehouse, or Room or other place, and, in case of Resistance, to break open Doors, Chests, Trunks, and other Package there, to seize, and from thence to bring, any Kind of Goods or Merchandize whatsoever prohibited or uncustomed, and to put and secure the same in his Majesty's Storehouse next to the Place where such Seizure shall be made: And whereas by an Act made in the seventh and eighth Years of the Reign of King William the Third, intituled, An Act for preventing Frauds, and regulating Abuses, in the Plantation Trade, it is, amongst other Things, enacted, that the Officers for collecting and

managing his Majesty's Revenue, and inspecting the Plantation Trade, in America, shall have the same Powers and Authorities to enter Houses or Warehouses, to search for and seize Goods prohibited to be imported or exported into or out of any of the said Plantations, or for which any Duties are payable, or ought to have been paid; and that the like Assistance shall be given to the said Officers in the Execution of their Office, as, by the said recited Act of the fourteenth Year of King Charles the Second, is provided for the Officers in England: But, no Authority being expressly given by the said Act, made in the seventh and eighth Year of the Reign of King William the Third, to any particular Court to grant such Writs of Assistants for the Officers of the Customs in the said Plantations, it is doubted whether such Officers can legally enter Houses and other Places on Land, to search for and seize Goods, in the Manner directed by the said recited Acts: To obviate which Doubts for the future, and in order to carry the Intention of the said recited Acts into effectual Execution, be it enacted, and it is hereby enacted by the Authority aforesaid, That from and after the said twentieth Day of November, one thousand seven hundred and sixty-seven, such Writs of Assistants, to authorise and impower the Officers of his Majesty's Customs to enter and go into any House, Warehouse, Shop, Cellar, or other Place, in the British Colonies or Plantations in America, to search for and seize prohibited or uncustomed Goods, in the Manner directed by the said recited Acts, shall and may be granted by the said Superior, or Supreme Court of Justice having Jurisdiction within such Colony or Plantation respectively.

* * *

Prominent among the draftsman's problems was that his phraseology could not allow it to appear, much less say outright, that customs search in the colonies was illegal. The law officers of the crown were free to say so in private exchanges with the Treasury and the customs commissioners [but] * * * care had to be taken that those notoriously litigious colonials were not given ideas. In Massachusetts searches with writ of assistance had been known for years; if the new legislation were so worded as to imply that every one of them had been unlawful, and therefore actionable as a trespass, the customs officers responsible would face ruinous liability in damages. Thus it was that section 10's recital of the preexisting law, while initially faithful to the Opinion of Attorney General De Grey—spelling out the 1662 enactment for writ of assistance search and bracketing the obscure 1696 text on to it—eased itself toward an altogether less hard-nosed position than De Grey's. In contrast to the law officers' unequivocal repudiation of colonial writs of assistance, section 10 did not close the door on all possibility of such writs having been valid. What appeared in intradepartmental files as a firm denial was presented to the public as a mere doubt. To the innocent reader section 10 would signify not a headlong rush to panic stations but rather a helpful, though not strictly necessary, clarification of the law as it already was. And to Bostonians and others who might otherwise have moved in on customs officers with writs for trespass it would mean nothing doing.

Legislation ostensibly "To obviate * * * Doubts" but in truth to head off certainty of trouble in the courts is an old trick of the lawsmith's trade. Section 10 of the Revenue Act of 1767 is a prize specimen.

NOTES AND QUESTIONS

1. Does this last excerpt suggest to you that English views on the legality of general writs of assistance were any clearer than American ones? The excerpt reveals that whatever may have been desired by the Lords of the Treasury and the Board of Trade, the English Attorney General believed in 1767 that general writs of assistance were illegal in the colonies, and that the English thought that a statute was necessary to "clarify" matters. Subsequent to the passage of this legislation, in 1768, the English Attorney General declared that such general warrants were legal, but, in 1771 a new Attorney General expressed the opinion that notwithstanding the legality of the writs, colonial courts which refused to grant them could not be ordered to do so by English courts.

2. As if the legal uncertainty in England were not enough, the local political situation also led to moves to counter the effect of the court's decision reached at the November hearing. The practice of plural office-holding, which was common in the colonies, seems to have aggravated the situation.

James Otis, Jr., serving in the Massachusetts House of Representatives, was a strong supporter of a 1762 bill that would have, in effect, forbidden Hutchinson's court to issue general writs of assistance. While there may have been some sympathy for the bill in the Governor's council as well, it is likely that the eventual veto of the bill by Governor Bernard was a result of persuasion by three of the Council members *who were also members of Hutchinson's court,* including Hutchinson himself! James Otis, Jr., "togeathere with a Number of Other firebrands" in the Assembly also saw to it that William Bollan was fired from his position as agent for the colonies in London.

Finally, shortly after the writs of assistance case, the Massachusetts House of Representatives, which set judicial salaries, reduced the salaries of the five judges of Hutchinson's court, and refused to vote Hutchinson the traditional extra payment for the Chief Justice. Smith, supra, at 434–437.

Plural office-holding was an aspect of colonial life that became an important grievance at the time of the American revolution, and which was subject to criticism much earlier, as you may have been able to discern from the materials regarding the Zenger trial. Do you understand why it was perceived as an "evil?"

3. Hutchinson's court upheld the issuance of the general writ of assistance in 1761, a decision favorable to the collection of English duties. What would happen, however, when a case involving compliance with British duties was to be decided by an American jury? You have seen how the Zenger jury responded to pleas on behalf of the government. How would you expect juries to behave in customs cases? Perhaps the most prominent student of this matter has declared that the civil traverse jury "especially in Massachusetts" was "perhaps the most unrenowned instrument the whigs possessed" in "their arsenal of legal warfare," and that "Naval officers who seized vessels for violating the trade or navigation statutes faced the prospect of being sued for large sums and having both their assets and their careers tied up for years in litigation." John Reid, In a Defiant Stance: The Conditions of Law in Massachusetts Bay, the Irish Comparison, and the Coming of the American Revolution 27–28 (1977). What was an American Governmental official who considered himself a loyal servant of the British Empire to make of this? In the next reading we find out.

D. MOVING TOWARD REVOLUTION

1. THE ATTITUDE OF THE LOYALISTS

BERNARD BAILYN, THE ORDEAL OF THOMAS HUTCHINSON*

70–107.

[We have already seen something of Thomas Hutchinson's activities as Chief Justice of Massachusetts, in the materials on the Writs of Assistance. He also served as the last Royal Governor of the colony of Massachusetts. He held this position at the time we read of him here.]

[A. THE SITUATION IN 1765]

* * *

There was no doubt by the summer of 1765 that the passions of the people had been aroused—aroused beyond anything Hutchinson, in his long career in public life, had ever seen before. Some great transformation had taken place. * * * "Patriots" who now would die rather than submit to the Stamp Act, he wrote in March 1766, had been angling for jobs with the stamp distributors just a few months earlier. When the inflammatory Virginia resolves** were received in Boston "a new spirit appeared at once. An act of Parliament against our natural rights was ipso facto void

* Copyright © 1974 by Bernard Bailyn. Published by the Belknap Press of Harvard University Press. Reprinted with the permission of the publisher and the author.

** The "Virginia Resolutions" were introduced by Patrick Henry before the Virginia House of Burgesses with his famous "treason" speech on May 29, 1765. The gist of the "Resolutions" or "Resolves" was that the colonists' legislatures had the sole legal and constitutional right to regulate internal affairs, and that there should be no Parliamentary taxation of Americans without American representation in Parliament.

and the people were bound to unite against the execution of it * * * it is the universal voice of all people, that if the Stamp Act must take place we are absolute slaves. There is no reasoning with them, you are immediately pronounced an enemy to your country." * * * He knew a country gentleman * * * whose servant on a dark night said he was afraid to go out to the barn: "Afraid of what," asked the gentleman. "Of the Stamp Act," replied the servant. * * *

What had set off this madness of the people? Not, Hutchinson believed, an understanding of the intrinsic impolicy of the Stamp Act, which had troubled him and other experienced public people. And not the existence of an actual threat to liberty. No such threat existed. Americans were the freest people on earth, and the acts that they said threatened them had been undertaken, however mistakenly, to strengthen the bond between them and the homeland, which was the ultimate guarantor of liberty. The ostensible motivations behind the wild opposition therefore could not possibly be the real ones. Another explanation must be sought.

* * * The common run of the people, lacking the necessary education, leisure, and economic independence to make an impartial assessment of public problems, were mercurial playthings of leaders who could profit by exciting their fears. Some of these leaders were pure demagogues, lovers of power adept at manipulating the mob, men who "have nothing to lose and * * * will hold out, for, from public mischief and confusion they may have a chance for private advantage." But some of the leaders had only too much to lose—by certain policies. These men were impelled by a close sense of their own selfish interests as against the public good: they were "the illicit traders" whose animosity * * * had been excited by the threat of efficient enforcement of the customs laws and the renewal of writs of assistance. * * *

Together, these demagogues and malcontents had deliberately raised the fears of a people bred to liberty and set them against the government. Together, they had released the latent forces of anarchy, always threatening from below, and unraveled the fabric of civic order.

* * * The ministry in England, blinded to the realities of life in America and unable or unwilling to see the need to redefine the terms of Anglo–American relations, had blundered badly and created conditions ideal for the purposes of selfish commercial operators and ruthless demagogues. As late as 1764, * * * no one would have dreamt of defying Parliament; everyone would have agreed that such defiance was high treason. But the Sugar Act, which had suddenly posed the question of "how far the Parliament of right might impose taxes upon them"; the threat, immediately following, of internal taxes; and the failure of Parliament to distinguish between petitions that acknowledged its right to tax and those that did not—all of this had given the hard-core demagogues and the selfish opportunists the occasion they sought, of rallying to them the

respectable, well-meaning, public-spirited part of the population. With this liberal support they had succeeded in making defiance of law and order respectable. * * * "Authority is in the populace," Hutchinson wrote, "no law can be carried into execution against their mind." No custom house officer would now dare make a seizure, and no law was safe from challenge. * * *

What was to be done? * * *

[B. THE ISSUES AT STAKE]

Hutchinson had no illusions about the limits of his own wisdom, but in the five years after the Stamp Act riots he undertook * * * a thoroughgoing study of the fundamental issues at stake in the Anglo–American controversy and of the courses of action open to the administration. * * *

* * *

One catches a glimpse of the theoretical presumptions that underlay his conclusions and recommendations in his enthusiastic praise of Allan Ramsay's Thoughts on the Origin and Nature of Government [(1769)] * * * a handbook of applied Hobbesianism, cold, harsh, and disillusioned. Men are in actuality unequal, Ramsay had written. The idea of human equality is a dangerous fiction which, when taken up by the "very lowest class of men" at the urging of demagogues, has in the end always resulted in slaughter and the plunder of property. And society, Ramsay wrote, far from being the voluntary compact conjured up in "the idle dreams of metaphysicians" was in real life an inescapable organism created by the flight for survival of weak and solitary men to the protection of the strong. From this natural origin flowed the equally natural and inevitable division between rulers and ruled and the necessity for the ruler's ultimate power to be supreme and absolute, though never arbitrary. Taxing? It was a necessary power of any government that sought to serve society, and in fact it did not—could not—rest * * * on the explicit consent of the governed, expressed either directly or through representatives. Taxing was simply an attribute of supreme authority, a mechanism necessary for its survival, and "sovereignty admits of no degrees, it is always supreme, and to level it is in effect to destroy it." For Britain, Ramsay concluded, this "absolute and supreme," this "uncontrollable" authority lay in Parliament, the ultimate proof of whose authority would be found in the coercive forces it could exert, force alone being the final, uncontrollable source of all law: "those," Ramsay said, "who try to separate law from force attempt impiously to put asunder whom God has been pleased to join."

* * * [Hutchinson agreed] with Ramsay's view of sovereignty, representation, and taxation. But he was not, like Ramsay, committed to basic notions systematically at variance with the liberal thought of the time. While he shared Ramsay's cold view of human nature * * * he shared too

the common premise of eighteenth-century British thought: that mankind was endowed in its original pre-social state with unlimited rights to actions of all kinds but that these rights had been restricted upon entrance into organized society. From that original abridgment of natural rights, he believed, derived the compelling authority of law and the rightful power of government. * * *

* * * Though Hutchinson spoke of the abridgment of natural rights that takes place upon entrance into society, he stressed not its voluntary and hence its reversible character (which would become the theoretical justification for the American Revolution) but its "necessity." * * * And he believed that if one understood the political nature of the British empire one would see how reasonable Parliament's actions really were, and that therefore, though orderly protests were proper, extralegal agitation against the government was criminal.

* * * Hutchinson felt that Parliament fused, expressed, and protected all the liberties of Britons, and, because in its essence it was benign and freedom-enhancing, it justified its use of unlimited power. * * * For Hutchinson as for Ramsay and the ruling Whig governments of England, the ultimate fact of all political life * * * was the logical necessity for an absolute and unitary authority to exist somewhere in every government; in its essential definition, that is what government was: a unit of absolute and indivisible authority. Absolute, supreme authority, for Hutchinson, was neither good nor bad, neither a desirable nor an undesirable thing: it simply was. * * * [I]n the case of Britain that power, marvelously restricted by the balances of "mixed" government, was entrusted to Parliament in its totality: that is, to King, Lords, and Commons operating together as sovereign.

* * * [T]here were certain times when the effective use of state power was peculiarly urgent. His own time, he believed, was one such moment in history. If one understood the delicate balance of power and liberty in free states and understood too the movement of history in the eighteenth century, one must conclude, Hutchinson believed, that the age he lived in was "an age of liberty." Since the time of the Glorious Revolution the thirst for liberty had become so intense as to threaten stability everywhere. If the threat of despotism had been deflected, the threat of anarchy was rising. * * * He never doubted that in certain circumstances—in governments under the arbitrary rule of despots, for example—the drive to reinforce and enlarge the sphere of liberty could have a most salutary effect; but in the British colonies, "where as much freedom is enjoyed as can consist with the ends of government"—where * * * the laxness of government was known to be so extreme as to be positively embarrassing to pro-Americans in Parliament—the heedless enthusiasm for liberty "must work anarchy and confusion unless there be some external power to restrain it." * * * If, therefore, the delicate balance of Britain's famed mixed

constitution * * * was to be preserved, it was the power element, not, as was the case before 1688, the liberty element, that needed most carefully to be protected.

[C. SOLUTIONS TO THE CRISIS]

* * * [Following the working-out of these theoretical presumptions, Hutchinson went on] first to work out a program of action to deal with the immediate crisis, and then, beyond that, to sketch the terms of a rational system of imperial relations. * * *

Hutchinson's program of reconstruction and reordering was conceived as a series of stages. There was no doubt in his mind of the proper way to handle the immediate crisis. The Stamp Act must be repealed, he said, promptly and resoundingly. A stupidly conceived act in the first place * * * it had proved unenforceable: if allowed to remain on the books and not enforced it would destroy confidence in government; if attempts were made to enforce it, "there is no determining what desperate men will not attempt."

* * * But nothing more, he felt, should be done immediately after the repeal. There would have to be a pause * * * "until the minds of the people are somewhat calmed and the effect of the repeal * * * shall appear." * * * Strenuous efforts would then have to be made by the government to reach the great majority of moderate, sensible people—the "many good men among us who abhor the present anarchy"—and to rally their support for the steps that would be necessary. They must be made to see the basic fact of life, that the colonies must be subject to some power; if their protector were not Great Britain it could only be some other European state "which would allow them less liberty than they are sure of always enjoying whilst they remain English subjects." * * * [T]hen efforts could be taken to strengthen the effective power of government. And this would have to be done by measures "which shall evidently appear to be intended to preserve to [the colonies] all the rights and liberties which can consist with their connection with their mother country" * * *. Finally, when the government was thus strengthened and free to use its power to support the authority it claimed—then and only then * * * a coherent, rational, and mutually beneficial political reconstruction of the English-speaking world could be created.

[In order to restabilize relations disturbed in the crisis, Hutchinson was even prepared to be coldly cynical] * * * [H]e believed that Lord Chatham's distinction in the powers of Parliament, between the power to tax and the power to legislate, was as specious as all the other fanciful distinctions in parliament's power that had been suggested. But it was nevertheless true * * * that most of the colonists in fact believed in that distinction, even though it made no sense: therefore Parliament should act on it as if it did make sense; it should pass legislation on the basis of this distinction as soon as possible, before Americans became impressed with the logic of claiming that among their rights as Britishers was freedom from all laws, not only tax laws, to which they had not consented. * * * Use anything reasonable that comes to hand to create the stability that is needed: exploit division within and among the colonies if doing so will help maintain authority, for though in some situations such duplicity would be criminal, when the aim is to prevent greater mischief, it may be laudable.

* * *

Parliament must act, he wrote again and again; it must not only enforce the rule of law but articulate the principles of colonial dependency. One could already see the outlines of the future if Parliament failed in this. One could see it in the popular misreading of Lord Coke's maxim that "an act of Parliament against Magna Carta or the peculiar rights of Englishmen is *ipso facto* void": the opposition, taught by Otis, now took that quite traditional doctrine of judicial discretion to mean that the people had the right to say what laws they would and would not obey. When people feel justified in taking the law into their own hands * * * society will revert to the rules of the jungle; the fear of brutality will sweep across the community and terror will make savages of civilized men. * * * The thin membrane of law and civil discourse that constrained the natural forces of anarchy would be worn away slowly, in successive outbreaks of disorder, and reach the breaking point before men generally realized what was happening. * * * Riots, for some reason, Hutchinson said, do not seem to "strike the mind with so much abhorrence as some other offenses do"; yet they are self-intensifying, feeding upon themselves, and no one can predict where they will end. * * * The more frequently disorders occurred, the less they would seem unnatural and unthinkable and the less the public at large would react with effective repulsion, though riotous disorders, he said again and again, necessarily "sap the foundation of all government."

* * * Of course, he said, there were reasons for protest; of course some laws were offensive to some groups, others to other groups, and no doubt some actions of the government were generally offensive. But somehow people must be made to see that if the government offends, if the law is felt to be oppressive, remedies must be sought in law and not in illegality. * * *

* * *

* * * [Hutchinson] disagreed with almost all of the long-term programs of reform suggested by his correspondents * * *.

[One of Hutchinson's correspondents with plans for reform and for dealing with the current crisis was Sir Francis Bernard, Hutchinson's predecessor as Governor of Massachusetts] * * * Bernard * * * recommended, as a possible expedient, the granting of Parliamentary representation as a special privilege to certain colonies, and suggested that Parliament consider turning over the levying of "internal" taxes to the colonial Assemblies, so long as they continued to provide sums sufficient to maintain a dependable financial basis for the executive branch of the government. But his chief ideas had to do with plans for a permanent recasting of colonial institutions and society. The present colonies in America, he argued, were too many in number, too small, and too weakly structured internally. They should be combined into a smaller number of larger units so that the financial bases of the governments might be strengthened and the forms of their constitutions brought closer to the pattern of England's. These enlarged colonies should have not only financially autonomous executive branches but also—what they had so far completely lacked—"a real and distinct third legislative power mediating between the King and the people, which is the peculiar excellence of the British constitution." This independent middle order of society was to be created by the appointment of American life peers, and the resulting colonial nobility would not only complete the classic triad of "mixed" government but also eliminate the need for the anomalous and obstructive Councils that then existed, some of which, like that of Massachusetts, Bernard said, had thrown the whole weight of the constitution to the popular side and had paralyzed the operation of government. * * *

* * *

[Another of Hutchinson's correspondents who addressed these issues was Thomas Pownall, who was also a former Governor of Massachusetts.] His main point was simply that Britain must reorganize the structure of its empire into a "grand marine dominion" with efficient, forceful administrative direction at the center. A single colonial office, combining the work of the Board of Trade and the secretary of state's office, should be created. Trade, justice, law must all center in Britain and be controlled by Britain. * * * [T]he existing administrative structure of the empire was intolerable; sweeping changes must be made which would replace the present hodgepodge of disparate offices and scattered responsibilities that had evolved through the accidents of history with a streamlined, logical, and efficiently centralized organization.

* * *

[A third correspondent was Richard Jackson,] formerly secretary to the chancellor of the exchequer and then a Member of Parliament, agent for Connecticut, Pennsylvania, and Massachusetts * * *. [In November 1766, Jackson] sought Hutchinson's opinion * * * of an intricate argument. * * * Having opposed the Stamp Act, Jackson, like many Americans, was seeking to define some kind of limitation on Parliament's rightful power. Was it truly necessary, he asked Hutchinson, for governments to exercise both legislative and taxing powers? Neither, he said, was an inevitable attribute of government. Sparta after the Lycurgan laws, he pointed out, had had no legislative body at all, and innumerable perfectly stable and viable if despotic governments had raised money by simple fiat or by "plunder, rapine, or the spoils of a disgraced minister." Only free states raise money by acts of representative legislatures, but they succeed in doing so only because of the confidence of the people in the legislature. The American colonists, however, had clearly proved that they had no confidence in Parliament as a legislature for them, for the very good reason that they were not represented in it. Even if Parliament rightly had the power to tax, therefore, it "was manifestly inconsistent with policy and the principles of our constitution to exercise it until the Parliament itself was improved to the perfection the principles of the constitution require." Someday perhaps the irregular constitution of England with respect to America would be improved to the point where the necessary confidence would exist, and at that point taxation might begin. At the moment its imperfections stood out—imperfections the more difficult to change, Jackson said, because of the total ignorance in England of the nature of government in the colonies.

In his lengthy reply Hutchinson sketched the parameters of his own thought. Legislation, he insisted, is a fundamental attribute of government, notwithstanding the example of Sparta * * *. And if by rectifying the inadequacies of the imperial constitution Jackson had meant introducing colonial representation into Parliament, he was—like both Bernard and Pownall—ignoring logical as well as political difficulties. Logically, colonial representation was irrelevant since the power to tax did not rest on representation; politically, it was clearly unacceptable to Americans since they quite correctly understood that it would only lend a specious approval to acts over which they would still have no control and of which they would still disapprove. Direct representation was one of the privileges enjoyed by some (and only some) Englishmen, and it simply could not be enjoyed by the colonists. This limitation was not a matter of will or desire or policy; it was certainly not something he personally advocated. It was, he wrote, simply a matter of evident logic and palpable fact.

For himself, he told Jackson * * * there was no mystery about the grounds for constructing a sensible colonial policy and a rational imperial constitution. Everything flowed from one simple but inescapable and undeniable fact: The American colonies were too weak to survive independently in a world of rival nation-states. * * * As a consequence of this necessary dependence, compounded by the colonists' remoteness, certain privileges enjoyed by Englishmen could not be held by them. It was simply a matter * * * of what was and what was not possible, not of what was theoretically good or bad. No amount of theorizing or wishful thinking could change the necessity for "an abridgment of what is called English liberty." * * *

The colonists' necessary and limiting dependence did not mean, however, that they need be victims of oppression. "I am as much against arbitrary government," he wrote to a correspondent in England in 1769, "as any person living. The more favor you show the colonies in freeing them from taxes of every sort and indulging them in such forms of constitution, civil and ecclesiastical, as they have been used to, the more agreeable it will be to me, provided you do not wholly relinquish us and take away the claim we have to your protection." Not only as a matter of sensible policy should the parent state allow the colonies every possible liberty * * * but * * * the parent state should compensate for the inescapable restrictions on liberty in overseas territories with extraordinary indulgences, so as to bring the condition of colonists and Englishmen into as close a general equality as possible. This * * * would merely formalize traditional practices. If partisans on both sides would put aside their passions, their delusions, and ambitions, they would see, he believed, that for over a century precisely such a balance had been struck and had proved workable and liberty-preserving. It had been this balance, established in many spheres, that had accounted for the prosperity, indeed the continuing existence, of the Anglo–American empire. For four generations there had been a major limitation on liberty in America in the restrictions on colonial trade, but Americans had not objected because there had been a compensating indulgence in freedom from Parliamentary taxation. * * *

What was needed to regain this long-successful set of balances between inescapable limitations and wise indulgences was not institutional restructuring, as Bernard, Pownall, and so many facile theoreticians claimed, but statesmanship. * * * He openly condemned the proposal of Chief Justice William Smith of New York that a single vice-regal government be created in America, including an American parliament, not only because he thought such an arrangement would be impracticable but because it would destroy the existing structure of authority * * *. Even the simpler and apparently more sensible idea, rapidly gaining popularity in America, that the colonies be associated with England through the King alone and not through Parliament—what later generations would call dominion status—he felt sacrificed reality to an attractive theory. For in such an arrangement, he pointed out, there would be a withdrawal of effective governmental power from communities already beset by civil disorder, and the result would simply be chaos. If order was to be restored and maintained, the ultimate power of the King-in-Parliament must remain as unitary and total over the colonies as it was over England. * * *

* * *

* * * [The proper course] was the most difficult and the most complicated: it was, simply, "to bear with their disorderly behavior until they have distressed themselves so as to bear their distresses no longer. Encourage the animosities already begun between the colonies, and distinguish one colony from another by favor for good behavior and frowns for the contrary. Lay aside taxation, not upon the principle that it is to be distinguished from legislation in general but because it is inexpedient. Keep up every other part of legislation and familiarize every colony to acts of Parliament. This may in time bring the colonies to their old state."

* * * Let the House of Commons appoint a permanent committee for America, and let that committee generate enactments that are manifestly to the colonists' advantage. Show Americans the favorable aspects of Parliament's authority; provide them with instruments and powers that they need and would welcome, and that might also have political support in England. * * * Only in that way would the colonists learn to respect English authority—indeed, all authority; authority as such—and see the folly of resistance. If such steps had been taken five years ago, he wrote in 1770, all the trouble would have been nipped in the bud.

* * *

* * * The whole mess, he exploded uncharacteristically to an English friend and business associate of thirty years standing, was the result of gross errors in high places. "You have brought all this trouble upon yourselves and upon us by your own imprudence. You never ought to have made any concessions from your own power over the colonies, and you ought not to have attempted an exertion of power which caused such a general dissatisfaction through the colonies. God only knows when the ill effects of this mistake will cease."

* * * [In the summer of 1768] as the Massachusetts House defied the ministry's order to rescind its inflammatory circular letter; as mobs assaulted the customs officers who had seized John Hancock's sloop Liberty and drove them to the refuge of the harbor fort; as the nonimportation committees tightened their boycott of British goods; and as plans were almost publicly made to oppose the landing of the two regiments of troops known to be en route to Boston—Thomas Hutchinson retired to the peace of his house in Milton to write what he hoped would be a definitive refutation of all the mistaken notions that had been circulating since the Stamp Act resistance had begun. * * *

[D. HUTCHINSON'S DEFINITIVE STATEMENT]

[The Document Hutchinson produced during this summer] may be called "A Dialogue between Europe and America" and it is written entirely as a dramatic exchange * * *. The purpose of the piece was not to set out new terms of imperial relations but to demonstrate the irrationality of the arguments of the American opposition, the impossibility of constructing a workable imperial system on the principles that the opposition had suggested, and the inescapable necessity of settling the current controversy on terms dictated by the historical tradition that Britain and America had inherited.

* * *

[The most important matters addressed in the Dialogue were] the central and universal questions of the grounds of personal obedience to the state and the limits, if any, of this obligation. * * * What kind of a society, *Europe* asks, would there be if individuals were empowered to tell judges and executives when to enforce the law and when not?

Judges themselves, *America* replied, should decide not to enforce immoral laws or laws contrary to the purposes of the government. *Europe:* but if judges were to select which laws to enforce and which to ignore they would be making, not enforcing, the law, and that would violate a primary precept of free government. * * * For there is no agreed-on, absolute, and objective definition of morality and immorality that judges or anyone else can simply invoke. Justice and morality are relative to the circumstances and culture. * * *

Let us suppose, *Europe* says, that a person believes his government is engaged in an immoral war. * * * Is he thereby free to refuse to pay taxes in support of that war? Perhaps not, *America* replied, but the British constitution does not provide for "an umpire or judge" to determine when the government has exceeded its authority—the courts, which were in fact as well as in name "executive courts," had never been given that power—and since that is the case, "every man's own conscience must be the judge, and he must follow the evidence of truth in his own mind, and submit or not accordingly." This, Europe replies, would be a constitution that is no constitution at all but "a mere rope of sand." No government in the history of the world has ever survived for long on the principle that individuals may claim an exemption to the law when they decide their rights have been infringed. Nor, indeed, has the definition of fundamental rights been constant in any nation's history. The British constitution—every constitution ever known—has been in flux at all times, and it is in fact through successive alterations of the British constitution that, historically, adjustments have been made to accommodate personal or group grievances. Instead of individuals personally defying the government in order to right wrongs they claim have been committed, the supreme authority itself has modified its own actions, "and such alterations become to all intents and purposes parts of the constitution." For constitutions are not immutable blueprints of government inscribed on parchment at a particular point in time; they are living, growing, malleable arrangements of things, and it is a contradiction in terms to think that an agency of government could serve as umpire to rule the government itself out of order when it impinged on individual rights. Courts are part of the law enforcement procedure, not a check upon it. The only restraint on the action of the state is the state's *self*-restraint, and in a balanced, "mixed" constitution that is an effective limitation indeed on the abuse of power.

Well, *America* replies, you may use any argument you wish, but it is still true that the government is wrong to take my property without my consent, expressed either directly or through a personally chosen representative. * * * the same immutable principles are embedded in English history and immemorial English law.

How "obstinately tenacious" you are, *Europe* replies. Let us indeed turn to the history of the English constitution. Does it justify an individual's refusal to obey the law? No—and more important, it does not contain immutable principles that might serve as the basis for such resistance. True, it is one of the glories of the English constitution that there are "certain fundamental principles, plain and intelligible," which can guide the courts in deciding difficult and uncertain cases, but these principles are far from being or having been immutable; they have always changed when circumstances changed. Magna Carta, surely, is a fundamental document in the English constitution. Yet it provides for the continuing jurisdiction of the then-existing Church, from which it follows at the very least that there should be a bishop of the Church in America. But is there one? And how have Americans in fact responded to the suggestion that there be one? If the Church really occupied the role conceded to it in Magna Carta, consider what a deplorable state we Protestants would all be in. Consider how many other provisions of that great charter of constitutional liberty have also been repealed by acts of Parliament. In fact there is only one absolutely immutable principle in the British constitution and certain to remain such: "that no act can be made or passed in any Parliament which it shall not be in the power of a subsequent Parliament to alter and repeal." No government or constitution on earth is immutable: "the power which established it may dissolve it." Yes, the British government has fundamental principles, "but if King, nobles, and people agree to make an alteration in what were before fundamentals, who is there to complain"?

The people, *America* replies, may complain, for they alone, as opposed to the other two elements of the constitution, do not personally participate in such decisions but act only through representatives. If these representatives exercise a power they were never given, they may be repudiated. Nor need this be only a majority's action: a *minor* part of the people may feel themselves free to repudiate such irresponsible actions by representatives. *Europe:* but it is an historical fact that the government was formed by representatives; surely it can be altered by representatives. *America:* I never gave my representative unlimited power; for him to give away my rights is to assume a power he never had, and any act of that sort "is void." If it is void, *Europe* replies, then there is an end to all organized government.

* * *

What must be done in the present circumstances? *Europe* asks. If America is exempt from any law, it is exempt from all laws. The law as it stands must be enforced, though the supreme authority may ultimately wish to alter the law. "I would not give up the least iota of our right, but I would exercise this right with discretion, with equity, and even with a degree of partiality, but when I had once determined how far I would exercise it * * * such determination should never be departed from." If such a policy were now followed it would easily succeed, for the extremists among the colonial leaders are simply desperadoes who stand to gain by reducing everything to chaos and then starting things over again. But the generality of the people, "who are in easy circumstances," will not risk their property and security for the benefit of a few irresponsible agitators. The present popular frenzy will pass, for "you are Englishmen. * * * No people upon the globe have been oftener in a frenzy and none return sooner to their senses than Englishmen."

2. A MIDDLE VIEW

OXENBRIDGE THACHER, THE SENTIMENTS OF A BRITISH AMERICAN*

(1764).

It well becomes the wisdom of a great nation, having been highly successful in their foreign wars and added a large extent of country to their dominions, to consider with a critical attention their internal state lest their prosperity should destroy them.

Great Britain at this day is arrived to an heighth of glory and wealth which no European nation hath ever reached since the decline of the Roman Empire. Everybody knows that it is not indebted to itself alone for this envied power: that its colonies, placed in a distant quarter of the earth, have had their share of efficiency in its late successes, as indeed they have also contributed to the advancing and increasing its grandeur from their very first beginnings.

In the forming and settling, therefore, the internal policy of the kingdom, these have reason to expect that *their* interest should be considered and attended to, that *their* rights, if they have any, should be preserved to them, and that *they* should have no reason to complain that they have been lavish of their blood and treasure in the late war only to bind the shackles of slavery on themselves and their children.

* Reprinted in 1 B. Bailyn, ed. Pamphlets of the American Revolution 490–498 (1965).

* * *

The writer of this, being a native of an English colony, will take it for granted that the colonies are not the mere property of the mother state; that they have the same rights as other British subjects. He will also suppose that no design is formed to enslave them, and that the justice of the British Parliament will finally do right to every part of their dominions.

These things presupposed, he intends to consider the late act made in the fourth year of his present Majesty entitled *An Act for Granting Certain Duties in the British Colonies and Plantations in America,* etc., to show the real subjects of grievance therein to the colonists, and that the interest of Great Britain itself may finally be greatly affected thereby. * * *

[I.] The first objection is that a tax is thereby laid on several commodities, to be raised and levied in the plantations, and to be remitted home to England. This is esteemed a grievance inasmuch as the same are laid without the consent of the representatives of the colonists. It is esteemed an essential British right that no person shall be subject to any tax but what in person or by his representative he hath a voice in laying. The British Parliament have many times vindicated this right against the attempts of Kings to invade it. And though perhaps it may be said that the House of Commons, in a large sense, are the representatives of the colonies as well as of the people of Great Britain, yet it is certain that these have no voice in their election. Nor can it be any alleviation of their unhappiness that if this right is taken from them, it is taken by that body who have been the great patrons and defenders of it in the people of Great Britain.

Besides, the colonies have ever supported a subordinate government among themselves.

* * * Now the colonies have always been taxed by their own representatives and in their respective legislatures, and have supported an entire domestic government among themselves. Is it just, then, they should be doubly taxed? * * *

The reason given for this extraordinary taxation, namely, that this war was undertaken for the security of the colonies, and that they ought therefore to be taxed to pay the charge thereby incurred, it is humbly apprehended is without foundation. For—

(1) It was of no less consequence to Great Britain than it was to the colonies that these should not be overrun and conquered by the French. * * * Put the case that the town of Portsmouth or any other seaport had been besieged and the like sums expended in its defense, could any have thought that town ought to be charged with the expense?

(2) The colonies contributed their full proportion to those conquests which adorn and dignify the late and present reign. One of them in particular raised in one year seven thousand men * * *. All of them by their expenses and exertions in the late war have incurred heavy debts, which it will take them many years to pay.

(3) The colonies are no particular gainers by these acquisitions. None of the conquered territory is annexed to them. All are acquisitions accruing to the crown. * * * It is true they have more security from having their throats cut by the French while the peace lasts; but so have also all His Majesty's subjects.

(4) Great Britain gaineth immensely by these acquisitions. The command of the whole American fur trade and the increased demand for their woolen manufactures from their numerous new subjects in a country too cold to keep sheep: these are such immense gains as in a commercial light would refund the kingdom, if every farthing of the expense of reducing Canada were paid out of the exchequer.

But to say the truth, it is not only by the taxation itself that the colonists deem themselves aggrieved by the act we are considering. For—

II. The power therein given to courts of admiralty alarms them greatly. The common law is the birthright of every subject, and trial by jury a most darling privilege. * * * Many struggles had [our ancestors] * * * with courts of admiralty, which, like the element they take their name from, have divers times attempted to innundate the land. Hence the statutes of *Richard* II, of *Henry* IV, and divers other public acts. Hence the watchful eye the reverend sages of the common law have kept over these courts. Now by the act we are considering, the colonists are deprived of these privileges: of the common law, for these judges are supposed to be connusant only of the civil law; of juries, for all here is put in the breast of one man. He judges both law and fact, and his decree is final; at least it cannot be reversed on this side of the Atlantic. In this particular the colonists are put under a quite different law from all the rest of the King's subjects: jurisdiction is nowhere else given to courts of admiralty of matters so foreign from their connusance. In some things the colonists have been long subject to this cruel yoke, and have indeed fully experienced its galling nature. Loud complaints have been long made by them of the oppressions of these courts, their exhorbitant fees, and the little justice the subject may expect from them in cases of seizures. Let me mention one thing that is notorious: these courts have assumed (I know not by what law) a commission of five per cent to the judge on all seizures condemned. What chance does the subject stand for his right upon the best claim when the judge, condemning, is to have an hundred or perhaps five hundred pounds, and acquitting, less than twenty shillings? * * *

* * *

But in the act we are considering, the power of these courts is even much enlarged and made still more grievous. For it is thereby enacted that the seizor may inform in any court of admiralty for the particular colony, or in any court of admiralty to be appointed over all America, at his pleasure. Thus a malicious seizor may take the goods of any man, ever so lawfully and duly imported, and carry the trial of the cause to a thousand miles distance, where for mere want of ability to follow, the claimer shall be incapable of defending his right. * * *

III. The empowering commanders of the King's ships to seize and implead, as is done in this act and a former act and by special commission from the commissioners of the customs, is another great hardship on the colonies. The knowledge of all the statutes relating to the customs, of the prohibitions on exports and imports, and of various intricate cases arising on them, requires a good lawyer. How can this science ever be expected from men educated in a totally different way, brought up upon the boisterous element and knowing no law aboard their ships but their own will? * * * [While this power in the captains might work less damage in England because there] no jurisdiction is given to any other than the common law courts; there too the subjects are near the throne, where, when they are oppressed, their complaints may soon be heard and redressed; but with respect to the colonies, far different is the case! Here it is their own courts that try the cause! Here the subject is far distant from the throne! His complaints cannot soon be heard and redressed. The boisterous commander may take for his motto, *Procul a Jove, a fulmine procul.* [Far from Jove, far from his thunder.]

* * *

There is yet another very great objection the colonists make to this act, of no less weight than the other three. It is this:

IV. Whereas it is good law that all officers seizing goods seize at their peril, and if the goods they seize are not liable to forfeiture they must pay the claimant his cost, and are liable to his action besides, which two things have been looked upon as proper checks of exorbitant wanton power in the officer: both these checks are taken off. They, the officers, may charge the revenue with the cost, with the consent of four of the commissioners of the customs. And if the judge of admiralty will certify that there was probable cause of seizure, no action shall be maintained by the claimant though his goods on trial appear to be ever so duly imported and liable to no sort of forfeiture, and he hath been forced to expend ever so much in the defense of them. * * *

* * *

Now everybody knows that the greatest part of the trade of Great Britain is with her colonies. This she enjoyeth, exclusive of any other European county, and hath entirely at her own command. Further, it may be made out that the greatest part of the profits of the trade of the colonies, at least on the continent, centers in Great Britain. The colonists, settled in a wide and sparse manner, are perpetually demanding the linen, woolen, and other manufacturers of Great Britain. * * * Great Britain, besides, is the mart which supplieth the colonies with all the produce of the other countries in Europe which the colonies use.

Considering the vast numbers supported by these manufactures vended in the colonies, and by the articles of foreign trade brought into the kingdom and thence exported and consumed in the plantations, doubtless even the luxury of the colonists is the gain of Great Britain. So thought wise ministers in the late reign: on which ground they repealed two or three sumptuary laws made in the colonies for restraining that luxury.

Now as the colonies have no gold or silver mines in them, it is certain that all their remittances they make must be from their trade. * * *

One grand source of these remittances is the fishery, which by the duty of three pence a gallon on molasses must entirely be at an end. That branch can never bear the high duties imposed, nor subsist without the molasses which the trade to the foreign islands furnisheth. Not only by their connection with this but by the mere effect of the new regulations, all the other trade of the colonists must be at an end. * * *

Hence, one or other of these consequences will follow: either (1) the colonies will universally go into such manufactures as they are capable of doing within themselves, or (2) they will do without them, and being reduced to mere necessaries, will be clothed like their predecessors the Indians with the skins of beasts, and sink into like barbarism. * * *

Now, either of these events taking place, how will it affect the island of Great Britain? The answer is obvious. The exports to the colonies wholly stopped or greatly diminished, the demands for those manufactures in Great Britain must be in proportion lessened. The substance of those manufacturers, merchants, and traders whom this demand supports is then gone. They who live from supplying these manufacturers, etc., must decay and die with them. Lastly, as trade may be compared to a grand chain made up of innumerable links, it is doubtful whether the British trade, great as it is, can bear the striking out so many without greatly endangering the whole.

What now is the equivalent for all this to the nation? A tenth part of one year's tax, at the extent two years' tax upon the colonies (for after that time all their money will be gone) to be lodged in the exchequer and thence issued as the Parliament shall direct. Doth not this resemble the conduct of the good wife in the fable who killed her hen that every day laid her a *golden egg?*

* * *

NOTES AND QUESTIONS

1. With these last two readings we open up the area of the immediate causes of the American Revolution and we continue our exploration, begun in the Writs of Assistance case, of the importance of law to the Whigs and the Loyalists. We cannot, of course, solve the problem of causation of the American Revolution here; it is still the subject of heated debate among American historians. There is no agreement about whether the primary causes were legal, economic, social, or political. For a summary of important historiography on the American Revolution see Jack P. Greene, ed., The Reinterpretation of the American Revolution, 1763–1789 (1968). For further efforts at coming to grips with the philosophical underpinnings of the American Revolution see Henry Steele Commager, The Empire of Reason (1977), Morton White, The Philosophy of the American Revolution (1978), Garry Wills, Inventing America: Jefferson's Declaration of Independence (1978) and Gordon Wood, The Radicalism of the American Revolution (1992). For the assertion of the importance of strictly "legal" arguments see the works of John Reid, cited in Note 5, pp. 83–84, supra.

2. One way of approaching the problem of American revolutionary ideology is to study what there was to rebel against. Governor Hutchinson was one of the most articulate theorists of the loyalist cause, even if his theoretical formulations were not generally known at the time. One writer has even tried to make out a case that Hutchinson ought to be bracketed with the greatest philosophical conservative of them all. See William Pencak, America's Burke: The Mind of Thomas Hutchinson (1982). Why doesn't Hutchinson sympathize with the popular critics of the Royal administration? Is it simply that he is the King's officer in the colony of Massachusetts, or does his hostility to what was to become the patriot cause run deeper?

3. Does Hutchinson believe that the majority of the American people are dissatisfied with royal rule? Who, then, is causing the disaffection that he is able to perceive on all sides? What does Hutchinson mean when he refers to "popular demagogues?"

4. Hutchinson is greatly troubled by recent riots and popular disturbances in Massachusetts. As indicated earlier, in 1765 a savage mob wrecked and torched his house, destroying virtually all of his belongings. There has been something of an explosion in the scholarship on the American Revolutionary mob. See, e.g., Pauline Maier, "Popular Uprisings and Civil Authority in Eighteenth–Century America," 27 Wm. & Mary Q. 3 (1970). It is clear that American mobs played a prominent role in the agitation against royal policy, and that some of them destroyed property and physically abused royal officials. Popular mobs had been fixtures in the colonial political process at least since the late 1600's. Mob activity extended over a wide range, including rioting, tarring and feathering, obstructing customs enforcement and service of

process, and highly selective damaging of property, such as brothels, private dwellings, or ships.

Still, is it correct to describe most American mobs as "lawless?" Were they really undisciplined and anarchic? John Reid argues that while Whig mobs in the 1760's and 1770's may have been "unlawful," they were not "lawless." Does the following discussion shed any light on the differences of opinion among Hutchinson, Otis, and Oxenbridge Thacher?*

> We must not demand precise rules or definitive principles. In the fluid rivalry of two competing governments what is "legal" may be as often a subjective as an objective judgment. * * *
>
> Consider the possibility that there are often two sides to lawlessness. A tory conscious of how the Massachusetts whigs departed from traditional principles of English common law by employing the civil traverse jury and the writ system to impose a criminal-law type sanction upon customs officials would have said that they abused the judicial process. Yet that same tory might not have thought it an abuse when the commissioners of the customs departed from similar principles of English common law and attempted to use the admiralty jurisdiction to impose a criminal-law type sanction upon John Hancock.** The tory who saw a violation of the constitution when whig juries ignored admiralty judgments and rendered common-law verdicts despite being instructed that the admiralty decree had settled all legal questions, probably did not recognize a comparable violation of the constitution in that section of the Sugar Act freeing customs officers from common-law damage suits whenever an admiralty court in a non-jury *ex parte* hearing ruled that they had acted with "probable cause." * * * Should Hutchinson concede that Whigs acted within the law when their grand jurors refused to indict the rioters who destroyed his house, yet assert they acted without principle, the complaint could with equal fairness be made about him, for Hutchinson kept imperial officials informed about secret grand jury proceedings and when men such as Gage or Bernard were indicted he saw to it that the law did not take its normal course.
>
> The judicial process was such in eighteenth-century British North America that it could be used by the political process, and each side of the controversy was willing to take whatever advantages fell its way. Most dropped on the whig side, but the whigs should not be accused of unlawful manipulations merely because the tories thought them unlawful. The whigs, for their part, believed that the British were altering an

* From John Phillip Reid, In a Defiant Stance: The Conditions of Law in Massachusetts Bay, The Irish Comparison, and the Coming of the American Revolution 162–163, Copyright © 1977 The Pennsylvania State University, Published by the Pennsylvania State University Press, University Park and London, reprinted with the permission of the publisher and the author.

** Hancock's sloop, The Liberty, was seized by royal customs officials in 1768, on charges of illegal trading.

immutable constitution and Hutchinson's "manipulations" were part of their story.

A more serious charge, as it troubled Americans who accepted implicitly the whig tale of constitutional abuse yet retained a conservative's respect for the rule of law, was the assertion that much of whig violence was lawless. We have seen whigs reject this contention yet none has articulated a satisfactory argument for the legality of their use of force. Implicit in their legal theory—in John Adams's distinction between legitimate and illegitimate mobs and his praise of the Boston Tea Party—was the concept that what is "unlawful" under imperial law is not always "lawless." "Lawlessness" in the whig sense implied that the act complained of—such as a riot—was not only in violation of constituted law but was performed either for an irrational purpose or for personal gain or had a negative or antisocial aim. "Lawful" or "semilawful" in the whig sense was an act contrary to statutory or common law, but when tory or imperial law was broken and the purpose was to defend whig constitutional principles the act was not necessarily "lawless." * * *

It is fair to say that Governor Francis Bernard was one high tory who never understood what whigs were up to. That rebels might be governed by a legal theory was beyond his imagination. Yet even Bernard grasped the whig distinction between the lawless rioters who sacked Hutchinson's house and the semilawful rioters who forced Andrew Oliver to resign as stamp agent. It was this legal theory—a theory that apparently had no limits as it led directly to mob rule—that persuaded other Americans to recoil from the whig program. * * *

5. Thacher was reacting against the "Sugar Act" of 1764, 4 George III, c. 15, VII Statutes at Large 457 (1764). The principal substantive provision of the act was a three pence per gallon duty on molasses imported into the colonies. This duty, which was of primary concern to rum distillers, was not thought to be excessively harsh by Parliament, and was approximately half of the former duty on molasses. Still, since this duty was to be enforced, and the former duty had been all but ignored, because of the importance of the trade in rum, many in America believed that the duty would cripple American commerce. See, e.g., Lawrence H. Gipson, The Coming of the Revolution 65–68 (1954). For Thacher, however, the *governmental philosophy* that appeared to be behind some of the enforcement provisions of the Sugar Act may have suggested a greater threat than the immediate economic impact. Here is how Professor Bernard Bailyn describes these provisions:

> To facilitate prosecution of violators of the navigation laws, the burden of proof was shifted to the defendant in cases brought by the customs officials; whatever the outcome of such cases, the defendant was obliged to pay costs; and the defendant was, in effect, prevented from entering retaliatory suits against customs officials. Above all, the law allowed all suits involving alleged violations of the navigation laws to be tried, if the "informer or prosecutor" wished, in the juryless admiralty courts: either

> the vice-admiralty court in the colony concerned "or in any court of vice-admiralty which may * * * be appointed over all *America*"—an alternative that referred to a projected new tribunal with jurisdiction over all the colonies, concurrent with that of the provincial vice-admiralty courts, which was created in fact in June 1764 in the remote hamlet of Halifax, Nova Scotia.

B. Bailyn, ed., 1 Pamphlets of the American Revolution 487 (1965).*

6. Thacher refers to some British statutes that restricted the jurisdiction of the English Admiralty courts. Bailyn's notes on these state that the statutes were "[1.] 13 Richard II c. 5, which declared that 'admirals and their deputies shall not meddle from henceforth of anything done within the realm, but only of a thing done upon the sea'; [2.] 15 Richard II c. 3, which added that over all matters 'rising within the bodies of the counties, as well by land as by water, and also of wreck of the sea, the admiral's court shall have no jurisdiction' and [3.] 2 Henry IV c. 11, which confirmed 13 Richard II c. 5." Bailyn, supra note 5, at 726–727. Can one reconcile Parliament's motives in passing and maintaining this legislation restricting admiralty jurisdiction in England and its passage of the Sugar Act expanding admiralty jurisdiction in the colonies?

7. The formal break with Great Britain did not come until 1776, approximately ten years after the events discussed in these excerpts. By that time, in the wake of the Boston Tea Party, Parliament had passed the infamous "Coercive Acts," closing Boston's port and severely restricting popular participation in the governance of Massachusetts. See, e.g., Gipson, supra note 5, at 223–225. These measures led directly to the convening of the Continental Congress which, following the failure of attempts at reconciliation, issued the Declaration of Independence. Compare the Declaration, which follows, with Hutchinson's, Otis's, and Thacher's comments.

> When in the Course of human events, it becomes necessary for one people to dissolve the political bands which have connected them with another, and to assume among the powers of the earth, the separate and equal station to which the Laws of Nature and of Nature's God entitle them, a decent respect to the opinions of mankind requires that they should declare the causes which impel them to the separation. We hold these truths to be self-evident, that all men are created equal, that they are endowed by their Creator with certain unalienable Rights, that among these are Life, Liberty and the pursuit of Happiness. That to secure these rights governments are instituted among Men, deriving their just powers from the consent of the governed, That whenever any Form of Government becomes destructive of these ends it is the Right of the People to alter or to abolish it, and to institute new Government, laying its foundation on such principles and organizing its powers in such form, as to them shall seem most likely to effect their Safety and Happiness.

Prudence, indeed, will dictate that Governments long established should not be changed for light and transient causes; and accordingly all experience hath shewn, that mankind are more disposed to suffer, while evils are sufferable, than to right themselves by abolishing the forms to which they are accustomed. But when a long train of abuses and usurpations, pursuing invariably the same Object evinces a design to reduce them under absolute Despotism, it is their right, it is their duty, to throw off such Government, and to provide new Guards for their future security. Such has been the patient sufferance of these Colonies; and such is now the necessity which constrains them to alter their former Systems of Government. The history of the present King of Great Britain is a history of repeated injuries and usurpations, all having in direct object the establishment of an absolute Tyranny over these States. To prove this, let Facts be submitted to a candid world. He has refused his Assent to Laws, the most wholesome and necessary for the public good. He has forbidden his Governors to pass Laws of immediate and pressing importance, unless suspended in their operation till his Assent should be obtained; and when so suspended, he has utterly neglected to attend to them. He has refused to pass other Laws for the accommodation of large districts of people, unless those people would relinquish the right of Representation in the Legislature, a right inestimable to them and formidable to tyrants only. He has called together legislative bodies at places unusual, uncomfortable, and distant from the depository of their public Records, for the sole purpose of fatiguing them into compliance with his measures. He has dissolved Representative Houses repeatedly, for opposing with manly firmness his invasions on the rights of the people. He has refused for a long time, after such dissolutions, to cause others to be elected; whereby the Legislative powers, incapable of Annihilation, have returned to the People at large for their exercise; the State remaining in the mean time exposed to all the dangers of invasion from without, and convulsions within. He has endeavoured to prevent the population of these States; for that purpose obstructing the Laws for Naturalization of Foreigners; refusing to pass others to encourage their migrations hither, and raising the conditions of new Appropriations of Lands. He has obstructed the Administration of Justice, by refusing his Assent to Laws for establishing Judiciary powers. He has made Judges dependent on his Will alone, for the tenure of their offices, and the amount and payment of their salaries. He has erected a multitude of New Offices, and sent hither swarms of Officers to harass our people, and eat out their substance. He has kept among us, in times of peace, standing Armies without the Consent of our legislatures. He has affected to render the Military independent of and superior to the Civil power. He has combined with others to subject us to a jurisdiction foreign to our constitution, and unacknowledged by our laws; giving his Assent to their Acts of pretended Legislation: For Quartering large bodies of armed troops among us: For protecting them, by a mock Trial, from punishment for any Murders which they should commit on the Inhabitants of these States: For cutting off our Trade with all parts of the world: For imposing Taxes on us without our Consent: For depriving us in many cases of the benefits of Trial by Jury: For transporting us beyond Seas to be tried for pretended offences: For abolishing the free System of English Laws in a neighbouring Province, establishing therein an Arbitrary government, and enlarging its Boundaries so as to render it at once an example and fit instrument for introducing the same absolute rule into these Colonies: For taking away our Charters, abolishing our most valuable Laws, and altering fundamentally the Forms of our Governments: For suspending our own Legislatures, and declaring themselves invested with power to legislate for us in all cases whatsoever. He has abdicated Government here, by declaring us out of his Protection and waging War against us. He has plundered our seas, ravaged our Coasts, burnt our towns, and destroyed the Lives of our people. He is at this time transporting large Armies of foreign Mercenaries to compleat the works of death, desolation and tyranny, already begun with circumstances of Cruelty & perfidy scarcely paralleled in the most barbarous ages, and totally unworthy the Head of a civilized nation. He has constrained our fellow Citizens taken Captive on the high Seas to bear Arms against their Country, to become the executioners of their friends and Brethren, or to fall themselves by their Hands. He has excited domestic insurrections amongst us, and has endeavoured to bring on the inhabitants of our frontiers, the merciless Indian Savages, whose known rule of warfare, is an undistinguished destruction of all ages, sexes and conditions. In every stage of these Oppressions We have Petitioned for Redress in the most humble terms: Our repeated Petitions have been answered only by repeated injury. A Prince, whose character is thus marked by every act which may define a Tyrant, is unfit to be the ruler of a free people. Nor have We been wanting in attentions to our Brittish brethren. We have warned them from time to time of attempts by their legislature to extend an unwarrantable jurisdiction over us. We have reminded them of the circumstances of our emigration and settlement here. We have appealed to their native justice and magnanimity, and we have conjured them by the ties of our common kindred to disavow these usurpations, which, would inevitably interrupt our connections and correspondence. They too have been deaf to the voice of justice and of consanguinity. We must, therefore, acquiesce in the necessity, which denounces our Separation, and hold them, as we hold the rest of mankind, Enemies in War, in Peace Friends.

We, therefore, the Representatives of the United States of America, in General Congress, Assembled, appealing to the Supreme Judge of the world for the rectitude of our intentions, do, in the Name, and by Authority of the good People of these Colonies, solemnly publish and declare, That these United Colonies are, and of Right ought to be Free and Independent States; that they are Absolved from all Allegiance to the British Crown, and that all political connection between them and the State of Great Britain, is and ought to be totally dissolved; and that as Free and Independent States, they have full Power to levy War, conclude Peace, contract Alliances, establish Commerce, and to do all other Acts and

Things which Independent States may of right do. And for the support of this Declaration, with a firm reliance on the protection of divine Providence, we mutually pledge to each other our Lives, our Fortunes and our sacred Honor.

8. Note, for example, that Thacher's pamphlet seems to be directed against parliament and the British government generally while Jefferson's Declaration singles out the King as the villain. Why? Note the reference in the beginning of the Declaration to the "Laws of Nature and of Nature's God" which are said to guarantee "separate and equal" stations to the peoples of the world. Note, as you probably have frequently, the ideas that "all men are created equal," that their "Creator" endows them with "certain unalienable Rights," that governments are instituted to secure these rights and that these governments derive "their just powers from the consent of the governed." Do these political premises have any bearing on the debate between Hutchinson and Thacher? Note also that while the King is accused of dissolving "Representative Houses repeatedly," the "Legislative Powers, incapable of Annihilation, have returned to the People at large for their exercise." How could this be? And why is it critical that Jefferson establish this point in the Declaration? See generally Carl Becker's little classic, The Declaration of Independence (1922), and see also the provocative treatment by the contemporary political commentator Garry Wills, Inventing America: Jefferson's Declaration of Independence (1978).

9. Part of what was ultimately at stake here, as American historians seem increasingly to recognize, was the idea of constitutionalism, that there are certain fundamental principles or laws which are sacred, transcendent, and immutable, and which circumscribe the activities of the Government. How would Hutchinson have reacted to this idea? Does he suggest that there are any inherent limits on the powers of Parliament? Does Thacher? Does Jefferson? What about Hutchinson's ideas on the allegiance of the subject? Would Jefferson agree with these? Note that Hutchinson indicates toward the close of his dialogue that there could be no organ of government capable of declaring that the actions of the government are "unconstitutional." Why is that? Do you agree with Hutchinson?

10. We have now acquired some sense of how problems of legality and constitutionalism figured in the American Revolution. These were to become perennial American difficulties. In the next set of readings and in Chapter Two we will attempt to come to grips with some of the practical problems of constitutionalism in the early American republic. One such problem of American constitutionalism is whether the Declaration of Independence, which you have just read, set forth principles or doctrines which of necessity were incorporated in other fundamental documents, such as the federal Constitution of 1789. On this question compare Scott Douglas Gerber, To Secure These Rights: The Declaration of Independence and Constitutional Interpretation (1995), and Michael P. Zuckert, The Natural Rights Republic: Studies in the Foundation of the American Political Tradition (1996) (suggesting that this was the intention of the framers) with Thomas B. McAffee, Inherent Rights,

The Written Constitution and Popular Sovereignty: The Founders' Understanding (2000), and Thomas B. McAffee, "Does the Federal Constitution Incorporate the Declaration of Independence?", 1 Nev. L.J. 138 (2001) (arguing that no such incorporation is proper).

E. TOWARDS POPULAR SOVEREIGNTY AND CONSTITUTIONALISM

We begin our examination of the political, constitutional, and legal philosophies in the early American republic with the Pennsylvania Constitution of 1776, generally believed to have been the most "democratic" or "radical" frame of government to emerge out of the American revolution. We will then compare and contrast the relatively "moderate" constitutional and legislative experience in Virginia, as described by Thomas Jefferson. Finally, in the beginning of the next Chapter, we will examine the "conservative" thought of the "Federalists," the political group which dominated the national government for twelve years after the adoption of the United States Constitution in 1789. As you examine these materials, see if you can discern some of the same concerns and themes to be found in the readings dealing with Hutchinson, Thacher, and the Declaration of Independence.

1. THE PENNSYLVANIA CONSTITUTION OF 1776

THE PROCEEDINGS RELATIVE TO THE CALLING OF THE CONVENTIONS OF 1776 AND 1790 * * *

54–65 (1825).

WHEREAS all government ought to be instituted and supported for the security and protection of the community as such, and to enable the individuals who compose it, to enjoy their natural rights, and the other blessings which the author of existence has bestowed upon man; and whenever these great ends of government are not obtained, the people have a right by common consent to change it, and take such measures as to them may appear necessary, to promote their safety and happiness. And whereas the inhabitants of this commonwealth, have, in consideration of protection only, heretofore acknowledged allegiance to the king of Great Britain, and the said king has not only withdrawn that protection, but commenced and still continues to carry on with unabated vengeance, a most cruel and unjust war against them, employing therein not only the troops of Great Britain, but foreign mercenaries, savages and slaves, for the avowed purpose of reducing them to a total and abject submission to the despotic domination of the British parliament * * * whereby all allegiance and fealty to the said king and his successors are dissolved and at an end, and all power and authority derived from him ceased in these colonies. And whereas it is absolutely necessary for the welfare and safety of the inhabitants of said colonies, that they be henceforth free and independent states, and that just, permanent and proper forms of government exist in every part of them, derived from, and founded on the authority of the people only, agreeable to the directions of the honorable American congress. WE, the representatives of the freemen of Pennsylvania, in general convention met, for the express purpose of framing such a government, * * * and being fully convinced, that it is our indispensible duty to establish such original principles of government, as will best promote the general happiness of the people of this state and their posterity, and provide for future improvements, without partiality for, or prejudice against, any particular class, sect or denomination of men whatsoever, do, by virtue of the authority vested in us by our constituents, ordain, declare and establish the following declaration of rights, and frame of government, to be the constitution of this commonwealth, and to remain in force therein for ever unaltered, except in such articles as shall hereafter, on experience, be found to require improvement, and which shall by the same authority of the people, fairly delegated, as this frame of government directs, be amended or improved for the more effectual obtaining and securing the great end and design of all government, herein before mentioned.

CHAPTER I

A DECLARATION OF THE RIGHTS OF THE INHABITANTS OF THE COMMONWEALTH OR STATE OF PENNSYLVANIA

I. That all men are born equally free and independent, and have certain natural, inherent and unalienable rights, amongst which are the enjoying and defending life and liberty, acquiring, possessing and protecting property, and pursuing and obtaining happiness and safety.

II. That all men have a natural and unalienable right to worship Almighty God, according to the dictates of their own consciences and understanding, and that no man ought, or of right can be compelled to attend any religious worship, or erect or support any place of worship, or maintain any ministry, contrary to, or against his own free will and con sent, nor can any man who acknowledges the being of a God, be justly deprived or abridged of any civil right as a citizen, on account of his religious sentiments, or peculiar mode of religious worship; and that no authority can, or ought to be vested in, or assumed by any power whatever, that shall in any case interfere with, or in any manner controul the right of conscience in the free exercise of religious worship.

* * *

IV. That all power being originally inherent in, and consequently derived from the people; therefore all officers of government, whether legislative or executive, are their trustees and servants, and at all times accountable to them.

V. That government is, or ought to be, instituted for the common benefit, protection, and security of the people, nation or community; and not for the particular emolument or advantage of any single man, family, or set of men, who are a part only of that community; and that the community hath an indubitable, unalienable and indefeasible right to reform, alter or abolish government, in such manner as shall be by that community judged most conducive to the public weal.

VI. That those who are employed in the legislative and executive business of the state, may be restrained from oppression, the people have a right, at such periods as they may think proper, to reduce their public officers to a private station, and supply the vacancies by certain and regular elections.

VII. That all elections ought to be free, and that all free men, having a sufficient evident common interest with and attachment to the community, have a right to elect officers, or to be elected into office.

VIII. That every member of society hath a right to be protected in the enjoyment of life, liberty and property, and therefore is bound to contribute his proportion towards the expense of that protection, and yield his personal service when necessary, or an equivalent thereto; but no part of a man's property can be justly taken from him or applied to public uses, without his own consent or that of his legal representatives; nor can any man who is conscientiously scrupulous of bearing arms be justly compelled thereto if he will pay such equivalent; nor are the people bound by any laws but such as they have in like manner assented to, for their common good.

IX. That in all prosecutions for criminal offences, a man hath a right to be heard by himself and his council; to demand the cause and nature of his accusation; to be confronted with the witnesses, to call for evidence in his favor, and a speedy public trial by an impartial jury of the country, without the unanimous consent of which jury he cannot be found guilty; nor can he be compelled to give evidence against himself; nor can any man be justly deprived of his liberty, except by the laws of the land or the judgment of his peers.

X. That the people have a right to hold themselves, their houses, papers and possessions free from search and seizure; and therefore warrants, without oaths or affirmations first made, affording a sufficient foundation for them, and whereby any officer or messenger may be commanded or required to search suspected places, or to seize any person or persons, his or their property not particularly described, are contrary to that right, and ought not to be granted.

XI. That in controversies respecting property, and in suits between man and man, the parties have a right to trial by jury, which ought to be held sacred.

XII. That the people have a right to freedom of speech, and of writing and publishing their sentiments; therefore the freedom of the press ought not to be restrained.

XIII. That the people have a right to bear arms for the defence of themselves, and the state; and as standing armies in the time of peace, are dangerous to liberty, they ought not to be kept up; and that the military should be kept under strict subordination to, and governed by the civil power.

XIV. That a frequent recurrence to fundamental principles and a firm adherence to justice, moderation, temperance, industry and frugality, are absolutely necessary to preserve the blessings of liberty and keep a government free. The people ought therefore to pay particular attention to these points in the choice of officers and representatives, and have a right to exact a due and constant regard to them from their legislatures and magistrates, in the making and executing such laws as are necessary for the good government of the state.

XV. That all men have a natural inherent right to emigrate from one state to another that will receive them, or to form a new state in vacant countries, or in such countries as they can purchase, whenever they think that thereby they may promote their own happiness.

XVI. That the people have a right to assemble together to consult for their common good, to instruct their representatives, and to apply to the legislature for redress of grievances by address, petition or remonstrance.

CHAPTER II

PLAN OR FRAME OF GOVERNMENT FOR THE COMMONWEALTH OR STATE OF PENNSYLVANIA

[*A. General Provisions*]

Section 1. The commonwealth or state of Pennsylvania shall be governed hereafter by an assembly of the representatives of the freemen of the same, and a president and council, in manner and form following:—

Sect. 2. The supreme legislative power shall be vested in a house of representatives of the freemen of the commonwealth or state of Pennsylvania.

Sect. 3. The supreme executive power shall be vested in a president and council.

Sect. 4. Courts of justice shall be established in the city of Philadelphia, and in every county of this state.

Sect. 5. The freemen of this commonwealth and their sons shall be trained and armed for its defence, under such regulations, restrictions and exceptions as the general assembly shall by law direct; preserving always to the people the right of choosing their colonels and all commissioned officers under that rank, in such manner, and as often as by the said laws shall be directed.

Sect. 6. Every freeman of the full age of twenty-one years, having resided in this state for the space of one whole year next before the day of election for representatives, and paid public taxes during that time, shall enjoy the right of an elector: Provided always, That sons of freeholders of the age of twenty-one years shall be entitled to vote, although they have not paid taxes.

[*B. The House of Representatives*]

Sect. 7. The house of representatives of the freemen of this commonwealth shall consist of persons most noted for wisdom and virtue, to be chosen by the freemen of every city and county of this commonwealth respectively, and no person shall be elected unless he has resided in the city or county for which he shall be chosen two years immediately before the said election, nor shall any member, while he continues such, hold any other office except in the militia.

Sect. 8. No person shall be capable of being elected a member to serve in the house of representatives of the freemen of this commonwealth more than four years in seven.

Sect. 9. The members of the house of representatives shall be chosen annually by ballot, by the freemen of the commonwealth * * * and shall have power to choose their speaker, the treasurer of the state, and their other officers; sit on their own adjournments; prepare bills and enact them into laws; judge of the elections and qualifications of their own members; they may expel a member, but not a second time for the same cause; they may administer oaths or affirmations on examination of witnesses; redress grievances; impeach state criminals; grant charters of incorporation; constitute towns, boroughs, cities and counties; and shall have all other powers necessary for the legislature of a free state or commonwealth; but they shall have no power to add to, alter, abolish or infringe any part of this constitution.

Sect. 10. A quorum of the house of representatives shall consist of two-thirds of the whole number of members elected, and having met and chosen their speaker, shall each of them, before they proceed to business, take and subscribe as well the oath or affirmation of fidelity and allegiance hereinafter directed, as the following oath or affirmation, viz.

I _______ _______ do swear (or affirm) that as a member of this assembly, I will not propose or assent to any bill, vote or resolution, which shall appear to me injurious to the people, nor do or consent to any act or thing whatever, that shall have a tendency to lessen or abridge their rights and privileges as declared in the constitution of this state, but will in all things conduct myself as a faithful honest representative and guardian of the people, according to the best of my judgment and abilities.

And each member, before he takes his seat, shall make and subscribe the following declaration, viz.

I do believe in one God, the creator and governor of the universe, the rewarder of the good and punisher of the wicked, and I do acknowledge the scriptures of the Old and New Testament to be given by Divine Inspiration.

And no further or other religious test shall ever hereafter be required of any civil officer or magistrate in this state.

Sect. 11. Delegates to represent this state in congress shall be chosen by ballot by the future general assembly at their first meeting, and annually for ever afterwards as long as such representation shall be necessary. Any delegate may be superseded at any time, by the general assembly appointing another in his stead. No man shall sit in congress longer than two years successively, nor be capable of re-election for three years afterwards; and no person who holds any office in the gift of the congress shall hereafter be elected to represent this commonwealth in congress.

* * *

Sect. 13. The doors of the house in which the representatives of the freemen of this state shall sit in general assembly, shall be and remain open for the admission of all persons, who behave decently, except only when the welfare of this state may require the doors to be shut.

Sect. 14. The votes and proceedings of the general assembly shall be printed weekly, during their sitting, with the yeas and nays on any question, vote or resolution, where any two members require it, except when the vote is taken by ballot; and when the yeas and nays are so taken, every member shall have a right to insert the reasons of his vote upon the minutes, if he desires it.

Sect. 15. To the end that laws before they are enacted, may be more maturely considered, and the inconvenience of hasty determinations as much as possible prevented, all bills of a public nature shall be printed for the consideration of the people, before they are read in general assembly the last time for debate and amendment; and except on occasions of sudden necessity, shall not be passed into laws until the next session of assembly; and for the more perfect satisfaction of the public, the reasons and motives for making such laws shall be fully and clearly expressed in the preambles.

* * *

Sect. 17. * * * as representation in proportion to the number of taxable inhabitants is the only principle which can at all times secure liberty and make the voice of a majority of the people the law of the land; therefore the general assembly shall cause complete lists of the taxable inhabitants in the city and each county in the commonwealth respectively, to be taken and returned to them on or before the last meeting of the assembly elected in the year one thousand seven hundred and seventy-eight, who shall appoint a representation to reach in proportion to the number of taxables in such returns, which representation shall continue for the next seven years afterwards, at the end of which, a new return of the taxable inhabitants shall be made, and a representation agreeable thereto appointed by the said assembly, and so on septennially for ever.

* * *

[*C. The Executive*]

Sect. 19. For the present the supreme executive council of this state shall consist of twelve persons chosen in the following manner: The freemen of the city of Philadelphia, and of the counties of Philadelphia, Chester and Bucks respectively, shall choose by ballot one person for the city and one for each county aforesaid, to serve for three years and no longer, at the time and place for electing representatives in general assembly. The freemen of the counties of Lancaster, York, Cumberland, and Berks, shall in like manner elect one person for each county respectively, to serve as councillors for two years and no longer. And the counties of Northampton, Bedford, Northumberland and Westmoreland respectively, shall in like manner elect one person for each county, to serve as councillors for one year and no longer: And at the expiration of the time for which each councillor was chosen to serve, the freemen of the city of Philadelphia and of the several counties in this state respectively, shall elect one person to serve as councillor for three years and no longer, and so on every third year for ever. By this mode of election and continual rotation more men will be trained to public business, there will in every subsequent year be found in the council a number of persons acquainted with the proceedings of the foregoing years, whereby the business will be more consistently conducted, and moreover the danger of establishing an inconvenient aristocracy will be effectually prevented. * * * No member of the general assembly or delegate in Congress, shall be chosen a member of the council. The president and vice-president shall be chosen annually by the joint ballot of the general assembly and council, of the members of the council. Any person having served as a councillor for three successive years, shall be incapable of holding that office for four years afterwards. Every member of the council shall be a justice of the peace for the whole commonwealth, by virtue of his office.

The council shall meet annually, at the same time and place with the general assembly.

The treasurer of the state, trustees of the loan-office, naval officers, collectors of customs or excise, judge of the admiralty, attornies-general, sheriffs and prothonotaries, shall not be capable of a seat in the general assembly, executive council or continental congress.

Sect. 20. The president, and in his absence the vice-president, with the council, five of whom shall be a quorum, shall have power to appoint and commissionate judges, naval officers, judge of the admiralty, attorney-general and all other officers, civil and military, except such as are chosen by the general assembly or the people * * *. They are to correspond with other states, and transact business with the officers of government, civil and military, and to prepare such business as may appear to them necessary, to lay before the general assembly. They shall sit as judges, to hear and determine on impeachments, taking to their assistance, for advice only, the justices of the supreme court. And shall have power to grant pardons and remit fines in all cases whatsoever, except in cases of impeachment; and in cases of treason and murder shall have power to grant reprieves, but not to pardon, until the end of the next session of assembly, but there shall be no remission or mitigation of punishment on impeachments, except by act of the legislature; they are also to take care that the laws be faithfully executed; they are to expedite the execution of such measures as may be resolved upon by the general assembly; and they may draw upon the treasury for such sums as shall be appropriated by the house. They may also lay embargoes, or prohibit the exportation of any commodity, for any time, not exceeding thirty days, in the recess of the house only. They may grant such licences as shall be directed by law, and shall have power to call together the general assembly when necessary, before the day to which they shall stand adjourned. The president shall be commander in chief of the forces of the state, but shall not command in person, except advised thereto by the council, and then only so long as they shall approve thereof. * * *

* * *

Sect. 22. Every officer of state, whether judicial or executive, shall be liable to be impeached by the general assembly, either when in office or after his resignation or removal for mal-administration. All impeachments shall be before the president or vice-president and council, who shall hear and determine the same.

[*D. The Judiciary*]

Sect. 23. The judges of the supreme court of judicature shall have fixed salaries, be commissioned for seven years only, though capable of re-appointment at the end of that term, but removable for misbehaviour at any time by the general assembly; they shall not be allowed to sit as members in the continental congress, executive council or general assembly, nor to hold any other office, civil or military, nor take or receive fees or perquisites of any kind.

* * *

Sect. 25. Trials shall be by jury as heretofore, and it is recommended to the legislature of this state to provide by law against every corruption or partiality in the choice, return or appointment of juries.

Sect. 26. Courts of sessions, common pleas and orphans' courts shall be held quarterly in each city and county, and the legislature shall have power to establish all such other courts as they may judge for the good of the inhabitants of the state; all courts shall be open, and justice shall be impartially administered without corruption or unnecessary delay: All their officers shall be paid an adequate but moderate compensation for their services, and if any officer shall take greater or other fees than the laws allow him, either directly or indirectly, it shall ever after disqualify him from holding any office in this state.

* * *

[*E. Other*]

* * *

Sect. 32. All elections, whether by the people or in general assembly, shall be by ballot, free and voluntary: And any elector, who shall receive any gift or reward for his vote, in meat, drink, monies or otherwise, shall forfeit his right to elect for that time, and suffer such other penalty as future laws shall direct. And any person who shall directly or indirectly give, promise or bestow any such rewards to be elected, shall be thereby rendered incapable to serve for the ensuing year.

* * *

Sect. 35. The printing presses shall be free to every person, who undertakes to examine the proceedings of the legislature, or any part of government.

Sect. 36. As every freeman, to preserve his independence, (if without a sufficient estate,) ought to have some profession, calling, trade or farm, whereby he may honestly subsist, there can be no necessity for nor use in establishing offices of profit, the usual effects of which are dependence and servility, unbecoming freemen, in the possessors and expectants, faction, contention, corruption, and disorder among the people: but if any man is called into public service to the prejudice of his private affairs, he has a right to a reasonable compensation: And whenever an office, through increase of fees, or otherwise becomes so profitable as to occasion many to apply for it, the profits ought to be lessened by the legislature.

Sect. 37. The future legislature of this state shall regulate entails in such manner as to prevent perpetuities.

Sect. 38. The penal laws as heretofore used, shall be reformed by the future legislature of this state, as soon as may be, and punishments made in some cases less sanguinary, and in general more proportionate to the crimes.

Sect. 39. To deter more effectually from the commission of crimes, by continued visible punishment of long duration, and to make sanguinary punishments less necessary, houses ought to be provided for punishing by hard labour, those who shall be convicted of crimes not capital; wherein the criminals shall be employed for the benefit of the public, or for reparation of injuries done to private persons. And all persons at proper times shall be admitted to see the prisoners at their labour.

* * *

Sect. 41. No public tax, custom or contribution shall be imposed upon, or paid by the people of this state, except by a law for that purpose; and before any law be made for raising it, the purpose for which any tax is to be raised, ought to appear clearly to the legislature to be of more service to the community than the money would be, if not collected, which being well observed, taxes can never be burthens.

* * *

Sect. 44. A school or schools shall be established in each county by the legislature for the convenient instruction of youth, with such salaries to the masters paid by the public as may enable them to instruct youth at low prices: And all useful learning shall be duly encouraged and promoted in one or more universities.

Sect. 45. Laws for the encouragement of virtue, and prevention of vice and immorality, shall be made and constantly kept in force, and provision shall be made for their due execution: And all religious societies or bodies of men heretofore united or incorporated for the advancement of religion and learning, or for other pious and charitable purposes, shall be encouraged and protected in the enjoyment of the privileges, immunities and estates which they were accustomed to enjoy or could of right have enjoyed under the laws and former constitution of this state.

* * *

[*F. Council of Censors*]

Sect. 47. In order that the freedom of this commonwealth may be preserved inviolate for ever, there shall be chosen, by ballot, by the freemen in each city and county respectively, on the second Tuesday in October, in the year one thousand seven hundred and eighty-three, and on the second Tuesday in October, in every seventh year thereafter, two persons in each city and county of this state, to be called THE COUNCIL OF CENSORS, who shall meet together on the second Monday of November next ensuing their election; the majority of whom shall be a quorum in every case, except as to calling a convention, in which two-thirds of the whole number elected shall agree, and whose duty it shall be to enquire whether the constitution has been preserved inviolate in every part; and whether the legislative and executive branches of government have performed their duty, as guardians of the people, or assumed to themselves or exercised other or greater powers than they are entitled to by the constitution; they are also to enquire whether the public taxes have been justly laid and collected in all parts of this commonwealth, in what manner the public monies have been disposed of, and whether the laws have been duly executed: For these purposes they shall have power to send for persons, papers and records; they shall have authority to pass public censures, to order impeachments, and to recommend to the legislature the repealing such laws as appear to them to have been enacted contrary to the principles of the constitution. These powers they shall continue to have for and during the space of one year, from the day of their election, and no longer. The said council of censors shall also have power to call a convention, to meet within two years after their sitting, if there appear to them an absolute necessity of amending any article of the constitution, which may be defective, explaining such as may be thought not clearly expressed, and of adding such as are necessary for the preservation of the rights and happiness of the people; but the articles to be amended, and the amendments proposed, * * * shall be promulgated at least six months before the day appointed for the election of such convention, for the previous consideration of the people, that they may have an opportunity of instructing their delegates on the subject.

NOTES AND QUESTIONS

1. Of all the state constitutions, Pennsylvania's was the purest application of revolutionary political theory to government; it also reflects many of the experiences and concerns of the colonists in the 1760's and 1770's. Do you see, for example, any similarities in the preamble to the Pennsylvania Constitution and the Declaration of Independence? Can you explain any specific provisions of the Constitution by reference to other readings in the course?

2. Note what rights the Pennsylvania Constitution-makers deemed to be fundamental. For example, in Section VIII of Chapter I (the Declaration of Rights), the right of Pennsylvanians to enjoy "life, liberty, and property" is

acknowledged. Also in that section the Constitution suggests that none of these rights, especially property, are to be infringed except by consent of the individual involved or by that of his legal representatives. How effective a protection is this? Who would be his "legal representatives?"

3. Why is this constitution thought to be so democratic? Examine, for example, the section of the Declaration of Rights which refers to the franchise (Section VII), but see the qualification to this principle in the Constitution itself (Chapter II, Section 6). Note that elections to the House of Representatives are to be held annually. Why is this? Note also the provision prohibiting any persons from serving in the House of Representatives for more than four years out of seven. Why? Do these provisions strike you as attempts to deal with political difficulties that are still with us today?

4. Examine the powers of the House of Representatives, and compare these to the powers of the other branches of government (Executive Council, Judiciary, Council of Censors). Which do you regard as the most important? How are representatives to the Continental Congress to be chosen?

5. Note that the Executive powers (Section 20 of Chapter II) are vested in a council, originally to consist of twelve persons elected to represent respectively the counties of the state and the city of Philadelphia. Why do you suppose the Pennsylvanians thought it wise to place executive powers in plural hands? Do the provisions for rotation in office of the members of the Executive Council (Section 19 of Chapter II) give you any clues?

6. In connection with the philosophy behind the concept of a plural executive, consider several other bold provisions in Chapter II. Section 36 discourages "offices of profit." What are these? Section 37 discourages "entails." Why? What about the philosophy of crimes limned in Sections 38 and 39? Do you suppose that the resolution of criminal matters in Pennsylvania was to follow the same course as in England?

7. Finally, consider this body to be called the "Council of Censors," created by Section 47. Why is there a need for such a body? What institution would today perform their function of scrutinizing the constitutionality of the activities of the other branches of government?

8. The Pennsylvania Constitution of 1776 lasted only fourteen years. Why do you suppose it had such a short lifespan? The Pennsylvania Constitution of 1790, which replaced the document which you have just read

> * * * [W]as exceedingly reactionary and undid much of the work of the early framers. In the new Constitution the legislative, executive, and judicial powers were distinguished and defined according to the now classic American method. Provision was made for a governor, an assembly, and a senate. A judiciary serving during good behavior was also established—an ideal strongly opposed in the Convention of 1776 as entirely too aristocratic.

J. Paul Selsam, The Pennsylvania Constitution of 1776: A Study in Revolutionary Democracy 259 (1971). The United States Constitution of 1787 (reproduced as an Appendix to this book) has been labelled by some historians as a "counter revolution" or "a revolution of conservatism." Can something similar be said of the revised Pennsylvania Constitution?

For a very provocative meditation on the meaning of the short-lived Pennsylvania Constitution of 1776, and, in particular, its creation of the Council of Censors, see Matthew J. Herrington, "Popular Sovereignty in Pennsylvania 1776–1791," 67 Temple L.Rev. 575 (1994). Herrington seeks to present events in Pennsylvania as a case study in "constitutional politics," extraordinary political activity of a kind posited and described by Bruce A. Ackerman in his We the People: Foundations (1992), and by Akhil Reed Amar in "Philadelphia Revisited: Amending the Constitution Outside Article V," 55 U.Chi.L.Rev. 1043 (1988). Ackerman's and Amar's important works explore the interaction between popular politics and constitutional meaning and order. There has been an increasing interest in state-constitution making, as scholars have sought to compare the constitutions in the states with developments regarding the Federal Constitution. See, for two such notable efforts, Marc W. Kruman, Between Authority and Liberty: State Constitution Making in Revolutionary America (1997), and, for the slightly later period, Laura Scalia, America's Jeffersonian Experiment: Remaking State Constitutions 1820–1850 (1999).

9. As you read the excerpts from Jefferson's Notes on Virginia which follow, see if you can determine to what extent he favors the political philosophy behind the Pennsylvania Constitution of 1776. You should also try to determine how closely the government of Virginia in 1776 corresponds to the Pennsylvania institutions.

2. THOMAS JEFFERSON, NOTES ON THE STATE OF VIRGINIA (1781)

[Thomas Jefferson was admitted to the Virginia bar in 1767 after graduating from the College of William and Mary and studying law under George Wythe. He was a young man of 33 when he served as a Virginia delegate to the Second Continental Congress and drafted the Declaration of Independence in Philadelphia in the summer of 1776. Like John Adams, he had a scholarly bent and gravitated quickly to the "whig" or "American" side of the dispute over the nature and extent of British colonial rule in the 1770s. He served in the Virginia House of Burgesses, where he interacted with Patrick Henry and other rising patriots in the colony. He was a brilliant writer although more convincing in his written than spoken advocacy. He wrote "A Summary View of the Rights of British America" in 1774, an early and radical statement challenging the necessity of loyalty to Parliament.

From 1776 to 1779 he was a representative in Virginia's House of Delegates, and in 1779 was elected governor, serving until 1781. He was responsible for the eventual abolition of an established (Anglican) church in the new state. He also was instrumental in ending Virginia's English-based system of primogeniture (where land was inherited entire by the eldest son) and entail (which required that property be kept in the family), the foundation in England of patriarchy and landed estates. From 1783 to 1784 Jefferson was a member of the Continental Congress, and at that time drafted the decree for the system of government in the trans-Appalachian Northwest Territory that became the basis of the Northwest Ordinance of 1787.

During the Philadelphia Convention of 1787, Jefferson was living in Paris as the American minister to France (1784–1789). He was in regular communication with James Madison during this time, and was a proponent of the proposed new national government though he wished to see the addition of a "bill of rights." A first-hand observer of the unfolding events leading up to the French Revolution, he became a quick friend of that cause that he saw as inevitable and necessary, albeit bloody.

He assumed the position of Secretary of State in President George Washington's first administration. The differences among the "Federalists" (supporters of Washington who coalesced around Treasury Secretary Alexander Hamilton) and a faction of national "Republicans" that began organizing around Jefferson and Madison put a strain on relations in the new national government. In 1793 Jefferson resigned his position; his conflict with Hamilton, inter alia, over policies that favored manufacturing, banking, and urban interests at the expense of agrarian proved insurmountable. Behind these disagreements was a deeper difference over the extent of national authority: Jefferson came to favor a more limited role for the national government if not government altogether; his vision of the future was one of independent yeomen farmers spreading out across the land.

Jefferson was elected Vice President in the election that elevated John Adams as President (1796). The passage by Congress and the implicit endorsement by Adams of the Federalist-inspired Alien and Sedition Acts of 1798 (which you will soon encounter) led, as you will see, to Jefferson and Madison's drafting of the Kentucky and Virginia Resolutions that set forth a purported right of the states to reject federal legislation. This became the basis of the "compact" theory of the Constitution, and the theory of "states rights" that would later be invoked by the Southern States which seceded from the Union following the election of Abraham Lincoln in 1860. This was in the future, though, and while no other state legislatures endorsed Jefferson's and Madison's resolutions, Jefferson was elected President, defeating the Federalist John Adams, in 1800.

In the excerpt which follows from his Notes on the State of Virginia, Jefferson is describing the Government of Virginia under the Virginia Constitution of 1776. Jefferson wrote Notes on the State of Virginia in 1781 after his retirement as governor and while at his home in Monticello. He revised his Notes and published them in 1787, on the eve of the Constitutional Convention. As you will see, the Jefferson who writes these Notes is not yet the critic of the national government and the proponent of states' rights he would eventually become. Indeed, can you find in these Notes the precise thinking of the author of the Declaration of Independence?]

* * *

* * * The executive powers are lodged in the hands of a governor, chosen annually, and incapable of acting more than three years in seven. He is assisted by a council of eight members. * * * Legislation is exercised by two houses of assembly, the one called the house of Delegates, composed of two members from each county, chosen annually by the citizens, possessing an estate for life in one hundred acres of uninhabited land, or twenty-five acres with a house on it, or in a house or lot in some town: the other called the Senate, consisting of twenty-four members, chosen quadrennially by the same electors, who for this purpose are distributed into twenty-four districts. The concurrence of both houses is necessary to the passage of a law. They have the appointment of the governor and council, the judges of the superior courts, auditors, attorney-general, treasurer, register of the land office, and delegates to Congress. * * *

This constitution was formed when we were new and unexperienced in the science of government. It was the first, too, which was formed in the whole United States. No wonder then that time and trial have discovered very capital defects in it.

1. The majority of the men in the State, who pay and fight for its support, are unrepresented in the legislature, * * *.

2. Among those who share the representation, the shares are very unequal. Thus the county of Warwick, with only one hundred fighting men, has an equal representation with the county of Loudon, which has one thousand seven hundred and forty-six. * * *

* * * [N]ineteen thousand men, living below the falls of the rivers, [occupying only 10% of the land] possess half the senate, and want four members only of possessing a majority of the house of delegates; a want more than supplied by the vicinity of their situation to the seat of government, and of course the greater degree of convenience and punctuality with which their members may and will attend in the legislature. These nineteen thousand, therefore, living in one part of the country, give law to upwards of thirty thousand living in another, and appoint all their chief officers, executive and judiciary. * * *

3. The senate is, by its constitution, too homogenous with the house of delegates. Being chosen by the same electors, at the same time, and out of the same subjects, the choice falls of course on men of the same descrip-

tion. The purpose of establishing different houses of legislation is to introduce the influence of different interests or different principles. Thus in Great Britain it is said their constitution relies on the house of commons for honesty, and the lords for wisdom; which would be a rational reliance, if honesty were to be bought with money, and if wisdom were hereditary. In some of the American States, the delegates and senators are so chosen, as that the first represent the persons, and the second the property of the State. But with us, wealth and wisdom have equal chance for admission into both houses. We do not, therefore, derive from the separation of our legislature into two houses, those benefits which a proper complication of principles are capable of producing, and those which alone can compensate the evils which may be produced by their dissensions.

4. All the powers of government, legislative, executive, and judiciary, result to the legislative body. The concentrating these in the same hands is precisely the definition of despotic government. It will be no alleviation that these powers will be exercised by a plurality of hands, and not by a single one. One hundred and seventy-three despots would surely be as oppressive as one. Let those who doubt it turn their eyes on the republic of Venice. * * * An elective despotism was not the government we fought for, but one which should not only be founded on free principles, but in which the powers of government should be so divided and balanced among several bodies of magistracy, as that no one could transcend their legal limits, without being effectually checked and restrained by the others. For this reason that convention which passed the ordinance of government, laid its foundation on this basis, that the legislative, executive, and judiciary departments should be separate and distinct, so that no person should exercise the powers of more than one of them at the same time. But no barrier was provided between these several powers. The judiciary and executive members were left dependent on the legislative, for their subsistence in office, and some of them for their continuance in it. If, therefore, the legislature assumes executive and judiciary powers, no opposition is likely to be made * * *. They have, accordingly, in many instances, decided rights which should have been left to judiciary controversy; and the direction of the executive, during the whole time of their session, is becoming habitual and familiar. * * * The views of the present members are perfectly upright. When they are led out of their regular province, it is by art in others, and inadvertence in themselves. * * * The public money and public liberty, intended to have been deposited with three branches of magistracy, but found inadvertently to be in the hands of one only, will soon be discovered to be sources of wealth and dominion to those who hold them * * *. Nor should our assembly be deluded by the integrity of their own purposes, and conclude that these unlimited powers will never be abused, because themselves are not disposed to abuse them. They should look forward to a time, and that not a distant one, when a corruption in this, as in the country from which we derive our origin, will

have seized the heads of government, and be spread by them through the body of the people * * *. Human nature is the same on every side of the Atlantic, and will be alike influenced by the same causes. The time to guard against corruption and tyranny, is before they shall have gotten hold of us. It is better to keep the wolf out of the fold, than to trust to drawing his teeth and talons after he shall have entered. * * *

5. That the ordinary legislature may alter the constitution itself. [The 1776 "constitution" was actually a statute passed by the Virginia "Convention" of 1776, a body of elected officials then serving as the new state's legislature.] * * * [T]his very convention, meeting as a house of delegates in general assembly with the Senate in the autumn of that year, passed acts of assembly in contradiction to their ordinance of government; and every assembly from that time to this has done the same. * * * [Jefferson proceeds to indicate his belief that a special convention should be called to approve a new state constitution and to make clear that it is not amendable by ordinary legislatures.] True it is, this is no time for deliberating on forms of government. While an enemy is within our bowels, the first object is to expel him. But when this shall be done, when peace shall be established, and leisure given us for intrenching within good forms, the rights for which we have bled, let no man be found indolent enough to decline a little more trouble for placing them beyond the reach of question. * * *

6. That the assembly exercises a power of determining the quorum of their own body which may legislate for us. After the establishment of the new form they adhered to the *Lex majoris partis,* founded in common law as well as common right. It is the natural law of every assembly of men, whose numbers are not fixed by any other law. They continued for some time to require the presence of a majority of their whole number, to pass an act. But the British parliament fixes its own quorum; our former assemblies fixed their own quorum; and one precedent in favor of power is stronger than an hundred against it. The house of delegates, therefore, have lately voted that, during the present dangerous invasion, forty members shall be a house to proceed to business. * * * But this danger could not authorize them to call that a house which was none; and if they may fix it at one number, they may at another, till it loses its fundamental character of being a representative body. * * *

* * *

* * * In December 1776, our circumstances being much distressed, it was proposed in the house of delegates to create a dictator, invested with every power legislative, executive, and judiciary, civil and military, of life and of death, over our persons and over our properties; and in June 1781, again under calamity, the same proposition was repeated, and wanted a few votes only of being passed. One who entered into this contest from a

pure love of liberty, and a sense of injured rights, who determined to make every sacrifice, and to meet every danger, for the re-establishment of those rights on a firm basis, who did not mean to expend his blood and substance for the wretched purpose of changing this matter for that, but to place the powers of governing him in a plurality of hands of his own choice, so that the corrupt will of no one man might in future oppress him, must stand confounded and dismayed when he is told, that a considerable portion of that plurality had mediated the surrender of them into a single hand, and, in lieu of a limited monarchy, to deliver him over to a despotic one! * * * In God's name, from whence have they derived this power? * * * Is it from any principle in our new constitution expressed or implied? Every lineament, expressed or implied, is in full opposition to it. Its fundamental principle is, that the State shall be governed as a commonwealth. It provides a republican organization, proscribes under the name of prerogative the exercise of all powers undefined by the laws; places on this basis the whole system of our laws * * *. Our ancient laws expressly declare, that those who are but delegates themselves shall not delegate to others powers which require judgment and integrity in their exercise. * * * They never admit the idea that [the people] like sheep or cattle, may be given from hand to hand without an appeal to their own will. Was it from the necessity of the case? Necessities which dissolve a government, do not convey its authority to an oligarchy or a monarchy. They throw back, into the hands of the people, the powers they had delegated, and leave them as individuals to shift for themselves. A leader may offer, but not impose himself, nor be imposed on them. * * * The necessity which should operate these tremendous effects should at least be palpable and irresistible. Yet in both instances, where it was feared, or pretended with us, it was belied by the event. * * *

In this State alone did there exist so little virtue, that fear was to be fixed in the hearts of the people, and to become the motive of their exertions, and principle of their government? The very thought alone was treason against the people; was treason against mankind in general; as rivetting forever the chains which bow down their necks, by giving to their oppressors a proof, which they would have trumpeted through the universe, of the imbecility of republican government, in times of pressing danger, to shield them from harm. * * * What a cruel moment was this for creating such an embarrassment, for putting to the proof the attachment of our countrymen to republican government! Those who meant well, of the advocates of this measure, (and most of them meant well, for I know them personally * * *) had been seduced in their judgment by the example of an ancient republic, whose constitution and circumstances were fundamentally different. They had sought this precedent in the history of Rome * * *. They had taken it from a republic rent by the most bitter factions and tumults where the government was of a heavy-handed unfeeling aristocracy, over a people ferocious, and rendered desperate by poverty and wretchedness; tumults which could not be allayed under the most trying circumstances, but by the omnipotent hand of a single despot. Their constitution, therefore, allowed a temporary tyrant to be erected, under the name of a dictator; and that temporary tyrant, after a few examples, became perpetual. They misapplied this precedent to a people mild in their dispositions, patient under their trial, united for the public liberty, and affectionate to their leaders. * * * Searching for the foundations of this proposition, I can find none which may pretend a color of right or reason, but the defect before developed, that there being no barrier between the legislative, executive, and judiciary departments, the legislature may seize the whole; that having seized it, and possessing a right to fix their own quorum, they may reduce that quorum to one, whom they may call a chairman, speaker, dictator, or by any other name they please. * * *

NOTES AND QUESTIONS

1. Based on what you have just read, do you think Thomas Jefferson would have voted for the adoption of the *Pennsylvania* Constitution of 1776? What does Jefferson see as the chief defect of the Virginia Constitution of 1776? What does he mean when he suggests several times that the Virginia Assembly has the potential to be despotic? Why does he believe that there must be different houses in a legislature, and they must be differently chosen? Would the framers of the Pennsylvania Constitution of 1776 have agreed with him?

2. Why is Jefferson disturbed that the Virginia legislature possesses the power to amend the constitution? What might he prefer as an alternative means of amendment? Why do you suppose, in an explanation of the workings of the Virginia Constitution, Jefferson feels that it is necessary to discuss the two bizarre episodes when the Virginia Assembly considered the creation of a "Dictator?" What heuristic purpose is to be served by the allusion to the practice in ancient Rome? What does it reveal about Jefferson's attitude toward the American people? You will have noticed that America as an example of "Republican" governments is of fundamental importance to him. Can you understand what Jefferson's ideal "Republic" would look like, how it might differ from that envisioned in the 1776 Pennsylvania Constitution, and how it might differ from ancient Rome? For the most influential, although most difficult treatment comparing European and American "Republican" thought see J.G.A. Pocock, The Machiavellian Moment: Florentine Political Thought and the Atlantic Republican Tradition (1975).

The notion of "republicanism," of creating and conducting government through the disinterested virtue of a self-sacrificing community had enormous appeal to the founding generation. It has enjoyed a renaissance among constitutional theoreticians seeking an alternative to the individualistic rights-based theories dominant in the sixties, seventies, and eighties. See, e.g., Cass R. Sunstein, The Partial Constitution (1993). Republicanism had its critics then and still does now. Do you think that Jefferson, for example, really believed that Americans possessed the virtue necessary to bring off republican government? Do you?

3. Jefferson's thoughts on the nature of Americans are perhaps more clearly stated in the excerpt which follows, from the next section of the Notes on Virginia, dealing with the revision of the Virginia substantive laws undertaken in 1776. Jefferson was the leading figure in the revisal.

3. JEFFERSON'S NOTES ON THE STATE OF VIRGINIA (CONTINUED)

The plan of the revisal was this. The common law of England, by which is meant, that part of the English law which was anterior to the date of the oldest statutes extant, is made the basis of the work. It was thought dangerous to attempt to reduce it to a text; it was therefore left to be collected from the usual monuments of it. Necessary alterations in that, and so much of the whole body of the British statutes, and of acts of assembly, as were thought proper to be retained, were digested into one hundred and twenty-six new acts, in which simplicity of style was aimed at, as far as was safe. The following are the most remarkable alterations proposed:

To change the rules of descent, so as that the lands of any person dying intestate shall be divisible equally among all his children, or other representatives, in equal degree.

To make slaves distributable among the next of kin, as other movables.

* * *

To establish religious freedom on the broadest bottom.

To emancipate all slaves born after the passing the act. The bill reported by the revisers does not itself contain this proposition; but an amendment containing it was prepared, to be offered to the legislature whenever the bill should be taken up, and farther directing, that they should continue with their parents to a certain age, then to be brought up, at the public expense, to tillage, arts, or sciences, according to their geniuses, till the females should be eighteen, and the males twenty-one years of age, when they should be colonized to such place as the circumstances of the time should render most proper, sending them out with arms, implements of household and of the handicraft arts, seeds, pairs of the useful domestic animals, & c., to declare them a free and independent people, and extend to them our alliance and protection, till they have acquired strength; and to send vessels at the same time to other parts of the world for an equal number of white inhabitants; to induce them to migrate hither, proper encouragements were to be proposed. It will probably be asked, Why not retain and incorporate the blacks into the State, and thus save the expense of supplying by importation of white settlers, the vacancies they will leave? Deep-rooted prejudices entertained by the whites; ten thousand recollections, by the blacks, of the injuries they have sustained; new provocations; the real distinctions which nature has made; and many other circumstances, will divide us into parties, and produce convulsions, which will probably never end but in the extermination of the one or the other race. To these objections, which are political, may be added others, which are physical and moral. The first difference which strikes us is that of color. * * * And is this difference of no importance? Is it not the foundation of a greater or less share of beauty in the two races? Are not the fine mixtures of red and white, the expressions of every passion by greater or less suffusions of color in the one, preferable to that eternal monotony, which reigns in the countenances, that immovable veil of black which covers the emotions of the other race? Add to these, flowing hair, a more elegant symmetry of form, their own judgment in favor of the whites, declared by their preference of them * * *. The circumstance of superior beauty, is thought worthy attention in the propagation of our horses, dogs, and other domestic animals; why not in that of man? * * * They have less hair on the face and body. They secrete less by the kidneys, and more by the glands of the skin, which gives them a very strong and disagreeable odor. This greater degree of transpiration, renders them more tolerant of heat, and less so of cold than the whites. * * * They seem to require less sleep. A black after hard labor through the day, will be induced by the slightest amusements to sit up till midnight, or later, though knowing he must be out with the first dawn of the morning. They are at least as brave, and more adventuresome. But this may perhaps proceed from a want of forethought, which prevents their seeing a danger till it be present. When present, they do not go through it with more coolness or steadiness than the whites. They are more ardent after their female; but love seems with them to be more an eager desire, than a tender delicate mixture of sentiment and sensation. Their griefs are transient. * * * In general, their existence appears to participate more of sensation than reflection. To this must be ascribed their disposition to sleep when abstracted from their diversions, and unemployed in labor. * * * Comparing them by their faculties of memory, reason, and imagination, it appears to me that in memory they are equal to the whites: in reason much inferior, as I think one could scarcely be found capable of tracing and comprehending the investigations of Euclid; and that in imagination they are dull, tasteless, and anomalous. * * * It will be right to make great allowances for the difference of condition, of education, of conversation, of the sphere in which they move. Many millions of them have been brought to, and born in America. Most of them, indeed, have been confined to tillage, to their own homes, and their own society; yet many have been so situated, that they might have availed themselves of the conversation of their masters * * *. Some have been liberally educated, and all have lived in countries where the arts and sciences are cultivated to a considerable degree, and all have had before their eyes samples of the best works from abroad. The Indians, with no advantages of this kind, will often carve figures on their pipes not destitute of design and merit. They will crayon out an animal, a plant, or a country, so as to prove the existence of a germ in their minds which only wants cultivation. They astonish you with strokes of the most sublime oratory; such as prove their reason and sentiment strong, their imagination glowing and elevated. But never yet could I find that a black had uttered a thought above the level of plain narration; never saw even an elementary trait of painting or sculpture. In music they are more generally gifted than the whites with accurate ears for tune and time, and they have been found capable of imagining a small catch. Whether they will be equal to the composition of a more extensive run of melody, or of complicated harmony, is yet to be proved. Misery is often the parent of the most affecting touches in poetry. Among the blacks is misery enough, God knows, but no poetry. Love is the peculiar oestrum of the poet. Their love is ardent, but it kindles the senses only, not the imagination. * * * The improvement of the blacks in body and mind, in the first instance of their mixture with the whites, has been observed by everyone, and proves that their inferiority is not the effect merely of their condition of life. We know that among the Romans, about the Augustan age especially, the condition of their slaves was much more deplorable than that of the blacks on the continent of America. The two sexes were confined in separate apartments, because to raise a child cost the master more than to buy one. Cato, for a very restricted indulgence to his slaves in this particular, took from them a certain price. But in this country the slaves multiply as fast as the free inhabitants. Their situation and manners place the commerce between the two sexes almost without restraint. The same Cato, on a principle of economy, always sold his sick and superannuated slaves. * * * The American slaves cannot enumerate this among the injuries and insults they receive. It was the common practice to expose in the island Aesculapius, in the Tyber, diseased slaves whose cure was like to become tedious. The emperor Claudius, by an edict, gave freedom to such of them as should recover, and first declared that if any person chose to kill rather than to expose them, it should not be deemed homicide. The exposing them is a crime of which no instance has existed with us; and were it to be followed by death, it would be punished capitally. We are told of a certain Vedius Pollio, who, in the presence of Augustus, would have given a slave as food to his fish, for having broken a glass. With the Romans, the regular method of taking the evidence of their slaves was under torture. Here it has been thought better never to resort to their evidence. When a master was murdered, all his slaves, in the same house or within hearing, were condemned to death. Here punishment falls on the guilty only, and as precise proof is required against him as against a freeman. Yet notwithstanding these and other discouraging circumstances among the Romans, their slaves were often their rarest artists. They excelled too in science, insomuch as to be usually employed as tutors to their master's children. Epictetus, Terence, and Phaedrus, were slaves. But they were of the race of whites. It is not their condition then, but nature, which has produced the distinction. Whether further observation will or will not verify the conjecture, that nature has been less bountiful to them in the endowments of the head, I believe that in those of the heart she will be found to have done them justice. That disposition to theft with which they have been branded, must be ascribed to their situation, and not to any depravity of the moral sense. The man in whose favor no laws of property exist, probably feels himself less bound to respect those made in favor of others. When arguing for ourselves, we lay it down as a fundamental, that laws, to be just, must give a reciprocation of right; that, without this, they are mere arbitrary rules of conduct, founded in force, and not in conscience; and it is a problem which I give to the master to solve, whether the religious precepts against the violation of property were not framed for him as well as his slave? And whether the slave may not as justifiably take a little from one who has taken all from him, as he may slay one who would slay him? * * * Notwithstanding these considerations which must weaken their respect for the laws of property, we find among them numerous instances of the most rigid integrity, and as many as among their better instructed masters, of benevolence, gratitude, and unshaken fidelity. The opinion that they are inferior in the faculties of reason and imagination, must be hazarded with great diffidence. To justify a general conclusion, requires many observations, even where the subject may be submitted to the anatomical knife, to optical glasses, to analysis by fire or by solvents. How much more then where it is a faculty, not a substance, we are examining; where it eludes the research of all the senses * * * let me add too, as a circumstance of great tenderness, where our conclusion would degrade a whole race of men from the rank in the scale of beings which their Creator may perhaps have given them. To our reproach it must be said, that though for a century and a half we have had under our eyes the races of black and of red men, they have never yet been viewed by us as subjects of natural history. I advance it, therefore, as a suspicion only, that the blacks, whether originally a distinct race, or made distinct by time and circumstances, are inferior to the whites in the endowments both of body and mind. It is not against experience to suppose that different species of the same genus, or varieties of the same species, may possess different qualifications. * * * This unfortunate difference of color, and perhaps of faculty, is a powerful obstacle to the emancipation of these people. Many of their advocates, while they wish to vindicate the liberty of human nature, are anxious also to preserve its dignity and beauty. Some of these, embarrassed by the question, "What further is to be done with them?" join themselves in opposition with those who are actuated by sordid avarice only. Among the Romans emancipation required but one effort. The slave, when made free, might mix with, without staining the blood of his master. But with us a second is necessary, unknown to history. When freed, he is to be removed beyond the reach of mixture.

The revised code further proposes to proportion crimes and punishments.

This is attempted on the following scale:

I. Crimes whose punishment extends to LIFE.

1. High treason.	Death by hanging.	
	Forfeiture of lands and goods to the commonwealth.	
2. Petty treason.	Death by hanging. Dissection.	
	Forfeiture of half the lands and goods to the representatives of the party slain.	
3. Murder.	1. By poison.	Death by poison.
		Forfeiture of one-half, as before.
	2. In duel.	Death by hanging. Gibbeting, if the challenger.
	Forfeiture of one-half as before, unless it be the party challenged, then the forfeiture is to the commonwealth.	
	3. In any other way.	Death by hanging.
	Forfeiture of one-half as before.	
4. Manslaughter.	The second offence is murder.	

II. Crimes whose punishment goes to LIMB

1. Rape.	)
2. Sodomy.	) Dismemberment.
	)
3. Maiming.	) Retaliation, and the forfeiture of half) of the lands and goods to the suf-) ferer.
4. Disfiguring.	

III. Crimes punishment by LABOR.

1. Manslaughter, 1st offence.	Labor VII. years for the public.	Forfeiture of half, as in murder.

2. Counterfeiting money.	Labor VI. years.	Forfeiture of lands and goods to the commonwealth.
3. Arson.	) Labor V. years.	Reparation three-fold
4. Asportation of vessels.	)	
5. Robbery.	)	
6. Burglary.	) Labor IV. years.	Reparation double.
	)	
7. House-breaking.	)	
	) Labor III. years.	Reparation.
8. Horse-stealing.	)	
9. Grand larceny.	Labor II. years.	Reparation. Pillory.
10. Petty Larceny.	Labor I. year.	Reparation. Pillory.
11. Pretensions to witch-craft, &c.	Ducking.	Stripes.

* * *

Another object of the revisal is, to diffuse knowledge more generally through the mass of the people. This bill proposes to lay off every county into small districts of five or six miles square, called hundreds, and in each of them to establish a school for teaching, reading, writing, and arithmetic. The tutor to be supported by the hundred, and every person in it entitled to send their children three years gratis, and as much longer as they please, paying for it. These schools to be under a visitor who is annually to choose the boy of best genius in the school, of those whose parents are too poor to give them further education, and to send him forward to one of the grammar schools, of which twenty are proposed to be erected in different parts of the country, for teaching Greek, Latin, Geography, and the higher branches of numerical arithmetic. Of the boys thus sent in one year, trial is to be made at the grammar schools one or two years, and the best genius of the whole selected, and continued six years, and the residue dismissed. By this means twenty of the best geniuses will be raked from the rubbish annually, and be instructed, at the public expense, so far as the grammar schools go. At the end of six years instruction, one half are to be discontinued (from among whom the grammar schools will probably be supplied with future masters); and the other half, who are to be chosen for the superiority of their parts and disposition, are to be sent and continued three years in the study of such sciences as they shall choose, at William and Mary college. * * * The ultimate result of the whole scheme of education would be the teaching all the children of the State reading, writing, and common arithmetic; turning out ten annually, of superior genius, well taught in Greek, Latin, Geography, and the higher branches of arithmetic; turning out ten others annually, of still superior parts, who, to those branches of learning, shall have added such of the sciences as their genius shall have led them to; the furnishing to the wealthier part of the people convenient schools at which their children may be educated at their own expense. The general objects of this law are to provide an education adapted to the years, to the capacity, and the condition of everyone, and directed to their freedom and happiness. * * * The first stage of this education being the schools of the hundreds, wherein the great mass of the people will receive their instruction, the principal foundations of future order will be laid here. Instead, therefore, of putting the Bible and Testament into the hands of the children at an age when their judgments are not sufficiently matured for religious inquiries, their memories may here be stored with the most useful facts from Grecian, Roman, European and American history. The first elements of morality too may be instilled into their minds; such as, when further developed as their judgments advance in strength, may teach them how to work out their own greatest happiness, by showing them that it does not depend on the condition of life in which chance has placed them, but is always the result of a good conscience, good health, occupation, and freedom in all just pursuits. Those whom either the wealth of their parents or the adoption of the State shall destine to higher degrees of learning, will go on to the grammar schools, which constitute the next stage, there to be instructed in the languages. The learning Greek and Latin, I am told, is going into disuse in Europe * * * it would be very ill judged in us to follow their example in this instance. There is a certain period of life, say from eight to fifteen or sixteen years of age, when the mind like the body is not yet firm enough for laborious and close operations. * * * The memory is then most susceptible and tenacious of impressions; and the learning of languages being chiefly a work of memory, it seems precisely fitted to the powers of this period, which is long enough too for acquiring the most useful languages, ancient and modern. * * * that time is not lost which is employed in providing tools for future operation; more especially as in this case the books put into the hands of the youth for this purpose may be such as will at the same time impress their minds with useful facts and good principles. * * * As soon as they are of sufficient age, it is supposed they will be sent on from the grammar schools to the university, which constitutes our third and last stage, there to study those sciences which may be adapted to their views. By that part of our plan which prescribes the selection of the youths of genius from among the classes of the poor, we hope to avail the State of those talents which nature has sown as liberally among the poor as the rich, but which perish without use, if not sought for and cultivated. But of the views of this law none is more important, none more legitimate, than that of rendering the people the safe, as they are the ultimate, guardians of their own liberty. For this purpose the reading in the first stage, where they will receive their whole education, is proposed, as has been said, to be chiefly historical. History, by apprizing them of the past, will enable them to judge of the future; it will avail them of the experience of other times and other nations; it will qualify them as judges of the actions and designs of men; it will enable them to know ambition under every disguise it may assume; and knowing it, to defeat its views. In every government on earth is some trace of human weakness, some germ of corruption and degeneracy, which cunning will discover, and wickedness insensibly open, cultivate and improve. Every government degenerates when trusted to the rulers of the people alone. The people themselves therefore are its only safe depositories. And to render even them safe, their minds must be improved to a certain degree. * * * An amendment of our constitution must here come in aid of the public education. The influence over government must be shared among all the people. If every individual which composes their mass participates of the ultimate authority, the government will be safe; because the corrupting the whole mass will exceed any private resources of wealth * * *. The government of Great Britain has been corrupted, because but one man in ten has a right to vote for members of parliament. The sellers of the government, therefore, get nine-tenths of their price clear. It has been thought that corruption is restrained by confining the right of suffrage to a few of the wealthier of the people; but it would be more effectually restrained by an extension of that right to such numbers as would bid defiance to the means of corruption.

* * *

NOTES AND QUESTIONS

1. Why is it that the basis of Virginia law is still principally to be the English common law? Why is it that Jefferson wishes to change some parts and not others? Why, for example, change the common law rules of descent? Did the old common law rules reflect principles "inconsistent with republicanism?" Why was Jefferson opposed to the reducing of law "to a text," an enterprise which he regarded as "dangerous?"

2. While Jefferson appears to have hoped for eventual emancipation of slaves, the Committee of Revisors reported a draft bill to the legislature which, in effect, perpetuated bondage. On the substance of the proposed law, see J. Noonan, Persons and Masks of the Law 51–54 (1976). Can you determine from this excerpt why Jefferson favored emancipation? What do you make of Jefferson's explanation of the necessity for "colonizing" emancipated Blacks? What conclusions does Jefferson reach regarding differences between the races? Do you find him consistent on this point throughout this passage? How, if at all, do you reconcile Jefferson's comments on Blacks with his assertion in the Declaration of Independence that "all men are created equal?"

Ought race to be a factor in the administration of "Republican" governments? For a recent provocative treatment of Jefferson as a slave-owner, which casts some heat and some light on these issues, see Henry Wiencek, Master of the Mountain: Thomas Jefferson and His Slaves (2012).

3. Can it be said that Jefferson thinks little of the qualities of Blacks when he suggests that if "nature has been less bountiful to them in the endowments of the head, I believe that in those of the heart she will have been found to have done them justice?" What does Jefferson mean by "justice?"

4. Why do you suppose that in this section of the Notes on Virginia, a section that is supposed to be concerned with the substantive revisions in Virginia law, Jefferson spends most of his time discussing slaves? Of what scientific, moral, or political relevance is the discussion contrasting American practice regarding slaves with that of Greece and Rome?

5. Do you find any philosophical similarities among Jefferson's comments on the nature of American slaves, his ideas on the appropriate punishments for crimes, and his views on public education? What is the reasoning behind the plan to "proportion crimes and punishments?" Is there an ideological dimension to this plan as well? Does it have any bearing on Jefferson's conception of humankind and the proper ends of government amplified in the Declaration of Independence? What does it mean that the plan of the proposed educational system "is to provide an education adapted to the years, to the capacity, and the condition of everyone?" What does "condition" mean? Does Jefferson's suggestion that by means of his scheme "twenty of the best geniuses will be raked from the rubbish annually" tell you anything about his social views? Yet can these views necessarily be described as "anti-republican?" What value, then, was education? Why, by the way, does Jefferson want Americans to learn Greek and Latin if Europeans have found it no longer necessary?

6. Jefferson is one of the most intriguing of America's historical figures. At one time or another he expressed an opinion on almost everything, and he has been cited to support innumerable causes, many of them in opposition to each other. Merrill Peterson's Jeffersonian Image in the American Mind (1960), Daniel Boorstin's The Lost World of Thomas Jefferson (1948), and Edmund Morgan's American Slavery—American Freedom (1975) are good starting places for understanding Jefferson as an eighteenth century enlightenment product. Fawn Brodie's popular analysis of Jefferson's supposed relationship with his slave, Sally Hemings, helps illuminate the complexities and contradictions in Jefferson's thinking about Blacks, Thomas Jefferson: An Intimate History (1974). Edward Dumbauld, Thomas Jefferson and the Law (1978), and John T. Noonan, Jr., Persons and Masks of the Law (1976), contain valuable materials on Jefferson's legal activities and social views during the Revolutionary era. Jefferson's rationalism in his proposals for reforming criminal law follows the thinking of the Italian, Cesare Beccaria, whose influence extended throughout Europe and influenced Blackstone, Bentham, and John Adams. For an important scholarly translation of Beccaria, see Cesare Beccaria, "On Crimes and Punishments" and Other

Writings, translated by Richard Davies, edited by Richard Bellamy (Cambridge Texts in the History of Political Thought, 1995). The publisher indicates that "Drawing on recent Italian scholarship, Richard Bellamy shows how Beccaria wove together the various political languages of the Enlightenment into a novel synthesis, and argues that his political philosophy, often regarded as no more than a precursor of Bentham's, combines republican, contractarian, romantic and liberal as well as utilitarian themes. The result is a complex theory of punishment that derives from a sophisticated analysis of the role of the state and the nature of human motivation in commercial society." Do you find some of these purported themes of Beccaria in these Notes on Virginia? For an exposition and an evaluation of the "Republican" character of the thought of Jefferson and his contemporaries, see, e.g., Drew McCoy, The Elusive Republic: Political Economy in Jeffersonian America (1980).

Until recently, Jefferson was most frequently portrayed as a mainstream thinker, indeed, as a virtual symbol of the founding generation. Recent historical treatment of Jefferson has spun him somewhat differently. In his own time Jefferson was a figure of fiery controversy, with his opponents viewing him as a dangerous radical. It is still possible to understand his philosophy as a self-consciously radical one. See, e.g., Richard K. Matthews, The Radical Politics of Thomas Jefferson: A Revisionist View (1984). Most recently, however, Jefferson, particularly taking into account his words on African–Americans and slavery in the Notes on Virginia, has been portrayed as more reactionary than radical, at least where slavery was concerned. See for additional scholarship on Jefferson, Joseph J. Ellis, American Sphinx: The Character of Thomas Jefferson (1997), Conor Cruise O'Brien, The Long Affair: Thomas Jefferson and the French Revolution 1785–1800 (1996), Annette Gordon–Reed, Thomas Jefferson and Sally Hemings: An American Controversy (1997; exp. ed., 1999), Roger G. Kennedy, Mr. Jefferson's Lost Cause (2003), Jan Ellen Lewis & Peter S. Onuf, eds., Sally Hemings and Thomas Jefferson: History, Memory, Civic Culture (1999), Peter S. Onuf, Jefferson's Empire: The Language of American Nationhood (2000) and Garry Wills, "Negro President": Jefferson and the Slave Power (2003). On the difficulties facing a Jefferson biographer, see, e.g., Richard B. Bernstein, "Wrestling with Jefferson: The Struggles of a Biographer," 46 N.Y.L.Sch.L.Rev. 757 (2003) (Professor Bernstein's biography is titled simply "Thomas Jefferson" (2003)).

4. A CONSTITUTION OR FRAME OF GOVERNMENT, AGREED UPON BY THE DELEGATES OF THE PEOPLE OF THE STATE OF MASSACHUSETTS–BAY (1780)

PREAMBLE.

The end of the institution, maintenance and administration of government, is to secure the existence of the body-politic; to protect it; and to furnish the individuals who compose it, with the power of enjoying, in safety and tranquillity, their natural rights, and the blessings of life: And whenever these great objects are not obtained, the people have a right to alter the government, and to take measures necessary for their safety, prosperity and happiness.

The body-politic is formed by a voluntary association of individuals: It is a social compact, by which the whole people covenants with each citizen, and each citizen with the whole people, that all shall be governed by certain laws for the common good * * *.

We, therefore, the people of Massachusetts, acknowledging, with grateful hearts, the goodness of the Great Legislator of the Universe, in affording us, in the course of His providence, an opportunity, deliberately and peaceably, without fraud, violence or surprise, of entering into an original, explicit, and solemn compact with each other; and of forming a new Constitution of Civil Government, for ourselves and posterity; and devoutly imploring His direction in so interesting a design, DO agree upon, ordain and establish, the following Declaration of Rights, and Frame of Government, as the CONSTITUTION of the COMMONWEALTH of MASSACHUSETTS.

PART THE FIRST. A DECLARATION OF THE RIGHTS * * *

Art. I.—All men are born free and equal, and have certain natural, essential, and unalienable rights; among which may be reckoned the right of enjoying and defending their lives and liberties; that of acquiring, possessing, and protecting property; in fine, that of seeking and obtaining their safety and happiness.

II.—It is the right as well as the duty of all men in society, publicly, and at stated seasons, to worship the SUPREME BEING, the great creator and preserver of the universe. * * *

III.—As the happiness of a people, and the good order and preservation of civil government, essentially depend upon piety, religion and morality, and as these cannot be generally diffused through a community, but by the institution of the public worship of GOD, and of public instructions in piety, religion and morality: Therefore, to promote their happiness and to secure the good order and preservation of their government, the people of this Commonwealth have a right to invest their legislature with power to authorize and require, and the legislature shall, from time to time, authorize and require, the several towns, parishes, precincts, and other bodies-politic, or religious societies, to make suitable provision, at their own expense, for the institution of the public worship of GOD, and for the support and maintenance of public protestant teachers of piety, religion and morality, in all cases where such provision shall not be made voluntarily.

* * *

V.—All power residing originally in the people, and being derived from them, the several magistrates and officers of government, vested with authority, whether legislative, executive, or judicial, are their substitutes and agents, and are at all times accountable to them.

VI.—No man, nor corporation, or association of men, have any other title to obtain advantages, or particular and exclusive privileges, distinct from those of the community, than what arises from the consideration of services rendered to the public; and this title being in nature neither hereditary, nor transmissible to children, or descendants, or relations by blood, the idea of a man born a magistrate, lawgiver, or judge, is absurd and unnatural.

VII.—Government is instituted for the common good; for the protection, safety, prosperity and happiness of the people; and not for the profit, honor, or private interest of any one man, family, or class of men; Therefore the people alone have an incontestible, unalienable, and indefeasible right to institute government; and to reform, alter, or totally change the same, when their protection, safety, prosperity and happiness require it.

VIII.—In order to prevent those, who are vested with authority, from becoming oppressors, the people have a right, at such periods and in such manner as they shall establish by their frame of government, to cause their public officers to return to private life; and to fill up vacant places by certain and regular elections and appointments.

* * *

XI.—Every subject of the Commonwealth ought to find a certain remedy, by having recourse to the laws, for all injuries or wrongs which he may receive in his person, property, or character. He ought to obtain right and justice freely, and without being obliged to purchase it; completely, and without any denial; promptly, and without delay; conformably to the laws.

XII.—No subject shall be held to answer for any crime or offence, until the same is fully and plainly, substantially and formally, described to him; or be compelled to accuse, or furnish evidence against himself. And every subject shall have a right to produce all proofs, that may be favorable to him; to meet the witnesses against him face to face, and to be fully heard in his defence by himself, or his council, at his election. * * *

* * *

XIV.—Every subject has a right to be secure from all unreasonable searches, and seizures of his person, his houses, his papers, and all his possessions. All warrants, therefore, are contrary to this right, if the cause or foundation of them be not previously supported by oath or affirmation * * *.

XV.—In all controversies concerning property, and in all suits between two or more persons, except in cases in which it has heretofore been otherways used and practised, the parties have a right to a trial by jury. * * *

XVI.—The liberty of the press is essential to the security of freedom in a state: it ought not, therefore, to be restrained in this Commonwealth.

XVII.—The people have a right to keep and to bear arms for the common defence. And as in time of peace armies are dangerous to liberty, they ought not to be maintained without the consent of the legislature; and the military power shall always be held in an exact subordination to the civil authority, and be governed by it.

* * *

XIX.—The people have a right, in an orderly and peaceable manner, to assemble to consult upon the common good; give instructions to their representatives; and to request of the legislative body, by the way of addresses, petitions, or remonstrances, redress of the wrongs done them, and of the grievances they suffer.

* * *

XXIV.—Laws made to punish for actions done before the existence of such laws, and which have not been declared crimes by preceding laws, are unjust, oppressive, and inconsistent with the fundamental principles of a free government.

* * *

XXVIII.—No person can in any case be subjected to law-martial, or to any penalties or pains, by virtue of that law, except those employed in the army or navy, and except the militia in actual service, but by authority of the legislature.

XXIX.—It is essential to the preservation of the rights of every individual, his life, liberty, property and character, that there be an impartial interpretation of the laws, and administration of justice. It is the right of every citizen to be tried by judges as free, impartial and independent as the lot of humanity will admit. It is therefore not only the best policy, but for the security of the rights of the people, and of every citizen, that the judges of the supreme judicial court should hold their offices as long as they behave themselves well; and that they should have honorable salaries ascertained and established by standing laws.

XXX.—In the government of this Commonwealth, the legislative department shall never exercise the executive and judicial powers, or either of them: The executive shall never exercise the legislative and judicial powers, or either of them: The judicial shall never exercise the legislative and executive powers, or either of them: to the end it may be a government of laws and not of men.

PART THE SECOND. THE FRAME OF GOVERNMENT.

The people, inhabiting the territory formerly called the Province of Massachusetts–Bay, do hereby solemnly and mutually agree with each other, to form themselves into a free, sovereign, and independent body-politic or state, by the name of THE COMMONWEALTH OF MASSACHUSETTS.

Chapter I. The Legislative Power.

Section I. The General Court.

Art. I.—The department of legislation shall be formed by two branches, a Senate and House of Representatives: each of which shall have a negative on the other.

The legislative body shall assemble every year, on the last Wednesday in May, and at such other times as they shall judge necessary; and shall dissolve and be dissolved on the day next preceding the said last Wednesday in May; and shall be styled, The General Court of Massachusetts.

II.—No bill or resolve of the Senate or House of Representatives shall become a law, and have force as such, until it shall have been laid before the Governor for his revisal: And if he, upon such revision, approve thereof, he shall signify his approbation by signing the same. But if he have any objection to the passing of such bill or resolve, he shall return the same, together with his objections thereto, in writing, to the Senate or House of Representatives, in which soever the same shall have originated; who shall enter the objections sent down by the Governor, at large, on their records, and proceed to reconsider the said bill or resolve: But if, after such reconsideration, two thirds of the said Senate or House of Representatives, shall, notwithstanding the said objections, agree to pass the same, it shall, together with the objections, be sent to the other branch of the legislature, where it shall also be reconsidered, and if approved by two thirds of the members present, shall have the force of a law. * * *

III.—The General Court shall forever have full power and authority to erect and constitute judicatories and courts of record, or other courts, to be held in the name of the Commonwealth, for the hearing, trying, and determining of all manner of crimes, offences, pleas, processes, plaints, actions, matters, causes and things, whatsoever, arising or happening within the Commonwealth, or between or concerning persons inhabiting, or residing, or brought within the same. * * *

IV.—And further, full power and authority are hereby given and granted to the said General Court, from time to time, to make, ordain, and establish, all manner of wholesome and reasonable orders, laws, statutes, and ordinances, directions and instructions, either with penalties or without; so as the same be not repugnant or contrary to this Constitution, as they shall judge to be for the good and welfare of this Commonwealth, and for the government and ordering thereof. * * *

Section II. Senate.

Art. I.—There shall be annually elected by the freeholders and other inhabitants of this Commonwealth, qualified as in this Constitution is provided, forty persons to be Counsellors and Senators for the year ensuing their election; to be chosen by the inhabitants of the districts, into which the Commonwealth may from time to time be divided by the General Court for that purpose. * * *

II.—The Senate shall be the first branch of the legislature; and the Senators shall be chosen in the following manner, viz: There shall be a meeting on the first Monday in April annually, forever, of the inhabitants of each town in the several counties of this Commonwealth * * * for the purpose of electing persons to be Senators and Counsellors: And at such meetings every male inhabitant of twenty-one years of age and upwards, having a freehold estate within the Commonwealth, of the annual income of three pounds, or any estate of the value of sixty pounds, shall have a right to give in his vote for the Senators for the district of which he is an inhabitant. * * *

* * *

V.—Provided nevertheless, that no person shall be capable of being elected as a Senator, who is not seized in his own right of a freehold within this Commonwealth, of the value of three hundred pounds at least, or possessed of personal estate to the value of six hundred pounds at least, or of both to the amount of the same sum, and who has not been an inhabitant of this Commonwealth for the space of five years immediately preceding his election, and, at the time of his election, he shall be an inhabitant in the district, for which he shall be chosen.

* * *

Section III. House of Representatives.

Art. I.—There shall be in the Legislature of this Commonwealth, a representation of the people, annually elected, and founded upon the principle of equality.

II.—And in order to provide for a representation of the citizens of this Commonwealth, founded upon the principle of equality, every corporate town, containing one hundred and fifty rateable polls, may elect one Representative: Every corporate town, containing three hundred and seventy-five rateable polls, may elect two Representatives: Every corporate town, containing six hundred rateable polls, may elect three Representatives; and proceeding in that manner, making two hundred and twenty-five rateable polls the mean increasing number for every additional Representative. * * *

III.—Every member of the House of Representatives shall be chosen by written votes; and for one year at least next preceding his election shall have been an inhabitant of, and have been seized in his own right of a freehold of the value of one hundred pounds within the town he shall be chosen to represent, or any rateable estate to the value of two hundred pounds; and he shall cease to represent the said town immediately on his ceasing to be qualified as aforesaid.

IV.—Every male person, being twenty-one years of age, and resident in any particular town in this Commonwealth for the space of one year next preceding, having a freehold estate within the same town, of the annual income of three pounds, or any estate of the value of sixty pounds, shall have a right to vote in the choice of a Representative or Representatives for the said town.

* * *

VII.—All money-bills shall originate in the House of Representatives; but the Senate may propose or concur with amendments, as on other bills.

VIII.—The House of Representatives shall have power to adjourn themselves; provided such adjournment shall not exceed two days at a time. * * *

* * *

Chapter II. Executive Power.

Section I. Governor.

Art. I.—There shall be a Supreme Executive Magistrate, who shall be styled, THE GOVERNOR OF THE COMMONWEALTH OF MASSACHUSETTS; and whose title shall be—HIS EXCELLENCY.

II.—The Governor shall be chosen annually: And no person shall be eligible to this office, unless at the time of his election, he shall have been an inhabitant of this Commonwealth for seven years next preceding; and unless he shall, at the same time, be seized in his own right, of a freehold within the Commonwealth, of the value of one thousand pounds; and unless he shall declare himself to be of the Christian religion.

III.—Those persons who shall be qualified to vote for Senators and Representatives within the several towns of this Commonwealth, shall, at a meeting, to be called for that purpose, on the first Monday of April annually, give in their votes for a Governor, to the Selectmen, who shall preside at such meetings. * * *

IV.—The Governor shall have authority, from time to time, at his discretion, to assemble and call together the Counsellors of this Commonwealth for the time being; and the Governor, with the said Counsellors, or five of them at least, shall, and may, from time to time, hold and keep a Council, for the ordering and directing the affairs of the Commonwealth, agreeably to the Constitution and the laws of the land.

* * *

VII.—The Governor of this Commonwealth, for the time being, shall be the commander-in-chief of the army and navy, and of all the military forces of the State, by sea and land; and shall have full power, by himself, or by any commander, or other officer or officers, from time to time, to train, instruct, exercise and govern the militia and navy; and, for the special defence and safety of the Commonwealth, to assemble in martial array, and put in warlike posture, the inhabitants thereof, and to lead and conduct them, and with them. * * *

* * *

IX.—All judicial officers, the Attorney–General, the Solicitor–General, all Sheriffs, Coroners, and Registers of Probate, shall be nominated and appointed by the Governor, by and with the advice and consent of the Council; and every such nomination shall be made by the Governor, and made at least seven days prior to such appointment.

* * *

XIII.—As the public good requires that the Governor should not be under the undue influence of any of the members of the General Court, by a dependence on them for his support—that he should, in all cases, act with freedom for the benefit of the public—that he should not have his attention necessarily diverted from that object to his private concerns—and that he should maintain the dignity of the Commonwealth in the character of its chief magistrate—it is necessary that he should have an honorable stated salary, of a fixed and permanent value, amply sufficient for those purposes. * * *

Permanent and honorable salaries shall also be established by law for the Justices of the Supreme Judicial Court.

And if it shall be found, that any of the salaries aforesaid, so established, are insufficient, they shall, from time to time, be enlarged, as the General Court shall judge proper.

Section II. Lieutenant–Governor.

Art. I.—There shall be annually elected a Lieutenant–Governor of the Commonwealth of Massachusetts, whose title shall be HIS HONOR—and who shall be qualified, in point of religion, property, and residence in the Commonwealth, in the same manner with the Governor * * *.

* * *

III.—Whenever the chair of the Governor shall be vacant, by reason of his death, or absence from the Commonwealth, or otherwise, the Lieutenant–Governor, for the time being, shall, during such vacancy, perform all the duties incumbent upon the Governor, and shall have and exercise all the powers and authorities, which by this Constitution the Governor is vested with, when personally present.

Section III. Council, and the Manner of Settling Elections by the Legislature.

Art. I.—There shall be a Council for advising the Governor in the executive part of government, to consist of nine persons besides the Lieutenant–Governor, whom the Governor, for the time being, shall have full power and authority, from time to time, at his discretion, to assemble and call together. And the Governor, with the said Counsellors, or five of them at least, shall and may, from time to time, hold and keep a council, for the ordering and directing the affairs of the Commonwealth, according to the laws of the land.

II.—Nine Counsellors shall be annually chosen from among the persons returned for Counsellors and Senators, on the last Wednesday in May, by the joint ballot of the Senators and Representatives assembled in one room. * * *

Chapter III. Judiciary Power.

Art. I.—The tenure that all commission officers shall by law have in their offices, shall be expressed in their respective commissions. All judicial officers, duly appointed, commissioned and sworn, shall hold their offices during good behaviour, excepting such concerning whom there is different provision made in this Constitution: Provided, nevertheless, the Governor, with consent of the Council, may remove them upon the address of both Houses of the Legislature.

II.—Each branch of the Legislature, as well as the Governor and Council, shall have authority to require the opinions of the Justices of the

Supreme Judicial Court, upon important questions of law, and upon solemn occasions.

* * *

V.—All causes of marriage, divorce and alimony, and all appeals from the Judges of Probate, shall be heard and determined by the Governor and Council until the Legislature shall, by law, make other provisions.

* * *

Chapter V. The University at Cambridge, and Encouragement of Literature, etc.

Section I. The University.

Art. I.—Whereas our wise and pious ancestors, so early as the year one thousand six hundred and thirty six, laid the foundation of Harvard–College, in which University many persons of great eminence have, by the blessing of GOD, been initiated in those arts and sciences, which qualified them for public employments, both in Church and State: And whereas the encouragement of Arts and Sciences, and all good literature, tends to the honor of God, the advantage of the Christian religion, and the great benefit of this, and the other United States of America—It is declared, That the PRESIDENT AND FELLOWS OF HARVARD–COLLEGE, in their corporate capacity, and their successors in that capacity, their officers and servants, shall have, hold, use, exercise and enjoy, all the powers, authorities, rights, liberties, privileges, immunities and franchises, which they now have, or are entitled to have, hold, use, exercise and enjoy: And the same are hereby ratified and confirmed unto them, the said President and Fellows of Harvard–College, and to their successors, and to their officers and servants, respectively, forever.

* * *

III.—And whereas by an act of the General Court of the Colony of Massachusetts–Bay, passed in the year one thousand six hundred and forty-two, the Governor and Deputy–Governor, for the time being, and all the magistrates of that jurisdiction, were, with the President, and a number of the clergy in the said act described, constituted the Overseers of Harvard–College: * * * IT IS DECLARED, That the Governor, Lieutenant–Governor, Council and Senate of this Commonwealth, are, and shall be deemed, their successors. * * * PROVIDED, that nothing herein shall be construed to prevent the Legislature of this Commonwealth from making such alterations in the government of the said university, as shall be conducive to its advantage, and the interest of the republic of letters, in as full a manner as might have been done by the Legislature of the late Province of the Massachusetts–Bay.

Section II. The Encouragement of Literature, etc.

Wisdom, and knowledge, as well as virtue, diffused generally among the body of the people, being necessary for the preservation of their rights and liberties; and as these depend on spreading the opportunities and advantages of education in the various parts of the country, and among the different orders of the people, it shall be the duty of legislators and magistrates, in all future periods of this Commonwealth, to cherish the interests of literature and the sciences, and all seminaries of them; especially the university at Cambridge, public schools, and grammar schools in the towns; to encourage private societies and public institutions, rewards and immunities, for the promotion of agriculture, arts, sciences, commerce, trades, manufactures, and a natural history of the country; to countenance and inculcate the principles of humanity and general benevolence, public and private charity, industry and frugality, honesty and punctuality in their dealings; sincerity, good humour, and all social affections, and generous sentiments among the people.

* * *

* * *.—Any person chosen Governor, Lieutenant–Governor, Counsellor, Senator, or Representative, and accepting the trust, shall, before he proceed to execute the duties of his place or office, make and subscribe the following declaration, viz.—

"I, A. B. do declare, that I believe the christian religion, and have a firm persuasion of its truth; and that I am seized and possessed, in my own right, of the property required by the Constitution as one qualification for the office or place to which I am elected."

And the Governor, Lieutenant–Governor, and Counsellors, shall make and subscribe the said declaration, in the presence of the two Houses of Assembly; and the Senators and Representatives first elected under this Constitution, before the President and five of the Council of the former Constitution, and, forever afterwards, before the Governor and Council for the time being.

And every person chosen to either of the places or offices aforesaid, as also any person appointed or commissioned to any judicial, executive, military, or other office under the government, shall, before he enters on the discharge of the business of his place or office, take and subscribe the following declaration, and oaths or affirmations, viz.—

"I, A. B. do truly and sincerely acknowledge, profess, testify and declare, that the Commonwealth of Massachusetts is, and of right ought to be, a free, sovereign and independent State; and I do swear, that I will bear true faith and allegiance to the said Commonwealth, and that I will defend the same against traitorous conspiracies and all hostile attempts whatsoever: And that I do renounce and adjure all allegiance, subjection and obedience to the King, Queen or Government of Great Britain, (as the case may be) and every other foreign power whatsoever: And that no foreign Prince, Person, Prelate, State or Potentate, hath, or ought to have, any jurisdiction, superiority, preeminence, authority, dispensing or other power, in any matter, civil, ecclesiastical or spiritual, within this Commonwealth; except the authority and power which is or may be vested by their Constituents in the Congress of the United States: And I do further testify and declare, that no man or body of men hath or can have any right to absolve or discharge me from the obligation of this oath, declaration or affirmation; and that I do make this acknowledgment, profession, testimony, declaration, denial, renunciation and abjuration, heartily and truly, according to the common meaning and acceptation of the foregoing words, without any equivocation, mental evasion, or secret reservation whatsoever. So help me GOD."

* * *

Provided always, that when any person, chosen or appointed as aforesaid, shall be of the denomination of the people called Quakers, and shall decline taking the said oaths, he shall make his affirmation in the foregoing form, and subscribe the same, omitting the words "I do swear," "and adjure," "oath or," "and abjuration," in the first oath; and in the second oath, the words "swear and;" and in each of them the words "So help me GOD;" subjoining instead thereof, "This I do under the pains and penalties of perjury."

* * *

No person shall be capable of holding or exercising at the same time, within this State, more than one of the following offices, viz:—Judge of Probate—Sheriff—Register of Probate—or Register of Deeds—and never more than any two offices which are to be held by appointment of the Governor, or the Governor and Council, or the Senate, or the House of Representatives, or by the election of the people of the State at large, or of the people of any county, military offices and the offices of Justices of the Peace excepted, shall be held by one person.

No person holding the office of Judge of the Supreme Judicial Court—Secretary—Attorney General—Solicitor General—Treasurer or Receiver General—Judge of Probate—Commissary General—President, Professor, or Instructor of Harvard College—Sheriff—Clerk of the House of Representatives—Register of Probate—Register of Deeds—Clerk of the Supreme Judicial Court—Clerk of the Inferior Court of Common Pleas—or Officer of the Customs, including in this description Naval Officers—shall at the same time have a seat in the Senate or House of Representatives; but their being chosen or appointed to, and accepting the same, shall operate as a resignation of their seat in the Senate or House of Representatives; and the place so vacated shall be filled up.

* * *

And no person shall ever be admitted to hold a seat in the Legislature, or any office of trust or importance under the Government of this Commonwealth, who shall, in the due course of law, have been convicted of bribery or corruption in obtaining an election or appointment.

* * *

* * * In order the more effectually to adhere to the principles of the Constitution, and to correct those violations which by any means may be made therein, as well as to form such alterations as from experience shall be found necessary—the General Court, which shall be in the year of our Lord one thousand seven hundred and ninety-five, shall issue precepts to the Selectmen of the several towns, and to the Assessors of the unincorporated plantations, directing them to convene the qualified voters of their respective towns and plantations for the purpose of collecting their sentiments on the necessity or expediency of revising the Constitution * * *.

And if it shall appear by the returns made, that two thirds of the qualified voters throughout the State, who shall assemble and vote in consequence of the said precepts, are in favor of such revision or amendment, the General Court shall issue precepts, or direct them to be issued from the Secretary's office to the several towns, to elect Delegates to meet in Convention for the purpose aforesaid.

* * *

NOTES AND QUESTIONS

1. The Massachusetts Constitution was ratified seven years before the drafting of the Federal Constitution, and it is the only one of the 13 original state constitutions to survive to the present day. It is possible to argue that this state constitution, more so than the Federal Constitution, embodies the principles of the Revolution as well as the uniquely American principles of republican government. Do you agree? It has been amended many times, but why do you suppose it has essentially remained in force?

2. John Adams was the principal drafter of the Massachusetts Constitution. Does this surprise you, after reading it? Why, or why not? Adams and Jefferson, though in agreement on the Declaration, later fell out over the scope of federal authority. Can you see why?

3. The Massachusetts Constitution is unique among the state constitutions in its both establishing religion, and singling out education and literature as the keys to the future happiness of the people. Does this focus seem unusual or out-of-keeping for the time? Is it a consideration that Harvard

was founded as a Puritan seminary, and continued as a source of ministers for New England towns? Thomas Jefferson considered two of his greatest contributions to be the Statute of Religious Freedom in Virginia, which limited the authority of the established Anglican Church, and the founding of the University of Virginia, which he envisioned as purely secular. We also read about Jefferson's proposal to educate the "talented tenth" at state expense. Are Jefferson and Adams at odds here, or not?

4. You have now read three sources of early constitutionalism: the Pennsylvania Constitution, Jefferson's reflections on the defects of the Virginia Constitution, and the Massachusetts Constitution. Whose approach do you find most appealing, and why? Which is least appealing? What does it mean that there could be such variance, among three critical states, in the ways they chose to govern themselves? You will next encounter the federal government, created by the adoption of the United States Constitution in 1789. Whose ideas, those of the framers of the Pennsylvania Constitution, Jefferson's, or Adams's seem most consistent with the new national Constitution?

CHAPTER 2

FEDERALISM VERSUS REPUBLICANISM IN THE COURTS: CONCEPTIONS OF NATIONAL LAW

■ ■ ■

A. THE FEDERALIST PERSUASION

If the conflict between colonial patriots and high-handed Parliamentarians taught the Americans anything, it was that absolute power corrupted absolutely. At the root of the perceived oppression of the colonies was the "sovereign" Parliament, a body answerable only to itself. The state and national governments erected during the War for Independence reflected this new political wisdom. The Pennsylvania Constitution, as we have seen, practically obliterated the executive authority in the name of liberty. Still, most of the new state constitutions followed Virginia's example, allowing governors, but hedging executive power. Many restricted their governors to one-year terms; some denied governors the veto power over legislation; and, in eight states, governors were selected by members of the legislature. Real power in the new United States thus resided in the assemblies, the branches of government ostensibly closest to the people. Unlike the case of the allegedly unrepresentative, corrupt, and uncontrolled English Parliament, it was believed, the American people themselves would be able to maintain their sovereignty over their legislative bodies.

The Articles of Confederation formed the basis of the new national government, and were ratified by the states in 1781. The Articles recognized that "Each state" was to "retain its sovereignty, freedom, and independence." The new national government lacked coercive powers, could merely request funds from the states, had no control over interstate commerce or the money supply, and had no powerful chief executive or effective judiciary. The national government implemented under the Articles was to be more an advisory than a ruling body. If effective national government under the Articles was difficult, however, it was so by design. Few wished to see a strong central government while memories of the English abuses that led to the Revolution were still fresh.

Events in the 1780's forced some to alter their opinions about the virtues of limited central power. Post-war periods are usually times of economic turmoil and adjustment. The war had disrupted agriculture, interrupted trade, and raised staggering public debts. States attempted to finance the Revolutionary War by selling securities to their citizens. But, after the war, the new states were reluctant to levy unpopular taxes to repay their obligations. The Treaty of Paris (1783), which ended the war, required the states to recognize the pre-war claims of British citizens and to compensate loyalists for their property which had been confiscated by patriot state governments. Following the treaty, an unfavorable balance of trade (as imports far overtook exports) aggravated the economic situation, as gold and silver flowed from the country. Under these circumstances few foreign governments or banks were willing to grant American state or national governments the loans needed to rekindle the economy. The states responded by issuing paper currency with each negative fluctuation of the business cycle, in such quantities that the currencies depreciated almost daily. "Rag money," it came to be called; in effect it allowed debtors to repay loans at a reduced rate, but the uncertain value of money badly hampered American trade.

Agrarian and backcountry elements removed from the market economy and from centers of commerce and transportation saw no great cause for alarm in these developments. A certain amount of economic disorganization may have been seen as the price of liberty. But when economic instability began to mix with the spectre of popular rebellion, the situation took on an alarming aspect. In 1786–1787, one Daniel Shays, a former officer in Washington's Continental Army, gathered a force in excess of one thousand men (many former revolutionary soldiers) and proceeded to close down the courts in the western counties of Massachusetts. Law enforcement in that area ceased.

The "Shaysites" acted because they resented the high burden of taxes imposed on already distressed farmers and the zeal of courts in collecting private debts. See, e.g., Claire Priest, "Colonial Courts and Secured Credit: Early American Commercial Litigation and Shays' Rebellion," 108 Yale L.J. 2413 (1999). Merchants in Boston raised money for a military expedition to restore order, but only after seven months were the insurgents routed. Similar, though less spectacular, incidents occurred in other states. Added to the disorder was a growing cacophony of criticism directed at the young state assemblies. "We daily see laws repealed or suspended," went one charge, "before any trial can be made of their merits, and even before a knowledge of them can have reached the remoter districts within which they were to operate." A prominent New York politician exclaimed that "the people do not exhibit the virtue that is necessary to support a republican government." An observer of North Carolina politics was more blunt. He described that state's session laws as "the vilest collection of trash ever framed by a legislative body." Much of this criticism was prompted by state legislative attempts to suspend or obliterate contractual debts. In the turmoil, moderates and conservatives alike began to fear that the great republican experiment was on the verge of collapsing.

Some historians now doubt that affairs in America were as precarious as they seemed. Most of the states appear to have experienced modest growth and comparative prosperity despite the economic difficulties, while social discontent may never have run as deeply as alarmists claimed. Nor did the young state legislatures compile only abysmal records. Virginia's revisal of her colonial laws, for example, was a model of circumspection. Nevertheless, contemporaries did see these years as a "critical period," and a growing number of nationalists called for a new central government that could arrest the perceived decline. They sought a structure with the military might to preserve the social order, a government sufficiently strong to bring the economy under control, to negotiate favorable trade agreements with foreign nations, and to tap the collective resources of the states.

In Philadelphia, in May of 1787, with news of Shays abroad, a meeting of delegates from every state but Rhode Island took place. The conferees were charged with finding a way to amend the Articles of Confederation to make the government more effective. Instead, the convention reported out an entirely new plan of government, a written Constitution, which created a national republic. The proposed Constitution was the product of many compromises, especially between smaller and larger and between slave-holding and free states. Still, there was a central vision of government implicit in the document which has led some historians to refer to the Philadelphia Constitutional Convention as a "second American Revolution." The new Constitution provided for a bicameral national legislature and co-equal executive and judicial branches of government. It gave the national legislature, Congress, the power to levy taxes, to coin and borrow money, to regulate interstate commerce, to raise an army, to create a federal court system, and to "make all Laws which shall be necessary and proper for carrying into execution" its enumerated powers. The document also circumscribed the workings of the state legislatures, forbidding them, *inter alia,* from abridging existing contractual rights.

The Constitution, reproduced in the Appendix, created a national chief executive with a veto power over legislation, command of the national armed forces, freedom to conduct foreign affairs, and vast appointive powers. The Constitution, then, rejected the assumptions of the political theory which had generated the "first" American Revolution, when it placed considerable power in the hands of a centralized government.

The struggle for ratification of the proposed national Constitution occupied national political life for the next several months. The so-called "Anti–Federalists" opposed ratification. They objected to the proposal for a strong central government, and railed against the absence of any Bill of Rights. Some Anti–Federalists also accused the Convention delegates of harboring monarchical and aristocratic sympathies. Nor were these opponents confident that an American national republic could survive free. The conventional political wisdom, supplied principally from ancient history, limited the successful operation of free republics to small geographical areas; to attempt a large-scale republic, they feared, would risk anarchy or despotism, and might thus spell the end of liberty.

The "Federalists," the proponents of ratification, at first claimed that a Bill of Rights was unnecessary, since the powers of the new national government were to be limited and enumerated. Nevertheless, they eventually pledged their support for constitutional amendments to guarantee basic liberties. To the charge of secretly harboring anti-republican sympathies, the Federalists responded that by separating, checking, and disbursing power, as their Constitution would, a balanced republican polity could be created. James Madison, in the Federalist (excerpts from which you will soon read), turned the conventional position of republican theory on its head when he argued that a national republic would actually better preserve liberty, because the clash of interests in as vast a land as America would prevent any faction from dominating the government. Finally, the Federalists reminded their critics that they were simply proposing a constitution. They were leaving to "the people," meeting in popularly constituted state conventions, the task of ratification of the document. The Federalists argued that the people ought to accept their proposal, because their Constitution would implement a government strong enough to meet the needs of the times, but limited enough to ensure the preservation of individual liberty and essential state sovereignty. The best compendium of the arguments for and against the proposed Constitution is Bernard Bailyn, editor, The Debate on the Constitution (2 vols., 1993).

The Constitution was finally ratified by the requisite number of states in 1789. But the political divisions which were manifest in the debate over ratification persisted, although in somewhat altered forms. Thomas Jefferson and Alexander Hamilton both served in President Washington's first cabinet, but held divergent views on national priorities. The differences between these two men, and the factions that formed around them (the Jeffersonian "Republicans" and the Hamiltonian "Federalists") were more than political. Hamiltonian policies favored commerce and manufacturing as well as a vigorous central government. Jeffersonian desires were more in the direction of limited government in a prosperous but stable agrarian economy. These differences determined these groups' differing visions of the future, their attitudes toward popular authority, and their regard for the functions of a judicial system in a republic. For the 1790's the Federalists held the balance of power: they occupied the Presidency and appointed Federalists to the national bench. In the following documents we will study these divergent views in the context of the early operation of the national judiciary. We begin with an excerpt from the Federalist, authored by Alexander Hamilton, and directed at the voters of New York. This material concerns judicial tenure under the proposed Federal Constitution.

1. ALEXANDER HAMILTON ON THE FEDERAL JUDICIARY

"PUBLIUS" [ALEXANDER HAMILTON], THE FEDERALIST PAPERS*

464–491; 520–527 (Clinton Rossiter, ed. 1961).

NO. 78

* * *

* * * [A]ll judges who may be appointed by the United States are to hold their offices during good behavior; which is conformable to the most approved of the State constitutions, and among the rest, to that of this State. Its propriety having been drawn into question by the adversaries of that plan is no light symptom of the rage for objection which disorders their imaginations and judgments. The standard of good behavior for the continuance in office of the judicial magistracy is certainly one of the most valuable of the modern improvements in the practice of government. In a monarchy it is an excellent barrier to the despotism of the prince; in a republic it is a no less excellent barrier to the encroachments and oppressions of the representative body. And it is the best expedient which can be devised in any government to secure a steady, upright, and impartial administration of the laws.

Whoever attentively considers the different departments of power must perceive that, in a government in which they are separated from each other, the judiciary, from the nature of its functions, will always be the least dangerous to the political rights of the Constitution; because it will be least in a capacity to annoy or injure them. The executive not only dispenses the honors but holds the sword of the community. The legislature not only commands the purse but prescribes the rules by which the duties and rights of every citizen are to be regulated. The judiciary, on the contrary, has no influence over either the sword or the purse; no direction either of the strength or of the wealth of the society, and can take no active resolution whatever. It may truly be said to have neither FORCE nor WILL but merely judgment; and must ultimately depend upon the aid of the executive arm even for the efficacy of its judgments.

* * * [T]he judiciary is beyond comparison the weakest of the three departments of power; * * * it can never attack with success either of the

other two; and * * * all possible care is requisite to enable it to defend itself against their attacks. * * * [T]hough individual oppression may now and then proceed from the courts of justice, the general liberty of the people can never be endangered from that quarter; I mean so long as the judiciary remains truly distinct from both the legislature and the executive. For I agree that "there is no liberty if the power of judging be not separated from the legislative and executive powers."* [F]rom the natural feebleness of the judiciary, it is in continual jeopardy of being overpowered, awed, or influenced by its co-ordinate branches; and * * * as nothing can contribute so much to its firmness and independence as permanency in office, this quality may therefore be justly regarded as an indispensable ingredient in its constitution, and, in a great measure, as the citadel of the public justice and the public security.

The complete independence of the courts of justice is peculiarly essential in a limited Constitution. By a limited Constitution, I understand one which contains certain specified exceptions to the legislative authority; such, for instance, as that it shall pass no bills of attainder, no *ex post facto* laws, and the like. Limitations of this kind can be preserved in practice no other way than through the medium of courts of justice, whose duty it must be to declare all acts contrary to the manifest tenor of the Constitution void. Without this, all the reservations of particular rights or privileges would amount to nothing.

Some perplexity respecting the rights of the courts to pronounce legislative acts void, because contrary to the Constitution, has arisen from an imagination that the doctrine would imply a superiority of the judiciary to the legislative power. It is urged that the authority which can declare the acts of another void must necessarily be superior to the one whose acts may be declared void. As this doctrine is of great importance in all the American constitutions, a brief discussion of the grounds on which it rests cannot be unacceptable.

There is no position which depends on clearer principles than that every act of a delegated authority, contrary to the tenor of the commission under which it is exercised, is void. No legislative act, therefore, contrary to the Constitution, can be valid. To deny this would be to affirm that the deputy is greater than his principal; that the servant is above his master; that the representatives of the people are superior to the people themselves * * *.

If it be said that the legislative body are themselves the constitutional judges of their own powers and that the construction they put upon them is conclusive upon the other departments it may be answered that this cannot be the natural presumption where it is not to be collected from any particular provisions in the Constitution. It is not otherwise to

* 1 Montesquieu, Spirit of the Laws 181.

be supposed that the Constitution could intend to enable the representatives of the people to substitute their *will* to that of their constituents. It is far more rational to suppose that the courts were designed to be an intermediate body between the people and the legislature in order, among other things, to keep the latter within the limits assigned to their authority. The interpretation of the laws is the proper and peculiar province of the courts. A constitution is, in fact, and must be regarded by the judges as, a fundamental law. It therefore belongs to them to ascertain its meaning as well as the meaning of any particular act proceeding from the legislative body. If there should happen to be an irreconcilable variance between the two, that which has the superior obligation and validity ought, of course, to be preferred; or, in other words, the Constitution ought to be preferred to the statute, the intention of the people to the intention of their agents.

Nor does this conclusion by any means suppose a superiority of the judicial to the legislative power. It only supposes that the power of the people is superior to both, and that where the will of the legislature, declared in its statutes, stands in opposition to that of the people, declared in the Constitution, the judges ought to be governed by the latter rather than the former. They ought to regulate their decisions by the fundamental laws rather than by those which are not fundamental.

* * *

It can be of no weight to say that the courts, on the pretense of a repugnancy, may substitute their own pleasure to the constitutional intentions of the legislature. This * * * might as well happen in every adjudication upon any * * * statute. The courts must declare the sense of the law; and if they should be disposed to exercise WILL instead of JUDGMENT, the consequence would equally be the substitution of their pleasure to that of the legislative body. The observation, if it proved anything, would prove that there ought to be no judges distinct from that body.

* * *

This independence of the judges is equally requisite to guard the Constitution and the rights of individuals from the effects of those ill humors which the arts of designing men, or the influence of particular conjunctures, sometimes disseminate among the people themselves, and which, though they speedily give place to better information, and more deliberate reflection, have a tendency, in the meantime, to occasion dangerous innovations in the government, and serious oppressions of the minor party in the community. Though [we would never question] * * * that fundamental principle of republican government which admits the right of the people to alter or abolish the established Constitution whenever they find it inconsistent with their happiness; yet it is not to be inferred from this principle that the representatives of the people, whenever a momentary inclination happens to lay hold of a majority of their constituents incompatible with the provisions in the existing Constitution would, on that account, be justifiable in a violation of those provisions; or that the courts would be under a greater obligation to connive at infractions in this shape than when they had proceeded wholly from the cabals of the representative body. Until the people have, by some solemn and authoritative act, annulled or changed the established form, it is binding upon themselves collectively, as well as individually; and no presumption, or even knowledge of their sentiments, can warrant their representatives in a departure from it prior to such an act. But it is easy to see that it would require an uncommon portion of fortitude in the judges to do their duty as faithful guardians of the Constitution, where legislative invasions of it had been instigated by the major voice of the community.

* * * The benefits of the integrity and moderation of the judiciary have already been felt in more States than one; and though they may have displeased those whose sinister expectations they may have disappointed, they must have commanded the esteem and applause of all the virtuous and disinterested. Considerate men of every description ought to prize whatever will tend to beget or fortify that temper in the courts; as no man can be sure that he may not be tomorrow the victim of a spirit of injustice, by which he may be a gainer today. And every man must now feel that the inevitable tendency of such a spirit is to sap the foundations of public and private confidence and to introduce in its stead universal distrust and distress.

* * * Periodical appointments, however regulated, or by whomsoever made, would, in some way or other, be fatal to [the judges'] necessary independence. If the power of making them was committed either to the executive or legislature there would be danger of an improper complaisance to the branch which possessed it; if to both, there would be an unwillingness to hazard the displeasure of either; if to the people, or to persons chosen by them for the special purpose, there would be too great a disposition to consult popularity to justify a reliance that nothing would be consulted but the Constitution and the laws.

* * * It has been frequently remarked with great propriety that a voluminous code of laws is one of the inconveniences necessarily connected with the advantages of a free government. To avoid an arbitrary discretion in the courts, it is indispensable that they should be bound down by strict rules and precedents which serve to define and point out their duty in every particular case that comes before them; and it will readily be conceived from the variety of controversies which grow out of the folly and wickedness of mankind that the records of those precedents must unavoidably swell to a very considerable bulk and must demand long and laborious study to acquire a competent knowledge of them. Hence it is that

there can be but few men in the society who will have sufficient skill in the laws to qualify them for the stations of judges. And making the proper deductions for the ordinary depravity of human nature, the number must be still smaller of those who unite the requisite integrity with the requisite knowledge. These considerations apprise us that the government can have no great option between fit characters; and that a temporary duration in office which would naturally discourage such characters from quitting a lucrative line of practice to accept a seat on the bench would have a tendency to throw the administration of justice into hands less able and less well qualified to conduct it with utility and dignity. * * *

* * * The experience of Great Britain affords an illustrious comment on the excellence of the institution [of good behavior tenure.]

NO. 79

NEXT to permanency in office, nothing can contribute more to the independence of the judges than a fixed provision for their support. * * * In the general course of human nature, *a power over a man's subsistence amounts to a power over his will.* And we can never hope to see realized in practice the complete separation of the judicial from the legislative power, in any system which leaves the former dependent for pecuniary resources on the occasional grants of the latter. * * * The plan of the convention accordingly has provided that the judges of the United States "shall at *stated times* receive for their services a compensation which shall not be *diminished* during their continuance in office."

* * *

The precautions for their responsibility are comprised in the article respecting impeachments. They are liable to be impeached for malconduct by the House of Representatives and tried by the Senate; and, if convicted, may be dismissed from office and disqualified for holding any other. This is the only provision on the point which is consistent with the necessary independence of the judicial character, and is the only one which we find in our own Constitution in respect to our own judges.

* * *

The constitution of New York, to avoid investigations that must forever be vague and dangerous, has taken a particular age as the criterion of inability. No man can be a judge beyond sixty. I believe there are few at present who do not disapprove of this provision. There is no station in relation to which it is less proper than to that of a judge. The deliberating and comparing faculties generally preserve their strength much beyond that period in men who survive it; and when, in addition to this circumstance, we consider how few there are who outlive the season of intellectual vigor and how improbable it is that any considerable portion of the bench, whether more or less numerous, should be in such a situation at the same time, we shall be ready to conclude that limitations of this sort have little to recommend them. In a republic where fortunes are not affluent and pensions not expedient, the dismission of men from stations in which they have served their country long and usefully, on which they depend for subsistence, and from which it will be too late to resort to any other occupation for a livelihood, ought to have some better apology to humanity than is to be found in the imaginary danger of a superannuated bench.

NO. 80

[OBJECTS OF THE FEDERAL JUDICIARY]

* * *

It seems scarcely to admit of controversy that the judiciary authority of the Union ought to extend to these several descriptions of cases: 1st, to all those which arise out of the laws of the United States * * *; 2nd, to all those which concern the execution of the provisions expressly contained in the articles of Union; 3rd, to all those in which the United States are a party; 4th, to all those which involve the PEACE of the CONFEDERACY, whether they relate to the intercourse between the United States and foreign nations or to that between the States themselves; 5th, to all those which originate on the high seas, and are of admiralty or maritime jurisdiction; and lastly, to all those in which the State tribunals cannot be supposed to be impartial and unbiased.

* * * The States, * * * are prohibited from doing a variety of things, some of which are incompatible with the interests of the Union and others with the principles of good government. The imposition of duties on imported articles and the emission of paper money are specimens of each kind. No man of sense will believe that such prohibitions would be scrupulously regarded without some effectual power in the government to restrain or correct the infractions of them. This power must either be a direct negative on the State laws, or an authority in the federal courts to overrule such as might be in manifest contravention of the articles of Union. There is no third course that I can imagine. The latter appears to have been thought by the convention preferable to the former, and I presume will be most agreeable to the States.

* * * If there are such things as political axioms, the propriety of the judicial power of a government being coextensive with its legislative may be ranked among the number. The mere necessity of uniformity in the interpretation of the national laws decides the question. Thirteen independent courts of final jurisdiction over the same causes, arising upon the same laws, is a hydra in government from which nothing but contradiction and confusion can proceed.

* * * Controversies between the nation and its members or citizens can only be properly referred to the national tribunals. Any other plan would be contrary to reason, to precedent, and to decorum.

* * *

A method of terminating territorial disputes between the States, under the authority of the federal head, was not unattended to, even in the imperfect system by which they have been hitherto held together. But there are many other sources, besides interfering claims of boundary, from which bickerings and animosities may spring up among the members of the Union. * * * It will readily be conjectured that I allude to the fraudulent laws which have been passed in too many of the States. And though the proposed Constitution establishes particular guards against the repetition of those instances which have heretofore made their appearance, yet it is warrantable to apprehend that the spirit which produced them will assume new shapes that could not be foreseen nor specifically provided against. Whatever practices may have a tendency to disturb the harmony between the States are proper objects of federal superintendence and control.

* * * [I]f it be a just principle that every government ought to possess the means of executing its own provisions by its own authority it will follow that in order [for] * * * the inviolable maintenance of that equality of privileges and immunities to which the citizens of the Union will be entitled, the national judiciary ought to preside in all cases in which one State or its citizens are opposed to another State or its citizens. To secure the full effect of so fundamental a provision against all evasion and subterfuge, it is necessary that its construction should be committed to that tribunal which, having no local attachments, will be likely to be impartial between the different States and their citizens and which, owing its official existence to the Union, will never be likely to feel any bias inauspicious to the principles on which it is founded.

* * * The most bigoted idolizers of State authority have not thus far shown a disposition to deny the national judiciary the cognizance of maritime cases. These so generally depend on the laws of nations and so commonly affect the rights of foreigners that they fall within the considerations which are relative to the public peace. * * *

The reasonableness of the agency of the national courts in cases in which the State tribunals cannot be supposed to be impartial speaks for itself. No man ought certainly to be a judge in his own cause, or in any cause in respect to which he has the least interest or bias. * * * Claims to land under grants of different States, founded upon adverse pretensions of boundary, are of this description. The courts of neither of the granting States could be expected to be unbiased. The laws may have even prejudged the question and tied the courts down to decisions in favor of the grants of the State to which they belonged. And even where this had not been done, it would be natural that the judges, as men, should feel a strong predilection to the claims of their own government.

* * *

NOTES AND QUESTIONS

1. Why is it true that "there is no liberty if the power of judging be not separated from the legislative and executive powers?" What exactly is *good behavior* tenure? What was the role of judicial tenure in the colonies? Why would good behavior tenure be popular then, and perhaps less so later among groups such as the Anti–Federalists? Note the idea of the judiciary serving as a barrier to both the monarchy (in England) and the legislature (in America). In a republic, why do you need a barrier between the people and the legislature? What view does Hamilton have of humankind, and what bearing does this have on his thinking about a national judiciary?

For the origins and development of judicial review in America see, respectively, Gordon S. Wood, "The Origins of Judicial Review," 22 Suffolk U.L.Rev. 1293 (1988), and Christopher Wolfe, The Rise of Modern Judicial Review: From Constitutional Interpretation to Judge–Made Law (1986). For Hamilton's rather unique conception of "Republican" theory, see the brilliant Alexander Hamilton and the Idea of Republican Government, by Gerald Stourzh (1970). See also Forrest McDonald, Alexander Hamilton: A Biography (1979). Hamilton appears to believe that the judiciary is the weakest and the least dangerous branch of government. Why might he think this, and what does he offer as proof? Do you agree?

2. Why is the necessity for judicial review a self-evident truth in a society with a "limited Constitution?" Incidentally, can you understand what would be meant by a Constitution that would be "unlimited?" What, if anything, does judicial review have to do with popular sovereignty? According to Hamilton, what kind of men should staff the national judiciary? What rules and procedures ought to guide their decision-making? What objections might an Anti–Federalist or a radical republican theorist have to Hamilton's proposals? Is judicial review necessarily a conservative or a liberal doctrine? The Bicentennial of the drafting of the 1787 United States Constitution produced an orgy of writing on judicial review and the intention of the Constitution's framers. See generally, for a spirited treatment that cites the work of many others, Leonard W. Levy, Original Intent and the Framers' Constitution (1988). For some other notable highlights in the Bicentennial-inspired reflection on Constitutional theory see Bruce Ackerman, We The People: Foundations (1991), Hans W. Baade, " 'Original Intent' in Historical Perspective: Some Critical Glosses," 69 Tex.L.Rev. 1001 (1991), Raoul Berger, Federalism: The Founders' Design (1987), Robert Bork, The Tempting of America: The Political Seduction of the Law (1990), Harry V. Jaffa et al., Original Intent and the Framers of the Constitution: A Disputed Question (1994), Paul W. Kahn, "Reason and Will in the Origins of American Constitutionalism," 98

Yale L.J. 449 (1989), Charles A. Lofgren, "The Original Understanding of Original Intent?" 5 Const. Comm. 77 (1988), Joseph M. Lynch, Negotiating the Constitution: The Earliest Debates Over Original Intent (1999), H. Jefferson Powell, "The Original Understanding of Original Intent," 98 Harv.L.Rev. 885 (1985), Stephen B. Presser, Recapturing the Constitution: Race, Religion and Abortion Reconsidered (1994), Jack N. Rakove, Original Meanings: Politics and Ideas in the Making of the Constitution (1996), Jack N. Rakove, "The Madisonian Moment," 55 U.Chi.L.Rev. 473 (1988), Suzanna Sherry, "The Founders' Unwritten Constitution," 54 U.Chi.L.Rev. 1127 (1987), Cass R. Sunstein, The Partial Constitution (1993), and William Michael Treanor, "The Original Understanding of the Takings Clause and the Political Process," 95 Colum. L. Rev. 782 (1995).

3. Do you agree with Hamilton's argument in Federalist 78 that the process of impeachment is a sufficient guarantee of judicial "competence?" What else does it guarantee? Do you think that Hamilton would have it apply *only* to questions of competence? Why does Hamilton note in this connection that the United States is a republic "where fortunes are not affluent and pensions not expedient?" Do you think that Hamilton expects the United States to remain this kind of a republic for very long?

4. In Federalist 80, Hamilton argues, *inter alia,* the need for national tribunals to resolve controversies between the nation and its members or citizens, but his argument seems not very detailed, relying instead on first principles. Do you think that jurisdiction would be necessarily so limited as Hamilton implies? Why might this trouble an Anti–Federalist? Concerning the controversies between the nation and its members or citizens, why would it be contrary "to reason, to precedent, and to decorum" to have state courts resolve these matters? What does Hamilton mean by "decorum"? What do you take to be Hamilton's opinion of state courts? Why? Would Hamilton's arguments be weaker or stronger if it turned out that Federal district judges were usually citizens of the states in which their courts sat?

5. The Federalist papers which are excerpted here were originally published in New York newspapers and were designed to persuade the New Yorkers to approve the proposed Federal Constitution. Why do you think that Alexander Hamilton and his co-authors, Madison and Jay, instead of signing their own names, wrote as "Publius?" In this connection, note that much of these Federalist papers was devoted to stressing the need for quick action of approval of the proposed constitution, as it then existed, leaving the constitutional amendment process to correct remaining errors. Why the rush? Consider these excerpts from the concluding paper, Federalist 85, and see if they sound familiar:

> The additional securities to republican government, to liberty, and to property, to be derived from the adoption of the plan under consideration, consist chiefly in the restraints which the preservation of the Union will impose on local factions and insurrections, and on the ambition of powerful individuals in single States who might acquire credit and influence enough from leaders and favorites to become the despots of the peo-

ple; in the diminution of the opportunities to foreign intrigue, which the dissolution of the Confederacy would invite and facilitate; in the prevention of extensive military establishments, which could not fail to grow out of wars between the States in a disunited situation; in the express guaranty of a republican form of government to each; in the absolute and universal exclusion of titles of nobility; and in the precautions against the repetition of those practices on the part of the State governments which have undermined the foundations of property and credit, have planted mutual distrust in the breasts of all classes of citizens, and have occasioned an almost universal prostration of morals.

* * *

I shall not dissemble that I feel an entire confidence in the arguments which recommend the proposed system [but,] * * * I am persuaded that it is the best which our political situation, habits, and opinions will admit, and superior to any the revolution has produced.

Concessions on the part of the friends of the plan that it has not a claim to absolute perfection have afforded matter of no small triumph to its enemies. "Why," say they, "should we adopt an imperfect thing? Why not amend it and make it perfect before it is irrevocably established?" * * * This, as far as I have understood the meaning of those who make the concessions, is an entire perversion of their sense. No advocate of the measure can be found who will not declare as his sentiment that the system, though it may not be perfect in every part, is, upon the whole, a good one * * *; and is such a one as promises every species of security which a reasonable people can desire.

* * *

The zeal for attempts to amend, prior to the establishment of the Constitution, must abate in every man who is ready to accede to the truth of the following observations * * * "To balance a large state or society * * * whether monarchical or republican, on general laws, is a work of so great difficulty that no human genius, however comprehensive, is able, by the mere dint of reason and reflection, to effect it. The judgments of many must unite in the work; EXPERIENCE must guide their labor; TIME must bring it to perfection, and the FEELING of inconveniences must correct the mistakes which they *inevitably* fall into in their first trials and experiments."* These judicious reflections * * * ought to put [us] upon [our] guard against hazarding anarchy, civil war, a perpetual alienation of the States from each other, and perhaps the military despotism of a victorious demagogue, in the pursuit of what [we] are not likely to obtain, but from TIME and EXPERIENCE. It may be in me a defect of political fortitude but I acknowledge that I cannot entertain an

* David Hume, I Essays 128, "The Rise of Arts and Sciences."

equal tranquility with those who affect to treat the dangers of a longer continuance in our present situation as imaginary. A NATION, without a NATIONAL GOVERNMENT, is, in my view, an awful spectacle. The establishment of a Constitution, in time of profound peace, by the voluntary consent of a whole people, is a PRODIGY, to the completion of which I look forward with trembling anxiety. * * * I dread the more the consequences of new attempts because I KNOW that POWERFUL INDIVIDUALS, in this and in other States, are enemies to a general national government in every possible shape.

The Federalist continues to be the most influential text in American politics, at least where appeals to original understanding are involved. For a sample of scholarship on these essays, see, e.g., Alan Brinkley, Nelson W. Polsby, and Kathleen M. Sullivan, New Federalist Papers: Essays in Defense of the Constitution (1997), Ira C. Lupu, "The Most–Cited Federalist Papers," 15 Const. Comm. 403 (1998), Ira C. Lupu, "Textualism and Original Understanding: Time, The Supreme Court, and the Federalist," 66 Geo. Wash. L. Rev. 1324 (1998), J. Michael Martinez and William D. Richardson, "The Federalist Papers and Legal Interpretation," 45 S.D.L.Rev. 307 (2000), and Seth Barrett Tillman, "The Federalist Papers as Reliable Historical Source Material for Constitutional Interpretation," 105 W. Va. L. Rev. 601 (2003).

6. With the next group of selections we begin to find out whether the national judiciary evolved along the lines Hamilton promised. As you read these materials, determine whether the federal judges were performing according to the theory of popular sovereignty that seems to underlie Federalist 78.

2. A SELECTION FROM THE UNITED STATES DISTRICT COURT FOR THE DISTRICT OF PENNSYLVANIA

(a) The Nature of Admiralty Jurisprudence

RICE ET AL. V. THE POLLY & KITTY

United States Circuit Court, District of Pennsylvania, 1789.
20 Fed.Cas. 666.

BY THE COURT. The libellants had been cruelly beaten and abused both by the captain and one Shirtliff, the mate * * * insomuch that on account of extreme illusage and dangerous threats, they were obliged to leave the brig at Lisbon in the midst of her voyage, and return to Philadelphia in another vessel; and the principal question was, whether this desertion did not incur a forfeiture of wages under the articles.

* * *

When mariners enter into articles for a voyage, they do not thereby put themselves out of the protection of the laws, or subject their limbs and lives to the capricious passions of a master or his mate. On account of the great charge entrusted to the master, and for the benefit of commerce, the law holds his office in high estimation, and vests him with a great extent of discretionary power. It gives him absolute command over the seamen in all matters concerning their duty and the object of their service, but not an absolute command over their persons. The master has a right to correct a refractory, disobedient mariner; but wherever this right is recognized in the books, moderate chastisement is always express or intended. For the law always watches the exercise of discretionary power with a jealous eye. The relation between a master and his servant or apprentice is such, that of necessity a discretionary authority is allowed by law to the master, yet nothing is more frequent than the intervention of the civil power to dissolve this connection, when the master is found to abuse his authority by undue severity and cruelty. Under such circumstances, the servant is justified in leaving his master. Keeping a servant from meat and drink, or battery, are good causes for a departure from the service. Fitzh.Nat.Brev. 391; 1 Bl.Comm. 428. The shipping articles, indeed, declare that forty-eight hours absence from the vessel, during the voyage, without leave, shall be deemed a total desertion, and incur a forfeiture of wages. But * * * although the sole contract mentioned in these articles on the part of the master or owner, is the payment of wages, yet law and reason will imply other obligations—such as, that the vessel shall be sea-worthy and properly fitted for navigation—that the mariners shall be supplied with sufficient meat and drink, and that they shall be treated with, at least, decent humanity.

From a general review of the testimony, and indeed from the mate's own account, it is manifest that the libellants have been cruelly beaten and abused on board this brig at sundry times, and especially in the port of Lisbon, where the captain found it necessary to take one of them on shore and put him under the care of a surgeon to be cured of the wounds and bruises he had suffered under the chastisement given him by the captain and his mate. The only justifications alleged for this great severity, are a general charge against the mariners of disobedience and insufficiency in their duty, without specifying any particulars, and an appearance of a mutinous combination between them in the port of Lisbon. * * * But what I principally look to, is the general conduct of the mariners on this occasion. Finding themselves so cruelly treated by the mate, they first made their complaint to the captain; instead of obtaining the redress they expected, the captain joined the mate in punishing them still more severely for making this complaint. This extreme severity, together with the declaration of the mate, that he would make them glad to jump overboard before they got to America, seems to have taken away all hope of redress or even safety on board, and the whole crew left the vessel. When on shore, they did not secrete themselves, but frequently sought for and met the captain, and openly demanded their wages and clothes; and finally, they applied to the legal authority at Lisbon, and obtained a process against the captain. This conduct on the part of the mariners, seems to remove every appearance of an intended mutiny or a voluntary desertion. If the suspicion of either had been well founded, why did not the captain apply to the courts of law at Lisbon, to have them secured and tried for their offences. This he did not do, but on the contrary, promised to pay them their wages, and anxiously avoided the process they had taken out against him.

* * * The libellants have not voluntarily deserted, but have been forced from a service in which neither the rights of humanity nor personal safety could be depended upon or even expected.

I adjudge that the libellants have and receive their wages to the time of their leaving the vessel at Lisbon (for this is all the libellants ask for), and that the respondent pay the costs of suit.

(b) The Sources of Admiralty Jurisprudence

THOMPSON ET AL. V. THE CATHARINA

United States Circuit Court, District of Pennsylvania, 1795.
23 Fed.Cas. 1028.

[This case, by Judge Richard Peters, relates the American law of admiralty to that of other countries. Pay particular attention to the footnotes; do not memorize the details, but note the scope of authorities cited.]

This was the case of a foreign ship, which came before the court on a claim for wages by her seamen * * * who by their contracts had engaged to return to the port from which they shipped. * * *

An objection is made * * * to my decision on a point, on which our own municipal laws are silent. This objection * * * obliges me to give my sentiments on the question, "What laws or rules shall direct or govern the decisions of maritime courts here, in points on which we have no regulations established by our own national legislature?" There are, in most nations concerned in commerce, municipal and local laws relative to contracts with mariners, and other maritime covenants and agreements; though the great leading principles, or outlines, are in all nearly the same. On this account among others, I have avoided taking cognizance, as much as possible, of disputes in which foreign ships and seamen, are concerned. * * * But where the voyage of a foreign ship ended here, or was broken up, and no treaty or compact designated the mode of proceeding, I have permitted suits to be prosecuted. In such cases, I have determined according to the laws of the country to which the ship belonged, if there existed any peculiar variance of difference from those generally prevailing. I have seldom found any very material difference in principle. The laws and customs of Spain, relating to mariners, are more rigid than those of other nations, on similar points. Among other points of variance from other laws, those of Spain grant the master a lien on the ship, for his wages. In the present case, the contract was, in part, with mariners of the United States; and these seamen were to be discharged in an American port. I apply the authority of this court to the case of our own citizens. If by our own municipal laws, there are rules established, our courts are bound exclusively to follow them. But in cases where no such rules are instituted, we must resort to the regulations of other maritime countries, which have stood the test of time and experience, to direct our judgments, as rules of decision. We ought not to betray so much vanity, as to take it for granted, that we could establish more salutary and useful regulations than those which have, for ages, governed the most commercial and powerful nations, and led them to wealth and greatness.

The laws of the Rhodians were followed and adopted by the Romans, in their most prosperous state of commerce and power. Those in the celebrated Consolato del Mare,[3] prevailing in the Mediterranean, and established, in concert with other trading states and countries, by the Venetians and Genoese, in the periods of their naval power and commercial prosperity, are collections of, and improvements on, more ancient customs and laws. Of these, the Amalfitan Code * * * furnished the predominant and most generally received principles.[4] The laws of Oleron occupy now a portion of the famous Black Book of the British Admiralty, which is consulted by all their courts on subjects of maritime and commercial controversy. These laws of Oleron were not entirely of British growth. They were compiled at first * * * by Queen Eleonora, Duchess of Guienne, for her continental dominions, and afterwards improved and enlarged by her son Richard the First, of England, in no small degree from the maritime laws and customs, not only of his own country, but also from the laws and customs prevailing among the continental trading nations. Of these, the Saxons were, at an early period, the most conspicuous and practically intelligent in nautical affairs. They introduced into England their maritime

[3] Consolato del Mare. These are the most ancient, celebrated and authentic sea laws, after those of the Rhodians, Greeks, and Romans. * * * As a respectable part of the laws of nations, they have always been received in the English courts of admiralty, and those of this country. Their origin is enveloped in obscurity, though attributed to several nations * * *. Their influence, value and authority, have been appreciated by claims to their origin, set up by various people of maritime countries. Those laws have prevailed in the countries occupying the coasts of the Mediterranean, and in the neighbouring parts of Southern Europe, for centuries. * * * This body of maritime law is a compilation of the best maritime laws then existing, comprising judicial proceedings, principles and decisions, settled by men of great experience and consummate prudence; who, having reason and custom for their guides, established these excellent regulations * * *.

[4] The city of Amalfi was situate in what is now called the province of Salerno, in the kingdom of Naples. Nothing great remains of it, but its celebrity for the most extensive commerce of its time, its immense wealth and magnificence, and its great weight in all questions of maritime concern. * * *

knowledge, as they did some valuable principles of the common law. * * * The maritime ordinances of France (where also the laws of Oleron, or Roll d'Oleron, are in force, and claimed, as of French origin) are very much grounded on the sea laws of other nations, mixed with their own. * * * The laws of the Hanse Towns,[5] are nearly in substance the same with those called the laws of Wisbuy, and both are principally founded on those of Oleron. The sea laws of Spain are, in no small degree, collections from those of other nations. There is a striking similarity in the leading principles of all these laws. So far from sound principles becoming obsolete, or injured by time, that it will be found, on careful investigation, that the oldest sea laws we know, those of the Rhodians,[6] have furnished the outline and leading character of the whole. With such examples before us, we need not hesitate to be guided by the rules and principles, established in the maritime laws of other countries. * * *

I shall not contend with those who say, we ought to have a maritime code of our own, about the binding force of all these laws on us. By the general laws of nations we certainly are bound. These apply, most frequently, in the prize court; but there are many cases of salvage, wreck, & c. on the instance or civil side of the court, which necessarily must be determined under the general law. The wisdom and experience, evidenced in the particular maritime institutions of other commercial countries, ought at least to be greatly respected. If they serve only as faithful guides, and tried and long established rules of decision, in similar cases, they are of high and exemplary importance. It must be granted, that it is safer to follow them, than to trust entirely to the varying and crooked line of discretion.[7]

Where a reciprocity of decision, in certain cases, is necessary, the court of one country is often guided by the customs, laws, and decisions of the tribunals of another, in similar cases. But the change in the form of our government has not abrogated all the laws, customs and principles of jurisprudence we inherited from our ancestors and possessed at the peri-

---

[5] The laws of the Hanse Towns were published first in 1591, and reviewed in 1614, and posterior to those of Wisbuy or Oleron. The history of this commercial confederacy is well known. Although in itself and its dependencies, it consisted of 62 cities, originally, it is now reduced to six, consisting of Lubeck, Hamburgh, Dantzig, Brenten, Rostock, and Cologne. * * *

[6] * * * The Rhodians applied themselves exclusively to commerce, and avoided every idea of extension of territory. Their fleet was so powerful, and their naval regulations so excellent, that they were courted by the most mighty nations of their time. They held the empire of the sea, and by confining their strength and resources to maritime objects, they not only protected and extended their own commerce, but scoured the ocean of pirates who annoyed the trade of all countries. Alexander the Great treated them with marked distinction. * * * Their superiority, in mercantile and naval talent and enterprise, gained them the admiration and respect of their contemporaries; when a spirit of monopoly, jealousy and plunder, would have handed them down to us, not to be imitated, but detested.

[7] The foregoing enumeration of some of the maritime codes, is not intended to comprehend the whole, which would swell the account too extensively. It is given merely to show, that the most renowned maritime nations always adopted the principles, when long tried and tested, of their predecessors or contemporaries. * * *

od of our becoming an independent nation. The people of these states, both individually and collectively, have the common law,[8] in all cases, consistent with the change of our government, and the principles on which it is founded. They possess, in like manner, the maritime law, which is part of the common law, existing at the same period; and this is peculiarly within the cognizance of courts, invested with maritime jurisdiction; although it is referred to, in all our courts on maritime questions. It is, then, not to be disputed, on sound principles, that this court must be governed in its decisions, by the Maritime Code we possessed at the period before stated; as well as by the particular laws since established by our own government, or which may hereafter be enacted. * * * Whatever may, in strictness, be thought of their binding authority, I shall always be ready to hear the opinions of the learned and wise jurisprudents or judicial characters of any country on subjects agitated in this court * * *. I am not so confident in my own judgment, as not to wish for all the lights and information, it may be in my power to obtain, from any respectable sources. * * * [Peters proceeded, apparently on the basis of many maritime authorities discussed, to determine that the plaintiffs, American seamen, were entitled to the wages they sought from the foreign owner of their ship. According to admiralty practice, the ship was to be sold to pay the wages if the owner did not.]

(c) The Aim of Admiralty Jurisprudence

WILLINGS ET AL. V. BLIGHT

United States Circuit Court, District of Pennsylvania, 1800.
30 Fed.Cas. 50.

This was a petition to permit the majority of owners to proceed with the brig Amelia on a voyage, after giving stipulation for value of the recusant owner's share. In this case the proceedings will shew the course originally taken by the parties. The court was clearly of opinion that the cause was one of admiralty jurisdiction; and that it had power to authorize the majority of owners to fit out and expedite the vessel on a voyage to be designated in the stipulation, and it directed accordingly. The question of freight was accommodated; and the court gave no final judgment. An opinion was however intimated that no freight was legally demandable by

---

[8] The feudal parts of this law, and such as are inconsistent with the principles of our government are not, nor can they be, in force. Those who are best acquainted with its wise and just principles, as they relate to contracts, and the property, as well as the personal rights of individuals, admire the common law as the venerable and solid bulwark of both liberty and property. Statute laws innovating upon it, have seldom been found, on experience, to be real improvements. Those who do not know the common law suppose it to be everything, that it is not. Its rules and principles are not arbitrary, but fixed and settled by the wisdom and decisions of the most respectable and intelligent sages, of both ancient and modern times. Many of the objections raised against it shew a want of acquaintance with its system and principles. Some of these objections are founded in innovation made by statutes altering or obscuring, the common law. Others have nothing in either common or statute law to support them.

a recusant owner, who would neither sell at a reasonable appraisement, nor make advances for outfit; but his share of the vessel should be secured to him, that as he gains no profit, he may incur no loss. It appeared unreasonable, that those who were prepared, and desirous to put their property into a state of activity, should use their funds disproportionably for the benefit of a delinquent owner.

During the progress of the cause the following opinion was given by the court.

Whether the minority shall or shall not be compelled to sell, has not, in the opinion of the court, been here judicially determined. It is asserted (Beawes, Lex.Merc. 49) that if the majority of owners refuse to fit out, they are compellable to sell at a valuation; and so are part-owners, deficient and unable to fit out the vessel. This majority or minority, means those who hold the greater or less proportion of property. In the Sea Laws (3d Ed. 442), it is said, that "upon any probable design, the major part of the owners may, even against the consent, though not without the privity and knowledge of the rest, freight out their vessel to sea." "If it should so fall out that the major part, in number, protest against the voyage, and but one left that is for the voyage, yet the same may be effected by that party, if there be equality in partnership." "If it falls out that one is so obstinate, that his consent cannot be had, the law will enforce him either to hold or to sell his proportion; but if he will set no price, the rest may rig her out, at their own costs and charges, and whatsoever freight she earns, he is not to have any share or benefit in the same. But if such vessel happens to miscarry, or to be cast away, the rest must answer him his part, or proportion, in the vessel. But if it should fall out, that the major part of the owners in value, refuse to set out the vessel to sea; there by reason of the inequality, they may not be compelled; but then such vessel is to be valued and sold: the like, whether part of the owners become deficient, or unable to set her forth to sea." The sixth article of the twenty-third section of the ordinances of Louis XIV of France, enacts, that "no person may constrain his partner to proceed to the sale of a ship, except the opinions of the owners be equally divided about the undertaking of the voyage." Here "equally" means equality of property.

It is a principle discernable in all maritime codes, that every encouragement and assistance should be afforded to those, who are ready to give to their ships constant employment; and this, not only for the particular profit of owners, but for the general interests and prosperity of commerce. If agriculture be, according to the happy allusion of the great Sully,* "one of the breasts from which the state must draw its nourishment," commerce is certainly the other. The earth, the parent of both, is the immedi-

* Maximilian de Béthune, duc de Sully (1560–1641), a brilliant administrator and visionary, was superintendent of finances for Henry IV of France. Sully helped make France prosperous in the late sixteenth and seventeenth centuries by his encouragement of agriculture, roads and canals.

ate foundation and support of the one, and ships are the moving powers, instruments and facilities of the other.—Both must be rendered productive by industry and ingenuity. The interests and comforts of the community will droop, and finally perish, if either be permitted to remain entirely at rest. The former will less ruinously bear neglect, and throw up spontaneous products; but the latter require unremitted employment, attention and enterprize, to ensure utility and profit. A privation of freight, the fruit and crop of shipping, seems therefore to be an appropriate mulct, on indolent, perverse, or negligent part-owners. The drones ought not to share in the stores, acquired and accumulated by the labour, activity, foresight and management of the bees. Although the hive may be common property, it is destructively useless to all, if not furnished with means of profit and support by industry and exertion; which should be jointly applied by all, before they participate in beneficial results. Nor should the idle and incompetent be permitted to hold it vacant and useless to the injury and ruin of the industrious and active.

NOTES AND QUESTIONS

1. The Constitution and the Judiciary Act of 1789 gave admiralty jurisdiction to the federal courts, but did not spell out what substantive maritime law the federal courts were to apply. On the judiciary act of 1789 see generally Maeva Marcus et al., Origins of the Federal Judiciary: Essays on the Judiciary Act of 1789 (1992), and Wythe Holt, " 'To Establish Justice': Politics, The Judiciary Act of 1789, and the Invention of the Federal Courts," 1989 Duke L.J. 1421. On the admiralty jurisdiction conferred by the 1789 Act see William R. Casto, "The Origins of Federal Admiralty Jurisdiction in an Age of Privateers, Smugglers, and Pirates," 27 Am.J.Leg.Hist. 117 (1993). Some of the cases you have just read are addressed to the problem of whose admiralty law our federal courts should use. In the first one, Rice v. The Polly, you will notice that there is very little citation of authority. The law of the case seems to be drawn from the "shipping articles" and also from "law and reason," or the "rights of humanity." Does this strike you as a wise approach? The federal admiralty courts, following the English practice, proceeded without a jury. In light of the American objections to the colonial English Vice–Admiralty courts on the grounds of their lack of juries, such as those made by Oxenbridge Thacher and Thomas Jefferson, was this a sensible manner of proceeding in America? In some states, immediately after the revolution, admiralty courts were created which functioned *with* juries. Why were the *federal* courts which replaced them juryless? For a brief history of American admiralty jurisdiction with some thoughts on its possible modern demise, see John R. Brown, "Tribute: Admiralty Judges: Flotsam on the Sea of Maritime Law?", 25 Hous.J.Int.L. 257 (2003).

2. In Thompson v. The Catharina, the second case, Judge Peters displays his knowledge of the maritime laws of ancient and modern nations. Much of this knowledge he acquired from his own translations of ancient and modern authorities from many European nations. Peters indicates that these

authorities will be used in his decisions. Does this seem correct? Why? Reread footnote 8 of the *Thompson* case, and its accompanying text. Does the attitude that one should reject the "feudal" parts of the common law, but keep its provisions with regard to contract, property, and individual rights make sense to you? How do you explain the attitude in the footnote that statutes, more often than not, miss the mark? Is this attitude dominant today? Should it be?

3. What does *Willings v. Blight,* the third case, tell you about its author's (Judge Peters) ideas about the aims of admiralty jurisprudence? In another admiralty case, Hollingsworth v. The Betsey, 12 Fed.Cas. 348 (D.C.D.Pa.1795), Judge Peters found his court asked to assess damages for the unlawful capture and detention of the brigantine *Betsey* and her cargo. Peters ordered the clerk of his court "to associate with him three intelligent and disinterested merchants of this district, who, or any two of them with the clerk, shall examine into all circumstances relative to the vessel and cargo and the losses and damages consequent thereon, and ascertain the amount thereof, according to justice and good conscience * * *." Why would Peters make such an order? Would you have approved of it? During most of American history most Americans were engaged in the practice of agriculture. Do *Willings* and *Hollingsworth* seem consistent with the spirit of American agrarianism? Is the Constitutional theory that seems implied by the Federalist consistent with this spirit?

4. In the two cases that follow, you will see a clash between rural agrarian Americans and the Federalist judges, growing out of two actual rebellions in Pennsylvania in the late eighteenth century. Does the attitude of the Federalist judges in these two cases seem different from that displayed in the three admiralty opinions?

B. THE FIRST FEDERAL TREASON TRIALS

1. THE TRIAL OF THE WESTERN INSURGENTS (1794–1795)

In 1794 the United States Government sought to collect long overdue revenues under a 1791 excise tax on whiskey in several western Pennsylvania counties. The tax struck hard at the economy of this region, as the manufacture of whiskey was viewed as the best means of preserving the grain crop. The tax was figured on the basis of quantity, and since the selling price of whiskey was lowest in Western Pennsylvania, the tax burden was especially great. Many of the residents of that region engaged in attacks on federal excise officials in the summer of 1794, often resorting to the use of tar and feathers. For several months federal authority was suspended. Federal commissioners sent to observe the situation concluded that "nothing less than the physical strength of the nation could enforce the law." Several thousand men of Western Pennsylvania took up arms in opposition to the federal statute, and President Washington finally dispatched a contingent of 15,000 federal troops, under the command of treasury secretary Alexander Hamilton, which restored the authority of the national government. Several of the ringleaders were brought to trial in Philadelphia before the United States Circuit Court.

THE UNITED STATES v. VIGOL

United States Circuit Court, District of Pennsylvania, 1795.
28 Fed.Cas. 376.

Indictment for High Treason, in levying war against the United States. The prisoner was one of the most active insurgents in the Western counties of Pennsylvania, and had accompanied the armed party, who attacked the house of the excise officer (Reigan's) in Westmoreland with guns, drums, & c., insisted upon his surrendering his official papers, and extorted an oath from him, that he would never act again in the execution of the excise law. The same party then proceeded to the house of Wells, the excise officer, in Fayette county, swearing that the excise law should never be carried into effect, and that they would destroy Wells and his house. On their arrival, Wells had fled, and concealed himself; whereupon they ransacked the house, burned it, with all its contents, including the public books and papers, and afterwards discovering Wells, seized, imprisoned, and compelled him to swear that he would never act again as excise officer. Witnesses were likewise examined to establish that the general combination and scope of the insurrection, were to prevent the execution of the excise law by force * * *.

Paterson, Justice: [charging the jury] The first point for consideration, is the evidence, which has been given to establish the case stated in the indictment; the second point turns upon the criminal intention of the party; and from these points (the evidence and intention) the law arises.

With respect to the evidence, the current runs one way. It harmonizes in all its parts. It proves that the prisoner was a member of the party, who went to Reigan's house, and afterwards to the house of Wells, in arms, marshalled and arrayed, and who, at each place, committed acts of violence and devastation.

With respect to the intention, likewise, there is not, unhappily, the slightest possibility of doubt. To suppress the office of excise, in the fourth survey of this State, and particularly in the present instance, to compel the resignation of Wells, the excise officer, so as to render null and void, in effect, an act of Congress, constituted the apparent, the avowed object of the inspection, and of the outrages which the prisoner assisted to commit.

Combining these facts, and this design, the crime of High Treason is consummate in the contemplation of the Constitution and law of the United States.

The counsel for the prisoner have endeavoured, in the course of a faithful discharge of their duty, to extract from the witnesses some testimony, which might justify a defence upon the ground of duress and terror, but in this they have failed, for the whole scene exhibits a disgraceful unanimity; and, with regard to the prisoner, he can only be distinguished for a guilty pre-eminence in zeal and activity. It may not, however, be useless on this occasion, to observe, that the fear, which the law recognizes as an excuse for the perpetration of an offence, must proceed from an immediate and actual danger, threatening the very life of the party. The apprehension of any loss of property, by waste or fire; or even an apprehension of a slighter remote injury to the person, furnish no excuse. If, indeed, such circumstances could avail, it would be in the power of every crafty leader of tumults and rebellions to indemnify his followers, by uttering previous menaces; an avenue would be forever open for the escape of unsuccessful guilt; and the whole fabric of society must inevitably be laid prostrate.

* * * Verdict guilty.

THE UNITED STATES V. MITCHELL

United States Circuit Court, District of Pennsylvania, 1795.
26 Fed.Cas. 1277.

Indictment for High Treason for levying war against the United States. * * *

[Following the testimony of witnesses] The attorney of the district (Mr. Rawle) [began his argument on the law of the case:] * * * Kings, it is true, have endeavoured to augment the number, and to perplex the descriptions of treasons, as an instrument to enlarge their powers, and to oppress their subjects; but in republics, and particularly in the American Republic, the crime of treason is naturally reduced to a single head, which divides itself into these constitutional propositions. 1st. Levying war against the government; and 2d. Adhering to its enemies and giving them aid and comfort. In other words, exciting internal, or waging external war against the State. * * *

What constitutes a levying of war, however, must be the same in technical interpretation, whether committed under a republican or a regal form of government, since either institution may be assailed and subverted by the same means. Hence we are enabled * * * to acquire precise and satisfactory ideas upon the subject, from the matured experience of another government * * *. By the English authorities it is uniformly and clearly declared, that raising a body of men to obtain by intimidation or violence the repeal of a law, or to oppose and prevent by force or terror the execution of the law, is an act of levying war. Doug. 570. Again; an insurrection with an avowed design to suppress public offices, is an act of levying war, and, although a bare conspiracy to levy war may not amount to that species of treason; yet, if any of the conspirators actually levy war, it is treason in all the persons that conspired * * *. Those, likewise, who join afterwards, though not concerned at first in the plot, are as guilty as the original conspirators; for in treason all are principals * * *.

The evidence, unfortunately, leaves no room for excuse or extenuation, in the application of the law to the prisoners' cases. The general and avowed object of the conspiracy at Couche's Fort, was to suppress the offices of excise in the Fourth Survey. As an important measure for that purpose, it was agreed to go to Gen. Neville's house, and to compel him to surrender his office and official papers. Some of the persons who were at Couche's Fort went, accordingly, to General Neville's and terminated a course of lawless and outrageous proceedings, by burning his house. The prisoner is proved by four witnesses to have been at Couche's Fort; and so far from opposing the expedition to General Neville's, he offered himself to reconnoitre. Being thus originally combined with the conspirators, in a treasonable purpose, to levy war, it was unnecessary that the purpose should be afterwards executed, in order to convict them all of treason, and much less is it necessary to his conviction, that he should have been present at the burning of General Neville's house, which was the consummation of their plot, or that the burning should be proved by two witnesses. But he is, likewise, discovered, by one of the witnesses at least, within a few rods of the General's, at the moment of the conflagration, and he is seen marching in the cavalcade, which escorted the dead body of their leader, in melancholy triumph, from the scene of action to Barclay's house. * * *.

The counsel for the prisoner * * * premised, that they did not conceive it to be their duty to show, that the prisoner was guiltless of any description of crime against the United States, or the State of Pennsylvania. But they contended, that he had not committed the crime of high treason, and ought, therefore, to be acquitted upon the present indictment. The adjudications in England upon the various descriptions of treason, have been worked, incautiously, into a system, by the destruction of which, at this day, the government itself would be seriously affected; but even there, the best judges, and the ablest commentators, while they acquiesce in the decisions that have already taken place, furnish a strong caution against the too easy admission of future cases, which may seem to have a parity of reason. Constructive, or interpretative treasons, must be the dread and scourge of any nation that allows them. 1 Hale P.C. 132, 259; 4 Bl.Com. 85. Take then, the distinction of treason by levying war, as laid down by the attorney of the district, and it is a constructive or interpretative weapon, which is calculated to annul all distinctions heretofore wisely established in the grades and punishments of crimes; and by whose magic power a mob may easily be converted into a conspiracy; and a riot aggravated into high treason. Such, however, is not the sense which Congress has expressed upon this very subject; for, if a bare opposition to the execution of a law can be considered as constituting a traitorous offence, as levying war against the government, it must be equally so, in relation to every other law, as well as in relation to the excise law * * *. And yet, in the penal code of the United States, the offence of wilfully obstructing, resisting or opposing, any officer, in serving, or attempting to serve any process, is considered and punished merely as a misdemeanour. * * * Let it be granted, that to compel Congress to repeal a law, by violence, or intimidation, is treason, (and the English authorities rightly construed, claim no greater concession,) it does not follow, that resisting the execution of a law, or attempting to coerce an officer into the resignation of his commission, will amount to the same offence. Let it be granted, also that an insurrection for an avowed purpose of suppressing all the excise offices in the United States, may be construed into an act of levying war against the government * * * it does not follow that an attempt to oblige one officer to resign, or to suppress all the offices in one district, will be a crime of the same denomination. 1 Hal.P.C. 135. * * * [A] bare conspiracy to levy war, does not amount to treason; but, it is contended, that if, at any time afterwards, a part of the conspirators should execute the plot, the whole of them will be involved in the guilt and punishment. Thus, no opportunity is left for repentance * * *. The state of the evidence, however, renders it unavoidable, that this ground should be taken; for, unless the proceedings at Couche's Fort, and at General Neville's house, can be so combined and interwoven, as to form one action, there are not two witnesses to prove that the prisoner was at the latter place; and the conduct at the former, could only amount, under the most rigid construction, to a conspiracy to levy war, not to an actual levying of war against the government. With the necessity for two witnesses to an overt act of treason, it is not in the power of the judge or juries to dispense; it is a shield from oppression, with which the constitution furnishes the prisoner * * *.

If this view of the law is correct, it will be easy to show, that its operation upon the facts, will entitle the prisoner to an acquittal. * * * With respect to the criminal proceedings at General Neville's house, (which after all, amount to the crime of arson, not of treason,) it is agreed that only one positive witness proves the fact of his having been there; but, even that Witness states, that the prisoner was alone, at the distance of thirty or forty rods; and it is not recollected whether he had a gun. Then it only remains to consider of the prisoner's presence at Couche's Fort * * *. It does not, then, appear by the testimony of two witnesses, that the meeting at Couche's Fort was convened for the purpose of accomplishing a compulsory repeal of the excise laws, or a suppression of the excise offices. The meeting seems to have originated merely in a wish to consider what it was best to do in the actual state of the country. On this point a committee was chosen, or rather was self-created, and the members determined to send a flag to General Neville. It does not appear with what view the flag was to be sent; but it will not be presumed, when the evidence is silent, to be with a view to attack the General's house, to force a repeal of the excise law, or to compel the officer's resignation; and even the fact itself is only proved by one witness. Besides, the conduct of the Committee, however culpable, will not be sufficient to involve the whole assembly in the guilt of treason. It is true, that the prisoner expressed his willingness to reconnoitre General Neville's house; but this expression, likewise, is only proved by one witness; and even if it were proved by fifty witnesses, it does not amount to an overt act of treason by levying war; nor does it appear that he even did reconnoitre, or furnish intelligence to the Committee. * * *

The Attorney General of the United States (Mr. Bradford) in reply. * * * If * * * the principles asserted in the course of the prisoner's defence should prevail, a flagrant attempt to obstruct the legitimate operations of the government, to prevent the execution of its laws, and to coerce its officers into a dereliction of their trusts, must no longer be regarded as high treason. * * *

[I]t has been argued, that Congress has provided a specific punishment, for the offence of resisting or obstructing the service of process, obviously distinguishing it from treason; and that it is as much treason to resist the execution of one law as another; to resist the marshal of a court, as much as the supervisor of a district. The analogy is, in a great measure, just; in either case, if the resistance is made by a few persons, in a particular instance, and under the impulse of a particular interest, the offence would not amount to high treason; but if, in either case, there is a general rising of a whole county, to prevent the officer from discharging his duty in relation to the public at large, the offence is unquestionably high treason. * * *

Again, it has been urged, that the criminal intention must point to the suppression of all the excise offices in the United States, or it cannot amount to high treason. * * * [I]f it was intended that, by their lawless career and example, Congress should be forced into a repeal of the obnoxious law, it necessarily followed, that from the same cause, the offices of excise would be suppressed throughout the Union. * * *

The truth is, however, that the insurgents did not entertain a personal dislike for General Neville, but in every stage of their proceedings * * * they were actuated by one single traitorous motive, a determination if practicable, to frustrate and prevent the execution of the excise law. The whole was one great insurrection, and it is immaterial at what point of time or place, from its commencement to its termination, any man became an agent in carrying it on. * * * To render any man criminal, he must not only have been present, but he must have taken part with the insurgents; yet, whether he was present at Couche's Fort, or the march to General Neville's, or at the burning of the General's house, if his intention was traitorous, his offence was treason. 3 Inst. 9. The overt act laid in the indictment (which is drawn from the most approved precedents) is levying war; and war may be levied, though not actually made. Fost. 218. It is agreed that this overt act must be proved by two witnesses; but there is a difference as to what constitutes the act itself. Now it is manifest from every authority, that to assemble in a body armed and arrayed for some treasonable purpose, is an act of levying war; this was the case at Couche's Fort, and the prisoner's active attendance there is proved by a number of witnesses. * * * The conspiracy to levy war being effected, all the conspirators are guilty, though they did not all attend at General Neville's house. 1 Hale P.C. 132. Fost. 213, 215. * * *

The charge of the Court was delivered to the jury * * *:

Paterson, Justice. The first question to be considered is, what was the general object of the insurrection? If its object was to suppress the excise offices and to prevent the execution of an act of Congress, by force and intimidation, the offence in legal estimation is high treason; it is an usurpation of the authority of government; it is high treason by levying of war. Taking the testimony in a rational and connected point of view, this was the object. It was of a general nature, and of national concern. * * * With what view was the attack made on General Neville's house? Was it to gratify a spirit of revenge against him as a private citizen, as an individual? No! as a private citizen he had been highly respected and beloved; it was only by becoming a public officer that he became obnoxious, and it was on account of his holding the excise office alone, that his house had been assailed, and his person endangered. On the first day of attack, the insurgents were repulsed, but they rallied, returned with greater force, and fatally succeeded in the second attempt. They were arrayed in a military manner; they affected the military forms of negotiation by a flag; they pretended no personal hostility to General Neville; but they insisted on the surrender of his commission. Can there be a doubt, then, that the object of the insurrection was of a general and public nature?

The second question to be considered is, how far was the prisoner traitorously connected with the insurgents? It was proved by four witnesses, that he was at Couche's Fort, at a great distance from his own home, and that he was armed. One witness proves, positively, that he was at the burning of General Neville's house; and another says, "it runs in his head, that he also saw the prisoner there." On this state of the facts, a difficulty has been suggested. It is said, that no act of treason was committed at Couche's Fort; and that however treasonable the proceedings at General Neville's may have been, there are not two witnesses who prove that the prisoner was there. Of the overt act of treason, there must, undoubtedly, be proof by two witnesses * * *. But let us consider the prisoner's conduct in a regular and connected course. He is proved, by a competent number of witnesses, to have been at Couche's Fort. At Couche's Fort the conspiracy was formed, for attacking General Neville's house; and the prisoner was actually passed on the march thither. Now, in Foster, 213, the very act of marching is considered as carrying the traitorous intention into effect; and the jury * * * will consider how far this aids the doubtful language of the second witness, even as to the fact of the prisoner's being at General Neville's house.

On the personal motives and conduct of the prisoner, it would be superfluous to make a particular commentary. He was armed, he was a volunteer, he was a party to the various consultations of the insurgents; and in every scene of the insurrection, from the assembly at Couche's Fort to the day prescribed for submission to the government, he makes a conspicuous appearance * * *. Upon the whole, whether the conspiracy at Couche's Fort may of itself be deemed treason, or the conspiracy there, and the proceedings at General Neville's house, are considered as one act, (which is, perhaps, the true light to view the subject in,) the prisoner must be pronounced guilty. The consequences are not to weigh with the jury:—it is their province to do justice; the attribute of mercy is placed by our Constitution in other hands. *Verdict—Guilty.*

NOTES AND QUESTIONS

1. These were the first trials for treason in the federal courts, and established the precedent that widespread armed opposition to execution of a United States statute amounted to "levying war" against the United States, and thus came within the Constitutional definition of treason. Are you satisfied with this definition of treason? What of the distinction, made by counsel for the prisoner, between resisting or opposing any officer attempting to serve process, which was only a misdemeanor, and the treatment of Neville, which Justice Paterson defines as "levying war?" Has the prosecutor satisfactorily met this argument? The prosecutor, William Rawle, argues that "What constitutes a levying of war * * * must be the same, in technical interpretation, whether committed under a republican, or a regal form of government; since either institution may be assailed and subverted by the same means." What force should the English common-law rule of conspiracy to commit treason have in a republic? Is Rawle sensitive enough to the differences between regal and republican governments? What might those differences be, and what bearing might they have on the concept of "treason"?

2. The prosecution of the insurgents was not particularly smooth. In the first trial, United States v. Porter, 27 Fed.Cas. 597 (C.C.D.Pa.1795) a verdict of not guilty was directed when the court discovered that another man having the same name as the defendant was the culprit sought by the government. In some other early skirmishing, Judge Peters advanced his opinion that the federal judiciary should not be hamstrung by delicate niceties of state procedure. Counsel for some of the prisoners had argued that the prosecutions were not being carried on in conformity with the requirements of section 29 of the Judiciary Act, which ordered that certain matters of jury selection should be in accordance with state practice. Peters diplomatically ac-

cepted some of these objections, and accordingly postponed the trials until compliance with state law could be accomplished, but he rejected arguments based on other technical infractions of state law:

> Although, in ordinary cases, it would be well to accommodate our practice with that of the state, yet the judiciary of the United States should not be fettered and controlled in its operations, by a strict adherence to state regulations and practice * * *. The legislature of a state have in their consideration a variety of local arrangements, which cannot be adapted to the more expanded policy of the nation. It never could have been in the contemplation of congress, by any reference to state regulations, to defeat the operation of the national laws.

United States v. Insurgents, 26 Fed.Cas. 499, 511–12 (C.C.D.Pa.1795). Peters cited no authority in support of these propositions.

3. Consider Justice Paterson's jury charges in the two cases that resulted in treason convictions. In both these cases Paterson makes extensive comments on the credibility of the evidence, and, in *Mitchell,* the second case, he goes so far as to say, "Upon the whole, * * * the prisoner must be pronounced guilty." Is this what a judge is supposed to do? Note, by the way, that these treason trials were held before benches consisting of the district court judge and a Supreme Court Justice, "riding circuit." Pursuant to the 1789 Judiciary Act, as revised in 1792 and 1793, one Supreme Court Justice (it had originally been two) was to preside with the district court judge over important criminal and some civil trials and some matters on appeal from the district courts. The Justices rotated service on what was initially three circuits. The idea was to save the expense of hiring a different group of circuit judges, to promulgate uniform rules, to allow the Supreme Court Justices to extol the virtues of the new system of national law, and to ensure that the Supreme Court Justices did not lose touch with local concerns. Circuit-riding was exceptionally arduous, however, and several of the Justices resisted it mightily though unsuccessfully. One may even have died prematurely at the age of 49, exhausted from his circuit riding. See generally the rich detail provided in Wythe Holt, " 'The Federal Courts Have Enemies in All Who Fear Their Influence on State Objects': The Failure to Abolish Supreme Court Circuit–Riding in the Judiciary Acts of 1792 and 1793," 36 Buff.L.Rev. 301 (1987).

4. To what degree was Justice Paterson's and Judge Peter's intolerance of social upheaval a reflection of changed attitudes toward mob behavior since the Revolution? In colonial America the mob, as we have seen, might have often functioned as an extra-legal arm of the community. In particular, where mob action was taken in resistance to imperial authority, mob actions might have been generally perceived by colonials as emanations of the popular will in support of liberty. Moreover, mob actions might have been resorted to generally only after the normal remedies for legal redress had been exhausted, when other means of preserving liberty did not exist, or when royal policies (and royal courts) were prepared to ignore colonial law. While the

means adopted by colonials who took to the streets might be condemned as an "evil," in the language of Jefferson, mobs were "productive of good," since they held rulers "to the true principles of their institutions;" they provided a "medicine necessary for the sound health of the government." XII Boyd et. al., The Papers of Thomas Jefferson 356. Even Lt. Governor Thomas Hutchinson could state in 1768 that "mobs * * * are constitutional." Hutchinson to Grant, XXVI Massachusetts Archives, 317. Both Hutchinson and Jefferson are quoted in Pauline Maier's important article on the post-revolutionary mobs, "Popular Uprisings and Civil Authority in Eighteenth–Century America," 27 Wm. & Mary Q. 3 (3rd Ser.1970).

Professor Maier suggests that after 1776 "changing attitudes toward popular uprisings turned upon fundamental transformations in the political perspective of Americans," and that many Americans

> began to see domestic turbulence not as indictments but as insults to government that were likely to discredit American republicanism in the eyes of European observers. "Mobs are a reproach to Free Governments," where all grievances could be legally redressed through the courts or the ballot box, it was argued in 1783. They originated there "not in Oppression, but in Licentiousness," an "ungovernable spirit" among the people. Under republican governments even that distrust of power colonists had found so necessary for liberty, and which uprisings seems to manifest, could appear outmoded.

27 Wm. & Mary Q. (3rd Ser.) at 34. Yet, Ms. Maier urges that this change in attitude toward popular uprisings might not be a distinctly American phenomenon:

> a century earlier, when England passed beyond her revolutionary era and progressed toward political "stability," radical ideology with its talk of resistance and revolution was gradually left behind. A commitment to peace and permanence emerged from decades of fundamental change. In America as in England this stability demanded that operative sovereignty, including the right finally to decide what was and was not in the community's interest, and which laws were and were not constitutional, be entrusted to established governmental institutions. The result was to minimize the role of the people at large, who had been the ultimate arbiters of those questions in English and American revolutionary thought.*

Id., at 34–35. Do these observations make it any easier to understand why President Washington might have pardoned the convicted defendants? Would you have recommended such a pardon if you were one of Washington's advisors? For some of the best writing on the Whiskey Rebellion see T. Slaughter, The Whiskey Rebellion: Frontier Epilogue to the American Revolution (1986), and S. Boyd, ed., The Whiskey Rebellion: Past and Present Perspectives (1985), particularly the essay by R. Ifft, *Treason in the Early Republic: The Federal Courts, Popular Protest, and Federalism During the Whiskey Insur-*

---

* Reprinted by permission of the author and the publisher.

rection, at 165–182. For more background on Justice Paterson, who presided over this first federal treason trial, who thus expounded on the definition of treason, and who was one of the principal architects of the 1789 Judiciary Act which set up the first federal courts, see J. O'Conner, William Paterson: Lawyer and Statesman, 1775–1806 (1979), and Daniel A. Degnan, "Justice William Paterson—Founder," 16 Seton Hall L.Rev. 313 (1986).

2. THE FIRST TRIAL OF JOHN FRIES**

PRESSER, A TALE OF TWO JUDGES: RICHARD PETERS, SAMUEL CHASE, AND THE BROKEN PROMISE OF FEDERALIST JURISPRUDENCE

73 Nw.L.Rev. 83–88 (1978).

* * * Five years after the Whiskey Rebellion, the "Fries Rebellion" took place in eastern Pennsylvania. The levy which was the object of the Fries Rebellion, a tax on houses, had become necessary because of the high cost of troops used to quell the Whiskey Rebellion, and also because of the expenditures for anticipated hostilities against France. The yeomen of [three] counties in eastern Pennsylvania organized protests against the new federal taxes and succeeded in preventing their collection. While there was no real bloodshed, there was, during the months of 1799, much marching around by armed troops in uniform, and at least one overt act of rebellion—the liberation of prisoners from the custody of a federal marshal * * *.

The chief perpetrators of agitation, including John Fries, who led the freeing of the federal prisoners, were brought to trial for treason before Judge Peters and Justice Iredell in 1799. The case aroused interest in the Pennsylvania press, and the trial immediately took on dramatic political overtones. Acting as lawyers for the defense were William Lewis, a former federal judge, and Alexander James Dallas, fast becoming the kingpin of the emerging Pennsylvania Republican organization. Their arguments * * * were clearly designed to stir popular sympathies.

* * * On April 30, 1799, Lewis moved for the Fries trial to be removed from Philadelphia to Northampton County, the place where Fries's offense was alleged to have been committed. His motion was made pursuant to section 29 of the Judiciary Act, which mandated trial in the county where the offense had occurred. The motion was denied by Iredell and Peters. In his opinion Peters announced, considering fairness to the prosecution, that "a fair and impartial trial ought to be had, which he was certain could not be held in the county of Northampton." Similarly, Iredell questioned: "If nearly one whole county has been in state of insurrection, can it be said that a fair trial can be had there?" * * *

** As the official report of this trial runs to hundreds of pages, this summary is provided instead.

Most of the arguments of Fries's counsel at trial went to the law of the case. The thrust of their defense was to persuade the jury that armed resistance to a federal officer's execution of a federal statute was not the crime of treason. Lewis and Dallas, in short, were exhorting the jurors in Fries's case to arrive at the opposite conclusion from that laid down by Justice Paterson, Judge Peters, and by the jurors in the trials of the Whiskey Rebels.

The technique of arguing the law to the jury was tacitly approved by Peters and Iredell. Peters was later to write that the latitude permitted counsel in this trial was "unbounded" or even "unjustifiable" as to "both Law & Fact." Indeed, Peters remembered five years later that defense counsel was permitted to charge that the law laid down in the [Whiskey Rebels Trials] * * * was as "unsound as the worst opinion, delivered in the worst of times in England."

Fries's counsel did not argue that their client was innocent of all crimes, but simply that he was not guilty of the heinous crime of treason. The strategy of Lewis and Dallas was to parade before the jury a series of "horribles" drawn from the English common law to show that a broad definition of "treason" led to gross tyranny. Judge Peters's reflection on this tactic was: "All the abominable and reprobated cases of constructive treason in England were suffered to be read." * * *.

Two such examples were cited with great enthusiasm. For one, defense counsel described how once, in the "dark ages of English jurisprudence" when the king killed a yeoman's stag, the yeoman, in a fit of anger "wished the horns of the stag in the king's belly." The yeoman was swiftly, and apparently successfully, prosecuted for treason. As an even more egregious travesty, for the second example, the case was given of an innkeeper who kept an inn called "the sign of the crown." He had bragged that he would make his son "heir to the crown," and so he was convicted of treason. * * *

Lewis and Dallas used these abuses from the English common law to distinguish the only English precedent holding that the "rescue" of prisoners from official hands could amount to treason. Since it came from the time of the absolute monarchy of Henry VIII, [they argued that] it should be ignored by the jury as reflective of despotic excess. * * *

In contrast to the abuses of the treason doctrine they cited from England, they argued that in a "free republic" like America, the application of the doctrine of treason should be so limited that the phrase "levying war" would only apply to cases where armed men sought "to put an end to the government," where a part of "the Union" sought to "throw off the authority of the United States," or where rebels actually marched on the legislature or the executive. It should not be treason, they argued, where insurgents simply opposed the implementation of the republic's laws. The latter activity, they urged, might constitute "sedition" or common law "rescue," but not the capital crime of treason. * * *

After more than a week of impassioned arguments by Lewis and Dallas, Iredell and Peters charged the jury. Peters stated his opinion first. He maintained that the *Vigol* and *Mitchell* cases (the Whiskey Rebellion trials) governed: "It is treason to oppose or prevent by force, numbers or intimidation, a public and general law of the United States, with intent to prevent its operation or compel its repeal." By opposing a law, said Peters, "the rights of all are invaded by the force and violence of a few" and "a deadly blow is aimed at the government, when its fiscal arrangements are forcibly destroyed, distracted and impeded; for on its revenues its very existence depends." * * * Justice Iredell opened his charge by declaring, in sharp contrast to the attitude of Justice Paterson in the trials of the Whiskey Rebels, * * * that he would not usurp the role of the jury. * * * "[I]t is not for the court," he stated, "to say whether there was treasonable intention or act as charged in the indictment; that is for the jury to determine; we have only to state the law, we therefore should have no right to give our opinion on it." * * *

A verdict of "guilty" was rendered. Given the latitude that Lewis and Dallas were allowed by the judges in arguing the law to the jury, and given the force of their arguments that their client at most had committed sedition, but not treason, the verdict is somewhat surprising. It may be that public opinion in the city of Philadelphia, where the trial took place, was strongly against the rural insurgents and influenced the jury. It may be, however, that the federal marshal, who had some discretion in picking the jury, was careful to choose members sensitive to the need for peace and good order. * * *

The possibility of a biased jury is strongly suggested * * * by subsequent events. Five days after the verdict was announced, Mr. Lewis moved for a new trial for Fries on the ground that a Mr. John Rhoad, one of the jurors, had "declared a prejudice against the prisoner after he was summoned as a juror on the trial. [Though Rhoad denied it under oath, five sworn witnesses stated that after Rhoad was summoned for jury duty but before the trial, he had said that Fries 'ought to be hung' and that 'it would not be safe at home unless they hung them all.'] Justice Iredell, probably much relieved, issued an opinion that Fries was entitled to a new trial. [Justice Iredell had earlier written his wife that when the jury's verdict was announced, 'I could not bear to look upon the poor man, but I am told he fainted away * * * I dread the task I have before me in pronouncing sentence on him.'] Judge Peters gave his opinion that there was no reason to grant a new trial. * * * Peters implied that even if Rhoad had made the statement attributed to him, Rhoad only reflected 'the facts' as they 'appeared then to the public.' In any event, Peters finally concluded that 'as a division in the court might lessen the weight of the judgement if finally pronounced and the great end of the law in punishments being example,' " he reluctantly went along with Iredell's opinion, and the new trial was granted.

NOTES AND QUESTIONS

1. Do you have any difficulties with the conception of "fair trial" invoked by Judge Peters and Justice Iredell in rejecting Fries's motion for a trial in Northampton? On the other hand, why did Peters and Iredell allow Fries's counsel such latitude in arguing that the law set down in the Whiskey Rebels' case should be rejected? Do the trials of Zenger and the Seven Bishops shed any light here? Compare the attitude toward the prerogatives of the jury of Peters and Iredell to that of Justice Chase (in the case which follows). How do Iredell's comments on the roles of judge and jury compare to the comments by Justice Paterson in the trials of the Whiskey Rebels?

2. Though the Fries trial lasted for nine or ten days, Justice Iredell seemed quite ready to subject the federal courts to repeating the process once it was discovered that a juror was prejudiced. Why didn't Peters reach the same initial conclusion? Peters commented:

> I am in sentiment against granting the motion for a new trial, Because:
>
> 1. The juror said no more than all friends to the laws and the government were warranted in thinking and saying as the facts appeared then to the public. Fries being generally alleged to be the most prominent character, it was on this account, and not with special or particular malice, that Rhoad's declaration was made.
>
> 2. If a juror was rejected on account of such declarations, trials, where the community at large are intimately affected by crimes of such general importance and public notoriety, must be had, in all probability, by those who only openly or secretly approved of the conduct of the criminals. This would be unjust and improper, as it affects the government in its public prosecutions. Little success could be expected from proceedings against the most atrocious offenders, if great multitudes were implicated in their delusions or guilt.
>
> 3. It is natural for all good citizens, when atrocious crimes, of a public nature, are known to have been committed, to express their abhorrence and disapprobation both of the offences and the perpetrators. It is their duty so to express themselves. This is not like the case of murder, or any offence against an individual; or where several are charged, and none remarkably prominent. In this latter case, selecting one out of the mass might evince particular malice.
>
> 4. I have no doubt that declarations of an opposite complexion could be proved; and yet the jurors were unanimous in their verdict. The defendant has had a fair, and I think an impartial trial.

9 Fed.Cas., at 923. Does this seem persuasive to you? How could Peters then turn around and vote with Iredell for a retrial? As indicated, Justice Iredell may have been quite relieved at the opportunity to declare a new trial in the case. Indeed, among the first Supreme Court justices Iredell appears to have had a unique hesitance to allow the exercise of federal power at the expense of the States. Perhaps it does not go too far to say that he may have been the most Antifederalist of the Federalist Justices. See, e.g., Christopher T. Graebe, "The Federalism of James Iredell in Historical Context," 69 N.Car.L.Rev. 252 (1990), and see also Stephen B. Presser, The Original Misunderstanding: The English, The Americans and the Dialectic of Federalist Jurisprudence (1991), for further exploration of the jurisprudence of Peters, Iredell and their contemporaries, particularly Samuel Chase, whom we will meet next.

3. As you read the next excerpts, dealing with the retrial, decide whether you would have found Fries guilty of treason.

3. THE SECOND TRIAL OF JOHN FRIES* (1800)

Fries was tried again in April of 1800, when Justice Samuel Chase was sitting on Circuit with Judge Peters. Before the trial, Chase had indicated to Peters that the Judges needed to devise some way to "get through all the business which had accumulated on the civil side" as a result of the great amount of time spent in the last session with the criminal trials resulting from the Fries Rebellion. Chase had heard an account of the first Fries trial and believed that what then took 10 days should have taken no more than "one third" of the time. Chase was determined that *this* time there should not be so much leeway in citing "irrelevant authorities & unnecessary discussions." Chase therefore drafted an opinion, which he hoped to use as the opinion of the court on the law, and thus prevent counsel from straying. He showed the draft opinion to Peters, who approved of it, later indicating that "he had expressed what I had before delivered as my opinion better than I had done it myself." At this point Chase had not settled on the manner of delivering this opinion, and Peters had told him that it should be done with "Prudence." Peters was left with the impression that Chase would consult him about the "time & manner of delivery" of the opinion. Peters, who believed in circumspection, had begun to be uneasy, "lest a premature Declaration of the Opinion of the Court might be made."

* The quoted portions of the introductory account of the second Fries trial are from a letter from Richard Peters to Timothy Pickering (Jan. 24, 1804), 10 Peters Papers 91 (Historical Society of Pennsylvania).

SAMUEL CHASE

The day assigned to the Fries trial arrived, and as the proceedings opened, a juror came up to Judge Peters on the bench "to make some excuses for non attendance." Peters then noticed some commotion and discovered that while his "attention had been thus engaged," Chase had distributed copies of his opinion, one for the defense counsel, one for the District attorney, and one for the Jury. "I felt uneasy," Peters later wrote, "& silently waited to see the effect, which did not surprize me." Chase had apparently engaged in the very "premature" conduct that Peters had feared. At the time he passed out this opinion, which he said was the opinion of the court, Chase told defense counsel that the opinion contained the court's view of the law of treason, which was the same as that of Justice Paterson in the "Whiskey Rebels" case and Judge Peters and Justice Iredell in the first *Fries* trial: that armed opposition to United States statutes was treason. Since this was the law, Chase went on, the court would not permit arguments that such conduct was not treason to be made to the jury. In particular, Chase was determined that the jury not be distracted with odious English treason cases like that of the yeoman who wished the stag's horns in the King's belly, or the boastful innkeeper.

When Mr. Lewis, one of Fries's two lawyers, realized that the tactics he and his co-counsel, Dallas, had used in the first Fries trial would be foreclosed, he threw down Chase's opinion in anger. Peters then whispered to Chase that he believed the two Fries counsel would "take the studs & abandon the Cause, or take advantage of [the delivery of this statement of Chase's view] to operate on public opinion, or on that of the jury at least." Peters reprimanded Chase, and reminded him of "my having 'told him so' or 'predicted it'." Chase replied that "[H]e did not think the counsel would quit the Cause," and that "it was only a *Threat*, or some such expression." Peters was right. Lewis and Dallas announced their intention of withdrawing from the case, since the court had prejudged what they wished to argue.

Chase and Peters then repaired to the office of Mr. Rawle, the prosecutor. Rawle (who was present for this discussion) and Peters then persuaded Chase that his opinion "should be recalled." Chase "readily consented, declaring his intention to be merely to save time & accelerate business."

The next morning Lewis and Dallas were again in court, and Peters told them that "they might proceed in the Cause." He assured them expressly that "you may, & I *hope* will, proceed in your own way, as if nothing had happened." Chase was not as conciliatory as Peters, and though he did not contradict Peters, Chase "administered no emolients." Chase, said Peters later, appeared "animated—if not irritated. He declared 'The council could not embarrass him. He knew what it was about'." Chase agreed that he was *"willing* and *desirous to hear"* counsel's opinion on the law, and that "it might be controverted either with the Jury or any other Way." He cautioned Lewis and Dallas, however, that "he would not permit improper or irrelevant authorities," and he probably told them that if they stepped out of bounds in their citation of authority they would be proceeding "at the hazard of [their] reputation." Dallas later said that "This had the contrary effect rather than to induce me to proceed," and he and Lewis remained firm in their determination to leave the case.

Chase and Peters then offered to appoint other counsel for Fries, and gave him a day to think it over. Fries declined other counsel, however, having been persuaded by Lewis and Dallas that to proceed without counsel would generate sympathy for him that might result in a Presidential pardon. Chase then informed the prisoner that since he refused to accept other counsel, but was instead relying on the court "to be his counsel," he, Chase, would take it upon himself to serve as attorney for the defense, as well as judge.

UNITED STATES V. JOHN FRIES

United States Circuit Court, District of Pennsylvania, 1800.
9 Fed.Cas. 924.

* * *

Thursday, April 24.—Before the jurors were sworn in, they were individually asked (upon oath) * * * "Have you ever formed or delivered an opinion as to the guilt or innocence of the prisoner, or that he ought to be punished?" * * * Some of the jurors said they had given their sentiments generally, disapprobatory of the transaction, but not as to the prisoner particularly. These were admitted.

One of the jurors (Mr. Taggert) after he was sworn, expressed himself to the court to be very uneasy under his oath; he then meant that he never had made up his mind that the prisoner should be hung, but very often had spoken his opinion that he was very culpable; he did not, when he took the oath, conceive it so strict, and therefore wished, if possible, to be excused. The court informed the juror it was impossible to excuse him, now he was sworn.

The court informed the prisoner, that he had a right to challenge thirty-five without showing cause, and as many more as he could show cause for. Thirty-four were challenged * * *.

* * *

Mr. Rawle then * * * observed that the jury must be aware of the very unpleasant duty he had to perform: he felt an extreme difficulty of situation—called forth by his duty to exhibit a charge against the prisoner at the bar of the highest magnitude, who now stood to answer, unattended by any legal advice * * *.

Mr. Rawle then proceeded to open the charge. He said, he should be able to prove, that John Fries, the prisoner at the bar, did oppose the execution of two laws of the United States, to effectuate which he was provided with men, who, as well as himself, were armed with guns, swords, and other warlike weapons [and that Fries and his accomplices also did] release from the custody of the Marshal of Pennsylvania a number of persons who were held in prison by the said marshal, and * * * prevent him executing process upon others * * *.

Mr. Rawle then proceeded, under the direction of the court, to state the law. The treason whereof the prisoner was charged was, "levying war against the United States." U.S. Const., Art. 3, Sec. 3.

He conceived himself authorized, upon good authority, to say, levying war did not only consist in open, manifest, and avowed rebellion against the government, with a design of overthrowing the Constitution; but it may consist in assembling together in numbers, and by actual force, or by terror, opposing any particular law or laws. * * * The endeavor, by intimidation, to do the act, whether it be accomplished or not, amounts to treason, provided the object of those concerned in the transaction, is of a general nature, and not applied to a special or private purpose.

* * * If a particular friend of the party had been in the custody of the marshal; if even a number sufficient for the purpose should step forward and rescue such a person, if it was not with a view to rescue prisoners generally, it would amount to no more than a rescue; but, if general, it is treason. * * *

* * * [In the cases of Vigol and Mitchell, said Rawle,] the attack on Gen. Neville's house was of this general nature, because he was an officer appointed to execute the obnoxious law; and being to the officer and not to the man that they objected, it was thought to be treason * * *.

He observed, that the clause in our Constitution was founded on a statute which was passed in England, to prevent the ever-increasing and ever-varying number of treasons, upon the general and undefined opposition to royal prerogative: the situation of things was such, previous to that period, as to call forth from the statesman, from the philosopher, and from the divine, even in those dark ages, the most vehement complaints: in attendance to these reasonable and just murmurs, the statute was passed.

Mr. Rawle was then producing an authority, when Judge Chase said, the court would admit, as a general rule, of quotations which referred to what constituted actual or constructive levying war against the King of Great Britain, in his regal capacity; or, in other words, of levying war against his government, but not against his person * * *—they may, any of them, be read to the jury, and the decisions thereupon—not as authorities whereby we are bound, but as the opinions and decisions of men of great legal learning and ability. But even then, the court would attend carefully to the time of the decisions, and in no case must it be binding upon our juries.

Mr. Rawle quoted Hawkins, b. 1, chap. 17, sec. 23, as an authority of authenticity to prove that * * * those who withstood [The King's] lawful authority, and who endeavoured to oppose his government; who withstood the king's forces, or attacked any of his fortresses * * * were guilty of high treason. He also read Sir John Friend's case from Holt, 681, and Damarree and Pinchases' case, 8 State Trials, 289.

Judge Chase begged the counsel to read only those parts of the cases which referred to what could be treason in the United States, and nothing which related to compassing the king's death. It would be found, he observed, by an attention to the last case, that because the intention was a rising to demolish ALL meeting-houses, generally, it was considered to be an insurrection against the Toleration Act, by numbers and open force, setting the law at defiance. * * *

Mr. Rawle said, that he conceived that, even if the matter made a grievance of, was illegal, the demolition of it in this way was, nevertheless, high treason, because of the people so assembled taking the law into their own hands; thus, in *Foster,* it would be seen that demolishing all bawdy-houses, as such, was high treason * * *. He also read Douglas, 570, Lord George Gordon's case, when it was Lord Mansfield's opinion that any attempt, by violence, to force the repeal of a law, or to prevent its execution, is levying war, and treason.

* * *

Mr. Rawle then proceeded to state the most prominent facts * * * in which it would fully appear, he presumed, that John Fries, the prisoner, * * * in every instance showed his aversion of, and opposition to, the assessors, and determination by threats and menaces to prevent them doing their duty, and that whenever any force was used, * * * he was the commander, * * * and that finally, by threats and intimidation, equally the same in the eyes of the law as force, he, the prisoner, did attain his object, to wit, the release of a number of prisoners who were confined for opposing the execution of the law, and were actually in custody of the marshal in a house at Bethlehem, which, by reason of his having prisoners there, and his having an armed posse to protect his lawful authority, was to all intents a fortress of the United States; and further, that he did, completely for a time, prevent the execution of the laws intended * * *.

Judge Chase then said to the prisoner:

John Fries, you will attend to all the evidence * * * and ask any questions you please of the several witnesses, or of the court; but be careful to ask no questions wherein you may possibly criminate yourself, for remember, whatever you say to your own crimination, is evidence with the jury; but if you say anything to your justification, it is not evidence. The court will be watchful of you; they will check anything that may injure yourself: they will be your counsel, and give you every assistance and indulgence in their power.

[The prosecution proceeded to call witnesses who testified as to the facts on which the prosecution relied. The testimony was substantially identical to that in Fries's first trial. The defendant produced no testimony.]

Mr. Rawle said he felt himself so very peculiarly situated in this case, that he would wish the opinion of the court. The unfortunate prisoner at the bar appeared to answer to a charge, the greatest that could be brought against him, without the assistance of counsel, or any friend to advise with. * * * I believe it will be found that in no *material* point have I failed to substantiate what I first gave notice that I could prove. I therefore conceive the charges are fully confirmed.

But although, if this trial was conducted in the usual way * * * it would now be proper, on my part, to sum up the evidence as produced to the jury, and apply it to the law, in order to see whether the crime was fixed or not. Under the present circumstances, I feel very great reluctance to fulfil what would, in other circumstances, be my bounden duty, lest it should appear to be going further than the rigid requisition of my office compels me to. I therefore shall rest the evidence and the law here, unless the court think that my office as public prosecutor, demands of me to do it * * *.

Judge Chase.—It is not unfrequent for a prisoner to appear in a court of justice without counsel, but it is uncommon for a prisoner not to accept of legal assistance. It is the peculiar lenity of our laws that makes it the duty of a court to assign counsel to the person accused. With respect to your situation, sir, it is a matter entirely discretionary with you whether you will state the evidence and apply it to the law or not. There is great justice due to a prisoner arraigned on a charge so important as the present: there is great justice also due to the government. * * * If you do not please to proceed, I shall consider it my duty to apply the law to the facts. The prisoner may therefore offer what he pleases to the jury.

Prisoner.—I submit to the court to do me that justice which is right.

Judge Chase.—That I will, by the blessing of God, do you every justice.

Judge Peters.—Mr. Attorney, while you are justifiable in considering this situation of the prisoner * * * there is another consideration deserving attention—there is justice due to the United States. * * * I wish it to be done for the due execution of public justice, and, God knows, I do it not with a desire to injure the prisoner, for I wish not the conviction of any man. It is a painful task, but we must do our duty. Still I think you are at liberty to fulfil your own pleasure.

Mr. Rawle [then stated that he would give a brief summary of the facts and the law of the case.]

As he stated before, Mr. Rawle said * * * in relation to the republican form of government existing among us, [levying war] could only consist in an opposition to the will of the society * * * declared and established by a majority; in short, an opposition to the acts of Congress, in whole or in part, so as to prevent their execution * * * to procure a repeal or a suspension of the law, by rendering it impracticable to carry such law or laws into effect * * *.

The question, then, is, how far the case of the prisoner and his conduct merit this definition? * * *

It will first be observed by the testimony of several respectable witnesses * * * that attempts were made and executed, by a combination, in which, unfortunately for him, the prisoner at the bar was very active, to prevent the assessors from doing the duty required of them when they accepted their office, and that this combination existed both in Northampton and Bucks counties, and to such a degree that it was impossible to carry the law into effect * * *. This spirit of opposition to the laws, as exhibited generally, is also related by Mr. Henry and Col. Nichols, the marshal, wherein it appears that process could not be served, and that witnesses could not be subpoenaed, being deterred from the threats made to them by this extensive combination; and that, in the serving of process, personal abuse was given, as well as to the assessors who attempted to execute the law. In short the law was *prostrate* at the feet of a powerful combination.

Mr. Rawle here called to view the occurrences in Bucks county, as deposed by Messrs. Foulke, Rodrick, Chapman, Thomas, Mitchell, and Wiedner, exhibiting a disposition to insurrection by a great number of persons, and who engaged in its acts; he referred to the meeting at Jacob Fries', where John Fries, the prisoner at the bar, expressed himself as determining to oppose and continue hostile to the laws; also to the circumstance afterwards near Singmaster's, where Mr. Rodrick made his escape, and where, as well as at other times, the prisoner forbade those officers to proceed, under threats of personal danger. * * * However, the assessors met the next day, but were stopped at Quaker town, where they were extremely abused. To be sure, while the prisoner at the bar was in the room, and whenever he was present, their abuse was suspended; when he absented himself, it was renewed. * * * Here it must be observed, in justice to the prisoner, that one more of his few good actions appeared, which Mr. Rawle wished in his heart had been more numerous. Fries assisted Mr. Foulke to get out of the house the back way, and advised him to keep out of the way of the men.

* * * The next morning they met and went on as far as Ritters, where it appeared they were stopped for a short period by young Marks, who had been sent forward, with information that the prisoners were gone on to Bethlehem: a doubt being stated whether they would not be too late, it

was debated, and at last determined to go forward: of this latter opinion was the prisoner at the bar. It was in evidence that none of those people knew the prisoners whom they were going to release * * * this, Mitchel and others swore.

Here Mr. Rawle thought commenced the overt act in the indictment. * * * They proceeded to Bethlehem, and here the officer of militia, the man who derived his power from the people, the prisoner, Captain John Fries, whose duty it was to support the law and Constitution of the United States, made a most distinguished figure. At Bethlehem it appeared that the prisoner was to step forward to effect the surrender of the prisoners, and of course to lay prostrate the legal arm of the United States. * * * The prisoner with an armed force arrived at Bethlehem, and proceeded on his mission to the marshal * * * to wit, demanding the surrender of the prisoners; the marshall answered, that he could not deliver them up. John Fries then returned to his men; and * * * said, "They must be taken by force; the marshal says he cannot deliver them up; if you are willing, we will take them by force: I will go foremost; if I drop, then take your own command." Words were followed by actions; they went into the house, and the prisoners were given up.

This, Mr. Rawle thought, was an unquestionable, full and complete proof of the commission of the overt act; and that overt act is high treason * * *.

To him, Mr. Rawle said, there was no doubt but the act of levying war was completed in the county of Bucks, independently of all those actions at Bethlehem; for there the prisoner and others were armed, and arrayed with all the appearances of war—with drums and fifes, and at times firing their pieces; and this to oppose the laws and prevent their execution * * *.

Gentlemen, said Mr. [Rawle], you will consider how far the individual witnesses are deserving your credit. If you consider them worthy of being believed, and if the facts related apply to the law which I submitted to your consideration * * * there can be but little doubt upon your minds, that the prisoner is guilty: if it be not so, in your opinion, you must find him otherwise.

* * *

Court. John Fries, you are at liberty to say anything you please to the jury.

Prisoner. It was mentioned, that I collected a parcel of people to follow up the assessors; but I did not collect them. They came and fetched me out from my house to go with them.

I have nothing to say, but leave it to the court.

Judge Chase then addressed the jury * * *.

Too much praise cannot be given to [the] constitutional definition of treason, and the requiring such full proof for conviction; and declaring, that no attainder of treason shall work corruption of blood or forfeiture, except during the life of the person attainted.

This constitutional definition of treason is a question of law. * * * What is the true meaning and true import of any statute, and whether the case stated comes within it, is a question of law, and not of fact. The question in an indictment for levying war against * * * the United States, is, whether the facts stated do, or do not amount to levying war, within the contemplation and construction of the Constitution.

It is the duty of the court in this case, and in all criminal cases, to state to the jury their opinion of the law arising on the facts; but the jury are to decide on the present, and in all criminal cases, both the law and the facts, on their consideration of the whole case.

It is the opinion of the court, that any insurrection or rising of any body of the people, within the United States, to attain or effect by force or violence any object of a great public nature, or of public and general (or national) concern, is a levying of war against the United States, within the contemplation and construction of the Constitution.

* * *

The true criterion to determine whether acts committed are treason, or a less offence (as a riot), is the *quo animo,* or the intention, with which the people did assemble. When the intention is universal or general, as to effect some object of a general public nature, it will be treason, and cannot be considered, construed, or reduced to a riot. * * *

The court are of opinion, that if a body of people conspire and meditate an insurrection to resist or oppose the execution of any statute of the United States by force, that they are only guilty of a high misdemeanour; but if they proceed to carry such intention into execution by force, that they are guilty of the treason of levying war, and the quantum of the force employed neither lessens nor increases the crime * * *.

* * * [I]t is altogether immaterial whether the force used is sufficient to effectuate the object—any force connected with the intention will constitute the crime of levying war.

This opinion of the court is founded on the same principles, and is, in substance, the same as the opinion of the Circuit Court for this district, on the trials (in April, 1795) of Vigol and Mitchell, who were both found guilty by the jury, and afterwards pardoned by the late President.

At the Circuit Court for the district (April term, 1799), on the trial of the prisoner at the bar, Judge Iredell delivered the same opinion, and Fries was convicted by the jury.

To support the present indictment against the prisoner at the bar, two facts must be proved to your satisfaction:

First. That some time *before* the finding of the indictment, there was an insurrection (or rising) of a body of people in the *County of Northampton,* in this State, *with intent* to oppose and prevent, by means of *intimidation* and *violence,* the execution of a law of the United States * * * and that *some acts of violence* were committed by *some* of the people so assembled, *with intent* to oppose and prevent, by means of intimidation and violence, the execution * * * of the said law of Congress.

* * *

If, from a careful examination of the evidence, you shall be convinced that the real object and intent of the people assembled at Bethlehem was of a *public nature* (which it certainly was), if they assembled with intent to prevent the execution of * * * the above-mentioned laws * * *, it must then be proved to your satisfaction, that the prisoner at the bar incited, encouraged, promoted, or *assisted* in the insurrection, or rising of the people, at Bethlehem * * * and that *some force* was used by *some* of the people assembled at Bethlehem.

In the consideration of this fact, the court think proper to assist your inquiry by giving you their opinion.

In treason, all the *participes criminis* are principals; there are no accessories to this crime. * * * All persons *present,* aiding, assisting, or abetting any *treasonable act,* are *principals.* All persons, who are present and countenancing, and are ready to afford assistance, if necessary, to those who actually commit any *treasonable act,* are also *principals.* If a number of persons assemble and set out upon a *common design,* as to resist and prevent, by force, the execution of any law, and some of them commit acts of force and violence, *with intent* to oppose the execution of any law, and others are present to aid and assist, if necessary, they are all *principals.* * * * If persons collect together to act *for one and the same common end,* any act done by any one of them, with intent to effectuate such common end, is a fact that may be given in evidence against all of them; the act of each is evidence against ALL concerned.

* * *

If, upon consideration of the whole matter (law as well as fact), you are *not* fully satisfied, *without any doubt,* that the prisoner is guilty of the treason charged in the indictment, you will find him *not guilty;* but if, upon consideration of the *whole* matter (law as well as *fact*), you are convinced that the prisoner is guilty of the treason charged in the indictment, you will find him guilty.

The jury retired, for the space of two hours, and brought in their verdict, GUILTY.

After the verdict was given, Judge Chase with great feeling and sensibility, addressed the prisoner, observing that, as he had no counsel on the trial, if he, or any person for him, could point out any flaw in the indictment, or legal ground for arrest of judgment, ample time would be allowed for that purpose.

* * *

The prisoner being set at the bar, Judge CHASE * * * proceeded:—

John Fries—* * * You have had a LEGAL, FAIR, and IMPARTIAL trial, with every indulgence that the law would permit. Of the whole panel, you PEREMPTORILY challenged thirty-four, and with truth I may say, that the jury who tried you were of your *own selection and choice.* Not one of them *before* had ever formed and delivered any opinion respecting your guilt or innocence. The verdict of the jury against you was founded on the testimony of many creditable and unexceptionable witnesses. It was apparent from the conduct of the jury * * * that they pronounced their verdict against you with great concern and reluctance, from a sense of duty to their country, and a *full conviction* of your guilt.

The crime of which you have been found guilty is *treason;* a crime considered, in the most civilized and the most free countries in the world, as the *greatest* that any man can commit. * * *

You are a *native* of this country—you live under a constitution (or form of government) framed by the people themselves; and under laws made by *your* representatives, faithfully executed by independent and impartial judges. Your government secures to every member of the community *equal liberty* and *equal rights;* * * * every person, without any regard to wealth, rank, or station, may enjoy an *equal* share of *civil liberty,* and *equal* protection of *law,* and an *equal* security for his *person* and *property.* * * *

If experience should prove that the *Constitution* is defective, *it* provides a mode to *change* or *amend* it, without any danger to public order, or any injury to *social* rights.

If Congress * * * should pass any law in violation of the Constitution, or burdensome or oppressive to the people, a peaceable, safe and *ample* remedy is provided by the *Constitution.* * * * If Congress should pass a law contrary to the *Constitution,* such law would be *void,* and the courts of the United States possess complete authority, and are the only tribunal to decide, whether any law is contrary to the *Constitution.* If Congress should pass *burdensome* or *oppressive* laws, the remedy is with their constituents, from whom they derive their existence and authority. If any law is made repugnant to the voice of a *majority* of their constituents, it is in their power to make choice of persons to repeal it; but until it is repealed, it is the duty of every citizen to submit to it, and to give up his *private* sentiments to the *public will.* If a law which is burdensome, or even oppressive in its *nature* or *execution,* is to be opposed by *force;* and obedience cannot be compelled, there must soon be an end to all government in this country. * * * The most ignorant man must know, that Congress can make *no law* that will not affect them *equally, in every respect,* with their constituents. Every law that is detrimental to their constituents must prove hurtful to themselves. From these considerations, every one may see, that Congress can have *no interest in oppressing their fellow-citizens.*

It is almost incredible, that a people living under the best and mildest government in the whole world, should not only be dissatisfied and discontented, but should break out into open resistance and opposition to its laws.

The insurrection in 1794 * * * is still fresh in memory * * *. Either persons disaffected to our government, or wishing to aggrandize themselves, deceived and misled the ignorant and uninformed class of the people. The opposition commenced in meetings of the people, with threats against the officers, which ripened into acts of outrage against *them* * * * Committees were formed to systematize and inflame the spirit of opposition. Violence succeeded to violence, and the collector of Fayette county was compelled to surrender his commission and official books; the dwelling house of the inspector * * * was attacked and burnt; and the marshal was seized, and obtained his liberty on a promise to serve no other process on the *west side of the Alleghany mountain.* To compel submission to the laws, the government were obliged to march an army against the insurgents, and the expense was above one million one hundred thousand dollars. Of the whole number of insurgents (many hundreds) only a *few* were brought to trial; and of them only *two* were sentenced to die (Vigol and Mitchell,) and they were pardoned by the late President. Although the insurgents made no resistance to the army sent against them, yet not a few of our troops lost their lives, in consequence of their great fatigue, and exposure to the severity of the season.

This great and remarkable clemency of the government had no effect upon *you,* and the deluded people in your neighbourhood. The rise, progress, and termination of the *late* insurrection bear a strong and striking analogy to the former; and it may be remembered that it has cost the United States 80,000 dollars. It cannot escape observation, that the ignorant and uninformed are taught to complain of taxes, which are necessary for the support of government, and yet they permit themselves to be seduced into insurrections which have so enormously increased the public burthens * * *.

* * * The expense, and all the consequences, therefore, are not imputable to the government, but to the insurgents. The mildness and lenity of our government are as striking on the *late* as on the *former* insurrection. Of nearly one hundred and thirty persons who might have been put on their trial for *treason,* only five have been prosecuted and tried for that crime.

* * * It was the height of folly in you to suppose that the great body of our citizens, blessed in the enjoyment of a free republican government of their own choice * * * and conscious that the laws are the only security for their preservation from violence, would not rise up as one man to oppose and crush so ill-founded, so unprovoked an attempt to disturb the public peace and tranquility. If you could see in a proper light your own *folly* and *wickedness,* you ought now to bless God that your insurrection was so happily and speedily quelled by the vigilance and energy of our government * * *.

The annual, necessary expenditures for the support of any extensive government like ours must be great; and the sum required can only be obtained by *taxes,* or loans. In all countries the levying taxes is unpopular, and a subject of complaint. * * * [I]t becomes you to reflect that the time you chose to rise up in arms to oppose the laws of your country, was when it stood in a very critical situation with regard to France, and on the eve of a rupture with that country.

* * *

The end of all *punishment* is *example;* and the enormity of your crime requires that a severe example should be made to deter others from the commission of *like* crimes in future. You have forfeited your life to justice. Let me, therefore, earnestly recommend to you most seriously to consider your situation—to take a review of your past life, and to employ the very little time you are to continue in this world in endeavors to make your peace with that God whose mercy is equal to his justice. I suppose that you are a Christian; and as *such* I address you. Be assured, my guilty and unhappy fellow-citizen, that without serious repentance of *all* your sins, you cannot expect happiness in the world to come * * *. Your *day* of *life* is almost spent; and the *night* of *death* fast approaches. Look up to the Father of mercies, and God of comfort. You have a great and immense work to perform, and but little time in which you must finish it. There is no repentance in the grave, for after death comes judgment; and as you die, so you must be judged. * * * If you will sincerely repent and believe, God has pronounced his forgiveness; and there is no crime too great for his mercy and pardon.

Although you must be strictly confined for the very short remainder of your life, yet the mild government and laws which you have endeavoured to destroy, permit you (if you please) to converse and commune with ministers of the gospel; to whose pious care and consolation, in fervant prayers and devotion, I most cordially recommend you.

What remains for me is a very painful but, a very necessary part of my duty. It is to pronounce that judgment, which the law has appointed for crimes of this magnitude. The judgment of the law is, and this Court doth award "that you be hanged by the neck *until dead*:" and I pray God Almighty to be merciful to your soul!

NOTES AND QUESTIONS

1. Judge Peters worried that Chase's hasty opinion-giving would have an adverse affect on public opinion. Why was he concerned with this? Should he have been?

2. Note that Chase cautioned the jury that English authority was not binding on them. This came right after the prosecutor, Rawle, praised the English treason statute, on which Article 3, Section 3, of the United States Constitution was modelled. Was Chase's comment favorable to the prosecution? How good a job overall did Chase do as both defense counsel *and* judge? By the way, incongruous though it may seem to us today, the notion that a judge would serve as the prisoner's counsel and protect his rights to a fair trial was a longstanding one in English law, where for many years criminal defendants had been forbidden the aid of any other counsel. How do you suppose such a system could be tolerated? The prosecutor, William Rawle, probably embarrassed by Fries's lack of counsel, indicated a willingness to go easy on Fries, and to decline summing up the evidence against him. *Both* Peters *and* Chase then indicated that the interests of the United States called for a summing up of the facts against Fries. Which should be more jealously guarded—the rights of the defendant or the rights of the government? Would your answer have been different in 1800?

3. What is Chase's attitude toward the jury? Chase says to the jury that they are to decide on both "the law and the facts." Is this consistent with his attempted delivery of an opinion to them at the beginning of the trial and his refusal to let certain legal arguments be made to them? Is there any other conduct of Chase's that you found to be improper? Were you surprised that Fries was convicted again?

4. Is Chase some kind of ogre? He has been described as "A hanging judge," and has often been called an "American Jeffreys," a derogatory reference, likening him to a brutal jurist who served James II. See, e.g., J. Miller, The Federalist Era 248 (1960). Is his political and judicial philosophy the work of the devil? What did you make of his remarks to John Fries after Fries's conviction? Compare Chase's thinking on American political principles and the importance of judicial review to that of John Marshall in Marbury v. Madison. For some elaboration of the political and religious elements in

Chase's jurisprudence *see* Stephen B. Presser, The Original Misunderstanding (1991). For strong dissents from Presser's essentially benign view of Chase's jurisprudence, see Raoul Berger, "The Transfiguration of Samuel Chase: A Rebuttal," 1992 Brigham Young U.L.Rev. 559 and Stewart Jay, "The Rehabilitation of Samuel Chase," 41 Buff.L.Rev. 273 (1993). Presser remains essentially unrepentant. See Stephen B. Presser, "Et tu Raoul? or the Original Misunderstanding Misunderstood," 1991 Brigham Young L.Rev. 1476, and Stephen B. Presser, Recapturing the Constitution: Race, Religion and Abortion Reconsidered 86–97, 111–128 (1994).

5. Shortly after the Second Fries trial, President Adams, against the advice of Alexander Hamilton, pardoned John Fries and all others who had taken part in the 1799 insurrection. This helped destroy the Federalist party from within. Instead of going to the gallows, then, Fries walked away a free man. How could Adams do this? Even more remarkable than Adams's pardon of Fries, was Fries's attitude toward Chase. Shortly after his pardon, Fries journeyed to Chase's home in Maryland, and thanked the justice "for his impartial, fair, and equitable conduct" during the trial. 9 J. Sanderson, Biography of the Signers to the Declaration of Independence 230 (1827). Was Fries completely unhinged, or did people behave differently at the turn of the eighteenth century? What might account for this behavior?

6. Recall Jefferson's proposals for reforming the law of crime and punishment. Contrast these with Chase's statement at the end of the Fries trial that "the end of all punishment is example." Does this suggest anything about Chase's view of the purpose of government in general and criminal law in particular? As part of the burgeoning spate of scholarship on American legal history, there has been increased attention paid to the early cases in the federal courts, and the workings of our earliest federal Justices, judges and juries, particularly insofar as the administration of law was influenced by politics or political philosophy. See, for further reading which illuminates many of the criminal trials that we study here, e.g., Daniel D. Blinka, " 'The Germ of Rottedness': Federal Trials in the New Republic 1789–1807," 36 Creighton L.Rev. 135 (2003), William R. Casto, "The Early Supreme Court Justices' Most Significant Opinion," 29 Ohio N.U.L.Rev. 173 (2002), William R. Casto, The Supreme Court in the Early Republic: The Chief Justiceships of John Jay and Oliver Ellsworth (1995), Scott Douglas Gerber, ed., Seriatim: The Supreme Court Before John Marshall (1998), Joshua Glick, "On the Road: The Supreme Court and the History of Circuit Riding," 24 Cardozo L.Rev. 1753 (2003), Stewart Jay, Most Humble Servants: The Advisory Role of Early Judges (1997), Andrew C. Lenner, The Federal Principle in American Politics, 1790–1833 (2001), and Eduardo C. Robreno, "Learning to do Justice: An Essay on the Development of the Lower Federal Courts in the Early Years of the Republic," 29 Rutgers L. J. 555 (1998).

C. THE FEDERAL COMMON LAW OF CRIMES

By late 1798 the question of whether there were federal nonstatutory crimes that could be punished in the federal courts was a hot political issue. The Federalists, with one significant exception (as you will soon see), unanimously maintained that the federal bench could punish "common law crimes" in the same manner as could the state courts. The Republicans, again almost without exception, felt equally strongly that to allow the federal courts to punish common law crimes would be an unconstitutional and unwarranted usurpation of power. These materials are to illustrate the divergent approaches to the problem of common law crimes. Your task is to determine which view or views you find convincing, and to determine whether the positions of the Federalist judges, and particularly Judge Peters and Justice Chase, seem consistent with what you have seen of them so far.

1. JAY'S AND WILSON'S JURY CHARGES

PRESSER, A TALE OF TWO JUDGES: RICHARD PETERS, SAMUEL CHASE, AND THE BROKEN PROMISE OF FEDERALIST JURISPRUDENCE

73 Nw.U.L.Rev. 48–52 (1978)

The Judiciary Act of 1789 gave the federal circuit courts jurisdiction over "crimes and offenses cognizable under the authority of the United States," but the statute did not specify what acts were "crimes and offenses," nor did it specify the extent of the "authority" of the United States. Much of the prevailing jurisprudence can be derived from contemporary jury charges. The first official interpretation of federal criminal jurisdiction, in 1790, signalled that it was to be broadly construed. Chief Justice John Jay charged the Grand Juries of the Eastern Circuit in the spring of that year as follows: * * * "Your province and your duty extend * * * to the enquiry and presentment of all offenses of every kind, committed against the United States in this district, or on the high seas by persons in it." Jay did not define the term "offenses," * * * Nevertheless, Jay did provide some clues * * *.

First, he suggested that the jurors

> would recollect that the laws of nations make part of the laws of this, and of every other civilized nation. They consist of those rules for regulating the conduct of nations towards each other, which, resulting from right reason, receive their obligation from that principle and from general assent and practice.

The jurors were thus to use their own common sense and their knowledge of world and national history to guide them in their search for criminal acts.

Second, Jay acknowledged that some federal statutes defined crimes, but he maintained that these statutes would not serve alone as indicators of what offenses the jurors should present:

> The penal statutes of the United States are few and principally respect the revenue. The right ordering and management of this important business is very essential to the credit, character, and prosperity of our country. On the citizens at large is placed the burden of providing for the public exigencies. Whoever therefore fraudulently withdraws his shoulder from the common burthen necessarily leaves his portion of the weight to be born by the others, and thereby does injustice not only to the government, but to them.

Here Jay's focus would seem to be not on particular violations of the terms of revenue statutes but more broadly on "whoever fraudulently withdraws his shoulder from the common burthen."

Finally Jay told the grand jurors * * * to "direct your conduct also to the conduct of the national officers, and let not any corruptions, frauds, extortions or criminal negligence with which you may find any of them justly chargeable pass unnoticed." Jay thus seemed to be defining "offenses against the United States" [at least as committed by government officials] to include virtually any examples of [what the grand jurors might conceive as] wrongdoing against the government or the public. * * *

Three years later, in a charge to the Grand Jury for the Middle Circuit in the District of Virginia, Jay * * * seemed most concerned with violations of the "law of nations." This was a result of the outbreak of war between England and France in January 1793, which had violently split American public opinion and had just resulted in the "Neutrality Proclamation" issued by President Washington. Jay quoted extensively from the Proclamation and indicated that Washington's instructions to prosecute persons who committed, aided, or abetted hostilities against any of the belligerents, or who furnished them contraband, were "exactly consistent with and declaratory of the conduct enjoined by the law of nations." Jay closed his charge with comments indicating that the United States' treaties of "firm and perpetual peace" also enjoined American citizens from aiding the belligerent powers, and that such conduct, as a violation of a treaty, was punishable as a crime [but it appears clearly from Jay's charge that an offense against the "law of nations" would be criminal even without a treaty.]

Later, in July 1793, Justice James Wilson of the Supreme Court charged a Grand Jury for the Middle Circuit in Philadelphia. One of the matters which this grand jury was to investigate involved one Gideon

Henfield, who was accused of engaging in acts hostile to nations at peace with the United States. Henfield had allegedly assisted in the capture of an English prize ship by a French privateer. [In Wilson's charge he stressed that] * * * the basis of the American judicial system, and indeed, the basis of any civilized system of jurisprudence was what he called the "common law." * * * Unlike the contemporary English common law * * * Wilson suggested, American common law was closer to the common law of the ancient Saxons than it was to that of the Normans. The Saxons, like the Americans, had a more expansive notion of individual liberty and popular sovereignty. Nevertheless, Wilson went on, the American common law, like every other, was "a social system of jurisprudence; and associates to herself those who can give her information, or advice, or assistance." Thus, when a court was faced with a problem involving the law of other countries, the law of merchants, or the law of nations, those bodies of doctrine would become assimilated into the common law and would be used in the disposition of particular cases.

In this manner Wilson arrived at the same point Jay started with in his jury charge two months earlier—the United States law incorporated the law of nations. Unlike Jay, however, Wilson carefully explained that he had arrived at this destination through the vehicle of what he called the "common law." For Wilson, the "law of nations" (and by implication, "the common law") was not simply a set of arbitrary rules. The "law of nations" was "the law of nature," it was "of obligation indispensible" and "of origin divine." Moreover, the "law of nations" was not simply limited to regulating the affairs of one nation with another. By becoming a nation, citizens created certain duties which they owed to each other and to the nation itself, duties specified by the "law of nations." Among these duties which devolved on individuals (and on nations) was that of keeping "peace on earth," of living in amity with one's neighbors. * * * [G]iven the primary duty of citizens to be peaceful [, Wilson told the jurors,] "[A] citizen, who in our state of neutrality, and without the authority of the nation, takes an hostile part with either of the belligerent powers, violates thereby his duty, and the laws of his country * * *."

Five days later, on July 27, 1793, the grand jury returned an indictment against Henfield. The indictment said that his conduct was "to the evil example of all others in like cases offending, in violation of the laws of nations, against the laws of the United States in such case made and provided, and against the Constitution of the United States, and against the peace and dignity of the said United States." * * *

* * *

2. HENFIELD'S TRIAL

INTRODUCTION: British, French, and American Foreign Relations

The Americans and the French enjoyed good relations during the Revolutionary War. French aid and military support had helped Americans in the difficult early years of the war, and French ships assisted in containing the British at the decisive victory of Yorktown in 1781. The Marquis de Lafayette, a magnificent general who volunteered his services (and his private fortune) in aid of the American Revolution symbolized the Franco–American fraternity. The French Revolution of 1789, however, polarized Americans. Those with strong democratic sympathies, such as Jefferson, saw the excesses of the Revolution as inevitable release of resentment stored up by the oppressed as a result of monarchial absolutism and extreme aristocratic privilege of nobles and clergy. The Federalists saw in French revolutionary violence the worst excesses of "license," an abandonment of the restraint of religion, and a complete breakdown of law.

The split in local opinion in the states reflected the conflict between the Jeffersonian Republicans and the Federalists at the national level. Britain and France were at war, and the British refused to respect the neutrality of the American merchant marine. Britain flagrantly seized American ships and impressed American citizens into British service at sea, on the theory that the American revolution was illegal and Americans still owed allegiance to the Crown. There were further tensions from the failure of each side fully to comply with the Peace Treaty of 1783. The British were angry that states were not honoring pre-war debts, and that Loyalists were being mistreated. The Americans were irked that the British had not fulfilled their treaty promises to evacuate their fortresses in the Northwest and to pay recompense for the slaves that British troops took with them when the Revolutionary War concluded.

The Washington Federalists did not want to lose the advantages of international trade and commerce with Britain, and many valued friendship with Britain above all else. In 1794 President Washington sent John Jay, Chief Justice of the Supreme Court and avowedly pro-British, on a special mission to Britain to negotiate a treaty that would respond to American complaints. In return for American assurances that it would not trade with the French during war time, the British agreed to live up to the terms of the 1783 treaty. The British proved tough negotiators, and the treaty submitted to Congress barely passed. With memories of the Revolutionary War still fresh, many Americans, and, in particular the Jeffersonian Republicans, were angered at what they saw as a lopsided win for the British, and they blamed the Federalists. In many towns, Jay was burned in effigy.

The French saw the Jay Treaty as reneging on America's 1778 agreements with France, and retaliated from 1798 to 1800 by attacking American ships. In coastal towns, especially those with Irish immigrant populations who hated the British, street fighting broke out between pro-French and pro-British groups. In a near-war atmosphere, Congress passed the Alien and Sedition laws of 1798 that lengthened the naturalization period, authorized deportations of aliens, and, as you will soon see, sought to protect the federal government from defamation. These Acts also authorized new taxes so that President Adams could create a navy to protect the coast. As you will soon learn, when you read about *U.S. v. Cooper* in the next section, at this time there were also soldiers in the field mopping up the results of the rebellion in Western Pennsylvania, of which you have just read, and the creation of the navy and the continued funding for these troops led some Jeffersonian Republicans to worry about a dreaded "standing army" at home.

UNITED STATES V. HENFIELD

United States Circuit Court, District of Pennsylvania, 1793.
11 Fed.Cas. 1099.

* * *

It appeared in evidence that Gideon Henfield was a citizen of the United States and that his family resided in Salem, Massachusetts. Being a sea-faring man he had been absent from them some time, and about the 1st of May, 1793, being then at Charleston, South Carolina, and desirous of coming to Philadelphia * * * he entered on board the Citizen Genet, a French privateer, commissioned by the French Republic and commanded by Pierre Johannen. Captain Johannen, it appeared, promised him the berth of prize-master on board the first prize they should capture, and the ship William belonging to British subjects, having been captured about the 5th of May, he was put on board her as prize-master, with another person, and arrived in that capacity at Philadelphia. It appeared that on his examination before the magistrate, he protested himself an American, that as such he would die, and therefore could not be supposed likely to intend anything to her prejudice. He declared if he had known it to be contrary to the President's proclamation, or even the wishes of the President, for whom he had the greatest respect, he would not have entered on board. About a month afterwards, being before the same magistrate, he declared he had espoused the cause of France, that he now considered himself as a Frenchman, and meant to move his family within their dominions.

Mr. Rawle, District Attorney [argued that:] * * *

1. *Every* member is accountable to society for those actions which may affect the *interest* of that society.

2. The United States being in perfect peace with *all* nations, and allied in friendly bonds with *some,* their national situation requires a *perfect neutrality* from *every* motive applicable to our *common interest.*

3. An aggression on the subjects of other nations done in an *hostile* manner and under *colour of war* is a violation of that neutrality.

4. If *not* under the colour of war it would be an act of *piracy.*

But by the laws of nations if one of the belligerent powers should capture a neutral subject fighting under a commission from the other belligerent powers he could not punish him as a pirate, but must *treat him as an enemy,* and it would be a good cause of declaring war against the nation to which he belonged; and if treated as an enemy without *just* cause it is the duty of the nation to which he belongs to interfere in his behalf; and thus arises another cause of war.

Hence the act of the individual is an *injury* to the nation, and the *right of punishment* follows the existence of the *injury.*

5. The right of peace and war is always vested in the government.

In the United States, but Congress alone possesses it.

By the formation of the society every individual has consented to its being thus exclusively deposited for the general benefit.

No individual, therefore, can assume the exercise of this right.

* * *

6. If *one* individual has a right to associate with the subjects of one of the belligerent powers, *another* individual has an equal right to do the same with the other belligerent power; thus the citizens of the neutral nation might be fighting *with each other.*

Under this unhappy prospect, the national *character* and *existence* of America are lost; and instead of being members of a *great nation,* we become a band of *miserable Algerines.*

* * *

France is at war with Austria, Spain, Portugal, and Sardinia, with whom we are at peace; with Great Britain, with whom a treaty of peace exists; and with the United Netherlands and Prussia, with whom there is peace, amity, and commerce.

* * *

With Great Britain is a treaty of peace, by Article 7 of which it is provided that there shall be a *firm* and *perpetual peace* between his Britannic Majesty and the United States, and the subjects of the one and the citizens of the other.

* * *

Thus, an infraction of *this kind,* unless punished, becomes a good cause of war on the part of the *offended* nation.—Vat. b. 4, § 52; Bynk, Jus.Pub. b. 1, c. 8, p. 178.

It is an offence against *our own* country, at common law, because the right of war is vested in the *government* only.—Puffendorf, b. 8, c. 6, sec. 8; Vat. b. 3, § 4; b. 4, § 223.

In a *state of nature* the right adhered to the individual.

It is lost by *joining* society.

* * *

Nor are these only the speculations of the closet. We see them carried into effect in England in affirmation of national common law, i.e., *the law of nations.*—4 Black.Com. 69.

The English statute is not in force here, because the specific remedy for which alone it was made cannot be had, but the *law* which it aided, not introduced, is in force.

The law of nations is part of the law of the land.—4 Black.Com. 66; 1 Dallas 111; C.L. 11 b.

This is an offence against the laws of nations. It is punishable by indictment on information as such.—1 Dallas, 114, & c.; 3 Burr. 1480.

* * *

* * * That the Executive should be inadequate to sudden and unusual exertions of power is our pride and happiness; and that our Courts should, with that impartial and unbiased dignity which characterizes their judicial investigations of truth, apply the law of nations to men, of which nations are composed, and substitute the scales of justice for the sword of war.

But it is said that there is a want of *precedent* for this prosecution.

The first answer is, that it is demonstrated that the law of nations is part of the law of the land.

The second answer is, that in numerous other instances, enumerated by Blackstone, the law of nations is enforced by the judiciary. * * *

It is urged, also, that the right of emigration is natural to freemen. It is no crime to become a French subject, and being a French subject, the defendant may lawfully enlist in this command.

The answer is, that when a man has fairly and deliberately emigrated * * * *previously* to the commission of the hostile act, and *without a view to it,* there is no offence in an act *of this kind.* * * *

But, at all events, if *at the time* the act was committed, the party was unquestionably a citizen, had *not renounced* his country, and was not domiciliated elsewhere, he cannot escape punishment by becoming a citizen *afterwards.* * * *

Is not the defendant's *family* still at Massachusetts?

Is he not *still* upon the *roll* of their citizens; were his family in want, would they not be entitled to public relief?

Did he not declare that, as an American he would die?

* * *

Let us suppose America engaged in war, and that one of her faithless children prefers the other party, joins an hostile detachment which has already invaded his own country, or enters on board a foreign privateer lying in our bay, and commits those acts, which in war are lawful, in peace, crimes. Does the right to emigrate, the right to choose his country, to renounce his former allegiance protect him here?

* * *

Let it not be said that this doctrine violates the rights of man. It is on the rights of man that it is established. The rights of man are the rights of all men in relation to each other, and when voluntarily assumed in society founded on principles of genuine freedom, they form a useful, benevolent and endearing system, in which as much is received as is given. Perfect equality is one of those rights. We render ourselves equal when we all submit to the laws. That equality is destroyed if one man can set himself above them. That equality is destroyed if one man with impunity may involve three millions in war.

* * *

Is it not fair to ask * * * by what authority have you or I delegated to an individual the right of subjecting us to the pressure of heavy taxes, to the desolation of property, to the destruction of agriculture and of commerce, to the dangers of military service, in short, to the havoc and miseries of war? * * * Our excellent constitution has wisely vested this solemn, awful step in the collected wisdom and patriotism of the whole country. There the necessity of the war and the means of defence will be compared by men selected by their country and responsible to it, but not by men who involve us in what they profess they will not share with us, and in the very act which draws on us the greatest political affliction renounce the very connexion which has alone rendered us liable for their conduct. * * *

Mr. Duponceau, Mr. Ingersoll and Mr. Sergeant addressed the jury at great length; and insisted—

1. That the indictment did not include an offence at common law.

2. That if the President's proclamation created such an offence, the case before the Court was committed before the proclamation was made.

3. That though the treaty with Morocco prohibited the enlisting of American citizens under such circumstances as the present, yet there was no such provision in the treaty with France, and hence the inference from its express introduction into the former treaty is that it was intentionally omitted from the latter.

4. That independently on these grounds, as there was no statute giving jurisdiction, the Court could take no cognizance of the offence.

* * *

Judge Wilson, (with whom were Judge Iredell and Judge Peters,) charged the jury as follows: * * *

It has not been contended, on the present occasion, that the defendant has any peculiar exclusive right to take a part in the present war between the European powers, in relation to all whom the United States are in a state of peace and tranquillity.

If he has no peculiar or exclusive right, it naturally follows, that what he may do every other citizen of the United States may also do * * * and thus thousands of our fellow-citizens may associate themselves with different belligerent powers, destroying not only those with whom we have no hostility, but destroying each other. In such a case, can we expect peace among their friends who stay behind? And will not a civil war, with all its lamentable train of evil, be the natural effect?

* * *

Two principal questions of fact have arisen, and require your determination. The first is, that the defendant, Gideon Henfield, has committed an act of hostility against the subjects of a power with whom the United States are at peace: this has been clearly established by the testimony. The second object of inquiry is, whether Gideon Henfield was at that time a citizen of the United States. This he explicitly acknowledged to Mr. Baker; and if he declared true, it was at that time the least of his thoughts to expatriate himself.

The questions of law coming into joint consideration with the facts, it is the duty of the Court to explain the law to the jury, and give it to them in direction.

It is the joint and unanimous opinion of the Court, that the United States, being in a state of neutrality relative to the present war, the acts of hostility committed by Gideon Henfield are an offence against this country, and punishable by its laws.

It has been asked by his counsel, in their address to you, against what law has he offended? The answer is, against many and binding laws. As a citizen of the United States, he was bound to act no part which could injure the nation; he was bound to keep the peace in regard to all nations with whom we are at peace. This is the law of nations; not an *ex post facto* law, but a law that was in existence long before Gideon Henfield existed. There are, also, positive laws, existing previous to the offence committed, and expressly declared to be part of the supreme law of the land. The Constitution of the United States has declared that all treaties made, or to be made, under the authority of the United States, shall be part of the supreme law of the land. * * *

The seventh article of the definitive treaty of peace between the United States and Great Britain, declares that there shall be a firm and perpetual peace between His Britannic Majesty and the United States, and between the subjects of the one and the citizens of the other.

* * *

These treaties were in the most public, the most notorious existence, before the act for which the prisoner is indicted was committed.

* * *

* * * [T]he Judge concluded by remarking, that the jury, in a general verdict must decide both law and fact, but that this did not authorize them to decide it as they please;

They were as much bound to decide by law as the judges: the responsibility was equal upon both.

The jury retired about nine on Saturday evening, and came into court again about half-past eleven, when they informed the Court they had not agreed. They were desired to retire again which they did, and returned on Monday morning * * *.

One of the jurymen now expressed some doubts, which occasioned the judges separately to deliver their sentiments on the points of law adverted to in the charge on Saturday evening, each of them assenting to the same, particularly as to the change of political relation in the defendant, from his having been some time absent from home previous to his entering on board the privateer.

The jury again retired, and the Court adjourned. At half-past four the Court was convened, and the jury presented a written verdict, which the

Court refused to receive, as being neither general nor special. Another adjournment took place, and about seven o'clock a verdict of "Not Guilty" was delivered.

NOTES AND QUESTIONS

1. As indicated in these materials, shortly before Henfield's alleged offense, President Washington issued a proclamation urging citizens *not* to get involved in the current French revolutionary war. The relevant text of this proclamation was:

> Whereas, it appears that a state of war exists between Austria, Prussia, Sardinia, Great Britain, and the United Netherlands of the one part, and France of the other, and the duty and interest of the United States, require that they should with sincerity and good faith, adopt and pursue a conduct friendly and impartial towards the belligerent powers:
>
> I have, therefore, thought fit by these presents, to declare the disposition of the United States to observe the conduct aforesaid towards these powers respectively, and to exhort and warn the citizens of the United States, carefully to avoid all acts and proceedings whatsoever, which may in any manner tend to contravene such disposition.
>
> I do hereby make known, that whosoever of the citizens of the United States, shall render himself liable to punishment or forfeiture, under the law of nations, by committing, aiding, or abetting hostilities against any of the said powers, or by carrying to them those articles which are deemed contraband, by the modern usage of nations, will not receive the protection of the United States against such punishment or forfeiture; and further, that I have given instructions to those officers to whom it belongs, to cause prosecutions to be instituted against all persons who shall within the cognizance of the Courts of the United States, violate the law of nations, with respect to the powers at war, or any of them.

Was it true, as Henfield's counsel maintained and as the anti–Federalist, "Democratic," or "Republican" press urged, that the Proclamation created a new crime? Does Washington's proclamation remind you of any aspect of the *Writs of Assistance* case, which you encountered in Chapter One?

2. The prosecutor, William Rawle, and the judges, notably Justice Wilson, indicate that the law Henfield violated was in existence long before Henfield. Where exactly did this law come from?

3. What is the difference between "the law of nations," as that term is used by the authors in this section, and the "common law?"

4. How would you have voted if you were a juror in *Henfield's* case? The opposition press hailed the acquittal of Henfield. See, e.g., John Marshall, II Life of Washington 273–274 (1807). Indeed, these newspapers suggested that the Henfield victory was as great a triumph for liberty as the verdict in the *Seven Bishops'* case. Do you agree? What is the connection between

the two trials? Does it help to know that there was no doubt that Henfield had done the acts charged against him? Is it of any significance that the ambassador from France, the famed "citizen Genet," paid for Gideon Henfield's legal defense? See Stewart Jay, "Origins of the Federal Common Law: Part One," 133 U.Pa.L.Rev. 1003, 1050 (1985).

5. Immediately below is the report of a case decided a year after Henfield's, United States v. Ravara, 27 Fed.Cas. 714 (C.C.D.Pa.1793). Note the verdict. What is the difference between the issue in the *Henfield* case and the issue in *Ravara's* case? Why the difference in the verdicts?

> The defendant, a Consul from Genoa, was indicted for a misdemeanour, in sending anonymous and threatening letters to Mr. Hammond, the British Minister, to Mr. Holland, a citizen of Philadelphia, and to several other persons, with a view to extort money. * * *
>
> The defendant was tried in April Session, 1794, before Jay, Chief Justice, and Peters, Justice; and was defended * * * on the following points: 1st. That the matter charged in the indictment was not a crime by the Common Law, nor is it made such by any positive law of the United States. In England it was once treason; it is now felony; but in both instances it was the effect of positive law. It can only, therefore, be considered as a bare menace of bodily hurt; and, without a consequent inconvenience, it is no injury public or private. 4 Bl.C. 5; 8 Hen. VI. cc. 6, 9; Geo. I. c. 22; 4 Bl.C. 144; 3 Bl.C. 120. 2d. That considering the official character of the defendant, such a proceeding ought not to be sustained, nor such a punishment inflicted. The law of nations is a part of the law of the United States; and the law of nations seems to require, that a counsel should be independent of the ordinary criminal justice of the place where he resides. Vat. b. 2, c. 2, s. 34. 3d. But that, exclusive of the legal exceptions, the prosecution had not been maintained in point of evidence; for, it was all circumstantial and presumptive, and that too, in so slight a degree, as ought not to weigh with a jury on so important an issue. * * *
>
> Mr. Rawle, in reply, insisted that the offence was indictable at common law; that the consular character of the defendant gave jurisdiction to the Circuit Court, and did not entitle him to an exemption from prosecution agreeably to the law of nations; and that the proof was as strong as the nature of the case allowed, or the rules of evidence required. * * *
>
> The Court were of opinion in the charge, that the offence was indictable, and that the defendant was not privileged from prosecution, in virtue of his consular appointment.
>
> The Jury, after a short consultation, pronounced the defendant guilty; but he was afterwards pardoned, on condition (*as stated by Mr. Dallas*) that he surrendered his commission * * *.

For a powerful and detailed argument that the *Ravara* case should be understood as a statement of a "supple" and "elastic" federal common law jurisprudence committed "to the attainment of substantial justice," see John D. Gordan III, *"United States v. Joseph Ravara:* 'Presumptuous Evidence,' 'Too Many Lawyers,' and a Federal Common Law Crime," in Maeva Marcus, ed., Origins of the Federal Judiciary: Essays on the Judiciary Act of 1789, 106, 140 (1992).

3. WORRALL'S CASE

UNITED STATES V. ROBERT WORRALL

United States Circuit Court, District of Pennsylvania, 1798.
28 Fed.Cas. 774.

[The defendant had been indicted for attempting to bribe Tench Coxe, the United States Commissioner of Revenue. Pursuant to federal legislation Coxe had been authorized to let a contract for the building of a lighthouse on Cape Hatteras, in North Carolina. The relevant part of the indictment charged that Robert Worrall] * * * yeoman, being an ill-disposed person, and wickedly contriving and contending to bribe and seduce the * * * Commissioner of the Revenue, from the performance of the trust and duty so in him reposed, on the said 28th day of September, 1797 * * * wickedly, advisedly and corruptly, did compose, write, utter and publish, and cause to be delivered to the said Tench Coxe, a letter * * *:

DEAR SIR:

Having had the honour of waiting on you, at different times, on the light house business, and having delivered a fair, honest estimate, and I will be candid to declare, that with my diligent and industrious attendance, and sometimes taking an active part in the work, and receiving a reasonable wages for attending the same, I will be bold to say, that when the work is completed in the most masterly manner, the job will clear at the finishing, the sum of £1400. * * *

* * * [G]ood sir, as having always been brought up in a life of industry, [I] should, be happy in serving you in the executing this job, and always content with a reasonable profit; therefore, every reasonable person would say that £1400 was not unreasonable * * *. If I should be so happy in your recommendation of this work, I should think myself very ungrateful, if I did not offer you one-half of the profits as above stated, and would deposit in your hand at receiving the first payment £350, and the other £350 at the last payment, when the work is finished and completed. * * * In the mean time I shall subscribe myself to be, your obedient and very humble servant to command.

ROBERT WORRALL

* * *

* * * On the receipt of the letter Mr. Coxe immediately consulted Mr. Ingersoll (the Attorney General of the State), communicated the circumstance that had occurred to the President, and invited the defendant to a conference at Burlington. In this conference, the defendant acknowledged having written and sent the letter; declared that no one else knew its contents, for "in business done in his chamber, he did not let his left hand know what his right hand did;" and repeated the offer of allowing Mr. Coxe a share in the profits of the contract. * * *

[The two counts of the indictment charged Mr. Worrall with (1) offering the bribe in the letter, and (2) repeating the offer orally.] On these facts, Mr. M. Levy, for the defendant, observed, that it was not sufficient for the purpose of conviction to prove that the defendant was guilty of an offence, but the offence must also appear to be legally defined * * *.

The attorney of the district (Mr. Rawle) * * * To show that the offer of a bribe is indictable, though the bribe is not accepted, * * * referred to 4 Burr. 2494, 1 Ld.Raym. 1377.

* * * Verdict—*guilty* on both counts of the indictment.

Mr. Dallas, (who had declined speaking on the facts before the jury) now moved in arrest of judgment, alleging that the Circuit Court could not take cognizance of the crime charged in the indictment. * * * It will be admitted, [Dallas stated,] that all the judicial authority of the Federal Courts, must be derived, either from the Constitution of the United States, or from the Acts of Congress made in pursuance of that Constitution. It is, therefore, incumbent upon the prosecutor to show, that an offer to bribe the Commissioner of the Revenue, is a violation of some constitution, or legislative prohibition. The Constitution contains express provisions in certain cases, which are designated by a definition of the crimes; by a reference to the characters of the parties offending; or by the exclusive jurisdiction of the place where the offences were perpetrated: but the crime of attempting to bribe, the character of a Federal officer, and the place where the present offence was committed, do not form any part of the constitutional express provisions, for the exercise of judicial authority in the courts of the Union. The judicial power, however, extends, not only to all cases, in law and equity, arising under the Constitution; but, likewise, to all such as shall arise under the laws of the United States, (Art. 3, § 2,) and besides the authority, specially vested in Congress, to pass laws for enumerated purposes, there is a general authority given "to make all laws which shall be necessary and proper for carrying into execution all the powers vested by the Constitution in the government of the United States, or in any department or office thereof." Art. 1, Sect. 8. Whenever, then, Congress think any provision necessary to effectuate the constitutional power of the government, they may establish it by law; and whenever it is so established, a violation of its sanctions will come within the jurisdiction of this Court, under the 11th Section of the Judicial Act, which declares, that the Circuit Court "shall have exclusive cognizance of all crimes and offences cognizable under the authority of the United States," & c. * * * Thus, Congress have provided by law, for the punishment of treason, misprision of treason, piracy, counterfeiting any public certificate, stealing or falsifying records, & c.; for the punishment of various crimes, when committed within the limits of the exclusive jurisdiction of the United States; and for the punishment of bribery itself in the case of a judge, an officer of the customs, or an officer of the excise. * * * But in the case of the Commissioner of the Revenue, the act constituting the office does not create or declare the offence; * * * it is not recognized in the act, under which proposals for building the light house were invited; * * * and there is no other act that has the slightest relation to the subject.

* * * A case arising under a law, must mean a case depending on the exposition of a law, in respect to something which the law prohibits, or enjoins. There is no characteristic of that kind in the present instance. But, it may be suggested, that the office being established by a law of the United States, it is an incident naturally attached to the authority of the United States, to guard the officer against the approaches of corruption, in the execution of his public trust. It is true, that the person who accepts an office may be supposed to enter into a compact to be answerable to the government, which he serves, for any violation of his duty; and, having taken the oath of office, he would unquestionably be liable, in such case, to a prosecution for perjury in the Federal Courts. But because one man, by his own act, renders himself amenable to a particular jurisdiction, shall another man, who has not incurred a similar obligation, be implicated? If, in other words, it is sufficient to vest a jurisdiction in this court, that a Federal officer is concerned; if it is a sufficient proof of a case arising under a law of the United States to affect other persons, that such officer is bound, by law, to discharge his duty with fidelity;—a source of jurisdiction is opened, which must inevitably overflow and destroy all the barriers between the judicial authorities of the state and the general government. Any thing which can prevent a Federal officer from the punctual, as well as from an impartial performance of his duty; an assault and battery; or the recovery of a debt, as well as the offer of a bribe, may be made a foundation of the jurisdiction of this court; and, considering the constant disposition of power to extend the sphere of its influence, fictions will be resorted to, when real cases cease to occur. A mere fiction, that the defendant is in the custody of the marshal, has rendered the jurisdiction of the King's Bench universal in all personal actions. Another fiction, which states the plaintiff to be a debtor of the crown, gives cognizance of all kinds of personal suits to the Exchequer * * *. If, therefore, the disposition to amplify the jurisdiction of the Circuit Court exists, precedents of the means to do so are not wanting; and it may hereafter be sufficient to

suggest, that the party is a Federal officer, in order to enable this court to try every species of crime, and to sustain every description of action.

But another ground may, perhaps, be taken to vindicate the present claim of jurisdiction: it may be urged, that though the offence is not specified in the Constitution, nor defined in any act of Congress; yet, that it is an offence at common law; and that the common law is the law of the United States, in cases that arise under their authority. The nature of our Federal compact will not, however, tolerate this doctrine. The twelfth article of the amendment stipulates, that "the powers not delegated to the United States by the Constitution, nor prohibited by it to the States, are reserved to the States respectively, or to the people." In relation to crimes and punishments, the objects of the delegated power of the United States are enumerated and fixed. Congress may provide for the punishment of counterfeiting the securities and current coin of the United States; and may define and punish piracies and felonies committed on the high seas, and offences against the law of nations. Art. 1, § 8. And, so likewise Congress may make all laws which shall be necessary and proper for carrying into execution the powers of the general government. But here is no reference to a common law authority: Every power is matter of definite and positive grant; and the very powers that are granted cannot take effect until they are exercised through the medium of a law. Congress had undoubtedly a power to make a law, which should render it criminal to offer a bribe to the Commissioner of the Revenue; but not having made the law the crime is not recognized by the Federal code, constitutional or legislative; and, consequently, it is not a subject on which the judicial authority of the Union can operate.

The cases that have occurred, since the establishment of the Federal Constitution, confirm these general principles. The indictment against Henfield, an American citizen, for enlisting and serving on board a French privateer, while she captured a Dutch merchant ship, & c., expressly charged the defendant with a violation of the treaties existing between the United States and the United Netherlands, Great Britain, & c., which is a matter cognizable under the Federal authority by the very words of the Constitution. The jurisdiction in the indictment against Ravara, was sustained by reason of the defendant's official character as Consul. * * *

Mr. Rawle (the attorney of the district) observed, that the exception, taken in support of the motion in arrest of judgment, struck at the root of the whole system of the national government; for, if opposition to the pure, regular and efficient administration of its affairs could thus be made by fraud, the experiment of force might next be applied; and doubtless with equal impunity and success. He concluded, however, that it was unnecessary to reason from the inconveniency and mischief of the exception; for, the offence was strictly within the very terms of the Constitution, arising under the laws of the United States. If no such office had been created by the laws of the United States, no attempt to corrupt such an officer could have been made; and it is unreasonable to insist, that merely because a law has not prescribed an express and appropriate punishment for the offence, therefore, the offence, when committed, shall not be punished by the Circuit Court, upon the principles of common law punishment. The effect, indeed, of the position is still more injurious; for, unless this offence is punishable in the Federal courts, it certainly is not cognizable before any State tribunal. The true point of view for considering the case, may be ascertained, by an inquiry whether, if Mr. Coxe had accepted the bribe, and betrayed his trust, he would not have been indictable in the courts of the United States? If he would be so indictable, upon the strongest principles of analogy, the offence of the person who tempted him, must be equally the subject of animadversion before the same judicial authority. The precedents cited by the defendant's counsel, are distinguishable from the present indictment. The prosecution against Henfield was not expressly on the treaty, but on the law of nations, which is a part of the common law of the United States; and the power of indicting for a breach of treaty, not expressly providing the means of enforcing performance in the particular instance, is itself a common law power. Unless the judicial system of the United States justified a recourse to common law against an individual guilty of a breach of treaty, the offence, where no specific penalty was to be found in the treaty, would therefore remain unpunished. So, likewise, with respect to Ravara, although he held the office of a Consul, he was indicted and punished at the common law. * * *

Chase, Justice. Do you mean, Mr. Attorney, to support this indictment solely at common law? If you do, I have no difficulty upon the subject: The indictment cannot be maintained in this Court.

Mr. Rawle, answering in the affirmative, Chase * * * delivered an opinion to the following effect.

Chase, Justice. This is an indictment for an offence highly injurious to morals, and deserving the severest punishment; but, as it is an indictment at common law, I dismiss, at once, everything that has been said about the Constitution and laws of the United States.

In this country, every man sustains a twofold political capacity; one in relation to the State, and another in relation to the United States. In relation to the State, he is subject to various municipal regulations, founded upon the State Constitution and policy, which do not affect him in his relation to the United States: For, the Constitution of the Union is the source of all the jurisdiction of the national government; so that the departments of the government can never assume any power, that is not expressly granted by that instrument, nor exercise a power in any other manner than is there prescribed. Besides the particular cases, which the

8th section of the 1st article designates, there is a power granted to Congress to create, define, and punish crimes and offences, whenever they shall deem it necessary and proper by law to do so, for effectuating the objects of the government; and although bribery is not among the crimes and offences specifically mentioned, it is certainly included in this general provision. The question, however, does not arise about the power; but about the exercise of the power:—Whether the courts of the United States can punish a man for any act, before it is declared by a law of the United States to be criminal? Now, it appears to my mind, to be as essential, that Congress should define the offences to be tried, and apportion the punishments to be inflicted, as that they should erect courts to try the criminal, or to pronounce a sentence on conviction.

It is attempted, however, to supply the silence of the Constitution and statutes of the Union by resorting to the common law for a definition and punishment of the offence which has been committed: but, in my opinion, the United States, as a Federal government, have no common law; and, consequently, no indictment can be maintained in their courts, for offences merely at the common law. If, indeed, the United States can be supposed, for a moment, to have a common law, it must, I presume, be that of England; and, yet, it is impossible to trace when, or how, the system was adopted, or introduced. With respect to the individual States, the difficulty does not occur. When the American colonies were first settled by our ancestors, it was held, as well by the settlers, as by the judges and lawyers of England, that they brought hither, as a birth-right and inheritance, so much of the common law as was applicable to their local situation and change of circumstances. But each colony judged for itself what parts of the common law were applicable to its new condition; and in various modes by legislative acts, by judicial decisions, or by constant usage, adopted some parts, and rejected others. Hence, he who shall travel through the different States, will soon discover, that the whole of the common law of England has been nowhere introduced; that some States have rejected what others have adopted; and that there is, in short, a great and essential diversity in the subjects to which the common law is applied, as well as in the extent of its application. The common law, therefore, of one State, is not the common law of another; but the common law of England, is the law of each State, so far as each State has adopted it; and it results from that position, connected with the judicial act, that the common law will always apply to suits between citizen and citizen, whether they are instituted in a Federal or State court.

But the question recurs, when and how have the courts of the United States acquired a common law jurisdiction in criminal cases? The United States must possess the common law themselves, before they can communicate it to their judicial agents: Now, the United States did not bring it with them from England; the Constitution does not create it; and no act of Congress has assumed it. Besides, what is the common law to which we are referred? Is it the common law entire, as it exists in England; or modified, as it exists in some of the States; and of the various modifications, which are we to select, the system of Georgia or New Hampshire, of Pennsylvania or Connecticut?

Upon the whole it may be a defect in our political institutions, it may be an inconvenience in the administration of justice, that the common law authority, relating to crimes and punishments, has not been conferred upon the government of the United States, which is a government in other respects also of a limited jurisdiction; but judges cannot remedy political imperfections, nor supply any legislative omission. * * * [C]ertainly, Congress might have provided by law for the present case, as they have provided for other cases, of a similar nature; and yet if Congress had ever declared and defined the offence, without prescribing a punishment, I should still have thought it improper to exercise a discretion upon that part of the subject.

Peters, Judge. Whenever a government has been established, I have always supposed, that a power to preserve itself, was a necessary and an inseparable concomitant. But the existence of the Federal government would be precarious, and it could no longer be called an independent government, if, for the punishment of offences of this nature, tending to obstruct and pervert the administration of its affairs, an appeal must be made to the State tribunals, or the offenders must escape with absolute impunity.

The power to punish misdemeanours is originally and strictly a common law power; of which I think the United States are constitutionally possessed. It might have been exercised by Congress in the form of a legislative act; but it may also, in my opinion, be enforced in a course of judicial proceeding. Whenever an offence aims at the subversion of any Federal institution, or at the corruption of its public officers, it is an offence against the well-being of the United States; from its very nature, it is cognizable under their authority; and, consequently, it is within the jurisdiction of this court, by virtue of the 11th section of the judicial act.

The court being divided in opinion, it became a doubt, whether sentence could be pronounced upon the defendant; and a wish was expressed by the judges and the attorney of the district, that the case might be put into such a form, as would admit of obtaining the ultimate decision of the Supreme Court, upon the important principle of the discussion: But the counsel for the prisoner did not think themselves authorized to enter into a compromise of that nature. The court, after a short consultation, and declaring that the sentence was mitigated in consideration of the defendant's circumstances, proceeded to adjudge,

That the defendant be imprisoned for three months; that he pay a fine of two hundred dollars; and that he stand committed until this sentence be complied with, and the costs of prosecution paid.

NOTES AND QUESTIONS

1. This case is probably our most important case on the federal common law of crimes because it involved *both* Peters and Chase, whom we are able to study in a variety of contexts. Does Peters's opinion in this case, that there *is* a federal common law of crimes, seem consistent with his opinions in the other cases which you have seen? What of Justice Chase? In *Worrall,* Chase states his opinion that there is *no* federal common law of crimes. Does this seem consistent with his conduct in the *Fries* trial? Chase's opinion in *Worrall,* according to a compiler of early federal criminal cases, Francis Wharton, "greatly surprised not only the bar but the community." Wharton suggests that Chase's opinion might have sprung from "the 'persuasions' of the 'metaphysical' Virginia lawyers, who led Judge Chase into the belief that the United States had no common law." "But the oddest part of the case," says Wharton, "is that though Judge Chase expressly denied that there was jurisdiction, and though there must have been at best a divided bench, the court, 'after a short consultation' imposed a sentence of unequivocally common law stamp." Wharton's theory is that "Judge Chase had used this 'short consultation' to acquaint himself with the views of his brethren on the supreme bench, about which after Henfield's case, there could then have been no doubt." Wharton, State Trials 199 n. (1849).

2. What is the nature of the dispute between those who believed in a federal common law of crimes and those who did not? Is the issue over the constitutional extent of Federal sovereignty? Could something more basic be involved? What is meant by Chase's suggestion that it is "as essential, that Congress should define the offences to be tried, and apportion the punishments to be inflicted, as that they should erect courts to try the criminal, or to pronounce a sentence on conviction"? Professor Morton Horwitz believes that something deeper *is* involved in the split between Chase and Peters. It is his opinion that the attack on common law crimes "emerged from a distinctively post-revolutionary conviction that the common law was both uncertain and unpredictable." Morton Horwitz, The Transformation of American Law 1780–1860, 14 (1977). Horwitz suggests that the opposition to the federal common law of crimes was part of a larger movement against common law crimes even at the state level. Here is Horwitz's analysis of the views of two anti-state common law men, Justices Chipman and Swift:

> * * * In his "Dissertation on the Act adopting the Common and Statute Laws of England" (1793), Vermont Chief Justice Nathaniel Chipman "lay[s] it down as an unalterable rule that no Court, in this State, ought ever to pronounce sentence of death upon the authority of a common law precedent, without the authority of a statute." And two years later, in his treatise on Connecticut law, Zepheniah Swift, soon to be that state's chief justice, indicated that he too was troubled by the doctrine "that every crime committed against the law of nature may be punished at the discretion of the judge, where the legislature has not appointed a particular punishment." Distinguishing between "crimes which are expressly defined by statute or common law" and those actions over

> which "courts of law have assumed a discretionary power of punishing," he warned that judges "ought to exercise [the latter] power with great circumspection and caution," since "the supreme excellency of a code of criminal laws consists in defining every act that is punishable with such certainty and accuracy, that no man shall be exposed to the danger of incurring a penalty without knowing it." It would be unjust, he continued, for "a man [to] do an act, which he knows has never been punished, and against which there is no law, yet upon a prosecution for it, the court may by a determination subsequent to the act, judge it to be a crime, and inflict on him a severe punishment." * * * Swift * * * was no longer prepared to assume that even the first judicial pronouncement of a legal rule was merely a declaration of some known and preexisting standard of natural law. Indeed, his entire discussion assumed the inability of individuals to know their legal duties without some express legislative or judicial pronouncement. * * * Swift's * * * preoccupation with the unfairness of administering a system of judge-made criminal law was a distinctly postrevolutionary phenomenon, reflecting a profound change in sensibility. For the inarticulate premise that lay behind Swift's warnings against the danger of judicial discretion was a growing perception that judges no longer merely discovered law; they also made it.*

Horwitz, supra, at 14–15 (footnotes omitted). Do you agree with Horwitz that this deeper philosophical view on the nature of the common law is what motivated Chase? How, then, do you explain Chase's ultimately agreeing to punish Worrall? Did Chase reverse himself on the issue of common law crimes? If so, why?

3. The last two excerpts in this section on the federal common law of crimes are, respectively, the clearest articulation of the Jeffersonian Republican position on the issue, and the Supreme Court's ultimate resolution of the problem. As you read them ask yourself again whether they seem to be concerned with the constitutional dimensions of the problem or whether they seem to be addressed to deeper questions about the nature of the American polity or the nature of law itself. The debate over the existence of the federal common law of crimes, as indicated, *was* resolved by the Supreme Court, but scholars continue to wonder whether the Federalists or the Jeffersonians had the better legal arguments. For a sampling of the scholarly debate, see Stewart Jay, "Origins of the Federal Common Law: Part One," 133 U.Pa.L.Rev. 1003 (1985), and the articles by Robert Palmer, Kathryn Preyer, and Stephen Presser in the Symposium on the Federal Common Law of Crimes, 4 Law and History Review 223, 267, 325 (1986). For the clearest and most far-ranging explanation of the Constitutional theory on which the Jeffersonian opposition to the federal common law of crimes ultimately rested, see H. Jefferson Pow-

* Reprinted from Morton J. Horwitz, The Transformation of American Law 1780–1860 Copyright © 1977 by the President and Fellows of Harvard University, published by the Harvard University Press, in association with the American Society for Legal History. Reprinted by permission of the Harvard University Press and the author.

ell, "The Principles of '98: An Essay in Historical Retrieval," 80 U.Va.L.Rev. 689 (1994).

4. VIRGINIA "INSTRUCTION"

INSTRUCTION FROM THE GENERAL ASSEMBLY OF VIRGINIA TO THE SENATORS FROM THAT STATE IN CONGRESS, JANUARY 11, 1800

I St. George Tucker, ed., Blackstone's Commentaries 438 (1803).

The general assembly of Virginia would consider themselves unfaithful to the trust reposed in them, were they to remain silent, whilst a doctrine has been publicly advanced, novel in its principle, and tremendous in its consequences: That the common law of England is in force under the government of the United States. It is not at this time proposed to expose at large the monstrous pretentions resulting from the adoption of this principle. It ought never, however, to be forgotten, and can never be too often repeated, that it opens a new tribunal for the trial of crimes never contemplated by the federal compact. It opens a new code of sanguinary criminal law, both obsolete and unknown, and either wholly rejected or essentially modified in almost all its parts by state institutions. It arrests, or supercedes, state jurisdictions, and innovates upon state laws. It subjects the citizen to punishment, according to the judiciary will, when he is left in ignorance of what this law enjoins as a duty, or prohibits as a crime. It assumes a range of jurisdiction for the federal courts, which defies limitation or definition. In short it is believed, that the advocates for the principle would, themselves, be lost in an attempt to apply it to the existing institutions of federal and state courts, by separating with precision their judiciary rights, and thus preventing the constant and mischievous interference of rival jurisdictions.

Deeply impressed with these opinions, the general assembly of Virginia, instruct the senators, and request the representatives from this state, in congress, to use their best efforts * * *.

To oppose the passing of any law, founded on, or recognizing the principle lately advanced, "that the common law of England, is in force under the government of the United States;" excepting from such opposition, such particular parts of the common law, as may have a sanction from the constitution, so far as they are necessarily comprehended in the technical phrases which express the powers delegated to the government; * * * and excepting, also, such other parts thereof as may be adopted by congress as necessary and proper for carrying into execution the powers expressly delegated.

5. THE SUPREME COURT ON THE FEDERAL COMMON LAW

UNITED STATES V. HUDSON & GOODWIN

Supreme Court of the United States, 1812.
11 U.S. (7 Cranch) 32, 3 L.Ed. 259.

This was a case certified from the Circuit Court for the district of Connecticut, in which, upon argument [over] * * * an indictment for a libel on the president and congress of the United States, contained in the Connecticut Currant, of the 7th of May 1806, charging them with having in secret voted $2,000,000 as a present to Bonaparte, for leave to make a treaty with Spain, the judges of that court were divided in opinion upon the question, whether the circuit court of the United States had a common-law jurisdiction in cases of libel?

Pinkney, Attorney–General, in behalf of the United States, and *Dana,* for the defendants, declined arguing the case.

The Court, * * * by JOHNSON, J.—The only question which this case presents is, whether the circuit courts of the United States can exercise a common-law jurisdiction in criminal cases. * * *

Although this question is brought up now, for the first time, to be decided by this court, we consider it as having been long since settled in public opinion. In no other case, for many years, has this jurisdiction been asserted; and the general acquiescence of legal men shows the prevalence of opinion in favor of the negative of the proposition.

The course of reasoning which leads to this conclusion is simple, obvious, and admits of but little illustration. The powers of the general government are made up of concessions from the several states—whatever is not expressly given to the former, the latter expressly reserve. The judicial power of the United States is a constituent part of those concessions; that power is to be exercised by courts organized for the purpose; and brought into existence by an effort of the legislative power of the Union. Of all the courts which the United States may, under their general powers, constitute, one only, the supreme court, possesses jurisdiction derived immediately from the constitution, and of which the legislative power cannot deprive it. All other courts created by the general government possesses no jurisdiction but what is given them by the power that creates them, and can be vested with none but what the power ceded to the general government will authorize them to confer.

It is not necessary to inquire, whether the general government, in any and what extent, possesses the power of conferring on its courts a jurisdiction in cases similar to the present; it is enough, that such jurisdiction has not been conferred by any legislative act, if it does not result to those courts as a consequence of their creation. And such is the opinion of the majority of this court: for the power which congress possess to create courts of inferior jurisdiction, necessarily implies the power to limit the jurisdiction of those courts to particular objects; and when a court is created, and its operations confined to certain specific objects, with what propriety can it assume to itself a jurisdiction, much more extended, in its nature very indefinite, applicable to a great variety of subjects, varying in every state in the Union and with regard to which there exists no definite criterion of distribution between the district and circuit courts of the same district.

The only ground on which it has ever been contended that this jurisdiction could be maintained is, that, upon the formation of any political body, an implied power to preserve its own existence and promote the end and object of its creation, necessarily results to it. But, without examining how far this consideration is applicable to the peculiar character of our constitution, it may be remarked that it is a principle by no means peculiar to the common law. It is coeval, probably, with the first formation of a limited government; belongs to a system of universal law, and may as well support the assumption of many other powers as those more peculiarly acknowledged by the common law of England.

But if admitted as applicable to the state of things in this country, the consequence would not result from it, which is here contended for. If it may communicate certain implied powers to the general government, it would not follow, that the courts of that government are vested with jurisdiction over any particular act done by an individual, in supposed violation of the peace and dignity of the sovereign power. The legislative authority of the Union must first make an act a crime, affix a punishment to it, and declare the court that shall have jurisdiction of the offence.

Certain implied powers must necessarily result to our courts of justice, from the nature of their institution. But jurisdiction of crimes against the state is not among those powers. To fine for contempt, imprison for contumacy, enforce the observance of order, & c., are powers which cannot be dispensed with in a court, because they are necessary to the exercise of all others: and so far our courts, no doubt, possess powers not immediately derived from statute; but all exercise of criminal jurisdiction in common-law cases, we are of opinion, is not within their implied powers.

NOTES AND QUESTIONS

1. Why did the lawyers decline to argue the case? In a bold piece, the title of which is drawn from this failure of counsel to argue the case, Gary D. Rowe argues that *Hudson & Goodwin* represented the triumphant popular acceptance of Jeffersonian Constitutionalism. Rowe, "The Sound of Silence: *United States v. Hudson & Goodwin,* the Jeffersonian Ascendancy, and the Abolition of Federal Common Law Crimes," 101 Yale L.J. 919 (1992). In his

attempt to suggest how the people can alter the meaning of the Constitution without invoking the formal amendment process, Rowe, as do several other scholars currently working in constitutional theory, draws on the increasingly seminal work of Bruce Ackerman, We the People: Foundations (1991). Do you think that the Constitution's framers would approve of such changes in Constitutional meaning? Do you?

2. The Supreme Court in *Hudson* says that no "legislative act" has conferred common law jurisdiction on the lower Federal Courts. What about the 1789 Judiciary Act itself, which gave the Circuit Court jurisdiction, presumably over *all* "crimes and offenses cognizable under the authority of the United States?" Judge Peters, you may remember, thought those words granted a federal common law crimes jurisdiction. Why didn't Justice Johnson agree? For further reading on the issue of common law crimes, apparently concluding that by the time of *Hudson v. Goodwin* there was a consensus that criminal punishments should be meted out by statutes, see Michael Conant, "Federal Common–Law Crimes and Non–Statutory Crimes Against the Law of Nations," 4 Anglo–American L. Rev. 456 (1995).

3. What decided the question in "public opinion?" Could it have been the seditious libel cases which you will encounter in the next section?

D. THE TRIALS FOR SEDITIOUS LIBEL

INTRODUCTION: The Adams Administration and Political Dissent

The administration of the Federalist John Adams (1797–1801), the second person to serve as an American president, was problematic from the beginning. Adams was alarmed at the machinations of Alexander Hamilton, Washington's Secretary of the Treasury, who was secretly communicating with Adams's Secretary of State (John Pickering) and his Secretary of the Treasury (Oliver Wolcott) to thwart some of Adams plans, and to exercise an influence over national policy. The relation between Adams and Thomas Jefferson, the leader of the Republicans elected Vice President in 1796, was about to experience a total breakdown. This was a personally painful development for Adams, and for his wife, Abigail. The three had become close during their ministerial years representing the United States in Europe during the Articles of Confederation period. But in the vice grip of new party differences, each suspected the other of behind-the-scenes maneuvering for personal advantage.

Adams inherited the diplomatic crises of the Washington administration (1789–1797). Pro–British and pro-French factions were crying for war and Adams was called on to take sides. He chose a middle ground, electing to enhance the army and build a navy to protect American shipping interests. To the Republicans, the President and the Federalists were seen as pro-British nationalists who harbored monarchial designs of their own. As indicated earlier, the military expenditures, even though purely for national defense, also laid Adams open to the Republican charge that he was creating a "standing army," the Revolutionary patriots' greatest fear. The Fries Rebellion, as we have seen, was an outgrowth of the Federal property taxes imposed by the government to pay for the expansion of the army and navy.

His own party was not particularly satisfied with Adams's policies. If he was not exactly pro-French, then he was blamed for being undecided. The Jacobean excesses in the French Revolution were fresh—the guillotine was becoming a universal symbol of what some French meant by *egalité*. Especially after the Whiskey and Fries rebellions, it was not difficult for Federalists to imagine an American version of full-scale bloody domestic rebellion, with concomitant threats to property and order. Desperate times, it was believed, called for desperate responses, and Federalists saw war with France as a necessary response.

Because political parties and the concept of a loyal opposition were as yet unaccepted in politics, Federalists and Republicans saw each other as motivated by personal agendas and a selfish lust for power. Newspapers, whose attacks were poisonous, were seen as little better than paid mouthpieces of factional interests. The depth of the animosity pointed to a very troubling disturbance in the nation's government, and raised serious questions about whether the United States could survive.

In a republic, what, if any, ought to be the limits imposed on the press, and on individuals, from attacking the integrity of a sitting president? How did one distinguish between a legitimate criticism of national policy and seditious behavior? In a system where the judicial establishment was appointed by the party in power, to what extent could courts be trusted? In short, how was the line between politics and law to be drawn? What interests (political, business, economic, and ideological) should the nation pursue in the conduct of its foreign relations? These were all questions of first impression in the new nation, and even in the best of circumstances, the development of a consensus was no easy matter. As both a reform and a hoped-for cure, Congress passed the Alien and Sedition Acts of 1798.

ACT FOR THE PUNISHMENT OF CERTAIN CRIMES,* JULY 14, 1798

1 Stat. 596.

* * *

§ 2. * * * if any person shall write, print, utter, or publish; or shall cause or procure to be written, printed, uttered, or published, or shall knowingly and willingly assist or aid in writing, printing, uttering, or publishing, any false, scandalous, and malicious, writing or writings,

* The act, by its own terms, expired on March 3, 1801.

against the government of the United States, or either house of the congress of the United States, or the president of the United States, with intent to defame the said government, or either house of the said congress, or the said president, or to bring them, or either of them, into contempt or disrepute; or to excite against them, or either or any of them, the hatred of the good people of the United States, or to stir up sedition within the United States; or to excite any unlawful combinations therein, for opposing or resisting any law of the United States, or any act of the president of the United States, done in pursuance of any such law, or of the powers in him vested by the constitution of the United States; or to resist, oppose, or defeat, any such law or act; or to aid, encourage, or abet any hostile designs or any foreign nation against the United States, their people, or government, then such person, being thereof convicted before any court of the United States having jurisdiction thereof, shall be punished, by a fine not exceeding two thousand dollars, and by imprisonment not exceeding two years.

§ 3. * * * if any person shall be prosecuted under this act, for the writing or publishing any libel aforesaid, it shall be lawful for the defendant, upon the trial of the cause, to give in evidence in his defense, the truth of the matter contained in the publication charged as a libel. And the Jury who shall try the cause, shall have a right to determine the law and the fact, under the direction of the court, as in other causes.

UNITED STATES V. MATTHEW LYON

United States Circuit Court, District of Vermont, 1798.
15 Fed.Cas. 1183.

[Lyon was charged in an indictment with committing the offense specified in § 2 of the Act. The first count charged him with publishing the following allegedly criminal matter:]

> As to the Executive, when I shall see the efforts of that power bent on the promotion of the comfort, the happiness, and accommodation of the people, that executive shall have my zealous and uniform support: but whenever I shall, on the part of the Executive, see every consideration of the public welfare swallowed up in a continual grasp for power, in an unbounded thirst for ridiculous pomp, foolish adulation, and selfish avarice; when I shall behold men of real merit daily turned out of office, for no other cause but independency of sentiment; when I shall see men of firmness, merit, years, abilities, and experience, discarded in their application for office, for fear they possess that independence, and men of meanness preferred for the ease with which they take up and advocate opinions, the consequence of which they know but little of—when I shall see the sacred name of religion employed as a state engine to make mankind hate and persecute one another, I shall not be their humble advocate.

The second count consisted of having * * * published a letter [said to be from a French diplomat, including these words:] * * *

> The misunderstanding between the two governments (France and the United States), has become extremely alarming; confidence is completely destroyed, mistrusts, jealousy, and a disposition to a wrong attribution of motives, are so apparent, as to require the utmost caution in every word and action that are to come from your Executive. I mean, if your object is to avoid hostilities. Had this truth been understood with you before the recall of Monroe, before the coming and second coming of Pinckney; had it guided the pens that wrote the bullying speech of your President, and stupid answer of your Senate, at the opening of Congress in November last, I should probably had no occasion to address you this letter.
>
> —But when we found him borrowing the language of Edmund Burke, and telling the world that although he should succeed in treating with the French, there was no dependence to be placed on any of their engagement, that their religion and morality were at an end, that they would turn pirates and plunderers, and it would be necessary to be perpetually armed against them, though you were at peace: We wondered that the answer of both Houses had not been an order to send him to a mad house. Instead of this the Senate have echoed the speech with more servility than ever George III. experienced from either House of Parliament. * * *

Several witnesses were called to show that the defendant, both in public and in private, had extensively used the letter for political purposes, and in doing so had frequently made use of language highly disrespectful to the administration. * * *

The prosecution having closed its case, the defendant stated his defence to consist in three points: first, that the court had not jurisdiction of the offence, the act of Congress being unconstitutional and void, * * * second, that the publication was innocent; and third, that the contents were true.

On the first two points he offered no testimony, but on the third he proposed to call Judge Paterson, the presiding judge, and Judge Israel Smith.

Judge Paterson being then on the bench, was then asked by the defendant, whether he had not frequently "dined with the President, and observed his ridiculous pomp and parade?"

Judge Paterson replied, that he had sometimes, though rarely, dined with the President, but that he had never seen any pomp or parade; he had seen, on the contrary, a great deal of plainness and simplicity.

The defendant then asked whether he (the judge) had not seen at the President's more pomp and servants there, than at the tavern at Rutland? To this no answer was given.*

No other witness was * * * called.

* * * The defendant addressed the jury at great length, insisting on the unconstitutionality of the law, and the insufficiency of the evidence to show anything more than a legitimate opposition.

PATERSON, J., CIRCUIT JUDGE, * * * charged the jury substantially as follows:

> You have nothing whatever to do with the constitutionality or unconstitutionality of the sedition law. Congress has said that the author and publisher of seditious libels is to be punished; and until this law is declared null and void by a tribunal competent for the purpose, its validity cannot be disputed. Great would be the abuses were the constitutionality of every statute to be submitted to a jury, in each case where the statute is to be applied. The only question you are to determine is * * * Did Mr. Lyon publish the writing given in the indictment? Did he do so seditiously?

On the first point * * * he himself concedes the fact of publication * * *. As to the second point, you will have to consider whether language such as that here complained of could have been uttered with any other intent than that of making odious or contemptible the President and government, and bringing them both into disrepute. If you find such is the case, the offense is made out, and you must render a verdict of guilty. Nor should the political rank of the defendant,* his past services, or the dependent condition of his family, deter you from this duty. Such considerations are for the court alone in adjusting the penalty they will bestow. * * * In order to render a verdict of guilty, you must be satisfied beyond all reasonable substantial doubt that the hypothesis of innocence is unsustainable. * * *

At about eight o'clock in the evening of the same day, after about an hour's absence, the jury returned with a verdict of guilty.

The defendant being called up for sentence * * * Judge Paterson addressed him as follows:

> Matthew Lyon, as a member of the federal legislature, you must be well acquainted with the mischiefs which flow from an unlicensed

* A report of this part of the trial in the Philadelphia *Aurora,* a Republican newspaper, states that "The judge, conscious that there was some difference between the table at Braintree, and the humble fare of a country tavern, with the privileges of half a bed, made no reply, but smoked a cigar."

* The defendant was a feisty Irish member of the United States Congress from Vermont. A stout Republican, the Federalists said of him, "a strange offensive brute, too wild to tame, too base to shoot." Quoted in Roger Butterfield, The American Past 28 (2nd. ed. 1966).

abuse of government, and of the motives which led to the passage of the act under which this indictment is framed. * * * What, however, has tended to mitigate the sentence which would otherwise have been imposed, is, what I am sorry to hear of, the reduced condition of your estate. The judgment of the court is, that you stand imprisoned four months, pay the cost of prosecution, and a fine of one thousand dollars * * *.

UNITED STATES V. THOMAS COOPER

United States Circuit Court, District of Pennsylvania, 1800.
25 Fed.Cas. 631.

JUDGE CHASE * * * charged the jury as follows: * * *

Thomas Cooper * * * stands charged with having published a false, scandalous and malicious libel against the President of the United States, in his official character as President. There is no civilized country that I know of, that does not punish such offences; and it is necessary to the peace and welfare of this country, that these offenses should meet with their proper punishment, since ours is a government founded on the opinions and confidence of the people. The Representatives and the President are chosen by the people. It is a government made by themselves; and their officers are chosen by themselves; and, therefore, if any improper law is enacted, the people have it in their power to obtain the repeal of such law, or even of the Constitution itself, if found defective, since provision is made for its amendment. Our government, therefore, is really republican; the people are truly represented, since all power is derived from them: it is a government of representation and responsibility: all officers of the government are liable to be displaced or removed, or their duration in office limited by elections at fixed periods * * *. All governments which I have ever read or heard of punish libels against themselves. If a man attempts to destroy the confidence of the people in their officers, their supreme magistrate, and their legislature, he effectually saps the government. A republican government can only be destroyed in two ways; the introduction of luxury, or the licentiousness of the press. This latter is the more slow, but most sure and certain, means of bringing about the destruction of the government. The legislature of this country, knowing this maxim, has thought proper to pass a law to check this licentiousness of the press * * *.

Thomas Cooper, then, stands indicted for having published a false, scandalous and malicious libel upon the President of the United States, with intent to defame the President, to bring him into contempt and disrepute, and to excite against him the hatred of the good people of the United States. * * * The traverser has pleaded not guilty, and that he has not published, & c., with these views: he has also pleaded in justification (which the law provides for), that the matters asserted by him are true, and that he will give the same in evidence.

It is incumbent on the part of the prosecution to prove * * * that he did publish with intent to defame, & c.

For the intent * * * must be proved in the same manner as other facts; and must be proved as stated in the law of Congress—the mere publication is no offence; and in making up your verdict, though you consider them separately, you must take the whole tenor and import of the publication * * *.

* * *

The fact of writing and publishing is clearly proved; nay, in fact, it is not denied * * *. It appears from the evidence that the traverser went to the house of a justice of the peace with this paper, whom, of all others, he ought to have avoided: for he must know that it was duty of the justice of the peace to deliver it immediately to those who administer the government. * * * It was indecent to deliver such a paper to a justice of the peace, and the manner in which it was delivered was yet more outrageous—if it was done in joke, as the traverser would wish to imply, it was still very improper—but there was the same solemnity in his expression, "this is my name, and I am the author of this handbill," as if the traverser was going to part with an estate. This conduct showed that he intended to dare and defy the government, and to provoke them, and his subsequent conduct satisfies my mind that such was his disposition. For he justifies the publication in all its parts, and declares it to be founded in truth: it is proved most clearly to be his publication. It is your business to consider the intent as coupled with that, and view the whole together. * * * If there are doubts as to the motives of the traverser, he has removed them; for, though he states in his defence that he does not arraign the motives of the President, yet he has boldly avowed that his own motives in this publication were to censure the conduct of the President * * *. Now, gentlemen, the motives of the President, in his official capacity, are not a subject of inquiry with you. Shall we say to the President, you are not fit for the government of this country? It is no apology for a man to say, that he believes the President to be honest, but that he has done acts which prove him unworthy the confidence of the people, incapable of executing the duties of his high station, and unfit for the important office to which the people have elected him * * *.

Now we will consider this libel as published by the defendant, and observe what were his motives. You will find the traverser speaking of the President in the following words: "Even those who doubted his capacity, thought well of his intentions." This the traverser might suppose would be considered as a compliment as to the intentions of the President; but I have no doubt that it was meant to carry a sting with it which should be felt; for it was in substance saying of the President, "you may have good intentions, but I doubt your capacity."

He then goes on to say, "Nor were we yet saddled with the expense of a permanent navy, nor threatened, under his (the President's) auspices, with the existence of a standing army. Our credit was not yet reduced so low as to borrow money at eight per cent, in *time of peace*." Now, gentlemen, if these things were true, can any one doubt what effect they would have on the public mind? * * * What! the President of the United States saddle us with a permanent navy, encourage a standing army, and borrow money at a large premium? * * * If you believe this to be true, what opinion can you, gentlemen, form of the President? * * * The President is further charged for that "the unnecessary violence of his official expressions might *justly* have provoked a war." * * * I say, gentlemen, again, if you believe this, what opinion can you form of the President? Certainly the worst you can form: you would certainly consider him totally unfit for the high station which he has so honourably filled, and with such benefit to his country.

The traverser states that, under the auspices of the President, "our credit is so low that we are obliged to borrow money at eight per cent. in time of peace." I cannot suppress my feelings at this gross attack upon the President. Can this be true? Can you believe it? Are we now in time of peace? Is there no war? No hostilities with France? Has she not captured our vessels and plundered us of our property to the amount of millions? Has not the intercourse been prohibited with her? Have we not armed our vessels to defend ourselves, and have we not captured several of her vessels of war? Although no formal declaration of war has been made, is it not notorious that actual hostilities have taken place? And is this, then, a time of peace? The very expense incurred, which rendered a loan necessary, was in consequence of the conduct of France. The traverser, therefore, has published an untruth, knowing it to be an untruth.

The other part of the publication is much more offensive * * *. The part to which I allude is that where the traverser charges the President with having influenced the judiciary department. * * * [T]he judicature of the country is of the greatest consequence to the liberties and existence of a nation. If your Constitution was destroyed, so long as the judiciary department remained free and uncontrolled, the liberties of the people would not be endangered. Suffer your courts of judicature to be destroyed: there is an end to your liberties. * * *

The traverser goes on thus—"This melancholy case of Jonathan Robbins, a native of America, forcibly impressed by the British, and delivered, with the advice of Mr. Adams, to the mock trial of a British court-martial, had not yet astonished the republican citizens of this free country. A case too little known, but of which the people ought to be fully apprised before the election, and they SHALL be." Now, gentlemen, there are circumstances in this publication which greatly aggravate the offence. The traverser [states that] the President interfered * * * in order to deliver up a native American citizen to be executed by a British court-martial under a mock trial, against law and against mercy. * * * I can scarcely conceive a charge can be made against the President of so much consequence, or of a more heinous nature. * * * It appears then that this is a charge on the President, not only false and scandalous, but evidently made with intent to injure his character, and the manner in which it is made is well calculated to operate on the passions of Americans, and I fear such has been the effect. If this charge were true, there is not a man amongst you but would hate the President; I am sure I should hate him myself if I had thought he had done this. Upon the purity and independence of the judges depend the existence of your government and the preservation of your liberties. They should be under no influence—they are only accountable to God and their own consciences * * *.

There is a little circumstance which the attorney-general, in his observations to you, omitted to state, but which I think it right to recall to your recollection, as it appears with what design the traverser made this publication. In this allusion to Jonathan Robbins he expressly tells you this is "a case too little known, but of which the people ought to be fully apprised before the election, and they shall be." Here, then, the evident design of the traverser was, to arouse the people against the President so as to influence their minds against him on the next election. I think it right to explain this to you, because it proves, that the traverser was actuated by improper motives to make this charge against the President. * * *

Now, gentlemen, with regard to this delivery of Jonathan Robbins, I am clearly of opinion that the President could not refuse to deliver him up. This same Jonathan Robbins, whose real name appears to have been Nash, was charged with murder committed on board the *Hermione* British ship of war. This Nash being discovered in America, the British Minister made a requisition to the President that he should be delivered up. * * * By the 27th article of the treaty with Great Britain, it is stipulated, "that either of the contracting parties will deliver up to justice all persons who, being charged with murder or forgery committed within the Jurisdiction of either, shall seek an asylum within any of the countries of the other, provided this shall be done only on such evidence of criminality as, according to the laws of the place where the fugitive or person so charged shall be found, would justify his apprehension and commitment for trial, if the offence had been there committed." If the President, therefore, by this treaty, was bound to give this Nash up to justice, he was so bound by law; for the treaty is the law of the land: if so, the charge of interference to influence the decisions of a court of justice, is without foundation. * * * Nash was charged with having committed murder on board a British ship of war: now a dispute has arisen whether murder committed on board such a ship of war, was committed within the jurisdiction of Great Britain: I have no doubt as to the point. All vessels, whether public or private, are part of the territory and within the jurisdiction of the nation to which they belong. This is according to the law of nations. * * * The President was the only person to take the proper steps, and to take cognizance of the business. He represents the United States in their concerns with foreign powers: this affair could not be tried before a court of law. No court of justice here has jurisdiction over the crime of murder committed on board a British ship of war. Now, as the requisition was made to the President on the part of the British government to deliver this man up, it became necessary to know whether there was sufficient evidence of his criminality pursuant to the treaty. The judge of the court of Carolina was therefore called upon to inquire into the evidence of his criminality: he was the instrument made use of by the President, which he was by the treaty and the law of the land, bound to perform; and had he not done so, we should have heard louder complaints from the party who are incessantly opposing and calumniating the government, that the President had grossly neglected his duty by not carrying a solemn treaty into effect. Was this, then, an interference on the part of the President with the judiciary without precedent, against law and against mercy; for doing an act which he was bound by the law of the land to carry into effect, and over which a court of justice had no jurisdiction? Surely not; neither has it merited to be treated in the manner in which the traverser has done in his publication. * * *

Take this publication in all its parts, and it is the boldest attempt I have known to poison the minds of the people. He asserts that Mr. Adams has countenanced a navy, that he has brought forward measures for raising a standing army in the country. * * * [T]o assert, as he has done, that we have a standing army in this country, betrays the most egregious ignorance, or the most wilful intentions to deceive the public. We have two descriptions of armies in this country—we have an army which is generally called the Western army, enlisted for five years only—can this be a standing army? Who raises them? Congress. Who pays them? The people. We have also another army, called the provisional army, which is enlisted during the existence of the war with France—neither of these can, with any propriety, be called a standing army. In fact, we cannot have a standing army in this country, the Constitution having expressly declared that no appropriation shall be made for the support of any army longer than two years. * * *

There is no subject on which the people of America feel more alarm, than the establishment of a standing army. Once persuade them that the government is attempting to promote such a measure, and you destroy their confidence in the government. * * *

It is too much to press this point on the traverser. But he deserves it. This publication is evidently intended to mislead the ignorant, and inflame their minds against the President, and to influence their votes on the next election.

* * *

The traverser has, to prove these points, read to you many extracts from the addresses and answers to the President. He has selected a number of passages, which, he asserts, prove the approbation of the President to the creation of a navy, and forming a standing army. But we are to recollect gentlemen, that when in consequence of the unjust proceedings of France, the great mass of the people thought proper to address the President, expressing in those addresses, sentiments of attachment and confidence in the President, and their determination to resist the oppression of the French government: the President replied to them, in answers which generally were the echo of their sentiments, and in fact, his expressions were as general as the nature of the addresses would permit—therefore, the traverser ought to have blamed the addressers, and not the President. * * *

* * *

You will please to notice, gentlemen, that the traverser in his defence must prove every charge he has made to be true; he must prove it to the marrow. * * * If he were to prove, that the President had done everything charged against him in the first paragraph of the publication—though he should prove to your satisfaction, that the President had interfered to influence the decisions of a court of justice, that he had delivered up Jonathan Robbins without precedent, against law and against mercy, this would not be sufficient, unless he proved at the same time, that Jonathan Robbins was a native American, and had been forcibly impressed, and compelled to serve on board a British ship of war. If he fails, therefore, gentlemen, in this proof, you must then consider whether his intentions in making these charges against the President were malicious or not. It is not necessary for me to go more minutely into an investigation of the defence. You must judge for yourselves—you must find the publication, and judge of the intent with which that publication was made, whether it was malice or not? If you believe that he has published it without malice, or an intent to defame the President of the United States, you must acquit him; if he has proved the truth of the facts asserted by him, you must find him Not Guilty.

After the jury had returned with a verdict of Guilty:—

Judge Chase. Mr. Cooper, as the jury have found you guilty, we wish to hear any circumstances you have to offer in point of the mitigation of the fine the court may think proper to impose on you, and also in extenuation of your punishment. We should therefore wish to know your situation in life, in regard to your circumstances. * * *

Mr. Cooper. * * * I think it right to say, that my property in this country is moderate. That some resources I had in England, commercial failures there have lately cut off: that I depend principally on my practice: that practice, imprisonment will annihilate. Be it so. I have been accustomed to make sacrifices to opinion, and I can make this. As to circumstances in extenuation, not being conscious that I have set down aught in malice, I have nothing to extenuate.

Judge Chase. * * * I am sorry you did not think proper to make an affidavit in regard to your circumstances * * *. I do not know you personally—I know nothing of you, more than having lately heard your name mentioned in some publication. Every person knows the political disputes which have existed amongst us. It is notorious that there are two parties in the country; you have stated this yourself. You have taken one side—we do not pretend to say, that you have not a right to express your sentiments, only taking care not to injure the characters of those to whom you are opposed.

* * *

If we were to indulge our own ideas, there is room to suspect that in cases of this kind, where one party is against the government, gentlemen, who write for that party, would be indemnified against any pecuniary loss; and that the party would pay any fine which might be imposed on the person convicted. * * * If the fine were only to fall on yourself, I would consider circumstances; but, if I could believe you were supported by a party inimical to the government, and that they were to pay the fine, not you, I would go the utmost extent of the power of the court. I understand you have a family, but you have not thought proper to state that to the court. From what I can gather from you, it appears that you depend on your profession for support; we do not wish to impose so rigorous a fine as to be beyond a person's abilities to support, but the government must be secured against these malicious attacks. You say that you are not conscious of having acted from malicious motives. It may be so; saying so, we must believe you; but, the jury have found otherwise. You are a gentleman of the profession, of such capacity and knowledge, as to have it more in your power to mislead the ignorant. I do not want to oppress, but I will restrain, as far as I can, all such licentious attacks on the government * * *.

Mr. Cooper. * * * Sir, I solemnly aver, that throughout my life, here and elsewhere, among all the political questions in which I have been concerned, I have never so far demeaned myself as to be a party writer. * * * The exertions of my talents, such as they are, have been unbought, and so they shall continue; they have indeed been paid for, but they have been paid for by myself, and by myself only, and sometimes dearly. The public is my debtor, and what I have paid or suffered for them, if my duty should again call upon me to write or to act, I shall again most readily submit to. I do not pretend to have no party opinions, to have no predilection for particular descriptions of men or of measures; but I do not act upon minor considerations; I belong here, as in my former country, to the great party of mankind. With regard to any offers which may have been made to me, to enable me to discharge the fine which may be imposed, I will state candidly to the court what has passed * * *. [M]any of my friends have, in the expectation of a verdict against me, come forward with general offers of pecuniary assistance; these offers I have, hitherto, neither accepted nor rejected. If the court should impose a fine beyond my ability to pay, I shall accept them without hesitation; but if the fine be within my circumstances to discharge, I shall pay it myself. But the insinuations of the court are ill founded, and if you, sir, from misapprehension or misinformation have been tempted to make them, your mistake should be corrected.

Judge Peters. I think we have nothing to do with parties; we are only to consider the subject before us. I wish you had thought proper to make an affidavit of your property. I have nothing to do, sitting here, to inquire whether a party in whose favour you may be, or you, are to pay the fine. I shall only consider your circumstances, and impose a fine which I think adequate; we ought to avoid any oppression. It appears that you depend chiefly upon your profession for support. Imprisonment for any time would tend to increase the fine, as your family would be deprived of your professional abilities to maintain them.

Judge Chase. We will take time to consider this. [The following day the court sentenced Cooper to pay a fine of four hundred dollars and to be imprisoned for six months. It appears that Cooper was aided financially by Thomas Jefferson himself. One historian has described him as the then vice-president's "paid hireling." Merrill Peterson, Adams and Jefferson: A Revolutionary Dialogue 98 (1976). Jefferson's support of Cooper, of Callender (whose case we read next), and of "a host of Republican libellers," led President John Adams to terminate his long-standing friendship with Jefferson. Adams believed that Jefferson's backing of such as Cooper and Callender "was not only a blot on his moral character but proof he was a captive of party." Id., at 78, 98, 100.]

* * *

UNITED STATES V. JAMES THOMPSON CALLENDER

United States Circuit Court, District of Virginia, 1800.
25 Fed.Cas. 239.

The matter set out in the indictment as libellous was as follows:

The reign of Mr. Adams has been one continued tempest of malignant passion. As President, he has never opened his lips, or lifted his pen without threatening and scolding; the grand object of his administration has been to exasperate the rage of contending parties, to calumniate and destroy every man who differs from his opinions. Mr. Adams has laboured, and with melancholy success, to break up the bonds of social affection, and under the ruins of confidence and friendship, to extinguish the only gleam of happiness that glimmers through the dark and despicable farce of life. [The allegedly libelous publication proceeds in this vein, accusing Adams of "corruption," "malignant designs," and of being Pro–Aristocrat, Anti–French, Pro–British, "grossly prejudiced," and a "hoary headed incendiary."]

* * *

[We enter the trial at the conclusion of the presentation of the prosecutor, Mr. Nelson.]

* * * [I]t is the peculiar privilege of every citizen of this happy country to place confidence in whom he pleases, and at the constitutional periods of making new elections, to withdraw his confidence from a former representative, and place his trust in another; and even expatiate on the virtues of the new candidate; but this does not warrant him to vilify, revile, and defame another individual, who is a candidate. Cannot a good thing be said of one individual, without saying black and damnable things of another? * * *

The attorney for the United States having concluded, the counsel for the traverser introduced Colonel John Taylor (of Caroline county) as a witness, and he was sworn; but at the moment the oath was administered, the Judge called on them, and desired to know what they intended to prove by the witness.

They answered that they intended to examine Colonel Taylor to prove that he [Adams] had avowed principles in his presence which justified Mr. Callender in saying that the President was an aristocrat; that he [Adams] had voted against the sequestration law, and the resolutions concerning the suspension of commercial intercourse with Great Britain, by which he defeated every effort of those who were in favour of those beneficial measures which were well calculated to promote the happiness of their country.

The Judge demanded a statement in writing of the questions intended to be put to the witness.

Mr. Nicholas remarked, that * * * this requisition had not been made of the attorney, when he introduced witnesses on behalf of the United States, nor was it according to the practice of the State courts; that he wished the witness to state all he knew that would apply to the defence of his client; that he did not know what the witness would precisely prove, but that if the court insisted upon it, he would furnish a statement of the question which he should first propound, but requested that he might not be considered as confined, in the examination of the witness, to the question so stated.

Judge Chase. It is right to state the questions intended to be propounded to witnesses, in all cases, and the reason is extremely plain. Juries are only to hear legal evidence, and the court are the only judges of what is or is not legal evidence, to support the issue joined between the parties. To say that you will correct improper evidence, after it shall have been given, is improper, because illegal evidence, once heard, may make an undue impression, and, therefore, ought not to be heard at all by the jury; and the attorney for the United States had, in opening the cause, stated the purpose for which he introduced the witnesses.

Judge Chase, having received a statement of the questions meant to be put,* and which were propounded by Mr. Nicholas, declared Colonel Taylor's evidence to be inadmissible. No evidence, said the Judge, is admissible that does not go to justify the whole charge. The charge you mean to justify by this witness, as I understand you, is, that the President is a professed aristocrat; and that he has proved serviceable to the British interest. You must prove both these points, or you prove nothing. Now as you do not attempt to prove the whole of one specific charge, but only a part of it, your evidence cannot be received. * * * It may be said that this will preclude the party from the privilege of his testimony; but this will only be a misrepresentation, it precludes them from no legal benefit. My country has made me a judge, and you must be governed now by my opinion, though I may be mistaken; but if I am not right, it is an error in judgment, and you can state the proceedings on the record so as to show any error, and I shall be the first man to grant you the benefit of a new trial by granting you a writ of error in the Supreme Court. * * * The very argument assigned by the young gentleman who spoke last, has convinced my mind that I am right. The offered testimony has no direct and proper application to the issue; it would deceive and mislead the jury; an argumentative justification of a trivial, unimportant part of a libel, would be urged before a jury as a substantial vindication of the whole. * * *

Mr. Nicholas suggested that it might be proper to prove one part of a specific charge by one witness, and another part by another, and thereby prove the charge.

---

* Ques. 1st. Did you ever hear Mr. Adams express any opinion favourable to monarchy and aristocracy: and what were they?

Ques. 2d. Did you ever hear Mr. Adams, whilst Vice President, express his disapprobation of the funding system?

Ques. 3d. Do you know whether Mr. Adams did not, in the year 1794, vote against the sequestration law, and the bill for suspending commercial intercourse with Great Britain?

Judge Chase, in answer, repeated some of his former arguments, and added, that the very argument suggested by the young gentleman who spoke last, convinced his mind that it would be improper to admit the testimony now offered to the court; that to admit evidence, which went to an argumentative establishment of the truth of a minute part of the charge by one witness, and another minute part by another witness, would be irregular, and subversive of every principle of law; that it had no relation to the issue; that it was a popular argument, calculated to deceive the people, but very incorrect. * * *

* * * This is a new doctrine, inculcated in Virginia. You have all along mistaken the law, and press your mistakes on the court. The United States must prove the publication, and the fallacy of it. When these things are done, you must prove a justification, and this justification must be entire and complete, as to any one specific charge; a partial justification is inadmissible. * * *

Mr. Hay spoke thus. * * * One specific charge is twofold; that the President is an aristocrat; and that he proved serviceable to the British interest. The evidence, we suppose, will support this charge; we wish to prove the truth of the whole charge if we can, though I do not know that it is in our power. The evidence, we have reason to believe, goes first to prove that he is an aristocrat, and secondly, that he *did* prove serviceable to the British interest; if the testimony *will* in fact prove these two points, whatever may be the opinion of the court, I do not hesitate to say that, in my estimation, it will fully excuse and justify the traverser * * *. As to the first part, I can prove by the words of Mr. Adams, published by himself, in his book called A Defence of the American Constitution, that he thinks a government of three parts, a king, lords, and commons, the best in the world. Suppose, in addition to this it could be proved that a law passed the House of Representatives of the United States, to sequester British property; and suppose that one-half the Senate of the United States were in favour of it; and that the policy of passing the law was advocated by the best and wisest men in this country, who have the same pretensions to patriotism and virtue that Mr. Adams has, but that its passage was prevented by the casting vote of Mr. Adams as speaker of the Senate, would not the traverser be justified as to this charge? Would it not demonstrate that he proved serviceable to the British interest? By the answers to the first and third questions we expect to prove both these points.

Here *Mr. Nelson* objected to the introduction of such testimony, as being altogether inadmissible * * *, that it would be a departure from the universal principle of law, which required the production of the best testimony which the nature of every case admitted, and that the journals and records of Congress were the best evidence of what votes had been given on any subject discussed before that body.

Judge Chase then addressed himself to Mr. Nelson thus:—Being very much pressed, by the young gentlemen who defend the traverser, to admit this testimony, I was going to recommend to you to permit those questions to be put to the witness, though they are certainly irregular. I wish you could consent that they should be propounded.

Mr. Nelson declared that he did not feel himself at liberty to consent to such a departure from legal principles.

Mr. Wirt then rose and addressed the jury.—He premised that the situation of the defendant and his counsel was extremely embarrassing; that as Mr. Callender had been presented, indicted, arrested and tried, during this term, he had not been able to procure the testimony essential to his defence, nor was his counsel prepared to defend him; and he insinuated that the conduct of the court was apparently precipitate, in not postponing the trial until the next term.

Judge Chase told him he must not reflect on the court.

* * *

Mr. Wirt.—Gentlemen of the jury, I am prevented from explaining to you the causes which have conspired to weaken our defence, and it is no doubt right that I should be prevented, as the court have so decided * * *. You will find that a material part of your inquiry will relate to the power of a jury over the subject committed to them, whether they have the right to determine the law, as well as the fact. In Virginia, an act of the assembly has adopted the common law of England; that common law, therefore, possesses in this state all the energy of a legislative act. By an act of Congress, the rules of proceedings in the federal courts, in the several states, are directed to conform to the rules of the states in which such court may be in session; by that act of Congress, it is therefore provided, that the practice of the courts of Virginia shall be observed in this court: to ascertain your power, therefore, as a jury, we have only to refer to the common law of England, which has been adopted in the laws of this state, and which defines the powers of juries in the state courts. By the common law of England, juries possess the power of considering and deciding the law as well as the fact in every case which may come before them. * * * If, then, a jury in a court of the state would have a right to decide the law and the fact, so have you. The federal Constitution is the supreme law of the land; and a right to consider the law, is a right to consider the Constitution: if the law of Congress under which we are indicted, be an infraction of the Constitution, it has not the force of a law, and if you were to find the traverser guilty, under such an act, you would violate your oaths.

Here *Judge Chase*—Take your seat sir, if you please. If I understand you rightly, you offer an argument to the petit jury, to convince them that the statute of Congress, entitled, "An act, & c., commonly called the Sedition Law," is contrary to the Constitution of the United States, and, therefore, void. Now I tell you that this is irregular and inadmissible; it is not competent to the jury to decide on this point; but if you address yourself, gentlemen, to the court, they will with pleasure hear any reason you may offer, to show that the jury have the right contended for. * * *

Here the Judge then read part of a long opinion, to show that the jury had not the right contended for * * *.

* * *

Judge Chase. * * * [W]e all know that juries have the right to decide the law, as well as the fact—and the Constitution is the supreme law of the land, which controls all laws which are repugnant to it.

Mr. Wirt.—Since, then, the jury have a right to consider the law, and since the constitution is law, the conclusion is certainly syllogistic, that the jury have a right to consider the Constitution.

Judge Chase.—A *non sequitur,* sir.

Here Mr. Wirt sat down.

Mr. Nicholas then addressed the court. * * * I intend to defend Mr. Callender by the establishment of two points.

First, that a law contrary to the Constitution is void; and, secondly, that the jury have a right to consider the law and the fact. First, it seems to be admitted on all hands, that, when the legislature exercise a power not given them by the Constitution, the judiciary will disregard their acts. The second point, that the jury have a right to decide the law and the fact, appears to me equally clear. In the exercise of the power of determining law and fact, a jury cannot be controlled by the court. The court have a right to instruct the jury, but the jury have a right to act as they think right; and if they find contrary to the directions of the court, and to the law of the case, the court may set aside their verdict and grant a new trial.

Judge Chase.—Courts do not claim the right of setting aside the verdict in criminal cases.

Mr. Nicholas.—From this right of the jury to consider law and fact in a general verdict, it seems to follow, that counsel ought to be permitted to address a jury on the constitutionality of the law in question;—this leads me back to my first position, that if an act of Congress contravene the Constitution of the United States, a jury have a right to say that it is null * * *; if this jury believed that the Sedition Act is not a law of the land, they cannot find the defendant guilty. The Constitution secures to every man a fair and impartial trial by jury * * *. If ever a precedent is established, that the court can control the jury so as to prevent them from finding a general verdict, their important right, without which every other right is of no value, will be impaired, if not absolutely destroyed. Juries are to decide according to the dictates of conscience and the laws of the country * * *.

* * * I do not deny the right of the court to determine the law, but I deny the right of the court to control the jury; though I have not bestowed a very particular attention on this subject, I am perfectly convinced that the jury have the right I contend for; and, consequently that counsel have a right to address them on that subject.

The act of Congress to which I have alluded, appears to have given to the jury the power of deciding on the law and the fact * * *.

Mr. Hay * * * I entertained doubts at first; but a calm and dispassionate inquiry, and the most temperate investigation and reflection, have led me to believe and to say, that the jury have a right to determine every question which is necessary to determine, before sentence can be pronounced upon the traverser. I contend that the jury have a right to determine whether the writing charged in the indictment to be false, scandalous and malicious, be libel or not. If this question should be decided in the affirmative by the court, I shall endeavour to convince the jury that it is not a libel, because there is no law in force, under the government of the United States, which defines what a libel is, or prescribes its punishment. It is a universal principle of law, that questions of law belong to the court, and that the decision of facts belongs to the jury; but a jury have a right to determine both law and fact in all cases.

Judge Chase * * * interrupted Mr. Hay, and briefly expressed his opinion of the law. And then Mr. Hay folded up and put away his papers, seeming to decline any further argument.

Judge Chase observed, that though he thought it his duty to stop the counsel when mistaking the law, yet he did not wish to interrupt them improperly; that there was no occasion to be captious * * *.

Judge Chase then proceeded. * * *

* * *

To support this indictment on behalf of the government of the United States, it must be proved to the jury; first, that the traverser did write, print, utter or publish * * * a false and scandalous writing against the President of the United States; secondly, that the said writing is false, scandalous, and malicious; and thirdly, that it was published with intent to defame the President, & c., as stated in the statute and charged in the indictment.

If these three facts shall be established to the satisfaction of the jury they must find the traverser guilty, generally, unless he can prove to them the truth of the matter contained in the publication * * *. If all the twenty sets of words, stated in the indictment as charges against the traverser, shall not be proved against him * * *, the jury will acquit him of such of them as shall not be established against him, and also of such of them as he can prove to be true; and they will find him guilty of the residue.

* * * The issue joined, therefore, is, whether the traverser is guilty of the several offences charged in the indictment; and to this issue no evidence is admissible * * * but what is pertinent or applicable to it. The petit jury, to discharge their duty, must first inquire, whether the traverser committed all or any of the facts alleged in the indictment to have been done by him some time before the indictment. If they find that he did commit all or any of the said facts, their next inquiry is, whether the doing such facts have been made criminal and punishable by the statute of the United States, on which the traverser is indicted. * * *

* * * The statute, on which the traverser is indicted, enacts "that the jury who shall try the cause shall have a right to determine the law and the fact, under the direction of the court, as in other cases." By this provision, I understand that a right is given to the jury to determine what the law is in the case before them; and not to decide whether a statute of the United States produced to them, is a law or not, or whether it is void, under an opinion that it is unconstitutional, that is, contrary to the Constitution of the United States. I admit that the jury are to compare the statute with the facts proved, and then to decide whether the acts done are prohibited by the law * * *. This power the jury necessarily possesses, in order to enable them to decide on the guilt or innocence of the person accused. It is one thing to decide what the law is, on the facts proved, and another and a very different thing, to determine that the statute produced is no law. * * *

* * * To determine the validity of the statute, the Constitution of the United States must necessarily be resorted to and considered, and its provisions inquired into. It must be determined whether the statute alleged to be void, because contrary to the Constitution, is prohibited by it expressly or by necessary implication. Was it ever intended, by the framers of the Constitution, or by the people of America, that it should ever be submitted to examination of a jury, to decide what restrictions are expressly or impliedly imposed by it on the national legislature? I cannot possibly believe that Congress intended, by the statute, to grant a right to a petit jury to declare a statute void. * * *

* * * Congress had no authority to vest it in any body whatsoever; because, by the Constitution, * * * this right is expressly granted to the judicial power of the United States, and is recognized by Congress by a perpetual statute. * * *

* * *

It never was pretended, as I ever heard, before this time, that a petit jury in England (from whence our common law is derived,) or in any part of the United States ever exercised such power. If a petit jury can rightfully exercise this power over one statute of Congress, they must have an equal right and power over any other statute, and indeed over all the statutes; for no line can be drawn, no restriction imposed on the exercise of such power; it must rest in discretion only.

If this power be once admitted, petit jurors will be superior to the national legislature, and its laws will be subject to their control. The power to abrogate or to make laws nugatory, is equal to the authority of making them. The evident consequences of this right in juries will be, that a law of Congress will be in operation in one state and not in another. A law to impose taxes will be obeyed in one state and not in another, unless force be employed to compel submission.

* * *

The effects of the exercise of this power by petit jurors may be readily conceived. It appears to me that the right now claimed has a direct tendency to dissolve the Union of the United States, on which, under Divine Providence, our political safety, happiness, and prosperity depend.

* * *

Every man must admit that the power of deciding the constitutionality of any law of the United States, or of any particular state, is one of the greatest and most important powers the people could grant.

Such power is * * * not absolute and unlimited, but confined to such cases only where the law in question shall clearly appear to have been prohibited by the Federal Constitution, and not in any doubtful case. On referring to the ninth section of the first article of the Constitution, there may be seen many restrictions imposed on the powers of the national legislature, and also on the powers of the several state legislatures. Among the special exceptions to their authority, is the power to make ex post facto laws, to lay any capitation, or other direct tax, unless in proportion to the census; to lay any tax or duty on articles exported from any state, & c. & c.

It should be remembered that the judicial power of the United States is co-existent, co-extensive, and co-ordinate with, and altogether independent of, the Federal legislature, or the executive. By the sixth article of the Constitution, among other things, it is declared that the Constitution shall be the supreme law of the land. By the third article, it is established "that the judicial power of the United States shall be vested in one supreme court, and in such other inferior courts as Congress may from time to time ordain and establish; and that the judicial power shall extend to all cases in law and equity, arising under the Constitution and laws of the United States."

Among the cases which may arise under the Constitution, are all the restrictions on the authority of Congress, and of the state legislatures.

It is very clear, that the present case arises under the Constitution, and also under a law of the United States, and therefore it is the very case to which the Constitution declares the judicial powers of the United States shall extend.

* * *

From these considerations I draw this conclusion, that the judicial power of the United States is the only proper and competent authority to decide whether any statute made by Congress (or any of the state legislatures) is contrary to, or in violation of, the Federal Constitution.

* * * [A provision of the Federal Judiciary Act of 1789 states] "that the justices of the Supreme Courts, and the district judges, shall take an oath or affirmation in the following words, to wit:

"I, A.B., do solemnly swear or affirm, that I will administer justice without respect to persons, and do equal right to the poor and to the rich, and that I will faithfully and impartially discharge and perform all the duties incumbent on me as ______, according to the best of my abilities and understanding, agreeably to the Constitution and laws of the United States."

No position can be more clear than that all the federal judges are bound by the solemn obligation of religion, to regulate their decisions agreeably to the Constitution of the United States, and that it is the standard of their determination in all cases that come before them.

I believe that it has been the general and prevailing opinion in all the Union, that the power now wished to be exercised by a jury, properly belonged to the federal courts.

It was alleged that the tax on carriages was considered by the people of this commonwealth to be unconstitutional, and a case was made to submit the question to the Supreme Court of the United States, and they decided that the statute was not unconstitutional, and their decision was acquiesced in.

I have seen a report of a case (Kamper v. Hawkins) decided in 1793, in the general court of this commonwealth, respecting the constitutionality of a law which gave the district courts a power of granting injunctions in certain cases, in which case the judges of the general court [four to one] determined that the law was unconstitutional and void. * * *

* * * It is now contended, that the constitutionality of the laws of Congress should be submitted to the decision of a petit jury. May I ask,

whence this change of opinion? I declare that the doctrine is entirely novel to me, and that I never heard of it before my arrival in this city. * * *

It must be evident, that decisions in the district or circuit courts of the United States will be uniform, or they will become so by the revision and correction of the Supreme Court; and thereby the same principles will pervade all the Union; but the opinions of petit juries will very probably be different in different states.

The decision of courts of justice will not be influenced by political and local principles, and prejudices. If inferior courts commit error, it may be rectified; but if juries make mistakes, there can be no revision or control over their verdicts, and therefore, there can be no mode to obtain uniformity in their decisions. Besides, petit juries are under no obligation by the terms of their oath, to decide the constitutionality of any law; their determination, therefore, will be extra judicial. I should also imagine, that no jury would wish to have a right to determine such great, important, and difficult questions; and I hope no jury can be found, who will exercise the power desired over the statutes of Congress, against the opinion of the federal courts.

I have consulted with my brother, Judge Griffin, and I now deliver the opinion of the court, "That the petit jury have no right to decide on the constitutionality of the statute on which the traverser is indicted; and that, if the jury should exercise that power, they would thereby usurp the authority entrusted by the Constitution of the United States to this court." * * *

The gentlemen of the profession know, that questions have sometimes occurred in state courts, whether acts of assembly had expired, or had been repealed; but no one will say that such questions were ever submitted to a jury.

* * *

Judge Chase concluded with observing, that, if he knew himself, the opinion he had delivered and the reasons offered in its support, flowed not from political motives, or reasons of state, with which he had no concern, and which he conceived never ought to enter courts of justice; but from a deliberate conviction of what the Constitution and the law of the land required. "I hold myself equally bound," said he, "to support the rights of the jury, as the rights of the court." I consider it of the greatest consequence to the administration of justice, that the powers of the court, and the powers of the petit jury, should be kept distinct and separate. I have uniformly delivered the opinion, "that the petit jury have a right to decide the law as well as the fact, in criminal cases;" but it never entered into my mind that they, therefore, had a right to determine the constitutionality of any statute of the United States. * * *

After two hours, the jury returned with a verdict of guilty, upon which the court sentenced the traverser to a fine of two hundred dollars, and an imprisonment of nine months.

JAMES MORTON SMITH, FREEDOM'S FETTERS: THE ALIEN AND SEDITION LAWS AND AMERICAN CIVIL LIBERTIES*

270–274 (1956).

* * * After Congress adjourned in July, 1798, President John Adams made preparations for his usual retreat from the summer heat of Philadelphia for the cool shade of his home in Quincy, Massachusetts. On the twenty-seventh, he and Mrs. Adams passed through Newark, New Jersey, which celebrated the event as a festive occasion. * * * "The Association of Young Men" manned an artillery piece and paraded at the flagstaff while awaiting the president's arrival.

As the Chief magistrate entered Broad Street about eleven o'clock, he was greeted by the firing of the artillery piece, the ringing of church bells, and, as he passed the flagstaff, a chant by the young men who had fired the salute: "Behold the Chief who now commands." Three cheers followed, bells again pealed forth, and as the president's party withdrew into the distance the cannon boomed a sixteen-gun salute.

There was one inebriated Republican, however, who took no delight in the festival. Luther Baldwin happened to be coming toward John Burnet's dram shop when one of the tavern's plain-spoken customers, noting that the cannon was firing after the president had passed, observed to Baldwin: "There goes the President and they are firing at his a__." * * *

Luther, a little merry, replies, that he did not care if they fired thro' [sic] his a__: Then exclaims the dram seller, that is seditious—a considerable collection gathered—and the pretended federalists, being much disappointed that the president had not stopped that they might have had the honor of kissing his hand, bent their malice on poor Luther and the cry was, that he must be punished.

Not until two months after these unguarded remarks did Supreme Court Justice William Cushing arrive in New Jersey to instruct the grand jury of the Circuit Court on the intricacies of the new sedition statute. After hearing his charge, [and after being informed of the remarks of Baldwin and his cronies by the tavernkeeper] the grand jury not only accused Baldwin but also indicted two of his tavern cronies, Brown Clark and a person identified only as Lespenard. [All three eventually pleaded guilty.] * * * For speaking "seditious words tending to defame the President and Government of the United States," both were fined, assessed court costs and expenses, and committed to federal jail until fine and fees were paid.

Baldwin's trial afforded the Republican papers a field day. * * *

"Here's *Liberty* for you," jeered a Newark newspaper in reporting Baldwin's arrest. "When we heard that Luther Baldwin was indicted for sedition," the New York *Argus* agreed, "we supposed that he had been guilty of something criminal. * * * When cognizance is taken of such a ridiculous expression," it concluded, every Republican could see "the extraordinary malignancy of the federal faction."

According to the Argus * * * Royalists in Europe would be pleased to read an account of this curious trial as evidence that their cause "might yet succeed in this country." * * * The editor bluntly charged that "the federalists are resolved that if they cannot force the republicans to admire John Adams, they shall not speak what they think of him." Happily, he concluded, the Democratic–Republicans at least could think their thoughts to themselves without being controlled.

Nothing about the case was overlooked; its every feature became grist for the Republican mill. The only power which the Federalists now lacked, the Newark Centinel asserted, was that of prosecuting and treading underfoot all those who refused "to be duped into their measures." Other opposition newspapers pointed to the rise of the "useful profession of informers" and recommended the tavernkeeper in Newark to any person needing such services. * * *

The Argus [called the tavernkeeper] * * * a "wretched tool, who, for the sake of a little patronage, we need not add, a little pelf, would sacrifice a neighbour, and at the same time know him to be a good citizen, an honest man and a friend to his country." A correspondent from Newark strengthened this hypothesis when he reported that "the *dram-seller,* the celebrated John Burnet," was being considered as the Federalist candidate for coronor. In an ironical letter, the writer, obviously a Republican, argued somewhat facetiously that since the tavernkeeper had risked so much for the president he ought to be rewarded with any office that the people of Newark could bestow on him. Not only had he turned informer; he had "nobly persevered in prosecuting the old fellow for daring to utter such a contemptuous expression of our beloved president, whom every one knows is one of the best of men, and thank God, we have shewn the cursed democrats that we will let none of them speak disrespectfully of any part of that dear man."

* * *

NOTES AND QUESTIONS

1. Historians have argued over whether the Federalist attempts to punish seditious libel represented, as Jefferson reportedly stated, a "reign of

terror," (See, e.g., J. Miller, Crisis in Freedom: The Alien and Sedition Laws and American Civil Liberties (1956)) or whether, instead, these measures were a "natural reaction" to an "extremely indecent campaign of public mendacity" on the part of the Republicans. (See 2 W.W. Crosskey, Politics and the Constitution 767 (1953).) That there *was* such a campaign of public mendacity seems to be confirmed by a brilliant careful study of the Jonathan Robbins matter, involved in the Cooper trial, which clearly demonstrates that Adams was innocent of the charges Cooper made regarding Robbins/Nash. Ruth Wedgwood, "The Revolutionary Martyrdom of Jonathan Robbins," 100 Yale L.J. 229 (1990). The term "reign of terror", of course, is taken from the nearly universal description of the contemporary acts during the French Revolution, where more than 20,000 people lost their lives. Are the efforts of the Federalists comparable?

2. You have studied seditious libel before, in the cases of the Seven Bishops and John Peter Zenger. The two key legal issues in those cases were 1) whether truth was to be a defense to a charge of seditious libel, and 2) whether the jury was to decide on anything other than the question of publication *vel non*. Does the 1798 Act work any change in the common law? Why, incidentally, was a statute needed? Why not simply proceed to prosecute seditious libel under the federal common law of crimes? For writing on the origins and development of the law of libel in America see Leonard W. Levy, Emergence of a Free Press (1985); David M. Rabban, The Ahistorical Historian: Leonard Levy on Freedom of Expression in Early American History, 37 Stan.L.Rev. 795 (1985); and Norman L. Rosenberg, Protecting the Best Men: An Interpretive History of the Law of Libel (1986).

3. Compare the standard of proof of guilt used by Justices Paterson (in *Lyon*) and Chase (in *Cooper*). Paterson, whom we observed dictating conclusions to the jury in the Whiskey Rebels case, told the *Lyon* jury that to return a guilty verdict the jury must be satisfied "beyond all reasonable substantial doubt that the hypothesis of innocence is unsustainable." Chase told the *Cooper* jury that Cooper had the burden of proving his defense, truth, "beyond a marrow." Is this the same standard? Which is correct? How would the different standards affect the outcome of verdicts? Do the different standards suggest different conceptions of government or liberty? Which standard would be most compatible with the Republican theory of the American revolution?

4. One thing on which both Paterson (in *Lyon*) and Chase (in *Callender*) agreed was that it was improper for arguments to be made to the jury on the alleged unconstitutionality of the Sedition Act. Given that the Sedition Act itself said that the jury "shall have a right to determine the law and the fact, under the direction of the court, as in other cases," were the Justices correct? Is Chase's view on this question consistent with his statement in *Cooper* that "If your Constitution was destroyed, so long as the judiciary department remained free * * * the liberties of the people would not be endangered?" What would be the consequences for "national law" if juries could rule on constitutionality? Why might *Virginians* advance such a theory?

What sort of constitutional jurisprudence might you expect a Virginia jury to implement? As you will soon see, Samuel Chase's rulings with regard to the scope of the jury's rights and power were to be made part of the impeachment articles brought against him. What do you believe is the proper assignment of authority regarding facts, law, and constitution in a jury trial? This remains a troubling area of American Law. The difficulty of satisfactorily resolving this issue has been a problem in this country since its founding. See generally, Albert W. Alschuler and Andrew G. Deiss, "A Brief History of the Criminal Jury in the United States," 61 U.Chi.L.Rev. 867 (1994).

5. In each of the cases where we have observed Chase there has been some debate about the province of the jury. Can you determine Chase's attitude with regard to the competence and reliability of jurors? Does his attitude suggest anything about his views regarding the role which he believes the citizenry generally should play in government? If the Republican printers whom Chase excoriates were making such notorious, scurrilous, and unfounded accusations; if, in short, they were so wide of the mark; how can Chase be concerned that they will have a negative effect on popular attitudes toward government? Who, or what, does Chase fear?

6. Consider the conduct of Justice Chase in the *Callender* trial. You are not given the full report of the case, but you have enough to give you the flavor of the proceedings. Do you agree with the legal rulings made by Chase? What about Chase's attitude during this trial? Do you notice anything unusual? Chase indicated that the opinions on the law which he delivered "flowed not from political motives, or reasons of state, with which he had no concern, and which he conceived never ought to enter courts of justice; but from a deliberate conviction of what the Constitution and the law of the land required." Do you agree? The court, after the guilty verdict in *Callender,* fined the defendant $200, and sentenced him to a term of nine months. Was this a severe penalty? For a spirited argument that the *Callender* case had "nothing to do with democrats versus aristocrats, or liberals versus republicans," and involved instead a conflict between a nationalizing judiciary and "the far older and more powerful tradition of localism," see Kathryn Preyer, "*United States v. Callender:* Judge and Jury in a Republican Society," in Maeva Marcus, editor, Origins of the Federal Judiciary: Essays on the Judiciary Act of 1789, 173, 188–189 (1992). Do you agree with Ms. Preyer?

7. What does the material on the *Baldwin* case reveal about the good faith of the Federalists? Can you relate the attitude of the *Baldwin* court to the attitude of the courts in the treason trials? Do the facts surrounding the *Baldwin* prosecution differ from the facts of the other cases in this section? If you were a Republican, over which trials would you be the most upset? On the other hand, since all you have to go on, regarding the *Baldwin* trial, are accounts from the Jeffersonian–Republican press, can you be certain that you have the full story? Whom do you find more trustworthy, Chase, Adams, Paterson, and their "Federalist" brethren, or Lyons, Cooper, Callender, Wirt, Hay, Nicholas, and their Jeffersonian colleagues?

8. Were the Alien and Sedition Acts unconstitutional, as Jefferson and Madison argued? For a fine history of antebellum developments in the area of free speech, see the acclaimed Michael Kent Curtis, Free Speech, "The People's Darling Privilege": Struggles for Freedom of Expression in American History (2000). In a review essay on Curtis's book Mark A. Graber concludes that "[p]lausible Arguments were made in 1798 that the Alien and Sedition Acts were unconstitutional, the most famous being the Virginia and Kentucky Resolutions. The problem from the perspective of 1791 is that, in 1798, equally plausible arguments could be made that the Alien and Sedition Acts were constitutional." Following Curtis, Graber suggests that "the Fourteenth Amendment helped settle the meaning of the First Amendment. Reconstruction Republicans constitutionalized one plausible interpretation of the antebellum Constitution [The Alien and Sedition Acts were unconstitutional] while rejecting what had previously been an alternative plausible interpretation of that text." Mark A. Graber, "Antebellum Perspectives on Free Speech," 10 Wm. & Mary Bill of Rights J. 779 (2002). See also, for an incisive review of Curtis's book which compares governmental attempts to suppress speech in the past with contemporary efforts connected to the war on terrorism, Paul Finkelman, Book Review, 10 Wm. & Mary. Bill of Rts. J. 813 (2002). For a comment on the perplexing nature of Jefferson's views regarding seditious political expression, see Michael P. Downey, Note: "The Jeffersonian Myth in Supreme Court Sedition Jurisprudence," 76 Wash. U.L.Q. 683 (1998). For a spirited account of the controversy over seditious libel in the early republic in general and the *Cooper* Trial in particular, see Peter Charles Hoffer, The Free Press Crisis of 1800: Thomas Cooper's Trial for Seditious Libel (2011). Professor Hoffer, one of the most prolific and talented of American legal historians, while seeking objectively to evaluate the controversy, still stoutly maintains that were he alive at the time, he would have felt compelled to write a check to the legal defense fund for Cooper. Id., at xi. Nevertheless, it is noteworthy that Hoffer concludes with regard to Chase's treatment of the defendant, "one can say that the trial was, on balance, fair. It was the law that was censurable." Id., at 110. Do you agree?

9. Soon after the *Callender* case, the event which all God-fearing Federalists had been dreading, the Presidential election of the man they believed to be a shameless atheist and vivisectionist, Thomas Jefferson, occurred. One of the most prominent targets of the new rulers of the federal government was to be Samuel Chase. The following materials are drawn from his trial pursuant to an impeachment for "high crimes and misdemeanors." As you examine these materials, determine how you would have voted if you were a member of the Senate which tried Chase.

E. THE IMPEACHMENT OF SAMUEL CHASE

1. CHASE'S CHARGE TO THE BALTIMORE GRAND JURY (1803)

SAMUEL H. SMITH AND THOMAS LLOYD, II TRIAL OF SAMUEL CHASE, AN ASSOCIATE JUSTICE OF THE SUPREME COURT OF THE UNITED STATES, IMPEACHED BY THE HOUSE OF REPRESENTATIVES, FOR HIGH CRIMES AND MISDEMEANORS, BEFORE THE SENATE OF THE UNITED STATES*

Appendix, pp. v–viii (1805).

* * *

It is essentially necessary at all times, but more particularly at the present, that the public mind should be truly informed; and that our citizens should entertain correct principles of government, and fixed ideas of their social rights. It is a very easy task to deceive or mislead the great body of the people by propagating plausible, but false doctrines; for the bulk of mankind are governed by their passions and not by reason.

Falsehood can be more readily disseminated than truth, and the latter is heard with reluctance if repugnant to popular prejudice. From the year 1776, I have been a decided and avowed advocate for a representative or republican form of government, as since established by our state and national constitutions. It is my sincere wish that freemen should be governed by their representatives, fairly and freely elected by that class of citizens described in our bill of rights, who have property in, a common interest with, and an attachment to, the community.

* * * [T]he history of mankind (in ancient and modern times) informs us "that a monarchy may be free, and that a republic may be a tyranny." The true test of liberty is in the practical enjoyment of protection to the person and the property of the citizen, from all enquiry. Where the same laws govern the whole society without any distinction, and there is no power to dispense with the execution of the laws; where justice is impartially and speedily administered, and the poorest man in the community may obtain redress against the most wealthy and powerful, * * * in that country the people are free. This is our present situation.—Where law is uncertain, partial or arbitrary; where justice is not impartially administered to all; where property is insecure, and the person is liable to insult and violence without redress by law, the people are not free, whatever

* Hereafter cited as "CHASE TRIAL."

may be their form of government. To this situation, I greatly fear we are fast approaching.

* * * [T]he late alteration of the federal judiciary by the abolition of the office of the sixteen circuit judges, and the recent change in our state constitution by the establishing of universal suffrage, * * * will, in my judgment, take away all security for property and personal liberty. The independence of the national judiciary is already shaken to its foundation, and the virtue of the people alone can restore it. The independence of the judges of this state will be entirely destroyed, if the bill for the abolition of the two supreme courts [is enacted]. The change of the state constitution, by allowing universal suffrage, will, in my opinion, certainly and rapidly destroy all protection to property, and all security to personal liberty; and our republican constitution will sink into a mobocracy, the worst of all possible governments.

* * *

I cannot but remember the great and patriotic characters by whom your state constitution was framed. I cannot but recollect that attempts were then made in favor of universal suffrage; and to render the judges dependent upon the legislature. You may believe that the gentlemen who framed your constitution, possessed the full confidence of the people of Maryland, and that they were esteemed for their talents and patriotism, and for their public and private virtues. You must have heard that many of them held the highest civil and military stations, and that they, at every risk and danger, assisted to obtain and establish your independence. * * * With great concern I observe, that the sons of some of these characters have united to pull down the beautiful fabric of wisdom and republicanism that their fathers erected!

The declarations respecting the natural rights of man, which originated from the claim of the British parliament to make laws to bind America in all cases whatsoever; the publications since that period, of visionary and theoretical writers, asserting that men in a state of society, are entitled to exercise rights which they possessed in a state of nature; and the modern doctrines by our late reformers, that all men in a state of society, are entitled to enjoy equal liberty and equal rights, have brought this mighty mischief upon us; and I fear that it will rapidly progress, until peace and order, freedom and property shall be destroyed. * * *

I have long since subscribed to the opinion, that there could be no rights of man in a state of nature, previous to the institution of society; and that liberty properly speaking, could not exist in a state of nature. I do not believe that any number of men ever existed together in a state of nature, without some head, leader or chief, whose advice they followed, and whose precepts they obeyed. * * * The great object for which men establish any form of government is to obtain security to their persons and property from violence; destroy the security to either and you tear up society by the roots. It appears to me that the institution of government is really no sacrifice made, as some writers contend, to natural liberty, for I think that previous to the formation of some species of government, a state of liberty could not exist. It seems to me that personal liberty and rights can only be acquired by becoming a member of a community, which gives the protection of the whole to every individual. * * * From thence I conclude that liberty and rights, (and also property) must spring out of civil society, and must be forever subject to the modification of particular governments. * * * I cheerfully subscribe to the doctrine of equal liberty and equal rights, if properly explained. I understand by equality of liberty and rights, only this, that every citizen, without respect to property or station, should enjoy an equal share of civil liberty; an equal protection from the laws, and an equal security for his person and property. Any other interpretation of these terms, is in my judgment, destructive of all government and all laws. * * * Will justice be impartially administered by judges dependant on the legislature for their continuance in office, and also for their support? Will liberty or property be protected or secured, by laws made by representatives chosen by electors, who have no property in, a common interest with, or attachment to the community?

NOTES AND QUESTIONS

1. It was the delivery of this charge which inexorably led to Chase's impeachment by the Jeffersonian-controlled House of Representatives, and his trial in the Senate. Have you encountered any of these thoughts on government previously in your reading for this course? What was so exceptionable about this charge? Is it Chase's statement that "the bulk of mankind are governed by their passions and not by reason?" Could it be his idea of "representative or republican" form of government? Do not forget that the party which opposed Chase often called themselves "Republican." How did their ideas on government differ from Chase's? Would they have shared Chase's notion that those who should vote to elect representatives should be those "who have property in, a common interest with, and an attachment to, the community?" Who are the true "Republicans?" See on this point Stephen B. Presser, Recapturing the Constitution 32–49 (1994).

2. Chase seems to have been agitated by three recent developments. The first was at the national level, the repeal of the Judiciary Act of 1801 by the Jeffersonian Congress. This repeal resulted in the abolition of the sixteen Federal Circuit judgeships which the 1801 Act had created, and which the Federalist President, John Adams, had filled in the closing days of his administration. Since that time, as you may know, the 1801 Act has been known as the "Midnight Judges' Act." See generally the classic account, Kathryn Turner, The Midnight Judges, 109 U.Pa.L.Rev. 494 (1961). Adams had filled the new judgeships with the party faithful, and the new administration was anxious to repeal the act (and get rid of the new judges) even though the act contained many provisions which made access to the federal courts speedier

and more efficient. Was the repeal constitutional? Was the repeal a wise measure?

3. The second and third new thorns in Chase's side were the attempts to circumscribe the judiciary in Maryland and the recent change in the Maryland Constitution to provide for "universal sufferage." Why would Chase regard these changes as dangerous? For an analysis of suffrage and the American Revolution see Robert J. Steinfeld, "Property and Suffrage in the Early American Republic," 41 Stan.L.Rev. 335 (1989). Consider how Chase would define "liberty" and "equality," and his discussion of "civil society" and the "state of nature." Whose set of attitudes about liberty, equality, and natural rights was Chase attacking?

2. THE POLITICS OF THE IMPEACHMENT OF SAMUEL CHASE

RICHARD E. ELLIS, THE JEFFERSONIAN CRISIS: COURTS AND POLITICS IN THE YOUNG REPUBLIC*

76–82 (1971).

* * *

* * * A prominent and militant proponent of colonial rights in the Maryland legislature during the 1760s, [Chase] had signed the Declaration of Independence and served as an active member of the Continental Congress between 1775–1778. His congressional career was suddenly cut short in 1778, when Alexander Hamilton denounced him for using privileged information to speculate in the flour market. Chase returned to Baltimore, where he continued to speculate in mercantile and land ventures, practiced law, rebuilt his political reputation, and became an influential Anti–Federalist leader.

After the ratification of the Constitution, for reasons that are obscure, Chase became an ardent Federalist. A hard worker, willing to fight uncompromisingly for his beliefs, his turbulent disposition made him an ally who often proved more of a liability than an asset. * * *

In the years immediately following Chase's promotion to the nation's highest tribunal, he conducted himself well and delivered several influential and learned decisions. But at the same time he was becoming increasingly aroused by vitriolic Republican attacks upon the Adams administration, until, finally, when he made his circuit ride in 1800, his partisan nature got the better of him. * * *

* * *

Yet, despite the popular groundswell against Chase and the desire of radical Republicans for impeachment proceedings, Jefferson, after becoming President, adopted a cautious attitude toward the Judge. This was part of his larger policy to establish a live-and-let-live arrangement with the judiciary, and it implied the administration's willingness to forget past excesses in return for good behavior in the future. * * *

Chase, however, increasingly bitter, adopted the hard line policy of the High Federalists and totally rejected any kind of accommodation with the administration. * * *

Less than two months later, on 2 May 1803, Chase delivered his charge to the federal grand jury in Baltimore, a charge that was soon to be famous. * * *

Chase's charge was published in a Baltimore newspaper, and an outraged Republican member of the Maryland legislature sent a copy to Jefferson. * * * Jefferson reacted immediately. He wrote to [Republican Congressman] Joseph Hooper Nicholson, asking "Ought the seditious and official attack on the principles of our Constitution and of a State to go unpunished? And to whom so pointedly as yourself will the public look for the necessary measures?" Because Republican conversations about Chase almost always turned to impeachment, and because Nicholson had definite Old Republican sympathies * * * there can be no doubt that the President was giving his consent to having Chase removed. It appears that Jefferson expected the impeachment of Chase to be hazardous politically, for he added, significantly, "for myself, it is better that I should not interfere."

* * * Nicholson * * * requested the opinion of the Speaker of the House, Nathaniel Macon. Macon indicated his own dislike for the Judge, but pointed out that since Nicholson would probably be appointed to the Supreme Court if Chase were convicted, it would be impolitic for him to prosecute. He then questioned the legitimacy of impeaching Chase for his political opinions. Thinking, undoubtedly, of the increasing number of Republicans using the state benches for partisan purposes, he warned, "it deserves the most serious consideration before a single step be taken." * * *

Throughout the spring and summer of 1803, the Republican press, led by the National Intelligencer, assailed Chase, but no official action was taken. * * * Then, suddenly, on 5 January 1804, John Randolph rose in the House and demanded an investigation of Chase's conduct. Only after three days of debate and the extension of the investigation of Chase to encompass the activities of Richard Peters, district judge of Pennsylvania, did the House pass the motion. The inclusion of Peters, made at the request of Pennsylvania's militant Republicans, was designed to discredit him, but no one seriously expected his impeachment. The committee, headed by Randolph, reported its findings on 6 March. It cleared Peters, but recommended impeachment proceedings against Chase. Five days later the report was approved by a vote of 73 to 32. * * *

Meanwhile, Chase, though publicly silent, was busy. He appointed Robert Goodloe Harper his chief counsel, and between them they began to solicit the aid of the most distinguished Federalist lawyers in the country. "Fees, of course," wrote Harper, "are out of the question."

> If you concur with me in opinion, that this is a great public cause, in which the honour of the federal party, the independence of the judiciary, and even the personal safety of the judges are involved, you will require no further motives for uniting with those who place themselves in the breach, and endeavor to resist the terror which threatens us with ruin. * * *

Chase, never an easy opponent, was under these circumstances formidable. True, he had acted with partiality in the courtroom. Richard Peters, for example, admitted that he "never sat with him without pain, as he was forever getting into some intemperate and unnecessary squabble." But it was one thing to accuse a Supreme Court justice of excessive partisanship, and another to convict him of criminal behavior. * * *

3. THE TEXT OF THE IMPEACHMENT ARTICLES*

I Chase Trial 5–8

Article I

That, unmindful of the solemn duties of his office, and contrary to the sacred obligation by which he stood bound to discharge them "faithfully and impartially, and without respect to persons," the said Samuel Chase, on the trial of John Fries, charged with treason * * * did, in his judicial capacity, conduct himself in a manner highly arbitrary, oppressive, and unjust, viz.

1. In delivering an opinion, in writing, on the question of law, on the construction of which the defense of the accused materially depended, tending to prejudice the minds of the jury against the case of the said John Fries, the prisoner, before counsel had been heard in his defense.

2. In restricting the counsel for the said Fries from recurring to such English authorities as they believed apposite, or from citing certain statutes of the United States, which they deemed illustrative of the positions upon which they intended to rest the defense of their client.

3. In debarring the prisoner from his constitutional privilege of addressing the jury (through his counsel) on the law, as well as on the fact, which was to determine his guilt, or innocence, and at the same time en-

* In the materials which follow, references to Articles II, V, VI, and VII of the Impeachment Articles are omitted. These were principally concerned with arcane procedural matters, and the final vote on them in the Senate was decidedly in favor of Chase.

deavoring to wrest from the jury their indisputable right to hear argument, and determine upon the question of law, as well as on the question of fact, involved in the verdict which they were required to give.

In consequence of which irregular conduct of the said Samuel Chase, as dangerous to our liberties, as it is novel to our laws and usages, the said John Fries was deprived of the right, secured to him by the eighth article amendatory of the constitution, and was condemned to death without having been heard by counsel, in his defense, to the disgrace of the character of the American bench, in manifest violation of law and justice, and in open contempt of the rights of juries, on which, ultimately, rest the liberty and safety of the American people.

Article III*

That, with intent to oppress and procure the conviction of the prisoner, the evidence of John Taylor * * * was not permitted by the said Samuel Chase to be given in, on pretence that the said witness could not prove the truth of the whole of one of the charges, contained in the indictment, although the said charge embraced more than one fact.

Article IV

That the conduct of the said Samuel Chase, was marked, during the whole course of the said trial, by manifest injustice, partiality, and intemperance; viz.

1. In compelling the prisoner's counsel to reduce to writing, and submit to the inspection of the court, for their admission, or rejection, all questions which the said counsel meant to propound to the above named John Taylor, the witness.

2. In refusing to postpone the trial, although an affidavit was regularly filed, stating the absence of material witnesses on behalf of the accused; and although it was manifest, that, with the utmost diligence, the attendance of such witnesses could not have been procured at that term.

3. In the use of unusual, rude, and contemptuous expressions towards the prisoner's counsel; and in falsely insinuating that they wished to excite the public fears and indignation, and to produce that insubordination to law, to which the conduct of the judge did, at the same time, manifestly tend:

4. In repeated and vexatious interruptions of the said counsel, on the part of the said judge, which, at length, induced them to abandon their cause and their client, who was thereupon convicted and condemned to fine and imprisonment:

5. In an indecent solicitude, manifested by the said Samuel Chase, for the conviction of the accused, unbecoming even a public prosecutor,

* Articles III and IV dealt with Chase's conduct in the Callender trial.

but highly disgraceful to the character of a judge as it was subversive of justice.

Article VIII

And whereas mutual respect and confidence between the government of the United States and those of the individual states, and between the people and those governments, respectively, are highly conducive to that public harmony, without which there can be no public happiness, yet the said Samuel Chase * * * did, at a circuit court, * * * held at Baltimore, * * * pervert his official right and duty to address the grand jury then and there assembled * * * for the purpose of delivering to the said grand jury an intemperate and inflammatory political harangue, with intent to excite the fears and resentment of the said grand jury, and of the good people of Maryland against their state government, and constitution, a conduct highly censurable in any, but peculiarly indecent and unbecoming in a judge of the supreme court of the United States: and moreover, that the said Samuel Chase * * * did, in a manner highly unwarrantable, endeavor to excite the odium of the said grand jury, and of the good people of Maryland, against the government of the United States, by delivering opinions, which, even if the judicial authority were competent to their expression, on a suitable occasion and in a proper manner, were at that time and as delivered by him, highly indecent, extra-judicial, and tending to prostitute the high judicial character with which he was invested, to the low purpose of an electioneering partizan.

And the House of Representatives * * * do demand that the said Samuel Chase may be put to answer the said crimes and misdemeanors, and that such proceedings, examinations, trials, and judgments may be thereupon had and given, as are agreeable to law and justice * * *.

4. CHASE'S ANSWER TO THE ARTICLES OF IMPEACHMENT

I Chase Trial 25–103

[Chase begins with a defense of his delivery of his written opinion in the *Fries* case. Chase refers to himself in the third person.]

* * *

With respect to the opinion, which is alleged to have been delivered by this respondent, at the above-mentioned trial, he begs leave to lay before this honorable court, the true state of that transaction, and to call its attention to some facts and considerations, by which his conduct on that subject will, he presumes, be fully justified.

The constitution of the United States, in the third section of the third article, declares that "treason against the United States, shall consist only in levying war against them, or in adhering to their enemies, giving them aid and comfort."

* * *

[Chase proceeds to explain the action he took after considering "with great care and deliberation" the indictment against Fries;]

* * * [F]inding from the three overt facts of treason which it charged, that the question of law arising upon it, was the same question which had already been decided twice in the same court, on solemn argument and deliberation, and once in that very case, he considered the law as settled by those decisions, with the correctness of which on full consideration he was entirely satisfied; and by the authority of which he should have deemed himself bound, even had he regarded the question as doubtful in itself. They are moreover in perfect conformity with the uniform tenor of decisions in the courts of England and Great Britain, from the revolution, in 1688, to the present time, which, in his opinion, added greatly to their weight and authority.

And surely he need not urge to this honorable court, the correctness, the importance, and the absolute necessity of adhering to principles of law once established, and of considering the law as finally settled, after repeated and solemn decisions by courts of competent jurisdiction. A contrary principle would unsettle the basis of our whole system of jurisprudence, hitherto our safeguard and our boast; would reduce the law of the land, and subject the rights of the citizen, to the arbitrary will, the passions, or the caprice of the judge in each particular case; and would substitute the varying opinions of various men, instead of that fixed, permanent rule, in which the very essence of law consists. * * *

Under the influence of these considerations, this respondent drew up an opinion on the law arising from the overt acts stated in the * * * indictment * * * conformable to the decisions before given as above mentioned, and which he sent to his colleague the said Richard Peters, for his consideration. That gentleman returned it to this respondent, with some amendments * * *, but not in any manner touching the substance.

The opinion thus agreed to, this respondent thought it proper to communicate to the prisoner's counsel * * *.

In the first place, this respondent considered himself and the court, as bound by the authority of the former decisions; especially the last of them, which was on the same case. * * * It was not suggested or understood, that any new evidence was to be offered; and he knew that if any should be offered, which could vary the case, it would render wholly inapplicable both the opinion and the former decisions on which it was founded. And he could not and did not suppose, that the prisoner's counsel would be desirous of wasting very precious time, in addressing to the court an useless argument, on a point which that court held itself precluded from deciding in their favor. He therefore conceived that it would be rendering the counsel a service and a favor, to apprise them before hand of the view which the court had taken of the subject; so as to let them see in time, the necessity of endeavoring to produce new testimony, which might vary the case, and take it out of the authority of former decisions.

Secondly, There were more than one hundred civil causes then depending in the said court * * *. Many of those causes had already been subjected to great delay, and it was the peculiar duty of this respondent, as presiding judge, to take care, that as little time as possible should be unnecessarily consumed * * *. He did believe, that an early communication of the court's opinion, might tend to the saving of time * * *.

Thirdly, As the court held itself bound by the former decisions, and could not therefore alter its opinion in consequence of any argument; and as it was the duty of the court to charge the jury on the law, in all cases submitted to their consideration, he knew that this opinion must not only be made known at some period or other of the trial, but must at the end of the trial be expressly delivered to the jury by him * * * and he could not suppose and cannot yet imagine, that an opinion * * * could make any additional impression on their minds, from the circumstance of its being intimated to the counsel before the trial began, in the hearing of those who might be afterwards sworn on the jury.

And, lastly, it was then his opinion, and still is, that it is the duty of every court of this country * * * to guard the jury against erroneous impressions respecting the laws of the land. He well knows, that it is the right of juries in criminal cases, to give a general verdict of acquittal, which cannot be set aside on account of its being contrary to law, and that hence results the power of juries, to decide on the law as well as on the facts, in all criminal cases. This power he holds to be a sacred part of our legal privileges, which he never has attempted, and never will attempt to abridge or to obstruct. But he also knows, that in the exercise of this power, it is the duty of the jury to govern themselves by the laws of the land, over which they have no dispensing power; and their right to expect and receive from the court, all the assistance which it can give, for rightly understanding the law. To withhold this assistance, in any manner whatever; to forbear to give it in that way, which may be most effectual for preserving the jury from error and mistake; would be an abandonment or forgetfulness of duty * * *. In this case, therefore, where the question of law arising on the indictment, had been finally settled by authoritative decisions, it was the duty of the court * * * early to apprise the counsel and the jury of these decisions, and their effect, so as to save the former from the danger of making an improper attempt, to mislead the jury in a matter of law, and the jury from having their minds preoccupied by erroneous impressions.

* * *

[Chase's long argument explaining the legal accuracy of his opinion is omitted.]

If, however, this opinion were erroneous, this respondent would be far less censurable than his predecessors, by whose example he was led astray, and by whose authority he considered himself bound. Was it an error to consider himself bound * * *? If it were, he was led into the error by the uniform course of judicial proceedings, in this country and in England * * *. Can such an error be a crime or misdemeanor?

If, on the other hand, the opinion be in itself correct * * * could the expression of a correct opinion on the law, wherever and however made, mislead the jury, infringe their rights, or give an improper bias to their judgments? Could truth excite improper prejudice? * * * And is not that a new kind of offence, in this country at least, which consists in telling the truth, and giving a correct exposition of the law.

As to the second specific charge * * * "of restricting the counsel for the said Fries, from recurring to such English authorities as they believed apposite * * * " this respondent admits that he did * * * express it as his opinion to the * * * counsel * * * "that the decisions in England, in cases of indictments for treason at common law, against the person of the king, ought not to be read to the jury, on trials for treason under the constitution and statutes of the United States; because such decisions could not inform, but might mislead and deceive the jury: that any decisions on cases of treason, in the courts of England, before the revolution of 1688, ought to have very little influence in the courts of the United States * * *."

* * * The counsellors admitted to practice in any court of justice are, in his opinion, and according to universal practice, to be considered as officers of such courts, and ministers of justice therein, and as such subject to the direction and control of the court, as to their conduct in its presence, and in conducting the defence of criminals on trial before it.—As counsel, they owe to the person accused diligence, fidelity, and secrecy, and to the court and jury, due and correct information, according to the best of their knowledge and ability * * *. The court * * * is bound in duty, to decide and direct what evidence, whether by record or by precedents of decisions in courts of justice, is proper to be admitted for the establishment of any matter of law or fact. Consequently, should counsel attempt to read to a jury, as a law still in force, a statute which had been repealed, or a decision which had been reversed, or the judgments of courts in countries whose laws have no connection with ours, it would be the duty of the court to interpose, and prevent such an imposition from being practised

on the jury. For these reasons, this respondent thinks that his conduct was correct, in expressing to the counsel for Fries, the opinions stated above. He is not bound to answer here for the correctness of those principles * * * but merely for the correctness of his motives * * *. A contrary opinion would convert this honorable court, from a court of impeachment into a court of appeals; and would lead directly to the strange absurdity, that whenever the judgment of an inferior court should be reversed on appeal or writ of error, the judges of that court must be convicted of high crimes and misdemeanors, and turned out of office * * * and that crimes may be committed without any criminal intention. * * *

* * * [The correctness of motives in delivering opinions] ought to be presumed, unless the contrary appear by some direct proof, or by some violent presumption, arising from his general conduct on the trial, or from the glaring impropriety of the opinion itself. * * *

Do the opinions now under consideration bear any of these marks? * * * [T]here has existed in England, no such thing as treason at common law, since the year 1350, when the statute of the 25th Edward III, chap. 2 * * * was passed. Is it perfectly clear that decisions made before that statute, 450 years ago, when England, together with the rest of Europe, was still wrapped in the deepest gloom of ignorance and barbarism * * * when law, justice and reason, were perpetually trampled under foot by feudal oppression and feudal anarchy; when, under an able and vigorous monarch, every thing was adjudged to be treason which he thought fit to call so, and under a weak one, nothing was considered as treason which turbulent, powerful, and rebellious nobles thought fit to perpetrate: is it perfectly clear that decisions, made at such a time, and under such circumstances, ought to be received by the courts of this country as authorities to govern their decisions, or lights to guide the understanding of juries? * * *

* * * [A]fter the above mentioned proceedings had taken place in the said trial, it was postponed until the next day * * * when at the meeting of the court, this respondent told both the above mentioned counsel for the prisoner, "that to prevent any misunderstanding of any thing that had passed the day before, he would inform them, that although the court retained the same opinion of the law * * * yet the counsel would be permitted to offer arguments to the court, for the purpose of shewing them that they were mistaken in the law * * * and also that the counsel would be permitted to argue before the petit jury, that the court were mistaken in the law." * * *

After some observations by the said William Lewis and Alexander James Dallas, they both declared to the court, "that they did not any longer consider themselves as the counsel for John Fries the prisoner." This respondent then asked the said John Fries, whether he wished the court to appoint other counsel for his defense? He refused to have other counsel assigned; in which he acted, as this respondent believes and charges, by the advice of the said William Lewis and Alexander James Dallas; whereupon the court ordered the said trial to be had on the next day * * *.

And this respondent * * * saith, that * * * the * * * charge * * * "that the said Fries was thereby deprived of the benefit of counsel for his defence," is not true. He insists that the said Fries was deprived of the benefit of counsel, not by any misconduct of this respondent, but by the conduct and advice of the above mentioned William Lewis and Alexander James Dallas, who * * * withdrew from his defence, and advised him to refuse other counsel when offered to him by the court, under pretence that the law had been prejudged, and their liberty of conducting the defence, according to their own judgment, improperly restricted by this respondent; but in reality because they knew the law and the facts to be against them, and the case to be desperate, and supposed that their withdrawing themselves under this pretence, might excite odium against the court; might give rise to an opinion that the prisoner had not been fairly tried; and in the event of a conviction * * * might aid the prisoner in an application to the President for a pardon. * * *

As little can this respondent be justly charged with having by any conduct of his, endeavored to "wrest from the jury their indisputable right to hear argument, and determine upon the question of law as well as the question of fact involved in the verdict which they were required to give." * * * It was expressly stated in the copy of his opinion delivered as above set forth to William Lewis, that the jury had a right to determine the law as well as the fact * * *. This respondent believes that the said William Lewis did not read the opinion delivered to him as aforesaid, except a very small part at the beginning of it, and of course, acted upon it without knowing its contents: and that the said Alexander James Dallas read no part of the said opinion until about a year ago * * *.

* * *

[Chase then turns to the charge that he improperly refused to admit testimony by John Taylor in the Callender trial.]

The indictment against James Thompson Callender * * * consisted of two distinct and separate counts, each of which contained twenty distinct and independent charges * * *. Each of those sets of words was charged as a libel against John Adams, as President of the United States, and the twelfth charge embraced the following words, "He (meaning President Adams) was a professed aristocrat; he proved faithful and serviceable to the British interest." The defence set up was confined to this charge, and was rested upon the truth of the words. * * * It was to prove the truth of these words, that John Taylor, the person mentioned in the article of impeachment now under consideration, was offered as a witness. It can hardly be necessary to remind this honorable court, that when an indictment for a libel contains several distinct charges, founded on distinct sets of words, the party accused, who in such cases is called the "traverser," must be convicted, unless he makes a sufficient defence against every charge. His innocence on one, does not prove him innocent on the others. * * * This conviction on nineteen charges, would put the traverser as completely in the power of the court, by which the amount of the fine and the term of the imprisonment were to be fixed, as a conviction upon all the twenty charges. * * * If then this respondent were desirous of procuring the conviction of the traverser, he was sure of his object, without rejecting the testimony of John Taylor. * * *

That the court did not feel this vindictive spirit, is clearly evinced by the moderation of the punishment, which actually was inflicted on the traverser, after he was convicted of the whole twenty charges. Instead of two thousand dollars, he was fined only two hundred, and was sentenced to only nine months imprisonment, instead of two years. And this respondent avers * * * that in this decision, as well as in every other given in the course of the trial, he fully and freely concurred with his colleague, Judge Griffin.

[Chase next defends the correctness of his ruling.]

* * * It is clear that no words are indictable as libellous, except such as expressly, or by plain implication, charge the person against whom they are published, with some offence either legal or moral. To be an "aristocrat," is not in itself an offence, either legal or moral * * * neither was it an offence either legal or moral, for Mr. Adams to be "faithful and serviceable to the British interest," unless he thereby betrayed or endangered the interests of his own country; which does not necessarily follow, and is not directly alleged in the publication. These two phrases, therefore, taken separately, charge Mr. Adams with no offence of any kind; and, consequently, could not be indictable as libellous: but taken together, they convey the implication that Mr. Adams, being an "aristocrat," that is, an enemy to the republican government of his own country, had subserved the British interest, against the interest of his own country; which would, in his situation, have been an offence both moral and legal; to charge him with it was, therefore, libellous.

Admitting, therefore, these two phrases to constitute one distinct charge, and one entire offence, this respondent considers and states it to be law, that no justification which went to part only of the offence, could be received. The plea of justification must always answer the whole charge, or it is bad * * *; for this plain reason, that the object of the plea is to shew the party's innocence; and he cannot be innocent, if the accusation against him be supported in part. * * * Evidence, therefore, which goes only to justify the charge in part, cannot be received. It is not indeed necessary, that the whole of this evidence should be given by one witness.

The justification may consist of several facts, some of which may be proved by one person, and some by another. But proof, in such cases, must be offered as to the whole, or it cannot be received.

In the case under consideration, no proof was offered as to the whole matter contained in the twelfth article [because no evidence was offered to support the implication that John Adams intended to betray the interests of his own country in favor of British interests.] No witness except the above mentioned John Taylor, was produced or mentioned.

* * *

For these reasons this respondent did concur with his colleague, the said Cyrus Griffin, in rejecting the three above mentioned questions; but not any other testimony that the said John Taylor might have been able to give. * * *

If his error was an honest one, which as his colleague also fell into it, might in charity be supposed; and, as there is not a shadow of evidence to the contrary, must in law be presumed; he cannot, for committing it, be convicted of any offence, much less a high crime and misdemeanor, for which he must, on conviction, be deprived of his office.

* * *

The fourth article of impeachment alleges, that during the whole course of the trial of James Thompson Callender, above mentioned, the conduct of this respondent was marked by "manifest injustice, partiality, and intemperance;" and five particular instances of the "injustice, partiality, and intemperance," are adduced.

* * *

This respondent, in answer to this part of the article now under consideration, admits that the court, consisting of himself and the above mentioned Cyrus Griffin, did require the counsel for the traverser, on the trial of James Thompson Callender, above mentioned, to reduce to writing the questions which they intended to put to the said witness. But he denies that it is more his act than the act of his colleague, who fully concurred in this measure. The measure, as he apprehends and insists, was strictly legal and proper; * * * if he, in common with his colleague, committed an error, it was an error into which the best and wisest men might have honestly fallen.

* * * [A]ccording to our laws, evidence, whether oral or written, may be rejected and prevented from going before the jury, on various grounds.—1st, For incompetency: where the source from which the evidence is attempted to be drawn, is an improper source: as if a witness were to be called who was infamous, or interested in the event of the suit

* * *. 2d, For irrelevancy: when the evidence offered is not such, as in law will warrant the jury to infer the fact intended to be proved; or where that fact, if proved, is immaterial to the issue. * * *

It being thus the right and duty of a court before which a trial takes place, to inform itself of the nature of the evidence offered, so as to be able to judge whether such evidence be proper, it results necessarily that they have a right to require, that any question intended to be put to a witness, should be reduced to writing, for that is the form in which their deliberation upon it may be most perfect, and their judgment will be most likely to be correct. * * * When the testimony of John Taylor was offered, the court enquired of the traverser's counsel, what that witness was to prove. The statement of his testimony given in answer, induced the court to suspect that it was irrelevant and inadmissible. They therefore, that they might have an opportunity for more careful and accurate consideration, called upon the counsel to state in writing, the questions intended to be put to the witness. * * *

The next circumstance * * * is [the] refusal to postpone the trial of the said James Thompson Callender, "although an affidavit was regularly filed, stating the absence of material witnesses on behalf of the accused, and although it was manifest that with the utmost diligence, the attendance of such witnesses could not have been procured at that term."

This respondent * * * admits, that * * * the traverser's counsel did move the court * * * for a continuance of the case until the next term * * * and did file as the ground work of their motion, an affidavit of the traverser * * * but he denies that any sufficient ground for a continuance until the next term, was disclosed by this affidavit * * *.

The affidavit * * * states, that the traverser wished to procure, as material to his defence, authentic copies of certain answers made by the President of the United States, Mr. Adams, to addresses from various persons; and also, a book entitled "an Essay on Canon and Feudal Law," * * * which was ascribed to the President, and which the traverser believed to have been written by him; and also, evidence to prove that the President was in fact the author of that book.

[Chase goes on to explain that defendant did *not* allege that the evidence and witnesses in question *could* be produced if a continuance or a postponement had been granted.]

* * *

But in order to afford every accommodation to the traverser and his counsel, which it was in his power to give, this respondent did offer to postpone the trial for a month or more, in order to afford them full time for preparation, and for procuring such testimony as was within their reach. This indulgence they thought proper to refuse. * * *

To the third charge adduced in support of the article now under consideration, the charge of using "unusual, rude, and contemptuous expressions, towards the prisoner's counsel," * * * he cannot answer otherwise than by a general denial. A charge so vague, admits not of precise or particular refutation. He denies that there was any thing unusual or intentionally rude or contemptuous in his conduct * * *.

On the contrary, it was his wish and intention, to treat the counsel with the respect due to their situation and functions, and with the decorum due to his own character. He thought it his duty to restrain such of their attempts as he considered improper, and to overrule motions made by them, which he considered as unfounded in law; but this it was his wish to accomplish in the manner least likely to offend * * *. He did indeed think * * * that the conduct of the traverser's counsel * * * was disrespectful, irritating, and highly incorrect. That conduct which he viewed in this light, might have produced some irritation in a temper naturally quick and warm, and that this irritation might, not withstanding his endeavors to suppress it, have appeared in his manner and in his expressions, he thinks not improbable; for he has had occasions of feeling and lamenting the want of sufficient caution and self-command, in things of this nature. But he confidently affirms, that his conduct in this particular was free from intentional impropriety; and this respondent denies, that any part of his conduct was such as ought to have induced the traverser's counsel to "abandon the cause of their client," nor does he believe that any such cause did induce them to take that step. On the contrary, he believes that it was taken by them under the influence of passion * * *. And this respondent admits, that the said traverser was convicted and condemned to fine and imprisonment, but not by reason of the abandonment of his defence by his counsel; but because the charges against him were clearly proved, and no defence was made or attempted against far the greater number of them.

The fourth charge in support of this article, attributes to this respondent, "repeated and vexatious interruptions of the said counsel, which at length induced them to abandon the cause of their client, who was therefore, convicted, and condemned to fine and imprisonment." To this charge also, it is impossible to give any other answer but a general denial. * * *

Lastly, this respondent is charged under this article, with an "indecent solicitude, manifested by him, for the conviction of the accused, unbecoming even a public prosecutor, but highly disgraceful to the character of a judge, as it was subversive of justice." * * * He denies that he felt any solicitude whatever for the conviction of the traverser; other than the general wish natural to every friend of truth, decorum, and virtue, that persons guilty of such offences * * * should be brought to punishment, for the sake of example. He has no hesitation to acknowledge, that his indignation was strongly excited, by the atrocious and profligate libel which the traverser was charged with having written and published. This indignation, he believes, was felt by every virtuous and honorable man in the community, of every party, who had read the book in question, or become acquainted with its contents * * *.

And this respondent thinks it his duty, on this occasion, to enter his solemn protest against the introduction in this country, of those arbitrary principles, at once the offspring and the instruments of despotism, which would make "high crimes and misdemeanors" to consist in "rude and contemptuous expressions," in "vexatious interruptions of counsel," and in the manifestation of "indecent solicitude" for the conviction of a most notorious offender. Such conduct is no doubt, improper and unbecoming in any person, and much more so in a judge: but, it is too vague, too uncertain, and too susceptible of forced interpretations, according to the impulse of passion or the views of policy, to be admitted into the class of punishable offences, under a system of law whose certainty and precision in the definition of crimes, is its greatest glory, and the greatest privilege of those who live under its sway.

* * *

[What follows is Chase's response to the eighth article, regarding his charge to the Baltimore Grand jury in 1803.]

In answer to this charge this respondent admits, that he did * * * deliver a charge to the grand jury, and express in the conclusion of it some opinions as to certain public measures, both of the government of Maryland and of that of the United States. But he denies that in thus acting, he disregarded the duties and dignity of his judicial character, perverted his official right and duty to address the grand jury, or had any intention to excite the fears or resentment of any person whatever, against the government and constitution of the United States or of Maryland. * * * He denies that he did any thing that was unusual, improper or unbecoming in a judge, or expressed any opinions, but such as a friend to his country, and a firm supporter of the governments both of the state of Maryland and of the United States, might entertain. For the truth of what he here says, he appeals confidently to the charge itself * * *.

* * *

Admitting these opinions to have been incorrect and unfounded, this respondent denies that there was any law which forbid him to express them * * *. The very essence of despotism consists, in punishing acts which, at the time when they were done, were forbidden by no law. Admitting the expression of political opinions by a judge, in his charge to a jury, to be improper and dangerous; there are many improper and very dangerous acts, which not being forbidden by law cannot be punished.

Hence the necessity of new penal laws; which are from time to time enacted for the prevention of acts not before forbidden, but found by experience to be of dangerous tendency. It has been the practice in this country, ever since the beginning of the revolution, which separated us from Great Britain, for the judges to express from the bench, by way of charge to the grand jury, and to enforce to the utmost of their ability, such political opinions as they thought correct and useful. There have been instances in which the legislative bodies of this country, have recommended this practice to the judges; and it was adopted by the judges of the supreme court of the United States, as soon as the present judicial system was established. If the legislature of the United States considered this practice as mischievous, dangerous, or liable to abuse, they might have forbidden it by law * * *. By not forbidding it, the legislature has given to it an implied sanction; and for that legislature to punish it now by way of impeachment, would be to convert into a crime, by an ex post facto proceeding * * *. Such conduct would be utterly subversive of the fundamental principles on which free government rests; and would form a precedent for the most sanguinary and arbitrary persecutions, under the forms of law.

Nor can the incorrectness of the political opinions thus expressed, have any influence in deciding on the guilt or innocence of a judge's conduct in expressing them. For if he should be considered as guilty or innocent, according to the supposed correctness or incorrectness of the opinion, thus expressed by him, it would follow, that error in political opinion however honestly entertained, might be a crime; and that a party in power might, under this pretext, destroy any judge, who might happen in a charge to a grand jury, to say something capable of being construed by them, into a political opinion adverse to their own system. * * *

* * * Confiding in the impartiality, independence and integrity of his judges, and that they will patiently hear, and conscientiously determine this case, without being influenced by the spirit of party, by popular prejudice, or political motives, he cheerfully submits himself to their decision. * * *

This respondent now stands not merely before an earthly tribunal, but also before that awful Being whose presence fills all space, and whose all-seeing eye more especially surveys the temples of justice and religion. In a little time, his accusers, his judges, and himself, must appear at the bar of Omnipotence, where * * * every human being shall answer for his deeds done in the body, and shall be compelled to give evidence against himself, in the presence of an assembled universe. To his Omniscient Judge, at that awful hour, he now appeals for the rectitude and purity of his conduct, as to all the matters of which he is this day accused.

He hath now only to adjure each member of this honorable court, by the living GOD, and in his holy name, to render impartial justice to him, according to the constitution and laws of the United States. He makes this solemn demand of each member, by all his hopes of happiness in the world to come, which he will have voluntarily renounced by the oath he has taken; if he shall wilfully do this respondent injustice, or disregard the constitution or laws of the United States, which he has solemnly sworn to make the rule and standard of his judgment and decision.

5. CONGRESSMAN RANDOLPH'S OPENING ARGUMENT FOR THE CONVICTION OF JUSTICE CHASE

I Chase Trial 108–127

It is a painful but indispensible task which we are called upon to perform:—to establish the guilt of a great officer of government, of a man, who, if he had made a just use of those faculties which God and Nature bestowed upon him, would have been the ornament and benefactor of his country, would have rendered her services as eminent and useful as he has inflicted upon her outrages and wrongs deep and deadly. * * * Base is that heart which could triumph over him.

* * * [Chase's] answer to the first of these charges is by evasive insinuation and misrepresentation, by an attempt to wrest the accusation from its true bearing, the manner and time of delivering the opinion, and the intent with which it was delivered, to the correctness of the opinion itself, which is not the point in issue. * * * It is not for the opinion itself, that the respondent is impeached; it is for a daring inroad upon the criminal jurisprudence of his country, by delivering that opinion at a time and in a manner (in writing) before unknown and unheard of. The criminal intent is to be inferred from the boldness of the innovation itself * * *. The admission of the respondent ought to secure his conviction on this charge. * * *

* * * For the truth of this opinion, and, as it would seem, for the propriety of this proceeding, the respondent takes shelter under precedent. He tells you, sir, this doctrine had been repeatedly decided on solemn argument and deliberation, twice in the same court, and once in that very case.—What is this, but a confession, that he himself hath been the first man to venture on so daring an innovation on the forms of our criminal jurisprudence? To justify himself for having given a written opinion *before* counsel had been heard for the prisoner, he resorts to the example set by his predecessors, who had delivered the customary verbal opinion, after solemn argument and deliberation. And what do these repeated arguments and solemn deliberations prove, but that none of his predecessors ever arrogated to themselves the monstrous privilege of breaking in upon those sacred institutions, which guard the life and liberty of the citizen from the rude inroads of powerful injustice? * * *

* * * I beg this honorable court never to lose sight of the circumstance, that this was a *criminal* trial, for a *capital* offence, and that the offence charged was *treason*. The respondent also admits, that the counsel for Fries, not meaning to contest the truth of the facts charged in the indictment, rested their defence altogether upon the law, which he declared to have been settled in the cases of Vigol and Mitchel: a decision which, although it might be binding on the court, the jury were not obliged to respect, and which the counsel had a right to controvert before them, the sole judges, in a case of that nature, both of the *law* and the *fact*. * * * If they verily believed that the overt acts charged in the indictment, did not amount to treason, they could not without a surrender of their consciences into the hands of the court, without a flagrant violation of all that is dear and sacred to man, bring in a verdict of Guilty. * * * In civil cases, indeed, the verdict may be set aside and a new trial granted—but in a criminal prosecution, the verdict, if not guilty, is final and conclusive. * * * When I concede the right of the court to explain the law to the jury in a criminal, and especially in a capital case, I am penetrated with a conviction that it ought to be done, if at all, with great caution and delicacy. * * * There is, in my mind, a material difference between a naked definition of law, the application of which is left to the jury, and the application by the court, of such definition to the particular case * * *. But it is alleged, on behalf of the respondent, that the law in this case was settled, and upon this he rests his defence. Will it be pretended by any man that the law of treason is better established than the law of murder? * * * And because what constitutes murder has been established and settled through a long succession of ages and adjudications, has any judge for that reason, been ever daring enough to assert that counsel should be precluded from endeavoring to convince the jury that the overt acts, charged in the indictment, did not amount to murder? * * *

* * *

* * * [Chase] confesses that he would not permit the prisoner's counsel to cite certain cases, "because they could not inform but might deceive and mislead the jury." Mr. President, * * * in criminal prosecutions * * * the jury are the sole judges, and where they acquit the prisoner, the judges, without appeal, both of law and fact. And what is the declaration of the respondent but an admission that he wished to take from the jury their indisputable privilege to hear argument and determine upon the law, and to usurp to himself that power, which belonged to them, and to them only? It is one of the most glorious attributes of jury trial, that in criminal cases (particularly such as are capital) the prisoner's counsel may (and they often do) attempt "to deceive and mislead the jury." It is essential to the fairness of the trial, that it should be conducted with perfect freedom. * * * Hence, a greater latitude is allowed to the accused, than is permitted to the prosecutor. The jury, upon whose verdict the

event is staked, are presumed to be men capable of understanding what they are called upon to decide, and the attorney for the state, a gentleman learned in his profession, capable of detecting and exposing the attempts of the opposite counsel to mislead and deceive. * * * [T]o what purpose has treason been defined by the constitution itself, if overbearing arbitrary judges are permitted to establish among us the odious and dangerous doctrine of constructive treason? The acts of Congress which had been referred to on the former trial, but which the respondent said he would not suffer to be cited again, tended to shew that the offence committed by Fries did not amount to treason. That it was a misdemeanor, only, already provided for by law and punishable with fine and imprisonment. * * * And are the laws of our own country (as well as foreign authorities) not to be suffered to be read in our courts, in justification of a man whose life is put in jeopardy!

* * *

The 3d article relates to the rejection of John Taylor's testimony. * * * [A]n attempt is made to justify it, on the ground of its "*irrelevancy,*" on the pretext that the witness could not prove the whole of a particular charge [which] * * * consists of two distinct sentences. Taken separately the respondent asserts that they mean nothing; taken together, a great deal. And because the respondent undertook to determine (without any authority as far as I can learn) that Col. Taylor could not prove the whole, that is both sentences, he rejected his evidence entirely, for "*irrelevancy.*" Might not his testimony have been relevant to that of some other witness, on the same, or on another charge? I appeal to the learning and good sense of this honorable court, whether it is not an unheard of practice (until the present instance) in a criminal prosecution, to declare testimony inadmissible because it is not expected to go to the entire exculpation of the prisoner? * * * Suppose for instance that the testimony of two witnesses would establish all the facts, but that each of those facts are not known by either of them. According to this doctrine the evidence of both might be declared inadmissible, and a man whose innocence, if the testimony in his favor were not rejected, might be clearly proved to the satisfaction of the jury, may thus be subjected by the verdict of that very jury to an ignominious death. Shall principles so palpably cruel and unjust be tolerated in this free country? I am free to declare that the decision of Mr. Chase, in rejecting Col. Taylor's testimony, was contrary to the known and established rules of evidence * * *. There is one ground of defence taken by the respondent, which I did suppose, a gentleman of his discernment would have sedulously avoided. That although the traverser had justified nineteen out of twenty of the charges, contained in the indictment, if he could not prove the truth of the twentieth, it was of little moment, as he was, "thereby, put into the power of the court." Gracious God! Sir, what inference is to be drawn from this horrible insinuation?

* * * Sir, in the famous case of Logwood, whereat the chief justice of the United States presided, I was present, being one of the grand jury who found a true bill against him. It must be conceded that the government was as deeply interested in arresting the career of this dangerous and atrocious criminal, who had aimed his blow against the property of every man in society, as it could be in bringing to punishment a weak and worthless scribbler. And yet, although much testimony was offered by the prisoner, which did, by no means, go to his entire exculpation, although much of that testimony was of a very questionable nature, none of it was declared inadmissible; it was suffered to go to the jury, who were left to judge of its weight and credibility, nor were any interrogatories to the witnesses required to be reduced to writing. And I will go farther, and say that it never has been done before, or since Callender's trial, in any court of Virginia, (and I believe I might add in the United States) whether state or federal. * * *

The respondent also acknowledges his refusal to postpone the trial of Callender, although an affidavit was regularly filed stating the absence of material witnesses on his behalf * * *. The dispersed situation of the witnesses, which he alleges to have been the motive of his refusal, is, to my mind, one of the most unanswerable reasons for granting a postponement. * * *

The 8th and last article remains to be considered. [article read.] I ask this honorable court whether the prostitution of the bench of justice to the purposes of an hustings is to be tolerated? We have nothing to do with the politics of the man. * * * If he must electioneer and abuse the government under which he lives, I know no law to prevent or punish him, provided he seeks the wonted theatres for his exhibition. * * * Shall he not put off the political partizan when he ascends the tribune; or shall we have the pure stream of public justice polluted with the venom of party virulence? In short, does it follow that a judge carries all the rights of a private citizen with him upon the bench * * *?

But, Sir, we are told that this high court is not a court of errors and appeals, but a court of impeachment, and that however incorrectly the respondent may have conducted himself, proof must be adduced of criminal intent, of wilful error, to constitute guilt. * * * It is not an indictable offence under the laws of the United States for a judge to go on the bench in a state of intoxication—it may not be in all the state courts. But it is indictable no where, for him to omit to do his duty, to refuse to hold a court. And who can doubt that both are impeachable offences, and ought to subject the offender to removal from office? But in this long and disgusting catalogue of crimes and misdemeanors (which he has in a great measure confessed) the respondent tells you he had accomplices and that what was guilt in him could not be innocence in them. I must beg the court to consider the facts alleged against the respondent in all their accumulated atrocity;—not to take them, each in an insulated point of view, but as a chain of evidence indissolubly linked together, and establishing the indisputable proof of his guilt. Call to mind his high standing and character, and his superior age and rank, and then ask yourselves whether he stands justified in a long course of oppression and injustice, because men of weak intellect, and yet feebler temper—men of far inferior standing to the respondent, have tamely acquiesced in such acts of violence and outrage? * * * But, sir, would the establishment of their guilt prove his innocence? At most it would only prove that they too ought to be punished. * * *

I have endeavored, Mr. President, in a manner, I am sensible, very lame and inadequate, to discharge the duty incumbent on me * * *. We shall bring forward in proof, such a specimen of judicial tyranny, as, I trust in God, will never be again exhibited in our country.

The respondent hath closed his defence by an appeal to the great Searcher of hearts for the purity of his motives. For his sake, I rejoice, that, by the timely exercise of that mercy, which, for wise purposes, has been reposed in the executive, this appeal is not drowned by the blood of an innocent man crying aloud for vengeance; that the mute agony of widowed despair and the wailing voice of the orphan do not plead to heaven for justice on the oppressor's head. * * * On that awful day the blood of a poor, ignorant, friendless, unlettered German, murdered under the semblance and color of law, sent without pity to the scaffold, would have risen in judgment at the Throne of Grace, against the unhappy man arraigned at your bar. But the President of the United States by a well timed act, at once of justice and of mercy, (and mercy like charity covereth a multitude of sins,) wrested the victim from his grasp, and saved him from the countless horrors of remorse, by not suffering the pure ermine of justice to be dyed in the innocent blood of John Fries.

* * *

NOTES AND QUESTIONS

1. You have now been given enough materials (the reports in *Fries*, *Cooper* and *Callender;* the charge to the Baltimore Grand Jury; the Articles of Impeachment; Chase's Answer; and Randolph's argument) to permit you to understand how law in the early republic might be freighted with ideological baggage, and how otherwise reasonable men might so vehemently disagree over questions of jurisprudence, the rules of evidence, or the roles of judge and jury. By now you should also be able to arrive at some conclusion whether or not Chase should have been found guilty of high crimes and misdemeanors at his Senate Trial. Let's take the charge relating to Chase's early opinion-giving in Fries's case. Why was this regarded as criminal by Randolph? Consider Chase's defense to this charge. He believed that the law on the matter was settled; he wanted to save time so that the court could get on

to its overcrowded civil docket, and he believed that it was his duty to prevent the jury from straying from what had been previously found to be the law. Are these reasons persuasive? Do they meet Randolph's criticisms? Do Chase and Randolph even agree on the meaning of the word "law?" In this connection what do you make of Chase's suggestion that the jury has no "dispensing power" over "the laws of the land?" You will remember that it was the controversy over the "dispensing power" that lost James II the throne of England. Are the issues the same whether the "dispensing power" is regarded as a prerogative of crown or jury?

2. What about the charges relating to Chase's conduct during the Callender trial? Some of these are very technical, but the thrust of all of the charges is that Chase's bias against the defendant led him to deprive the defendant of a chance adequately to defend himself in court. Do you agree with this charge? Do you understand how Chase could believe he was simply neutrally applying legal rules, such as the rules of evidence? How effective is Chase's defense that the other Judge, Griffin, acquiesced in Chase's rulings? Note that Chase makes the same defense (substituting Judge Peters for Judge Griffin) with regard to the *Fries* trial. Why do you suppose there were no impeachments of Peters and Griffin?

3. Note, especially in the case of the eighth count, the Baltimore Grand Jury charge, Chase comes down hard on the notion that while what he did may have been improper or inappropriate it was *not* a crime. Is this a good defense? What is the meaning of the Constitutional provision (Article II, Section 4) which states that "The President, Vice President and all Civil Officers of the United States, shall be removed from Office on Impeachment for, and Conviction of, Treason, Bribery, or other high Crimes and Misdemeanors?" Former President Gerald Ford, who when a Congressman sought the impeachment of former Justice William O. Douglas, stated that an impeachable offense was "whatever a majority of the House of Representatives considers it to be . . ." 116 Cong.Rec. H 3113–3114 (daily ed., April 15, 1970). Imagine, if you can, with what joy Mr. Ford's definition was cited to former President Nixon's lawyers who attempted to argue to the House of Representatives, in 1974, that Nixon could only be impeached for a criminal offense. One scholar has concluded that while Mr. Ford may not have been entirely correct, the phrase "high crimes and misdemeanors" at least when it refers to the conduct of a judge, *is* much broader than criminal acts, and probably extends to anything that could be construed as *not* good behavior. See Raoul Berger, Impeachment: The Constitutional Problems 53–102 (1973). Raoul Berger believes that Chase's "rabid partisanship" and his "implacable intention to convict" Callender should have resulted in his conviction by the Senate. Berger, supra, at 229, 250–251. For more analyses of the Chase impeachment see the fine accounts by Richard Ellis, "The Impeachment of Samuel Chase," in Michael Belknap, ed., American Political Trials 57–76 (Revised, Expanded Edition, 1994), Peter Charles Hoffer and N.E.H. Hull in their Impeachment in America 1635–1805, 228–255 (1984), William H. Rehnquist, Grand Inquests: The Historic Impeachments of Justice Samuel Chase and President Andrew Johnson (1992), Keith E. Whittington, "Reconstructing the Federal Judiciary:

The Chase Impeachment and the Constitution," 9 Studies in Am. Pol Dev. 55 (1995) (Later incorporated as Chapter 2 of Keith E. Whittington, Constitutional Construction: Divided Powers and Constitutional Meaning (1999)). For the current leading authority on impeachment generally, see Michael J. Gerhardt, The Federal Impeachment Process: A Constitutional and Historical Analysis. (2d ed. 2000).

4. In order for Chase to have been convicted by the Senate, twenty-three Senators would have to have voted against him on any one charge. On the first count of the impeachment (improper conduct in delivering his opinion in the *Fries* case) sixteen senators voted *guilty* and eighteen *not guilty*. On the third and fourth counts (events at Callender's trial) eighteen voted *guilty* and sixteen *not guilty*. On the eighth count (the Baltimore Grand Jury charge) nineteen voted *guilty* and fifteen voted *not guilty*. On the other four charges there were never more than ten votes of guilty, and on one charge there were no guilty votes at all. Accordingly, Chase was acquitted and continued in office, though he was reported to be somewhat subdued by the experience. Wharton, State Trials, at 46. Most commentators have believed that Chase's acquittal was the proper result, and have suggested that since the time of the Chase impeachment, never again has the impeachment remedy been used as a means of punishing merely errant politics on the part of judges. See, e.g. 1 Charles Warren, The Supreme Court in United States History 292–95 (rev. ed. 1947). Do you agree with Warren or Berger? Should impeachment be a means of keeping judges' politics in line? What, if anything, was resolved by the trial of Chase?

5. How do you explain the closing references to God and an afterlife made by *both* Chase and Randolph? Which is more persuasive? Why?

CHAPTER 3

SECURING THE REVOLUTION OF 1800 THROUGH THE COMMON LAW

■ ■ ■

Jefferson styled his victory over the Federalists in the election of 1800 a "Revolution." The new President and his supporters believed that they had recaptured the spirit of '76, but the defeated Federalists expected Jefferson's election, like the recent French Revolution, to result in bloody purges, anarchy, and rampaging hordes ravishing Federalist women and private property. This never occurred, but in retrospect Jefferson's election was like a revolution. It marked the first peaceful transfer of power between opposing factions under the new Constitution. Still, Jefferson attempted to steer a middle course between radical and Federalist interests. "We are all Federalists, we are all Republicans," he had said in his inaugural. Eventually he broke with the radical agrarian wing of his party; he tolerated the first National Bank, a Hamiltonian creation; he grudgingly accepted the Federalist Supreme Court, and he came to acknowledge the importance of commercial and manufacturing interests to the life of the nation. He even unwittingly supported the Federalist principles of centralization and promotion of American industry, when he went beyond express Constitutional executive powers to purchase the Louisiana Territory in 1803. While some political divisiveness persisted for much of his Presidency, there was a pronounced movement in the direction of American consensus. Administrations after the War of 1812 flourished in an atmosphere of "Good Feeling." Lasting until the mid–1820s, this period is characterized by a relative absence of political rancor, a decline of agrarian and Federalist stridency and the emergence of widespread agreement on basic values of democracy, economic progress, and social mobility.

The generation coming of age in the 1820s could look back in wistful wonder at the achievements of the Founding Fathers. Some grand old men of that time still lingered. After years of political enmity, Adams the Federalist and Jefferson the Republican once again engaged in a lively correspondence on all manner of things, but in particular on their mutual sense of alienation from the bustling society of the early nineteenth century. Their eerily-timed deaths (both on the fourth of July in 1826) soon symbolized for the rising generation the irrevocable passage of the old order.

The new generation of Americans found new heroes: Daniel Webster, Henry Clay, and especially Andrew Jackson, who captured the Presidency in 1828 on a tidal wave of popular support. These men and others like them had temporarily resolved many of their political differences and were embarked on the common enterprise of national expansion.

The rate of demographic, territorial and economic growth during these years was astounding. The population of the United States grew from less than 4 million in 1790 to more than 31 million in 1860. This growth sprang not only from a prolific birth rate, but also from an influx of European immigrants who sought to farm western land and to fill the demand for labor in the expanding cities. The percentage of urban population climbed from a meager 3.3 percent in 1790 to 16.1 percent in 1860. The construction of turnpikes, canals and, after 1830, the railroads, facilitated internal migration and the westward movement. In 1790 most Americans were clustered east of the Alleghenies. By the Civil War, settlements had spread from the Atlantic to the Pacific. The new transportation network aided in the development of an internal economy by linking the regions of the country and by creating vast new markets for goods and services. Americans learned to look less and less to Europe for commercial progress. The Northeastern states supplied the rest of the country with manufactured commodities; the Western regions concentrated on agricultural production for both national and international trade; the Southern states grew cotton for the New England finishing mills and for export. State and local governments promoted growth by encouraging immigration, by liberalizing land policy, and by subsidizing transportation, manufacturing and education. The national government constructed tariff barriers, removed impediments to interstate commerce, and opened up new reserves of land.

A new national ideology of the antebellum era equated material progress with the fulfillment of the principles of the Revolution of 1776. Mining America's vast human and physical resources, spreading out across the face of the continent was seen as a patriotic mission, the realization of a providentially ordained "manifest destiny."

Often, of course, such chauvinism barely concealed crass materialism. Still, national growth revealed an important intellectual change, at the root of which was a new conception of man. The Americans of the Founding generation feared authority and the inherent tendency toward corruption in humankind, and thus built checks, balances, and separations of power into government. Most clung to the Calvinist belief that people were born in sin; their capacity for doing evil, their lust for power, could be thwarted only by the erection of earthly restraints. In antebellum America, however, people were more often seen as innately good, even perfectible. Traditional institutions which had been used to restrain men and women and thus preserve what freedom remained, gave way before a new regard for liberty that sought instead to enlarge the opportunities for action. The national policy was not only to voice platitudes of popular sovereignty, but actually to place power in the hands of the people. This new spirit was most clearly revealed in the "ferment of reform." The removal of property qualifications for voting, the improvements in the status of women and children, the establishment of free public schools, abolitionism, temperance, and religious revivalism were but another side of expansionism: both expansionism and reform were born of an optimistic faith in humankind, and both ostensibly sought to expand the boundaries of opportunity for all.

The transformation of American values was carried through in the changing social structure of society. The Jacksonian Era has been called the Age of the Common Man, and has been supposed to have been characterized by boundless opportunity. Quantitative studies seem to bear out the existence of substantial fluidity between classes, and of great economic potential, at least compared to the contemporary situation in other countries. Millions of acres of cheap, fertile farmland in the West operated as a steady lure for restless Easterners and for immigrants. Developments in transportation, the expansion of capital, and the growth of consumer demand also insured that farmers would profit as never before. Businessmen benefitted as the proliferation of banks, the relaxation of debtor laws, liberal lending policies, and the willingness of Western Europeans to invest here spurred risk-taking, entrepreneurial ventures.

The new manufacturing industries made the city a center of economic activity, a new "urban frontier." There was a continual demand for skilled and for semi-skilled labor. Diligent working men and women might eventually save enough to buy a farm in the West, or at least to provide their children with hopes for the future. Manufacturing also gave rise to a new class of white collar employees—salesmen, accountants, clerks, draftsmen, engineers, and managers. New public schools and relatively inexpensive colleges became available to many seeking the skills to advance in the urban world.

Not all Americans shared in these new opportunities. Most women, nearly all Blacks, and many unskilled laborers remained poor and powerless. But the rest could hope, and often expect, to rise or fall according to their individual initiative and abilities.

The materials of this chapter are designed to suggest how the spirit of expansion permeated American law and produced new rules to govern private economic behavior. There was a broad consensus that material progress would benefit all of American society. In practice, however, clear formulations of these legal rules were not easily drawn. It gradually became apparent that there were divisions in the economy and advocates for differing approaches to legal problems. There were disagreements between industrial developers and agrarian users of property, between groups of developers or industries, between competitors for some scarce resources, and between some advocates of change and some forces of conservatism. How American courts perceived these divisions, the legal conclusions they reached, and the manner in which private judicial decision-making became clothed in the language of public policy is the subject of this chapter.

A. THE LAW AND AMERICAN DEMOCRACY

INTRODUCTION: The Legal Profession in England and America to 1860

Between 1100 and 1200, during the earliest years of English law, the legal profession was made up of clergy who "spoke" for litigants in cases before the king's courts. The clergy were ideal candidates because they were literate, fluent in Latin and French (the language of the Norman and Angevin kings), and loyal to the king. As hinted at in our materials on Sir Edward Coke and James I, the evolution of the English legal profession into a learned and highly skilled body of professionals is a story of the differentiation among practitioners. As early as 1200, there was a group of lay persons not clerics, whose expertise lay in the common law, and whose practice was regulated to some extent by the king. By 1350, this community of lawyers, numbering between 12 and 15 men at any one time, became a distinct order of "sergeants." They were installed by the king in a special ceremony; their dress included a robe and a cap, or coif; and they alone eventually enjoyed the privilege of pleading before the most important civil court in the land, the Court of Common Pleas.

Apprentices at law, the sergeants in training, enjoyed a special privilege of pleading before the prerogative courts, such as Star Chamber and Chancery. Between 1400 and 1550 the apprentices expanded their practice to include the other royal courts, excepting Common Pleas which continued to be the exclusive domain of sergeants-at-law. The apprentices were known as "pleaders" and "counselors at law." By 1600 the pleaders and sergeants had come to constitute the learned profession of law. Entry into this profession was highly controlled by the Inns of Court in London, where apprentices served for a set number of years, usually seven, before being called to the Bar. By 1700 the members of this upper branch were commonly referred to as barristers-at-law. Functioning much like a guild, the Inns recruited their apprentices from among the landed gentry and the sons of gentlemen who had completed at least one year of study at Oxford or Cambridge, and carefully managed the number called to the Bar each year. Barristers alone could represent clients in court. The judges of the royal courts and King's Counsel (attorneys representing the interests of the crown in legal affairs) were appointed from within this group of trained practitioners and served at the pleasure of the king.

A second or "lower" branch of the legal profession were those who served as clerks and officers of the courts, where they advised clients, offered assistance to attorneys, and prepared and filed legal documents—in short, they did everything except the actual argument of a case in court. This somewhat vague assemblage of practitioners by 1650 was now being recognized as a distinct order of "solicitors." Although they fell outside of the strict control and appointment that ruled membership in the Bar, they handled most of the legal business outside of appearing in courts, and, in the manner that they advised and served clients, functioned very much like lawyers do today.

The legal profession in the British colonies was far less structured. The formalities and jurisdictions of the English court system that evolved from medieval complexities and the Norman Conquest, and the distinctions among kinds of legal professionals that grew up around royal courts, were essentially bypassed in the New World. The materials of Seventeenth century colonial law were meager. They included the Charters which established the colonies, associated royal instructions and legal opinions of the crown's attorneys, and any Parliamentary legislation that specifically applied, such as the Navigation Acts. Initially, at least, there was no professional colonial judiciary, and what passed for law was whatever knowledge colonials actually possessed of the English common law and local custom. There were few among the early colonists who had any experience at all in the practice of law. The officers of the local courts that were eventually established in order to resolve disputes, and the justices of the peace, typically were lay persons, and they were called upon to meet the inevitable legal needs of town, parish, and county. Furthermore, legal fora were not the only venue for the resolution of conflicts. More often than not, town leaders or local churches stepped in informally to resolve disputes or complaints among neighbors.

Between 1700 and 1750 the political and legal infrastructure grew and diversified according to each colony's unique needs, its relations with the crown, its business and commercial practices, and its particular local customs. Still, as a general rule, as we have seen in the Writs of Assistance case, the court systems in the colonies mimicked English practices, and, as we saw in the Zenger trial, judges and lawyers cited English cases and law books as authority. Again as we saw in *Zenger*, judges in the colonies often lacked the training and deep knowledge of their English counterparts. American colonial courts and proceedings were simpler than those employed in England's central courts, and the language of law was the English vernacular rather than Latin or Law French.

The method of training for the practice of law in each colony was apprenticeship, as it was in England. Nothing comparable to the Inns of

Court developed, however. An aspiring practitioner simply "read" law in the offices of another lawyer, and after a period of time was admitted to the local bar following an examination by a judge and a letter of endorsement from a member of the bar. The only course on law taught by a skilled professional was at William and Mary College in Virginia, and that (offered by George Wythe) was intended as to provide general background for gentlemen and not professional preparation. Both Thomas Jefferson and John Marshall were Wythe's students. A few colonials did attend the Inns of Court in London. The British distinction among the branches of the profession (barristers and solicitors) was out of place in the colonies, where colonial courts merged jurisdictions and lacked supervisory authority of attorneys. The attempts on a few occasions in the colonies to recognize this distinction failed.

Bar associations did come to exist at the local level, though they were more informal than professional. They offered the occasion for mutual learning, social intercourse, and the discussion of concerns regarding professional practice (including fees and bar requirements). The first was the New York Bar Association founded in the city of New York in 1747.

As the colonies expanded in population and achieved greater economic status in the British Empire and the Atlantic world, the demands upon law accelerated and the practice of law gained in profitability. In the mid–1700s lawyers with thriving practices had become much better acquainted with the nuances of English law, were familiar with the English treatises and reports, and had grown cosmopolitan in their professional outlook. New York, Boston, Philadelphia, Baltimore, and Charleston were important centers of trade in the Atlantic world, and relied upon lawyers for counsel, drafting of legal documents, and representation in lawsuits. To an aspiring son of a merchant, farmer, planter, or city-dwelling family, the inducements of law practice were not small, and hence the attractions of the legal profession to upwardly mobile aspirants such as John Adams, whose father was a shoemaker and farmer, and wanted his son to go to Harvard to train for the ministry. Adams went to Harvard, but opted for law and politics.

By the eve of the American Revolution in 1776, colonial lawyers comprised an important, informed, and literate class. They followed the news and public affairs of their region, the mother country, and other European nations. Some, like Adams and Jefferson, read deeply in literature and philosophy, were fluent in Latin and Greek, and prided themselves on their knowledge of history—especially English constitutional history and the history of political institutions stretching back to classical Greece and Rome. Lawyers sat in the provincial legislatures, served a growing clientele of legal consumers, received appointments as judges (though legal experience was not a requirement), and gravitated to leadership positions in local affairs.

If stirred, these lawyers could be dangerous. Of the 56 signers of the Declaration of Independence, 24 were lawyers or judges. Their common profession formed a bond of familiarity and language that not only spanned the colonies, but provided the legal and intellectual framework for the radical break with the Crown. The influence of those with experience in law was even more in evidence at the Philadelphia convention of 1787. Of the 55 members present, 31 were lawyers. In the first Congress, 10 of the 29 senators were lawyers, and in the house, 17 of 56 representatives were lawyers.

From 1800 to 1860 the democratization of American society dramatically altered the American legal profession. In a nation where legal demands were being multiplied by population, geographic, and economic transformations, restrictions on entry into the legal profession practically disappeared. Some states did away with requirements for admission to the bar altogether. Where they already existed, local bar associations declined in influence or ceased operations.

While these changes made law and its practice more accessible to everyone, class-based resentments also played a role. Expressions of anti-lawyer sentiment were not uncommon in the colonies; indeed, ill-will toward lawyers in England went hand in hand with the profession's rise. As an outgrowth of 1776 Revolutionary ideals, some states considered instituting arbitration as a substitute for the adversarial legal process. Lawyers were accused of stirring up legal disputes and making the law more complicated (and expensive) than necessary, as will be argued in the piece you will soon read written by a Boston merchant. Massachusetts, in 1790, took aim at the legal profession when it passed a law making it possible for anyone to represent another in a court of law. Other states later adopted similar statutes.

During the presidency of Andrew Jackson (1828–1836) and the "age of the common man," anti-lawyer sentiment grew still further, and was related to the criticism voiced even by some progressive lawyers, like Robert Rantoul, whose attack on the common law as unduly beholden to a class-based English social system you will soon see. Certainly the movement toward an elective judiciary, which you will encounter in a subsequent chapter, revealed a distrust of lawyers and the skilled professional. Because successful lawyers enjoyed often substantial wealth and tended to represent, among others, wealthy clients, they were liable to be tarred by the same brush of privilege and monopoly as other entrenched interests. Lawyers were especially unpopular during periods of economic stress and depression, for it was the legal process that protected landlords and creditors and seemed often to crush the common man.

Still, as you will see in the reading from Tocqueville, there was an uneasy and paradoxical alliance between lawyers and the American people. Lawyers constituted a public profession, but engaged in a private practice. They were the defense and the prosecution, judges and legislators, the gatekeepers of a "mysterious science," yet were subject to few if any regulations. They were trained with a habit of mind and outlook that contrasted with the day's values of individualism and the emerging reformist concept of humankind as perfectible. They were entrusted with law, but servants of clients. And yet, they were often perceived as the guardians of liberty and basic constitutional rights. Whether these opposing forces—the conservative instincts of the lawyer and the radical democratic desires for the transformation of American society—could work in harmony for a greater American good was the question Tocqueville addresses and is still a concern.

Further Reading:

Richard Abel, *American Lawyers*, 1989

Jerold S. Auerbach, *Unequal Justice: Lawyers and Social Change in Modern America,* 1976

J.H. Baker, *The Legal Profession and the Common Law. Historical Essays*, 1986

A.G. Roeber, *Faithful Magistrates and Republican Lawyers: Creators of Virginia Legal Culture, 1680–1810*, 1981

John Dos Passos, *The American Lawyer: As He Was—As He Is—As He Can Be,* 1907

Robert Stevens, *Law School: Legal Education in America from the 1850s to the 1980s,* 1983

Roscoe Pound, *The Lawyer from Antiquity to Modern Times, with Particular Reference to the Development of Bar Associations in the United States,* 1953

HONESTUS [BENJAMIN AUSTIN, JR.], OBSERVATIONS ON THE PERNICIOUS PRACTICE OF THE LAW, AS PUBLISHED OCCASIONALLY IN THE INDEPENDENT CHRONICLE, IN THE YEAR 1786

7–10 (1819).

The following observations are meant, in general, to apply to the practitioners of the law in their malpractice, and not intended to reflect on them in their particular character, as many individuals among them are gentlemen of high esteem and confidence. But as it has lately been asserted * * * that they are a "necessary order in a republic," it is presumed the subject is open to inquiry, and consequently there can be no objection in applying the general practice to support a contrary hypothesis.

Among the multiplicity of evils which we at present suffer, there are none more justly complained of, than those we labor under by the many pernicious practices in the profession of the law. It has therefore become a subject of serious inquiry whether this body of men, in a young republic, ought not to be controuled in their pleas.

Laws are necessary for the safety and good order of society, and consequently the execution of them is of great importance to be attended to. When therefore, *finesse* and gross impositions are practised, and under sanction of the law, every principle of equity and justice is destroyed, the persons concerned in such pernicious measures ought to be brought forward, and their conduct arraigned before the impartial tribunal of the people.

The study and practice of the law are doubtless an honourable employment; and when a man acts becoming the dignity of the profession, he ought to be esteemed by every member in the community. But when any number of men under sanction of this character are endeavouring to perplex and embarrass every judicial proceeding; who are rendering intricate even the most simple principles of law; who are involving individuals, applying for advice, in the most distressing difficulties; who are practising the greatest art in order to delay every process; who are taking the advantage of every accidental circumstance which an unprincipled person might have, by the lenity and indulgence of an honest creditor; who stand ready to strike up a bargain, (after rendering the property in a precarious state) to throw an honest man out of three quarters of his property. When such men pretend to cloak themselves under the sacredness of law, it is full time the people should inquire, "by what authority they do these things."

* * *

The distresses of the people are now great, but if we examine particularly, we shall find them owing, in a great measure, to the conduct of some practitioners of the law. Seven-eighths of the causes which are now in their hands might have been settled by impartial referees. Why cannot the disputes of the merchant, & c. be adjusted by reference, rather than by a long tedious Court process? Or why should we engage lawyers who are wholly unacquainted with all mercantile concerns? Is it to swell the cost and then by a rule of Court have them finally determined by referees, which is generally the case? * * * [I]f we look through the different counties throughout the Commonwealth, we shall find that the troubles of the people arise principally from debts enormously swelled by tedious lawsuits.

The many pernicious modes of judiciary process which have taken place within a few years, are too notorious to mention; scarcely a petty office but has become a little distinct tribunal. What flagrant impositions are daily practised under sanction of law! The distressed individual is often reduced to the humiliating state of submitting to the extortion of official fees without any remedy. Is it not a disgrace to a free republic that the citizens should dread appealing to the laws of their country? To what purpose have we laws? * * *

It has, therefore, become necessary for the welfare and security of the Commonwealth, that some mode be adopted in order to render the laws a blessing, instead of an evil. For this purpose, it is requested that some acts should be passed, declaring that in all cases left to reference in future, the decision of the referees should be binding on the parties. In all judiciary processes, the Jury, to receive the evidence from the parties, and the Judges to give their opinion on any controverted points of law. The Jury in this manner would be possessed of all that was necessary to determine on the cause, viz. Law and Evidence, without the false glosses and subterfuges too often practised by lawyers.

If such regulations were made in our Courts, the Judges could determine with more precision; the Jury by taking the evidence, and points of law from the Judges, could, with more clearness, determine the cause; as in many instances, a Jury becomes puzzled in their judgment by the variety of sentiments advanced by lawyers. By this method the laws would be more justly executed, as the judges are under no influence from either party, their salaries being independent. But by our present mode, the lawyers become parties by their fees, and are too apt to delay the business while there is any prospect of further profit.

I would ask, whether there are many cases, that absolutely require the assistance of this "order?" Or if they were not admitted, whether any great inconvenience could arise? The law and evidence are all the essentials required, and are not the Judges with the Jury competent for these purposes? Why then this intervening "order?" The important study of law should be followed solely with a view of doing justice; and gentlemen of talents, who meant to serve their country as Judges, should make the public good their chief object. They would not take up the profession as a set of needy persons, who meant by chicanery and finesse, to get a living by their practice; but they would make it a point of duty, so to understand the laws, as to distribute equal justice to the rich and poor; each individual would receive the benefit of the laws, and by a speedy and impartial determination, every man would have his cause decided without the imposition of enormous Court charges, and lawyers' fees. There would be no great danger of the Judges converting their authority to any destructive purposes, "as the municipal institutions are so fixed and determined, in this Commonwealth, that it must be difficult for the Judicial Authority to trample upon them with impunity." The perplexity of our laws, therefore, are chiefly owing to the embarrassments thrown in the way by many in the profession.

* * *

NOTES AND QUESTIONS

1. What is the meaning of this piece? Note that this was first published in 1786, the year of Shay's rebellion, which sought to put an end to debt collection in Massachusetts, and the year before the convention that drafted the Federal Constitution. Honestus takes issue with those who have "lately * * * asserted" that "lawyers are a necessary order in a republic." With whom might he be disagreeing? Why might lawyers be referred to as an "order?" Why might anyone think them "necessary?" Why should it make a difference that America is a "republic?"

2. Honestus advocates that lawyers be "controlled in their pleas." Does he mean by this that page limits on court documents should be established? Concerning lawyers, he rails against "finesse," "the greatest art," and, in general, against the lawyers' ability to make the simple complex. These have been perennial complaints about lawyers, but is Honestus's complaint just with the "lawyers," or does his disaffection cut much deeper? Where would you place him in the political spectrum we observed in the last Chapter? Note that he comments on the high judicial fees, and suggests that most matters ought to be handled by referees instead of courts. Could Honestus be correct when he argues that at present the courts and lawyers are "wholly unacquainted with all mercantile concerns?" If Honestus was correct on this matter, how could such a situation have come about?

3. Note Honestus's observation that it would be desirable if, for the most part, we did without lawyers, and "In all judiciary processes, the Jury to receive the evidence from the parties, and the Judges to give their opinion on any controverted points of law." Is this a radical proposal? Do you share Honestus's confidence that judges and juries, functioning without lawyers, would consistently arrive at equitable results? What evidence from earlier in the course can you cite to support your answer?

ROBERT RANTOUL, JR., ORATION AT SCITUATE, DELIVERED ON THE FOURTH OF JULY, 1836

The Common Law sprung from the dark ages; the fountain of justice is the throne of the Deity. The Common Law is but the glimmering taper by which men groped their way through the palpable midnight in which learning, wit, and reason were almost extinguished; justice shines with the splendor of that fulness of light which beams from the Ineffable Presence. The Common Law had its beginning in time, and in the time of ignorance; justice is eternal, even with the eternity of the allwise and just Lawgiver and Judge. The Common Law had its origin in folly, barbarism, and feudality; justice is the irradiance of divine wisdom, divine truth, and the government of infinite benevolence. * * * Older, nobler, clearer, and more glorious, then, is everlasting justice, than ambiguous, baseborn, purblind, perishable Common Law. That which is older than the creation may indeed be extolled for its venerable age; but among created things, the argument from antiquity is a false criterion of worth. Sin and death are older than the Common Law; are they, therefore, to be preferred to it? * * *

Judge-made law is *ex post facto* law, and therefore unjust. An act is not forbidden by the statute law, but it becomes void by judicial construction. The legislature could not effect this, for the Constitution forbids it. * * *

Judge-made law is special legislation. The judge is human, and feels the bias which the coloring of the particular case gives. If he wishes to decide the next case differently, he has only to distinguish, and thereby make a new law. The legislature must act on general views, and prescribe at once for a whole class of cases.

No man can tell what the Common Law is; therefore it is not law: for a law is a rule of action; but a rule which is unknown can govern no man's conduct. Notwithstanding this, it has been called the perfection of human reason.

The Common Law is the perfection of human reason,—just as alcohol is the perfection of sugar. The subtle spirit of the Common Law is reason double distilled, till what was wholesome and nutritive becomes rank poison. * * *

The judge makes law, by extorting from precedents something which they do not contain. He extends his precedents, which were themselves the extension of others, till, by this accommodating principle, a whole system of law is built up without the authority or interference of the legislator.

The judge labors to reconcile conflicting analogies, and to derive from them a rule to decide future cases. No one knows what the law is, before he lays it down; for it does not exist even in the breast of the judge. * * *

No man knows what the law is after the judge has decided it. Because, as the judge is careful not to decide any point which is not brought before him, he restricts his decision within the narrowest possible limits; and though the very next case that may arise may seem, to a superficial observer, and even upon a close inspection by an ordinary mind, to be precisely similar to the last, yet the ingenuity of a thorough-bred lawyer may detect some unsuspected shade of difference upon which an opposite decision may be founded. * * *

Statutes, enacted by the legislature, speak the public voice. Legislators, with us, are not only chosen because they possess the public confidence, but after their election, they are strongly influenced by public feeling. They must sympathize with the public, and express its will: should they fail to do so, the next year witnesses their removal from office, and others are selected to be the organs of the popular sentiment. The older portions of the Common Law are the work of judges, who held their places during the good pleasure of the king, and of course decided the law so as to suit the pleasure of the king. In feudal times it was made up of feudal principles, warped, to be sure, according to the king's necessities. Judges now are appointed by the executive, and hold their offices during good behavior,—that is, for life, and are consequently out of the reach of popular influence. They are sworn to administer Common Law as it came down from the dark ages, excepting what has been repealed by the Constitution and the statutes, which exception they are always careful to reduce to the narrowest possible limits. With them, wrong is right, if wrong has existed from time immemorial: precedents are everything: the spirit of the age is nothing. And suppose the judge prefers the Common Law to the Constitutions of the State and of the Union; or decides in defiance of the statute; what is the remedy? * * * Impeachment is a bugbear, which has lost its terrors. We must have democratic governors, who will appoint democratic judges, and the whole body of the law must be codified.

It is said, that where a chain of precedents is found running back to a remote antiquity, it may be presumed that they originated in a statute which, through lapse of time, has perished. Unparalleled presumption this! To suppose the legislation of a barbarous age richer and more comprehensive than our own. It was without doubt a thousand times more barren. But what if there were such statutes? The specimens which have survived do not impress us with a favorable opinion of those that may have been lost. Crudely conceived, savage in their spirit, vague, indeterminate, and unlimited in their terms, and incoherent when regarded as parts of a system, the remains of ancient legislation are of little use at present, and what is lost was probably still more worthless. If such laws were now to be found in our statute book, they would be repealed at once; the innumerable judicial constructions which they might have received would not save them. * * *

These objections to the Common Law have a peculiar force in America, because the rapidly advancing state of our country is continually presenting new cases for the decision of the judges; and by determining these as they arise, the bench takes for its share more than half of our legislation, notwithstanding the express provisions of the Constitution, that the judiciary shall not usurp the functions of the legislature. If a Common Law system could be tolerable anywhere, it is only where every thing is stationary. With us, it is subversive of the fundamental principles of a free government, because it deposits in the same hands the power of first making the general laws, and then applying them to individual cases; powers distinct in their nature, and which ought to be jealously separated.

* * * All American Law must be statute law.

NOTES AND QUESTIONS

1. Compare Robert Rantoul's attitude toward the common law with that of Alexander Hamilton expressed in the Federalist. Would Hamilton have agreed with the position that the common law is reason "double distilled" and that judge-made law is "*ex post facto law*?" Would Hamilton have agreed that impeachment is a "bugbear, which has lost its terrors?" The Oxford English Dictionary defines "bugbear" as "A sort of hobgoblin, presumably in the shape of a bear, supposed to devour naughty children; hence, generally, any imaginary being invoked by nurses to frighten children. *Obs.*" When and how did impeachment lose its terrors?

2. Rantoul especially objects to the common law because it is unsuited to "the rapidly advancing state of our country." He then says that if it "could be tolerable anywhere, it is only where every thing is stationary." What does this mean? Could you advance a counter argument?

3. Do you see any common thread which runs through Honestus's criticism of American lawyers as non-commercially oriented and Rantoul's criticism of the common law based on its affinity with "folly, barbarism, and feudality?" Do you agree with Rantoul that the only sensible law is statute law? Why might he say this? Would Richard Peters have agreed? Robert Rantoul, incidentally, was a Jacksonian Democrat from Massachusetts, a spokesman for reformist causes, and an advocate of the urban workingman. Is this evident from this excerpt?

4. Rantoul advocates the "codification" of the law, and seems to be suggesting that it would be possible for comprehensive legislation enacted on the basis of reasoned principles to replace what he perceives to be the outmoded common law. Did Rantoul's views win wide acceptance? Of what does "law" primarily consist today, statutes or court decisions?

5. Was the lawyer "order" abolished? Why not? Consider the argument in the next few excerpts, the famous analysis of American law and lawyers by Alexis de Tocqueville.

I ALEXIS DE TOCQUEVILLE, DEMOCRACY IN AMERICA*

48–56, 102–107, 247–250, 256–258, 282–290 (1840).

[(A) THE SOCIAL AND POLITICAL CONDITIONS OF AMERICA]

* * *

* * * The social condition of the Americans is eminently democratic; this was its character at the foundation of the colonies, and it is still more strongly marked at the present day.

---

* Henry Reeve translation, as revised by Francis Bowen, edited by Phillips Bradley. Copyright © 1945 and renewed 1973 by Alfred A. Knopf, Inc. Reprinted by permission of Alfred A. Knopf, Inc.

* * * [G]reat equality existed among the immigrants who settled on the shores of New England. Even the germs of aristocracy were never planted in that part of the Union. The only influence which obtained there was that of intellect * * *. Some of their fellow citizens acquired a power over the others that might truly have been called aristocratic if it had been capable of transmission from father to son.

* * * In most of the states situated to the southwest of the Hudson some great English proprietors had settled who had imported with them aristocratic principles and the English law of inheritance. * * * In the South one man, aided by slaves, could cultivate a great extent of country; it was therefore common to see rich landed proprietors. But their influence was not altogether aristocratic, as that term is understood in Europe, since they possessed no privileges; and the cultivation of their estates being carried on by slaves, they had no tenants depending on them, and consequently no patronage. Still, the great proprietors south of the Hudson constituted a superior class, having ideas and tastes of its own and forming the center of political action. This kind of aristocracy sympathized with the body of the people, whose passions and interests it easily embraced; but it was too weak and too shortlived to excite either love or hatred. This was the class which headed the insurrection in the South and furnished the best leaders of the American Revolution.

At this period society was shaken to its center. The people, in whose name the struggle had taken place, conceived the desire of exercising the authority that it had acquired; its democratic tendencies were awakened; and having thrown off the yoke of the mother country, it aspired to independence of every kind. * * *

But the law of inheritance was the last step to equality. * * * It is true that these laws belong to civil affairs; but they ought, nevertheless, to be placed at the head of all political institutions; for they exercise an incredible influence upon the social state of a people, while political laws show only what this state already is. * * * Through their means man acquires a kind of preternatural power over the future lot of his fellow creatures. When the legislator has once regulated the law of inheritance, he may rest from his labor. The machine once put in motion will go on for ages * * *. When framed in a particular manner, this law unites, draws together, and vests property and power in a few hands; it causes an aristocracy, so to speak, to spring out of the ground. If formed on opposite principles, its action is still more rapid; it divides, distributes, and disperses both property and power. * * * When the law of inheritance permits, still more when it decrees, the equal division of a father's property among all his children, its effects are of two kinds: it is important to distinguish them from each other, although they tend to the same end.

As a result of the law of inheritance, the death of each owner brings about a revolution in property; not only do his possessions change hands, but their very nature is altered, since they are parceled into shares, which become smaller and smaller at each division. This is the direct and as it were the physical effect of the law. In the countries where legislation establishes the equality of division, property, and particularly landed fortunes, have a permanent tendency to diminish. * * *

* * *

Among nations whose law of descent is founded upon the right of primogeniture, landed estates often pass from generation to generation without undergoing division; the consequence of this is that family feeling is to a certain degree incorporated with the estate. The family represents the estate, the estate the family, whose name, together with its origin, its glory, its power, and its virtues, is thus perpetuated in an imperishable memorial of the past and as a sure pledge of the future.

When the equal partition of property is established by law, the intimate connection is destroyed between family feeling and the preservation of the paternal estate; the property ceases to represent the family * * *. The sons of the great landed proprietor, if they are few in number, or if fortune befriends them, may indeed entertain the hope of being as wealthy as their father, but not of possessing the same property that he did; their riches must be composed of other elements than his. Now, as soon as you divest the landowner of that interest in the preservation of his estate which he derives from association, from tradition, and from family pride, you may be certain that, sooner or later, he will dispose of it; for there is a strong pecuniary interest in favor of selling, as floating capital produces higher interest than real property and is more readily available to gratify the passions of the moment.

* * *

And now, after a lapse of a little more than sixty years, the aspect of society is totally altered; the families of the great landed proprietors are almost all commingled with the general mass. * * *

I do not mean that there is any lack of wealthy individuals in the United States; I know of no country, indeed, where the love of money has taken stronger hold on the affections of men and where a profounder contempt is expressed for the theory of the permanent equality of property. But wealth circulates with inconceivable rapidity, and experience shows that it is rare to find two succeeding generations in the full enjoyment of it.

* * *

It is not only the fortunes of men that are equal in America; even their acquirements partake in some degree of the same uniformity. I do not believe that there is a country in the world where, in proportion to the population, there are so few ignorant and at the same time so few learned individuals. Primary instruction is within the reach of everybody; superior instruction is scarcely to be obtained by any. This is not surprising; it is, in fact, the necessary consequence of what I have advanced above. Almost all the Americans are in easy circumstances and can therefore obtain the first elements of human knowledge.

In America there are but few wealthy persons; nearly all Americans have to take a profession. Now, every profession requires an apprenticeship. The Americans can devote to general education only the early years of life. At fifteen they enter upon their calling, and thus their education generally ends at the age when ours begins. If it is continued beyond that point, it aims only towards a particular specialized and profitable purpose * * *.

In America most of the rich men were formerly poor; most of those who now enjoy leisure were absorbed in business during their youth; the consequence of this is that when they might have had a taste for study, they had no time for it, and when the time is at their disposal, they have no longer the inclination.

There is no class, then, in America, in which the taste for intellectual pleasures is transmitted with hereditary fortune and leisure and by which the labors of the intellect are held in honor. Accordingly, there is an equal want of the desire and the power of application to these objects.

* * *

It is impossible to believe that equality will not eventually find its way into the political world, as it does everywhere else. To conceive of men remaining forever unequal upon a single point, yet equal on all others, is impossible; they must come in the end to be equal upon all.

Now, I know of only two methods of establishing equality in the political world; rights must be given to every citizen, or none at all to anyone. For nations which are arrived at the same stage of social existence as the Anglo–Americans, it is, therefore, very difficult to discover a medium between the sovereignty of all and the absolute power of one man * * *.

There is, in fact, a manly and lawful passion for equality that incites men to wish all to be powerful and honored. This passion tends to elevate the humble to the rank of the great; but there exists also in the human heart a depraved taste for equality, which impels the weak to attempt to lower the powerful to their own level and reduces men to prefer equality in slavery to inequality with freedom. Not that those nations whose social condition is democratic naturally despise liberty; on the contrary, they have an instinctive love of it. But liberty is not the chief and constant object of their desires; equality is their idol: they make rapid and sudden efforts to obtain liberty and, if they miss their aim, resign themselves to their disappointment; but nothing can satisfy them without equality, and they would rather perish than lose it.

On the other hand, in a state where the citizens are all practically equal, it becomes difficult for them to preserve their independence against the aggressions of power. No one among them being strong enough to engage in the struggle alone with advantage, nothing but a general combination can protect their liberty. Now, such a union is not always possible.

* * *

The Anglo–Americans are the first nation who, having been exposed to this formidable alternative, have been happy enough to escape the dominion of absolute power. They have been allowed by their circumstances, their origin, their intelligence, and especially by their morals to establish and maintain the sovereignty of the people.

* * *

[At the time before the American Revolution, the principle of popular sovereignty was not yet established.] * * * Intelligence in New England and wealth in the country to the south of the Hudson * * * long exercised a sort of aristocratic influence, which tended to keep the exercise of social power in the hands of a few. Not all the public functionaries were chosen by popular vote, nor were all the citizens voters. The electoral franchise was everywhere somewhat restricted and made dependent on a certain qualification, which was very low in the North and more considerable in the South.

The American Revolution broke out, and the doctrine of the sovereignty of the people came out of the townships and took possession of the state. Every class was enlisted in its cause; battles were fought and victories obtained for it; it became the law of laws.

A change almost as rapid was effected in the interior of society, where the law of inheritance completed the abolition of local influences.

As soon as this effect of the laws and of the Revolution became apparent to every eye, victory was irrevocably pronounced in favor of the democratic cause. All power was, in fact, in its hands, and resistance was no longer possible. The higher orders submitted without a murmur and without a struggle to an evil that was thenceforth inevitable. The ordinary fate of falling powers awaited them; each of their members followed his own interest; and as it was impossible to wring the power from the hands of a people whom they did not detest sufficiently to brave, their only aim was to secure its goodwill at any price. The most democratic laws were consequently voted by the very men whose interests they impaired: and thus, although the higher classes did not excite the passions of the people against their order, they themselves accelerated the triumph of the new state of things; so that, by a singular change, the democratic impulse was found to be most irresistible in the very states where the aristocracy had the firmest hold. The state of Maryland, which had been founded by men of rank, was the first to proclaim universal suffrage and to introduce the most democratic forms into the whole of its government.

When a nation begins to modify the elective qualification, it may easily be foreseen that, sooner or later, that qualification will be entirely abolished. There is no more invariable rule in the history of society * * * for after each concession the strength of the democracy increases, and its demands increase with its strength. The ambition of those who are below the appointed rate is irritated in exact proportion to the great number of those who are above it. The exception at last becomes the rule, concession follows concession, and no stop can be made short of universal suffrage.

* * *

[(B) JUDICIAL POWER IN THE UNITED STATES, AND ITS INFLUENCE ON POLITICAL SOCIETY]

* * * Confederations have existed in other countries besides America; I have seen republics elsewhere * * *; the representative system of government has been adopted in several states of Europe; but I am not aware that any nation of the globe has hitherto organized a judicial power in the same manner as the Americans. The judicial organization of the United States is the institution which a stranger has the greatest difficulty in understanding. He hears the authority of a judge invoked in the political occurrences of every day, and he naturally concludes that in the United States the judges are important political functionaries; nevertheless, when he examines the nature of the tribunals, they offer at the first glance nothing that is contrary to the usual habits and privileges of those bodies * * *.

* * *

The first characteristic of judicial power in all nations is the duty of arbitration. But rights must be contested in order to warrant the interference of a tribunal; and an action must be brought before the decision of a judge can be had. * * * When a judge in a given case attacks a law relating to that case, he extends the circle of his customary duties, without, however, stepping beyond it, since he is in some measure obliged to decide upon the law in order to decide the case. But if he pronounces upon a law without proceeding from a case, he clearly steps beyond his sphere and invades that of the legislative authority.

The second characteristic of judicial power is that it pronounces on special cases, and not upon general principles. If a judge, in deciding a particular point, destroys a general principle by passing a judgment which tends to reject all the inferences from that principle, and consequently to annul it, he remains within the ordinary limits of his functions. But if he directly attacks a general principle without having a particular case in view, he leaves the circle in which all nations have agreed to confine his authority * * *.

The third characteristic of the judicial power is that it can act only when it is called upon, or when, in legal phrase, it has taken cognizance of an affair. * * *

[Americans have adopted these three judicial principles. Why, then are their judiciaries regarded as more powerful than those of other nations?] * * * The cause of this difference lies in the simple fact that the Americans have acknowledged the right of judges to found their decisions on the Constitution rather than on the laws. In other words, they have permitted them not to apply such laws as may appear to them to be unconstitutional.

I am aware that a similar right has been sometimes claimed, but claimed in vain, by courts of justice in other countries; but in America it is recognized by all the authorities; and not a party, not so much as an individual, is found to contest it. This fact can be explained only by the principles of the American constitutions. In France the constitution is, or at least is supposed to be, immutable; and the received theory is that no power has the right of changing any part of it. In England the constitution may change continually, or rather it does not in reality exist; the Parliament is at once a legislative and a constituent assembly. * * * An American constitution is not supposed to be immutable, as in France; nor is it susceptible of modification by the ordinary powers of society, as in England. It constitutes a detached whole, which, as it represents the will of the whole people, is no less binding on the legislator than on the private citizen, but which may be altered by the will of the people in predetermined cases, according to established rules. In America the Constitution may therefore vary; but as long as it exists, it is the origin of all authority, and the sole vehicle of the predominating force.

* * *

Whenever a law that the judge holds to be unconstitutional is invoked in a tribunal of the United States, he may refuse to admit it as a rule; this power is the only one peculiar to the American magistrate, but it gives rise to immense political influence. In truth, few laws can escape the searching analysis of the judicial power for any length of time, for there are few that are not prejudicial to some private interest or other, and none that may not be brought before a court of justice * * *. But as soon as a judge has refused to apply any given law in a case, that law immediately loses a portion of its moral force. Those to whom it is prejudicial learn that means exist of overcoming its authority, and similar suits are multiplied until it becomes powerless. The alternative, then, is, that the people must alter the Constitution or the legislature must repeal the law. The political power which the Americans have entrusted to their courts of justice is therefore immense, but the evils of this power are considerably diminished by the impossibility of attacking the laws except through the courts of justice. * * * It will be seen, also, that by leaving it to private interest to censure the law, and by intimately uniting the trial of the law with the trial of an individual, legislation is protected from wanton assaults and from the daily aggressions of party spirit * * *.

I am inclined to believe this practice of the American courts to be at once most favorable to liberty and to public order. If the judge could attack the legislator only openly and directly, he would sometimes be afraid to oppose him; and at other times party spirit might encourage him to brave it at every turn. The laws would consequently be attacked when the power from which they emanated was weak, and obeyed when it was strong * * *. But the American judge is brought into the political arena independently of his own will. He judges the law only because he is obliged to judge a case. The political question that he is called upon to resolve is connected with the interests of the parties, and he cannot refuse to decide it without a denial of justice. * * * It is true that, upon this system, the judicial censorship of the courts of justice over the legislature cannot extend to all laws indiscriminately, inasmuch as some of them can never give rise to that precise species of contest which is termed a lawsuit; and even when such a contest is possible, it may happen that no one cares to bring it before a court of justice. The Americans have often felt this inconvenience; but they have left the remedy incomplete, lest they should give it an efficacy that might in some cases prove dangerous. Within these limits the power vested in the American courts of justice of pronouncing a statute to be unconstitutional forms one of the most powerful barriers that have ever been devised against the tyranny of political assemblies.

[(C) AMERICAN LAWS]

[Tocqueville proceeds from a discussion of the judiciary to a discussion of American Laws.] * * * The laws of the American democracy are frequently defective or incomplete; they sometimes attack vested rights, or sanction others which are dangerous to the community; and even if they were good, their frequency would still be a great evil. How comes it, then, that the American republics prosper and continue? * * *

Democratic laws generally tend to promote the welfare of the greatest possible number * * *. The laws of an aristocracy tend, on the contrary, to concentrate wealth and power in the hands of the minority * * *. It may therefore be asserted, as a general proposition, that the purpose of a democracy in its legislation is more useful to humanity than that of an aristocracy. This, however, is the sum total of its advantages.

Aristocracies are infinitely more expert in the science of legislation than democracies ever can be. They are possessed of a self-control that protects them from the errors of temporary excitement; and they form far-reaching designs, which they know how to mature till a favorable opportunity arrives. Aristocratic government proceeds with the dexterity of art; it understands how to make the collective force of all its laws converge at the same time to a given point. Such is not the case with democracies, whose laws are almost always ineffective or inopportune. The means of democracy are therefore more imperfect than those of aristocracy, and the measures that it unwittingly adopts are frequently opposed to its own cause; but the object it has in view is more useful.

Let us now imagine a community so organized by nature or by its constitution that it can support the transitory action of bad laws, and that it can await, without destruction, the general tendency of its legislation: we shall then conceive how a democratic government, notwithstanding its faults may be best fitted to produce the prosperity of this community. This is precisely what has occurred in the United States * * *.

* * *

No political form has hitherto been discovered that is equally favorable to the prosperity of the development of all the classes into which society is divided. These classes continue to form, as it were, so many distinct communities in the same nation; and experience has shown that it is no less dangerous to place the fate of these classes exclusively in the hands of any one of them than it is to make one people the arbiter of the destiny of another. * * * The advantage of democracy does not consist, therefore, as has sometimes been asserted, in favoring the prosperity of all, but simply in contributing to the well-being of the greatest number.

The men who are entrusted with the direction of public affairs in the United States are frequently inferior, in both capacity and morality, to those whom an aristocracy would raise to power. But their interest is identified and mingled with that of the majority of their fellow citizens. They may frequently be faithless and frequently mistaken, but they will never systematically adopt a line of conduct hostile to the majority; and they cannot give a dangerous or exclusive tendency to the government.

* * *

The common purpose which in aristocracies connects the interest of the magistrates with that of a portion of their contemporaries identifies it also with that of future generations; they labor for the future as well as for the present. The aristocratic magistrate is urged at the same time towards the same point by the passions of the community, by his own, and,

I may almost add, by those of his posterity. Is it, then, wonderful that he does not resist such repeated impulses? And, indeed, aristocracies are often carried away by their class spirit without being corrupted by it; and they unconsciously fashion society to their own ends and prepare it for their own descendants.

The English aristocracy is perhaps the most liberal that has ever existed, and no body of men has ever, uninterruptedly, furnished so many honorable and enlightened individuals to the government of a country. It cannot escape observation, however, that in the legislation of England the interests of the poor have often been sacrificed to the advantages of the rich, and the rights of the majority to the privileges of a few. * * *

In the United States, where public officers have no class interests to promote, the general and constant influence of the government is beneficial, although the individuals who conduct it are frequently unskillful and sometimes contemptible. There is, indeed, a secret tendency in democratic institutions that makes the exertions of the citizens subservient to the prosperity of the community in spite of their vices and mistakes; while in aristocratic institutions there is a secret bias which, notwithstanding the talents and virtues of those who conduct the government, leads them to contribute to the evils that oppress their fellow creatures. * * *

* * *

[(D) RESPECT FOR LAW IN THE UNITED STATES]

* * *

In the United States, except slaves, servants, and paupers supported by the township, there is no class of persons who do not exercise the elective franchise and who do not indirectly contribute to make the laws. Those who wish to attack the laws must consequently either change the opinion of the nation or trample upon its decision.

* * * [I]n the United States everyone is personally interested in enforcing the obedience of the whole community to the law; for as the minority may shortly rally the majority to its principles, it is interested in professing that respect for the decrees of the legislator which it may soon have occasion to claim for its own. However irksome an enactment may be, the citizen of the United States complies with it, not only because it is the work of the majority, but because it is his own, and he regards it as a contract to which he is himself a party.

In the United States, then, that numerous and turbulent multitude does not exist who, regarding the law as their natural enemy, look upon it with fear and distrust. It is impossible, on the contrary, not to perceive that all classes display the utmost reliance upon the legislation of their country and are attached to it by a kind of parental affection.

I am wrong, however, in saying all classes; for as in America the European scale of authority is inverted, there the wealthy are placed in a position analogous to that of the poor in the Old World, and it is the opulent classes who frequently look upon law with suspicion. * * * In the United States, where the poor rule, the rich have always something to fear from the abuse of their power. This natural anxiety of the rich may produce a secret dissatisfaction; but society is not disturbed by it, for the same reason that withholds the confidence of the rich from the legislative authority makes them obey its mandates: their wealth, which prevents them from making the law, prevents them from withstanding it. Among civilized nations, only those who have nothing to lose ever revolt; and if the laws of a democracy are not always worthy of respect, they are always respected; for those who usually infringe the laws cannot fail to obey those which they have themselves made and by which they are benefited; while the citizens who might be interested in their infraction are induced, by their character and station, to submit to the decisions of the legislature, whatever they may be. * * *

[(E) THE TEMPER OF THE LEGAL PROFESSION IN THE UNITED STATES, AND HOW IT SERVES AS A COUNTERPOISE TO DEMOCRACY]

* * *

* * * Men who have made a special study of the laws derive from occupation certain habits of order, a taste for formalities, and a kind of instinctive regard for the regular connection of ideas, which naturally render them very hostile to the revolutionary spirit and the unreflecting passions of the multitude.

The special information that lawyers derive from their studies ensures them a separate rank in society, and they constitute a sort of privileged body in the scale of intellect. This notion of their superiority perpetually recurs to them in the practice of their profession: they are the masters of a science which is necessary, but which is not very generally known; they serve as arbiters between the citizens; and the habit of directing to their purpose the blind passions of parties in litigation inspires them with a certain contempt for the judgment of the multitude. * * *

Some of the tastes and the habits of the aristocracy may consequently be discovered in the characters of lawyers. They participate in the same instinctive love of order and formalities; and they entertain the same repugnance to the actions of the multitude, and the same secret contempt of the government of the people. I do not mean to say that the natural propensities of lawyers are sufficiently strong to sway them irresistibly; for they, like most other men, are governed by their private interests, and especially by the interests of the moment.

* * * When an aristocracy excludes the leaders of that profession from its ranks, it excites enemies who are the more formidable as they are independent of the nobility by their labors and feel themselves to be their equals in intelligence though inferior in opulence and power. But whenever an aristocracy consents to impart some of its privileges to these same individuals, the two classes coalesce very readily and assume, as it were, family interests.

I am in like manner inclined to believe that a monarch will always be able to convert legal practitioners into the most serviceable instruments of his authority. * * *

Lawyers are attached to public order beyond every other consideration, and the best security of public order is authority. It must not be forgotten, also, that if they prize freedom much, they generally value legality still more: they are less afraid of tyranny than of arbitrary power; and, provided the legislature undertakes of itself to deprive men of their independence, they are not dissatisfied.

I am therefore convinced that the prince who, in presence of an encroaching democracy, should endeavor to impair the judicial authority in his dominions, and to diminish the political influence of lawyers, would commit a great mistake: he would let slip the substance of authority to grasp the shadow. He would act more wisely in introducing lawyers into the government; and if he entrusted despotism to them under the form of violence, perhaps he would find it again in their hands under the external features of justice and law.

The government of democracy is favorable to the political power of lawyers; for when the wealthy, the noble, and the prince are excluded from the government, the lawyers take possession of it, in their own right, as it were, since they are the only men of information and sagacity, beyond the sphere of the people, who can be the object of the popular choice. If, then, they are led by their tastes towards the aristocracy and the prince, they are brought in contact with the people by their interests. They like the government of democracy without participating in its propensities and without imitating its weaknesses; whence they derive a twofold authority from it and over it. The people in democratic states do not mistrust the members of the legal profession, because it is known that they are interested to serve the popular cause; and the people listen to them without irritation, because they do not attribute to them any sinister designs. The lawyers do not, indeed, wish to overthrow the institutions of democracy, but they constantly endeavor to turn it away from its real direction by means that are foreign to its nature. Lawyers belong to the people by birth and interest, and to the aristocracy by habit and taste; they may be looked upon as the connecting link between the two great classes of society.

The profession of the law is the only aristocratic element that can be amalgamated without violence with the natural elements of democracy and be advantageously and permanently combined with them. I am not ignorant of the defects inherent in the character of this body of men; but without this admixture of lawyer-like sobriety with the democratic principle, I question whether democratic institutions could long be maintained; and I cannot believe that a republic could hope to exist at the present time if the influence of lawyers in public business did not increase in proportion to the power of the people.

* * *

The French codes are often difficult to comprehend, but they can be read by everyone; nothing, on the other hand, can be more obscure and strange to the uninitiated than a legislation founded upon precedents. The absolute need of legal aid that is felt in England and the United States, and the high opinion that is entertained of the ability of the legal profession, tend to separate it more and more from the people and to erect it into a distinct class. The French lawyer is simply a man extensively acquainted with the statutes of his country; but the English or American lawyer resembles the hierophants of Egypt, for like them he is the sole interpreter of an occult science * * * [since most of American law is based on judicial precedent.]

* * *

In America there are no nobles or literary men, and the people are apt to mistrust the wealthy; lawyers consequently form the highest political class and the most cultivated portion of society. They have therefore nothing to gain by innovation, which adds a conservative interest to their natural taste for public order. * * *

The more we reflect upon all that occurs in the United States, the more we shall be persuaded that the lawyers, as a body, form the most powerful, if not the only, counterpoise to the democratic element. In that country we easily perceive how the legal profession is qualified by its attributes, and even by its faults, to neutralize the vices inherent in popular government. When the American people are intoxicated by passion or carried away by the impetuosity of their ideas, they are checked and stopped by the almost invisible influence of their legal counselors. These secretly oppose their aristocratic propensities to the nation's democratic instincts, their superstitious attachment to what is old to its love of novelty, their narrow views to its immense designs and their habitual procrastination to its ardent impatience.

The courts of justice are the visible organs by which the legal profession is enabled to control the democracy. * * *

* * * I am aware that a secret tendency to diminish the judicial power exists in the United States; and by most of the constitutions of the several states the government can, upon the demand of the two houses of the legislature, remove judges from their station. Some other state constitutions make the members of the judiciary elective, and they are even subjected to frequent re-elections. I venture to predict that these innovations will sooner or later be attended with fatal consequences; and that it will be found out at some future period that by thus lessening the independence of the judiciary they have attacked not only the judicial power, but the democratic republic itself.

It must not be supposed, moreover, that the legal spirit is confined in the United States to the courts of justice; it extends far beyond them. As the lawyers form the only enlightened class whom the people do not mistrust, they are naturally called upon to occupy most of the public stations. They fill the legislative assemblies and are at the head of the administration; they consequently exercise a powerful influence upon the formation of the law and upon its execution. The lawyers are obliged, however, to yield to the current public opinion, which is too strong for them to resist; but it is easy to find indications of what they would do if they were free to act. The Americans, who have made so many innovations in their political laws, have introduced very sparing alterations in their civil laws, and that with great difficulty, although many of these laws are repugnant to their social condition. The reason for this is that in matters of civil law the majority are obliged to defer to the authority of the legal profession, and the American lawyers are disinclined to innovate when they are left to their own choice.

The influence of legal habits extends beyond the precise limits I have pointed out. Scarcely any political question arises in the United States that is not resolved, sooner or later, into a judicial question. Hence all parties are obliged to borrow, in their daily controversies, the ideas, and even the language, peculiar to judicial proceedings. As most public men are or have been legal practitioners, they introduce the customs and technicalities of their profession into the management of public affairs. The jury extends this habit to all classes. The language of the law thus becomes, in some measure, a vulgar tongue; the spirit of the law, which is produced in the schools and courts of justice, gradually penetrates beyond their walls into the bosom of society, where it descends to the lowest classes, so that at last the whole people contract the habits and the tastes of the judicial magistrate. The lawyers of the United States form a party which * * * acts upon the country imperceptibly, but finally fashions it to suit its own purposes.

NOTES AND QUESTIONS

1. It is the conventional wisdom that Tocqueville understood America better than most Americans before or since. Do you agree? Do his words still ring true? Why do you suppose that following the November 1994 congressional elections Newt Gingrich, newly-crowned Republican speaker-to-be of the United States House of Representatives, immediately advised his victorious colleagues to prepare for their coming legislative agenda by reading Tocqueville? Tocqueville was a French aristocrat, lawyer, and legislator who was sent to America to study penal reform. He proceeded to write a wide-ranging survey of American social and political life. For a short and penetrating analysis of his work, see Richard Hofstadter, Alexis de Tocqueville, in L. Kronenberger, ed., Atlantic Brief Lives 795 (1971). For the continuing validity of Tocqueville's social and political observations see the remarkable reproduction of Tocqueville and Beaumont's trip to America in Richard Reeves, American Journey: Travelling with Tocqueville in Search of Democracy in America (1982). Tocqueville believed that the world was moving in the direction of democracy, and that America was in the vanguard. He was not overwhelmingly pleased with what the future offered, and believed that modern pressures for equality would extinguish some excellence that the *ancien regime* had encouraged. Can you discern, from these excerpts, Tocqueville's personal attitude toward American law and lawyers?

2. Your excerpts begin with Tocqueville's views on the general social and political conditions in America. His major premise is that America seems to have moved furthest towards a classless society. What part did American law play in this movement? Would Tocqueville have approved of Thomas Jefferson's efforts to do away with entail and primogeniture? Was Tocqueville correct when he predicted that either all Americans would come to have all rights or all but one man would have no rights? Why or why not?

3. What about the established American political institutions Tocqueville describes? He suggests that the overriding principle in American politics is the "sovereignty of the people?" Can you discern what is meant by this phrase? Would you agree with Tocqueville that it was the aristocrats in Maryland who led the way toward universal suffrage? What relevance does Samuel Chase's attitude toward universal suffrage have here?

4. What relevance does American judicial power have to the principle of popular sovereignty? Why doesn't an American "turbulent multitude" regard law as its enemy? Or does one? Why is it, as Tocqueville observes, that in America the judiciary has more power than in other countries? How does it come about that in America nearly every political dispute sooner or later winds up in the courts? You are probably familiar with this phenomenon, but note that Tocqueville was describing it almost two centuries ago.

5. What relationship is there between the prominence of judicial power in America and the prominence of American lawyers? Why is it that Tocqueville believes that the only true American aristocracy is the lawyers? Compare with Toqueville's views those of Alva Hugh Maddox, a Justice of the Su-

preme Court of Alabama, "Lawyers: The Aristocracy of Democracy or 'Skunks, Snakes, and Sharks?'," 29 Cumb.L.Rev. 323 (1998). How does one reconcile the ideas that the American lawyers are aristocrats, the spirit of equality of Americans, and Tocqueville's notion that Americans have a special veneration and respect for the law? Are Tocqueville's observations on lawyers consistent with those of Honestus? Does he explain the anti-lawyer sentiment in America? Note that Tocqueville suggests that while it is the special province of lawyers to be well-informed and sagacious, they also have a tendency to gravitate toward the centers of power, and can just as easily serve a monarchy as a democracy. Towards what center of power would Tocqueville suggest that American lawyers would eventually gravitate? Consider his comments on the inevitability of another American aristocracy:

> As the conditions of men constituting the nation become more and more equal, the demand for manufactured commodities becomes more general and extensive, and the cheapness that places these objects within the reach of slender fortunes becomes a great element of success. Hence there are every day more men of great opulence and education who devote their wealth and knowledge to manufactures and who seek, by opening large establishments and by a strict division of labor, to meet the fresh demands which are made on all sides. Thus, in proportion as the mass of the nation turns to democracy, that particular class which is engaged in manufactures becomes more aristocratic. * * *
>
> But this kind of aristocracy by no means resembles those kinds which preceded it. * * * To tell the truth, though there are rich men, the class of rich men does not exist; for these rich individuals have no feelings or purposes, no traditions or hopes, in common; there are individuals, therefore, but no definite class.
>
> Not only are the rich not compactly united among themselves, but there is no real bond between them and the poor. Their relative position is not a permanent one; they are constantly drawn together or separated by their interests. The workman is generally dependent on the master, but not on any particular master; these two men meet in the factory, but do not know each other elsewhere; and while they come into contact on one point, they stand very far apart on all others. The manufacturer asks nothing of the workman but his labor; the workman expects nothing from him but his wages. The one contracts no obligation to protect nor the other to defend, and they are not permanently connected either by habit or by duty. * * *
>
> The territorial aristocracy of former ages was either bound by law, or thought itself bound by usage, to come to the relief of its serving-men and to relieve their distresses. But the manufacturing aristocracy of our age first impoverishes and debases the men who serve it and then abandons them to be supported by the charity of the public. * * *

I am of the opinion, on the whole, that the manufacturing aristocracy which is growing up under our eyes is one of the harshest that ever existed in the world; but at the same time it is one of the most confined and least dangerous. Nevertheless, the friends of democracy should keep their eyes anxiously fixed in this direction; for if ever a permanent inequality of conditions and aristocracy again penetrates into the world, it may be predicted that this is the gate by which they will enter.

II Democracy in America 169–171 (Vintage Books ed. 1945).

6. Perhaps you can sense, reading between the lines (as it were) of Toqueville's masterpiece, an ambivalence about the American democratic experiment. The ambivalence that characterized Tocqueville's work, and the manner in which he was uneasily poised between an aristocratic past and a democratic future, are the themes in two recent powerful studies of his life and his writing, Leo Damrosch, Tocqueville's Discovery of America (2010), and Sheldon S. Wolin, Toqueville Between Two Worlds: The Making of a Political and Theoretical Life (2001).

7. Tocqueville, and, for that matter, Robert Rantoul, suggest that the American common law is essentially conservative. Is this correct? How do these two men divide over the value placed on conservatism? "Honestus" was a Boston merchant, Tocqueville a French Aristocrat. Do their different backgrounds lead to a different evaluation of American lawyers? As you read the cases on contracts, property, torts, and corporations which follow, and which are ostensibly American common-law decisions, see if you find "essentially conservative" results in the cases.

B. THE RISE OF THE "CLASSICAL THEORY" OF CONTRACTS

INTRODUCTION: The Colonial Background of American Law: Contracts, Property, and Torts

Twelve of the thirteen English colonies in North America were established in the seventeenth century, and Georgia, the last, was founded in 1732. The creation of a legal system—a mechanism, however rudimentary, for the adjudication of disputes and enforcement of authority—was an elemental need from the beginning. Each colony eventually provided local courts with jurisdiction over criminal and civil matters. Here trials were conducted, usually at the county level. The courts in the colony of New Jersey were typical. At the local level there was the Justice of the Peace, the inferior Court of Common Pleas (civil jurisdiction) and the Court of General Sessions of the Peace (criminal jurisdiction), as well as a few more specialized courts. There was a single Supreme Court of Judicature. The highest court, while it mainly dealt with appeals, was also a court of original jurisdiction in some instances, depending on the seriousness of the case. The Supreme Court of Judicature of New Jersey included a chief justice and four associate judges. Colonial trial courts, in many cases, sat with juries. At the lowest trial court level outside of New England were those presided over by justices of the peace, commissioners, and sheriffs where petty complaints were resolved, and local governmental administration implemented. In New England, township governments played that role.

The sources of law in each colony depended on local circumstances. The terms of royal charters were important, as well as the instructions from royal officials, provincial legislation (which, as we saw in the Parsons' Cause, required approval by royal ministers in London acting on behalf of the King), Parliamentary enactments, and local custom. The English common law was a basis of law in the colonies, though the wide variation of conditions in the colonies from the mother country inevitably meant that laws were adapted to local needs. As we have indicated, by 1760, when the colonists numbered about 1.5 million, lawyers were an important, and even thriving, order of professionals. They were fully aware of the variations in law, jurisdiction, and practices between the colonies and England, which were many. These differences they were also willing to exploit when it was to the advantage of a client.

In the mid–1750s Sir William Blackstone gave a series of lectures at Oxford on the history of English law. Between 1761 and 1765 he arranged them into a treatise of four volumes that were published as *Commentaries on the Laws of England*. You will soon read some excerpts from that work, and it is one of the most influential set of law books in English history. Its impact in the English colonies was extraordinary. Colonial lawyers sent for copies, and in 1771–1772 a special edition was published in Philadelphia that quickly sold out. The *Commentaries* examined the totality of English law and offered lucid summaries based on Blackstone's readings of case and statutory law. While the colonists' grasp of common law was reasonably good in 1765, as also was the awareness of the differences between colony and mother country, after the publication of the *Commentaries* no lawyer could plead ignorance of the state of the law in England.

As indicated, though, if there were broad legal similarities between colonies and mother country, there were also profound differences. For settlers in the North American colonies, ever-present was the reality of life on the fringes of a vast continent, far removed from English control and protection. Physical security was a more or less constant concern. From the beginning the colonists and native inhabitants clashed, and the further removed from coastal areas of settlement, the greater the dangers for settlers. England was not alone in its colonizing ambitions. The Spanish, from their foothold in Florida, had designs on Georgia; colonial coastal fortifications were a necessity in the young English colony. From the holdings they claimed stretching from Canada to Louisiana, the

French freely navigated the Eastern interior along the Mississippi, where they entered into trade agreements and protective alliances with Native Americans. Brewing antagonisms in the trans-Appalachian Ohio River Valley between the British and the French erupted into armed conflict in 1754. The "French and Indian War" was the costliest war in English history up to that time, and it seemed only fair to the crown that the Americans should help pay for it, since they stood to benefit and shouldered none of the direct costs. The controversial decisions by the British ministry to impose new taxes and tighten up the collection of customs and revenue in the colonies through the Writs of Assistance, the Sugar Act of 1763, and the Stamp Act of 1765 were a direct consequence. As we saw in the readings on the Writs of Assistance case and Thomas Hutchinson in an earlier chapter, these legal developments stimulated a decade-long patriot movement from which the British government never recovered.

Cultural and ideological differences between colonies and the mother country also were evident. The colonies did not arise from a feudal tradition, and there was no landed aristocracy or monarchy in the new world. Among white males at least, a rough equality existed in a land where farmers, merchants, tavern owners, blacksmiths, ironworkers, shoemakers, carpenters, and lawyers mingled. The contrasts between the makeup of the provincial legislative assemblies and Parliament flowed naturally from this demographic fact. While the bulk of colonists were English, there were also settlers of German, Swedish, French, Portuguese, Italian, and Dutch descent.

There were also religious differences. In the mother country the established Protestant Church of England dominated, but in New England (except Rhode Island) it was the Puritan Congregational churches, the dissenters and nonconformists in the England of 1600, that constituted the establishment. In Southern colonies, like England, the established church was the Church of England. Still, none of the churches North or South wielded the same authority and legal jurisdiction over local affairs as did England's. Moreover, not every colony had an established church. Quakers were prominent in Pennsylvania, Catholics in parts of Maryland, New York and Pennsylvania, and Protestant Huguenot dissenters from Catholic France settled in the Carolinas. The Scots–Irish brought Presbyterianism to the piedmont of the Middle and Southern colonies. Jewish Synagogues were founded in Newport, New Amsterdam, Savannah, Charleston, and Philadelphia.

Protestant denominational practices and even beliefs were made yet more diverse during the Great Awakening beginning in the 1720s, America's first great religious revival. In stark contrast with the European continent and the mother country, by 1760 the hallmark of American religion was its variety joined with a general spirit of tolerance, at least by European standards. The great majority of colonial inhabitants were united by common Judeo–Christian precepts and beliefs, and these infused not only institutions, but also perceptions of law and law's purposes. There was little doubt about what constituted right values and behavior, and colonists brought these perceptions with them when serving on juries or as justices of the peace, sitting as judges, or serving in assemblies.

It was colonial perceptions and needs, combined with the inheritance of law and custom from England and elsewhere in Europe, that dictated the development of law. Contract law in the colonies applied mainly to the exchange of title to land, and did not exist as a distinct branch of law. Contract law, as it developed in America in the nineteenth century, as you will soon understand, transformed to enforce speculative bargains made to secure future gains. A market economy based on competition requires the freedom to enter into such risking bargains, and to reap accordingly. The colonial economy was rural, agricultural, and pre-industrial. While it is the case that trade and commerce were important, market relations tended to be locally based, and in more remote areas subsistence agriculture and barter was the rule. An agreement might be concluded with a handshake or merely a verbal assurance. Its performance, written or otherwise, was immediate and not based on a future expectation. The community frowned upon idiosyncratic agreements that might threaten the peace or upset the social order. In this category were agreements whose terms suggested shady dealing, or exploiting an advantage.

As you will see in *Searight v. Calbraith*, infra, juries gave voice to a community's values, and in cases involving contract disputes, they were expected closely to scrutinize the terms and exercise moral judgment regarding the appropriateness of damages for nonperformance. As you will see when you encounter *White v. Flora & Cherry*, in some cases courts of equity were called upon to enforce the contract's performance, which was most easily secured in the case of title to land.

"There is nothing which so generally strikes the imagination, and engages the affections of mankind, as the right of property; or that sole and despotic dominion which one man claims and exercises over the external things of the world, in total exclusion of the right of any other individual in the universe." With these words Blackstone captured the English common law's reverence for private property. Colonists carried these values with them to the New World, but circumstances here worked changes. For one, land was readily available, and simple devices for its ownership and transfer evolved. The complexities of English tenure were left behind when the first settlers crossed the ocean. In the absence of a class of legal professionals in the seventeenth century, communities resorted to plain common sense and moral and pragmatic solutions to problems which arose concerning property and commerce. Thus towns regulated the quality and price of merchandise sold in markets, and forbad price gouging.

Efforts were made in the middle and Southern colonies to regulate the quality and price of tobacco sold for export, knowing it would effect marketability abroad. This was simply viewed as part of the larger responsibilities communities had to maintain order and protect their inhabitants.

Nor were colonials free to use their property in ways that damaged others. Following the English common law as you will soon see set forth in Blackstone, tanneries, and other local industries that produced noxious odors or dangers were potential nuisances that were regulated; colonial assemblies required tippling houses and taverns to obtain a license to operate, and sometimes stipulated standards of care for overnight guests. Again as you will later read in Blackstone, the law also accorded privileges, when those privileges served important community needs. Ferry owners, for example, operated with legislative grants of monopoly and could sue competitors for infringement. (Ferries were absolutely essential to travel and commerce in the colonies, where few roads existed.) While courts protected rights and privileges, the enforcement of regulations always presented a problem, for it was the informal local rule of colonial life, and not central governmental administration, that most distinguished the Americans from their English counterparts. In a community where no one was a total stranger, the persuasions and judgments of one's neighbors carried much weight, and it was difficult if not impossible to impose a regime of central planning and regulation.

As indicated earlier, in another area of property, inheritance, colonial patterns varied from the mother country. The English rule of primogeniture ensured that estates would be passed down to the eldest son on the death of the father. In this manner, land and family were perpetuated intact as the symbol of an aristocratic order. In the New England colonies, the law was changed to permit partible inheritance (splitting up the landed property) among the surviving spouse and children. In the Middle and Southern colonies, while primogeniture remained the law, it declined in importance as land owners used wills to provide for the distribution of property among their wives and children. The availability of land helped, of course, and colonies encouraged its settlement and development up to a point. These developments also grew from a decidedly more egalitarian attitude toward family and authority than existed in England—hardly surprising given that the opportunity permanently to relocate in the New World was one that attracted the middling ranks of society.

Property law in the colonies also took its measure from the possibilities as well as the limits of life in the New World. By 1750 a crude economy based on markets and production had begun to distinguish each of the regions, with ship building and fishing centering in the New England colonies, fur trade and crops in the Middle Colonies, and plantation-based production of tobacco, rice, and indigo in the Chesapeake and Carolinas. There were also challenges. Certainly the existence of an imperial and mercantile system of administration by the Crown prevented developmental and manufacturing interests from gaining a hold in local economies. No less a limiting factor was the prevailing moral system, rooted in religious orthodoxies and communitarian traditions that made little room for materialism. (Wealth won by hard work and thrift, on the other hand, was a just reward.)

Geography presented its own challenges. Colonial society was overwhelmingly agrarian; most people lived along the Atlantic coast and rivers, extending to the edge of a backcountry that was often hostile. Europeans came to the colonies seeking something—greater religious freedoms, opportunity, the prospect of land ownership, even escape. Africans were the great exception, the first of whom were forcibly transported to Virginia by Dutch ship as early as 1619. For all who successfully made the journey to the New World, the demands for security were great, and good security translated into good order and cohesion. The law of property, contract, and nuisance recognized these realities.

Private property and its uses were important everywhere in the English colonies. Blackstone's voice was readily heard across the Atlantic, and he might have been speaking directly to colonial lawyers and community pillars when he wrote that "the peace and security of individuals" is promoted by "steadily pursuing that wise and orderly maxim, of assigning to every thing capable of ownership a legal and determinate owner." If colonials grew accustomed to security in their property, they also recognized that there were limits to property's use. Perhaps the grandest limits of all were their own conflicting expectations.

Further Reading:

Daniel Boorstin, *The Mysterious Science of the Law: An Essay on Blackstone's Commentaries*, 1941

Jon Butler, *Becoming America: The Revolution before 1776*, 2000

Paul Finkelman and David Cobin, eds., *Tucker's Blackstone*, 1996

Lawrence M. Friedman, *A History of American Law*, 3d edition, 2005

Robert A. Gross, *The Minutemen and Their World*, 1976

Kermit L. Hall, *The Magic Mirror*, 1989

Peter Charles Hoffer, *Law and People in Colonial America*, 2d ed., 1998

Morton J. Horwitz, *The Transformation of American Law: 1780–1860*, 1977

Kenneth Lockridge, John J. McCusker and Russell R. Menard, *The Economy of British America, 1607–1789*, 1985

Gary Nash, *The Urban Crucible: Social Change, Political Consciousness, and the Origins of the American Revolution*, 1979

William Nelson, *The Americanization of the Common Law*, 1975

Carol Shammas, Marylynn Salmon, and Michel Dahlin, *Inheritance in America, From Colonial Times to the Present,* 1987

Edward G. White, *Tort Law in America: An Intellectual History*, 1980

Michael Zuckerman, *Peaceable Kingdoms: New England Towns in the Eighteenth Century,* 1983

SEARIGHT V. CALBRAITH

United States Circuit Court, District of Pennsylvania, 1796.
21 Fed.Cas. 927.

[In February 1792, Mr. Searight sold Calbraith & Co. a bill of exchange (a negotiable piece of paper, like a check, which entitles the bearer to receive from a person or bank a certain sum of money) for 150,000 *livres tournois* (French units of currency). The bill of exchange was payable in Paris, six months from the date of sale. Calbraith & Co. promised to pay £10,625 in Pennsylvania currency for the Bill of Exchange, on or after July 1, 1792. The agent of Calbraith & Co. presented the bill of exchange for payment at the appointed time in Paris. The bank which was to pay on the bill of exchange offered payment in "assignats" (French paper currency) "which, by the then existing laws of France, were made a lawful tender, in payment of debts." Calbraith & Co.'s agent refused to accept the offered assignats, "declaring at the same time, that he would receive no other money than French crowns" (specie). Following these events Calbraith & Co., which had not yet paid Searight for the Bill of Exchange, refused to do so. Searight then sued Calbraith & Co. for their failure to pay the £10,625. Calbraith & Co., in turn, sued Searight for damages because of the French bank's failure to pay in specie. There was apparently no *explicit* agreement regarding whether the French bank would pay in paper money or in specie.]

* * *

On the trial of the cause, evidence was produced, on both sides, to ascertain and fix the precise terms of the original contract, for the sale and purchase of the bill of exchange * * * as to the knowledge and view of the parties, relative to the existence of assignats, or the law of France, making them a legal tender in payment of debts. And the great question of fact for decision, was, whether the parties contracted for a payment in gold and silver; or tacitly left the medium of payment, to the laws of France, where the bill was payable? The law arising from the fact, was discussed at large, according to the different positions of the parties in interest.

For Searight, it was shown, by the decrees of the French government, that assignats were established as a circulating medium for the payment of debts, before, and at the time of, the contract for the bill of exchange. * * * And this fact being known, it was contended, that the purchase of a bill payable in France, must in itself import an agreement to receive in satisfaction, the lawful current medium of that country, unless the contract expressly provides against it, which, on the present occasion, was controverted and denied. * * *

For Calbraith and Co. it was contended, that an express contract had been proved to pay the bill in specie; that the very terms of the bill import the same understanding of the parties; that however binding the law of France may be on cases between French citizens, or between American and French citizens, it did not affect contracts between Americans; that, in legal contemplation, there has been neither a payment, nor a tender of payment; and that Searight has sustained no damage, nor shown any right to recover. * * *

Before IREDELL, CIRCUIT JUSTICE, and PETERS, DISTRICT JUDGE.

IREDELL, CIRCUIT JUSTICE. * * * The sole question * * * is, whether the tender of assignats in payment of the bill, was a compliance with that contract? * * *

* * *

* * * Every man is bound to know the laws of his own country; but no man is bound to know the laws of foreign countries.

In two cases, indeed, (and, I believe, only in two cases) can foreign laws affect the contracts of American citizens: 1st. Where they reside, or trade, in a foreign country; and 2d. Where the contracts, plainly referring to a foreign country for their execution, adopt and recognize the lex loci. The present controversy, therefore, turns upon the fact, whether the parties meant to abide by the law of France? And this fact the jury must decide.

As to the damages, if the verdict should be for Searight, though it is true that in actions for a breach of contract, a jury should, in general, give the whole money contracted for and interest; yet, in a case like the present, they may modify the demand, and find such damages, as they think adequate to the injury actually sustained. * * *

Peters, District Judge. The decision depends entirely on the intention of the parties, of which the jury must judge. If a specie payment was meant, a tender in assignats was unavailing. But if the current money of France was in view, the tender in assignats was lawfully made, and is sufficiently proved.

When the jury were at the bar, ready to deliver verdicts, the plaintiff in each action voluntarily suffered a nonsuit. It was afterwards declared, however, that in Searight v. Calbraith and Co. the verdict would have been, generally, for the defendants; and that in Calbraith and Co. v. Searight, the verdict would have been for the plaintiffs, but with only six pence damages.

NOTES AND QUESTIONS

1. "Livres Tournois" were French coins in use before the French Revolution of 1789. What effect would you have given the use of that term in the contract if you were a member of this jury, and you knew that the coins were no longer in use? By the way, what do you take to be the reason for the transaction in the case? Does the fact that at this time the political situations in both France (the creation in 1792 of the French Republic and the outbreak of the French Revolutionary Wars in Europe) and America (the experiment with the new national government) were somewhat uncertain help in interpreting the deal?

2. How much discretion does the jury have to find the law and the facts in this case? Does this discretion seem to be more or less than that which you saw the jury exercise in criminal cases? In which type of case, criminal or civil, is it more important that the jury be given great discretion? Why? Why do you suppose that *after* the judges' instructions to the jury, but *before* "a verdict was rendered," the plaintiff in each action voluntarily suffered a nonsuit? What is the meaning of the verdict that the jury would have delivered? Does it support Honestus's arguments?

3. In the beginning of the nineteenth century, in many states, efforts were undertaken to modernize legal procedure, and to improve the overall efficiency of courts. In Massachusetts, Theodore Sedgwick, a prominent Federalist, advanced many proposals for judicial reform. What follows is the description in Richard E. Ellis, The Jeffersonian Crisis: Courts and Politics in the Young Republic 190–191, 198 (1971) of Sedgwick's opinions on the jury, and the political reaction to his ideas. Do these excerpts help to understand what the jury was up to in Searight v. Calbraith? Have you encountered anything like the controversy between Sedgwick and "Republican writers" before?

> Sedgwick * * * counseled that under no circumstances should juries be permitted to interpret the law. Allowing juries, as was sometimes done in post-revolutionary Massachusetts, to mingle law with fact in arriving at their decisions, he believed, had contributed greatly to the disastrous inefficiency of the state's legal system. "In all instances where trial by jury has been practiced, and a separation of the law from the fact has taken place, there have been expedition, certainty, system and their consequences, general approbation. Where this has not been the case, neither expedition, certainty nor system have prevailed."
>
> He also argued that the quality of juries had to be improved. Under an existing act justices of the peace, "men of the first consideration and weight of character in their counties," were exempted from jury duty. He advised that the act be repealed, otherwise the community would be de-

nied the services of educated men upon whose "intelligence, integrity and independence," a successful administration of justice was so dependent.

* * *

> Republican writers, on the other hand, defended the jury's right to interpret the law and to bring in a decision contrary to that ordered by the court. * * * [One wrote] that on points of law the greatest attention should be given the opinion of the court, but went on to argue that the question still remained: "suppose a difference in sentiment between the judges and the jury with regard to the law . . . What is to be done?—The jury must do their duty, and their whole duty; they must decide upon the law as well as upon the fact." To do otherwise would be to ask a man "to judge against his own judgment; in other words to sacrifice his honor and conscience—who would willingly be a juror upon these degrading terms?"

4. Consider the implications for national or international trade of the behavior of the judges and jury in this case and the implications of Sedgwick's comments. If you were involved in such trade would you have confidence about the decision American courts might render if you were forced to litigate? Is it relevant that the American economy was capital-scarce until about the middle of the nineteenth century? Technological development, internal improvements, and manufacturing enterprise in America depended upon the availability of vast sums of venture capital, and much of it had to come in the form of investment by Europeans. See generally Stuart Bruchey, The Roots of American Economic Growth 1607–1861 (1965). Would you expect the scarcity of capital to affect American law?

WHITE V. FLORA AND CHERRY

Supreme Court of Tennessee, 1815.
2 Tenn. (2 Overt.) 426.

In Equity—COOKE, J., delivered the following opinion of the Court:—The bill charges that a grant issued to Lazarus Flora by the State of North Carolina for 274 acres of land, by whom previous to his death the same was devised to the defendant, Jesse Flora; that Jesse Flora, not knowing where the land was situated, applied to the complainant [White], and proposed to give him the one-half of the tract if he would find it and be at the expense of investigating the title, and to sell him the other half at a price to be fixed by valuers chosen for that purpose, payable in horses, and that a contract was made and reduced to writing in pursuance of such proposition; that the complainant made search in the land office and other places, and found the situation of the land; that afterwards Jesse Flora, with a view to cheat the complainant, sold and conveyed the whole tract to the defendant, Daniel Cherry, who at the same time had full knowledge of the equity on the part of the complainant. It is also charged that the complainant let Flora have a horse, bridle, and saddle at the price of one hundred dollars, and that it was agreed that, should the land be found, it was to stand as so much paid towards the purchase of half of the tract according to the agreement.

The bill prays that the land may be conveyed to the complainant.

Flora answers, in substance, that the agreement was made as set forth in the bill, but that White was guilty of great fraud and concealment in the transaction; that the land did not lie more than three miles from White's house, and that the situation of it was well known to White at the time the contract was made, although he represented himself to be entirely ignorant upon the subject; and indeed caused Flora to believe it would require great labor and influence to ascertain where the land lay. Flora admits that he sold and conveyed the land to Cherry, believing that White could not compel a performance of the contract, in consequence of the fraud and misrepresentation which he used; that he is willing to pay White the hundred dollars mentioned in the bill upon application, but denies that the horse, bridle, and saddle were received in part payment of the land.

Cherry's answer contains the same allegations as to the fraud practised by White, of which transaction he admits he was well informed when he took the deed from Flora. * * *

The proof in the cause shows that young Flora and a man by the name of Biggs had been hunting for the land, and, being unsuccessful, came to White's and inquired of him if he knew any thing of the land; he replied that he did not. Flora then pressed him to take a part of the land for finding it and paying the expense of investigating the title, which White at first refused to do; but finally, after much persuasion, the contract was closed as set forth in the bill. The parties then went to an attorney to have writings drawn; and the attorney is particular in stating that he was careful in making Flora understand the nature of the agreement. Flora said he was illiterate, and a stranger in the country, and was willing to make a liberal allowance for finding and securing the land. * * * The agreement was signed on the 18th day of August, 1807, and both parties went on to Nashville, which was only a few miles, to search the register's office. White got a copy of the grant, and the next day, on application to one Thomas Bradley, White found where the land was, and that it lay within two or three miles of his own house. * * *

There is no satisfactory proof going to show that White knew where the land was situated, before he made the contract with Flora.

The purchase of the horse, bridle, and saddle was proved to be in the manner set forth in the bill; and that the day after Bradley told White where the land lay, White and Flora went together on the land, and verbally agreed that the half to be purchased by White should be valued by Bradley. Flora seemed then well pleased with the contract he had made. Some short time after this, Cherry made propositions to Flora, to get a deed for the land, which were at first rejected, but finally agreed to, and the deed made as set forth by Cherry in his answer. Cherry at the same time gave Flora a bond of indemnity against the claim of White.

To the specific execution of the contract sought by the complainant, the defendant's counsel in the argument objected * * *:

1st. The fraud alleged to have been practised by the complainant upon Flora.

2d. The inadequacy of the consideration given by the complainant.

* * *

1st. There is no proof of fraud on the part of White. It is true, when he was first applied to by the defendant Flora, he represented himself as wholly ignorant of the situation of the land, but it is equally true that no proof has been shown to us that this representation was false. If the fact had been with the defendant upon that point, we should have no hesitation in saying the complainant ought not to have a decree. When the complainant was applied to, with a view to ascertain his knowledge upon the subject of this land, if he then knew where it was, a representation on his part that he did not know, would have been a fraud, inasmuch as by means of it Flora would, in all probability, have been induced to give a greater price for the trouble and labor of searching, and the expenses incident to an investigation of the title. In all cases of contract, any representation of a falsehood or concealment of a truth, which, if correctly known, would probably be a reason for making the terms of the contract different, will be a good ground for rescinding the agreement in a court of equity. Equity delights in doing justice, it delights in compelling men, by means of an appeal to the conscience, to do those things which ought to be done. To effect so desirable an object, strict regard must be had that no one is permitted to enjoy property which has been procured through means of an unreal appearance of things, more particularly if that appearance is the result of the fraudulent machinations of the person who seeks to be availed of it.

* * *

Had White known where to find the land, and apprised Flora of such knowledge, it is more than probable that Flora would not have given so much for the information as if he imagined that White was as ignorant of its situation as himself, and would most likely be put to some considerable trouble and expense in finding it. Therefore the representation on the part of White, that he knew not where the land was, if he did know, was a fraud; but there is no proof that he concealed any fact within his knowledge, or made any suggestion inconsistent with truth.

2d. It is also urged that there is in this case great inadequacy of consideration; and that therefore the Court ought not to decree a specific performance of the contract with Flora. * * *

When a complainant comes into a court of equity for the purpose of having a contract rescinded on the ground of mere inadequacy of consideration, all the books agree that relief cannot be afforded. The mere circumstance of the sum paid being greatly inferior in value to the thing contracted to be purchased, will not, of itself, be sufficient to set aside an agreement; but it is in many instances strong evidence of fraud and imposition, and, coupled with other matters, such as the embarrassment of one of the parties, or the like, may frequently occasion the interference of a court of equity. But the situation of a complainant seeking to enforce the execution of an unreasonable and unconscientious bargain is placed on a ground very different. In such cases, the Court has a discretionary power; it will either cause the agreement to be executed or not, depending upon the equity of the whole case. * * *

What cases of mere inadequacy of consideration will authorize the Court to refuse lending its aid to enforce an agreement, is not now necessary to be specified, as we are of opinion this is not one of them.

The sum it really cost White to find this land is, as we conceive, not the proper question; the bargain was clearly a risking one; it might cost only a few dollars to find the land, or it might cost the worth of the land itself. At the time the contract was made, it was utterly unknown to the parties, and impossible to tell which had the advantage; for any thing then known, the result might prove equally valuable, or much more advantageous to one than to the other. Every fact, tending to remove uncertainty, was wholly unknown. If White had in the end been put to an expense more than sufficient to absorb the whole value of the land, an event which no man can say was impossible, could a court of equity have relieved him? Could Flora be compelled to pay him for his trouble and expense, and rescind the contract as to land? Clearly not. Why not, then, make the situation of the parties reciprocal? Here, White found this land at a cost much beneath what probably would have been given, had the trouble and expense been previously known. But is that any reason why the contract ought not to be specifically executed? When we are asked not to enforce an agreement merely upon the ground of the consideration being inadequate, in a case where that consideration was to be performed in services of an uncertain and dubious value, it is impossible for us not to look at what might have been the amount. When we look at that, we believe there is nothing in it to prevent the interference of this court.

* * *

The complainant is therefore entitled to a decree * * * [that will compel Cherry to deed him the land] upon his paying up to the defendant, Daniel Cherry, the value of the one-half * * * in horses, agreeably to the contract made with Flora.

NOTES AND QUESTIONS

1. As you have learned if you have had a course in contracts, courts of equity are ancient institutions borrowed from England and used for relaxing the rigors of the common law. For example, as suggested by the first defense in this case, if Mr. White had defrauded Mr. Flora by representing that he (White) knew nothing about the location of the land in question, this fraud would have been "a good ground for rescinding the agreement [to sell the land to White] in a court of equity." As this court remarks, this is because the equity court "delights in doing justice," and "in compelling men * * * to do those things which ought to be done." Of more importance to us at this point, however, is the discretion to refuse specific enforcement of land sale contracts possessed by equity court judges. By this time, the beginning of the nineteenth century, it had been clear for many years that inadequacy of consideration was *not a legal* defense to a contract; what do you understand from this case to be the *equity* judge's discretion to refuse enforcement of a land sale contract on the grounds of inadequacy of consideration? Why was the contract enforced in this case?

2. An important case on this issue arose in New York, Seymour v. Delancey, 6 Johns Ch. 222 (1822), and was first heard by that state's great Chancellor, James Kent. The case involved a contract for an exchange of two country farms for a one-third interest in two city lots. The action for specific performance of the exchange was brought by a descendant of the party who was to receive the two farms. According to Chancellor Kent's interpretation of the "weight of the testimony" the two farms were worth $14,000 at the date of the agreement, and the one-third interest in the lots was worth $5,000. There was great disagreement among the witnesses called for valuation, however, with some putting the disparity within about $2,000 or less. Still Kent stated that "I am satisfied, that * * * the village lots were not worth half the value of the country farms * * * ".

Kent proceeded to announce that "It is a settled principle, that a specific performance of a contract of sale is not a matter of course, but rests entirely in the discretion of the Court, upon a view of all the circumstances." "A Court of Equity," Kent went on, "must be satisfied that the claim for a deed is fair and just, and reasonable, and the contract equal in all its parts, and founded on an adequate consideration, before it will interpose with this extraordinary assistance." After examining a nearly interminable series of English and Roman decisions, Kent confessed that in the most recent cases "there is a doubt thrown over the question, whether inadequacy of price alone, though not so great as to be evidence of fraud, will be sufficient * * * to withhold the decree for specific performance." Apparently, however, Kent was more struck with the preponderance of earlier cases in which no such doubts were raised. Said he:

> There is a very great weight of authority against enforcing a contract, where the consideration is so inadequate as to render it a hard bargain, and an unequal and an unreasonable bargain; the argument is exceedingly strong against it in such cases, when it is considered that if equity acts at all, it must act *ex vigore,* and carry the contract into execution, with unmitigated severity: Whereas, if the party be sent to law, to submit his case to a jury, relief can be afforded in damages, with a moderation agreeable to equity and good conscience, and when the claims and pretensions of each party can be duly attended to, and be admitted to govern the assessment.

What did Kent mean when he suggested that if an equity court declined specific enforcement, the party seeking such enforcement could then "be sent to law" where the jury could offer "relief * * * agreeable to equity and good conscience"? Does the proposed jury verdict in Searight v. Calbraith & Co. help in understanding this? Suppose Sedgwick's views on jury discretion were to predominate. Would this undercut Kent's reasoning?

3. After observing that under the civil law contracts for sale of land were rescinded by judicial authority if the price was below half the value of the land, and that even under the Code Napoleon rescission could be granted if the price was 7/12ths below the "real value", Kent refused specific performance. Kent's refusal was reversed by a vote of 14–10 of the New York Court for the Trial of Impeachment and the Correction of Errors, a unique New York judicial institution, now extinct, which consisted of the Members of the New York Senate, the Chief Judge of the New York Supreme Court, and the Equity Chancellor. Seymour v. Delancey, 3 Cow. 445 (1824).

Senator Sudam, who wrote the opinion for the majority, stated that Kent was wrong because his holding amounted to an assertion that *mere inequality* in value, which is not so gross as to strike the moral feeling of an indifferent man, would be sufficient to warrant the Chancellor in withholding a decree for specific performance. Sudam acknowledged the "sound discretion" of the equity court in its decision on granting the decree, but stated that "sound legal discretion" was not to be used as "an arbitrary power, interfering with the contracts of individuals, and sporting with their vested rights." Sudam brought out some facts that Kent had failed to mention, in particular that the owner of the two farms against whom the action was brought had previously purchased the two-thirds interest in the city lots, and that he might have suspected that the city lots would dramatically rise in value if a proposed Navy Yard were built in town.

Sudam went on to suggest that where there was inadequacy of consideration which was "so flagrant and palpable as to convince a man at the first blush that one of the contracting parties had been imposed on by some false pretence" no equity court should enforce a contract. For Sudam, however, this was not such a case. Sudam observed that "There is no question so well calculated to generate a variety of opinion, as that which regards the value of a village lot, or a farm in the country," and that the wide variance in witness valuations illustrated this. Sudam concluded that people will always disagree on the value of land and on the wisdom of particular speculative purchases. Here, said Sudam, the parties were entering into a transaction which none was really capable of evaluating, and there was no evidence to suggest "fraud, surprise, misrepresentation, or deceit." "What right have we," asked Sudam, "to sport with the contracts of parties fairly and deliberately entered into and prevent them from being carried into effect?"

4. With whom do you agree, Kent or Sudam? You have already seen, from Tocqueville, that fortunes in America tended to rise and fall with astonishing rapidity. It should come as no surprise to learn that land values could similarly fluctuate. Indeed, the entire nineteenth century economy in America could be viewed as careening up and down, from boom to bust, as wildly as a roller-coaster. See e.g., Charles Warren, Bankruptcy in United States History (1935), Douglass C. North, The Economic Growth of the United States 1790–1860, 66–71 (Norton library ed. 1966). What should have been the effect of this fluctuation in economic value on contract law? Can you imagine what contract law would have been like in a society where economic values were stable? Once you conclude that economic values will always be in a state of fluctuation, however, to whom is it wisest for the law to turn for determinations of value?

5. By now you have probably suspected that the rules of American contract law reflected *social* as well as economic values. Whose interests would be promoted by the rule of equity discretion to refuse to enforce specific performance of unfair contracts? Is there anything in the reading from Tocqueville which sheds light on why this rule was weakened in the nineteenth century?

GOULDING V. SKINNER

Supreme Judicial Court of Massachusetts, 1822.
18 Mass. (1 Pick.) 162.

In an action of *assumpsit* to recover damages for the breach of a warranty made on the sale of certain machine cards, the declaration alleged, that the defendants warranted them to be good and merchantable, and that in truth they were not so, but were of little or no value. At the trial * * * before Wilde, J., the plaintiffs, to prove the warranty, read to the jury an advertisement stating that machine cards were manufactured by the defendants, warranted equal to any in America. The judge instructed the jury, that a warranty in these terms was equivalent to the warranty set forth in the declaration. The jury having returned a verdict for the plaintiffs, the defendants moved for a new trial, partly on the ground of the misdirection of the judge in this particular.

Phinney, for the defendants. A warranty should be proved as it is set forth in the declaration. * * * A warranty that the cards should be equal to any in America cannot be considered the same with a warranty that they should be good and merchantable, although an article agreeing with the former warranty might be superior to one agreeing with the latter. Proof which would support one of these warranties might not support the other. The best cards in America might not be merchantable.

Webster, for the plaintiffs. * * * The object of the plaintiffs was to purchase good cards; they did not want the very best. Neither did the defendants want to sell any but such as were of the ordinary quality. The expression in the advertisement is equivalent to the word *warranted* simply; which means that the article should be of the ordinary quality. What would have been the result, if the defendants had proved that the cards sold were as good as other cards usually are, and the plaintiffs had proved, that, in some particular place in America, cards of an extraordinary good quality were manufactured? Would this show that the warranty had been broken? A common advertisement is not to be viewed with as much strictness as a deed * * *. It was a question for the jury to determine, whether the cards were not warranted to be of the ordinary quality, and they have found for the plaintiffs. The warranty, indeed, set out in the declaration is not so strong as that in the advertisement, but it is not for the defendants to make this an objection. The plaintiffs have taken the substantial part, and a recovery here will be a bar to any future action on the warranty.

The cause was continued *nisi* for advisement, and at the following March term, at Concord, the Court granted a new trial, on account of variance between the warranty alleged in the declaration and the contract proved.

NOTES AND QUESTIONS

1. Who won in this decision? What sort of an attitude toward businessmen does the ruling of the court reveal? How might you explain that attitude? Would Honestus have been pleased with the result? The jury, in the first trial, found for the plaintiff. Note that a new trial is granted. What does this tell us about the jury's role in decisions on the law in contract cases? Would Sedgwick have been pleased?

2. Goulding v. Skinner arrives at a result that is not inconsistent with one of the great maxims in the nineteenth century American law of contract, *caveat emptor.* The legal principle behind this maxim gained widespread acceptance in the course of the first half of the century. Why? What does the rise of *caveat emptor* have to do with the ultimate result in White v. Flora & Cherry and Seymour v. Delancey? Consider these comments on the doctrine taken from Horwitz, Historical Foundations of Modern Contract Law, 87 Harv.L.Rev. 945–946 (1974):

The nineteenth century departure from the equitable conceptio contract is particularly obvious in the rapid adoption of the doctrine o *caveat emptor.* * * * [D]espite the supposed ancient lineage of *caveat emptor,* eighteenth century English and American courts embraced the doctrine that "a sound price warrants a sound commodity." It was only after Lord Mansfield declared in 1778, in one of those casual asides that seem to have been so influential in forging the history of the common law, that the only basis for an action for breach of warranty was an express contract, that the foundation was laid for reconsidering whether an action for breach of an implied warranty would lie. In 1802 the English courts finally considered the policies behind such an action deciding that no suit on an implied warranty would be allowed. Two years later, in the leading American case of Seixas v. Woods, the New York Supreme Court, relying on a doubtfully reported seventeenth century English case, also held that there could be no recovery against a merchant who could not be proved knowingly to have sold defective goods. Other American jurisdictions quickly fell into line.

While the rule of caveat emptor established in Seixas v. Woods seems to be the result of one of those frequent accidents of historical misunderstanding, this is hardly sufficient to account for the widespread acceptance of the doctrine of caveat emptor elsewhere in America. Nor are the demands of a market economy a sufficient cause. Although the sound price doctrine was attacked on the ground that there "is no standard to determine whether the vendee has paid a sound price," the most consistent legal theorist of the market economy, Gulian Verplanck, devoted his impressive analytical talents to an elaborate critique of the doctrine of caveat emptor. The sudden and complete substitution of caveat emptor in place of the sound price doctrine must therefore be understood as a dramatic overthrow of an important element of the eighteenth century's equitable conception of contract.

* * *

I have not meant to assert that *caveat emptor* is more conducive to a market economy than the contrary doctrine of *caveat venditor,* though this might be independently demonstrated. Rather, I have argued that the importance of caveat emptor lies in its overthrow of both the sound price doctrine and the latter's underlying conception of objective value.

We can best see the nature of the attack on the "sound price" doctrine in South Carolina, the only state in which it persisted well into the nineteenth century. Urging reversal of the sound price doctrine and adoption in its place of a rule of *caveat emptor,* the Attorney General of South Carolina argued in 1802 that "[s]uch a doctrine * * * if once admitted in the formation of contracts, would leave no room for the exercise of judgment or discretion, but would destroy all free agency; every transaction between man and man must be weighed in the balance like the pre-

l if found wanting in * * * adequacy, must be made good
farthing * * *." Whitefield v. McLeod, 2 Bay 380, 382,
nent of counsel). If a court should refuse to enforce a
a man who has had "an equal knowledge of all the cir-
ell as "an opportunity of informing himself, and the
g information * * *," he maintained, "good faith and
would be at an end * * *." * * * According to South
ıgh Legare, the rule of caveat emptor was desirable
it rejected the "refined equity" of the civil law in favor of "the policy of society." Though there was "something captivating in the equity of the principle, that a sound price implies a warranty of the soundness of the commodity," he was "certain that this rule is productive of great practical inconveniences * * *." 2 Writings of Hugh Swinton Legare 110 (M. Legare ed. 1845). * * *

Copyright © 1974 by the Harvard Law Review Association, reprinted with the permission of that Association and of the author. Perhaps the most important aspect of this excerpt from Horwitz's work to us is his assertion that nineteenth century contract law rejected the dominant notion of eighteenth century contract law, that there were "objective" values in contracting that might be implemented by judges or juries in deciding which contracts ought to be enforced. Suppose Horwitz is right. Would this change in the law be approved of by Honestus, Rantoul, or Tocqueville? By you?

If you are interested in pursuing this question further, see, in addition to Horwitz's article, the criticism in A.W.B. Simpson, The Horwitz Thesis and the History of Contracts, 46 U.Chi.L.Rev. 533 (1979). Simpson argues that Horwitz has a "romanticized view" of eighteenth century English contract law, because that law was not as committed to concepts of enforcing "the inherent justice or fairness of an exchange," as Horwitz suggests. Id. at 533–34. Nevertheless, even a critic of Horwitz, such as Simpson, concedes that Horwitz is correct about the change in American contract law that removed the jury's ability to undo the parties' contractual arrangements. Horwitz decries this development, and appears to suggest that it removed a democratic check on the unscrupulous. Simpson isn't so sure. What about you?

C. PROPERTY: FROM ASCRIPTION TO UTILIZATION

III WILLIAM BLACKSTONE, COMMENTARIES ON THE LAWS OF ENGLAND

216–221 (1768).

* * * Nuisance, *nocumentum,* or annoyance, signifies any thing that worketh hurt, inconvenience, or damage. And nuisances are of two kinds; *public* or *common* nuisances, which affect the public, and are an annoyance to all the king's subjects; for which reason we must refer them to the

class of public wrongs, or crimes and misdemeanors: and *private* nuisances, which are the objects of our present consideration, and may be defined, any thing done to the hurt or annoyance of the lands, tenements, or hereditaments of another. * * *

I. In discussing the several kinds of nuisances, we will consider, first, such nuisances as may affect a man's corporeal hereditaments, and then those that may damage such as are incorporeal.

SIR WILLIAM BLACKSTONE

1. FIRST, as to *corporeal* inheritances. If a man builds a house so close to mine that his roof overhangs my roof, and throws the water off his roof upon mine, this is a nuisance, for which an action will lie. Likewise to erect a house or other building so near to mine, that it obstructs

my ancient lights and windows, is a nuisance of a similar nature. But in this latter case it is necessary that the windows be *ancient;* that is, have subsisted there time out of mind; otherwise there is no injury done. For he hath as much right to build a new edifice upon his ground, as I have upon mine: since every man may erect what he pleases upon the upright or perpendicular of his own soil, so as not to prejudice what has long been enjoyed by another; and it was my folly to build so near another's ground. Also, if a person keeps his hogs, or other noisome animals, so near the house of another, that the stench of them incommodes him and makes the air unwholesome, this is an injurious nuisance, as it tends to deprive him of the use and benefit of his house. A like injury is, if one's neighbour sets up and exercises any offensive trade; as a tanner's, a tallow-chandler's or the like; for though these are lawful and necessary trades, yet they should be exercised in remote places; for the rule is, *"sic utere tuo, ut alienum non laedas:"* this therefore is an actionable nuisance. So that the nuisances which affect a man's dwelling may be reduced to these three: 1. Overhanging it: which is also a species of trespass, for *cujus est solum ejus est usque ad coelum:* 2. Stopping ancient lights: and, 3. Corrupting the air with noisome smells: for light and air are two indispensable requisites to every dwelling. But depriving one of a mere matter of pleasure, as of a fine prospect, by building a wall, or the like; this, as it abridges nothing really convenient or necessary, is no injury to the sufferer, and is therefore not an actionable nuisance.

As to nuisance to one's *lands:* if one erects a smelting house for lead so near the land of another, that the vapor and smoke kills his corn and grass, and damages his cattle therein, this is held to be a nuisance. And by consequence it follows, that if one does any other act, in itself lawful, which yet being done in that place necessarily tends to the damage of another's property, it is a nuisance: for it is incumbent on him to find some other place to do that act, where it will be less offensive. * * *

With regard to *other* corporeal hereditaments: it is a nuisance to stop or divert water that used to run to another's meadow or mill; to corrupt or poison a water-course, by erecting a dye-house or a lime-pit for the use of trade, in the upper part of the stream; or in short to do any act therein, that in its consequences must necessarily tend to the prejudice of one's neighbour. So closely does the law of England enforce that excellent rule of gospel-morality, of "doing to others, as we would they should do unto ourselves."

2. As to *incorporeal* hereditaments, the law carries itself with the same equity. If I have a way, annexed to my estate, across another's land, and he obstructs me in the use of it, either by totally stopping it, or putting logs across it, or ploughing over it, it is a nuisance: for in the first case I cannot enjoy my right at all, and in the latter I cannot enjoy it so commodiously as I ought. Also, if I am entitled to hold a fair or market,

and another person sets up a fair or market so near mine that he does me a prejudice, it is a nuisance to the freehold which I have in my market or fair. But in order to make this out to be a nuisance, it is necessary, 1. That my market or fair be the elder, otherwise the nuisance lies at my own door. 2. That the market be erected within the third part of twenty miles from mine. For sir Matthew Hale construes the *dieta,* or reasonable day's journey mentioned by Bracton, to be twenty miles * * *. So that if the new market be not within seven miles of the old one, it is no nuisance: for it is held reasonable that every man should have a market within one-third of a day's journey from his own home; that the day being divided into three parts, he may spend one part in going, another in returning, and the third in transacting his necessary business there. If such market or fair be on the same day with mine, it is *prima facie* a nuisance to mine, and there needs no proof of it, but the law will intend it to be so; but if it be on any other day, it *may be* a nuisance; though whether it *is* so or not, cannot be intended or presumed, but I must make proof of it to the jury. If a ferry is erected on a river, so near another ancient ferry as to draw away its custom, it is a nuisance to the owner of the old one. For where there is a ferry by prescription, the owner is bound to keep it always in repair and readiness, for the ease of all the king's subjects; otherwise he may be grievously amerced: it would be therefore extremely hard, if a new ferry were suffered to share his profits, which does not also share his burden. But where the reason ceases, the law also ceases with it: therefore it is no nuisance to erect a mill so near mine, as to draw away the custom unless the miller also intercepts the water. Neither is it a nuisance to set up any trade, or a school, in neighbourhood or rivalship with another: for by such emulation the public are like to be gainers; and, if the new mill or school occasion a damage to the old one, it is *damnum absque injuria.*

II. Let us next attend to the remedies, which the law has given for this injury of nuisance. * * *

The remedies by suit are, 1. By action *on the case* for damages; in which the party injured shall only recover a satisfaction for the injury sustained; but cannot thereby remove the nuisance. Indeed every continuance of a nuisance is held to be a fresh one; and therefore a fresh action will lie, and very exemplary damages will probably be given, if, after one verdict against him, the defendant has the hardiness to continue it. Yet the founders of the law of England did not rely upon probabilities merely, in order to give relief to the injured. They have therefore provided two other actions; the *assize of nuisance,* and the writ of *quod permittat prosternere:* which not only give the plaintiff satisfaction for his injury past, but also strike at the root and remove the cause itself, the nuisance that occasioned the injury. * * *

* * *

Both these actions, of *assize of nuisance,* and of *quod permittat prosternere,* are now out of use, and have given way to the action on the case * * *. [T]he effect will be much the same, unless a man has a very obstinate as well as an ill-natured neighbour: who had rather continue to pay damages, than remove his nuisance. For in such a case, recourse must at last be had to the old and sure remedies, which will effectually conquer the defendant's perverseness, by sending the sheriff with his *posse comitatus,* or power of the county, to level it.

NOTES AND QUESTIONS

1. "In the history of American institutions, no other book—except the Bible—has played so great a role as Blackstone's Commentaries on the Laws of England." D. Boorstin, The Mysterious Science of the Law iii (Peter Smith, ed. 1973). When he was training as a lawyer, Lincoln is said to have read his *Blackstone* (and his Coke) by candlelight. While Blackstone's books, composed of his Oxford lectures, and originally published from 1765 to 1769, were to be a major source of American private law for roughly fifty years after the American Revolution, and were continually updated by American editors, there were some Americans, for example, Thomas Jefferson, who opposed the influence of Blackstone. Jefferson felt that Blackstone and those nurtured on him were "Tories," and that Blackstone's influence was harmful in America, where more attention needed to be paid to the needs of "whiggism" or "republicanism." See generally Julian S. Waterman, Thomas Jefferson and Blackstone's Commentaries, 27 Illinois Law Review (now the "Northwestern University Law Review") 629 (1933), reprinted in Flaherty, ed. Essays in the History of Early American Law 451 (1969), and see also Edward Dumbauld, Thomas Jefferson and the Law (1979). What did Jefferson mean by this criticism of Blackstone? Can you make out anything in this excerpt that causes you to agree or disagree with Jefferson? Ask yourself again whether you agree or disagree with Jefferson after you have considered the following questions. For some reflections on Blackstone and/or his conception of property rights, see, e.g., George Anastaplo, "Law and Popular Culture: Nature and Convention in Blackstone's Commentaries: The Beginning of an Inquiry," 22 Legal Stud. Forum 161 (1998), Douglas H. Cook, "Sir William Blackstone: A Life and Legacy Set Apart for God's Work," 13 Regent U.L. Rev. 169 (2001), Duncan Kennedy, "The Structure of Blackstone's Commentaries," 28 Buff. L. Rev. 205 (1979), Dennis R. Nolan, "Sir William Blackstone and the New American Republic: A Study of Intellectual Impact," 51 New York U. L. Rev. 731 (1976), and Carol M. Rose, "Canons of Property Talk, or Blackstone's Anxiety," 108 Yale L.J. 601 (1998). Finally, for the fullest biography to date of Blackstone, which makes out a convincing case that he has a claim to be regarded as a radical reformer for his work on behalf of the Oxford University Press and for his work in the creation of penitentiaries in England, and, further, that Blackstone might justly be ranked among the four greatest figures of the European Enlightenment (along with Montesquieu, Beccaria, and Voltaire), see the absorbing account by Wilfrid Prest, William Blackstone: Law and Letters in the Eighteenth Century 308 (2008).

2. Blackstone begins his discussion of nuisance by a discussion of the doctrine of "ancient lights." Why must the lights be "ancient" for them to be preserved? What impact would this doctrine have on societal "progress?"

3. Two Latin maxims are of primary importance to Blackstone in this excerpt:

> (1) *sic utere tuo, ut alienum non laedas* ("Use your own property in such a manner as not to injure that of another") and
>
> (2) *cujus est solem ejus est usque ad coelum* ("The owner of the soil owns to the sky.").

These maxims are said to be the central principles of Blackstonian property law. Do you see any conflict between them? Consider, for example, how you reconcile the doctrine of "ancient lights" with these two maxims.

4. Why, if blocking off "ancient lights" is a nuisance, is it not a nuisance to block off a "fine prospect?" What, exactly, is a "nuisance?"

5. Note that Blackstone says that it may be a nuisance for one person to erect a "market" in a manner that draws off the trade of another's market. Similarly, it may be a nuisance to operate a ferry that competes with another's ferry. When is it such a nuisance, and why? Why is it never a nuisance merely to compete with an already existing mill or school?

6. Why, in the "action on the case" for nuisance, was there no injunctive relief? What about Blackstone's idea that the action will be effective simply because of the availability of "exemplary damages" for repeat offenders—do you agree? "Exemplary damages," or "punitive damages" as they are sometimes called, are not unknown in modern American private actions, although, until recently, they were nearly unknown in breach of contract cases. Why not allow them in contract cases if we allow them in property and tort actions?

VAN NESS V. PACARD

Supreme Court of the United States, 1829.
27 U.S. (2 Pet.) 137, 7 L.Ed. 374.

MR. JUSTICE STORY delivered the opinion of the Court.

* * *

The original was an action on the case brought by the plaintiffs in error against the defendant for waste committed by him, while tenant of the plaintiffs, to their reversionary interest, by pulling down and removing from the demised premises a messuage or dwelling-house erected thereon and attached to the freehold. [The tenant won below, the landlords have brought the case to the Supreme Court for review.] * * *

By the bill of exceptions, filed at the trial, it appeared that the plaintiffs in 1820 demised to the defendant, for seven years, a vacant lot in the city of Washington, at the yearly rent of one hundred and twelve dollars and fifty cents, with a clause in the lease that the defendant should have a right to purchase the same at any time during the term for one thousand eight hundred and seventy-five dollars. After the defendant had taken possession of the lot, he erected thereon a wooden dwelling-house, two stories high in front, with a shed of one story, a cellar of stone or brick foundation and a brick chimney. The defendant and his family dwelt in the house from its erection until near the expiration of the lease, when he took the same down and removed all the materials from the lot. The defendant was a carpenter by trade; and he gave evidence, that upon obtaining the lease he erected the building above mentioned, with a view to carry on the business of a dairyman, and for the residence of his family and servants engaged in his said business; and that the cellar, in which there was a spring, was made and exclusively used for a milk cellar, in which the utensils of his said business were kept and scalded, and washed and used; and that feed was kept in the upper part of the house, which was also occupied as a dwelling for his family. That the defendant had his tools as a carpenter, and two apprentices in the house, and a work-bench out of doors; and carpenter's work was done in the house, which was in a rough unfinished state, and made partly of old materials. That he also erected on the lot a stable for his cows of plank and timber fixed upon posts fastened into the ground, which stable he removed with the house before the expiration of his lease.

* * *

The first exception raises the important question, what fixtures erected by a tenant during his term are removable by him?

The general rule of the common law certainly is, that whatever is once annexed to the freehold becomes part of it, and cannot afterwards be removed, except by him who is entitled to the inheritance. The rule, however, never was, at least as far back as we can trace it in the books, inflexible, and without exceptions. It was construed most strictly between executor and heir in favour of the latter; more liberally between tenant for life or in tail, and remainderman or reversioner, in favour of the former; and with much greater latitude between landlord and tenant, in favour of the tenant. But an exception of a much broader cast, and whose origin may be traced almost as high as the rule itself, is of fixtures erected for the purposes of trade. Upon principles of public policy, and to encourage trade and manufactures, fixtures which were erected to carry on such business were allowed to be removed by the tenant during his term, and were deemed personalty for many other purposes. [In a leading English case,] * * * Elwes v. Maw, 3 East's R. 38, [it was] * * * decided, that in the case of landlord and tenant, there had been no relaxation of the general rule in cases of erections, solely for agricultural purposes, however beneficial or important they might be as improvements of the estate. Being once annexed to the freehold by the tenant, they became a part of the realty, and could never afterwards be severed by the tenant. The distinction is certainly a nice one between fixtures for the purposes of trade, and fixtures for agricultural purposes; at least in those cases where the sale of the produce constitutes the principal object of the tenant, and the erections are for the purpose of such a beneficial enjoyment of the estate. But that point is not now before us; and it is unnecessary to consider what the true doctrine is or ought to be on this subject. * * *

The common law of England is not to be taken in all respects to be that of America. Our ancestors brought with them its general principles, and claimed it as their birthright; but they brought with them and adopted only that portion which was applicable to their situation. There could be little or no reason for doubting, that the general doctrine as to things annexed to the freehold, so far as it respects heirs and executors, was adopted by them. The question could arise only between different claimants under the same ancestor, and no general policy could be subserved, by withdrawing from the heir those things, which his ancestor had chosen to leave annexed to the inheritance. But, between landlord and tenant, it is not so clear that the rigid rule of the common law, at least as it is expounded in 3 East, 38, was so applicable to their situation, as to give rise to necessary presumption in its favour. The country was a wilderness, and the universal policy was to procure its cultivation and improvement. The owner of the soil, as well as the public, had every motive to encourage the tenant to devote himself to agriculture and to favour any erections which should aid this result; yet, in the comparative poverty of the country, what tenant could afford to erect fixtures of much expense or value, if he was to lose his whole interest therein by the very act of erection? His cabin or log-hut, however necessary for any improvement of the soil would cease to be his the moment it was finished. It might, therefore, deserve consideration, whether, in case the doctrine were not previously adopted in a state by some authoritative practice or adjudication, it ought to be assumed by this Court as a part of the jurisprudence of such state, upon the mere footing of its existence in the common law. At present, it is unnecessary to say more, than that we give no opinion on this question. The case, which has been argued at the bar may well be disposed of without any discussion of it.

It has been already stated, that the exception of buildings and other fixtures, for the purpose of carrying on a trade or manufacture, is of very ancient date, and was recognised almost as early as the rule itself. The very point was decided in 20 Henry VII. 13, a. and b., where it was laid down, that if a lessee for years made a furnace for his advantage, or a dyer made his vats or vessels to occupy his occupation, during the term, he may afterwards remove them. That doctrine was recognised by Lord Holt, in Poole's case, 1 Salk. 368, in favour of a soap-boiler, who was tenant for years. He held that the party might well remove the vats he set up in relation to trade; and that he might do it by the common law (and not by virtue of any custom) in favour of trade, and to encourage industry. In Lawton v. Lawton, 2 Atk.R. 13, the same doctrine was held in the case of a fire engine, set up to work a colliery by a tenant for life. Lord Hardwicke, there said, that since the time of Henry the Seventh, the general ground the Courts have gone upon of relaxing the strict construction of law is, that it is for the benefit of the public to encourage tenants for life to do what is advantageous to the estate during the term. * * *

It has been suggested at the bar, that this exception in favour of trade has never been applied to cases like that before the Court, where a large house has been built and used in part as a family residence. But the question, whether removable or not, does not depend upon the form or size of the building, whether it has a brick foundation or not, or is one or two stories high, or has a brick or other chimney. The sole question is, whether it is designed for purposes of trade or not. * * *

Then, as to the residence of the family in the house, this resolves itself into the same consideration. If the house were built principally for a dwelling-house for the family, independently of carrying on the trade, then it would doubtless be deemed a fixture, falling under the general rule, and immovable. But if the residence of the family were merely an accessory for the more beneficial exercise of the trade, and with a view to superior accommodation in this particular, then it is within the exception. There are many trades, which cannot be carried on well, without the presence of many persons by night as well as by day. It is so in some valuable manufactories. It is not unusual for persons employed in a bakery to sleep in the same building. Now, what was the evidence in the present case? It was, "that the defendant erected the building before mentioned, with a view to carry on the business of a dairyman, and for the residence of his family and servants engaged in that business." The residence of the family was then auxiliary to the dairy; it was for the accommodation and beneficial operations of his trade.

Surely it cannot be doubted, that in a business of this nature, the immediate presence of the family and servants was, or might be, of very great utility and importance. The defendant was also a carpenter, and carried on his business, as such, in the same building. It is no objection that he carried on two trades instead of one. There is not the slightest evidence of this one being a mere cover or evasion to conceal another, which was the principal design; and, unless we were prepared to say (which we are not) that the mere fact, that the house was used for a dwelling-house, as well as for a trade, superseded the exception in favour of the latter, there is no ground to declare that the tenant was not entitled to remove it. * * * In our opinion, the Circuit Court was right in refusing the first instruction.

The second exception proceeds upon the ground, that it was not competent to establish a usage and custom in the city of Washington for tenants to make such removals of buildings during their term. We can perceive no objection to such proof. Every demise between landlord and tenant in respect to matters, in which the parties are silent, may be fairly open to explanation by the general usage and custom of the country or of the district where the land lies. Every person under such circumstances is supposed to be cognizant of the custom, and to contract with a tacit reference to it. * * * In the very class of cases now before the Court the custom of the country has been admitted to decide the right of the tenant to remove fixtures. * * *

The third exception turns upon the consideration, whether the parol testimony was competent to establish such a usage and custom. Competent it certainly was, if by competent is meant that it was admissible to go to the jury. Whether it was such as ought to have satisfied their minds on the matter of fact was solely for their consideration, open indeed to such commentary and observation, as the Court might think proper in its discretion to lay before them for their aid and guidance. We cannot say, that they were not at liberty, by the principles of law, to infer from the evidence the existence of the usage. * * *

The last exception professes to call upon the Court to institute a comparison between the testimony introduced by the plaintiff and that introduced by the defendant against and for the usage. It requires from the Court a decision upon its relative weight and credibility, which the Court were not justified in giving to the jury in the shape of a positive instruction.

Upon the whole, in our judgment there is no error in the judgment of the Circuit Court; and it is affirmed with costs.

* * *

NOTES AND QUESTIONS

1. Mr. Justice Story, who wrote the opinion of the Court in Van Ness v. Pacard, has often been described as the "American Blackstone." He, and the other towering figure of early nineteenth century law, James Kent, are usually thought to have been orthodox, or conservative legal thinkers, and to have been concerned with serving "the interests of the wealthy, and the powerful." See, e.g. Morton Horwitz, The Transformation of American Law 1780–1860, 257–259 (1977), and John Horton, James Kent, A Study in Conservatism, 1763–1847 (1939). Does Story's opinion in this case fit this description?

2. Why was it a "general rule of the common law" (of England) that "whatever is once annexed to the freehold becomes part of it, and cannot afterwards be removed, except by him who is entitled to the inheritance?" What

does the rule mean? Does Story believe that the rule is in effect in America? Why or why not?

3. What, exactly, is the holding in Van Ness v. Pacard? Does it necessarily involve the question of whether or not the English common law rule regarding "waste," that is, the removal of fixtures, is in force in America? If not, why does Story discuss it at all? Does it turn on more narrow concerns relating to the "trade fixtures" exception to the "waste" doctrine? What is this "trade fixtures" exemption? Is a building which houses the defendant's family (and also his dairy operations) necessarily a "trade fixture?" Does Story say it is? Are you persuaded?

4. What is the importance of the "custom" in the District of Columbia to the holding in this case? Should these matters turn on local custom? What would you expect to be the economic effect of Story's decision? Do you approve or disapprove of the consequences? For a fine discussion of the economic effects of nineteenth century law, and criticism of the leading historical interpreters of that law, see Herbert Hovenkamp, "The Economics of Legal History," 67 Minn.L.Rev. 645 (1983).

PARKER V. FOOTE

Supreme Court of New York, 1838.
19 Wend. 309.

This was an action on the case for stopping lights in a dwelling house. * * *

In 1808 the defendant being the owner of two village lots situate in the Village of Clinton, adjoining each other, sold one of them to Joseph Stebbins, who in the same year erected a dwelling house thereon on the line adjoining the other lot with windows in it overlooking the other lot. The defendant also, in the same year, built an addition to a house which stood on the lot which he retained, leaving a space of about 16 feet between the house erected by Stebbins and the addition put up by himself. This space was subsequently occupied by the defendant as an alley leading to buildings situate on the rear of his lot, and was so used by him until the year 1832, when (24 years after the erection of the house by Stebbins) he erected a store on the alley, filling up the whole space between the two houses, and consequently stopping the lights in the house erected by Stebbins. At the time of the erection of the store, the plaintiffs were the owners of the lot originally conveyed to Stebbins, by title derived from him, and were in the actual possession thereof, and brought this action for the stopping of the lights. Stebbins, the original purchaser, from the defendants, was a witness for the plaintiffs, and on his cross examination, testified that he never had any written agreement, deed or writing granting permission to have windows overlook the defendant's lot, and that nothing was ever said upon the subject. * * * On motion for a nonsuit, the defendant's counsel insisted that there was no evidence of a user authorizing the presumption of a grant as to the windows; that the user in this case was merely permissive, which explained and rebutted all presumption of a grant. That if the user, in the absence of other evidence, authorized the presumption of a grant, still that here the presumption was rebutted by the proof that, in fact, there never had been a grant. The circuit judge expressed a doubt whether the modern English doctrine in regard to stopping lights, was applicable to the growing villages of this country, but said he would rule in favor of the plaintiffs, and leave the question to the determination of this court. He also decided that the fact, whether there was or was not a grant in writing as to the windows, was not for the jury to determine; that the law presumed it from the user, and it could not be rebutted by proving that none had in truth been executed. After the evidence was closed, the judge declined leaving to the jury the question of presumption of right, and instructed them that the plaintiffs were entitled to their verdict. The jury accordingly found a verdict for the plaintiffs, with $225 damages. The defendant having excepted to the decisions of the judge, now moved for a new trial.

* * *

By the Court, BRONSON, J. The modern doctrine of presuming a right, by grant or otherwise, to easements and incorporeal hereditaments after 20 years of uninterrupted adverse enjoyment, exerts a much wider influence in quieting possession, than the old doctrine of title by prescription, which depended on immemorial usage. The period of 20 years has been adopted by the courts in analogy to the statute limiting an entry into lands; but as the statute does not apply to incorporeal rights, the adverse user is not regarded as a legal bar, but only as a ground for presuming a right, either by grant or in some other form. * * *

To authorize the presumption, the enjoyment of the easement must not only be uninterrupted for the period of 20 years, but it must be adverse, not by leave or favor, but under a claim or assertion of right; and it must be with the knowledge and acquiescence of the owner. * * * It is said that there may be cases relating to the use of water, which form exceptions to the rule that the enjoyment must be adverse to authorize the presumption of a grant. See Bealey v. Shaw, 6 East, 208; Ingraham v. Hutchinson, 2 Conn. 584. To this doctrine I cannot subscribe. * * * I think it sufficient at this time to say, that in whatever manner the water may be appropriated or enjoyed, it must, of necessity, be either rightful or wrongful. The use of the stream must be such as is authorized by the title of the occupant to the soil over which the water flows, or it must be a usurpation on the rights of another. If the enjoyment is rightful, there can be no occasion for presuming a grant. The title of the occupant is as perfect at the outset, as it can be after the lapse of a century. If the user be wrongful, a usurpation to any extent upon the rights of another, it is then adverse; and if acquiesced in for 20 years, a reasonable foundation is laid for presuming a grant. If the enjoyment is not according to the title of the occupant, the injured party may have redress by action. His remedy does not depend on the question whether he has built on his mill site or otherwise appropriated the stream to his own use. It is enough that his right has been invaded; and although in a particular case he may be entitled to recover only nominal damages, that will be a sufficient vindication of his title, and will put an end to all ground for presuming a grant. * * *

The presumption we are considering is a mixed one of law and fact. The inference that the right is in him who has the enjoyment, so long as nothing appears to the contrary, is a natural one—it is a presumption of fact. But adverse enjoyment, when left to exert only its natural force as mere presumptive evidence, can never conclude the true owner. No length of possession could work such a consequence. Hence the necessity of fixing on some definite period of enjoyment, and making that operate as a presumptive bar to the rightful owner. This part of the rule is wholly artificial; it is a presumption of mere law. In general, questions depending upon mixed presumptions of this description must be submitted to the jury, under proper instructions from the court. The difference between length of time which operates as a bar to a claim and that which is only used by way of evidence was very clearly stated by Ld. Mansfield, in the Mayor, etc., v. Horner, Cowp., 102. "A jury is concluded," he says, "by length of time that operates as a bar, as where the Statute of Limitations is pleaded in bar to a debt; although the jury is satisfied that the debt is due and unpaid, it is still a bar. So in the case of prescription, if it be time out of mind, a jury is bound to conclude the right from that prescription, if there could be a legal commencement of the right. But length of time used merely by way of evidence may be left to the consideration of a jury to be credited or not, and to draw their inference one way or the other, according to circumstances." In Darwin v. Upton, 2 Saund. 175, n. 2, the question related to lights, and it was said by the same learned judge that "Acquiescence for 20 years is such decisive presumption of a right by grant or otherwise, that unless contradicted or explained, the jury ought to believe it; but it is impossible that length of time can be said to be an absolute bar, like a Statute of Limitations; it is certainly a presumptive bar which ought to go to the jury." * * *

Some of the cases speak of the presumption as conclusive. Bealey v. Shaw, 6 East 208; Tyler v. Wilkinson, 4 Mas., 397. This can only mean that the presumption is conclusive where there is no dispute about the facts upon which it depends. It has never been doubted that the inference arising from 20 years' enjoyment of incorporeal rights might be explained and repelled; nor, so far as I have observed, has it ever been denied that questions of this description belong to the jury. The presumption we are considering has often been likened to the inference which is indulged that a bond or mortgage has been paid, when no interest has been demanded within 20 years. Such questions must be submitted to the jury to draw the proper conclusion from all the circumstances of each particular case. * * *

In a plain case, where there is no evidence to repeal the presumption arising from 20 years' uninterrupted adverse user of an incorporeal right, the judge may very properly instruct the jury that it is their duty to find in favor of the party who has had the enjoyment; but still it is a question for the jury. The judge erred in this case in wholly withdrawing that question from the consideration of the jury. On this ground, if no other, the verdict must be set aside.

The bill of exceptions presents another question which may probably arise on a second trial, and it seems proper, therefore, to give it some examination.

As neither light, air nor prospect can be the subject of a grant, the proper presumption, if any, to be made in this case, is that there was some covenant or agreement not to obstruct the lights. * * *

Most of the cases on the subject we have been considering relate to ways, commons, markets, water-courses, and the like, where the user or enjoyment, if not rightful, has been an immediate and continuing injury to the person against whom the presumption is made. His property has either been invaded, or his beneficial interest in it has been rendered less valuable. The injury has been of such a character that he might have immediate redress by action. But in the case of windows overlooking the land of another, the injury, if any, is merely ideal or imaginary. The light and air which they admit are not the subjects of property beyond the moment of actual occupancy; and for overlooking one's privacy no action can be maintained. The party has no remedy but to build on the adjoining land, opposite the offensive window. * * * Upon what principle the courts in England have applied the same rule of presumption to two classes of cases so essentially different in character, I have been unable to discover. If one commit a daily trespass on the land of another, under a claim of right to pass over, or feed his cattle upon it; or divert the water from his mill, or throw it back upon his land or machinery; in these and the like cases long continued acquiescence affords strong presumptive evidence of right. But in the case of lights there is no adverse user, nor, indeed, any use whatever of another's property; and no foundation is laid for indulging any presumption against the rightful owner.

Although I am not prepared to adopt the suggestion of Gould, J., in Ingraham v. Hutchinson, 2 Conn., 597, that the lights which are protected may be such as project over the land of the adjoining proprietor, yet it is not impossible that there are some considerations connected with the subject which do not distinctly appear in the reported cases. * * *

The learned judges who have laid down this doctrine have not told us upon what principle or analogy in the law it can be maintained. They tell us that a man may build at the extremity of his own land, and that he may lawfully have windows looking out upon the lands of his neighbor. * * * The reason why he may lawfully have such windows must be because he does his neighbor no wrong; and, indeed, so it is adjudged, as we have already seen; and yet, somehow or other, by the exercise of a lawful right in his own land for 20 years, he acquires a beneficial interest in the land of his neighbor. The original proprietor is still seised of the fee, with the privilege of paying taxes and assessments; but the right to build on the land, without which city and village lots are of little or no value, has been destroyed by a lawful window. How much land can thus be rendered useless to the owner remains yet to be settled. * * * Now what is the acquiescence which concludes the owner? * * * How, then, has he forfeited the beneficial interest in his property? He has neglected to incur the expense of building a wall 20 or 50 feet high, as the case may be—not for his own benefit, but for the sole purpose of annoying his neighbor. That was his only remedy. A wanton act of this kind, although done in one's own land, is calculated to render a man odious. Indeed, an attempt has been made to sustain an action for erecting such a wall. Mahan v. Brown, 13 Wend., 261.

There is, I think, no principle upon which the modern English doctrine on the subject of lights can be supported. It is an anomaly in the law. It may do well enough in England * * *. But it cannot be applied in the growing cities and villages of this country, without working the most mischievous consequences. It has never, I think, been deemed a part of our law. 3 Kent, Com., 446, n.a. Nor do I find that it has been adopted in any of the States. * * * It cannot be necessary to cite cases to prove that those portions of the common law of England which are hostile to the spirit of our institutions, or which are not adapted to the existing state of things in this country, form no part of our law. And besides, it would be difficult to prove that the rule in question was known to the common law previous to Apr. 19, 1775. Const.N.Y., art. 7, sec. 13. * * *

There is one peculiar feature in the case at bar. It appears affirmatively that there never was any grant, writing or agreement about the use of the lights. A grant may under certain circumstances be presumed, although, as Ld. Mansfield once said, the court does not really think a grant has been made. Eldridge v. Knott, Cowp., 214. But it remains to be decided that a right by grant or otherwise can be presumed when it plainly appears that it never existed. If this had been the case of a way, common, or the like, and there had actually been an uninterrupted adverse user for 20 years under a claim of right, to which the defendant had submitted, I do not intend to say that proof that no grant was, in fact, made would have overturned the action. It will be time enough to decide that question when it shall be presented. But in this case the evidence of Stebbins, who built the house, in connection with the other facts which appeared on the trial, proved most satisfactorily that the windows were never enjoyed under a claim of right, but only as a matter of favor. If there was anything to leave to the jury, they could not have hesitated a moment about their verdict. But I think the plaintiffs should have been nonsuited.

THE CHIEF JUSTICE concurred on both points.

COWEN, J., only concurred in the opinion that the question of presumption of a grant should have been submitted to the jury.

New trial granted.

NOTES AND QUESTIONS

1. It has become a cliché in American legal history to say that the English common law or at least the English common law method of deciding cases won wide acceptance in the United States during the early nineteenth century. While some, like Robert Rantoul, whom we have already met, advocated the creation of statutes to encompass all of American law, nineteenth century American private law was primarily the work of courts. Rantoul, as you saw, resisted this trend. Why? Do the decisions in the last two cases suggest that Rantoul was correct or incorrect in his objections to the "common law?"

2. Parker v. Foote, and particularly the majority opinion that there should be no conclusive presumption of a grant to the plaintiff, present problems of understanding. How would Blackstone have decided the case? Defense counsel had argued that since there was no "adversity" in plaintiff's possession, he should lose. Much of the difficulty here comes from the fact that by this time (1838), there had been many cases involving prescription in the area of water rights. In those cases it had been held that there was no requirement of "adversity" for one seeking to establish prescriptive rights to an undiminished flow of water. See, e.g. Ingraham v. Hutchinson, 2 Conn. 584 (1818), and Professor Horwitz's discussion of that case, Horwitz, Transformation of American Law, at 44–45. Consistently with most of the doctrinal analysis in the rest of his book, Horwitz reads the water rights cases as unfairly favoring emerging commercial interests. There seems to be no doubt that the change in water rights law was economically motivated, but precisely whose interests were favored is a difficult question. See John S. Martin, "Water Law and Economic Power: A reinterpretation of Morton Horwitz's Subsidy Thesis," 77 Va.L.Rev. 397 (1991).

We most commonly think of the doctrine of "prescription" as adverse possession; one who adversely possesses a piece of land for a certain number of years (often twenty) thereby gains legal title. The water-rights prescription cases granted legal rights after twenty years' possession with no requirement of *adverse* possession. Can you understand why? How would you adversely possess a naturally flowing body of water? Why should adversity be an element of prescription? What, if anything does this have to do with the idea that title by "prescription" is said to involve a "lost grant?"

3. Does Judge Bronson decide Parker v. Foote on the law regarding presumptions of grants, or on the unsuitability of the doctrine of "ancient

lights" to America? Why do you suppose that Cowen, J. "only concurred in the opinion that the question of presumption of a grant should have been submitted to the jury?" Does it strike you as strange that a question of "legal" presumptions should go to the jury? Is this case atavistic?

4. You have probably sensed, from the *Van Ness* and the *Parker* cases, that the concept of property in America was being radically transformed from the pre-Revolutionary English notions. This change in the nature of property has resulted in some of the most interesting work by legal historians. See, e.g., Hendrik Hartog, Public Property and Private Power: The Corporation of the City of New York in American Law 1730–1870 (1983), James W. Ely, Jr., The Guardian of Every Other Right: A Constitutional History of Property Rights (3d ed., 2007), Jennifer Nedelsky, Private Property and the Limits of American Constitutionalism: The Madisonian Framework and Its Legacy (1990), Carol M. Rose, "Property as the Keystone Right?", 71 Notre Dame L. Rev. 329 (1996). Much of the writing on property law has sought to explore whether the transformation in property law described by Professor Horwitz in his Transformation of American Law 1780–1860 (1977) was one that furthered or frustrated the development of republican idealism, democracy, and justice. Horwitz appears to have thought the key theme was the frustration of these goals, but the evidence he presents and the nineteenth century record are clearly subject to differing interpretations. See e.g., Gregory S. Alexander, "Time and Property in the American Republican Legal Culture," 66 N.Y.U. L.Rev. 273 (1991), James W. Ely, Jr., " 'That due satisfaction may be made:' The Fifth Amendment and the Origins of the Compensation Principle," 26 Am.J.Leg.Hist. 1 (1992), William J. Novak, "Public Economy and the Well-ordered Market: Law and Economic Regulation in 19th Century America," 18 Law & Social Inquiry 1 (1993), Jed Rubenfeld, "Usings," 102 Yale L.J. 1077 (1993).

D. THE FALL OF NUISANCE AND RISE OF NEGLIGENCE

III WILLIAM BLACKSTONE, COMMENTARIES ON THE LAWS OF ENGLAND

165–166 (1768).

* * *

The last class of contracts, implied by reason and construction of law, arises upon this supposition, that every one who undertakes any office, employment, trust, or duty, contracts with those who employ or intrust him, to perform it with integrity, diligence, and skill. And, if by his want of either of those qualities any injury accrues to individuals, they have therefore their remedy in damages by a special action on the case. A few instances will fully illustrate this matter. If an officer of the public is guilty of neglect of duty, or a palpable breach of it, of non-feasance or of misfeasance, as, if the sheriff does not execute a writ sent to him, or if he wilfully makes a false return thereof; in both these cases the party aggrieved shall have an action on the case, for damages to be assessed by a jury. If a sheriff or gaoler suffers a prisoner * * * during the pendency of a suit * * * to escape, he is liable to an action on the case. But if, after judgment, a gaoler or a sheriff permits a debtor to escape, who is charged in execution for a certain sum; the debt immediately becomes his own, and he is compellable by action of debt, being for a sum liquidated and ascertained, to satisfy the creditor his whole demand * * *. An advocate or attorney that betray the cause of their client, or, being retained, neglect to appear at the trial, by which the cause miscarries, are liable to an action on the case for a reparation to their injured client. There is also in law always an implied contract with a common inn-keeper, to secure his guest's goods in his inn; with a common carrier, or bargemaster, to be answerable for the goods he carries; with a common farrier, that he shoes a horse well, without laming him; with a common tailor, or other workman, that he performs his business in a workmanlike manner: in which if they fail, an action on the case lies to recover damages for such breach of their general undertaking. But if I employ a person to transact any of these concerns, whose common profession and business it is not, the law implies no such general undertaking; but, in order to charge him with damages, a special agreement is required. Also, if an inn-keeper, or other victualler, hangs out a sign and opens his house for travellers, it is an implied engagement to entertain all persons who travel that way; and upon this universal *assumpsit* an action on the case will lie against him for damages, if he without good reason refuses to admit a traveller. If any one cheats me with false cards or dice, or by false weights and measures, or by selling me one commodity for another, an action on the case also lies against him for damages upon the contract which the law always implies, that every transaction is fair and honest. In contracts likewise for sales, it is constantly understood that the seller undertakes that the commodity he sells is his own; and if it proves otherwise, an action on the case lies against him, to exact damages for this deceit. In contracts for provisions it is always implied that they are wholesome; and, if they be not, the same remedy may be had. * * *

Besides the special action on the case, there is also a peculiar remedy, entitled an action of deceit, to give damages in some particular cases of fraud; and principally where one man does any thing in the name of another, by which he is deceived or injured; as if one brings an action in another's name, and then suffers a nonsuit, whereby the plaintiff becomes liable to costs: or where one obtains or suffers a fraudulent recovery of lands, tenements, or chattels, to the prejudice of him that hath right. As when by collusion the attorney of the tenant makes default in a real action, or where the sheriff returns that the tenant was summoned when he was not so, and in either case he loses the land, the writ of deceit lies against the demandant, and also the attorney or the sheriff and his officers; to annul the former proceedings, and recover back the land. * * *

* * *

PATTEN V. HALSTED

Supreme Court of New Jersey, 1795.
1 N.J.Law 277.

This was an action on the case against defendant as sheriff, for the escape of one Freeman. The declaration charged that the plaintiff in November Term, 1790, had sued out a writ of *capias ad respondendum* against Clarkson, Freeman and others, by virtue of which Halsted, the sheriff, on the 10th of March, 1791, arrested Freeman only, and in April Term succeeding returned him in custody * * *; that in November Term, there was a *nol. pros.* as to the other defendants, and plaintiff recovered against Freeman the sum of £1526 19s. 6d. for his damages, costs and charges; and that afterwards the defendant suffered Freeman to escape.

There were two counts in the declaration, one for a voluntary, and the other for a negligent escape.

After having proved the writ, the arrest, the judgment roll, and the escape, plaintiff rested his cause.

Aaron Ogden, for defendant, moved for a non-suit, on the following grounds:

1. That special bail could not be required in the action against Freeman; and the sheriff, therefore, had a right to discharge him from custody on the entering of an appearance, which had been done. The writ in this case was to answer a plea of trespass on the case, and agreeably to the practice in the English courts, which has ever been adopted as the rule for our government, unless expressly altered or repealed, special bail is not required except in actions of debt. 3 Bl.Com. 292. * * *

If, therefore, the writ was erroneous, and Freeman himself might have been relieved from the arrest, the sheriff was entitled to assume the risk himself, to release the prisoner, and to avail himself in his defence of every defect which the person arrested would have been permitted to urge against its sufficiency. * * *

* * *

R. Stockton, contra * * * contended that the sheriff was obliged to look only to the writ placed in his hands, and to comply with its directions; if defendant had been improperly arrested, let him make his application to the court in a regular manner for his discharge. It was not to be endured, that the sheriff was to assume upon himself an authority to decide in what cases bail was required, and when it might be dispensed with. His own interests were in no degree jeopardized by executing the arrest, and it was a business in which he had no concern, and no right to interfere. Nor was it a matter of which the sheriff could avail himself, that an appearance had been entered. That was a proceeding in the court under his own eye, and the legal operation of it could not be inquired into and determined by the sheriff. He contended, that if Freeman was arrested without sufficient authority, or upon defective process, an application should have been made to the court to have him discharged on a common appearance. * * *

The court overruled the motion * * *. On the question as to the right of taking bail, Kinsey, C.J., observed, that the writ was directory to the sheriff * * *. That when the writ was put in his hands, he was not to determine whether it was a case in which special bail was required; he was bound to imprison the defendant, unless sufficient bail was found.

The ground of defence adopted by the defendant, was to prove that there was no want of attention on his part; that every precaution consistent with humanity, and sometimes even bordering on rigor, had been adopted with regard to Freeman. This was made out by several witnesses, and it was proved that the escape was occasioned by circumstances not to be foreseen, and which could not be prevented by even more than ordinary exertions and caution.

On the trial, John Gifford was offered as a witness on the part of the defendant, and objected to by Stockton, on the ground of his being the gaoler and sheriff's deputy, and consequently interested to exonerate himself, as well as Halsted, from responsibility. * * * A release, however, from the sheriff being produced, he was admitted by the court.

The court, in their charge to the jury, said that there appeared to be no evidence warranting a suspicion that the escape was collusive or voluntary, so far as it was within their authority to express an opinion on the subject. This, however, was a subject exclusively for the decision of the jury, who were to consider and weigh all the circumstances that had been proved. If they should be of opinion that the escape was connived at by the sheriff, it was their duty to find the whole amount of the judgment against Freeman as the damages.

On the count for a negligent escape, the court said that every escape not happening by the act of God, or the public enemies, was, in the eye of the law, considered a negligent escape. The law admits no other excuse, and if the prisoner is rescued by a mob, whose power the sheriff is unable to withstand, even with the aid of his *posse comitatus,* yet he is answerable for an escape; he must keep him, at all events. The reasons are obvious. If it were otherwise, the creditor would be exposed to imposition and hardship. He must be constantly watching the conduct of the sheriff, and guarding against any collusion between him and the debtor; always liable to deceptions, which it would be impossible to thwart in their progress, or to unravel after their accomplishment. It does not, therefore, lie in the mouth of the sheriff to say that the gaol was insufficient, or that he took all possible care; that the prisoner escaped by means of a false key, or that he was rescued by a mob. He knows at the time of his election, before he enters upon the execution of his office, upon what terms and conditions he is to hold it, and how far the law makes him answerable for any accidents that may occur. He can examine the gaol, but if, after having done what it behooves a prudent man to do, he takes the office and enjoys its benefits, he must submit to the inconveniences, and be answerable for escapes, however innocent he may be of any connivance. O'Niel v. Marson, 5 Burr. 2812.

In cases, however, where the action is for a negligent escape, the jury are not bound to make the original debt the measure of damages against the sheriff. They may take into consideration the circumstances of the case, and find such a measure of damages as the more or less favorable view of the facts which appear in evidence will warrant. On the point, therefore, of the *quantum* of damages in this case, it is a matter upon which the jury are to exercise their own discretion and judgment, and the court ought not, nor will they, direct you.

The jury found a verdict in favor of the plaintiff for £1545 6d. 6s.

* * *

A rule to show cause why a new trial should not be awarded had been obtained in May, and came on for argument in September Term, 1795.

In support of the motion, it was argued * * *. * * * That the court misdirected the jury in stating that the insufficiency of the gaol was not a bar to the action. In England there can be no doubt that the law is as stated by the court; but there the sheriff provides the gaol as well as keeps it, and in case of its weakness, the original and real cause of the escape is his own negligence and inattention. In this country, the county is bound to build the gaol and keep it in repair, and the sheriff should not be made answerable for their remissness in preparing a suitable place for the reception and safe custody of prisoners.

It was further stated that in this case it appeared on the trial that Halsted had made a regular protest against the sufficiency of the gaol. * * *

Stockton, contra * * *. * * * The distinction attempted to be drawn between the different extent to which the sheriff's responsibility ought to be carried in this country and in England, from the circumstance that with us the county is obliged to build and repair the gaol, is without foundation; and this is the first time that it has been thought of. The sheriff was bound to keep his prisoners safely, and if he suffered any injury from the insufficiency of the prison, it was his own loss, and a question between him and the county; but it cannot affect the interests of the plaintiff, who has a right to look immediately to him in case of a loss by an escape.

PER CURIAM * * * Until our own legislature change the common law in this particular, we must adopt it as the rule for our government; and by that the sheriff is answerable for an escape under circumstances like the present.

* * *

Rule discharged.

NOTES AND QUESTIONS

1. The excerpt from Blackstone is from his discussion of the law of "contract." Does it seem to you that he is talking about "contracts?" When Blackstone uses the word "neglect," for example, as in the case he describes of a lawyer guilty of "neglect to appear at the trial," what does he mean, and how would you describe the cause of action?

2. Does the law that is applied in Patten v. Halsted (a case which occurs approximately a generation after Blackstone) follow Blackstone? Note that Blackstone is cited by defendant's attorney in his unsuccessful attempt to have the action dismissed because of procedural irregularities. In particular, the defendant's claim is that "special bail" should not have been required, and thus, there was no original right to imprison the defendant for his failure to make bail. It is argued that since this case called for no "special bail," the sheriff should have dismissed the defendant on personal recognizance. The court holds that the writ given to the sheriff made no express mention that it was not a case requiring special bail, and merely directed the sheriff to imprison the defendant. The court held that the sheriff was not at liberty "to determine whether it was a case in which special bail was required," and that thus unless the defendant himself posted sufficient bail (which he apparently did not) it was the sheriff's duty to imprison him without asking questions. Does this sound right to you? Once the procedural objections are defeated, what becomes the defendant's defense?

3. Note that the judge takes it upon himself to tell the jury that "there appeared to be no evidence warranting a suspicion that the escape was collusive or voluntary * * *." Was it appropriate for the judge so to comment on the evidence? What about the liability on the count for "negligent escape?" According to the judge, what would be the resultant liability of the sheriff if the escape is caused by mob action "whose power the sheriff is unable to withstand, even with the aid of his *posse comitatus*?" Why is the reason for this result so "obvious" to the judge?

4. Is the operation of this rule, liability for "negligent escape," necessarily unjust? What about the operation of the rule in this particular case? What was the measure of damages used here? Note that there was a motion for a new trial. Do you agree with the court's position on disposition of this

motion, that "Until our own legislature change the common law in this particular, we must adopt it as the rule for our government * * *." Does this square with the cases you have read before? Would you expect this attitude of not changing the English common law of torts to continue for very long? What does the next case suggest about American willingness to examine English precedent?

5. Thirty years after *Patten v. Halsted,* the issue of the sheriff's liability for a "negligent" escape was still a live one. In *Commissioners of Brown County v. Butt,* 2 Ohio 348 (1826), the Ohio Supreme Court was asked to decide whether a county "can be made responsible for the escape of a prisoner, confined for debts where the escape happens in consequence of the want of a jail, or where the jail furnished by the county commissioners is insufficient." The precise question which the Supreme Court was addressing was whether, instead of the county itself, the county commissioners, as individuals, should have been liable for the debtor's escape. Curiously, the Supreme Court declared that it could not deviate from the rule that the sheriff himself should be liable in the first instance to the creditor, so that all it was concerned with was whether, once the sheriff was found liable to the creditor, he could look to the county or to the individual commissioners for indemnification.

In declaring that the Ohio Supreme Court could not abandon the English rule that the sheriff was liable in the first instance, Judge Hitchcock, for the court, noted that while it was correct as a general rule for American courts to follow "settled" questions of law in England, there were exceptions to the rule. It was the job of American courts, Hitchcock explained, to seek to discover the reasons for the English rules, and see if they applied in America, because "It is a useful maxim that when the reason of a law ceases, the law itself should cease." In England, Hitchcock noted, the sheriff was liable for an escape, without redress against the county, because he could confine the debtor wherever he pleased, and if the public jail needed repairs, he could make them himself, and then be indemnified by the county. Thus, said Hitchcock, "The escape will not happen without a violation or neglect of duty on his part, and whenever an individual sustains an injury in consequence of the violation or neglect of duty on the part of a public officer, justice requires that the officer should make reparation for the injury." Is this, by the way, the same use of the concept of "neglect" that you saw at work in *Patten v. Halsted*? In any event, Hitchcock observed that in Ohio the sheriff could not imprison the debtor any place he pleased, nor could he make expenses to alter the jail and expect reimbursement without the prior consent of the county commissioners. To deny him redress when the county had failed to provide a proper jail, then, said Hitchcock, "would be to inflict a penalty on an officer who had violated no law, who had been guilty of no violation or neglect of duty. It would, in fact, be to punish him for neglect of duty on the part of others." Concluding, Hitchcock observed that "When the escape is voluntary, or where it happens in consequence of the negligence of the sheriff, he ought to be liable. But where it happens in consequence of circumstances not within his control, the principles of justice require that he should be exonerated." Does this go beyond *Patten*? Curiously, the majority in *Brown County,* while declaring that the county itself was liable to the sheriff, imposed no personal liability on the commissioners for neglect of their duties, since the court believed that it was the duty of the *county* to furnish an adequate prison, and the escape had happened as a consequence of the neglect of the *county's* duty.

Judge Burnet, dissenting in the case, believed that there could be no liability imposed on the county, and that, instead, the individual commissioners ought to be liable. Said he, "The statute made it the duty of the commissioners to provide a sufficient jail, and gave them the means [through taxation] of doing so. They voluntarily accepted the trust, and if they have neglected to execute it, and by that negligence the plaintiff has been injured, the injury has not proceeded from the county, but has been occasioned by the illegal conduct of the commissioners for which they are personally responsible." Was Judge Burnet using "negligence" in the same manner as the majority? As the court in *Patten*? Judge Burnet also noted that there had been no other American case which had imposed liability on the county without a statute specifically so requiring. Indeed, he pointed out, such a rule had been promulgated by Ohio's territorial governor and its judges, but that early statute was repealed by the first Ohio territorial legislature. If the county was to be made liable, in its official capacity, he believed, it should be a decision for the Ohio legislature, and not for the Ohio courts. Who was right on this, Burnet or Hitchcock?

6. Seven years after the *Brown County* case, the Ohio Supreme Court held again in Richardson v. Spencer, 6 Ohio 13 (1833) that a sheriff could not escape from liability for negligent escape by showing that the jail was insufficient, even if his county would be liable to indemnify him if the escape resulted from such insufficiency. Nevertheless, the Supreme Court did suggest that where "the escape was not voluntary on the part of the officer," the sheriff might present evidence that the escaped debtor was insolvent, and thus limit his initial liability. The court held that the evidence of the involuntary or voluntary nature of the escape *and* the insolvency of the debtor were all facts which should go to the jury, which should receive instructions on the law from the trial judge and then reach a damage figure on its own. Would the Patten v. Halsted court sympathize with the notion of differentiating between voluntary and involuntary escapes?

GREGORY, TRESPASS TO NEGLIGENCE TO ABSOLUTE LIABILITY*

37 Virginia Law Review 359, 360–370 (1951).

In this essay I am concerned * * * with liability for harm which defendants caused to others under circumstances where they did not intend to indulge in behavior directed in any way at the interests of such others. On the contrary, these defendants are minding their own business and get involved with the interests of others either because things get out of hand or because they are negligent. Nevertheless, those others sustain damage in some way because of the defendants' behavior; and the task of the courts is to decide whether or not there shall be compensation for such damage. * * *

Civil liability in the common law was originally based on a fairly simple concept—trespass. The King's Court in early England issued the writ of trespass to any litigant who could show that he had sustained a physical contact on his person or property, due to the activity of another. If this litigant-plaintiff could then convince the court that the defendant had intentionally brought about this contact, he had judgment for damages because of the trespass—unless the defendant could justify his act. But if the plaintiff could not establish intent, then in order to recover he had to go ahead and show that he had sustained some actual damage * * *. [T]his ancient concept of trespass had reference to any contact achieved as the consequence of one's conduct against the interest of another, no matter under what circumstances it occurred, as long as the defendant's causative conduct was his voluntary act.

In the early days of the King's Court, the only available writ was that of trespass. Plaintiffs who sustained harm under non-trespassory circumstances were not able to bring suit in the King's Court. Thus, suppose the defendant in a particular instance was building a house adjacent to the highway. As he was carrying a beam along a scaffold, he stumbled and unintentionally dropped the beam on the sidewalk, so that it hit a passerby named White on the head, causing him severe harm. White could easily procure a writ of trespass and recover damages. It was immaterial that the defendant dropped the beam unintentionally; and it made no difference whether or not the defendant was negligent or otherwise at fault. This was a trespass under the early law; and this primitive conception of trespass implied all the fault that was necessary for liability.

Shortly thereafter, let us assume, Black came walking along and stumbled over the beam, falling so that his head hit the beam, with the result that he sustained identically the same harm as that suffered by White. Suppose that the defendant had not had time to remove the beam from the sidewalk nor to post warnings; and also assume that Black neither saw the beam as he walked along nor was careless in having failed to see it. When Black sought a writ entitling him to sue the defendant, there was none available which was appropriate for his case; and he was unable to recover damages. That was because there was no trespass by the defendant against him, since the force initiated by the defendant had come to rest before Black was hurt. Indeed, the only force involved in Black's case was that supplied by Black himself when he came walking along and stumbled.

Poor Black never could understand why White was allowed recovery and he was denied it. Each had sustained the same hurt from the same unintended conduct of the same defendant—the dropping of the beam. The only difference Black could perceive was that White was "lucky" enough to get hit by the beam, so that he was allowed to recover with no questions asked. In the meantime, there were people who were accidentally hit by arrows shot at targets and by limbs cut off trees—all of whom were allowed to recover; while others who were hurt "consequentially"—that is, on whose person there had been no direct contact resulting from unexpended forces initiated by others—were denied recovery. This apparent unbalance of justice was no doubt responsible for the creation of a new writ, to be issued in situations where harm had occurred otherwise than by a "direct" or trespassory contact. The new writ was called "trespass in a similar case"—a misnomer, because it was intended to function in the absence of trespassory contact. Lawyers, however, soon came to refer to this new writ as the action on the case and nicknamed it "case", in contradistinction to trespass.

This development occurred in the thirteenth and fourteenth centuries. Thereafter, people in Black's position were enabled to bring their suits before the King's Court. But that did not mean that they were necessarily entitled to recover. Since they could not show a trespassory contact, they had to supply some other element justifying the imposition of liability on the people who had been instrumental in causing their harm. For by this time even an unintended trespassory contact was regarded as tantamount to *a trespass;* and a trespass of any kind was accepted as a wrong in itself, without inquiry into the circumstances leading up to it. Those who sued in case, therefore, because they could not show a trespassory contact, had to submit some item of illegality or fault to take the place of the missing element of trespass in order to establish liability. In actions on the case for inadvertently caused harm to person or property, this new item of illegality or fault ultimately became what we now speak of as negligence. For negligence, as it has operated during the past century or so to afford a basis of liability, is a fairly modern concept. Certainly its modern significance was completely unknown at the time when the action on the case was developing. But something of the sort no doubt operated to furnish the basis for liability during these early times in the absence of the trespassory contact.

At any rate, as the centuries rolled around, it became apparent that Black's descendants in the law were not much better off than they had been when only the writ of trespass was available—certainly in comparison with litigants who fell into White's category. For plaintiffs like White found trespassory contacts so easy to prove; and legal fault or the early counterpart of negligence was not at all easy to establish. To illustrate, let us return to the instance of the defendant who dropped the beam which hit White and over which Black stumbled. Whatever the circumstances were which governed the defendant's dropping of the beam, they were by hypothesis identically the same as far as the two hurt litigants were concerned. Yet all White has to do under this new development is still merely to show contact and damages, while Black has to undertake the burden of proving fault, at the risk of losing his suit if he cannot do so. If we assume that there was some explanation of the incident showing that defendant's conduct was reasonable and not due to his fault, then if Black cannot offer convincing evidence to the contrary, defendant will get the judgment in his case. But White, on the other hand, will still recover damages.

The frequent recurrence of this state of affairs was bound to irritate litigants in Black's position—not so much because they failed to recover as that White did recover without any real showing of fault. And they were not satisfied with the explanation that the unintended contact was trespassory and that such trespass implied fault in itself. To them the courts seemed to be maintaining a double standard for determining liability to govern unintentionally caused harm—that of fault or social inadequacy in cases like Black's and absolute liability without fault in cases like White's.

Moreover, defendants themselves began to notice this double standard and to complain bitterly about it. Builders whose non-negligently dropped beams hit plaintiffs before they came to rest on the ground felt themselves unfairly treated under a system of alleged justice which excused other builders from liability for harm caused after their beams had reached the ground. Such a capricious and one-sided administration of civil liability might even become a factor tending to discourage them from enterprise and investment!

This very consideration began to worry American judges during the first half of the nineteenth century. They disliked the imposition of liability without fault and reacted against any manifestation of this notion. * * * [M]any of our judges believed that the development of this young country under a system of private enterprise would be hindered and delayed as long as the element of chance exposed enterprisers to liability for the consequences of pure accident, without fault of some sort. * * *

Chief Justice Lemuel Shaw, of the Massachusetts Supreme Court, gets most of the credit for the establishment of a consistent theory of liability for unintentionally caused harm. The case in which he marked the departure from the past was Brown v. Kendall, decided in 1850. There it appeared that two dogs, belonging respectively to the plaintiff and defendant, were engaged in mortal combat. Defendant undertook to separate the dogs by beating them with a stick. Of course, the dogs moved about a good deal as they fought; and both plaintiff and defendant anxiously followed them around. At a certain point defendant raised his stick over his shoulder to strike the dogs, and the end of the stick then happened to hit the plaintiff in the eye while he was standing behind the defendant, causing him serious damage. * * * It does not appear from the report that either the defendant or the plaintiff was in any way negligent * * *.

The plaintiff sued the defendant in trespass for damages. After all, he had been hit in the eye by a stick set in motion by the defendant—a clear case of direct contact. He thought that this contact or, as he called it, this trespass entitled him to recover damages for the resulting harm, without showing anything else. Such a theory of liability, he claimed, was historically traditional * * *.

But the Massachusetts Supreme Court turned the plaintiff down cold. Shaw denied that the contact between defendant's stick and plaintiff's eye had any substantive significance at all. Certainly he did not believe that this unintended contact amounted to the tort of trespass, on which liability could be established. He admitted that the contact had procedural significance, enabling the plaintiff to bring his suit under the action of trespass rather than in case. And he declared that all of the old precedents cited by the plaintiff, in which it appeared that unintentionally caused direct physical contacts amounted to trespass, meant no more than that. They did not imply that any such contact was a trespass in the sense that it was a tort, in itself. Apparently that would be true only if the contact were intentionally inflicted. He then stated as a general principle that when harm occurs as the consequence of an unintended contact, it is actionable only on the basis of negligence, just as if there had been no contact at all in the causing of the harm. Thus, according to Shaw's principle, White and Black in the hypothetical case discussed above, would henceforth be treated exactly the same and White would have no advantage over Black merely because he sustained his harm by a direct hit while Black suffered consequentially.

Now Shaw, of course, had indicated in his opinion that White and Black had always been treated the same—that one who had been hurt by an unintended contact had never enjoyed any advantage over others whose unintentionally caused harm had not resulted from a direct hit. The available evidence, however, indicates that this was not so. * * *

As an alternative basis of liability in the absence of available evidence of negligence, the plaintiff in this dog fight case sought a ruling to the effect that one who sustained harm as the consequence of an unintended direct hit resulting from another's conduct, was entitled to a sort of presumption that such other was negligent and that the burden of disproving negligence was on such other. Thus, he wanted to have the jury instructed that, in view of the direct contact resulting from the defendant's act, even though it was not intended, the defendant must offer convincing evidence that he was not negligent in order to escape liability and that otherwise he would be liable. But Shaw and his court refused to compromise their new principle in this way. They said that the burden of proving negligence in a case of this type always lay on the plaintiff and that it never shifted, leaving the defendant free to sit tight and wait for the plaintiff to show that he had been negligent. For if the burden of disproving negligence were placed on the defendant, simply because of the chance that plaintiff's harm had occurred as the result of a direct hit, then the courts would be lending the element of contact or "trespass" a substantive significance similar to that which they had already denied. Whenever the defendant in such a case was unable to convince the jury of his due care or lack of negligence, liability would be imposed on him in the absence of any proof of fault. He would thus have lost the benefit of the doubt which was still accorded to the defendant whose conduct allegedly harms another, but not under the circumstances of a direct hit. Such a result would go far to cancel out the consistency in theory of liability which the Massachusetts court was endeavoring to establish.

BROWN v. KENDALL, the dog-fight case, quickly became a landmark in the law of torts. * * * If he wanted to win thereafter, a plaintiff hurt by an unintended contact would have to prove the commission of a tort based on negligence, just as if there had been no trespassory contact at all. And with this consistency of theory came another basic notion: no longer was there any theory of absolute liability without fault in our common law to govern the disposition of cases where one sustained harm unintentionally inflicted as the result of another's conduct.

While it is pure speculation, one of Chief Justice Shaw's motives underlying his opinion appears to have been a desire to make risk-creating enterprise less hazardous to investors and entrepreneurs than it had been previously at common law. Certainly that interpretation is consistent with his having furthered the establishment of the fellow servant doctrine and expansion of the assumption-of-risk defense in actions arising out of industrial injuries. Judicial subsidies of this sort to youthful enterprise removed pressure from the pocket-books of investors and gave incipient industry a chance to experiment on low-cost operations without the risk of losing its reserve in actions by injured employees. Such a policy no doubt seems ruthless; but in a small way it probably helped to establish industry, which in turn was essential to the good society as Shaw envisaged it. And, of course, he also had in mind the obvious advantages of consistency in legal theory.

Seven years earlier, in 1843, the highest New York court had enunciated a principle similar to that promulgated in Massachusetts.* There it appeared that a six-year old defendant had thrown a stone at random and it had struck the plaintiff's five-year old daughter in the eye, causing serious damage. The evidence indicated, however, that the young defendant was not at fault, which presumably meant that he did not intend to hit

* Harvey v. Dunlop, Hill & Denio 193 (N.Y.1843). Morton Horwitz has argued that this case "merely represented the culmination of a uniform course of New York decisions which since 1820 had assumed that carelessness had to be shown in both trespass and case." Transformation of American Law 1780–1860 91 (1977). [Ed.]

the little girl and was not to be held negligent in having done so. In any event, the jury seems to have found it to be a case of inevitable accident; and following the instructions of the trial court, it gave the verdict to the defendant. In his appeal the plaintiff assigned error in these instructions. After all, he contended, the defendant had thrown the stone, which had hit his daughter's eye. And while a child of six could hardly be held for negligence, at least he could be made liable at common law for his trespasses.

But the highest New York court affirmed the judgment for defendant, the Chief Judge declaring: "No case or principle can be found, or if found can be maintained, subjecting an individual to liability for an act done without fault on his part." He then went on to say, however, that where harm is inflicted by the defendant, "it should be presumed to have been done wrongfully or carelessly," the burden of proving the contrary to be placed on him. * * *

A somewhat similar instance, illustrating the difficulty with which a few of our state courts made the break from the past, occurred in 1835. The Vermont Supreme Court then declared the law to be that a plaintiff who was run down by a horse and buggy driven by the defendant, could not recover damages if this occurrence was the "result of unavoidable accident" and if "there was no want of prudence or care on the part of the defendant." But then the court went on to say something inconsistent with this statement. "Therefore," its Chief Justice observed, "where a person is doing a voluntary act, which he is under no obligation to do, he is held answerable for any injury which may happen to another, either by carelessness or accident." Now much the same idea was later expressed, in a slightly different way, in the trial court's instructions to the jury in Brown v. Kendall, the Massachusetts dog-fight case. There the trial court said that if what the defendant did "was not a necessary act, and [he] was not in duty bound to part the dogs, but might with propriety interfere or not as he chose, [he] was responsible for the consequences of the blow, unless it appeared that he was in the exercise of extraordinary care, so that the accident was inevitable, using the word not in a strict but a popular sense."

The meaning of this kind of language is hard to grasp. But whatever it means, it runs counter to the main principle that Shaw ultimately stated in the dog-fight case. Certainly Shaw recognized it as drivel, since its validity depended upon drawing a distinction between human conduct which was "necessary," or performed pursuant to some duty, on the one hand, and that which the defendant merely had a right to engage in, on the other hand. Naturally the defendant in Brown v. Kendall didn't have to separate the fighting dogs. It was not a necessary act, in the sense that there was any compulsion on him to perform it. Shaw said, rather, that it "was a lawful and proper act, which he might do by proper and safe means." And he then made it clear that his new principle applied to all human conduct lawfully embarked upon, whether it was driving a horse for pleasure or profit, shooting at targets, building houses or anything else. The only test was to be whether or not such lawful conduct was carefully or negligently performed. Otherwise his new principle would not mean very much, since most human conduct is not compulsory or necessary but is undertaken either for economic gain, for personal value ends, including recreation, or just for something to do.

Perhaps judges using the kind of language which Shaw disapproved were somewhat uncertain about the relatively new concept of negligence. After all, that concept did not then have a very long tradition; and its career in the modern sense was entirely in the future. It is fairly apparent from the examples cited by these judges in their opinions that they were confusing so-called unnecessary conduct with what clearer-headed judges like Shaw would have called conduct from which a jury might be permitted to infer negligence. Again, it is barely possible that they were in this fashion attempting to explain away some of the older precedents which Shaw had preferred simply to ignore—that is, the earlier English decisions in which liability for unintentionally caused harm resulting from direct contacts was based on trespass regardless of the absence of negligence.

* * *

NOTES AND QUESTIONS

1. Gregory gives Shaw much of the credit (albeit unclaimed by Shaw) for changing the rule which imposed a different standard for liability in actions of trespass and case. Before Brown v. Kendall, according to Gregory, one seeking to recover on a writ in trespass need only prove that he was *directly injured* by the conduct of the defendant (e.g. by being hit by defendant's baseball bat wielded at the time by defendant). One seeking to recover in an action on the case (the action brought for indirect injuries—one hurt for example by stumbling over defendant's baseball bat left on the floor by defendant), however, needed to prove some "fault," e.g. a lack of "due care" on the part of defendant. Shaw is said to have swept all this away, and to have applied the same "fault" standard in trespass and case. If Shaw's opinion was such a novel development, why did he claim it wasn't? Consider Professor Horwitz's statements in The Transformation of American Law 1780–1860 (1977) where he comments on the importance of the trespass/case distinction. Do they accord with those of Gregory? What follows is the footnote (number 146, on pages 297–298) which Horwitz uses to support his statement (p. 90) that " * * * there is no indication that American judges, unlike their English brethren, * * * ever regarded the substantive law governing the two writs as turning on a distinction between strict liability and negligence.":

> In Taylor v. Rainbow, 2 H & M (12 Va.) 423 (1808) we find the court reporter observing of the difference between trespass and case that "the

law says there is a nice distinction, but the reason * * * is often difficult to discover." Id. at 423. And the defendant's counsel, in arguing that the plaintiff brought the wrong action, declared: "It is unnecessary to reason on the propriety of keeping up the boundaries of action: it is a settled rule of law that they must be preserved." Id. at 430. Of the three judges who wrote opinions in the case, none puts the distinction on substantive law. Judge Fleming, for example, emphasized that he saw no substantive difference between the two writs, since the ends of justice would be served by either, yet he felt "tied down, and bound by precedents" establishing the direct-indirect distinction. Id. at 444.

* * * In Gates v. Miles, 3 Conn. 64, 67 (1819), the Connecticut Supreme Court also spelled out only procedural reasons for preserving the difference between the actions: "As no suit can be maintained for trespass *vi et armis* after three years, and as in trespass on the case there is no limitation, it becomes highly important to preserve the established boundaries between these actions."

An 1817 case in New York, Foot v. Wiswall, 14 Johns. 304, marks a significant turning point because it emphasizes how late it was before lawyers came to regard even the allegation of negligence in an action on the case as limiting liability. In a ship collision case, the plaintiff's counsel still argued the strict liability doctrine that the defendant had "acted at his peril." The action was brought in case, he pointed out, only because that form of action was required when a servant brought about an injury. "If the defendant had been at the helm of his boat at the time," he concluded, "there is no doubt that the plaintiffs could have recovered in an action of trespass; and there is no reason why they should not be equally entitled to recover in an action of trespass on the case, or for negligence; the distinction between the two actions being purely technical." Id. at 306. Nevertheless, the New York Supreme Court upheld the verdict for the defendant, clearly indicating for the first time it was for the plaintiff to prove and for the jury to determine whether the defendant had violated some standard of care. Three years later the court also upheld a trespass action for a collision only after minutely examining the evidence for proof of carelessness. Percival v. Hickey, 18 Johns. 257, 289–90 (1820). Thus, it is not surprising that by 1826, when the New York court elaborately explained why "it is still important to preserve the distinction between the actions" it failed to discuss any differences in substantive law, mentioning only technical differences in costs and pleadings. M'Allister v. Hammond, 6 Cow. 342, 344 (N.Y.1826). For within a few short years, actions in both trespass and case had been simultaneously put to the test of negligence.

Outside New York, Benjamin L. Oliver, Jr., of Massachusetts was the first clearly to state that "without any negligence or fault whatever, it seems no action can be maintained" in either trespass or case. B. Oliver, Forms of Practice; or American Precedents 619 (1828).

2. Still, Horwitz believes that the substantive law of both trespass and case did change from the application of a *strict liability* standard in both to the application of a "fault" or "due care" (modern "negligence") standard in both. Horwitz might well agree with Gregory on the reasons for such a change. What do you suppose that those reasons would be? Could they be the same ones that led, for example, to a change in the American common law regarding ancient lights? For other studies of the development of nineteenth century American tort law and/or its English antecedents, which address the question of whether the common law judges were seeking to subsidize American industry and which offer conclusions or approaches different from those of Horwitz, see Morris S. Arnold, "Introduction" to Select Cases of Trespass from The King's Courts, 1307–1399 (Morris S. Arnold ed., 1985), John H. Baker, An Introduction to English Legal History 456–59 (3d ed. 1990), Stephen G. Gilles, "Inevitable Accident in Classical English Tort Law," 43 Emory L.J. 575 (1994), Peter Karsten, Heart versus Head: Judge–Made Law in Nineteenth–Century America (1997), Jerrilyn Marston, "Comment, The Creation of a Common Law Rule: The Fellow–Servant Rule, 1837–1860," 132 U. Pa. L. Rev. 579 (1984), Robert L. Rabin, "The Historical Development of the Tort Principle: A Reinterpretation," 15 Ga. L. Rev. 925 (1981), Gary Schwartz, "Tort Law and the Economy in Nineteenth Century America: A Reinterpretation," 90 Yale L.J. 1717 (1981), and "The Character of Early American Tort Law," 36 U.C.L.A.L.Rev. 641 (1989), G. Edward White, Tort Law in America: An Intellectual History (1980), Stephen F. Williams, "Transforming American Law: Doubtful Economics Makes Doubtful History," 25 U.C.L.A.L.Rev. 1187 (1978), and Robert J. Kaczorowski, "The Common–Law Background of Nineteenth–Century Tort Law," 51 Ohio St. L.J. 1127 (1990).

3. In Callender v. Marsh, 18 Mass. (1 Pick.) 418 (1823), a homeowner whose foundation walls were seriously weakened by the lowering of a street adjacent to his property brought an action of trespass on the case against Boston's surveyor of highways, who had ordered the "improvement" in the road. The plaintiff had owned his property for more than twenty years, and the original road had been in existence some time before that. Massachusetts statutes gave the surveyor of highways the "power and duty" to make the public ways "safe and convenient." The court stated that "[i]f the public safety and convenience require a levelling of the road, [the surveyor] must do it with as much care in relation to property bordering on the road, as it is possible for him to use; and if he should abuse his authority by digging down or raising up, where it might not be necessary for the reasonable repair and amendment of the road, he would be amenable to any suffering party for his damages." In *Callender,* however, there was no allegation that the surveyor had failed to use "as much care * * * as it is possible for him to use." The plaintiff

seems rather to have relied on his argument that the statute giving the surveyor the power to lower the roads in a manner that injured his foundations was unconstitutional, and thus could not be relied on by the surveyor. The Massachusetts Declaration of Rights provided, in pertinent part, that "whenever the public exigencies require that the property of any individual should be appropriated to public uses, he shall receive a reasonable compensation therefor," and there was no provision made by the surveyor for compensating homeowners whose foundations were weakened. *Held,* by the Supreme Court, *per* Parker, C.J., the plaintiff must be nonsuited. There was no problem with the constitutionality of the statute, since the provision of the Declaration of Rights could not be construed "to extend the benefit of it to one who suffers an indirect or consequential damage or expense, by means of the right use of property already belonging to the public." "Those who purchase house lots bordering upon streets," said the court, "are supposed to calculate the chances of such elevations and reductions as the increasing population of a city may require * * * [and] may indemnify themselves in the price of the lot which they buy, or take the chance of future improvements, as they shall see fit."

The surveyor, was, of course, a public official, and the plaintiff a citizen damaged by the conduct of such an official. How is it that in Patten v. Halsted there is relief for such damage, but not in Callender v. Marsh?

HENTZ V. THE LONG ISLAND RAILROAD CO.

Supreme Court of New York, 1852.
13 Barb. 646.

S.B. STRONG, J. The plaintiff alleges in his complaint that he has been for the last five years, and is, lawfully possessed of a lot in the village of Hempstead, in the county of Queens * * * comprising half an acre; on which there are a dwelling house and shop fronting on Main-street * * *. That while he has been so possessed of the said premises, the defendants having previously, and in or about the year 1837, laid down and along Main-street, and upon such premises, certain timbers and iron rails, constituting their railroad track, continued them thereon, running over the same with passenger and freight cars drawn by horses, greatly to his injury * * *. That about the 5th of last August, the defendants took up the old timbers and rails and tore up the soil of his land, and laid down in their place other timbers and iron rails, and have at various times since * * * run upon the said rails * * * with their locomotives, propelled by steam; that "by the coming of the said locomotives upon and running the same over his said close, the health and lives of his family, tenants and inmates, are prejudiced and endangered, and the value of his property lessened; that an offensive smoke has filled his dwelling house; that the same is a nuisance of the most flagrant character," and that the continuance thereof would be an irreparable injury to his said property and the enjoyment thereof; and that his tenants are likely to abandon the same.

That the defendants have since such 5th of August last, run upon and over the said premises certain freight cars loaded with manure and merchandise, propelling the same by means of their steam engine and horses, often without agents to watch and conduct them, and to the danger, nuisance and inconvenience of himself and family; and that from the contiguity of his land to the depot, the locomotives frequently stop opposite to his premises, and he is thus injured more than the rest of mankind.

He therefore claims two thousand dollars damages, and prays for an order of injunction restraining the defendants during the pendency of this suit from running their locomotives or cars of any description upon or over his said premises, and that a judgment may be given him for his damages, and for a perpetual injunction.

* * *

The only remaining question is whether the road where it passes the plaintiff's premises is a nuisance. * * * The legislature has expressly authorized various companies to lay and use their track through many of our cities and villages, and cars are now drawn by locomotives propelled by steam through Albany, Schenectady, Utica, Syracuse, Rochester, Buffalo, Poughkeepsie, Brooklyn, Jamaica, and many other cities and villages. It was held in the case of Drake v. The Hudson River Railroad Company, (7 Barb. 509,) that a road passing through the streets in the city of New York, and when the cars are drawn by steam-power into a crowded part of the city (although not to the terminus of the road) was not a nuisance. Similar decisions were made in the cases of Hamilton v. The New York and Harlem Railroad Company, (9 Paige, 171); The Lexington and Ohio Railroad Co. v. Applegate, (8 Dana, 289); and Chapman v. The Albany and Schenectady Railroad Company, (10 Barb. 360). Is there then any thing peculiar to Main-street, or in the management of the defendants, which makes the railroad where it passes the plaintiff's house a nuisance? It is not averred in the complaint that the railroad constitutes any serious impediment to the travel, along the highway. It no where appears that the rails are badly laid down, so as to create any obstruction on the surface, and it is apparent that the street is of sufficient width for carriages to pass each other without danger or difficulty, on either side of the railway. Besides, a number of respectable inhabitants of the place deposed that the condition of the street as a passway has been considerably improved by the defendants' works upon it.

Is there any thing in the management of the road and its appendages which renders it offensive to the plaintiff, to such an extent as to justify the interposition of this court by way of restraint upon the action of the defendants? * * * The plaintiff complains that about two years ago, and for about a year, the track was disused and suffered "to go to ruin," its shattered state embarrassing the travel upon the highway, causing the breaking of vehicles, and hindering their passage to and from his premises. There were no doubt serious grievances at the time, but they resulted from the then impaired condition of the track. The cause has since been removed, and the papers furnish us no reasons to apprehend a recurrence of the same or similar evils. None of the papers mention any serious accidents since the track has been relaid and the locomotive has passed over it, and if there had been any, they would no doubt have been discovered by the plaintiff, or the learned member of the bar who has resided during the past summer with him, who acts as one of his counsel in this action, and has shown a laudable zeal, and made strenuous exertions in behalf of his client. The plaintiff complains also of the smoke from the locomotive, on the ground that it is prejudicial to the health and comfort of himself and his family, and he alleges that the establishment as now conducted is a "nuisance of the most flagrant character," and the lives of his family, tenants and inmates are endangered. The general charge that it is a flagrant nuisance, cannot be taken into consideration, any further than as it may be supported by the facts. In this case there are none except those which I have mentioned. The smoke must undoubtedly be annoying to some extent, but not more disagreeable or prejudicial than what may proceed from many lawful establishments in the village, nor is the inconvenience so constant or continuous. There may be some danger to human life from the rapid passage of a railroad train, but in the opinion of many, not more than what results from the passage of ordinary carriages. Accidents to children, or to adults who are not grossly careless, from the locomotives when passing through our most populous cities, are very rare. The times of their passage are generally known, and the noise made by the movement over the rails, and the engineer's whistle, give timely notice of the approach of the train. When the usual precautions are practiced the danger is very slight, and when there is any carelessness or mismanagement the company and its officers are very properly held to a rigid accountability. It is true that there can be no satisfaction for the loss of life, nor any adequate remuneration for the deprivation of a limb, but the strong probability that the company will encounter a serious loss of property, and that a careless or notoriously incompetent conductor, or engineer, will undergo a disgraceful punishment where serious injuries are inflicted, must necessarily lead to great caution and to consequent security. The evils of which the plaintiff complains are by no means peculiar to himself. They are the necessary concomitants of this species of locomotion, whether in the city or in the country. They cannot be prevented without an entire suspension of one of the greatest improvements of modern times.

Private rights should undoubtedly be effectually guarded, but the courts cannot extend the protection of the interest of any one so far as to restrict the lawful pursuits of another. The maxim *sic uteri tuo ut non alienum laedas* is true when correctly construed. It extends to all damages for which the law gives redress, but no further. If it should be applied literally, it would deprive us to a great extent of the legitimate use of our property, and impair, if not destroy its value. A man who sets up a new store or hotel in the vicinity of an old one, or who discovers and makes a new machine which wholly supersedes a prior invention, or who erects a new dwelling house so near that of his neighbor as to endanger it from the cinders which may escape from the chimney, or as to interrupt some fine prospect, or who plants a grove so near the boundary line of another as to shade a valuable garden, or prevent the free circulation of air around a dwelling house, inflicts an injury for which the law gives no redress, and which cannot be averted by the tribunals intrusted with its administration. So too there are some useful employments which endanger the lives of human beings which cannot and ought not to be prohibited. Lives are sometimes destroyed by an omnibus, a carman's cart, a stage or a steamboat, but so long as they are not imminently dangerous they cannot be prohibited. We cannot enjoy our private rights, nor can we avail ourselves of the many advantages resulting from modern discoveries, without encountering some risk to our lives, or our property, or to some extent endangering the lives or injuring the property of others. The questions in all such cases are, is the business a lawful one, and is the injury or danger to others by or from its legitimate pursuit inevitable? If they are, the law furnishes no remedy either by way of indemnity or prevention.

* * *

Upon the whole I am satisfied that the case presented in behalf of the plaintiff does not call for, or warrant, the interposition of this court by way of restriction upon the future action of the defendants.

The motion for an injunction must therefore be denied, and the order temporarily restraining the defendants must be vacated.

NOTES AND QUESTIONS

1. How would Blackstone have decided this case, and why?

2. As noted by this court, its opinion, that a railroad was *not* a nuisance *per se,* followed earlier cases. In one of the first of these, Lexington & Ohio Railroad Co. v. Applegate, 38 Ky. (8 Dana.) 289 (1839), there are some poignant comments about the implications of declaring steam locomotives *not* nuisances:

> * * * [E]ven though some persons owning property on the railroad street may be subjected to some inconvenience, and even loss, by the construction and use of the road, yet, if the use made of the road be consistent with the purpose for which the street was established, and also consistent with the just rights of all, such persons have no right either to damages or to an injunction; because they purchased their property, and must hold it—as all others purchase and must hold town lots—subject to

any consequences that may result, whether advantageously or disadvantageously, from any public and authorized use of the streets, in any mode promotive of, and consistent with, the purposes of establishing them as common highways in town, and compatible with the reasonable enjoyment by all others entitled thereto.

* * *

Main street, in Louisville, was established as a common highway for the universal public; and, as said in Rex v. Russel, "the right of the public is not confined to the purposes of passage; trade and commerce are the chief objects, and the right of passage is chiefly subservient to those ends."

* * *

The onward spirit of the age must, to a reasonable extent, have its way. The law is made for the times, and will be made or modified by them. The expanded and still expanding genius of the common-law should adapt it here, as elsewhere, to the improved and improving condition of our country and our countrymen. And, therefore, railroads and locomotive steam-cars—the offsprings, as they will also be the parents, of progressive improvement—should not, in themselves, be considered as nuisances, although, in ages that are gone, they might have been so held, because they would have been comparatively useless, and, therefore, more mischievous.

We know that a zealous and inconsiderate spirit of innovation and improvement requires the vigilance and restraint of both reason and law. We are fully aware, also, of the fact that, when such a spirit is abroad, private rights are in peculiar danger, unless sternly guarded by the judiciary; and we are not sure that such guardianship is not most needed in a government where whatever is popular is apt to prevail at first, and often at last, only because it is the *vox populi.*

* * *

Note the comments of this court that when a spirit of "innovation and improvement" is abroad in a situation where the *vox populi* tends to prevail, the court's task is the vigilant protection of private rights. Based on what you have seen of the law of torts in the early nineteenth century, how well did nineteenth century American courts perform this task? Would you say that tort liability increased or decreased? What implications would this have for the bearing of the costs of industrial and commercial development? Do you think this is a "democratic," or "anti-democratic" result? Does it further the ends of justice or republicanism? Lest you should conclude that the Blackstonian concept of nuisance simply withered away, you can find a useful corrective in Louise A. Halper, "Nuisance, Courts and Markets in the New

York Court of Appeals, 1850–1915," 54 Albany L. Rev. 301 (1990). Ms. Halper finds that nuisance doctrine was alive and well and living in New York throughout the nineteenth century.

E. THE EVOLUTION OF THE AMERICAN BUSINESS CORPORATION

INTRODUCTION: The Corporation in English Law and Early America

The corporation has a long and varied history. Its essential character is as a government-sanctioned enterprise that has the authority to raise funds through the organization of shareholders. Though it is not human, it is given an artificial legal personality, and often perpetual life, and this unique status was traditionally conferred, as you will soon see in *Currie's Administrator*, to serve a public purpose. The corporation was recognized under classical Roman law, and Roman law's incorporation into the Canon law in Europe is nowhere so obvious as in the corporate conception of the early Christian Church, which was conceived as more than the sum of its members and capable of an existence continuing indefinitely into the future.

One of the early examples of a successful European business corporation was the Dutch East India Company chartered by the Estates–General of the Netherlands in 1602. The charter granted the company a state-protected monopoly in colonial activities in Asia. The company was the first to issue stocks and bonds to raise money for its trading expeditions, and it became a model for future development. In England, only the Crown could grant a charter of incorporation, often to reward a Royal favorite. The Crown also used such charters as a means of implementing mercantilist policy. Mercantilism was a political and economic theory that equated the state's prosperity with the level of capital holdings, especially gold and silver. Spain's sixteenth century conquests in the New World set the tone for European colonization, and fueled French and English monarchial visions of vast wealth, especially gold. Following the Dutch example, the English crown in 1606 granted charters of incorporation to English merchants who formed the Virginia Companies of London and Plymouth. The objective was to establish colonial outposts in the New World. Influenced by the stories of the Aztecs and Incas, the Englishmen hoped to cash in.

Raising funds through selling stock, in December 1606 the Virginia Company of London launched three small ships with 106 settlers; they landed in Jamestown almost five months later. A crew of colonists less suited to the work would be hard to imagine. A colony was established, but not before much hardship, starvation, illness, and death, and a rethinking of what kinds of people were most likely to succeed. Of course there was no gold, and "gentlemen" unwilling to work were no longer welcomed. Unable to turn a profit, the company's corporate charter was revoked by the king in 1624, but the company did leave a lasting mark on the colony's future when it decided to encourage the planting of tobacco as a cash crop, and to import Africans as a labor source. Tobacco became British North America's gold. By the time of the Revolution, Virginia's annual tobacco trade accounted for 60% of all colonial exports to the mother country.

The Virginia Companies were the first, and the last, corporate charters used to found a British colony. Nevertheless the corporate charter was a not uncommon presence within the settled colonies, and was granted to churches, cities, or boroughs. Only seven charters of incorporation were issued to business corporations before 1776. Does this help you understand the confusion about the nature of a corporate charter which you will see reflected below in *Currie's Administrator* and *Dartmouth College*?

After the Revolution the number of corporate business charters took off, with 227 grants made from 1780 to 1800. In the colonies, charters were granted by the governor. In the new states, it was the legislature that made the grants "specially" on a case-by-case basis. At this time the legislation granting corporate charters usually stated that the corporation was to end after a set period of years, usually five, ten, or twenty. Like colonial corporations, state-granted charters characteristically made shareholders personally liable for the corporation's debts, although as you will see, the state legislatures began setting limits on shareholder liability in the first third of the nineteenth century. By about 1840 this trend was nearly universal.

The granting of charters continued to be linked to some public purpose, even in the case of business corporations. Thus charters were issued for raising capital to build or operate public conveyances, such as canals, turnpikes, stage lines, bridges, and, later, railroads. The charter often granted broad monopoly privileges, including a right to condemn lands and to collect tolls. This eminent domain privilege remains highly controversial today, as demonstrated by the reaction to the United States Supreme Court's recent decision in *Kelo v. New London*, 545 U.S. 469 (2005). In the case of banks, charters were established to give subsidies in the form of state investments that banks then loaned to private developers. For the young states, the advancement of commercial agriculture, transportation, and manufacturing depended upon the ability to raise capital, and incorporation met that need.

Though it was establishing a place for itself in commercial affairs, the corporation was not an overwhelmingly popular form of business organization before 1860. Tensions and contradictions existed. The process of granting special charters on a case-by-case basis was burdensome alike for legislators and those seeking charters. There was a popular distrust of monopolistic rights granted to a privileged few by special charters. In the era of President Andrew Jackson, anti-monopolistic sentiment found its way into mainstream politics when in 1832 Jackson vetoed the re-chartering of the Second Bank of the United States. The special charter also exposed the state to risks. Investments of public funds in private ventures went sour in periods of economic panic, when businesses failed and projects collapsed. The worst was the Panic of 1837, followed by a depression. When this happened, the state was open to charges of favoritism and even corruption in its choice of corporate partners. A safer route for the state was to avoid public-private entanglements entirely, and this was the direction that states began to take, for a while, after 1840.

The obvious advantages of the corporate form won advocates too, however, and the pre-Civil War example that many states set in replacing special with "general" incorporation statutes greatly democratized access. The old belief dating back to the colonial era that specially granted charters ensured accountability of stockholders to their communities was losing credibility; it was also not a point of view with much appeal to developers and entrepreneurs. In place of state control was a preference for individual initiative. In place of accountability was a preference for freedom from restraints. In opposition to cumbersome access to the corporate charter was a desire for ready availability. Even in 1860, America remained a predominantly agricultural society, and most engaged in business pursuits did so as sole proprietors or as members of a partnership. Still, it was also evident that the "onward spirit of the age" pointed to advancing technologies, new industries, and the opening up of far-flung markets. In the Gilded Age, decades after the Civil War, it was the device of the corporation that made possible the growth of the new commercial empires including railroads, steel, iron, rubber, automobiles, food processing, and oil. The corporation allowed for the pooling of vast sums of capital, an essential requirement for industries with large fixed-cost components: track, locomotives, railway cars, buildings, factories, furnaces, and machines. With enormous sums of capital at risk, the limitation on liability worked as the perfect inducement to investors.

During the Progressive Era, it was not the corporate form *per se* that attracted the attention of reformers, state legislators, the Congress, and the ill-will of labor organizers. Even by 1930, the corporate form was used by less than half of all American businesses. It was the existence of large-scale enterprise on so vast a scale, and all the informal power that implied; the fact that the private corporation was able to shed its public responsibility that again raised questions about whether the corporation was a tool of virtue or vice. As we will see when we turn to Antitrust law, at issue were questions of the limits of private power and the responsibilities of government to act to enforce those limits. Even so, the development of the modern business corporation is generally regarded as the most innovative and enduring creation of American law, and is now imitated throughout the world. As you contemplate the materials that follow, ask yourself whether you believe this to be a benign or dangerous development.

Further Reading:

J. Willard Hurst, *Law and the Conditions of Freedom in Nineteenth Century America,* 1964

J. Willard Hurst, *The Growth of American Law: The Law Makers*, 1950

Morton Horwitz, The *Transformation of American Law*, 1780–1860, 1977

Lawrence M. Friedman, *A History of American Law*, 3rd ed. 2005

Kermit L. Hall, *The Magic Mirror: Law in American History*, 1989

John Micklethwait, Adrian Wooldridge, *The Company: A Short History of a Revolutionary Idea*, 2003

Ronald E. Seavoy, *The Origins of the American Business Corporation, 1784–1855: Broadening the Concept of Public Service During Industrialization*, 1982

Harry L. Watson, *Liberty and Power: The Politics of Jacksonian America*, 1990

1. THE STATE AND THE CORPORATION

CURRIE'S ADMINISTRATORS V. THE MUTUAL ASSURANCE SOCIETY

Supreme Court of Virginia, 1809.
4 Hen. & M. 315.

[This case concerns an attempt by an early insurance ("assurance") company to rationalize its risk/reward calculations by allocating premiums from owners of town dwellings to pay only for damage to town dwellings, and "country" premiums for "country" damages. Formerly there had been only one pool. The change, made pursuant to an 1805 statute, had the effect of raising the plaintiff town dweller's premium. He sued to have the 1805 Act declared void. The plaintiff lost in the Virginia District Court, and appealed to the Virginia Supreme Court.]

JUDGE ROANE. In the year 1794, the legislature passed an act, at the suggestion of an individual, "for establishing a Mutual Assurance Society against fire, upon buildings in this state." It provided for a subscription to the scheme, by individuals, and declared that the principle of the assurance should be, "that the citizens of this state may insure their buildings against losses and damages occasioned accidentally by fire, and that the insured pay the losses and expenses, each his share, according to the sum insured." * * * The act further provided, that as soon as three millions of dollars should be subscribed, the subscribers should meet together, examine the system submitted to the legislature, and conclude on such rules and regulations, as to a majority of the subscribers might seem best; and that the said society should be at liberty, from time to time, to alter and amend the said rules and regulations, as they may judge necessary; and in particular, that they should agree upon the premiums to be paid. The act also provided, that as soon as the society should have acted in the premises, and elected their agents and officers, it should be considered as incorporated by virtue of the act.

It is evident, that every thing touching the question before us, is left to the pleasure of the society itself by this act * * * and that some of the powers expressly recognized by the act, as appertaining to the society itself, (that of fixing and altering the premiums for example,) are equally as important and as liable to be abused as the principle in question; which, it is urged, has been infringed by the act of 1805, effecting a separation between the interests of the towns and those of the country. * * * The true question, therefore, before us is, whether any fundamental principle exists in the case at bar, interdicting the separation of the interests in question—and if there be, whether the subsequent legislature had power to invade it?

* * *

In order to show that the act in question is no law, and therefore, it is further urged, is a compact, and as such is beyond the power of a succeeding legislature, Blackstone's definition of municipal law has been relied on. Municipal law is defined by him to be "a rule of civil conduct prescribed by the supreme power of the state, commanding what is right, and prohibiting what is wrong;" and it is argued, that the act in question is no law, under this definition, for want of the generality implied by the term "rule," and because it is said to be not so much in the nature of a command by the legislature, as of a promise or contract proceeding from it. When we consider, that mere private statutes and acts of parliament, are (even by this writer himself) universally classed among the municipal laws of England; nay, even that the particular customs of that kingdom, are admitted to form a part of the municipal code, it is evident, that this definition of municipal law, is by far too limited and narrow. I would rather adopt the definition of Justinian, that civil (or municipal) law, is, "*quoad quisque sibi populus constituit*," bounded only in this country in relation to legislative acts, by the constitutions of the general and state governments; and limited also by considerations of justice. It was argued by a respectable member of the bar, that the legislature had a right to pass any law, however just, or unjust, reasonable, or unreasonable. This is a position which even the courtly Judge Blackstone was scarcely hardy enough to contend for, under the doctrine of the boasted omnipotence of parliament. What is this, but to lay prostrate, at the footstool of the legislature, all our rights of person and of property, and abandon those great objects, for the protection of which, alone, all free governments have been instituted?

For my part, I will not outrage the character of any civilized people, by supposing them to have met in legislature, upon any other ground, than that of morality and justice. In this country, in particular, I will never forget, "that no free government, or the blessing of liberty, can be preserved to any people, but by a firm adherence to justice, moderation, temperance, frugality, and virtue, and by frequent recurrence to fundamental principles."[a] I must add, however, that when any legislative act is to be questioned, on the ground of conflicting with the superior acts of the people, or of invading the vested rights of individuals, the case ought to be palpable and clear: in an equivocal or equiponderant case, it ought not easily to be admitted, that the immediate representatives of the people, representing as well the justice as the wisdom of the nation, have forgotten the great injunctions under which they are called to act. In such case, it ought rather to be believed, that the judging power is mistaken.

With respect to acts of incorporation, they ought never to be passed, but in consideration of services to be rendered to the public. This is the principle on which such charters are granted even in England; (1 Bl.Com. 467,) and it holds *a fortiori* in this country, as our bill of rights interdicts all "exclusive and separate emoluments or privileges from the community, but in consideration of public services." (Art. 4.) It may be often convenient for a set of associated individuals, to have the privileges of a corporation bestowed upon them; but if their object is merely private or selfish; if it is detrimental to, or not promotive of, the public good, they have no adequate claim upon the legislature for the privilege. But as it is possible that the legislature may be imposed upon in the first instance; and as the public good and the interests of the associated body, may, in the progress of time, by the gradual and natural working of events, be thrown entirely asunder, the question presents itself, whether, under such and similar circumstances, the hands of a succeeding legislature are tied up from revoking the privilege. My answer is, that they are not. In the first case, no consideration of public service ever existed, and in the last, none continues to justify the privilege. It is the character of a legislative act to be repealable by a succeeding legislature; nor can a preceding legislature limit the power of its successor, on the mere ground of volition only. That effect can only arise from a state of things involving public utility, which includes the observance of justice and good faith towards all men.

These ideas are not new; they are entirely sanctioned by the sublime act of our legislature, "for establishing religious freedom." That act, after having declared and asserted certain self-evident principles, touching the rights of religious freedom, concludes in this manner: "And though we well know that this assembly, elected by the people for the ordinary pur-

[a] Virginia Bill of Rights, art. 15.

poses of legislation only, have no power to restrain the acts of succeeding assemblies, constituted with powers equal to our own, and that, therefore, to declare this act irrevocable, would be of no effect in law, yet we are free to declare, that the rights hereby asserted, are of the natural rights of mankind, and that if any act shall be hereafter passed, to repeal the present, or to narrow its operation, such act will be an infringement of natural right." Conforming to the principles declared in this luminous exposition, I infer, irresistibly, that the power of a succeeding legislature is bounded only, (and that in cases of no equivocal complexion,) by the principles and provisions of the constitution and bill of rights, and by those great rights and principles, for the preservation of which all just governments are founded. * * *

Under the actual case before us, I might, perhaps have spared myself the necessity of this discussion. The principle stated in the act of 1794, which is supposed to have interdicted the separation in question, is couched in terms extremely abstract and general. While other principles declared by this act, have clearly and expressly confined the benefits of the institution to citizens of this state, and limited insurances to losses occasioned accidentally by fire; while it is clearly provided that retribution is to be made by the insured, and that according to the sum insured, the principle now immediately in question does not seem to prohibit a division or distribution of the members, or their interests into classes, or districts. * * *

From these considerations, it would, perhaps, result, that the regulation in question did not require legislative aid to carry it into operation, but might have been effected by the society itself. That, however, is taking a broader ground than is necessary to be maintained on the present occasion. That aid having been afforded by the legislature, it is enough for our purpose that the act of 1805, if it has produced any injustice at all to any class of subscribers, has fallen short of the crying grade of injustice, which alone can disarm the act of its operation. The society itself, at least, considered this, on the contrary, as a measure essential to the equalization of the risks; and, in this respect, I see no cause to differ from them in opinion.

By referring to the principle of our law respecting corporations, the foregoing results will be fully justified. Those artificial persons are rendered necessary in the law from the inconvenience, if not impracticability of keeping alive the rights of associated bodies, by devolving them on one series of individuals after another. The effect of them is, to consolidate the will of the whole, which is collected from the sense of the majority of those who constitute them. This decision by a majority is a fundamental law of corporations in this country and in England * * *. It is also a fundamental principle of corporations, that this majority may establish rules and regulations for the corporation, (which are considered as a sort of municipal law for the body corporate,) subject only to a superior and fundamental law which may have been prescribed by the founder thereof, or by the legislature which grants the privilege perhaps, also, these petty legislatures ought further to be limited by all those considerations, (including the due observance of justice,) which I have endeavoured to shew, ought to bound the proceedings of all legislatures whatsoever. If, however, there be no such paramount law, or overruling principle, the mere will of the majority is competent to any regulation. * * * But further, a corporation may be extinguished by the surrender of its rights and franchises; as to which the unanimous assent of every individual is not requisite. The will of the majority must prevail in this, as in other cases. It is not to be expected that this kind of suicide will be committed for light causes; and where cases of greater exigency require it, the corporation should not hesitate to make the surrender.

* * *

As it is not expected, that corporations shall exist for ever, when the reasons for granting them shall have passed away, and no public utility can ensue from their continuance, this right of surrender must incontrovertibly exist, even in derogation of the fundamental laws and principles. In the case before us, the resolution of the society, on which the act of 1805 was bottomed, may be considered as such surrender, and that act as the acceptance thereof. The interest of the institution commenced thereafter, as it were, *de novo;* and provision was made for a revision, and revaluation of the houses in the towns and in the country, as thus separated. Whether, therefore, the measure adopted by the society in 1805, and sanctioned by the legislature, be considered as a legitimate change, by the society itself, of an ordinary regulation, or as a surrender which destroyed a fundamental one, the effect as to the question before us, is precisely the same.

* * *

In every view of this case, therefore, I am of opinion, that the judgment of the District Court is correct, and ought to be affirmed.

NOTES AND QUESTIONS

1. Why do you suppose Judge Roane finds it necessary to suggest that "morality and justice" are the only grounds on which a legislature would ever choose to act? Is there something suspect in what the legislature did here? Do you believe that there is anything inherently wrong with the idea that the legislature has the power to alter an insurance company's charter in order to alter the rates it charges?

2. Surely one of the core ideas in Judge Roane's opinion is the notion that incorporation is only to be allowed when the corporation will operate in

the public interest. Corporations are still chartered by the fifty states today, and the rationale for granting charters is that corporations serve the public interest. Do you see how the notion that corporations are to operate in the public interest leads to the conclusions that legislatures may alter corporate charters? For the history of nineteenth century conceptions of business corporations operating in the public interest, see generally, Ronald E. Seavoy, The Origins of the American Business Corporation 1784–1855 (1982). Herbert Hovenkamp, Enterprise and American Law 1836–1937 (1991), and Note, "Incorporating the Republic: The Corporation in Antebellum Political Culture," 102 Harv. L. Rev. 1883 (1989).

3. When Judge Roane is speaking of the power that legislatures have to undo the work of their predecessors, he suggests that the only "bounds" on the action of a successor legislature are set "by the principles and provisions of the constitution and bill of rights, and by those great rights and principles, for the preservation of which all just governments are founded." What are "those great rights and principles, for the preservation of which all just governments are founded"? Where do those "great rights and principles" come from, and where have you encountered this notion before? Do they have anything at all to do with corporations? Was any of this discussion of the power of legislatures necessary to the resolution of this case?

4. What purposes of corporations does Judge Roane recognize as legitimate? Does he make incorporation sound very attractive to you? What about Judge Roane's suggestion that corporate charters are like "fundamental law"? With what is Judge Roane thereby comparing corporate charters? Does that suggest that legislatures should feel free about changing charters? Compare Roane's attitude toward corporations and corporate charters with that of Justices Marshall and Story in the case which follows.

DARTMOUTH COLLEGE V. WOODWARD

Supreme Court of the United States, 1819.
17 U.S. (4 Wheat.) 518, 4 L.Ed. 629.

[Acts of the New Hampshire Legislature sought to change the terms of the corporate charter of Dartmouth College. The Dartmouth Trustees argued that a corporate charter was a "contract," and that a legislative act unilaterally changing that "contract" violated the United States Constitution. We begin with an edited version of the opinion of the Court, delivered by Chief Justice Marshall.]

* * *

* * * [T]his Court has * * * declared, that, in no doubtful case, would it pronounce a legislative act to be contrary to the constitution. But the American people have said, in the constitution of the United States, that "no State shall pass any bill of attainder, *ex post facto* law, or law impairing the obligation of contracts." In the same instrument they have also said, "that the judicial power shall extend to all cases in law and equity

arising under the constitution." On the judges of this Court, then, is imposed the high and solemn duty of protecting, from even legislative violation, those contracts which the constitution of our country has placed beyond legislative control; and, however irksome the task may be, this is a duty from which we dare not shrink.

* * *

It can require no argument to prove, that the circumstances of this case constitute a contract. An application is made to the crown for a charter to incorporate a religious and literary institution. In the application, it is stated that large contributions have been made for the object, which will be conferred on the corporation, as soon as it shall be created. The charter is granted, and on its faith the property is conveyed. Surely in this transaction every ingredient of a complete and legitimate contract is to be found.

* * *

Is this contract protected by the constitution of the United States?

* * *

* * * [I]t has been argued, that the word "contract," in its broadest sense, would comprehend the political relations between the government and its citizens, would extend to offices held within a State for State purposes, and to many of those laws concerning civil institutions, which must change with circumstances, and be modified by ordinary legislation; which deeply concern the public, and which, to preserve good government, the public judgment must control. That even marriage is a contract, and its obligations are affected by the laws respecting divorces. That the clause in the constitution, if construed in its greatest latitude, would prohibit these laws. * * * That as the framers of the constitution could never have intended to insert in that instrument a provision so unnecessary, so mischievous, and so repugnant to its general spirit, the term "contract" must be understood in a more limited sense. That it must be understood as intended to guard against a power of at least doubtful utility, the abuse of which had been extensively felt; and to restrain the legislature in future from violating the right to property. That anterior to the formation of the constitution, a course of legislation had prevailed in many, if not in all, of the States, which weakened the confidence of man in man, and embarrassed all transactions between individuals, by dispensing with a faithful performance of engagements. To correct this mischief, by restraining the power which produced it, the State legislatures were forbidden "to pass any law impairing the obligation of contracts," that is, of contracts respecting property, under which some individual could claim a right to something beneficial to himself; and that since the clause in the

constitution must in construction receive some limitation, it may be confined, and ought to be confined, to cases of this description * * *.

The general correctness of these observations cannot be controverted. That the framers of the constitution did not intend to restrain the States in the regulation of their civil institutions, adopted for internal government, and that the instrument they have given us, is not to be so construed, may be admitted. The provision of the constitution never has been understood to embrace other contracts, than those which respect property, or some object of value, and confer rights which may be asserted in a court of justice. * * *

The parties in this case differ less on general principles, less on the true construction of the constitution in the abstract, than on the application of those principles to this case, and on the true construction of the charter of 1769. This is the point on which the cause essentially depends. If the act of incorporation be a grant of political power, if it create a civil institution to be employed in the administration of the government, or if the funds of the college be public property, or if the State of New Hampshire, as a government, be alone interested in its transactions, the subject is one in which the legislature of the State may act according to its own judgment, unrestrained by any limitation of its power imposed by the constitution of the United States.

But if this be a private eleemosynary institution, endowed with a capacity to take property for objects unconnected with government, whose funds are bestowed by individuals on the faith of the charter; if the donors have stipulated for the future disposition and management of those funds in the manner prescribed by themselves; there may be more difficulty in the case * * *. Those who are no longer interested in the property, may yet retain such an interest in the preservation of their own arrangements, as to have a right to insist, that those arrangements shall be held sacred. Or, if they have themselves disappeared, it becomes a subject of serious and anxious inquiry, whether those whom they have legally empowered to represent them forever, may not assert all the rights which they possessed, while in being * * *.

* * *

From the [original charter] itself, it appears, that about the year 1754, the Rev. Eleazer Wheelock established at his own expense, and on his own estate, a charity school for the instruction of Indians in the christian religion. The success of this institution inspired him with the design of soliciting contributions in England for carrying on, and extending, his undertaking. In this pious work he employed the Rev. Nathaniel Whitacker, who, by virtue of a power of attorney from Dr. Wheelock, appointed the Earl of Dartmouth and others, trustees of the money, which had been, and should be, contributed; which appointment Dr. Wheelock confirmed by a deed of trust authorizing the trustees to fix on a site for the college. They determined to establish the school on Connecticut river, in the western part of New Hampshire * * * and the proprietors in the neighborhood * * * made large offers of land, on condition, that the college should there be placed. Dr. Wheelock then applied to the crown for an act of incorporation; and represented the expediency of appointing those whom he had, by his last will, named as trustees in America, to be members of the proposed corporation. "In consideration of the premises," "for the education and instruction of the youth of the Indian tribes," & c. "and also of English youth, and any others," the charter was granted, and the trustees of Dartmouth College were by that name created a body corporate, with power, for the use of the said college, to acquire real and personal property, and to pay the president, tutors, and other officers of the college, such salaries as they shall allow.

The charter proceeds to appoint Eleazer Wheelock, "the founder of said college," president thereof, with power by his last will to appoint a successor, who is to continue in office until disapproved by the trustees. In case of vacancy, the trustees may appoint a president, and in case of the ceasing of a president, the senior professor or tutor, being one of the trustees, shall exercise the office, until an appointment shall be made. The trustees have power to appoint and displace professors, tutors, and other officers, and to supply any vacancies which may be created in their own body, by death, resignation, removal, or disability; and also to make orders, ordinances, and laws, for the government of the college, the same not being repugnant to the laws of Great Britain, or of New Hampshire, and not excluding any person on account of his speculative sentiments in religion, or his being of a religious profession different from that of the trustees.

This charter was accepted, and the property both real and personal, which had been contributed for the benefit of the college, was conveyed to, and vested in, the corporate body.

* * * [I]t is apparent, that the funds of the college consisted entirely of private donations. * * *

The origin of the institution was, undoubtedly, the Indian charity school, established by Dr. Wheelock, at his own expense. It was at his instance, and to enlarge this school, that contributions were solicited in England. The person soliciting these contributions was his agent; and the trustees, who received the money, were appointed by, and act under, his authority. It is not too much to say, that the funds were obtained by him, in trust, to be applied by him to the purposes of his enlarged school. The charter of incorporation was granted at his instance. The persons named by him in his last will, as the trustees of his charity school, compose a part of the corporation, and he is declared to be the founder of the college, and its president for life. Were the inquiry material, we should feel some hesitation in saying, that Dr. Wheelock was not, in law, to be considered as the founder of this institution, and as possessing all the rights appertaining to that character. But be this as it may, Dartmouth College is really endowed by private individuals, who have bestowed their funds for the propagation of the christian religion among the Indians, and for the promotion of piety and learning generally. * * * It is then an eleemosynary, and, as far as respects its funds, a private corporation.

Do its objects stamp on it a different character? * * *

That education is an object of national concern, and a proper subject of legislation, all admit. That there may be an institution founded by government, and placed entirely under its immediate control, the officers of which would be public officers, amenable exclusively to government, none will deny. But is Dartmouth College such an institution? Is education altogether in the hands of government? Does every teacher of youth become a public officer, and do donations for the purpose of education necessarily become public property, so far that the will of the legislature, not the will of the donor, becomes the law of the donation? * * *

Doctor Wheelock, as the keeper of his charity school, instructing the Indians in the art of reading, and in our holy religion; sustaining them at his own expense, and on the voluntary contributions of the charitable, could scarcely be considered as a public officer, exercising any portion of those duties which belong to government; nor could the legislature have supposed, that his private funds, or those given by others, were subject to legislative management, because they were applied to the purposes of education. * * *

A corporation is an artificial being, invisible, intangible, and existing only in contemplation of law. Being the mere creature of law, it possesses only those properties which the charter of its creation confers upon it, either expressly, or as incidental to its very existence. These are such as are supposed best calculated to effect the object for which it was created. Among the most important are immortality, and, if the expression may be allowed, individuality; properties, by which a perpetual succession of many persons are considered as the same, and may act as a single individual. They enable a corporation to manage its own affairs, and to hold property without the perplexing intricacies, the hazardous and endless necessity, of perpetual conveyances for the purpose of transmitting it from hand to hand. It is chiefly for the purpose of clothing bodies of men, in succession, with these qualities and capacities, that corporations were invented, and are in use. By these means, a perpetual succession of individuals are capable of acting for the promotion of the particular object, like one immortal being. But this being does not share in the civil government of the country, unless that be the purpose for which it was created. Its immortality no more confers on it political power, or a political character, than immortality would confer such power or character on a natural person. It is no more a State instrument, than a natural person exercising the same powers would be. If, then, a natural person, employed by individuals in the education of youth * * * would not become a public officer, or be considered as a member of the civil government, how is it, that this artificial being, created by law, for the purpose of being employed by the same individuals for the same purposes, should become a part of the civil government of the country? Is it because its existence, its capacities, its powers, are given by law? Because the government has given it the power to take and to hold property in a particular form, and for particular purposes, has the government a consequent right substantially to change that form, or to vary the purposes to which the property is to be applied? This principle has never been asserted or recognized, and is supported by no authority. Can it derive aid from reason?

The objects for which a corporation is created are universally such as the government wishes to promote. They are deemed beneficial to the country; and this benefit constitutes the consideration, and, in most cases, the sole consideration of the grant. In most eleemosynary institutions, the object would be difficult, perhaps unattainable, without the aid of a charter of incorporation. Charitable, or public spirited individuals, desirous of making permanent appropriations for charitable or other useful purposes, find it impossible to effect their design securely, and certainly, without an incorporating act. They apply to the government, state their beneficient object, and offer to advance the money necessary for its accomplishment * * *. The proposition is considered and approved. The benefit to the public is considered as an ample compensation for the faculty it confers, and the corporation is created. If the advantages to the public constitute a full compensation for the faculty it gives, there can be no reason for exacting a further compensation, by claiming a right to exercise over this artificial being a power which changes its nature, and touches the fund, for the security and application of which it was created. There can be no reason for implying in a charter, given for a valuable consideration, a power which is not only not expressed, but is in direct contradiction to its express stipulations.

* * *

* * * It requires no very critical examination of the human mind to enable us to determine, that one great inducement to these gifts is the conviction felt by the giver, that the disposition he makes of them is immutable. It is probable, that no man ever was, and that no man ever will be, the founder of a college, believing at the time, that an act of incorporation constitutes no security for the institution; believing, that it is immediately to be deemed a public institution, whose funds are to be governed and applied, not by the will of the donor, but by the will of the legislature. * * * If every man finds in his own bosom strong evidence of the universality of this sentiment, there can be but little reason to imagine, that the

framers of our constitution were strangers to it, and that, feeling the necessity and policy of giving permanence and security to contracts, of withdrawing them from the influence of legislative bodies, whose fluctuating policy, and repeated interferences, produced the most perplexing and injurious embarrassments, they still deemed it necessary to leave these contracts subject to those interferences. The motives for such an exception must be very powerful, to justify the construction which makes it.

The motives suggested at the bar grow out of the original appointment of the trustees, which is supposed to have been in a spirit hostile to the genius of our government, and the presumption, that, if allowed to continue themselves, they now are, and must remain forever, what they originally were. Hence is inferred the necessity of applying to this corporation, and to other similar corporations, the correcting and improving hand of the legislature.

It has been urged repeatedly * * * that the trustees deriving their power from a regal source, must, necessarily, partake of the spirit of their origin; and that their first principles, unimproved by that resplendent light which has been shed around them, must continue to govern the college, and to guide the students. * * * The first trustees were undoubtedly named in the charter by the crown; but at whose suggestion were they named? * * * The charter informs us. Dr. Wheelock had represented, "that, for many weighty reasons, it would be expedient, that the gentlemen whom he had already nominated, in his last will, to be trustees in America, should be of the corporation now proposed." * * * Some were probably added by the crown, with the approbation of Dr. Wheelock. Among these is the Doctor himself. If any others were appointed at the instance of the crown, they are the governor, three members of the council, and the speaker of the house of representatives, of the colony of New Hampshire. The stations filled by these persons ought to rescue them from any other imputation than too great a dependence on the crown. If in the revolution that followed, they acted under the influence of this sentiment, they must have ceased to be trustees; if they took part with their countrymen, the imputation, which suspicion might excite, would no longer attach to them. * * *

The only evidence which we possess of the character of Dr. Wheelock is furnished by this charter. The judicious means employed for the accomplishment of his object, and the success which attended his endeavours, would lead to the opinion, that he united a sound understanding to that humanity and benevolence which suggested his undertaking. It surely cannot be assumed, that his trustees were selected without judgment. With as little probability can it be assumed, that, while the light of science, and of liberal principles, pervades the whole community, these originally benighted trustees remain in utter darkness, incapable of participating in the general improvement; that, while the human race is rapidly advancing, they are stationary. Reasoning *a priori,* we should believe, that learned and intelligent men, selected by its patrons for the government of a literary institution, would select learned and intelligent men for their successors; men as well fitted for the government of a college as those who might be chosen by other means. Should this reasoning ever prove erroneous in a particular case, public opinion, as has been stated at the bar, would correct the institution. The mere possibility of the contrary would not justify a construction of the constitution, which should exclude these contracts from the protection of a provision whose terms comprehend them.

The opinion of the Court, after mature deliberation, is, that this is a contract, the obligation of which cannot be impaired, without violating the constitution of the United States. * * *

* * *

NOTES AND QUESTIONS

1. Pursuant to the legislative acts mentioned in Justice Marshall's opinion, the New Hampshire legislature sought to change the method of appointment of trustees of Dartmouth College, in order to have appointments made by the state government. Since the trustees had the power to hire and fire Dartmouth instructors and officers, the acts of the legislature were an attempt to change Dartmouth from what we would consider to be a "private" college to a "public" one. This case is one of the great old "chestnuts" of American constitutional law. For the rich personal, political, and social background of the case, the lawyers, and the Justices, see Francis N. Stites, Private Interest and Public Gain: The Dartmouth College Case, 1819 (1972).

"It is a small college," Daniel Webster is supposed to have said in his argument on behalf of the trustees, "but there are those who love it." There was, however, much more to the case than love of *alma mater*. Consider some of the closing remarks which Webster made to the Supreme Court:

> The case before the court is not of ordinary importance, nor of everyday occurrence. It affects not this college only, but every college, and all the literary institutions of the country. They have flourished, hitherto, and have become in a high degree respectable and useful to the community. They have all a common principle of existence, the inviolability of their charters. It will be a dangerous, a most dangerous experiment, to hold these institutions subject to the rise and fall of popular parties, and the fluctuations of political opinions. If the franchise may be at any time taken away, or impaired, the property also may be taken away, or its use perverted. Benefactors will have no certainty of effecting the object of their bounty; and learned men will be deterred from devoting themselves to the service of such institutions, from the precarious title of their offices. Colleges and halls will be deserted by all better spirits, and become a theatre for the contention of politics. Party and faction will be cherished

> in the places consecrated to piety and learning. These consequences are neither remote nor possible only. They are certain and immediate.

Webster's argument is from Timothy Farrar, Report of the Case of the Trustees of Dartmouth College against William H. Woodward 282–283 (1819). Do you discern any similarities between Webster's argument here and Justice Chase's charge to the Baltimore grand jury in 1803, the charge which led to his impeachment? There has been a boomlet in the study of Daniel Webster by legal historians, made possible in part by the publication of his Legal Papers in a readable and wonderfully-annotated edition by Alfred S. Konefsy and Andrew J. King (3 vols., 1982, 1983, 1989). Those wishing to pursue Webster's massive presence at the bar should begin with William W. Fisher III, Webster's Legal Legacy, 18 Reviews in American History 44 (1990) and Robert Gordon, "The Devil and Daniel Webster," 94 Yale L.J. 445 (1984). See also Paul Erikson, The Poetry of Events (1986), and Robert Ferguson, Law and Letters in American Culture (1984).

2. Justice Marshall holds that the Dartmouth College charter is a contract. Can you follow his reasoning? Are you impressed with the number and scope of authorities which Justice Marshall cites in support of his arguments? Do you agree with the following assessment of Justice Marshall by Professor G. Edward White:

> The ability to "master the most complicated subjects with facility" was joined in Marshall with a certain disinclination toward academic learning and "some little propensity for indolence." His legal education consisted of a six-week lecture course given by George Wythe at William & Mary College in 1780, during which, if Marshall's notebook may be trusted, he devoted at least as much thought to the pursuit of his future wife, Polly Ambler (whose name was scrawled at prominent places throughout his law notes), as to the offerings of Mr. Wythe. As a lawyer in Virginia, and later as a judge, he was not prone to the use of legal authorities, and on several occasions his arguments in Virginia rested on no precedents at all. On the Supreme Court his "original bias," according to his colleague Story, "was to general principles and comprehensive views, rather than to technical or recondite learning."

White, The American Judicial Tradition 11 (1976) (footnotes omitted) copyright © 1976 by Oxford University Press, Inc. Reprinted by permission. If this is correct, why is Justice Marshall nearly universally regarded as the greatest Supreme Court justice? For a provocative article claiming that Marshall's opinion in *Dartmouth College* was a precursor of the great Civil Rights cases of the twentieth century, see Bruce Campbell, "Dartmouth College as a Civil Liberties Case: The Formation of Constitutional Policy," 70 Ky.L.J. 643 (1982). For White's celebrated book-length study of Marshall's jurisprudence in the period in which *Dartmouth College* was decided, see his volume in the Holmes Devise History of the Supreme Court of the United States, The Marshall Court and Cultural Change, 1815–35 (1988).

3. As the 200th anniversary of Marbury v. Madison, 5 U.S. (1 Cranch) 137 (1803), the decision many wrongly regard as having initiated judicial review in America, came and went in 2003, there were many symposia on the decision and the Justice who wrote it. For a sampling of the debunking of the decision's (and, by implication, Marshall's) significance see, e.g. Davison M. Douglas, "The Rhetorical Uses of Marbury v. Madison: The Emergence of a 'Great Case'", 38 Wake Forest L. Rev. 375 (2003), Michael Klarman, "How Great Were the Great Marshall Court Decisions?," 87 Va. L. Rev. 1111 (2001), Jack N. Rakove, "The Origins of Judicial Review: A Plea for New Contexts", 49 Stan.L.Rev. 1031 (1997). For arguments that Marshall was indeed as impressive as his reputation suggests see, e.g. Charles F. Hobson: The Great Chief Justice: John Marshall and the Rule of Law (1996), Herbert A. Johnson, The Chief Justiceship of John Marshall, 1801–1835 (1997), R. Kent Newmyer, John Marshall and the Heroic Age of the Supreme Court (2001)(called by the New York Times "the most sophisticated one-volume treatment we now have of the great chief justice"), Jean Edward Smith, John Marshall: Definer of a Nation (1996), and Jack M. Balkin, "The Use that the Future Makes of the Past: John Marshall's Greatness and Its Lessons for Today's Supreme Court Justices," 43 Wm and Mary L. Rev. 1321 (2002). Balkin acknowledges Klarman's argument that Marshall gets more credit for [his] opinions than he deserves, and that "the prevalent assumption that they fundamentally shaped the course of American national development is almost certainly wrong," id. at n. 6, but still regards Marshall as great because of the vision that he had for the country and what it means. Id. at 1335. Newmyer's conclusion is similar. The current conventional wisdom is probably well-expressed by veteran legal historian John V. Orth, who, in an incisive review of the Hobson, Johnson, and Smith volumes concludes that "On the record of these three books, the great Chief Justice kept faith with his own ideal in all cases, large and small. Marshall listened to the arguments on both sides, considered the cases fairly and fully, and then exercised his best judgment. He was always disinterested, in the sense that he sought the best outcome, not for himself, but for the litigants the court, and the nation." John V. Orth, "John Marshall and the Rule of Law," 49 S.Car.L.Rev. 633, 649 (1998).

4. After reading Marshall's opinion in this case can you explain why he decided it in the manner he did? See, e.g., R. Kent Newmyer, "John Marshall as a Transitional Jurist: Dartmouth v. Woodward and the Limits of Omniscient Judging," 32 Conn.L.Rev. 1665 (2000). Do you detect any sympathy for Webster's arguments?

DARTMOUTH COLLEGE V. WOODWARD

(continued)

[We next consider the opinion of Mr. Justice Story. As the excerpt from his opinion begins, he is discussing the different types of corporations. Many citations are here omitted.]

* * *

* * * Eleemosynary corporations are such as are constituted for the perpetual distribution of the free alms and bounty of the founder, in such manner as he has directed; and in this class are ranked hospitals for the relief of poor and impotent persons, and colleges for the promotion of learning and piety, and the support of persons engaged in literary pursuits.

Another division of corporations is into public and private. Public corporations are generally esteemed such as exist for public political purposes only, such as towns, cities, parishes, and counties; and in many respects they are so, although they involve some private interests; but strictly speaking, public corporations are such only as are founded by the government for public purposes, where the whole interests belong also to the government. If, therefore, the foundation be private, though under the charter of the government, the corporation is private * * *. For instance, a bank created by the government for its own uses, whose stock is exclusively owned by the government, is, in the strictest sense, a public corporation. * * * But a bank, whose stock is owned by private persons, is a private corporation, although it is erected by the government, and its objects and operations partake of a public nature. The same doctrine may be affirmed of insurance, canal, bridge, and turnpike companies. In all these cases, the uses may, in a certain sense, be called public, but the corporations are private * * *.

This reasoning applies in its full force to eleemosynary corporations. A hospital founded by a private benefactor is, in point of law, a private corporation, although dedicated by its charter to general charity. So a college, founded and endowed in the same manner, although, being for the promotion of learning and piety, it may extend its charity to scholars from every class in the community, and thus acquire the character of a public institution. * * *

It was indeed supposed at the argument, that if the uses of an eleemosynary corporation be for general charity, this alone would constitute it a public corporation. But the law is certainly not so. * * * That the mere act of incorporation will not change the charity from a private to a public one, is most distinctly asserted in the authorities. Lord Hardwicke * * * says, "the charter of the crown cannot make a charity more or less public, but only more permanent than it would otherwise be; but it is the extensiveness, which will constitute it a public one. A devise to the poor of the parish is a public charity. Where testators leave it to the discretion of a trustee to choose out the objects, though each particular object may be said to be private, yet in the extensiveness of the benefit accruing from them, they may properly be called public charities. A sum to be disposed of by A.B. and his executors, at their discretion, among poor housekeepers, is of this kind." The charity, then, may, in this sense, be public, although it may be administered by private trustees; and, for the same reason, it may thus be public, though administered by a private corporation. The fact, then, that the charity is public, affords no proof that the corporation is also public; and, consequently, the argument, so far as it is built on this foundation, falls to the ground. If, indeed, the argument were correct, it would follow, that almost every hospital and college would be a public corporation * * *.

When, then, the argument assumes, that because the charity is public, the corporation is public, it manifestly confounds the popular, with the strictly legal sense of the terms. * * * But it is on this foundation, that a superstructure is erected, which is to compel a surrender of the cause. When the corporation is said at the bar to be public, it is merely meant, that the whole community may be the proper objects of the bounty, but that the government have the sole right, as trustees of the public interests, to regulate, control, and direct the corporation, and its funds and its franchises, at its own good will and pleasure. Now, such an authority does not exist in the government, except where the corporation is in the strictest sense public; that is, where its whole interests and franchises are the exclusive property and domain of the government itself. If it had been otherwise, Courts of law would have been spared many laborious adjudications in respect to eleemosynary corporations * * *. Nay, more, private trustees for charitable purposes would have been liable to have the property confided to their care taken away from them without any assent or default on their part, and the administration submitted, not to the control of law and equity, but to the arbitrary discretion of the government. Yet, who ever thought before, that the munificent gifts of private donors for general charity became instantaneously the property of the government; and that the trustees appointed by the donors, whether corporate or unincorporated, might be compelled to yield up their rights to whomsoever the government might appoint to administer them? If we were to establish such a principle, it would extinguish all future eleemosynary endowments * * *.

* * *

When a private eleemosynary corporation is * * * created by the charter of the crown, it is subject to no other control on the part of the crown, than what is expressly or implicitly reserved by the charter itself. Unless a power be reserved for this purpose, the crown cannot, in virtue of its prerogative, without the consent of the corporation, alter or amend the charter, or divest the corporation of any of its franchises, or add to them, or add to, or diminish, the number of the trustees, or remove any of the members, or change, or control the administration of the charity, or compel the corporation to receive a new charter. This is the uniform language of the authorities, and forms one of the most stubborn, and well settled doctrines of the common law.

* * *

We are now led to the consideration of * * * whether this charter is a contract, within the clause of the constitution prohibiting the States from passing any law impairing the obligation of contracts. In the case of Fletcher v. Peck, [6 Cranch 87 (1810)] this Court [stated] * * * "A contract is a compact between two or more persons, and is either executory or executed. An executory contract is one, in which a party binds himself to do or not to do a particular thing. A contract executed is one in which the object of the contract is performed; and this, says Blackstone, differs in nothing from a grant. A contract executed, as well as one that is executory, contains obligations binding on the parties. A grant in its own nature amounts to an extinguishment of the right of the grantor, and implies a contract not to reassert that right. A party is always estopped by his own grant." This language is perfectly unambiguous, and was used in reference to a grant of land by the Governor of a State under a legislative act. It determines, in the most unequivocal manner, that the grant of a State is a contract within the clause of the constitution now in question, and that it implies a contract not to reassume the rights granted. *A fortiori,* the doctrine applies to a charter or grant from the king.

But it is objected, that the charter of Dartmouth College is not a contract contemplated by the constitution, because no valuable consideration passed to the king as an equivalent for the grant * * * and further, that no contracts merely voluntary are within the prohibitory clause. It must be admitted, that mere executory contracts cannot be enforced at law, unless there be a valuable consideration to sustain them; and the constitution certainly did not mean to create any new obligations, or give any new efficacy to nude pacts. But it must, on the other hand, be also admitted, that the constitution did intend to preserve all the obligatory force of contracts, which they have by the general principles of law. Now, when a contract has once passed, *bona fide,* into grant, neither the king nor any private person, who may be the grantor, can recall the grant of the property, although the conveyance may have been purely voluntary. A gift, completely executed, is irrevocable. * * * And a gift by the crown of incorporeal hereditaments, such as corporate franchises, when executed, comes completely within the principle, and is, in the strictest sense of the terms, a grant. Was it ever imagined that land, voluntarily granted to any person by a State, was liable to be resumed at its own good pleasure? Such a pretension would, under any circumstances, be truly alarming; but in a country like ours, where thousands of land titles had their origin in gratuitous grants of the States, it would go far to shake the foundations of the best settled estates. And a grant of franchises is not, in point of principle, distinguishable from a grant of any other property. If, therefore, this charter were a pure donation * * * it involved a contract, that the grantees should hold, and the grantor should not reassume the grant, as much as if it had been founded on the most valuable consideration.

But it is not admitted that this charter was not granted for what the law deems a valuable consideration. For this purpose it matters not how trifling the consideration may be; a pepper corn is as good as a thousand dollars. Nor is it necessary that the consideration should be a benefit to the grantor. It is sufficient if it import damage or loss, or forbearance of benefit, or any act done, or to be done, on the part of the grantee. * * *

With these principles in view, let us now examine the terms of this charter. * * * [The charter] on its face, purports to be granted in consideration of the premises in the introductory recitals. Now, among these recitals it appears, that Dr. Wheelock had founded a charity school at his own expense, on his own estate; that divers contributions had been made in the colonies, by others, for its support; that new contributions had been made, and were making, in England for this purpose * * * that Dr. Wheelock had consented to have the school established at such other place as the trustees should select; that offers had been made by several of the governments in America, inviting the establishment of the school among them; that offers of land had also been made by divers proprietors of lands in the western parts of New Hampshire, if the school should be established there; that the trustees had finally consented to establish it in New Hampshire; and that Dr. Wheelock represented that, to effectuate the purposes of all parties, an incorporation was necessary. Can it be truly said that these recitals contain no legal consideration of benefit to the crown, or of forbearance of benefit on the other side? Is there not an implied contract by Dr. Wheelock, if a charter is granted, that the school shall be removed from his estate to New Hampshire? and that he will relinquish all his control over the funds collected, and to be collected, in England, under his auspices, and subject to his authority? that he will yield up the management of his charity school to the trustees of the college? that he will relinquish all the offers made by other American governments, and devote his patronage to this institution? * * *

* * *

This is not all. A charter may be granted upon an executory, as well as an executed or present consideration. * * * Upon the acceptance there is an implied contract on the part of the grantees, in consideration of the charter, that they will perform the duties; and exercise the authorities conferred by it. This was the doctrine asserted by the late learned Mr. Justice Buller, in a modern case. He there said, "I do not know how to reason on this point better than in the manner urged by one of the relator's counsel, who considered the grant of incorporation to be a compact between the crown, and a certain number of the subjects, the latter of whom undertake, in consideration of the privileges which are bestowed, to exert themselves for the good government of the place," (i.e. the place incorporated.) It will not be pretended, that if a charter be granted for a bank, and the stockholders pay in their own funds, the charter is to be deemed a grant without consideration, and, therefore, revocable at the pleasure of the grantor. Yet here, the funds are to be managed, and the services performed exclusively for the use and benefit of the stockholders themselves. And where the grantees are mere trustees to perform services without reward, exclusively for the benefit of others, for public charity, can it be reasonably argued, that these services are less valuable to the government, than, if performed for the private emolument of the trustees themselves? * * *

There is yet another view of this part of the case, which deserves the most weighty consideration. The corporation was expressly created for the purpose of distributing in perpetuity the charitable donations of private benefactors. * * * The crown, then, upon the face of the charter, pledged its faith that the donations of private benefactors should be perpetually devoted to their original purposes, without any interference on its own part, and should be forever administered by the trustees of the corporation, unless its corporate franchises should be taken away by due process of law. From the very nature of the case, therefore, there was an implied contract on the part of the crown with every benefactor, that if he would give his money, it should be deemed a charity protected by the charter * * *. As soon, then, as a donation was made to the corporation, there was an implied contract springing up, and founded on a valuable consideration, that the crown would not revoke, or alter the charter, or change its administration, without the consent of the corporation. There was also an implied contract between the corporation itself, and every benefactor upon a like consideration, that it would administer his bounty according to the terms, and for the objects stipulated in the charter.

* * *

The principal objections having been thus answered satisfactorily, at least to my own mind, it remains only to declare, that my opinion, after the most mature deliberation is, that the charter of Dartmouth College, granted in 1769, is a contract within the purview of the constitutional prohibition.

* * *

The remaining inquiry is, whether the acts of the legislature of New Hampshire now in question, or any of them, impair the obligations of the charter of Dartmouth College * * *.

[As you might have suspected, Justice Story finds that the Acts, in changing the methods of choosing trustees and administering the corporation, impair the obligations of the original charter.]

* * *

If these are not essential changes, impairing the rights and authorities of the trustees, and vitally affecting the interests and organization of Dartmouth College under its old charter, it is difficult to conceive what acts, short of an unconditional repeal of the charter, could have that effect. If a grant of land or franchises be made to A., in trust for special purposes, can the grant be revoked, and a new grant thereof be made to A., B., and C., in trust for the same purposes, without violating the obligation of the first grant? If property be vested by grant in A. and B., for the use of a college, or a hospital, of private foundation, is not the obligation of that grant impaired when the estate is taken from their exclusive management, and vested in them in common with ten other persons? * * * If a bank, or insurance company, by the terms of its charter, be under the management of directors, elected by the stockholders, would not the rights acquired by the charter be impaired if the legislature should take the right of election from the stockholders, and appoint directors unconnected with the corporation? These questions carry their own answers along with them. The common sense of mankind will teach us, that all these cases would be direct infringements of the legal obligations of the grants to which they refer; and yet they are, with no essential distinction, the same as the case now at the bar.

In my judgment it is perfectly clear, that any act of a legislature which takes away any powers or franchises vested by its charter in a private corporation or its corporate officers, or which restrains or controls the legitimate exercise of them, or transfers them to other persons, without its assent, is a violation of the obligations of that charter. If the legislature mean to claim such an authority, it must be reserved in the grant. The charter of Dartmouth College contains no such reservation; and I am, therefore, bound to declare, that the acts of the legislature of New Hampshire, now in question, do impair the obligations of that charter, and are, consequently, unconstitutional and void.

In pronouncing this judgment, it has not for one moment escaped me how delicate, difficult, and ungracious is the task devolved upon us. The predicament in which this Court stands in relation to the nation at large, is full of perplexities and embarrassments. It is called to decide on causes between citizens of different States, between a State and its citizens, and between different States. It stands, therefore, in the midst of jealousies and rivalrics of conflicting parties, with the most momentous interests confided to its care. Under such circumstances, it never can have a motive to do more than its duty; and, I trust, it will always be found to possess firmness enough to do that.

Under these impressions I have pondered on the case before us with the most anxious deliberation. I entertain great respect for the legislature, whose acts are in question. I entertain no less respect for the enlightened tribunal whose decision we are called upon to review. In the examination, I have endeavoured to keep my steps *super antiquas vias* of the law, under the guidance of authority and principle. It is not for judges to listen to the voice of persuasive eloquence or popular appeal. We have nothing to do but to pronounce the law as we find it; and having done this, our justification must be left to the impartial judgment of our country.

NOTES AND QUESTIONS

1. Which opinion strikes you as the more lawyer-like, that of Marshall or that of Story? For Marshall's role in helping to establish the "grammar" of Constitutional interpretation, see H. Jefferson Powell, "The Political Grammar of Early Constitutional Law," 71 N. Car. L. Rev. 949 (1993), and for Story's, see H. Jefferson Powell, "Joseph Story's Commentaries on the Constitution: A Belated Review," 94 Yale L.J. 1285 (1985). Which opinion would you rather have written? Are Story's reasons for deciding the case the same as Marshall's? What is the importance of Story's distinction between public and private corporations? Why is a bank a public or a private corporation? Why does Story make so many references to banks and other types of business corporations in this opinion? For the early history of American corporations, and Justice Story's Dartmouth College opinion's role in that history see, e.g., Douglas Arner, "Article in Tribute: Development of the American Law of Corporations to 1832," 55 SMU L.Rev. 23 (2002).

2. Once Story and Marshall's opinions pass into law, is there no way that a state legislature can alter corporate charters? Do these opinions really affect the ability of state legislatures to amend corporate charters of corporations not yet in existence? If, as Story suggests, future corporate charters may contain a clause reserving to the state legislature the right to amend or alter the charter, isn't the *Dartmouth College* case much ado about nothing? What is the meaning of the last two paragraphs of Story's opinion, where he suggests that the task of the Supreme Court is "difficult" and "ungracious"? You will have been able to discern that both for Story and Marshall much of what is at stake concerns the ability of the state legislature to restrict what can be done with private property. This "takings" issue continues to be an important one in constitutional jurisprudence. The literature on it is vast, but for a very readable short introduction, with citations to important cases and scholarship on the "takings" question see, by the dean of legal historians of property, James W. Ely, Jr., "Property Rights and Judicial Activism," 1 Geo. J. of Law & Pub. Pol. 125 (2002). Ely's piece is part of an important symposium in the inaugural issue (Fall 2002) of The Georgetown Journal of Law & Public Policy, "The Eleventh Amendment, Federalism, and Judicial Activism: Questions and Answers."

3. Justice Joseph Story began his political career as a Jeffersonian Republican, and was appointed to the Supreme Court by Jefferson's political heir, James Madison, in 1811. Once on the court, however, Story's views were

perceived to be of a similar nationalist character to those of John Marshall, and Story's view on the common law of crimes was probably not different from those of the hard-line Federalist judges we saw in Chapter Two. See United States v. Coolidge, 25 Fed.Cas. 619 (C.C.D.Mass.1813), reversed 14 U.S. (1 Wheat.) 415, 4 L.Ed. 124 (1816). What political views, if any, are reflected in Story's *Dartmouth College* opinion? A biographer of Story states that this opinion was "displayed [by him] with pride to confidants both on and off the bench." Gerald Dunne, Justice Joseph Story and the Rise of the Supreme Court 180 (1970). Mr. Dunne appears to hint that this might have had something to do with the fact that Story was, at the time he wrote this opinion, not only a Justice on the Supreme Court, but the President of the Merchants' Bank of Salem, Massachusetts. Id. at 181. Can you see the connection? "[B]y the standards of the day," writes Dunne of Story's presidency of the bank, "it involved no conflict with his judicial duties." Id. at 268. Would this be true today? Why the change? For more on Story and his times see the magisterial biography by R. Kent Newmyer, Supreme Court Justice Joseph Story: Statesman of the Old Republic (1985).

2. THE CORPORATION AND ITS SHAREHOLDERS

ELLIS V. MARSHALL

Supreme Judicial Court of Massachusetts, 1807.
2 Mass. 269.

[By an 1804 Statute the Massachusetts legislature chartered a "corporation" for the purpose of making a street. The defendant, Mr. Marshall, was named as one of the "members" of the corporation, but he apparently had never consented to join. He was, however, one of the landowners adjoining the road that the corporation was to build, and a majority of such landowners *had* agreed to become members of the corporation. The Act of the legislature authorized the corporation to assess its members for the costs of building the road, and to sell the lands of members who refused to pay their assessments. Marshall refused to pay his assessments, and the corporation sold his land to the plaintiff, Ellis. Ellis brought an action in Ejectment to get possession of the property from Marshall. The court's opinion follows. Is the "corporation" involved in this case anything like what you understand by the term "corporation"? You will soon see that the court decides that Mr. Marshall could not be compelled to be a member of the corporation, and thus doesn't have to give up his land; but this raises the interesting question: why did the plaintiff and the other members of the corporation think that he *could* be compelled to be a member?]

PARKER, J. * * * [Addressing himself to the plaintiff's two arguments: (1) that the legislature had the power to compel Marshall to become a member of the corporation, and (2) that the facts show Marshall's consent.]

* * *

The determination of the first point requires that we should ascertain the true nature and character of this legislative proceeding. If it were a public act, predicated upon a view to the general good, the question would be more difficult. If it be a private act, obtained at the solicitation of individuals, for their private emolument, or for the improvement of their estates, it must be construed, as to its effect and operation, like a grant. We are all of opinion that this was a grant or charter to the individuals who prayed for it, and those who should associate with them; and all incorporations to make turnpikes, canals, and bridges, must be so considered.

Can then one, whose name is, by mistake or misrepresentation, inserted in such an act, refuse the privileges it confers, and avoid the burdens it imposes? If he cannot, then the legislature may, at all times, press into the service of such corporations those whose lands may be wanted for such objects, whenever they may be prevailed on to insert the names of such persons by the intrigue or mistake of those more interested in the success of the object. No apprehension exists in the community that the legislature has such power. That the land of any person, over or through which a turnpike or canal may pass, may be taken for that purpose, if the legislature deem it proper, is not doubted. The constitution gives power to do this, provided compensation is made. But it was never before known that they have power over the person, to make him a member of a corporation, and subject him to taxation, *nolens volens,* for the promotion of a private enterprise.

That a man may refuse a grant, whether from the government or an individual, seems to be a principle too clear to require the support of authorities. That he may decline to improve his land, no one will doubt. Although the legislature may wisely determine that a certain use of his property will be highly beneficial to him, he has a right to judge for himself on points of this nature. The fact therefore in the case, that *Marshall* is benefited equally with the other owners by the making of this street, is of no importance. In *Bagg's* case[3] it seems to be agreed by the Court, that a patent procured by some persons of a corporation shall not bind the rest, unless they assent. And in *Brownlow's* Reports, 100, there is this passage: "It was said that inhabitants of a town cannot be incorporated without the consent of the major part of them, and an incorporation without their consent is void."

In *Comberbach,* 316, *Holt,* speaking of a new charter made to the city of *Norwich* by *Henry* 4, and confirmed by *Charles* 2, says the new charter had been void if the corporation had refused it; but when they accept it, and put it in execution, it is good.

---

[3] Roll's Rep. 224.

If these principles were correct in *England* in times when prerogative ran high,—and the crown or the Parliament could not force charters or patents upon the subject without his assent,—surely in this free country, where the legislature derives its power from the people, such authority cannot be contended for.

It being, then, the opinion of the Court that this act is of a nature to require the assent of *Marshall,* either express or implied, before it can operate upon him, it is necessary to inquire into the second point, *viz.,* whether the facts agreed on in this case furnish evidence of such assent.

It is contended that the act itself, as it contains *Marshall's* name, furnishes such evidence, since it must be presumed that the legislature were satisfied on this point before they passed the act.

* * * It appearing that Marshall did not sign the petition; that he did not, in word or writing, assent to it, or to the act founded upon it; that he did not attend before the committee; and that, in the only transaction in which he noticed the corporation, he protested against its authority over him,—the presumption arising from his name being in the act is weakened, if not destroyed.

It is then said that, public notice having been given of the hearing intended by the committee, his silence is evidence of his tacit assent to the passage of the act. As we are bound to presume every thing in favor of the doings of the legislature, we should think this a strong, if not a conclusive argument, if the notice given had been such as necessarily to signify to *Marshall* that he was to be included in the act prayed for. But on perusing the petition, which probably was published in the papers, we find nothing in it from which he could infer that his property or rights were to be affected, in the manner contemplated by this act. He may be considered as notified that a street was intended to be built over his ground; and all that he could infer from this was, that so much of his land as the street would pass over would be taken for this purpose, and that he would receive indemnity for it in the usual way; and that any opposition to it would be unavailing. He certainly could never have understood that it was intended to make him a member of the corporation without his consent. * * *

Upon the whole, therefore, we are of opinion that the act under which the plaintiff sets up his title could not bind Marshall without his assent; that he, having uniformly, whenever opportunity occurred, signified his dissent, is not a member of the corporation it created, was not liable to their assessments, and therefore that the sale of his land was without authority of law, and is void. According to the agreement of the parties, therefore, the plaintiff must become nonsuit, and judgment be given for costs to the defendant.

It having been said in argument that the acts relative to fencing common fields, and the act providing for the appointment of commissioners of common sewers, are within the principle of this act, it is proper to observe that we do not consider this decision as involving principles which militate with the provisions of those acts.

Those are public acts, promotive of general convenience, and operating equally upon all citizens whose property is intended to be secured or improved by them.

This is a private act, obtained at the solicitation of individuals, for their emolument or advantage.

The act relative to common fields, also, is predicated upon the assent of all who are to be affected by it; and that which provides for the appointment of commissioners of sewers gives an eventual trial by jury of all questions arising under it. These circumstances so materially vary those laws from the act under consideration, that our decisions upon the latter can by no means be considered as questioning the validity of the former.

* * *

Plaintiff nonsuit.

ANDOVER AND MEDFORD TURNPIKE CORP. V. ABRAHAM GOULD

Supreme Judicial Court of Massachusetts, 1809.
6 Mass. 40.

This was an action of *assumpsit*, to recover the amount of certain assessments upon the share in the said turnpike owned by the defendant, who was one of the original associates for making the same.

The cause was tried * * * and a verdict found for the defendant, which was to be set aside, and a new trial granted, if the Court should be of opinion, that upon the evidence, as reported by the judge, the defendant was liable in this action.

The report states that there was regular evidence of the several assessments, and of a demand made on the defendant for payment. The only evidence produced by the plaintiffs of any promise or engagement on the part of the defendant to pay such sums as should be assessed on his share, was the subscription paper, which was in the following form, *viz.:—*

"*Whereas the legislature has, at the last session, granted leave for making a turnpike road from,*" & *c.,* [describing the course.] "*We, the subscribers, desirous of having the same completed as soon as possible, agree to take in said road the number of shares set against our names, and be proprietors therein.*"

"*Medford,* Sept. 9, 1805."

To this paper the defendant, among others, had set his name, and against it had set "*one share*."

This being considered by the judge as insufficient to maintain the action, he directed the jury that no promise was proved in the case, either express or implied; and that the sale of the shares, as provided for by the act of incorporation, was the only remedy the corporation had for the delinquency of the defendant.

* * *

PARSONS, C.J. The question submitted to us in this case is, whether the direction of the judge to the jury was, or was not, legal.

This corporation was created by the statute of 1805, c. 14, by which six persons named, with such others as might afterwards associate with them, and their successors and assigns, are made a body corporate for the purpose of making the turnpike road. * * *

The expenses of making a turnpike road are certain, and frequently very great; and the money to defray them must be advanced, before any profit can be derived from the road; while the future toll to be received depends on the travel of passengers, and must be uncertain. The value of the shares will always depend on the expenses of making the road, compared with the expected profits from the toll. Although, when the incorporation is procured, the presumption is, that the toll will be an indemnity,—otherwise the undertakers would act a very unwise part,—yet, as this presumption may fail, it may be very reasonable for the corporation not to trust to the sale of the shares for a reimbursement of the expense, but, before any expense be incurred, to require an express undertaking from the corporators, that they will pay the several assessments on their shares. Where this express agreement has been made, we have decided that it may be enforced by action, there being a legal consideration for the contract.

Where no express agreement has been made by the corporators to pay their assessments, it has not been determined that the corporation can maintain an action to recover them, upon an implied *assumpsit* arising from their being voluntarily members of the corporation. That point is now before us, and if this should be decided against the plaintiffs, another point is made, that the subscription signed by the defendant, upon a fair construction of it, is evidence of an express agreement with the plaintiffs to pay the assessments.

If the plaintiffs can maintain this action, as upon an implied promise, it must be on the principle that the defendant is obliged by law to pay his assessment. * * *

Let us now consider whether the defendant is in law bound to pay his assessments. If he is, this obligation must result from the powers of the corporation, and the due execution of those powers. The statute creating it refers, for its powers and duties, to the statute of 1804, c. 125. All the powers and duties of the plaintiffs result from this statute, or are incident to it at common law. But very clearly a corporation has not power, as incident to it at common law, to assess for its own use a sum of money on the corporators, and compel them, by action at law, to the payment of it. To authorize this assessment, the power must be derived from the general statute. In the twelfth section, power is expressly given to choose the necessary officers, and to establish rules and regulations for the well-ordering of the affairs of the corporation.

The power to make assessments on the shares of the corporators for the use of the corporation is not in that act expressly given; but it impliedly results from the construction of the tenth section. It is there enacted that, whenever any proprietor shall neglect or refuse to pay a tax or assessment agreed on by the corporation to their treasurer in sixty days after the time set for payment, the treasurer may sell the share of the delinquent proprietor at public auction for the payment of the tax and the charges for sale. From this section we must conclude that the corporation have power to agree on a tax on the shares of the proprietors.

But it is a rule founded in sound reason, that when a statute gives a new power, and at the same time provides the means of executing it, those who claim the power can execute it in no other way. When we find a power in the plaintiffs to make the assessments, they can enforce the payment in the method directed by the statute, and not otherwise; and that method is by the sale of the delinquent's shares. This rule applies to all taxes, public and private. No action can be maintained to compel the payment of state, county, or town taxes, except in the particular cases in which an action is expressly given by the statute of 1789, c. 4. The same rule applies to taxes assessed by parishes, and also, by statute of 1785, c. 53, § 3, by the proprietors of general fields.

* * *

This rule of law is, in cases like the present, reasonable. Persons not interested in having the turnpike, either from their situation or private property, may be requested to associate and become corporators. They may not be able to judge of the probable expenses or profits. But if they know, that if the assessments become grievous, they may abandon the enterprise by suffering their shares to be sold, they may on this principle join the association. And it may be observed that it must be presumed that the legislature considered the sale of the shares as an adequate remedy to recover the assessments; for it is not to be supposed that corporate powers were applied for, to subject the adventurers to a probable loss.

As we are of opinion that the plaintiffs cannot maintain this action on an implied promise, we shall now consider whether the subscription paper, upon a fair construction, is evidence of an express promise.

The agreement there expressed is, that the subscribers will take in the said road the number of shares set against their names, and will be proprietors therein. These words certainly cannot amount, upon any reasonable construction, to a promise to pay the assessments that shall be made on their shares.

But the plaintiffs rely on the motives, expressed by the subscribers, of their taking shares and becoming proprietors. The words are, "We the subscribers, desirous of having the said turnpike road completed as soon as possible, agree," & c. Now, perhaps no man ever associated in a turnpike corporation without some hope of profit; and if so, he must be desirous of having the road completed as soon as possible, that he may be in the reception of the supposed profits. Whether this motive to make the agreement is, or is not, expressed, it can have no effect in the construction of the contract.

We are therefore satisfied that the terms of the association do not in law amount to an agreement to pay the assessments that may be made on the shares.

* * *

Judgment on the verdict.

NOTES AND QUESTIONS

1. In the course of its opinion holding that Mr. Marshall could not be compelled to be a member of the road corporation, the court in Ellis v. Marshall quotes a passage from Brownlow's Reports: "It was said that inhabitants of a town cannot be incorporated without the consent of the major part of them, and an incorporation without their consent is void." What relevance does a case involving a "town" have to a road corporation? Does this statement from Brownlow's Reports suggest that it was correct or incorrect to decide that Mr. Marshall could not be compelled to become a member of the road corporation?

2. Do you agree with the *Ellis* court that the situation of the corporation for construction of a road by private property holders is different in kind from the acts for fencing common fields and for commissioners of common sewers, or other corporations formed for purposes "promotive of general convenience?" Do you agree that the road corporation in *Ellis* is no different in kind from "all incorporations to make turnpikes, canals, and bridges?" Why the distinctions? Does the Ellis court classify corporations in the same manner Story did? Is the distinction between "public" and "private" corporations an artificial one?

3. In the *Andover* case, the court indicates that it will strictly construe the powers of the corporation, and will not find a power to sue members for unpaid assessments, but will limit the corporation's remedy for unpaid assessments to sale of the delinquent member's shares. What policy does the court believe that it is encouraging by this holding? Incidentally, does the method of raising funds by assessment of members strike you as a reasonable way for a corporation to raise funds? Was it correct to rely on the analogy provided by Massachusetts statutes regarding state, county, or town taxes and general fields? Do corporations still raise funds in this way? Why or why not?

4. Is the Massachusetts court correct about the limitation on the powers of corporations at common law? In Cucullu v. Union Ins. Co., 2 Rob. 573 (La.1842), plaintiff was a judgment creditor of the Union Insurance Co., the defendant, and sought to compel one of the company's shareholders to pay money previously subscribed on shares, so that the money could be used to satisfy the judgment. The shareholder was itself a corporation, the Atchafalya Rail Road and Banking Company. When Atchafalya and the other shareholders of Union Insurance Co. originally received their shares, pursuant to the legislative charter, they each paid five dollars for each share, and gave notes for additional sums to be paid in installments until a total of $50.00 per share had been paid by each shareholder. Another provision of the charter, an act passed by the Louisiana legislature, stated that "any subscriber or stockholder who shall neglect to pay any installment * * * shall forfeit to the Company all previous payments, and shall cease to be a stockholder in said corporation, unless the Board of Directors, in their discretion, should determine to compel the payment of said subscription by suit." Atchafalya had never paid anything other than the initial $5, and argued that since the Board of Directors had never sued for additional payments, it could simply forfeit its shares and have its liability to the corporation end. The court held for the plaintiff, explaining its decision in the following language:

> A person who, with others, signs an agreement or promise to take stock in an incorporated company, thereby promises to pay the corporation the sum necessary to cover every share set opposite to his name, and an action will lie to recover it. This point has been repeatedly decided, both in England and the United States, and rests upon the plainest principles of law and justice. 6 Barn. & Cress. 341. 1 Maule & Selwyn, 569. 9 Johns.Rep. 217. 14 Ibid. 238. 16 Mass. 94. Angel on Corporations, 293. This action may be maintained for the purpose of getting in the stock to carry on the business, or to execute the purposes for which the corporation was created, and also to pay the debts it may contract.
>
> We are, further, of opinion, that whenever the stockholders in an incorporated company neglect or refuse to elect Directors to manage its affairs, and keep it in operation, or elect persons who will not call in the stock to pay the debts which may have been contracted, the creditors will have an action to compel them to pay, and that each will be responsible

> for the amount subscribed, if so much be necessary to pay the debts. It is not to be permitted to any number of individuals to get up incorporated companies for insurance, banking, or other operations, and, after enabling them to get in debt, to throw the loss upon the creditors, by refusing to pay their stock, or forfeiting it, or dissolving the corporation and releasing themselves by non-user. 2 Rob., at 202.

Is this decision consistent with Andover and Medford Turnpike Corp. v. Gould?

5. Selma and Tennessee Rail Road Co. v. Tipton, 5 Ala. 787, 39 Am.Dec. 344 (1843), involved another corporation's charter which provided a remedy for failure to pay amounts subscribed. The charter provision in question was:

> "if any stockholder shall fail, or neglect to pay any instalment required to be paid, for the period of ninety days next after the same shall be due and payable, the stock on which it is demanded, shall be forfeited to the company, together with the instalments which may have been paid thereon, and a new subscription may be opened to make up such deficiency as may be caused by the nonpayment aforesaid: *Provided,* that nothing in this section shall be so construed as to prevent the President and Directors of [the company] from offering for sale the stock of any defaulting stockholder, or so much thereof as may be necessary to pay such defalcation, after giving twenty days notice of the time and place of said sale, in some newspaper, and out of the proceeds of said sale, after paying the amount of such defalcation, * * * the residue, if any, shall be paid over to the said defaulting stockholder."

The defendant paid an initial $5.00 for his shares, but refused to pay additional amounts when the Board of Directors, pursuant to the plan eventually to collect an additional $95.00 on each share, made a call for a second installment. The defendant, who had originally been a director in the corporation, argued that the corporation's only remedy was to declare his shares forfeited, and sell them pursuant to the charter provision. The remaining directors disagreed, and sued him for the unpaid assessments. At the time of becoming a shareholder, the defendant had signed a "book of subscription" which indicated that he undertook to pay the full $100.00 per share, as required by the Board of Directors in installments. The exact language of the book, however, was: "We the undersigned agree to pay the sums annexed to our respective names, towards the capital stock of the Selma and Tennessee rail road company, in conformity with the provisions of the act incorporating said company." For whom would you have decided this case?

Quoting language from previous decisions, the *Selma* court declared that "it is a maxim of the common law, that an affirmative statute does not take away the common law," and that thus "the provision of the act giving to the company the right to sell the shares of a delinquent subscriber does not amount to a negative of their right to any other remedy * * *." This meant, said the court, that the company was still perfectly free to sue the subscriber, in a contract action, upon his original promise to pay the full subscription price. "A subscriber," said the court "cannot speculate upon the chances of a rise in stocks, and if the enterprise promises to be unprofitable, elect at his pleasure, to avoid a direct promise to pay by failing to meet calls made under the authority of the charter." 5 Ala. at 798–799. Does this attitude toward risk-taking by shareholders seem consistent or inconsistent with that of the court in *Andover?*

6. Suppose that you owned 100 shares of International Business Machines (IBM) and that IBM owed the Bank of America several billion dollars on an outstanding loan. If IBM defaulted, could the Bank of America come after you? Why or why not? The answer to this question turns on the widespread acceptance of the principle of limited liability of shareholders for corporate debts, which swept the states in the first half of the Nineteenth Century. Who wins and who loses as a result of such limited liability? The controversy over this issue among legal historians is one of the hottest topics in historiography, and, intriguingly enough, the debate over the justice of shareholder limited liability has recently become an important contemporary topic as well. Should limited liability for corporate shareholders be abolished for torts committed by corporations, for example? For the contracts they enter into? For the historiographical debate over the meaning of corporate concepts such as limited liability and corporate personality, compare, e.g., Morton J. Horwitz, The Transformation of American Law 1870–1960: The Crisis of Legal Orthodoxy 65–107 (1992) with Herbert Hovenkamp, Enterprise and American Law 1836–1937 (1991) and Richard A. Posner, Overcoming Law 271–286 (1995). For the contemporary debate over shareholder limited liability, compare and contrast, e.g., Frank H. Easterbrook and Daniel R. Fischel, The Economic Structure of Corporate Law 40–62 (1991), Theresa A. Gabaldon, "The Lemonade Stand: Feminist and Other Reflections on the Limited Liability of Corporate Shareholders," 45 Vand. L. Rev. 1 (1992), Henry Hansmann & Reinier Kraakman, "Toward Unlimited Shareholder Liability for Corporate Torts," 100 Yale L.J. 1879 (1991), Stephen B. Presser, "Thwarting the Killing of the Corporation: Limited Liability, Democracy, and Economics," 87 Nw. U. L. Rev. 148 (1992), and Robert B. Thompson, "Unpacking Limited Liability: Direct and Vicarious Liability of Corporate Participants for Torts of the Enterprise," 47 Vand. L. Rev. 1 (1994).

CHAPTER 4

LAW AND SOCIETY IN THE MID–NINETEENTH CENTURY

■ ■ ■

INTRODUCTION: American Society at Mid–Century

In 1790 the population of the thirteen States was 3.9 million. Approximately half the population lived in the Southern States, and about 25% each lived in the New England and Middle States. About 3% of this population lived in urban areas, the largest of which were Philadelphia (42,444), New York (33,131), Boston (18,038), Charleston (16,359), and Baltimore (13,503). By 1860, New York's population had grown to 1.1 million and the total of the nation's urban residents constituted 16% of the national population, which now was 31.4 million. In 1790, 97% of the population lived along the East Coast. By 1860, that percentage was 51. The number of States had grown from thirteen to thirty-seven with the admission of Nebraska in 1867. California (admitted in 1850) and Oregon (admitted in 1859) created a continuous expanse of American territory to the Pacific.

Regional variations became more obvious from 1800–1865. In the South, plantation agriculture and the development of staple crops through slave labor dominated. Slavery shaped not only the South's economy, but the patterns of settlement, land usage, social relations, and the region's wealth and education. As tobacco production waned (it had ruinous effects on the soil), the development of the cotton gin in 1793 suddenly made the planting of cotton profitable. The cultivation of cotton soon displaced the growing of grain and rice as well. Cotton continued to be the most important product of the Southern States into the twentieth century, fueling the westward expansion of slavery onto the Piedmont and into the southwest. The South's cotton exports supplied an abundance of raw materials for the new textile mills of the Northeastern States and of Europe.

The percentage of population engaged in agricultural pursuits in the Middle and New England States gradually declined, reflecting the trend toward urbanization in these more settled areas. This phenomenon of urbanization accounts for much of the spatial distribution of population and its growth in the nineteenth century: While population grew through immigration and natural increase, its spread west lagged far behind the concentration of population both in old and new urban centers. Population distribution in turn grew from a transportation revolution that saw, successively, the development of roads and turnpikes, bridges, canals, steam boats, and the railroad. The new urban centers sprouted up along junctures of rivers and lake regions, and these centers became distribution points for the westward movement of population and land settlement, and for trade within the region and with the East. A new national market system was emerging that made the New England and Middle states manufacturers and shippers of finished products; the South suppliers of raw material; and the Mid–Western and Western regions suppliers of grain and meat products for consumption in the East.

The contours of a rising commercial economy shaped work, family, labor, and socio-economic classes. In the South, the plantation system of agriculture and the institution of slavery meant that a significant percentage of the population was illiterate and unskilled for anything except manual labor. The presence of an enslaved class also tied Southern capital to a plantation system of production. The rise of the free public school in the Northeast did not have an analogy in the South, and the lack of an independent class of bankers, workers, mechanics, teamsters, shopkeepers, tailors, merchants and so forth on the scale of that to be found in the Northeast meant that Southern society remained strongly agrarian in occupation and outlook, and local in orientation. The Northeast, on the other hand, experienced a diversification and stratification of labor and expertise as a result of its move away from household production. New manufacturing establishments led to specialization and a division of labor that created an urban-based working class; financial institutions produced a class of middlemen who facilitated loans and investments, and mercantile establishments depended on individuals with management, clerical, marketing, sales, and financial skills. The growth of a middle class and a consumer population in the North went hand in hand with urbanization, rising literacy rates and increased personal income.

As dramatic as economic growth, particularly in the Northeast, was the democratization of society. Indeed, one fed the other. By 1860 all states had removed property qualifications for voting, though these laws did not grant the franchise to women nor, in some Northern states, to free people of color. The emergence of political parties mobilized participation of the public in the political process, created new political aspirations, and often gave concrete effect to popular will. Americans showed themselves to be peculiarly inclined to form voluntary associations, to borrow Tocqueville's phrasing. These were informal combinations and assemblies freely entered into to accomplish some religious, moral, civic or charitable purpose. In the colonies, these included hospitals and fire departments, though few in number. In the nineteenth century, the voluntary association was a symbol of emerging democracy. Certainly the formation of a revitalized political party system in the 1820s was a prime new example of such voluntary associations. Perhaps nowhere was voluntary association as important as in the proliferation of reform efforts. "Freedom's ferment," as it has been described, spilled over into reform movements that envisioned new possibilities in human achievement and perfectibility. The penitentiary movement certainly was one example, based on a new confidence in the idea that character could be molded and improved. Other examples of reform, some of which will be treated here, were the antislavery movement, reforms in the care of the mentally-challenged and the blind, the movement to abolish the death penalty, the founding of homes for orphans, the rise of legal adoption, and the push for universal free public education. Increased development of women's rights were an outgrowth of many of these reforms, as the widespread participation of women in reformist efforts brought new attention to their roles and to the legal inequities that women, especially married women, suffered. Many of the women involved in reform came from non-farm, middle class urban families with access to education, information and political power.

The greatest voluntary associations of the nineteenth century were the churches. The religious impulse as an element in reform—indeed, as the underpinning of much of public life—cannot be overemphasized. The clergy and their congregations were activists in many social movements, and especially in the struggle for the abolition of slavery. Religious revivals of the Second Great Awakening of the 1830s splintered denominations but also ignited reformist energies that led to the founding of denominational schools and colleges, foreign missions, and agencies of philanthropy for the poor, especially the urban poor. Another religion-influenced crusade was the temperance movement, hinted at in the excerpt you read earlier from Robert Rantoul. The consumption of alcohol, temperance advocates argued, was at the root of problems sweeping through the young Republic: crime, family abandonment, vagrancy, and destitution. If alcohol was the great threat to the future of the family, taking the "abstinence pledge" was the family's best guarantee of survival. Church pulpits became platforms for the promotion of temperance, and congregations its foot soldiers. As many as 6,000 local temperance associations were in existence in the 1830s, many of whose members were women.

America's economic growth rate in the century after the Revolution was nothing short of phenomenal. In 1840, the United States had a per capita product that was about one-fourth less than the British, and about one-third larger than France's, giving the American economy a world stature after barely 60 years of nationhood. The rapidity of growth was leaving another kind of mark. Territorial expansion kept issues of sectional conflict alive with each new state admitted to the union, holding the balance between slave and non-slaveholding states in suspension. The growth in immigration spurred by the young nation's high labor demands, and the opening of new lands for settlement on a moving frontier, introduced "strangers in the land." As a byproduct, a reactionary xenophobic and anti-Catholic movement reared its head in American politics in the 1840s and 1850s. The nation's more settled landscapes and its urban areas were both changing. Mills sprouted up in New England; steamboats plied rivers; canals, and later railroads cut through the countryside. The process of urbanization was also making cities home to a new class of poor. They were part of the anonymous "dangerous classes" that worried community pillars and reformers throughout the nineteenth century. The creation of the modern urban police force in the 1850s was in part a response to those fears. Moreover, though new factory establishments were still in an early development phase, they were unfriendly to labor. Workers, most often women and children, sat or stood for long hours in enclosed structures, and around new-fangled machines that were unpredictable, and often dangerous.

If America at mid-century was a magnetic and growing nation imbued with a patriotic confidence about its national destiny, it was also a nation with emerging problems. The beginnings of industrialization in the East and the accelerating growth of cities were disturbing to some citizens. The image of consensual communities that dotted the colonial landscape, closely knit families where the husband ruled, and the security of knowing where one stood in the local social order still held a powerful appeal for many as an antidote to an increasingly rootless individualism. Others worried about the impact on the young Republic of giving the franchise to so many people who lacked property, or who seemed unready, or unwilling, to accept their responsibilities as productive members of society. Still, to others, the promise of 1776 was interpreted as an optimistic opening into the future, to a world where change was not threatening at all, but liberating, and where the disruption of the traditional social order was a sign of good things to come.

If these two perceptions were in competition with each other, they still shared a common recognition that the United States was an experiment in liberty. Two places where these conflicting understandings of what was appropriate for the young nation played out were American courts and legislatures. As Tocqueville observed in *Democracy in America* (1835–40), the range of individual ambitions and expectations often was displayed in litigation, and thus it was that law in the United States attained a remarkable scope that left almost no societal issue uncontested in court. As you have seen, Tocqueville saw this as a safety-valve for American democracy, one that made the legal profession an important counterweight to popular passions and impulses. Rather than having to resort to revolution, violence or anarchy, as often occurred in contemporary Europe, social and political issues could be settled through the orderly unfolding of law in America's courts. Still, there were limits to what the legal process could accomplish; there were threads in the American experiment that were simply not spun into whole cloth. Occasionally, when intractable problems were brought to court, old ways or habits might be discarded in light of new knowledge, as newer understandings prevailed. Some wrenching national issues simply could not be resolved by litigation, however, and, as we shall soon see, slavery was one of those.

Further Reading:

Paul Boyer, *Urban Masses and Moral Order in America, 1820–1920*, 1978

Alfred D. Chandler, *Scale and Scope: The Dynamics of Industrial Capitalism*, 1990

Thomas C. Cochran, *Frontiers of Change: Early Industrialism in America,* 1981

Roger Daniels, *Coming to America: Immigration and Ethnicity in American Life*, 2002

Milton Derber, *The American Ideal of Industrial Democracy, 1865–1965,* 1970

John Higham, *Strangers in the Land: Patterns of American Nativism, 1860–1925,* 1955

Russell Kirk, *The Conservative Mind: From Burke to Eliot*, 1953

Edwin Mansfield, *The Economics of Technological Change*, 1968

Eric H. Monkkonen, *America Becomes Urban: The Development of U.S. Cities and Towns,* 1780–1980, 1988

Daniel J. Monti, Jr., *The American City: A Social and Cultural History,* 1999

Daniel Nelson, *Shifting Fortunes: The Rise and Decline of American Labor from the 1820s to the Present*, 1997

David M. Potter, *The Impending Crisis, 1848 1861*, 1976

Alice Felt Tyler, *Freedom's Ferment: Phases of American social history from the Colonial period to the outbreak of the Civil War, 1944*

Richard C. Wade, *The Urban Frontier: The Rise of Western Cities, 1790–1830*, 1996

Ronald Walters, *American Reformers, 1815–1860*, 1996

Sam Bass Warner, Jr., *The Urban Wilderness: A History of the American City,* 1972

Sean Wilentz, *Chants Democratic: New York City and the Rise of the American Working Class, 1788–1850,* 1984

Bertram Wyatt–Brown, *The Shaping of Southern Culture: Honor, Grace, and War, 1760s–1880s,* 2001

A. THE NATURE OF NINETEENTH CENTURY LAW

SWIFT V. TYSON

Supreme Court of the United States, 1842.
41 U.S. (16 Pet.) 1, 10 L.Ed. 865.

MR. JUSTICE STORY delivered the opinion of the Court.

* * *

There is no doubt, that a bonâ fide holder of a negotiable instrument for a valuable consideration, without any notice of facts which impeach its validity as between the antecedent parties, if he takes it under an endorsement made before the same becomes due, holds the title unaffected by these facts, and may recover thereon, although as between the antecedent parties the transaction may be without any legal validity. * * *

In the present case, the plaintiff is a bonâ fide holder without notice for what the law deems a good and valid consideration, that is, for a pre-existing debt; and the only real question in the cause is, whether, under the circumstances of the present case, such a pre-existing debt constitutes a valuable consideration in the sense of the general rule applicable to negotiable instruments. We say, under the circumstances of the present case, for the acceptance having been made in New York, the argument on behalf of the defendant is, that the contract is to be treated as a New York contract, and therefore to be governed by the laws of New York, as expounded by its Courts, as well upon general principles, as by the express provisions of the thirty-fourth section of the judiciary act of 1789, ch. 20. And then it is further contended, that by the law of New York, as thus expounded by its Courts, a pre-existing debt does not constitute, in the sense of the general rule, a valuable consideration applicable to negotiable instruments. * * *

JOSEPH STORY

[Justice Story's discussion of individual New York cases is omitted.]

But, admitting the doctrine to be fully settled in New York, it remains to be considered, whether it is obligatory upon this Court, if it differs from the principles established in the general commercial law. It is observable that the Courts of New York do not found their decisions upon this point upon any local statute, or positive, fixed, or ancient local usage: but they deduce the doctrine from the general principles of commercial law. It is, however, contended, that the thirty-fourth section of the judiciary act of 1789, ch. 20, furnishes a rule obligatory upon this Court to follow the decisions of the state tribunals in all cases to which they apply. That section provides "that the laws of the several states, except where the Constitution, treaties, or statutes of the United States shall otherwise require or provide, shall be regarded as rules of decision in trials at common law in the Courts of the United States, in cases where they apply." In order to maintain the argument, it is essential, therefore, to hold, that the word "laws," in this section, includes within the scope of its meaning the decisions of the local tribunals. In the ordinary use of language it will hardly be contended that the decisions of Courts constitute laws. They are, at most, only evidence of what the laws are; and are not of themselves laws. They are often reexamined, reversed, and qualified by the Courts themselves, whenever they are found to be either defective, or ill-founded, or otherwise incorrect. The laws of a state are more usually understood to mean the rules and enactments promulgated by the legislative authority thereof, or long established local customs having the force of laws. In all the various cases which have hitherto come before us for decision, this Court have uniformly supposed, that the true interpretation of the thirty-fourth section limited its application to state laws strictly local, that is to say, to the positive statutes of the state, and the construction thereof adopted by the local tribunals, and to rights and titles to things having a permanent locality, such as the rights and titles to real estate, and other matters immovable and intraterritorial in their nature and character. It never has been supposed by us, that the section did apply, or was designed to apply, to questions of a more general nature, not at all dependent upon local statutes or local usages of a fixed and permanent operation, as, for example, to the construction of ordinary contracts or other written instruments, and especially to questions of general commercial law, where the state tribunals are called upon to perform the like functions as ourselves, that is, to ascertain upon general reasoning and legal analogies, what is the true exposition of the contract or instrument, or what is the just rule furnished by the principles of commercial law to govern the case. And we have not now the slightest difficulty in holding, that this section, upon its true intendment and construction, is strictly limited to local statutes and local usages of the character before stated, and does not extend to contracts and other instruments of a commercial nature, the true interpretation and effect whereof are to be sought, not in the decisions of the local tribunals, but in the general principles and doctrines of commercial jurisprudence. Undoubtedly, the decisions of the local tribunals upon such subjects are entitled to, and will receive, the most deliberate attention and respect of this Court; but they cannot furnish positive rules, or conclusive authority, by which our own judgments are to be bound up and governed. The law respecting negotiable instruments may be truly declared in the language of Cicero, adopted by Lord Mansfield in Luke v. Lyde, 2 Burr.R. 883, 887, to be in a great measure, not the law of a single country only, but of the commercial world. * * *

It becomes necessary for us, therefore, upon the present occasion to express our own opinion of the true result of the commercial law upon the question now before us. And we have no hesitation in saying, that a pre-existing debt does constitute a valuable consideration in the sense of the general rule already stated, as applicable to negotiable instruments. Assuming it to be true * * * that the holder of a negotiable instrument is unaffected with the equities between the antecedent parties, of which he has no notice, only where he receives it in the usual course of trade and business for a valuable consideration, before it becomes due; we are prepared to say, that receiving it in payment of, or as security for a pre-existing debt, is according to the known usual course of trade and business. And why upon principle should not a pre-existing debt be deemed such a valuable consideration? It is for the benefit and convenience of the commercial world to give as wide an extent as practicable to the credit and circulation of negotiable paper, that it may pass not only as security for new purchases and advances, made upon the transfer thereof, but also in payment of and as security for pre-existing debts. The creditor is thereby enabled to realize or to secure his debt, and thus may safely give a prolonged credit, or forbear from taking any legal steps to enforce his rights. The debtor also has the advantage of making his negotiable securities of equivalent value to cash. But establish the opposite conclusion, that negotiable paper cannot be applied in payment of or as security for pre-existing debts, without letting in all the equities between the original and antecedent parties, and the value and circulation of such securities must be essentially diminished, and the debtor driven to the embarrassment of making a sale thereof, often at a ruinous discount, to some third person, and then by circuity to apply the proceeds to the payment of his debts. What, indeed, upon such a doctrine would become of that large class of cases, where new notes are given by the same or by other parties, by way of renewal or security to banks, in lieu of old securities discounted by them, which have arrived at maturity? Probably more than one-half of all bank transactions in our country, as well as those of other countries, are of this nature. The doctrine would strike a fatal blow at all discounts of negotiable securities for pre-existing debts.

This question has been several times before this Court, and it has been uniformly held, that it makes no difference whatsoever as to the rights of the holder, whether the debt for which the negotiable instrument is transferred to him is a pre-existing debt, or is contracted at the time of the transfer. In each case he equally gives credit to the instrument. * * *

In England the same doctrine has been uniformly acted upon. * * *

* * *

In the American Courts, so far as we have been able to trace the decisions, the same doctrine seems generally but not universally to prevail. In

Brush v. Scribner, 11 Conn.R. 388, the Supreme Court of Connecticut, after an elaborate review of the English and New York adjudications, held, upon general principles of commercial law, that a pre-existing debt was a valuable consideration, sufficient to convey a valid title to a bonâ fide holder against all the antecedent parties to a negotiable note. There is no reason to doubt, that the same rule has been adopted and constantly adhered to in Massachusetts; and certainly there is no trace to be found to the contrary. In truth, in the silence of any adjudications upon the subject, in a case of such frequent and almost daily occurrence in the commercial states, it may fairly be presumed, that whatever constitutes a valid and valuable consideration in other cases of contract to support titles of the most solemn nature, is held à fortiori to be sufficient in cases of negotiable instruments, as indispensable to the security of holders, and the facility and safety of their circulation. Be this as it may, we entertain no doubt, that a bonâ fide holder, for a pre-existing debt, of a negotiable instrument, is not affected by any equities between the antecedent parties, where he has received the same before it became due, without notice of any such equities. * * *

NOTES AND QUESTIONS

1. A complete understanding of the arcane legal point involved in this case is not crucial to an appreciation of the importance of Swift v. Tyson. You need only appreciate that everyone agreed that by the law of negotiable instruments, in order for an endorsee to have the legal rights to sue on a bill of exchange, free from any legal disabilities of the previous holders of the bill, the endorsee had to furnish valuable consideration. The question in the case then became, simply, whether a pre-existing debt constituted such valuable consideration. The court decisions on this point differed. There had been some decisions of New York courts which had held that a pre-existing debt could *not* constitute the requisite consideration. Our real interest is in answering the question, "Why wasn't Story inclined to follow the New York decisions?" What's *your* answer?

2. Most law students know the case of Swift v. Tyson chiefly as a decision that was "correctly" overruled by the United States Supreme Court in Erie Railroad Co. v. Tompkins, 304 U.S. 64, 58 S.Ct. 817, 82 L.Ed. 1188 (1938). For a work placing these two cases in the context of American legal and economic history see Tony Allan Freyer, Harmony and Dissonance: the *Swift* and *Erie* cases in American Federalism (1981). See also William R. Casto, "The Erie Doctrine and the Structure of Constitutional Revolutions," 62 Tul.L.Rev. 907 (1998), and Jack Goldsmith & Steven Walt, "Essay: Erie and the Irrelevance of Legal Positivism," 84 Va.L.Rev. 673 (1998). Law students usually learn that Erie v. Tompkins not only overruled a case, but also overruled a particular way of looking at the common law. In *Swift,* it has been said, Justice Story was reflecting the position that "there is one august corpus" of law; "a transcendental body of law outside of any particular state but obligatory within it unless and until changed by statute * * * " Black &

White Taxicab & Transfer Co. v. Brown & Yellow Taxicab & Transfer Co., 276 U.S. 518, 532–34, 48 S.Ct. 404, 408, 409, 72 L.Ed. 681 (1928) (Holmes, J. dissenting). In other words, so the critics of Swift v. Tyson were once given to arguing, Story believed in a "brooding omnipresence" of the law, a common law that existed like some Platonic form, of which certain state courts could see only dim shadows, like the men in Plato's cave. Have you encountered such a belief before? Is this characterization of Story's opinion accurate? Would Story apply the conceptions in his *Swift* opinion in any other contexts?

3. You have already read Story's opinion in *Dartmouth College*. Are there similar jurisprudential principles being applied by Story in that case? Would Story consider most of the private law developments reviewed in Chapter Three to be "local law," or emanations of "general principles and doctrines?" What, by the way, do you suppose would be the sources of "general principles and doctrines," and who might determine their content?

MORTON HORWITZ, THE RISE OF LEGAL FORMALISM*

19 Am.J.Leg.Hist. 251–253 (1975).

For seventy or eighty years after the American Revolution the major direction of common law policy reflected the overthrow of eighteenth century pre-commercial and anti-developmental common law values. As political and economic power shifted to merchant and entrepreneurial groups in the post-revolutionary period, they began to forge an alliance with the legal profession to advance their own interests through a transformation of the legal system.

By around 1850, that transformation was largely complete. Legal rules providing for the subsidization of enterprise and permitting the legal destruction of old forms of property for the benefit of more recent entrants had triumphed. Anti-commercial legal doctrines had been destroyed or undermined and the legal system had almost completely shed its eighteenth century commitment to regulating the substantive fairness of economic exchange. Legal relations that had once been conceived of as deriving from natural law or custom were increasingly subordinated to the disproportionate economic power of individuals or corporations that were allowed the right to "contract out" of many existing legal obligations. Law, once conceived of as protective, regulative, paternalistic and, above all, a paramount expression of the moral sense of the community, had come to be thought of as facilitative of individual desires and as simply reflective of the existing organization of economic and political power.

This transformation in American law both aided and ratified a major shift in power in an increasingly market-oriented society. By the middle of the nineteenth century the legal system had been reshaped to the ad-

* Published in the American Journal of Legal History, Copyright © 1975 by Temple University. Reprinted with the permission of the publisher and the author. Reprinted as Chapter VIII of Morton Horwitz, The Transformation of American Law 1780–1860 (1977).

vantage of men of commerce and industry at the expense of farmers, workers, consumers and other less powerful groups within the society. Not only had the law come to establish legal doctrines that maintained the new distribution of economic and political power, but, wherever it could, it actively promoted a legal redistribution of wealth against the weakest groups in the society.

The rise of legal formalism can be fully correlated with the attainment of these substantive legal changes. If a flexible, instrumental conception of law was necessary to promote the transformation of the postrevolutionary American legal system, it was no longer needed once the major beneficiaries of that transformation had obtained the bulk of their objectives. Indeed, once successful, those groups could only benefit if both the recent origins and the foundations in policy and group self-interest of all newly established legal doctrines could be disguised. There were, in short, major advantages in creating an intellectual system which gave common law rules the appearance of being self-contained, apolitical, and inexorable, and which, by making "legal reasoning seem like mathematics," conveyed "an air * * * of * * * inevitability" about legal decisions.

* * *

The sources of legal formalism as it developed after 1850 can be traced to a much earlier bifurcation of American legal thought, for in reality two competing ideological tendencies operated on American law after the Revolution. The first, which dominated the law until around 1850, was largely shaped by the efforts of mercantile and industrial groups to capture and transform the system of private law that existed in 1776.

In commercial law, entrepreneurial groups from the beginning sought to change the law inherited from the colonial period and to restrict the power of the state to enforce substantive standards of fair dealing. They also regularly sought the state's aid in creating a more efficient system of debt collection, and, after the Panic of 1819, they strongly increased their enthusiasm for bankruptcy legislation, seeking, however, to limit its benefits to "merchants and traders." In general, the course of commercial law during the nineteenth century was to perfect the remedial system while circumscribing the power of courts—and, far more importantly, legislatures—to intervene substantively.

In property and tort law, the interventionist state was inseparably linked to the earliest goals of low cost development. In this area, it was the constant aspiration of the developers first to seek as much support for change as they could from the courts, while only involving the more politically volatile legislatures when they could not. It is remarkable how well they succeeded. The basic system of tort and property law (other than rules of inheritance and systems of title recordation) was judicially created. And, by and large, it was strongly geared to the aspirations of those that benefited most from low cost economic development.

These efforts to overthrow pre-commercial and anti-developmental legal doctrines and institutions powerfully supported the instrumentalist character of private law before the Civil War. A second, seemingly contradictory, tendency, however, was also established quite early in post-revolutionary constitutional law. By forging constitutional doctrines under the Contracts Clause barring retroactive laws and giving constitutional status to "vested rights," this line of intellectual development sought basically to limit the ability of the legal system—more specifically of the legislature—to bring about redistributions of wealth. * * *

While commercial and entrepreneurial interests thus saw the private law shaped to their own needs and interests, they managed also to derive the benefits of an anti-distributive ideology developed in public law. One cannot but be struck by the sharp contrast between the utilitarian and instrumentalist character of early nineteenth century private law and the equally emphatic anti-utilitarian, formalistic cast of public law. If public law during this period was dominated by a conservative fear that legislatures might invade "vested property rights"—that is, that it might be used to redistribute wealth for equalitarian ends—the reality of the private law system was that it invariably tolerated and occasionally encouraged disguised forms of judicially sanctioned economic redistribution that actually increased inequality.

More than any other jurist of the nineteenth century, Joseph Story brought each of these two contradictory tendencies to their highest fulfillment. His private law opinions are, by and large, highly utilitarian and self-consciously attuned to the goals of promoting pro-commercial and developmental legal doctrines. By contrast, his public law opinions are usually starkly formalistic, often antiquarian, and therefore have frequently puzzled historians by running contrary to the supposed "prevailing economic needs" of his day.

These differences between the character of public and private law, however, can be traced directly to an underlying conviction held by all orthodox nineteenth century legal thinkers that the course of American legal change should, if possible, be developed by courts and not by legislatures. The persistent formalism of public law, in short, was related to the infinitely greater threat of redistribution that statutory interferences with the economy represented.

* * *

R. RANDALL BRIDWELL, THEME V. REALITY IN AMERICAN LEGAL HISTORY*

53 Ind.L.J. 450, 473–487 (1978).

* * *

In the context of Horwitz's thesis, the basic issue is this: was there a growing body of transcendent legal rules known as the "general commercial law" which was acknowledged by the federal courts and which would literally supercede otherwise applicable state rules of law, and if this is so, is this evidence of a willingness of the federal courts, like their state brethren, to engage in self conscious, interest-oriented judicial legislation?

* * *

In order to deal with this dual question it is necessary to first consider the true scope of the federal power in regard to diversity jurisdiction. In Swift v. Tyson, Mr. Justice Story construed § 34 of the Judiciary Act of 1789 to make certain local laws obligatory in the federal courts, but to exclude certain kinds of laws from its operation. Justice Story regarded as obligatory "the positive statutes of the state * * * " and state cases construing them, and laws pertaining "to things having a permanent locality," such as real estate, *and* other "matters * * * intraterritorial in their nature." Contrariwise, nothing required the federal courts to follow state laws applicable "to questions of a more general nature." Furthermore, Story clearly did not make the distinction between statutes and case law determinative of what was obligatory, but rather included both within the scope of the obligation to follow local law. The obligation was determined by the nature of the question and not by the nature of the legal pronouncement.

In the first place, Story referred not only to statutes as obligatory but also [to] "established local customs having the force of laws." Further it was clear that there was a distinct interplay between extra-territorial matters and local customs, which could become sufficiently developed and certain to counteract the general principles, in which case they would control. Additionally, commercial cases arising under the diversity jurisdiction were by definition extraterritorial to the sovereignty of any single state. Clearly Justice Story recognized that this implicated a pool of case law including but not limited to that of any given states, and called for an independent judgment on the part of the federal courts. In such cases "the state tribunals are called upon to perform the like function as ourselves, that is, to ascertain upon general reasoning and legal analogies, what is the true exposition of the contract or instrument, or what is the just rule furnished by the principles of commercial law to govern the case." To have done otherwise would have been to abdicate their primary function in diversity cases—to insure impartial justice between citizens of different states.

Equally important, however, was the recognition of a variety of subject matters which were or could be "localized" by a state, so that the local rule could be obligatory on the federal courts. Most importantly, "localization" required a *particular form* of local pronouncement about the legal issue in question *and* a congruity between the commercial and private international law conflict principles. A body of interstate common law rules dictated when and under what circumstances one state could localize a transaction *vis a vis* another. The case law taken as a whole reveals that federal courts would defer to localization, by statute or judicial decision, only in accordance with general conflict of laws principles. * * * Under these conceptions, sufficiently clear local laws—either statutes or decisions—would be obligatory when they pertained to matters local per se, such as real property within the state, and where they pertained to certain features of commercial transactions as well. The federal case law makes it clear that the judges were concerned with determining which set of potentially relevant rules the private parties may legitimately have assumed were relevant to their transaction. In cases where an articulate localization had taken place, even if the rule thereby promulgated differed from the general rules of the law merchant, and the shared extraterritorial rules of sovereignty—the conflict of laws rules—pointed to the state where the localization had occurred, the rule would be followed, but not otherwise. Thus, rather than the "either-or" conflict between the transcendent and instrumental general law and applicable local law, the pattern that *actually* emerged was one in which parties to commercial transactions were obligated under the conflict of laws principles which controlled commercial cases to look to the appropriate state, in order to determine whether there had been a localization by statute or custom, of the relevant controlling law. If none was found, it could be presumed that the general custom prevailing in the commercial world would be applied, at least in the federal courts in cases within the diversity jurisdiction. This did not, of course, eliminate all uncertainty from interstate commercial dealings; but it did provide a regularized, relatively coherent system within which the expectations of the parties to various commercial transactions could be generally preserved intact. Moreover, it provided ample space for local variations from general commercial jurisprudence, enforceable in both state and federal courts, thus securing the only important state and party interests in the application of local rules.

* * *

Critical to the understanding of the actual significance of the general commercial law and conflict of laws principles as employed by the federal judiciary and their relationship to the source of legal obligation is an understanding of the relationship between these subjects and the law of nations generally. Just as the law of nations must deal with multinational transactions, the creation of a federal government in the United States required a means of dealing with multistate transactions. The means employed were not novel in that they followed the pattern set by international law, and followed a pattern of judicial decision-making which repeated the earlier incorporation of multi-national principles in the English common law. In understanding the role of commercial law as a part of the law of nations, it is important to recognize that there was originally no sharp distinction drawn between civil admiralty and maritime jurisprudence and commercial law. They were one and the same jurisprudence, and only after the passage of time did they become thought of as separate parts of international law. Consequently, because commercial law was originally customary law, and because it was also a branch of private international law, it was dealt with in the same fashion by the courts as cases within the general customary system of common law adjudication.

Similarly there was eventually a clear identity of function between substantive commercial law rules and conflict of laws rules which governed their application. It was thus quite appropriate for eminent writers on these subjects to describe conflict of laws doctrine as but a "branch of commercial law." The conflict of laws rules designed to serve legitimate party expectations and intentions by making it universally obvious which of the potentially involved substantive rules applied to any given case. The commercial law rules interacted with the conflict of laws rules to serve this end. This was possible because of the increasingly regular, stereotyped forms which the commercial law had in many of its aspects assumed. It had become, as it were, a sort of international or interstate language, which enabled the parties to engage in "reciprocal orientation of their actions" across state lines.

For example, it was clear to parties in commerce from the facts of a transaction, particularly the forms by which it was conducted, whether or not it pertained to an extraterritorial as opposed to a purely municipal or local set of governing rules. Various sets of rules, including customary ones both recorded and unrecorded in precedent, were present to govern or control [al]most any transaction, and the conflict of laws principles when logically applied to a given transaction revealed whether it was confined to a particular sovereign or not. Thus, in creating a negotiable bill of exchange, certain commonly recognized features were necessary before the instrument became negotiable, a quality considered to be the very essence of such an instrument, and to constitute "its true character." Such terms as "or order" and "or bearer" were, according to the general or extraterritorial methods of commerce, essential to negotiability. The form which the transaction assumed according to the common multistate language of commerce determined whether its consequences were to be measured by one set of rules or another, that is by particular, or local, as opposed to general, or multistate rules.

* * * Indeed, the employment of common rules either implicitly or explicitly observed by all concerned sovereigns to mitigate the inevitable differences in the substantive rules and their application among different nations and states, was essential to the successful settlement of multistate problems. The form in which a particular multistate transaction was conducted would in the contemplation of *both* the state and federal courts implicate a body of law which no state alone was constitutionally competent to supply because of the limiting conception of sovereign authority embodied in private international law rules.

This will, if properly understood, explain why the various state cases were not thought to be in direct conflict with some obligatory pronouncement about the correct rule of general commercial law by a federal diversity court and why most state decisions were not in any case obligatory on the federal diversity courts. Professor Horwitz's "Federal Court v. Local Rule" metaphor is, it will be observed, entirely inaccurate. To fully understand the litigation in the early federal cases, it must be understood that the ability to discern in advance which body of rules and usages would be deemed relevant to a transaction was the key to understanding the early commercial decisions. * * *

The value of a judicial decision as precedent in extraterritorial cases was determined with reference to a wider field of data and by different standards than was the case with purely municipal rules, and this was so without affecting any considerations of federalism whatsoever. It is enough for our present purpose to note the implication of prevailing extraterritorial custom through the use of well understood transactional forms and the role this played in judicial settlement of private disputes. Quite naturally the federal court sitting in a diversity case which *per se* involved *some* multistate elements (and usually in the commercial law cases actually involved in interstate or multistate transaction) would have to determine what the appropriate source of the governing rule was, and by adverting to the presumptively applicable multistate rules of a customary origin in such cases should not be confused with a pretension to "make" the governing law by blatantly ignoring a local state rule. Further, in deciding controversies within the context of this multistate customary system, state judges would thus resort to extraterritorial considerations, and in so doing they did not manifest the act of a sovereign "freezing" a rule within its geographical power to do so, but rather acted in a cooperative fashion in an area over which they could not pretend absolute authority. The originally non-sovereign origin of commercial rules in the common law process, of course, accounts for the fact that judicial opinions were not referred to as laws but only as evidence of the law, and this aphorism was even more apt in the state cases admittedly dealing with transactions over which the state involved could not pretend any absolute authority, that is in cases involving extraterritorial or multistate rules. Thus, if a large portion of the common law rules involved "interstate common law," then federal judicial exegesis of the principles contained in these rules posed no direct conflict with state sovereignty at all. And more to the point, such cases cannot be construed as examples of judicial creativity in conflict with presumptively applicable state rules, because under such an interpretation the conflict is absent. * * *

Under this view of the commercial law as originally customary law, and as subject to the common law process, the nature of diversity jurisdiction in commercial cases should be apparent. In a customary law system in which the purpose of a grant of subject matter jurisdiction is to protect nonresidents from local bias, it would be essential that the intentions and expectations of the parties to every dispute be determined by a tribunal independent of the apprehended local prejudice. The law applied would be determined by the exercise of independent judgment by the impartial tribunal, just as factual disputes between the parties would be resolved by a presumptively unbiased trier of fact. * * *

* * *

NOTES AND QUESTIONS

1. Professor Horwitz sees two potentially conflicting tendencies in antebellum legal development. The one concerns the "utilitarian and instrumentalist character" of private law, such as torts and contracts, and the other the "anti-utilitarian, formalistic cast of public law." In what ways are these tendencies contradictory? What explanation does Horwitz offer for their existence? How does Story bring them to their "highest fulfillment"? For what Story was actually up to, see, in addition to the biography by R. Kent Newmyer, supra, Stephen Presser, "Resurrecting the Conservative Tradition in American Legal History," 13 Reviews in American History 526 (1985).

2. Who benefits most from Story's resolution of these legal issues? Are you persuaded by Horwitz in light of the development of private law reviewed in Chapter 3? Incidentally, as you have seen, Horwitz suggests that the "policy and group self-interest of all newly established legal doctrines" were "disguised" through "judicial forms." Do you understand how this could be? Why do you suppose it would be necessary to disguise them?

3. How does *Swift v. Tyson* fit Horwitz's model? What, precisely, does Bridwell see as dictating the decision in *Swift v. Tyson* and how, exactly, does he differ with Horwitz? What does Bridwell mean when he speaks of "private international law"?

4. Consider the title of Bridwell's piece from which these excerpts are taken, "Theme v. Reality in American Legal History." What do you suppose that this means with regard to Bridwell's analysis of Horwitz's work? For the

elaboration of Bridwell's differences with Horwitz see generally R. Bridwell and R. Whitten, The Constitution and the Common Law (1977). For another blast at Horwitz, see Richard A. Posner, Overcoming Law 270–286 (1995), and for spirited appreciations of Horwitz's work see Stephen B. Presser, Revising the Conservative Tradition: Towards a New American Legal History, 52 N.Y.U. L. Rev. 700 (1977), and Robert Gordon, Critical Legal Histories, 36 Stan. L. Rev. 57 (1984). By now you might have come to suspect that much of the legal history written in the late seventies and early eighties was a critical dialogue with Professor Horwitz, and for that reason his work has been emphasized here. It should be stressed, however, that Horwitz stood on the shoulders of giants, particularly Willard Hurst and Roscoe Pound. For a review of Hurst's work, see Aviam Soifer, "In Retrospect: Willard Hurst, Consensus History, and *The Growth of American Law*," 20 Reviews in American History 124 (1992), Robert Gordon, "Introduction: J. Willard Hurst and the Common Law Tradition in American Legal Historiography," 10 Law & Society Review 9 (1975), Harry Scheiber, "Federalism and the American Economic Order, 1789–1910," 10 Law & Society Review 57 (1975), and Morton Keller, "The Varieties of American Legal History: Hurst's History," 6 Reviews in American History 1 (1978). For Pound, read his classic, albeit dated, The Formative Era of American Law (1938).

5. In light of all you have read up to this point, what meaning would *you* give to antebellum legal change? See if your opinion remains the same after the consideration of the substantive legal topics which follow. We now turn from the rather technical doctrinal considerations with which we have been engaged to a broader consideration of the impact of culture and society on the law. First we will look briefly at a still-simmering political topic, the appropriate means of choosing the judiciary. We will then consider some differences between law and society in the Antebellum North and South, examine events before, during, and after the Civil War, and we will conclude with an examination of criminal law and the law of domestic relations.

B. THE MOVEMENT FOR AN ELECTIVE JUDICIARY

ROBERT M. IRELAND, "AN INDEPENDENT JUDICIARY": THE POPULAR ELECTION OF JUDGES IN AMERICAN HISTORY*

[In the mid-nineteenth century there was a nationwide movement for state constitutional reform and for the popular election of state judges. According to Professor Ireland:]

States which converted wholly to an elective judiciary [were] * * * Illinois (1848), Indiana (1851), Kentucky (1850), Louisiana (1852), Maryland (1851), Michigan (1850), Missouri (1851), Ohio (1851), Pennsylvania (1850), Tennessee (1853), and Virginia (1851). Two newly admitted

* Unpublished paper by Professor Ireland, of the University of Kentucky Department of History, reprinted with the permission of the author.

states, California (1849) and Wisconsin (1848) adopted elective judiciaries. Five others, Alabama (1850), Arkansas (1848), Connecticut (1850), Iowa (1846), and Vermont (1850) began electing inferior court judges. In 1852, Georgia's general assembly provided for popularly elected superior court judges leaving only the newly created Supreme Court subject to legislative appointment. Voters in New Hampshire (1851) and Massachusetts (1853) bucked the American mainstream and rejected proposed constitutions with reformed judiciaries. * * *

* * *

[The following excerpt from the preface to Professor Ireland's study gives some of the background for the movement towards an elective judiciary. Do you find it supports or challenges the conclusions you have reached about nineteenth-century law?]

Almost from their beginning Americans have brooded about the problem of how to select their judges and for what period of time. During the colonial era the principal question was that of tenure; the Crown insisted that colonial judges be chosen for a period at the pleasure of the King, while certain colonists, most often speaking from assemblies, demanded that jurists be appointed for life on the condition of good behavior. Before 1701 most English judges were appointed for a tenure at the pleasure of the King. After more than a century of turmoil which saw some of the Stuart kings, especially James II, implement a type of judicial tyranny, English reformers in the Act of Settlement of 1701 secured the appointment of judges for the life of the monarch on the condition of good behavior. In 1760, Parliament specified that the death of the monarch would not terminate judicial tenure. But the mother country refused to extend these reforms to her colonies * * *.

Colonists argued that it was unfair for the royal government (most often acting through the governors) both to appoint judges and be able to remove them at pleasure. * * * Only life tenure could protect the judiciary and the people from a dependent judiciary acting under the influence of the Crown and its agents, the governors. The royal government disputed this argument, noting that the legislatures maintained leverage over the judiciary by controlling its salaries * * *. [The Governors also argued that] lack of legal talent in the colonies necessitated tenure at the pleasure of the King * * * to remove incompetent jurists.

* * *

The Revolution may have rendered most judiciaries independent of the executive, but in most cases it did not completely remove their dependence upon the legislature. The new state constitutions generally codified the colonial conception of the ideal judiciary; legislatures most often had the right to appoint judges, usually for life and seldom had to provide them with permanent and sufficient salaries. Furthermore, they often won a right rarely recognized during the colonial period, to remove judges by impeachment or by joint address. * * * [In] the first decade of independence legislatures added to their newly gained authority by trespassing on territory traditionally occupied by the courts, overturning judicial decisions by special statutes and the like.

But the judiciary did not sit by idly * * *. The period 1776–1800 also witnessed the emergence of the judiciary as a powerful constitutional institution regarded by increasing numbers of influential * * * thinkers as an essential check on legislative power. With this transformation of the judiciary came new appreciation for judicial independence and power. State appellate courts even before the Constitution of 1787 began to claim the right to declare unconstitutional legislative statutes. By 1790 trial judges also commenced claiming more authority at the expense of juries. And finally, judges, however gradually, began to regard the common law as an instrument of social and economic change rather than simply fixed doctrine. * * * [A]ll three states entering the Union between 1780 and 1800 provided for good behavior judicial tenure, and by the latter date eleven of sixteen states had lifetime judges. Delegates to the [Federal] Constitutional Convention of 1787 generally endorsed the newly found significance of the judiciary and without much debate provided for good behavior judicial tenure and salaries that could not be diminished.

Alexander Hamilton * * * in his Federalist Paper Number Seventy–Eight * * * submitted that an independent judiciary was essential to a republican government and was best achieved by good behavior tenure. Hamilton's devotion to judicial independence resulted in large part from his fear of the legislature which he believed would exceed its powers under the constitution should the courts not have the power to declare its statutes unconstitutional. Furthermore, unless checked by an independent judiciary, a legislature might do "injury" to the "private rights of particular classes of citizens, by unjust and partial laws." Thus by 1787 many political leaders applauded the newly asserted power of judges, but most discussed this power and its foundation, judicial independence, only in the narrow terms of preventing legislative tyranny. * * * Hamilton and others believed that the people [should involve] themselves only by their selection of delegates to constitutional conventions and their indirect ratification of constitutions. Constitutions represented the supreme embodiment of the will of the people and the courts upheld this will against legislative usurpation. But the people could not claim the power to elect those charged with interpreting constitutions.

Even critics of the new Constitution did not [seriously] question the newly [derived notions about the need for an] independent judiciary. During the debate over the constitution in 1787 and 1788, antifederalists rarely attacked the proposed provisions regarding judicial tenure and selection and when they did so, most often suggested that federal judges would not be independent enough. Pennsylvania's John Smilie contended that the mere existence of an impeachment power would seriously compromise the judicial will, whereas Patrick Henry and Luther Martin implied that state judges were more secure from undue pressure. * * *

If antifederalists were generally silent regarding the new nation's general allegiance to non-popular life-tenured judges, so-called "radical republicans" of the early national period were not. Eager to reform the bar and bench in drastic ways, a few radicals wrote detailed pamphlets calling for an elective judiciary for limited terms. Typical was the effort in 1805 of John Leland, Protestant minister of western Massachusetts, who called for an elective judiciary both federal and state, issuing an elaborate denial that the people were incompetent to choose their judges and that popular selection would impair the independence of the judiciary. Yet Leland, not confident of success, ended his tract with the standard radical plea for the masses to ignore judges and lawyers and to settle their own disputes. More withdrawn and philosophical was Thomas Jefferson whose antipathy toward the judiciary, especially that of the federal government, deepened in retirement at Monticello. In letters to friends and in his autobiography, he castigated federal judges as "miners and sappers" and seemed to call for an elective judiciary for a term of years.

Leland's pessimism was well-placed, for his and Jefferson's diatribes did not spark national debate on judicial selection and tenure, and few states seriously entertained the notion of an elective judiciary before 1830. * * * [Why not, do you suppose?]

SAMUEL M. SMUCKER, POPULAR ARGUMENTS IN FAVOR OF AN ELECTIVE JUDICIARY*

(1850).

The Statesmen of this Commonwealth [Pennsylvania] have at length arrived at the assertion of a very important and fundamental principle, which belongs to the great system of rational and republican freedom under which we live; we mean the Election of the Judiciary at the polls. The minds of thinking men and patriots are, however, divided, as to the desirableness of anything in the structure of our Constitution with reference to this point. This difference of opinion among men of equal sagacity, experience and patriotism, shows that the question must be involved in serious difficulty. * * *

We invite the attention, therefore, of both the approvers and opposers of this measure, to the consideration of the following brief and popular

* This, and the following two readings, are taken from some of the debates in the states which arose as a result of Constitutional Conventions and reforms.

arguments, which, as we think, powerfully commend its unqualified adoption.

§ I. The selection of the Judges, when chosen by the people will be accomplished with less mercenary motive and influence *on the part of the electors themselves,* than is the case under the present system of appointment by the Governor.

* * *

How, then, have most of the Judges in this Commonwealth been chosen, for the last thirty years? Have not the majority of them been the relations—the brothers, the cousins, or the sons-in-law of the acting executive? Or else, if the Cornucopia of official abundance has not poured out its riches upon these, probably because none such were in existence; have not many of the vacant Judgeships been conferred upon those faithful, but obscure friends of the Executive, who, for many long years, had groped with him, shoulder to shoulder, amid the obscure drudgery of some country law-office, or worked up with him the petty county politics of some remote section of the state? Such has been the fact. Faithful to the often bitter memories of the past, the successful aspirant after the supreme seat in the Commonwealth, casts his eye, from his lofty eminence, upon his ancient, less fortunate allies, who still grope among the subterranean shades below; he dips the Executive arm far down the declivity, and heaves up his expectant friends to the elevation of the Judiciary.

Now, we maintain that this is not the way to elect suitable wise and able Judges; that this is the very way to fill the bench with the most incompetent incumbents. And we maintain that the election of the Judges, by the people, would entirely remove this evil. In the election of their legislators, the people are not under the influence of any selfish or improper motive. They uniformly choose men who, if they are not always able and enlightened, are at the least the object of no personal or family partiality; and they are generally men well adapted to the part which they are called upon to perform. If they are under any obligations whatever, it is not one of individual favors, but only those which they owe their party, whose principles they have publicly espoused, and are supposed, in common honor and honesty, faithfully to maintain.

But this partial kind of obligation for party preferences, however it may operate in inducing legislators to vote for party measures in the halls of legislation, cannot possibly operate upon the Bench, where the whole sphere of the incumbent is one altogether professional, scientific, and extra-popular. No Judge can rule a cause in favor of a party. Corruption, in such cases, is utterly impossible. And therefore, when the people assemble at the polls, to choose the men who are to hold offices, which afford so little opportunity to reward those to whose votes they owe their election, they will vote under the influence of no selfish bias whatever. * * * The people would at once be thrown upon the necessity of voting for men whose only recommendation was their legal distinction and their personal worth.

§ II. From this first position necessarily follows our second one; that by the election of the Judges by the people, there will be less subserviency, less timeserving, and less mercenary place-hunting on the part of the applicants.

The reason for this will be, because it will be impossible for the candidates, from the nature of the case, to display the same degree of unprincipled subserviency to the countless members of a vast community, which they can and will display toward one single and all-potent individual. That the applicants for the Judgeship under the proposed change, will make all possible efforts to secure their aims, is of course to be expected. But what means can they employ to attain those ends? None which savor of bribery or corruption. None which can result in benefits unjustly and unfairly bestowed by the successful applicant, upon those who lift him up to power; because they are too numerous. The only way by which the popular favor could be courted, with reference to election to the Judiciary, is by the attainment of general popularity; by the display of those qualities which will commend men, as Judges, to the people. For will the people elect to that high responsible office, men who are notoriously corrupt or mercenary; or men who are notoriously irascible or selfish or incompetent? * * *

* * *

AN ELECTIVE JUDICIARY

Baltimore Sun, June 4, 1851, page 1, col. 4.

A writer in the Georgetown Reporter has the following excellent remarks on the great principle of an elective Judiciary. He is a native of Maryland and speaks with reference to the new Constitution:

" * * * That which is most novel to us, and most calculated to strike our attention, is in the organization of the Judiciary department. The change here proposed, I suppose, may safely be regarded as one of the most material points upon which its opponents will turn the thunder of their batteries. The bare idea of allowing the people to elect the Judges of their courts, has filled with a sort of magical apprehension the minds of some * * *.

"The masses of the people must be a singular and rather strange intellectual and moral compound, to be held universally to be capable of self-government, and yet have that capability limited, so as to exempt from the exercise of the elective franchise the Judges of our courts. * * *

The people are either capable of self-government, or they are not. To admit that they are, is to be consistent, not only with the idea of liberty, but also with the theory which runs throughout the framework of that stupendous government which unites into one republic the thirty States of which it is composed. To deny it, is but a bold declaration that the whole is but one magnificent falsehood.

"What, then, is the effect of this limitation of the right of the people to govern in the judiciary department? It is that the people are qualified to govern in the legislative and executive departments of the government, but not there; as if qualifications of a high order, and purity of character were not as necessary in the two, as in the other grand department of government. We are told, that in order to keep the ermine pure, and to secure the efficient administration of justice, the Judge must be independent of, and not accountable to the people. This is a doctrine which belongs to the ages that have past and gone—certainly not to this in which we live.

"It is this doctrine alone, of 'irresponsibility to the people' which has spotted the annals of our race with so many instances of wanton and odious cruelty. It is the prolific parent of all kinds and modes of tyranny. Place your fellow man in a position wholly independent of you, invest him with the attribute of irresponsibility, and that *human sympathy* which stimulates to virtuous actions, and guides one on to the accomplishment of a noble and praiseworthy destiny, will certainly be extinguished. In its stead, selfishness, with all its little, bigoted, and concomitant auxiliaries, will enthrone itself * * *.

"Why, then, shall the people of Maryland retain such an antagonistical doctrine in the organization of their Judiciary department? Now that they have an opportunity to do so peacefully, I hope that on the 4th of June next they will vote to strike down into the dust this modern Moloch of unreasonable power, which has been so long enthroned in the very Temples of Justice."

* * *

J.M. LOVE, THE ELECTION OF JUDGES BY THE PEOPLE FOR SHORT TERMS OF OFFICE

3 So.L.Rev. (New Series) 18 (1877).

The inevitable tendency of all free institutions is to radicalism. Free thought and free discussion bring two great forces into perpetual conflict—the one radical, the other conservative. The former is positive and aggressive; the latter, negative and defensive. The first assails, the last resists. It is a conflict of ideas, in which there can be no doubtful result. The active, positive, moving force ever prevails against the negative, quiescent, resisting force. This active force in a free country is democratic sentiment, the constant tendency of which is to carry all established institutions irresistibly forward in the direction of radicalism. * * *

There is nothing more natural to the human mind than to accept abstract propositions and follow them to their logical consequences, without regard to the existing conditions to which they are to be applied. * * * The shallow thinker imagines that he sees in this logical process profound philosophy. The lazy investigator finds in it a ready solution of all difficult problems, without the painstaking labor required by the process of induction from innumerable facts. * * * But to determine truly with what modifications abstract truths are to be applied to existing conditions, so as to avert possible evils and promote the well-being of society, demands the profoundest insight into men and things, as well as careful investigation and thorough knowledge. A great scholar and legist has said with sententious wisdom that "many things which are true in the abstract are not true in the concrete." The founders of our institutions understood the full truth of this apothegm, and they acted upon it in laying the foundations of the system which they established. They were not mere theorists, nor *doctrinaires,* nor utopian legislators. They were great lawyers, practical philosophers, and wise statesmen, experienced in affairs. They recognized the principle of popular sovereignty. They were too wise not to know that the will of the people must needs be a great factor—nay, the greatest factor in any system of government to be established in a state of society where neither military power nor traditional rights exists. Hence, they skillfully wrought into the framework of our institutions the principle that the consent of the governed is the only legitimate source of human authority over the people. But in framing our early constitutions the fathers did by no means blindly follow the doctrine of popular sovereignty to its logical consequences. On the contrary * * * they carefully and studiously erected powerful barriers to arrest, control, and sometimes defeat, the popular will. * * * The fathers evidently believed that between the tyranny of one man and the tyranny of an unrestrained popular majority, the balance of evil would be largely with the latter. Did they recognize the absurd dogma that all men, all women, and all children, at the age of discretion, have an inalienable right, without experience or training, to participate in the government of the country? Did they for a moment assent to the proposition that to fight and to vote are correlative rights, and that the bullet and the ballot must be wielded by the same hand? On the contrary, they postponed universal suffrage for many years after the close of the Revolution, and until the people who had been living under monarchical form, without the training required to vote intelligently in a republic, became, to a certain extent, politically educated. * * * Little did they dream of perpetuating the monstrous and criminal folly of introducing, without the least preparation, into the body politic vast hordes of ignorant, illiterate, and semi-barbarous men, to vote away the property of their fellow-men, and subvert all civil order! If the fathers had been called upon to consider the question of negro suffrage under the same circumstances in which this generation of statesmen had to deal with that problem, they would probably have reasoned thus: "Let us by no means establish a constitution excluding these four millions of freedmen absolutely from the suffrage, lest we make the whole race enemies of the government under which they are to live. It is not consistent with the true idea of a republican commonwealth to exclude by arbitrary designation large numbers of people from all participation in the government. The deprivation of essential rights tends inevitably to make those who are thus excluded, enemies of the government. Let us, therefore, take measures to prepare these people, by education and political training, for the great duties of citizenship; and let us introduce them slowly and gradually as members of the political community. Thus may we at once satisfy the just and natural aspirations of the colored race, and prevent them from becoming the victims of demagogues and designing politicians, who will otherwise mislead them to their own injury, and to the irreparable detriment of society."

Many were the barriers which the wise fathers erected * * *. Consider the Senate of the United States. The people are not represented in that body at all. Its members are not elected by the people.* * * * Two senators, speaking for that little commonwealth [Delaware] of one hundred thousand people, may negative the voice of the great state of New York, with its five millions of inhabitants. * * * The Senate was intended to be, and is, an obstruction to the popular will; yet what American citizen would consent to abolish the Senate? * * *

Again, in the organization of the executive department our ancestors sought to raise restraining obstacles to the will of popular majorities. It is well known that it was not their purpose that the president should be elected directly by the people. On the contrary, they intended so to organize the electoral colleges as to place the election of president in the hands of the small number of independent men elected, indeed, by the people, but free to exercise their own judgment and discretion in the choice of the chief magistrate of the nation. * * * Thus they made it quite possible that a president should be chosen by a popular minority, and it is a familiar fact of our history that several of our presidents were elected in opposition to a majority of the popular vote. * * *

* * *

The fathers were too wise and too honest to give assent to the false and blasphemous dogma, that "the voice of the people is the voice of God." They had read history, and from its "pictured page" they had learned that the voice of the people is not unfrequently the voice of the devil! They had heard the voice of the people in the enlightened, polite, and art-loving Athenian democracy, condemning to death without cause their wisest citizen, and banishing another equally illustrious, because they were "vexed" to hear him everywhere called "the just." They had heard that potential voice in the Roman forum—now applauding one usurper, now another; today following with shouts of approbation the tyrant Sylla, tomorrow the tyrant Marius! They had heard it uttered in the streets of the great city at the death of the usurper in wild cries for vengeance against their own deliverers! They had heard the voice of the people in the mother country, demanding the burning of witches and heretics, sustaining the accursed slave trade, and approving of the judicial murder of many illustrious men. * * * The fathers well knew what history, ancient and modern, but too clearly reveals that faction and party spirit not frequently prevail in republics over truth, reason, and justice * * *.

* * * It was evidently their purpose to make the judiciary perfectly independent of the people, as well as the government. This they sought to accomplish by the manner of their appointment, the tenure of office, and the mode of compensation.

* * * They would not consent even to allow the House, in which the people are directly represented, to participate in the appointment of the judges. * * * They withheld from the whole government the power to remove a judge except by impeachment. They forbade any reduction of the salary of a judge during the time of his continuance in office. But in a large number of the states of the Federal Union this wise policy respecting the judiciary has been swept away by the drift of public sentiment toward radicalism. The judges in many states are now elected by universal suffrage for a short term of office, and the manifest tendency in all the states is strongly in the same direction. This is a momentous change! Is it a wise one? Or, on the contrary, is it but another proof, of which history furnishes so many, that all change is not progress—all innovation not improvement.

The fathers had read the history of the mother country * * *. They had noted the corruption, the craft, the self-abasement of English judges when it became their interest to conciliate that power in the state upon which they depended for their continuance in office and their salaries. They had seen exhibited in English history the amazing and humiliating spectacle of illustrious magistrates, judges of the highest dignity, crawling to the footstool of kingly power, like prostrate slaves before some eastern despot! * * *

Then, again, the founders of the government had seen a great change in the history of English jurisprudence. At the Revolution of 1688 the judges were made partially independent. * * * [By the time of the American Revolution, Parliament had] provided that the commissions of the judges should continue during good behavior, notwithstanding any demise of the crown, and that their full salaries should be absolutely secured to them during the continuance of their commissions. The great and salutary change which resulted from these facts in the administration of English law is well known to every student of the judicial history of England. * * *

* * * We have in our day and generation taken a vast stride in the opposite direction. We have in a great number of states made the judges dependent, not upon the executive government, but upon the popular will. Is the change a wise one? The American bar certainly does not approve of it; and the members of the bar are not only the best judges of such a matter, but they have had the best possible opportunities of observing the results of the change, and of forming a correct judgment concerning it. What is the difference in the principle and practice between making the judges dependent upon the people and dependent upon the executive head of the government? In my judgment it would be far better to make them dependent, if dependent at all, upon the executive than upon the people. It is only in political questions sometimes, though rarely involved in private litigation, that the executive government takes any special interest in the administration of justice by the courts. Even the kings of England desired to see the laws impartially administered between private litigants. * * * They rarely interfered with the courts, except in cases involving the interests and prerogatives of the crown. But how is it with King Public Opinion? Does he not interest himself in a vast variety of cases, involving mere individual right and private litigation? Does he not often, as well in the remote corners of the land as at the seat of government, assume to influence, revise, and sometimes overrule, judges as well as juries? Is he not often arbitrary, one-sided, prejudiced, ill-informed, yet violent and dominating? * * * [I]t is equally well known that public opinion is not seldom influenced and controlled by party spirit, religious bigotry, and personal prejudices. Now, a judge sitting to administer justice in the midst of an excited populace, upon whose will his future judicial existence depends, must be elevated above ordinary human nature not to be removed or affected by such influence. * * *

Nothing surely could be more shocking to our sense of justice and propriety than that a court of justice should be influenced in its judgments between man and man by outside popular opinion. * * * Yet, with strange inconsistency, our people have in many states * * exposed their judges to such temptations that nothing but that lofty virtue and independence of personal character, which cannot be expected in the ordinary incumbent of judicial office, can give assurance that the courts will not be influenced by the prevailing popular opinion. * * *

The fundamental objection to an elective judiciary is that the people have no right to be represented in a judicial proceeding. * * On the contrary, if all the people in all America should demand judgment against the humblest individual, yet, if right and justice were with him, a court of justice should, in disregard of universal opinion, give judgment in his favor. * * * The people ought of right to be represented in the making of the laws, but not in their administration by the courts. The legislator enacts a general law, the burdens and obligations of which fall alike upon his friends and foes, and in this we have a sufficient guaranty that the legislator will not pass oppressive laws. But the judge pronounces sentence in a particular case between individuals, or between the government and individuals, and he may therefore, if so disposed, without wounding his own friends and supporters, give judgment in favor of the party who controls the greater power or commands the greater number of votes. * * *

Since all men reject without the least hesitation the idea that the popular voice should be heard in a court of justice * * * what are the reasons which have induced the change in our state constitutions by which the judges are made elective by the people? It is surely not that judges should be responsible to the people for decisions made by them in the administration of justice; for how are the great mass of the people to know whether the decisions of the judge are right or wrong—in accordance with law or otherwise? Perhaps the idea underlying the great change of policy respecting the mode of appointing judges may be found in the belief that the people are capable of making a wiser choice of judges than the executive head of the state would be. There are many demagogues who affect to believe, and some honest people who, by dint of repetition, have brought themselves to believe, that the popular judgment of men and things is well nigh infallible. * * *

But without questioning the infallibility of the popular mind, let us for a moment enquire what are the inevitable consequences of making the judiciary subject to popular election. Is it not notorious that it brings the judicial office into direct connection with party politics and all the bad methods and influences of faction? Who will deny the somewhat startling assertion that, under the elective system, the party caucus does, in fact, appoint the judges of the land? Wherever either party is dominant, it makes the election of judges strictly partisan, and uses the judicial office as a part of its patronage. * * * And who is the man most likely to get a caucus nomination? Is the thoughtful, studious, and upright lawyer, the man of ideas and books and nice scruples, or the man of inflexible love of right, truth, and justice, likely to prove acceptable to a party caucus? Is such a candidate likely to succeed in getting a nomination in opposition to the adroit wire-puller, the man of popular ways and manners, voluble tongue, and little law? * * *

* * * Now, what would be said of a law or constitution enacted in these terms: Be it ordained, or enacted, that the party caucus of the majority faction shall choose the judges of the state! Such a statute or constitution, made in direct terms, would startle everybody, and meet probably with universal reprobation; yet such is the undoubted practical result of making the judges elective.

And here I may remark that it is one of the singular and, it seems to me, anomalous workings of our free institutions that the country is practically deprived by party usage of the services of nearly one-half its citizens. All the offices and honors of the state are engrossed by the majority. The minority, without respect to their own merits and qualifications, and often in utter disregard of the interests of the public service, are excluded by a rigid and inflexible party usage. * * * Now, it would seem to be to the highest degree unjust and impolitic in a free republican commonwealth that the community should not be perfectly free to choose from the entire body of its citizens the individual best qualified for the public service in a given capacity; and, theoretically, our American republics enjoy this liberty, but practically it is not so. Could a democrat in Iowa or republican in Missouri, by any conceivable means, be chosen as a supreme judge of the state in the face of existing party usages and organizations, which rule elections with a rod of iron? * * *

* * * With respect to executive and legislative offices, the majority have at least the entire body of their own partisans and followers from whom to make their selection. But judges have to be chosen from the very small number of citizens who form the body of a learned profession * * *.

* * * To say nothing of the evil influence that such a relation to party must exert upon the mind of the judge himself, it is obvious that he is, more or less, an object of distrust to his political opponents, and that he takes his seat without that full and unreserved confidence which would attend him if freely chosen by the whole people instead of a faction. There is, perhaps, no mode of election in this country by which the evil in question could be entirely cured. By whomsoever appointed, party views would, perhaps, have undue influence in the choice of judges, but the incumbent himself, if the old plan of appointment by the executive and senate prevailed, would be, to a considerable extent, removed from popular and partisan influences, and the candidate for judge would certainly, under that mode of selection, be less exposed to the temptation of plying the arts of popularity in obtaining and administering his high office.

Again, it is evident that the sense of responsibility is lessened as you divide and diffuse it. * * * Now, the appointment of a judge imposes upon the appointing power a heavy responsibility, and if this responsibility could be concentrated upon the executive head of the state, that officer would, I think, very rarely provoke the censure of the legal profession, and the indignation of the whole community, by the appointment of a bad or incompetent judge.

But what sense of responsibility can be brought home to an entire people for the election of a bad judge? * * *

I do not myself believe that the law for the popular election of judges can be changed. Popular privileges, once granted, are not likely to be surrendered, especially where the people are taught to believe themselves an unfailing source of all political wisdom. The only practicable remedy consists, in my judgment, in greatly enlarging the terms of judicial office, and in making the incumbent ineligible to a second election. To this, I think, the people would consent, and it would place the judge in a position of *quasi* independence. * * *

Finally, let me say, that although the election of judges for short terms by the people is not, in my judgment, a wise institution, and although we have certainly taken a wrong step in that direction, yet the system does not seem to work as badly as one would be led to suppose, reasoning from cause to effect. There is, I think, far less ground of complaint than might be expected, since private justice is, in the main, administered in the states which have adopted the elective system with at least tolerable ability and impartiality. The reason is obvious. The offence of judicial corruption or partiality is so heinous a crime in the eyes of all men, and especially of the legal profession, that few judges would have the hardihood to face the community and the bar under a sense of judicial delinquency. There is very little intemperance among women, because the public sentiment will not tolerate drunkenness in a woman. A female inebriate is a spectacle shocking to behold. The same stern and inexorable sentiment of condemnation against judicial delinquencies stares every judge in the face, and deters him in general, even if so inclined, from the commission of any serious offences against the rights of litigants, and the usages, traditions, and proprieties of his station.

NOTES AND QUESTIONS

1. There were efforts in many jurisdictions, especially in states where there were effective political machines, to end judicial selection by popular election. Until approximately the middle of the twentieth century, however, there were virtually no changes, and elected judiciaries were to be found in a clear majority of the states. In the beginning of the twentieth century, debate on judicial reform began to focus on the "merit plan" as an alternative to popular election. A merit plan was first adopted in Missouri, in 1949, following some particularly egregious conduct on the part of the Pendergast machine in Kansas City. The way that such a merit plan worked was that a commission, normally consisting of jurists, lawyers, and laymen, would recommend several names to governors, who would then appoint judges from the recommended list. The judges so appointed would serve for a term of years, and their terms would be subject to renewal in periodic non-competitive elections. According to Professor Ireland's unpublished study, as of late 1976, 13 states used some variant of the merit plan, 28 elected judges (14 by partisan nominations, 14 by non-partisan), five had their judges appointed by governors, and four had the legislature appoint judges. In recent years several states have grappled with judicial selection machinery and at least three—New York, North Carolina and Pennsylvania—have weighed abandoning the election of judges. The United States appears to be the only country pretty thoroughly committed to judicial elections for most of its judges (though federal

judges, as provided in the federal constitution, are still appointed for good behavior tenure). For a provocative meditation on the American practice, concluding that in the nineteenth century the movement for election of judges was designed to secure judicial independence, but the practice as it now exists has resulted in a judicial "plutocracy," where judicial elections are decided by enormous expenditures of campaign funds, often by parties with a financial stake in the outcome of judicial decisions, see Jed H. Shugerman, The People's Courts: Pursuing Judicial Independence in America (2012). Shugerman concludes that the "merit system" of selection is now the best means of preserving judicial independence. Which plan of judicial selection do you favor, and why? Does the merit plan solve the difficulties that are inherent in the other schemes? How do you explain the pervasiveness and tenacity of popular election for the judiciary? On the other hand, why do you suppose that the United States constitution was never amended to provide for election of judges?

2. You may remember that Alexis de Tocqueville, in *Democracy in America,* predicted that if Americans changed to the election of judges they would fatally undermine the foundation on which the rule of law and popular sovereignty rested. Has this happened? Based on your acquaintance with the judiciary in your own state, is there reason for fear? Is there more or less cause for alarm because of the decisions by the federal courts construing the federal Voting Rights Act of 1965? These require the creation of new state and federal legislative districts in order to give minorities representation in legislatures to an extent closer to their representation in the population, and extend that logic to the election of judges. See, e.g., *Chisom v. Roemer,* 501 U.S. 380, 111 S.Ct. 2354, 115 L.Ed.2d 348 (1991). The beginning of the Court's rewriting of the constitutional law involved was *Shaw v. Reno,* 509 U.S. 630, 113 S.Ct. 2816, 125 L.Ed.2d 511 (1993), which placed a heavy burden on states seeking to argue the constitutionality of racially-based redistricting, but failed to specify precisely how that burden was to be met. Future decisions can be expected to clarify that question, and there is even a chance that the Supreme Court might outlaw racially-based redistricting altogether. Would you favor such a color-blind constitutional approach? On this point see generally Andrew Kull, The Color–Blind Constitution (1992), and Stephen B. Presser, Recapturing the Constitution: Race, Religion, and Abortion Reconsidered 219–225 (1994).

3. Some United States Supreme Court appointments (those of Justices O'Connor, Thomas, Ginsburg, Sotomayor, and Kagan, for examples) have also been made to a greater or lesser degree in order to represent particular constituencies on the Court. Is this a good idea? Would Tocqueville approve? Would any of the three commentators you have just read? The source of much of the late twentieth century feeling that particular minority or previously-disadvantaged groups ought to receive increased representation in courts and legislatures was their experience under the legal system that prevailed until the nineteenth century. We next turn to what must be regarded as the most distinctive aspect of American nineteenth century law, the law of slavery. Could popular sovereignty in America ever really be said to have existed until

slavery was abolished? How could slavery have flourished until the Civil War? Was it simply racism, or was something more involved, and what role did the law play in supporting or undermining the system of chattel slavery? Bear these questions in mind as you review the materials which follow, and try to imagine what it must have been like not only to live as a slave, but to live as an owner of other human beings.

4. For further reading on the Constitutional reform that led to elected judiciaries, and the debate over whether what fueled the movement was "the clash between populism and paternalism," or an attempt "to strengthen the judiciary at the expense of the legislatures," "to weaken officialdom as a whole," or "to rein in the power of all officials to act independently of the people," see Caleb Nelson, "A Re–Evaluation of Scholarly Explanations for the Rise of the Elective Judiciary in Antebellum America," 37 Am.J.Leg.Hist. 191 (1993), and see also several articles by Kermit L. Hall, to which Nelson was responding, "The Judiciary on Trial: State Constitutional Reform and the Rise of an Elected Judiciary, 1846–1860," 45 HISTORIAN 337 (1983), "Constitutional Machinery and Judicial Professionalism: The Careers of Midwestern State Appellate Court Judges, 1861–1899," in the New High Priests: Lawyers in Post–Civil War America 29 (Gerald W. Gawalt, ed., 1984), and "The 'Route to Hell' Retraced: The Impact of Popular Election on the Southern Appellate Judiciary, 1832–1920," in Ambivalent Legacy: A Legal History of the South 229 (David J. Bodenhamer & James W. Ely, Jr., eds., 1984), and "Progressive Reform and the Decline of Democratic Accountability: The Popular Election of State Supreme Court Judges, 1850–1920," 9 Am.B.Found.Res.J. 345 (1984).

For further reading regarding the still-continuing controversy over selection of judges, much of it prompted by an exceptionally contentious judicial election in Ohio in 2000, see, e.g., Kelley Armitage, "Denial Ain't Just a River in Egypt: A Thorough Review of Judicial Elections, Merit Selection and the Role of State Judges in Society," 29 Cap. U.L.Rev. 625 (2002), Kara Baker, "Is Justice For Sale in Ohio? An Examination of Ohio Judicial Elections and Suggestions for Reform Focusing on the 2000 Race for the Ohio Supreme Court," 35 Akron L.Rev. 159 (2001), Mark A. Behrens & Cary Silverman, "The Case for Adopting Appointive Judicial Selection Systems for State Court Judges," 11 Cornell J. L. & Pub. Pol'y 273 (2002), Paul D. Carrington & Adam R. Long, "The Independence and Democratic Accountability of the Supreme Court of Ohio," 30 Cap.U.L.Rev. 455 (2002), The Federalist Society Judicial Selection White Paper Task Forces, "Judicial Selection White Papers: The Case for Judicial Appointments and the Case for Partisan Judicial Elections," 22 U. Tol. L. Rev. 353, 393 (2002) (part of a symposium on state judicial selection in the Winter 2002 issue of that journal), Alex B. Long, "An Historical Perspective on Judicial Selection Methods in Virginia and West Virginia," 18 J. L. & Politics (2002), and John Copeland Nagle, "Choosing the Judges Who Choose the President," 30 Cap. U.L.Rev. 499 (2002).

C. SLAVERY

The Practice of Slavery in the Colonies and States

The first record of African labor in the colonies was in Virginia in 1619. These early arrivals were bound to labor by indenture (a contract to labor for a set number of years, after which one became free of obligation) which made them not much different from the typical white English immigrant (between a third and one-half of whites came as indentured servants). By the late seventeenth century in Virginia and Maryland, that had changed. There was no blinding moment of transformation, just a slow accumulation of practices that set Africans apart from white servants. These practices eventually evolved into a system of law that recognized African servitude as perpetual. As you will soon see, this change in Africans' legal status came about as a result of colonial legislation, since English common law and Parliament did not recognize the institution of slavery. Virginians borrowed from the code provisions of the Caribbean island of Barbados, where British-owned tobacco and sugar plantations also relied on Africans for forced labor. The emerging institution of slavery in the Chesapeake colonies was tied to the production of tobacco, and in the low country of South Carolina, rice. Both were forms of cultivation that relied heavily on labor, and both were supported by a vigorous market demand in England and Europe that made slavery profitable. In 1709, the Chesapeake colonies exported 29 million pounds of tobacco to England. In the year 1775, annual exports had risen to 100 million pounds.

The institution of slavery was not restricted to the South. Slaves were present and legal, at one time or another, in all thirteen colonies. By 1750, most slaves in New England worked as domestic servants, laborers in towns and sea ports, or as field hands on small farms. The largest slave-holding colony in New England was Rhode Island, where 3% of its population was African. The business of the Atlantic slave trade was by far the greatest source of profit for New Englanders. In New York in 1750, 15% of the residents (about 10,000) were slaves. Slaves were also present in New Jersey and Pennsylvania, though in fewer numbers.

It was in the Southern colonies, however, that slavery took root. About 88% of the almost 250,000 slaves in the colonies in 1750 lived in Maryland, Virginia, North Carolina, South Carolina, and Georgia. By this time a body of law in these colonies worked out in minute detail the slave's status. This legislation also mandated extremely harsh forms of discipline, in part a reflection of a growing white fear of slave uprisings, the first of which occurred at Stono River in South Carolina in 1739. There were common elements, from colony to colony, in what was to become known as the "peculiar institution." All slaves were people of African descent. They were categorized as property, and like property, could be inherited or devised by will, bought and sold, and taxed. Slave status was passed on through the mother, a sign of the law's intent to create a permanent class, even when the children were those of the slave owner. As we will see reflected in Judge Ruffin's opinion in *State v. Mann*, Slaves were to be under the complete dominion of the master and others in the master's place, and their intercourse with whites was regulated. Slaves were forbidden to learn to read or write; their assembly was outlawed without the express approval of a master; and the master was forbidden from freeing his slaves during the master's life time. Slaves could not own weapons or firearms. Codes also provided for the punishment of slaves, listing in great detail the kinds and amount of punishment that could be administered (lashes, mutilation, castration, branding, and death). Slaves running away were to be apprehended and punished, or killed. Slaves were not permitted to legally marry, nor could a white person marry a black person. There were variations in these laws from colony to colony, but as Judge Ruffin notes in *Mann*, the intent was to do all that was necessary to ensure the complete dominion of the master and the complete subservience of the slave. While provisions in these laws offered some protections for slaves from mistreatment, it was up to local authorities to enforce them or not.

Criticisms of slavery were not uncommon in the colonies. The Quakers were prominent in their resistance to slavery in Pennsylvania, New Jersey, Virginia, and in New England. In the 1760s, Blacks petitioned colonial governments for greater privileges, and in colonies like Pennsylvania and Massachusetts, sometimes were successful. Their petitions often were couched as appeals to Christian charity, dignity, and virtue, and were prepared by influential attorneys and community pillars, such as Benjamin Franklin (who at one time owned a slave). With independence, two Northern states, Massachusetts and New Hampshire, abolished slavery. Five other Northern states adopted laws that made future children born of slave mothers free.

At the time of independence there were also Southern voices questioning the viability of slavery. A few of the South's leading revolutionaries, including Thomas Jefferson and George Washington, were embarrassed by the obvious contradiction of slavery to the Patriot cause and privately expressed hope of its eventual disappearance. Here and there Baptist, Presbyterian, and Methodist ministers labeled slavery as un-Christian. Southern states also softened their stance on elements of slavery, enacting laws that prohibited the importation of slaves, giving owners the authority to free their slaves, and offering slaves greater protections from mistreatment. The Continental Congress took the important step of prohibiting the spread of slavery into new land when it enacted the Northwest Ordinance of 1787, drafted by Jefferson.

The colonization movement was another approach to the problem of slavery, as we have seen promoted by Jefferson in his *Notes on the State of Virginia*. It eventually came to fruition in the American Colonization

Society of 1817 that counted among its founders influential figures from North and South (its efforts would lead to the colonization of Monrovia by free blacks from the U.S. and West Indies, later part of the free state of Liberia in West Africa). These efforts did not add up to a real social movement for change, however. After a century and a half of existence, the institution of slavery in the South was ineradicable. Law, customs, social mores, expectations, a code of behavior, religious beliefs, agricultural practices, and economic necessities—all were converging in making race and slavery the lynchpins of Southern life.

At the Constitutional Convention of 1787, the delegates of the Southern states (25 of the 55 in attendance owned slaves) made the acceptance of slavery a condition of their approval of any final proposal of government. They succeeded. Three separate provisions worked in favor of slavery's continued existence: the counting of each slave as three-fifths of one person for apportioning seats in the House and the number of Electors in the Electoral College, and the protection of the Atlantic slave trade for another twenty years. Two more provisions guaranteed Federal support for the institution (the suppression of insurrections and the return of runaway slaves), and one made the approval of three-fourths of the states a requirement for the amendment of the constitution. It would take an overwhelming majority that the North did not have to amend the constitution to eliminate slavery. Moreover, the fact that the words "slave" and "slavery" are nowhere mentioned in the document would indicate an intention to make slavery part of local law, putting its regulation beyond the reach of a national legislature. Plainly, there was ample Constitutional protection for slavery's continuation.

One possibility, held out by Washington and others, was that slavery would wither and die of its own. As indicated earlier, tobacco was hard on the land. In Virginia, the most prosperous of the Southern states, more than a century of intense tobacco cultivation left the soil exhausted and damaged from erosion. To a planter pulled into debt, slave labor was often an economic curse, frequently costing more than it made. Slavery was less hospitable in the mountainous regions of North and South Carolina, and western Virginia, where livestock and produce were more commonly grown on smaller farms. Cotton was an option as a staple crop, and the demand for it was growing in English and European textile mills. On the other hand, cotton was expensive to grow because of the difficulty of removing the seeds. The only profitable location for cotton was the coastal islands of Georgia and South Carolina, because there the long-fiber variety could be grown without the problem of seeds. As also indicated earlier, Eli Whitney's cotton gin in 1793 was about to change everything.

The cotton gin was a machine that used a comb to separate seeds from cotton. With a gin, one slave now could do the work of 50. Overnight the cultivation of short-staple cotton became profitable. The Louisiana

Purchase of 1803 opened up tremendously fertile lands in the west, and just as important, access to the Mississippi. The river and its tributaries, with the city of New Orleans at its mouth, and further up, Memphis (founded in 1819), offered a natural system for the movement of cotton to markets in the U.S. and abroad. Louisiana joined the union in 1812, bringing with it the rich lowlands of the delta. Contiguous with the old Southern states was the "black belt" region (named for its land) of western Georgia, the Mississippi Territory (out of which Mississippi and Alabama would be carved in 1817 and 1819) and the Missouri Territory (contributing the states of Missouri and Arkansas in 1821 and 1836). All that was needed were developers and a labor force. The old Southern states had both, and a process of migration onto the Piedmont and Southwest began in earnest before 1800 and continued through 1863. Eventually as cotton became king in these new lands slavery was revived.

The remarkable expansion in cotton production rippled through the national economy. By 1850, the South produced 40% of the world's cotton; this cotton accounted for 55% of all U.S. exports. As we have observed, Southern cotton supplied the raw material for New England's textile mills (and New England's industrial revolution), and met three-quarters of the raw-material demand in England. The price of a slave field hand rose from $500 in 1794 to $1,500 in 1825. The slave owners and traders in older states also benefited. Virginia's economy flourished as it assumed a new status of "breeder" and exporter of slaves, a practice that made the separation of slave families commonplace. Between 1800 and 1820 the slave population in the South increased by 62%. In 1810 the South held about 1.2 million slaves; by 1860 that number was 3.8 million. Most of this increase was natural, by far the highest rate of increase of all New World slavery. While it is the case that the South lagged behind the North on many economic indicators, individual wealth may not have been one of them. Of the richest 1% of the U.S. population, more than half lived in the South. Of the European nations, only England had greater personal wealth than the South. Compared to the North, the stratification of wealth in the South was probably greater in the decades leading up to 1860. In the South in 1850, about 17% of the population owned 66% of the acreage. If slave wealth was concentrating in fewer hands, it is also the case that slave ownership in the South remained widespread. Among those who did not own slaves, the poorest whites, perceptions varied. Some gladly took from the institution of slavery the advantages that came from being part of a superior caste. However, opinion in the South was by no means solid. Those removed from large plantation regions saw in slavery an alien system, one for which they had no great love. And still others, including more than a few who owned slaves, saw in the institution an abiding and problematic evil.

As slavery expanded west, its legal regulation and policing grew stricter. Greater limits were placed on free blacks living in Southern states, and on their entry; manumission was restricted, and greater controls were placed on the movements of slaves. Partly this was a result of the more intensive, backbreaking labor in the new states where overseers worked dozens, and even hundreds of slaves on a single plantation. The harsh conditions and severity of field work, especially in the summer months in the Deep South, made life for the slave vicious and short. Not surprisingly, the fear of insurrection was never far from the slave owner's mind. All were aware of the slave uprising in Saint–Domingue in the 1790s that produced the new state of Haiti. While nothing remotely similar occurred in the U.S., there may have been as many as 200 planned or attempted uprisings in the South before 1861. The four best known were Gabriel's Rebellion in Richmond in 1800, an 1811 uprising outside of New Orleans, Denmark Vesey's planned uprising in Charleston (betrayed by informers in 1822), and the rebellion in Virginia led by Nat Turner in 1831. Slaves resisted in dozens of other ways, perhaps most frequently by simply running away. Estimates are that as many as 100,000 slaves escaped from the Southern states during the Revolutionary War (compensation for slaves liberated by the British during the war was one of the demands of the Americans in negotiating a treaty of peace). As many as 80,000 slaves may have escaped into Ohio between 1830 and 1850. The presence of the Underground Railroad in the Border States, with "stations" stretching to Canada, funneled thousands of slaves to freedom.

The expansion of slavery in the South—indeed its very existence—continued to attract criticism in the North. Though Northern racism was widespread and certainly evident in the restrictions, harsh treatment, and sometimes violence aimed at free black persons, the reform movement to end slavery, "Abolition," was attracting greater attention and support. Free blacks themselves were establishing associations in the North for mutual assistance and abolition. The most radical advocate of abolition was William Lloyd Garrison, whose newspaper *The Liberator,* first published in 1831, graphically portrayed the horrors of slavery and called for its immediate end. As we will see, Frederick Douglass, an escaped slave, was a powerful spokesman for the cause of freedom and a galvanizing presence for audiences. His autobiography, *Narrative of the Life of Frederick Douglass*, published in 1845, had the credibility of a first-hand account and gained a wide audience. It is estimated that as many as 2,000 local abolitionist societies were founded in the North by the 1840s. While the radical abolitionists did have a splintering effect because of their legal defiance and open resistance (Garrison attacked the Constitution as a "covenant with death and an agreement with Hell"), the net result was to contribute to the demise of slavery. The abolitionists strengthened opposition to slavery by pushing it into more accepted legal and political channels, such as personal liberty laws in Pennsylvania (see infra, *Prigg v. Pennsylvania* (1842)) and New York, electioneering, and more concrete efforts such as the Underground Railroad. *Uncle Tom's*

Cabin created a sensation when it was published in book form in 1852; it crystallized an image of slavery in the popular mind that made indifference in the North increasingly difficult. The Fugitive Slave Act of 1850 brought others in the North face to face with the reality of slavery, as slave catchers roamed through Free States and as far north as the boundaries of Canada in search of run-away slaves. As we will see in the narrative purportedly written by Solomon Northrup, a free person of color who did not have in his possession official documentation testifying to his freedom was at risk of being legally detained and sold into slavery. For the runaway slave, and many free people of color, the slave catcher armed with guns, cuffs, ropes, chains, and the backing of the law was a terrifying specter.

The intensification of slavery's legal restrictions in the South, and the South's furious objections to the portrayal of its "peculiar institution" by abolitionists was part of an unfolding paternalistic ethos taking shape in the white Southern mind. This proslavery formulation was promoted by advocates and defenders of slavery in the 1830s and after, who broke with the apologetic "necessary evil" explanation of earlier times. As we will see, under the new portrayal, slavery was viewed as a positive good—a humane system of labor that contrasted with exploitative Northern employers who took from their "wage slaves" toiling in industrial dungeons, and gave nothing in return. Slavery, in this conception, was a superior social, economic, and religious way of life that bound the master and the slave in a compact of mutual responsibility. Presented as a uniquely American agrarian tradition, and rather paradoxically adopting Washington and Jefferson as its symbols, proslavery advocates scorned the capitalism of factory and city in favor of a more personal social world of plantation and farm. The protective, paternalistic shield of "my family black and white," as many owners and advocates put it, gave slavery its new meaning. This concept found its way into slave codes as expressions of legal protection for the slave from criminal mistreatment, and there are numerous instances of cases in Southern courts where law seemed to cast a protective arm around the slave. The characterization of slavery as a benign paternalistic system (which even Northrup alludes to) does not, of course, obscure the plain and simple reality that law reinforced and supported the master's often brutal dominion over his or her slaves, and the absolute maintenance of that dominion became the personal responsibility of masters and their neighbors backed up by the force of the state.

Divisions between North and South were most evident—and public—in the debate over the admission of states to the union. The Missouri Compromise of 1820, the subject of the infamous *Dred Scott* decision which you will soon read, involved an unprecedented level of congressional negotiating and accommodation. The result of admitting Maine as a Free State and Missouri as a slave state, the 1820 law drew a latitudinal line across Missouri's southern border and into the Louisiana Territory as the future divide between free and slave states. Intended as a long-term solution, Jefferson in his retirement at Monticello saw it as the reverse: it was "the knell of the union." The thorny issues around the admission of new states kept national politics off balance and drew deep fracture lines in the Congress and within political parties. With each new solution came new rules: The Compromise of 1850 admitted California as a free state and strengthened the fugitive slave law; the Kansas–Nebraska Act of 1853 left the choice of "free soil" or slavery to "popular sovereignty." The entire process broke down when antislavery and proslavery forces fought pitched battles in "bleeding Kansas" for seven years (1854–1861). To each side, loss was unacceptable, and compromise impossible.

What began as a labor system in 17th century Virginia not much different from white indentured servitude expanded into a Southern social system, with impact all over the nation. The contradictions in the two novel American experiments, one in slavery and one in freedom were carefully negotiated as the nation expanded into new lands, but there came a breaking point. In 1856, Rep. Preston Brooks of South Carolina caned abolitionist Massachusetts Sen. Charles Sumner on the floor of the Senate, leaving him near death, in retaliation for Sumner's criticism of slavery and the implied insult of a Brooks family member. In 1857 the *Dred Scott* decision diminished future prospects for compromise when it declared that Congress did not have the authority to prohibit slavery in the territories. John Brown's raid on the U.S. military arsenal at Harper's Ferry in 1859, conducted with military precision and with the express purpose of provoking slave rebellion in the vicinity and then conducting guerilla campaigns from the safety of mountain hide outs, was the slave owner's worst nightmare. Brown's hanging made him a martyr in the North. The Whig Party experienced a total collapse in the 1850s, and was replaced by a new Republican Party that nominated ex-Whig Abraham Lincoln as its presidential candidate in the 1860 election. Lincoln was on record as opposing the extension of slavery into western territory, but he also pledged to do nothing that threatened slavery where it already existed. The candidate for the Democrats, John Breckinridge, took the Southern position of protecting slavery. Absent that assurance from a sitting president, he favored secession. John Bell of the Union Party was a compromise candidate.

Lincoln won the election of November 6 with less than 40% of the popular vote. He carried none of the Southern or border slave states. Painted as an abolitionist, Lincoln's election prompted South Carolina, as you will soon see, to convene a state convention in December of 1860. Within a few days of meeting, it issued an "Ordinance of Secession" that dissolved its ties to the United States. Southern newspapers urged other states to follow quickly, believing that their presence in the union left them legally and militarily helpless. By early February of 1861, seven lower-South states seceded and formed the Confederate States of America. On March 6, Lincoln became the 16th President of the United States. On April 12, the federal Fort Sumter in South Carolina was barraged by Confederate batteries and surrendered. The union was falling apart. Lincoln declared South Carolina in rebellion, and issued a call-up of troops. By May, the upper-South states of Virginia, North Carolina, Tennessee, and Arkansas joined the Confederacy. The Civil War was the result, and we will explore the legal and constitutional aspects of that war in the section which follows.

Further Reading:

Ira Berlin, *Many Thousands Gone: The First Two Centuries of Slavery in North America*, 1998

David Brion Davis, *The Problem of Slavery in Western Culture*, 1996

Paul Finkelman, *Defending Slavery: Proslavery Thought in the South*, 2003

Robert Fogel, *Without Consent or Contract: The Rise and Fall of American Slavery*, 1989

Eugene D. Genovese, *Roll, Jordan, Roll: The World the Slaves Made*, 1976

James O. Horton, Lois E. Horton, *In Hope of Liberty: Culture, Community, and Protest Among Northern Free Blacks, 1700–1860*, 1997

James O. Horton, Lois E. Horton, *Slavery and the Making of America*, 2005

Peter Kolchin, *American Slavery, 1619–1877*, 1993

Lawrence W. Levine, *Black Culture and Black Consciousness*, 1977

Edmund S. Morgan, *American Slavery, American Freedom*, 1975

James Oakes, *The Ruling Race: A History of American Slaveholders*, 1982

Kenneth M. Stampp, *The Peculiar Institution: Slavery in the Antebellum South*, 1956

Sterling Stuckey, *Slave Culture: Nationalist Culture and the Foundations of Black America*, 1987

Michael Tadman, *Speculators and Slaves: Masters, Traders, and Slaves in the Old South*, 1989

Shane White, *Somewhat More Independent: The End of Slavery in New York City, 1770–1810*, 1991

Peter Wood, *Strange New Land: Africans in Colonial America*, 2003

1. THE EXPERIENCE OF SLAVERY

KENNETH STAMPP, THE PECULIAR INSTITUTION*

206–216 (1956).

Every slave state had a slave code. Besides establishing the property rights of those who owned human chattels, these codes supported masters in maintaining discipline and provided safeguards for the white community against slave rebellions. In addition, they held slaves, as thinking beings, morally responsible and punishable for misdemeanors and felonies.

Fundamentally the slave codes were much alike. Those of the Deep South were somewhat more severe than those of the Upper South, but most of the variations were in minor details. * * *

After a generation of liberalization following the American Revolution, the codes underwent a reverse trend toward increasing restrictions. This trend was clearly evident by the 1820's, when rising slave prices and expansion into the Southwest caused more and more Southerners to accept slavery as a permanent institution. * * *

In practice the slave codes went through alternating periods of rigid and lax enforcement. Sometimes slaveholders demanded even more rigorous codes, and sometimes they were remiss in enforcing parts of existing ones. When the danger of attack from without or of rebellion from within seemed most acute, they looked anxiously to the state governments for additional protection. * * *

At the heart of every code was the requirement that slaves submit to their masters and respect all white men. The Louisiana code of 1806 proclaimed this most lucidly: "The condition of the slave being merely a passive one, his subordination to his master and to all who represent him is not susceptible of modification or restriction * * * he owes to his master, and to all his family, a respect without bounds, and an absolute obedience, and he is consequently to execute all the orders which he receives from him, his said master, or from them." A slave was neither to raise his hand against a white man nor to use insulting or abusive language. Any number of acts, said a North Carolina judge, may constitute "insolence"—it may be merely "a look, the pointing of a finger, a refusal or neglect to step out of the way when a white person is seen to approach. But each of such acts violates the rules of propriety, and if tolerated, would destroy that subordination, upon which our social system rests."

The codes rigidly controlled the slave's movements and his communication with others. A slave was not to be "at large" without a pass which he must show to any white man who asked to see it; if he forged a pass or free papers he was guilty of a felony. Except in a few localities, he was prohibited from hiring his own time, finding his own employment, or living by himself. A slave was not to preach, except to his master's own slaves on his master's premises in the presence of whites. A gathering of more than a few slaves (usually five) away from home, unattended by a white, was an "unlawful assembly" regardless of its purpose or orderly decorum.

No person, not even the master, was to teach a slave to read or write, employ him in setting type in a printing office, or give him books or pamphlets. A religious publication asked rhetorically: "Is there any great moral reason why we should incur the tremendous risk of having our wives slaughtered in consequence of our slaves being taught to read incendiary publications?" * * *

Farms and plantations employing slaves were to be under the supervision of resident white men, and not left to the sole direction of slave foremen. Slaves were not to beat drums, blow horns, or possess guns; periodically their cabins were to be searched for weapons. They were not to administer drugs to whites or practice medicine. "A slave under pretence of practicing medicine," warned a Tennessee judge, "might convey intelligence from one plantation to another, of a contemplated insurrectionary movement; and thus enable the slaves to act in concert."

A slave was not to possess liquor, or purchase it without a written order from his owner. He was not to trade without a permit, or gamble with whites or with other slaves. He was not to raise cotton, swine, horses, mules, or cattle. Allowing a slave to own animals, explained the North Carolina Supreme Court, tended "to make other slaves dissatisfied * * * and thereby excite * * * a spirit of insubordination."

* * * Richmond required Negroes and mulattoes to step aside when whites passed by, and barred them from riding in carriages except in the capacity of menials. Charleston slaves could not swear, smoke, walk with a cane, assemble at military parades, or make joyful demonstrations. In Washington, North Carolina, the town Commissioners prohibited "all disorderly shouting and dancing, and all disorderly * * * assemblies * * * of slaves and free Negroes in the streets, market and other public places." In Natchez, all "strange slaves" had to leave the city by four o'clock on Sunday afternoon.

Violations of the state and local codes were misdemeanors or felonies subject to punishment by justices, sheriffs, police, and constabulary. Whipping was the most common form of public punishment for less than capital offenses. Except in Louisiana, imprisonment was rare. By midnineteenth century branding and mutilation had declined, though they had not been abolished everywhere. South Carolina did not prohibit branding until 1833, and occasionally thereafter slave felons still had their ears cropped. Mississippi and Alabama continued to enforce the penalty of "burning in the hand" for felonies not capitally punished.

But most slave offenders were simply tied up in the jail or at a whipping post and flogged. Some states in the Upper South limited to thirty nine the number of stripes that could be administered at any one time, though more could be given in a series of whippings over a period of days or weeks. In the Deep South floggings could legally be more severe. Alabama permitted up to one hundred stripes on the bare back of a slave who forged a pass or engaged in "riots, routs, unlawful assemblies, trespasses, and seditious speeches."

State criminal codes dealt more severely with slaves and free Negroes than with whites. In the first place, they made certain acts felonies when committed by Negroes but not when committed by whites; and in the second place, they assigned heavier penalties to Negroes than whites convicted of the same offense. Every southern state defined a substantial number of felonies carrying capital punishment for slaves and lesser punishments for whites. In addition to murder of any degree, slaves received the death penalty for attempted murder, manslaughter, rape and attempted rape upon a white woman, rebellion and attempted rebellion, poisoning, robbery, and arson. A battery upon a white person might also carry a sentence of death under certain circumstances. In Louisiana, a slave who struck his master, a member of the master's family, or the overseer, "so as to cause a contusion, or effusion or shedding of blood," was to suffer death as was a slave on a third conviction for striking a white.

The codes were quite unmerciful toward whites who interfered with slave discipline. Heavy fines were levied upon persons who unlawfully traded with slaves, sold them liquor without the master's permission, gave them passes, gambled with them, or taught them to read or write. North Carolina made death the penalty for concealing a slave "with the intent and for the purpose of enabling such slave to escape." Aiding or encouraging a bondsman to rebel was the most heinous crime of all. "If a free person," said the Alabama code, "advise or conspire with a slave to * * * make insurrection, * * * he shall be punished with death, whether such rebellion or insurrection be made or not."

Every slave state made it a felony to say or write anything that might lead, directly or indirectly, to discontent or rebellion. In 1837, the Missouri legislature passed an act "to prohibit the publication, circulation, and promulgation of the abolition doctrines." The Virginia code of 1849 provided a fine and imprisonment for any person who maintained "that owners have not right of property in their slaves." Louisiana made it a capital offense to use "language in any public discourse, from the bar, the bench, the stage, the pulpit, or in any place whatsoever" that might produce "insubordination among the slaves." Most southern states used their police power to prohibit the circulation of "incendiary" material through the United States mail; on numerous occasions local postmasters, public officials, or mobs seized and destroyed antislavery publications.

* * *

Southern slave codes protected the owners of bondsmen who attempted to abscond by requiring officers to assist in their recapture and by giving all white men power to arrest them. Every state required the owner of a fugitive to compensate the captor for his trouble. Because of the magnitude of the problem, Kentucky obligated masters to pay a reward of one hundred dollars for runaways taken "in a State where slavery is not tolerated by law." In an effort to induce the return of fugitives escaping to Mexico, Texas promised a reward of one third the value of a slave who fled "beyond the limits of the slave territories of the United States." * * *

North Carolina authorized the outlawing of a "vicious" runaway. For example, two justices of New Hanover County gave notice that the slave London was "lurking about" and "committing acts of felony and other misdeeds." London was therefore outlawed; unless he surrendered immediately, "any person may KILL and DESTROY the said slave by such means as he or they may think fit, without accusation or impeachment of any crime or offense for so doing." At the same time, London's master offered a reward of fifty dollars for his confinement in jail, or one hundred dollars for his head. Louisiana permitted a person to shoot a runaway who would not stop when ordered to do so. * * *

Occasionally a band of runaways was too formidable to be dispersed by volunteers, and the governor called upon the militia to capture or destroy it. Ordinarily, however, this and other organized police activity was delegated to the slave patrols. A system of patrols, often more or less loosely connected with the militia, existed in every slave state. Virginia empowered each county or corporation court to "appoint, for a term not exceeding three months, one or more patrols" to visit "all negro quarters and other places suspected of having therein unlawful assemblies," and to arrest "such slaves as may stroll from one plantation to another without permission." Alabama compelled every slaveowner under sixty and every nonslaveholder under forty five to perform patrol duty. The justices of each precinct divided the eligible males into detachments which had to patrol at least one night a week during their terms of service. Everywhere the patrols played a major role in the system of control.

* * *

* * * The nonslaveholding whites, to whom most patrol service was relegated, frequently disliked the masters almost as intensely as the Negroes, and as patrollers they were in a position to vent their feelings toward both. Slaveholders repeatedly went to the courts with charges that patrollers had invaded their premises and whipped their slaves excessively or illegally. The slaves in turn both hated and feared the patrollers and retaliated against them when they could. Yet masters looked upon the patrol as an essential police system, and none ever seriously suggested abolishing it.

The final clauses in the southern legal codes relating directly to the control of slaves were those governing free Negroes. The laws reflected the general opinion that these people were an anomaly, a living denial "that nature's God intended the African for the status of slavery." They "embitter by their presence the happiness of those who remain slaves. They entice them and furnish them with facilities to elope." They were potential allies of the slaves in the event of a rebellion. In 1830, David Walker, a free Negro who moved from North Carolina to Boston, wrote and attempted to circulate in the South a pamphlet which urged the slaves to fight for their freedom. He thus aroused southern legislatures to the menace of the free Negro.

The trend of antebellum legislation was toward ever more stringent controls. Free Negroes could not move from one state to another, and those who left their own state for any purpose could not return. In South Carolina and the Gulf states Negro seamen were arrested and kept in custody while their vessels were in port. Though free Negroes could make contracts and own property, in most other respects their civil rights were as circumscribed as those of slaves. They were the victims of the white man's fears, of racial prejudice, and of the desire to convince slaves that winning freedom was scarcely worth the effort.

Many Southerners desired the complete expulsion of the free Negroes, or the reenslavement of those who would not leave. Petitions poured in to the state legislatures demanding laws that would implement one or the other of these policies. In 1849, a petition from Augusta County, Virginia, asked the legislature to make an appropriation for a program of gradual removal; all free Negroes who refused to go to Liberia should be expelled from the state within five years. In 1859, the Arkansas legislature required sheriffs to order the state's handful of free Negroes to leave. Those who remained were to be hired out as slaves for a year, after which those who still remained were to be sold into permanent bondage.

* * *

NOTES AND QUESTIONS

1. This first excerpt drawn from Kenneth Stampp's "Landmark in American Historical Writing," is to give you an overview of conditions under the American slavery laws. For appreciations of Stampp's contribution and evaluations of his perspective on the South and its "peculiar institution," see Don E. Fehrenbacker, "A Stampp Collection," 8 Reviews in American History 511 (1980), and Robert W. Johannsen, "A Nation on the Brink," 19 Reviews in American History 499 (1991). For some of the most detailed and absorbing descriptions of Southern slave society see Eugene D. Genovese, Roll, Jordan, Roll: The World the Slaves Made (Vintage paperbacks, 1976), and Solomon Northrup, Twelve Years a Slave (Sue Eakin and Joseph Logsdon, eds. 1968). For an analysis of the complexities and contradictions of Southern case and statute law on slavery see Mark V. Tushnet, The American Law of Slavery 1810–1860 (1981). For an account of contemporary African–American responses to those complexities, see Jon–Christian Suggs, Whispered Consolations: Law and Narrative in African–American Life (2000). Finally, for a study of slaves' awareness of the importance of law in their lives, which makes extensive use of slave narratives and former slaves' recollections, see Ariela Gross, Double Character: Slavery and Mastery in the Southern Courtroom, 1800–1860 (2000).

2. Note that the author of this excerpt comments on the reversal of a "generation of liberalization" in slavery legislation which followed the American Revolution. What would have caused this liberalization, and what does Professor Stampp suggest brought about the reversal?

3. You may have noticed that as the nineteenth century progressed, some aspects of the slave laws seem to reflect humanitarian concerns; for example, there is less toleration for mutilation of slaves. Still, the harshness of the laws which aimed to prevent runaways or slave rebellions tended to increase until the Civil War. Why? Note, in particular, that much of the enforcement of these laws may have been in the hands of the "slave patrols," many members of which were not themselves slaveowners. Does this strike you as an intelligent system? How do you explain the preeminence of the slave patrols?

4. One of your most difficult tasks, in evaluating these materials, is to try to understand how the system of slavery could have existed for so long in the South. The evils of slavery are obvious to people of our century. What then could have been said in its defense? In 1837 Senator John C. Calhoun of South Carolina responded to abolitionist critics of slavery by claiming that slavery, instead of being an "evil", had proved to be a "good." Calhoun observed that "there never has yet existed a wealthy and civilized society in which one portion of the community did not, in point of fact, live on the labor of the other." Calhoun explained that each society had concocted its own devices for ensuring the inevitable and necessary unequal division of wealth between the laboring and consuming classes, and that they ranged "from the brute force and gross superstition of ancient times, to the subtle and artful fiscal contrivances of modern." Turning to the South's own solution, Calhoun

claimed that "the more direct, simple and patriarchal mode by which the labor of the African race is * * * commanded by the European" compared favorably with the means of maldistribution in other societies. Calhoun concluded by stating that "I fearlessly assert that the existing relation between the two races in the South, against which these blind fanatics [the abolitionists] are waging war, forms the most solid and durable foundation on which to rear free and stable political institutions." I Calhoun, Works 630–632 (R.K. Cralle, ed. 1853–1855, repr. 1968), quoted in H.W. Farnam, Chapters in the History of Social Legislation in the United States to 1860 173–174 (1938). How could Calhoun believe such things? Would you have subscribed to these views in 1837? For discussions of Calhoun's acumen as a political theorist, see "John C. Calhoun: The Marx of the Master Class," Chapter IV of Richard Hofstadter, The American Political Tradition and The Men Who Made It (Vintage Books ed., 1974) and Lacy K. Ford, Jr., "Toward A Divided Union," 18 Reviews in American History 349 (1990), and, for a readable and informative biography of "the Old South's foremost political strategist and political thinker," see John Niven, John C. Calhoun and the Price of Union: A Biography (1988). How inhuman was the overall system of slavery? Consider the following continuation of Stampp's discussion.

KENNETH STAMPP, THE PECULIAR INSTITUTION

217–222 (1956).

"A slave," said a Tennessee judge, "is not in the condition of a horse. * * * He has mental capacities, and an immortal principle in his nature." The laws did not "extinguish his highborn nature nor deprive him of many rights which are inherent in man." * * * Many state constitutions required the legislature "to pass such laws as may be necessary to oblige the owners of slaves to treat them with humanity; to provide for them necessary clothing and provisions; [and] to abstain from all injuries to them, extending to life or limb."

The legislatures responded with laws extending some protection to the persons of slaves. Masters who refused to feed and clothe slaves properly might be fined; in several states the court might order them to be sold, the proceeds going to the dispossessed owners. Those who abandoned or neglected insane, aged, or infirm slaves were also liable to fines. In Virginia the overseers of the poor were required to care for such slaves and to charge their masters.

Now and then a master was tried and convicted for the violation of one of these laws. In 1849, the South Carolina Supreme Court upheld the conviction of a slaveholder who "did not give his negroes enough even of [corn] meal, the only provision he did give." In such a case, said the court, the law had to be enforced for the sake of "public sentiment, * * * and to protect property from the depredation of famishing slaves." But prosecutions were infrequent. * * *

Some of the codes regulated the hours of labor. As early as 1740, South Carolina limited the working day to fifteen hours from March to September and fourteen hours from September to March. All the codes forbade field labor on Sunday. * * * It was permissible, however, to let slaves labor on the Sabbath for wages * * *. With rare exceptions, masters who were so inclined violated these laws with impunity.

The early colonial codes had assessed only light penalties, or none at all, for killing a slave. * * *

After the American Revolution there was a drastic change of policy. Virginia, in 1788, and North Carolina, in 1791, defined the malicious killing of a slave as murder subject to the same penalty imposed upon the murderer of a freeman. In 1817, North Carolina applied this principle to persons convicted of manslaughter. Georgia's Constitution of 1798 contained a clause that was copied, in substance, into the constitutions of several states in the Southwest: "Any person who shall maliciously dismember or deprive a slave of life shall suffer such punishment as would be inflicted in case the like offence had been committed on a free white person."

Eventually all the southern states adopted laws of this kind. * * * In Alabama a person who, "with malice aforethought," caused the death of a slave "by cruel whipping or beating, or by any inhuman treatment, or by the use of any weapon in its nature calculated to produce death," was guilty of murder in the first degree. A master or overseer causing death by cruel whipping or by other cruel punishment, "though without any intention to kill," was guilty of murder in the second degree.

By the 1850's, most of the codes had made cruelty a public offense even when not resulting in death. * * * Louisiana prohibited the owner from punishing a slave with "unusual rigor" or "so as to maim or mutilate him." Georgia more explicitly prohibited "cutting, or wounding, or * * * cruelly and unnecessarily biting or tearing with dogs." In Kentucky, a slave who was treated cruelly might be taken from his master and sold.

But these laws invariably had significant qualifications. For example the accidental death of a slave while receiving "moderate correction" was not homicide. Killing a slave in the act of rebellion or when resisting legal arrest was always "justifiable homicide." South Carolina permitted a white person to "apprehend and moderately correct" a slave who was at large without a pass and refused to submit to examination; "and, if any such slave shall assault and strike such white person, such slave may be lawfully killed." * * *

Under most circumstances a slave was powerless to defend himself from an assault by a white man. According to the Tennessee Supreme Court, severe chastisement by the master did not justify resistance. If a master exercised his right to punish, "with or without cause, [and] the slave resist and slay him, it is murder * * * because the law cannot recognize the violence of the master as a legitimate cause of provocation." According to the Georgia Supreme Court, even if the owner should "exceed the bounds of reason * * * in his chastisement, the slave must submit * * * unless the attack * * * be calculated to produce death."

* * *

In a few notable cases the courts enforced the laws against the killing of slaves. A North Carolinian was sentenced to death for the murder of his own female chattel. * * * The Virginia Court of Appeals, in approving a similar conviction, explained precisely how far a master could go before the law would intervene. For the sake of securing "proper subordination and obedience" the master would not be disturbed even though his punishment were "malicious, cruel and excessive." But he "acts at his peril; and if death ensues in consequence of such punishment, the relation of master and slave affords no ground of excuse or palliation." In Mississippi, too, a white man was hanged for killing another man's slave. "In vain," argued the state Supreme Court, "shall we look for any law passed by the * * * philanthropic legislature of this state, giving even to the master, much less to a stranger, power over the life of a slave."

Decisions such as these were exceptional. Only a handful of whites suffered capital punishment for murdering slaves, and they were usually persons who had committed the offense upon slaves not their own. * * *

* * *

NOTES AND QUESTIONS

1. Does this second excerpt from Stampp make you feel any more sanguine about the laws of slavery? Stampp seems to suggest that the laws offered relatively little protection, and that convictions were rare. Does this necessarily mean that the laws were ineffective? For a compelling argument that Southern courts were often committed to recognizing the essential "humanity" of slaves in the antebellum years see A.E. Keir Nash, A More Equitable Past? Southern Supreme Courts and the Protection of the Antebellum Negro, 48 North Carolina Law Review 197 (1970). Do you note any trend in this legislation discussed in this second excerpt that seems to run counter to the trends discussed in the first excerpt from Professor Stampp?

2. You will remember that John C. Calhoun thought otherwise, but is the existence of slavery inconsistent with the existence of principles of political freedom? This problem is addressed in David Brion Davis, The Problem of Slavery in Western Culture (1966). Turning to the ancient past, Davis observes:

> Though actual slaves never formed a significant percentage of the populations of China or ancient Egypt, in Greece, where they were treated as commodities and put to industrial and commercial employments,

> the number kept increasing from the Persian Wars to the time of Alexander. Historians disagree on the exact percentage of slaves in the total population of fourth-century Athens, but Moses Finley states that the proportion was as great as in the combined slave states of America in 1860, and that the ownership of slaves in Greece was even more widely distributed among the free population than in America. * * * Finley argues persuasively that the institution was an integral element in Hellenic society. Moreover, "the cities in which individual freedom reached its highest expression—most obviously Athens—were cities in which chattel slavery flourished." Thus the history of ancient Greece presents the same paradox that has perplexed Americans since the eighteenth century: freedom and slavery seemed to advance together.*

Id., at 35–36. How might we go about expressing and solving the American paradox? Virginia, for example, had been the source of much of the Revolutionary ideology and doctrines of political equality, and yet Virginia had one of the largest slave populations. Were slaveholding Virginians mere hypocrites? Was Jefferson? For an intriguing explanation of how an increasingly democratic South could still cling to slavery, see Michael Wayne, "An Old South Morality Play: Reconsidering the Social Underpinnings of the Proslavery Ideology," 77 Journal of American History 838 (1990). On the debate that Davis's work continues to generate, see Thomas Bender, ed., Capitalism and Abolitionism as a Problem in Historical Interpretation (1992) and the review of the Bender book by Morton J. Horwitz, "Reconstructing Historical Theory from the Debris of the Cold War," 102 Yale L.J. 1287 (1993). For some further perspective on the law of slavery see the much heralded Ira Berlin, Many Thousands Gone: The First Two Centuries of Slavery in North America (1998), and see also the articles in the "Symposium on the Law of Slavery," 68 Chicago Kent–Law Review 1009 (1993), edited and introduced by Paul Finkelman and with articles by Derrick Bell, William W. Fisher III, Sanford Levinson, Michael Kent Curtis, James Oliver Horton & Lois E. Horton, Andrew Kull, Thomas D. Morris, Thomas D. Russell, Judith K. Schafer, Alan Watson, Jacob Corre, and Ruth Wedgewood. For the continuing opportunities for the legal history of slavery and an incisive piece on legal historiography generally, see Jenni Parrish, "A Guide to American Legal History Methodology with an Example of Research in Progress," 86 Law. Lib. J. 105 (1994).

One way of coming to a better understanding of the history of American slavery is to compare it to that of other nations. For a pioneering work in this regard see Robert J. Cottrol, "The Long, Lingering Shadow: Law, Liberalism, and Cultures of Racial Hierarchy and Identity in the Americas," 76 Tulane L. Rev. 11 (2001) (Contrasting the law of race and slavery in Brazil, Columbia, and Venezuela, with the parallel history of the United States, and concluding that "liberalism helped create a system of castelike separation between black and white in the United States," which was "far more rigid than found elsewhere in the hemisphere and was enforced by discriminatory laws," but that

* Reprinted from David Brion Davis: The Problem of Slavery in Western Culture. Copyright 1966 by Cornell University.

nevertheless liberalism in the United States "has also helped produce a more thorough North American civil rights revolution than has, to date, occurred in Latin America.")

3. Does the following material from Eugene Genovese suggest a means of reconciling the ideal of political liberty and the realities of slavery? As you study this excerpt, from Genovese's celebrated work on plantation slavery, bear in mind John Calhoun's praise for the "direct, simple, and patriarchal" mode of Southern slavery. Does Genovese help you to understand what Calhoun meant?

EUGENE D. GENOVESE, ROLL, JORDAN, ROLL: THE WORLD THE SLAVES MADE*

97–99, 102–103, 105–112 (Vintage Books, ed. 1976).

The slaveholders' understanding of themselves and their world suffered a severe shock during and immediately after the war, when "their black family" appeared in a new light. * * * Their behavior presented their masters with a terrible moment of truth. Could it be that they had never known "their people" at all? that they had been deceiving themselves? * * *

The masters had expected more than obedience from their slaves; they had expected faithfulness obedience internalized as duty, respect, and love. They had had little choice, for anything less would have meant a self-image as exploitative brutes. This insistence on the slaves' constituting part of the family and these expressions of belief in their loyalty lay at the heart of the masters' worldview and, abolitionist criticism notwithstanding, embraced little insincerity. Thus the leading southern ideologues, who wrote the proslavery polemics of the late antebellum period, were deceiving none so much as themselves. In 1837, Chancellor Harper blithely wrote of docile and faithful slaves adding greatly to southern military strength. * * * In 1850, a young aristocratic South Carolinian gloomily told Fredrika Bremer, "The world is against us, and we shall be overpowered by voices and condemned without justice, for what we are, and for what we are doing on behalf of our servants." And as late as 1864, with the cause lost, a lawyer in Memphis lamented, "I believe too that a very large number of the negroes will not accept their freedom and that, by one name or another, pretty much of the old relations will be reestablished." * * *

The wartime and immediate postwar trauma derived less from the sudden confrontation with the true attitudes of their slaves than from the enforced confrontation with themselves. The experience proved all the more bitter since that organic relationship of master and slave which the

* Reprinted from Eugene D. Genovese, Roll, Jordan, Roll: The World the Slaves Made, Copyright 1972, 1974 by Eugene D. Genovese, published originally by Pantheon Books, a division of Random House, Inc., in 1974, with the permission of the publisher.

slaveholders always celebrated had so clearly rebounded against them: any change in their perception of the slaves intrinsically meant a bitter change in their perception of themselves. The freedmen often had a better sense of this relationship and of the nature of the slaveholders' reaction than did the slaveholders. They spoke of masters and mistresses who died of broken hearts both for the loss of their property and for their sense of having been betrayed. * * *

The great shock to the planters came with the defection of their most trusted and pampered slaves-the drivers and especially the more intimate of the house servants. That many of these remained loyal did not offset the shock at the behavior of those who did not. The slaveholders might reconcile themselves to the defection of their field hands, for it struck at their pocketbooks but not necessarily at their self-esteem. They could explain the exodus from the fields by reasoning that these were inexperienced, simple people whom the Yankees could mislead. No such reasoning would serve to explain the behavior of the house slaves or the drivers. Their desertion, in the minds of the slaveholders, constituted the essence of ingratitude, of unfaithfulness, of disloyalty, of treason.

* * *

Eliza Frances Andrews noted in her diary for January 16, 1865, that the most well-behaved and docile blacks became increasingly unruly as Yankee troops got close. On May 27, she celebrated the loyalty of her own servants, whom she called "treasures": "I really love them for the way they have stood by us." A month later she told of the adventures of a neighbor's favorite pampered, loyal, religiously devout, superannuated slave. One day, as usual without the slightest provocation so far as the slaveholders were concerned, he slandered his white family, which had sheltered and befriended him, and of all things had the temerity to claim the plantation as his own. Years later, when Miss Andrews had grown into a woman of considerable intellectual sophistication, she reflected on these pages of her diary and recalled how her aunt, who had had no children of her own, had compensated by spoiling a "pet" servant. The boy had been orphaned by the death of his mother, the aunt's favorite maid. As soon as the war ended he "deserted." "The kind-hearted old lady never ceased to mourn over his ingratitude." Miss Andrews recalled this story along with another. Arch, her father's favorite dining room servant, was the first black to leave the plantation. Yet he had not sneaked off. He had asked his old master's permission, which could hardly have been refused, and had expressed all possible respect. But the time had come. For many years afterwards he visited the white family, which continued to employ his sister.

This ambivalence in the Big House often broke into its antagonistic components, with some white families experiencing only the slaves' "loyalty" and others only their "desertion." And for many whites the fact of freedom itself constituted a desertion. One planter in Georgia burned his slave cabins to the ground and expelled his people. He had no use for them any longer, he said, nor they for him. In 1871 a hysterical old white man "denounced, with bitter curses, his negroes, saying that they had abandoned him when set free and left him to starve in his old age, knowing as they did what he had intended to do for them [that is, to care for them] if he could have had his own way."

* * *

Several entries in the journal of Mrs. Mary Jones during January, 1865, taken together, reveal the deepening despair and sense of abandonment and betrayal:

> [Jan. 6, 1865.] The people are all idle on the plantations, most of them seeking their own pleasure. Many servants have proven faithful, others false and rebellious against all authority and restraint. Susan, a Virginia Negro and nurse to my little Mary Ruth, went off with Mac, her husband, to Arcadia the night after the first day the Yankees appeared, with whom she took every opportunity of conversing, informing them that the baby's father was Colonel Jones. She has acted a faithless part as soon as she could. Porter left three weeks since. * * * Gilbert, Flora, Lucy, Tenah, Sue, Rosetta, Fanny, Little Gilbert, Charles, Milton, and Elsie and Kate have been faithful to us. Milton has been a model of fidelity. He will not even converse with the Yankees. * * * His brother, Little Pulaski * * * took himself off a week since.
>
> [Jan. 21, 1865.] Kate daughter's servant who has been cooking for us, took herself off today, influenced, as we believe, by her father. Sent for cook Kate to Arcadia. She refuses to come.
>
> Their condition is one of perfect anarchy and rebellion. They have placed themselves in perfect antagonism to their owners and to all government and control.
>
> [Jan. 24, 1865.] Nearly all the house servants have left their homes, and from most of the plantations they have gone in a body.

* * * After receiving more reports of the awful behavior of trusted servants, Mrs. Mary Jones pronounced herself "thoroughly disgusted with the whole race." By November, 1865, despite continued affectionate references to some of the old servants, she burst out:

> My life long (I mean since I had a home) I have been laboring and caring for them, and since the war have labored with all my might to supply their wants, and expended everything I had upon their support, directly or indirectly; and this is their return.

* * *

> It is impossible to get at any of their intentions, and it is useless to ask them. I see only a dark future for the whole race.

A month later, with cotton stolen, Mrs. Mary Jones's "heart is pained and sickened with their vileness and falsehood in every way. I long to be delivered from the race." * * *

The struggle of the members of the Jones family to keep faith with their past in the face of what they regarded as the most severe provocations emerges from two letters with which we may close our account of them. Charles C. Jones wrote to his mother from New York in May, 1866:

> I regret deeply to hear that you have been subjected to "severe trials" at Montevideo, and heartily unite with you in the hope that they are now overpassed. The transition in the status of the Negro has been such a marked and violent one that we cannot wonder that he does not at once adapt himself rationally and intelligently to the change. He has always been a child in intellect-improvident, incapable of appreciating the obligations of a contract, ignorant of the operation of any law other than the will of his master, careless of the future, and without the most distant conception of the duties of life and labor now devolved upon him. Time alone can impart the necessary intelligence; and the fear of the law, as well as kindness and instruction, must unite in compelling an appreciation and discharge of the novel duties and responsibilities resting upon him.

But his mother had remained on the plantation and could not manage to be quite so philosophical. On May 28, she replied with news about a strike over contract terms that had been put down by Federal troops:

> I have told the people that in doubting my word they have offered me the greatest insult I ever received in my life; that I had considered them friends and treated them as such, giving them gallons of clabber every day and syrup once a week with rice and extra dinners; but that now they were only laborers under contract, and only the law would rule between us, and I would require every one of them to come up to the mark in their duty on the plantation. The effect has been decided, and I am not sorry for the position we hold mutually. They have relieved me of the constant desire and effort to do something to promote their comfort. * * *

Everything lies bare in these letters and in numerous others like them. The "ingratitude" of the blacks. But then, we must try to understand that their condition opens them to temptation and error. Still, how could they do this to us? What about Cato—a favorite, wonderful at ingratiating himself? Why was he the one to stir up trouble among the slaves so much earlier than the bad characters among them? They are hateful. But we cannot hate them, for we are good Christians. And, they really still do love us. Of course they do-some of them. They must. They are confused. They will come to their senses. Some of the old affection remains. How are we supposed to live without it? They do love us, in their own irritating childish, perverse way. The ungrateful wretches. What can they be thinking of? What is in their enigmatic heads? * * *

* * *

* * * Three ex-slaves from Texas said their own piece, in terms essentially the same as those used everywhere else. Anderson Edwards had been a slave on a small unit of three black families. His master had treated them with kindness and as part of his own family but could not cope with their emancipation. "Gawd," he exploded, "never did 'tend to free niggers.' " Isaac Martin described how his master grieved himself to death, although his own slaves had remained loyal and had cried when freedom came. And Anne Miller watched her master go mad when emancipation came. He left the area, screaming that he would not live in a country in which blacks were free. A year later he committed suicide.

The blacks knew what they saw. They saw the trauma and often felt compassion despite their determination to assert themselves. Jane Simpson of Kentucky was stern: "I never heard of white folks giving niggers nothing. * * * Dey was so mad 'cause dey had to set 'em free, dey just stayed mean as dey would allow 'em to be anyhow, and is yet, most of 'em." Willis of Georgia, who had been foreman of a plow gang, recalled that he had wanted to stay with his former master but that his wife had insisted on leaving. Naturally, he chose his wife. But his master had trouble understanding the decision. He burst out crying: "I didn't thought I could raise up a darkey dat would talk dataway." Robert Falls of Tennessee told of his good master's announcement that his slaves had been freed:

> "Sit down there all of you and listen to what I got to tell you. I hates to do it but I must. Youall ain't my niggers no more. You is free. Just as free as I am. Here I have raised you all to work for me, and now you are going to leave me. I am an old man, and I can't get along without you. I don't know what I am going to do." Well, sir, it killed him. He was dead in less than ten months.

The Memphis Argus, a conservative southern newspaper, summed up part of the story in 1865:

> The events of the last five years have produced an entire revolution in the social system of the entire Southern country. The old arrangement of things is broken up. The relation of master and servant is severed. Doubt and uncertainty pervade the mind of both. * * * The transition state of the African from the condition of slaves to that of freemen has placed him in a condition where he cannot avoid being suspicious of his newly acquired privilege of freedom. He looks with a jealous eye upon anything like an encroachment on what he esteems

> his rights. * * * We fear that too many of the former masters of the negro, forced by the events of a mighty revolution to relinquish their rights in the persons of slaves as property, do it with a bitter reluctance, amounting to absolute hatred.

* * *

For many, the old paternalism died hard. * * *

But for many, especially those whose spirit had shaped the old ruling class, the defection of so many blacks had spelled the end. No matter that 80 percent or more had stood fast. More would have gone if they had had the chance or the courage. Many others wisely waited for the end of the war to go their own way. They were faithless. The "loyalty" of the many could never, in any case, have compensated for the "betrayal" of so many trusted others. Betrayal! For that was the point. The slaveholders had been deserted in their time of need. Abandoned. * * *

The old paternalistic sensibility, in its best and basest manifestations, withered. In some cases it died quickly, with screams of most foul and bloody murder; in others, it declined slowly, with brave attempts to forget and forgive or with pathetic groans. To a decreasing extent it lingered on well into the twentieth century * * *.

The temper of the times may be discerned in a deposition filed by a Louisiana planter with the Union army: "When I owned niggers, I used to pay medical bills. I do not think I shall trouble myself." * * *

And above all, it may be discerned in a letter to the New York Tribune, written in 1865 by Augustin L. Taveau of Charleston, South Carolina * * * :

> Apart from religious considerations, by the loss of the cause and the institution I have suffered like the rest, yet am I content, for the conduct of the Negro in the late crisis of our affairs has convinced me that we were all laboring under a delusion. Good masters and bad masters all alike, shared the same fate—the sea of the Revolution confounded good and evil; and, in the chaotic turbulence, all suffer in degree. Born and raised amid the institution, like a great many others, I believed it was necessary, to our welfare, if not to our very existence. I believed that these people were content, happy, and attached to their masters. But events and reflection have caused me to change these opinions; for if they were necessary to our welfare, why were four-fifths of the plantations of the Southern States dilapidated caricatures of that elegance and neatness which adorn the Country-seats of other people? If as a matter of profit they were so valuable, why was it that nine-tenths of our planters were always in debt and at the mercy of their factors? If they were content, happy and attached to their masters, why did they desert him in the moment of

his need and flock to an enemy, whom they did not know; and thus left their perhaps really good masters whom they did know from infancy?

NOTES AND QUESTIONS

1. On the notion that slaves were simply considered members of the "household" of their owners, see also Elizabeth Fox–Genovese, Within the Plantation Household: Black and White Women of the Old South 37–99 (1988). What do you infer about this from Genovese's own description of the way masters behaved following the Civil War and the emancipation of their slaves? Still, Genovese seems to argue that the plantation owners were deluding themselves about the nature of their "organic" relationship with their slaves, but do you read his data in the same way? One means of gaining further perspective on this question–just what was the nature of the relationship between slaveowner and slave—is to study the "Slave Narratives," the recorded remembrances of slaves, which sometimes took the form of autobiographies, and other times were in the form of recollections given to third party recorders. These Slave Narratives have the advantage of reflecting first-hand experience, but they must be read cautiously, since human memory is not completely accurate. Still, many of them are striking in the manner that they reflect the humanity and the paradoxes that both masters and their slaves exhibited in the ante-bellum South.

Most historians of slavery now champion the use of the slave narratives as both appropriate and necessary to paint a complete and historically accurate picture of the "peculiar institution." Among other things, slave narratives can demonstrate how "stories become the appropriate vehicle for analyzing moral/ethical dilemmas." See Nancy L. Cook, Symposium on Law, Literature and the Humanities: Outside the Tradition: Literature as Legal Scholarship: The Call to Stories: Speaking In and About Stories, 63 U. Cin. L. Rev. 95, 99 (1994). See also, Jerome McCristal Culp, Jr., Response: Telling a Black Legal Story: Privilege, Authenticity, "Blunders," and Transformation in Outsider Narratives, 82 Va. L. Rev. 69 (1994). More importantly, perhaps, the slave narratives aspire to "put a human face on an inhuman social system that ended in the United States not so many generations ago." See Ira Berlin, et al., Remembering Slavery xlvii (1998). Most importantly, slave narratives have contributed to an emerging revisionist account of slavery. In an earlier period, it was not uncommon for slaves to be thought of as passive, simple, and child-like beings. This view has given way to an understanding that the slaves had their own active and complex culture. On the emergence of these revisionist views see, e.g., Thomas D. Russell, A New Image of the Slave Auction: An Empirical Look at the Role of Law in Slave Sales and a Conceptual Reevaluation of Slave Property, 18 Cardozo L. Rev. 473, 492 (1996). See also Guyora Binder, Did the Slaves Author the Thirteenth Amendment? An Essay in Redemptive History, 5 Yale J.L. & Human. 471 (1993), and James Oliver Horton, Links to Bondage: Northern Free Blacks and the Underground Railroad, 24 Rutgers L.J. 667 (1993).

2. The slave narratives, in particular, offer some rebuttal to the claim of John C. Calhoun and others that the lot of slaves was a relatively happy one, and help us understand something about the interaction between plantation life and the law. One of the best narratives for this purpose is that of Solomon Northrup, Twelve Years a Slave, originally published in 1853, and now widely available in an edition prepared by Sue Eakin & Joseph Logsdon (L.S.U. Press, 1968, paperback edition available). Northrup was a free Black living in New York, who was enticed to come to Washington, D.C., and was there drugged, and sold into slavery. He labored in Louisiana for twelve years until he was able to make contact with friends in New York, who travelled to Louisiana, and, using the Louisiana and New York legal institutions, gained his freedom. The facts of Northrup's account have been corroborated to an extent that virtually all commentators on slavery accept it as authentic, although the actual words of the narrative are probably often those of a New York lawyer and novelist named David Wilson, who seems to have served as Northrup's ghostwriter. One main theme of Northrup's account is his suggestion that slavery could never be an acceptable system. Replying to Calhoun and those like him, Northrup states "I came not to the conclusion, even once, that the southern slave, fed, clothed, whipped and protected by his master, is happier than the free colored citizen of the North. To that conclusion I have never since arrived. There are many, however, even in the Northern States, benevolent and well-disposed men, who will pronounce my opinion erroneous, and gravely proceed to substantiate the assertion with an argument. Alas! They have never drunk, as I have from the bitter cup of slavery." Northrup, Twelve Years a Slave, at 88 (Hereafter cited as "Northrup." Citations are to the 1968 edition of the 1853 work). As you read the four narratives which follow, bear in mind Northrup's comments, see whether the experience of slavery they describe is that of the institution described by Calhoun, by Stampp, or by Genovese.

3. The first of the slave narratives that we will consider is that of Frederick Douglass, from one of his celebrated autobiographies. His "Narrative" is one of the most famous and frequently republished, and these excerpts are taken from a posting on the Internet of Douglass's Chapter X, from a Website maintained by the University of Southern California:

http://www.usc.edu/isd/archives/ethnicstudies/historicdocs/Douglass/douglass_chap10.txt. The Douglass materials also can be found at pages 293–299 in Henry Louis Gates, Jr., ed. The Classic Slave Narratives (1987), a widely-available paperback.

4. Following Douglass's, the next three narratives are from the collection put together by the Federal Writers Project during the Great Depression, and subsequently published, in edited form, in the book, Lay My Burden Down: A Folk History of Slavery, edited by B.A. Botkin, first published in 1945, by the University of Chicago Press. Lay My Burden Down has been republished subsequently by the University of Georgia Press (1989), and by Dell Publishing (1994), from which edition these excerpts are taken. They appear with the permission of the University of Georgia Press. Another use-

ful collection of excerpts from the slave narratives (with accompanying recordings) is Ira Berlin, Marc Favreau, and Steven F. Miller, eds. Remembering Slavery (New Press, in association with the Library of Congress, 1998).

NARRATIVE OF THE LIFE OF FREDERICK DOUGLASS, AN AMERICAN SLAVE (1845)

Chapter 10.

* * *

If at any one time of my life more than another, I was made to drink the bitterest dregs of slavery, that time was during the first six months of my stay with Mr. Covey. [Mr. Covey was a relatively pecunious farmer with the reputation of a "slave-breaker," to whom recalcitrant slaves were sent to become more docile. Douglas was leased to Covey by his master, Thomas, with this purpose in mind.–Ed.] We were worked in all weathers. It was never too hot or too cold; it could never rain, blow, hail, or snow, too hard for us to work in the field. Work, work, work, was scarcely more the order of the day than of the night. The longest days were too short for him, and the shortest nights too long for him. I was somewhat unmanageable when I first went there, but a few months of this discipline tamed me. Mr. Covey succeeded in breaking me. I was broken in body, soul, and spirit. My natural elasticity was crushed, my intellect languished, the disposition to read departed, the cheerful spark that lingered about my eye died; the dark night of slavery closed in upon me; and behold a man transformed into a brute!

Sunday was my only leisure time. I spent this in a sort of beast-like stupor, between sleep and wake, under some large tree. At times I would rise up, a flash of energetic freedom would dart through my soul, accompanied with a faint beam of hope, that flickered for a moment, and then vanished. I sank down again, mourning over my wretched condition. I was sometimes prompted to take my life, and that of Covey, but was prevented by a combination of hope and fear. My sufferings on this plantation seem now like a dream rather than a stern reality.

* * *

I have already intimated that my condition was much worse, during the first six months of my stay at Mr. Covey's, than in the last six. The circumstances leading to the change in Mr. Covey's course toward me form an epoch in my humble history. You have seen how a man was made a slave; you shall see how a slave was made a man. On one of the hottest days of the month of August, 1833, Bill Smith, William Hughes, a slave named Eli, and myself, were engaged in fanning wheat. Hughes was clearing the fanned wheat from before the fan. Eli was turning, Smith was feeding, and I was carrying wheat to the fan. The work was simple, requiring strength rather than intellect; yet, to one entirely unused to such work, it came very hard. About three o'clock of that day, I broke down; my strength failed me; I was seized with a violent aching of the head, attended with extreme dizziness; I trembled in every limb. Finding what was coming, I nerved myself up, feeling it would never do to stop work. I stood as long as I could stagger to the hopper with grain. When I could stand no longer, I fell, and felt as if held down by an immense weight. The fan of course stopped; every one had his own work to do; and no one could do the work of the other, and have his own go on at the same time.

Mr. Covey was at the house, about one hundred yards from the treading-yard where we were fanning. On hearing the fan stop, he left immediately, and came to the spot where we were. He hastily inquired what the matter was. Bill answered that I was sick, and there was no one to bring wheat to the fan. I had by this time crawled away under the side of the post and rail-fence by which the yard was enclosed, hoping to find relief by getting out of the sun. He then asked where I was. He was told by one of the hands. He came to the spot, and, after looking at me awhile, asked me what was the matter. I told him as well as I could, for I scarce had strength to speak. He then gave me a savage kick in the side, and told me to get up. I tried to do so, but fell back in the attempt. He gave me another kick, and again told me to rise. I again tried, and succeeded in gaining my feet; but, stooping to get the tub with which I was feeding the fan, I again staggered and fell. While down in this situation, Mr. Covey took up the hickory slat with which Hughes had been striking off the half-bushel measure, and with it gave me a heavy blow upon the head, making a large wound, and the blood ran freely; and with this again told me to get up. I made no effort to comply, having now made up my mind to let him do his worst. In a short time after receiving this blow, my head grew better.

Mr. Covey had now left me to my fate. At this moment I resolved, for the first time, to go to my master, enter a complaint, and ask his protection. In order to do this, I must that afternoon walk seven miles; and this, under the circumstances, was truly a severe undertaking. I was exceedingly feeble; made so as much by the kicks and blows which I received, as by the severe fit of sickness to which I had been subjected. I, however, watched my chance, while Covey was looking in an opposite direction, and started for St. Michael's. I succeeded in getting a considerable distance on my way to the woods, when Covey discovered me, and called after me to come back, threatening what he would do if I did not come. I disregarded both his calls and his threats, and made my way to the woods as fast as my feeble state would allow; and thinking I might be over-hauled by him if I kept the road, I walked through the woods, keeping far enough from the road to avoid detection, and near enough to prevent losing my way.

I had not gone far before my little strength again failed me. I could go no farther. I fell down, and lay for a considerable time. The blood was yet oozing from the wound on my head. For a time I thought I should bleed to death; and think now that I should have done so, but that the blood so matted my hair as to stop the wound. After lying there about three quarters of an hour, I nerved myself up again, and started on my way, through bogs and briers, barefooted and bareheaded, tearing my feet sometimes at nearly every step; and after a journey of about seven miles, occupying some five hours to perform it, I arrived at master's store. I then presented an appearance enough to affect any but a heart of iron. From the crown of my head to my feet, I was covered with blood. My hair was all clotted with dust and blood; my shirt was stiff with blood. I suppose I looked like a man who had escaped a den of wild beasts, and barely escaped them.

In this state I appeared before my master, humbly entreating him to interpose his authority for my protection. I told him all the circumstances as well as I could, and it seemed, as I spoke, at times to affect him. He would then walk the floor, and seek to justify Covey by saying he expected I deserved it. He asked me what I wanted. I told him, to let me get a new home; that as sure as I lived with Mr. Covey again, I should live with but to die with him; that Covey would surely kill me; he was in a fair way for it. Master Thomas ridiculed the idea that there was any danger of Mr. Covey's killing me, and said that he knew Mr. Covey; that he was a good man, and that he could not think of taking me from him; that, should he do so, he would lose the whole year's wages; that I belonged to Mr. Covey for one year, and that I must go back to him, come what might; and that I must not trouble him with any more stories, or that he would himself *get hold of me*. After threatening me thus, he gave me a very large dose of salts, telling me that I might remain in St. Michael's that night, (it being quite late,) but that I must be off back to Mr. Covey's early in the morning; and that if I did not, he would *get hold of me*, which meant that he would whip me.

I remained all night, and, according to his orders, I started off to Covey's in the morning, (Saturday morning,) wearied in body and broken in spirit. I got no supper that night, or breakfast that morning. I reached Covey's about nine o'clock; and just as I was getting over the fence that divided Mrs. Kemp's fields from ours, out ran Covey with his cowskin, to give me another whipping. Before he could reach me, I succeeded in getting to the cornfield; and as the corn was very high, it afforded me the means of hiding. He seemed very angry, and searched for me a long time. My behavior was altogether unaccountable. He finally gave up the chase, thinking, I suppose, that I must come home for something to eat; he would give himself no further trouble in looking for me. I spent that day mostly in the woods, having the alternative before me,—to go home and be whipped to death, or stay in the woods and be starved to death.

That night, I fell in with Sandy Jenkins, a slave with whom I was somewhat acquainted. Sandy had a free wife who lived about four miles from Mr. Covey's; and it being Saturday, he was on his way to see her. I told him my circumstances, and he very kindly invited me to go home with him. I went home with him, and talked this whole matter over, and got his advice as to what course it was best for me to pursue. I found Sandy an old adviser. He told me, with great solemnity, I must go back to Covey; but that before I went, I must go with him into another part of the woods, where there was a certain *root*, which, if I would take some of it with me, carrying it *always on my right side*, would render it impossible for Mr. Covey, or any other white man, to whip me. He said he had carried it for years; and since he had done so, he had never received a blow, and never expected to while he carried it. I at first rejected the idea, that the simple carrying of a root in my pocket would have any such effect as he had said, and was not disposed to take it; but Sandy impressed the necessity with much earnestness, telling me it could do no harm, if it did no good. To please him, I at length took the root, and, according to his direction, carried it upon my right side.

This was Sunday morning. I immediately started for home; and upon entering the yard gate, out came Mr. Covey on his way to meeting. He spoke to me very kindly, bade me drive the pigs from a lot near by, and passed on towards the church. Now, this singular conduct of Mr. Covey really made me begin to think that there was some-thing in the *root* which Sandy had given me; and had it been on any other day than Sunday, I could have attributed the conduct to no other cause than the influence of that root; and as it was, I was half inclined to think the *root* to be something more than I at first had taken it to be.

All went well till Monday morning. On this morning, the virtue of the *root* was fully tested. Long before daylight, I was called to go and rub, curry, and feed, the horses. I obeyed, and was glad to obey. But whilst thus engaged, whilst in the act of throwing down some blades from the loft, Mr. Covey entered the stable with a long rope; and just as I was half out of the loft, he caught hold of my legs, and was about tying me. As soon as I found what he was up to, I gave a sudden spring, and as I did so, he holding to my legs, I was brought sprawling on the stable floor.

Mr. Covey seemed now to think he had me, and could do what he pleased; but at this moment—from whence came the spirit I don't know—I resolved to fight; and, suiting my action to the resolution, I seized Covey hard by the throat; and as I did so, I rose. He held on to me, and I to him. My resistance was so entirely unexpected that Covey seemed taken all aback. He trembled like a leaf. This gave me assurance, and I held him uneasy, causing the blood to run where I touched him with the ends of my fingers. Mr. Covey soon called out to Hughes for help.

Hughes came, and, while Covey held me, attempted to tie my right hand. While he was in the act of doing so, I watched my chance, and gave him a heavy kick close under the ribs. This kick fairly sickened Hughes, so that he left me in the hands of Mr. Covey. This kick had the effect of not only weakening Hughes, but Covey also. When he saw Hughes bending over with pain, his courage quailed. He asked me if I meant to persist in my resistance. I told him I did, come what might; that he had used me like a brute for six months, and that I was determined to be used so no longer. With that, he strove to drag me to a stick that was lying just out of the stable door. He meant to knock me down. But just as he was leaning over to get the stick, I seized him with both hands by his collar, and brought him by a sudden snatch to the ground.

By this time, Bill came. Covey called upon him for assistance. Bill wanted to know what he could do. Covey said, "Take hold of him, take hold of him!" Bill said his master hired him out to work, and not to help to whip me; so he left Covey and myself to fight our own battle out. We were at it for nearly two hours. Covey at length let me go, puffing and blowing at a great rate, saying that if I had not resisted, he would not have whipped me half so much. The truth was, that he had not whipped me at all. I considered him as getting entirely the worst end of the bargain; for he had drawn no blood from me, but I had from him. The whole six months afterwards, that I spent with Mr. Covey, he never laid the weight of his finger upon me in anger. He would occasionally say, he didn't want to get hold of me again. "No," thought I, "you need not; for you will come off worse than you did before."

This battle with Mr. Covey was the turning-point in my career as a slave. It rekindled the few expiring embers of freedom, and revived within me a sense of my own manhood. It recalled the departed self-confidence, and inspired me again with a determination to be free. The gratification afforded by the triumph was a full compensation for whatever else might follow, even death itself. He only can understand the deep satisfaction which I experienced, who has himself repelled by force the bloody arm of slavery. I felt as I never felt before. It was a glorious resurrection, from the tomb of slavery, to the heaven of freedom. My long-crushed spirit rose, cowardice departed, bold defiance took its place; and I now resolved that, however long I might remain a slave in form, the day had passed forever when I could be a slave in fact.

I did not hesitate to let it be known of me, that the white man who expected to succeed in whipping, must also succeed in killing me. From this time I was never again what might be called fairly whipped, though I remained a slave four years afterwards. I had several fights, but was never whipped. It was for a long time a matter of surprise to me why Mr. Covey did not immediately have me taken by the constable to the whipping-post, and there regularly whipped for the crime of raising my hand against a white man in defence of myself. And the only explanation I can now think of does not entirely satisfy me; but such as it is, I will give it. Mr. Covey enjoyed the most unbounded reputation for being a first-rate overseer and negro-breaker. It was of considerable importance to him. That reputation was at stake; and had he sent me—a boy about sixteen years old—to the public whipping-post, his reputation would have been lost; so, to save his reputation, he suffered me to go unpunished.

NOTES AND QUESTIONS

1. Frederick Douglass drew blood when he refused to submit to the chastisement of the man to whom his master had leased him. This should have been a major criminal offense, one, as Stampp tells us, that would have been punished by death in some Southern states. If Douglass is right about the reason that Covey did not have him punished, what does this tell us about the effectiveness of the law of slavery? Does Douglass's behavior suggest the difficulty of maintaining that state of "absolute subordination" slavery is supposed to require? How much use is the law here? Douglass fled his servitude, escaped to the North, and, though a fugitive slave, became one of the most articulate and leading abolitionists. Could it be that his victory over Covey, the act that made him a "man" rather than a slave, made it impossible to keep him in servitude? Why didn't more slaves do what Douglass did? Does Genovese provide an answer? Does Stampp?

2. For further reading on Frederick Douglass see, e.g., Frederick Douglass, Autobiographies (Modern Library Edition, Henry Louis Gates, ed., 1994), Frederick Douglass, The Oxford Frederick Douglass Reader (William S. Andrews, ed. 1997), William S. Andrews, Critical Essays on Frederick Douglass (Critical Essays on American Literature Series, 1991), Narrative of the Life of Frederick Douglass, An American Slave, Written by Himself: Authoritative Text, Contexts, Criticism (Norton Critical Edition, William S. Andrews, William S. McFeeley, eds. 1997), William S. McFeeley, Frederick Douglass (1995).

3. There is a similar story told in Solomon Northrup's narrative of a time when he administered a beating to a person to whom his master had given him to pay off a debt, while still holding a mortgage on the slave [so that he still could be said to be the ultimate owner]. As was true in the case of Douglass, Northrup was never really severely punished for this incredible breach of discipline, nor was the law invoked against him. Instead, when the person to whom the slave had been mortgaged, a man named Tibbets, threatened to kill Northrup for his insolence, Tibbets and his friends were reminded, by another white overseer, one Chapin, that if they destroyed Northrup (whose slave name was "Platt") they would incur his wrath and the wrath of the law:

> Gentlemen, I have a few words to say. You had better listen to them. Whoever moves that slave another foot from where he stands is a dead man. In the first place, he does not deserve this treatment. It is a shame

> to murder him in this manner. I never knew a more faithful boy than Platt. You, Tibbets, are in the fault yourself. You are pretty much of a scoundrel, and I know it, and you richly deserved the flogging you have received [from Platt/Northrup]. In the next place, I have been overseer of this plantation seven years, and in the absence of William Ford [Northrup's owner], am master here. My duty is to protect his interests, and that duty I shall perform. You are not responsible–you are a worthless fellow. Ford holds a mortgage on Platt of four hundred dollars. If you hang him, he loses his debt. Until that is canceled you have no right to take his life. You have no right to take it any way. There is a law for the slave as well as for the white man. You are no better than a murderer.

Northrup, at 83–85. Does this excerpt from Northrup's narrative support Stampp's analysis? Does it help explain why Covey didn't retaliate against Douglass?

TINES KENDRICKS: GEORGIA

Lay my Burden Down, supra, pp. 81–85.

My old marse, Arch Kendricks, I will say this, he certainly was a good fair man. Old Miss and the young marse, Sam, they was strictly tough and, boss, I is telling you the truth, they was cruel. The young marse, Sam, he never taken at all after he pa. He got all he meanness from Old Miss, and he sure got plenty of it, too. Old Miss, she cuss and rare worse'n a man. "Way 'fore day she be up hollering loud enough for to be heared two miles, 'rousing the niggers out for to git in the fields ever 'for light. Marse Sam, he stand by the pots handing out the grub and giving out the bread, and he cuss loud and say: 'Take a sop of that grease on your hoecake and move along fast 'fore I lashoo you.' " Marse Sam, he was a big man too, that he was. He was nigh on to six and a half feet tall. Boss, he certainly was a child of the devil. All the cooking in them days was done in pots hanging on the pot racks. They never had no stoves enduring the times what I is telling you 'bout. At times they would give us enough to eat. At times they wouldn't—just 'cording to how they feeling when they dishing out the grub. The biggest what they would give the field hands to eat would be the truck what us had on the place, like greens, turnips, peas, side meat, and they sure would cut the side meat awful thin too, boss. Us always had a heap of corn-meal dumplings and hoecakes. Old Miss, her and Marse Sam, they real stingy. You better not leave no grub on your plate for to throw away. You sure better eat it all iffen you like it or no. Old Miss and Marse Sam, they the real bosses, and they was wicked. I's telling you the truth, they was. Old Marse, he didn't have much to say 'bout the running of the place or the handling of the niggers. You know, all the property and all the niggers belonged to Old Miss. She got all that from her peoples. That what they left to her on their death. She the real owner of everything.

Just to show you, boss, how 'twas with Marse Sam and how contrary and factious and wicked that young white man was, I wants to tell you 'bout the time that Aunt Hannah's little boy Mose died. Mose, he sick 'bout a week. Aunt Hannah, she try to doctor on him and git him well, and she tell Old Miss that she think Mose bad off and ought to have the doctor. Old Miss she wouldn't git the doctor. She say Mose ain't sick much, and bless my soul, Aunt Hannah she right. In a few days from then Mose is dead. Marse Sam, he come cussing and told Gabe to get some planks and make the coffin and sont some of them to dig the grave over there on the far side of the place where they had a burying-ground for the niggers. Us toted the coffin over to where the grave was dug and gwine bury little Mose there, and Uncle Billy Jordan, he was there and begun to sing and pray and have a kind of funeral at the burying. Everyone was moaning and singing and praying, and Marse Sam hear 'em and come sailing over there on he hoss and lit right in to cussing and raring and say that if they don't hurry and bury that nigger and shut up that singing and carrying on, he gwine lash every one of them, and then he went to cussing worser and 'busing Uncle Billy Jordan. He say iffen he ever hear of him doing any more preaching or praying round 'mongst the niggers at the graveyard or anywheres else, he gwine lash him to death. No, sir, boss, Marse Sam wouldn't even 'low no preaching or singing or nothing like that. He was wicked. I tell you he was.

* * *

Before the war broke out, I can 'member there was some few of the white folks what said that niggers ought to be sot free, but there was just one now and then that took that stand. One of them that I 'member was the Rev. Dickey what was the parson for a big crowd of the white peoples in that part of the county. Rev. Dickey, he preached freedom for the niggers and say that they all should be sot free and gived a home and a mule. That preaching the Rev. Dickey done sure did rile up the folks—that is, the most of them, like the Kendricks and Mr. Eldredge and Dr. Murcheson and Nat Walker and such as them what was the biggest of the slaveowners. Right away after Rev. Dickey done such preaching, they fired him from the church and 'bused him, and some of them say they gwine hang him to a limb or either gwine ride him on a rail out of the country. Sure enough, they made it so hot on that man he have to leave clean out of the state, so I heared. No, sir, boss, they say they ain't gwine divide up on land with the niggers or give them no home or mule or their freedom or nothing. They say they will wade knee deep in blood and die first.

* * *

It was this way, boss, how come me to be in the war. You see, they 'quired all of the slaveowners to send so many niggers to the army to work digging the trenches and throwing up the breastworks and repairing the railroads what the Yankees done 'stroyed. Every marse was 'quired to send one nigger for every ten that he had. * * * I was one of them that my marse 'quired to send. That was the worst times that this here nigger ever seen, and the way them white men drive us niggers, it was something awful. The strap, it was going from 'fore day till 'way after night. The niggers, heaps of 'em, just fall in they tracks–give out–and them white men laying the strap on they backs without ceasting. That was 'zacly way it was with them niggers like me what was in the army work. I had to stand it, boss, till the war was over.

* * *

Slavery time was tough, boss. You just don't know how tough it was. I can't 'splain to you just how bad all the niggers want to get they freedom. With the free niggers it was just the same as it was with them that was in bondage. You know there was some few free niggers in that time even 'fore the slaves taken outen bondage. It was really worse on them than it was with them what wasn't free. The slaveowners, they just despised them free niggers and make it just as hard on them as they can. They couldn't get no work from nobody. Wouldn't ary man hire 'em or give 'em any work at all. So because they was up against it and never had any money or nothing, the white folks make these free niggers 'sess the taxes. And 'cause they never had no money for to pay the tax with, they was put up on the block by the court man or the sheriff and sold out to somebody for enough to pay the tax what they say they owe. So they keep these free niggers hired out all the time 'most, working for to pay the taxes. I 'member one of them free niggers mighty well. He was called Free Sol. He had him a little home and a old woman and some boys. They was kept bounded out nigh 'bout all the time working for to pay they tax. Yes, sir, boss, it was heap more better to be a slave nigger than a free one. And it was really a heavenly day when the freedom come for the race.

In the time of slavery another thing what make it tough on the niggers was them times when a man and he wife and their children had to be taken 'way from one another. This separation might be brung 'bout 'most any time for one thing or another, such as one or t'other, the man or the wife, be sold off or taken 'way to some other state like Louisiana or Mississippi. Then when a marse die what had a heap of slaves, these slave niggers be divided up 'mongst the marse's children or sold off for to pay the marse's debts. Then at times when a man married to a woman that don't belong to the same marse what he do, then they is liable to git divided up and separated 'most any day. They was heaps of nigger families that I know what was separated in the time of bondage that tried to find they folkses what was gone. But the mostest of 'em never git together again even after they sot free 'cause they don't know where one or the other is.

After the war over and the slaves taken out of they bondage, some of the very few white folks give them niggers what they liked the best, a small piece of land for to work. But the mostest of them never give 'em nothing, and they sure despise them niggers what left 'em. Us old marse say he want to 'range with all his niggers to stay on with him, that he gwine give 'em a mule and a piece-a ground. But us know that Old Miss ain't gwine agree to that. And sure enough she wouldn't. I's telling you the truth, every nigger on that place left. They sure done that; and Old Marse and Old Miss, they never had a hand left there on that great big place, and all that ground laying out.

The government seen to it that all of the white folks had to make contracts with the niggers that stuck with 'em and they was sure strict 'bout that too. The white folks at first didn't want to make the contracts and say they wasn't gwine to. So the government filled the jail with 'em, and after that everyone make the contract.

When my race first got they freedom and begin to leave they marses, a heap of the marses got raging mad and just tore up truck. They say they gwine kill every nigger they find. Some of them did do that very thing, boss, sure enough. I's telling you the truth. They shot niggers down by the hundreds. They just wasn't gwine let 'em enjoy their freedom. That is the truth, boss.

NOTES AND QUESTIONS

1. Does the system that Tines Kendricks describes sound like the one John C. Calhoun championed? Note the horrific system of discipline imposed by the wicked son and his mother, and the ineffective head of the family who was unable to ameliorate the discipline. Is this patriarchy, or something else? It is often said that the common law system of the nineteenth century gave women no property rights. Does Kendricks's narrative suggest other possibilities? Note also that Kendricks seems to suggest that the desire for freedom was never absent from the slaves, even though they could see that the lot of free blacks was not a pleasant one. How do you explain this?

2. Solomon Northrup's narrative also deals with the effect of slavery on the children of slaveowners. He poignantly describes how a cruel slaveowner to whom he was eventually sold passed on his views to his son:

> Young Master Epps possessed some noble qualities, yet no process of reasoning could lead him to comprehend, that in the eye of the Almighty there is no distinction of color. He looked upon the black man simply as an animal, differing in no respect from any other animal, save in the gift of speech and the possession of somewhat higher instincts, and therefore the more valuable. To work like his father's mules—to be whipped and kicked and scourged through life—to address the white man with hat in hand, and eyes bent servilely on the earth, in his mind, was the natural and proper destiny of the slave. Brought up with such ideas—in the no-

tion that we [slaves] stand without the pale of humanity—no wonder the oppressors of my people are a pitiless and unrelenting race.

Northrup, supra, at 201–202. As did Kendricks, Northrup also gives an account of a white man living in the South who argued for the freedom of slaves, but who was regarded as a curiosity at best and a fool at worst by his fellow whites. Id., at 205–207.

CATO _______: ALABAMA

Lay My Burden Down, supra, pp. 94–99.

* * *

Back in Alabama, Missy Angela took me when I was past my creeping days to live in the big house with the white folks. I had a room built on the big house, where I stayed, and they was always good to me, 'cause I's one of their blood. They never hit me a lick or slapped me once, and they told me they'd never sell me away from them. They was the best-quality white folks and lived in a big, two-story house with a big hall what run all the way through the house. They wasn't rough as some white folks on their niggers.

* * *

Talking 'bout victuals, our eating was good. Can't say the same for all places. Some of the plantations half-starved their niggers and 'lawanced out their eating till they wasn't fitting for work. They had to slip about to niggers on other places to piece out their meals. They had field calls and other kinds of whoops and hollers, what had a meaning to 'em.

* * *

I was trained for a houseboy and to tend the cows. The bears was so bad then, a 'sponsible person who could carry a gun had to look after them.

My massa used to give me a little money * * * to buy what I wanted. I always bought fine clothes. In the summer when I was a little one, I wore lowerings, like the rest of the niggers. That was things made from cotton sacking. Most of the boys wore shirttails till they was big yearlings. When they bought me red russets from the town, I cried and cried. I didn't want to wear no rawhide shoes. So they took 'em back. They had a weakness for my crying. I did have plenty fine clothes, good woolen suits they spinned on the place, and doeskins and fine linens. I druv in the carriage with the white folks and was 'bout the most dudish nigger in them parts.

* * *

They whupped the women and they whupped the mens. I used to work some in the tannery, and we made the whups. They'd tie them down to a stob, and give 'em the whupping. Some niggers, it taken four men to whup 'em, but they got it. The nigger driver was meaner than the white folks. They'd better not leave a blade of grass in the rows. I seed 'em beat a nigger half a day to make him 'fess up to stealing a sheep or a shoat. Or they'd whup 'em for running away, but not so hard if they came back of their own 'cordance when they got hungry and sick in the swamps. But when they had to run 'em down with the nigger dogs, they'd git in bad trouble.

My massa never did have any real 'corrigible niggers, but I heard of 'em plenty on other places. When they was real 'corrigible, the white folks said they was like mad dogs and didn't mind to kill them so much as killing a sheep. They'd take 'em to the graveyard and shoot 'em down and bury 'em face downward with their shoes on. I never seed it done, but they made some the niggers go for a lesson to them that they could git the same.

But I didn't even have to carry a pass to leave my own place, like the other niggers. I had a cap with a sign on it: "Don't bother this nigger, or there will be hell to pay." I went after the mail, in the town. It come in coaches and they put on fresh hosses at Pineapple. The coachman run the hosses into Pineapple with a big to-do and blowing the bugle to get the fresh hosses ready. I got the mail. I was a trusty all my days and never been 'rested by the law to this day.

I never had no complaints for my treatment, but some the niggers hated syrup-making time, 'cause when they had to work till midnight making syrup, it's four o'clock up, just the same. Sunup to sundown was for field niggers.

* * *

'Course niggers had their serious side, too. They loved to go to church and had a little log chapel for worship. But I went to the white folks' church. In the chapel some nigger mens preached from the Bible but couldn't read a line no more than a sheep could. My white folks didn't mind their niggers praying and singing hymns, but some places wouldn't 'low them to worship a-tall, and they had to put their heads in pots to sing or pray.

Most the niggers I know, who had their marriage put in the book, did it after the breaking-up, plenty after they had growed children. When they got married on the places, mostly they just jumped over a broom and that made 'em married. Sometimes * * * the white folks read a little out of the Scriptures to 'em and they felt more married.

* * *

They used to cry the niggers off just like so much cattle, and we didn't think no different of it. I seed them put them on the block and brag on them something big. Everybody liked to hear them cry off niggers. The crier was a clown and made funny talk and kept everybody laughing.

When Massa and the other mens on the place went off to war, he called me and said, "Cato, you's always been a 'sponsible man, and I leave you to look after the women and the place. If I don't come back, I want you to always stay by Missy Angela!" I said, "Fore God, I will, Massa Cal." He said, "Then I can go away peaceable."

* * *

Massa Cal come back, and he was all wore out and ragged. He soon called all the niggers to the front yard and says, "Mens and womens, you are today as free as I am. You are free to do as you like 'cause the damned Yankees done 'creed you are. They ain't a nigger on my place what was born here or ever lived here who can't stay here and work and eat to the end of his days, as long as this old place will raise peas and goobers. Go if you wants, and stay if you wants." Some of the niggers stayed and some went, and some what had run away to the North came back. They always called, real humble-like, at the back gate to Missy Angela, and she always fixed it up with Massa Cal they could have a place.

Near the close of the war I seed some folks leaving for Texas. They said if the Federals won the war, they'd have to live in Texas to keep slaves. So plenty started drifting their slaves to the West. They'd pass with the womens riding in the wagons and the mens on foot. Some took slaves to Texas after the Federals done 'creed the breaking-up.

Long as I lived, I minded what my white folks told me, 'cept one time. They was a nigger working in the field, and he kept jerking the mules and massa Cal got mad, and he give me a gun and said, "Go out there and kill that man." I said, "Massa Cal, please don't tell me that. I ain't never kilt nobody, and I don't want to." He said, "Cato, you do what I tell you." He meant it. I went out to the nigger and said, "You has got to leave this minute, and I is, too, 'cause I is 'spose to kill you, only I ain't, and Massa Cal will kill me." He drops the harness, and we run and crawled through the fence and ran away.

I hated to go 'cause things was so bad, and flour sold for $25 a barrel, and pickled pork for $15 a barrel. You couldn't buy nothing lessen with gold. I had plenty of 'Federate money, only it wouldn't buy nothing.

But today I is an old man, and my hands ain't stained with no blood. I is always been glad I didn't kill that man.

Mules run to a terrible price then. A right puny pair of mules sold for $500. But the Yankees give me a mule, and I farmed a year for a white man and watched a herd of mules, too. I stayed with them mules till four o'clock even Sundays. So many scoundrels was going 'bout, stealing mules.

That year I was bound out by 'greement with the white man, and I made $360. The bureau came by that year looking at niggers' contracts, to see they didn't git skunt out their rightful wages. My white folks didn't stay mad at me, and every Sunday they come by to see me and brung me little delicate things to eat.

They said a hundred times they regretted they never larned me to read or write, and they said my daddy done put up $500 for me to go to the New Allison school for colored folks. Miss Benson, a Yankee, was the teacher. I was twenty-nine years old and just starting in the blue-back speller. I went to school a while, but one morning at ten o'clock my poor old mammy come by and called me out. She told me she got put out, 'cause she too old to work in the field. I told her not to worry, that I'm the family man now, and she didn't never need to git any more three-quarter hand wages no more.

So I left school and turnt my hand to anything I could find for years. I never had no trouble finding work, 'cause all the white folks knowed Cato was a good nigger. I left my mammy with some fine white folks, and she raised a whole family of children for them. Their name was Bryan, and they lived on a little bayou. Them younguns was crazy 'bout Mammy, and they'd send me word not to worry about her, 'cause she'd have the best of care and when she died they'd tend to her burying.

* * *

NOTES AND QUESTIONS

1. To what extent is the system that Cato describes the same as that Douglass, Northrup, and Kendricks remember? If the North had not won the war and decreed freedom for the slaves, would Cato have been likely to flee, as did Douglass? And yet, what is the meaning of the episode where Cato is asked to kill for his master? What precisely was the relationship that Cato had with "[m]y white folks," as he called them? Both Douglass and Cato were apparently mulattos. Does that tell us anything about their experience in slavery?

2. Cato's experience, perhaps the result of his white parentage, or the kindliness of a particular master, was occasionally shared by Solomon Northrup. In a moving passage of his Narrative, Northrup writes of his first master, Ford:

> In many northern minds, perhaps, the idea of a man holding his brother man in servitude, and the traffic in human flesh, may seem altogether incompatible with their conceptions of a moral or religious life. From descriptions of such men [as the cruel slave-traders Northrup encountered], and others hereinafter mentioned, they are led to dispise and exe-

> crate the whole class of slaveholders indiscriminately. But I was some time his slave, and had an opportunity of learning well his character and disposition, and it is but simple justice to him when I say, in my opinion, there never was a more kind, noble, candid, Christian man than William Ford. The influences and associations that had always surrounded him, blinded him to the inherent wrong at the bottom of the system of Slavery. He never doubted the moral right of one man holding another in subjection. Looking through the same medium with his fathers before him, he saw things in the same light. Brought up under other circumstances and other influences, his notions would undoubtedly have been different. Nevertheless, he was a model master, walking uprightly, according to the light of his understanding, and fortunate was the slave who came to his possession. Were all men such as he, Slavery would be deprived of more than half its bitterness.

Northrup, at 62. Northrup even concludes, with regard to Ford, "During my residence with Master Ford I had seen only the bright side of slavery. His was no heavy hand crushing us to the earth. *He* pointed upwards, and with benign and cheering words addressed us as his fellow-mortals, accountable, like himself, to the Maker of us all. I think of him with affection, and had my family been with me, could have borne his gentle servitude, without murmering, all my days." Id., at 74. Do you understand John C. Calhoun a bit better, now? Compare these last words of Northrup's and those of Cato, with those of the next narrative.

JENNY PROCTOR: ALABAMA

Lay My Burden Down, supra, pp. 99–103.

I's hear tell of them good slave days, but I ain't never seen no good times then. * * * My mother, she was cook, and I don't recollect nothing 'bout my father. If I had any brothers and sisters I didn't know it. We had old ragged huts made out of poles and some of the cracks chinked up with mud and moss and some of them wasn't. We didn't have no good beds, just scaffolds nailed up to the wall out of poles and the old ragged bedding throwed on them. That sure was hard sleeping, but even that feel good to our weary bones after them long hard day's work in the field. * * *

* * *

Weddings? Uh-uh! We just steps over the broom and we's married. Ha! Ha! Ha!

* * *

Sometimes [Old Master] would sell some of the slaves off of that big auction block to the highest bidder when he could git enough for one.

When he go to sell a slave, he feed that one good for a few days, then when he goes to put 'em up on the auction block he takes a meat skin and greases all round that nigger's mouth and makes 'em look like they been eating plenty meat and such like and was good and strong and able to work. Sometimes he sell the babes from the breast, and then again he sell the mothers from the babes and the husbands and the wives, and so on. He wouldn't let 'em holler much when the folks be sold away. He say, "I have you whupped if you don't hush." They sure loved their six children though. They wouldn't want nobody buying them.

We might-a done very well if the old driver hadn't been so mean, but the least little thing we do he beat us for it and put big chains round our ankles and make us work with them on till the blood be cut out all around our ankles. Some of the masters have what they call stockades and puts their heads and feet and arms through holes in a big board out in the hot sun, but our old driver he had a bull pen. That's only thing like a jail he had. When a slave do anything he didn't like, he takes 'em in that bull pen and chains 'em down, face up to the sun, and leaves 'em there till they nearly dies.

None of us was 'lowed to see a book or try to learn. They say we git smarter than they was if we learn anything, but we slips around and gits hold of that Webster's old blue-back speller and we hids it till 'way in the night and then we lights a little pine torch, and studies that spelling book. We learn it too. I can read some now and write a little too.

They wasn't no church for the slaves, but we goes to the white folks' arbor on Sunday evening, and a white man he gits up there to preach to the niggers. He say, "Now I takes my text, which is, Nigger obey your master and your mistress, 'cause what you git from them here in this world am all you ever going to git, 'cause you just like the hogs and the other animals—when you dies you ain't no more, after you been throwed in that hole." I guess we believed that for a while 'cause we didn't have no way finding out different. We didn't see no bibles.

Sometimes a slave would run away and just live wild in the woods, but most times they catch 'em and beats 'em, then chains 'em down in the sun till they nearly die. The only way any slaves on our farm ever goes anywhere was when the boss sends him to carry some news to another plantation or when we slips [away] in the night. Sometimes after all the work was done a bunch would have it made up to slip out down to the creek and dance. We sure have fun when we do that, most times on Saturday night.

* * *

Lord, Lord, honey! It seems impossible that any of us ever lived to see that day of freedom, but thank god we did.

When Old Master comes down in the cotton patch to tell us 'bout being free, he say, "I hates to tell you, but I knows I's got to—you is free, just as free as me or anybody else what's white." We didn't hardly know what he means. We just sort of huddle round together like scared rabbits, but after we knowed what he mean, didn't many of us go, 'cause we didn't know where to of went. Old Master he say he give us the woods land and half of what we make on it, and we could clear it and work it or starve. Well, we didn't know hardly what to do 'cause he just gives us some old dull hoes and axes to work with; but we all went to work, and as we cut down the trees and the poles he tells us to build the fence round the field and we did, and when we plants the corn and the cotton we just plant all the fence corners full too, and I never seen so much stuff grow in all my born days. Several ears of corn to the stalk, and them big cotton stalks was a-laying over on the ground. Some of the old slaves they say they believe the Lord knew something 'bout niggers after all. He lets us put corn in his crib, and then we builds cribs and didn't take long 'fore we could buy some hosses and some mules and some good hogs. Them mangy hogs what our master give us the first year was plumb good hogs after we grease them and scrub them with lye soap. He just give us the ones he thought was sure to die, but we was a-gitting going now, and 'for long we was a-building better houses and feeling kind of happy-like. After Old master dies, we keeps hearing talk of Texas, and me and my old man—I's done been married several years then and had one little boy—well, we gits in our covered wagon with our little mules hitched to it, and we comes to Texas. We worked as sharecroppers around Buffalo, Texas, till my old man he died. My boy was nearly grown then, so he wants to come to San Angelo and work, so here we is. He done been married long time now and git six children. Some of them work at hotels and cafes and filling stations and in homes.

NOTES AND QUESTIONS

1. Jenny Proctor and Cato both lived in antebellum Alabama as slaves, and then both experienced freedom. Did they escape from the same "peculiar institution?" Which of the two had an experience of slavery closer to that which Genovese describes? Is Jenny Proctor's experience consistent with any notion that the law of slavery in the years immediately before the civil war ameliorated the lot of slaves?

2. The role of religion in the lives of the slaves is a complex topic. Jenny Proctor suggests that the White minister told the slaves they could expect no relief in the hereafter, but this was not Solomon Northrup's experience. Here is his description of Sundays with his kind master, Ford:

> [On Sundays] our master would gather all his slaves about him, and read and expound the Scriptures. He sought to inculcate in our minds feelings of kindness towards each other, of dependence upon God—setting forth the rewards promised unto those who lead an upright and prayerful life. Seated in the doorway of his house, surrounded by his man-servants and his maid-servants, who looked earnestly into the good

> man's face, he spoke of the loving kindness of the Creator, and of the life that is to come. Often did the voice of prayer ascend from his lips to heaven, the only sound that broke the solitude of the place.

Northrup, supra, at 69. Ford believed that his slaves would be better off if they were permitted to have the consolation of religion, and he didn't even object to their having Bibles to read. This met with derision from his neighbors. Said Northrup, about one such of Ford's slaves, Sam, who was devoted to his bible, "Sam's piety was frequently observed by white men who came to the mill and the remark it most generally provoked was, that a man like Ford, who allowed his slaves to have Bibles, was 'not fit to own a nigger.' " Id., at 69.

3. Kendricks', Cato's, and Proctor's narratives were gathered many years after the Civil War, but the pre-Civil War narratives, such as Douglass's and Northrup's, tend to tell a similar story, particularly with regard to the use of the lash and the consummate cruelty of the institution. One can find in many of the narratives the notion that the slaves could only be made to produce sufficiently if they were severely whipped. Northrup gives accounts of several masters and overseers who adhered to this practice, but he questions it:

> It is a fact I have more than once observed, that those who treated their slaves most leniently, were rewarded by the greatest amount of labor. I know it from my own experience. It was a source of pleasure to surprise Master Ford with a greater day's work than was required, while, under subsequent [more cruel] masters, there was no prompter to extra effort but the overseer's lash.

Northrup, supra, at 70.

4. In what follows we will consider discussions of the law of slavery in the Courts, both at the state court and federal court level. As you read these cases, once again consider whether the institution described by the judges accords with the institution described by the former slaves themselves, by Calhoun, by Stampp, and by Genovese.

2. SLAVERY IN THE STATE COURTS

ROBERT M. COVER, JUSTICE ACCUSED*

67–75 (1975).

Prior to 1782, manumission of slaves within Virginia, without special act of the legislature, was forbidden. The Quakers, led by Robert Pleasants, mounted a campaign of correspondence to major liberal Virginians

* Reprinted from Justice Accused: Antislavery and the Judicial Process, Copyright 1975 by Yale University, published by the Yale University Press, New Haven and London, with the permission of the publisher and the author.

to change that law. In 1782 these efforts were successful. The Act of 1782 provided:

> That it shall hereafter be lawful for any person by his or her last will and testament, or by any other instrument in writing, under his or her hand and seal attested and proved in the county court by two witnesses, or acknowledged by the party in the court of the county where he or she resides, to emancipate and set free his or her slaves, or any of them. * * *

* * *

* * * Undoubtedly, for many of the moving forces behind the original statute, this act was meant to be only the first step in the gradual vitiation of slavery in Virginia. They hoped that the combined force of private manumission, prohibitions against importation, and public distaste for slavery would lead to withering away of the institution. The cotton gin was still eleven years away, and almost everybody seemed agreed that prohibitions against importation ought to be strictly enforced. The hope for a relatively painless end to slavery was not quixotic. Quakers and others knew that the key to public acceptance of emancipation was public tolerance of the free black. In a real sense, therefore, the private manumission law was a trial balloon. The free black population would increase and with it the opportunity to test public reaction to such a class.

Not all of the support for the Act of 1782 came from those who imperfectly programmed an ultimate emancipation. There were many who simply felt that the property rights of a master ought to extend to the power of liberating his property if he so chose. * * *

In construing this apparently simple statute, courts could choose from a variety of interpretive principles. Clearly, they ought to effectuate legislative intent. However, * * * the larger purposes of the act were not clear. Was this simply tolerance for whim or an invitation to the end of slavery? The courts could also choose to appeal to the normal principles of construction for the instruments of gratuitous transfers: wills and trusts. * * * Appeal to such principles carried with it the question of whether and how the normal limits on the capacity of a testator or settlor would be effectuated. Were there public policy limitations? Did the Rule against Perpetuities apply? How should formalities be treated? * * *

At the outset, in the first cases under the act decided at the turn of the century, the Virginia court made eclectic use of equitable, common law and statutory devices all informed by and infused with a favorable attitude toward manumission. * * * Later judges came to implicitly and explicitly reject the earlier cases and—most important—the interpretive principles on which they rested.

The first of the Virginia cases was Pleasants v. Pleasants, decided in 1799. * * *

John Pleasants died before passage of the Act of 1782. He provided in his will that his slaves "shall be free if they chose it when they arrive at the age of thirty years, and the laws of the land will admit them to be set free. * * * " He provided further that should the laws not so permit, the slaves were to be bequeathed to various members of the family subject to the condition that they allow the slaves to be set free "if the laws of the land would admit of it." The *Pleasants* litigation was instituted by John's son, Robert, as executor under his father's will. Robert sought to enforce the slaves' rights to freedom as against various legatees and their successors in interest who had refused to free the Negroes after the Act of 1782.

From a legal standpoint, Pleasants's will presented a number of difficulties. Most important, when executed and when probated, the will could not legally operate to free these slaves, for manumission was prohibited. Thus, if it were to have effect at all, the will would have to be construed as creating a trust with the legatees as trustees who would be under a duty to effectuate the freedom of the slaves "if the laws allow." Such an appointment, however, presented two problems. First, if construed to affect unborn generations of blacks, it would violate the rule against perpetuities. The "Rule," as stated in the roughly contemporaneous Dane's *Abridgment,* provided:

> that all * * * executory interests whatever, including executory devises, must * * * cease to become contingent, and become vested within a life or lives in being, * * * with a mother's pregnancy and the child's minority added; this rule applies not only to inheritances in lands, * * * but to personal estate and chattels real.

The contingency contemplated in the Pleasants will was the passage of a statute or some other change in Virginia law that would permit manumission. There was no certainty, then, that the interest in freedom provided for in the will would vest within lives in being plus twenty-one years nine months, at least as to the interest in freedom of remote generations. Second, perpetuities aside, the question remained whether the 1782 Act would operate to posthumously ratify a settlor's act for which no capacity existed at the time of his death. * * *

The *Pleasants* case was first heard by Chancellor George Wythe. Wythe, not surprisingly, ruled in favor of the slaves, requiring the legatees and their successors to do their duty under the instrument. * * * On appeal, the Supreme Court of Appeals upheld Wythe * * *.

Judge Spencer Roane thought that if an analogy to ordinary property and trust principles would arguably suffice to validate the Negroes' interests, then the result "will hold with increased force, when the case is considered in its true point of view, as one which involves human liberty."

Thus, the preference for liberty is an explicit principle of construction * * *. This preference goes hand-in-hand with a reading of the animus of the statute as not simple toleration, but a "policy of authorizing or *encouraging* emancipation." Pendleton and Carrington, the other two judges, agreed that the major goal ought to be effectuating the object of the testator and of the Negroes. They, too, read the act to be applied to retroactively ratify Pleasants's will.

The judges were equally expansive in dealing with the Rule against Perpetuities. Roane stated his respect for the public policy behind the Rule—the refusal to let the disposition of property be governed too long by the dead—however, he doubted "whether the doctrine of perpetuities is applicable to cases in which human liberty is challenged." The policy of freedom is of greater weight. Carrington agreed that devises respecting liberty are not subject to the limitations on those respecting chattel interests. And Pendleton thought, "That it would be too rigid to apply that rule, with all its consequences, to the present case."

* * *

The *Pleasants* case was extended four years later in Charles v. Hunnicutt. * * * The Quaker testator, Gloister Hunnicutt, died in 1781 leaving a will that provided

> that the following negroes should be manumitted on or before the first month next 1782. * * * I give the above named Negroes to the monthly meeting, of which I am a member, to be manumitted by such members of the said meeting, as the meeting shall appoint.

This provision differed significantly from *Pleasants* in that it purported not to direct a manumission when the laws should allow, but to direct a manumission on a date certain; which date, unfortunately, was prior to the effective date of the Act of 1782.

The *Pleasants* case was relied on by the plaintiff, one of the named Negroes, in suing for his freedom. His counsel * * * asserted that *Pleasants* stood for application of the broad proposition that "subsequent statutes will embrace anterior dispositions made with a view to the existence of future laws." The opposition claimed that *Pleasants,* by its own terms, explicitly distinguished the case of a bequest that purported to make a manumission when it was not permitted by law.

St. George Tucker read the language of the will as not being an immediate act of manumission, but rather the settling of a trust. Accordingly, the trust instrument should be read to effectuate the settlor's intent "and that such intention be construed, if it be possible, not to be repugnant to the law, or the policy of the law." He construed the will as if it had been written like that of Pleasants, supplying the phrase "if the laws allow." Roane embraced a similar reading. The president of the court, Peter Lyons, brought the preference for liberty to the fore:

> Devises in favor of charities, and particularly those in favor of liberty, ought to be liberally expounded: and upon the present occasion, it is fair to infer, that the testator meant that the deed of manumission should not take place, until an act of assembly, to authorize it, should pass * * *.

As in the case of *Pleasants,* the court also deemed it advisable to take a very flexible view of procedure. The plaintiff had sued for his freedom in an action at law. There was some doubt as to whether the common law court ought to apply rules and standards involving the obligations of the "Quakers meeting" as trustee as against the claim of an executor of the estate, or whether such relief would be available only in a Court of Equity. Roane argued strongly that "The courts of law will rather stand in the place of courts of equity in relation to the principles of their decision." Roane thought that even the more rigid of common law judges "would have approved that system in relation to the case before us: a case involving human liberty."

* * *

By 1821 decisions in the area of conflict of laws already foretold a decisive shift in the attitude and technique of the Virginia court. In 1824, in Maria v. Surbaugh that shift manifested itself in a private manumission case with the disclaimer that principles of interpretation favoring liberty have any place in decisions on private emancipation. * * *

In *Maria* the court held that an instrument providing for the manumission of a slave upon her reaching a specific age would not have the effect of rendering free children born to her between the effective date of the instrument and her attainment of the given age. Spencer Roane had reached the opposite conclusion in *Pleasants* and on natural rights grounds, though the rest of that court had chosen other inconclusive reasoning. Even more significant than the result, for purposes of this analysis, is Judge Green's perception of the interpretive process:

> in deciding upon questions of liberty and slavery, * * * it is the duty of the Court, uninfluenced by considerations of humanity on the one hand, or of policy (except so far as the policy of the law appears to extend) on the other, to ascertain and pronounce what the law is: leaving it to the legislature, * * * to deal * * * with a subject involving * * * such important moral and political considerations.

If any doubt might have remained about an explicit rejection of earlier standards, they were certainly dispelled by the court in Gregory v. Baugh in 1831:

> But all who have examined the earlier cases in our books, must admit, that our judges (from the purest motives, I am sure) did, *in favorem libertatis,* sometimes relax, rather too much, the rules of law. * * * Of this, the court in later times, has been so sensible, that it has felt the propriety of gradually returning to the legal standard, and of treating these precisely like any other questions of property.

* * *

NOTES AND QUESTIONS

1. Why was there no legislation permitting "private manumission" in Virginia until 1782? How do you explain the fact that the pressure for manumission came from a "Quaker-dominated" antislavery upper class? Wouldn't that class have benefited the most from slavery? How do you explain the increasing trend toward libertarian slavery decisions in Virginia, and then the shift away from that attitude after 1821? Did you notice anything similar in Stampp's account of the development of slavery legislation generally?

2. In the Virginia case of Maria v. Surbaugh, 23 Va. 228, 2 Rand (23 Va.) 228 (1824), as you have seen, the judge stated that the court must remain "uninfluenced by considerations of humanity on the one hand, or of policy (except so far as the policy of the law appears to extend) on the other * * *." Rather the court was supposed to leave "such important moral and political considerations" to the legislature. Why? Why did this attitude not appear earlier? Does this attitude seem consistent with the opinions you read in Chapter Three involving contracts, property, torts and corporations? For an exploration of the Southern Judges' dilemma see Mark V. Tushnet, The American Law of Slavery 1810–1860: Considerations of Humanity and Interest (1981).

3. How free were judges to decide slavery cases according to their consciences? We can perhaps derive some perspective on this problem by comparing the decisions of Judges Ruffin and Shaw, which follow.

STATE V. MANN

Supreme Court of North Carolina, 1829.
13 N.C. (2 Dev.) 263.

The Defendant was indicted for an assault and battery upon *Lydia,* the slave of one *Elizabeth Jones.*

On the trial it appeared that the Defendant had hired the slave for a year-that during the term, the slave had committed some small offence, for which the Defendant undertook to chastise her-that while in the act of so doing, the slave ran off, whereupon the Defendant called upon her to stop, which being refused, he shot at and wounded her.

His honor JUDGE DANIEL charged the Jury, that if they believed the punishment inflicted by the Defendant was cruel and unwarrantable, and disproportionate to the offence committed by the slave, that in law the Defendant was guilty, as he had only a special property in the slave.

A verdict was returned for the State, and the Defendant appealed.

No Counsel appeared for the Defendant.

The Attorney General contended, that no difference existed between this case and that of the State v. Hale, (2 Hawks, 582.) In this case the weapon used was one calculated to produce death. He assimilated the relation between a master and a slave, to those existing between parents and children, masters and apprentices, and tutors and scholars, and upon the limitations to the right of the Superiors in these relations, he cited Russell on Crimes, 866.

RUFFIN, JUDGE. A Judge cannot but lament when such cases as the present are brought into judgment. It is impossible that the reasons on which they go can be appreciated, but where institutions similar to our own, exist and are thoroughly understood. The struggle, too, in the Judge's own breast between the feelings of the man, and the duty of the magistrate is a severe one, presenting strong temptation to put aside such questions, if it be possible. It is useless however, to complain of things inherent in our political state. And it is criminal in a Court to avoid any responsibility which the laws impose. With whatever reluctance therefore it is done the Court is compelled to express an opinion upon the extent of the dominion of the master over the slave in North Carolina.

The indictment charges a battery on *Lydia,* a slave of Elizabeth Jones. Upon the face of the indictment, the case is the same as the State v. Hale, (2 Hawks, 582.) No fault is found with the rule then adopted; nor would be, if it were now open. But it is not open; for the question, as it relates to a battery on a slave by a stranger, is considered as settled by that case. But the evidence makes this a different case. Here the slave had been hired by the Defendant, and was in his possession and the battery was committed during the period of hiring. * * * The inquiry here is, whether a cruel and unreasonable battery on a slave, by the hirer, is indictable. The Judge below instructed the Jury, that it is. He seems to have put it on the ground, that the Defendant had but a special property. Our laws uniformly treat the master or other person having the possession and command of the slave, as entitled to the same extent of authority. The object is the same-the services of the slave; and the same powers must be confided. In a criminal proceeding, and indeed in reference to all other persons but the general owner, the hirer and possessor of a slave, in relation to both rights and duties, is, for the time being, the owner. * * *

[U]pon the general question, whether the owner is answerable *criminaliter,* for a battery upon his own slave, or other exercise of authority or force, not forbidden by statute, the Court entertains but little doubt.—That he is so liable, has never yet been decided; nor, as far as is known, been hitherto contended. There have been no prosecutions of the sort. The established habits and uniform practice of the country in this respect, is the best evidence of the portion of power, deemed by the whole community, requisite to the preservation of the master's dominion. If we thought differently, we could not set our notions in array against the judgment of everybody else, and say that this, or that authority, may be safely lopped off. This has indeed been assimilated at the bar to the other domestic relations; and arguments drawn from the well established principles, which confer and restrain the authority of the parent over the child, the tutor over the pupil, the master over the apprentice, have been pressed on us. The Court does not recognize their application. There is no likeness between the cases. They are in opposition to each other, and there is an impassable gulf between them. The difference is that which exists between freedom and slavery—and a greater cannot be imagined. In the one, the end in view is the happiness of the youth, born to equal rights with that governor, on whom the duty devolves of training the young to usefulness, in a station which he is afterwards to assume among freemen. To such an end, and with such a subject, moral and intellectual instruction seem the natural means; and for the most part, they are found to suffice. Moderate force is superadded, only to make the others effectual. If that fails, it is better to leave the party to his own headstrong passions, and the ultimate correction of the law, than to allow it to be immoderately inflicted by a private person. With slavery it is far otherwise. The end is the profit of the master, his security and the public safety; the subject, one doomed in his own person, and his posterity, to live without knowledge, and without the capacity to make any thing his own, and to toil that another may reap the fruits. What moral considerations shall be addressed to such a being, to convince him what, it is impossible but that the most stupid must feel and know can never be true-that he is thus to labor upon a principle of natural duty, or for the sake of his own personal happiness, such services can only be expected from one who has no will of his own; who surrenders his will in implicit obedience to that of another. Such obedience is the consequence only of uncontrolled authority over the body. There is nothing else which can operate to produce the effect. The power of the master must be absolute, to render the submission of the slave perfect. I most freely confess my sense of the harshness of this proposition, I feel it as deeply as any man can. And as a principle of moral right, every person in his retirement must repudiate it. But in the actual condition of things, it must be so.—There is no remedy. This discipline belongs to the state of slavery. They cannot be disunited, without abrogating at once the rights of the master, and absolving the slave from his subjection. It constitutes the curse of slavery to both the bond and free portions of our population. But it is inherent in the relation of master and slave.

That there may be particular instances of cruelty and deliberate barbarity, where, in conscience the law might properly interfere, is most probable. The difficulty is to determine, where *a Court* may properly begin. Merely in the abstract it may well be asked, which power of the master accords with right. The answer will probably sweep away all of them. But we cannot look at the matter in that light. The truth is, that we are forbidden to enter upon a train of general reasoning on the subject. We cannot allow the right of the master to be brought into discussion in the Courts of Justice. The slave, to remain a slave, must be made sensible, that there is no appeal from his master; that his power is in no instance, usurped; but is conferred by the laws of man at least, if not by the law of God. The danger would be great indeed, if the tribunals of justice should be called on to graduate the punishment appropriate to every temper, and every dereliction of menial duty. No man can anticipate the many and aggravated provocations of the master, which the slave would be constantly stimulated by his own passions, or the instigation of others to give; or the consequent wrath of the master, prompting him to bloody vengeance, upon the turbulent traitor—a vengeance generally practised with impunity, by reason of its privacy. The Court therefore disclaims the power of changing the relation, in which these parts of our people stand to each other.

We are happy to see, that there is daily less and less occasion for the interposition of the Courts. The protection already afforded by several statutes, that all powerful motive, the private interest of the owner, the benevolences towards each other, seated in the hearts of those who have been born and bred together, the frowns and deep execrations of the community upon the barbarian, who is guilty of excessive and brutal cruelty to his unprotected slave, all combined, have produced a mildness of treatment, and attention to the comforts of the unfortunate class of slaves, greatly mitigating the rigors of servitude, and ameliorating the condition of the slaves. The same causes are operating, and will continue to operate with increased action, until the disparity in numbers between the whites and blacks, shall have rendered the latter in no degree dangerous to the former, when the police now existing may be further relaxed. This result, greatly to be desired, may be much more rationally expected from the events above alluded to, and now in progress, than from any rash expositions of abstract truths, by a Judiciary tainted with a false and fanatical philanthropy, seeking to redress an acknowledged evil, by means still more wicked and appalling than even that evil.

I repeat, that I would gladly have avoided this ungrateful question. But being brought to it, the Court is compelled to declare, that while slavery exists amongst us in its present state, or until it shall seem fit to the Legislature to interpose express enactments to the contrary, it will be the imperative duty of the Judges to recognize the full dominion of the owner over the slave, except where the exercise of it is forbidden by statute. And this we do upon the ground, that this dominion is essential to the value of slaves as property, to the security of the master, and the public tranquility, greatly dependent upon their subordination; and in fine, as most effectually securing the general protection and comfort of the slaves themselves.

PER CURIAM. Let the judgment below be reversed and judgment entered for the Defendant.

NOTES AND QUESTIONS

1. This opinion "has both attracted and repulsed commentators for over a century." Robert Cover, Justice Accused: Anti–Slavery and the Judicial Process 77n (1975). Were you attracted or repulsed? Cover quotes Harriet Beecher Stowe's comments:

> "No one can read this decision, so fine and clear in expression, so dignified and solemn in its earnestness, and so dreadful in its results, without feeling at once deep respect for the man and horror for the system. The man, judging him from this short specimen, * * * has one of that high order of minds, which looks straight through all verbiage and sophistry to the heart of every subject which it encounters. He has, too, that noble scorn of dissimulation, that straight forward determination not to call a bad thing by a good name, even when most popular and reputable and legal, which it is to be wished could be more frequently seen, both in our Northern and Southern States. There is but one sole regret; and that is that such a man, with such a mind, should have been merely an *expositor,* and not a *reformer* of law."

Id., at 77–78n, *quoting* Harriet Beecher Stowe, The Key to Uncle Tom's Cabin 78–79 (1853). Do you agree with her analysis? Mark Tushnet has argued that Ruffin believed that those reading his opinion, on reflection, ought to be able to "appreciate how the apparently inhumane doctrine [he] announced is compatible with true humanity." Tushnet, *supra,* at 57. Who is right, Stowe or Tushnet? See also, for an examination of Harriet Beecher Stowe's and Judge Ruffin's views, Alfred L. Brophy, "Humanity, Utility and Logic in Southern Legal Thought: Harriet Beecher Stowe's Vision in *Dred: A Tale of the Great Dismal Swamp,*" 78 Boston U.L.Rev. 113 (1998), and Alfred L. Brophy, " 'Over and Above . . . There Broods a Portentous Shadow,—the Shadow of *Law,*': Harriett Beecher Stowe's Critique of Slave Law in *Uncle Tom's Cabin,*" 12 J. Law & Religion 457 (1996).

For further thoughts on State v. Mann and the world of the slaveholding South, see James Oakes, Slavery and Freedom: An Interpretation of the Old South (1990). For still more commentary on this case, on Harriet Beecher Stowe, and on slavery, law, religion, and literature generally, see the splendid and provocative study by Mark Tushnet, Slave Law in the American South: *State v. Mann* in History and Literature (2003). Tushnet states that "Judge Ruffin plainly did not think that slavery was immoral, even though he believed that absolute dominion was indeed morally repugnant." Id., at 63. Do you agree?

2. Does it seem to you that Ruffin's attitude toward slavery, or his legal analysis, supports Stampp's or Genovese's descriptions of the relationship between slaves and masters? In particular, does the excerpt from Frederick Douglass's "Narrative," which you read earlier in this section, cast any doubt on, or does it support Ruffin's analysis? How, by the way, do you explain the note of optimism that creeps into Ruffin's opinion at the end? Was it justified?

3. Was Ruffin even correct in his theories about what would best make the system of slavery work, or what the purposes of slavery were? Ruffin says it exists simply for the profit of the master. Would Calhoun have agreed? With regard to how best to make the system work, recall that Solomon Northrup believed that kindly masters, rather than those who used brutal discipline, would get the most work out of their slaves. Is that Ruffin's view? Ruffin appears to suggest that giving masters legal permission to wield absolute authority would be best for masters and slaves, but Solomon Northrup, as we have seen, as did many others, believed that the system of slavery had a brutalizing effect on masters, and as for what it did to slaves, Northrup remarked that there were some slaves who "scarcely knew that there was such a word as freedom. Brought up in the ignorance of a brute [they] possessed but little more than a brute's intelligence." Speaking of one such creature, Northrup continued, "She was one of those, and there are very many, who fear nothing but their master's lash, and know no further duty than to obey his voice." Northrup, supra, at 39. Such a one sounds a bit like Ruffin's ideal slave, or does she? Curiously, in other parts of his narrative, Northrup seems to deny that slaves ever relinquished the notion of freedom:

> They are deceived who flatter themselves that the ignorant and debased slave has no conception of the magnitude of his wrongs. They are deceived who imagine that he arises from his knees, with back lacerated and bleeding, cherishing only a spirit of meekness and forgiveness. A day may come–it *will* come, if his prayer is heard–a terrible day of vengeance, when the master in his turn will cry in vain for mercy.

Northrup, supra, at 191. Did that day ever come? Again, was the note of optimism in Ruffin's opinion justified?

COMMONWEALTH V. AVES

Supreme Judicial Court of Massachusetts, 1836.
35 Mass. (18 Pick.) 193.

SHAW, C.J., delivered the opinion of the Court. * * *

* * *

The precise question presented by the claim of the respondent is, whether a citizen of any one of the United States, where negro slavery is established by law, coming into this State, for any temporary purpose of business or pleasure, staying some time, but not acquiring a domicil here, who brings a slave with him as a personal attendant, may restrain such slave of his liberty during his continuance here, and convey him out of this State on his return, against his consent. * * *

* * *

It is now to be considered as an established rule, that by the constitution and laws of this Commonwealth, before the adoption of the constitution of the United States, in 1789, slavery was abolished, as being contrary to the principles of justice, and of nature, and repugnant to the provisions of the declaration of rights, which is a component part of the constitution of the State.

* * *

How, or by what act particularly, slavery was abolished in Massachusetts, whether by the adoption of the opinion in Sommersett's case, as a declaration and modification of the common law, or by the Declaration of Independence, or by the constitution of 1780, it is not now very easy to determine, and it is rather a matter of curiosity than of utility; it being agreed on all hands, that if not abolished before, it was so by the declaration of rights. In the case of Winchendon v. Hatfield, 4 Mass.R. 123, which was a case between two towns respecting the support of a pauper, Chief Justice Parsons, in giving the opinion of the Court, states, that in the first action which came before the Court after the establishment of the constitution, the judges declared, that by virtue of the declaration of rights, slavery in this State was no more. * * *

It has recently been stated as a fact, that there were judicial decisions in this State prior to the adoption of the present constitution, holding that negroes born here of slave parents were free. A fact is stated in the above opinion of Chief Justice Parsons, which may account for this suggestion. He states that several negroes, born in this country, of imported slaves, had demanded their freedom of their masters by suits at law, and obtained it by a judgment of court. The defence of the master, he says, was faintly made, for such was the temper of the times, that a restless, discontented slave was worth little, and when his freedom was obtained in a course of legal proceedings, his master was not holden for his support, if he became poor. It is very probable, therefore, that this surmise is correct, and that records of judgments to this effect may be found; but they would throw very little light on the subject.

Without pursuing this inquiry farther, it is sufficient for the purposes of the case before us, that by the constitution adopted in 1780, slavery was abolished in Massachusetts, upon the ground that it is contrary to natural right and the plain principles of justice. The terms of the first article of the declaration of rights are plain and explicit. "All men are born free and equal, and have certain natural, essential, and unalienable rights, which are, the right of enjoying and defending their lives and liberties, that of acquiring, possessing, and protecting property." It would be difficult to select words more precisely adapted to the abolition of negro slavery. According to the laws prevailing in all the States, where slavery is upheld, the child of a slave is not deemed to be born free, a slave has no right to enjoy and defend his own liberty, or to acquire, possess, or protect property. That the description was broad enough in its terms to embrace negroes, and that it was intended by the framers of the constitution to embrace them, is proved by the earliest contemporaneous construction, by an unbroken series of judicial decisions, and by a uniform practice from the adoption of the constitution to the present time. The whole tenor of our policy, of our legislation and jurisprudence, from that time to the present, has been consistent with this construction, and with no other.

Such being the general rule of law, it becomes necessary to inquire how far it is modified or controlled in its operation; either,

1. By the law of other nations and states, as admitted by the comity of nations to have a limited operation within a particular state; or

2. By the constitution and laws of the United States.

In considering the first, we may assume that the law of this State is analogous to the law of England, in this respect; that while slavery is considered as unlawful and inadmissible in both, and this because contrary to natural right and to laws designed for the security of personal liberty, yet in both, the existence of slavery in other countries is recognized, and the claims of foreigners, growing out of that condition, are, to a certain extent, respected. Almost the only reason assigned by Lord *Mansfield* in Sommersett's case was, that slavery is of such a nature, that it is incapable of being introduced on any reasons moral or political, but only by positive law; and, it is so odious, that nothing can be suffered to support it but positive law.

The same doctrine is clearly stated in the full and able opinion of Marshall C.J., in the case of the *Antelope,* 10 Wheat. 120. He is speaking of the slave trade, but the remark itself shows that it applies to the state of slavery. "That it is contrary to the law of nature will scarcely be denied. That every man has a natural right to the fruits of his own labor, is generally admitted, and that no other person can rightfully deprive him of those fruits, and appropriate them against his will, seems to be the necessary result of the admission."

But although slavery and the slave trade are deemed contrary to natural right, yet it is settled by the judicial decisions of this country and of England, that it is not contrary to the law of nations. * * * The consequence is, that each independent community, in its intercourse with every other, is bound to act on the principle, that such other country has a full and perfect authority to make such laws for the government of its own subjects, as its own judgment shall dictate and its own conscience approve, provided the same are consistent with the law of nations; and no independent community has any right to interfere with the acts or conduct of another state, within the territories of such state, or on the high seas, which each has an equal right to use and occupy; and that each sovereign state, governed by its own laws, although competent and well authorized to make such laws as it may think most expedient to the extent of its own territorial limits, and for the government of its own subjects, has no authority to enforce her own laws, or to treat the laws of other states as void, although contrary to its own views of morality.

This view seems consistent with most of the leading cases on the subject.

Sommersett's case, 20 Howell's State Trials, 1, as already cited, decides that slavery, being odious and against natural right, cannot exist, except by force of positive law. But it clearly admits, that it may exist by force of positive law. And it may be remarked, that by positive law, in this connection, may be as well understood customary law as the enactment of a statute; and the word is used to designate rules established by tacit acquiescence or by the legislative act of any state, and which derive their force and authority from such acquiescence or enactment, and not because they are the dictates of natural justice, and as such of universal obligation.

Le Louis, 2 Dodson, 236. This was * * * the case of a French vessel seized by an English vessel in time of peace, whilst engaged in the slave trade. It proceeded upon the ground, that a right of visitation, by the vessels of one nation, of the vessels of another, could only be exercised in time of war, or against pirates, and that the slave trade was not piracy by the laws of nations, except against those by whose government it has been so declared by law or by treaty. And the vessel was delivered up.

* * *

Two cases are cited from the decisions of courts of common law, which throw much light upon the subject.

Madrazo v. Willes, 3 Barn. & Ald. 353. It was an action brought by a Spaniard against a British subject, who had unlawfully, and without justifiable cause, captured a ship with three hundred slaves on board. The only question was the amount of damages. Abbott C.J., who tried the cause, in reference to the very strong language of the acts of Parliament, declaring the traffic in slaves a violation of right and contrary to the first principles of justice and humanity, doubted whether the owner could recover damages, in an English court of justice, for the value of the slaves as property, and directed the ships and the slaves to be separately valued. On further consideration, he and the whole court were of opinion, that the plaintiff was entitled to recover for the value of the slaves. That opinion went upon the ground, that the traffic in slaves, however wrong in itself, if prosecuted by a Spaniard between Spain and the coast of Africa, and if permitted by the laws of Spain, and not restrained by treaty, could not be lawfully interrupted by a British subject, on the high seas, the common highway of nations. * * *

Forbes v. Cochrane, 2 Barn. & Cressw. 448; S.C. 3 Dowl. & Ryl. 679. * * * The plaintiff, a British subject, domiciled in East Florida, where slavery was established by law, was the owner of a plantation, and of certain slaves, who escaped thence and got on board a British ship of war on the high seas. It was held, that he could not maintain an action against the master of the ship for harbouring the slaves after notice and demand of them. * * * Best, J. declared * * * "Slavery is a local law, and therefore if a man wishes to preserve his slaves, let him attach them to him by affection, or make fast the bars of their prison, or rivet well their chains, for the instant they get beyond the limits where slavery is recognized by the local law, they have broken their chains, they have escaped from their prison, and are free."

* * *

This view of the law applicable to slavery, marks strongly the distinction between the relation of master and slave, as established by the local law of particular states, and in virtue of that sovereign power and independent authority which each independent state concedes to every other, and those natural and social relations, which are everywhere and by all people recognized, and which, though they may be modified and regulated by municipal law, are not founded upon it, such as the relation of parent and child, and husband and wife. Such also is the principle upon which the general right of property is founded, being in some form universally recognized as a natural right, independently of municipal law.

This affords an answer to the argument drawn from the maxim, that the right of personal property follows the person, and therefore, where by the law of a place a person there domiciled acquires personal property, by the comity of nations the same must be deemed his property everywhere. It is obvious, that if this were true, in the extent in which the argument employs it, if slavery exists anywhere, and if by the laws of any place a property can be acquired in slaves, the law of slavery must extend to every place where such slaves may be carried. The maxim, therefore, and the argument can apply only to those commodities which are everywhere, and by all nations, treated and deemed subjects of property. But it is not speaking with strict accuracy to say, that a property can be acquired in human beings, by local laws. Each state may, for its own convenience, declare that slaves shall be deemed property, and that the relations and laws of personal chattels shall be deemed to apply to them. * * * But it would be a perversion of terms to say, that such local laws do in fact make them personal property generally; they can only determine, that the same rules of law shall apply to them as are applicable to property * * *.

* * *

The conclusion to which we come from this view of the law is this:

That by the general and now well established law of this Commonwealth, bond slavery cannot exist, because it is contrary to natural right, and repugnant to numerous provisions of the constitution and laws * * *.

* * *

That, as a general rule, all persons coming within the limits of a state, become subject to all its municipal laws, civil and criminal, and entitled to the privileges which those laws confer; that this rule applies as well to blacks as whites, except in the case of fugitives, to be afterwards considered; that if such persons have been slaves, they become free, not so much because any alteration is made in their *status,* or condition, as because there is no law which will warrant, but there are laws, if they choose to avail themselves of them, which prohibit, their forcible detention or forcible removal.

That the law arising from the comity of nations cannot apply; because if it did, it would follow as a necessary consequence, that all those persons, who, by force of local laws, and within all foreign places where slavery is permitted, have acquired slaves as property, might bring their slaves here, and exercise over them the rights and power which an owner of property might exercise, and for any length of time short of acquiring a domicil; that such an application of the law would be wholly repugnant to our laws, entirely inconsistent with our policy and our fundamental principles, and is therefore inadmissible.

* * *

The question has thus far been considered as a general one, and applicable to cases of slaves brought from any foreign state or country; and it now becomes necessary to consider how far this result differs, where the person is claimed as a slave by a citizen of another State of this Union. * * *

In art. 4, par. 2 the constitution declares that no person held to service or labor in one State, under the laws thereof, escaping into another, shall in consequence of any law or regulation therein, be discharged from such service or labor, but shall be delivered up on claim of the party to whom such service or labor may be due.

The law of congress made in pursuance of this article provides, that when any person held to labor in any of the United States, & c. shall escape into any other of the said States or Territories, the person entitled, & c. is empowered to arrest the fugitive, and upon proof made that the person so seized, under the law of the State from which he or she fled, owes service, & c. Act of February 12, 1793, c. 7, par. 3.

In regard to these provisions, the Court are of opinion, that as by the general law of this Commonwealth, slavery cannot exist, and the rights and powers of slave owners cannot be exercised therein; the effect of this provision in the constitution and laws of the United States, is to limit and restrain the operation of this general rule, so far as it is done by the plain meaning and obvious intent and import of the language used, and no further. The constitution and law manifestly refer to the case of a slave escaping from a State where he owes service or labor, into another State or Territory. He is termed a fugitive from labor; the proof to be made is, that he owed service or labor, under the laws of the State or Territory *from which he fled,* and the authority is given to remove such fugitive to the State *from which he fled.* This language can, by no reasonable construction, be applied to the case of a slave who has not fled from the State, but who has been brought into the State by his master.

The same conclusion will result from a consideration of the well known circumstances under which this constitution was formed. Before the adoption of the constitution, the States were to a certain extent, sovereign and independent, and were in a condition to settle the terms upon which they would form a more perfect union. It has been contended by some overzealous philanthropists, that such an article in the constitution could be of no binding force or validity, because it was a stipulation contrary to natural right. But it is difficult to perceive the force of this objection. It has already been shown, that slavery is not contrary to the laws of nations. It would then be the proper subject of treaties among sovereign and independent powers. * * * Now the constitution of the United States partakes both of the nature of a treaty and of a form of government. It regards the States, to a certain extent, as sovereign and independent communities, with full power to make their own laws and regulate their own domestic policy, and fixes the terms upon which their intercourse with each other shall be conducted. * * * It is well known that when this constitution was formed, some of the States permitted slavery and the slavetrade, and considered them highly essential to their interest, and that some other States had abolished slavery within their own limits, and from the principles deduced and policy avowed by them, might be presumed to desire to extend such abolition further. * * * Under these circumstances the clause in question was agreed on and introduced into the constitution; and as it was well considered, as it was intended to secure future peace and harmony, and to fix as precisely as language could do it, the limit to which the rights of one party should be exercised within the territory of the other, it is to be presumed that they selected terms intended to express their exact and their whole meaning; and it would be a departure from the purpose and spirit of the compact to put any other construction upon it, than that to be derived from the plain and natural import of the language used. Besides, this construction of the provision in the constitution, gives to it a latitude sufficient to afford effectual security to the owners of slaves. The States have a plenary power to make all laws necessary for the regulation of slavery and the rights of the slave owners, whilst the slaves remain within their territorial limits; and it is only when they escape, without the consent of their owners, into other States, that they require the aid of other States, to enable them to regain their dominion over the fugitives.

In the case of Butler v. Hopper, 1 Wash.C.C.Rep. 499, it was held * * * that the provision in the constitution which we are now considering, does not "extend to the case of a slave voluntarily carried by his master into another State, and there leaving him under the protection of some law declaring him free." In this case, however, the master claimed to hold the slave in virtue of a law of Pennsylvania, which permitted members of congress and sojourners, to retain their domestic slaves, and it was held that he did not bring himself within either branch of the exception, because he had, for two years of the period, ceased to be a member of congress, and so lost the privilege; and by having become a resident could not claim as a sojourner. The case is an authority to this point, that the claimant of a slave, to avail himself of the provisions of the constitution and laws of the United States, must bring himself within their plain and obvious meaning, and they will not be extended by construction; and that the clause in the constitution is confined to the case of a slave escaping from one State, and fleeing to another.

But in a more recent case, the point was decided * * *. Ex parte Simmons, 4 Wash.C.C.R. 396. It was an application for a certificate under par. 3, of the act of February 12, 1793. [The court] held that both the constitution and laws of the United States apply only to fugitives, escaping from one State and fleeing to another, and not to the case of a slave voluntarily brought by his master.

Another question was made in that case, whether the slave was free by the laws of Pennsylvania, which, like our own in effect, liberate slaves voluntarily brought within the State, but there is an exception in favor of members of congress, foreign minister and consuls, and *sojourners:* but this provision is qualified as to sojourners and persons passing through the State, in such manner as to exclude them from the benefit of the exception, if the slave was retained in the State longer than six months. The slave in that case having been detained in the State more than six months, was therefore held free.

This case is an authority to this point; the general rule being, that if a slave is brought into a State where the laws do not admit slavery, he will be held free, the person who claims him as a slave under any exception or limitation of the general rule, must show clearly that the case is within such exception.

* * *

In Louisiana, it has been held, that if a person with a slave, goes into a State to reside, where it is declared that slavery shall not exist, for ever so short a time, the slave *ipso facto* becomes free, and will be so adjudged and considered afterwards in all other States; and a person moving from Kentucky to Ohio to reside, his slaves thereby became free, and were so held in Louisiana. This case also fully recognizes the authority of States to make laws dissolving the relation of master and slave; and considers the special limitation of the general power, by the federal constitution, as a forcible implication in proof of the existence of such general power. Lunsford v. Coquillon, 14 Martin's Rep. 403.

* * *

The constitution and laws of the United States, then, are confined to cases of slaves escaping from other States and coming within the limits of this State without the consent and against the will of their masters, and cannot by any sound construction extend to a case where the slave does not escape and does not come within the limits of this State against the will of the master, but by his own act and permission. The provision is to be construed according to its plain terms and import, and cannot be extended beyond this, and where the case is not that of an escape, the general rule shall have its effect. It is upon these grounds we are of opinion, that an owner of a slave in another State where slavery is warranted by law, voluntarily bringing such slave into this State, has no authority to detain him against his will, or to carry him out of the State against his consent, for the purpose of being held in slavery.

* * *

NOTES AND QUESTIONS

1. In a classic of American Legal historiography, Shaw's biographer, Leonard W. Levy, has written that Northern Abolitionists greeted the opinion in Commonwealth v. Aves with great joy, and that Boston's Columbian Centinel "called the decision 'THE MOST IMPORTANT' ever made in any one of the free states." The opinion in the South, however, was considerably less sanguine:

> The Baltimore *Chronicle* fumed over judicial confiscation of property and declared that whereas the Constitution had provided for the restoration of slaves fleeing from one state to another, "the decision of Chief Justice Shaw virtually annuls this security * * *." * * * The *Augusta Sentinel* * * * exclaimed that the Union was worthless if its members were able to destroy the right of private property and to deprive the people of the

> South "of what is justly theirs." "This is the strongest and boldest step ever yet taken against the rights of the South, and leaves the puny efforts of the abolitionists at an immeasureable distance in the rear," the paper trumpeted, as it demanded of Southerners whether they would submit to the outrage.

Levy, The Law of the Commonwealth and Chief Justice Shaw 67–68 (1957).* Were the Southerners overreacting? Can you think of a legal basis for deciding the case differently? How do you suppose Thomas Ruffin would have resolved the issue?

2. Were the Southerners hypocrites when they accused Northern judges, such as Shaw, of failing to implement the Constitution's principles? This was a problem that lingered until the Civil War, and only that conflagration settled the issue. As late as 1859, there was some authority for the notion that state courts could issue writs of habeas corpus to take runaway slaves out of the custody of federal authorities and, presumably, allow sympathetic Northern state officials to aid them in escaping from bondage. In *Ableman v. Booth*, 21 How. (62 U.S.) 506 (1859), the Supreme Court finally ruled that the federal fugitive slave law trumped state habeas corpus jurisdiction, reversing a decision of the Wisconsin Supreme Court, and dashing the hope of any constitutional restraints on Southern slavery.

Until *Ableman*, though, there was some doubt about the extent to which state procedures could interfere with federal enforcement of the process for returning fugitive slaves. Southern legal thinkers maintained that it was the constitutional duty of their Northern countrymen to enforce the constitutional provisions regarding fugitive slaves, but for them to be consistent in their constitutional arguments, one would have expected the South to respect the freedom of Blacks who were freemen in the North, and who found themselves in the South. Interestingly enough, Justice Shaw, in *Aves*, relies on a Louisiana case that did indeed affirm that by the law of Louisiana, a slave brought willingly into a free state became free, and that the Louisiana courts had to honor that freedom. Solomon Northrup was a free Black, living in New York, who was kidnapped and forced to be a slave in Louisiana. Does this belie the sincerity of Southerners on this point?

Indeed, Northrup believed that hundreds of free Blacks from the North had been kidnapped and forced into Southern servitude, as he was. Northrup, supra, at 252. Northrup's twentieth century editors doubt that the figure of free Blacks kidnapped and forced into Southern slavery was as high as Northrup suggests, though his case may not have been unique. Indeed, they note that "Even Harriet Beecher Stowe acknowledged that the known cases of such crimes were rare, and when discovered by Southern authorities, were 'generally tried with great fairness and impartiality.' " Northrup, supra at x, citing Harriet Beecher Stowe, The Key to Uncle Tom's Cabin 345 (1853).

---

* Reprinted from The Law of the Commonwealth and Chief Justice Shaw: The Evolution of American Law, 18301860, copyright 1957 by the President and Fellows of Harvard College, originally published by the Harvard University Press, with the permission of the author.

Northrup himself seems to support the Southern legal institutions' good faith on this point. While he claims that he feared for his safety if he tried to assert his right to freedom, early in his narrative he reports on the case of a fellow kidnapped free Black who was rescued in New Orleans, and whose kidnappers were arrested and confined in a Norfolk prison. Northrup, supra, at 48.

What finally happened in Northrup's own case is further evidence that Louisiana authorities were prepared to enforce the law of freedom as well as the law of slavery. While it took twelve years for Northrup to communicate with his friends and relatives in New York precisely where he had been forced to toil as a slave in Louisiana, once those acting on his behalf made contact with those administering Louisiana law, they uniformly supported his quest for freedom. Northrup himself noted that once he got his hands on "free papers" proving his status as a free citizen of New York, even if his master objected to his leaving his service, it would have been no crime for Northrup to flee the plantation in the company of another white who had agreed to help him. "It would be no infringement of law, however much it might provoke individual hostility," Northrup observes, "to assist a freeman to regain his freedom." Id., at 213.

Once Northrup's New York friends were able to secure proof of his freedom in New York, one of them proceeded to Washington, to enlist the aid of the federal government. Northrup explains what happened next:

> * * * The Hon. Pierre Soule, Senator in Congress from Louisiana, Hon. Mr. Conrad, Secretary of War, and Judge Nelson, of the Supreme Court of the United States, upon hearing a statement of the facts, and examining [Northrup's friend's documentation of his freedom], furnished [Northrup's friend] with open letters to gentlemen in Louisiana, strongly urging their assistance in accomplishing the object [of Northrup's freedom].
>
> Senator Soule especially interested himself in the matter, insisting, in forcible language, that it was the duty and interest of every planter in his State to aid in restoring me to freedom, and trusted the sentiments of honor and justice in the bosom of every citizen of the commonwealth [of Louisiana] would enlist him at once in my behalf. * * *

Northrup, supra, at 227.

Senator Soule's prediction turned out to be more or less accurate. One Louisiana lawyer in particular, one John P. Waddill, a Louisiana state senator, became the ultimate instrument by which Northrup's freedom was finally secured:

> After reading the documents presented him, and listening to a representation of the circumstances under which I had been carried away into captivity, Mr. Waddill at once proffered his services, and entered into the affair with great zeal and earnestness. He in common with others of like elevated character, looked upon the kidnapper with abhorrence. The title of his fellow parishioners and clients to the property [in slaves] which

> constituted the larger proportion of their wealth, not only depended upon the good faith in which slave sales were transacted, but he was a man in whose honorable heart emotions of indignation were aroused by such an instance of injustice.

Northrup, supra, at 228. Is it now a bit easier to understand the Baltimore and Augusta editorialists' ire at Justice Shaw? Total candor demands, however, that it be noted that Louisiana lawyer Waddill was not completely a disinterested public servant. The editors of the 1968 edition of Northrup's narrative report that Waddill was paid the sum of $50.00 for his services. Id., at 242, n. 6. For evaluation of Waddill's fee, consider that Northrup reported that his own worth at the time, as a slave, was probably around $1700. Id., at 219.

3. Consider Shaw's explanation for the lack of positive law to support slavery in Massachusetts. Shaw concedes that slavery once existed in the state, but it has since become illegal. What led to the changed legal status for slavery? Shaw offers three possibilities: (1) *Sommersett's* case, a British opinion written in 1772; (2) the Declaration of Independence, adopted by the Continental Congress in 1776; and (3) The Massachusetts Constitution of 1780 (Article One of the Declaration of Rights). Do you have any problems with using the first two as authorities for the abolition of slavery in Massachusetts? What about the third? The Massachusetts Declaration of Rights provided in article one that "All men are born free and equal, and have certain natural, essential, and unalienable rights; which are, the right of enjoying and defending their lives and liberties, that of acquiring, possessing, and protecting property." Shaw says that "It would be difficult to select words more properly adjudged to the abolition of negro slavery." Can you come up with words "more properly adjudged" for that purpose?

4. Are the cases construing Pennsylvania's statute authorizing the temporary transit of slaves through the state, Butler v. Hopper and Ex Parte Simmons, good authority for Shaw to cite in support of his opinion that Med [the slave at issue in the case] was freed by her being brought to Massachusetts? Consider Shaw's construction of the fugitive slave clause of the Constitution. Shaw says that the clause's "plain meaning" is the only acceptable construction. Why should this be so? In any event, could it be argued that its "plain meaning" could be extended to include the case of a slave who comes willingly with his or her master to Massachusetts and then refuses to go home?

5. How can Shaw suggest that one of the bases for his decision is that slavery is contrary to "natural right and to laws designed for the security of personal liberty," and yet dismiss as "overzealous philanthropists" abolitionists like William Lloyd Garrison who argued that the fugitive slave provisions of federal law were void because they were "contrary to natural right?" Garrison, incidentally, was apparently "thrilled" by this decision of Shaw's, but a few years later, when Shaw participated in a Massachusetts decision which upheld the federal law regarding fugitive slaves, Garrison denounced Shaw

as willing " * * * to act the part of Pilate in the Crucifixion of the Son of God" or " * * * the slave pirate on the African coast," and complained that Shaw "had betrayed the honor of Massachusetts 'when Liberty lay bleeding.' " Levy, supra, at 67, 82. Would you have predicted, on the basis of the *Aves* opinion, that Shaw would be willing to suffer the vilest personal abuse to support the apprehension of fugitive slaves? Compare the sophistication and subtlety of Shaw's analysis of the state and federal laws regarding slavery with those of Justices Story and Taney which you will soon read.

3. DISUNION, WAR, AND RECONSTRUCTION

The Slide to Disunion

We have seen in previous sections of this book that the young Republic of 1789 had never truly resolved the question debated during the ratification of the U.S. Constitution: Exactly what kind of "new nation" was the United States to be? The absence of a fundamental guarantee of liberties in the 1787 draft of the Constitution was, to patriots like Patrick Henry, a tip-off that the delegates meeting in Philadelphia were up to something. For Henry, the goings-on were part of a monarchist plot to subvert the Revolution waged for "home rule." These concerns, to a greater or lesser degree, were not isolated. New Hampshire, New York, Virginia, and North Carolina were slow to ratify. One state, Rhode Island, stayed out until 1790. These recalcitrant states acted only after receiving assurances from other states that a first order of business in the Congress would be consideration of a series of amendments (what became the Bill of Rights) that would guarantee the rights stipulated as God-given and natural in the Declaration of Independence, and that a provision would be adopted (what subsequently became the 10th Amendment) reserving to the states powers not "expressly delegated" to the national government. The government was off to a rocky start.

The addition of a Bill of Rights did not resolve the question of the nature of the new nation. The controversial and highly politicized interpretations of the rationale for prosecuting the Whisky Rebels, as we have seen, spoke fundamentally to a disagreement over the purposes of a national government. The Alien and Sedition Acts of 1798 only amplified these differences; this Federalist-sponsored legislation in fact was opposed by the "Father of the Constitution," James Madison, and by his close colleague Thomas Jefferson, who, as we have seen, together secretly coauthored the Kentucky and Virginia Resolutions of 1798. In them they argued that the Constitution was a "compact" and that the states had a right to nullify or "interpose" upon Federal laws when and if these laws exceeded the specific powers granted to the national government by the Constitution. According to Madison and Jefferson, then, the determination that the federal government had gone too far was a matter for each state to determine for itself.

As we have seen, there were divisions even inside President Washington's first and second Administrations, pitting Jefferson's vision of a yeoman-centered, locally-oriented set of agrarian republics aligned under a national constitution, against Hamilton's vision of a potent "national system" anchored by a National Bank, a vital national military force and navy, and tariff protections for New England and mid-Atlantic "infant industry." These clashes are evidence of early cracks along North–South, frontier-settled, city-country, and manufacturing-agricultural axes that energized competing factions and led eventually to the formation of a modern political party system: Federalists (1792–1805) v. Democratic Republicans (1792–1824), then Democrats v. Whigs (1829–1856), and, on the eve of the Civil War and after, the Democrats v. Republicans (1856–present).

Exactly what power would the new Federal Government have over the states? With the loss of John Adams and the Federalists to Jefferson and the emerging Democratic–Republican Party in the election of 1800, a choice was made: With a few major exceptions, such as the Louisiana Purchase, for the next few decades the power would gravitate to the states and local economies. Tariffs would not be abandoned, nor would support for the Navy cease, though in 1811 Congress scuttled the First Bank of the United States and its charter. Still, the dynamism, enterprise, capital formation, and "release of energy" that Hamilton and the Federalists envisioned would, in the pre-Civil War era, be primarily at the state level. And the principal organs of policy development, with some notable exceptions, were the state legislatures and courts.

The national government was not exactly relegated to irrelevance. The sectional divides implicit in the ratification controversy over the Constitution, the emergence of Jeffersonian Republicans as rivals to the Federalists, and the rise in 1828–1852 of two new national parties as part of the second American party system (the Democrats and Whigs) were all *national* phenomena. Contests over the presidency and the balance of power in the U.S. Congress became defining issues for the young nation. Those who favored a strong national government, energetic Congressional leadership, and national economic development (advocates of the "American system," a phrase coined by Henry Clay in an 1824 speech) won modest victories for tariff, port, road, and canal-building projects in the 1820s. In 1834 these pro-national commercial interests coalesced to form the new Whig Party in opposition to the Jacksonian Democrats. (Abraham Lincoln ran successfully as a Whig in his 1846 bid for a seat in Congress.)

Conservative in orientation and inheritors of the mantel of the now-dead Federalist Party, the Whigs, like the Federalists, believed in rule by the "better sort," placed great value on education, gravitated toward the professions, and favored a national system of banking and commerce that included internal improvements. Unlike the Federalists, however, the

Whigs made their peace with democracy, but they worried about an egalitarian nation's vulnerability to demagogues and autocrats. "King Andrew" Jackson terrified them.

Jackson's presidency (1829–1837) marked the birth of the modern Democratic Party, which defined itself in popular terms as the alternative to the rule of "money men," "monopolies," and elites with "special privileges." The Jacksonian diatribe against the re-chartering of the Second Bank of the United States became a war on the beneficiaries of state deal-making: Bankers, industrialists, road and canal builders. While he did believe that there were proper responsibilities for the Federal government, and while his loyalty to the Union was never in question, Jackson's orientation as a frontiersman and Westerner suggested that he believed in the primacy of the "common man," the citizen of the state or locality.

The face of democracy, then, symbolized by Jackson as the war-hero commoner on horseback, was ruddy if not actually rude. Liquor flowed freely on Election Day and most especially in Jackson's inauguration day White House, as the franchise was expanded to include practically all white males. The new politics were rough and tumble, extending to the most humble of households. Candidates on the hustings were liable to be hooted down or worse and the badge of ordinariness worn by a candidate was often the best guarantee of success. (The Whigs quickly learned how to out-Jackson the Democrats, touting their candidates as men born in log cabins, Indian fighters, and war heroes, whether or not they actually were.) The transformation of society into a democracy mirrored the consuming passion of the rising nation, which was politics. Electioneering in the days before mass communication was a more or less constant state of affairs, as the most vital issues of the time were parried before crowds crowing for sport and entertainment. Affairs of state, the Constitutional order, party politics, elections at every level, and the contests between factions eclipsed all else.

The primary destabilizing element in the newly emerging two-party democracy was territorial expansion. This had always been a touchy issue, since the Northwest Ordinance of 1787 that banned slavery from the Northwest Territory (inclusive of all or part of the future states of Indiana, Ohio, Illinois, Michigan, Wisconsin, and Minnesota). The successful conclusion of the War of 1812 accelerated the removal of Woodland Indians in the North and Creeks in the South and created new opportunities for settlement in the Mississippi Valley (Indiana, Mississippi, Illinois, and Alabama all became states between 1816 and 1820). State expansion, however, also became the flash-point of sectional divide. Issues of land seemed to influence every other national issue as well. For example, the war with Mexico in 1848 was viewed by the Whigs (including Lincoln) as an unwise imperialist adventure, but was seen by the Democrats as deserved reprisal for Mexican incursions in Texas and, indeed, an aspect of the nation's "manifest destiny" to occupy the land from the Atlantic to the Pacific. Visions of empire undeniably guided some expansionists too, especially in the South, where cotton magnates were eyeing Cuba and Mexico as ripe for the plucking for the territorial expansion of slavery.

America in the decades before the Civil War might best be understood as a nation of "two democracies," one in the North founded on free labor, and one in the South whose planters and common people passionately prized their liberties, but whose wealth depended on the subordination of a race made permanently unfree. As new lands came into the Union, what was to be done about slavery? What was to become of the "two democracies" whose incompatibility and ever-expanding need for land was becoming so obvious?

The generation of the Revolution and the Constitution were not blind to the potential of division over slavery. The Constitution, after all, was a series of compromises among thirteen independent republics (as they in fact were under the Articles of Confederation), but the one issue that all recognized as troubling was that of slavery. While slavery was yet to be abolished in many of the Northern States, the fact is that in 1787 slavery already had emerged as a regional phenomenon highly identified with the South's plantation-based economy. Compromises over issues of "service" (the word "slave" appears nowhere in the U.S. Constitution) were sectional ones, and many of the South's leaders, such as Washington and Jefferson, understood as well as anyone that the days of slavery's profitability were slipping by. The South in the 1780s was a region wracked with debt; its land was bleached of its fertility by ruinous cash-crop agriculture (tobacco especially) and it declined steadily in value. The ownership of slaves, then, was often a liability. Southerners in 1787 who saw slavery in these terms chose to leave to the next generation the decision about what to do about the "peculiar institution," confident that slavery's eventual demise was just a matter of time. Such expectations helped make compromise at the Philadelphia convention palatable to all sides.

What no one anticipated in 1787 was Eli Whitney's development of the "cotton gin" (or cotton engine). The "gin," introduced in 1796, overnight made the cultivation of short-staple cotton in the Southern climate profitable, and introduced an extraordinary dynamism into the previously idyllic, if declining, landscape of the South. The national picture of "sections" was about to change. Before the gin, the effort of separating the seeds by hand from the harvested cotton fiber was too laborious to make large-scale planting profitable. (The harvesting of long-staple cotton was simpler, but it could be cultivated only on plantations that hugged the coastal areas of Georgia and South Carolina, where climate and rainfall was favorable.)

The gin's ingenious simplicity solved this problem with a mechanical cranking device that "combed" the seeds from the tuft with wire teeth.

What once took fifty slaves could now be done by one or two operating a gin. Cotton quickly became "king" as slaves cleared and planted new lands in the lower South, extending quickly into the fertile Louisiana Purchase territories with their favorable climate. So productive, large-scale and profitable was the new plantation system that by 1850 the South had become the foremost supplier of cotton for the textile mills of England and New England. At the time, 75% of the 3.9 million slaves in the U.S. were engaged in cotton agriculture, while the value of a healthy male slave field hand had increased 500 per cent between 1800 and 1860. No longer was the ownership of slaves a financial liability, and the new economy of slavery benefited all of the Southern states, including even the older ones like Virginia and South Carolina, that found it profitable to "breed" and sell slaves to the new states and territories. Indeed, it is quite possible that slavery could be seen to benefit the entire national economy, and to have played a role in fueling the Industrial Revolution in New England.

The opening of these new territories to slavery in the early nineteenth century exposed the fractures in the young Republic, and pushed to center stage questions about the nature of the Union itself. The Missouri Compromise of 1820, as we have seen, was the first in a series of statutes that attempted to balance the power of slaveholding and non-slaveholding states in the admission of new states to the Union (Maine and Missouri). Maintaining the precise balance of Congressional seats was critical to each section, given the growing divergence of markets, economic interests, tariffs, and labor systems. Despite these differences, before 1850 it was still possible to talk about the national political system as integrating sectional interests, for the most part—and at times welding the regions together.

Senators Daniel Webster of Massachusetts, Henry Clay of Kentucky, and John C. Calhoun of South Carolina could each lay claim to truly national leadership and vision. Both the Whigs and the Democrats drew their voters from the North and South. Jackson, the founder of the egalitarian Democratic Party, after all, was a national war hero and Southerner who owned slaves and who convincingly won two national elections, while his Democratic successor, Martin Van Buren, was a prominent attorney from New York. Indeed, among Whigs and Democrats the issues were as much ones of political economy as of sectionalism. Large plantation owners, bankers, developers of technology, merchants, and advocates of internal improvement and westward expansion were, for a while, united in their vision for the nation and their understanding of national political culture.

Democrats and proponents of the "common man" tended to be drawn from the majority of the population—small farmers, "mechanics," laboring men, shopkeepers, frontiersmen and settlers, sailors, craftsmen, and others. For these, the pace of life was felt locally and Democrats North and South found more to agree on than not. Tariffs certainly were an aggravating sectional issue, with Southern planters favoring a policy of free trade to support cotton markets and importation of cheap manufactures, and Northern interests seeking protection from outside competition in technology and industry. These interests were not beyond compromise, however.

After 1830, the economic success of the slave-system in the South, combined with its insatiable need for new cotton-growing land, put enormous pressure on the national government to renegotiate the Missouri Compromise as settlers moved further west of the Mississippi. The Mexican War (1846–48) followed in the wake of the admission of Texas into the Union in 1845 as a slave state. Northerners, some of whom were awakened to the evils of slavery and others who were more interested in maintaining a balance of power among the sections, reacted strongly to what they saw as the spread of the "slave power" west toward the Pacific.

In 1846, Rep. David Wilmot, a Democrat from Pennsylvania, quietly tacked a rider onto an appropriations bill (the "Wilmot Proviso") that would exclude slavery from any lands gained from Mexico in the war. When it passed the House, the Wilmot Proviso resounded like a clap of thunder. An alerted Senate foiled its passage. The 1848 Treaty of Hidalgo that concluded the Mexican War ceded one million square miles of territory covering the American Southwest to California. How suitable these lands were for slavery was unknown. That decision would be left to those who settled the land.

The Wilmot Proviso had support among Whigs and Democrats in the North and South, but it also signaled to Southerners that anti-slavery views were not limited to a handful of radicals. To moderate Northerners, the suddenness of the storm of controversy was highly disturbing, showing the extent to which the South was committed to defending the spread of slavery and its power in the Congress. Southerners, in their turn, taken off guard by Wilmot's proposal, saw conspiracies in the North to strike at their very way of life. The nature and future of the Union itself and the ends of national government were once again at issue.

A first victim of the Mexican War and the Pandora's land box it opened was the Whig Party itself, one of whose members, as indicated earlier, was Abraham Lincoln of Springfield, Illinois. While its leaders, both Northern and Southern, generally opposed the War with Mexico, the coalition split and fell apart over the question of slavery's expansion into new territories. The Compromise of 1850 admitted California as a free state, postponed for a time the matter of slavery in the remaining lands ceded by Mexico, and led to the passage of a strict Fugitive Slave Law that applied to all states without regard to the legality of slavery in any jurisdiction. The rise of the short-lived Free Soil Party in response (1848–

52) and the growth of the anti-Catholic and nativist "Know–Nothing" Party (1854–56) in eastern urban areas further siphoned off support from the Whigs, while the deaths of Webster and Clay in 1852 left the party rudderless. The Kansas–Nebraska Act of 1854 sounded the death knell for the Whigs. That 1854 statute, a compromise brokered by the Democratic Party Senator Stephen A. Douglas of Illinois, opened the heartlands to settlement and left to "popular sovereignty" the fate of slavery in both territories. At the time, it seemed like a definitive solution and was celebrated as such in the Congress.

Instead, the 1854 Kansas–Nebraska Act was the stimulus for the formation of the all-new Republican Party, among whose first organizers in Illinois was Abraham Lincoln. Unlike the Southwestern territorial acquisition, the Kansas–Nebraska Act struck deep into the American heartland, apparently thrusting the reach of the "slaveocracy" north toward Canada. With slave owners from Border States like Missouri now flooding into the Great Plains, the spread of slavery seemed unstoppable. The *Dred Scott* decision of 1857, which ruled that Congress lacked the power to prohibit slavery in the territories, and was rendered by a court whose Chief Justice was a slave owner (he eventually freed his slaves), added to the North's paranoia.

The sectional crisis of 1861 was triggered when the eleven Confederate states seceded from the Union after Lincoln's election as President with barely 40 percent of the popular vote. The crisis is astounding for the misapprehensions that it revealed. Whether secession was Constitutional (and, remember, the North's early justification for the Civil War was that it was not) was much in debate. Precedents for the Southern States' action were not lacking. Threats of nullification and even secession were practically commonplace in the first eighty years of the nation's existence. The Whiskey Rebels of Western Pennsylvania, we have seen, in openly repudiating the taxing power of the federal government, acted in a manner they believed consistent with the protection of their "rights and liberties." Indeed, the drums, fifes, and uniforms they donned were living remnants of the 1776 rebellion against an earlier distant and insensitive power.

Defendants in the Federalist prosecutions for seditious libel, we saw earlier, propounded the theory of jury nullification of Federal legislation. Jefferson's and Madison's Virginia and Kentucky Resolutions, clearly advanced a conception of union as highly conditional and contingent; a "compact" subject to interpretation and rejection by sovereign state republics. How else were these disagreements to be resolved, if not by the states themselves? Wrote Madison of "interposition" in his draft of the Virginia Resolution:

> "That this Assembly doth explicitly and peremptorily declare, that it views the powers of the federal government, as resulting from the

> compact, to which the states are parties; as limited by the plain sense and intention of the instrument constituting the compact; as no further valid that they are authorized by the grants enumerated in that compact; and that in case of a deliberate, palpable, and dangerous exercise of other powers, not granted by the said compact, the states who are parties thereto, have the right, and are in duty bound, to interpose for arresting the progress of the evil, and for maintaining within their respective limits, the authorities, rights and liberties appertaining to them."

Jefferson's draft of the Kentucky Resolution addresses "nullification" as an act of a sovereign state (in this case, Kentucky) invalidating a Federal law that on its face violates the Constitution. The reaction of Northern states against the Virginia and Kentucky resolutions was swift, but Kentucky responded, at that time, with a clarification that was unambiguous: Nullification was the "rightful remedy." In the midst of that war of words, however, neither Kentucky and nor Virginia actually took any action against the Alien and Sedition Acts.

In 1814–15 delegates from three New England states met in Hartford, Connecticut to consider responses to President James Madison's conduct of the War of 1812. The continuing effects of the war (especially the non-importation and embargo restrictions) had devastated New England's economy, which depended on trade with the English. Some New Englanders called for a separation from the Federal government, and a separately-negotiated peace with the British; others expressed sentiments in favor of nullification of the despised federal laws. Andrew Jackson's important victory in the Battle of New Orleans in 1815, occurring just as a delegation from Massachusetts had arrived in Washington, D.C. to negotiate terms with the Federal government, embarrassed New Englanders, and eventually led to the collapse of the already-weak Federalist Party. Still, the fragile quality and ambiguous meaning of the concept of "union" had been exposed.

Perhaps the most serious threat to Federal authority before the Civil War, because it introduced the concept of indivisible state sovereignty, was the crisis brought on by Governor George Troup of Georgia in 1823. That *contretemps* grew out of the cession of lands belonging to Native Americans—Cherokees and Creeks. Georgia was politically divided in 1819. One faction, in the Atlantic and Piedmont regions, comprised merchant and planter interests. In Georgia's Western backcountry, however, were small farmers and frontier settlers who had organized politically behind one John Clark. They sought to change the state constitution, which had placed election of the governor in the hands of the Eastern-dominated legislature. The Western Democrats did succeed in expanding the franchise and making elections more dependent on the popular vote, but Clark unexpectedly lost to Troup, who outmaneuvered his opponent by tying the slavery issue to the ever-popular nostrum of Native American removal.

On the heels of his election, Governor Troup manufactured the fraudulent "Treaty of Indian Springs," with a few hand-picked Cherokee "representatives" (one of whom was his relative) that purportedly ceded five million acres of prime farm land to the state. The Governor somehow managed to win U.S. Senate approval of the transfer at a time when President John Quincy Adams was distracted with his Inauguration. When the new President Adams learned of the fraud, he negotiated and received Senate approval of a second treaty (the Treaty of Washington) that restored some of the land to the Cherokees. In a defiant stance, Governor Troup and the Georgia legislature dared Adams to enforce the treaty while charging the Georgia militia to repel any hostile Federal armed intrusion across its borders. Troup sent a letter to Secretary of War James Barbour that made his intentions clear:

> "From the first decisive act of hostility, you will be considered and treated as a public enemy; and with the less repugnance, because . . . you, to whom we might constitutionally have appealed for our own defense against invasion, are yourselves the invaders, and what is more, the unblushing allies of the savages whose cause you have adopted."

The Northern press compared Georgia's opportunistic land grab to the machinations of the Hartford Convention and its disparagement of the Union. In the end, President John Quincy Adams and the Senate backed down, thereby delivering the first "states rights" victory for Southern sectionalism, and setting a precedent for other challenges.

One such challenge came four years later. In part a response to New England's economic hardships, beginning in 1816, Congress began passing stronger protective tariffs in order to encourage American industry and to generate further federal revenue for payment of debts incurred in the War of 1812. The Tariff of 1824, however, became linked with some politicians' desire for expansion and internal improvements—a controversial subject—and it was becoming increasingly evident that the woeful conditions of transportation networks among the states were both a logistical military weakness (one of the lessons of the War of 1812) and an impediment to economic growth. Whatever benefits New England manufacturers derived from the Tariff of 1824, however, and whatever revenues it raised, tariffs were not popular in the South.

The subsequent Tariff of 1828 was given the epithet in the South "Tariff of Abominations," because it placed even greater duties on imports, thus clearly favoring Northern industry and trade, and operating to the disadvantage of agrarian Southern exports.

In late 1828, Andrew Jackson's newly elected Vice President, John C. Calhoun of South Carolina, penned a then anonymous "Exposition and Protest," that questioned whether the Constitution gave the federal government the authority to impose unequal benefits of taxation—and whether the national government could deny a state from exercising its sovereign "right of judging" whether it would obey a prejudicial law:

> "If it be conceded, as it must be by every one who is the least conversant with our institutions, that the sovereign powers delegated are divided between the General and State Governments, and that the latter hold their portion by the same tenure as the former, it would seem impossible to deny to the States the right of deciding on the infractions of their powers, and the proper remedy to be applied for their correction. The right of judging, in such cases, is an essential attribute of sovereignty, of which the States cannot be divested without losing their sovereignty itself. . . . [T]o reserve such exclusive right to the General Government (it matters not by what department to be exercised), is to convert it, in fact, into a great consolidated government, with unlimited powers, and to divest the States, in reality, of all their rights. . . . "

Calhoun's "Exposition," then, was in perfect harmony with Jefferson's and Madison's statements in 1798, and with Georgia's late assertion that it fell to the states to judge when Federal sovereign assertions wrongly negated legitimate state sovereignty. The "Exposition" was also an ominous portent of a seismic political rift, as only five years earlier the Southerner Calhoun had been a pro-nationalist in the Senate, in league with Senator Henry Clay of Missouri and Senator Daniel Webster of Massachusetts. With memories of the Missouri Compromise's effort to cement the tear in the fabric of the Union still fresh, the effect of Calhoun's defense of states' rights was electric.

The dispute over the natures of state and federal sovereignty sparked a national debate about the Union that drew in judicial lights such as Harvard Professors Joseph Story and Nathan Dane, Senator Daniel Webster, former President John Quincy Adams, and others on the nationalist side. What was the nature of the Union? What kind of "compact" held the states together? How were values of "Our federal Union" (in Jackson's words) to be balanced with "our Liberty, most dear" (in the words of Calhoun)? Was sovereignty lodged in a remote generation of "We the people" who ratified the Constitution of 1789, creating once and for all an unbreakable agreement about where ultimate sovereignty was lodged (as Lincoln was to argue)? Or was sovereignty divisible, ongoing and contingent upon the "will of the people" in each state who, to protect their liberties from an encroaching power beyond their borders, needed to remain vigilant and proactive? What was the role of the Supreme Court as an arbiter between the state and federal governments?

President Jackson managed to nip the crisis prompted by Calhoun's "Exposition" in the bud by the stoutness of his response—made tolerable by his own identity as a man of the South. He declared nullification an "impractical absurdity" that would be dealt with as "treason" if force were to be used to resist the tariff of abominations by South Carolinians. Jackson gained Congressional approval for a "Force Bill" in 1831 (opposed in the Senate by Calhoun) that authorized the President to use the military to enforce tariff laws.

Jackson boasted that he would come to Charleston himself and "hang traitors." Meanwhile, a compromise tariff bill (ameliorating the "tariff of abominations") was making its way through the House and passed the Senate, with Calhoun's support. Jackson signed the Force Bill and the compromise Tariff Bill on the same day, March 2. Declaring itself satisfied with the new tariff law, South Carolina's constitutional convention rescinded its nullification of the "tariff of abominations," but enjoyed the last word when it declared the Force Bill null and void.

Inspired by the Fugitive Slave Act of 1850 (as part of the Compromise of 1850), Harriet Beecher Stowe's profoundly anti-slavery *Uncle Tom's Cabin* (1852) was a smash success in the North and did more to polarize relations between the regions than any other single event up to that time. To Southerners, the rise of the Republican Party in 1854, its inclusion of the pro-freedom wing of the dying Whig party, and its incorporation of former adherents to the Free Soil party and some Northern anti-slavery Democrats, signaled a threatening coalescence of common causes against their region. The historic function and capacity of American political parties to bridge sectional divides was breaking down.

The Kansas–Nebraska Act of that same year fanned the flames, and eventually became the principal issue in a series of seven extraordinary and eloquent Illinois Senatorial campaign debates (the "Great Debate") between the Republican Abraham Lincoln and the Illinois Democrat, Senator Stephen Douglas, in 1858. Never before had a campaign so engaged a state's voters on the question of slavery. Lincoln's performance caught the attention of Republican Party leaders and of Southerners too, for Lincoln's "House divided" speech could be read to say that a showdown was inevitable:

> "Mr. President and Gentlemen of the [Illinois Republican Party State] Convention. If we could first know where we are, and whither we are tending, we could then better judge what to do, and how to do it.
>
> We are now far into the fifth year, since a policy was initiated, with the avowed object, and confident promise, of putting an end to slavery agitation. Under the operation of that policy, that agitation has not only not ceased, but has constantly augmented.

In my opinion, it will not cease, until a crisis shall have been reached, and passed. 'A house divided against itself cannot stand.'

I believe this government cannot endure, permanently half slave and half free. I do not expect the Union to be dissolved—I do not expect the house to fall—but I do expect it will cease to be divided. It will become all one thing or all the other. Either the opponents of slavery, will arrest the further spread of it, and place it where the public mind shall rest in the belief that it is in the course of ultimate extinction; or its advocates will push it forward, till it shall become alike lawful in all the States, old as well as new—North as well as South."

News of the fanatical abolitionist John Brown's 1859 Harper's Ferry raid the next year riveted the nation; the audaciousness of the attack on a federal munitions depot, and Brown's stated goal of encouraging a mass slave insurrection confirmed the South's deepest fears that the North would seek to end slavery by force of arms, while the glorification of the raid by Abolitionists was taken by Southerners as a clear throwing down of the gauntlet. Was Lincoln's prediction coming true?

In the 1860 campaign for the presidency, the only one of the four national candidates utterly unacceptable to the South was the Republican, Lincoln. The Democratic Party had splintered, with Sen. Douglas as the Northern and John Breckinridge the Southern candidates. John Bell of Tennessee ran on the Constitutional Union Party ticket. Breckinridge carried the South in the election; Douglas carried only Missouri, and Lincoln won solidly in the remaining Northern states. As the South absorbed the news of Lincoln's geographically lopsided presidential victory, South Carolina hastily convened a state constitutional convention.

On December 20, 1860, the convention passed by unanimous vote an Ordinance of Secession, announcing that "the union now subsisting between South Carolina and the other States, under the name of the 'United States of America,' is hereby dissolved." Four days later the South Carolina convention issued its "Declaration of Immediate Causes," which you will soon read, that elaborated on South Carolina's conception of state powers and justified its decision to secede by claiming that the President-elect was presiding over a party whose sole purpose was to further the interests of the North, and "whose opinions and purposes are hostile to slavery."

As he rode the train with his family from Springfield to Washington in February for his March 4th, 1861 inauguration, Lincoln worried about the latest news of yet another Southern state secession. The lame duck Democrat, President James Buchanan, seemed utterly paralyzed. Two months earlier, on the advice of his Attorney General, Buchanan had stated in a message to Congress (in which still sat Southern Congressional representatives) that the U.S. government was helpless to prevent any state from seceding, as the national government could not respond with force. By Lincoln's Inaugural five Southern states had seceded, with some Border States undecided, and the great prize of Virginia still wavering.

In February, the seceding states organized a provisional government with a Confederate Constitution and elected former Mississippi U.S. Senator Jefferson Davis President. There was still hope, however, that cooler heads in the South (you'll soon read the speech of one, Alexander Stephens of Georgia) could stem the secession fever and coax the seceded states back in. In actuality, some Southerners might have understood that they were, for the time being at least, perfectly secure in their right of slave ownership; at no point had Lincoln or any other prominent Republican actually taken steps to abolish slavery, though Lincoln's "House Divided" speech and other utterances could certainly be interpreted as showing hostility to the peculiar institution. Nevertheless, it was believed in some quarters that the old-time loyalists to the Union in the South would eventually recognize that ties of language, friendship, blood, shared memories, and shared sacrifices in times of war and peace should not be torn asunder. If only he could keep the balance tipped in favor of the non-seceding states for a while longer, Lincoln believed, something perhaps could be worked out.

Lincoln tried to prepare himself for what lay ahead. He had reason to be optimistic: The South's perspective was not really alien to him. In his years in Springfield and on the circuit as a lawyer he was surrounded by fellow Illinoisans (many, like himself, migrants from the South) whose resentment of slaves and freedmen alike, and whose opposition to the spread of slavery was profound. But still, Lincoln and his neighbors were repulsed by "hot head" Abolitionists. Indeed, at no time in his political career up to 1861 or during the presidential campaign did he directly express any views other than respect for the rights of slaveholders in states where slavery already existed. Congress, he believed, was powerless to change that fact.

Even so, it was true that he disagreed with Chief Justice Roger Taney's opinion in *Dred Scott*, that you will soon encounter, that Congress was powerless to forbid slavery in the territories. Like most white Americans, however, Lincoln believed that blacks were members of an inherently inferior race, and therefore, as we have seen Jefferson did as well, Lincoln supported a policy of colonization of freedmen. Lincoln disapproved strongly of John Brown's raid on the federal arsenal at Harper's Ferry, and he did not object to Brown's eventual hanging, following Brown's trial for treason against the state of Virginia.

It cannot be denied, however, that Lincoln did believe that the institution of slavery was odious, that it was an affront to American principles of liberty and the natural instinct of humanity for freedom. Where slavery already existed in law, Lincoln placed his hope in the power of gradual emancipation (as did many Southern Founding Fathers, he pointed out) to resolve the dilemma once and for all—what Lincoln imagined as the course of slavery's "ultimate extinction." In the meantime, Lincoln wished only to stop slavery's spread, but this put him on a collision course with the South.

If Lincoln recognized that the coming clash between North and South was not about slavery exactly (and in the beginning of the struggle he characterized the Civil War as a battle over the nature of the Union), Lincoln also believed that somehow, slavery lay behind everything; that two kinds of societies were rising in the nation but of such contrary essence that eventually one must consume the other—that was, after all the thrust of his "House Divided" speech. For the Lincoln of 1861, though, the issue of the moment was not slavery. By his reasoning and reckoning, "No State, upon its own mere action, can lawfully get out of the Union."

And yet, looking back, were disunion and war inevitable? Could Lincoln or anyone else have avoided the Civil War? If there were obvious differences between North and South dating back to debates at the Constitutional Convention of 1787, there were more things that drew them together or at least made them fraternal, a fact that blurs the boundaries between slave-holding and free, North and South. Certainly important is the economic transformation of both the North and South after 1800, that made the two regions interdependent. This was a fact appreciated by merchants, planters, bankers, manufacturers, shippers, and textile mill owners everywhere. For them, war was a horrid specter, and their diplomacy had for decades helped each section to cool off after a crisis and to push back from the brink.

On matters of race, if slavery was the South's "peculiar institution," most whites in the North subscribed to white supremacy, and certainly this was evident in the Union Army. The New York City anti-draft riots of 1863 (the First Conscription Act went into effect that year) caused great destruction to property and roving bands targeted free blacks, killing perhaps as many as 100. Lincoln himself was vilified and hounded in the Northern press, whose stories became General Lee's most convincing source of information about the North's war fatigue.

But cooler heads, if such there were, did not prevail, and once the war began, Lincoln's generals seemed unwilling to fight and unable to win when they occasionally did. As the war dragged on, the North's peace movement swelled, leaving Northern opinion divided and desperate. Lincoln's own General-in-Chief of the Union Army, George McClellan, after a demotion for his inaction and insubordination, accepted a draft as the Democratic Party's "peace" candidate in the 1864 presidential election (he did not resign his commission until election day). The Democrats' platform was reunion with the South and a return to the *status quo antebellum*. Within the Republican Party itself, there was a move by malcontents to replace Lincoln on the ticket with Salmon P. Chase, his Secretary of the Treasury. So gloomy was Northern opinion on the war's prospects that the Republicans fully expected to lose the White House and possibly the Congress in the 1864 election—an outcome that probably would have brought the war to a quick and negotiated conclusion. It was averted only at the eleventh hour with Sherman's summertime victory in the Battle of Atlanta, that decisively changed the war's momentum.

Southerners showed great loyalty to their region, which they believed to have been invaded by a hostile power. While there was no longer sympathy with even gradual compensated emancipation anywhere in the South (the fear was slave insurrection), the fact is that the war was never very popular with many Southerners. Not all slave-holding states joined the Confederacy (Delaware, Maryland, Kentucky, and Missouri did not). Even in the Deep South, the popular vote on secession yielded uncertain outcomes, and in Georgia, for example, the majority of voters actually appear to have voted against secession (though the Georgia Constitutional Convention voted otherwise). In Atlanta, more people voted for Lincoln in the election of 1860 than any other presidential candidate.

Col. Robert E. Lee, a relative by marriage of the father of his nation, George Washington, agonized over the decision whether to accept the invitation tendered personally by General Winfield Scott to lead the Union Army. When Virginia seceded in April, Lee made his decision. As you will see, Alexander Stephens of Georgia, one of the country's foremost Constitutional law experts (and a valued acquaintance of Lincoln's from their days of service together in the House of Representatives as fellow Whigs), and later a Vice President of the Confederacy, opposed secession on legal grounds. Only with great reluctance did Stephens sign the Georgia Ordinance of secession, and only after its passage was a *fait accompli*. When Lincoln was assassinated, Stephens suffered "horrid dreams" and fasted and mourned his friend's loss.

The Confederate firing on the Federal Fort Sumter on April 12, 1861 and its surrender the next day was a decisive event for many Southerners and Northerners alike. (Whether Lincoln "tricked" the South Carolinians into taking the first shot is still a subject of some debate, but there is no doubt that Lincoln made the decision to go to war to defend federal prerogatives following the firing on the federal fort—was he in the right or wrong on that?) Long into the war, pockets of Unionist support dotted the South from Mississippi, through Appalachia, and into East Tennessee and North Carolina.

Some Southerners, especially from the Border States, joined the Union Army: One in four "Yankee" soldiers were born in the South. The majority of Southerners were not slave owners, and the average Confederate foot soldier's disgruntlement with the war as an enterprise to defend the mandarins of the slaveocracy crops up constantly in Confederate letters home. Southern boys, these missives suggested, were starved and fighting for their lives while some planter-aristocrats were making a fortune in the cotton harvests at home. Still, the fact that Confederate forces were fighting on their own ground made the war a defense of hearth and home.

In perhaps the most telling irony of all, the Commander-in-Chief of the Union Army, the President, was a Southerner by birth and temperament. Lincoln had even participated in a duel, and was as moved by sentiments of honor as the most Southern of gentlemen (this may explain his immovability on the issue of Union: for him, it was an affair of honor). Lincoln was married to a Southern woman whose family members owned slaves. Although Kentucky was a Border State that did not join the Confederacy, First Lady Mary Todd Lincoln lost two brothers and one brother-in-law to combat, each in service to the Confederacy. Lincoln felt the death of a Southern lad in uniform as deeply as one of his own.

We can also look back from the vantage point of knowing how the war came out. For Lincoln and his fellow Republicans, the first outlines of a new idea of the nature of the American Union began to form in 1859 and 1860, one that in the run-up to the Civil War and in the course of the conflict would build on old Whig and Democratic Party principles to form a new Republican Party synthesis of a *United* States of America (as opposed to the United *States* of America—only after the Civil War, after all, would it be common to speak of the United States as a single noun.). The Republican platform of 1860, that you will soon read, and that Lincoln ran on, favored an expansive central governmental role in internal improvements, a tariff policy to promote "the development of the industrial interests of the whole country," construction of a railroad to the Pacific, a homestead law that encouraged settlement of the West by ordinary farmers, and a fundamental commitment to free labor and unbridled opportunity, which in large measure was Lincoln's own story. (Were the South's fears justified?)

The new concept of Union at the end of the war placed unprecedented power in the national government, in the executive branch, and in the Congress. As the North's war aims lurched from the preservation of the Union, to the emancipation of slaves in the seceded states, and then to the abolition of slavery everywhere, Lincoln fused the liberty-loving principles and social idealism of the Declaration of Independence with the new nationalist power. For the Republicans, waging war would enhance both liberty and idealism in ways previously unimaginable and from which there could be no definitive "turning back." (Again, can you understand how this might have looked different to the South?)

Democracy would remain a shibboleth in post–1865 America, but it would now be transformed—if in fact it was talked about at all. Reconstruction, Reunion, Populism, trade unionism, social Darwinism, economic laissez-faire, monopoly and trust-busting, Progressivism, white supremacy at home and *noblesse oblige* abroad, world wars and "new deals," became the new channels for debating and creating meaning in politics and society. Antebellum democracy's tumultuous, rebellious, glorious quality, its romantic individualism and its orientation to the events of local life, its rough equality and open disdain for the refinement of manners and "social betters," its prizing of politics as entertaining machinations of ordinary people who defined, and filled, the public space—these would eventually become dim memories. In their place, after 1865, would be new industrial, technological, and economic realities, new manifestations of national corporate power, new amalgamations of working classes in teeming cities on the edge of disorder, new national associations of rising professional and commercial classes, new kinds of immigrants, and a new locus of politics in the national capital city of Washington, D.C.

Drawing from the reservoirs fed by the Revolutionary era's fervor for liberty, secessions and nullifications were always a rattling possibility in pre-Civil War America, tolerated to some degree as patriotic excesses of the "Spirit of '76." But after the Union victory of 1865, such threats were made almost unthinkable by a war that fundamentally redefined the obligations of government and citizens. Suggestions for revolution would be uttered, calls for reform and so forth would be made and even demanded, and in the South there would be a "Lost Cause" movement that resurrected a romanticized version of the Old South and the "War Between the States"—but there would be few calls for separation and withdrawal. ("States rights" would emerge again in the second half of the 20th century, an issue again linked with race, but it would never again be a serious threat to national sovereignty).

Looking back in 1900, Americans would see the Age of Jacksonian Democracy and the remonstrances of states-centered politicians as almost antique symbols of the flowering of the Republic, the era of innocence and the American Adam, a time of the individual and the frontier, when opportunity beckoned even for the lowliest. The allure of this view would exert itself in different ways even up to the present. Yet the fact remains: The behemoth of the Northern nation and its centralized government that won the war utterly supplanted that vision. A hardness, a toughness, a realism crept in. Precisely what kind of society and what kind of polity was to replace the eclipsed Age of Democracy, however, would become a fierce subject of political debate, which debate still continues. The ultimate meaning of the Civil War and the legacy of Abraham Lincoln, then, is still being worked out in our own time.

Further Reading:

Irving H. Bartlett, *John C. Calhoun: A Biography* (New York, 1993)

Donald W. Crofts, *Reluctant Confederates: Upper South Unionists in the Secessionist Crisis* (Chapel Hill, 1989)

Richard N. Current, *Lincoln and the First Shot* (Philadelphia, 1963)

Charles B. Dew, *Apostles of Disunion: Southern Secession Commissioners and the Causes of the Civil War* (Charlottesville, 2002)

David H. Donald, *Charles Sumner and the Coming of the Civil War* (New York, 1960)

David H. Donald, *Lincoln* (New York, 1995)

Dwight L. Dumond, *The Secessionist Movement, 1860–1861* (New York, 1931)

William W. Freehling, *Prelude to Civil War: The Nullification Controversy in South Carolina, 1816–1836* (New York, 1966)

William W. Freehling, *The Road to Disunion: Secessionists at Bay, 1776–1854* (New York, 1990)

Charles Buxton Going, *David Wilmot, Free–Soiler: A Biography of the Great Advocate of the Wilmot Proviso* (New York, 1924)

Joan Hedrick, *Harriet Beecher Stowe: A Life* (New York, 1994)

Richard Hofstadter, *The American Political Tradition and the Men Who Made It* (New York, 1948)

Michael F. Holt, *The Rise and Fall of the American Whig Party: Jacksonian Politics and the Onset of the Civil War* (New York, 1999)

Harold Holzer, *Lincoln at Cooper Union: The Speech That Made Abraham Lincoln President* (New York, 2004)

Daniel Walker Howe, *What Hath God Wrought: The Transformation of America, 1815–1848* (New York, 2007)

Harry V. Jaffa, *The Crisis of the House Divided: An Interpretion of the Issues in the Lincoln–Douglas Debates* (Chicago, 1982)

Jon Meacham, *American Lion: Andrew Jackson in the White House* (New York, 2008)

William S. McFeely, *Frederick Douglass* (New York, 1991)

James M. McPherson, *Battlecry of Freedom: The Civil War Era* (New York, 1988)

Frederick Merk, *Slavery and the Annexation of Texas* (New York, 1972)

John C. Niven, *John C. Calhoun and the Price of the Union* (Baton Rouge, 1988)

Merryll D. Peterson, *The Great Triumvirate: Webster, Clay, and Calhoun* (New York, 1987)

David Potter, *The Impending Crisis, 1848–1861* (New York, 1976)

Robert V. Remini, *Henry Clay: Statesman for the Union* (New York, 1991)

David S. Reynolds, *John Brown, Abolitionist: The Man Who Killed Slavery, Sparked the Civil War, and Seeded Civil Rights* (New York, 2005)

Thomas E. Schott, *Alexander Stephens: A Biography* (Baton Rouge, 1988)

Sean Wilentz, *The Rise of American Democracy: Jefferson to Lincoln* (New York, 2005)

Charles S. Sydnor, *The Development of Southern Sectionalism, 1819–1848* (Baton Rouge, 1948)

J. Mills Thornton III, *Politics and Power in a Slave Society: Alabama, 1800–1860* (Baton Rouge, 1978)

Slavery and the U.S. Constitution

Slavery before the Constitution

As we have seen, in the middle of the eighteenth century, slavery was legal in every English colony, though the practice of slavery was more expansive in the Southern colonies of Virginia, South Carolina, and Georgia where tobacco and rice plantations flourished. While a handful of Colonial Americans and British (especially Quakers) expressed doubts about the propriety of slavery in America before the era of the Revolution, the catalyst for delving more deeply into the multiple meanings of the word "slavery" was, ironically, the debate over Parliament's power to govern the colonies. The trigger was the Crown's desire to pay off its enormous debt generated by the French and Indian War (1759-1763), known in Europe as the Seven Years War. Because the war was fought in part to protect the colonies, Parliament thought it logical to ask the colonies to help pay "their share." The political strategy adopted initially was to lower the tax burden on the colonies, but to more strictly enforce its collection, mainly through duties on imports. After the colonials protested, Parliament upped the ante in 1765 with the "internal" Stamp Act tax, which, as we have seen already, raised in the minds of colonials questions about their "taxation without representation" in Parliament. After a half-century of "benign neglect" in which the corruption of Royal customs officials combined with widespread evasion and lax enforcement, the English colonies now fell under a Parliamentary boot of strict enforcement.

In a land where African slavery was commonplace, the Americans protested with a rhetorical vigor striking for the many references to their own enslavement. Again as we have seen, James Otis in 1761, in arguing against the legitimacy of the Writs of Assistance used by customs officials to ferret out smuggling, said that British trade laws were "instruments of slavery" and by them, Boston's Englishmen were being turned into "Negroes."

Benjamin Franklin, who represented colonial interests in London and pushed for the repeal of the Stamp Act, is reputed to have said to the English Undersecretary of State for the British Colonies that Parliament's taxation of Pennsylvania is "equivalent of an authority to declare all white persons in that province Negroes."

In 1768, in the wake of a spreading colonial resistance to Parliamentary taxation, John Dickinson of Delaware coined the "Liberty Song":

"Come join hand in hand, brave Americans all,

And rouse your bold hearts at fair Liberty's call;

No tyrannous acts, shall suppress your just claim,

Or stain with dishonor America's name.

In freedom we're born, and in freedom we'll live;

Our purses are ready,

Steady, Friends, steady,

Not as SLAVES but as FREEMEN our money we'll give."

When the public discussion of "slavery" in any guise was launched, as it was at the time of our Revolutionary War, the inevitable next question for some was: If "white slavery" is an abomination, is "black slavery" wrong too? Blacks in the colonies, some of whom were free, were alive to these implications, and became outspoken advocates of slave emancipation as consistent with developing American doctrines of liberty and self-government.

Phyllis Wheatley was a slave whose master lived in Boston. She was eventually emancipated. Below is an excerpt from a letter she wrote at age 20 that found its way into the *Connecticut Gazette* in March, 1774. Wheatley, born in Gambia, Senegal, was a published poet with an international reputation at the time of the American Revolution and was a devout Christian, whose religious beliefs influenced her writing. In this passage, she talks about the spirit of "civil and religious liberty" that, she believes, with God's help, is "chasing away the thick darkness" of racism and oppression:

> "I have this day received your obliging kind epistle, and am greatly satisfied with your reasons respecting the negroes, and think highly reasonable what you offer in vindication of their natural rights: Those that invade them cannot be insensible that the divine light is chasing away the thick darkness which broods over the land of Africa; and the chaos which has reigned so long, is converting into beautiful order, and reveals more and more clearly the glorious dispensation of civil and religious liberty, which are so inseparably united, that there is little or no enjoyment of one without the other: Otherwise, perhaps, the Israelites had been less solicitous for their freedom from Egyptian slavery; I do not say they would have been contented without it, by no means; for in every human breast God has implanted a principle, which we call - it is impatient of oppression, and pants

> for deliverance; and by the leave of our modern Egyptians I will assert, that the same principle lives in us. God grant deliverance in his own way and time, and get him honour upon all those whose avarice impels them to countenance and help forward the calamities of their fellow creatures. This I desire not for their hurt, but to convince them of the strange absurdity of their conduct, whose words and actions are so diametrically opposite. How well the cry for liberty, and the reverse disposition for the exercise of oppressive power over others agree - I humbly think it does not require the penetration of a philosopher to determine."

By 1776, as indicated earlier, many Americans, even slaveholders in the South, were taking a second look at the institution of slavery. Certainly an atmosphere of protest raised broad questions about social hierarchies of all kinds, as did the doctrines of American religion. As we have noted, concerns about slavery were strongest among Quakers in the colonies. Others also were beginning to express a glimmer of doubt about "what to do" with slavery in an era that was making "inalienable rights," "liberty" and "revolution" the new watchwords. In Philadelphia and New York, a nascent anti-slavery movement was finding its voice. How odd, in the eyes of many of the British, were those Americans who "yelped" incessantly about their "liberty" but still countenanced, for the most part, slavery.

Thinking about the wisdom and justice of slavery was difficult in the Southern colonies. Many slaveholders who were beginning to question the institution also were confronted by the most obvious of facts that their wealth and social standing were products of a slave-based economy. Certainly Jefferson was in this category, as was Patrick Henry, George Washington, George Mason, and later, James Madison. An early draft of the Declaration of Independence, penned by Jefferson, reveals a decidedly anti-slavery orientation when he blames the King of England for imposing slavery upon Africans, and then preventing the colonies from eliminating the slave trade. Jefferson continues in this vein, in this draft, castigating the King for using slaves as pawns when he made slave emancipation a war strategy. The delegates of the Continental Congress edited out both references and instead accused the King of promoting "insurrections."

While the advocacy of American liberty among slaveholders struck some across the sea as the purest hypocrisy, British philosopher and Parliamentarian Edmund Burke had a more subtle understanding. He saw American slavery and American freedom as joined at the hip: Slavery made Southern planters "proud and jealous of their freedom. Freedom to them is not only an enjoyment, but a kind of rank and privilege. . . In such a people, the haughtiness of domination combines with the spirit of freedom, fortifies it, and renders it invincible."

The coexistence of freedom and un-freedom in an era remarkable for the advancement of liberty and self-government led some to understand that there must be a future reckoning. Benjamin Franklin of Pennsylvania, once himself an owner of slaves, and John Adams of Massachusetts, whose cousin Samuel Adams owned a slave, by 1776 had come to see slavery as a dark cloud on the nation's distant horizon. They were not alone. When so much depended on national unity, how were the Patriots to deal with an issue that was foundational in the economic development of the colonies, not to mention in the Atlantic world itself?

The Constitutional Convention of 1787

Before the publication of James Madison's notes on the debates in the Constitutional Convention in the summer of 1787, little was known about the give-and-take on the issue of slavery among the delegates. (Madison delayed release of his notes until fifty years after the convention, when most of the participants were long dead.) Certainly by 1787, American slavery had become identified with the Southern states though slaves were still held in all states but one (Vermont). Above what became the Mason-Dixon Line, the movement was in the direction of gradual emancipation.

Surprisingly little was said about the presence of slavery in the draft of what eventually became the Constitution. As we have previously noted, three items attracted the most attention: 1) the Three-Fifths compromise over representation in the Congress, and for purposes of taxation and apportionment of presidential electors, 2) the abolition of the slave trade in twenty years, and 3) the return of fugitive slaves to their owners. Even these provisions, however, attracted relatively minor (though intense) dialogue.

The *Federalist Papers* brushed lightly on slavery, adopting a somewhat stilted anti-slavery tone that hinted of defensiveness. (Madison argued that the elimination of the slave trade in 20 years was an anti-slavery advance over the Articles of Confederation, which said nothing of the slave trade and thereby approved of it in perpetuity.)

In the course of the all-important Ratification debates in 1787 and 1788, two facts became obvious. One was that the delegates who signed the draft Constitution were not eager to discuss slavery. Although the words "slavery" and "slave" appear nowhere in the draft Constitution, Madison's notes report that the topic surfaced early in their proceedings and was a heated one that required the appointment of special committees whose terms of compromise became embedded and interwoven throughout the document. And second, the drafters were adamant that the Constitution's text and provisions not be tinkered with. Both positions suggest a deliberate post-Convention strategy to remain publically silent on the subject of slavery and, in the face of Anti-Federalist opposition to a strong national government, to insist on the speedy adoption of the draft Constitution *as a whole or not at all.*

It is worth remembering that the very act of creating a new form of government in the summer of 1787 was a departure from the agreement of the States at the outset, which was simply to send delegates to revise the Articles of Confederation. Moreover, the self-imposed black-out on any public discussion of their deliberations while in Philadelphia added an air of mystery to the proceedings. The accusation of back-room deal-making in Philadelphia and the rumors of "something afoot" (a monarchial plot?) that surfaced constantly in the Anti-Federalist critique of the draft Constitution are not surprising.

Still, in some respects, at least to those engaged in the political discourse of the era, there was nothing disruptive or overt about the treatment of slavery in the draft Constitution. After all, the Articles of Confederation stipulated the return of runaway slaves to their owners, as did the draft Constitution, and the Articles of Confederation also used the same "Federal ratio" of counting three-fifths of all slaves for the apportionment of representation in Congress. (John Adams said then that if the slave-holding states were permitted to count slaves, then New England states should be able to count cows.) Though the draft Constitution obviously treats of slavery in multiple places and guarantees its protection, the legalisms, the circuitous language, and the lapses into double-negatives naturally stoked the Anti-Federalists' distrust.

Moreover, the generation that produced the Constitution had its own impressions of the future of slavery that undoubtedly disposed them to accommodate the institution to the degree that they did, and ever so delicately by indirection. Whether as wishful thinking or as a frank assessment, many from North *and* South believed that slavery was destined to disappear because it was not economically viable, and among those most convinced of this eventuality were the Virginians themselves. The willingness to end the slave trade in twenty years would be, they thought, slavery's death knell. It is notable that Jefferson was the principal author of the "Northwest Ordinance," enacted by the Confederation Congress in 1787 and affirmed by the U.S. Congress in 1789, prohibiting slavery in the Northwest Territory, the domain most identified with America's future. In 1791, Virginia's College of William and Mary made the extraordinary gesture of giving the British abolitionist Granville Sharp an honorary degree. Perhaps the drafters of the Constitution saw whatever compromises were made as the cost of maintaining unity during a national crisis—9 states were required for ratification—trusting that the thorny matter of human bondage would eventually topple out of the Constitution of its own weight.

As we have observed earlier, what they could not have foreseen was Eli Whitney's invention of the "cotton engine" just five years later at Mulberry Grove Plantation, in Georgia, that gave slavery a new lease on life; nor could they possibly have imagined that 530 million acres of some of the world's most fertile soil would be added to the national domain (the 1803 Louisiana Purchase). To what must have been the surprise of these framers, Slavery did not die – it flourished. It was left to later generations to wrestle with that new nineteenth century reality that played out along a North-South divide spreading ever westward. As you will soon learn, wrestle they did through the Missouri Compromise of 1820, the Mexican-American War and the Wilmot Proviso of 1846, the Great Compromise of 1850, the Kansas-Nebraska Act of 1854, the Dred Scott decision of 1857, the Lincoln-Douglas debates of 1858, Lincoln's "house divided" speech that electrified the young Republican Party in 1860, and ultimately, the decision of eleven Slave-states to secede from the Union after Lincoln's election to the presidency, convinced that the agreements originally written into the Constitution had now been abandoned by those charged with their enforcement.

David Waldstreicher in his strongly argued book, *Slavery's Constitution: From Revolution to Ratification* (2009) concludes that it was not slavery that caused the Civil War, but slavery's Constitution. The 1787 Constitution "nationalized" and "republicanized" slavery, making it impossible to root out because of the degree to which slavery was embedded and protected throughout the Supreme Law of the land. Lawrence Goldstone, author of *Dark Bargain: Slavery, Profits, and the Struggle for the Constitution* (2006) believes there was never any real choice: "Of all the issues that would arise in Philadelphia, the one that evoked the most passion, the one that left the least possibility of compromise, the one that would most pit morality against pragmatism, was the question of slavery." Only war could cleanse the Constitution believed John Brown and Frederick Douglass. In this critical thread of scholarship that portrays the Constitution as leaning toward, if not committed to slavery, the Founders were deliberate in sacrificing liberty to the expediency of politics, with cataclysmic results. Neither Waldstreicher nor Goldstone are the first to point to the contradictions and paradox of slavery in the Revolutionary and Constitutional periods. Their work rests on a rich body of historical study beginning in the 1970s through the present day. Indeed, one of the earliest historians of the Constitution, Hermann Von Holst, saw slavery as a driving element of the founding generation in his *Constitution and Political History of the United States* (1876).

For much of the twentieth century the Constitution's Founders have been under the microscope. Charles Beard's *Economic Interpretation of the Constitution of the United States* (1913) placed monetary and other types of property interests at the center of the Constitutional Convention's deliberations, a point of view that infused much of the historiography for the next half-century. Gordon Wood and his mentor, Bernard Bailyn, in *The Ideological Origins of the American Revolution* (1967) rescued the Patriot Generation from accusations of crass self-interest by reinterpreting their work in the unfolding tradition of republicanism. Wood's highly influential book, *The Creation of the American Republic: 1776-1787* (1967), is mostly silent on the subject of slavery. To judge or analyze the Founders using the lens of recent history carries with it the danger of presentism, he contends. We cannot "read their minds" and "we have to try to rid ourselves of our knowledge of what happened in the succeeding decades" following the Constitution's ratification. According to Wood, the Founders' great accomplishment was to treat the subjects of liberty, political theory, the track record of corruption in prior republics, the eternal problem of corruption in politics generally, and the newly emerging European science of government with utmost seriousness. In so doing, the Founders did not so much dodge the issue of slavery, as focus their energy on the ultimate act of *creating* an entirely new form of government which used power to protect, rather than thwart, the liberty of the citizenry – the first and most successful government of its kind in history. From this vantage point, if the Constitution left slavery undisturbed, the republicanism and liberty at the Constitution's core inevitably implied silent disapproval that in time led to slavery's ultimate destruction.

With the arrival of the 150th anniversary of the Civil War, and with the modern Civil Rights movement itself now part of history (2011 was the 50th Anniversary of the Freedom Rides), perhaps Waldstreicher's provocative conclusion will continue the conversation first begun in Philadelphia in 1787: Did the U.S. Constitution owe its existence to slavery? Did slavery owe its existence to the U.S. Constitution? Was the conflict surrounding slavery that resulted in the Civil War ultimately the responsibility of the Constitution? The judiciary? The Congress and the presidency? The political party system? Abolitionists? A new generation of apologists for Southern slavery? The willingness of American society to engage the discussion openly and vigorously in the 21st century is a measure of the seriousness of America's experiment with liberty and government – then and now. If the Founders bequeathed anything to the future, perhaps it is that. Consider these questions as you read the materials on slavery in the federal courts, which follow.

Further Reading:

Bernard Bailyn, *The Ideological Origins of the American Revolution* (1967)

Alfred W. Blumrosen and Ruth G. Blumrosen, *Slave Nation: How Slavery United the Colonies and Sparked the American Revolution* (2005)

Don E. Fehrenbacher, *The Slaveholding Republic* (2001)

Paul Finkelman, *Slavery and the Founders* (2001)

Paul Finkelman, *An Imperfect Union: Slavery, Federalism, and Comity* (1981)

Staughton Lynd, *Class Conflict, Slavery, and the United States Constitution* (1967)

Gary Nash, *Forgotten Fifth: African Americans in the Age of Revolution* (2006)

Leonard L. Richards, *The Slave Power* (2000)

David Waldstreicher, *Slavery's Constitution: From Revolution to Ratification* (2009)

Garry Wills, *"Negro President": Jefferson and the Slave Power* (2003)

William M. Wiecek, The Sources of Antislavery Constitutionalism In America, 1760–1848 (1977)

Gordon S. Wood, "Reading the Founders' Minds," *New York Review of Books* (June 28, 2007)

Gordon S. Wood, *The Creation of the American Republic: 1776–1787* (1967)

PRIGG V. PENNSYLVANIA

Supreme Court of the United States, 1842.
41 U.S. (16 Pet.) 539, 608, 10 L.Ed. 1060.

* * *

MR. JUSTICE STORY delivered the opinion of the Court.

* * *

The facts are briefly these: The plaintiff in error was indicted, * * * for having, with force and violence, taken and carried away from [York] county [Pennsylvania] to the state of Maryland, a certain negro woman, named Margaret Morgan, with a design and intention of selling and disposing of, and keeping her as a slave or servant for life, contrary to a statute of Pennsylvania, passed on the 26th of March, 1826. That statute in the first section, in substance, provides, that if any person or persons shall from and after the passing of the act, by force and violence take and carry away * * * [or] shall by fraud or false pretence, seduce, or cause to be seduced * * * any negro or mulatto from any part of that commonwealth, with a design and intention of selling and disposing of * * * or of keeping and detaining * * * such negro or mulatto as a slave or servant for life * * * every such person or persons, his or their aiders or abettors, shall, on conviction thereof, be deemed guilty of a felony, and shall forfeit and pay a sum not less than five hundred, nor more than one thousand dollars; and moreover, shall be sentenced to undergo a servitude for any term or terms of years, not less than seven years nor exceeding twenty-one years; and shall be confined and kept to hard labour, & c. * * *

The plaintiff in error pleaded not guilty to the indictment; and at the trial the jury found a special verdict * * * that the negro woman, Margaret Morgan, was a slave for life, and held to labour and service under and according to the laws of Maryland, to a certain Margaret Ashmore, a citizen of Maryland; that the slave escaped and fled from Maryland into Pennsylvania in 1832; that the plaintiff in error, being legally constituted the agent and attorney of the said Margaret Ashmore, in 1837, caused the said negro woman to be taken and apprehended as a fugitive from labour by a state constable, under a warrant from a Pennsylvania magistrate; that the said negro woman was thereupon brought before the said magistrate, who refused to take further cognisance of the case; and thereupon the plaintiff in error did remove, take, and carry away the said negro woman and her children out of Pennsylvania into Maryland, and did deliver the said negro woman and her children into the custody and possession of the said Margaret Ashmore. * * *

Upon this special verdict, the Court of Oyer and Terminer of York county adjudged that the plaintiff in error was guilty of the offence charged in the indictment. * * *

There are two clauses in the Constitution upon the subject of fugitives, * * * They are both contained in the second section of the fourth article, and are in the following words: "A person charged in any state with treason, felony, or other crime, who shall flee from justice, and be found in another state, shall, on demand of the executive authority of the state from which he fled, be delivered up, to be removed to the state having jurisdiction of the crime."

"No person held to service or labour in one state under the laws thereof, escaping into another, shall in consequence of any law or regulation therein, be discharged from such service or labour; but shall be delivered up, on claim of the party to whom such service or labour may be due."

The last clause is that, the true interpretation whereof is directly in judgment before us. Historically, it is well known, that the object of this clause was to secure to the citizens of the slaveholding states the complete right and title of ownership in their slaves, as property, in every state in the Union into which they might escape from the state where they were held in servitude. The full recognition of this right and title was indispensable to the security of this species of property in all the slaveholding states; and, indeed, was so vital to the preservation of their domestic interests and institutions, that it cannot be doubted that it constituted a fundamental article, without the adoption of which the Union could not have been formed. Its true design was to guard against the doctrines and principles prevalent in the nonslaveholding states, by preventing them from intermeddling with, or obstructing, or abolishing the rights of the owners of slaves.

By the general law of nations, no nation is bound to recognise the state of slavery, as to foreign slaves found within its territorial dominions, when it is in opposition to its own policy and institutions, in favour of the subjects of other nations where slavery is recognised. If it does it, it is a matter of comity, and not as a matter of international right. The state of slavery is deemed to be a mere municipal regulation, founded upon and limited to the range of the territorial laws. * * *

It is manifest from this consideration, that if the Constitution had not contained this clause, every nonslaveholding state in the Union would have been at liberty to have declared free all runaway slaves coming within its limits, and to have given them entire immunity and protection against the claims of their masters; a course which would have created the most bitter animosities, and engendered perpetual strife between the different states. * * *

The clause manifestly contemplates the existence of a positive, unqualified right on the part of the owner of the slave, which no state law or regulation can in any way qualify, regulate, control, or restrain. The slave is not to be discharged from service or labour, in consequence of any state law or regulation. Now, certainly, without indulging in any nicety of criticism upon words, it may fairly and reasonably be said, that any state law or state regulation, which interrupts, limits, delays, or postpones the right of the owner to the immediate possession of the slave, and the immediate command of his service and labour, operates, pro tanto, a discharge of the slave therefrom. The question can never be, how much the slave is discharged from; but whether he is discharged from any, by the natural or necessary operation of state laws or state regulations. * * *

We have said, that the clause contains a positive and unqualified recognition of the right of the owner in the slave, unaffected by any state law or regulation whatsoever, because there is no qualification or restriction of it to be found therein; and we have no right to insert any which is not expressed, and cannot be fairly implied. * * * If this be so, then all the incidents to that right attach also. The owner must, therefore, have the right to seize and repossess the slave, which the local laws of his own state confer upon him as property; and we all know that this right of seizure and recaption is universally acknowledged in all the slaveholding states. * * * Upon this ground we have not the slightest hesitation in holding, that, under and in virtue of the Constitution, the owner of a slave is clothed with entire authority, in every state in the Union, to seize and recapture his slave, whenever he can do it without any breach of the peace, or any illegal violence. In this sense, and to this extent this clause of the Constitution may properly be said to execute itself, and to require no aid from legislation, state or national.

But the clause of the Constitution does not stop here * * *. Many cases must arise in which, if the remedy of the owner were confined to the mere right of seizure and recaption, he would be utterly without any adequate redress. He may not be able to lay his hands upon the slave. * * * He may be restricted by local legislation as to the mode of proofs of his ownership; as to the Courts in which he shall sue, and as to the actions which he may bring; or the process he may use to compel the delivery of the slave. Nay, the local legislation may be utterly inadequate to furnish the appropriate redress, by authorizing no process in rem, or no specific mode of repossessing the slave, but a mere remedy in damages; and that perhaps against persons utterly insolvent or worthless. * * *

And this leads us to the consideration of the other part of the clause, which implies at once a guaranty and duty. It says, "But he (the slave) shall be delivered up on claim of the party to whom such service or labour may be due." Now, we think it exceedingly difficult, if not impracticable, to read this language and not to feel, that it contemplated some farther remedial redress than that, which might be administered at the hands of the owner himself. A claim is to be made. What is a claim? It is, in a just juridical sense, a demand of some matter as of right made by one person upon another, to do or to forbear to do some act or thing as a matter of duty. [This means, said Story, that there must be] * * * legislation to protect the right, to enforce the delivery, and to secure the subsequent possession of the slave. If, indeed, the Constitution guarantees the right * * * the natural inference certainly is, that the national government is clothed with the appropriate authority and functions to enforce it. * * * The clause is found in the national Constitution, and not in that of any state. It does not point out any state functionaries, or any state action to carry its provisions into effect. The states cannot, therefore, be compelled to enforce them; and it might well be deemed an unconstitutional exercise of the power of interpretation, to insist that the states are bound to provide means to carry into effect the duties of the national government, nowhere delegated or intrusted to them by the Constitution. * * *

Congress has taken this very view of the power and duty of the national government. As early as the year 1791, the attention of Congress was drawn to it * * *. The result of their deliberations, was the passage of the act of the 12th of February, 1793, ch. 51, (7,) which * * * proceeds, in the third section, to provide, that when a person held to labour or service in any of the United States, shall escape into any other of the states or territories, the person to whom such labour or service may be due, his agent or attorney, is hereby empowered to seize or arrest such fugitive from labour, and take him or her before any judge of the Circuit or District Courts of the United States * * * or before any magistrate of a county, city, or town corporate, wherein such seizure or arrest shall be made; and upon proof to the satisfaction of such judge or magistrate, either by oral evidence or affidavit, & c., that the person so seized or arrested, doth, under the laws of the state or territory from which he or she fled, owe service or labour to the person claiming him or her, it shall be the duty of such judge or magistrate, to give a certificate thereof to such claimant, his agent or attorney, which shall be sufficient warrant for removing the said fugitive from labour, to the state or territory from which he or she fled. The fourth section provides a penalty against any person, who shall knowingly and willingly obstruct or hinder such claimant, his agent, or attorney, in so seizing or arresting such fugitive from labour, or rescue such fugitive from the claimant, or his agent, or attorney when so arrested * * *.

In a general sense, this act may be truly said to cover the whole ground of the Constitution * * * because it points out fully all the modes of attaining those objects, which Congress, in their discretion, have as yet deemed expedient or proper to meet the exigencies of the Constitution. If this be so, then it would seem, upon just principles of construction, that the legislation of Congress, if constitutional, must supersede all state legislation upon the same subject; and by necessary implication prohibit it. For, if Congress have a constitutional power to regulate a particular subject, and they do actually regulate it in a given manner, and in a certain form, it cannot be that the state legislatures have a right to interfere, and, as it were, by way of complement to the legislation of Congress, to prescribe additional regulations, and what they may deem auxiliary provisions for the same purpose. In such a case, the legislation of Congress, in what it does prescribe, manifestly indicates, that it does not intend that there shall be any further legislation to act upon the subject matter. Its silence as to what it does not do, is as expressive of what its intention is as the direct provisions made by it.

* * *

But it has been argued, that the act of Congress is unconstitutional, because it does not fall within the scope of any of the enumerated powers of legislation confided to that body; and therefore it is void. Stripped of its artificial and technical structure, the argument comes to this, that although rights are exclusively secured by, or duties are exclusively imposed upon, the national government, yet, unless the power to enforce these rights, or to execute these duties can be found among the express powers of legislation enumerated in the Constitution, they remain without any means of giving them effect by any act of Congress; * * * even although, in a practical sense, they may become a nullity from the want of a proper remedy to enforce them, or to provide against their violation. * * * Such a limited construction of the Constitution has never yet been adopted as correct, either in theory or practice. No one has ever supposed that Congress could, constitutionally, by its legislation, exercise powers, or enact laws beyond the powers delegated to it by the Constitution. But it has, on various occasions, exercised powers which were necessary and proper as means to carry into effect rights expressly given, and duties expressly enjoined thereby. The end being required, it has been deemed a just and necessary implication, that the means to accomplish it are given also * * *.

* * *

[Story then proceeds to give two instances where Congress exercised implied powers in order to accomplish express constitutional ends: apportionment of Congressional representatives among the states and preventing the suspension of the writ of habeas corpus.]

* * *

The very act of 1793, now under consideration, affords the most conclusive proof, that Congress has acted upon a very different rule of interpretation, and has supposed that the right as well as the duty of legislation on the subject of fugitives from justice, and fugitive slaves, was within the scope of the constitutional authority conferred on the national legislature. In respect to fugitives from justice, the Constitution, although it expressly provides, that the demand shall be made by the executive authority of the state from which the fugitive has fled, is silent as to the party upon whom the demand is to be made, and as to the mode in which it shall be made. This very silence occasioned embarrassments in enforcing the right and duty at an early period after the adoption of the Constitution; and produced a hesitation on the part of the executive authority of Virginia to deliver up a fugitive from justice, upon the demand of the executive of Pennsylvania, in the year 1791; and as we historically know from the message of President Washington and the public documents of that period, it was the immediate cause of the passing of the act of 1793, which designated the person (the state executive) upon whom the demand should be made, and the mode and proofs upon and in which it should be made. From that time down to the present hour not a doubt has been breathed upon the constitutionality of this part of the act; and every executive in the Union has constantly acted upon and admitted its validity. * * * This very acquiescence, under such circumstances, of the highest state functionaries, is a most decisive proof of the universality of the opinion that the act is founded in a just construction of the Constitution, independent of the vast influence, which it ought to have as a contemporaneous exposition of the provisions by those, who were its immediate framers, or intimately connected with its adoption.

The same uniformity of acquiescence in the validity of the act of 1793, upon the other part of the subject matter, that of fugitive slaves, has prevailed throughout the whole Union until a comparatively recent period. * * * So far as the judges of the Courts of the United States have been called upon to enforce it, and to grant the certificate required by it, it is believed that it has been uniformly recognised as a binding and valid law, and as imposing a constitutional duty. Under such circumstances, if the question were one of doubtful construction, such long acquiescence in it, such contemporaneous expositions of it, and such extensive and uniform recognition of its validity, would in our judgment entitle the question to be considered at rest * * *.

But we do not wish to rest our present opinion upon the ground either of contemporaneous exposition, or long acquiescence * * *. On the contrary, our judgment would be the same, if the question were entirely new, and the act of Congress were of recent enactment. We hold the act to be clearly constitutional in all its leading provisions, and, indeed, with the exception of that part, which confers authority upon state magistrates, to be free from reasonable doubt and difficulty upon the grounds already stated. As to the authority so conferred upon state magistrates, while a difference of opinion has existed, and may exist still on the point, in different states, whether state magistrates are bound to act under it, none is entertained by this Court, that state magistrates may, if they choose, exercise that authority, unless prohibited by state legislation.

The remaining question is, whether the power of legislation upon this subject is exclusive in the national government, or concurrent in the states, until it is exercised by Congress. In our opinion it is exclusive * * *. "Wherever," said Mr. Chief Justice Marshall, in delivering the opinion of the Court [in Sturgis v. Crowninshield, 4 Wheat.Rep. 122, 193,] "the terms in which a power is granted to Congress, or the nature of the power require, that it should be exercised exclusively by Congress, the subject is as completely taken from the state legislatures, as if they had been forbidden to act." * * *

In the first place, it is material to state * * * that the right to seize and retake fugitive slaves, and the duty to deliver them up, * * * and of course the corresponding power in Congress to use the appropriate means to enforce the right and duty, derive their whole validity and obligation exclusively from the Constitution of the United States * * *. Before the adoption of the Constitution, no state had any power whatsoever over the subject, except within its own territorial limits, and could not bind the sovereignty or the legislation of other states. * * * Under the Constitution it is recognized as an absolute, positive, right and duty, pervading the whole Union with an equal and supreme force, uncontrolled and uncontrollable by state sovereignty or state legislation. * * * The natural inference deducible from this consideration certainly is, in the absence of any positive delegation of power to the state legislatures, that it belongs to the legislative department of the national government, to which it owes its origin and establishment. It would be a strange anomaly, and forced construction, to suppose, that the national government meant to rely for the due fulfillment of its own proper duties and the rights, which it intended to secure, upon state legislation, and not upon that of the Union. * * *

In the next place, the nature of the provision and the objects to be attained by it, require that it should be controlled by one and the same will, and act uniformly by the same system of regulations throughout the Union. If, then, the states have a right, in the absence of legislation by Congress, to act upon the subject, each state is at liberty to prescribe just such regulations as suit its own policy, local convenience, and local feelings. * * * One state may require the owner to sue in one mode, another in a different mode. One state may make a statute of limitations as to the remedy, in its own tribunals, short and summary; another may prolong the period, and yet restrict the proofs. * * * The duty might be enforced in some states; retarded, or limited in others; and denied, as compulsory in many, if not in all. Consequences like these must have been foreseen as very likely to occur in the nonslaveholding states, where legislation, if not silent on the subject, and purely voluntary, could scarcely be presumed to be favorable to the exercise of the rights of the owner.

It is scarcely conceivable, that the slaveholding states would have been satisfied with leaving to the legislation of the nonslaveholding states, a power of regulation, in the absence of that of Congress, which would or might practically amount to a power to destroy the rights of the owner. * * * Surely such a state of things never could have been intended, under such a solemn guarantee of right and duty. On the other hand, construe the right of legislation as exclusive in Congress, and every evil, and every danger vanishes. The right and the duty are then coextensive and uniform in remedy and operation throughout the whole Union. The owner has the same security, and the same remedial justice, and the same exemption from state regulation and control, through however many states he may pass with his fugitive slave in his possession, in transit, to his own domicile. * * *

These are some of the reasons, but by no means all, upon which we hold the power of legislation on this subject to be exclusive in Congress. To guard, however, against any possible misconstruction of our views, it is proper to state, that we are by no means to be understood in any manner whatsoever to doubt or to interfere with the police power belonging to the states in virtue of their general sovereignty. * * * We entertain no doubt whatsoever, that the states, in virtue of their general police power, possess full jurisdiction to arrest and restrain runaway slaves, and remove them from their borders, and otherwise to secure themselves against their depredations and evil example, as they certainly may do in cases of idlers, vagabonds, and paupers. * * * But such regulations can never be permitted to interfere with or to obstruct the just rights of the owner to reclaim his slave, derived from the Constitution of the United

States, or with the remedies prescribed by Congress to aid and enforce the same.

Upon these grounds, we are of opinion that the act of Pennsylvania upon which this indictment is founded, is unconstitutional and void. It purports to punish as a public offence against that state, the very act of seizing and removing a slave by his master, which the Constitution of the United States was designed to justify and uphold. * * *

NOTES AND QUESTIONS

1. What do you understand to have been the purpose of the Pennsylvania Act of March 26, 1826, described in the second paragraph of Story's opinion? Many of these "personal liberty laws," passed at about this time, did not expressly reject the Constitution's fugitive slave clause, but did require certain safeguards, such as jury trials or a certificate from a state officer before a fugitive could be taken. Is such legislation consistent with the text of the clause of Article IV, Section 2 of the U.S. Constitution which provides that "No person held to service or labour in one state under the laws thereof, escaping into another, shall in consequence of any law or regulation therein, be discharged from such service or labour * * *." Would you have voted for such a "personal liberty law" if you were a Pennsylvania state legislator?

2. Consider a somewhat different type of statute. On May 14, 1840, the New York Legislature passed "An act more effectively to protect the free citizens of this State from being kidnapped, or reduced to Slavery." That 1840 act was the one used to free Solomon Northrup, and its text follows:

> 1. Whenever the Governor of this State shall receive information satisfactory to him that any free citizen or any inhabitant of this State has been kidnapped or transported away out of this State, into any other State or Territory of the United States, for the purpose of there being held in slavery; or that such free citizen or inhabitant is wrongfully seized; imprisoned or held in slavery in any of the States or Territories of the United States, on the allegation or pretence that such a person is a slave, or by color of any usage or rule of law prevailing in such State or Territory, is deemed or taken to be a slave, or not entitled of right to the personal liberty belonging to a citizen; it shall be the duty of the said Governor to take such measures as he shall deem necessary to procure such person to be restored to his liberty, and returned to this State. The Governor is hereby authorized to appoint and employ such agent or agents as he shall deem necessary to procure such person to be restored to his liberty, and returned to this State. The Governor is hereby authorized to appoint and employ such agent or agents as he shall deem necessary to effect the restoration and return of such person and shall furnish the said agent with such credentials and instructions as will be likely to accomplish the object of his appointment. The Governor may determine the compensation to be allowed to such agent for his services besides his necessary expenses.

> 2. Such agent shall proceed to collect the proper proof to establish the rights of such person to his freedom, and shall perform such journeys, take such measures, institute and procure to be prosecuted such legal proceedings, under the direction of the Governor, as shall be necessary to procure such person to be restored to his liberty and returned to this State.
>
> 3. The accounts for all services and expenses in carrying this act into effect shall be audited by the Comptroller, and paid by the Treasurer on his warrant, out of any moneys in the Treasury of this State not otherwise appropriated. The Treasurer may advance, on the Warrant of the Comptroller, to such agent, such sum or sums as the Governor shall certify to be reasonable advances to enable him to accomplish the purposes of his appointment, for which advance such agent shall account, on the final audit of his warrant.

Reproduced in Northrup, supra, at 254–255. Would you have voted for this statute, if you had been a New York legislator in 1840? Would the statute pass constitutional muster under Story's opinion in *Prigg*?

3. How do you explain that it is not until 1842 that the United States Supreme Court passes on the constitutionality of the Fugitive Slave Act of 1793? What was the argument that the Act was unconstitutional and did you find it persuasive? Can you imagine how this argument could be advanced by anyone who took seriously the idea that the United States Constitution was to be the "supreme law" of the land? Do you see any similarities in this argument and the debate over the federal common law of crimes which we studied in Chapter Two? Are the problems of conceptions of the allocation of powers between the state and federal governments similar? How would you have dealt with the argument, also made, that the federal fugitive slave act was unconstitutional because it deprived alleged fugitives of their freedom without a jury trial. Is the problem of the constitutionality of the 1793 Act confined to fugitive *slaves?* Suppose Story had decided that the federal legislation on fugitive slaves was unconstitutional. What would have been the effect on other fleeing felons?

4. Is Story necessarily correct that the power to legislate regarding fugitive slaves is exclusively vested in congress? Is this necessarily a proslavery holding? Chief Justice Taney dissented from this part of Story's opinion:

> The language used in the Constitution does not, in my judgment, justify the construction given to it by the Court. It contains no words prohibiting the several states from passing laws to enforce this right. They are in express terms forbidden to make any regulation that shall impair it. But, there the prohibition stops. And according to the settled rules of construction for all written instruments, the prohibition being confined to laws injurious to the right, the power to pass laws to support and enforce it, is necessarily implied. And the words of the article which direct that the fugitive "shall be delivered up," seem evidently designed to impose it as a duty upon the people of the several states to pass laws

> to carry into execution, in good faith, the compact into which they thus solemnly entered with each other. The Constitution of the United States, and every article and clause in it, is a part of the law of every state in the Union; and is the paramount law. * * * And why may not a state protect a right of property, acknowledged by its own paramount law? Besides, the laws of the different states, in all other cases, constantly protect the citizens of other states in their rights of property, when it is found within their respective territories; and no one doubts their power to do so. And in the absence of any express prohibition, I perceive no reason for establishing, by implication, a different rule in this instance; where, by the national compact, this right of property is recognized as an existing right in every state of the Union.

41 U.S. (16 Pet.) at 627–633. Who is correct on this point, Justice Story or Justice Taney? In an important study of the federal slavery cases, Professor Earl M. Maltz points out that the fugitive slave clause "is included not in Article I, which defines the power of Congress, but in Article IV, section 2, which is primarily concerned with defining the rights and obligations of states towards other states and citizens of those states." He goes on to suggest that "To infer from the provision a limitation on state authority to enforce the right described therefore seems entirely inappropriate." Maltz's piece, "Slavery, Federalism, and the Structure of the Constitution," 36 Am.J.Leg.Hist. 466 (1992) is a powerful reminder that the great federal slavery cases (*Prigg* and *Dred Scott* among others) were not only about slavery but about the most basic issues of federalism.

Was it necessary for Story to decide the question of whether a state could pass legislation to aid in the enforcement of the fugitive slave act? What are we to make of Story's offhand suggestions that state magistrates may have the right to "choose" whether to act pursuant to the 1793 Act, and that states might "prohibit" them from doing so? Based on this part of Justice Story's opinion, his son and biographer, William Wetmore Story, claimed that his father's opinion could actually be read as an antislavery document. How could Story's son claim that this opinion was a "charter of freedom"? See II William W. Story, Life and Letters of Joseph Story 381–98 (1851). Whether Story was "unduly proslavery" in *Prigg* remains a hot historiographical topic. Maltz, supra, at 479 n. 5. See also, for Professor Maltz's further thoughts on *Prigg*, Earl M. Maltz, "Majority, Concurrence, and Dissent: Prigg v. Pennsylvania and the Structure of Supreme Court Decisionmaking," 31 Rut.L.J. 345 (2000). There is one defense of Story in Note, "Justice Story, Slavery, and the Natural Law Foundations of American Constitutionalism," 55 U.Chi.L.Rev. 273 (1988), but most modern commentators have railed against him. See, e.g., Robert Cover, Justice Accused: Antislavery and the Judicial Process 240–241 (1975), Ronald Dworkin, "The Law of the Slavecatchers," Times Literary Supplement 1427 (December 5, 1975), Paul Finkelman, An Imperfect Union: Slavery, Federalism and Comity (1981), Barbara Holden–Smith, "Lords of Lash, Loom, and Law: Justice Story, Slavery, and *Prigg v. Pennsylvania*," 78 Cornell L. Rev. 1086 (1993).

5. Story's son was defending his father against the rage his opinion prompted among the more rabid of the abolitionists. The leading abolitionist newspaper greeted Story's decision in the following manner: "*It is not law* * * * It is to be spit upon, hooted at, trampled in the dust resolutely and openly." The Liberator, March 11, 1842. This prompted Story himself to rail "from his Harvard classroom at the 'madmen' who would pull down the house of Union to exorcise its defects." Gerald T. Dunne, Justice Joseph Story and the Rise of the Supreme Court 401 (1970). Imagine the effect of the next case on these "madmen."

6. In his masterful study of the events leading up to the *Dred Scott* case and its aftermath, Professor Maltz notes the significance of the fact that three of the Supreme Court justices from the South -- John Catron of Tennessee, John McKinley of Alabama, and James Moore Wayne of Georgia, unlike the position taken by Taney, concurred in Justice Story's opinion that the states were not required to aid in recapture of fugitive slaves, and that this could be left to the federal government. Maltz theorizes that "the concurrence of the three Southern justices in *Prigg* is most plausibly viewed as a reflection of a decision to sacrifice some of the interests of slaveowners in the hope of minimizing the sectional friction created by the dispute over fugitive slaves." Earl M. Maltz, Dred Scott and the Politics of Slavery 33 (2007). Is the majority decision in *Dred Scott*, written by Taney, reflective of the same spirit? If not, why not?

SCOTT V. SANDFORD

Supreme Court of the United States, 1856.
60 U.S. (19 How.) 393, 400, 15 L.Ed. 691.

[In this suit Dred Scott sought to assert "the title of himself and his family to freedom." Chief Justice Taney's opinion begins with a discussion of whether or not the United States Circuit Court had diversity jurisdiction over this case. Diversity jurisdiction exists when the parties are "citizens" of different states. The first point to be addressed is whether the plaintiff, who then lived in Missouri, and who had once been held by the defendant as a slave in Missouri, could be considered to be a "citizen" of Missouri. If so, then the requisite diversity was present, since the defendant was a citizen of New York.]

[(A) IS A NEGRO A "CITIZEN"?]

* * *

The words "people of the United States" and "citizens" are synonymous terms, and mean the same thing. They both describe the political body who, according to our republican institutions, form the sovereignty, and who hold the power and conduct the Government through their representatives. They are what we familiarly call the "sovereign people," and every citizen is one of this people, and a constituent member of this sovereignty. The question before us is, whether [Negroes] compose a portion of this people, and are constituent members of this sovereignty? We think they are not, and that they are not included, and were not intended to be included, under the word "citizens" in the Constitution, and can therefore claim none of the rights and privileges which that instrument provides for and secures to citizens of the United States. On the contrary, they were at that time considered as a subordinate and inferior class of beings, who had been subjugated by the dominant race, and, whether emancipated or not, yet remained subject to their authority, and had no rights or privileges but such as those who held the power and the Government might choose to grant them.

It is not the province of the court to decide upon the justice or injustice, the policy or impolicy, of these laws. The decision of that question belonged to the political or lawmaking power; to those who formed the sovereignty and framed the Constitution. The duty of the court is, to interpret the instrument they have framed, with the best lights we can obtain on the subject, and to administer it as we find it, according to its true intent and meaning when it was adopted.

* * *

* * * The Constitution has conferred on Congress the right to establish an uniform rule of naturalization, and this right is evidently exclusive, and has always been held by this court to be so. Consequently, no State, since the adoption of the Constitution, can by naturalizing an alien invest him with the rights and privileges secured to a citizen of a State under the Federal Government, although, so far as the State alone was concerned, he would undoubtedly be entitled to the rights of a citizen, and clothed with all the rights and immunities which the Constitution and laws of the State attached to that character.

It is very clear, therefore, that no State can, by any act or law of its own, passed since the adoption of the Constitution, introduce a new member into the political community created by the Constitution of the United States. * * *

The question then arises, whether the provisions of the Constitution, in relation to the personal rights and privileges to which the citizen of a State should be entitled, embraced the negro African race, at that time in this country, or who might afterwards be imported, who had then or should afterwards be made free in any State; and to put it in the power of a single State to make him a citizen of the United States, and endue him with the full rights of citizenship in every other State without their consent? * * *

The court think the affirmative of these propositions cannot be maintained. * * *

* * * In the opinion of the court, the legislation and histories of the times, and the language used in the Declaration of Independence, show, that neither the class of persons who had been imported as slaves, nor their descendants, whether they had become free or not, were then acknowledged as a part of the people, nor intended to be included in the general words used in that memorable instrument.

It is difficult at this day to realize the state of public opinion in relation to that unfortunate race, which prevailed in the civilized and enlightened portions of the world at the time of the Declaration of Independence, and when the Constitution of the United States was framed and adopted. But the public history of every European nation displays it in a manner too plain to be mistaken.

They had for more than a century before been regarded as beings of an inferior order, and altogether unfit to associate with the white race, either in social or political relations; and so far inferior, that they had no rights which the white man was bound to respect; and that the negro might justly and lawfully be reduced to slavery for his benefit. * * * This opinion was at that time fixed and universal in the civilized portion of the white race. It was regarded as an axiom in morals as well as in politics, which no one thought of disputing, or supposed to be open to dispute * * *.

And in no nation was this opinion more firmly fixed or more uniformly acted upon than by the English Government and English people. They not only seized them on the coast of Africa, and sold them or held them in slavery for their own use; but they took them as ordinary articles of merchandise to every country where they could make a profit on them, and were far more extensively engaged in this commerce than any other nation in the world.

The opinion thus entertained and acted upon in England was naturally impressed upon the colonies they founded on this side of the Atlantic. And, accordingly, a negro of the African race was regarded by them as an article of property, and held, and bought and sold as such, in every one of the thirteen colonies which united in the Declaration of Independence, and afterwards formed the Constitution of the United States. * * *

The legislation of the different colonies furnishes positive and indisputable proof of this fact. * * * They show that a perpetual and impassable barrier was intended to be erected between the white race and the one which they had reduced to slavery, and governed as subjects with absolute and despotic power, and which they then looked upon as so far below them in the scale of created beings, that intermarriages between white persons and negroes or mulattoes were regarded as unnatural and immoral, and punished as crimes, not only in the parties, but in the person who joined them in marriage. * * *

We refer to these historical facts for the purpose of showing the fixed opinions concerning that race, upon which the statesmen of that day spoke and acted. It is necessary to do this, in order to determine whether the general terms used in the Constitution of the United States, as to the rights of man and the rights of the people, was intended to include them, or to give to them or their posterity the benefit of any of its provisions.

The language of the Declaration of Independence is equally conclusive. * * *

The general words [of the Declaration] would seem to embrace the whole human family, and if they were used in a similar instrument at this day would be so understood. But it is too clear for dispute, that the enslaved African race were not intended to be included, and formed no part of the people who framed and adopted this declaration; for if the language, as understood in that day, would embrace them, the conduct of the distinguished men who framed the Declaration of Independence would have been utterly and flagrantly inconsistent with the principles they asserted * * *.

Yet the men who framed this declaration were great men—high in literary acquirements—high in their sense of honor, and incapable of asserting principles inconsistent with those on which they were acting. They perfectly understood the meaning of the language they used, and how it would be understood by others; and they knew that it would not in any part of the civilized world be supposed to embrace the negro race, which, by common consent, had been excluded from civilized Governments and the family of nations, and doomed to slavery. * * *

This state of public opinion had undergone no change when the Constitution was adopted, as is equally evident from its provisions and language.

* * * It speaks in general terms of the people of the United States, and of citizens of the several States, when it is providing for the exercise of the powers granted or the privileges secured to the citizen. It does not define what description of persons are intended to be included under these terms, or who shall be regarded as a citizen and one of the people. * * *

But there are two clauses in the Constitution which point directly and specifically to the negro race as a separate class of persons, and show clearly that they were not regarded as a portion of the people or citizens of the Government then formed.

One of these clauses reserves to each of the thirteen States the right to import slaves until the year 1808, if it thinks proper. * * * And by the other provision the State pledge themselves to each other to maintain the right of property of the master, by delivering up to him any slave who may have escaped from his service, and be found within their respective territories. * * * And these two provisions show, conclusively, that neither the description of persons therein referred to, nor their descendants, were embraced in any of the other provisions of the Constitution; for certainly these two clauses were not intended to confer on them or their posterity the blessings of liberty, or any of the personal rights so carefully provided for the citizen.

No one of that race had ever migrated to the United States voluntarily; all of them had been brought here as articles of merchandise. The number that had been emancipated at that time were but few in comparison with those held in slavery; and they were identified in the public mind with the race to which they belonged, and regarded as a part of the slave population rather than the free. * * *

Indeed, when we look to the condition of this race in the several States at the time, it is impossible to believe that these rights and privileges were intended to be extended to them.

It is very true, that in [some states] * * * few slaves were held at the time of the Declaration of Independence; and when the Constitution was adopted, it had entirely worn out in one of them, and measures had been taken for its gradual abolition in several others. But this change had not been produced by any change of opinion in relation to this race; but because it was discovered, from experience, that slave labor was unsuited to the climate and productions of these States: for some of the States, where it had ceased or nearly ceased to exist, were actively engaged in the slave trade * * *. And it can hardly be supposed that, in the States where it was then countenanced in its worst form—that is, in the seizure and transportation—the people could have regarded those who were emancipated as entitled to equal rights with themselves.

[Even in Massachusetts, said Taney,] The law of 1786, like the law of 1705, forbids the marriage of any white person with any negro, Indian, or Mulatto * * *. And this mark of degradation was renewed, and again impressed upon the race, in the careful and deliberate preparation of their revised code published in 1836. [And the same law can be found in Connecticut and Rhode Island at the time of framing the Federal Constitution.]

* * *

By the laws of New Hampshire, collected and finally passed in 1815, no one was permitted to be enrolled in the militia of the State, but free white citizens * * *. Nothing could more strongly mark the entire repudiation of the African race. The alien is excluded, because, being born in a foreign country, he cannot be a member of the community until he is naturalized. But why are the African race, born in the State, not permitted to share in one of the highest duties of the citizen? The answer is obvious; he is not, by the institutions and laws of the State, numbered among its people. He forms no part of the sovereignty of the State, and is not therefore called on to uphold and defend it.

* * *

* * * Chancellor Kent, whose accuracy and research no one will question, states in the sixth edition of his Commentaries, (published in 1848, 2 vol., 258, note b.) that in no part of the country except Maine, did the African race, in point of fact, participate equally with the whites in the exercise of civil and political rights.

The legislation of the States therefore shows, in a manner not to be mistaken, the inferior and subject condition of that race at the time the Constitution was adopted * * *. [It] is hardly consistent with the respect due to these States, to suppose that they regarded at that time, as fellow-citizens and members of the sovereignty, a class of beings whom they had thus stigmatized * * *, or, that when they met in convention to form the Constitution, they looked upon them as a portion of their constituents, or designed to include them in the provisions so carefully inserted for the security and protection of the liberties and rights of their citizens.

* * *

[Furthermore,] no State was willing to permit another State to determine who should or should not be admitted as one of its citizens, and entitled to demand equal rights and privileges with their own people, within their own territories. The right of naturalization was therefore, with one accord, surrendered by the States, and confided to the Federal Government. And this power granted to Congress to establish an uniform rule of *naturalization* is, by the well-understood meaning of the word, confined to persons born in a foreign country, under a foreign Government. It is not a power to raise to the rank of a citizen any one born in the United States, who, from birth or parentage, by the laws of the country, belongs to an inferior and subordinate class. And when we find the States guarding themselves from the indiscreet or improper admission by other States of emigrants from other countries, by giving the power exclusively to Congress, we cannot fail to see that they could never have left with the States a much more important power—that is, the power of transforming into citizens a numerous class of persons, who in that character would be much more dangerous to the peace and safety of a large portion of the Union, than the few foreigners one of the States might improperly naturalize. * * *

* * *

To all this mass of proof we have still to add, that Congress has repeatedly legislated upon the same construction of the Constitution that we have given. Three laws, two of which were passed almost immediately after the Government went into operation, will be abundantly sufficient to show this. * * *

The first of these acts is the naturalization law, which was passed at the second session of the first Congress, March 26, 1790, and confines the right of becoming citizens "to aliens being free white persons."

Now, the Constitution does not limit the power of Congress in this respect to white persons. And they may, if they think proper, authorize the naturalization of any one, of any color, who was born under allegiance to another Government. But the language of the law above quoted, shows that citizenship at that time was perfectly understood to be confined to the white race; and that they alone constituted the sovereignty in the Government.

Another of the early laws of which we have spoken, is the first militia law, which was passed in 1792, at the first session of the second Congress. The language of this law is equally plain and significant with the one just mentioned. It directs that every "free ablebodied white male citizen" shall be enrolled in the militia. The word white is evidently used to exclude the African race, and the word "citizen" to exclude unnaturalized foreigners; the latter forming no part of the sovereignty, owing it no allegiance, and therefore under no obligation to defend it. The African race, however, born in the country, did owe allegiance to the Government, whether they were slave or free; but it is repudiated, and rejected from the duties and obligations of citizenship in marked language.

The third act to which we have alluded is even still more decisive; it was passed as late as 1813, (2 Stat., 809,) and it provides: "That from and after the termination of the war in which the United States are now engaged with Great Britain, it shall not be lawful to employ, on board of any public or private vessels of the United States, any person or persons except citizens of the United States, or persons of color, natives of the United States."

* * *

And even as late as 1820, (chap. 104, sec. 8,) in the charter to the city of Washington, the corporation is authorized "to restrain and prohibit the nightly and other disorderly meetings of slaves, free negroes, and mulattoes," thus associating them together * * *. And in a subsequent part of the same section, the act authorizes the corporation "to prescribe the terms and conditions upon which free negroes and mulattoes may reside in the city."

This law, like the laws of the States, shows that this class of persons were governed by special legislation directed expressly to them, and always connected with provisions for the government of slaves, and not with those for the government of free white citizens. * * *

The conduct of the Executive Department of the Government has been in perfect harmony upon this subject with this course of legislation. The question was brought officially before the late William Wirt, when he was the Attorney General of the United States, in 1821, and he decided that the words "citizens of the United States" were used in the acts of Congress in the same sense as in the Constitution; and that free persons of color were not citizens, within the meaning of the Constitution and laws; and this opinion has been confirmed by that of the late Attorney General, Caleb Cushing, in a recent case, and acted upon by the Secretary of State, who refused to grant passports to them as "citizens of the United States."

* * *

No one, we presume, supposes that any change in public opinion or feeling, in relation to this unfortunate race, in the civilized nations of Europe or in this country, should induce the court to give to the words of the Constitution a more liberal construction in their favor than they were intended to bear when the instrument was framed and adopted. Such an argument would be altogether inadmissible in any tribunal called on to interpret it. If any of its provisions are deemed unjust, there is a mode prescribed in the instrument itself by which it may be amended; but while it remains unaltered, it must be construed now as it was understood at the time of its adoption. * * * Any other rule of construction would abrogate the judicial character of this court, and make it the mere reflex of the popular opinion or passion of the day. This court was not created by the Constitution for such purposes. Higher and graver trusts have been confided to it, and it must not falter in the path of duty.

* * *

And upon a full and careful consideration of the subject, the court is of opinion, that, upon the facts stated * * * Dred Scott was not a citizen of Missouri within the meaning of the Constitution of the United States, and not entitled as such to sue in its courts; and, consequently, that the Circuit Court had no jurisdiction of the case * * *.

[(B) WAS SCOTT FREE?]

[Taney proceeds to note that if Scott *was* a slave he certainly could not have been a citizen, and since he (Taney) has just proven that even free Blacks are not citizens, there is no jurisdiction, and the case must be dismissed. Still, because the lower court's holding that Scott was no longer a slave might be treated as precedent, Taney goes on to evaluate Scott's assertion of his right to freedom.]

* * *

The plaintiff was a negro slave, belonging to Dr. Emerson, who was a surgeon in the army of the United States. In the year 1834, he took the plaintiff from the State of Missouri to the military post at Rock Island, in the State of Illinois, and held him there as a slave until the month of April or May, 1836. At the time last mentioned, said Dr. Emerson removed the plaintiff from said military post at Rock Island to the military post at Fort Snelling * * * in the Territory known as Upper Louisiana * * * north of the State of Missouri. Said Dr. Emerson held the plaintiff in slavery at said Fort Snelling, from said last-mentioned date until the year 1838. [Scott argued that he had become free, *inter alia,* because Congress had forbidden slavery in the part of the Louisiana territory where Fort Snelling was located.]

The act of Congress, upon which the plaintiff relies, declares that slavery and involuntary servitude, except as a punishment for crime, shall be forever prohibited in all that part of the territory ceded by France, under the name of Louisiana, which lies north of thirty-six degrees thirty minutes north latitude, and not included within the limits of Missouri. And the difficulty which meets us at the threshold of this part of the inquiry is, whether Congress was authorized to pass this law under any of the powers granted to it by the Constitution * * *.

The counsel for the plaintiff has laid much stress upon that article in the Constitution which confers on Congress the power "to dispose of and make all needful rules and regulations respecting the territory or other property belonging to the United States;" but, in the judgment of the court, that provision has no bearing on the present controversy, and the power there given, whatever it may be, is confined, and was intended to be confined, to the territory which at that time belonged to, or was claimed by, the United States, and was within their boundaries as settled by the treaty with Great Britain * * *.

It will be remembered that, from the commencement of the Revolutionary war, serious difficulties existed between the States, in relation to the disposition of large and unsettled territories which were included in the chartered limits of some of the States. And some of the other States, and more especially Maryland, which had no unsettled lands, insisted that as the unoccupied lands, if wrested from Great Britain, would owe their preservation to the common purse and the common sword, the money arising from them ought to be applied in just proportion among the several States to pay the expenses of the war * * *.

* * *

These fears and dangers were, however, at once removed, when the State of Virginia, in 1784, voluntarily ceded to the United States the immense tract of country lying northwest of the river Ohio, and which was within the acknowledged limits of the State. * * *

The example of Virginia was soon afterwards followed by other States * * *. The main object for which these cessions were desired and made, was on account of their money value, and to put an end to a dangerous controversy, as to who was justly entitled to the proceeds when the lands should be sold. * * *

Undoubtedly the powers of sovereignty and the eminent domain were ceded with the land. * * * But it must be remembered that, at that time, there was no Government of the United States in existence with enumerated and limited powers; what was then called the United States, were thirteen separate, sovereign, independent States, which had entered into a league or confederation for their mutual protection and advantage, and the Congress of the United States was composed of the representatives of these separate sovereignties, meeting together, as equals * * *. But this Confederation had none of the attributes of sovereignty in legislative, executive, or judicial power. It was little more than a congress of ambassadors, authorized to represent separate nations, in matters in which they had a common concern.

It was this Congress that accepted the cession from Virginia. They had no power to accept it under the Articles of Confederation. But they had an undoubted right, as independent sovereignties, to accept any cession of territory for their common benefit, which all of them assented to; and it is equally clear, that as their common property, and having no superior to control them, they had the right to exercise absolute dominion over it * * *. It was by a Congress, representing the authority of these several and separate sovereignties, and acting under their authority and command, (but not from any authority derived from the Articles of Confederation,) that the instrument usually called the ordinance of 1787 was adopted; regulating in much detail the principles and the laws by which this territory should be governed; and among other provisions, slavery is prohibited in it. We do not question the power of the States, by agreement among themselves, to pass this ordinance, nor its obligatory force in the territory, while the confederation or league of the States in their separate sovereign character continued to exist.

This was the state of things when the Constitution of the United States was formed. The territory ceded by Virginia belonged to the several confederated States * * *. They were about to dissolve this federative Union, and to surrender a portion of their independent sovereignty to a new Government, * * * but this Government was to be carefully limited in its powers, and to exercise no authority beyond those expressly granted by the Constitution, or necessarily to be implied from the language of the instrument, and the objects it was intended to accomplish; and as this league of States would, upon the adoption of the new Government, cease to have any power over the territory, and the ordinance they had agreed upon be incapable of execution, and a mere nullity, it was obvious that some provision was necessary to give the new Government sufficient power to enable it to carry into effect the objects for which it was ceded * * *. It was necessary that the lands should be sold to pay the war debt; that a Government and system of Jurisprudence should be maintained in it, to protect the citizens of the United States who should migrate to the territory, in their rights of person and of property. * * * [For these reasons,] the clause was inserted in the Constitution which gives Congress the power "to dispose of and make all needful rules and regulations respecting the territory or other property belonging to the United States." * * * It applied only to the property which the States held in common at that time, and has no reference whatever to any territory or other property which the new sovereignty might afterwards itself acquire.

* * * It does not speak of *any territory,* nor of *Territories,* but uses language which, according to its legitimate meaning, points to a particular thing. The power is given in relation only to the territory of the United States—that is, to a territory then in existence, and then known or claimed as the territory of the United States. It begins its enumeration of powers by that of disposing, in other words, making sale of the lands, or raising money from them, which, as we have already said, was the main object of the cession, and which is accordingly the first thing provided for in the article. It then gives the power which was necessarily associated with the disposition and sale of the lands—that is, the power of making needful rules and regulations respecting the territory. And whatever construction may now be given to these words, every one, we think, must admit that they are not the words usually employed by statesmen in giving supreme power of legislation. * * *

* * *

* * * The concluding words of the clause appear to render this construction irresistible; for, after the provisions we have mentioned, it proceeds to say, "that nothing in the Constitution shall be so construed as to prejudice any claims of the United States, or of any particular State."

Now, * * * all of the States, except North Carolina and Georgia, had made the cession before the Constitution was adopted * * *. The claims of other States, that the unappropriated lands in these two States should be applied to the common benefit, in like manner, was still insisted on, but refused by the States. And this member of the clause in question evidently applies to them, and can apply to nothing else. It was to exclude the conclusion that either party, by adopting the Constitution, would surrender what they deemed their rights. And when the latter provision relates so obviously to the unappropriated lands not yet ceded by the States, and the first clause makes provision for those then actually ceded, it is impossible, by any just rule of construction, to make the first provision general, and extend to all territories, which the Federal Government might in any way afterwards acquire, when the latter is plainly and unequivocally confined to a particular territory; which was a part of the same controversy, and involved in the same dispute, and depended upon the same principles. * * *

The Constitution has always been remarkable for the felicity of its arrangement of different subjects, and the perspicuity and appropriateness of the language it uses. But if this clause is construed to extend to territory acquired by the present Government from a foreign nation, outside of the limits of any charter from the British Government to a colony, it would be difficult to say, why it was deemed necessary to give the Government the power to sell any vacant lands belonging to the sovereignty which might be found within it; and if this was necessary, why the grant of this power should precede the power to legislate over it and establish a Government there; and still more difficult to say, why it was deemed necessary so specially and particularly to grant the power to make needful rules and regulations in relation to any personal or movable property it might acquire there. * * *

The words "needful rules and regulations" would seem, also, to have been cautiously used for some definite object. They are not the words usually employed by statesmen, when they mean to give the powers of sovereignty, or to establish a Government, or to authorize its establishment. Thus, in the law to renew and keep alive the ordinance of 1787, and to reestablish the Government, the title of the law is: "An act to provide for the government of the territory northwest of the river Ohio." And in the Constitution, when granting the power to legislate over the territory that may be selected for the seat of Government independently of a State, it does not say Congress shall have power "to make all needful rules and regulations respecting the territory;" but it declares that "Congress shall have power to exercise exclusive legislation in all cases whatsoever over such District * * * "

The words "rules and regulations" are usually employed in the Constitution in speaking of some particular specified power which it means to confer on the Government, and not, as we have seen, when granting general powers of legislation. * * * But if confined to a particular Territory, in which a Government and laws had already been established, but which would require some alterations to adapt it to the new Government, the words are peculiarly applicable and appropriate for that purpose.

* * * Consequently, the power which Congress may have lawfully exercised in this Territory, while it remained under a Territorial Government, and which may have been sanctioned by judicial decision, can furnish no justification and no argument to support a similar exercise of power over territory afterwards acquired by the Federal Government. We put aside, therefore, any argument, drawn from precedents, showing the

extent of the power which the General Government exercised over slavery in this Territory, as altogether inapplicable to the case before us.

* * *

This brings us to examine by what provision of the Constitution the present Federal Government, under its delegated and restricted powers, is authorized to acquire territory outside of the original limits of the United States, and what powers it may exercise therein over the person or property of a citizen of the United States * * *.

There is certainly no power given by the Constitution to the Federal Government to establish or maintain colonies bordering on the United States or at a distance, to be ruled and governed at its own pleasure; nor to enlarge its territorial limits in any way, except by the admission of new States. That power is plainly given; and if a new State is admitted, it needs no further legislation by Congress, because the Constitution itself defines the relative rights and powers, and duties of the State, and the citizens of the State, and the Federal Government. But no power is given to acquire a Territory to be held and governed permanently in that character.

* * *

We do not mean, however, to question the power of Congress in this respect. The power to expand the territory of the United States by the admission of new States is plainly given; and in the construction of this power by all the departments of the Government, it has been held to authorize the acquisition of territory, not fit for admission at the time, but to be admitted as soon as its population and situation would entitle it to admission. * * * All we mean to say on this point is, that, as there is no express regulation in the Constitution defining the power which the General Government may exercise over the person or property of a citizen in a Territory thus acquired, the court must necessarily look to the provision and principles of the Constitution, and its distribution of powers, for the rules and principles by which its decision must be governed.

Taking this rule to guide us, it may be safely assumed that citizens of the United States who migrate to a Territory belonging to the people of the United States, cannot be ruled as mere colonists, dependent upon the will of the General Government, and to be governed by any laws it may think proper to impose. The principle upon which our Governments rest, and upon which alone they continue to exist, is the union of States, sovereign and independent within their own limits in their internal and domestic concerns, and bound together as one people by a General Government, possessing certain enumerated and restricted powers * * *. Whatever it acquires, it acquires for the benefit of the people of the several States who created it. It is their trustee acting for them, and charged with the duty of promoting the interests of the whole people of the Union in the exercise of the powers specifically granted.

At the time when the Territory in question was obtained by cession from France, it contained no population fit to be associated together and admitted as a State; and it therefore was absolutely necessary to hold possession of it, as a Territory belonging to the United States, until it was settled and inhabited by a civilized community capable of self-government * * *.

* * * The form of government to be established necessarily rested in the discretion of Congress. It was their duty to establish the one that would be best suited for the protection and security of the citizens of the United States * * *.

[Taney proceeds to suggest the scope of permissible legislation for territories.]

* * *

For example, no one, we presume, will contend that Congress can make any law in a Territory respecting the establishment of religion, or the free exercise thereof, or abridging the freedom of speech or of the press, or the right of the people of the Territory peaceably to assemble, and to petition the Government for the redress of grievances.

Nor can Congress deny to the people the right to keep and bear arms, nor the right to trial by jury, nor compel any one to be a witness against himself in a criminal proceeding.

These powers, and others, in relation to rights of person, which it is not necessary here to enumerate, are, in express and positive terms, denied to the General Government; and the rights of private property have been guarded with equal care. Thus the rights of property are united with the rights of person, and placed on the same ground by the fifth amendment to the Constitution, which provides that no person shall be deprived of life, liberty, and property, without due process of law. And an act of Congress which deprives a citizen of the United States of his liberty or property, merely because he came himself or brought his property into a particular Territory of the United States, and who had committed no offence against the laws, could hardly be dignified with the name of due process of law.

* * *

The powers over person and property of which we speak are not only not granted to Congress, but are in express terms denied, and they are forbidden to exercise them. And this prohibition is not confined to the States, but the words are general, and extend to the whole territory over which the Constitution gives it power to legislate, including those portions of it remaining under Territorial Government, as well as that covered by States. * * * And if Congress itself cannot do this—if it is beyond the powers conferred on the Federal Government—it will be admitted, we presume, that it could not authorize a Territorial Government to exercise them. It could confer no power on any local Government, established by its authority, to violate the provisions of the Constitution.

It seems, however, to be supposed, that there is a difference between property in a slave and other property, and that different rules may be applied to it in expounding the Constitution of the United States. And the laws and usages of nations, and the writings of eminent jurists upon the relation of master and slave and their mutual rights and duties, and the powers which Governments may exercise over it, have been dwelt upon in the argument.

But in considering the question before us, it must be borne in mind that there is no law of nations standing between the people of the United States and their Government, and interfering with their relation to each other. The powers of the Government, and the rights of the citizen under it, are positive and practical regulations plainly written down. * * * It has no power over the person or property of a citizen but what the citizens of the United States have granted. And no laws or usages of other nations, or reasoning of statesmen or jurists upon the relations of master and slave, can enlarge the powers of the Government, or take from the citizens the rights they have reserved. And if the Constitution recognises the right of property of the master in a slave, and makes no distinction between that description of property and other property owned by a citizen, no tribunal, acting under the authority of the United States, whether it be legislative, executive, or judicial, has a right to draw such a distinction, or deny to it the benefit of the provisions and guarantees which have been provided for the protection of private property against the encroachments of the Government.

Now * * * the right of property in a slave is distinctly and expressly affirmed in the Constitution. The right to traffic in it, like an ordinary article of merchandise and property, was guaranteed to the citizens of the United States, in every State that might desire it, for twenty years. And the Government in express terms is pledged to protect it in all future time, if the slave escapes from his owner. * * * And no word can be found in the Constitution which gives Congress a greater power over slave property, or which entitles property of that kind to less protection than property of any other description. The only power conferred is the power coupled with the duty of guarding and protecting the owner in his rights.

Upon these considerations, it is the opinion of the court that the act of Congress which prohibited a citizen from holding and owning property of this kind in the territory of the United States north of the line therein mentioned, is not warranted by the Constitution, and is therefore void;

and that neither Dred Scott himself, nor any of his family, were made free by being carried into this territory; even if they had been carried there by the owner, with the intention of becoming a permanent resident.

* * *

[Taney concluded his opinion by holding that even though Scott temporarily resided in a free State, Illinois, this had no effect on his status in Missouri, since, as an independent State, Missouri was not required to give effect to Illinois law regarding slavery. By the relevant laws of Missouri, then, Scott was still a slave.]

NOTES AND QUESTIONS

1. Scott v. Sandford is one of the most important decisions ever rendered by the United States Supreme Court. It has been the subject of controversy and study since it was first decided. For a thorough treatment of the case, see Don E. Fehrenbacher, The Dred Scott Case: Its Significance in American Law and Politics (1978) and for some provocative scholarship on the case, see Eric T. Dean, Jr., "Reassessing *Dred Scott*: The Possibilities of Federal Power in the Antebellum Context," 60 Conn.L.Rev. 713 (1992), Earl M. Maltz, "Slavery, Federalism, and the Structure of the Constitution," 36 Am.J.Leg.Hist. 466 (1992), Earl M. Maltz, "Bondage, Freedom & the Constitution: The New Slavery Scholarship and Its Impact on Law and Legal Historiography: Slavery and the Constitution: The Unlikely Hero of Dred Scott: Benjamin Robbins Curtis and the Constitutional Law of Slavery," 17 Cardozo L. Rev. 1995 (1996), and Robert Meister, "The Logic and Legacy of *Dred Scott*: Marshall, Taney, and the Sublimation of Republican Thought," 3 Studies on American Political Development 199 (Yale University Press, 1989), and Tania Tetlow, "The Founders and Slavery: A Crisis of Conscience," 3 Loy.J.Pub.Int.L. 1 (2001). For further reading on the question of whether the United States Constitution of 1789 was a pro-slavery document, see generally Earl M. Maltz, "The Idea of the Proslavery Constitution," 17 J.Early Repub. 37 (1997), and sources there cited. There is a fine short collection of primary sources on *Dred Scott v. Sandford*, along with all the opinions in the case in Paul Finkelman, Dred Scott v. Sandford: A Brief History with Documents (1997). Finally, for what may well be the most dispassionate and balanced recent analysis of the case, see the volume in the wonderful Landmark Law Cases and American Society series by Earl M. Maltz, Dred Scott and the Politics of Slavery (2007), which suggests that the Court made a fundamental error by thinking that it could solve the political problem of slavery through constitutional analysis. Maltz's work is perhaps helpful in understanding what may be a continuing perception that the Court must always avoid inflaming the other branches of government, or sizeable numbers of the American people themselves. But how does one square that (perhaps wise) admonition with the traditional maxim *Fiat Justitia Ruat Caelum* ("Let justice be done, though the heavens fall")?

Generally speaking, without regard to the school of constitutional interpretation to which any individual scholar might subscribe, everyone who has written on Dred Scott's case, finds Taney's conclusions and analysis to be morally repugnant. Until relatively recently the trend in scholarly analysis, perhaps flowing from this moral repugnance, was further to suggest that Taney's legal analysis as well was fatally flawed. This may be changing, as some scholars have begun to argue that under the Constitution as it existed at the time of the *Dred Scott* decision (i.e., without the Thirteenth or Fourteenth Amendments), Taney's conclusions were, if not inevitable, then certainly within the range of acceptable Constitutional construction. This line of scholarship thus contends that the most important question raised by *Dred Scott* is not what flaws existed in the composition and reasoning of the Supreme Court which brought it to such a decision, but rather what should be done when the flaws which would lead to such a conclusion exist within the Constitution itself? On these points see Mark A. Graber, Desperately Ducking Slavery: *Dred Scott* and Contemporary Constitutional Theory, 14 Const. Comm. 271 (1997). We concentrate here on the legal implications of the Dred Scott case, but it must not be forgotten that there were human and emotional aspects to it as well. For an extraordinary investigation of these, see the remarkable reconstruction of the life of Harriet Scott, Lea VanderVelde, Mrs. Dred Scott: A Life on Slavery's Frontier (2009).

2. The crucial decision in the case, as you may have guessed, was not the determination of the personal status of Dred Scott, but was the ruling on Congress's ability to forbid slavery in the federal territories acquired after the Constitution of 1789, such as those of Louisiana. After the "era of good feelings" passed, during the years before the Civil War (1830–1860), the dominant national issues were those of allocation of power and wealth between the states of the North and South. To simplify matters, Southerners feared that the uncouth masses of the North were conspiring to end the aristocratic and noble Southern Civilization, while Northerners were worried that the mandarins of the Southern "slavocracy" were conspiring to impose slavery on the entire nation. Some sort of balance was struck by Congress in the "Missouri Compromise" of 1820, when legislation was passed admitting Missouri as a slave state, admitting Maine as a free state, and forbidding slavery in the territories North of the line 36 degrees and 30 minutes in latitude.

What do you suppose the Court's opinion in Dred Scott did to the delicate balance struck in 1820? The decision was the Supreme Court's first declaration since Marbury v. Madison (1803) that an Act of Congress was unconstitutional. President Buchanan had predicted in his inaugural address two days before the *Dred Scott* opinion was issued that the current controversy over the status of slavery in the territories would be "speedily and finally settled" by the Supreme Court. Immediately prior to his inaugural speech Buchanan was seen huddled with Chief Justice Taney, and from that time to this the Dred Scott decision has been seen as evidence of the Southern Conspiracy, which allegedly included Taney and Buchanan among the principals, and which amounted to the President's playing politics with the members of the Court. Whether or not Taney's whispering to Buchanan on the day of the

Inaugural revealed what the Supreme Court was to do two days later, it now seems clear that Buchanan *was* in correspondence with at least two of the judges of the Supreme Court, and that he did know exactly what the court was up to. Fehrenbacher, supra, at 305–314.

The abolitionist newspapers attacked the Dred Scott opinion in a manner that almost makes their comments about Prigg v. Pennsylvania seem like paeans. Horace Greeley's New York Tribune described the decision as "atrocious," "wicked," "abominable," and "no better than what might be obtained in any 'Washington barroom.' " He excoriated Taney, the " 'cunning chief' whose 'collation of false statements and shallow sophistries' revealed a 'detestable hypocrisy' and a 'mean and skulking cowardice.' " Fehrenbacher, supra, at 417. As late as 1865 Senator Charles Sumner declared that "the name of Taney is to be hooted down the page of history. Judgment is beginning now; and an emancipated country will fasten upon him the stigma which he deserves * * *. He administered justice at least wickedly, and degraded the age." Cong.Globe, 38th Cong.2d Sess. 1012 (1865). Taney has undergone some rehabilitation, and there are works which claim that Taney, his opinion in Dred Scott notwithstanding, was one of the greatest of American Chief Justices. See generally Carl Brent Swisher, Roger B. Taney (1935) and Walker Lewis, Without Fear or Favor, A Biography of Chief Justice Roger Brook Taney (1965). Were the critics right about the quality of the decision in *Dred Scott?* See on this point, Graber, supra, Maltz, supra, and Paul Finkelman, "The Constitution and the Intentions of the Framers: The Limits of Historical Analysis," 50 U.Pitt.L.Rev. 349, 390–96 (1989) for the argument that Taney was correct about the "original understanding" of the relevant constitutional provisions. See also, for an excellent study of Taney's jurisprudence, William W. Wiecek, Liberty Under Law: The Supreme Court in American Life 56–81 (1988).

3. If Missouri had the power, as Taney acknowledges, to make Dred Scott a "citizen" of Missouri, why exactly does Taney maintain that he was not to be considered a "citizen" of Missouri for the purposes of diversity jurisdiction? What bearing does Article 4, Section 2, of the United States Constitution, "The citizens of each state shall be entitled to all privileges and immunities of citizens in the several states," have on this problem?

4. Are you impressed with Taney's abilities as an historian? How accurately does he present English attitudes on Negroes and on slavery which were contemporary with the Constitution? How important is the intention of the Constitutional framers to Taney? Do you find his attitude towards effectuating the intentions or the understandings of the framers consistent throughout his opinion? Are you persuaded by Taney's proof that the authors of the Declaration of Independence could not have meant to have referred to the "African race" when it was written that "all men are created equal?" What about Taney's argument that even in the states where, at the time of the Constitution, no slaves or few slaves were held, Blacks were still regarded as an inferior race and *not* accorded the privileges of citizenship? Does it necessarily follow that if a race is regarded by many as "inferior" it cannot

contribute "citizens?" Robert Meister argues that "Much of the extreme language in [Taney's] opinion reflects not only his personal acceptance of the racism of his time but also a peculiarly modern perception that the Court must be prepared to give historical justifications for the view that certain political identities qualify for Constitutional protection and that others do not." Meister, supra note 1, at 256. Do you agree? Was Taney a racist?

5. What are the essential qualifications for United States citizenship under the Constitution? There is one Constitutional provision which refers to Blacks that Taney never discusses. Article One, Section Two of the Constitution provides that " * * * Representatives and direct Taxes shall be apportioned among the several States which may be included within this Union, according to their respective Numbers, which shall be determined by adding to the whole Number of free Persons, * * * three fifths of all other Persons." Does the provision affect Taney's argument?

6. Is Taney correct when he presumes that no one would suppose "that any change in public opinion or feeling in relation to this unfortunate race * * * should induce the court to give the words of the Constitution a more liberal construction in their favor than they were intended to bear when the instrument was framed and adopted?" Is this a proper view of the task of Constitutional exposition? Is this consistent with the Supreme Court's ultimate resolution of the issue of common law crimes in *Hudson & Goodwin*? If not, why the change?

7. What is the ground upon which Taney decides the second issue in this case, whether Scott was entitled to freedom? How is it that Taney believes it was permissible for the Continental Congress under the Articles of Confederation to forbid slavery in the Northwest Territory in 1787, but the United States Congress *after* the Constitution lacked Constitutional authority to prohibit slavery in the territories of the Louisiana Purchase? Why do you suppose it has been suggested that *Dred Scott* helped cause the Civil War? What do you suppose Taney would have had to say about the Constitutionality of President Lincoln's Emancipation Proclamation?

8. If Taney concedes the Constitutional power in Congress to acquire territories later to be admitted as states, and if, as Taney says, "[t]he power to acquire necessarily carries with it the power to preserve and apply to the purposes for which [territories are] acquired," then why, where Congress has decided that the preservation of the national union requires the prohibition of slavery in part of newly-acquired territories, does Taney say it is unconstitutional? Would Taney's analysis crumble if he is wrong in his assertion that "there is no law of nations standing between the people of the United States and their Government"? Is he wrong? What does it mean to suggest that a "law of nations" might "stand between" Americans and the government? Would you agree with this anthropomorphic notion? Does this notion have anything to do with the attitude reflected in Shaw's opinion in *Commonwealth v. Aves,* the early Virginia cases we studied, or even Story's opinion in *Prigg*? The two dissenters in *Dred Scott,* Justices Curtis and McLean, disagreed with Taney on this point. Curtis, relying on *Aves,* made clear *his* belief

that the relevant law to be applied in the case, the law of the state of Missouri, was "the common law," and "the common law, as Blackstone says (4 Comm. 67), adopts, in its full extent, the law of nations, and holds it to be a part of the land." Curtis went on to observe that "slavery, being contrary to natural right, is created only by municipal law," and Curtis took this fundamental principle of the law of nations to mean that unless there was a clear constitutional provision or congressional statute creating the status of slavery in the territories, there was nothing to stop Congress from there prohibiting it. McLean agreed. On these points see Stephen Presser, Recapturing the Constitution: Race, Religion, and Abortion Reconsidered 134 (1994). For further reading on *Dred Scott* and the principles of Southern Jurisprudence that may have influenced it, see three articles by Alfred L. Brophy, " 'A Revolution which Seeks to Abolish Law, Must End Necessarily in Despotism': Louisa McCord and Antebellum Southern Legal Thought," 5 Cardozo Women's L.J. 33 (1998), "Let Us Go Back and Stand upon the Constitution: Federal–State Relations in *Scott v.* Sandford," 90 Col. L.Rev. 192 (1990), and "The Rule of Law in Antebellum College Literary Addresses: The Case of William Greene," 31 Cumb.L.Rev. 231 (2001). For important surveys of slavery and law see, e.g., Thomas D. Morris, Southern Slavery and the Law 1619–1860 (1996), and Jenny Bourne Walh, The Bondsman's Burden: An Economic Analysis of the Common Law of Southern Slavery (1998). The Supreme Court slowly recovered from the drubbings it took as a result of Dred Scott, but, not unexpectedly, it found itself thrust into political controversy following the Civil War and Lincoln's assassination, during the era of Reconstruction. For this story see, e.g., Barry Friedman, "The History of the Countermajoritarian Difficulty, Part II: Reconstruction's Political Court," 91 Geo.L.J. 1 (2002).

REPUBLICAN PARTY PLATFORM, 1860

Source: http://facweb.furman.edu/?benson/docs/repplat6.htm.

[Compare the Republican Party Platform of 1860 with the 1776 Declaration of Independence. The 1776 document, targeted at a world audience, explained the reasons why the Americans were willing to shatter the bonds that had formerly tied them to Great Britain. To whom is the 1860 document addressed? Is it any way similar to the Declaration? Today's Republicans are often compared with the Federalists of the 1790's. Can the same be said of the Republicans of the 1860's? How would you describe the differences between the Republicans then and now, and the Federalists? Lincoln frequently quoted the words of Jefferson. Do you find any Jeffersonian aspects to this Republican party platform? Would you have voted for Lincoln in 1860? In 1864? The Republicans of 1860 saw the country as poised between two futures, one dominated by what they called "slaveocracy" and the other, the one they saw themselves as offering—"democracy." But was the "democracy" offered by the Republicans Jefferson's yeoman vision, or something else? If you were a Southerner, how would you have reacted to this document? Once the Republicans won the Presidential election of 1860, was secession inevitable? Could it be said that the conflict emerging between the North and the South was essentially a contest over the meaning of the Founding, with history on the side of the South, and the North creating a new synthesis of democratization with economic nationalism—a profoundly modern development (and the rebirth of the United States as we now know it)? Did the Republicans offer an essentially modern vision of a nation of free men bound together by a vigorous national government, while the South clung to the older ideal of a nation of little republics dedicated to personal liberty, including the liberty to own slaves? Which do you prefer, and why? In 1860, who was more "American," who was more committed to capitalism, who favored liberty, and who favored economic growth?]

Resolved, That we, the delegated representatives of the Republican electors of the United States, in Convention assembled, in discharge of the duty we owe to our constituents and our country, unite in the following declarations:

1. That the history of the nation, during the last four years, has fully established the propriety and necessity of the organization and perpetuation of the Republican party, and that the causes which called it into existence are permanent in their nature, and now, more than ever before, demand its peaceful and constitutional triumph.

2. That the maintenance of the principles promulgated in the Declaration of Independence and embodied in the Federal Constitution, "That all men are created equal; that they are endowed by their Creator with certain inalienable rights; that among these are life, liberty, and the pursuit of happiness; that to secure these rights, governments are instituted among men, deriving their just powers from the consent of the governed," is essential to the preservation of our Republican institutions; and that the Federal Constitution, the Rights of the States, and the Union of the States, must and shall be preserved.

3. That to the Union of the States this nation owes its unprecedented increase in population, its surprising development of material resources, its rapid augmentation of wealth, its happiness at home and its honor abroad; and we hold in abhorrence all schemes for Disunion, come from whatever source they may: And we congratulate the country that no Republican member of Congress has uttered or countenanced the threats of Disunion so often made by Democratic members without rebuke and with applause from their political associates; and we denounce those threats of Disunion, in case of a popular overthrow of their ascendency, as denying the vital principles of a free government, and as an avowal of contemplated treason, which it is the imperative duty of an indignant People sternly to rebuke and forever silence.

4. That the maintenance inviolate of the rights of the States, and especially the right of each State to order and control its own domestic institutions according to its own judgment exclusively, is essential to that

balance of powers on which the perfection and endurance of our political fabric depends; and we denounce the lawless invasion by armed force of the soil of any State or Territory, no matter under what pretext, as among the gravest of crimes.

5. That the present Democratic Administration has far exceeded our worst apprehensions, in its measureless subserviency to the exactions of a sectional interest, as especially evinced in its desperate exertions to force the infamous Lecompton Constitution [which would have provided for the legality of slavery] upon the protesting people of Kansas; in construing the personal relation between master and servant to involve an unqualified property in persons; in its attempted enforcement, everywhere, on land and sea, through the intervention of Congress and of the Federal Courts of the extreme pretensions of a purely local interest; and in its general and unvarying abuse of the power intrusted to it by a confiding people.

6. That the people justly view with alarm the reckless extravagance which pervades every department of the Federal Government; that a return to rigid economy and accountability is indispensible to arrest the systematic plunder of the public treasury by favored partisans, while the recent startling developments of frauds and corruptions at the Federal metropolis, show that an entire change of administration is imperatively demanded.

7. That the new dogma, that the Constitution, of its own force, carries Slavery into any or all of the Territories of the United States [what was the source of that "dogma"?], is a dangerous political heresy, at variance with the explicit provisions of that instrument itself, with contemporaneous exposition, and with legislative and judicial precedent; is revolutionary in its tendency, and subversive of the peace and harmony of the country.

8. That the normal condition of all the territory of the United States is that of freedom; That as our Republican fathers, when they had abolished Slavery in all our national territory, ordained that "no person should be deprived of life, liberty, or property, without due process of law," it becomes our duty, by legislation, whenever such legislation is necessary, to maintain this provision of the Constitution against all attempts to violate it; and we deny the authority of Congress, of a territorial legislature, or of any individuals, to give legal existence to Slavery in any Territory of the United States.

9. That we brand the recent re-opening of the African slave-trade, under the cover of our national flag, aided by perversions of judicial power, as a crime against humanity and a burning shame to our country and age; and we call upon Congress to take prompt and efficient measures for the total and final suppression of that execrable traffic.

10. That in the recent vetoes, by their Federal Governors, of the acts of the Legislatures of Kansas and Nebraska, prohibiting Slavery in those Territories, we find a practical illustration of the boasted Democratic principle of Non-Intervention and Popular Sovereignty, embodied in the Kansas–Nebraska bill, and a demonstration of the deception and fraud involved therein.

11. That Kansas should, of right, be immediately admitted as a State under the Constitution recently formed and adopted by her people [which rejected Lecompton and barred slavery], and accepted by the House of Representatives.

12. That, while providing revenue for the support of the General Government by duties upon imports, sound policy requires such an adjustment of these imposts as to encourage the development of the industrial interest of the whole country; and we commend that policy of national exchanges which secures to the working men liberal wages, to agriculture remunerative prices, to mechanics and manufactures an adequate reward for their skill, labor, and enterprise, and to the nation commercial prosperity and independence.

13. That we protest against any sale or alienation to others of the Public Lands held by actual settlers, and against any view of the Homestead policy which regards the settlers as paupers or supplicants for public bounty; and we demand the passage by Congress of the complete and satisfactory Homestead measure which has already passed the House. [That measure would have offered land at 25 cents an acre. It was opposed by the South, on the grounds that those buying lands would likely be free-soilers, and would frustrate the expansion of slavery into the West. The Bill eventually did pass, but was vetoed by President Buchanan.]

14. That the Republican party is opposed to any change in our Naturalization Laws or any State legislation by which the rights of citizenship hitherto accorded to immigrants from foreign lands shall be abridged or impaired; and in favor of giving a full and efficient protection to the rights of all classes of citizens, whether native or naturalized, both at home and abroad.

15. That appropriations by Congress for River and Harbor improvements of a National character, required for the accommodation and security of an existing commerce, are authorized by the Constitution, and justified by the obligations of Government to protect the lives and property of its citizens.

16. That a Railroad to the Pacific Ocean is imperatively demanded by the interest of the whole country; that the Federal Government ought to render immediate and efficient aid in its construction; and that, as preliminary thereto, a daily Overland Mail should be promptly established.

17. Finally, having thus set forth our distinctive principles and views, we invite the coöperation of all citizens, however differing on other questions, who substantially agree with us in their affirmance and support.

"DECLARATION OF THE IMMEDIATE CAUSES WHICH INDUCE AND JUSTIFY THE SECESSION OF SOUTH CAROLINA FROM THE FEDERAL UNION," DECEMBER 24, 1860

Source: The Avalon Project, Yale Law School: http://avalon.law.yale.edu/19th_century/csa_scarsec.asp.

[If one temporarily sets the matter of slavery aside, does this statement from South Carolina seem more or less faithful to the Declaration of Independence and the Federal Constitution of 1787 than the Republican Party Platform of 1860? Do you see any obvious reference to that Platform? Did the South Carolinians get their history right? Who could more honestly lay claim to the ownership of the legacy of Jefferson and Washington, South Carolina or the Republicans? Do these two documents—the Republican Platform and the South Carolina Declaration—suggest to you that the growing divergence in political economy and ideology between North and South made war or secession inevitable?]

The people of the State of South Carolina, in Convention assembled, on the 26th day of April, A.D., 1852, declared that the frequent violations of the Constitution of the United States, by the Federal Government, and its encroachments upon the reserved rights of the States, fully justified this State in then withdrawing from the Federal Union; but in deference to the opinions and wishes of the other slaveholding States, she forbore at that time to exercise this right. Since that time, these encroachments have continued to increase, and further forbearance ceases to be a virtue.

And now the State of South Carolina having resumed her separate and equal place among nations, deems it due to herself, to the remaining United States of America, and to the nations of the world, that she should declare the immediate causes which have led to this act.

In the year 1765, that portion of the British Empire embracing Great Britain, undertook to make laws for the government of that portion composed of the thirteen American Colonies. A struggle for the right of self-government ensued, which resulted, on the 4th of July, 1776, in a Declaration, by the Colonies, "that they are, and of right ought to be, FREE AND INDEPENDENT STATES; and that, as free and independent States, they have full power to levy war, conclude peace, contract alliances, establish commerce, and to do all other acts and things which independent States may of right do."

They further solemnly declared that whenever any "form of government becomes destructive of the ends for which it was established, it is the right of the people to alter or abolish it, and to institute a new government." Deeming the Government of Great Britain to have become destructive of these ends, they declared that the Colonies "are absolved from all allegiance to the British Crown, and that all political connection between them and the State of Great Britain is, and ought to be, totally dissolved."

In pursuance of this Declaration of Independence, each of the thirteen States proceeded to exercise its separate sovereignty; adopted for itself a Constitution, and appointed officers for the administration of government in all its departments—Legislative, Executive and Judicial. For purposes of defense, they united their arms and their counsels; and, in 1778, they entered into a League known as the Articles of Confederation, whereby they agreed to entrust the administration of their external relations to a common agent, known as the Congress of the United States, expressly declaring, in the first Article "that each State retains its sovereignty, freedom and independence, and every power, jurisdiction and right which is not, by this Confederation, expressly delegated to the United States in Congress assembled."

Under this Confederation the war of the Revolution was carried on, and on the 3rd of September, 1783, the contest ended, and a definite Treaty was signed by Great Britain, in which she acknowledged the independence of the Colonies in the following terms: "ARTICLE 1—His Britannic Majesty acknowledges the said United States, viz: New Hampshire, Massachusetts Bay, Rhode Island and Providence Plantations, Connecticut, New York, New Jersey, Pennsylvania, Delaware, Maryland, Virginia, North Carolina, South Carolina and Georgia, to be FREE, SOVEREIGN AND INDEPENDENT STATES; that he treats with them as such; and for himself, his heirs and successors, relinquishes all claims to the government, property and territorial rights of the same and every part thereof."

Thus were established the two great principles asserted by the Colonies, namely: the right of a State to govern itself; and the right of a people to abolish a Government when it becomes destructive of the ends for which it was instituted. And concurrent with the establishment of these principles, was the fact, that each Colony became and was recognized by the mother Country a FREE, SOVEREIGN AND INDEPENDENT STATE.

In 1787, Deputies were appointed by the States to revise the Articles of Confederation, and on 17th September, 1787, these Deputies recommended for the adoption of the States, the Articles of Union, known as the Constitution of the United States.

The parties to whom this Constitution was submitted, were the several sovereign States; they were to agree or disagree, and when nine of them agreed, the compact was to take effect among those concurring; and the General Government, as the common agent, was then invested with their authority.

If only nine of the thirteen States had concurred, the other four would have remained as they then were—separate, sovereign States, independent of any of the provisions of the Constitution. In fact, two of the States [North Carolina and Rhode Island] did not accede to the Constitution until long after it had gone into operation among the other eleven; and during that interval, they each exercised the functions of an independent nation.

By this Constitution, certain duties were imposed upon the several States, and the exercise of certain of their powers was restrained, which necessarily implied their continued existence as sovereign States. But to remove all doubt, an amendment was added [now the Tenth Amendment], which declared that the powers not delegated to the United States by the Constitution, nor prohibited by it to the States, are reserved to the States, respectively, or to the people. On the 23d May, 1788, South Carolina, by a Convention of her People, passed an Ordinance assenting to this Constitution, and afterwards altered her own Constitution, to conform herself to the obligations she had undertaken.

Thus was established, by compact between the States, a Government with definite objects and powers, limited to the express words of the grant. This limitation left the whole remaining mass of power subject to the clause reserving it to the States or to the people, and rendered unnecessary any specification of reserved rights.

We hold that the Government thus established is subject to the two great principles asserted in the Declaration of Independence; and we hold further, that the mode of its formation subjects it to a third fundamental principle, namely: the law of compact. We maintain that in every compact between two or more parties, the obligation is mutual; that the failure of one of the contracting parties to perform a material part of the agreement, entirely releases the obligation of the other; and that where no arbiter is provided, each party is remitted to his own judgment to determine the fact of failure, with all its consequences.

In the present case, that fact is established with certainty. We assert that fourteen of the States have deliberately refused, for years past, to fulfill their constitutional obligations, and we refer to their own Statutes for the proof.

The Constitution of the United States, in its fourth Article, provides as follows: "No person held to service or labor in one State, under the laws thereof, escaping into another, shall, in consequence of any law or regulation therein, be discharged from such service or labor, but shall be delivered up, on claim of the party to whom such service or labor may be due."

This stipulation was so material to the compact, that without it that compact would not have been made. The greater number of the contracting parties held slaves, and they had previously evinced their estimate of the value of such a stipulation by making it a condition in the Ordinance for the government of the territory ceded by Virginia, which now composes the States north of the Ohio River.

The same article of the Constitution stipulates also for rendition by the several States of fugitives from justice from the other States.

The General Government, as the common agent, passed laws to carry into effect these stipulations of the States. For many years these laws were executed. But an increasing hostility on the part of the non-slaveholding States to the institution of slavery, has led to a disregard of their obligations, and the laws of the General Government have ceased to effect the objects of the Constitution. The States of Maine, New Hampshire, Vermont, Massachusetts, Connecticut, Rhode Island, New York, Pennsylvania, Illinois, Indiana, Michigan, Wisconsin and Iowa, have enacted laws which either nullify the Acts of Congress or render useless any attempt to execute them. In many of these States the fugitive is discharged from service or labor claimed, and in none of them has the State Government complied with the stipulation made in the Constitution. The State of New Jersey, at an early day, passed a law in conformity with her constitutional obligation; but the current of anti-slavery feeling has led her more recently to enact laws which render inoperative the remedies provided by her own law and by the laws of Congress. In the State of New York even the right of transit for a slave has been denied by her tribunals; and the States of Ohio and Iowa have refused to surrender to justice fugitives charged with murder, and with inciting servile insurrection in the State of Virginia. Thus the constituted compact has been deliberately broken and disregarded by the non-slaveholding States, and the consequence follows that South Carolina is released from her obligation.

The ends for which the Constitution was framed are declared by itself to be "to form a more perfect union, establish justice, insure domestic tranquility, provide for the common defence, promote the general welfare, and secure the blessings of liberty to ourselves and our posterity."

These ends it endeavored to accomplish by a Federal Government, in which each State was recognized as an equal, and had separate control over its own institutions. The right of property in slaves was recognized by giving to free persons distinct political rights, by giving them the right to represent, and burthening them with direct taxes for three-fifths of their slaves; by authorizing the importation of slaves for twenty years; and by stipulating for the rendition of fugitives from labor.

We affirm that these ends for which this Government was instituted have been defeated, and the Government itself has been made destructive of them by the action of the non-slaveholding States. Those States have assumed the right of deciding upon the propriety of our domestic institutions; and have denied the rights of property established in fifteen of the States and recognized by the Constitution; they have denounced as sinful the institution of slavery; they have permitted open establishment among them of societies, whose avowed object is to disturb the peace and to eloign ["to remove or carry away"] the property of the citizens of other States. They have encouraged and assisted thousands of our slaves to leave their homes; and those who remain, have been incited by emissaries, books and pictures to servile insurrection.

For twenty-five years this agitation has been steadily increasing, until it has now secured to its aid the power of the common Government. Observing the forms of the Constitution, a sectional party [the Republicans] has found within that Article establishing the Executive Department, the means of subverting the Constitution itself. A geographical line has been drawn across the Union, and all the States north of that line have united in the election of a man to the high office of President of the United States, whose opinions and purposes are hostile to slavery. He is to be entrusted with the administration of the common Government, because he has declared that that "Government cannot endure permanently half slave, half free," and that the public mind must rest in the belief that slavery is in the course of ultimate extinction.

This sectional combination for the submersion of the Constitution, has been aided in some of the States by elevating to citizenship, persons who, by the supreme law of the land [Dred Scott?], are incapable of becoming citizens; and their votes have been used to inaugurate a new policy, hostile to the South, and destructive of its beliefs and safety.

On the 4th day of March next, this party will take possession of the Government. It has announced that the South shall be excluded from the common territory, that the judicial tribunals shall be made sectional, and that a war must be waged against slavery until it shall cease throughout the United States.

The guaranties of the Constitution will then no longer exist; the equal rights of the States will be lost. The slaveholding States will no longer have the power of self-government, or self-protection, and the Federal Government will have become their enemy. Sectional interest and animosity will deepen the irritation, and all hope of remedy is rendered vain, by the fact that public opinion at the North has invested a great political error with the sanction of more erroneous religious belief.

We, therefore, the People of South Carolina, by our delegates in Convention assembled, appealing to the Supreme Judge of the world for the rectitude of our intentions, have solemnly declared that the Union heretofore existing between this State and the other States of North America, is dissolved, and that the State of South Carolina has resumed her position among the nations of the world, as a separate and independent State; with full power to levy war, conclude peace, contract alliances, establish commerce, and to do all other acts and things which independent States may of right do.

ALEXANDER H. STEPHENS, SPEECH BEFORE THE LEGISLATURE OF GEORGIA

Delivered at Milledgeville, November 14th, 1860
Richard Malcolm Johnson and William Hand Browne,
Life of Alexander H. Stephens 580–582
(New and Revised edition, 1884).

[How representative was the action of South Carolina? This excerpt from Georgia statesman Alexander H. Stephens suggests that there was also in the slave South something of a progressive, forward-looking movement that found it possible to remain loyal to the Constitution and to a dynamic vision of the Union even while preserving the institution of slavery. Stephens is the perfect example of a pro-Union Confederate who also happened to be a masterful lawyer and expert on the Constitution. Even so, when the break came (a break he did not want) Stephens become Vice President of the Confederacy, but only after his home state voted for secession. Stephens' ultimate loyalty, then, was to his home state and not to the nation. This is precisely the situation of Robert E. Lee, who seriously considered taking the job of commanding general of the Union Army until his beloved state of Virginia seceded—then his decision, of course, was to oppose Lincoln. Was this affinity to state and locale unique to the South? Can Americans any longer understand a greater loyalty to state than nation? What, exactly, did the South stand for? Was slavery (in this context) "really the issue"? Is it fair to say that to Southerners the war and what led up to it was not about preserving slavery—but about preserving *all* the institutions which made up Southern tradition, family, agriculture, and a state-oriented political identity? Where does race fit into this picture? Can it really be separated? This excerpt from Stephens raises at least some of these questions. Like Lincoln's inaugural address, Stephens's speech manifests a mixing of law and politics. Were his assumptions, and particularly his assumptions about Lincoln, correct?]

FELLOW CITIZENS, I appear before you tonight at the request of members of the Legislature and others, to speak of matters of the deepest interest that can possibly concern us all of an earthly character. There is nothing—no question or subject connected with this life—that concerns a free people so intimately as that of the Government under which they live. We are now indeed surrounded by evils. Never since I entered upon the public stage, has the country been so environed with difficulties and dangers that threatened the public peace and the very existence of society as now. I do not appear before you at my own instance. It is not to gratify any desire of my own that I am here. Had I consulted my own ease and pleasure, I should not be before you; but believing that it is the duty of every good citizen when called on to give his counsels and views whenever the country is in danger as to the best policy to be pursued, I am here. For these reasons, and these only, do I bespeak a calm patient and attentive hearing.

My object is not to stir up strife, but to allay it; not to appeal to your passions, but to your reason. Good governments can never be built up or sustained by the impulse of passion. I wish to address myself to your good sense, to your good judgment, and if, after hearing, you disagree, let us agree to disagree, and part, as we met, friends. We all have the same object, the same interest. That people should disagree in republican governments upon questions of public policy is natural. That men should disagree upon all matters connected with human investigation, whether relating to science or human conduct, is natural. Hence, in free governments, parties will arise. But a free people should express their different opinions with liberality and charity, with no acrimony toward those of their fellows when honestly and sincerely given. These are my feelings tonight.

Let us therefore reason together. It is not my purpose to say aught to wound the feelings of any individual who may be present; and if, in the ardency with which I shall express my opinions, I shall say anything which may be deemed too strong, let it be set down to the zeal with which I advocate my own convictions. There is with me no intention to irritate or offend.

Fellow citizens, we are all launched in the same bark—we are all in the same craft in the wide political ocean,—the same destiny awaits as all for weal or woe. We have been launched in the good old ship that has been upon the waves for three quarters of a century, which has been in so many tempests and storms, has been many times in peril, and patriots have often feared that they should have to give it up; ay, have at times almost given it up; but, still, the gallant ship is afloat. Though new storms now howl around us, and the tempest beats heavily against us, I say to you, Don't give up the ship,—don't abandon her yet. If she can possibly be preserved, and our rights, interests, and security be maintained, the object is worth the effort. Let us not, on account of disappointment and chagrin at the reverse of an election, give up all as lost; but let us see what can be done to prevent a wreck. [A voice from the audience:] *"The ship has holes in her!"* [Stephens continues:] And there may be leaks in her, but let us stop them if we can; many a stout old ship has been saved with richest cargo after many leaks; and it may be so now.

I do not intend, on this occasion, to enter into the history of the reasons or causes of the embarrassments which press so heavily upon us all at this time. In justice to myself, however, I must barely state upon this point that I do think much of it depended upon ourselves. The consternation that has come upon the people is the result of a sectional election of a President of the United States, one whose opinions and avowed principles are in antagonism to our interests and rights, and, we believe, if carried out, would subvert the Constitution under which we now live. But are we entirely blameless in this matter, my countrymen? I give it to you as my opinion, that but for the policy the Southern people pursued, this fearful result would not have occurred. Mr. Lincoln has been elected, I doubt not, by a minority of the people of the United States. What will be the extent of that minority we do not yet know, but the disclosure, when made, will show, I think, that a majority of the constitutional conservative voters of the country were against him; and had the South stood firmly in the Convention at Charleston, on her old platform of principles of nonintervention, there is in my mind but little doubt that whoever might have been the candidate of the national Democratic party would have been elected by as large a majority as that which elected Mr. Buchanan or Mr. Pierce. Therefore, let us not be hasty and rash in our action, especially if the result be attributable at all to ourselves. Before looking to extreme measures, let us see, as Georgians, that everything which can be done to preserve our rights, our interests, and our honor, as well as the peace of the country in the Union, be first done.

The first question that presents itself is, "Shall the people of the South secede from the Union in consequence of the election of Mr. Lincoln to the Presidency of the United States?" My countrymen, I tell you frankly, candidly, and earnestly, that I do not think they ought. In my judgment, the election of no man constitutionally chosen to that high office is sufficient cause for any State to separate from the Union. It ought to stand by and aid still in maintaining the Constitution of the country. To make a point of resistance to the Government, to withdraw from it because a man has been constitutionally elected, puts us in the wrong. We are pledged to maintain the Constitution. Many of us have sworn to support it. Can we therefore, for the mere election of a man to the Presidency, and that too in accordance with the prescribed forms of the Constitution, make a point of resistance to the Government, without becoming the breakers of that sacred instrument ourselves by withdrawing ourselves from it? Would we not be in the wrong? Whatever fate is to befall this country, let it never be laid to the charge of the people of the South, and especially to the people of Georgia, that we were untrue to our national engagements. Let the fault and the wrong rest upon others. If all our hopes are to be blasted, if the Republic is to go down, let us be found to the last moment standing on the deck with the Constitution of the United States waving over our heads. Let the fanatics of the North break the

Constitution, if such is their fell purpose. Let the responsibility he upon them. * * * [L]et not the South—let us not be the ones to commit the aggression. We went into the election with this people. The result was different from what we wished, but the election has been constitutionally held. Were we to make a point of resistance to the Government, and go out of the Union on that account, the record would be made up hereafter against us.

But it is said that Mr. Lincoln's policy and principles are against the Constitution, and that if he carries them out, it will be destructive of our rights. Let us not anticipate a threatened evil. If he violates the Constitution, then will come our time to act. Do not let *us* break it, because forsooth, *he* may. If he does, that is the time for us to strike. I think it would be injudicious and unwise to do this sooner. I do not anticipate that Mr. Lincoln will do anything to jeopard[ize] our safety or security, whatever may be his spirit to do it; for he is bound by the constitutional checks which are thrown around him, which at this time render him powerless to do any great mischief. This shows the wisdom of our system. The President of the United States is no emperor, no dictator—he is clothed with no absolute power. * * *

* * *

ABRAHAM LINCOLN, FIRST INAUGURAL ADDRESS, 1861

Source: Project E—Guttenberg.

[Lincoln's first Inaugural is a masterful piece of legal and political argument, as Lincoln attempts to suggest that despite the rhetoric of the Republicans, nothing really has changed in the nation. Lincoln argues that the North really is law-abiding, so that the South has nothing to fear. He might be speaking directly to Stephens, and others like him. Are you convinced that Lincoln intends to be neutral on the issue of slavery? If you were a Southerner hearing this speech, would you be reassured? How accurate did Lincoln's statements in this First Inaugural turn out to be?

Just what were the burdens that Lincoln assumed when he took the oath to defend the Constitution (which provided for the protection of slavery) at a time when great numbers of people in the North were violently opposed to the institution, and Lincoln himself had fanned the flames of that discontent? Is Lincoln's statement on Constitutional law in this speech essentially a personal interpretation of the Constitution and the role of the states, or is it one that was rooted in history?

What, might we say, is the difference between a politician-lawyer, and a statesman? Which one is Lincoln? Does Lincoln really reveal his views on slavery? Does Lincoln fairly characterize the Republican party's Platform? Still, could Lincoln have said or done anything to mollify the

South at this point? Is he, indeed, drawing a kind of line in the sand? To put this slightly differently, how "American" was Lincoln, really? Do you get the impression from this speech that he believes in that most American creed, the rule of law? What was most important to Lincoln: the concept of Union, or the abhorrence of slavery?

As we will see, Radical Republicans during Reconstruction would assert that the war was about the liberation of slaves and the creation of a new Southern biracial democracy; the "unreconstructed" South would assume the war was about Union only, and that while the South may have had the better of the Constitutional argument, it was defeated by the superior military might of the North. Can you understand why the South simmered for decades?

Is this First Inaugural an opaque address in which one can hear what one wishes? Does that help explain why Lincoln's assassination was roundly repudiated by some Southerners and Confederates who considered him (still) a friend of their region? We might ask the question, why is Lincoln perennially voted by historians and others as America's second greatest president, vying with Washington? Do you agree with this characterization?]

March 4, 1861

Fellow citizens of the United States: in compliance with a custom as old as the government itself, I appear before you to address you briefly and to take, in your presence, the oath prescribed by the Constitution of the United States, to be taken by the President "before he enters on the execution of his office."

* * *

Apprehension seems to exist among the people of the Southern States that by the accession of a Republican administration their property and their peace and personal security are to be endangered. There has never been any reasonable cause for such apprehension. Indeed, the most ample evidence to the contrary has all the while existed and been open to their inspection. It is found in nearly all the published speeches of him who now addresses you. I do but quote from one of those speeches when I declare that "I have no purpose, directly or indirectly, to interfere with the institution of slavery where it exists. I believe I have no lawful right to do so, and I have no inclination to do so."

Those who nominated and elected me did so with full knowledge that I had made this and many similar declarations, and had never recanted them. And, more than this, they placed in the platform for my acceptance, and as a law to themselves and to me, the clear and emphatic resolution which I now read:

> "Resolved: that the maintenance inviolate of the rights of the States, and especially the right of each State to order and control its own domestic institutions according to its own judgment exclusively, is essential to that balance of power on which the perfection and endurance of our political fabric depend, and we denounce the lawless invasion by armed force of the soil of any State or Territory, no matter under what pretext, as among the gravest of crimes."

I now reiterate these sentiments; and, in doing so, I only press upon the public attention the most conclusive evidence of which the case is susceptible, that the property, peace, and security of no section are to be in any wise endangered by the now incoming administration. I add, too, that all the protection which, consistently with the Constitution and the laws, can be given, will be cheerfully given to all the States when lawfully demanded, for whatever cause—as cheerfully to one section as to another.

There is much controversy about the delivering up of fugitives from service or labor. The clause I now read is as plainly written in the Constitution as any other of its provisions:

> "No person held to service or labor in one State, under the laws thereof, escaping into another, shall in consequence of any law or regulation therein be discharged from such service or labor, but shall be delivered up on claim of the party to whom such service or labor may be due."

It is scarcely questioned that this provision was intended by those who made it for the reclaiming of what we call fugitive slaves; and the intention of the lawgiver is the law. All members of Congress swear their support to the whole Constitution—to this provision as much as to any other. To the proposition, then, that slaves whose cases come within the terms of this clause "shall be delivered up", their oaths are unanimous. Now, if they would make the effort in good temper, could they not with nearly equal unanimity frame and pass a law by means of which to keep good that unanimous oath?

There is some difference of opinion whether this clause should be enforced by national or by State authority; but surely that difference is not a very material one. If the slave is to be surrendered, it can be of but little consequence to him or to others by which authority it is done. And should any one in any case be content that his oath shall go unkept on a merely unsubstantial controversy as to HOW it shall be kept?

Again, in any law upon this subject, ought not all the safeguards of liberty known in civilized and humane jurisprudence to be introduced, so that a free man be not, in any case, surrendered as a slave?

And might it not be well at the same time to provide by law for the enforcement of that clause in the Constitution which guarantees that "the citizen of each State shall be entitled to all privileges and immunities of citizens in the several States?"

I take the official oath today with no mental reservations, and with no purpose to construe the Constitution or laws by any hypercritical rules. And while I do not choose now to specify particular acts of Congress as proper to be enforced, I do suggest that it will be much safer for all, both in official and private stations, to conform to and abide by all those acts which stand unrepealed, than to violate any of them, trusting to find impunity in having them held to be unconstitutional.

It is seventy-two years since the first inauguration of a President under our national Constitution. During that period fifteen different and greatly distinguished citizens have, in succession, administered the executive branch of the government. They have conducted it through many perils, and generally with great success. Yet, with all this scope of precedent, I now enter upon the same task for the brief Constitutional term of four years under great and peculiar difficulty. A disruption of the Federal Union, heretofore only menaced, is now formidably attempted.

I hold that, in contemplation of universal law and of the Constitution, the Union of these States is perpetual. Perpetuity is implied, if not expressed, in the fundamental law of all national governments. [Is this consistent with the Declaration of Independence?]

It is safe to assert that no government proper ever had a provision in its organic law for its own termination. Continue to execute all the express provisions of our National Constitution, and the Union will endure forever—it being impossible to destroy it except by some action not provided for in the instrument itself.

Again, if the United States be not a government proper, but an association of States in the nature of contract merely, can it, as a contract, be peaceably unmade by less than all the parties who made it?

One party to a contract may violate it—break it, so to speak; but does it not require all to lawfully rescind it?

Descending from these general principles, we find the proposition that in legal contemplation the Union is perpetual confirmed by the history of the Union itself. The Union is much older than the Constitution. It was formed, in fact, by the Articles of Association in 1774. It was matured and continued by the Declaration of Independence in 1776. It was further matured, and the faith of all the then thirteen States expressly plighted and engaged that it should be perpetual, by the Articles of Confederation in 1778. And, finally, in 1787 one of the declared objects for ordaining and establishing the Constitution was "TO FORM A MORE PERFECT UNION."

But if the destruction of the Union by one or by a part only of the States be lawfully possible, the Union is LESS perfect than before the Constitution, having lost the vital element of perpetuity.

It follows from these views that no State upon its own mere motion can lawfully get out of the Union; that Resolves and Ordinances to that effect are legally void; and that acts of violence, within any State or States, against the authority of the United States, are insurrectionary or revolutionary, according to circumstances.

I therefore consider that, in view of the Constitution and the laws, the Union is unbroken; and to the extent of my ability I shall take care, as the Constitution itself expressly enjoins upon me, that the laws of the Union be faithfully executed in all the States. Doing this I deem to be only a simple duty on my part; and I shall perform it so far as practicable, unless my rightful masters, the American people, shall withhold the requisite means, or in some authoritative manner direct the contrary.

I trust this will not be regarded as a menace, but only as the declared purpose of the Union that it WILL Constitutionally defend and maintain itself.

In doing this there needs to be no bloodshed or violence; and there shall be none, unless it be forced upon the national authority.

The power confided to me will be used to hold, occupy, and possess the property and places belonging to the government, and to collect the duties and imposts; but beyond what may be necessary for these objects, there will be no invasion, no using of force against or among the people anywhere. Where hostility to the United States, in any interior locality, shall be so great and universal as to prevent competent resident citizens from holding the Federal offices, there will be no attempt to force obnoxious strangers among the people for that object. While the strict legal right may exist in the government to enforce the exercise of these offices, the attempt to do so would be so irritating, and so nearly impracticable withal, that I deem it better to forego for the time the uses of such offices.

The mails, unless repelled, will continue to be furnished in all parts of the Union. So far as possible, the people everywhere shall have that sense of perfect security which is most favorable to calm thought and reflection. The course here indicated will be followed unless current events and experience shall show a modification or change to be proper, and in every case and exigency my best discretion will be exercised according to circumstances actually existing, and with a view and a hope of a peaceful solution of the national troubles and the restoration of fraternal sympathies and affections.

That there are persons in one section or another who seek to destroy the Union at all events, and are glad of any pretext to do it, I will neither affirm nor deny; but if there be such, I need address no word to them. To those, however, who really love the Union may I not speak?

Before entering upon so grave a matter as the destruction of our national fabric, with all its benefits, its memories, and its hopes, would it not be wise to ascertain precisely why we do it?

Will you hazard so desperate a step while there is any possibility that any portion of the ills you fly from have no real existence?

Will you, while the certain ills you fly to are greater than all the real ones you fly from—will you risk the commission of so fearful a mistake?

All profess to be content in the Union if all Constitutional rights can be maintained. Is it true, then, that any right, plainly written in the Constitution, has been denied? I think not. Happily the human mind is so constituted that no party can reach to the audacity of doing this.

Think, if you can, of a single instance in which a plainly written provision of the Constitution has ever been denied. If by the mere force of numbers a majority should deprive a minority of any clearly written Constitutional right, it might, in a moral point of view, justify revolution—certainly would if such a right were a vital one. But such is not our case. All the vital rights of minorities and of individuals are so plainly assured to them by affirmations and negations, guaranties and prohibitions, in the Constitution, that controversies never arise concerning them. But no organic law can ever be framed with a provision specifically applicable to every question which may occur in practical administration. No foresight can anticipate, nor any document of reasonable length contain, express provisions for all possible questions. Shall fugitives from labor be surrendered by national or State authority? The Constitution does not expressly say.

May Congress prohibit slavery in the Territories? The Constitution does not expressly say. MUST Congress protect slavery in the Territories?

The Constitution does not expressly say.

From questions of this class spring all our constitutional controversies and we divide upon them into majorities and minorities. If the minority will not acquiesce, the majority must, or the government must cease.

There is no other alternative; for continuing the government is acquiescence on one side or the other.

If a minority in such case will secede rather than acquiesce, they make a precedent which in turn will divide and ruin them; for a minority of their own will secede from them whenever a majority refuses to be controlled by such minority.

For instance, why may not any portion of a new confederacy a year or two hence arbitrarily secede again, precisely as portions of the present Union now claim to secede from it?

All who cherish disunion sentiments are now being educated to the exact temper of doing this.

Is there such perfect identity of interests among the States to compose a new Union, as to produce harmony only, and prevent renewed secession?

Plainly, the central idea of secession is the essence of anarchy.

A majority held in restraint by constitutional checks and limitations, and always changing easily with deliberate changes of popular opinions and sentiments, is the only true sovereign of a free people.

Whoever rejects it does, of necessity, fly to anarchy or to despotism. Unanimity is impossible; the rule of a minority, as a permanent arrangement, is wholly inadmissible; so that, rejecting the majority principle, anarchy or despotism in some form is all that is left.

I do not forget the position, assumed by some, that Constitutional questions are to be decided by the Supreme Court; nor do I deny that such decisions must be binding, in any case, upon the parties to a suit, as to the object of that suit, while they are also entitled to very high respect and consideration in all parallel cases by all other departments of the government. And while it is obviously possible that such decision may be erroneous in any given case, still the evil effect following it, being limited to that particular case, with the chance that it may be overruled and never become a precedent for other cases, can better be borne than could the evils of a different practice.

At the same time, the candid citizen must confess that if the policy of the government, upon vital questions affecting the whole people, is to be irrevocably fixed by decisions of the Supreme Court, the instant they are made, in ordinary litigation between parties in personal actions, the people will have ceased to be their own rulers, having to that extent practically resigned their government into the hands of that eminent tribunal. Nor is there in this view any assault upon the court or the judges. It is a duty from which they may not shrink to decide cases properly brought before them, and it is no fault of theirs if others seek to turn their decisions to political purposes.

One section of our country believes slavery is RIGHT, and ought to be extended, while the other believes it is WRONG, and ought not to be extended. This is the only substantial dispute.

The fugitive-slave clause of the Constitution, and the law for the suppression of the foreign slave-trade, are each as well enforced, perhaps, as any law can ever be in a community where the moral sense of the people imperfectly supports the law itself.

The great body of the people abide by the dry legal obligation in both cases, and a few break over in each. This, I think, cannot be perfectly cured; and it would be worse in both cases AFTER the separation of the sections than BEFORE. The foreign slave-trade, now imperfectly suppressed, would be ultimately revived, without restriction, in one section, while fugitive slaves, now only partially surrendered, would not be surrendered at all by the other.

Physically speaking, we cannot separate. We cannot remove our respective sections from each other, nor build an impassable wall between them. A husband and wife may be divorced, and go out of the presence and beyond the reach of each other; but the different parts of our country cannot do this. They cannot but remain face to face, and intercourse, either amicable or hostile, must continue between them. Is it possible, then, to make that intercourse more advantageous or more satisfactory after separation than before? Can aliens make treaties easier than friends can make laws? Can treaties be more faithfully enforced between aliens than laws can among friends? Suppose you go to war, you cannot fight always; and when, after much loss on both sides, and no gain on either, you cease fighting, the identical old questions as to terms of intercourse are again upon you.

This country, with its institutions, belongs to the people who inhabit it.

Whenever they shall grow weary of the existing government, they can exercise their CONSTITUTIONAL right of amending it, or their REVOLUTIONARY right to dismember or overthrow it. I cannot be ignorant of the fact that many worthy and patriotic citizens are desirous of having the national Constitution amended. While I make no recommendation of amendments, I fully recognize the rightful authority of the people over the whole subject, to be exercised in either of the modes prescribed in the instrument itself; and I should, under existing circumstances, favor rather than oppose a fair opportunity being afforded the people to act upon it. I will venture to add that to me the convention mode seems preferable, in that it allows amendments to originate with the people themselves, instead of only permitting them to take or reject propositions originated by others not especially chosen for the purpose, and which might not be precisely such as they would wish to either accept or refuse. I understand a proposed amendment to the Constitution—which amendment, however, I have not seen—has passed Congress, to the effect that the Federal Government shall never interfere with the domestic institutions of the States, including that of persons held to service. To avoid misconstruction of what I have said, I depart from my purpose not to speak of particular amendments so far as to say that, holding such a provision to now be implied Constitutional law, I have no objection to its being made express and irrevocable.

The chief magistrate derives all his authority from the people, and they have conferred none upon him to fix terms for the separation of the states. The people themselves can do this also if they choose; but the executive, as such, has nothing to do with it. His duty is to administer the present government, as it came to his hands, and to transmit it, unimpaired by him, to his successor.

Why should there not be a patient confidence in the ultimate justice of the people? Is there any better or equal hope in the world? In our present differences is either party without faith of being in the right? If the Almighty Ruler of Nations, with his eternal truth and justice, be on your side of the North, or on yours of the South, that truth and that justice will surely prevail, by the judgment of this great tribunal, the American people.

By the frame of the government under which we live, this same people have wisely given their public servants but little power for mischief; and have, with equal wisdom, provided for the return of that little to their own hands at very short intervals. While the people retain their virtue and vigilance, no administration, by any extreme of wickedness or folly, can very seriously injure the government in the short space of four years.

My countrymen, one and all, think calmly and WELL upon this whole subject. Nothing valuable can be lost by taking time.

If there be an object to HURRY any of you in hot haste to a step which you would never take DELIBERATELY, that object will be frustrated by taking time; but no good object can be frustrated by it. Such of you as are now dissatisfied, still have the old Constitution unimpaired, and, on the sensitive point, the laws of your own framing under it; while the new administration will have no immediate power, if it would, to change either.

If it were admitted that you who are dissatisfied hold the right side in the dispute, there still is no single good reason for precipitate action. Intelligence, patriotism, Christianity, and a firm reliance on Him who has never yet forsaken this favored land, are still competent to adjust in the best way all our present difficulty.

In YOUR hands, my dissatisfied fellow-countrymen, and not in MINE, is the momentous issue of civil war. The government will not assail YOU.

You can have no conflict without being yourselves the aggressors.

YOU have no oath registered in heaven to destroy the government, while I shall have the most solemn one to "preserve, protect, and defend it."

I am loathe to close. We are not enemies, but friends. We must not be enemies. Though passion may have strained, it must not break our bonds of affection. The mystic chords of memory, stretching from every battlefield and patriot grave to every living heart and hearthstone all over this broad land, will yet swell the chorus of the Union when again touched, as surely they will be, by the better angels of our nature.

The Civil War, Reconstruction, and Reunion

The conclusion of the Civil War in 1865 left the South in a state of utter devastation and ruin. With the exception of some battles in the free state of Pennsylvania, the land war was fought entirely on Southern soil. The Union policy of "total war," initiated with Ulysses S. Grant's rise to supreme commander of the Union forces in early 1864, targeted not only the Confederate forces but also the South's commercial, manufacturing, transportation, and agricultural infrastructures, which were keys to sustaining the Confederate war effort. Inevitably, civilians suffered. All war is ugly, but the American Civil War set a new standard for battlefield carnage and destruction when, for the first time, it brought modernizing weaponry and explosives technology to bear in closely-fought battle.

The Combatants probably believed that the war would be over quickly, but this was not to be. It lasted for years, and camp sicknesses and disease were rampant in the armies of both the North and South, food was at times scarce (and it was almost always so for the Confederate soldiers), and, in a time when medical instruments were rarely cleaned and sterilized, even the most superficial wound or scrape might become a gamble with death. By war's end the Union had lost 359,528; the Confederacy 258,000. Casualties were about 35% of the combined Union and Confederate military forces. One in ten of all white Southern males died. A byproduct of the North's new way of waging total war was the creation of refugees (both blacks and whites), whose numbers were in the millions.

Not until 1864 did it appear that the Union Army was finally grinding down the South's resistance, and that the North's war machine was probably unstoppable. But even if Northern victory were assured, the acute problem of managing the political, social, and economic reconstruction and reintegration of the South into the Union was evident before the war ended. The most immediate challenge involved what to do with slaves who had escaped to freedom. In 1861, with the first major Confederate–Union battlefield encounter (Bull Run) still two months away, General G.F. Butler of Fortress Monroe in Virginia refused to return slaves who had escaped to his lines. On the question of their status, and in response to their masters' demand for their return, General Butler declared them "contraband of war." In late August of 1861, General John C.

Fremont, commander of the Western department of the Union Army stationed in St. Louis, issued a proclamation announcing that the slaves of Missourians who took up arms with the Confederacy (Missouri did not secede) were free. Lincoln removed Fremont from his position and modified the order, as at that time he did not wish to antagonize Border States who so far had not left the Union.

What, then, to do with the "contraband of war?" Lincoln at first sought to make sure that the issue of slavery did not interfere with his war aims. The fact remained, however, that slaves were one of the most important assets of the Confederacy, and if slavery could be ended, the ability of the South to resist the North would diminish. Moreover, for a growing number of Northern newspaper editorialists, and an increasing number of people in the North—those on whose support Lincoln's war effort ultimately depended—freeing the slaves was becoming the *de facto* objective of the war, even if it had begun simply over the issue of whether the union was inviolable.

In July 1862 Congress, for the first time, provided for the emancipation of slaves held by Confederates and for the liberation of slaves coming within Union lines. The effectiveness of this act, however, would depend entirely on the president's willingness to enforce it. Lincoln himself was rethinking his position on emancipation, and began working secretly on an emancipation document, sharing a draft privately with his cabinet. Lincoln eventually determined to move forward on emancipation, but waited for the right opportunity. That opportunity came with a Union victory at the Battle of Antietam in September, 1862. A few days later, Lincoln circulated a Preliminary Emancipation Proclamation. Relying on the war powers provision of the Constitution as his authority, the proclamation was to take effect January 1, 1863. In it, as you will see, the President declared that all slaves in the states in rebellion were "then, thenceforward, and forever free."

The Emancipation Proclamation was a stunning development for those who knew Lincoln; his position announced a seismic shift in the North's stated war aims, from one of mere preservation of the Union, to the radical Abolitionist position of the liberation of slaves. These twin purposes were now joined, making of the war an idealistic reformist crusade. Lincoln's emancipation message was also intended for European powers whose neutrality he hoped to win by investing the war with a moral purpose. Yet even in the fall of 1862, between his announcement and the day the proclamation was to take effect, Lincoln worked behind the scenes, still hoping he could convince Border States to set an example by emancipating their slaves, for which Lincoln promised to pay compensation. Lincoln continued to hold out the option of colonization for freedman, a position that put him at loggerheads with many Abolitionists. His appeals were, however, rebuffed. On January 1, 1863, then, the Proclamation went into effect. Paradoxically, the Emancipation Proclamation would apply only to those states where the Union Army had no control (i.e., the seceded states), and therefore no slaves would actually be freed. Nevertheless, the issuance of the Proclamation, and the transformation of a war for union into a moral crusade would shape and dictate (and, alas, confuse and frustrate) the goals of Reunion and Reconstruction.

Lincoln's administration, with the support of Congressional Republicans, began taking steps in preparation for the end of the conflict and the era to come. They repealed racist laws, they included African American troops in the U.S. Army, and they passed the Thirteenth Amendment (ratified in 1865) abolishing slavery, once and for all, in all the states. Thornier questions loomed, however. What conditions should attach to the restoration of former Confederate states into the Union? What, exactly, was the status of the freedman? Did freedmen enjoy the same civil rights as all other citizens? Could they vote? Could the land of rebellious White Confederates be confiscated and redistributed to ex-slaves?

Because Lincoln saw secession as illegal, even though he continued to view the Southern states as members of the Union, he regarded the South as in a state of "insurrection." He relied on the provision in the Constitution that gave to the President "power to grant reprieves and pardons for offenses against the United States" for managing Reconstruction. (Was this appropriate?) In his December, 1863, Proclamation of Amnesty and Reconstruction he adopted a conciliatory tone, as he was often wont to do. The Confederates (with some exceptions) were to be welcomed back into "the family," and granted exceedingly liberal terms of amnesty that entailed making a simple pledge of loyalty. Lincoln enormously simplified the process of state and local government creation by specifying that only 10% of the population (based on 1860 figures) needed to swear loyalty to the U.S. Government for the state to initiate the restoration process. The only other requirement for the rebellious states to rejoin the Union was the acceptance of emancipation. As more Confederate land fell to Federal forces, the more urgent the process of effectuating Reconstruction became. The first state to be subjected to reconstruction was Louisiana, in 1864.

Congress and especially its radical Republican members (Rep. Thaddeus Stevens of Pennsylvania and Senator Charles Sumner of Massachusetts were the most prominent), for whom the war had always been an emancipationist crusade, found themselves bypassed by Lincoln's unilateral action. To them, the Southern states ceased to exist because of their "state suicide." Therefore restoring them back into the Union was more properly analogous to Congress's jurisdiction over the admission of territories; it was *Congress* and not the executive who should be managing the readmission of the secessionist states.

The Radicals also objected to Lincoln's failure to include protections for the civil rights of freedpeople and his too-lenient dependence on only 10 percent of former Confederates taking a simple loyalty oath. (The Radicals wanted an "iron clad" oath taken by no less than half the population.) The Wade–Davis Bill passed in July 1864 incorporated these concerns, putting the Congress and the President on a collision course. Lincoln pocket-vetoed the Bill and with the fall of Atlanta in the late summer of 1864—a disastrous loss for the South and a definitive turn in the war—Lincoln now rode a sudden wave of Northern popularity that propelled him back into office in the November presidential election. Lincoln's adroitness, good fortune, and overnight electoral popularity trumped Congress, at least for a time.

Then came the catastrophe of Lincoln's assassination. Eight days after Lee's surrender at Appomattox, John Wilkes Booth's botched conspiracy to decapitate the government by killing Lincoln, Vice President Johnson, and Secretary of State William Seward, actually came very close to success. Barely five weeks after Lincoln's festive second inauguration, Northerners mourned the assassination of their president. Lincoln's worn features, that so vividly reflected the nation's pain and anguish, his rock-steadiness, and his innate political caution combined with his boldness and essential humanity had seemed the perfect combination for winning the war and for building the peace. He was now gone.

The former Vice–President Johnson was completely unprepared and ill-equipped for the job he now assumed. Adopting Lincoln's executive-centered plan and Lincoln's stated intent of showing "malice toward none" and "charity toward all," the new President (between May and December 1865) managed Reconstruction. He recognized five states whose plans for reentry had already begun under Lincoln, all while Congress was in recess. Johnson worked with the remaining seven secessionist states to establish provisional governments. The process involved a presidentially appointed provisional governor who then was authorized to convene a state convention. Participants in the convention were elected by those citizens who took the loyalty oath (Lincoln's "10 percent") or who received a presidential pardon. The process of restoration was finalized when and if the convention amended the state constitution, repudiated the Confederate war debt, and abolished slavery. In December 1865, as part of his annual message to Congress, Johnson announced that the Union was officially restored for all but one state (Texas, which would be officially restored in April, 1866).

Though the military defeat of the Confederacy was conclusive only with the surrender of General Joseph E. Johnston's forces in the Carolina campaign of late April 1865, the South's subjection as a region was anything but certain. "Black Codes" in Southern states sprang up immediately after the cessation of hostilities. These systems of regulation deprived freedmen of their civil rights and liberties, and, though slavery was technically at an end, the Black Codes sought to perpetuate the South's racial caste system. In the countryside, Southern whites organized work regimens that mimicked slavery, as overseers and drivers rounded up freedmen under vagrancy and apprenticeship laws and put them to "service," often on the same lands and even with the same masters of former times. In early 1866, the Ku Klux Klan was formed and spread rapidly throughout the South, using tactics of terror, beatings, and murder against freedmen and supporters of the Southern Republican Party. By not acting, President Johnson, a Southerner and a Unionist Democrat who was the military governor of occupied Tennessee in 1864 before being elevated as Vice President, signaled his support.

When Congress reconvened in December 1865, it refused to endorse the new President's actions and took matters into its own hands, initiating a Congressional phase of Reconstruction. The 13th Amendment was ratified in December of 1865, abolishing slavery formally. In the opening months of 1866, Congress passed bills to beef up and extend the scope of the Freedmen's Bureau (created in 1864) for the protection of ex-slaves, especially in their negotiations with planters. Johnson vetoed the bill and the Congress overrode the veto. In April 1866, the Congress passed the Civil Rights Bill (the text of which you will soon read) that granted citizenship and civil rights to blacks and effectively overturned the *Dred Scott* decision. Johnson also vetoed this bill as an unwarranted intrusion into state affairs, and Congress again overrode the veto. In June Congress drafted what was to become the 14th Amendment, a measure designed to assure that the 1866 Civil Rights Act could be construed as within the powers granted by the Constitution. The Fourteenth Amendment (ratified in 1868) guaranteed the civil rights of blacks as citizens within each state, and its ratification was made conditional before a Southern state could be restored to the Union. As he had opposed other actions of the radically-dominated Congress, Johnson opposed the Fourteenth Amendment as an unwise overreaching of Federal power.

The war for reconstruction between the President and the Congress ended in a total melt-down. The diverging understandings of what the Civil War meant, the effect that emancipation was to have, the question whether the Southern states were to be simply "restored" to the Union or were to be "reconstructed," and who was to lead in the wake of the president's assassination, became the issues that drove the Congressional elections of 1866. Helped by Johnson's very poor performance on a national speaking tour to build a centrist National Union Party, the Radical Republicans were effective in framing the peace as the extension of war-time patriotism and reformist zeal. The Radicals added to their numbers in the House and Senate. Claiming a national mandate, they proceeded to launch their Congressional program of Reconstruction to rebuild Southern society in the image of the North.

In March of 1867, a new Reconstruction Act (once again passed over Johnson's veto) divided the South into military districts, each overseen by a commanding general who would supervise the entry of former Confederate states into the Union. The new law required new constitutional conventions, disenfranchised many former Confederate officials, enfranchised freedmen, and made entry into the union dependent on a state's ratification of the Fourteenth Amendment and granting the vote to freedmen. In opposition to Johnson's simple goal of restoring states to the Union as soon as possible, the Radicals endeavored to remake and reform post-war Southern society as a biracial democracy. The Radicals also possessed an activist vision of the national government and a free labor commitment to capitalism, in contrast to Johnson's solidly states-rights stand. For his intransigence, Johnson found himself impeached in the House. He escaped conviction by one vote and served out the remainder of what was left of his term as a virtual irrelevance.

The fratricidal relations between the executive and legislative branches was a distraction for the nation; with the 1868 election of Ulysses S. Grant, a war hero who ran for office as a Republican, the Radicals now had a friend in the White House. Grant endorsed the use of force in Southern states to support Radical Reconstruction. During his term, the Fifteenth Amendment, guaranteeing suffrage to freedmen, was passed and ratified. By 1870 all the Southern states were back in the Union under the Radicals' terms. In the Reconstructed Southern states, the Republican Party dominated politics, and a biracial coalition saw freedmen elected to local and state offices in every Southern state, and to Congress. Newly elected Republicans passed laws in support of public education, the rebuilding of state infrastructure, and promotion of economy and industry. For a brief moment, some promise of democracy shone.

Despite these early successes, the Republican Party in the South was under siege in the 1870s. Democrats (with some truth and some justice on their side) lambasted the Republicans as corrupt, bemoaned "Negro Rule," attacked "scalawags" (white Southerners who supported Reconstruction) as disloyal and branded "carpet baggers" (Northerners who had moved into the South, carrying their possessions in cloth luggage) as vile predators. The Ku Klux Klan continued to spread terror, and joined by other vigilante groups, acted, in effect, as a paramilitary arm of the South's Democratic Party.

The Southern economy was a pillaged and ruined wreck, and most of the region's people now lived in a state of poverty. Freedmen hoped to own land and farm, but instead became entrapped in sharecropping arrangements dictated by planters. While Grant and the Congress managed to reign in the Klan with The Enforcement Acts (1870–71), there was never enough federal military presence to do the job of enforcing Radical Reconstruction over the resistance that lingered in the former Confederate states. Meanwhile the Democratic Party drum-beat against "Black Republicans" was steady and corrosive. Other challenges intervened that diverted the Federal government's (and the nation's) attention. Indian wars were breaking out in the West and the Grant Administration found itself entangled in one scandal after another. Congress was changing too: The Democratic Party took advantage of white dissatisfaction in the South and a wounded president to pick up a majority in the House following the Panic of 1873. In 1878, the Democrats also took control of the Senate, and this was the first time since 1859 that the Democrats controlled the Congress.

The 1874 vote showed the nation's growing weariness with Reconstruction. An opportunity for closure presented itself in the 1876 presidential election. The Democrat, Samuel Tilden of New York, led the Republican, Rutherford B. Hayes, in the popular vote and in the electoral vote. There remained, however, 20 disputed electoral votes (those of Florida, Louisiana, and South Carolina), which were necessary to declare a winner in the Electoral College. The stalemate was broken when the Democrats quietly agreed to recognize Hayes as the winner, in return for the Republicans agreeing to withdraw all Federal troops from the South and declare an end to Reconstruction. The Republicans agreed, Hayes became president, and, beginning in 1877, Congressional Reconstruction came to an end, as Federal troops withdrew from the South.

If Reconstruction was to continue in the South without the direct oversight of the Federal government, what would it look like? Whose memories of the war and its purpose would fuel and guide these next steps in Reunion? Northern and Black hopes for Radical Reconstruction were not entirely dashed. The nation was left with the heritage of Lincoln's wartime Republican Party, some Radical advocates like Sen. Charles Sumner who remained in Congress, the Emancipation Proclamation, and three new Amendments, as well as a body of civil rights legislation. For all 4.2 million freedmen in the South, the memory of slavery was a living thing, as was their emancipation. Black intellectuals, political activists, former abolitionists, and journalists resisted efforts to diminish equality and civil rights. The post-war South also attracted Northern philanthropists, church groups, and reformers who sought to build schools for freedmen and to teach them mechanical trades.

For many White Southerners, however, the memory of the Civil War (or, as some would call it for decades, "The War of Northern Aggression") was that of a long nightmare that took the lives of their sons, fathers, brothers, and husbands. These losses, of course, they shared with Northerners, the absolute number of whose casualties was even greater. But, however the "War Between the States" was characterized, the South had lost. For many painful years, the bitter humiliation of defeat in a society that prized honor above all else, was daily symbolized by the "bayonet rule" of Union soldiers who were bivouacked in their towns and in the countryside. Perhaps inevitably, there gradually arose among Southern whites a "Lost Cause" movement, that memorialized the honorable stand of their slaveholding ancestors who fought with valor (though greatly outnumbered) against Yankee aggressors. For these Southerners, who did have some limited basis in fact for their claims, relations between slaves and their masters before the war were remembered as the peaceful and harmonic affairs of "plantation families," presided over by aristocratic and noble men like Washington and Jefferson. The War and its aftermath were regarded as an invasion of barbarians who, as the Visigoths had done to Rome, sacked Southern Civilization.

This dream of a Golden Age of the "Old South" died hard, but, in other quarters, in the midst of the reality of a modernizing "New South," eventually the reunion of North and South was viewed as creating opportunities for investors and entrepreneurs, for industrial development and for commercial expansion of a kind that had never been seen in the South before. The national message of the Compromise of 1877 was that the people of the nation might at last bind up their wounds and make money together, while leaving the Southerners to tend to matters of race in their own way. In this one area, the South would be left alone. The reunion, if there was one, might be seen as a reunion of whites.

Under the banner of "Redeemers" the region's Democratic Party set to work winning (and taking back) Southern state governments from the Republicans. By 1880 the "redemption" was complete as the South became a "solid" one-party region. The South now truly could be remade, in practice and in ideology, as the Democratic Party turned to legal institutions to perfect and secure into future generations its doctrine of white supremacy. Over the next two decades almost no sphere of Southern life would be left untouched.

Initially, towns, cities, and counties informally phased in separate facilities, schools, and accommodations for "colored" and "white." In time social practices hardened into legislation that mandated in the minutest detail the separation of the races. This new system of "Jim Crow" was inherently unequal, as basic services in communities of freedpeople, such as security of person and property, roads, schools, water, and sanitation were only minimally supported, if these services existed at all. Some blacks who dared to exercise their civil rights put themselves at risk of retaliation, including lynching, while local administrative processes were used to bar blacks from serving on juries. Criminal law and enforcement became not only a mechanism of social control but also a means of creating a work force. Imprisonment for even the slightest infraction, for petty offenses like vagrancy or violating curfew, resulted in prosecution and the offenders being sent to prison work camps. The innovation of putting prisoners to work on public projects like road building saved the state money, while "convict leasing," as we will explore later, was positively a financial boon for many rural counties, enforcement officials, and the turpentine, mining, brick-making, railroad, and lumber interests. Through lease agreements the state "hired out" prisoners who worked in dangerous and often life-threatening conditions, amassing a "debt" to their "bosses" (for clothing, shelter, food) that kept them in a new sort of perpetual bondage. Thousands died—their deaths often unrecorded.

By the late 1890s, most states had begun taking the ultimate formal step of constitutionally disenfranchising their black citizens and on occasion poor white citizens as well: Mississippi in 1890, Florida in 1885–91, South Carolina in 1895, Louisiana in 1898, North Carolina in 1900, Alabama in 1901, Texas in 1901 and 1923, Virginia in 1902, and Georgia in 1908. Poll taxes, literacy tests, grandfather clauses (provisions which tied the then-current generation's voting rights to those of their grandfathers, subsequently found unconstitutional by the Supreme Court in 1915), property requirements, and white primaries almost completely eliminated suffrage for most blacks. By 1910, the removal of freedmen from civic and political life was legally complete, while extralegal violence (lynching, horse whipping, beatings, shootings) was relied upon to ensure that the spirit of the law no less than the letter was enforced.

In the North and South, sadly, there came to be surprising agreement on matters of race. Segregation, inferior schools, Klan activity, anti-black violence, and the relegation of black workers to the most menial jobs were a pattern in most states or cities in the North, where blacks lived in concentration. As we will see in the work of Lambroso, scientific theories of hereditary traits (race was assumed to be one factor) dominated in the new criminology of the 1880s. Research in the emerging fields of the social sciences that "proved" (or assumed) the superiority of the white race was regular fare in professional conferences and journals, while attitudes of *noblesse oblige* and even, at times, racial virulence, drew from Americans' direct experience in the Philippine–American war of 1899.

These beliefs were propped up by generalized Victorian notions of Anglo–Saxon racial superiority and of the "white man's burden." Americans were influenced by Social Darwinism and its tenets of natural selection and survival of the fittest to explain the organization of their society—why some racial and ethnic groups found themselves on top and others on the bottom. For evidence, one needed only look to the presence of new immigrant populations crowding American cities (especially Asians, and Southern and Central Europeans) whose customs, practices, religions, and beliefs appeared strange and retrogressive. Efforts to stem the immigration of non-Western Europeans into the U.S. would pick up steam in the first three decades of the twentieth century.

The struggle to preserve and hold on to the Civil War's emancipationist agenda was not universal among black leaders. Booker T. Washington's speech at the Atlanta-based Cotton States and International Exposition in 1895 announced an acceptance of segregation and the diminishing of equal rights and political power, as he urged blacks to "pick themselves up" through industrial and agricultural trades. His speech mirrored a growing concern about the freedpeople's economic dislocation and an escalating cycle of violence and was instantly embraced by advocates of the New South as the way of the future. For other black intellectuals, like W.E.B. Dubois, Washington's public statement was a betrayal. The Niagara Movement, launched in 1905 in Buffalo, one of the end-points of the antebellum Underground Railroad, became a wedge of resistance for Northern and Southern black leaders, ministers, teachers, and leaders who decried Booker T. Washington's new direction. Symbolically, they held a second convention at Harper's Ferry in 1906 where they also memorialized John Brown's raid. In 1909, the National Association for the Advancement of Colored People (NAACP) emerged out of the Niagara Movement.

In their own history books, however, and most certainly in their popular lore, white Southerners would remember Reconstruction, in the words of one contemporary, as "that dismal period—massacres of the helpless, violations of the ballot, usurpations of force on the popular will and the independence of the States." The presence of Union troops was an example of "alien rule and federal domination by which sovereign states were reduced to the impotence of satrapies." The story went on, telling of a land that was eventually rescued from this nightmare, but only through its own heroic effort. Outside the African–American community, this legend of Reconstruction for a while triumphed to become the nation's dominant view, eclipsing the emancipationist story of the freedpeople and the purported crusading purpose of the North's moral war.

D.W. Griffith's silent film "Birth of a Nation" (1915), based on Thomas Dixon's triumphal *The Clansman* (1905), that glorified the Klan's rise, became Hollywood's first blockbuster. The runaway best seller and Hollywood film version of *Gone with the Wind* (1939) presented a transcendent vision of the "Old South" as a time of Cavaliers and Gentlemen tended to by faithful "darkies." Walt Disney's "Song of the South" (1946), though set in the post-Civil War era, presented on the big screen Joel Chandler Harris's "Uncle Remus" folk tales as the updated story of the happy slave. Through these and other countless examples of popular media as well as books, the South was not only reconciled with its Northern neighbors, but romanticized by them as well.

The encampment at Gettysburg Battlefield of almost 50,000 veterans of the Civil War in June and July of 1913—the fiftieth anniversary of the Battle of Gettysburg—was as fine a symbol of national unity as anyone could conjure. There were celebrations, commemorations, hand-shaking and posed pictures across stone fence lines that 50 years earlier marked bloody Northern and Southern battlements. Blue and gray uniforms rolled out in a sea of humanity, sweeping up the gentle slopes of the battlefield. Units of the Confederate and Union armies exchanged flags in ceremonies, and speeches were made. The youngest veteran there was 61, the oldest purportedly 112. The *Washington Post* reported: "Nothing could possibly be more impressive or more inspiring to the younger generation than this gathering. They feel the thrill of bygone days, without knowledge of its bitterness, which, thank God, has passed us all."

President Woodrow Wilson, the first Southern president since the Civil War, made an appearance, and in his speech posed the question of the meaning of the fiftieth anniversary and answered that it meant

> "Peace and union and vigor, and the maturity and might of a great nation. How wholesome and healing the peace has been! We have found one another again as brothers and comrades, in arms enemies no longer, generous friends rather, our battles long past, the quarrel forgotten—except that we shall not forget the splendid valor, the manly devotion of the men then arrayed against one another, now grasping hands and smiling into each other's eyes. How complete the union has become and how dear to all of us, how unquestioned, how benign and majestic, as state after state has been added to this, our great family of free men!"

A "forgotten quarrel" indeed it seemed to be. In the photos and journals of the event, there is not a single record documenting the presence of a participating African–American veteran, though about 200,000 were enlisted in the Union Army and Navy. The reunion was a strictly Jim Crow affair. As the president looked upon his audience, perhaps he was thinking about the excellence of President Lincoln's executive leadership (which he greatly admired) and the awesomeness of the twentieth century nation that Lincoln's presidency helped make possible.

Wilson must have appreciated, as well, that on those very grounds, in that very spot, Lincoln had delivered the greatest speech of his life (which appears below). What a moment! Finally, Wilson the Progressive reformer, was likely also thinking about his own preparation for facing the challenges that lay ahead. One of those challenges was a war that would burst upon the world a year later. It would become for Wilson the crusade of his life, not unlike Lincoln's: The opportunity to "make the world safe for democracy," but, alas, at that time, for whites only. African–Americans would also participate in that war in the hope (again) that one day democracy would spread in their own land too, though not until in our own time would those hopes come close to realization.

Further Reading:

Ira Berlin et. al, *Slaves No More: Three Essays on Emancipation and the Civil War* (New York, 1992)

Douglas A. Blackmon, *Slavery By Another Name: The Re–Enslavement of Black Americans From the Civil War to World War II* (New York, 2008)

David W. Blight, *Race and Reunion: The Civil War in American Memory* (Cambridge, MA, 2001)

William J. Cooper, *Jefferson Davis: American* (New York, 2001)

Thomas Cripps, *Slow Fade to Black: The Negro in American Film, 1900–1942* (New York, 1977)

Philip Dray, *Capitol Men: The Epic Story of Reconstruction Through the Lives of the First Black Congressmen* (New York, 2008)

W.E.B. DuBois, *The Souls of Black Folk* (1903, Boston reprint, 1997)

Drew Gilpin Faust, *This Republic of Suffering: Death and the American Civil War* (New York, 2009)

Charles Bracelen Floyd, *Grant and Sherman: The Friendship That Won the Civil War* (New York, 2005)

Eric Foner, *Reconstruction: America's Unfinished Revolution, 1863–1877* (New York, 1988)

Shelby Foote, *The Civil War: A Narrative* (3 vol., New York, 1958)

Gaines M. Foster, *The Ghosts of the Confederacy: Defeat, the Lost Cause, and the Emergence of the New South* (New York, 1987)

Gary W. Gallagher, *Causes Won, Lost, and Forgotten: How Hollywood and Popular Art Shape What We Know About the Civil War* (Chapel Hill, 2008)

Paul M. Gaston, *The New South Creed: A Study in Southern Mythmaking* (New York, 1970)

Doris Kearns Goodwin, *Team of Rivals: The Political Genius of Abraham Lincoln* (New York, 2006)

Allen C. Guelzo, *Lincoln's Emancipation Proclamation: The End of Slavery in America* (New York, 2006)

J. Morgan Kousser, *The Shaping of Southern Politics: Suffrage Restriction and the Establishment of the One–Party South, 1880–1910* (New Haven, 1974)

Charles Lane, *The Day Freedom Died: The Colfax Massacre, the Supreme Court, and the Betrayal of Reconstruction* (New York, 2008)

Nicholas Lemann, *Redemption: The Last Battle of the Civil War* (New York, 2007)

Gerald F. Linderman, *Embattled Courage: The Experience of Combat in the American Civil War* (New York, 1987)

William S. McFeely, *Grant: A Biography* (New York, 1981)

James M. McPherson, *This Mighty Scourage: Perspectives on the Civil War* (New York, 2007)

Elizabeth Brown Pryor, *Reading the Man: A Portrait of Robert E. Lee Through His Private Letters* (New York, 1908)

Emory M. Thomas, *Robert E. Lee: A Biography* (New York, 1997)

Emory M. Thomas, *The Confederacy as a Revolutionary Experience* (Columbia, SC, 1991)

Allen W. Trelease, *White Terror: The Ku Klux Klan Conspiracy and Southern Reconstruction* (New York, 1971)

Robert Penn Warren, *The Legacy of the Civil War: Meditations on the Centennial* (New York, 1961)

Edmund Wilson, *Patriotic Gore: Studies in the Literature of the American Civil War* (1962, reprint, Boston, 1984)

Thomas B. Wilson, *The Black Codes of the South* (University, AL, 1965)

C. Vann Woodward, *Reunion and Reaction: The Compromise of 1877 and the End of Reconstruction* (1951, reprint NY, 1956)

EMANCIPATION PROCLAMATION, JANUARY 1, 1863

[The Emancipation Proclamation, when Lincoln first unveiled it in draft in August 1862, was surprising to supporters and opponents alike. It explicitly tied the war's aims to the abolition of slavery. Lincoln's action was an exercise of presidential war powers, as he understood that in order to free slaves during peacetime a Constitutional Amendment would be necessary. Is there a powerful constitutional argument to be made that no Amendment is needed during wartime? Does Lincoln's action (proceeding without Constitutional Amendment) remind you of any actions you have seen Presidents take in the course of any other wars? How important was the elimination of slavery to Lincoln and the North at this stage of the war? The answer to this is not simple.

Arguably, the Proclamation was a political document to keep abolitionists (who were an important constituency for Lincoln's Republicans) mollified, and it was simultaneously a brilliant piece of military strategy, since it recognized that slaves were a resource that aided the South's war effort. Even so, many historians have suggested that the Proclamation was primarily symbolic, since it freed none of the slaves in the Border States that still remained in the Union, nor did it free any of the slaves in those pro-Union sections of the seceding states. It also did not, of course, actually free slaves in Confederate territory beyond Federal control—which was almost the entirety of the South. In effect, then, it applied only to slave "contraband" who escaped to Union lines. For all of that, the Proclamation remains a pivotal document, because it announced a seismic shift for Lincoln, who, in his 1861 Inaugural Address, as you have seen, had clearly accepted slavery as constitutionally protected in those states where it already existed.

In attaching abolition to the war effort, Lincoln (advertently or inadvertently) opened the deeply problematic question of what the peace would look like. It is also noteworthy that the Proclamation provides for freed slaves to serve in the U.S. armed forces, and also to undertake gainful employment. The policy debate around Reconstruction (1865–1876), which Lincoln foreshadowed in the Proclamation, lasted much longer than did the war itself and to black and white Southerners and Northerners, was often perceived as war by other means. The Proclamation is surely one of the most significant things for which President Lincoln is remembered. Would you have advised him to issue it? Is it appropriate to ignore the Constitution during wartime? (You will notice, for example, that Lincoln clearly indicates that the federal government will no longer be bound by the Constitution's fugitive slave clause with regard to slaves who escape from rebellious Southern states.) Is there something particularly suspect about the Constitution's provisions regarding slavery that might make them less binding than others? Is Commonwealth v. Aves relevant in answering this question?]

By the President of the United States of
America
A Proclamation.

* * *

That on the first day of January, in the year of our Lord one thousand eight hundred and sixty-three, all persons held as slaves within any State or designated part of a State, the people whereof shall then be in rebellion against the United States, shall be then, thenceforward, and forever free; and the Executive Government of the United States, including the military and naval authority thereof, will recognize and maintain the freedom of such persons, and will do no act or acts to repress such persons, or any of them, in any efforts they may make for their actual freedom.

That the Executive will, on the first day of January aforesaid, by proclamation, designate the States and parts of States, if any, in which the people thereof, respectively, shall then be in rebellion against the United States; and the fact that any State, or the people thereof, shall on that day be, in good faith, represented in the Congress of the United States by members chosen thereto at elections wherein a majority of the qualified voters of such State shall have participated, shall, in the absence of strong countervailing testimony, be deemed conclusive evidence that such State, and the people thereof, are not then in rebellion against the United States.

Now, therefore I, Abraham Lincoln, President of the United States, by virtue of the power in me vested as Commander-in-Chief of the Army and Navy of the United States in time of actual armed rebellion against the authority and government of the United States, and as a fit and necessary war measure for suppressing said rebellion, do, on this first day of January, in the year of our Lord one thousand eight hundred and sixty-three, and in accordance with my purpose so to do publicly proclaimed for the full period of one hundred days, from the day first above mentioned, order and designate as the States and parts of States wherein the people thereof respectively, are this day in rebellion against the United States, the following, to wit:

Arkansas, Texas, Louisiana, (except the Parishes of St. Bernard, Plaquemines, Jefferson, St. John, St. Charles, St. James Ascension, Assumption, Terrebonne, Lafourche, St. Mary, St. Martin, and Orleans, including the City of New Orleans) Mississippi, Alabama, Florida, Georgia, South Carolina, North Carolina, and Virginia, (except the forty-eight counties designated as West Virginia, and also the counties of Berkley, Accomac, Northampton, Elizabeth City, York, Princess Ann, and Norfolk, including the cities of Norfolk and Portsmouth[)], and which excepted parts, are for the present, left precisely as if this proclamation were not issued.

And by virtue of the power, and for the purpose aforesaid, I do order and declare that all persons held as slaves within said designated States, and parts of States, are, and henceforward shall be free; and that the Executive government of the United States, including the military and naval authorities thereof, will recognize and maintain the freedom of said persons.

And I hereby enjoin upon the people so declared to be free to abstain from all violence, unless in necessary self-defence; and I recommend to them that, in all cases when allowed, they labor faithfully for reasonable wages.

And I further declare and make known, that such persons of suitable condition, will be received into the armed service of the United States to garrison forts, positions, stations, and other places, and to man vessels of all sorts in said service.

And upon this act, sincerely believed to be an act of justice, warranted by the Constitution, upon military necessity, I invoke the considerate judgment of mankind, and the gracious favor of Almighty God.

* * *

LINCOLN'S GETTYSBURG ADDRESS (1863)

[This speech is one of the most famous in all American history. It was given at the dedication of the Soldiers' National Cemetery at Gettysburg on November 19, 1863, it lasted about two minutes, and it was composed of 10 sentences and 272 words. Lincoln suggested that the world would forget what was said on that occasion, although it would remember the sacrifices made by those interred there. Lincoln, was, of course, wrong. (Edward Everett, who also spoke, and whose speech lasted two hours and was billed as the event's main "Oration," spoke immediately before Lincoln.) Significantly, in his "dedicatory remarks" (as it was billed in the program) Lincoln made no distinction between Union and Confederate soldiers who died in the Battle of Gettysburg, approximately 10,000 in all. As you will see, Lincoln drew on the Declaration of Independence to announce that the war's aims were part of a "new birth of freedom," for Lincoln nothing less than a final fulfillment of the American Revolution itself. In fastening liberty to the cause of the Union, Lincoln thus fuses the Declaration with the Constitution to produce a "nation conceived in liberty." Was this an appropriate use of the Declaration?

Was this a new synthesis in American history—or at the least, a new emphasis? Surely the radical quality of Lincoln's words is evident when we think of Madison's justification of a national republic: One that allows contesting interests to freely compete in the political arena, thereby keeping any single selfish interest from dominating. In contrast, for Lincoln the national republic has a single aim—Liberty is best preserved by the existence of a centralized national power through which self-government operates and thereby affirms itself. In this formulation, it might be suggested that autonomous state entities become a disintegrative element. Would Thomas Jefferson, the author of the Declaration of Independence, have agreed?

We might say, considering Lincoln's words, with only a bit of tongue in cheek, that American history divides itself into two phases: one in which government is the problem (before 1861), and the other in which government is the solution (after 1865). The ultimate fulfillment of this modernist vision is the New Deal and the Welfare State that it enthroned. Can one trace a direct line from Abraham Lincoln to Barack Obama?

Lincoln was not the only "big government" man to turn to Jefferson for justification. By adopting Thomas Jefferson as his personal hero, FDR also claimed that Big Government was the friend of personal liberty. (The Lincoln and Jefferson memorials in Washington, D.C. are within a mile of each other, and symbolize this unity. Interestingly, the Lincoln memorial was dedicated in the Republican Administration of President Warren G. Harding, and the Jefferson Memorial by the Democrat FDR.) Can it be said that outside of academic economics and some pockets of conservative free market ideology, the fringe libertarian movement is all that remains of the pre-Civil War affection for liberty? With the exception of the appeal of religious fundamentalism in some societies, Lincoln's "nation conceived in liberty" appears to be the model replicated nearly everywhere, and seems to know no effective rival in the world. Or would you agree?]

Four score and seven years ago our fathers brought forth on this continent a new nation, conceived in Liberty, and dedicated to the proposition that all men are created equal.

Now we are engaged in a great civil war, testing whether that nation, or any nation, so conceived and so dedicated, can long endure. We are met on a great battle-field of that war. We have come to dedicate a portion of that field, as a final resting place for those who here gave their lives that that nation might live. It is altogether fitting and proper that we should do this.

But, in a larger sense, we can not dedicate—we can not consecrate—we can not hallow—this ground. The brave men, living and dead, who struggled here, have consecrated it, far above our poor power to add or detract. The world will little note, nor long remember what we say here, but it can never forget what they did here. It is for us the living, rather, to be dedicated here to the unfinished work which they who fought here have thus far so nobly advanced. It is rather for us to be here dedicated to the great task remaining before us—that from these honored dead we take increased devotion to that cause for which they gave the last full measure of devotion—that we here highly resolve that these dead shall not have died in vain—that this nation, under God, shall have a new birth of freedom—and that government of the people, by the people, for the people, shall not perish from the earth.

LINCOLN'S SECOND INAUGURAL ADDRESS (1865)

Fellow–Countrymen:

At this second appearing to take the oath of the Presidential office there is less occasion for an extended address than there was at the first. Then a statement somewhat in detail of a course to be pursued seemed fitting and proper. Now, at the expiration of four years, during which public declarations have been constantly called forth on every point and phase of the great contest which still absorbs the attention and engrosses the energies of the nation, little that is new could be presented. The progress of our arms, upon which all else chiefly depends, is as well known to the public as to myself, and it is, I trust, reasonably satisfactory and encouraging to all. With high hope for the future, no prediction in regard to it is ventured.

On the occasion corresponding to this four years ago all thoughts were anxiously directed to an impending civil war. All dreaded it, all sought to avert it. While the inaugural address was being delivered from this place, devoted altogether to saving the Union without war, urgent agents were in the city seeking to destroy it without war—seeking to dissolve the Union and divide effects by negotiation. Both parties deprecated war, but one of them would make war rather than let the nation survive, and the other would accept war rather than let it perish, and the war came.

One-eighth of the whole population were colored slaves, not distributed generally over the Union, but localized in the southern part of it. These slaves constituted a peculiar and powerful interest. All knew that this interest was somehow the cause of the war. To strengthen, perpetuate, and extend this interest was the object for which the insurgents would rend the Union even by war, while the Government claimed no right to do more than to restrict the territorial enlargement of it. Neither party expected for the war the magnitude or the duration which it has already attained. Neither anticipated that the cause of the conflict might cease with or even before the conflict itself should cease. Each looked for an easier triumph, and a result less fundamental and astounding. Both read the same Bible and pray to the same God, and each invokes His aid against the other. It may seem strange that any men should dare to ask a just God's assistance in wringing their bread from the sweat of other men's faces, but let us judge not, that we be not judged. The prayers of both could not be answered. That of neither has been answered fully. The Almighty has His own purposes. "Woe unto the world because of offenses; for it must needs be that offenses come, but woe to that man by whom the offense cometh." If we shall suppose that American slavery is one of those offenses which, in the providence of God, must needs come, but which, having continued through His appointed time, He now wills to remove, and that He gives to both North and South this terrible war as the woe due to those by whom the offense came, shall we discern therein any departure from those divine attributes which the believers in a living God always ascribe to Him? Fondly do we hope, fervently do we pray, that this mighty scourge of war may speedily pass away. Yet, if God wills that it continue until all the wealth piled by the bondsman's two hundred and fifty years of unrequited toil shall be sunk, and until every drop of blood drawn with the lash shall be paid by another drawn with the sword, as was said three thousand years ago, so still it must be said "the judgments of the Lord are true and righteous altogether."

With malice toward none, with charity for all, with firmness in the right as God gives us to see the right, let us strive on to finish the work we are in, to bind up the nation's wounds, to care for him who shall have borne the battle and for his widow and his orphan, to do all which may achieve and cherish a just and lasting peace among ourselves and with all nations.

NOTES AND QUESTIONS

1. This is another famous oration from Lincoln, but note the rather extraordinarily unworldly and existential quality of the piece. Lincoln, who had only a short time before being felled by an assassin (who exclaimed "*Sic Semper Tyranus*"—"Thus always to tyrants," as he shot the President), was in the midst of an internecine war of North against South. Who or what does he say is to blame for that war? Do you agree?

2. Note the strong religious element in the speech, and, in particular, that the war is explained, at least in part, by God's judgment on the institution of slavery. Lincoln justifies the war as a struggle undertaken to free the slaves, but when the war began, of course, the North argued, at least initially, that it was fighting the South simply to restore the Union, to defend the principle that no state had a right to secede. The South, indeed, to a greater extent than the North, maintained that if popular sovereignty meant anything, it meant that no state could be compelled to be a member of a polity sworn to obliterate its own institutions, and that the theory of the Declaration of Independence, if not the Constitution itself, was the primacy of the states, and not the central government. For generations many Southerners referred to the Civil War as the War of Northern Aggression, although many Northerners referred to it as the "Rebellion." Who got it right? Does Lincoln acknowledge this dispute? He certainly observes that both sides prayed to the same God, but does this really help explain the zeal on both sides?

3. Among the most famous of the words of the Second Inaugural are those of the last paragraph, and, in particular, its beginning with Lincoln's claim that he speaks and proceeds "With malice toward none, and with charity for all . . . " Why do you suppose the South, which mightily resisted the efforts that were to come at Reconstruction, found this so difficult to accept or believe? Does Lincoln forgive the South? He appears to suggest that the war's titanic death and devastation (more than 600,000 Americans lost their lives) was the necessary price for purging the evil of slavery. Does he view this in sadness or in anger? Reconstruction led to decades of hostility between North and South, remnants of which still exist in our own time. Had Lincoln lived, would the lasting resentment of that era have been less?

THE CIVIL RIGHTS ACT OF 1866

[The Civil Rights Act of 1866 was the response of a Congress controlled by what have usually been described as "Radical" Republicans committed to the "Reconstruction" of the former slave-holding South, and, in particular, the securing of Civil Rights for the former slaves. The Radicals believed that President Andrew Johnson (who, as Vice President, succeeded to the Presidency following Lincoln's assassination) was not sufficiently zealous in seeking to transform the South, following its military defeat. President Johnson, who thought the 1866 bill too strong and probably unconstitutional, vetoed it, but Congress overrode his veto (and, eventually, sought unsuccessfully to remove Johnson—he survived by just one vote in the Senate). The 1866 Act is probably the clearest indication that we have of the Radicals' goals for Reconstruction. Do you share them? Before you peruse the 1866 Act, quickly skim the Thirteenth, Fourteenth, and Fifteenth Amendments to the Constitution, known collectively as the "Reconstruction" Amendments. There is a body of scholarly opinion that suggests, in particular, that the Fourteenth Amendment is best understood as a means of providing a Constitutional foundation for the 1866 Act. Would you have voted for the 1866 Act? Would you have vetoed it, had you been President? Have you seen anything earlier in the course that influences your opinion about the wisdom of this Act?]

An Act to protect all Persons in the United States in their Civil Rights, and furnish the Means of their Vindication.

Sec. 1. Be it enacted by the Senate and House of Representatives of the United States of America in Congress assembled, That all persons born in the United States and not subject to any foreign power, excluding Indians not taxed, are hereby declared to be citizens of the United States; and such citizens, of every race and color, without regard to any previous condition of slavery or involuntary servitude, except as a punishment for crime whereof the party shall have been duly convicted, shall have the same right, in every State and Territory in the United States, to make and enforce contracts, to sue, be parties, and give evidence, to inherit, purchase, lease, sell, hold, and convey real and personal property, and to full and equal benefit of all laws and proceedings for the security of person and property, as is enjoyed by white citizens, and shall be subject to like punishment, pains, and penalties, and to none other, any law, statute, ordinance, regulation, or custom, to the contrary notwithstanding.

Sec. 2. And be it further enacted, That any person who, under color of any law, statute, ordinance, regulation, or custom, shall subject, or cause to be subjected, any inhabitant of any State or Territory to the deprivation of any right secured or protected by this act, or to different punishment, pains, or penalties on account of such person having at any time been held in a condition of slavery or involuntary servitude, except as a punishment for crime whereof the party shall have been duly convicted, or by reason of his color or race, than is prescribed for the punishment of white persons, shall be deemed guilty of a misdemeanor, and, on conviction, shall be punished by fine not exceeding one thousand dollars, or imprisonment not exceeding one year, or both, in the discretion of the court.

Sec. 3. And be it further enacted, That the district courts of the United States, within their respective districts, shall have, exclusively of the courts of the several States, cognizance of all crimes and offences committed against the provisions of this act, and also, concurrently with the circuit courts of the United States, of all causes, civil and criminal, affecting persons who are denied or cannot enforce in the courts or judicial tribunals of the State or locality where they may be any of the rights secured to them by the first section of this act; and if any suit or prosecution, civil or criminal, has been or shall be commenced in any State court, against any such person, for any cause whatsoever, or against any officer, civil or military, or other person, for any arrest or imprisonment, trespasses, or wrongs done or committed by virtue or under color of authority derived from this act or the act establishing a Bureau for the relief of Freedmen and Refugees, and all acts amendatory thereof, or for refusing to do any act upon the ground that it would be inconsistent with this act, such defendant shall have the right to remove such cause for trial to the proper [federal] district or circuit court . . . The jurisdiction in civil and criminal matters hereby conferred on the district and circuit courts of the United States shall be exercised and enforced in conformity with the laws of the United States, so far as such laws are suitable to carry the same into effect; but in all cases where such laws are not adapted to the object, or are deficient in the provisions necessary to furnish suitable remedies and punish offences against law, the common law, as modified and changed by the constitution and statutes of the State wherein the court having jurisdiction of the cause, civil or criminal, is held, so far as the same is not inconsistent with the Constitution and laws of the United States, shall be extended to and govern said courts in the trial and disposition of such cause, and, if of a criminal nature, in the infliction of punishment on the party found guilty.

Sec. 4. And be it further enacted, That the district attorneys, marshals, and deputy marshals of the United States, the commissioners appointed by the circuit and territorial courts of the United States, with powers of arresting, imprisoning, or bailing offenders against the laws of the United States, the officers and agents of the Freedmen's Bureau, and every other officer who may be specially empowered by the President of the United States, shall be, and they are hereby, specially authorized and required, at the expense of the United States, to institute proceedings against all and every person who shall violate the provisions of this act, and cause him or them to be arrested and imprisoned, or bailed, as the case may be, for trial before such court of the United States or territorial court as by this act has cognizance of the offence. And with a view to affording reasonable protection to all persons in their constitutional rights of equality before the law, without distinction of race or color, or previous condition of slavery or involuntary servitude, except as a punishment for crime, whereof the party shall have been duly convicted, and to the prompt discharge of the duties of this act, it shall be the duty of the circuit courts of the United States and the superior courts of the Territories of the United States, from time to time, to increase the number of commissioners, so as to afford a speedy and convenient means for the arrest and examination of persons charged with a violation of this act; and such commissioners are hereby authorized and required to exercise and discharge all the powers and duties conferred on them by this act, and the same duties with regard to offences created by this act, as they are authorized by law to exercise with regard to other offences against the laws of the United States.

Sec. 5. And be it further enacted, That it shall be the duty of all marshals and deputy marshals to obey and execute all warrants and precepts issued under the provisions of this act, when to them directed; and should any marshal or deputy marshal refuse to receive such warrant or other process when tendered, or to use all proper means diligently to execute the same, he shall, on conviction thereof, be fined in the sum of one thousand dollars, to the use of the person upon whom the accused is alleged to have committed the offense. And the better to enable the said commissioners to execute their duties faithfully and efficiently, in conformity with the Constitution of the United States and the requirements of this act, they are hereby authorized and empowered, within their counties respectively, to appoint, in writing, under their hands, any one or more suitable persons, from time to time, to execute all such warrants and other process as may be issued by them in the lawful performance of their respective duties; and the persons so appointed to execute any warrant or process as aforesaid shall have authority to summon and call to their aid the bystanders or posse comitatus of the proper county, or such portion of the land or naval forces of the United States, or of the militia, as may be necessary to the performance of the duty with which they are charged, and to insure a faithful observance of the clause of the Constitution which prohibits slavery [The Thirteenth Amendment], in conformity with the provisions of this act; and said warrants shall run and be executed by said officers anywhere in the State or Territory within which they are issued.

Sec. 6. And be it further enacted, That any person who shall knowingly and willfully obstruct, hinder, or prevent any officer, or other person charged with the execution of any warrant or process issued under the provisions of this act, or any person or persons lawfully assisting him or them, from arresting any person for whose apprehension such warrant or process may have been issued, or shall rescue or attempt to rescue such person from the custody of the officer, other person or persons, or those lawfully assisting as aforesaid, when so arrested pursuant to the authority herein given and declared, or shall aid, abet, or assist any person so arrested as aforesaid, directly or indirectly, to escape from the custody of the officer or other person legally authorized as aforesaid, or shall harbor or conceal any person for whose arrest a warrant or process shall have been issued as aforesaid, so as to prevent his discovery and arrest after notice or knowledge of the fact that a warrant has been issued for the apprehension of such person, shall, for either of said offences, be subject to a fine not exceeding one thousand dollars, and imprisonment not exceeding six months, by indictment and conviction before the district court of the United States for the district in which said offense may have been committed, or before the proper court of criminal jurisdiction, if committed within any one of the organized Territories of the United States.

Sec. 7. And be it further enacted, That the district attorneys, the marshals, their deputies, and the clerks of the said district and territorial courts shall be paid for their services the like fees as may be allowed to them for similar services in other cases; and in all cases where the proceedings are before a commissioner, he shall be entitled to a fee of ten dollars in full for his services in each case, inclusive of all services incident to such arrest and examination. The person or persons authorized to execute the process to be issued by such commissioners for the arrest of offenders against the provisions of this act shall be entitled to a fee of five dollars for each person he or they may arrest and take before any such commissioner as aforesaid, with such other fees as may be deemed reasonable by such commissioner for such other additional services as may be necessarily performed by him or them, such as attending at the examination, keeping the prisoner in custody, and providing him with food and lodging during his detention, and until the final determination of such commissioner, and in general for performing such other duties as may be required in the premises; such fees to be made up in conformity with the fees usually charged by the officers of the courts of justice within the proper district or county, as near as may be practicable, and paid out of the Treasury of the United States on the certificate of the judge of the district within which the arrest is made, and to be recoverable from the defendant as part of the judgment in case of conviction.

Sec. 8. And be it further enacted, that whenever the President of the United States shall have reason to believe that offences have been or are likely to be committed against the provisions of this act within any judicial district, it shall be lawful for him, in his discretion, to direct the judge, marshal, and district attorney of such district to attend at such place within the district, and for such time as he may designate, for the purpose of the more speedy arrest and trial of persons charged with a violation of this act; and it shall be the duty of every judge or other officer, when any such requisition shall be received by him, to attend at the place and for the time therein designated.

Sec. 9. And be it further enacted, that it shall be lawful for the President of the United States, or such person as he may empower for that purpose, to employ such part of the land or naval forces of the United States, or of the militia, as shall be necessary to prevent the violation and enforce the due execution of this act.

Sec. 10. And be it further enacted, That upon all questions of law arising in any cause under the provisions of this act a final appeal may be taken to the Supreme Court of the United States.

* * *

THE CIVIL RIGHTS ACT OF 1875

[The 1875 Act was designed to give further effect to the 14th Amendment, and was proposed by Sen. Charles Sumner of Massachusetts and Rep. Benjamin Butler of Pennsylvania, both of whom were committed Republicans who believed that the war's purpose was the conferring not only of political and civil rights to the ex-slaves, but also the securing of social equality with whites. Like the 1866 Act, the 1875 legislation was the work, then, of the Radical Republican advocates of Reconstruction. The act appears to have been sporadically enforced, if enforced at all. Would you have voted for the passage of the 1875 Act?]

Whereas it is essential to just government[,] we recognize the equality of all men before the law, and hold that it is the duty of government in its dealings with the people to mete out equal and exact justice to all, of whatever nativity, race, color, or persuasion, religious or political; and it being the appropriate object of legislation to enact great fundamental principles into law: Therefore,

Sec. 1. Be it enacted by the Senate and House of Representatives of the United States of America in Congress assembled, That all persons within the jurisdiction of the United States shall be entitled to the full and equal enjoyment of the accommodations, advantages, facilities, and privileges of inns, public conveyances on land or water, theaters, and other places of public amusement; subject only to the conditions and limitations established by law, and applicable alike to citizens of every race and color, regardless of any previous condition of servitude.

Sec. 2. That any person who shall violate the foregoing section by denying to any citizen, except for reasons by law applicable to citizens of every race and color, and regardless of any previous condition of servitude, the full enjoyment of any of the accommodations, advantages, facilities, or privileges in said section enumerated, or by aiding or inciting such denial, shall, for every offence, forfeit and pay the sum of five hundred dollars to the person aggrieved thereby, to be recovered in an action of debt, with full costs; and shall also, for every such offense, be deemed guilty of a misdemeanor, and, upon conviction thereof, shall be fined not less than five hundred nor more than one thousand dollars, or shall be imprisoned not less than thirty days nor more than one year: Provided, that all persons may elect to sue for the State under their rights at common law and by State statutes; and having so elected to proceed in the one mode or the other, their right to proceed in the other jurisdiction shall be barred. But this proviso shall not apply to criminal proceedings, either under this act or the criminal law of any State: And provided further, That a judgment for the penalty in favor of the party aggrieved, or a judgment upon an indictment, shall be a bar to either prosecution respectively.

Sec. 3. That the district and circuit courts of the United States shall have, exclusively of the courts of the several States, cognizance of all crimes and offenses against, and violations of, the provisions of this act; and actions for the penalty given by the preceding section may be prosecuted in the territorial, district, or circuit courts of the United States wherever the defendant may be found, without regard to the other party; and the district attorneys, marshals, and deputy marshals of the United States, and commissioners appointed by the circuit and territorial courts of the United States, with powers of arresting and imprisoning or bailing offenders against the laws of the United States, are hereby specially authorized and required to institute proceedings against every person who shall violate the provisions of this act, and cause him to be arrested and imprisoned or bailed, as the case may be, for trial before such court of the United States, or territorial court, as by law has cognizance of the offense, except in respect of the right of action accruing to the person aggrieved; and such district attorneys shall cause such proceedings to be prosecuted to their termination as in other cases: Provided, That nothing contained in this section shall be construed to deny or defeat any right of civil action accruing to any person, whether by reason of this act or otherwise; and any district attorney who shall willfully fail to institute and prosecute the proceedings herein required, shall, for every such offense, forfeit and pay the sum of five hundred dollars to the person aggrieved thereby, to be recovered by an action of debt, with full costs, and shall, on conviction thereof, be deemed guilty of a misdemeanor, and be fined not less than one thousand nor more than five thousand dollars: And provided further, That a judgment for the penalty in favor of the party aggrieved against any such district attorney, or a judgment upon an indictment against any such district attorney, shall be a bar to either prosecution respectively.

Sec. 4. That no citizen possessing all other qualifications which are or may be prescribed by law shall be disqualified for service as grand or petit juror in any court of the United States, or of any State, on account of race, color, or previous condition of servitude; and any officer or other person charged with any duty in the selection or summoning of jurors who shall exclude or fail to summon any citizen for the cause aforesaid shall, on conviction thereof, be deemed guilty of a misdemeanor, and be fined not more than five thousand dollars.

Sec. 5. That all cases arising under the provisions of this act in the courts of the United States shall be reviewable by the Supreme Court of the United States, without regard to the sum in controversy, under the same provisions and regulations as are now provided by law for the review of other causes in said court.

NOTES AND QUESTIONS

1. The "Freedman's Bureau" was an agency of the federal government set up by Congress in order to facilitate the noble goal of the transformation of the former slaves into productive citizens of the United States. This agency, formally known as "the Bureau of Refugees, Freedmen, and Abandoned Lands," was established on March 3, 1865, and was originally only to last for one year. The Bureau was actually a part of the United States Department of War, and was directed by Union Army General Oliver O. Howard. Its assignment was to provide food and medical care for the freedmen, to help them settle on property abandoned in the South during and after the war, and, in particular, to establish schools. The Bureau did have some success in its educational mission. Over 1000 schools were set up, and, indeed, many historically-black colleges which still exist today were founded (one of the most prominent, Howard University, was named after the Bureau's commissioner, General Howard). The Bureau's efforts at resettlement foundered, however, when President Andrew Johnson ordered the 850,000 acres of land which had been allotted to the freedmen returned to their original white owners. The Freedman's Bureau's efforts to find gainful employment for its charges eventually resulted in most of the freedmen returning to work on Southern plantations, and while these workers were no longer the chattels of the plantation's owners, the tenancy and sharecropping arrangements which resulted left many freedman in conditions not much better than those before the war. There never were funds provided to the Bureau adequate to do the tasks assigned to it, and in 1869, four years after the bureau was founded, Congress ended its other efforts, allowing it only to continue to seek to educate the freedmen. Finally, in July, 1872, the bureau's educational efforts were terminated by Congressional fiat. Would you have expected these noble efforts to end so quickly and so inconclusively? Why did they?

2. In the *Slaughter-House Cases*, 83 U.S. 36 (1873), the United States Supreme Court was asked to determine the reach of the recently-passed Fourteenth Amendment. At issue was an 1869 Louisiana statute law that permitted the city of New Orleans to set up a corporation which would consolidate slaughter-house operations in the city. Several Louisiana butchers, arguing that the new corporation was a blatant attempt to monopolize the slaughter-house industry in favor of politically-powerful operators, argued that the "due process, equal protection, and privileges and immunities" clauses of the Fourteenth Amendment, ratified in 1868, prevented this legislative favoritism of some butchers over others. In a five to four decision written by Justice Samuel Freeman Miller, the Court narrowly interpreted the Fourteenth Amendment to rule both that the privileges and immunities clause protected only United States Citizenship and not state citizenship, and that the Amendment did not alter the general police power possessed by the state. Further, the court noted that the Amendment was primarily intended to protect former slaves, and could not be stretched to be applicable to the protection of white Louisiana butchers. The Slaughter–House cases have generally been taken to stand for the proposition that individual citizens in

the separate states are not protected under the Thirteenth and Fourteenth amendments from the actions of their own state governments. Counsel for the butchers, former Supreme Court Justice John A. Campbell, had argued that the Thirteenth and Fourteenth Amendments constitutionalized common law property rights (in particular the right to practice a legitimate trade). While the majority of the court rejected this view, the powerful dissenting opinion of Justice Stephen Field accepted Campbell's argument. Field's view, that the "due process" clause of the Fourteenth Amendment should be understood as barring certain substantive actions of the state governments interfering with liberty of contract, eventually became the majority view of the Court in cases such as Allgeyer v. Louisiana, 165 U.S. 578 (1897) and Lochner v. New York, 198 U.S. 45 (1905). Was that development consistent with the aims of the radical Republican advocates of the Reconstruction era Constitutional Amendments and legislation? In connection with this query, see the brilliant and provocative David E. Bernstein, Rehabilitating Lochner: Defending Individual Rights against Progressive Reform (2011), which argues that *Lochner* and its progeny led the way to a vigorous defense of civil rights and civil liberties by the Court. For further reading on the *Slaughter-House Cases*, see the monograph by Ronald M. Labbe and Jonathan Lurie, The Slaughterhouse Cases: Regulation, Reconstruction, and the Fourteenth Amendment (Abridged edition, 2005).

3. The *Civil Rights Cases*, 109 U.S. 3 (1883) were several consolidated cases which challenged the Constitutionality of the 1875 Civil Rights Act, above. In an 8 to 1 decision, the Court held that the enforcement provisions of the Fourteenth Amendment forbade discrimination by state and local governments, but could *not* be construed to regulate the behavior of private citizens. (Would this be your interpretation of the text of the Fourteenth Amendment?) This meant that the 1875 Civil Rights Act was unconstitutional. Justice John Marshall Harlan dissented, because he believed that Congress's goal in the 1875 legislation was an appropriate and worthy one. As he put it, "What the nation, through Congress, has sought to accomplish in reference to [the Black] race is, what had already been done in every state in the Union for the white race, to secure and protect rights belonging to them as freemen and citizens; nothing more." Harlan understood and sympathized with the Radicals' Reconstruction goals. Still, eight of his brethren did not, and The Civil Rights cases signaled that the national doors were beginning to close on the Civil War era, and that the white North's and white South's desire for reunion would proceed without permitting the incredibly and sadly divisive matter of racial equality to come between them. In the words of most American historians "Reunion" rather than "Reconstruction" becomes the new goal—and the freedmen of the South, as it were, are left, at a disadvantage, to fend for themselves. Many of the states of the South responded to this 1883 decision by implementing discriminatory laws and by amending their state constitutions to mandate racial segregation at every level in society. As you will see, *Plessy v. Ferguson* soon addressed the constitutionality of that state legislation—and with that decision, the door finally slams shut on the Radical Reconstruction vision of a biracial democracy. As the essay that

opens this section makes clear, discrimination based on race was not merely a Southern phenomenon.

4. In *Plessy v. Ferguson*, 163 U.S. 537 (1896), the Court heard a challenge to a Louisiana statute passed in 1890, which required railroads to provide "equal but separate accommodations for the white and colored races," and barred passengers from occupying seats in cars that were not assigned to their particular race. The Louisiana statute was a prime example of the so-called "Jim Crow" laws which were passed by many Southern legislatures in order to reestablish white hegemony following Reconstruction. ["Jim Crow" had been a staple character in minstrel shows in the early nineteenth century, where whites in blackface presented stereotypical characters—the term had originally been one of derision for blacks, but this earlier use was superseded by the connotation of the new repressive legislation of the late Nineteenth Century.] The 1890 Louisiana statute imposed additional costs on railroads, and some were sympathetic to the plaintiff's argument, which was that the "equal but separate" legislative directive violated the Thirteenth and Fourteenth Amendments (can you understand what that argument would have been?). In a 7 to 1 decision (Justice Brewer did not participate) the United States Supreme Court held, in an opinion by Justice Henry Billings Brown, that the statute did not violate the Thirteenth Amendment, since it did not seek to reintroduce slavery, and that it was improper to construe the Amendment to bar all distinctions based on race. Justice Brown held that the Fourteenth Amendment was not violated because there was no violation of equal protection since equal accommodation was provided, and moreover, laws requiring separation of the races did not suggest that one race was inferior. In a dissent that has become a famous rallying cry, Justice Harlan stated that the Thirteenth Amendment was designed to bar all "badge[s] of servitude," not just slavery itself, and, even more important, that the "Constitution is color-blind, and neither knows nor tolerates classes among citizens." Do you find the holding in *Plessy* consistent with the aims of the Radical Republicans who passed the Reconstruction–Era civil rights acts? Did Harlan get it right? Is it fair to say that with *Plessy v. Ferguson* the reunion of North and South finally became complete—The South was permitted to deal with race without further Constitutional intrusion, and, for a while at least, in the popular memory, the cause of the Civil War was affirmed as a disagreement about state sovereignty, and not slavery. This was not, of course, true in the case of all Americans, particularly African Americans, who continued to see a particular conception of civil and human rights as integral to the North's waging of war and, indeed, as fundamental to the ongoing "waging the peace," which continues into our own time.

5. In *Berea College v. Kentucky*, 211 U.S. 45 (1908), the Supreme Court made clear how far it was prepared to go in permitting states to enforce racial segregation. Berea College had been founded in 1855 as a rare institution devoted to the teaching of blacks and whites without discrimination. In 1904, in a statute clearly targeted at Berea College, the Kentucky legislature prohibited any person, association of persons, or corporation from teaching black and white students in the same school, or from operating separate branches

of a school for the teaching of black and white students within twenty-five miles of each other. The provision forbidding teaching of the different races within twenty-five miles of each other was struck down by the Kentucky Court of Appeals, but that court upheld the provision barring teaching of the two races in the same school. The case was appealed to the United States Supreme Court, which proceeded to affirm the Kentucky court's decision that it was permissible to order separation of the races in education. Justice Brewer, writing for the Court, suggested that because Berea college held a corporate charter from the state, and because the charter contained a clause reserving to the state the power to alter the charter [remember the problem in *Dartmouth College*] the state had the power to control the education it provided to the different races. In Brewer's words, "In granting corporate powers, the legislature may deem that the best interests of the state would be subserved by some restriction . . . 'The granting of such right or privilege [the right or privilege to be a corporation] rests entirely in the discretion of the state, and, of course, when granted, may be accompanied with such conditions as its legislature may judge most befitting to its interests and policy.' [citation omitted]." All the justices, even Justice Holmes, save one, concurred in the judgment. Justice Harlan, who, you will remember, dissented in *Plessy* as well, disagreed. "I am of opinion," he wrote, "that, in its essential parts, the statute is an arbitrary invasion of the rights of liberty and property guaranteed by the 14th Amendment against hostile state action, and is, therefore, void." "If pupils, of whatever race,—certainly, if they be citizens,—choose, with the consent of their parents, or voluntarily, to sit together in a private institution of learning while receiving instruction which is not in its nature harmful or dangerous to the public," Harlan continued, "no government, whether Federal or state, can legally forbid their coming together, or being together temporarily, for such an innocent purpose." "Have we become so inoculated with prejudice of race," he asked, "that an American government, professedly based on the principles of freedom, and charged with the protection of all citizens alike, can make distinctions between such citizens in the matter of their voluntary meeting for innocent purposes, simply because of their respective races?" The answer to Justice Harlan given by the majority was "yes," and with the *Berea College* case it might be said that the overturning of the aims of Reconstruction was complete, and, in many ways, lasted until *Brown v. Board of Education* (1954), of which more soon.

D. CRIME AND JUSTICE IN NINETEENTH CENTURY AMERICA

MICHAEL HINDUS, PRISON AND PLANTATION: CRIME, JUSTICE, AND AUTHORITY IN MASSACHUSETTS AND SOUTH CAROLINA 1767–1878*

xxiii–xxviii, 125–127, 250–255 (1980).

Massachusetts and South Carolina are natural cases to use in order to illustrate regional differences. Both were founded as colonies in the seventeenth century, and their legal histories are indigenous. By the nineteenth century, however, they symbolized totally different ways of life. * * *

The differences between the two states were very real in terms of population, ethnicity, and culture. Massachusetts was the most heavily urbanized state in the country; South Carolina was one of the most rural. But even that contrast only touches the surface. Both states had major cities that were regional centers. But in addition Massachusetts had several lesser cities of considerable importance, such as Worcester, Salem, New Bedford, and Fall River. In South Carolina, beyond Charleston, there was only Columbia, a sleepy college town that was also the state capital. * * *

Massachusetts was also one of the major magnets for foreign and domestic migrants. In 1860, 21 percent of the population was foreign-born and 35 percent was born outside the state. South Carolina, by contrast, was no magnet at all. Only 3 percent of the white population was foreign-born; 8 percent were born out of state, and the most salient fact about the state's migration trends was that native South Carolinians were leaving in huge numbers. Of course, the ethnic component of the state's population was far less significant than its racial makeup. South Carolina was 59 percent black in 1860; no other state had that large a proportion. Individual districts were up to 86 percent black. In Massachusetts, by contrast, less than 1 percent of the population was black.

The economies of the two states were very different. Historically a commercial center, Massachusetts became the American prototype for industrialization. The labor system at Lowell attracted almost as many visitors as did the state's prisons. South Carolina, by contrast, had some of the most highly developed forms of plantation organization, and slavery, too, attracted the inquisitive visitor.

The two states can be contrasted culturally as well. In Massachusetts, Horace Mann established a uniform statewide system of public education. South Carolina had no free school system at all, although there were small state educational subsidies to the districts. Formal education in South Carolina was a class-based privilege. Massachusetts was a hotbed of agitation for all sorts of social issues; South Carolina had virtually no social reform societies. Yet, Nullification and secession galvanized the state into action. South Carolina citizens were the only ones in the Union who did not vote for presidential electors; the legislature chose the electors and the governor as well. With no opportunity for choice, South Carolina spawned no competing political parties.

* * *

Criminal justice evolved differently in the two states for three reasons: tradition, economic and social development, and slavery. From the days of Puritan holy watching in the seventeenth century, law played a significant role in the lives of Massachusetts citizens. Much of colonial South Carolina, by contrast, was a frontier society, where alternatives to formal authority had to be found. These traditions influenced subsequent developments in both states, causing Massachusetts authority to remain activist, while South Carolina valued a laissez-faire approach. This traditional pattern was suited not so much to the backcountry * * * but to the plantation areas where aristocrats could live like manor lords.

Tradition, evolving from conditions of settlement as well as from the ideas of those who settled each colony, explains why divergences between Massachusetts and South Carolina are clear even in the colonial era, preceding the massive social changes of the nineteenth century. For example, by the Revolution, South Carolina had ten times as many capital offenses in its criminal code as did Massachusetts. Massachusetts had been gradually (if slowly) revising its seventeenth-century Mosaic code, but South Carolina had already shown great reluctance to alter its 1712 penal code. Each state had a frontier rebellion over courts, the Regulators in South Carolina (1766–67) and Shay's Rebellion in Massachusetts (1785). But while the South Carolina protesters demanded more courts to tame the backcountry, the Massachusetts rebels wanted to stem the oppressive encroachment of centralized authority into the Berkshires. Each state's legal heritages, then, were significant in shaping their subsequent legal histories.

A second reason why criminal justice evolved differently can be found in the contrasting needs of the new economic order in Massachusetts and of the South Carolina plantation. The manorial authority of the planter was supported, not superseded, by the state. An ideology of deference—whether it be among whites or across races—obviated the need for meticulous legal regulation of the affairs of society. In Massachusetts, by contrast, the pace of social change outstripped the ability of traditional mechanisms of control and order. Family, church, and community proved inadequate guardians of virtue and morals in an increasingly transient and anonymous society. State authority was exercised on behalf of capital and property. A laboring class of immigrants and migrants required the inculcation of the new factory-inspired values of hard work, self-control, and self-denial.

The impersonal and complex society produced by social and economic change had to deal with deviance on a large-scale basis. Criminal justice had to be routinized. Institutional controls—permanent, universalistic, and dependable—were seen as the only way to keep the lid on crime and disorder.

Tradition and economic development are important to understanding differences in the use of extralegal authority, the rise of the penitentiary, and the like. But perhaps the single most important factor was slavery. Above all, as Charles Sydnor pointed out decades ago, slavery created a class that was virtually beyond the law. South Carolina whites became accustomed to dealing with a majority of that state's population without any serious restrictions. Moreover, slavery altered all class relations in the South. Rather than wishing to inculcate middle-class virtues in the criminal, dangerous, and laboring classes, as was the goal in Massachusetts, South Carolinians conceived of their dangerous and criminal class as one which by its innate inferiority could not be salvaged. This meant, of course, that no reformatory sentence was ever contemplated for South Carolina slaves.

But slavery altered relations among whites as well. Although a fifth of the state's white population was living at a subsistence level, no poor, dangerous, or laboring class of whites was ever officially recognized. The only serious notice taken of the mass of poor whites appeared in the ill-fated attempt to reopen the slave trade in the mid–1850's, the purpose being to broaden the slaveholding base, already the broadest in the nation. This plan would have taken care of the ambiguous status of the poor whites by ensuring that the society consisted solely of two classes, masters and slaves.

* * * Massachusetts consistently sought to bolster the role of formal authority by strengthening its courts, establishing police, and curbing extralegal violence. In South Carolina, however, plantation aristocrats mocked court laws, took their quarrels to the dueling field instead of the courthouse, belatedly established police, supported permanent vigilante organizations, and actually encouraged citizens to find extralegal accommodations rather than increase strife through lawsuits.

The pattern of crime, prosecution, and punishment in the two states shows how crime was related both to the social order and to the differences between the two societies. In Massachusetts, crimes against property and propriety were the most common. Both types of offenses challenged the demand for order in the new industrial era. In South Carolina, by contrast, crimes of violence were the most common among whites. Crime against property was seen almost exclusively as the work of slaves. Because white crime was seen as the product of passions, not hunger, it was hardly a cause for alarm or action. As a result, archaic statutes and conscience-stricken juries freed over two-thirds of those arraigned. In Massachusetts, where crime and disorder appeared to threaten the fragile new order, conviction rates were twice as high.

If white crime created little alarm in South Carolina, slave crime had almost the opposite effect. Slaves were prosecuted for crimes against property, convicted at rates comparable to those in Massachusetts, punished severely, and executed at shocking rates. On the other hand, slaves were afforded little protection against white abuse.

Slavery may not have been a "total institution," but it was still the one to which most black South Carolinians were confined. The only equivalent in the North was the penitentiary, repository for the most dangerous of the dangerous class. While the plantation represented commercial agriculture in a slave society in its most highly developed form, the Massachusetts State Prison took its cue (and its system of labor and discipline) from the new industrial order.

* * * In Massachusetts, efforts to render the legal and penal system rational, responsive, and predictable received widespread support. Proponents of statute reform, penal reform, and abolition of the death penalty realized many of their desired goals, although all stopped short of complete success. In South Carolina, even the most modest proposals for eliminating some of the more bizarre and antiquated features of the legal and penal systems were summarily rejected.

Reform failed in one state and gained a hearing in the other for many reasons. Chief among them was the existence (or absence) of a culture of reform, the extent to which the aims of reform varied from the status quo, and the views of society and of the classes in it held by each state. Environmentalist thought in Massachusetts, spurred by religious fervor, led to a penal policy that stressed rehabilitation. Only a small minority of even the dangerous class was considered beyond hope. In South Carolina, by contrast, the association of crime with race meant that rehabilitation was impossible, unnecessary, and undesirable. Ironically, Massachusetts began to move away from its optimistic posture after decades of penal reform failed to alter the crime problem. By the 1860s, environmentalism, with its promise of reclamation, began to yield to the less flexible and less optimistic tenets of heredity and stock.

It should be clear that, although I view the Massachusetts experience as the prototype of our modern criminal justice system, there is little in that system to cheer about. Furthermore, although the structure, laws, and institutions are those of Massachusetts, some of the values—particularly the association of crime with race or nativity—are those of

South Carolina. And that, most certainly, is nothing to cheer about. Massachusetts would hardly be eager to accept credit for the criminal justice system as we know it today, but the South Carolina experience clearly shows that there was no virtue in intransigence, nor in a legal and penal system based on extralegal terror, fatal notions of honor, and racial supremacy. By offering a contrasting model with which to view the institutions so familiar to us, this study demonstrates that there was nothing inevitable, linear, or progressive about our history of criminal justice. * * *

* * *

* * * Outwardly, South Carolina slavery and the Massachusetts State Prison hardly seem to be subjects for comparison. Neither had a clear counterpart in the other state; one was a penal institution, tangential to the social system, and the other was a labor system, central to the nature of society. But having conceded these fundamental contrasts, we can explore the realm of less obvious similarities.

Both prison and plantation confronted the most critical problems of crime and control in each state. Both institutions reflected the most important features of each state's demographic history: immigrants in Massachusetts, blacks in South Carolina. And both institutions confined those people seen to be the most threatening to the social order. The Massachusetts State Prison housed (and for long terms) only the most serious and incorrigible of the state's offenders. Reformation may have been the goal, but incarceration was the means, and incapacitation (that is, the inability to commit additional crimes while confined) was always a result. Similarly, in South Carolina, slavery was a method of confining the most threatening element of that state's population. White crime * * * was seen primarily as the result of personal animosities. With the exception of murder, white crime was not considered a vital social problem. Punishments were insubstantial, and few resources were devoted to improving courts or jails.

Yet control of the slave population—and particularly of slave criminality—was just the opposite. Slaves were not simply the state's labor source and most valued investment. The entire way of life in South Carolina depended upon the maintenance of race control, and that principle could not be allowed to be threatened. Unlike white offenders, whose crimes of violence were largely attributable to unchecked passions, slave criminals posed a threat not only to property, but also (in its extreme forms of insurrection and resistance to authority) to white hegemony. Prison and plantation, therefore, were where both states became serious about controlling their troublesome populations.

The absence of slavery was not the motive for building a penitentiary in Massachusetts, but it is not an exaggeration to argue that the presence of slavery prevented South Carolina from building one. In this sense the Palmetto State was not unique. Although some slave states did build penitentiaries, all the states that did not were southern. And almost nowhere in the South did prisons resemble the northern penitentiary. Southern prisons were like centralized state jails; secure confinement was the goal, not programmed reformation or disciplined labor. These institutions paid little more than lip service to the purposes of their northern counterparts, and public disillusionment with them was rampant. The Georgia state prison was abolished for a time, and Louisiana displayed similar skepticism. Because of slavery, the penitentiary never gained a strong foothold in the South before the Civil War.

Despite their obvious dissimilarities, then, the prison and the plantation had much in common. Obviously, this was not the intent of these institutions. Slavery was not primarily a penal institution, though that was one of its results. In addition to its role in the southern labor and social system, the plantation kept under confinement and control the one class that was most threatening to the social order. Similarly, the prison was not primarily a labor system, but it mandated labor for rehabilitation, profit, and internal order. The prison adopted many features of the factory system and justified forced labor of convicts because of the moral uplift it provided.

Despite the obvious and significant differences between the prison and the plantation, there are some similarities that reflect the salient features of each state's criminal justice systems. Prison and plantation confined at forced, unpaid, large-scale labor those people in society seen as threatening. Both inmates and slaves were deprived of basic political, civil, and human rights by a legal system sworn to uphold those rights for others. Both institutions relied on corporal and shaming punishments for discipline. In both states the internal workings of the institutions were shielded from external scrutiny. Finally, both institutions were linked to the productive systems of the states. The Massachusetts State Prison, with its labor and discipline, was a distorted model of the factory; the South Carolina plantation was the main productive unit in the state. * * *

* * * There is no doubt that the systems of crime, justice, and authority functioned differently in the two states. One state modified its penal code with regularity, built impressive institutions, if not for the reformation, at least for the incarceration of its miscreants, came close to abolishing the death penalty, and established professional police forces to put society's official imprimatur on the war against disorder and deviance. The other state built no prison, fiercely retained a criminal code that was more a lineal descendant of medieval times than a clear reflection of contemporary thought, and encouraged extralegal means of dispute settlement.

But this is not simply a study in contrasts; it is an attempt to determine how the fundamental sources of social cohesion and authority functioned in two ostensibly different societies. The structural contrasts are dramatic—the presence of slavery or a penitentiary, antiquated statutes or organized laws, high or low conviction rates—but such outward contrasts do not tell the entire story. In many ways more significant * * * are the similarities between the two states.

* * *

Although perhaps an oversimplification, to a great extent the function of law and authority was to channel the behavior of potentially threatening or dangerous segments of the population. But this channeling did not have to occur in a uniform fashion. Where personal relations and honor were important, as in South Carolina, elaborate institutional arrangements were unnecessary. In the increasingly impersonal world of nineteenth-century Massachusetts, routinized structures for the exercise of authority seemed most suitable. In both instances, developments in the legal system neatly paralleled those in the political and economic spheres. Massachusetts boasted well-organized political machines and forged a commercial law based on universalistic principles. South Carolina politics were based on deference, and its large-scale business was often conducted on the basis of a gentleman's honor and a handshake.

Obviously, in order to understand many of the structural arrangements of the South Carolina system of authority, it is necessary to look at race relations. Similarly, in Massachusetts, where the problem of crime was eventually seen as a matter of class, class relations are a key to understanding the nature of crime and authority. And here we see that when the vital interests of each state were at stake, formal guarantees of justice were subserved to what Eugene Genovese termed the hegemonic function of law.[1] Despite the law reform and the considerable capital expenditure in prisons and reformatories, enforcement of the criminal law in Massachusetts was frequently a matter of class control.

It does not take much imagination to see within the operation of the criminal law this class control motive. The largest single category of arrests in Massachusetts was liquor-related offenses. Arrests for vagrancy and the entire area of sex-related crimes also show that a particular value system was being upheld through law, rather than simply that limited list of crimes against persons and property, prosecution for which few people would object to. Class control as a motive, of course, is hard to pinpoint. Yet, there are definite indications that large-scale employers were most concerned about the effects of unchecked drunkenness on the working population of the state and only secondarily concerned about the disruptive impact of measures of harassment against honest and dependable

[1] Eugene D. Genovese, *Roll, Jordan, Roll,* p. 25.

laborers raucously enjoying their scarce free time. Furthermore, as no minimal effort was made toward prevention or rehabilitation of drunks and vagrants, it is hard to see in these perennial arrests anything other than a street-cleaning motive.

In South Carolina, the most threatening population—and one identified as the equivalent of the northern criminal class—was the state's slaves. Here the purpose of the legal system was unmistakable. * * * [T]he legal system formally sanctioned the exercise of police power solely on the basis of race.

In South Carolina, there is yet another part to this picture. Although this study has not attempted to determine the social attributes of the defendant class in that state, we can infer that the dominant interests were served in yet another fashion: they were left alone. Although, as we have seen, the notion of honor was widely shared among South Carolina whites, protection of honor took many forms. The gentleman class took the dueling ground, virtually immune from prosecution despite the legal proscription on dueling, and lesser classes responded to slurs and insults in a violent manner. In many cases, criminal prosecutions resulted from such violence, even though the offense itself was in part based on the South Carolina class system. Thus, by prosecuting people for assaults, riots, and brawls, but not duels, the double standard in South Carolina justice was not limited to blacks.

Finally, it is not too farfetched to see in both states a number of safety-valve mechanisms to ensure that the legal system, the legitimacy of which derives to a great extent from its formal autonomy from the political and social systems, did not get out of hand. The most obvious of such devices was the pardon. Again, impressionistic evidence must suffice, but the case for a pardon was strengthened if a person came from a stable family or had influential friends to support the application. Such was not always the case: Harvard professor John White Webster was executed. But pardons in both states served a crucial, double-edged corrective function; on the one hand, victims of the legal system were given a second chance; on the other hand, an opportunity was provided for certain offenders to escape the harshest rigors of the criminal justice system.

Therefore, despite the different economic systems, despite the vast demographic differences, and despite even the cultural traditions that led to the creation of certain different types of legal structures, the criminal justice systems of both states served similar functions.

Once we go beyond the obvious structural contrasts, when we abandon the litmus-test conviction rates and the disputes over courts and the proper posture of authority and populace, we find that somehow things were not as drastically different in the two states as they appeared. Deference and other forms of traditional authority operated to keep planters and patricians in power in both states. In the highly formalized, legalistic

Yankee society, control of political power was part and parcel of this accomplishment. In South Carolina, political control was significant but hardly determinative. That state systematically weakened or dismantled potentially competitive sources of power and authority. And so the courts were kept ineffectual, dueling was clandestinely promoted, and slaves were tried either on the plantation or before neighborhood slaveholders, never in courthouses.

As I have indicated, I believe that legal traditions are as important as economic and social evolution in fashioning a society's legal and criminal justice systems. And, to some extent, tradition has influenced the course of each state's legal development from the nineteenth century to today. By the 1870s the Massachusetts State Prison, now home for many displaced members of the new industrial proletariat, was modeled on a factory, with shops and contractors. But the South Carolina penitentiary, almost entirely black, with its chain gangs, field hands, work songs, and white overseers, resembled the plantation. Thus, even after the formal abolition of slavery, the equation of prison and plantation remained valid. The tradition of personal violence proved to be a persistent characteristic of the entire South; homicide and suicide rates in the decades after Reconstruction were higher than in any other region of the country.

The peculiarities of South Carolina law and justice remain. A few years ago, the legacy of South Carolina justice was revealingly described in two totally unrelated segments of a highly rated network television news show. One story was on Spartanburg, South Carolina, then the gun capital of the country, upholding the tradition of personal violence in the upcountry. The second story concerned part-time local peace justices, blissfully untrained in law, who settle disputes informally in remote lowcountry areas of the South Carolina coast. Like the untrained and ignorant magistrates who were the object of so many nineteenth-century grand jury complaints, these officials served a purpose while revealing the persistence of the state's ambivalence toward formal justice and authority.

Such vignettes point to a reassuring continuity in South Carolina history. The same cannot easily be said for Massachusetts. The Massachusetts of the nineteenth century was divided between Yankee and immigrant. * * *

Two things happened in Massachusetts to break the sort of continuity we saw in South Carolina. First, the Yankees and the Irish more or less came to terms with each other. Second, twentieth-century Massachusetts to a great extent accepted the same equation of class and race that characterized nineteenth-century South Carolina. Ceding politics and the police to the new immigrants, Yankees perceived no basic threat to their own position. But there was an interesting trade-off, one in sharp but fascinating contrast to the nineteenth-century quest for certainty and efficiency. No longer can the legal system of Massachusetts be seen as efficient. Its courts are among the most overcrowded in the country. Boston's city councillors risked jail in the 1970s rather than replace the Charles Street jail * * *. Lack of enforcement of traffic regulations has created a special form of anarchy which the state insurance commissioner once blamed for the state's high automobile insurance rates.

We should recognize some of these themes from nineteenth-century Massachusetts. The people who were in effect the victims of the periodic obsession of the police with minor vice and drunkenness are the ancestors of those [now] in formal control of the law enforcement apparatus. The minor illegalities so tolerated in Massachusetts represent the response to decades of class control.

And, though always class conscious, Massachusetts today is certainly one of the most race conscious of states, north or south. To no small degree, the recent history of race relations in Massachusetts shows that the class control measures of the nineteenth century have been applied to achieve race control in the twentieth. The anarchy in the streets and courts in Massachusetts is as misleading today as the absence of a penitentiary was in South Carolina. Just as nineteenth-century planters retained their hegemony without building legal and political structures to support it, so today in Massachusetts, formal control of the criminal justice system gives those groups who enjoy that control apparently only a tenuous foothold on the crucial ladder that leads to security and respectability.

Ironically, what seemed at first a clear study in contrasts must yield to an understanding of the essentially similar role of the system of authority and law in preserving, albeit in different forms, order and social cohesion. The purpose of law and authority, not the structures and institutions, becomes the point of comparison, rather than of contrast. And thus, if one society chose the prison and the other the plantation, it was the criteria for confinement and not the institutional setting with which we must contend. If we understand that fact, we will also understand that the same social, racial, and political antagonisms that fuel the sense of threat and danger will eventually create a prison or a plantation, no matter what institutional (or anti-institutional) form it takes, no matter what we call it.

NOTES AND QUESTIONS

1. In a compelling review of Hindus's book, Professor Paul Finkelman, the author of a celebrated work on Northern and Southern responses to the law of slavery, An Imperfect Union: Slavery, Federalism, and Comity (1981), observes that contrary to Hindus's claim, Massachusetts and South Carolina were *not* representative states for the North and South, but were probably the most extreme proponents of the differing cultures of the two regions.

Finkelman, Book Review, 129 Pa.L.Rev. 1485–1489 (1981). Nevertheless, Finkelman concludes that by picking such extremist states Hindus was able to do a better job of illuminating the starkness of the contrasts in the manner which the antebellum North and South dealt with criminal justice. For Professor Finkelman's further thoughts on how a "distinctive southern legal history" regarding "[c]rime, violence, prisons, local courts, legal education, institutional resistance to change, laws concerning divorce and child custody, and the nature of the southern bench" could be written, see his "Exploring Southern Legal History," 64 N.Car.L.Rev. 77 (1985).

Hindus suggests that "tradition" and the "economy" explain some of the differences in society and in approaches to criminal justice in these two states. What, exactly, does he mean, and, in particular, when he suggests that in South Carolina "aristocrats could live like manor lords," and in Massachusetts "State authority was exercised on behalf of capital and property," is he necessarily describing two radically different societies? Alternatively, can you articulate reasons for preferring or condemning, on the one hand, a society which "forged a commercial law based on universalist principles" (as you saw, for example, in *Swift v. Tyson,* in the beginning of this chapter), or, on the other hand, a society where "politics were based on deference, [with] large-scale business . . . often conducted on the basis of a gentleman's honor and a handshake?"

Whatever the influence of "tradition" and the economy, you will have noticed that the most important explanatory variable for Hindus, and, indeed, the most explanatory social characteristic for most analysts of antebellum North and South, is the presence of slavery in the South and its absence in the North. Indeed, as we have already seen, it was the Supreme Court's treatment of slavery in *Dred Scott* that was often said to have caused the Civil War. Do you agree that slavery is the most important determinant of the differences between North and South, or would you characterize regional culture more broadly? In particular, why was Massachusetts possessed of a "culture of reform" and South Carolina not? Is the contrast with South Carolina, and its treatment of criminal violence among white "lesser classes" instructive?

2. Consider Hindus's suggestion that both Massachusetts and South Carolina similarly faced a need to control their "criminal, dangerous, and laboring classes." Hindus believes that the Southern institution of the "plantation" incarcerated the members of this class, Southern slaves, just as Northerners incarcerated members of their troublesome class in "prisons." Is the comparison, the overarching theme of Hindus's book, persuasive? Or is there a difference in the Southern and Northern conceptions of these two groups of members of the "laboring class?" In particular, does the reading you have done so far on the law of slavery suggest to you that Southerners and Northerners were using the same models regarding "labor?" You have already had some exposure to the notion that Southern society and its treatment of slave labor was very different from the prevailing "wage-labor" system of the North, in the work of Eugene Genovese. For further developments of the con-

trast between a supposedly "bourgeois" North and a South which sought to reject the "undifferentiated individualism" of the "bourgeois" world-view, see Mark Tushnet, The American Law of Slavery, 1810–1860: Considerations of Humanity and Interest (1981).

3. Paul Finkelman, in his review of Hindus, rejects Hindus's assertion that one can construct a valid comparison between the plantation and the penitentiary because "both institutions confined those people seen to be the most threatening to the social order." Finkelman argues that "plantation slaves [in the South] were not considered the most dangerous class; rather, it was free blacks, urban slaves, and the skilled slaves in small towns who really threatened the system. Perceived as even more threatening, of course, were the abolitionists, who southerners believed were secretly infiltrating their society to foment a slave rebellion." 129 U.Pa.L.Rev., at 1497. With whom do you agree, Hindus or Finkelman, and of what significance is the disagreement?

4. Finkelman appears to agree with Hindus's characterization of Prison and Plantation insofar as Finkelman concludes that "Both the prison and the plantation exuded paternalism." Id., at 1501. What is "paternalism" in this context, and how does an institution "exude" it? Were there any alternatives in the nineteenth century criminal justice system to "paternalism?" Are such alternatives available now? Bear in mind the implications of a "paternalistic" approach to social problems, as we proceed to study some aspects of family law later in this Chapter, and, still later, when we consider the issues raised by the Feminist challenge to American law.

Hindus apparently believes that there was "no virtue" in the Southern "legal and penal system based on extralegal terror, fatal notions of honor, and racial supremacy." Obviously White Southerners disagreed, since they were willing, twice, to risk their lives, fortunes and their "sacred honor" in wars to preserve their society. Why? Does this have anything to do with Hindus's assertion that his study demonstrates that there was "nothing inevitable, linear, or progressive about our history of criminal justice?"

5. Hindus's overall conclusion is that "despite the different economic systems, despite the vast demographic differences, and despite even the cultural traditions . . . the criminal justice systems of both states served similar functions." Professor Finkelman and other reviewers have suggested that this conclusion obscures rather than clarifies Hindus's data, which, in its great descriptive power, tends more to suggest profound differences between North and South than it does to confirm similarities. If this is true, why do you suppose Hindus reached his baffling conclusions? Why the need to suggest that at bottom North and South were similar? Could it have something to do with the depressing parallel Hindus draws between the antebellum South and modern Massachusetts? In another incisive review of Hindus's book, legal historian and biographer Robert Jerome Glennon, probably referring to matters like Hindus's parallel drawn between modern Massachusetts and the Old South, notes that Hindus "asks important questions about the economic and social role of the criminal justice system as a form of class con-

trol. The ideological implications of his answers should disturb anyone who, unlike Hindus, thinks that the history of criminal justice was 'inevitable, linear, or progressive.' " Glennon, *Book Review,* 77 Nw.U.L.Rev. 906 (1983). Are you disturbed? Should you be?

6. We continue our exploration of the criminal justice systems in nineteenth century America with two more works, one, from which two excerpts are taken, on Southern approaches to the problem, and the next on the social philosophy behind Northern reforms, such as the penitentiary. To what extent do these readings support or challenge the assertion that prison and plantation served "similar functions?"

EDWARD L. AYERS, VENGEANCE AND JUSTICE: CRIME AND PUNISHMENT IN THE 19TH CENTURY AMERICAN SOUTH*

19–20 (1984).

* * *

Contemporaries who described Southerners as gracious and hospitable described men who adhered to honorable conduct, but so did those who described Southerners as touchy and even belligerent. Honor, the overweening concern with the opinions of others, led people to pay particular attention to manners, to ritualized evidence of respect. When that respect was not forthcoming between men, violence might be the result. A culture of honor thus tended to breed the extremes of behavior for which nineteenth-century Southerners were famous. Yet Southern culture was not so brittle that it could not absorb the usual range of human foibles and quirks. Honor did not create one temperament, one personality, any more than does any other culture. A sense of noblesse oblige and disciplined rectitude, as well as violence, could and did grow out of honor.

Any accurate description of Southern honor must be couched in qualified language and described with care, for it was simultaneously potent and elusive. No contemporary visitor saw the entirety of Southern honor, no Southern poet or philosopher described its workings from the inside. Historians must therefore reconstruct it out of fragments, glimpsed on counters, passing comments. Southern honor was an anomaly, a strange hybrid of Old World and New World.

But so was Northern culture, and by the mid-nineteenth century the Northern United States had generated the core of a culture antagonistic to honor. This Northern culture celebrated "dignity"—the conviction that each individual at birth possessed an intrinsic value at least theoretically equal to that of every other person. In practice, of course, this ideal was qualified, violated, and undermined. Women, blacks, and Irish immi-

---

* Reprinted from Vengeance and Justice: Crime and Punishment in the 19th–Century American South, by Edward L. Ayers, © 1984 by Oxford University Press, Inc. Reprinted by permission of the publisher and the author.

grants, to name the most obvious examples, were not treated as equals by native white men. Even those white men found their supposedly equal worth mocked by class distinctions. Nevertheless, from the perspective of world history few can fail to be struck at the public allegiance awarded dignity at every turn in the American North in the mid-nineteenth century. Dignity stood as the ideal, the goal, however often it was violated in practice. Deviations had to be explained away, rationalized.

In a culture of dignity, people were expected to remain deaf to the same insults that Southern men were expected to resent. "Call a man a liar in Mississippi," an old saying went, "and he will knock you down; in Kentucky, he will shoot you; in Indiana, he will say 'You are another.' " Dignity might be likened to an internal skeleton, to a hard structure at the center of the self; honor, on the other hand, resembles a cumbersome and vulnerable suit of armor that, once pierced, leaves the self no protection and no alternative except to strike back in desperation. Honor in the Southern United States cannot be understood without reference to dignity, its antithesis and adversary to the north.

Both honor and dignity had roots in Old World cultures but developed new strains in the bracing environment of the New World. Almost from the very beginning a subtle and reinforcing sifting process created regional cultures in North America. Once British settlers arrived in America in the seventeenth and eighteenth centuries, they inevitably drew upon different elements of their diverse and changing culture as increasingly different economies led the Northern and Southern colonies further and further apart. Just as Northern settlers tried to reestablish the "English ways" of the counties and towns from which they came, so did the slaveholding gentry of colonial Virginia consciously adopt the culture of the English aristocracy.

NOTES AND QUESTIONS

1. As mentioned before, so far you have probably assumed, along with many American historians, that what really distinguished the South from the North was the presence of slavery in the former and its absence in the latter. Edward Ayers attempts to make out a case, however, that the differences between North and South flow as much from differences between a culture of "honor" and a culture of "dignity." For another treatment of Southern culture, which strives to deny a strong connection between honor and slavery see Bertram Wyatt–Brown, Southern Honor: Ethics and Behavior in the Old South (1982). Ayers has been praised for carefully explaining the link between Southern honor and slavery. Mark Tushnet, Book Review, 17 U.C. Davis Law Review 1307 (1984). Whether intimately connected with slavery or not, obviously the culture of "honor" is now gone, and the culture of "dignity" has triumphed. Is this triumph an unqualified good?

Note that Ayers appears to suggest that there were "regional cultures" in North America. You may remember that Tocqueville, writing in the eighteen-thirties, seemed to find a common culture of American democracy, although his evidence may have been biased toward the Northeast. Ayers seems to be suggesting that a real culture of "aristocracy" attempted to take root in the South.

If there was such a thing as an American "aristocracy" apart from the lawyers Tocqueville described as American "aristocrats," what meaning would this have for the importance of law in Southern culture? In his brilliant and controversial *The American Law of Slavery, 1810–1860: Considerations of Humanity and Interest* (1981), for example, Tushnet argues that the law was really of secondary importance to Southern culture, which preferred to vest great discretion to administer the principles of slavery in the individual plantation owner rather than to work out the details of slave law in the courts. You will remember that Hindus reached a similar conclusion. Is a secondary role for law in a culture necessarily suspect?

2. In some important historical writing there has been much more attention paid to the notion of regional cultures, and an increasing awareness that the North may have been fundamentally different from the South. See, e.g. Finkelman, "Exploring Southern Legal History," 64 North Carolina Law Review 77 (1985). How does the rediscovery of fundamental cultural differences between North and South affect your evaluation of the legal practices in both "cultures?"

For further development of the idea that the South had a distinctly different culture from that of the North, see Eugene D. Genovese, The Southern Tradition: The Achievement and Limitations of an American Conservatism (1994). In his book Genovese explores what we might regard as a distinct Southern "Constitutional" culture. For earlier work on constitutional development during the mid-nineteenth century sectional struggle see the seminal account in Harold M. Hyman and William M. Wiecek, Equal Justice Under Law: Constitutional Development 1835–1875 (1982). Could it be that the Civil War was not just about slavery, but about even more basic cultural concerns?

3. How did the concept of "honor" and a culture of "aristocracy" translate into institutional means of dealing with criminal justice? Michael Hindus has suggested that prison and plantation served similar "functions," but if a culture of "honor" was truly different from a culture of "dignity," we would expect the manifestations of Southern Justice to be quite different from those of the North. This appears to be the conclusion of Ayers, who notes on page 137 that

> Justice was personal and concrete in the slave South, for whites and for blacks. Twice a year respectable citizens, wealthier and perhaps more upright than the usual run of rural white men, performed jury duty; they surveyed the moral condition of the county, chided its shortcomings, and periodically brought gamblers, liquor vendors, and fornicators to

mild justice. They dismissed most cases brought before them, though, and other cases disappeared of their own accord when offenders or witnesses left the county. Petit jurors, men of more diverse economic background than grand jurors and certainly of less visible stature in the county, judged the relatively few offenders sent before them with neither great leniency nor great harshness. Most convicted people left the courthouse a bit poorer after paying a fine, but had to spend no time in the ramshackle jail. Other people who might have eventually met trouble because of their drunkenness or fighting were disciplined by their church instead. Cases of theft by blacks that would otherwise have filled court dockets never went beyond the bounds of the plantation.

Southerners such as George Fitzhugh looked at the effect of these interlocking institutions and proclaimed that "at the slaveholding South all is peace, quiet, plenty and contentment. . . . We have but few in our jails, and fewer in our poor houses. Southerners who made these claims were not lying—but neither were they acknowledging the hidden costs of the antebellum order. As long as slavery held the vast majority of the region's poor under rigid control, the South could afford a weak state, could afford to leave most white men alone, could afford to treat even accused criminals with leniency."

Does this support or contradict the views of Hindus? In any event, one test of the depth of the cultural differences between North and South would be to take away slavery from the South, and see what happened to conceptions of justice. This is, of course, what happened. Ayers asks, further on page 137, "But what would happen if the unimaginable came to pass, if slavery should come to a sudden end, if the white South had to pay the price for the peace and security purchased by its centuries of slavery?"

4. Our remaining excerpts from Ayers deal with this "unimaginable" situation. The depth of Southern despair and cynicism in the aftermath of the Civil War was profound.

EDWARD L. AYERS, VENGEANCE AND JUSTICE: CRIME AND PUNISHMENT IN THE 19TH CENTURY AMERICAN SOUTH

182–186, 191–195, 218–222 (1984).

* * * Few people have been so buffeted by chaos and change as the blacks and whites of the South in the twenty years between 1860 and 1880. The suffering of those twenty years, as inevitable as it may have been, left a bitter legacy—a legacy more damaging in its effect on crime and punishment, perhaps, than on any other facet of Southern society. Looking back from the perspective of 1904, W.E.B. DuBois admitted that "there can be no doubt that crime among Negroes has sensibly increased in the last thirty years, and that there has appeared in the slums of great cities a distinct criminal class among the blacks." Black criminality did not merely grow inexorably out of black depravity, ignorance, and destitu-

tion, DuBois wanted to make clear. Black lawbreaking was the result of a distinct historical process in which whites had made crucial and disastrous decisions. After the war the freed-people's offenses "were those of laziness, carelessness, and impulse, rather than of malignity or ungoverned viciousness. Such misdemeanors needed discriminating treatment, firm but reformatory, with no hint of injustice, and full proof of guilt." Instead, Southern justice "erred on the white side by undue leniency and the practical immunity of red-handed criminals, and erred on the black side by undue severity, injustice, and lack of discrimination." The result was that "Negroes came to look upon courts as instruments of injustice and oppression, and upon those convicted in them as martyrs and victims." DuBois believed that when blacks committed more serious crimes in later years "the greatest deterrent to crime, the public opinion of one's own social caste, was lost, and the criminal was looked upon as crucified rather than hanged."

This lament echoed through the New South for generations, a lament of a society, once bound together by slavery, witnessing rampant fragmentation. The South's fragmentation began with secession, as whites suddenly saw their differences exposed. Classes, ethnic groups, and subregions found themselves at odds with their neighbors. The privation of war heightened the South's internal divisions, and mass theft, bread riots, and armed resistance were the results. The Civil War set the South adrift. Slaves and slaveowners confronted each other in a new light. Southerners of all classes and races became unsure of themselves and of each other.

When the Civil War destroyed slavery, it destroyed the basic structure that gave shape to the South. Slavery had sealed off vast numbers of people from the state and the market economy, and when the walls of slavery fell nothing stood ready to replace them. Neither slavery nor true free labor could prevail, neither the master nor the state exercised the control they wished. The Freedmen's Bureau tried to supply a rudimentary state and the framework for the beginning of free labor, but its efforts were temporary and soon overwhelmed. * * *

Slowly and haltingly, new institutions grew up. Ex-masters and ex-slaves settled on forms of labor and payment that contained enough control to mollify the planter and enough freedom to help mollify the laborer. For the freedman the control remained galling, and his freedom came at the price of subjection to the relentless pressures of the international market. Black farmers as well as white ones found new masters in liens and mortgages. Masters no longer felt bound by duty and investment to supply food to hungry blacks, and white farmers sacrificed their ability to feed themselves in order to grow cotton. Theft, already a problem, increased dramatically in country as well as city when the South suffered its first debilitating postwar depression in the 1870s.

The most dramatic battles during Reconstruction were fought over the control of the state. Radicals in Congress sought to guarantee republicanism by enfranchising the disenfranchised; the conservative white South sought to guarantee republicanism by restoring "home rule." The latter triumphed, and the criminal courts soon reflected the reassertion of local white control. In urban as well as rural areas, white officers arrested, prosecuted, and sentenced blacks accused of minor theft while neglecting white malefactors. Black property crime, fueled by widespread destitution and the special effort expended by white courts, suddenly superseded white violent crime in the court records. Whites made little attempt to disguise the injustice in their courts. Thousands of black people served long terms on chain gangs for petty theft and misdemeanors in the 1860s and 1870s. Thousands more went to the convict lease system, the most visible product of a society caught between the worst of the past and the worst of the future.

* * *

Convict labor * * * has become a symbol, even a cliché of the New South. The convict lease system is often perceived as merely a bald attempt by whites to resurrect slavery in a disguised form. But it was much more than this, an institution that reflected fundamental changes as well as continuities in the postwar South. The convict lease system emerged because Southern governments, still wedded to the antebellum innovation of centralized state penal institutions, suddenly found themselves responsible for millions of black people untouched by the state only a few years earlier. Convict labor also developed as an adjunct of a nascent industrial capitalism short of capital and labor. Once established, the South's network of convict labor became a force of its own in the region, shaping local justice, labor relations, and politics. The most lasting effect of the convict lease system was the role it played as the symbol, to blacks and whites alike, of the white South's injustice and inhumanity. * * *

For half a century following the Civil War, convict camps could be seen scattered over the Southern landscape. Thousands of Southern men and women, most of them black, passed years of their lives in the convict lease system, deep in mines or waist-high in swamps during the day, in wet clothes and filthy shacks during the night. Men with capital, from the North as well as the South, bought these years of convicts' lives. The largest mining and railroad companies in the region as well as small-time businessmen scrambled to win the leases. The crumbling antebellum penitentiaries, granite monuments of another social order, became mere outposts of the huge and amorphous new system of convict labor. Only a few white men convicted of murder, a few black men too sick to remain profitable at the work site, and a few women of both races remained in the dilapidated penitentiaries. Wardens had little to do; the state had become superfluous in the punishment and reclamation of its criminals.

* * *

The same forces impinged on every political group in the South and led them to tolerate, if not endorse, the convict lease system. Demands for governmental frugality, the necessity of avoiding competition between convict and free labor, political pressures for party unity, white unwillingness to support criminal blacks in apparent idleness, and the usual disregard of the law-abiding for the welfare of the criminal remained constant throughout the postwar years. Within fifteen years after the war, all the ex-Confederate states allowed businessmen to submit bids for the labor of the state's felons.

The labor that convicts performed varied from year to year and from place to place. In the late 1860s and early 1870s there was cautious experimentation with convict labor; leases ran for relatively short periods and convicts worked primarily as agricultural and railroad laborers. Railroad work on a larger scale dominated the penal labor of virtually every state throughout the 1870s. In the 1880s and 1890s convict labor became increasingly concentrated in mining, especially in the states leasing the largest number of convicts: Alabama, Georgia, Florida, and Tennessee.

The evolution of the convict lease system traces the contours of the evolving Southern economy in general. The early leases were inaugurated in a period of political and economic uncertainty, and neither the capitalist nor the state had a clear sense of the true value or utility of convict labor. To planters used to managing slaves, the bound labor of convicts must have seemed a welcome opportunity to return to accustomed ways, to a control of every facet of the worker's life impossible even in slavery. The lease system was part of a continuum of forced labor in the New South, a continuum that ran from the monopolistic company store, to the coercions of sharecropping, to peonage, to the complete subjugation of convict labor. Obviously, the roots of such forced labor reached into slavery, not only for the work force itself but also for the habits of thought that encouraged employers to turn so readily to such heavy-handed means of securing labor.

As Harold Woodman has observed, however, the "desire for a dependent, easily controlled, docile, and cheap labor force burns as fiercely in the heart of a thoroughly bourgeois factory owner as it does in the heart of a plantation owner." The convict lease system was not simply slavery reincarnated, and ex-slaveowners were not the only employers interested in convict labor. The lease system must be viewed in relation to the new demands of the postbellum South and not merely as the inertia of the antebellum South. The convict lease system, along with the other variations of forced labor, bridged the chasm between an agricultural slave economy and a society in the earliest states of capitalist industrial development. On railroads and then in mines, the convict lease system served as the entering wedge, as the only labor force capitalists investing in the South knew they could count on to penetrate dangerous swamps and to work in deadly primitive mines. Convict labor depended upon both the heritage of slavery and the allure of industrial capitalism.

Many parts of the postwar South suffered from a severe labor shortage, and planters and railroad builders found themselves in competition for scarce workers. The postwar South had no pool of displaced male agricultural laborers of the sort that fed industrialization in England and Europe. For decades, the new factories of the South would be dominated by women and children—but women and children could not be used in many of the South's more profitable and dangerous new industries. New Yorker Charles K. Dutton, head of a turpentine and naval stores company, leased Florida's convicts because "turpentine culture was exhausting work, and it was difficult to obtain enough labor for the proper cultivation of any great number of trees. Natives of Florida's piney woods would quickly abandon the work when any other type of livelihood became available." Phosphate mining was little better, and as one historian put it, the discovery of phosphate in Florida had "the same effect on convict leasing as the invention of the cotton gin had had on slavery." Colonel Arthur Colyar used convict labor in his Tennessee coal mines because, he said, he could not find 300 free men willing to work in the mines.

Railroad building presented the same problems of labor shortages; the South's antebellum rail network, in fact, had been built largely by companies using slaves instead of scarce, expensive, and unreliable free white labor. The postbellum railroads, therefore, seemed a natural place for convicts to labor. The railroads needed rebuilding, state governments had often invested heavily in the lines, the roads seemed to serve the entire state economy, and railroad laborers were unorganized and powerless. The work was backbreaking and took workers into the most remote and most dangerous reaches of the South. In the mid–1870s, for example, Tennessee leased its convicts to the Cincinnati Southern Railroad. Other contractors on the line had managed to entice some Italians, Irishmen, blacks, and perhaps even Chinese to labor in the mountain wilderness. These free laborers, not surprisingly, drank freely of the local moonshine whiskey sold in the log taverns that sprang up along the route, and fights broke out between gangs of workers. Employers discovered their free labor force was frequently decimated by desertions and injuries. But the convicts working on the railroad could not get whiskey, could not run away, could not brawl. They were guarded by young white men who practiced target shooting in their spare time; the convicts slackened their labor at the risk of a whipping or worse. Owners of a railroad in Mississippi also turned to convict labor. * * * As a legislative committee discovered, the convicts "were placed in the swamp in water ranging to their knees, and in almost nude state they spaded caney and rooty ground, their bare feet chained together by chains that fretted the flesh. * * * Eighteen convicts nearly died, and had to be transported through Vicksburg hidden in a wagon."

The lease system was tailor-made for capitalists concerned only with making money fast. Labor costs were fixed and low, problems of labor uncertainty were reduced to the vanishing point, lucrative jobs could be undertaken that others would not risk, convicts could be driven at a pace free workers would not tolerate. * * * The benefits of a captive workforce took on greater luster, too, when compared to the scene in the North in 1877, as the warden of the Alabama penitentiary pointed out: "considering the depression in business throughout the country, the frightful upheavings of labor against capital of some of our sister States, its consequent injury and derangement of the general business of the country, we have cause to congratulate ourselves as to our financial success."

Convict labor, not unlike slavery, insulated the lessee from "frightful upheavings of labor" and labor shortages. But as in slavery, laborers had to be supported during slack times; and convicts, unlike slaves, could not be sold. "Epidemics may prevail," a Tennessee official pointed out in 1867, "contagion may spread death and devastation all over the country—debtors may become insolvent, and cause the prison to sustain heavy losses—the labor market may be dull, and no remunerative employment be found for the convicts—but the State is indemnified against all these, and if any loss is sustained, it must be borne by the lessees, and not by the state." Similarly, if the lease decreed that the lessee must accept all hands in the prison, many of the advantages of convict labor disappeared. "Now, every convict, old or young, skilled or unpracticed, clumsy, indolent, or vicious, is at once turned over, at forty-three cents per day, and it is the lessee's business, to provide work profitable or otherwise, without regard to the character, condition, or competency of the laborer." Increasingly, lessees accepted only able-bodied men from the state, but another problem with convict labor persisted despite this winnowing. A visitor to a Tennessee coal-mining camp discovered that "some of those in charge spoke with great contempt of the value of this class of convict labor, and said that they grudged paying the twenty-five dollars for the recapture of such lazy loafers." Not unlike slaves, convicts resisted. Some loaded the bottoms of their coal wagons with stones to fill their quota. Others did not even bother resorting to such subterfuge: although a mandatory whipping followed "any shirking of the task, the men will sometimes lounge away the day and at its close take the punishment, rather than do the work."

Inefficiency and fixed costs in times of depression no doubt hurt the lessee's profits, but apparently most convict labor paid handsomely. Some of the largest mining companies and shrewdest entrepreneurs in the South avidly sought and used convict labor for decades. * * * The convict lease system, argued a Northern member of the American Iron and Steel

Association, was the major reason the South could produce such cheap iron. * * *

* * *

By 1881, however, the tide of public opinion had already begun to turn against the lease. Residents of Greene County, whose Superior Court sent so many convicts to the state penal system, read that a recent report on the convict lease system by a special committee of the legislature was "so full of horrors that it would furnish material for a thousand bloody shirt speeches." Although lobbyists had succeeded in convincing legislators to keep the lease, the *Herald* 's correspondent charged that the lease system was "already a reproach to us in the eyes of the nation and the Georgian who sees his state pointed out with the finger of scorn on this account may blush in silence for he can find no words with which to justify her or even palliate her dishonor." * * *

Just as a reading of antebellum newspapers would suggest, erroneously, that "public opinion" in the South favored penitentiaries, so might the newspapers of the New South give a misleading picture of popular attitudes toward the convict lease system. No state governments ever held referenda on the convict lease, but if they did, argued one defender of the lease system, no more than a quarter of the electorate would vote to abolish the system. Given the distinctly draconian attitudes white Southerners expressed in favor of public hangings, lynchings, and chain gangs, this claim may well be true. In any case, Southerners could not stand to hear their penal practices denounced by Northerners.

* * * "When a stately mansion is burned to the ground and the owner thereof is doing all in his power to rebuild his home," remarked one Southern delegate to a national prison convention, "it ill becomes him, who was, in part, responsible for its destruction, to stand by and deride his efforts and to criticize the style of architecture he had adopted." * * * Southern defensiveness led men to defend, well into the 1890s, an indefensible institution. Not unlike their antebellum slaveholding predecessors, apologists for the lease rationalized a "necessary evil" into a "positive good."

Forgetting or repudiating their own antebellum penal history, defenders of the lease attacked the more subtle yet equally powerful coercion inherent in the Auburn-style penitentiary still dominant in the North. The lack of discipline in the convict lease, so often deplored, was transfigured into a virtue. "We have not yet reached that point in refined cruelty," a Southerner bragged, "where the convict is kept in a solitary cell and not allowed to raise his eyes from his work or to speak to anyone but his keeper, until his mind, from constant communion with its own thoughts, is liable to become a wreck." In the lease, conversation was common, and even singing rang through the mines. "A happy contrast this," another philosopher of punishment rhapsodized, "with some prisons where convicts are struck dumb, and wear the shackles on their very eyelids; denied the last privilege of manhood, the privilege of looking up! Could punishment be more crushing? Could degradation be deeper?" Just as some defenders of slavery had been insightful critics of the hidden coercions of capitalism, so did defenders of the lease perceive the deep but less tangible cruelty of the penitentiary.

Defenders of the lease before national prison associations did find, however, a sympathetic audience among the adherents of the hardening "scientific" racial attitudes of the late nineteenth century. In the context of speeches by Northerners filled with references to recently "discovered" linkages between crime, race, and heredity, the old-fashioned racism of Southern speakers fell on sympathetic ears. A Tennessee physician would not apologize for the lease: "We have difficulties at the South which you at the North have not. We must not be held to too strict an accountability. We have a large alien population, an inferior race." Another Southern doctor asserted that one "fact beyond dispute" had to be kept in mind at all times: "as a race, the negro is physically and mentally inferior." No one at the national congress argued with the "fact." One woman thought that black convicts died with such frequency in the mines because "the blood of educated people can resist a great deal more than the blood of the uneducated classes." * * *

* * *

Although some states in the South—Virginia, Texas, Tennessee, Kentucky, and Missouri—had long used manufacturing prisons in addition to the lease system, as late as 1890 the majority of Southern convicts still passed their sentences in convict camps run by absentee businessmen. In 1890 Mississippi's constitutional convention decreed that such a system would end when the current lease expired in 1894; the convicts were to be worked on a state-owned farm instead. The nineties saw a gradual shift toward the compromise of such state farms, as Southern legislatures began to separate women, youths, and the ill from the prisoners in the camps and dilapidated prisons. These vulnerable convicts had been particularly brutalized (and unprofitable) in railroad and mining camps, but on the farms they could perform healthful labor, help pay their way, stay out of competition with free labor, and avoid contamination from more hardened criminals. The Carolinas had used this plan for part of their prisoners in the 1880s, and in the 1890s Alabama, Virginia, and Georgia adopted the state farm plan as a way to ameliorate what most observers considered the worst features of the lease system.

Despite these changes, and despite attacks from Greenbackers and Populists throughout the South, only two Southern states besides Mississippi completely abolished the lease before the end of the nineteenth century. Tennessee, reeling from the rebellion of free miners against the lease, abandoned the system in 1895. Louisiana saw a breakdown in the lessee's political control lead to the termination of the system there. In general, the Southern convict lease system ended the way it began—uncertainly, ambiguously. A federal commission found that in 1898 nine states still leased convicts, "but in almost every case the objectionable features of the system had been eradicated, as far as possible, by stringent laws, rules, and inspections; and in all but two of the states (Florida and Louisiana) the convicts were also worked under other systems in connection with the lease system."

The introduction of centralized state-operated prison farms and the imposition of stricter controls over the lessees seemed important victories at the time. Death rates declined and conditions improved, but many of the evils of the lease remained. Not until the first two decades of the twentieth century did the South finally dismantle the lease system. By 1920 only Alabama had failed to pass a law ending the control of state convicts by anyone other than the state. To the eyes of the world, however, the replacements for the convict lease system seemed virtually indistinguishable from their beleaguered predecessor. Southern states did not erect new penitentiaries, but instead worked their convicts on chain gangs on public roads or on huge state-owned prison farms. Dedicated individuals continued to agitate for juvenile reformatories and gradually they were established, along with prison schools, libraries, and commutation laws. But the image of black convicts in striped uniforms laboring under the gaze of armed white guards has endured as one of the most telling symbols of the American South.

The New South was no less an anomaly, no less an unstable mixture of contradictory elements, than the Old South had been. The convict lease system grew out of the unique hybrid of a republican past and undisguised minority rule, of the South's history of slavery and nascent capitalism. Had the Old South not built state penitentiaries, after all, the New South would have had little reason to erect centralized state-sanctioned convict lease systems. Had the abolition of slavery not opened the New South to the promise of industrial development, capitalists would not have sought convict labor to build new railroads and dig new coal mines. Convict labor helped forge crucial parts of a new industrial economy and thus make the South more like the North, but at the same time the lease system testified to the South's separate and tragic destiny. The flagrant racial injustice of the lease system, whites admitted, bred crime among alienated young blacks as it helped destroy any bonds of trust and mutual obligation that survived between the races. From every perspective, even that of prominent Southern whites, the convict camps were incontrovertible evidence of the New South's moral failure.

NOTES AND QUESTIONS

1. Ayers's analysis, like that of virtually all modern historians of the South, suggests that racist attitudes dominated the administration of criminal justice in the aftermath of the civil war, but that the differential between black and white crime, if there was one, is explained by social causes. What are these social causes, and were you convinced that the rise of black criminality was, as W.E.B. DuBois suggested, "a distinct historical process in which Whites had made crucial and disastrous decisions?" Is this itself a rather racist analysis? Or is there no way of getting around the fact that Whites were pulling the levers of social change in North and South, and that neither region's rulers had a monopoly on "crucial and disastrous" decision making? How much of "crucial and disastrous" decision making had to do with substituting the "new masters" of liens and mortgages for the slaveholders? How much of this flowed from a substitution of the (Northern) ways of the law for the traditional family-oriented ways of the South?

2. In particular, how does the rise of the "convict lease system" reflect the rise of the law as a means of organizing Southern slave society? If you were a black person living in the South in the heyday of the convict lease system would you have preferred a return to slavery? Would you have felt the same as a white Southerner? Why does Ayers suggest that the convict lease system was "much more" than a "bald attempt by whites to resurrect slavery in a disguised form?" In particular, what does Ayers think caused the large-scale acceptance of the "injustice and inhumanity" inherent in the convict lease system? What kind of a view about the causes of social and legal change is this?

3. If the widespread acceptance of the convict lease system can be explained by the economic efficiency of that form of labor, and by the increasing needs of a social system converting from slavery to Northern-style capitalism, how does one explain the ending of the convict lease system in the South? Ayers seems to suggest that some of this had to do with Northern criticism of the South's practices, and the wishes of Southerners not to appear evil in the eyes of the North. Ayers explains, however, that there were attempts by Southerners to argue that their convict lease system was superior to Northern penitentiary "reforms," to which we will turn shortly. Did you find any merit in these defenses of the Southern system? If the Northern prison was "refined cruelty" as the Southerners suggested, and if the Southern convict lease system was unjust and inhumane as its critics (particularly those in the North) maintained, how could either society adopt either set of criminal justice practices? Is the explanation to be found in the economic circumstances of North and South, is it to be found in the maintenance of rival cultures of honor and dignity, is it, perhaps, to be found in rival cultures of "tradition" and "reform" or is there some other explanation?

Does the final abandonment of the convict lease system tell us something about a change in racial views? A change in legal attitudes? Ayers concludes that Southern means of dealing with those convicted of crimes furnishes "incontrovertible evidence of the New South's moral failure." Is this, perhaps, a bit too glib? Why did the South move from the convict lease system to a preponderance of "chain gangs" and "huge state-owned prison farms?" Did this lessen any inherent "evil," "injustice," or "inhumanity" in the South? Why didn't the South find appealing the Northern-style penitentiary? In order to answer that question we probably need to know more about the philosophy of the Northern penitentiary. It is to a review of that criminal justice system, then, that we now turn.

Those curious about constitutional and legal development in the postbellum years should consult the voluminous literature on reconstruction and the reconstruction amendments. Some starting points include five books, Raoul Berger, Government by Judiciary: The Transformation of the Fourteenth Amendment (1977), Michael Kent Curtis, No State Shall Abridge: The Fourteenth Amendment and the Bill of Rights (1986), William Nelson, The Fourteenth Amendment: From Political Principle to Judicial Doctrine (1988), Eric Foner, Reconstruction: America's Unfinished Revolution, 1863–1877 (1988), and Earl M. Maltz, Civil Rights, The Constitution, and Congress, 1863–1869 (1990), and several articles, Aviam Soifer, "Protecting Civil Rights: A Critique of Raoul Berger's History," 54 N.Y.U.L.Rev. 651 (1979), Robert C. Palmer, "The Parameters of Constitutional Reconstruction: *Slaughter–House, Cruickshank,* and the Fourteenth Amendment," 1984 U.Ill.L.Rev. 739, Randall Kennedy, "Reconstruction and the Politics of Scholarship," 98 Yale L.J. 522 (1989), Barry Sullivan, "Historical Reconstruction History, and the Proper Scope of Section 1981," 98 Yale L.J. 541 (1989), Paul Kens, "Whose Intent and Which Purpose? The Origins of the Fourteenth Amendment," 20 Reviews in American History 59 (1992), and Richard L. Aynes, "On Misreading John Bingham and the Fourteenth Amendment," 103 Yale L.J. 57 (1993), Richard L. Aynes, "Constricting the Law of Freedom: Justice Miller, The Fourteenth Amendment, and the *Slaughter-House* Cases," 70 Chicago–Kent L.Rev. 627 (1994).

DAVID J. ROTHMAN, THE DISCOVERY OF THE ASYLUM: SOCIAL ORDER AND DISORDER IN THE NEW REPUBLIC*

70–71, xviii–xix, 79–88, 105–108 (1971).

[Rothman's book is an attempt to understand how Americans (particularly Northerners) in the period after about 1820 rather suddenly decided that deviant and dependent members of their communities should be placed in institutions, rather than being cared for by families, as had been done throughout earlier American history. Our reading from Rothman begins with his description of the still-remaining centrality of family life for would-be reformers, but notice that the assumption which the reformers are apparently making is that the pressures on some nineteenth-century families are simply too great for them to cope with by themselves.

Would this description of the failures of families fit the antebellum South as well as the North? Has it any relevance today?]

* * * American students of deviant behavior moved family and community to the center of their analysis. New York officials accumulated and published biographies because this technique allowed them to demonstrate to legislators and philanthropists the crucial role of social organizations. Accordingly, almost every sketch opened with a vivid description of an inadequate family life and then traced the effects of the corruptions in the community. While many a convict may possibly have come from a broken home or been prone to drink, no one ought to take the inspectors' findings as straight facts. They had a prior commitment to gathering and publicizing this type of information to explain the origins of crime. Interviewers probably induced the convicts to describe, whether accurately or not, their early life in grim terms. Sympathetic questioners, letting the criminal know that they thought that much of the blame for his fate rested with his parents, would soon hear him recount his father's drinking habits and the attraction of the tavern around the corner. These sketches reflected the ideas of the questioner, not some objective truth about the criminal. The doctrine was clear: parents who sent their children into the society without a rigorous training in discipline and obedience would find them someday in the prison. * * *

The pessimism and fear underlying this outlook pointed to the difficulty Americans had in fitting their perception of nineteenth-century society as mobile and fluid into an eighteenth-century definition of a well-ordered community. Their first reaction was not to disregard the inherited concept but to condemn present conditions. Hence, in these biographies a dismal picture emerged of a society filled with a myriad of temptations. It was almost as if the town, in a nightmarish image, was made up of a number of households, frail and huddled together, facing the sturdy and wide doors of the tavern, the gaudy opening into a house of prostitution or theater filled with dissipated customers; all the while, thieves and drunkards milled the streets, introducing the unwary youngster to vice and corruption. Every family was under siege, surrounded by enemies ready to take advantage of any misstep. The honest citizen was like a vigilant soldier, well trained to guard against temptation. Should he relax for a moment, the results would be disastrous. Once, observers believed, neighbors had disciplined neighbors. Now it seemed that rowdies corrupted rowdies.

Yet for all the desperation in this image, Americans shared an incredible optimism. Since deviant behavior was a product of the environment, the predictable result of readily observable situations, it was not inevitable. Crime was not inherent in the nature of man, as Calvinists had asserted; no theological devils insisted on its perpetuation. Implicit in this outlook was an impulse to reform. If one could alter the conditions breeding crime, then one could reduce it to manageable proportions and bring a new security to society.

One tactic was to advise and warn the family to fulfill its tasks well. By giving advice and demonstrating the awful consequences of an absence of discipline, critics would inspire the family to a better performance. * * * One might also organize societies to shut taverns and houses of prostitution, an effort that was frequently made in the Jacksonian period. But such measures, while important, were slow-working, and by themselves seemed insufficient to meet the pressing needs of this generation. Another alternative then became not only feasible but essential: to construct a special setting for the deviant. Remove him from the family and community and place him in an artificially created and therefore corruption-free environment. Here he could learn all the vital lessons that others had ignored, while protected from the temptations of vice. A model and small-scale society could solve the immediate problem and point the way to broader reforms.

The response in the Jacksonian period to the deviant and the dependent was first and foremost a vigorous attempt to promote the stability of the society at a moment when traditional ideas and practices appeared outmoded, constricted, and ineffective. The almshouse and the orphan asylum, the penitentiary, the reformatory, and the insane asylum all represented an effort to insure the cohesion of the community in new and changing circumstances. Legislators, philanthropists, and local officials, as well as students of poverty, crime, and insanity were convinced that the nation faced unprecedented dangers and unprecedented opportunities. The asylum, they believed, could restore a necessary social balance to the new republic, and at the same time eliminate long-standing problems. * * *

* * * Eighteenth-century procedures consistently reflected the colonists' concepts of the proper functioning of the society. Poverty and crime, in their estimation, did not indicate a basic defect in community organization, nor could they be eliminated through ameliorative action. Under these conditions, noninstitutional mechanisms of relief and correction seem logical and appropriate, and social realities did not compel a reexamination or revision of the program.

This situation was not maintained for long after the Revolution, and by the 1820's and 1830's, novel ideas and procedures abounded. The nation had a new sense of its society. Americans now wrote voluminously about the origins of deviant and dependent behavior, insisting that the causes of crime, poverty, and insanity lay in the faulty organization of the community. From this perspective they issued harsh and bleak judgments on the functioning of the society and the perils that citizens faced. Yet at the same time they shared a keen sense of the promise of social action, for the diagnosis seemed to contain the cure. This viewpoint led directly to the discovery of the asylum.

The asylum was to fulfill a dual purpose for its innovators. It would rehabilitate inmates and then, by virtue of its success, set an example of right action for the larger society. There was a utopian flavor to this first venture, one that looked to reform the deviant and dependent and to serve as a model for others. The well-ordered asylum would exemplify the proper principles of social organization and thus insure the safety of the republic and promote its glory.

* * *

Americans' understanding of the causes of deviant behavior led directly to the invention of the penitentiary as a solution. It was an ambitious program. Its design—external appearance, internal arrangement, and daily routine—attempted to eliminate the specific influences that were breeding crime in the community, and to demonstrate the fundamentals of proper social organization. Rather than stand as places of last resort, hidden and ignored, these institutions became the pride of the nation. A structure designed to join practicality to humanitarianism, reform the criminal, stabilize American society, and demonstrate how to improve the condition of mankind, deserved full publicity and close study.

In the 1820's New York and Pennsylvania began a movement that soon spread through the Northeast, and then over the next decades to many midwestern states. New York devised the Auburn or congregate system of penitentiary organization, establishing it first at the Auburn state prison between 1819 and 1823, and then in 1825 at the Ossining institution, familiarly known as Sing–Sing. Pennsylvania officials worked out the details of a rival plan, the separate system, applying it to the penitentiary at Pittsburgh in 1826 and to the prison at Philadelphia in 1829. In short order, the Connecticut legislature stopped using an abandoned copper mine to incarcerate offenders, and in 1827 built a new structure at Wethersfield. Massachusetts reorganized its state prison at Charlestown in 1829; that same year, Maryland erected a penitentiary, and one year later New Jersey followed suit. Ohio and Michigan built penitentiaries in the 1830's, and so did Indiana, Wisconsin, and Minnesota in the 1840's.

The results of all this activity deeply concerned Americans, so that annual reports to state legislators and popular journals as well contained long and detailed discussions and arguments on the merits of various enterprises. Europeans came to evaluate the experiment and the major powers appointed official investigators. France in 1831 dispatched the most famous pair, Alexis de Tocqueville and Gustave Auguste de Beaumont * * *. Tourists with no special interest in penology made sure to visit the institutions. Harriet Martineau, Frederick Marryat, and Basil Hall would no more have omitted this stop from their itinerary than they would have a southern plantation, a Lowell textile mill, or a frontier town. * * *

The focus of attention was not simply on whether the penitentiary accomplished its goals, but on the merits of the two competing modes of organization. The debate raged with an incredible intensity during these decades, and the fact that most prisons in the United States were modeled after the Auburn system did not diminish it. Even more startling, neither did the basic similarity of the two programs. In retrospect they seem very much alike, but nevertheless an extraordinary amount of intellectual and emotional energy entered the argument. The fervor brought many of the leading reformers of the period to frequently bitter recriminations, and often set one benevolent society against another. Periodicals regularly polled foreign visitors for their judgment or printed a vigorous defense by one school and then a critical rejoinder by the other. * * * Every report from the New York and Pennsylvania penitentiaries was an explicit apology for its procedures and an implicit attack on its opponents. And as soon as a state committed its prison organization to one side or the other then it too entered the controversy with the zeal of a recent convert.

The content of the debate between the Auburn and Pennsylvania camps points to the significance of the ideas on the causes of crime to the creation of the penitentiary, and the zeal reflects the expectations held about the innovation. To understand why men became so passionate about internal questions of design is to begin to comprehend the origins and popularity of institutionalization in this era. Under the Auburn scheme, prisoners were to sleep alone in a cell at night and labor together in a workshop during the day for the course of their fixed sentences in the penitentiary. They were forbidden to converse with fellow inmates or even exchange glances while on the job, at meals, or in their cells. The Pennsylvania system, on the other hand, isolated each prisoner for the entire period of his confinement. According to its blueprint, convicts were to eat, work, and sleep in individual cells, seeing and talking with only a handful of responsible guards and selected visitors. They were to leave the institution as ignorant of the identity of other convicts as on the day they entered. As both schemes placed maximum emphasis on preventing the prisoners from communicating with anyone else, the point of dispute was whether convicts should work silently in large groups or individually within solitary cells.

To both the advocates of the congregate and the separate systems, the promise of institutionalization depended upon the isolation of the prisoner and the establishment of a disciplined routine. Convinced that deviancy was primarily the result of the corruptions pervading the community, and that organizations like the family and the church were not counterbalancing them, they believed that a setting which removed the offender from all temptations and substituted a steady and regular regimen would reform him. Since the convict was not inherently depraved, but the victim of an upbringing that had failed to provide protection against the vices at loose in society, a well-ordered institution could successfully reeducate and rehabilitate him. The penitentiary, free of corruptions and dedicated to the proper training of the inmate, would inculcate the discipline that negligent parents, evil companions, taverns, houses of prostitution, theaters, and gambling halls had destroyed. * * *

The duty of the penitentiary was to separate the offender from *all* contact with corruption, both within and without its walls. There was obviously no sense to removing a criminal from the depravity of his surroundings only to have him mix freely with other convicts within the prison. * * * [o]fficials in the 1830's argued that the great mistake of the prisons of the 1790's had been their failure to separate inmates. Lacking an understanding of the forces of the environment and still caught up with the idea that humane and certain punishment would eradicate deviancy, they had neglected to organize or supervise the prisoners' immediate surroundings. Consequently their institutions became seminaries of vice. Now, however, reformers understood the need to guard the criminal against corruption and teach him the habits of order and regularity. Isolation and steady habits, the right organization and routine, would yield unprecedented benefits.

As a result of this thinking, prison architecture and arrangements became the central concern of reformers of the period. Unlike their predecessors, they turned all their attention inward, to the divisions of time and space within the institution. The layout of cells, the methods of labor, and the manner of eating and sleeping within the penitentiary were the crucial issues. The most influential benevolent organization devoted to criminal reform, the Boston Prison Discipline Society, appropriately considered architecture one of the most important of the *moral* sciences. "There are," the society announced, "principles in architecture, by the observance of which great moral changes can be more easily produced among the most abandoned of our race. * * * There is such a thing as architecture adapted to morals; that other things being equal, the prospect of improvement, in morals, depends, in some degree, upon the construction of buildings." * * *

As with any other science, the advocates of moral architecture anticipated that the principles which emerged from the penitentiary experiment would have clear and important applications to the wider society. An arrangement which helped to reform vicious and depraved men would also be effective in regulating the behavior of ordinary citizens in other situations. The penitentiary, by its example, by its discovery and verification of proper principles of social organization, would serve as a model for the entire society. Reformers fully anticipated that their work behind prison walls would have a critical significance beyond them. Since crime was symptomatic of a breakdown in traditional community practices, the penitentiary solution would point the way to a reconstitution of the social structure.

Tocqueville and Beaumont appreciated how significant both of these purposes were to the first penologists. The institutions, Americans believed, would radically reform the criminal and the society. "Philanthropy has become for them," observed the two visitors, "a kind of profession, and they have caught the *monomanie* of the penitentiary system, which to them seems the remedy for all the evils of society." Proponents described the penitentiary as "a grand theatre, for the trial of all new plans in hygiene and education, in physical and moral reform." The convict "surrendered body and soul, to be experimented upon," and the results, as the Boston Prison Discipline Society insisted, would benefit not only other custodial institutions like almshouses and houses of refuge, but also "would greatly promote order, seriousness, and purity in large families, male and female boarding schools, and colleges." Perhaps the most dramatic and unabashed statement of these views appeared in a memoir by the Reverend James B. Finley, chaplain at the Ohio penitentiary. "Never, no never shall we see the triumph of peace, of right, of Christianity, until the daily habits of mankind shall undergo a thorough revolution," declared Finley. And in what ways were we to achieve such a reform? "Could we all be put on prison fare, for the space of two or three generations, the world would ultimately be the better for it. Indeed, should society change places with the prisoners, so far as habits are concerned, taking to itself the regularity, and temperance, and sobriety of a good prison," then the grandiose goals of peace, right, and Christianity would be furthered. "As it is," concluded Finley, "taking this world and the next together . . . the prisoner has the advantage."

It is no wonder, then, that Auburn and Pennsylvania supporters held their positions staunchly, eager to defend every detail. With the stakes so high and the results almost entirely dependent upon physical design, every element in penitentiary organization assumed overwhelming importance. * * *

The Pennsylvania camp had no doubt of its superiority, defining in countless pamphlets, articles, and reports its conception of the model institution. It aggressively insisted that the separate design carried the doctrine of isolation to a logical and appropriate conclusion. The arrangements at the Philadelphia prison, as partisans described them, guaranteed that convicts would avoid all contamination and follow a path to reform. Inmates remained in solitary cells for eating, sleeping, and working, and entered private yards for exercise; they saw and spoke with only carefully selected visitors, and read only morally uplifting literature—the Bible. No precaution against contamination was excessive. Officials placed hoods over the head of a new prisoner when marching him to his cell so he would not see or be seen by other inmates.

Once isolated, the prisoner began the process of reform. "Each individual," explained Pennsylvania's supporters, "will necessarily be made the instrument of his own punishment; his conscience will be the avenger of society." Left in total solitude, separated from "evil society . . . the progress of corruption is arrested; no additional contamination can be received or communicated." At the same time the convict "will be compelled to reflect on the error of his ways, to listen to the reproaches of conscience, to the expostulations of religion." Thrown upon his own innate sentiments, with no evil example to lead him astray, and with kindness and proper instruction at hand to bolster his resolutions, the criminal would start his rehabilitation. Then, after a period of total isolation, without companions, books, or tools, officials would allow the inmate to work in his cell. Introduced at this moment, labor would become not an oppressive task for punishment, but a welcome diversion, a delight rather than a burden. The convict would sit in his cell and work with his tools daily, so that over the course of his sentence regularity and discipline would become habitual. He would return to the community cured of vice and idleness, to take his place as a responsible citizen.

The separate system of penitentiary organization promised to accomplish these ends with a minimum of distraction and complication. The ordinary guards would not have to be well-trained, for their contact with the inmates would be slight and superficial; prisoners continuously confined to their cells would not have to be herded to meals or supervised in workshops and common exercise yards. Security would be easily maintained, since escape plans would be difficult to plot and to fulfill. There would be little recourse to the whip—cruel punishment would be rare, since men in isolation would have little occasion to violate regulations. Finally, these arrangements would permit officials to treat prisoners as individuals, rewarding some with more frequent visitors and books for good behavior, depriving recalcitrant others of these privileges. The Pennsylvania penitentiary promised to be a secure, quiet, efficient, humane, well-ordered, and ultimately reformatory institution.

Advocates of the separate system dismissed the competing congregate program as an incomplete and inconsistent version of the Pennsylvania scheme. The basic imperfection of Auburn, insisted critics like Samuel Gridley Howe, was a failure to maintain a thorough isolation of inmates. New York knew enough to separate prisoners at night, but for misguided motives allowed them to work together during the day. One result was that convicts came to recognize the other inmates, making it that much more likely that they would meet after release to resume a life in crime. They would also influence one another while still within the penitentiary walls. So many possibilities for conversation occurred during work and meals and exercise that guards could not eliminate all communication. Auburn's procedures diabolically tempted the convicts. They were to sit together at mess tables and workbenches, and yet abstain from talking—an unnecessarily painful situation. Officials, compelled to enforce rules that were too easily broken, inevitably meted out frequent and harsh punishments without solving the problem. These basic defects, Pennsylvania's partisans concluded, made cruelty and corruption endemic to the congregate plan.

For its part, the Auburn school vigorously defended the principle of separation and the reformatory promise of the penitentiary, fully sharing the axioms and optimism of its rival. But in reply to criticism, Auburn was necessarily on the defensive, for its arrangements did not so totally isolate the inmates or so studiously aim to prevent all chance of contamination. Auburn's supporters, therefore, spent more time picking fault with their opponents than advancing the superiority of their own procedures. Wherever possible they moved the debate from the ideal to the real, insisting that New York had the more practical scheme, a balanced combination of commitment and flexibility. They argued that Pennsylvania did not carry out its program perfectly, and then went on to contend that the very consistency of the separate design was itself a grave fault. Auburn's partisans answered complaints of frequent inmate communication in congregate prisons by contending that the walls of the Philadelphia prison were not thick enough and its sewer pipes not arranged well enough to prevent convict conversations. * * *

One main thrust, however, of the congregate school came on the issue of the effects of constant and unrelieved isolation of prisoners. It was unnatural, the New York camp insisted, to leave men in solitary, day after day, year after year; indeed, it was so unnatural that it bred insanity. * * *

After asserting that the separate system was no more effective or perfect than the congregate one, the New York school presented what proved to be its most persuasive point: the added expenses of establishing the Pennsylvania program were unnecessary. Auburn-type institutions, their defenders flatly, and accurately, declared, cost less to construct and brought in greater returns from convict labor. Since the two systems were more or less equal, with faults and advantages fairly evenly distributed, states ought not to incur the greater costs of the separate plan. By having prisoners work together in shops, Auburn's cells did not have to be as large as those at Philadelphia; also, a greater variety of goods could be efficiently manufactured in congregate prisons. The New York program provided the best of both worlds, economy and reform.

The pamphlet warfare between the two camps dominated practically all thinking and writing about the problem of crime and correction. The advantages and disadvantages of Pennsylvania as against Auburn blocked out any other consideration. No one thought to venture beyond the bounds of defining the best possible prison arrangements, and this narrowness of focus was clear testimony to the widespread faith in institutionalization. People argued whether solitary should be continuous and how ducts ought to be arranged, but no one questioned the shared premise of both systems, that incarceration was the only proper social response to criminal behavior. * * *

* * *

The doctrines of separation, obedience, and labor became the trinity around which officials organized the penitentiary. They carefully instructed inmates that their duties could be "comprised in a few words"; they were "to *labor diligently,* to *obey all orders,* and preserve an *unbroken silence.*" Yet to achieve these goals, officers had to establish a total routine, to administer every aspect of the institution in accord with the three guidelines, from inmates' dress to their walk, from the cells' furnishings to the guards' deportment. The common solution was to follow primarily a quasi-military model. The regulations based on this model promised to preserve isolation, to make labor efficient, and to teach men lacking discipline to abide by rules; this regimented style of life would inculcate strict discipline, precision, and instantaneous adherence to commands. Furthermore, a military model in a correctional institution seemed especially suitable for demonstrating to the society at large the right principles of organization. Here was an appropriate example for a community suffering a crisis of order.

The first designers of the prison had few other useful models to emulate. In fact, the penitentiary was not the only institution in the 1820's and 1830's facing the dilemma of organization. Such a novel economic unit as the factory was also beginning to use rigorous procedures to bring an unprecedented discipline to workers' lives. Prison designers could find the factory an interesting but limited source of inspiration, appropriating that part of it which was most regulatory and precise. Both organizations were among the first to try to take people from casual routines to rigid ones.

Regimentation became the standard mode of prison life. Convicts did not walk from place to place; rather, they went in close order and single file, each looking over the shoulder of the man in front, faces inclined to the right, feet moving in unison, in lockstep. The lockstep became the trademark of American prisons in these years, a curious combination of march and shuffle that remained standard procedure well into the 1930's. Its invention and adoption exemplified the problems and responses of the first penitentiary officials. How were they to move inmates about? Prison officials with fixed ideas on convict communication and obedience, had to reject informal movement. Searching for greater discipline, they turned to the military march, crossed it with a shuffle to lessen its dignity, and pointed heads to the right, rather than facing straight ahead, to prevent conversation. The result, the lockstep, was an immediate success and became the common practice.

Wardens organized the convicts' daily schedule in military style. At the sound of a horn or bell, keepers opened the cells, prisoners stepped onto the deck, and then in lockstep marched into the yard. In formation they emptied their night pails, moved on and washed them, took a few more steps, and placed them on a rack to dry. Still in line they marched to the shops. There they worked at their tasks in rows on long benches until the bell rang for breakfast. They grouped again in single file, passed into the kitchen, picked up their rations (regulations admonished them not to break step), and continued on to their cells, or in some institutions, to a common messroom where they ate their meal. (Regulations again instructed them to sit erect with backs straight.) At the bell they stood, reentered formation, and marched back to the shops. They repeated this routine at noon, and again at six o'clock; then they returned to their cells for the night and at nine o'clock lights went out, as at a barracks. * * *

The furnishings of convicts' cells also indicates the relevance of the military model. A cot and pail and tin utensils were the basic objects. Prisoners now wore uniforms of a simple, coarse, striped fabric, and all had their hair cut short to increase uniformity. The military example affected keepers as well as convicts. Several wardens came to their positions directly from an army or navy career, legislators obviously eager to have them apply their former training to this setting. Guards wore uniforms, mustered at specific hours, and kept watch like sentries. Regulations ordered them to behave in a "gentlemanly manner," like officers, without laughter, ribaldry, or unnecessary conversation while on duty. As Sing–Sing's rules put it, in only a slight overstatement of a general sentiment: "They were to require from the convicts the greatest deference, and never suffer them to approach but in respectful manner; they are not to allow them the least degree of familiarity, nor exercise any towards them; they should be extremely careful to *command* as well as to compel their respect."

The military style also influenced the construction and appearance of the institutions. Some were modeled after medieval fortresses. An adaptation of a structure from the Middle Ages was necessarily monumental, appropriate in size to a noble experiment like the penitentiary, capable of stimulating a citizen's pride and a visitor's respect. It also had functional qualities, for thick walls promised security against prison breaks, and turrets became posts for guarding an enclosed space. Another popular alternative was to construct the prison along factory lines—a long and low building, symmetrically arranged with closely spaced windows, all very regular and methodical. Whatever it lacked in grandeur it tried to make up in fixity and order.

The functioning of the penitentiary—convicts passing their sentences in physically imposing and highly regimented settings, moving in lockstep from bare and solitary cells to workshops, clothed in common dress, and forced into standard routines—was designed to carry a message to the community. The prison would train the most notable victims of social disorder to discipline, teaching them to resist corruption. And success in this particular task should inspire a general reformation of manners and habits. The institution would become a laboratory for social improvement. By demonstrating how regularity and discipline transformed the most corrupt persons, it would reawaken the public to these virtues. The penitentiary would promote a new respect for order and authority.

Reformers never spelled out the precise nature and balance of this reformation. They hoped that families, instead of overindulging or neglecting their children, would more conscientiously teach limits and the need for obedience to them. Assuming that social stability could not be achieved without a very personal and keen respect for authority, they looked first to a firm family discipline to inculcate it. Reformers also anticipated that society would rid itself of corruptions. In a narrow sense this meant getting rid of such blatant centers of vice as taverns, theaters, and houses of prostitution. In a broader sense, it meant reviving a social order in which men knew their place. Here sentimentality took over, and critics in the Jacksonian period often assumed that their forefathers had lived together without social strain, in secure, placid, stable, and cohesive communities. In fact, the designers of the penitentiary set out to re-create these conditions. But the results, it is not surprising to discover, were startlingly different from anything that the colonial period had known. A conscious effort to instill discipline through an institutional routine led to a set work pattern, a rationalization of movement, a precise organization of time, a general uniformity. Hence, for all the reformers' nostalgia, the reality of the penitentiary was much closer to the values of the nineteenth than the eighteenth century.

NOTES AND QUESTIONS

1. Do you find anything familiar in the cast of mind of nineteenth-century reformers who saw the decline in family discipline as the source of deviance in society? Does Rothman believe that this was what produced criminals? If the reformers who sought to induce the deviants they studied to offer pre-packaged accounts of broken families, in order to fit within the reformers' penological theories, does this cast doubt upon their philosophy of institutional reform? Why do you suppose that Rothman describes the outlook of the "innovators" who "discovered" the asylum (by which is meant not only penitentiaries for the criminal, but also hospitals for the insane, almshouses for the poor, orphanages for homeless children, and reformatories for delin-

quents) as "utopian?" Do you agree? What, then, do you make of suggestions, such as that from the former Speaker of the House of Representatives, Newt Gingrich, that we ought to resurrect institutions such as orphanages as a means of dealing with the problem of disturbed and delinquent youth?

2. How do you account for the fact that in retrospect both the "Pennsylvania" and "New York" systems seem similar to us, but engendered such fierce debate on the part of their respective proponents? Why do you suppose the American prison so captured the European imagination? What do you make of the fact that the great rumination on American democracy which you dipped into earlier, by Alexis de Tocqueville, grew out of his visit to study American prisons? After having contemplated the differing cultural systems of North and South, do you now believe that Tocqueville's immersion in the philosophy and culture of Northern "reform" may have colored his view of America?

3. Southern critics of Northern prisons found the Auburn "reforms" to be a "refined cruelty." Do you agree? Do you find noble or base the idea of the reformers that there could be such things as a "moral science" of prison architecture? How about the notion that practices in the prison could serve as a moral beacon for the rest of society? From what you know of prison conditions today, how could the nineteenth century reformers believe what they did? Consider, for example, the good Reverend James B. Finley, who believed that all society could be significantly improved if put on "prison fare" for two or three generations. Are something of the ideals, and perhaps the limitations, of Finley's beliefs revealed by his suggestion that a world-wide prison regimen would hasten the achievement of the "grandiose goals" of "peace, right, and Christianity?" Why or why not would these be acceptable American goals today?

4. If you had to choose between the New York "Auburn" or "congregate" and the "Pennsylvania" or "separation" prison systems, which would you choose, and how would you go about justifying your position? Which system would you say was more in keeping with the spirit of the legal doctrinal reforms which you studied in the preceding chapters? In particular, do you find telling the criticism of the Pennsylvania plan on the grounds that "it was so unnatural that it bred insanity?" Why would the presumably sane Pennsylvania reformers advocate such a system? If it was true, however, that the New York or "Auburn" system promised basically the same reforms as the Pennsylvania system, and was cheaper in the bargain, which system would you have expected eventually to triumph? Is this consistent or inconsistent with the progress of criminal justice in the South? Does the philosophy that led to the "lockstep," a curious fusion of military discipline and social debasement, suggest any similarities between the convict lease system of the South and the "reforms" of the North? Did they, in Hindus's words, serve "similar functions?"

It appears that the Northern "reforms" may have eventually suffered a fate similar to the Southern attempts to create a perfect system for criminal justice. These are Edward L. Ayers's conclusions about the state of late-nineteenth century prison reform in the North:

> The Northern delegates to the national prison congresses of the late nineteenth century did not exude the confidence of their antebellum predecessors. The penitentiaries of the North, after all, had suffered their own decades of decline and scandal. "One string is harped upon *ad nauseum*—money, money, money," complained one reader of prison reports in the Gilded Age. "The directors of a bank or a railroad could hardly be more anxious for large dividends than these gentlemen are for good round incomes from the labor of their prisoners. Where one word is spoken for reformation, hundreds are spoken for revenue." The Pennsylvania penitentiary, which had built its worldwide reputation on strict isolation, began to pile prisoners into shared cells. Some reformers expressed interest in a new system of prison discipline from Ireland based on incentives for early release, but few Northern penitentiaries adopted the method. Legislators in Ohio remained unimpressed with this "mere theory," and invoked language used by their Southern contemporaries: most criminals, despite all the programs officials implemented for their reformation, left prison "as hardened and as dangerous to the State as they were when they were sentenced." * * *

Vengeance and Justice, at 220.

5. What does it mean to declare, as Rothman does, that "for all the reformers' nostalgia, the reality of the penitentiary was much closer to the values of the nineteenth than the eighteenth century?" In particular, does it suggest a flaw in the reformers' basic theory, that by using the "asylum," by placing deviants in specially-designed institutions, they could be rehabilitated, in model environments which the rest of society could then emulate? As we will see in the next chapter, social strife in America increased dramatically in the late nineteenth century, and it appeared that the promise of "asylums" for the treatment of social deviants was never fulfilled. One possible explanation for the failure of such institutions was that the reformers' basic assumptions about human nature, about the rehabilitative capacity of social deviants were incorrect. As the nineteenth century wore on, the view that there was something fundamentally different about criminals and social deviants gained ground, and our next topic is that particular theory. Does it seem, in its spirit, closer to the culture of the antebellum North or South?

6. Rothman's widely-praised and prize-winning study of the rise of the asylum has been recognized as a model work in intellectual history, although it has been subject to friendly criticism for neglecting the empirical and social data on which the reformers' assumptions rested. For thoughtful reflections on Rothman's work and for more on nineteenth-century "Prison Science," see Adam Jay Hirsch, The Rise of the Penitentiary: Prisons and Punishment in Early America (1992), and Samuel Walker, Exploring the Roots of Our Criminal Justice Systems, 81 Mich.Law Rev. 946 (1983).

CRAIG HANEY, CRIMINAL JUSTICE AND THE NINETEENTH CENTURY PARADIGM: THE TRIUMPH OF PSYCHOLOGICAL INDIVIDUALISM IN THE "FORMATIVE ERA"*

6 Law and Human Behavior 191, 209–218, 221–226 (1982).

For most of the nineteenth century, psychological individualism was part of a shared common sense, endorsed by the public, legal professionals, and social scientists alike. As a common and captivating world view it diverted attention away from the structural and situational causes of behavior. Ironically, the legal system came to understand human problems in exclusively individualistic terms at precisely that point in American history at which powerful social and economic forces were transforming and reshaping American society. The behavioral assumptions of nineteenth-century American law translated social conflict into matters of personal aspiration, ability, and deviance. Nowhere was this more apparent than in the legal response to crime.

The legal impact of psychological individualism could be discerned clearly in the criminal law and in the criminal justice policies that evolved during the nineteenth century. Free will doctrine had been the centerpiece of the common law of crimes since before the advent of English liberalism. But it was greatly strengthened in America. Roscoe Pound * * * observed that "in the individualist society of the last century the individual free will was made the central point in the theory of law". And Leonard Levy * * * has described the "pervasive individualism" that underpinned the influential decisions of Chief Justice Shaw of the Massachusetts Supreme Judicial Court: "The cardinal principal of criminal jurisprudence is that a crime is the act of a voluntary and responsible agent who chooses between the lawful and the unlawful. From this standpoint, guilt, like sin, is personal because each man is the captain of his own conduct" * * *. People were assumed to intend the natural and probable consequences of their actions and they were most assuredly responsible for the acts that they performed. Of course, if autonomous individuals are seen as the causal locus of their own behavior, and if that behavior is regarded as deviant or undesirable, then the law must focus exclusively on those people—to punish, treat, or change them. This assumption, so self-evident to individualistic nineteenth-century America, was the basis of a "prison science" whose legacies are with us still.

As a theory of behavior, free will functioned as undifferentiated assumption: people *were* autonomous and free. The general psychology of the day served to buttress and confirm this assumption. People who were factually guilty of committing criminal acts were virtually always found legally responsible. Holmes * * * wrote that legal standards "take no ac-

* Reprinted from volume 6 of Law & Human Behavior, 1982, by permission of the publisher, Plenum Publishing Corporation, and the author.

count of incapacities, unless the weakness is so marked as to fall into well-known exceptions such as infancy or madness. They assume that every man is as able as every other to behave as they command" * * *. Except in rare (but sometimes celebrated) trials in which insanity was at issue, the substantive criminal law was relatively oblivious to various debates occurring in academic psychology during the nineteenth century. Beyond the assumption that individuals were the causal locus of behavior—a fact virtually undisputed in nineteenth century psychology—the criminal law avoided questions of exact causation. However, the same could not really be said about criminal justice and penal policy during this period. Here the question of *whether* someone was criminally responsible was separated from the question of *what consequences* should befall those who were. This latter question, a concern of social policy as much as substantive law, was intimately connected to more specific nineteenth-century conceptions of human nature.

Especially during the second half of the nineteenth century, a growing number of people were united by the bond of professed expertise on matters of crime and prison. Clergy, judges, politicians, prison administrators, physicians, and social reformers all met to discuss the problem of crime and to propose solutions. In 1870 they formed the National Prison Association, whose members included luminaries like Teddy Roosevelt and William Jennings Bryan. The Association met in a yearly "congress" to hear papers and debate current issues of criminal justice policy. These "prison scientists" had close ties to the social scientists of the day. Indeed, the National Prison Association was an outgrowth of the American Social Science Association, and both groups were united by the mantle of "science" they had adopted. Together they believed that society's ills could be ameliorated by a stiff dose of "sound thinking." For them, the crises faced by late nineteenth-century America were ones of personal shortcoming and irrationality rather than social structure, politics, or economics.

In 1888, a standing committee on prison discipline told the members of the National Prison Association that

> . . . a new school of criminalists has arisen, moved equally by benevolence, broad enough to include society as well as the criminal, advocating more thorough and scientific treatment of offenders; a theory that finds expression in habitual criminal acts in several of the states, in the advocacy and enactment of the so-called indeterminant sentence laws, and in providing the modern reformatory prisons * * *.

Ten years later, Zebulon Brockway told this same body that "[p]rison science is working out as it can, in the present progress a methodical system of penology which is in accord with the true science of our common human nature" * * *

The perspectives which underlay this new criminal and prison science was a natural extension of nineteenth-century individualism: crime was seen as a product of the defective traits of individual criminals. At the annual meeting of the National Conference of Charities and Correction in 1910, Professor Maurice Parmlee was warmly received when he advocated what had by then become a familiar theme: "the sciences of sociology, physiology, medicine, and psychology furnish data and methods which cannot be ignored by the criminologist and penologist" since "the delinquent is what he is largely because of physical or mental abnormalities." And one reporter present at the meeting felt "the whole discussion rather tended toward the impression that the day may come when we shall consider all criminality as synonymous with feeble-mindedness".

The "scientific" inspiration for these beliefs was Cesare Lombroso and his theory of the "born criminal type." His best known work, first published in 1876, detailed his thesis that criminals were a distinct anthropological type, distinguishable from others by their inherited physical characteristics. In a well-known passage, he described his discovery:

> In 1870 I was carrying on for several months researches in the prisons and asylums of Pavia upon cadavers and living persons, in order to determine upon substantial differences between the insane and criminals, without succeeding very well. At last I found in the skull of a brigand a very long series of atavistic anomalies, above all an enormous middle occipital fossa and a hypertrophy of the vermis analogous to those that are found in inferior vertebrates. At the sight of these strange anomalies the problem of the nature and of the origin of the criminal seemed to me resolved; the characteristics of primitive men and of inferior animals must be reproduced in our times. Many facts seemed to confirm this hypothesis, above all the psychology of the criminal; the frequency of tattooing and of professional slang; the passions as much more fleeting as they are more violent, above all that of vengeance; the lack of foresight which resembles courage which alternates with cowardice, and idleness which alternates with the passion for play and activity * * *.

As a technical and seemingly scientific basis for the treatment of the socially unfit, Lombroso's "born criminal" theory meshed nicely with the prevailing social Darwinism. Consistent with the individualism of the times, both theories located the determinants of behavior almost exclusively within the persons who performed it. Although Lombroso's theory never won complete acceptance in the United States, its basic assumptions were highly influential. Even most of his ardent critics agreed that crime stemmed from the disordered character of criminals, and disputes centered only on technical matters like the origins of these defects or the specific kinds of physical deformities that separated the criminal type from normals. When William Noyes (1888) published a paper in the

Journal of Social Science allegedly documenting the cranial deformities of criminals, for example, the Prison Discipline Committee of the National Prison Association (1888) acknowledged his work by commenting:

> . . . Whatever may be thought of the particular points mentioned, all who have carefully observed criminals must agree with him that there are anatomical and physiological peculiarities of the real criminal, evidences of degeneration—possible atavistic degeneration that suggest traits of savagery in his habits and customs * * *.

Twenty-five years later, in a long-awaited and elaborate study of 3000 English convicts that was heralded as "devastating" to Lombroso's theory, Charles Goring (1913) essentially agreed that criminals were physically and mentally inferior, questioning only the extent of these inferiorities and whether they were measurable in the way Lombroso had claimed.

Even attempts to explicitly acknowledge the role of external, environmental variables in crime causation drifted invariably towards the dispositional and individualistic. For example, Richard Dugdale (1881) began an *Atlantic Monthly* article on the "origins of crime in society" by noting that "[i]n the study of the causes which regulate the existence of crime, the first influence to be taken into account is that of the environment". But here is his description of the "environmental" influence of unemployment:

> . . . Usually during the period of crises the operatives are selectively dismissed from employment, those turned off being less skillful, less reliable, less honest, less steady, or less industrious than the workmen who are retained. The discharged men thus approximate nearer to the savage type. Famine, an essential condition of savage life, looms up before them, and becomes to those most closely allied to the savage character their most effective temptation . . .

For the new prison scientists, especially in America, the origins of criminal characteristics mattered far less than their personal conviction that such criminal traits existed and that something could be done about them. As Brockway (1899) put it:

> . . . It is unimportant for any practical purpose to find the relation of heredity and environment to the degeneracy of prisoners. It is enough to know that they are defective. Their improvement must be accomplished by the same means and methods whether heredity or environment predominates as causes of criminal conduct.

Attention was thus focused on the *dimensions* of these defects rather than their origins. Prison scientists repeatedly emphasized the importance of systematically assessing the personalities, character, and dispositions of prisoners. For example, Gaylord B. Hubbell, warden of Sing Sing, wrote in his annual report to the New York Prison Association in 1866 that a "careful system of classification should be made, based on marks, honestly given according to their character, conduct, industry, and obedience * * *." Like all "sciences," the first step of this new penology was to be the classification of its subject matter. And as the law had classified crimes, so the prison scientists could classify criminals. For the next fifty years, prisons throughout the country adopted and implemented such systems. Prison scientists were sure that such data would reveal the similarities of character among persons who had committed similar kinds of crime. Eventually, they thought, certain kinds of treatment would be found to be effective for certain kinds of criminals, by virtue of their common characters.

By the turn of the century, it had become the search for psychological traits rather than physical anomaly that preoccupied most criminalists. Fink * * * suggests that the "tremendous activity in psychological research in America" helped to undermine the belief in a criminal type whose distinguishing marks were physical: "a criminal with certain mental characteristics . . . had replaced the physical type". The larger significance of Lombroso's "criminal type," however, was not diminished by this shift from the physical to the psychological. Indeed, Norval Morris (1951) has written that ". . . it is to Lombroso's everlasting credit that his work turned men's minds to the consideration of the criminal as an individual requiring scientific investigation" and suggested that it was this consideration that led to the "incursion of psychiatry into criminology". The incursion was not restricted to criminology. By 1915, for example, the New York City police department had developed a "Police Psychopathic Laboratory" staffed by psychological professionals to assess the personalities of suspected criminals even before they appeared in court.

* * *

The source of crime was in the nature of criminals. As Judge Charlton Lewis (1899) wrote in the pages of the *Yale Law Journal,* "[t]he convict is commonly defective in mind, often in body; and his particular defects must be studied by those who would supply or remove them". The modern reformatory, Lewis told his readers, focuses upon the "physical, intellectual and moral defects which mark its inmates and which have brought them there, and seeks to remove these by enforcing cleanliness, education, and habits of truth, self-control and industry". Brockway (1898), who was the recognized expert on these matters, asserted without qualification that "[p]risoners generally belong to the grade of humanity that is inferior. The whole prison population may be divided in this connection into two grades of inferiority, those whose defectiveness is very apparent and others whose mental and moral defects are concealed under good and sometimes quite brilliant capabilities".

Hereditarian and exclusively biological explanations for crime never entirely dominated American consciousness. For one, scientific attempts to document them continually failed. Perhaps more importantly, there was something overly exculpatory about them. If some persons were actually *born* criminal, then they couldn't really help what they did. Especially in a society that so highly valued individuals and autonomy, this was an unpopular prospect * * *. Finally, an hereditarian theory of criminality was a theory of despair, for how could one hope to purge defective genes of their criminal propensities? Such a theory would have left little for the enthusiastic new prison scientists to do in their increasingly populous and elaborate reformatories.

Instead, a kind of compromise was achieved in the idea that crime was *sickness*. This notion emphasized the extreme, even physical, differences between criminals and the rest of society, but implied also that the condition was a potentially curable one. This view also conveyed the appropriate measure of guarded ambivalence about the question of personal responsibility which seemed to turn then (as now) to some degree on the generality of the "illness" and the patient's complicity in contracting it. Disease theories of crime were not generally thought to be exculpatory, in part because of the individualistic way in which "disease" was regarded. Susan Sontag (1978) explains that "[i]n the nineteenth century the notion that the disease fits the patient's character, as the punishment fits the sinner, was abandoned for the notion that it expresses the character. It is a product of will". Sickness could be used to impute a heavy moral burden. "Ceasing to consider disease as a punishment which fits the objective moral character, making it an expression of the inner self, might seem less moralistic. But this view turns out to be just as, or even more, moralistic and punitive". Thus, criminals could be "sick" but they would also be "responsible." Little contradiction was felt in blaming and punishing criminals for contracting the disease at the same time as trying to cure them of it. Henry Boies (1901), for example, based his "science of penology" on the notion that crime was a manifestation of "the disease of criminality in the individual." Indeed, one of his central theorems or "positive laws of penology" was that "criminality is a diseased condition of the human character". But another central theorem was that "the cause of crime is the moral depravity of the criminal".

The term "moral insanity" was employed during this period for persons whose psychological defects rendered them unable to conform their conduct to the moral dictates of society. Charles Rosenberg (1968) notes that "[m]edical men and pioneer social scientists were, during the 1880's and 1890's, particularly devoted to biological and mechanistic explanations of human behavior. . . . The born epileptic, or insane, or atavistic criminal was becoming a cliche in the writings of 'progressive' sociologists, psychiatrists, and penologists". Both the public and the law accepted the individualism of these theories but resisted the implications of physiology. Biological theories of crime gave physical substance to individualism, not absolution to "offenders." The reactions of the public were not lost on the practitioners. Rosenberg reports that "[p]sychologists, while still anxious to have their specialty recognized as a science, must, one spokesman for the establishment warned, guard against the 'imputation of having contributed to the demoralization of society' ". Indeed, for most of the nineteenth century insanity itself was seen in terms of moral failure—"a result of willful disregard for widely shared moral norms".

The crime-as-sickness theory manifested itself at times in the form of explicit disease explanations, but more often in the use of medical metaphors in discussions of crime. For example, in his introduction to Beaumont and d'Tocqueville's report on the penitentiary in America, Francis Lieber captured the flavor of these metaphors:

> Prisons have been called hospitals for patients laboring under moral diseases, but until recently, they have been [more like] the plague houses of the East, in which every person afflicted with that mortal disorder is sure to perish, and he who is sent there without yet being attacked is sure to have it * * *.

Some years later, Zebulon Brockway (1869) developed this theme, absent its critical implication. In a report he made to the New York legislature when he was superintendent of the Detroit House of Correction, he wrote that all persons "whose moral deformity makes them a public offense" should be confined in institutions "until they are cured—when a relapse occurs, the patient may be placed under treatment again, as would be the case if he were afflicted with a relapse of contagious disease or mental malady". In a career that lasted another forty years, during which time he became the most highly respected and influential "prison scientist" in America, Brockway never deviated from this perspective. In 1898, for example, he told the Indianapolis Prison Congress that "[t]he criminal is the bacillus of society and the crime is the symptom of society's endemic disease". And in 1910, in his invited address to the International Prison Conference in Washington, he predicted that the

> reformatory of the future will be a "moral orthopedic institute" where deformed and wayward feet are straightened out and put in proper paths; and it will be a laboratory for the study of socially dangerous human defectiveness—a research station for discovering the anti-social bacilli and at the same time for searching for nature's counteracting serum.

* * *

Disease imagery emerged frequently in the discussion of the *indeterminate sentence*—a criminal justice reform that was first seriously proposed in the late nineteenth century and adopted in a number of jurisdictions in the early twentieth. In a speech given to the National Prison Association in 1902, for example, Justice John Franklin Fort told them that the "proper way to cure those who are really criminal is as you cure other diseased persons; namely, keep them under treatment until they are cured, or at least so nearly cured that they may be discharged safely" * * *. "A Prisoner," writing in the *Atlantic Monthly* told his lay audience that indeterminate sentencing would eliminate fixed prison terms. Instead he explained, prisoners would remain in prison "until cured, just as a person suffering from physical disease or infection is sent to a hospital or asylum, to remain for such period as may be necessary for his restoration to health" * * *

The debate over indeterminate sentencing made clear the extent to which the personality of the prisoner had become the focus of the criminal justice system. Charltan Lewis (1899) suggested that "[t]o the sound social thinker there are no degrees in crime, there are only grades of character". And in a letter to Professor John H. Wigmore concerning the National Conference on Criminal Law and Criminology, Lombroso had written

> . . . [i]f I could offer any suggestion to so competent a body of men, it would be to emphasize the importance of apportioning penalties, not according to the offense, but according to the offender. To this end the probation system, which it is the great credit of America to have introduced, should be extended so as to suit the offender's type and individuality * * *.

Since personality and not crime *per se* was at issue, it was not long before some prison scientists proposed that certain persons should be incarcerated because of their personal characteristics, in the absence of any criminal acts. Walter Fernald (1909), for example, hoped for the day when "criminals who have committed no crime" would be identified at a very early age, "before they have acquired facility in crime," so that they could be "permanently taken out of the community and given life-long care and supervision in special institutions, combining the educational and developmental methods of a school for the feeble-minded with the industry and security of a modern penal institution." Fernald was correct in observing that his proposal was "only a rational extension of the principal of indeterminate sentence". Both were the products of a psychological individualism that located the source of criminality exclusively in the nature of isolated individuals.

Debate over the indeterminate sentencing movement placed prison science in some conflict with legal science, however, for it sought to wrest sentencing discretion from judges and place it in the hands of prison administrators. The Prison Discipline Committee told the National Prison Association (1888) that they should be "studying the criminal instead of the crime." They proposed that prisoners be classified according to character type, so that they could be better rehabilitated. Legal formalities like the severity of the crime for which they were convicted were to be ignored:

> . . . But upon what basis shall such a classification be made? Shall it be upon the statutory grade or real gravity of their crimes? No. Upon their age? No. Upon their conduct as it relates to prison rules? No; not altogether. Shall it be upon their ascertained character? To this we answer, Yes. . . .

And C.R. Henderson, who would succeed Brockway as President of the National Prison Association, wrote about the "importance of basing all social treatment on the nature of the criminal rather than the artificial distinctions of the codes which notice only acts" * * *. When the Congress of Criminal Anthropology met in Paris in 1889, the connection of the indeterminate sentence to the prevailing social science was clear:

> Uniformity of punishment is a manifest absurdity . . . The old criminal law only recognized two terms, the *offence* and the *punishment.* The new criminology recognises three terms, the *crime,* the *criminal,* and the *method of repression.* Criminal laws . . . must not be treated as a detached and isolated science; it must be subordinated to psychology and anthropology, or it will be powerless to interpret and to determine, in any enlightened legislation, the true classification of criminals * * *.

By 1899 a criminal court judge could ask the readers of the *Yale Law Journal*

> If students of humanity trained in the work of searching the character . . . who are in daily, hourly intercourse with their wards for the sole purpose of preparing them to be free may still be deceived in them, what shall we say of the judge who sees the prisoner for an hour or a day at his bar and whose knowledge of him is carefully limited to the single act of which he is accused? * * *

* * *

By the late nineteenth century, not sterilization but imprisonment had become American society's response to serious crime. [In addition to its hereditarian basis, sterilization was sometimes advocated for criminals on simple punishment grounds (especially as retribution for sexual crimes) and also as a therapeutic (on the theory that sexual passion aroused in some persons a generalized excitement that resulted in crime).] The wrenching social changes and dislocations that occurred during the century produced a widespread "search for order" * * *. Deviation was less tolerated as it became more threatening. The task of Victorian culture in America, John Higham (1969) suggests, was to create "a framework of order within and—so to speak—around American individualism". There was no better way to do so than through law and prisons.

* * *

By the 1870s, however, widespread confidence that badly needed order and stability could be found or imposed through institutions had waned. The forces of social and economic change had gained significantly in magnitude and momentum. People were no longer as concerned with reversing or stopping the trend of urbanization and industrialization as they were with surviving it. The harder it became for everyone to adapt, the more important it became for deviants to conform. Mechanic (1969) writes that "[i]ndustrial and technological change . . . coupled with increasing urbanization brought decreasing tolerance for bizarre and disruptive behavior and less ability to contain deviant behavior within the existing social structure" * * *. Earlier in the century, the discipline, regularity, and routinization of institutional life promised to instill work habits required by the developing factory system. As the century progressed, however, this possibility declined in significance. The working classes had become increasingly accustomed to factory routines and, for many, public schools acted to instill factory work habits and ethics. It became more reasonable to assume that those who had not yet fit in, would not.

The nature of the criminal problem seemed increasingly intractable, despite the numerous "scientific" theories generated to account for it. At times, a seemingly confident rhetoric of change and rehabilitation existed side-by-side with theories that located the source of deviance in the blood or the genes. With habitual criminal statutes came the first signs that this new society was quite willing to "give up" on those it could not make conform. The most prevalent early theories had been more encouraging. But the century had witnessed a transition from early utopian aspirations in which reformatories would act as exemplars of order and regularity, to the enthusiasm of rehabilitation experts who would completely rid society of the disease of crime, and finally to an increased willingness to concede in many cases that containment and isolation were quite enough.[53]

Amid changes in the surface rhetoric of "prison science," however, its basic message remained constant. The very first prisons, like the ones that would follow, were expressions of an ultimately individualistic ideology. Their early advocates believed that society could be reformed by demonstrations of changes brought about in individuals. Of course, they had been naive about the momentum of social changes that were occurring in the society around them, and about the power of those persons in whose interest it was to promote such changes. To certain segments of society crime and deviance were a regrettable but certainly tolerable price to pay for the "release of energy" that preoccupied nineteenth-century economic developers. The price was all the more tolerable when its pay-

[53] This is not to say that the rehabilitative ideal was relinquished; it was merely modified. Rehabilitation continued to be the prevailing ideal, with practical provisions having been made for those who could not or would not respond. The distinction between "born" and "occasional" criminals permitted prison administrators to both claim credit for successes and eschew responsibility for failures.

ment could be localized in and upon the poor, who suffered doubly as targets of criminal justice processing and as the victims of its failures. And, contrary to the intentions of their earliest advocates, prisons conveyed a powerful lesson that quickly diverted attention away from the social structural causes of crime to exclusively person-centered causes. Armed with individualizing psychological theories, prison scientists convinced a receptive public that the ultimate solutions to the crime problem were to be found in the nature of criminals.

In fact, these first prisons had not only focused the attention of the community on individual criminals but required criminals to focus attention inwardly on themselves. In its emphasis on introspection, this form of punishment was supremely individualistic. The nineteenth century's "great debate" between competing schools of American penology—the Pennsylvania and Auburn camps—concerned the efficacy of complete isolation versus a system that allowed comingling but enforced silence. Not surprisingly, the idea that crime reflected rather than caused community disorder was soon forgotten. * * *

To be sure, "prison science" underwent several transformations during the nineteenth century; newly hypothesized causes of crime begat different forms of treatment. From solitude and religious reflection, to labor and hard work, followed by education and finally psychotherapy, the specific prescriptions continued to change. But each new phase retained the previous one's emphasis on order and discipline, since it was personal disorder and the lack of individual discipline that were the clearest symptoms of the crime problem. * * *

The most stable feature of nineteenth-century criminal justice policy was still the way in which the individual prisoner remained the exclusive focus of its cure. The terms employed for the prison form—"penitentiary," "reformatory," "house of correction"—reflected its person-changing perspective. Later in the century when classification or grading schemes divided prisoners into categories—"occasional criminals" susceptible to change, "habitual criminals" who were not—attention was still focused upon the actor. If only specific prison treatments could be better matched to the individual character of the offender, *then,* the public was told, imprisonment would work.

In the nineteenth century, American society embraced prisons as its solution to the problem of crime. Between 1850 and 1890 the *per capita* rate of persons confined to prisons increased *500* percent * * *. By 1894 the National Conference of Charities and Corrections listed 363 state benevolent, penal, and reformatory institutions in the United States. The institutional response was not confined to adults: the New York City House of Refuge, the first institution for children convicted of crime, was established in 1824 and by 1900 there were 65 such reformatories for children in the country * * *.

Proliferation of correctional institutions certainly cannot be explained in terms of their efficacy or success. Indeed, the evils and failures of prisons were apparent soon after their inception. Eventually prisoners themselves began to raise legal claims based on the adverse consequences of imprisonment. For example, an Iowa prisoner sued the county for injuries to his health allegedly sustained because of unsafe conditions in the jail where he had been kept * * *. And, in 1907, a California prisoner named Jacob Oppenheimer offered an insanity defense (to an assault charge that could have gotten him the death penalty) that was based on the psychological effects of the extreme conditions of his confinement in San Quentin prison.

As believers in the principle that deviance was the product of individual defect and degeneracy, however, prison administrators and criminal justice officials were largely insensitive to the deleterious effects that these institutional environments had on those locked inside. If a convict's behavior worsened, it was because his criminal "illness" was more serious than it had at first appeared. The public accepted this one-sided analysis, perhaps in part because of the psychological message such institutions convincingly conveyed. The larger, more intimidating, and more inhumane prisons became, the more deserving of such treatment became the persons kept within them. Taken to such dark and frightening places, prisoners must be that much in need of segregation and quarantine. This marriage of individual cause and institutional solution produced a cycle of self-justification that was impervious to effective critique and change. The problem of crime had been defined in such a way that it admitted to no alternative approach. As Foucault (1977) observes, "prison had always been offered as its own remedy; the reactivation of the penitentiary techniques as the only means of overcoming their perpetual failure; the realization of the corrective project as the only method of overcoming the impossibility of implementing it".

The continued and overwhelming acceptance of these institutions was based on several additional factors as well. During the nineteenth century, a class of criminal justice professionals was created whose status and wellbeing depended upon the existence of prisons. They were active and effective advocates of imprisonment, and facile at explaining away its apparent failures. For a short time, moreover, prisons even offered the promise of being profitable enterprises. By employing inmates, in the name of instilling the work ethic, prisons produced numerous goods that were later sold at a profit. Productivity was high enough that several states passed laws at the turn of the century restricting the sale of convict-made goods. Clearly, then, the expectation of personal gain motivated some advocates to sell and defend the idea of imprisonment. Once built, of course, considerable inertia attached to these institutions. Concrete and steel monuments to the individualist ideology on which they were premised, society developed a substantial economic investment in them. * * *

Perhaps more than an economic commitment, however, people developed an intellectual investment in prisons. Not long after the first prisons were built, people turned to them almost naturally, as though there was not, and could not be, any other solution to crime. Prisons have been called "the detestable solution, which one seems unable to do without" (Foucault, 1977 * * *); and it was during the nineteenth century that they rose to the level of a necessity. Our intellectual investment in them can only be understood in terms of the psychological individualism of this era.

Completion of the movement from status to contract signaled the individualization of legal relationships between people and it enabled the market system to better render human resources into economic commodities. Persons whose behavior undermined the productivity of others, or decreased the efficiency of the marketplace, could not be countenanced as easily. Thus, specialized institutions served another important function by relieving the burdens of working people who were not able to care for those who were inconvenient, troublesome, or who appeared unfit * * *. The death of local community meant that there were few other ways for these problems to be addressed on a widespread basis. The demands of productivity and efficiency would restrict the personal time family members could devote to any solutions that involved them directly. It soon seemed not only tolerable but necessary to confine deviants inside institutions.

Person-centered institutions like prisons also defined the problem of deviance in terms that restricted its social implication. By localizing crime in the personalities of those who committed it, a policy of political containment was virtually assured. Calvin Woodard (1962) summarizes the nature of this circumscription: "[T]his approach inevitably subordinated amoral aspects of worldly phenomena (including economic causes and consequences) to their moral aspects (the imprudent conduct, the lack of virtue and bad character) of man" * * *. The beneficiaries of this containment, of course, were those who controlled the "amoral aspects of worldly phenomena" and profited by their laissez-faire nonregulation.

In prisons the nineteenth century's theory of behavior had been literally institutionalized. By the time exacting and detailed critiques were offered, it was too late. Social scientists of the early twentieth century could decry the institutions their predecessors had helped to build, and reject the theories on which they had been premised, but to no avail. Too much had been invested in prisons, and the psychological lesson taught by their awesome presence was now too well learned to be abandoned.

NOTES AND QUESTIONS

1. Consider the concept of "psychological individualism," which is said to be the cornerstone of nineteenth-century criminal justice policy. Is it a concept you find congenial? What, if anything, are the alternatives? Is the idea of

individual social responsibility one which you found inherent in the antebellum criminal justice institutions of the North or South? Is it an idea that is now dominant in criminal justice? For a panoramic review of the foibles of American attempts to control crime, see Lawrence Friedman, Crime and Punishment in American History (1993), which should now be the standard reference on the history of American criminal law. Friedman's perspective is similar to that of Haney, but for a spirited statement of the philosophy that Haney and Friedman question—that individual morality is important, objective, and subject to a kind of orthopedics, see James Q. Wilson, The Moral Sense (1993).

2. You may have been a bit skeptical about the notion of a "born criminal type," the "scientific" conclusion reached by that giant of nineteenth century criminology Cesare Lombroso. Why do you suppose this notion is greeted with skepticism today? Have we abandoned the "scientific" basis on which it rested?

Haney suggests that the idea of "born criminals" meshed nicely with the prevailing "Social Darwinism" of the late nineteenth century. "Social Darwinism" was that set of beliefs which suggested that there ought to be a minimum of interference on the part of government with the economy and society, so that the fittest characters would have the freedom they needed to demonstrate their superiority. Social Darwinists believed that in this way the best men and women could prevail in the social world, as the fittest animal species were able to survive in the animal world. "Social Darwinism" owed its inspiration to the phenomenal popular success of Charles Darwin's Origin of Species (1859), his treatise on evolution and natural selection ("survival of the fittest" in Herbert Spencer's phrase) in the plant and animal kingdoms.

In late nineteenth century America and England the main thrust of Social Darwinist theory was to support the capitalist free market, and encourage a "laissez-faire" attitude on the part of American state and federal legislatures. Is this idea of "Social Darwinism," then, one that could co-exist comfortably with a "reformist" prison science? In particular, if it seemed that "criminals" were the product of physical defects, why were the prison scientists so optimistic that criminals could be cured? Why did the "physical defect" theory never really become fully accepted among Americans?

3. The alternative to Lombroso's theory and those like it, of course, is that the criminal is created not by heredity, but by the environment. Which seems more likely to you? Alas, this is a debate that still goes on today, with conflicting solutions to the problems of criminal justice. Do you think that those late nineteenth century "prison scientists" who believed that the "improvement" of prisoners "must be accomplished by the same means and methods whether heredity or environment predominates" were on the right track? Do you think that the approach of psychology or psychiatry, the idea that crime is somehow the product of a "social disease," holds any more promise for the treatment of criminals than does the "physical defect" approach of Lombroso? Do they share a common weakness in that both rely on the study of defects in the individual? Do you understand how late nineteenth and ear-

ly twentieth century penologists could claim that criminals were "sick," but at the same time find them "responsible" for their criminal conduct?

4. Do you find the great nineteenth century "prison scientist" Zebulon Brockway persuasive when he argues that prisons could be "moral orthopedic institutes," where "deformed and wayward feet are straightened out and put in proper paths?"

What did Brockway mean when he said that prisons could be "research station[s] for discovering the anti-social bacilli and at the same time for searching for nature's counteracting serum?" Is that view consistent or inconsistent with the supposedly dominant nineteenth century view that criminals are individually responsible for their actions? How about the idea of "indeterminate sentencing" and the reform of "parole" (letting prisoners out before their sentences had run if they seemed to have been sufficiently rehabilitated)? Are these notions consistent with the dominant individualism of the period? Are they consistent with your views on how criminal justice ought to be administered? Do such ideas lead ineluctably to the notion that we can and should identify, isolate, and treat "criminals" even before they commit any crimes? Is that a notion that has contributed positively to world history?

For a good discussion of the reforms of indeterminate sentencing, parole, and probation, and the manner in which they were administered in the late nineteenth and early twentieth century see Lawrence M. Friedman, History, Social Policy, and Criminal Justice, Chapter Seven of D. Rothman, and S. Wheeler, eds., Social History and Social Policy 203 (1981). Friedman noted that recent trends were "turning back the clock," since "Most of the nineteenth century reforms have fallen into disrepute." Id., at 212. He suggested that both those who believed our criminal justice system was too harsh and those who believed it was too soft had combined to undermine the work of the "criminal scientists" of the late nineteenth and early twentieth centuries:

> * * * The indeterminate sentence is out of favor with both sides. Reformers feel it is arbitrary, harsh, and discriminatory. Prisoners complain of the "constant mental torture of never knowing how long you'll be here." The hard-liners, in turn, are afraid that it holds out too much hope for the criminal; they want definite (and harsh) punishments. California abolished indeterminate sentencing effective 1 July 1977 * * *, and replaced it with a system of flat sentences. For habitual criminals, or those who commit crimes under "aggravating" circumstances, the sentences can be very severe. How the new law will work out remains to be seen.
>
> Parole too, is increasingly under attack. Hard-liners contend that parole is a "compromise" with "the thug, the gangster, the killer and racketeer," who win "cut-rate penitentiary sentences." In practice, the parole board never functioned as ideally pictured; it never made calm, precise, individual decisions. On the one hand, it developed "guidelines" and rules of thumb. The inmate's hearing was nasty, brutish, and short. And, on the other hand, decisions were influenced (it was said) by "ignorance, pure caprice, bigotry, and other abuses of discretion." If parole

> boards can not or will not distinguish between inmates who reform and those who do not, then the parole system has lost its premises and should not survive. At least one state, indeed, has abolished it.*

Id., at 212–213. Do you favor the retention of indeterminate sentencing and parole? Friedman's conclusion is that "Once again, the emphasis has shifted, this time back to the offense itself. Neither hard-liners nor soft-liners have much faith in rehabilitation, in treating the individual." Id., at 214.

5. Do you believe, as Haney suggests, that there may be an inherent conflict between "prison science" and "legal science?" Can a system that hopes to govern by an established "rule of law" which applies to all, coexist easily with a set of principles which suggest that the focus ought to be on "the criminal" and not the "crime?" Historically, in America, which view has prevailed? Which should? Recall the debate over the federal common law of crimes, and Justice Chase's difficulty in the *Worrall* case with a federal jurisdiction which would permit judges to determine crimes and fix punishments. Is there a problem in the "reforms" of parole and indeterminate sentencing that recalls the late-eighteenth century democratic criticism of common law crimes?

6. The last part of the reading from Haney is a summary of the path travelled by prison theory during the course of the nineteenth century, primarily from a utopian belief that prisons could serve as moral beacons for the rest of society to a saddened pragmatic conclusion that they ought to serve as warehouses for the congenitally unfit. If prisons failed to perform on their original promise, why do we keep them as our primary means of dealing with habitual criminals? What does the history of penology in the nineteenth century tell us about the underlying reasons for the existence of legal institutions? Bear this conclusion in mind when you read the excerpt from Oliver Wendell Holmes Jr.'s The Common Law (1881), in Chapter Six.

Note that Haney argues that whatever the shifting justifications for prisons in the course of the nineteenth century, there were certain common elements to "prison science," in particular the common "exclusive focus" on treating the individual. Note that Haney suggests that prison reformers maintained with rugged tenacity that as soon as they could latch onto the proper way of matching treatment with the particular individual character of the offender "*then,* the public was told, imprisonment would work." What do you suppose Haney believes was the flaw in the reasoning of the nineteenth century reformers? Why, in particular, according to Haney, did the public and the reformers fail to appreciate the deleterious effects on prisoners of prisons? You may be familiar with modern federal cases which have held that even a state's lowliest criminals are entitled to some civil rights, and that these include "humane treatment." As you may remember from your reading from Ayers, the failure of some states to accord these rights has resulted, in fact, in the virtual receivership of at least one state's prison system, which was, for a

* Reprinted from Chapter Seven of Social History and Social Policy, David J. Rothman and Stanton Wheeler, eds., © 1981 by Academic Press, Inc. by permission of the publisher and the author.

time, for all practical purposes, under the management of a federal court. Why do you suppose this came about, and is it of particular significance that it happened in the South?

7. In his concluding pages Haney quotes repeatedly from the then fashionable French social psychologist, historian, and philosopher Michel Foucault (1926–84). Foucault's turgid prose (translated from the French) is somewhat impenetrable, but there is a brilliant and exciting, powerful theoretical framework behind his analysis of prisons, expressed, for example, in the book Haney quotes from, Michel Foucault, Discipline and Punishment: The Birth of the Prison (A. Sheridan, Trans., 1977). Can you discern such a framework for criticism? Does it come from philosophy? From psychology? From Marxism? From all three? For an introductory analysis of Foucault's *oeuvre,* and, in particular, for an evaluation of the influence on him of Marx, Freud, and Nietzsche, see Barry Smart, Michel Foucault (1985).

8. When Haney concludes that "Completion of the movement from status to contract signalled the individualization of legal relationships between people and it enabled the market system to better render human resources into economic commodities," he is arguing in accordance with the theories of Foucault and other notable Marxist-influenced analysts of nineteenth century culture. Which "regional culture," North or South, had to travel the farthest in moving from "status to contract?" What is gained, and what is lost in such a move? Who wins and who loses? What, in Haney's views, are the "political" and "moral" implications of such legal and institutional change?

9. Consider further the work of Cesare Lombroso, the nineteenth century "scientist" of the "criminal type." Lombroso studied the physiognomy and other physical attributes of hundreds of criminals, and claimed that he had found that "born criminals" were physically different from most men, and were actually atavistic "throwbacks" to an earlier, less civilized period of human development. For an exhaustive treatment of Lombroso's theories, see the filiopietistic work by his daughter, Gina Lombroso Ferrero, Criminal Man According to the Classification of Cesare Lombroso (1911). Ms. Ferrero's paean to her father begins with praise for Cesare Beccaria, the great late-eighteenth century Italian jurist whose work was influential on Thomas Jefferson. You may remember the excerpt from Jefferson's Notes on Virginia you read, on criminal law, which was a direct result of Jefferson's absorption of Beccaria's ideas. Both sought to restrict the discretion of judges over punishment. Do you think that this is necessarily wise, or is this discretion itself a tool for accomplishing what apparently was Lombroso's goal, and that of many nineteenth century reformers, that the punishment fit the criminal rather than the crime? By the way, is this the goal which you think ought to be implemented in a system of criminal justice? What is the purpose of the criminal law? Is it to deter the commission of future crimes? Is it to segregate possible future offenders? Is it to "reform" the criminal, or is it, perhaps, to exact the "vengeance" of society?

These questions are still very live issues in public policy debates. Indeed, one of the important questions asked of the Presidential candidates in the fall of 1988 was whether they supported the death penalty in any cases. One candidate, Michael Dukakis, argued that the death penalty was not a significant deterrent, and, given our high regard for human life, ought not to be a permissible punishment. The other candidate, who won, George Bush, did not respond to the deterrence argument (although had he known about them, he could have cited some existing studies of the criminal law that do suggest the deterrent value of the death penalty), but simply argued that some crimes were so odious that the death penalty was justified. With whom do you agree?

10. Are you impressed with the approach of the group with which Lombroso identified himself, the "Modern, or Positive, School of Penal Jurisprudence," which "maintains that the anti-social tendencies of criminals are the result of their physical and psychic organization, which differs essentially from that of normal individuals?"

Do you share Cesare Lombroso's excitement at the discovery of the *median occipital fossa*, an unusual cavity, in the skull of Vilella, the "Italian Jack the Ripper?" Here, in his own words, is the thrill Cesare experienced as he sliced away at Vilella's corpse:

> At the sight of that skull, I seemed to see all of a sudden, lighted up as a vast plain under a flaming sky, the problem of the nature of the criminal—an atavistic being who reproduces in his person the ferocious instincts of primitive humanity and the inferior animals. Thus were explained anatomically the enormous jaws, high cheek-bones, prominent superciliary arches, solitary lines in the palms, extreme size of the orbits, handle shaped or sessile ears found in criminals, savages, and apes, insensitivity to pain, extremely acute sight, tattooing, excessive idleness, love of orgies, and the irresistible craving for evil for its own sake, the desire not only to extinguish life in the victim, but to mutilate the corpse, tear its flesh, and drink its blood.

"Introduction," by Cesare Lombroso, to Ferrero, supra, at xiv-xv. Do you believe there is a connection between things like "solitary lines in the palms, extreme size of the orbits, handle shaped or sessile ears" and "tattooing, excessive idleness, love of orgies, and the irresistible craving for evil for its own sake" that Lombroso seemed to suggest were linked in the life of criminals? Why did Lombroso believe what he did about "criminals?"

Alas, even Cesare Lombroso seems to have backed off from some of the more outlandish suggestions in this rich passage on Vilella's skull, eventually concluding, as his daughter reported, that "the criminal type" can be determined as well as by "disease and environment" as by atavism. Id., at 8. Nevertheless, to the end Lombroso believed in an atavistic "born criminal," such as Vilella, whose numbers made up fully one third "of the mass of offenders," and who, in fact, "constitute the most important part of the whole criminal army, partly because they are constantly appearing before the public and also because the crimes committed by them are of a particularly monstrous character." Ibid. Thus it is that Ms. Ferrero's book was still devoted to the "born criminal."

11. Do you believe in the notion of the "born criminal?" Can you cite your own anecdotal data which suggest, as Lombroso apparently believed, that a protruding lower facial area is common in criminal types, that dark hair and aquiline noses are common on murderers ("like the beak of a bird of prey"), that fleshy, swollen and protruding lips are to be found on murderers and the violators of women, or that long fingers, curly and woolly hair and thin straight lips are common on swindlers? How do you suppose all of this came to pass as science, and why does it not now? Are there some clues in Lombroso's casual linking of apes, "savages," "Negroes," and "born criminals?" In the idea of Lombroso's and other nineteenth century theorists that there are "existing inferior races of mankind?" At this point you might recall, as well, Michael Hindus's lament, at one point in the excerpts you read from Prison and Plantation, that "By the 1860's [even in the reform-minded Massachusetts], environmentalism, with its promise of reclamation, began to yield to the less flexible and less optimistic tenets of heredity and stock." Id., at xxviii. How do you explain the appeal of a thinker like Lombroso, even in Massachusetts?

12. A particular difficulty which seems to lie behind Lombroso's work is the problem of "evil." In the born criminal, he maintained, there are "outward and visible signs of a mysterious and complicated process of degeneration, which * * * evokes evil impulses that are largely of atavistic origin." Why should "evil" be atavistic in origin, and what does that particular view of evil mean for the treatment of crime? Under Lombroso's view of "criminal man," can the criminal be "cured?" For an alternative vision we have the work of another "modern" nineteenth century writer on criminal justice, Robert L. Dugdale.

13. Robert L. Dugdale's, The Jukes: A Study in Crime, Pauperism, Disease, and Heredity (1877), was a purportedly scientific study of seven generations of a family in New York, conducted pursuant to a resolution of the Prison Association of New York. Mr. Dugdale did exhaustive field work, including visits to thirteen county jails, and interviews with all available members of the clan he studied. His final data base included 709 people descended or married into the family of one "Max," born some time between 1720 and 1740, a descendant of the early Dutch settlers, "a hunter and fisher, a hard drinker, jolly and companionable, averse to steady toil," a man who worked hard "by spurts and idling by turns." He was reported to be the sire of many progeny, some of them illegitimate. His line continued in his ways, and illegitimacy, profligacy, licentiousness, and poverty were typical among his descendants. The flavor of Dugdale's analysis, and the manner in which Dugdale followed and charted the lines of descent in the family can be gathered by reproducing his comments on two "Cases" from the family, called the "Jukes":

> *Case 1.* Taking up the legitimate branch of Ada, which intermarried into Bell and Clara * * *, we follow the heredity of legitimacy in lines 6, 8, and 10, generation 5. They are three sisters, children of a legitimate father, * * * and a chaste and legitimate mother * * *, whose mother * * * was a chaste and legitimate daughter of Clara, who was chaste. Going

back to the father, we find his mother * * * was a chaste legitimate daughter of Clara. Both parents, therefore, of generation four, were of chaste descent on the mother's side. Thus the original characteristic of chastity seems to have descended from Clara through two branches * * * and cumulated in the three sisters under consideration. Further, we find * * * the sister of the above three to be a prostitute, and in going back upon the heredity we find that in generation 4 that the father's father was the licentious, though legitimate son of Ada, a harlot, and on the mother's side (generation 4) the father was the legitimate son of Bell, a prostitute. According to the law of heredity, it is a logical deduction to make, that line 7 [that of the fourth sister, a prostitute] has reverted to the ancestral types on the unchaste side of both parents. Respecting this case, very little reliable information has been gathered about the environment, but it must be noted that the mother in generation four was one of seven sisters, one of whom was idiotic, and no doubt licentious, and five others, harlots or prostitutes, one of them keeping a brothel; while, on the father's * * *, there was one sister who also kept a brothel. Whether this pair removed from the vicinity of their relations has not been learned, and what were the other particulars of their career are unknown. The case looks more like one of pure heredity than any that has been traced.

Case 2. Taking line 13, and following the heredity, we have (generation 6) two illegitimate children of a white woman. One of them was a mulatto girl, who died at one year old of syphilis, whose mother (generation 5) was a bastard prostitute, afflicted with the same disease, whose mother (generation 4) was a prostitute afflicted likewise in the constitutional form, inherited from her licentious father, whose mother Ada, was a harlot.

Now for the environment. The infant girl who died was conceived by the roadside, and born in the poor-house. Its mother (generation 5) was a vagrant child, her mother having no home for her. So neglected was she, that at seven years she was committed to the county jail for a misdemeanor. She was idle, disgustingly dirty, and for that reason could get no place as a servant, and as she must live, fell into the practice of prostitution. Her half-sister also had an illegitimate child, while other relations and acquaintances gave the example of profligacy. Her mother (generation 4) was married twice—then cohabited with the man who became this girl's father, and when he went to the war in 1863 and deserted her, she followed the example of her other four prostitute sisters, one of whom kept a brothel. Going back to the father (generation 3) we find him a soldier in the war of 1812, very licentious, whose two harlot sisters married mulattos. As this was a time when slavery existed in this State, the social condition under which this consorting took place is significant.

We have here an environment of three generations which corresponds to the heredity; this environment forming an example to the

> younger generation which must have been sufficient, without heredity, to stimulate licentious practices.

Id., at 20–21 (1877).

14. Even though Dugdale strongly suggested that licentious ancestors can end up influencing their descendants, he was not as pessimistic about "born criminals" as was Lombroso. Drawing on the theories about mental development from contemporary psychological treatises, Dugdale stated his belief that we can improve individuals' moral character, and thus society itself through education. Do you agree?

15. The introduction to the fourth edition of Dugdale's 1877 work, published in 1910, pointed out that *The Jukes* has "long been known as one of those important books that exert an influence out of all proportion to their bulk [it was only 120 pages long]. It is doubtful if any concrete study of moral forces is more widely known, or has provoked more discussion, or has incited a larger number of students to examine for themselves the immensely difficult problems presented by the interaction of 'heredity' with 'environment.' " Id., at iii. Why do you suppose that this study by Dugdale proved so immensely popular and influential? According to the 4th edition's introduction, by one Franklin H. Giddings, of Columbia University, "It is not too much to say that when the first edition of *The Jukes* was published, it was the best example of scientific method applied to a sociological investigation." Giddings states that Dugdale "had no hypothesis to verify, no theoretical antagonist to throw down. His mind was intent on discovering the truth, whatever it might turn out to be, and presenting it completely, clearly, and simply." Ibid. Do you agree with Giddings?

16. Giddings conceded, however, that many readers of *The Jukes* had taken Dugdale's work to be "a thorough-going demonstration of 'hereditary criminality,' 'hereditary pauperism,' 'hereditary degeneracy' and so on." Giddings sought to refute this reading of *The Jukes,* by declaring that "It is nothing of the kind, and its author never made such claim for it. He undoubtedly believed in the hereditary transmission of character tendencies, as of physical traits * * * [But, f]ar from believing that heredity is fatal, Mr. Dugdale was profoundly convinced that 'environment' can be relied on to modify, and ultimately to eradicate even such deep-rooted and wide-spreading growths of vice and crime as the 'Jukes' group exemplified." Id., at iv. Does the excerpt from Haney, or the work of Michel Foucault help you to understand why Dugdale might have believed that environment could eradicate the effects of heredity?

17. You may be able to catch, bubbling below the surface in the work of nineteenth century criminal scientists, like Dugdale or Lombroso, something like a tone of frenzied desperation, as a "cure" for crime is sought. The nineteenth century saw a radical rise in both private and public crime, with perhaps the most obvious manifestation being what was actually happening in the streets:

> The frequent riots that plagued antebellum American cities were the largest instances of social disorder crime. Between 1830 and 1860 at

least 35 major riots took place in the eastern cities of Baltimore, Philadelphia, New York, and Boston. During the same period Cincinnati, the largest midwestern city, experienced four equally destructive episodes of mob violence. The riots were ignited by social sparks including parades, lectures, elections, and even theatrical performances, as in the 1849 Astor Place riot in New York, which pitted followers of two rival Shakespearian actors and led to 31 deaths when police fired on rioters. However, if specific events set off social disorder, the riots themselves were amorphous affairs. In most instances unorganized mobs vented their frustrations on blacks, Irish Catholics and members of other minority groups. In the words of one historian, the riots were "brutal street plays in which gangs had acted out the fear and enmities of ordinary citizens by attacking their scapegoats."

Riots of this sort reached a midcentury peak in the frightening 1863 draft riots, which ravaged a half dozen cities from Boston to Detroit. The National Conscription Act, the federal government's first major attempt to raise and maintain an army without the aid of state authorities, prompted the riots. The act required all men between the ages of 20 and 45 to register for a draft lottery; particularly irksome to working-class registrants was a stipulation that anyone whose name was drawn could avoid service by paying $300 or by finding a substitute. The rioting began in most cases with attacks on lottery workers and offices, but shortly thereafter rioters forgot the draft and turned to other targets. In New York, where rioting extended over four days and nights and involved an estimated 70,000 participants, rioters first destroyed a Third Avenue lottery office. Fueled by excitement, mobs then raced through the city, burning orphanages, lynching Blacks, and looting establishments of the well-to-do, most notably the Brooks Brothers clothing store. Before troops ended the rioting, an estimated 500 people had died in "the longest, most widespread, and most destructive riots in American history, with by far the largest numbers of rioters."

Midcentury riots dramatically illustrate a major aspect of nineteenth century American crime. Like more commonplace social disorder crime, the riots were products of a rapidly changing and disorganized society. Confused instigators and participants longed for excitement and exhilaration. Frustrated and aided by only inchoate political views and vague goals, these criminals, as most perceived them, thrashed desperately about in what seemed like an anomic society. What were the social meanings of the world in which they found themselves?

David Ray Papke, Framing the Criminal: Crime, Cultural Work and the Loss of Critical Perspective 1830–1900 5–6 (1987). Reprinted by permission of the author, © 1987 David Ray Papke. Papke also suggests that "In the years immediately following the Civil War, criminal activity in the East and old Midwest quickly regained its antebellum levels and then rose to even higher levels. The daily papers reported a general crime wave, and court and prison authorities confirmed the development." Id., at 8. For a study of empirical data regarding homicide in Chicago which compliments Papke's analysis, and which offers many opportunities for future historians of criminal law see Leigh B. Bienen and Brandon Rottinghaus, "Learning from the Past, Living in the Present: Understanding Homicide in Chicago, 1870–1930," 92 J.Crim.L. & Criminology 437 (2003).

All of this accelerated what Papke describes as a search for "social meaning," which Papke seems to suggest spawned crime. This "Search for Order," as it has also been described by historians of the nineteenth century, seems also to have influenced the treatment of women and the family in the nineteenth century law. The family could, supposedly, serve as something of an antidote to the anomie of the rest of society, a place where "traditional values" could still be inculcated, a place where future "Jukes" could be prevented. We conclude our study of nineteenth century Law and Society, then, with a review of the treatment of nineteenth century family law. Does any of the urban disorder Papke describes strike a familiar note? How about the nineteenth century's linkage of criminal difficulties with domestic problems? What light does the nineteenth century experience cast on our own social pathologies? Our first reading, from nineteenth century radical abolitionist Sarah Grimke, addresses the status of women in the early nineteenth century, and compares it to the status of slaves. As you read the remainder of the materials in the following section, see if you tend further to agree or disagree with Ms. Grimke. For David Papke's fascinating study of the importance of dissenters to the development of American law, discussing several of the individuals whom we at least touch on in the course (including William Lloyd Garrison, Elisabeth Cady Stanton, and Eugene Debs) see David Ray Papke, Heretics in the Temple: Americans Who Reject the Nation's Legal Faith (1998).

E. WOMEN AND THE FAMILY IN NINETEENTH CENTURY AMERICAN LAW

Introduction: Women and the Family in Nineteenth Century American Law

When we think of the term "traditional family," we may perhaps imagine a husband and wife, and one or two children. We might also include a set of grandparents, but they are not essential to this picture—they may live nearby, or far away, but no longer in the same home. The husband-father is a worker, according to this "traditional" model, and the mother-wife a full-time homemaker. What is most striking about this notion, which may or may not represent reality even today, is that it is, in actuality, anything but traditional. Not until the 1920s did the "traditional" model begin to reflect the social reality of American society, and even then only for a short time. Today, fewer than 20% of all households fit that mold.

Before 1800 in America, the family was many-peopled. The household might consist of several generations, and just as likely include non-relatives as relatives. It was customary in New England towns for parents to apprentice young children to other families before the age of 10. It was also customary for New England families to include under the same roof the apprenticed or servant children of non-relatives. As you will soon see in the reading from Max Bloomfield, this was a Puritan concept of childrearing that recognized the overly-tender feelings of the natural parent as an impediment to the child's character development. The family might also include a member of the community too sick to care for him or herself, and one or both sets of elderly parents, depending on whether there were other grown children with their own homes who could share in the caretaking. There was no retirement from work as such. Life expectancy in eighteenth-century America was about 35 years, which was still higher than England's. This was more a reflection of high rates of infant mortality than anything else. One in three children born in the colonies would not live through the first year of life. Of those who lived to age twenty, the odds were good they would live for another thirty or forty years. In general, people worked until they were no longer physically capable. The elderly, the infirm, non-relatives, and the dependent of all ages and circumstances were cared for in the home, by family members.

The New England family was perhaps atypical in the colonies because of the dominance of Puritanism and the town-centered pattern of development. But in the main, New England family life shared common elements with the Middle, Chesapeake and Southern colonies. The mortality rate was higher in the Chesapeake colonies because of climate-related diseases and illnesses (malaria, dysentery, yellow fever). Simple survival was a priority for most families, and few people had the luxury of being able to live entirely alone. Children were economic assets, helping to plant and harvest. Wives would experience childbirth with regularity in most families. The average number of children born to married women in the colonies, regardless of region, was between 6 and 9. The function of marriage was procreation, if nature allowed that, and frequent and frequently-risky procreation still sustained the family and built the community.

Community provided protections for the family, resources and aid in times of need, companionship, and the benefit of collective experience. Community also provided houses of worship, the meeting place not only for the practice of religion but also for administering the proper training and oversight of personal conduct. Community leaders were mostly males—fathers and husbands. Their proper place in the community was at the head, just as in the family, where the husband-father was the ruler. This was not only a reflection of things as they were, but presumably also meant to be, because in accordance with biblical injunctions and a European worldview that said every corporate entity, whether state or family, must have a head. In the case of community and family, that head was almost exclusively male.

The law in the colonies reinforced this fact of family life. As we will soon observe, the English common law placed great powers in the husband-father's hands. It also recognized the legitimate family, one that in England was united by sacrament of marriage, as an important interest of the state. "Bastard" children brought shame to the mother (though not always to the father, if he were known), and shame to the child. The father-husband's dominion in practice meant that he was permitted to chastise his wife, if she was unruly or unwilling to abide by the marital vow of obedience. The father was also the owner of his children, in a sense. That meant that he was expected to administer whatever discipline was necessary to make the child an upright member of the family and of the community. That discipline might be physical. It also involved teaching the child to read, so that the child later could turn to the Bible for moral and practical guidance. Since male children were the likely heirs of the father's lands, it was natural that the father should have the highest claim to the child's custody and service. That which applied to the male child applied to female children too. The household head's right of custody extended to the wife. She was expected to live with and be available to her husband for the duration of the marriage. (In some cases of adultery, a person might be permitted to divorce.) Marriage in the eighteenth century was for life, at least in the eyes of law. The wife was not at liberty to live apart from the husband without his consent, and even then, she enjoyed no rights that she did not already have as the wife, which were few. Legally, her identity was submerged in his as *femme covert.*

If the husband-father was the ruler of the family, he was also expected to be ruler of his household. All who lived within his physical home were subject to the same authority as were immediate members of his family. Of course, an elderly parent, perhaps one who still owned the land that the husband-father farmed, retained considerable power. The core unit was the household, however, and its strict governance was essential to the wellbeing and good order of the community at large. The community reinforced and supported the husband-father's authority because its own authority structure mirrored it and depended upon it.

As we will see when we review some cases involving family law, religion was profoundly important in the structuring of familial relations. Common law took as its guide the Bible, Blackstone often reminded his readers. In colonial America, whether in New England town, Middle colony farm, or Chesapeake colony plantation, most people lived in a rural setting and made their living from the land. The seasons and rhythms of farm life reinforced the morally, legally, and biblically prescribed relations between husband and wife, parents and children, and relatives and strangers living in the household. The realities of life did so too.

Did the wife chafe under these restrictions? Did children rebel? Did husbands always live up to the high moral expectations heaped on their shoulders? You can guess at the answers; human folly and temptation, after all, are ever-present phenomena. The moral dilemmas of family life have long been a subject of American literature, and never with greater understanding than in the work of one of earliest and best writers, Nathaniel Hawthorne. The Salem witch trials of the late sixteenth century are another reminder that disturbances exist in every Peaceable Kingdom. Sometimes, resistance to old ways was a sign of how liberal life in the colonies was compared to European society. Indeed, whatever the common law maintained, the husband and the wife in the New World were thrown into a partnership that depended more on mutual support than coercion. The reality of survival dictated it. About 90% of Jamestown, Virginia's inhabitants died in the first two years of settlement. While the situation there was extreme, so too was the task of creating and maintaining a society where outside resources were few. In addition to building homes and founding community, colonial life involved the grave medical risks of childbirth, susceptibility to contracting diphtheria, tuberculosis, or small pox, dealing with hostile Native American tribes, surviving the extremes of climate, clearing and cultivating the land, praying for weather conditions that allowed (at the least) a harvest that would stave off starvation, dealing with the emotional strains of losing loved ones, especially young children, and passing the land down to the next generation. The creation of family units in the New World demanded resourcefulness in finding ways of living and working together that simply was not required in the Old World.

One typically resourceful American wife was Abigail Adams. When her husband John Adams was at the Continental Congress in Philadelphia, she reminded him to "Remember the Ladies" because they now were capable of doing the same work as men. She was not only referring to herself, but more broadly to the work that all women in the colonies had long-since taken on. Abigail Adams in particular did not shy away from discussing the political and social issues of the day with her husband and her neighbors; she engaged in a long-standing correspondence with Thomas Jefferson on all manner of political and public affairs; and like her husband, she held strong opinions about her beloved country. While she was a most remarkable person by any standard, Adams shared a hope with other women that the blessing of American liberty might be extended to the mothers and daughters of the new Republic, and eventually, with great struggle, it was.

The power of republican rhetoric, once unleashed, was not easily contained. By the early 19th century, restrictions on participation in the political process were removed for all white males. The anti-slavery movement of the 1830s was fed by the same love of liberty that prompted colonial radicals like John Adams and Benjamin Franklin to condemn the institution of slavery. The rise of infant and orphan asylums, and special homes for unwed mothers, was no less a part of the expanding spheres of freedom, as reformers "rescued" children and young women from lives of lost opportunity. In the law, the expansion of freedom challenged the traditional common-law construction of the family. As we will see in Bloomfield, Married women's property legislation appeared as a legal reform in the first half of the century, and by 1900 was present in most states. The first general adoption statute passed the legislature in Massachusetts in 1851. Legislation appeared in many states making divorce more accessible for relationships that ceased to exist because of abandonment, or for reasons of cruelty, abuse, or adultery. Custody disputes also began to appear between separated husbands and wives who were not divorced, and as we will soon observe in the *Mercein* case, in some decisions, in direct conflict with common law precedent, courts awarded custody to the mother-wife. Some couples anticipating marriage entered into prenuptial agreements, and a few courts enforced them. These were significant departures from English and colonial law and signaled a deep shift in concepts of family in America in the period after Independence. What were these concepts?

One was a new "cult of domesticity" that elevated the wife in the family's internal relations. Increasingly in the nineteenth century, the woman was seen as possessed of a special nurturing power. She was becoming the caretaker and source of sustenance for family members, the glue that held the unit tightly together. The husband, drawn off the farm and engaged in work away from his house, was removed from the daily interactions of the wife and children. Indirectly, he was delegating to the wife a new kind of authority. As we will see in the reading from Orestes Brownson, the husband himself was a beneficiary of this delegation, for the wife's comfort and support extended to him too.

The mother's special domain for which she was said to be uniquely equipped was child-rearing. In antebellum America children were becoming the central focus of the family and demanding more of the mother's attention. There were fewer in the family, for starters, as the birthrate for women fell to 3 by 1900. Extraneous members also were ejected as the confines of the home were redefined to include only immediate family members. By 1900, almost all children in the nation were subject to compulsory school attendance, and their presence in the home was thus extended even further. The family was becoming an emotionally rich conclave of husband, wife, and children, a haven from the world—or at least in the popular culture and literature of the time.

What today is described as the "traditional" family has its origins, then, in this image of the nuclear family that makes its appearance in the century after 1776. It is, at least in the idealization of the type, restricted to husband and wife who share a loving relationship, and the children who are linked to the parents as much by ties of affection as by blood. Gone are the peripheral members. While the creation of this family type does not expressly confer equality upon the members, it does negate the traditional power of the husband-father by replacing bonds of authority with bonds of feeling, and by the movement of the mother-wife to the center of the new family type.

If republican sentiments and a rising cult of domesticity were two sources of this idealized vision of the family, a third was the changing nature of work. The majority of Americans continued to inhabit an agrarian world in the nineteenth century, but it was not a world in isolation. Cities, in which one in four Americans lived in 1900, grew from commercial and industrial development. A rising middle class managed the nation's affairs. Per capita income in the nation was on the rise the entire century. Education was growing in stature and professionalism. A part of this change was a new class of women, many from urban areas, who were attracted to reform causes. Because women were seen as possessing special capacities as nurturing mothers and wives, and experienced in managing the "domestic economy," they were welcomed as the ideal organizers and foot soldiers in social movements and moral crusades to improve humanity. As indicated earlier, women were prominent in the anti-slavery movement, in the temperance movement and later the successful movement for Prohibition. They were prominent in the movement to reform the treatment of children, in prison reform and in opposition to capital punishment. Elizabeth Cady Stanton, whose life nearly spanned the nineteenth century (1815–1902), is perhaps an apt symbol of the dualism of the women's movement. She was empowered by the "separate sphere" of womanhood as a mother and wife, and as a feminist she fought against its limitations. She was the author of the Declaration of Sentiments of the Seneca Falls Convention of 1848, which you will soon read, an anti-slavery advocate, and after the Civil War, a suffragette. She was also the mother of 7 children, but in her marriage vows dropped the command to "obey" her husband, whom she saw as an equal.

Still, the transformation of woman's status was more gradual than revolutionary. Among the clergy, there were those who saw woman's place as biblically ordained and predicted dire consequences if nature's plan was disrupted. As you will see, Orestes Brownson adopted a more secular stance, and saw women's equality as a destructive branch of a corrupted individualism and extreme selfishness, from which no good ever could come. Influenced by the views of those such as Brownson, the legal system was slow to change, but eventually the law was revised in important ways that reflected a new and evolving consensus about the place of women in American life.

In particular, what the rise of the nuclear family and reform efforts share is a bestowing of new authority on women. Was the glass half-empty or half-full? The new qualities attributed to women contained elements of power, but also limitations. The cult of domesticity put woman on a pedestal, but pedestals could also be traps. Throughout the nineteenth century, women could not exercise the most basic prerogatives of citizenship: voting and serving on juries. Serving in public office and the professions, when it did occur, as you will see with Myra Bradwell's case, was more a novelty than a harbinger. Nevertheless, the cultural contrast with the colonial era is astonishing.

Not considered in the portrayal of this "traditional" family model are the families of poor, the families of working class immigrants, the families of slaves, and others. The development of the nuclear-family concept seems most rooted in depictions of the middle class, especially in urban settings. Perhaps that is to be expected, as it is this class that usually has had the greatest influence in shaping American culture and managing the American economy. In the nineteenth century, it is also the class from which lawyers and judges are most heavily drawn, and it is to their encounter with the changes in the "traditional" family that we now turn.

Further Reading:

Philippe Aries, *Centuries of Childhood: A Social History of Family Life*, 1962

Kathleen Barry, *Susan B. Anthony: A Biography*, 1988

Stephanie Coontz, *The Way We Never Were: American Families and the Nostalgia Trap,* 1992

Nancy F. Cott, *The Bonds of Womanhood: "Woman's Sphere" in New England, 1780–1835*

Carl N. Degler, *At Odds: Women and the Family in America from the Revolution to the Present,* 1980

John Demos, *A Little Commonwealth: Family Life in Plymouth Colony*, 1970

John Demos, *Past, Personal, and Present: The Family and Life Course in American History,* 1988

Jacques Donzelot, *The Policing of Families*, 1979

Lori D. Ginzberg, *Women and the Work of Benevolence: Morality, Politics, and Class in the Nineteenth–Century United States,* 1990

Philip J. Greven, Jr., *Four Generations: Population, Land, and Family in Colonial Andover, Massachusetts*, 1970

Tamara K. Hareven, *Family Time and Industrial Time: The Relationship between the Family and Work in a New England Industrial Community,* 1982

Linda Kerber, *Women of the Republic: Intellect and Ideology in Revolutionary America,* 1980

Christopher Lasch, *Haven in a Heartless World: The Family Besieged,* 1977

Suzanne M. Marilley, *Woman Suffrage and the Origins of Liberal Feminism in the United States, 1820–1920,* 1996

Steven Mintz and Susan Kellogg, *Domestic Revolutions: A Social History of American Family Life,* 1988

Nell Irvin Painter, *Sojourner Truth: A Life, a Symbol,* 1996

Mary P. Ryan, *Cradle of the Middle Class: The Family in Oneida County, New York, 1790–1865,* 1981

Mary P. Ryan, *Women in Public: Between Banners and Ballots, 1825–1880,* 1990

Kathrun Kish Sklar, *Catharine Beecher: A Study in American Domesticity,* 1973

Sandra F. VanBurkleo, *Belonging to the World: Women's Rights and American Constitutional Culture,* 2001

SARAH GRIMKÉ, "LEGAL DISABILITIES OF WOMEN," FROM LETTERS ON THE EQUALITY OF THE SEXES AND THE CONDITION OF WOMEN

74–83 (1837), reprinted in Wendy McElroy, ed., Freedom, Feminism, and the State 121–127 (1982).*

There are few things which present greater obstacles to the improvement and elevation of woman to her appropriate sphere of usefulness and duty, than the laws which have been enacted to destroy her independence, and crush her individuality; laws which, although they are framed for her government, she has had no voice in establishing, and which rob her of some of her *essential rights.* Woman has no political existence. With the single exception of presenting a petition to the legislative body, she is a cipher in the nation; or, if not actually so in representation governments, she is only counted, like the slaves of the South, to swell the number of law-makers who form decrees for her government, with little reference to her benefit, except so far as her good may promote their own. I am not sufficiently acquainted with the laws respecting women on the continent of Europe, to say anything about them. But Prof. Follen, in his essay on "The Cause of Freedom in our Country," says, "Woman, though fully possessed of that rational and moral nature which is the foundation of all rights, enjoys amongst us fewer legal rights than under the civil law of continental Europe." I shall confine myself to the laws of our country. These laws bear with peculiar rigor on married women. Blackstone, in the chapter entitled "Of husband and wife," says:—

> "By marriage, the husband and wife are one person in law; that is, *the very being, or legal existence of the woman* is suspended during the marriage, or at least is incorporated and consolidated into that of the husband under whose wing, protection and cover she performs everything." For this reason, a man cannot grant anything to his wife, or enter into covenant with her; for the grant would be to suppose her separate existence, and to covenant with her would be to covenant with himself; and therefore it is also generally true, that all compacts made between husband and wife, when single, are voided by the intermarriage. "A woman indeed may be attorney for her husband, but that implies no separation from, but is rather a representation of, her love."

Here now, the very being of a woman, like that of a slave, is absorbed in her master. All contracts made with her, like those made with slaves by their owners, are a mere nullity. Our kind defenders have legislated away almost all our legal rights, and in the true spirit of such injustice and oppression, have kept us in ignorance of those very laws by which we are governed. They have persuaded us, that we have no right to investigate the laws, and that, if we did, we could not comprehend them; they alone are capable of understanding the mysteries of Blackstone, & c. But they are not backward to make us feel the practical operation of their power over our actions.

> "The husband is bound to provide his wife with necessaries by law, as much as himself; and if she contracts debts for them, he is obliged to pay for them; but for anything besides necessaries, he is not chargeable."

Yet a man may spend the property he has acquired by marriage at the ale-house, the gambling table, or in any other way that he pleases. Many instances of this kind have come to my knowledge; and women, who have brought their husbands handsome fortunes, have been left, in consequence of the wasteful and dissolute habits of their husbands, in straitened circumstances, and compelled to toil for the support of their families.

> "If the wife be indebted before marriage, the husband is bound afterwards to pay the debt; for he has adopted her and her circumstances together."

The wife's property is, I believe, equally liable for her husband's debts contracted before marriage.

> "If the wife be injured in her person or property, she can bring no action for redress without her husband's concurrence, and his name as well as her own: neither can she be sued, without making her husband a defendant."

This law that "a wife can bring no action," & c., is similar to the law respecting slaves. "A slave cannot bring a suit against his master, or any other person, for an injury—his master, must bring it." So if any damages are recovered for an injury committed on a wife, the husband pockets it; in the case of the slave, the master does the same.

> "In criminal prosecutions, the wife may be indicted and punished separately, unless there be evidence of coercion from the fact that the offence was committed in the presence, or by the command of her husband. A wife is excused from punishment for theft committed in the presence, or by the command of her husband."

It would be difficult to frame a law better calculated to destroy the responsibility of woman as a moral being, or a free agent. Her husband is supposed to possess unlimited control over her; and if she can offer the flimsy excuse that he bade her steal, she may break the eighth commandment with impunity, as far as human laws are concerned.

> "Our law, in general, considers man and wife as one person; yet there are some instances in which she is separately considered, as inferior to him and acting by his compulsion. Therefore, all deeds executed, and acts done by her during her coverture (i.e. marriage,) are void, except it be a fine, or like matter of record, in which case she must be solely and secretly examined, to learn if her act be voluntary."

Such a law speaks volumes of the abuse of that power which men have vested in their own hands. Still the private examination of a wife, to know whether she accedes to the disposition of property made by her husband is, in most cases, a mere form; a wife dares not do what will be disagreeable to one who is, in his own estimation, her superior, and who makes her feel, in the privacy of domestic life, that she has thwarted him. With respect to the nullity of deeds or acts done by a wife, I will mention one circumstance. A respectable woman borrowed of a female friend a sum of money to relieve her son from some distressing pecuniary embarrassment. Her husband was from home, and she assured the lender, that as soon as he returned, he would gratefully discharge the debt. She gave her note, and the lender, entirely ignorant of the law that a man is not obliged to discharge such a debt, actually borrowed the money, and lent it to the distressed and weeping mother. The father returned home, refused to pay the debt, and the person who had loaned the money was obliged to pay both principal and interest to the friend who lent it to her. * * *

> "The husband, by the old law, might give his wife moderate correction, as he is to answer for her misbehavior. The law thought it reasonable to entrust him with this power of restraining her by domestic chastisement. The courts of law will still permit a husband to restrain a wife of her liberty, in case of any gross misbehavior."

What a mortifying proof this law affords, of the estimation in which woman is held! She is placed completely in the hands of a being subject like herself to the outbursts of passion, and therefore unworthy to be trusted with power. Perhaps I may be told respecting this law, that it is a dead letter, as I am sometimes told about the slave laws; but this is not true in either case. The slaveholder does kill his slave by moderate correction, as the law allows; and many a husband, among the poor, exercises the right given him by the law, of degrading woman by personal chastisement. And among the higher ranks, if actual imprisonment is not resorted to, women are not unfrequently restrained of the liberty of going to places of worship by irreligious husbands, and of doing many other things about which, as moral and responsible beings, *they* should be the *sole* judges. Such laws remind me of the reply of some little girls at a children's meeting held recently at Ipswich. The lecturer told them that God had created four orders of beings with which he had made us acquainted through the Bible. The first was angels, the second was man, the third beasts; and now, children, what is the fourth? After a pause, several girls replied, "WOMEN."

> "A woman's personal property by marriage becomes absolutely her husband's, which, at his death, he may leave entirely away from her."

And further, all the avails of her labor are absolutely in the power of her husband. All that she acquires by her industry is his; so that she cannot, with her own honest earnings, become the legal purchaser of any property. If she expends her money for articles of furniture, to contribute to the comfort of her family, they are liable to be seized for her husband's debts: and I know an instance of a woman, who by labor and economy had scraped together a little maintenance for herself and a do-little husband, who was left, at his death, by virtue of his last will and testament, to be supported by charity. I knew another woman, who by great industry had acquired a little money which she deposited in a bank for safe keeping. She had saved this pittance whilst able to work, in hopes that when age or sickness disqualified her for exertion, she might have something to render life comfortable, without being a burden to her friends. Her husband, a worthless, idle man, discovered this hid treasure, drew her little stock from the bank, and expended it all in extravagance and vicious indulgence. I know of another woman, who married without the least idea that she was surrendering her rights to all her personal property. Accordingly, she went to the bank as usual to draw her dividends, and the person who paid her the money, and to whom she was personally known as an owner of shares in that bank, remarking the change in her signature, withdrew the money, informing her that if she were married, she had no longer a right to draw her dividends without an order from her husband. It appeared that she intended having a little fund for private use, and had not even told her husband that she owned this stock, and she was not a little chagrined, when she found that it was not at her disposal. I think she was wrong to conceal the circumstance. The relation of husband and wife is too near and sacred to admit of secrecy about money matters, unless positive necessity demands it; and I can see no excuse for any woman entering into a marriage engagement with a design to keep her husband ignorant that she was possessed of property. If she was unwilling to give up her property to his disposal, she had infinitely better have remained single.

The laws above cited are not very unlike the slave laws of Louisiana.

> "All that a slave possesses belongs to his master; he possesses nothing of his own, except what his master chooses he should possess."
>
> "By the marriage, the husband is absolutely master of the profits of the wife's lands during the coverture, and if he has had a living child, and survives the wife, he retains the whole of those lands, if they are estates of inheritance, during his life; but the wife is entitled only to one third if she survives, out of the husband's estates of inheritance. But this she has, whether she has had a child or not." "With regard to the property of women, there is taxation without representation; for they pay taxes without having the liberty of voting for representatives."

And this taxation, without representation, be it remembered, was the cause of our Revolutionary war, a grievance so heavy, that it was thought necessary to purchase exemption from it at an immense expense of blood and treasure, yet the daughters of New England, as well as of all the other States of this free Republic, are suffering a similar injustice * * *.

The laws I have quoted, are, I believe, the laws of Massachusetts, and, with few exceptions, of all the States in this Union. * * * That the laws which have generally been adopted in the United States, for the government of women, have been framed almost entirely for the exclusive benefit of men, and with a design to oppress women, by depriving them of all control over their property, is too manifest to be denied. Some liberal and enlightened men, I know, regret the existence of these laws; and I quote with pleasure an extract from Harriet Martineau's Society in America, as a proof of the assertion. "A liberal minded lawyer of Boston, told me that his advice to testators always is to leave the largest possible amount to the widow, subject to the condition of her leaving it to the children; but that it is with shame that he reflects that any woman should owe that to his professional advice, which the law should have secured to her as a right." I have known a few instances where men have left their whole property to their wives, when they have died, leaving only minor children; but I have known more instances of "the friend and helper of many years, being portioned off like a salaried domestic," instead of having a comfortable independence secured to her, while the children were amply provided for.

As these abuses do exist, and women suffer intensely from them, our brethren are called upon in this enlightened age, by every sentiment of honor, religion and justice, to repeal these unjust and unequal laws, and restore to woman those rights which they have wrested from her. Such laws approximate too nearly to the laws enacted by slaveholders for the government of their slaves, and must tend to debase and depress the mind of that being, whom God created as a help meet for man, or "helper like unto himself," and designed to be his equal and his companion. Until such laws are annulled, woman never can occupy that exalted station for which she was intended by her Maker. And just in proportion as they are practically disregarded, which is the case to some extent, just so far is woman assuming that independence and nobility of character which she ought to exhibit.

The various laws which I have transcribed, leave women very little more liberty, or power, in some respects, than the slave. "A slave," says the civil code of Louisiana, "is one who is in the power of a master, to whom he belongs. He can possess nothing, nor acquire anything, but what must belong to his master." I do not wish by any means to intimate that the condition of free women can be compared to that of slaves in suffering, or in degradation; still, I believe the laws which deprive married women of their rights and privileges, have a tendency to lessen them in their own estimation as moral and responsible beings, and that their being made by civil law inferior to their husbands, has a debasing and mischievous effect upon them, teaching them practically the fatal lesson to look unto man for protection and indulgence.

* * * The men frame the laws, and, with few exceptions, claim to execute them on both sexes. In * * * courts, woman is tried and condemned, not by a jury of her peers, but by beings, who regard themselves as her superiors in the scale of creation. Although looked upon as an inferior, when considered as an intellectual being, woman is punished with the same severity as man, when she is guilty of moral offences. Her condition resembles, in some measure, that of the slave, who, while he is denied the advantages of his more enlightened master, is treated with even greater rigor of the law. * * *

NOTES AND QUESTIONS

1. Sarah Grimké argues, essentially, that the legal lot of the nineteenth century married American woman is basically the same as that of the slave. If this was the case, how did it come about? Ms. Grimké, and her younger sister Angelina Grimké, were leaders in the movement to free the slaves, but sought with equal vigor to educate women as to their own oppressed status through lectures, letters, and pamphlets. Some of the male

abolitionists, most notably Theodore Weld, like the Grimké sisters from Massachusetts, sought to restrain them from arguing the feminist cause until the slaves were free. Sarah Grimké (like her sister), refused, and castigated Weld. In a letter to him she complained that "I know the opposition to our views arises in part from the fact that women are habitually regarded as inferior beings," or worse, "from a desire to keep them in unholy subjection to man. . . . " From what you have seen of the culture of the Antebellum South, do you think it is likely that Southern white women were no better off than slaves? Was there a difference in the status of women in North and South?

2. Note that Ms. Grimké, in her close legal analysis (said to be her particular contribution to nineteenth century feminism), pinpoints one very disturbing feature of the early nineteenth century law. The property which a woman brings into marriage becomes, in effect, the property of her husband, and can be used by creditors to satisfy debts of the husband. As you will soon see, in the next reading, this particular problem was corrected by the "Married Women's Property Acts," which sought to give some legal protection to the resources women brought to their marriages. See generally Marylynn Salmon, Women and the Law of Property in Early America (1986), and Richard H. Chused, Married Women's Property Law: 1800–1850, 71 Georgetown Law Journal 1359 (1983), and "Late Nineteenth Century Married Women's Property Law: Reception of the Early Married Women's Property Acts by Courts and Legislatures," 29 Am.J.Leg.Hist. 3 (1985), and see also, for the definitive study of the New York State married women's property acts, Norma Basch, In the Eyes of the Law: Women, Marriage, and Property in Nineteenth Century New York (1982). Do you suppose that righting this particular "wrong" went very far in alleviating the situation Sarah Grimké decries? For the limited nature of the courts' and legislatures' recognition of women's property rights in nineteenth century America, see Reva B. Siegel, "Home as Work: The First Women's Rights Claims Concerning Wives' Household Labor, 1850–1880," 103 Yale L.J. 1073 (1994).

3. Ms. Grimké's authority for the "legal disabilities" of women is principally I Blackstone's Commentaries on the Law of England 430–433 (1765). She does a bit of pointed editing of Blackstone, particularly the part which deals with the husband's legal ability to chastise his wife. She omits, for example, some parts of Blackstone's explanation, in his first edition, for why the "old law" permitted such chastisement. Here it is, put somewhat better in context:

> The husband also (by the old law) might give his wife moderate correction. For, as he is to answer for her misbehaviour, the law thought it reasonable to intrust him with this power of restraining her, by domestic chastisement, in the same moderation that a man is allowed to correct his servants or children; for whom the master or parent is also liable in some cases to answer. But this power of correction was confined within reasonable bounds; and the husband was prohibited to use any violence to his wife, * * *. The civil law gave the husband the same, or a larger,

authority over his wife; allowing him, for some misdemeanors [to beat his wife]; for others, only [moderate chastisement]. But with us, in the politer reign of Charles the second, this power of correction began to be doubted: and a wife may now have security of the peace against her husband; or, in return, a husband against his wife. Yet the lower rank of people, who were always fond of the old common law, still claim and exert their antient privilege: and the courts of law will still permit a husband to restrain a wife of her liberty, in case of any gross misbehaviour.

I Blackstone's Commentaries 432–433 (1765). Does this fuller excerpt from Blackstone undercut or further support Ms. Grimké's arguments?

4. Similarly, if one looks to the full text of Blackstone for his remarks on the husband's control and ownership of his wife's property, a somewhat more complex picture emerges than that presented by Ms. Grimké. Consider, for example, Blackstone's remarks on the wife's real and personal property which she brings into marriage:

> * * * whatever personal property belonged to the wife, before marriage, is by marriage absolutely vested in the husband. In * * * real estate he only gains a title to the rents and profits during coverture [while the marriage continues]: for that, depending upon feodal principles, remains entire to the wife after the death of her husband, or to her heirs, if she dies before him; unless, by the birth of a child, he becomes tenant for life by the curtesy. But, in chattel interests, the sole and absolute property vests in the husband, to be disposed of at his pleasure, if he chooses to take possession of them: for, unless he reduces them to possession, by exercising some act of ownership upon them, no property vests in him, but they shall remain to the wife, or to her representatives * * *.

II Blackstone's Commentaries 433 (1766). Indeed, Blackstone seemed to suggest that English law gingerly sought to protect the really important things of a woman, as indicated in the following excerpt:

> And, as the husband may thus, generally, acquire a property in all the personal substance of the wife, so in one particular instance the wife may acquire a property in some of her husband's goods; which shall remain to her after his death, and shall not go to his executors. These are called her *paraphernalia;* which is a term borrowed from the civil law, and is derived from the Greek language, signifying something over and above her dower. Our law uses it to signify the apparel and ornaments of the wife, suitable to her rank and degree; which she becomes entitled to at the death of her husband over and above her jointure or dower, and preferably to all other representatives: and the jewels of a peeress, usually worn by her, have been held to be *paraphernalia.* Neither can the husband devise by his will such ornaments and jewels of his wife; though during his life perhaps he hath the power (if unkindly inclined to exert it) to sell them or give them away. But if she continues in the use of them till his death, she shall afterwards retain them against his executors and administrators, and all other persons except creditors where

> there is a deficiency of assets [in the husband's estate]. And her necessary apparel is protected even against the claim of creditors.

II Blackstone's Commentaries 436 (1766). Taking all of this into consideration, Blackstone concluded that "[E]ven the disabilities, which the wife lies under, are for the most part intended for her protection and benefit. So great a favourite is the female sex of the laws of England." I Blackstone's Commentaries 433 (1765). Do you agree? What sort of woman is protected and benefited by the common law of England, and what sort of woman is not?

5. Do you share Ms. Grimké's conception of what marriage should be like, and what "exalted station for which [woman] was intended by her maker?" Did Blackstone? In particular, why is it necessary for women to assume "independence and nobility of character?" What do those words mean in the context of nineteenth century society?

6. For further background in evaluating Ms. Grimké's arguments, consider the following summary of family law, including the English common law, the law of the American colonial period, and early nineteenth century American legal developments. For the earliest common-law foundations, see generally Thomas Lund, "Women in the Early Common Law," 1997 Utah L.Rev. 1.

MAXWELL BLOOMFIELD, AMERICAN LAWYERS IN A CHANGING SOCIETY*

92–99, 104–108, 112–122 (1976).

* * *

American family law in the seventeenth and eighteenth centuries derived from several distinct sources: the English common law, the marital regulations of the established Church of England, parliamentary and colonial statutes, and the workaday conditions of life on a transatlantic frontier. In general, it may be said that the doctrines and attitudes of common-law judges most strongly influenced the private law of domestic relations * * *. But any policy formulated in England, whether legislative or judicial in origin, inevitably suffered a marked sea change in its transit from the Old World to the New.

The marriage ceremony itself illustrates the point. Ecclesiastical courts had jurisdiction over marriage and divorce in England, where the law required that every marriage be solemnized by a minister of the Anglican church. No such church courts were ever established in the American colonies, however, and the religious Dissenters who settled New England and Pennsylvania had no intention of conforming to the ritual of a church they had long since repudiated. Instead, Puritans and Quakers tended to espouse the view of Continental religious reformers that marriage was properly a civil contract, whose validity did not depend upon any prescribed church service. Religious ceremonies were not discouraged, of course; in New England it became customary for parties to be married first by a lay magistrate, then by a minister in a church wedding. But the religious sanction added nothing to the legal efficacy of the marriage. By the time of the Revolution the civil ceremony had been introduced by statute into every colony outside the South as a legitimate secular form of marriage.

Even more responsive to the folkways of a rude pioneering society was the development in some jurisdictions of the so-called common-law marriage. No formal ceremony, civil or religious, was needed to validate this type of conjugal union. If a man and woman agreed to consider themselves husband and wife and thereafter lived together as such, the law would uphold their verbal contract and recognize their issue as legitimate. Probably no such institution was ever known to the English common law * * *. But there can be no doubt that informal marriages were prevalent throughout the colonies, for a number of reasons: a shortage of clergymen in many areas; the isolation and loneliness of backwoods settlements; an aversion to bureaucratic procedures on the part of half-educated frontiersmen; and the heavy expense that sometimes accompanied a faithful compliance with legal regulations. In eighteenth-century Virginia, for example, where ministers of the Church of England were alone authorized to celebrate marriages, the fees incident to securing a clergyman's services and a license from the county court equaled the cost of some 465 pounds of tobacco. The colonial judge who gave effect to common-law marriages thus sanctioned a widespread social practice that reflected the Spartan quality of life in an undeveloped country.

Daily experience in a New World environment likewise modified the legal relations that had traditionally existed between English husbands and wives. Those relations had been shaped by the needs of a male-dominated, feudal society, in which land was the chief form of wealth and vassals owed military service to their overlords. Feudal law did not recognize the family as such, or assign rights and duties to individuals in accordance with their respective family roles. Instead, property considerations prevailed over personal relationships or natural blood ties, and property rights alone were enforced by the king's courts in disputes involving husband and wife or father and son.

Under a manorial system geared to the omnipresent threat of war, it was scarcely surprising that male heirs were preferred by law or that women and their property were subjected to the protective custody of masculine guardians or husbands. But the decline of feudalism did little to relieve women of their legal disabilities or to weaken the hoary fiction of the "unity" of husband and wife, which was explained at length in a seventeenth-century law tract:

> In this consolidation which we call wedlock is a locking together. It is true, that man and wife are one person; but understand in what manner. When a small brooke or little river incorporateth with Rhodanus, Humber, or the Thames, the poor rivulet looseth her name; it is carried and recarried with the new associate; it beareth no sway; it possesseth nothing during coverture. A woman as soon as she is married, is called *covert;* in Latine *nupta,* that is, "veiled;" as it were, clouded and overshadowed; she hath lost her streame. I may more truly, farre away, say to a married woman, Her new self is her superior; her companion, her master . . . Eve, because she had helped to seduce her husband, had inflicted upon her a special bane. See here the reason of that which I touched before,—that women have no voice in Parliament. They make no laws, they consent to none, they abrogate none. All of them are understood either married, or to be married, and their desires are to their husbands. I know no remedy, that some can shift it well enough. The common laws here shaketh hand with divinitye.

In more mundane terms, the husband through marriage acquired absolute ownership of his wife's personal property and lifetime control of her lands. If a living child was born to them, the doctrine of "curtesy" furnished the husband with a continuing life estate in all lands owned by his wife at her death. Any other income that accrued to a wife during wedlock, such as wages earned by her labor, likewise fell into her husband's hands.

These extensive male prerogatives were not matched by any corresponding legal duties. Although a man was morally obligated to cherish and support his wife, the common law permitted him to squander her property with impunity, to deprive her at will of creature comforts, and, if she complained, to "chastise" her roundly. Judges would interfere in the sensitive area of domestic relations only to protect a married woman against the threat of death or serious bodily harm or to compel her husband to supply her with the necessities of life. Divorce was out of the question, too, for any cause. If certain canonical disabilities existed, such as marriage within prohibited degrees of blood kinship, an ecclesiastical court might issue a decree of annulment, but in most cases an unhappy spouse could secure only a qualified divorce from bed and board (*a mensa et thoro*), a form of legal separation that did not allow either party to remarry. The very wealthy did manage on rare occasions to squeeze a private bill of divorce out of Parliament; in such exceptional circumstances adultery invariably figured as a principal charge.

By the seventeenth century English equity courts had begun to concede limited proprietary rights to married women by enforcing premarital settlements or trust arrangements that earmarked certain property as a wife's separate estate and exempted it from husbandly control. Such protective devices, which generally reflected a father's desire to shield his daughter against future penury, benefited only the members of the landed aristocracy in practice. For other wives the standard disabilities that accompanied marriage remained fully operative. Unlike single women, they could not make contracts or wills, execute deeds, sue or be sued in court, administer estates, or act as guardians of minors. The one significant proprietary right that they possessed at common law was dower, the female equivalent of curtesy. Through dower a widow became entitled to a life estate in one-third of the lands owned by her deceased husband.

In the American colonies different social and economic conditions helped to enlarge the legal powers of married women in several notable respects. The institution of civil marriage, where it existed in the northern and middle colonies, accustomed people to think of mutual rights and duties on the part of the contracting spouses; a more egalitarian social structure and an abundance of free land diminished the importance of entail, primogeniture, and other discriminatory feudal doctrines (at least outside the South); and everywhere the spur of necessity forced pioneer women to assume occupational roles that in more stable and tradition-bound societies were reserved for men. Legislation in each colony authorized married women to act as "feme-sole traders" and to conduct businesses or manage landed estates in their own interest or on behalf of absent or disabled spouses. As independent entrepreneurs they were empowered to make and enforce their own contracts and could be sued separately by their creditors. Some also represented their husbands in lawsuits, although the practice seems to have died out by the end of the seventeenth century.

Colonial judges likewise proved more liberal than their counterparts in the home country in upholding postnuptial contracts between a man and wife. Even the Court of Chancery in England drew the line at premarital settlements, reasoning from the fiction of marital unity that spouses could not contract with each other or vary the terms of a property settlement they had agreed upon before marriage. But colonial courts were less doctrinaire, and enforced postnuptial, as well as prenuptial, contracts prior to the Revolution. In practice, as Richard B. Morris has remarked, this striking departure from English precedent often permitted a married couple contemplating separation to effect in advance a legally binding division of family property * * *.

Absolute divorce, too, could be obtained in some colonies. Courts and legislatures alike granted such divorces on occasion in New England, for causes that included desertion and cruelty as well as adultery. * * * Even in the southern colonies, which adhered closely to English divorce law, mistreated wives could secure a decree of separate maintenance under circumstances that would never have moved an English judge.

One must beware of exaggerating the impact of these legal changes in women's rights, however. At most it may be argued that in the colonial period the first tentative steps were taken toward recognizing the wife as a distinct legal personality, whose interests need not always be subordinated to quasi-religious norms of marital unity. Limited advances in the proprietary capacity of married women provoked no corresponding changes in their social or political status, and except where property claims were involved judges were reluctant to intervene in family affairs, even to protect a wife or child from physical abuse. In every colony the value of privacy in domestic relations received strong community support * * *. * * *

The common-law principles applicable to parent and child in the seventeenth and eighteenth centuries derived historically from the same set of feudal conditions that had dictated the subjection of married women to their husbands. To protect the integrity of landed estates, feudal law singled out one group of children—heirs and heiresses—for special treatment. The heir received his inheritance by virtue of feudal rules that could not be altered by an ancestor's will, and in other respects his interests as a person were subordinated to overriding economic considerations. Thus, by the law of wardship a father was normally entitled to the custody of his child's person and property. In the event of the father's death, however, guardianship devolved not upon the mother but upon the lord of the infant's land—a clear indication that the child's welfare was deemed of less consequence than the preservation of his estate. But paternal guardianship itself was no guarantee of incorruptibility, since many fathers were not above sordid profiteering in their management of a child's patrimony. While the law obliged them to maintain and educate their wards, it left them otherwise free to use the revenues of an estate as they pleased. * * *

For other children, such as the younger brothers or sisters of a minor heir or the offspring of the propertyless classes, the rules governing the parent-child relationship were drawn from English labor law. The child was regarded in certain contexts as a "servant," and the law pertaining to master and servant was applied to family situations. A father, for example, had a right to his child's services and could sue a third party for abducting, enticing away, or injuring the child, just as a master under similar circumstances could bring suit on behalf of an apprentice. But there the analogy pretty well ended, for the child, as against its parent, possessed none of the contractual rights—to wages, shelter, and maintenance during sickness and disability—that a servant habitually enjoyed. The law, to be sure, recognized certain primary duties, such as protection, support, and education, that every parent owed to his children, but these it held to be exclusively moral obligations. Providence, wrote Blackstone, enforced the claims of the child "more effectually than any laws, by implanting in the breast of every parent that . . . insuperable degree of affection which not even the deformity of person or mind, not even the wickedness, ingratitude, and rebellion of children, can totally suppress or extinguish." Long after feudal tenures had been abolished and the protective jurisdiction of chancery courts extended over wealthy young heirs, most children continued to be regarded, for legal purposes, as quasi servants who had no recourse against the mistreatment or neglect of their paternal "masters."

Nor did youngsters enjoy any greater rights in the American colonies. Indeed, in seventeenth-century New England, Puritan lawmakers invoked biblical sanctions against youthful insubordination that exceeded in severity anything known to English law. Thus, Massachusetts and Connecticut provided the death penalty for any rebellious son or for any child who should "smite or curse" its parents. It does not appear that these sanguinary laws were ever enforced, since happily an alternative method of disciplining the young existed in the widespread practice of "putting out," or apprenticeship.

The apprenticeship system, which was equally popular in England, affected all social classes, but its rationale and general utility varied with the economic condition of a child and its parents. Among the well-to-do and artisan groups, as Stephen B. Presser has noted, apprenticeship often served as a substitute for adoption, a mode of child care that did not exist at common law. Parents sometimes provided by will that a child should be placed in the home of a relative or friend for education and Christian upbringing, or arranged with a neighbor that he should take a youngster into his family and train him for a term of years in some special skill. (Girls were likely to be taught "manners" or household management.) The free consent of both natural and surrogate parents characterized such "putting out" agreements, in which a child's welfare was of paramount concern. Since, in the absence of more specialized civic agencies, a colonial family was expected to perform many semi-public functions of acculturation and job training, the apprenticeship experience could (and frequently did) prove invaluable to the young man or woman of "respectable" background. * * *

The Revolution did not alter the substantive content of American family law in any perceptible way. Despite the rhetoric of individualism and natural rights that accompanied the struggle, the legal aspects of domestic relations remained the same after the war as before. * * *

In the early Republic there was general agreement among jurists that the institution of marriage deserved every possible encouragement, for reasons of sound public policy. Kent, Hoffman, and other leading commentators borrowed heavily from the philosophical writings of William Paley to prove that Christian monogamy alone was suited to the needs of a progressive republican state. * * *

The plain-spoken clergyman from Yorkshire * * * espoused a unique brand of theological utilitarianism. "God wills the happiness of mankind," he declared, "and the existence of civil society, as conducive to that happiness." Lawmakers therefore were charged with a divine mandate to promote the general welfare, a mission they fulfilled by aiding population growth and encouraging productive employment. For Paley, as for Bentham, "happiness" was a democratic principle, capable of objective measurement: if you doubled the number of citizens you increased the quantity of national happiness in the same proportion, provided all classes enjoyed a reasonable level of subsistence. Conversely, population decline betokened spiritual as well as physical degeneracy and was "the greatest evil that a state can suffer."

Demographic considerations thus pointed up the need for sound marriage laws to regulate sexual intercourse in the public interest. Christian monogamy, argued Paley, possessed built-in pragmatic advantages that made it a superior policy tool: "It is only in the marriage union that this [sexual] intercourse is sufficiently prolific. Besides which, family establishments alone are fitted to perpetuate a succession of generations. The offspring of a vague and promiscuous concubinage are not only few, and liable to perish by neglect, but are seldom prepared for, or introduced into, situations suited to the raising of families of their own." The monogamous household further contributed to political stability by cutting off sexual contests for the possession of more than one woman. (Harem intrigues, Paley thought, sufficiently explained the frequency of palace revolts in the Arab world.) Within "civilized" Western societies marriage to a single spouse divided the community into more manageable subunits, each under the control of a responsible master; it also tied parents to fixed habitations and incited them to greater industry during the minority of their offspring. Enlightened statesmanship therefore called for the strengthening of man's naturally monogamous tendencies through the application of appropriate legal sanctions. The state might grant bounties or tax exemptions to the parents of a certain number of legitimate children, for instance, while imposing stiff punishments on adulterers and others guilty of deviant sexual behavior.

Such a utilitarian approach to the institution of marriage goes far to explain the continued judicial acceptance of common-law and other irregular marriages in a majority of American states. The courts that recognized these informal unions were not as a rule staffed by frontier mavericks, nor did they display much sympathy for theories of anarchic individualism. A strong community interest guided their decisions, which legitimized the position of wives and children for inheritance purposes and prevented them from becoming potential public charges. That social conservatism played a large part in shaping the marital policies of the judiciary may be inferred from the fact that the chief supporters of common-law marriage were all members of the upper middle class, cosmopolitan city dwellers who had little interest in, or sympathy for, frontier mores.

Chancellor James Kent of New York did more than any other to entrench self-marriage in American jurisprudence, despite state statutes requiring registration, parental consent for minors, and other procedural formalities. In the landmark case of *Fenton v. Reed* (1809) Kent stated his position unequivocally: "No formal solemnization of marriage was requisite. A contract of marriage *per verba de presenti* amounts to an actual marriage, and is as valid as if made *in facie ecclesiae*." Like any other civil contract, marriage depended for its validity solely on a meeting of minds, on the free consent of the parties. And proof of consent was almost axiomatic; for, as Kent made clear in his later *Commentaries:* "The consent of the parties may be declared before a magistrate, or simply before witnesses, or subsequently confessed or acknowledged, or the marriage may even be inferred from continual cohabitation, and reputation as husband and wife."

The Kent doctrine found its way into the leading law texts of the antebellum period. * * * In a majority of jurisdictions judges relied upon these authorities to sustain the most unorthodox matrimonial arrangements against repeated legislative prohibitions. Statutes that imposed uniform marriage requirements were merely directory, the courts held; they set up a legal mode of solemnization (as the established church had once done), but they did not affect the underlying contractual obligation. Hence, in the absence of an express statutory declaration of nullity, a marriage could at the same time violate state law through procedural infractions, yet remain a binding contract between the parties.

This happy logic—which would have delighted the paradoxical mind of a W.S. Gilbert—did not find favor with all American judges, however. A substantial minority, particularly in the New England states, enforced legislative regulations to the letter and charged that a contrary course would require the courts to condone behavior that would otherwise be punishable as adultery or fornication. * * *

The highest court of Tennessee * * * repudiated common-law marriages on moral grounds. In *Grisham v. State* (1831) a widow and widower agreed to cohabit as man and wife and swore an oath to that effect, in the presence of witnesses. They were subsequently indicted and convicted of "lewd acts of fornication and adultery . . . to the great scandal of . . . good and worthy citizens." The state supreme court upheld their conviction with little difficulty, remarking that the law must ever be the "guardian of the morals of the people."

But in states where informal marriages had long been recognized, the consequences of overturning a settled custom forced even the most conscientious jurists to swallow their scruples and bow to expediency. "A doctrine which would tend to vitiate a great proportion of the marriages of the country would result in incalculable evils," asserted the Kentucky Supreme Court in 1821, "and can not be admitted to be correct." * * *

* * *

Where postmarital domestic relations were concerned, the law materially improved the position of wives and children in the years before the Civil War. Married women secured a greater measure of economic (and ultimately social) independence with the passage of Married Women's Property Acts in a majority of states. Mississippi enacted the first such statute in 1839, and by mid-century about nineteen other states had followed her example. None of these early laws gave a wife full legal equality in economic matters, but they did enlarge her capacity to deal independently with her property in a number of specific situations. They also simplified conveyance procedures and made unnecessary the cumbersome trust arrangement that had characterized family property settlements in the colonial era. Indeed, as Lawrence M. Friedman has observed, a major, if not controlling, motive behind much of this legislation was the desire to rationalize land transactions so that creditors might be better able to collect debts out of real estate owned by husband, wife, or both. Lawmakers certainly did not intend to effect any radical changes in the relations between the spouses; they sought merely to codify and expand colonial precedents, and to make available to all women the protective devices formerly reserved for a wealthy elite. Even these paternalistic designs were sometimes frustrated by conservative judges, who tended to construe strictly any statutory provisions that threatened to impair the common-law rights of married men.

A sampling of representative cases suggests the variety of judicial responses elicited by the claims of antebellum wives under specific statutes. In New York Judge Platt Potter of the state supreme court ruled that legislation passed in 1848 and 1849 had effectively abolished a husband's common-law right of curtesy in his wife's lands. Remedial statutes ought to be interpreted liberally, Potter argued, * * *:

> Why, in this noon of the nineteenth century, and under a free government, are we solemnly warned against innovations upon the common law as it existed, and the legal precedents established in the days of the Norman conqueror? Did all knowledge exist in the past? . . . For theories which have no support but antiquity I have no veneration . . . I hold an honest, sensible construction of the statute, according to its true intent, to be practical wisdom; and that the spirit of justice, befitting the wants of the age, is the soundest philosophy in a system of law. I regard it as a humiliating admission of intellectual decline, and worse than weak superstition, to assume that

> all wisdom existed in the former common law of England, or that laws suited to the condition of a free government could only be framed by the ancient inhabitants of Britain, whom Blackstone with fond partiality calls "our Saxon princes;" nor do I believe that it is only in the annals of past ages that we shall look for the wisdom necessary to guide us in our own. As changes are wrought in the circumstances of a people, or country, it is necessary, not only that their laws themselves, but also the spirit of the laws should be accommodated.

The New York statutes were meant to eradicate such feudal excrescences as tenancy by the curtesy, the learned judge concluded, and, if properly construed, they "will become a kind of magna charta, in the restoration of natural rights, too long and too unreasonably withheld." Unhappily for the feminist cause, the same New York tribunal a few months later qualified Potter's opinion considerably and reasserted a husband's common-law rights of succession to his wife's property. Although admitting that state legislation empowered a married woman to dispose of her property absolutely during her lifetime, the court nevertheless held that if she failed to do so her husband's vested marital rights of succession would become enforceable at the time of her death.

In the neighboring state of New Jersey, where the law authorized a wife to "hold" lands "to her sole and separate use," the courts ruled that she had no power to convey such lands to a third party, since they remained subject to her husband's right of curtesy. She might manage her landed property in her own interest, however, free from the power of her husband or the claims of his creditors.

Careless draftsmanship and ambiguous legislative purpose marred many of the early property acts and invited judges to resist any changes which they feared might alter traditional sex roles within the family. The most glaring example of legislative ambivalence involved the earnings of married women. Virtually no antebellum statute provided in express terms that a wife was entitled to the money or other property that she earned during her marriage. The courts therefore tended to uphold the common-law rights of the husband while indulging in avuncular remarks on the nobility of the American female. In Pennsylvania a statute passed in 1848 declared that "all property, of whatever name or description, which shall accrue to any married woman, by will, descent, deed of conveyance, or otherwise, shall be owned, used, and enjoyed by such married woman as her own separate property." Deceived by such apparently comprehensive coverage, a married woman who ran a boardinghouse sued in *Raybold v. Raybold* (1853) to establish her equitable title to some real estate that her husband had purchased out of her rents and savings. But the court turned a deaf ear to her claim, explaining: "Meritorious as her industry and frugality were, they enured to the benefit of her husband

. . . He is still entitled to the person and labor of the wife, and the benefits of her industry and economy. Nor is she degraded to the condition of a hireling, which she would be if servants' wages could become her separate property."

From state to state other wifely wage earners lost out to their male protectors with monotonous regularity. Mississippi, the pioneer in women's economic legislation, had provided in 1839 that "any married woman may become seized or possessed of any property, real or personal, by direct bequest, demise [*sic*], gift, purchase, or distribution, in her own name, and as of her own property, provided the same does not come from her husband after coverture." In *Henderson v. Warmack* (1854) an overseer's wife sought unsuccessfully to recover a slave whom she had bought with her own money, given to her by the plantation owners in return for extra services that she performed about the place. Despite the fact that the bill of sale was made out in her name alone, her husband seized the slave against her wishes and mortgaged him to one of his creditors as security for a debt. The court informed the irate wife that she had no legal leg to stand on: since the act did not refer to money earned by a wife during coverture, "such means would, therefore, remain the property of the husband, and a purchase made therewith by the wife would vest in the husband." * * *

Judicial concern over the weakening of long-accepted family relationships, which ran as an undercurrent through many of the property decisions, received its most articulate expression in an unusual and protracted Maryland case. The complaining wife in *Schindel v. Schindel* (1858) was a tempestuous southern belle of the Scarlett O'Hara variety, who walked out on her husband after six months of marriage because he allegedly said unkind and cruel things to her. Not content with returning to her mother's home to live, she sought to take all of her property with her, relying upon the terms of several state laws that asserted the economic rights of married women. First she induced her brother-in-law to carry off her furniture, but the husband promptly sued him for trespass, and won. She then brought suit in her own name, asking for an accounting of the use hitherto made of her separate property as well as an injunction against her husband's further management of her estate. Judge Thomas Perry, in rejecting her demands at the circuit court level, made explicit the underlying sexual assumptions that guided most antebellum jurists in their approach to the emancipation of the American housewife.

> Is it proper [Perry queried] to give a construction to the law, by which a change is to be made in the social relations of husband and wife, unknown to the common law, and which requires from her that which would do violence to that delicacy and retirement which is so much admired and encouraged, and so essential to the happiness of the marriage state? To give her a title as a *feme sole,* a title inde-

> pendent of, and distinct from her husband, would, as an incident to such right, require her to make all contracts and agreements and perform all the duties usually expected from the other sex, forcing her from the domestic circle to go out into the community to protect the rights to, and secure the profits of her property.

The fear of any drastic reordering of sex roles that might impair the stability of family life manifested itself still more strongly in the argument of attorney Richard H. Alvey, who represented Ms. Schindel's husband in the final stage of the case before the Maryland Court of Appeals. Alvey's strident harangue forecast the difficulties that later generations of legal traditionalists would face in trying to separate limited economic concessions from more fundamental changes in the social and political status of women:

> The right sought to be established by this proceeding is an extraordinary one, and goes far beyond anything that has yet been conceded to the cause of woman's rights. To enable the wife to leave her husband at pleasure, and to take with her, in the retreat, all her property, of every kind and description, to be enjoyed by her, and managed and disposed of as her own, apart from and to the entire exclusion of the husband, and in total disregard of the marital rights, is a monstrous proposition, that, among all the wild theories of improvements, has never yet been advocated in a civilized, Christian community, until the bringing of this suit, except by a few erratic and fanatical women, composing what is known as the "Woman's Rights Society." It is true, our legislation for the protection of married women, is of a most liberal character, even to the extent of doubtful propriety; but that it has gone the length of cutting the cords that bind society together, and of virtually destroying the moral and social efficacy of the marriage institution, is a notion not to be entertained for a moment. But such would be the inevitable result, if such a proceeding as this could be sustained. For let it once be understood that a wife, whenever she may become tired of her husband, or moved by any whim or caprice, may leave him, and take with her the whole property that she ever owned, and enjoy it exclusively, and thus become independent of that superiority and controlling power which the law has always wisely recognized in the husband, what incentive would there be for such a wife ever to reconcile differences with her husband, to act in submission to his wishes, and perform the many onerous duties pertaining to her sphere? Would not every wife, with property enough to sustain herself independently of her husband, when becoming impatient of his restraint and control, however necessarily exercised over her, take the refuge such a law would give her, and abandon her husband and her home? And thus the community would be filled with persons maintaining the unenviable character of husbands without wives, and wives without husbands, indulging in mutual hatred and ani-

> mosity, bringing disgrace upon themselves, and mortification upon their families and friends.

The high court proved predictably responsive to Alvey's reasoning and ruled that Ms. Schindel's capricious separation from her husband gave her no statutory right to separate maintenance or to the independent management of her property.

In the cold light of historical hindsight, the manifold deficiencies of the early Married Women's Property Acts stand out all too plainly. Crudely drafted, ambiguous in important particulars, subjected to rough handling by unsympathetic judges, they yet represented a major turning point in the legal emancipation of American women. If the rights they conceded were limited, and generally agreed to by male lawmakers with a minimum of debate or publicity, they amounted nonetheless to tangible economic gains that were further enlarged with the passage of time. The process was piecemeal and erratic; it was also progressive and irreversible. By 1875 a majority of state legislatures had passed statutes that explicitly gave a wife control of her separate earnings. And, where paternalistic lawmakers led, militant suffragettes soon followed. The old Blackstonian unity of husband and wife, once shattered by antebellum legislation, proved impossible to repair * * *.

Changes in the legal rights of the child during the antebellum years were far less dramatic, but here too some significant inroads were made upon traditional common-law doctrines of paternal power. * * *

Although most courts continued to uphold a father's paramount claim to the custody of his minor children in the absence of a strong showing of misconduct or unfitness on his part, the development of a more child-centered theory of guardianship was clearly discernible among progressive jurists. The new view, destined to prevail in later times, guided the New York Court of Errors in its approach to one of the most famous custody cases that arose in the United States prior to the Civil War. In *Mercein v. People ex rel. Barry* (1840) a husband and wife had separated, pursuant to an agreement that left an infant daughter, in delicate health, permanently in the care of her mother. Later the husband sought to recover custody of the child through habeas corpus proceedings that came before the courts on five different occasions. At one point the court of errors, the highest state tribunal, ruled that the mother might retain possession of the girl, who was only two years old and required special care. "The interest of the infant is deemed paramount to the claims of both parents," declared Senator Alonzo C. Paige, who then went on to outline a theory of the state as *parens patriae* in custody situations:

> By the law of nature, the father has no paramount right to the custody of his child. By that law the wife and child are equal to the husband and father; but inferior and subject to their sovereign. The head of a family, in his character of husband and father, has no authority

> over his wife and children; but in his character of sovereign he has. On the establishment of civil societies, the power of the chief of a family as sovereign, passes to the chief or government of the nation. And the chief or magistrate of the nation not possessing the requisite knowledge necessary to a judicious discharge of the duties of guardianship and education of children, such portion of the sovereign power as relates to the discharge of these duties, is transferred to the parents, subject to such restrictions and limitations as the sovereign power of the nation thinks proper to prescribe. There is no parental authority independent of the supreme power of the state . . . The moment a child is born, it owes allegiance to the government of the country of its birth, and is entitled to the protection of that government. And such government is obligated by its duty of protection, to consult the welfare, comfort and interests of such child in regulating its custody during the period of its minority.

But matters did not end there, for two years later the husband secured another writ, and the New York Supreme Court then ordered his daughter to be returned to him. Exceptional circumstances no longer existed, since the child was now healthy and the father admittedly capable of giving her a proper upbringing. The qualifications of both spouses being equal, the court held that "by the law of the land the claims of the father are superior to those of the mother."

Despite the final outcome of the *Mercein* case, which was typical of custody decisions in other states, the willingness of antebellum judges to weigh the peculiar needs of the individual child against the claims of either parent marked a necessary transitional stage in the evolution of modern custody practices. Not all judges were so child-oriented, of course; some clung stubbornly to the old formulas of paternal omnipotence. But by 1860 the tide had set in the direction of more humane custody procedures as legislatures, too, began to recognize the importance of consulting a child's wishes and interests in matters of parental guardianship. Massachusetts lawmakers thus passed statutes in 1855 and 1856 that gave judges broad discretionary control over the award of custody in divorce and separation cases, "on the principle that the rights of the parents to their children, in the absence of misconduct, are equal, and the happiness and welfare of the children are to determine the care and custody."

A similar concern for child welfare led some antebellum courts to impose upon parents a legal obligation to support their minor children, where the common law had recognized only a nonenforceable moral duty. New York judges pioneered in the establishment of this principle, which took almost half a century to evolve fully out of scattered and tentative precedents. It was not until 1863 that the New York Supreme Court squarely held that a third party who supplied necessaries to a minor could recover his expenses from the child's delinquent parent in an action at common law. Parental liability in such circumstances, reasoned the court, was analogous to a husband's common-law obligation to provide for his wife: both derived from the essential nature of the marriage relation itself. * * *

* * *

Finally, with the passage of the first comprehensive adoption acts around the middle of the nineteenth century, a serious effort was made to give adopted children all of the legal rights formerly enjoyed by natural children alone, including a share of the estate of adoptive parents who died intestate. * * *

As in the case of marriage laws, the regulations governing divorce varied widely from state to state. South Carolina remained a divorceless society down to the Civil War; New York granted divorces for only one cause, adultery. But most states tended to enlarge upon the limited precedents set in colonial times in two ways: they broadened the range of acceptable legal grounds for divorce, and they democratized divorce procedures so as to bring legal action for the first time within the reach of every taxpayer.

Indiana went further than any other state in multiplying grounds for complaint. Besides the traditional ones, such as adultery, bigamy, and desertion, her statutes recognized cruel treatment, habitual drunkenness, conviction of a felony, and "any other cause for which the Court shall deem it proper that the divorce shall be granted." This open-ended "omnibus clause," coupled with lax residence requirements, made the Hoosier state the divorce capital of the country in the 1850s. She also served as a model for sister jurisdictions in one other respect: her new constitution of 1851 expressly forbade the legislature to meddle in any way with future divorce proceedings, which were left exclusively in the hands of the judiciary.

The shift from private divorce bills to court decrees granted pursuant to general statutes marked one of the most striking developments in antebellum jurisprudence. A nationwide phenomenon, it seems to have reflected in part a real increase in the demand for legal divorces. So much may be gleaned from the reasons officially given by the Georgia legislature in 1835 for vesting complete jurisdiction over divorces thereafter in the state courts. The number of divorce applications had increased alarmingly in recent years, the lawmakers reported, taxing the time and energies of the legislative body and unnecessarily swelling the statute books. * * * State legislators hoped to curb the trend by entrusting divorce matters to the more conservative administration of the courts, asserted Judge Eugenius A. Nisbet in an early decision interpreting the new legislation.

If conditions in Georgia were at all representative of those in other states, logistical considerations played a determining role in the abolition of legislative divorces. But other factors, of a less obvious nature, may also have been operative. Thus, a move toward general divorce laws arguably represented part of a larger crusade against special privilege that moved into high gear with the election of Andrew Jackson to the Presidency in 1828. Just as small businessmen in the antebellum period sometimes demanded and got general incorporation laws from their state legislatures to protect them against the expense and favoritism associated with individual legislative grants, so less affluent householders may have sought general divorce legislation to eliminate the need for costly private bills that catered to the interests of the upper classes. * * *

Despite the comparative ease with which divorces were made available to the masses in these years, however, there was no dramatic rush to take advantage of them. Statistics indicate only a slight rise in the national divorce rate to the time of the Civil War, when the figures leveled off at 0.3 divorces per 1,000 persons, a ratio that remained virtually constant for the next decade. There was much loose talk of a spreading "divorce evil" in newspapers and magazines * * *. But in retrospect the relaxation of divorce requirements, like the passage of the Married Women's Property Acts, appears rather a symbolic gesture—a concession to the temper of a democratic society—than the signal for any revolutionary assault upon the institution of the family.

NOTES AND QUESTIONS

1. One of the most interesting aspects of this pithy reading from Professor Bloomfield's provocative book is that he explores several different theories to account for historical change. For example, he begins his analysis by suggesting that "frontier" conditions in the colonies exerted an influence on the law of the family, in particular in the institution of common-law marriage. Is the notion of "common-law marriage," (one foreign, by the way, to the English common law) one of which you approve? Who benefits by the courts' holding spouses in a common-law marriage to have created the effect of a legally-binding marriage covenant?

Why would some courts have felt that giving legal force to "common law marriages" was morally repugnant? Can you draw any connections between the thought that would have refused enforcement to common law marriages, the reluctance to give legal effect to adoptions of children, and the reluctance to allow women to have the full enjoyment of private property rights in marriage? How much of this reluctance on the part of judges can be explained through a "frontier" theory of legal development? What accounts for it? See generally Ariela R. Dubler, "Governing through Contract: Common Law Marriage in the Nineteenth Century," 107 Yale L.J. 1885 (1998).

2. Another model, like the "frontier" idea based on economic factors, which Bloomfield relies on to explain legal change is the broad movement in Western European society from feudalism to capitalism which movement culminates in the nineteenth century. In particular Bloomfield notes how the

feudal tenures for property, and the related "family-law" doctrines such as dower, curtesy, primogeniture and entail were eroded in the nineteenth century. These doctrines were originally set up to keep real property intact and passed down from generation to generation. They quickly went by the board in America, as Americans came to feel that it was more important to turn land into a market commodity than it was to retain the stability and tradition of landed estates.

Blackstone is rather uneasily poised between the world of feudalism and the world of capitalism, and this explains the archaic nature of many of the doctrines of family law he explores. Does Bloomfield help you understand how American society came to differ from the English feudal model? At this point you might wish to turn back to our readings from Jefferson and Tocqueville to get their thoughts on the decline of feudalism and the rise of democracy in American property law.

3. Still another causal theme which Bloomfield explores, related, perhaps, to the decline of feudalism, is the increasing secularization of American law, the declining influence of religion in general and Christianity in particular on American family law. Which set of views, that which would have liberally enforced common law marriage, adoption, and married women's property acts, or that which would have been reluctant to enforce them is in accord with secularization? Which do you prefer?

Is there anything to be said for resisting the secularization of American family law? You will remember that the Old Testament was relied on to defend the institution of slavery in the South, just as the Old Testament was relied upon by allegedly patriarchal nineteenth century English and American judges who sought to defend the notion of the husband and wife being but "one person" at common law. How did such reliance work, and of what importance was the story of Eve and the apple to the legal analysis?

You will have noted that some nineteenth century judges almost seemed to prefer relying on "providence" to enforce the "moral obligations" of protection, support, and education that parents ought to owe children, instead of making these legally enforceable obligations. Why? It is pretty clear that today the state will step in and compel the performance of such obligations, to the extent that parents have available resources, and, indeed, that if parents are unable to support their children, there are means by which the state can remove them from the custody of the parents. The family unit, in short, is much less sacrosanct than it used to be. Is this necessarily progress? What are the costs of secularization of family law?

It is even doubtful just how far "secularization" was implemented by American judges in the antebellum years. You will have noticed, for example, that Bloomfield makes much of the influence on American family law of a man whom he describes as a "Christian utilitarian philosopher," the English theologian William Paley (1743–1805). How much of Paley's influence on American family law was "Christian," and how much was "utilitarian?" Bloomfield suggests that Paley's influence resulted in a conservative "community-oriented" antebellum jurisprudence of family law. Other scholars, evaluating the full sweep of the nineteenth century, however, have suggested that the law generally reflected the rise of American individualism. Which influence is better for family law?

4. Consider the "Married Women's Property Acts," chronicled by Bloomfield. Do you find that they reflect economic change, secularization, individualism, or some combination of these factors? Can you defend the resistance to those acts on the part of antebellum courts, if resistance it was? Why might they favor implementing the "patriarchal" rights of the husband? Could these judges have had a valid argument that they were preserving the family unit and combating some of the inherent evils of unbridled individualism? Were there alternatives to patriarchy that could still implement the view of the family as a unit? Does focus on the married women's property acts, or the status of women in marriage illuminate or obscure the important issues of the family in American society? See generally, Dianne Avery and Alfred S. Konefsky, "The Daughters of Job: Property Rights and Women's Lives in Mid–Nineteenth–Century Massachusetts," 10 Law & History Rev. 323 (1992).

How do you explain the fact that Mississippi, a Southern state, was in the vanguard of the protection for married women's property rights? What does this do to any theories you might have of the forces that resulted in those acts?

In any event, no matter what their source, note that Bloomfield does seem to see a slow, steady progress in the rights of women—first the Married Women's Property Acts that protected the property women brought into marriage, and then the legislative acts which reversed hostile court decisions, and protected women's earnings during coverture. Moreover, note that Bloomfield appears to find in the Married Women's Property Acts a desire democratically to expand ideas that were already in the common law. He suggests that these works of nineteenth century legislation were not intended to make radical changes in relations between spouses—"they sought merely to codify and expand colonial precedents, and to make available to all women the protective devices (e.g. the trust) formerly reserved for a wealthy elite."

Nevertheless, you will have noticed that some judges were so sympathetic to the democratizing goals of the acts that they saw them as an opportunity fundamentally to move away from the feudal sympathies of the English common law. Bloomfield's example of this trend is New York Judge Platt Potter, who championed the wisdom of nineteenth century legislation, and railed against the Blackstonian view of the ancient wisdom of the English common law. Platt's views are part of a massive intellectual movement in American law in the nineteenth century, called the codification movement, whose adherents believed that Americans ought democratically to fashion their own law by statutes, and ought to move away from dependence on an allegedly undemocratic and basically feudal English common law. For a very readable summary of this movement see another Chapter in Bloomfield's book, "William Sampson and the Codification Movement," at pages 59–90. See also

Charles M. Cook, The American Codification Movement, A Study of Antebellum Legal Reform (1981). The Married Women's Property Acts, and the legislation affecting divorce, adoption, and child custody are all products of this trend in American law.

5. Should all of this legislative reform be interpreted as a cup that is half-full or half-empty? For a provocative treatment of this and other issues, suggesting that the decline of the role of the father as patriarch in the family eroded in the nineteenth century only to surrender authority to a new class of super-patriarchs, the judges, see the prize-winning book by Michael Grossberg, Governing the Hearth: Law and the Family in Nineteenth–Century America 304–305 (1985):*

> Perhaps the most enduring product of the distinctive domestic-relations law hammered out in nineteenth-century America was the legal concept of the family as a collection of separate legal individuals rather than an organic part of the body politic. This occurred at the expense of traditional notions of paternal sovereignty and household legal unity. The older concept of the family, evident in the legal maxim "the husband and wife are one, and that one is the husband," gradually declined as the distinct legal personalities of married women and their children developed. In an analysis of family governance in France, sociologist Jacques Donzelot has persuasively argued that "[f]amily patriarchalism was destroyed only at the cost of a patriarchy of the State." In republican America, the state's new parental authority was delegated to the bench; judges used their patriarchal powers to forge direct relationships between each family member and the state. These legal identities breached the home's protective walls and vitiated its role as a buffer between the state and each occupant of the household.

As you consider the rest of these notes and questions, and as you read the rest of the materials in this section, see if you agree or disagree with Grossberg. For further development of Grossberg's views on the importance of Family and Legal History see his "Crossing Boundaries: Nineteenth Century Domestic Relations Law and the Merger of Family and Legal History," 1985 Am.Bar.Found.Res. J. 799. For a provocative suggestion that it might make more sense to reorder the Blackstonian patriarchal model with one suggested by Justice Ruth Bader Ginsburg, which might lead to a "new and more democratic family theory," see Allison Anna Tait, "A Tale of Three Families: Historical Households, Earned Belonging, and Natural Connections," 63 Hastings L.J. 1345 (2012).

6. We will return to the theme of the patriarchy of American law in the last chapter of the book, but it might be worth remarking, in passing, that the idea of the movement away from a patriarchal family order to one characterized more by a collection of relatively autonomous and equal individuals has even been suggested as a cause for the American Revolution. In

his extraordinary Prodigals and Pilgrims: The American Revolution Against Patriarchal Authority 1750–1800 (1982),* Jay Fliegelman observed that

> By the middle of the eighteenth century family relations had been fundamentally reconsidered in both England and America. An older patriarchal family authority was giving way to a new parental ideal characterized by a more affectionate and equalitarian relationship with children. This important development paralleled the emergence of a humane form of childrearing that accommodated the stages of a child's growth and recognized the distinctive character of childhood. Parents who embraced the new childrearing felt a deep moral commitment to prepare their children for a life of rational independence and moral self-sufficiency.

Fliegelman suggests that Americans had been prepared, by eighteenth century child rearing practices to "make a successful separation from their parents and to face with equanimity the prospect of living independently." This allowed them more easily to participate in "overthrowing the father figure of George III." The idea which Fliegelman explores is that the new non-patriarchal family had prepared Americans to think that they had "come of age" and that they were ready to take their own place in the greater family of nations, independent of any patriarchal authority at all, in the family, or in the British Empire. Fliegelman thus suggests that the American Revolution (and, presumably, by extension, the change in American family law) can be viewed, at least in part, as an outgrowth of the application of new, non-patriarchal psychological theories of child-rearing, such as those advanced by John Locke in his Essay Concerning Human Understanding (1690), or Jean Jacques Rousseau in his seminovelistic pedagogical work Emile (1762). For further work on the flexible discourse surrounding the American family in the early republican period see Linda K. Kerber, Women of the Republic: Intellect and Ideology in Revolutionary America (1980), Mary Beth Norton, Liberty's Daughters: The Revolutionary Experience of American Women, 1750–1850 (1980), and Sylvia A. Law, "The Founders on Families," 39 U.Fla.L.Rev. 583 (1987).

7. You will have noticed, as well as his concern with "patriarchy," the suggestion in the excerpt from Michael Grossberg, note 5, supra, that the new family law forged in the nineteenth century was for "republican" America. The emergence of "republican" theory as a force for legal change has also been made much of by legal scholars, and is advanced by Grossberg, among others, as another alternative cause for the changes in family law. For brief descriptions of the variant approaches to "republican" ideologies among nineteenth century Americans in general and an analysis of Grossberg's thought in particular see Emily Field Van Tassel, Judicial Patriarchy and Republican Family Law, 74 Georgetown Law Journal 1553 (1986). Do you think that changes in family law and society result from economics, politics, ideology, psychology, or some combination of these factors?

---

8. We began this section with a reading on the status of women in marriage, but Bloomfield and Grossberg have broadened our analysis to consider also issues related to divorce and child custody. For further reading on judicial attitudes toward divorce in antebellum law see Hendrik Hartog, "Marital Exits and Marital Expectations in Nineteenth Century America," 80 Geo.L.J. 95 (1991), which now appears, in a revised version, as Chapter 3 in Hartog's magisterial Man and Wife in America: A History (2000). Hartog's fascinating thesis is that family law in American changed over the course of "the long Nineteenth Century" (which is a term he uses to denote a period that ends shortly after World War II and begins in 1790), because of the pressures created by married couples who separated from each other. How do the developments in the law of antebellum divorce and child custody reflect the issues involved in the Married Women's Property Acts and their judicial interpretation?

To address divorce first, do you favor a liberal or a strict law of divorce? Consider the opinion of Judge Thomas Perry and the argument of the counsel for the husband in the *Schindel v. Schindel* case, discussed by Bloomfield. Do you find the idea that a wife could leave her husband (who allegedly verbally abused her), and seek to take her property with her, "monstrous?" Would you agree that in a "civilized Christian community" such behavior by a wife could only be advocated by "erratic and fanatical women?"

Our primary vehicle for considering nineteenth-century judicial attitudes toward child custody and husband-wife relations is the convoluted *Barry* case, which you have encountered in the reading from Bloomfield. Consider, to begin with, some comments from the New York Chancellor's, 1839 opinion in the case, *People ex rel. Barry v. Mercein,* 8 Paige 47, 56–57:

> * * * [I]t is contrary to public policy to allow the husband or the wife to withdraw from the duty of matrimonial cohabitation for any slight causes, which do not endanger the personal safety of the party; as such withdrawal is wholly repugnant to good morals and the injunctions of the divine lawgiver. The court, therefore, is bound to set its face against every attempt on the part of married persons, either by agreement or otherwise, to throw off the duties or the responsibilities which the marriage contract has imposed upon them. To use the language of a late distinguished judge, who certainly was well qualified to speak on this subject, and from experience, too, if his biographer is correct in supposing that his own matrimonial sky was not always clear, it is not difficult to show that the law in this respect is in accordance with its usual wisdom and humanity,—with that true wisdom and real humanity which regard the general interests of mankind.
>
> Though in particular cases the repugnance of the law to dissolve the obligations of matrimonial cohabitation may operate with great severity upon individuals, yet it must be remembered that the general happiness of the married life is secured by its indissolubility. When married people understand that they must live together, except for a very few reasons

> known to the law, they have to soften by mutual accommodation that yoke which they know they cannot shake off. They become good husbands and good wives from the necessity of remaining husbands and wives; for necessity is a powerful master in teaching the duties it imposes. Were it once understood that upon mutual disgust married persons might legally separate themselves from each other, many couples, who now pass through the world with mutual comfort, with attention to their common offspring and to the moral order of civil society, might have been at this moment living in a state of mutual unkindness; in a state of estrangement from their common offspring; and perhaps in a state of the most licentious and unreserved immorality. In this case, as in many others, therefore, the happiness of some individuals must be sacrificed to the greater and more general good. * * *

Do you see anything wrong with this reasoning? Is there a problem in the notion of sacrificing the happiness of some to the greater good of others? Is there a problem with compelling any two parties to a marriage contract who desire to alter it to stick to the state's understanding of the arrangement? Why might nineteenth century judges have believed that, in particular, giving a woman the freedom to leave her husband "for slight causes" (causes which we might now well regard as the intentional infliction of mental distress, and everywhere grounds for divorce) would destroy "the moral and social efficacy of the marriage institution?"

9. Somewhat later in his 1839 opinion, the New York Chancellor in the *Barry* case quoted Lord Eldon, a distinguished English jurist on the nature of the marriage contract:

> * * * [T]he marriage contract, whether it be considered as a civil contract only, or one which is both civil and religious, is a contract of a very peculiar nature. It is one which the parties cannot dissolve; one by which they impose duties upon themselves, and by which they engage to perform duties with respect to their offspring,—duties which are imposed as much for the sake of public policy as of private happiness.

Id., at 67. Do you believe that "the marriage contract" is different from other kinds of contracts? Do you believe that it is "both civil and religious?" Do you think that those whom God has joined together in holy matrimony, to paraphrase the traditional marriage ceremony, should easily be put asunder? On the other hand, do you favor the system of "divorce on demand," or "no-fault divorce," which is what, essentially, we have now? Why or why not? Have the dire predictions of the New York chancellor in 1839 come to pass for modern families? Unanticipated by Bloomfield, Lord Eldon, or the New York Chancellor, of course, was early twenty-first century controversy over whether to permit gay partners to marry, a controversy stirred to the boiling point by the United States Supreme Court's decision in Lawrence v. Texas, 539 U.S. 558 (2003), in which it ruled that criminal punishment of homosexual sodomy violated the Constitution. At least one dissenting opinion in that case predicted that the Court's holding could be construed to bar state authorities

invoked) provision of the seventeenth century New England Puritan legislation which provided the death penalty for a child who struck his parents?

14. Bloomfield suggests that the story of child custody procedures in the nineteenth century is one of a shift from the father having superior child custody rights to one in which the "best interests" of the child predominated. There seems to have been great uncertainty about the proper standards in child custody cases *both* in America and England. In *Blisset's* case, for example, decided by Lord Mansfield in 1774, a case in which the parents disagreed about who was best suited to care for a child, Mansfield declared, flatly, "If the parties disagree, the court will do what shall appear best for the child." By the early nineteenth century, however, a series of English judicial decisions had enunciated the rule that

> [T]he father of a child born in lawful wedlock was entitled to the entire and absolute control and custody of that child, and to exclude from any share in that control and custody the mother of that child. The mother might be the most virtuous woman that ever lived, amiable in her manners, fond and attached to her children; the father, on the other hand, might be profligate in character, brutal in manner, living in adultery, and yet would have the right, under the existing law, to the custody of the children of his marriage, to the exclusion of even access to them of his wife, their mother.

Remarks of Lord Lyndhurst, in the House of Lords July 30, 1838, 44th Vol.Parl.Debates, 8 series, at 774.

In 1839 the British Parliament modified these father-centered rules of child custody, in an act which authorized the English equity courts to enter orders for the access of the mother to her young children, and, if the child was under 7 years old, to require that it be delivered to and remain in the custody of the mother until reaching the age of 7. This rule, from a British statute, did not, of course, have any effect in America, where the father was still often favored in custody disputes. Nevertheless, the American courts seem to have struggled to avoid the worst excesses of English law, and to implement something of a spirit of reform, even if they tried to follow the rules requiring a preference for the father. For the difficulties of adjudicating child custody in the nineteenth century see the work by a leading historian of the American family, Michael Grossberg, A Judgment for Solomon: The D'Hauteville Case and Legal Experience in Antebellum America (1996).

15. In one of the opinions in the *Barry* case, delivered in 1840, the judge declared that he was bound to follow the nineteenth century rules requiring custody to be given to the father, but he noted there were exceptions, and he seemed to suggest that it was the interests of the child which governed, not the absolute right of the father:

> In these unhappy controversies between husband and wife, the former, if he chooses to assert his right, has the better title to the custody of their minor children. The law regards him as the head of the family; obliges

him to provide for its wants; and commits the children to his charge, in preference to the claims of the mother or any other person. * * *

* * * I deem it well settled that, in the absence of any positive disqualification on the part of the father, for the proper discharge of his parental duties, and when there is no other special reason, touching the welfare of the children, for preferring the mother, the father has a paramount right to the custody, which no court is at liberty to disregard.

In taking into consideration the probable welfare of the children, we do not presume, without proof, that it will be best promoted by preferring the mother. The law has settled that question the other way, by preferring the father. His claim cannot be set aside upon light grounds, or upon mere conjecture that the interests of the children require it. He must be chargeable with such grossly immoral conduct as shows him plainly disqualified for the proper discharge of parental duties; or else it must appear that, in consequence of disease or some other misfortune, he wants either the capacity or the means for the proper training of the children, according to their circumstances and expectations in life. And whatever may be the objections to the father, they cannot prevail, if the same objection, or others of the like magnitude can be urged against the mother. In short, the claim of the father is preferred, until it plainly appears that the interests of the children require it to be set aside.

Bronson, J., in Mercein v. People ex rel. Barry, 25 Wend. 64, 71–72 (1840). Bronson reversed the 1839 opinion of the New York Chancellor in the case, and suggested that no evidence had been offered to rebut the presumption of the appropriate parent for custody being the father.

16. Even so, under the "best interests of the child" standard, at least in the case of younger children, the child custody "rights" of the mother often were favored, just as they implicitly were in the 1839 British statute. Indeed, in the 1839 opinion in the *Barry* case, which was reversed by Judge Bronson, the Chancellor had declared, in the course of a decision awarding continuing legal custody of a two-year old daughter to its mother that:

* * * the mother, all other things being equal, is the most proper person to be entrusted with such a charge, in relation to an infant of this tender age. The law of nature has given to her an attachment for her infant offspring which no other relative will be likely to possess in an equal degree. And where no sufficient reasons exist for depriving her of the care and nurture of her child, it would not be a proper exercise of discretion in any court to violate the law of nature in this respect.

8 Paige's Chancery Reports, at 70. This seems to give a presumption of better fitness for custody of young children to the mother, according to "the law of nature."

17. The 1840 *Barry* opinion by Bronson, reversing the Chancellor, was itself reversed by another New York court. You have read an excerpt from

this opinion in the Bloomfield reading, a quote from Senator Alonzo C. Paige, writing in Mercein v. People ex rel. Barry (1840). There the Senator endorses the "interests of the infant" standard as "paramount to the claims of both parents." Somehow Paige manages to derive this from an analysis of the "law of nature." Does the New York Chancellor in the 1839 opinion, or Senator Paige in the 1840 opinion strike you as engaged in the kind of "law of nature" analysis you saw employed by the Federalist judge Richard Peters in Chapter Two, supra? Is it the law of nature referred to by Thomas Jefferson in the Declaration of Independence? Is the law of nature they describe one to which you are prepared to submit? Alternatively, are you comfortable with the notion, also expressed by Senator Paige, that all parental rights to child custody derive from the "supreme power of the state?"

18. By now you might well be curious to learn a bit more about the *Barry* case, which generated so many opinions on the law of child custody and marriage. Perhaps you are even intrigued about how it finally came out, since it was a rather stark pitting of the rights of father, mother, and child against each other. Your next reading is the final published opinion in that case, following the Chancellor's opinion, the opinion by Judge Bronson in 1839, and Senator Paige's opinion in 1840.

The matter still in dispute was ostensibly who was to have custody of the Barrys' daughter, who was then four and one-half. Complicating the case, and bringing in the problems as well of the legal relationship between husband and wife, the child's mother, Mrs. Barry, had, years earlier, left the child's father, Mr. Barry. She justified separating herself (and her daughter) from her husband, on the grounds that Barry had broken a promise he made to her to live near her own father, Mr. Mercein. Mrs. Barry's fondness for her father, and her unwillingness to be separated from *him* was an attachment that one of the courts referred to as close to a "mental illness." Mr. Barry had been quite exasperated with Mrs. Barry on occasion, and had, at least once, refused to sleep in the same bed with her. This was in a fit of temper when she refused to take some medicine prescribed by a doctor. Nevertheless, Barry's attachment to his wife probably had some of the same pathological features of her attachment to her father. Barry tried, for many years, to get her to come back with him and live in Nova Scotia, and leave her father in New York.

The New York Court for the Correction of Errors, as you may remember, a rather exotic and short-lived New York judicial appellate court which included among its members the body of the New York Senate, including Senator Paige, had, as you have seen, ordered in 1840 that the Barrys' little girl, then two, be allowed to remain with her mother, who still insisted on staying with Mr. Mercein.

19. What you will next read is the high-water mark of Mr. Barry's ill-fated attempt to get custody of his daughter, and, perhaps, indirectly to get back his wife. The person referred to as "the relator" in the court's opinion is Mr. Barry, the father and spurned husband. It is an obscure legal term used to designate the real party in interest when, as was the case here, the pro-

ceeding had to be brought in the name of the state, "the people." The proceeding is one called the writ of *habeas corpus* (literally "you have the body"), which was brought to force one confining another (here Mr. Barry's father-in-law, who was allegedly illegally confining Mr. Barry's daughter) to produce the person confined before the court, for the court to determine whether the confinement was lawful or not.

One more arcane aspect of the case flows from the fact that the question of appropriate custody for the daughter had already been considered in several opinions by three New York courts, some of which had clearly been against the custody of the father. Mr. Mercein, Mrs. Barry's father, raised as defenses the doctrines of *res judicata* and *estoppel,* which as applied here, simply meant that these matters had already been decided, and the parties ought to be bound by what had been decided before. See if you can understand why this defense was rejected. Professor Hendrik Hartog of Princeton discovered that the following opinion did not end the matter, and that although Mr. Barry was awarded custody by the New York Supreme Court, that award was immediately reversed by the Court of Errors, in an unreported decision. Barry then tried to get the Court of Errors opinion overturned by the federal courts, but lost there as well. Hartog's witty and exhaustive analysis of Mr. Barry's attempts to implement his patriarchal prerogatives is to be found in Hartog's "John Barry and American Fatherhood," Chapter 7 in his book, Man and Wife in America (2000).

THE PEOPLE *EX REL.* BARRY V. MERCEIN

3 Hill. 399 (1842).

Habeas *corpus ad subjiciendum,* issued and returned at the last term of this court. The writ commanded the respondent, Thomas R. Mercein, to bring into court Mary Mercein Barry, an infant child of John A. Barry, the relator; the said child, as alleged, being illegally detained by the respondent, and withheld from the relator's custody. The petition for the writ did not purport to be presented on behalf of the child, but by the relator in his right as father. From the petition and return it appeared that, at the time of awarding the writ, the child was about four years and six months old—that her mother, Eliza Anna Barry, wife of the relator, was a daughter of the respondent—that she, with the respondent's consent and countenance, was living at his house, in a state of voluntary separation from her husband, having the said child with her—that the relator had made repeated applications to his wife and the respondent for the custody of the child, but without success, & c.

The marriage between the relator and the said Eliza Anna took place in the spring of 1835, at her father's house in the city of New–York; she then being upwards of twenty-five years of age, the relator a British subject, born in Nova Scotia, where he was engaged in business. Shortly after this event he and his wife proceeded to Nova Scotia, and resided there for a year. They then, at her solicitation, removed to the city of New York, at which place he engaged in mercantile pursuits. His New York business proving unfortunate, however, in the winter of 1837, he found himself constrained to relinquish it. Previous to this, two children were born, the issue of the marriage; viz. a son, now between five and six years old, and a daughter, the child in question. In the spring of 1838 it was arranged between the relator, his wife and the respondent, that she and the two children should stay at the respondent's house, while the relator went to Nova Scotia with a view to re-establishing himself in business there. Nothing like a permanent separation was proposed or contemplated at this time; at least, there was no evidence of such having been the intent either of the relator or his wife. He embarked for Nova Scotia in April 1838, accompanied by his elder daughters, children of a former marriage; and, after an absence of three or four weeks, he returned, proposing to his wife certain measures preparatory to their permanent settlement in Nova Scotia. She strongly opposed his views on that subject, and finally told him she never would *consent* to go, & c.—that he might *force* her to go by taking her son—but rather than this, she would prefer *to part with the relator at once.* He expressed himself displeased and disappointed with her conduct; and, after some further conversation, left the respondent's house. Various letters then passed between the relator and his wife respecting their future views and intentions, the disposition to be made of their children, & c.; and the correspondence finally resulted in an agreement, executed under the hands and seals of the relator, his wife and the respondent, as follows: "Agreement made this 7th day of June, 1838, between John A. Barry of the first part, Eliza Anna Barry of the second part, and Thomas R. Mercein of the third part. Whereas *certain differences have existed* between John A. Barry and Eliza Anna, which it is their *mutual desire shall be amicably and peacefully arranged and reconciled;* and the said John A. Barry's business requiring him to be *absent from New York for a time; and neither individual at present wishing a final separation:* IT IS AGREED between the aforesaid John A. Barry of the one part, the said Eliza Anna his wife of the second part, and Thomas R. Mercein of the third part, that the said John A. Barry *shall leave in the care and keeping of his said wife, until the first day of May next ensuing,* their daughter Mary Mercein, and that on that day or so soon thereafter as may be, he shall relinquish to Eliza Anna, his said wife, *all his right existing at that or accruing at any then future period to their said daughter, provided his said wife shall then require him so to do.* The aforesaid parties also covenant and agree that Mercein, the son of the said John A. and Eliza Anna, shall be left in the care and keeping of his said mother until she shall be required by his said father to deliver him, the said Mercein, to him the said John A. Barry; the said mother having, at such time, the option to accompany him. *Finally,* it is agreed between the aforesaid parties, that this document may be *cancelled annulled and destroyed at any moment by the mutual consent of the said John A. Barry and Eliza Anna his wife* In witness" & c.

In the latter part of June, 1838, the relator again embarked for Nova Scotia, and returned on the 8th of September following. At this time he proposed to his wife that he would remain in New–York until spring, provided she would positively promise then to return with him to Nova Scotia. She refused; and, in the course of the interview, he spoke of taking their son from her in case she persisted in her refusal. She acknowledged his power of doing so, but admonished him that such a step *would seal their fate*. The son was afterward given up to the relator, and has since remained with him.

On the 18th of May, 1839, the relator instituted proceedings by *habeas corpus* before the recorder of the city of New–York, to obtain the custody of the child now in question. The writ was directed to the respondent, and he and the relator's wife united in making return to it. The result was, an order by the recorder "that the said Mary Mercein Barry do remain in the care and custody of the said Eliza Anna Barry, *until the said John A. Barry and the said Eliza Anna Barry shall make some arrangement or compromise, or until the custody of the said child shall be changed by a judicial decision*." This order was made on the 1st of July, 1839. On the 13th of the same month, the relator obtained another writ of *habeas corpus* from the chancellor. * * * The chancellor's order declared "that the said infant daughter of the relator *is not improperly restrained of her liberty* by the said Thomas R. Mercein, and that *no good reason now exists for taking the said infant child from the care and protection of the said Thomas R. Mercein,* & c.; and this court therefore will not make an order to take the said infant child from the custody and nurture of its mother & c., for the purpose of delivering it up to the relator," & c. This order was dated the 26th of August, 1839. On the 29th of October following, the relator instituted like proceedings before William Inglis, one of the associate judges of the common pleas of the city and county of New–York. The respondent interposed the same facts upon which he had prevailed before the chancellor and the recorder; insisting, moreover, that the orders made by those officers respectively, constituted a bar to further litigation as to the same subject matter. The final order of Judge Inglis was made on the 30th of April, 1840, refusing to deliver up the child to the relator. * * * The relator caused these proceedings to be removed by certiorari into this court; where they were reversed. * * * The respondent thereupon sued out a writ of error; and afterwards the court for the correction of errors *reversed* the decision of this court, and *affirmed* that of Judge Inglis, *with costs to be paid by the relator.* * * * Intermediate the decision by this court and that of the court for the correction of errors—viz. in October, 1840—the relator, on application to this court, obtained a fourth *habeas corpus,* returnable on the 30th of the same month, before Thomas J. Oakley, one of the associate justices of the superior court of the city of New–York; * * * this writ being directed to the respondent and the relator's wife, and having the like object with the others. A return was made, and the proceedings remained pending until March, 1841, when Judge Oakley decided "that said infant child, Mary Mercein Barry, is *not improperly restrained of her liberty by the said Thomas R. Mercein and the said Eliza Anna Barry, or either of them, and that the said infant child be not taken from its mother & c., to be given to the said John A. Barry,* and that the said writ of *habeas corpus* be discharged."

Soon after this, the relator returned to Nova Scotia, where he engaged in business and has continued to reside; having occasionally, however, during the interval, been in the city of New–York. The petition mentioned various fruitless efforts on his part since the decision of Judge Oakley, to obtain the custody of the child, and induce his wife to live with him.

The respondent denied that he detained or withheld the child from the relator, otherwise than by protecting the said Eliza Barry in her refusal to deliver it up, & c. In order to justify the latter in the position she had assumed with respect to the relator, the respondent gave a detailed account of various instances of domestic difficulty which had occurred between the relator and his wife, commencing shortly after the marriage. It is impossible to state these with any tolerable degree of accuracy, without occupying more space than their relative importance would warrant. An attempt was also made in the return to question the relator's qualifications and fitness for having the care and education of the child. The conclusions which the facts on this and the preceding topic tended to sustain, will be seen by the opinions delivered by the judges. The respondent annexed to his present return, full copies of the returns respectively made to each of the former writs of *habeas corpus;* re-asserting the truth of the facts therein set forth. It thus appeared that one main ground of defence urged in those proceedings was, the tender age and ill health of the child; its feeble constitution, & c. The present return, moreover, insisted upon the several decisions above set forth as constituting a bar to the claim now interposed by the relator. * * *

* * *

COWEN, J. * * *

The defendant claims that Mrs. Barry was lawfully at his house; and that, in her right, he is properly accessory to the detention of the child. This brings us to a consideration of the legal rights and powers of the relator and his wife in respect to their offspring. These rights and powers, like nearly all others when the claims of husband and wife come in conflict, depend upon a rule too elementary to require the adduction of authority; and too obvious to have been denied in the whole course of this particular controversy, from the hearing before the chancellor in the summer of 1839, * * * through the several hearings before commissioners, in this court, and the court for the correction of errors. The principle is thus stated in 1 *Black.Com.* 468: "The very being or legal existence of the woman is suspended during the marriage, or, at least, is incorporated and consolidated into that of the husband." Their relative power over the person of the child follows as a consequence, and is stated in the same book, (*p.* 478, 9,) to the following effect: The legal power of the father over his child is sufficient to keep the latter in order and obedience. The father is entitled to the benefit of his child's labor while it lives with and is maintained by him; while the mother, as such, is entitled to no power over it, but only to reverence and respect. The father's legal power ceases at the age of twenty-one. The extent of the rule is shown by the exceptions which the book mentions at *p.* 471. They are such as to shield the wife from corporal abuse, though "the courts of law will still permit the husband to restrain the wife of her liberty in case of any gross misbehavior."

One consequence necessarily resulting from the legal identity of husband and wife, answers Mrs. Barry's claim to the custody of the child; which, as counsel have insisted, arises out of the relator's written agreement that she should retain it. That upon a proper construction of its words, she could derive any such right as is now claimed for her, I do not admit. But, for the purposes of the argument, suppose it an agreement for permanent separation—a complete relinquishment by the relator of all claim whatever, and a transfer of his right to Mrs. Barry. A single passage from the law shews its futility. "A man cannot grant any thing to his wife, or enter into covenant with her; for the grant would be to suppose her separate existence; and to covenant with her would be only to covenant with himself." (1 *Black.Com.* 468.) As an agreement, therefore, the writing was void. As a delegation of power, it was revocable in its own nature, and in this instance has been actually revoked. Whatever latitude may have occasionally been allowed for the framing of bargains between husband and wife through trustees, I must be allowed to deny that it stands on any principle which can with propriety be applied to the case in question. I am aware that a separate maintenance may be settled by the husband on the wife, and that, incidentally, they may covenant for the separation of their persons; that this may, if you please, be done under such pretexts as the parties shall choose to allege, whether in consonance or not with the law of divorce; and the courts both of law and equity have sanctioned such arrangements, by carrying them into effect. The practice probably started on the principle I have mentioned, of protection against corporal abuse, without its being sought with sufficient care to distinguish the fact from the mere declaration of the parties. The courts do not seem to have foreseen that, in doing so much, they empowered the parties to be their own judges in a matter which may, in the end, vitally affect the interests of society. The practice is in itself by no means entitled to favor; and the courts are beginning to regret that they ever allowed it to any extent. It is at best letting into our system the doctrine of conventional divorce in its worst form. The advocates of that doctrine carry out their system to its proportional consequences. They would leave the parties at liberty to marry again; thus fulfilling the supposed law of nature with comparative decency. Our law still proclaims the obligation of the marriage contract, while it aids the parties in measures to evade that obligation, and thus to defraud both the law and one another. The whole is indeed matter of agreement between persons who are immediately interested; and the consequences, if confined to them, might be regarded as of little moment. The discouragement to enterprise in business, the wreck of private fortune and loss of character, might be placed to the account of retribution for such wickedness or weakness as cannot endure the trouble of becoming respectable. But the evil does not stop there. An innocent family and a wide circle of connections are perhaps brought to share in the misfortune and disgrace * * *. The sentiments of filial reverence are subverted, and the conjugal relation itself distrusted and traduced. Husbands and wives with feelings and appetites already too violent for the restraints of duty or of shame, are thrown into the highway of temptation. It is said that the husband's common law right to correct the wife began to be doubted in the politer reign of Charles the Second. (1 *Black.Com.* 471.) It has since ceased to exist. In asserting the principle on which the barbarous practice of correction was abolished, the courts should beware of the opposite extreme that characterized the same reign. Much as we may congratulate ourselves on the abolition of unreasonable severity, such an achievement would but poorly compensate for the general corruption of domestic morals.

I make these remarks because they come into the argument that the doctrine of separate maintenance cannot be made to bear on the agreement in question; which, as it seems to me, is neither within the original principle of the rule, nor the sphere of its most extended practice. If the husband has a right to transfer the marriage bed to his wife, I deny that he has, therefore, the right still farther to violate his duty by selling his children, with or without it. These he holds under the duty of a personal trust, inalienable even to another who is *sui juris; a fortiori* to his wife, with whom he can make no contract whatever.

We do not perceive with counsel, that in *Mercein v. The People,* * * * the court of errors differed from us upon this question. We understand that court, on the contrary, to have reversed our former decision upon the sole ground that the question before us, being *res judicata,* we had no right to take notice of the truth. * * *

I have, therefore, felt entirely warranted in withholding from the agreement that effect which two of the members of the court of errors seemed in the course of their arguments to have thought might possibly be due to it. The doctrine of the cases cited by Senator Paige, I have already conceded in all their force. * * * They were both cases of separate maintenance, on which it was held that the husband had lost his power over the person of his wife. Children were not in question. I have endeavored to show that such cases form an exception in the law of husband and wife; and have suggested some reasons why I think the principle should not be extended in its operation. I know the learning of that senator, and have great deference for his opinion; but I have in this instance felt less diffidence in my dissent, because I find the learned chancellor had before pronounced the agreement in question void. * * * Admitting that an agreement for present separation is valid as between the parties, (and I have supposed it to be a kind of divorce which the courts cannot very well gainsay at this day,) I am yet unable to see that, as a consequence, the husband may contract away the custody of his children. * * * Those countries in which the father has a general power to dispose of his children, have always been considered barbarous. Our own law never has allowed the exercise of such power except for some specific and temporary purpose, such as apprenticeship during the father's life, or guardianship after his death. But was it ever heard that during his lifetime, he could bind out his child to his own wife, even as an apprentice? * * * In the language of Lord Kenyon, applied by Chancellor Walworth to the agreement in question, (8 *Paige,* 67,) I ask, "how can it be in the power of any persons by their private agreement to alter the character and condition which by law results from the state of marriage while it subsists?"

The rights of the relator being clearly unimpaired by the alleged bargain between him and his wife, the case is, on its merits, brought down to the single point on which it was considered before the chancellor, (8 *Paige,* 47;) viz. whether, assuming that the wife resolves to continue in her state of separation, a due regard to the welfare of the child will warrant an order for its delivery to the relator; or whether we shall allow her and her father longer to oppose the supposed necessities of nurture to the demands of law. I say, demands of law, because the defendant's case was presented to the chancellor in its strongest possible aspect; and no doubt was entertained by him of the relator's right in legal strictness. This was in the summer of 1839, and could not have been long after the child was weaned. The chancellor then said, if delivered to its father, he had no apprehension it would be treated with unkindness; adding, "I have no doubt that his elder daughters, to whose good characters and amiable dispositions Mrs. Barry herself bears full and ample testimony, would endeavor faithfully to discharge the duties of a mother to their infant sister, as far as they were able to do so, as they have already done to the brother." After considerable hesitation, he refused an order in favor of the relator, on the sole ground of the child's then tender age. The case was again investigated before Judge Inglis, before this court, the court of errors, and, finally, on a *habeas corpus* issued in October, 1840, returnable before Mr. Justice Oakley. It is now three years since it was examined by the chancellor, and more than a year and a half since the suit was commenced before Mr. Justice Oakley. The case has at no stage appeared to be any stronger against the relator than it was when before the chancellor; and the inquiry seems to come with scarcely a plausible answer—why should his child be longer withheld? It is at present nearly five years old. The father's claim, if not stronger, is at least more apparent, for it is by no means unimportant that he has a right to train up this child as he has his other daughters, with dispositions to serve him affectionately in the business of his household, should its health become sufficiently stable. This may indeed be essential to the child's welfare; and, I am strongly inclined to believe, will be better attended to by the relator, than by the wife. It is equally his right and his duty to see that the child shall also be properly educated in other respects. The general allegation that a daughter may be well in the hands of a mother who chooses to leave her husband, would, if allowed, work an entire subversion of his right. When we are told in Mr. Mercein's return, that this child is still in such delicate health as to require a mother's care, the first answer which strikes the mind is the generality and unsatisfactory nature of the allegation—an allegation by which, if allowed, the relator may still be baffled till his child is twenty-one. Let it be taken, however, that evidence of a propensity on his part wilfully to withdraw his child beyond the reach of maternal care, should form a ground for our refusing to interfere in his favor: the attempt to make out such a case on the circumstances before us is a very extraordinary one. We have seen this man for years soliciting the woman to go with the child, and aid him in its nurture. Bating some matrimonial bickering, the state of his affections was not at all impeached before the chancellor; and there is now nothing left to impugn the sincerity of his attachment both to the mother and child. He has manifested an anxiety which nothing could repress, that they should both come to the home he has prepared and the table he has spread for them; or, if his wife's better feelings should revive and she were to follow after him and his child, he would no doubt joyfully receive her at any time, and strive to forget that she had ever left him. The argument has been urged as if there were, in the abstract, such an unfitness in a woman returning to the bed and board of her husband as can not be endured consistently with a proper sense of duty. I have listened in vain for a single lisp, even in argument, that there would be more danger in this woman returning to the relator, than in the return of any wife to any husband in christendom. From all we can collect, I am inclined to think she would stand in as little danger from his temper as from his morals. That the former has been well balanced and regulated in his intercourse with society at large, it is not necessary either to affirm or deny. Its general amenity in his family was expressly conceded by Chancellor Walworth, after a severe scrutiny. Before us there has been no attempt to impeach it. The chancellor was also of opinion that, as between him and his wife, nothing had occurred which was legally sufficient to authorize a decree of separation; and the promise of the relator during courtship, that she should continue near her parents, is not now interposed as a reason for her voluntary separation. To every thing else that was attempted in proof before the chancellor, we may well apply the remarks of Sir William Scott, in *Evans v. Evans,* * * * "Mere turbulence of temper, petulance of manners, infirmity of mind, are not to be numbered among the causes" of voluntary separation. No corporal violence, or menace of corporal violence, has, at any stage of the controversy, that I can see, been pretended; and looking at some disclosures in the course of it—the pecuniary embarrassment of the relator, the cause of that embarrassment, the manner in which it was met by the wife, and the irritating disputes which ensued concerning the rights and duties of the parties—it is rather a matter of surprise that we have not witnessed much greater displays of ill temper on his side than have as yet been charged. His affections have been unwarrantably trifled with; and it is by no means the least evidence in his favor, that during the course of a tedious litigation, he has been the more unwavering in his suit, from entertaining the hope that success would be tributary to a restoration of his conjugal rights. That he was habitually unfeeling, or even rude in language towards his wife during the time when they cohabited together, is now scarcely pretended. The utmost that can be imputed are occasional ebullitions of anger and vexation, arising from momentary excitement operating upon a temper naturally hasty, but by no means unrelenting. The children of his first marriage, it is still conceded, are intelligent and amiable, and have uniformly demeaned themselves towards Mrs. Barry with great attention and respect.

I entertain no fears, therefore, on what has seemed to me the whole stress of the argument upon the merits against the relator—the alternative between Mrs. Barry's returning to her husband, and abandoning the care of her child. I see nothing to furnish either a legal or moral excuse on her part for hesitating upon such an alternative.

Clearly, however, it should be enough for this part of the argument that the conduct of the relator has been such as to leave her without excuse. If she still continue in a state of separation, the consideration of a few facts will be sufficient to remove all objection against the child being restored to the husband; indeed, dispel all fear of its welfare in his hands. That he now commands a comfortable home with adequate means for supporting the child, is no longer denied. He is at the head of an interesting family, mostly I believe daughters, who have been bred under his care in the best manner; some of them from childhood to age. That he is qualified, and eminently so, for the moral and mental instruction of this child is clear. That in his family the child can and will derive from his daughters and other means, care and attention fully proportioned to its physical wants, we have reason to be confident. Besides, the next oldest child of the marriage with Mrs. Barry has, with her consent and that of her relatives, been left in the exclusive charge of the relator, from an age, I believe, still younger than that of the child whose custody she claims to withhold. The condition of the older child has been open to enquiry; and yet we hear not a pretence that its custody could have been more properly bestowed. In short, we know that the relator ranks well as a man of intellect and education. We have evidence that, though not affluent, he is yet a man of business and enterprize, in the prime of life and health, of sound morals and estimable character, with a comfortable, indeed, desirable home, and every means and disposition to take proper care of the child whose custody he sues for.

* * *

* * * A mother deserts her husband, with a child at her breast; and the father's claim is denied because it wants a wet nurse, which he cannot furnish. With what propriety, or what decent color can it be said, on the reason ceasing, that the point is the same? So where the father is a wanderer or his domestic affairs are in confusion, and the child is very young, he may well be required to postpone the exercise of his legal right till the courts see such a permanent change in his condition as shall insure its comfort. On such change occurring, and the claim being renewed, would it not be trifling with the party and the law to tell him that, on an alteration of the very circumstance which controlled the first decision, the point is still the same, and has been adjudged against him? It is matter of common experience, that an act rightful under some circumstances may be injurious under others. * * * Hardly any magistrate has denied the relator's legal and moral right to the custody of his child, at least it is impossible to see that such right has ever been questioned by any magistrate whose decision has been returned to us; nor should it be supposed, after seeing that the chancellor put the whole case on the fact that, at the time when he spoke, the mother was excused in not following her husband to Nova Scotia, and that the child not being then two years old, should remain with her for nurture. He did not see fit to extend even this temporary indulgence, except as a consequence of what he thought the relator's harsh, though not illegal conduct towards his wife—certain instances of unkindness without apparent cause. The moment we depart from legal causes of separation on account of temper, which never arise except from bodily injury either actual or menaced, the points of the controversy are illimitable. They extend to austerity of temper, petulance of manners, rudeness of language, a want of civil attention and accommodation, occasional sallies of passion, indeed through the whole chapter of family jars; matters which, it is generally agreed, the parties should decide as well as they can in their own domestic forum. They are moral offences, in respect to which both parties are often about equally blameable. Happily, they are commonly fleeting and evanescent, a sort of sinning and repenting business * * *. The very best men and best wives are not always in full command of their tempers. Sometimes where a good man's prospects in life are discouraging, as Mr. Barry's appears to have been, he may, for a time, fall into a state of habitual peevishness, annoying and tormenting

the very persons who are dearest to him. Such effects, especially between husband and wife, pass away like the summer cloud, unless aggravated by recrimination or desertion. It would surely be a harsh application of the rule of estoppel, to say that because a man stands convicted of being in bad temper, he should, therefore, be permanently deprived of his children. I do not believe that any magistrate has intended to convict Mr. Barry of more, unless indeed it be the crime of living in Nova Scotia * * *. All the points of mere convenience have ceased to be the same as formerly, by his having acquired a settled residence, and means perfectly equal to the comfort and welfare of the child at its present increased age.

* * * Where the entire right has been once litigated and passed upon, it should not be stirred again. To allow a second trial, would be against public policy, and therefore unjust; but it would be monstrously unjust to cut off substantial rights which have not and never could have been tried, for the reason that they either did not exist, or were disallowed at the moment for some fleeting cause which has ceased to exist; nay, though it have ceased to exist in the same form or degree which influenced the mind of the judge on the first trial.

On the right of the matter now before us, there never has been even an issue. That the relator is the husband and father, was never denied. The only issue was, on the expediency of leaving the child for nurture with a mother who had withdrawn from her husband and bade him defiance. Whether the same morbid excuse for desertion may continue, it is not necessary to enquire; but only whether the wrong should, under new circumstances, be allowed longer to suspend the assertion of right. The claim of the husband has throughout been allowed to be paramount by every body except the wife. It has not been denied that he is the legal head of the whole family, wife and children inclusive; and I have heard it urged from no quarter that he should be brought under subjection to a household democracy. All will agree, I apprehend, that such a measure would extend the right of suffrage quite too far. Yet I do not see how this defence can be sustained unless we are prepared to go that length. Marriage is indeed regarded by our law as a mere civil contract; but not such an one as is capable of repudiation by a majority of the family, or even the assent of the whole. Bating some slight amelioration, its obligations should be maintained in all their ancient rigor. There is scarcely a doubt that matrimony in the severe form of monogamy, with the prerogatives of the husband as they are announced by the common law, are no less according to the order of nature and providence, than of positive institution.

Where the child is of such tender years as to be incapable of election, it should be delivered to the father on his attending to receive it. That is this case.

BRONSON, J. * * *

* * *

* * * There has been no impeachment of the moral character of the relator, nor is there any thing to show a want of capacity on his part for the proper care and training of the child. He is in all respects as well qualified as the mother for the proper discharge of parental duties, and, so far as relates to a just sense of the obligation of marriage vows, he stands most decidedly on the vantage ground. The question then is, which of these parties, the father or the mother, has the best title to the custody of the child? * * *

We have been referred to a late English statute touching this question. But the British parliament has long since ceased to give laws to this country, and our legislature has not yet spoken. This statute proves, however, that in England even bad laws cannot be altered without the co-operation of both branches of the legislature. I say bad laws, for it cannot be denied that there had been one or two decisions of the English courts on this subject which fully justified the remark of Chief Justice Denman in the house of lords, that the judges "felt ashamed of the state of the law, and that it was such as to render it odious in the eyes of the country." We have been referred to this remark as one having a bearing upon the case under consideration. But as we have never followed, and never intend to follow the decision mentioned by the chief justice, we have no occasion to unite in the confession made by his lordship.

It is possible that our laws relating to the rights and duties of husband and wife have not kept pace with the progress of civilization. It may be best that the wife should be declared head of the family, and that she should be at liberty to desert her husband at pleasure and take the children of the marriage with her. But I will not enquire what the law ought to be. That prerogative belongs to others. I will however venture the remark, even at the hazard of being thought out of fashion, that human laws cannot be very far out of the way when they are in accordance with the law of God.

I think an order should be made that the child be delivered to the relator.

NELSON, CH. J. dissenting. * * *

* * *

* * * I am of opinion that the case has not been materially varied on the present occasion. The circumstance of a year and a half having been added to the age of the child since the former hearing, seems to me too unimportant to afford ground for changing the legal judgment of a court. It appears affirmatively, moreover, that the personal care and nurture of the mother were as necessary to the well being of the child at the period of the former hearing, as they are now. The subject matter therefore remains essentially the same; and if so, the same result should follow. My

brethren, however, have arrived at a different conclusion, and an order must therefore be entered that the child be delivered to the relator.

Ordered accordingly.

NOTES AND QUESTIONS

1. The opinions by Judges Cowen and Bronson give us an opportunity to review what we have learned about the rights of husband and wife, and the principles of nineteenth century child custody law. You have probably been able to figure out that the great legal problem in the case, aside from whether the previous decisions were binding for the future, is that Mr. and Mrs. Barry had entered into a written agreement which permitted her to keep custody of their daughter, and also permitted her to remain in her father's home, with the daughter. Why doesn't the court enforce that contract? How would you have decided the case, and what reasons would you have advanced in support of your decision? You should be aware that not only were contracts not binding between spouses, but they were also immune from tort suits brought against each other for personal injuries. See generally, Carl Tobias, "Interspousal Tort Immunity in America," 23 Ga.L.Rev. 359 (1989). Was this a wise policy? The doctrine of interspousal tort immunity has now eroded significantly, so it is no longer the majority rule in the states. Is this reassuring?

2. Do you have more sympathy for the idea of "household democracy" than did Judge Cowen? He apparently believed that there was a place where ideas of "democracy" should leave off, and ideas of patriarchy ought to hold sway. Is there a problem with this? Do you find any real difference between the opinions of Judge Cowen and Judge Bronson? What does Bronson mean by suggesting a) that current law may not have "kept pace with the progress of civilization" but b) his court is powerless to change that, and c) even if he, Bronson, is "out of fashion," "human laws cannot be very far out of the way when they are in accordance with the law of God?"

3. Compare the attitudes expressed on the relative positions of husband and wife and on the principles of child custody in this 1842 opinion with those of Blackstone, with those of English courts and English legislation in the nineteenth century, and with the excerpts you have read from the 1839 and 1840 opinions in the case. Particularly given the fact that Mr. Barry lost his fight to recover custody of his daughter, would you say that the course of the development of family law in general and child custody law in particular was a smooth one?

4. The "best interests" of the child standard is still dominant in the law of child custody, although ideas about the "best interests" of children have varied over time. In particular, the superior custodial interest of the father, a staple of the Blackstonian common law, has eroded, but so has the presumption current in the courts until recently that the mother was a better custodial parent for young children.

The child custody problem now most commonly occurs in the case of divorce, and, in most states, there is now a preference for the institution of "joint custody" arrangements, whereby the child spends some time in each parent's home. How would you go about determining principles for the law of child custody, and do you favor custody for the father, mother, or joint custody?

5. Much of Bloomfield's chapter on family law, from which the excerpt you recently read was taken, treats the law applied to "dependent" families, those poor without the resources to meet their own needs for food and shelter, who were, since the time of Queen Elizabeth I, provided for in whole or in part by the state. We have been considering principally the family law applied to families with property, and, unfortunately, a detailed description of the development of welfare law for the poor is outside the scope of this book.

Still, you should understand that the story that Bloomfield tells, for the eighteenth and nineteenth centuries, is one of increased "rights" for women and children in relatively wealthy families, and decreased legal powers for men, women, and children in poor families. Families on relief often had their mobility curtailed, they were required to work either in "poorhouses" or at other menial tasks, and their children were often taken from them and placed in service or apprenticeship to wealthier masters.

Has the lot of the poor improved any since the nineteenth century? Poor relief from the state was regarded in the nineteenth century as a "privilege," as a matter of governmental largess, to which no one could actually lay claim. Do you understand how our law has subtly developed in a direction more towards giving poor and dependent family members a package of "rights" and "entitlements" closer to that accorded propertied families in the nineteenth century? This has coincided with the increasing penetration of the federal government into welfare areas formerly reserved to the individual states, so that the increased "rights" of the poor have seemed to coincide with an increase in the power of the "sovereign" federal government. Is this healthy? Can you point to any relevance the nineteenth century experience has to current public policy debates on this issue? Are you sanguine about current efforts at welfare reform? In the summer of 1996 the Congress passed and President Clinton signed into law massive changes in the federal welfare program, designed to "require welfare recipients to work, limit benefits to five years and reduce spending by $54.1 billion over six years. The bill also denies most aid to most legal immigrants who are not citizens." Barbara Vobedja, "Welfare Bill Glides Through Senate: Approval Sends Overhaul to White House for Clinton Signature," The Washington Post, August 2, 1996, p. A08. The welfare reform legislation successfully reduced the nation's welfare rolls by more than 2 million people, but there is still debate about whether "ending the 60–year-old federal guarantee of minimal financial support for needy parents and children" was the right thing to do. David S. Broder, "A Party Split," The Washington Post, August 7, 1996, page A19.

6. While children and the poor have had more attention paid to their "rights" and their welfare of late, the most significant story of change in the

late nineteenth century law of the family is probably the change in the treatment of women, away from the Blackstonian notion, still accepted in the 1842 opinions in the *Barry* case, that the husband and wife are but "one person" at the common law, and that person is the husband. We continue our survey of the law and society of the nineteenth century with more materials from the struggle for the rights of women.

SENECA FALLS DECLARATION OF SENTIMENTS AND RESOLUTIONS

(1848).

DECLARATION OF SENTIMENTS

When, in the course of human events, it becomes necessary for one portion of the family of man to assume among the people of the earth a position different from that which they have hitherto occupied, but one to which the laws of nature and of nature's God entitle them, a decent respect to the opinions of mankind requires that they should declare the causes that impel them to such a course.

We hold these truths to be self-evident: that all men and women are created equal; that they are endowed by their Creator with certain inalienable rights; that among these are life, liberty, and the pursuit of happiness; that to secure these rights governments are instituted, deriving their just powers from the consent of the governed. Whenever any form of government becomes destructive of these ends, it is the right of those who suffer from it to refuse allegiance to it, and to insist upon the institution of a new government, laying its foundation on such principles, and organizing its powers in such form, as to them shall seem most likely to effect their safety and happiness. Prudence, indeed, will dictate that governments long established should not be changed for light and transient causes; and accordingly all experience hath shown that mankind are more disposed to suffer, while evils are sufferable, than to right themselves by abolishing the forms to which they were accustomed. But when a long train of abuses and usurpations, pursuing invariably the same object, evinces a design to reduce them under absolute despotism, it is their duty to throw off such government, and to provide new guards for their future security. Such has been the patient sufferance of the women under this government, and such is now the necessity which constrains them to demand the equal station to which they are entitled.

The history of mankind is a history of repeated injuries and usurpations on the part of man toward woman, having in direct object the establishment of an absolute tyranny over her. To prove this, let facts be submitted to a candid world.

He has never permitted her to exercise her inalienable right to the elective franchise.

He has compelled her to submit to laws, in the formation of which she had no voice.

He has withheld from her rights which are given to the most ignorant and degraded men—both natives and foreigners.

Having deprived her of this first right of a citizen, the elective franchise, thereby leaving her without representation in the halls of legislation, he has oppressed her on all sides.

He has made her, if married, in the eye of the law, civilly dead.

He has taken from her all right in property, even to the wages she earns.

He has made her, morally, an irresponsible being, as she can commit many crimes with impunity, provided they be done in the presence of her husband. In the covenant of marriage, she is compelled to promise obedience to her husband, he becoming, to all intents and purposes, her master—the law giving him power to deprive her of her liberty, and to administer chastisement.

He has so framed the laws of divorce, as to what shall be the proper causes, and in case of separation, to whom the guardianship of the children shall be given, as to be wholly regardless of the happiness of women—the law, in all cases, going upon the false supposition of the supremacy of man, and giving all power into his hands.

After depriving her of all rights as a married woman, if single, and the owner of property, he has taxed her to support a government which recognizes her only when her property can be made profitable to it.

He has monopolized nearly all the profitable employments, and from those she is permitted to follow, she receives but a scanty remuneration. He closes against her all the avenues to wealth and distinction which he considers most honorable to himself. As a teacher of theology, medicine, or law, she is not known.

He has denied her the facilities for obtaining a thorough education, all colleges being closed against her.

He allows her in Church, as well as State, but a subordinate position, claiming Apostolic authority for her exclusion from the ministry, and, with some exceptions, from any public participation in the affairs of the Church.

He has created a false public sentiment by giving to the world a different code of morals for men and women, by which moral delinquencies which exclude women from society, are not only tolerated, but deemed of little account in man.

He has usurped the prerogative of Jehovah himself, claiming it as his right to assign for her a sphere of action, when that belongs to her conscience and to her God.

He has endeavored, in every way that he could, to destroy her confidence in her own powers, to lessen her self-respect, and to make her willing to lead a dependent and abject life.

Now, in view of this entire disfranchisement of one-half the people of this country, their social and religious degradation—in view of the unjust laws above mentioned, and because women do feel themselves aggrieved, oppressed, and fraudulently deprived of their most sacred rights, we insist that they have immediate admission to all the rights and privileges which belong to them as citizens of the United States.

In entering upon the great work before us, we anticipate no small amount of misconception, misrepresentation, and ridicule; but we shall use every instrumentality within our power to effect our object. We shall employ agents, circulate tracts, petition the State and National legislatures, and endeavor to enlist the pulpit and the press in our behalf. * * *

RESOLUTIONS

WHEREAS, The great precept of nature is conceded to be, that "man shall pursue his own true and substantial happiness." Blackstone in his Commentaries remarks, that this law of Nature being coeval with mankind, and dictated by God himself, is of course superior in obligation to any other. It is binding over all the globe, in all countries and at all times; no human laws are of any validity if contrary to this, and such of them as are valid, derive all their force, and all their validity, and all their authority, mediately and immediately, from this original; therefore,

Resolved, That such laws as conflict, in any way, with the true and substantial happiness of woman, are contrary to the great precept of nature and of no validity, for this is "superior in obligation to any other."

Resolved, That all laws which prevent woman from occupying such a station in society as her conscience shall dictate, or which place her in a position inferior to that of man, are contrary to the great precept of nature, and therefore of no force or authority.

Resolved, That woman is man's equal—was intended to be so by the Creator, and the highest good of the race demands that she should be recognized as such.

Resolved, That the women of this country ought to be enlightened in regard to the laws under which they live, that they may no longer publish their degradation by declaring themselves satisfied with their present position, nor their ignorance, by asserting that they have all the rights they want.

Resolved, That inasmuch as man, while claiming for himself intellectual superiority, does accord to woman moral superiority, it is pre-eminently his duty to encourage her to speak and teach, as she has an opportunity, in all religious assemblies.

Resolved, That the same amount of virtue, delicacy, and refinement of behavior that is required of woman in the social state, should also be required of man, and the same transgressions should be visited with equal severity on both man and woman.

Resolved, That the objection of indelicacy and impropriety, which is so often brought against woman when she addresses a public audience, comes with a very ill-grace from those who encourage, by their attendance, her appearance on the stage, in the concert, or in feats of the circus.

Resolved, That woman has too long rested satisfied in the circumscribed limits which corrupt customs and a perverted application of the Scriptures have marked out for her, and that it is time she should move in the enlarged sphere which her great Creator has assigned her.

Resolved, That it is the duty of the women of this country to secure to themselves their sacred right to the elective franchise.

Resolved, That the equality of human rights results necessarily from the fact of the identity of the race in capabilities and responsibilities.

Resolved, therefore, That, being invested by the Creator with the same capabilities, and the same consciousness of responsibility for their exercise, it is demonstrably the right and duty of woman, equally with man, to promote every righteous cause by every righteous means; and especially in regard to the great subjects of morals and religion, it is self-evidently her right to participate with her brother in teaching them, both in private and in public, by writing and by speaking, by any instrumentalities proper to be used, and in any assemblies proper to be held; and this being a self-evident truth growing out of the divinely implanted principles of human nature, any custom or authority adverse to it, whether modern or wearing the hoary sanction of antiquity, is to be regarded as a self-evident falsehood, and at war with mankind.

Resolved, That the speedy success of our cause depends upon the zealous and untiring efforts of both men and women, for the overthrow of the monopoly of the pulpit, and for the securing to woman an equal participation with men in the various trades, professions, and commerce.

NOTES AND QUESTIONS

1. These "Declaration of Sentiments" and Resolutions, which track the thought of Sarah Grimké you encountered in our first reading for this section, grew out of what has been called "the official beginning of the women's movement," a meeting at Seneca Falls, New York on July 19 and 20, 1848.

Norma Basch, In the Eyes of the Law: Women Marriage and Property in Nineteenth Century New York 168 (1982). Two hundred and sixty women and forty men attended the Seneca Falls Convention, which concluded by issuing the Declaration of Sentiments and the Resolutions. Even before you encountered Grimké, you had read one other document, of course, that bears a strong resemblance to the Declaration of Sentiments. How would you compare and contrast the two "Declarations?" Why didn't the "Declaration of Independence," without editing, furnish the needed intellectual foundation for equality of the rights of women?

Consider the assertions that "the history of mankind" shows that its direct object is "the establishment of an absolute tyranny" over women, and that in the "eyes of the law," a married woman is "civilly dead." Given what you have learned about family law up until 1848, are these true? It is perhaps significant that the New York Married Women's Property Act of 1848 was passed just before the Seneca Falls meeting. That Act, for the first time, made it clear that women owned the property they brought into marriage and acquired during marriage, reversing the common law. Is that something less than absolute tyranny? The Seneca Falls feminists have been accused "of not being careful students of jurisprudence," Basch, supra, at 168. Do you see any evidence of this? On the other hand, is careful jurisprudence the issue, or is the Declaration of Sentiments, like the Declaration of Independence, to be permitted a bit of hyperbole for the sake of effectiveness?

2. How much of the "Declaration of Sentiments" do you feel remains true today? Note that it is not only concerned with the law, but with education and entry into the professions. Has the course of women's progress been at the same rate in all three of these endeavors? We will see a bit more of the difficulties women faced in the profession of law shortly.

Apparently there was something noble to be taken from the common law, however, as the long quote from Blackstone that begins the "Resolutions" shows. Would Blackstone have agreed with this interpretation of his thought? Norma Basch, the historian of women's legal rights in New York, remarks that

> Intellectual rigor and logical consistency were not requisite for [the Seneca Falls feminists'] immediate goals. In legal theory, moreover, they were self-educated, and the limited range of their legal sources was an indication of their exclusion from the upper levels of professional education. Thus even as they deplored Blackstone's classic formulation of common law marriage principles, making it the object of their most vitriolic rhetoric, they reverently cited his analysis of natural rights, selectively quoting passages from the *Commentaries* that they found relevant and appealing.

Basch, supra, at 170.

3. Would you have voted in favor of the "Resolutions?" If not, are there particular ones which you would have excised, and supported the others? Would you have expected the resolutions dealing with women's "moral supe-

riority," or the resolutions that spoke of public speaking, stage, and circus performances by women? How do these help you to a further understanding of the nature of "The Woman question" in the nineteenth century?

4. All but the last of the Resolutions were drafted by Elizabeth Cady Stanton, a brilliant, fiery and determined feminist. Before she was a fighter for women's rights she had been active in the abolitionist movement. Nevertheless, she was said to have welcomed support for the cause of women's rights from wherever it came, including, in at least one instance, the support of a "Copperhead and a racist." As Stanton explained, "if the Devil steps forward ready to help, I shall say good fellow come!" Letter from Stanton apparently addressed to E.A. Studwell of Buffalo, November 30, 1867, quoted from the Elizabeth Cady Stanton Papers, Vassar College, by Basch, supra, at 170. This is the second time, in this section, that we have encountered this problem of the movement for the rights of women clashing with the movement for better treatment for Blacks. Should there be priorities in these two struggles? Does the end of women's rights justify the means?

5. The formal struggle for women's rights is occasionally dated from these 1848 Resolutions and Declarations, but it certainly did not end with them. Compare with the 1848 document the following 1876 Declaration of Rights for women, written by leaders of the National Woman Suffrage Association, and read in its entirety by Susan B. Anthony "to a large audience of curious citizens, military and civil officers, and women's rights workers at Independence Hall, in Philadelphia, on July 4, 1876," Quoted language and the text of the 1876 Declaration are taken from the world-wide-web, in a version edited by Sandra F. Van Burkleo, *http://www.unl.edu/legacy/19cwww/books/elibe /documents/suffrage/INDE.HTM*. Ms. Burkleo worked from the reprint of the 1876 Declaration to be found in Elizabeth C. Stanton, et. al., III History of Woman Suffrage 31 (Originally published 1882, reprinted 1985). For a penetrating study of the struggle for women's rights in the nineteenth century, including an analysis of these 1848 and 1876 documents, see Van Burkleo's "Belonging to the World": Women's Rights and American Constitutional Culture (Oxford University Press, 2001). What are the differences between the 1848 and the 1876 formulations? Which do you prefer and why?

> While the nation is buoyant with patriotism, and all hearts are attuned to praise, it is with sorrow we come to strike the one discordant note, on this one-hundredth anniversary of our country's birth. When subjects of kings, emperors, and czars, from the old world join in our national jubilee, shall the women of the republic refuse to lay their hands with benedictions on the nation's head? Surveying America's exposition, surpassing in magnificence those of London, Paris, and Vienna, shall we not rejoice at the success of the youngest rival among the nations of the earth? May not our hearts, in unison with all, swell with pride at our great achievements as a people; our free speech, free press, free schools, free church, and the rapid progress we have made in material wealth, trade, commerce and the inventive arts? And we do rejoice in the success, thus far, of our experiment of self-government. Our faith is firm

and unwavering in the broad principles of human rights proclaimed in 1776, not only as abstract truths, but as the corner stones of a republic. Yet we cannot forget, even in this glad hour, that while all men of every race, and clime, and condition, have been invested with the full rights of citizenship under our hospitable flag, all women still suffer the degradation of disfranchisement.

The history of our country the past hundred years has been a series of assumptions and usurpations of power over woman, in direct opposition to the principles of just government, acknowledged by the United States as its foundation, which are:

First—The natural rights of each individual.

Second—The equality of these rights.

Third—That rights not delegated are retained by the individual.

Fourth—That no person can exercise the rights of others without delegated authority.

Fifth—That the non-use of rights does not destroy them.

And for the violation of these fundamental principles of our government, we arraign our rulers on this Fourth day of July, 1876,—and these are our articles of impeachment:

Bills of attainder have been passed by the introduction of the word "male" into all the State constitutions, denying to women the right of suffrage, and thereby making sex a crime—an exercise of power clearly forbidden in Article I, sections 9, 10, of the United States constitution.

The writ of habeas corpus, the only protection against *lettres de cachet* and all forms of unjust imprisonment, which the constitution declares "shall not be suspended, except when in cases of rebellion or invasion the public safety demands it," is held inoperative in every State of the Union, in case of a married woman against her husband—the marital rights of the husband being in all cases primary, and the rights of the wife secondary.

The right of trial by a jury of one's peers was so jealously guarded that States refused to ratify the original constitution until it was guaranteed by the sixth amendment. And yet the women of this nation have never been allowed a jury of their peers—being tried in all cases by men, native and foreign, educated and ignorant, virtuous and vicious. Young girls have been arraigned in our courts for the crime of infanticide; tried, hanged, convicted—victims, perchance, of judge, jurors, advocates—while no woman's voice could be heard in their defense. And not only are women denied a jury of their peers, but in some cases jury trial altogether. . . . During the last presidential campaign a woman, arrested for voting, was denied the protection of a jury, tried, convicted, and sentenced . . . , by the absolute power of a judge of the Supreme Court [See U.S. v. Anthony, infra] * * *

Taxation without representation, the immediate cause of the rebellion of the colonies against Great Britain, is one of the grievous wrongs the women of this country have suffered during this century. Deploring war, . . . we have been taxed to support standing armies, with their waste of life and wealth. Believing in temperance, we have been taxed to support the vice, crime and pauperism of the liquor traffic. While we suffer its wrongs and abuses infinitely more than man, we have no power to protect our sons * * * During the temperance crusade, mothers were arrested, fined, imprisoned, for even praying and singing in the streets, while men blockade the sidewalks with impunity, even on Sunday, with their military parades and political processions. Believing in honesty, we are taxed to support a dangerous army of civilians, buying and selling the offices of government and sacrificing the best interests of the people * * * [W]e are taxed to support the very legislators and judges who make laws, and render decisions adverse to woman. And for refusing to pay such unjust taxation, the houses, lands, bonds, and stock of women have been seized and sold * * * thus proving Lord Coke's assertion, that "The very act of taxing a man's property without his consent is, in effect, disfranchising him of every civil right."

Unequal codes for men and women. Held by law a perpetual minor, deemed incapable of self protection, even in the industries of the world, woman is denied equality of rights. The fact of sex, not the quantity or quality of work, in most cases, decides the pay and position; and because of this injustice thousands of fatherless girls are compelled to choose between a life of shame and starvation. Laws catering to man's vices have created two codes of morals in which penalties are graded according to the political status of the offender. Under such laws, women are fined and imprisoned if found alone in the streets, or in public places of resort, at certain hours. Under the pretense of regulating public morals, police officers seizing the occupants of disreputable houses, march the women in platoons to prison, while the men, partners in their guilt, go free * * *. Special legislation for woman has placed us in a most anomalous position. Women invested with the rights of citizens in one section—voters, jurors, office-holders—crossing an imaginary line, are subjects in the next. In some States, a married woman may hold property and transact business in her own name; in others, her earnings belong to her husband. In some States, a woman may testify against her husband, sue and be sued in the courts; in others, she has no redress in case of damage to person, property, or character. In case of divorce on account of adultery in the husband, the innocent wife is held to possess no right to children or property, unless by special decree * * * But in no State of the Union has the wife the right to her own person, or to any part of the joint earnings of the co-partnership during the life of her husband. In some States, women may enter the law schools and practice in the courts; in others they are forbidden. In some universities girls enjoy equal educational advantages with boys, while many of the proudest institutions in the land deny them admittance, though the sons of China, Japan and Africa are welcomed there. But the privileges already gained in the several States are by no means secure. The right of suffrage once exercised by women in certain States and territories has been denied by subsequent legislation. A bill is now pending in congress to disfranchise the women of Utah, thus interfering to deprive United States citizens of the same rights which the Supreme Court has declared the national government powerless to protect anywhere. Laws passed after years of untiring effort, guaranteeing married women certain rights of property, and mothers the custody of their children, have been repealed in States where we supposed all was safe. Thus have our most sacred rights been made the football of legislative caprice, proving that a power which grants as a privilege what by nature is a right, may withhold the same as a penalty when deeming it necessary for its own perpetuation.

Representation of woman has had no place in the nation's thought. Since the incorporation of the thirteen original States, twenty-four have been admitted to the Union, not one of which has recognized woman's right of self-government. On this birthday of our national liberties, July Fourth, 1876, Colorado, like all her elder sisters, comes into the Union with the invidious word "male" in her constitution. Universal manhood suffrage, by establishing an aristocracy of sex, imposes upon the women of this nation a more absolute and cruel despotism than monarchy; in that, woman finds a political master in her father, husband, brother, son. The aristocracies of the old world are based upon birth, wealth, refinement, education, nobility, brave deeds of chivalry; in this nation, on sex alone; exalting brute force over moral power, vice above virtue, ignorance above education, and the son above the mother who bore him.

The judiciary above the nation has proved itself but the echo of the party in power, by upholding and enforcing laws that are opposed to the spirit and letter of the constitution. When the slave power was dominant, the Supreme Court decided that a black man was not a citizen, because he had not the right to vote; and when the constitution was so amended as to make all persons citizens, the same high tribunal decided that a woman, though a citizen, had not the right to vote. Such vacillating interpretations of constitutional law unsettle our faith in judicial authority, and undermine the liberties of the whole people.

These articles of impeachment against our rulers we now submit to the impartial judgment of the people. To all these wrongs and oppressions woman has not submitted in silence and resignation. From the beginning of this century . . . until now, woman's discontent has been steadily increasing, culminating nearly thirty years ago in a simultaneous movement among the women of the nation, demanding the right of suffrage. In making our just demands, a higher motive than the pride of sex inspires us; we feel that national safety and stability depend on the complete recognition of the broad principles of our government. Woman's degraded, helpless position is the weak point in our institutions to-day [and] a disturbing force everywhere * * * It was the boast of the founders of the republic, that the rights for which they contended were the rights of human nature. If these rights are ignored in the case of one-half the people, the nation is surely preparing for its downfall. Governments try themselves. The recognition of a governing and a governed class is incompatible with the first principles of freedom. Woman has not been a heedless spectator of the events of this century, nor a dull listener to the grand arguments for the equal rights of humanity. From the earliest history of our country woman has shown equal devotion with man to the cause of freedom, and has stood firmly by his side in its defense. Together, they have made this country what it is. Woman's wealth, thought and labor have cemented the stones of every monument man has reared to liberty.

And now, at the close of a hundred years . . . , we declare our faith in the principles of self government; our full equality with man in natural rights; that woman was made first for her own happiness, with the absolute right to herself—to all the opportunities and advantages life affords for her complete development, and we deny that dogma of the centuries, incorporated in the codes of all nations—that woman was made for man—her best interests, in all cases, to be sacrificed to his will. We ask of our rulers, at this hour, no special favors, no special privileges, no special legislation. We ask justice, we ask equality, we ask that all the civil and political rights that belong to citizens of the United States, be guaranteed to us and our daughters forever. [Signed by Lucretia Mott, Elizabeth Cady Stanton, Pauline Wright Davis, Ernestine Rose, Clarina Nichols, Mary Ann McClintock, Mathilde Franceske Anneke, Sarah Pugh, Amy Post, Catharine Stebbins, Susan B. Anthony, Matilda Joslyn Gage, Clemence Lozier, Olympia Brown, Mathilde Wendt, Adeline Thomson, Ellen Clark Sargent, Virginia Minor, Catherine Waite, Elizabeth Schenk, Phoebe Couzins, Elizabeth Boynton Harbert, Laura DeForce Gordon, Sara Andres Spencer, Lillie Devereux Blake, Jane Graham Jones, Abigail Scott Duniway, Belva Lockwood, Isabella Beecher Hooker, Sara Williams, and Abby Ela.]

6. In case you are now puzzled how anyone could object to the spirit of and the arguments of these 1848 and 1876 documents, consider the following.

ORESTES A. BROWNSON, THE WOMAN QUESTION, ARTICLES I AND II

Reprinted from XVIII Henry F. Brownson, ed., The Works of Orestes A. Brownson 388–89, 403 (1885).*

The conclusive objection to the political enfranchisement of women is, that it would weaken and finally break up and destroy the Christian family. The social unit is the family, not the individual; and the greatest danger to American society is, that we are rapidly becoming a nation of isolated individuals, without family ties or affections. The family has already been much weakened, and is fast disappearing. We have broken away from the old homestead, have lost the restraining and purifying associations that gathered around it, and live away from home in hotels and boarding-houses. We are daily losing the faith, the virtues, the habits, and the manners without which the family cannot be sustained; and when the family goes, the nation goes too * * *.

Extend now to women suffrage and eligibility; give them the political right to vote and to be voted for; render it feasible for them to enter the arena of political strife, to become canvassers in elections and candidates for office, and what remains of family union will soon be dissolved. The wife may espouse one political party, and the husband another, and it may well happen that the husband and wife may be rival candidates for the same office, and one or the other doomed to the mortification of defeat. Will the husband like to see his wife enter the lists against him, and triumph over him? Will the wife, fired with political ambition for place or power, be pleased to see her own husband enter the lists against her, and succeed at her expense? Will political rivalry and the passions it never fails to engender increase the mutual affection of husband and wife for each other, and promote domestic union and peace, or will it not carry into the bosom of the family all the strife, discord, anger, and division of the political canvass? * * *

Woman was created to be a wife and a mother; that is her destiny. To that destiny all her instincts point, and for it nature has specially qualified her. Her proper sphere is home, and her proper function is the care of the household, to manage a family, to take care of children, and attend to their early training. For this she is endowed with patience, endurance, passive courage, quick sensibilities, a sympathetic nature, and great executive and administrative ability. She was born to be a queen in her own household, and to make home cheerful, bright, and happy.

We do not believe women, unless we acknowledge individual exceptions, are fit to have their own head. The most degraded of the savage

* These articles were originally published in the *Catholic World,* May 1869 and Brownson's *Quarterly Review,* October 1873. They were reprinted again in Aileen S. Kraditor, ed., Up From the Pedestal: Selected Writings in the History of American Feminism 191–194 (1968). Reprinted with the permission of Ms. Kraditor.

tribes are those in which women rule, and descent is reckoned from the mother instead of the father. Revelation asserts, and universal experience proves that the man is the head of the woman, and that the woman is for the man, not the man for the woman; and his greatest error, as well as the primal curse of society is that he abdicates his headship, and allows himself to be governed, we might almost say, deprived of his reason, by woman. It was through the seductions of the woman, herself seduced by the serpent, that man fell, and brought sin and all our woe into the world. She has all the qualities that fit her to be a help-meet of man, to be the mother of his children, to be their nurse, their early instructress, their guardian, their life-long friend; to be his companion, his comforter, his consoler in sorrow, his friend in trouble, his ministering angel in sickness; but as an independent existence, free to follow her own fancies and vague longings, her own ambition and natural love of power, without masculine direction or control, she is out of her element, and a social anomaly, sometimes a hideous monster, which men seldom are, excepting through a woman's influence. This is no excuse for men, but it proves that women need a head, and the restraint of father, husband, or the priest of God.

NOTES AND QUESTIONS

1. Do you have any difficulty taking the thoughts of Orestes Brownson seriously? Was it ever possible to make out a logical or convincing case that women should be denied the right to vote or to hold political office? Was Brownson some kind of nut? Or is it possible that, placed in social, economic, and political context his thought made a certain kind of sense? In particular, is there anything to be said for his fear that the "Christian family" would soon be destroyed, and with that destruction could come the triumph of "isolated" individualism and the loss of the "faith, the virtues, the habits and manners" of the family?

Women now have the vote and can hold political office. Did these evils come to pass? Do you find Brownson's arguments more or less sophisticated than those of the New York judges in the *Barry* case? How would you compare his thinking to that expressed in the *Seneca Falls* document?

2. Where does Brownson get his notions about the unfitness of women "to have their own head?" What does he mean by "Revelation" and "universal experience?" Are his arguments anthropological, sociological, religious, or some combination of all of them? Do women need special restraints? How can you explain the hostility of many men to female suffrage?

Is the male reaction to the demand for women's rights simply jealous hoarding of power, or is something more involved? Consider the remarks made on the floor of the United States Senate by Senator George G. Vest (Democrat, Missouri), on January 25, 1887:

> I pity the man who can consider any question affecting the influence of woman with the cold, dry logic of business. What man can, without

> aversion, turn from the blessed memory of that dear old grandmother, or the gentle words and caressing hand of that dear blessed mother gone to the unknown world, to face in its stead the idea of a female justice of the peace or township constable? For my part I want when I go to my home—when I turn from the arena where man contends with man for what we call the prizes of this paltry world—I want to go back, not to be received in the masculine embrace of some female ward politician, but to the earnest, loving look and touch of a true woman. I want to go back to the jurisdiction of the wife, the mother; and instead of a lecture upon finance or the tariff, or upon the construction of the Constitution, I want those blessed, loving details of domestic life and domestic love.

Reprinted in Aileen S. Kraditor, ed., Up From the Pedestal: Selected Writings in the History of American Feminism 195 (1968).

Does the Senator have a handle on what makes a "true woman?" Later in his speech Senator Vest said that "I believe that they [women] are better than men, but I do not believe that they are adopted to the political work of this world. I do not believe that the Great Intelligence ever intended them to invade the sphere of work given to men, tearing down and destroying all the best influences for which God has intended them." How could women be "better than men" and yet not fit for the franchise or the professions?

What happened when women tried to get relief for their inability to vote or to practice law, for example, from the courts? We conclude our examination of nineteenth-century domestic relations law with Myra Bradwell's attempt to practice law, and Susan Anthony's attempt to vote.

MYRA BRADWELL

BRADWELL V. ILLINOIS

Supreme Court of the United States, 1872.
83 U.S. (16 Wall.) 130, 21 L.Ed. 442.

Mrs. Myra Bradwell, residing in the State of Illinois, made application to the judges of the Supreme Court of that State for a license to practice law. She accompanied her petition with the usual certificate from an inferior court of her good character, and that on due examination she had been found to possess the requisite qualifications. Pending this application she also filed an affidavit, to the effect "that she was born in the State of Vermont; that she was (had been) a citizen of that State; that she is now a citizen of the United States, and has been for many years past a resident of the city of Chicago, in the State of Illinois." And with this affidavit she also filed a paper asserting that, under the foregoing facts, she was entitled to the license prayed for by virtue of the second section of the fourth article of the Constitution of the United States, and of the fourteenth article of amendment of that instrument.

The statute of Illinois on the subject of admissions to the bar, enacts that no person shall be permitted to practice as an attorney or counsellor-at-law, or to commence, conduct, or defend any action, suit, or plaint, in which he is not a party concerned, in any court of record within the State, either by using or subscribing his own name or the name of any other person, without having previously obtained a license for that purpose from some two of the justices of the Supreme Court, which license shall constitute the person receiving the same an attorney and counsellor-at-law, and shall authorize him to appear in all the courts of record within the State, and there to practice as an attorney and counsellor-at-law, according to the laws and customs thereof.

On Mrs. Bradwell's application first coming before the court, the license was refused, and it was stated as a sufficient reason that under the decisions of the Supreme Court of Illinois, the applicant—"as a married woman would be bound neither by her express contracts nor by those implied contracts which it is the policy of the law to create between attorney and client." After the announcement of this decision, Mrs. Bradwell, admitting that she was a married woman * * * filed a printed argument in which her right to admission, notwithstanding that fact, was earnestly and ably maintained. The [Illinois Supreme] court thereupon gave an opinion in writing. Extracts are here given:

> "[In most respects] it is left to our discretion to establish the rules by which admission to this office shall be determined. But this discretion is not an arbitrary one, and must be held subject to at least two limitations. One is, that the court should establish such terms of admission as will promote the proper administration of justice; the second, that it should not admit any persons or class of persons who

are not intended by the legislature to be admitted, even though their exclusion is not expressly required by the statute."

* * *

"Whether, in the existing social relations between men and women, it would promote the proper administration of justice, and the general well-being of society, to permit women to engage in the trial of cases at the bar, is a question opening a wide field of discussion, upon which it is not necessary for us to enter. It is sufficient to say that, in our opinion, the other implied limitation upon our power, to which we have above referred, must operate to prevent our admitting women to the office of attorney at law. If we were to admit them, we should be exercising the authority conferred upon us in a manner which, we are fully satisfied, was never contemplated by the legislature.

"It is to be remembered that at the time this statute was enacted we had, by express provision, adopted the common law of England, and, with three exceptions, the statutes of that country passed prior to the fourth year of James the First, so far as they were applicable to our condition.

"It is to be also remembered that female attorneys at law were unknown in England, and a proposition that a woman should enter the courts of Westminster Hall in that capacity, or as a barrister, would have created hardly less astonishment than one that she should ascend the bench of bishops, or be elected to a seat in the House of Commons.

"It is to be further remembered, that when our act was passed, that school of reform which claims for women participation in the making and administering of the laws had not then arisen, or, if here and there a writer had advanced such theories, they were regarded rather as abstract speculations than as an actual basis for action.

"That God designed the sexes to occupy different spheres of action, and that it belonged to men to make, apply, and execute the laws, was regarded as an almost axiomatic truth.

"In view of these facts, we are certainly warranted in saying that when the legislature gave to this court the power of granting licenses to practice law, it was with not the slightest expectation that this privilege would be extended to women."

The court having thus denied the application, Mrs. Bradwell brought the case here * * *.

MR. JUSTICE MILLER delivered the opinion of the court.

* * * [T]he plaintiff asserted her right to a license on the grounds, among others, that she was a citizen of the United States, and that having been a citizen of Vermont at one time, she was, in the State of Illinois, entitled to any right granted to citizens of the latter State.

* * *

As regards the provision of the Constitution that citizens of each State shall be entitled to all the privileges and immunities of citizens in the several States, [U.S. Constitution, Article IV, § 2] the plaintiff in her affidavit has stated very clearly a case to which it is inapplicable.

The protection designed by that clause * * * has no application to a citizen of the State whose laws are complained of. If the plaintiff was a citizen of the State of Illinois, that provision of the Constitution gave her no protection against its courts or its legislation.

The plaintiff seems to have seen this difficulty, and attempts to avoid it by stating that she was born in Vermont.

While she remained in Vermont that circumstance made her a citizen of that State. But she states, at the same time, that she is a citizen of the United States, and that she is now, and has been for many years past, a resident of Chicago, in the State of Illinois.

The fourteenth amendment declares that citizens of the United States are citizens of the State within which they reside; therefore the plaintiff was, at the time of making her application, a citizen of the United States and a citizen of the State of Illinois.

We do not here mean to say that there may not be a temporary residence in one State, with intent to return to another, which will not create citizenship in the former. But the plaintiff states nothing to take her case out of the definition of citizenship of a State as defined by the first section of the fourteenth amendment.

In regard to that amendment counsel for the plaintiff in this court truly says that there are certain privileges and immunities which belong to a citizen of the United States as such; otherwise it would be nonsense for the fourteenth amendment to prohibit a State from abridging them, and he proceeds to argue that admission to the bar of a State of a person who possesses the requisite learning and character is one of those which a State may not deny.

In this latter proposition we are not able to concur with counsel. We agree with him that there are privileges and immunities belonging to citizens of the United States, in that relation and character, and that it is these and these alone which a State is forbidden to abridge. But the right to admission to practice in the courts of a State is not one of them. This right in no sense depends on citizenship of the United States. It has not, as far as we know, ever been made in any State, or in any case, to depend on citizenship at all. Certainly many prominent and distinguished lawyers have been admitted to practice, both in the State and Federal courts, who were not citizens of the United States or of any State. But, on whatever basis this right may be placed, so far as it can have any relation to citizenship at all, it would seem that, as to the courts of a State, it would relate to citizenship of the State, and as to Federal courts, it would relate to citizenship of the United States.

* * * [T]he right to control and regulate the granting of license to practice law in the courts of a State is one of those powers which are not transferred for its protection to the Federal government, and its exercise is in no manner governed or controlled by citizenship of the United States in the party seeking such license.

* * *

Judgment affirmed.

MR. JUSTICE BRADLEY:

I concur * * *.

The claim of the plaintiff, who is a married woman, to be admitted to practice as an attorney and counsellor-at-law, is based upon the supposed right of every person, man or woman, to engage in any lawful employment for a livelihood. The Supreme Court of Illinois denied the application on the ground that, by the common law, which is the basis of the laws of Illinois, only men were admitted to the bar, and the legislature had not made any change in this respect * * *.

The claim that, under the fourteenth amendment of the Constitution, which declares that no State shall make or enforce any law which shall abridge the privileges and immunities of citizens of the United States, the statute law of Illinois, or the common law prevailing in that State, can no longer be set up as a barrier against the right of females to pursue any lawful employment for a livelihood (the practice of law included), assumes that it is one of the privileges and immunities of women as citizens to engage in any and every profession, occupation, or employment in civil life.

It certainly cannot be affirmed, as an historical fact, that this has ever been established as one of the fundamental privileges and immunities of the sex. On the contrary, the civil law, as well as nature herself, has always recognized a wide difference in the respective spheres and destinies of man and woman. Man is, or should be, woman's protector and defender. The natural and proper timidity and delicacy which belongs to the female sex evidently unfits it for many of the occupations of civil life. The constitution of the family organization, which is founded in the divine ordinance, as well as in the nature of things, indicates the domestic sphere as that which properly belongs to the domain and functions of womanhood. The harmony, not to say identity, of interests and views which belong, or should belong, to the family institution is repugnant to the idea of a woman adopting a distinct and independent career from that of her husband. So firmly fixed was this sentiment in the founders of the common law that it became a maxim of that system of jurisprudence that a woman had no legal existence separate from her husband, who was regarded as her head and representative in the social state; and, notwithstanding some recent modifications of this civil status, many of the special rules of law flowing from and dependent upon this cardinal principle still exist in full force in most States. One of these is, that a married woman is incapable, without her husband's consent, of making contracts which shall be binding on her or him. This very incapacity was one circumstance which the Supreme Court of Illinois deemed important in rendering a married woman incompetent fully to perform the duties and trusts that belong to the office of an attorney and counsellor.

It is true that many women are unmarried and not affected by any of the duties, complications, and incapacities arising out of the married state, but these are exceptions to the general rule. The paramount destiny and mission of woman are to fulfil the noble and benign offices of wife and mother. This is the law of the Creator. And the rules of civil society must be adapted to the general constitution of things, and cannot be based upon exceptional cases.

The humane movements of modern society, which have for their object the multiplication of avenues for woman's advancement, and of occupations adapted to her condition and sex, have my heartiest concurrence. But I am not prepared to say that it is one of her fundamental rights and privileges to be admitted into every office and position, including those which require highly special qualifications and demanding special responsibilities. In the nature of things it is not every citizen of every age, sex, and condition that is qualified for every calling and position. It is the prerogative of the legislator to prescribe regulations founded on nature, reason, and experience for the due admission of qualified persons to professions and callings demanding special skill and confidence. This fairly belongs to the police power of the State; and, in my opinion, in view of the peculiar characteristics, destiny, and mission of woman, it is within the province of the legislature to ordain what offices, positions, and callings shall be filled and discharged by men, and shall receive the benefit of those energies and responsibilities, and that decision and firmness which are presumed to predominate in the sterner sex.

For these reasons I think that the laws of Illinois now complained of are not obnoxious to the charge of abridging any of the privileges and immunities of citizens of the United States.

MR. JUSTICE SWAYNE and MR. JUSTICE FIELD concurred in the foregoing opinion of MR. JUSTICE BRADLEY.

THE CHIEF JUSTICE dissented from the judgment of the court, and from all the opinions.

NOTES AND QUESTIONS

1. Why did the Supreme Court of Illinois refuse to admit Myra Bradwell to the practice of law? Was the Supreme Court's action justified as a matter of then currently correct social practice, or did the action of the Judges have a narrower basis? Do you find the argument of legislative intent a persuasive one? Have you encountered it before in this section? How much of the Illinois court's action is based in the common law, and how much of that derives not from America, but from England?

Myra Bradwell (1831–94) was the editor of the *Chicago Legal News,* a well-regarded professional publication. She had also "read law under the guidance of her husband, a practitioner and then judge in Chicago." Charles Fairman, VI History of the Supreme Court of the United States: Reconstruction and Reunion 1864–88, Part One 1364 (1971).

There was no doubt about Myra Bradwell's objective qualifications to practice law except for the fact that she was a woman. Indeed, it is perhaps significant that in the argument before the United States Supreme Court no counsel appeared to oppose her appeal. Still, her efforts to gain admission to the bar, even in Chicago, were "commonly treated as somewhat whimsical." Fairman, supra, at 1365.

2. Justice Miller's opinion, for the court, has not gone down as one of the great works of constitutional exegesis, but do you find anything wrong with his disposing of Ms. Bradwell's constitutional arguments? In particular, what are we to make of her invocation of the "privileges and immunities" clause (Article IV, Section 2) based on the fact that she was born in Vermont? Do you find Miller persuasive in his rejection of Ms. Bradwell's argument based on the Fourteenth Amendment? Do you think, by the way, that barring women from the practice of law would violate the Fourteenth Amendment today?

3. It is Justice Bradley's concurring opinion which has generated more interest among historians. Why do you suppose that is? Why do you suppose Bradley found it necessary to write a concurrence? Could it be his view of "nature herself?" How does this view lead to the common law rule that a married woman can make no contracts on her own, and that therefore she is unfit for the practice of law? Do you suppose Bradley would be willing to find a Fourteenth Amendment violation if single women were barred from the practice of law? Whose law is it that "The paramount destiny and mission of woman are to fulfil the noble and benign offices of wife and mother," and is it a law that ought to receive constitutional sanction?

How do you explain Bradley's suggestion that "The humane movements of modern society, which have for their object the multiplication of avenues for woman's advancement, and of occupations adapted to her condition and sex" have his "heartiest concurrence?" If being an attorney is not suited to a woman's condition and sex, which occupations are? What are the "peculiar characteristics, destiny, and mission of woman," to which Bradley refers? Is there a particular problem in Bradley's view that the legislature is the proper agency to determine what professions are fit for men and which for women if there are no women in the legislature (or even entitled to vote for legislators)? Why does Bradley call men "the sterner sex?"

What are we to make of the fact that Chief Justice Chase dissented, but filed no opinion? Apparently the Chief Justice was in declining health, and this prevented him from writing. For a draft of an opinion which he might have written, and for the argument that Chase dissented because "like many another father, [he] may have thought that his daughter Kate deserved the right to function up to her abilities and not be rigidly constrained by gender roles, whether it be in politics, business or even law . . ." see Richard L. Aynes, "*Bradwell v. Illinois*: Chief Justice Chase's Dissent and the 'Sphere of Women's Work,' " 59 La.L.Rev. 521 (1999).

4. One year before the Supreme Court rendered its opinion in the *Bradwell* case, the legislature of Illinois enacted:

> That no person shall be precluded or debarred from any occupation, profession or employment (except military) on account of sex: *Provided,* that this Act shall not be construed to affect the eligibility of any person to an elective office.

Laws of 1870–71, page 578.

This statute would have probably required Myra Bradwell to be admitted to the Bar of Illinois, but she did not choose to take advantage of it, although she continued to publish her journal. Nevertheless, on its own motion, upon the basis of her original application, some years later, the Illinois Supreme Court directed that a license to practice law be issued to her. It must have been some satisfaction to Ms. Bradwell that *both* her surviving son *and* daughter were to become practicing lawyers.

5. In 1892, on the motion of the Attorney General, Myra Bradwell was admitted, as well, to the bar of the United States Supreme Court. Sadly, Justice Bradley didn't live to see that day, since he died two months before. One can't help but wonder what Bradley must have thought six years after his opinion in *Bradwell,* however, when the first woman *was* admitted to practice before the Supreme Court. That honor belonged to Mrs. Belva Ann Lockwood, a member of the District of Columbia Bar since 1873, who was admitted to practice before the United States Supreme Court on March 3, 1879. Her admission was only made possible after she had spearheaded the enactment of a federal statute authorizing women to be admitted to the Supreme Court Bar. Fairman, supra, at 1367. For further reading on Myra Bradwell, see Jane M. Friedman, America's First Woman Lawyer: The Biography of Myra Bradwell (1993). For her sister lawyer, the first woman to be admitted to the practice of law in California, Clara Shortridge Foltz (1849–1934, admitted to the California Bar, 1878), see three articles by Foltz's biographer, Barbara Allen Babcock, "Reconstructing the Person: The Case of Clara Shortridge

Foltz," in Revealing Lives: Autobiography, Biography, and Gender 131 (Susan Groag Bell & Marilyn Yalom eds., 1990), "Clara Shortridge Foltz: Constitution–Maker," 66 Ind.L.J. (1991), and "Clara Shortridge Foltz: 'First Woman,' " 30 Ariz.L.Rev. 673 (1988). See also the articles in the Volume 28, Number 4, Summer 1994, symposium in the Valparaiso University Law Review, "First Women: The Contribution of American Women to the Law" by Sandra Day O'Connor, Ruth Bader Ginsburg, Illana Diamond Rovner, Vivian Sue Shields & Suzanne Melanie Buchko, Barbara Allen Babcock, Jane M. Friedman, Sylvia A. Law, and Jo Ellen Lind. For an exploration of the complexities facing the feminist biographer of early women lawyers see Carol Sanger, "Curriculum Vitae (feminae): Biography and Early American Women Lawyers," 46 Stan.L.Rev. 1245 (1994). For a feminist perspective on writing about women and the practice of law, see Cynthia Grant Bowman, "Bibliographical Essay: Women and the Legal Profession," 7 J.of Gender, Social Policy & the Law 149 (1998–1999).

6. By the late nineteenth century, then, the formal barriers against women practicing law were crumbling. As we have seen, though, this was not the case with regard to female suffrage. Myra Bradwell's lawyer, arguing before the United States Supreme Court, tried to distinguish her case from that of women seeking the vote. "Female suffrage," he conceded, might "overthrow Christianity, defeat the ends of modern civilization, and upturn the world." Quoted in Fairman, supra, at 1365. For what happened when a woman tried to vote in a Congressional election, and found herself prosecuted for a federal crime, consider the next case.

UNITED STATES V. ANTHONY

United States Circuit Court, Northern District of New York, 1873.
24 Fed.Cas. 829.

HUNT, CIRCUIT JUSTICE * * *

The defendant is indicted under the act of congress of May 31st, 1870, for having voted for a representative in congress, in November, 1872. Among other things, that act makes it an offence for any person knowingly to vote for such representative without having a lawful right to vote. It is charged that the defendant thus voted, she not having a right to vote, because she is a woman. The defendant insists that she has a right to vote; and that the provision of the constitution of this state, limiting the right to vote to persons of the male sex, is in violation of the fourteenth amendment of the constitution of the United States, and is void.

The thirteenth, fourteenth and fifteenth amendments were designed mainly for the protection of the newly emancipated negroes, but full effect must, nevertheless, be given to the language employed. The thirteenth amendment provides, that "neither slavery nor involuntary servitude, except as a punishment for crime, whereof the party shall have been duly convicted, shall exist within the United States or any place subject to their jurisdiction." If honestly received and fairly applied, this provision would have been enough to guard the rights of the colored race. In some states it was attempted to be evaded by enactments cruel and oppressive in their nature—as, that colored persons were forbidden to appear in the towns, except in a menial capacity; that they should reside on and cultivate the soil without being allowed to own it; that they were not permitted to give testimony in cases where a white man was a party. They were excluded from performing particular kinds of business, profitable and reputable, and they were denied the right of suffrage. To meet the difficulties arising from this state of things, the fourteenth and fifteenth amendments were enacted.

The fourteenth amendment creates and defines citizenship of the United States. It had long been contended, and had been held by many learned authorities, and had never been judicially decided to the contrary, that there was no such thing as a citizen of the United States, except as that condition arose from citizenship of some state. No mode existed, it was said, of obtaining a citizenship of the United States, except by first becoming a citizen of some state. This question is now at rest. The fourteenth amendment defines and declares who shall be citizens of the United States, to wit, "all persons born or naturalized in the United States, and subject to the jurisdiction thereof." * * *

After creating and defining citizenship of the United States, the fourteenth amendment provides, that "no state shall make or enforce any law which shall abridge the privileges or immunities of citizens of the United States." This clause is intended to be a protection, not to all our rights, but to our rights as citizens of the United States only: that is, to rights existing or belonging to that condition or capacity. The expression, citizen of a state, used in the previous paragraph, is carefully omitted here. In article 4, § 2, subd. 1, of the constitution of the United States, it had been already provided, that "the citizens of each state shall be entitled to all privileges and immunities of citizens in the several states." The rights of citizens of the states and of citizens of the United States are each guarded by these different provisions. * * * The rights of citizens of the state, as such, are not under consideration in the fourteenth amendment. They stand as they did before the adoption of the fourteenth amendment, and are fully guaranteed by other provisions. The rights of citizens of the states * * * are the fundamental privileges and immunities belonging of right to the citizens of all free governments, such as the right of life and liberty, the right to acquire and possess property, to transact business, to pursue happiness in his own manner, subject to such restraint as the government may adjudge to be necessary for the general good. In Crandall v. Nevada, 6 Wall. [73 U.S.] 35, 44, is found a statement of some of the rights of a citizen of the United States, viz., to come to the seat of government to assert any claim he may have upon the government, to transact any business he may have with it, to seek its protection, to share its offices, to engage in administering its functions, and to have free access to its seaports, through which all the operations of foreign commerce are conducted, to the sub-treasuries, the land offices, the revenue offices, and the courts of justice in the several states. "Another privilege of a citizen of the United States," says Mr. Justice Miller * * * "is to demand the care and protection of the federal government over his life, liberty, and property, when on the high seas or within the jurisdiction of a foreign government." "The right to peaceably assemble and petition for redress of grievances, the privilege of the writ of habeas corpus," he says, "are rights of the citizen guaranteed by the federal constitution."

The right of voting, or the privilege of voting, is a right or privilege arising under the constitution of the state, and not under the constitution of the United States. The qualifications are different in the different states. Citizenship, age, sex, residence, are variously required in the different states, or may be so. If the right belongs to any particular person, it is because such person is entitled to it by the laws of the state where he offers to exercise it, and not because of citizenship of the United States. If the state of New York should provide that no person should vote until he had reached the age of thirty years, or after he had reached the age of fifty, or that no person having gray hair, or who had not the use of all his limbs, should be entitled to vote, I do not see how it could be held to be a violation of any right derived or held under the constitution of the United States. We might say that such regulations were unjust, tyrannical, unfit for the regulation of an intelligent state, but, if rights of a citizen are thereby violated, they are of that fundamental class, derived from his position as a citizen of the state, and not those limited rights belonging to him as a citizen of the United States * * *.

The United States rights appertaining to this subject are those, first, under article 1, § 2, subd. 1, of the United States constitution, which provides, that electors of representatives in congress shall have the qualifications requisite for electors of the most numerous branch of the state legislature; and second, under the fifteenth amendment, which provides, that "the right of citizens of the United States to vote shall not be denied or abridged by the United States, or by any state, on account of race, color, or previous condition of servitude." If the legislature of the state of New York should require a higher qualification in a voter for a representative in congress than is required for a voter for a member of the house of assembly of the state, this would, I conceive, be a violation of a right belonging to a person as a citizen of the United States. That right is in relation to a federal subject or interest, and is guaranteed by the federal constitution. The inability of a state to abridge the right of voting on account of race, color, or previous condition of servitude, arises from a federal guaranty. Its violation would be the denial of a federal right—that is, a right belonging to the claimant as a citizen of the United States. This right, however, exists by virtue of the fifteenth amendment. If the fifteenth amendment had contained the word "sex," the argument of the defendant would have been potent. She would have said, that an attempt by a state to deny the right to vote because one is of a particular sex is expressly prohibited by that amendment. The amendment, however, does not contain that word. It is limited to race, color, or previous condition of servitude. The legislature of the state of New York has seen fit to say, that the franchise of voting shall be limited to the male sex. In saying this, there is, in my judgment, no violation of the letter, or of the spirit, of the fourteenth or of the fifteenth amendment.

This view is assumed in the second section of the fourteenth amendment, which enacts, that, if the right to vote for federal officers is denied by any state to any of the male inhabitants of such state, except for crime, the basis of representation of such state shall be reduced in a proportion specified. Not only does this section assume that the right of male inhabitants to vote was the especial object of its protection, but it assumes and admits the right of a state, notwithstanding the existence of that clause under which the defendant claims to the contrary, to deny to classes or portions of the male inhabitants the right to vote which is allowed to other male inhabitants. The regulation of the suffrage is thereby conceded to the states as a state's right.

The case of Bradwell v. State, 16 Wall. [83 U.S.] 130, decided at the recent term of the supreme court, sustains both of the positions above put forth, viz., first, that the rights referred to in the fourteenth amendment are those belonging to a person as a citizen of the United States and not as a citizen of a state; and second, that a right of the character here involved is not one connected with citizenship of the United States. Mrs. Bradwell made application to be admitted to practice as an attorney and counsellor at law in the courts of Illinois. Her application was denied, and, upon a writ of error, it was held by the supreme court, that, to give jurisdiction under the fourteenth amendment, the claim must be of a right pertaining to citizenship of the United States, and that the claim made by her did not come within that class of cases. Justices Bradley, Swayne, and Field held that a woman was not entitled to a license to practice law. It does not appear that the other judges passed upon that question. The fourteenth amendment gives no right to a woman to vote, and the voting by Miss Anthony was in violation of law.

* * *

Upon the foregoing ruling, the counsel for the defendant requested the court to submit the case to the jury on the question of intent, and with the following instructions: (1) If the defendant, at the time of voting, believed that she had a right to vote, and voted in good faith in that belief, she is not guilty of the offence charged. (2) In determining the question whether the defendant did or did not believe that she had a right to vote, the jury may take into consideration, as bearing upon that question, the advice which she received from the counsel to whom she applied, and, also, the fact, that the inspectors of the election considered the question and came to the conclusion that she had a right to vote. (3) The jury have a right to find a general verdict of guilty or not guilty, as they shall believe that the defendant has or has not committed the offence described in the statute.

THE COURT declined to submit the case to the jury, on any question, and directed the jury to find a verdict of guilty. A request, by the defendant's counsel, that the jury be polled, was denied by THE COURT, and a verdict of guilty was recorded. On a subsequent day, a motion for a new trial was made, on the part of the defendant, before HUNT, CIRCUIT JUSTICE.

HUNT, CIRCUIT JUSTICE, in denying the motion, said, in substance:

The whole law of the case has been reargued, and I have given the best consideration in my power to the arguments presented. But for the evident earnestness of the learned counsel for the defendant, for whose ability and integrity I have the highest respect, I should have no hesitation. Still I can entertain no doubt upon any point in the case. I do not doubt the correctness of my decision, that the defendant had no right to vote, and that her belief that she had a right to vote, she knowing all the facts and being presumed and bound to know the law, did not relieve her from the penalty for voting, when in truth she had no right to vote.

The learned counsel insists, however, that an error was committed in directing the jury to render a verdict of guilty. This direction, he argues, makes the verdict that of the court and not of the jury, and it is contended that the provisions of the constitution looking to and securing a trial by jury in criminal cases have been violated.

The right of trial by jury in civil as well as in criminal cases is a constitutional right. The second section of the first article of the constitution of the state of New York provides, that "the trial by jury, in all cases in which it has been heretofore used, shall remain inviolate forever." Articles six and seven of the amendments to the constitution of the United States contain a similar provision. Yet, in cases where the facts are all conceded, or where they are proved and uncontradicted by evidence, it has always been the practice of the courts to take the case from the jury and decide it as a question of law. No counsel has ever disputed the right of the court to do so. No respectable counsel will venture to doubt the correctness of such practice, and this in cases of the character which are usually submitted to a jury. * * * The right of a trial by jury in a criminal case is not more distinctly secured than it is in a civil case. In each class of cases this right exists only in respect of a disputed fact. To questions of fact the jury respond. Upon questions of law, the decision of the court is conclusive, and the jury are bound to receive the law as declared by the court. People v. Bennett, 49 N.Y. 137, 141. Such is the established practice in criminal as well as in civil cases, and this practice is recognized by the highest authorities. It has been so held by the former supreme court of this state, and by the present court of appeals of this state.

At a circuit court of the United States, held by Judges Woodruff and Blatchford, upon deliberation and consultation, it was decided, that, in a criminal case, the court was not bound to submit the case to the jury, there being no sufficient evidence to justify a conviction, and the court accordingly instructed the jury to find a verdict of not guilty. U.S. v. Fullerton [Case No. 15,176]. The district attorney now states, that, on several occasions, since he has been in office, Judge Hall, being of opinion that the evidence did not warrant a conviction, has directed the jury to find a verdict of not guilty.

In the case of People v. Bennett, 49 N.Y. 137, 141, the court of appeals of the state of New York, through its chief justice, uses the following language: "Contrary to an opinion formerly prevailing, it has been settled that the juries are not judges of the law, as well as the facts, in criminal cases, but that they must take the law from the court. All questions of law during the trial are to be determined by the court, and it is the duty of the jury to regard and abide by such determination. * * * I can see no reason, therefore, why the court may not, in a case presenting a question of law only, instruct the jury to acquit the prisoner, or to direct an acquittal, and enforce the direction, nor why it is not the duty of the court to do so. This results from the rule, that the jury must take the law as adjudged by the court, and I think it is a necessary result."

In these cases the question, in each instance, was, whether the court had power to direct a verdict of not guilty to be rendered. But, the counsel for defendant expressly admits that the authority which justifies a direction to acquit will, in a proper case, justify a direction to convict; that it is a question of power; and that, if the power may be exercised in favor of the defendant, it may be exercised against him. As I now state this proposition, the counsel again signifies his assent. The reason given by Chief Justice Church in the case just cited, shows that there is no distinction between the cases in this respect. He says the rule results from the principle, that the jury must take the law from the court. The duty of the jury to take the law from the court is the same, whether it is favorable to the defendant, or unfavorable to him.

It is laid down in Colby, Cr.Law, c. 12, § 125, that no jury shall in any case be compelled to give a general verdict, so that they find the facts and require the court to give judgment thereon. 2 Rev.St. c. 421, § 68. "A special verdict is given when the jury find certain facts to exist, and leave the court to determine whether, according to law, the prisoner is guilty." "It is not necessary that the jury should, after stating the facts, draw any legal conclusion. If they do so, the court will reject the conclusion as superfluous, and pronounce such judgment as they think warranted by the facts." Colby, Cr.Law, c. 12, § 125.

All the authorities tend to the same result. It is the duty of the jury to act upon the facts. It is the duty of the court to decide the law. The facts being specially found by the jury, it is the duty of the court, and not of the jury, to pronounce the judgment of guilty or not guilty. The facts being fully conceded, it is the duty of the court to announce and direct what the verdict shall be, whether guilty or not guilty. Therefore, I cannot doubt the power and the duty of the court to direct a verdict of guilty, whenever the facts constituting guilt are undisputed.

In the present case, the court had decided, as matter of law, that Miss Anthony was not a legal voter. It had also decided, as matter of law, that, knowing every fact in the case, and intending to do just what she did, she had knowingly voted, not having a right to vote, and that her belief did not affect the question. Every fact in the case was undisputed. There was no inference to be drawn or point made on the facts, that could, by possibility, alter the result. It was, therefore, not only the right, but it seems to me, upon the authorities, the plain duty of the judge to direct a verdict of guilty. The motion for a new trial is denied.

The defendant was thereupon sentenced to pay a fine of $100 and the costs of the prosecution.

NOTES AND QUESTIONS

1. Do you understand the subtle distinctions Circuit Justice Hunt draws between the rights of citizens of the United States, and citizens of the individual states? Why is the right to vote a right of "state" citizenship, and not of federal citizenship? Do you understand how Susan Anthony could believe that such a right was hers as a *United States* citizen, and how she could argue that by depriving her of the right to vote for representatives in Congress the state of New York would be depriving her of a federal Constitutionally-guaranteed right? Which do you find more persuasive, the arguments of Ms. Anthony, or the constitutional analysis of Justice Hunt?

Note that Hunt believes that if New York wished to bar from voting those with gray hair, those over fifty, or those not having the use of all of their limbs, "I do not see how it could be held to be a violation of any right derived or held under the constitution of the United States." Do you?

You will have noticed that Justice Hunt makes plain his belief that depriving a person of the vote on account of sex involves "no violation of the letter, or of the spirit, of the fourteenth or of the fifteenth amendment." Hunt is clearly right about the "letter" of the amendments, but what about their "spirit?"

2. Notice that the *Bradwell* case is relied upon as authority to support Justice Hunt's upholding of Ms. Anthony's conviction. Is this an appropriate use of precedent? Even more interesting than Hunt's constitutional analysis

is what he did with the jury in this case. As a criminal trial it was before a jury, which was, apparently, perfectly prepared to sift the evidence, and pronounce as to Ms. Anthony's guilt or innocence. You will have probably understood that the jury was never allowed to deliberate on its own whether it would find a verdict of "guilty" or "not guilty." Instead, the jury was *directed,* by Justice Hunt, to bring in a verdict of guilty.

There can be no doubt that Ms. Anthony and her attorneys felt that this was an obscene mockery of justice. When Justice Hunt asked Ms. Anthony whether she had anything to say why sentence shall not be pronounced, she replied that

> [I]n your ordered verdict of guilty you have trampled under foot every vital principle of our government. My natural rights, my civil rights, my political rights, my judicial rights, are all alike ignored. Robbed of the fundamental principle of citizenship, I am degraded from the status of a citizen to that of a subject; and not only myself individually but all of my sex are, by your honor's verdict, doomed to political subjection under this so-called republican form of government.

Was she right?

3. Do you find such a practice, of a directed verdict, in accordance with the *Seven Bishops* case and the *Zenger* trial, which you studied earlier in the course? Was it even in accordance with the practices under the Alien and Sedition Acts, which you studied in Chapter Two? Do you suppose, for example, that Samuel Chase would have directed a verdict in this case? Do you find the directing of a verdict of guilty in a criminal case to violate the "spirit," if not the "letter" of the Sixth Amendment to the United States Constitution, which guarantees those accused of crimes trial "by an impartial jury?"

In an absolutely delightful, absorbing, and thorough account of the trial of Ms. Anthony and the biographies of the principals involved, N.E.H. Hull notes that a few years after Justice Hunt's decision, in U.S. v. Taylor, Chief Judge McCrary, of the 8th Circuit, after consultation with Mr. Justice Miller (Justice Hunt's onetime colleague on the United States Supreme Court), declared that Justice Hunt improperly deprived Ms. Anthony of her constitutional right to trial by jury by directing a guilty verdict in her case. N.E.H. Hull The Woman Who Dared to Vote: The Trial of Susan B. Anthony 184 (2012) (citing U.S. v. Taylor, 11 F. 470 (Circuit Ct., D. Kan., 1882)). It is probably significant that in Judge McCrary's opinion, he also notes that "upon reflection," Justice Hunt himself seems to have thought better of what he did in *U.S. v Anthony*, because "on the subsequent trial of the officers of election indicted with Miss Anthony for the same offence, and in which substantially the same testimony was introduced, he stated that instead of ordering a verdict of guilty he would submit the case to the jury with the instructions that there was no justification for the act of the defendants, and that in effect they were all guilty." 11. F., at 473. The jury, after some hesitance, did actually find all of the officials who allegedly impermissibly allowed Ms. Anthony to cast her ballot guilty as charged. Hull, supra, at 167–169. It is interesting to speculate whether Ms. Anthony's jury would have done the same if permitted to do so, but it is, perhaps, equally likely, as Ms. Hull appears to hint, that the public relations campaign conducted by Anthony in upstate New York to influence potential jurors would have resulted in a "not guilty" verdict in her case. Id., at 158-159. The election officials were later pardoned by President U.S. Grant. Id., at 185. Judge McCrary acknowledged that allowing cases such as Ms. Anthony's to go to the jury would inevitably recognize "that the right to render a general verdict includes the power to decide both law and fact, and therefore necessarily the power to decide independently of the court." 11 F., at 472. Is this a wise power to vest in the jury? Ms. Anthony was able, following Justice Hunt's action, to present herself as a martyr. Should Hunt have allowed the jury to decide the case? In Minor v. Happersett, 88 U.S. 162 (1875), the United States Supreme Court addressed the argument made by Ms. Anthony that the privileges and immunities clause of the 14th Amendment gave women the right to vote, which no state could abridge. The Court rejected the argument unanimously. For an analysis of that case see Hull, supra, at 185–208.

4. How wicked an oppressor was Justice Hunt? The statute under which Ms. Anthony was convicted provided for a fine not exceeding five hundred dollars, or for imprisonment for a term not exceeding three years. Justice Hunt ordered Ms. Anthony to pay a fine of $100, and the costs of the prosecution. Ms. Anthony's reply:

> May it please your honor, I will never pay a dollar of your unjust penalty. All the stock in trade I possess is a debt of $10,000, incurred by publishing my paper—*The Revolution*—the sole object of which was to educate all women to do precisely as I have done, rebel against your man-made, unjust, unconstitutional forms of law which tax, fine, imprison and hang women, while denying them the right of representation in the government; and I will work on with might and main to pay every dollar of that honest debt [which, by the way, through speaking tours lasting six years, she did], but not a penny shall go to this unjust claim. And I shall earnestly and persistently continue to urge all women to the practical recognition of the old Revolutionary maxim, "Resistance to tyranny is obedience to God."

What would you have expected Justice Hunt's reaction to be to this speech? Apparently he said, simply, "Madam, the Court will not order you to stand committed until the fine is paid." Why did he refuse to put her in jail until her fine was paid? See generally Rayne L. Hammond, "Trial and Tribulation: The Story of *United States v. Anthony*," 48 Buff. L. Rev. 981 (2000).

5. For further reading on the struggles for the rights of women in the nineteenth century see, for primary sources, the valuable collection by Aileen S. Kraditor, ed., Up From the Pedestal: Selected Writings in the History of American Feminism 195 (1968). See also, for representative secondary works, Eleanor Flexner, Century of Struggle: The Woman's Rights Movement in the United States (rev. ed., 1975); W.L. O'Neill, Everyone Was Brave: The Rise

and Fall of Feminism in America (1970); Miriam Gurko, The Ladies of Seneca Falls: The Birth of the Women's Rights Movement (1974); Alma Lutz, Susan B. Anthony: Rebel, Crusader, Humanitarian (1959), and, for a biography of Ms. Anthony, Kathleen Barry, Susan B. Anthony: A Biography of a Singular Feminist (1988).

6. The struggle for the formal rights of women was a long one. Not until 1920, for example, did the Nineteenth Amendment become law. That Amendment to the United States Constitution provided that "The right of citizens of the United States to vote shall not be denied or abridged by the United States or by any State on account of sex." Why did it take so long for women even to receive the constitutional guarantee of the vote? Susan Anthony and Myra Bradwell thought that the Fourteenth Amendment should have guaranteed women equal rights, though a majority of the contemporary Court was unconvinced. How far did the framers of that Amendment intend to go in protecting the rights of women? See generally Ward Farnsworth, "Women Under Reconstruction: The Congressional Understanding," 94 Nw.U.L.Rev. 1229 (2000). As we move into the next chapter, eventually to consider the treatment of economic issues in the last part of the nineteenth century, see if you can understand the social and cultural forces which kept women (and many men) in a legally subordinate position.

CHAPTER 5

COMPETITION AND LABOR LAW IN ANTE–BELLUM AND LATE NINETEENTH CENTURY AMERICA

■ ■ ■

INTRODUCTION: The New Competition: Individualism, Technology, and Private Power, 1800–1920

Individualism is such a powerful theme in American history that we are rarely aware how unique American individualism is. In the eighteenth century, when many colonial Americans, like Benjamin Franklin, were busy becoming exemplars of European-based Enlightenment thought, what Europeans found most charming about them was that they were not Europeans. Franklin lived in France as the ambassador to the court of Louis XVI during the American Revolution, where he successfully worked to obtain French support for the patriots' cause. In his coonskin hat, he symbolized to the people of France a rustic individuality born of pristine nature. Franklin was not exactly a noble savage, a concept made popular among the French by Rousseau, but he was something of a new world analogue. His practical manners, his casual style and dress, his erudition that showed through a plain and humorous turn of speech, these all announced the presence of an alternative to the traditional European subject of a monarch.

What was unique about this new kind of man, this American? Franklin was interested in science, and his experiments in electricity brought him international attention. As a young man, he was a reader of serious English literature. He was a master artisan who made his living operating a printing press in Philadelphia, and owned the *Pennsylvania Gazette.* He worked with an apprentice in his shop, which was located on the ground floor of his home. He was also the printer of *Poor Richard's Almanack,* completely American in its outlook and enormously popular. First published in 1733, *Poor Richard* encouraged the financial success of his readers, and Franklin titled the preface to his 1758 edition "The Way to Wealth." His writings are filled with practical prescriptions for self-improvement. Franklin's famous Autobiography—a classic of American literature—is especially revealing for the manner in which Franklin portrays himself continually seeking a state of individual perfection ("Imitate Jesus and Socrates"). Without question, Franklin's was a new kind of voice in the colonies. For him, the goal of perfection was not the anticipation of life in the hereafter, as would have been true for his New England predecessors, but rather the improvement of his worldly circumstances. It was not luxury he wanted, and most certainly not a life of leisure. The traits he personifies are thrift, inventiveness, practicality, and hard work, and material reward is the goal, one that he amply achieved. Having risen above his humble beginnings, he was an early exemplar of the American "self-made man."

American individualism was not necessarily inconsistent with contributions to the community. If Franklin saw individual self-interest as an enlightened approach to the business of life, he was anything but self-absorbed. He involved himself in his city's community affairs, encouraged enlightened reform, took a serious interest in technology (he developed the "Franklin stove" and bifocals, which he deliberately chose not to patent in order to make their benefits freely available), and took part in the founding of a hospital, fire company, insurance company, and an academy (later the University of Pennsylvania). He served his country as a delegate to the Continental Congress and to the Constitutional Convention. If Franklin did not rise to the stature of Augustinian hero, as did Washington, he became a hero of another kind. He showed that private gain and public good could live happily together. Indeed, and here he broke decisively with the Puritan clergy of his Boston boyhood, and became an American icon when he indicated his belief that enlightened self-interest *was* the public good.

Tocqueville, writing in the 1830s, might have had Franklin in mind when he commented that that the key to the future of America was keeping alive the connection between individual spirit and public good. Tocqueville saw them each, together, as a necessity for the maintenance of vigor in the nation. Individual energies released by democracy promoted economic improvements, individual achievement, and lively and dynamic communities where liberties and opportunities were continuously expanded. Still, this dynamism and expansion had its darker side. A free people of equals who cared little about their responsibility to the larger society might incline toward selfishness, and selfishness could lead to new forms of tyranny. As we have seen, Tocqueville was captivated by the progress and future of democracy. Still, he saw tyranny as an unfortunate though ubiquitous natural byproduct of the human condition, and he worried that this might yet become America's fate.

The history of technology, labor, and the trusts in the nineteenth century is the story of conflicts between individualism and the responsibilities of public life, and the evolving meaning of justice under law. Determining the limits of private pursuit, fashioning an evolving understanding of the public good and seeking to apply 18th century conceptions of liberty to new realities of 19th century democracy and economic life was a challenge that fell largely to the courts and legislatures. How well did they do? What values guided them? Was the transformation of the economy in the 19th century an inevitable outcome of the secular, business-oriented individualism embodied by Franklin, or an aberration that he would have disapproved of? Was Tocqueville accurate in suspecting that excessive self-interest would lead to another form of tyranny? Are competition and freedom the same things? What exactly was the "American dream?" Was it economic? Some of the answers to these questions may be revealed by considering the development of new technologies in nineteenth century America, and how technological developments altered the character of Americans and their economy and society.

Technology in the colonial era was limited to finding new ways of doing old things. As we have indicated earlier, the Crown discouraged production, manufacturing, and invention in the colonies; the purpose of the colonies was, instead, to provide raw material to the mother country, which turned it into commodities to be sold back to the colonies. There were practical developments in agriculture, some borrowed from the traditions that African slaves brought with them to the New World. Native Americans modified the musket in their daily use (they eliminated the need to use flint), and Americans borrowed from them when it fitted their needs. The most important technological projects were water-powered grist mills, some very limited iron production, and the building of two canals and some turnpikes. But these products relied on age-old technology.

Soon, however, the interaction between invention, work force, and business organization altered the characteristics of the American economy. By looking at one example we have already considered, the cotton gin, we can appreciate how a single technological innovation in pre-Civil War America rippled through the economy, stimulated collateral developments and created new opportunities for further invention and application, as did many similar inventions.

Eli Whitney's 1793 device, the most basic of technology innovations, transformed agriculture in the South. Cotton agriculture led to the expansion in the South of new lands for cultivation, and, as we have seen, a revival of the institution of slavery and the plantation economy during the period 1800–60 (22 times more cotton was produced in 1860 than in 1810). The spread of cotton cultivation created a need for new forms of transport to move the cotton to market. The cities of Savannah, Charleston, and Baltimore were adequate points of shipment for cotton producers near the Atlantic coast, but impossible to reach as cultivation moved deeper South and westward. Because roads were in poor condition throughout the South, waterways were the natural option. The Mississippi and its tributaries extending North, East, and West was a natural transportation system, and also one made better by the introduction of steam-powered boats (in full use by the 1830s) able to travel upstream at a remarkable 20 miles per hour, and downstream at an even more impressive 30. An agricultural invention, westward settlement, and the development of steam-technology on vessels transformed the national economy: by 1850, cotton accounted for 50% of the nation's export trade. The distribution of cotton created new urban centers, such as Memphis and Mobile, and made New Orleans an international port.

Cotton from the South also fueled the textile mills in Waltham, Massachusetts, opened in 1813, and the Lowell mills opened in the 1820s. There cotton was spun for wholesale and retail. The new textile mills in New England were a novelty in America. They ran on waterpower, and were the first businesses in the New World to operate as what we would now recognize as factories. The mills were run by professional managers whose job was to generate as much output as possible from the labor of workers, who worked for wages, instead of sharing in the profits of the undertaking. Because textile mills competed with each other, and with European mills, economy and productivity could not be divorced: Keeping as many employees as could be used in the factory, working as constantly and long as possible, became the enterprise's object. The mills, which were very good at spinning cotton, also became good at making other machines, especially other spinning wheels which could be marketed to individual homes throughout New England where piece-work could still be done. The existence of mills was a stimulus to inventors like Isaac Singer, whose sewing machine of the 1850s led to the mass production of clothing, shoes, and book binding. The sewing machine itself became an object of mass production in factories: 1.5 million machines were sold from 1856–69 and 4.8 million from 1869–1878.

Moving the raw cotton from seaport to mill and from mill to wholesalers, manufacturers, and retailers depended on a well-developed system of transportation. Overland transportation was important, especially in the mid-West and West. Early in the nineteenth century, and with some Federal governmental support, canal building linked rivers and lakes. Canal building, the grandest of which was the Erie completed in 1825, involved dozens of small technological innovations that were transferable to the building of other canals, and also to other forms of manufacture. Canals stimulated urban growth in cities like Rochester, Syracuse, Buffalo, Cleveland, Akron, Toledo, and Dayton. Paralleling the canal was the turnpike, and in 1820, 40,000 miles of graded roads were in use, and over these roads passed still more innovations like the Concord Coach, a mass-produced conveyance that stayed in use until the next century, and was first manufactured in New Hampshire in 1826.

Railroads were another beneficiary of technological improvement. The first railway was the Quincy Tramway of Massachusetts, built in 1827. The tramway used horses to haul cars over wooden rails. The first self-propelled railroad engine was used by the Delaware and Hudson

Railroad, a steam engine fixed to a wheeled platform to haul cars on iron-covered wooden rails. Passenger railroad service began in South Carolina in 1831. Continuous advances in steam technology and the use of solid iron track allowed for faster speeds and travel over longer distances. The railroad turned out to be a particularly economical form of transportation. It could carry passengers at one-third the cost of a Concord Coach (the finest American horse-driven stagecoach) fare.

In each case—textile mills, the factory, canal building, road building, railroads—the Americans borrowed from European models and made innovations that fit local circumstances. In some cases, the final product was a distinct improvement over the European original. For example, the steam locomotive had its origin in England, but the Americans added moveable truck wheels that made it better suited to negotiating curved track, which was more typical of American topography.

Building locomotives was not work to be done by traditional craftsman, such as carpenters, mechanics, coopers, ironworkers, and blacksmiths. They could do it using traditional means, but the great demand for the product called for alternative and innovative approaches. Just as the factory arose to meet changing needs of production, building engines led to the creation of the "machine shop." It too used workers who performed skilled tasks, and operated in separate departments. Each department was capable of producing many parts of the same kind, with assembly done at the final stage. The locomotive and the railway depend ed on the science of metallurgy, since boilers for steam engines imposed strict requirements, and iron for track needed to be of a quality and quantity to sustain punishing widespread daily use by locomotives and their cargos. Advances in metallurgy also benefited bridge design and construction, which were needed to convey trains. Investments and refinements in iron production (and later steel) grew with the demands from railroads.

All of these forms of technology depended for their success upon human labor. In the case of cotton, slave labor was used. Technology change was evident in other agricultural fields, however. The greatest influence on technology is the availability of lands. As western lands opened up for cultivation in the Ohio valley and western territories, farmers faced a new challenge of how to bring the maximum amount of land under cultivation. Colonial agriculture was fueled by animal and hand-use implements, such as the hoe and the rake. Harvesting was done by hand. The productive potential of a typical colonial farm family more or less depended on the number of helping hands. By 1850 this had changed dramatically. The development of the steel plow, cultivator, and the horse-drawn reaper meant that more land could be brought under cultivation and harvested in a fraction of the time, using the same number of workers as before. The development of the first grain elevators in 1842 ensured that large quantities of grain could be stored, loaded and unloaded for quick shipment. Access to railroad lines was also key to an expanding commercial agriculture: The train followed the farm and the city in its movement west. In 1869, the transcontinental railroad was completed, and thousands of small communities, and millions of farmers, gained markets for their yields.

A necessity for the railroads, and other sources that used steam-generated power, was coal. The need for coal sustained the rise of mining as a major new American industry. Iron making, and later the manufacturing of steel, was heavily dependent on coal to fuel blast and open-hearth furnaces. The transportation network of railroads, roadways and rivers transported coal to market, where it was sold both to businesses and the homes of consumers in newly developing cities.

In the nineteenth century America's population growth accelerated to its highest levels. The increased population was important for the development of factory-based systems of labor, and for cultivation of new land. Many of the new immigrants, especially those from Western Europe who arrived before 1860, came with ambitions of owning land, and moved west to fulfill their dreams. Others, especially those in the latter decades of the nineteenth century who came from Southern and Eastern Europe to escape poverty and national dislocations, saw in America an opportunity for a new start. Many of these gravitated to cities. In 1860, the foreign born population accounted for 40% of New York City's residents, 60% of St. Louis', and 50% of Pittsburgh's and Chicago's. These cities became new centers of manufacturing and after 1870 bore little resemblance to the urban mills and factories of the antebellum era. The factories of the Gilded Age were larger, involved better machinery, used electricity, and employed many more laborers. The new industrial cities were also transportation hubs, suited not only for the shipment of product, but also for the transportation of people, on whom new factories depended. Chicago, for example, was served by shipping on the Great Lakes that connected the city with other states and the Atlantic; its Illinois River gave the city access to the Mississippi, and its strategic location made it a North–South and East–West railway hub.

The industrial revolution of the nineteenth century, then, was part of a massive economic transformation, and both proceeded from changes in technology. A system of values that encouraged and rewarded individual enterprise, a patriotism that equated economic development with national destiny, the growth of population, the emergence of markets, and the availability of land and natural resources fuelled these changes. The economic transformation generated wealth, and per capita income grew steadily in every decade of the nineteenth century, averaging 1.5% each year after 1820, an unprecedented (and unmatched) rate of increase in human history. Per capita production also exploded. One person in 1900 produced the same volume as four in 1780. A new middle class emerged, and with it, as we have seen, a new family form that introduced changes in the roles of women and children. Education gained in value, both for its contribution to the work force of the future, and its contribution to civic virtue. Concentrations in wealth grew through the century, tracking the development of new industries and markets for products. There were 50 millionaires in 1848, 1000 in 1875, and 4047 in 1892.

Not until 1920 did more than half of the population reside in cities, but the dominance of the city and its manufacturing economy was evident long before then. The city and its supporting and neighboring town and villages now included a new kind of labor, the largest classes of which were unskilled and semi-skilled workers. Beginning with the first textile mills, labor was becoming virtually mechanized. Manufacturing was no longer the product of a single home-based working unit (the artisan and his journeymen or apprentice), but the coordination and synchronization of many who worked in an impersonal environment, the factory, and under the supervision of a manager. The decades after 1820 saw the gradual disappearance of the master artisan who created and owned his own products, which he sold directly to customers, often on special order. They had been tailors, coopers, chandlers, hat makers, printers, blacksmiths, shoemakers, glassblowers, and others. By 1900 they were relics, the nostalgic symbols of a more personal meaning that manufacturing once held.

The change in the nature of work occurred on several levels. Laborers in factories enjoyed little immediate control over what they did on their jobs. The rhythms of their machines and the pacing of the clock ruled the workplace. Any skills employed by the new industrial worker did not count for a great deal. More important was the willingness to work steadily, to perform the same repetitive tasks for up to 12 hours per day, six days per week. The extremely competitive nature of industry kept wages low. Conditions in the work place became an important social and political issue, particularly since many women and children worked in factories in the nineteenth century. The use of machinery and processes that involved long hours of repetitive cutting, slicing, stitching, pounding, and lifting involved dangers to life and limb; the possibility of malfunctioning equipment was an ever-present threat. The most dangerous work often was reserved for the newest immigrants, who were willing to work for the least.

Along with changes in the nature of work came changes in the nature of business. Though its origin is in the antebellum era, it is not until after the Civil War that the corporate form became well-established as a part of the American economy. The Corporation was tailor made for the new industries of the Gilded Age because it allowed for the organization of business activity across state and international boundaries; it facilitated wealth accumulation, a critical feature given the large fixed-costs of new industrial forms, such as the railroad, the manufacture of steel, and the production of petroleum. The shareholder limited liability provided by the corporate form encouraged widespread investment. As we have seen, corporations were treated as artificial persons by the courts, and were even accorded some constitutional protections, such as those provided by the Fourteenth Amendment. The perpetual life of the corporation, however, allowed it to accomplish things mere humans could not.

While in the course of the nineteenth century the nation saw spectacular economic, commercial, and industrial progress, nevertheless, beginning around the middle of the century, the growth of business was marred by periodic failures, perhaps the inevitable consequence of multiplying opportunities in a largely unregulated environment of competition. Breaking points usually came during periods of panic and contractions in the economy, when prices dropped, unemployment grew, and bankruptcies climbed. The Panic of 1873, which lasted through the decade, was severe. It fell heaviest on those industries given to gross overproduction, wasteful practice, and non-existent quality controls. Difficulties with the railroads were examples of what could go wrong in a free-wheeling, shoot-it-out economy with roller-coaster businesses cycles. Railroads were expensive to build and operate. They had laid 160,500 miles of track by 1880, but many of the dozens of railroad companies established before then were gone—made obsolete, failed, or gobbled up by competitors. The average rail line owned between 100 and 500 miles of track. The wide variance in railway gauges, the disruptions of passenger service along a continuous line of track, the incompatibility of rail equipment, and wild fluctuations in pricing led companies to adopt new survival and growth strategies, foremost of which were non-competitive agreements such as "pooling." From the industry's standpoint, this was understandable, and also profitable. In 1887 Congress stepped in and created the Interstate Commerce Commission to bring order to the industry and to protect the interests of interstate rail users. The ICC was the first national regulatory commission, and the railroads the first large-scale business to be supervised by a regulatory agency. You'll read about it soon in connection with a great railroad antitrust case, *U.S. v. Trans–Missouri Freight Association*.

The railroad was a unique industry, seen by Americans as a "natural monopoly;" and, eventually, public dismay over pricing called for a unique response. For other industries, the survival-and-growth strategy was vertically to integrate production and distribution of products in a given industry, allowing management control over an entire range of costs; and horizontally to integrate different product types with markets, under a single group of professional managers. Integration allowed control over all aspects of production, distribution, and pricing. It was the solution to the problem of cut-throat competition, and this is precisely what "trust" agreements accomplished. After the passage of the Sherman Anti–Trust Act of 1890, to which we will soon turn, these "trust" agreements were discarded and the device of holding companies–corporations who owned other corporations–was substituted. In the absence of state centralized management of the economy, the private reorganization of industry into amalgamations managed by holding companies created a new kind of "big business," such as Carnegie Steel, Standard Oil, McCormick Harvester, and G. Swift and Company.

The trend toward consolidation and integration accelerated through the decade: In 1897, there were 67 new combinations through mergers, in 1898, 300 mergers; and in 1899, 1208 mergers. Through mergers, to use one example, a single meat processing company was able vertically to integrate its markets by taking control over the production of hogs and cattle, transporting them in their own refrigerated rail cars to slaughterhouses in Chicago, which they also owned. The meat was prepared for packaging in plants, belonging to the company, and shipped in their own freight cars to wholesalers. Only a very few meat-packing plans could compete at this large scale of operation. Often such large and monopolistic organizations enjoyed almost complete freedom in managing every aspect of business, including the wages, working conditions, and hours of employees; and they enjoyed further leverage in working with buyers and suppliers. You'll learn more about this when you read *U.S. v. E.C. Knight Co.*, a case involving the "sugar trust," and *NLRB v. Jones & Laughlin*, a case involving "big steel," below.

Another new approach to labor was the company town, which did for the work force what integration did for production. The Pullman Palace Car company, owned by George Pullman, about which you will soon read, maintained a virtual monopoly in the production of railroad sleeping cars from the mid–1860s until the 1920s. The Pullman sleeper, known for its luxurious appointments and full-service attendants, typically was leased to a railroad company and operated on the line by Pullman employees. Its cars were painted dark green and prominently labeled as Pullman property. The factory employed about 6,000 workers at its plants on Lake Calumet, just south of Chicago, and Pullman built a town, named after him, next to the factory. In a day when many workers lived in tenements, the company's planned community appeared to set a new standard for workers, who paid rent to the company. The town included markets, churches, and a hotel for visitors, and even entertainment (alcohol was barred, however). As you will see, Pullman had almost complete control over his workers and their families, on the job and off. When the panic of 1895 hit, Pullman laid off employees and cut wages without reducing rent. His purported workers utopia was attacked as "un-American," and called by some of his employees "Pullman's hell."

Thus, though many Americans may have embraced technology and economic and industrial development, equating national material growth with patriotic duty, there were also strong undercurrents of tension. Culturally, the concept of the individual in the first half of the century evoked a romantic image of humanity in nature, best exemplified in the life of Henry David Thoreau and his meditations on Walden Pond. The intellectual movement of transcendentalism, the utopian experiment in cooperative living of Brook Farm, and the celebration of the young nation's natural beauty by artists, clashed with the increasing materialism of the marketplace, the noxious smoke of steam engines, and the metallic sound of clanging railway carriages (as you saw in the *Long Island Railroad v. Hentz* case). The concerns were not simply aesthetic. Changes in work, growth of cities, the loss of a sense of community, and the worship of the almighty dollar seemed to many a corrupt worship of Mammon. Some clergy saw in the rush to wealth a dangerous competitive spirit let loose, a "bloodless heart" that threatened American social bonds.

The experience of war, a hardening experience in any time, took on a special meaning when the Union Army and the national government mobilized the entire Northern population and its industries in the world's first "total war" effort. The human toll of the Civil War was great. More military personnel were killed in that conflict (estimated at 620,000) than in all other U.S. wars combined. Whatever idealism survived the war, it was not for the innocence, or the beauty, of humanity.

The war effort stimulated manufacturing and industrial growth that continued unabated until the Great Depression, but the patriotic echo of the antebellum era's economic take-off sounded hollow in the heavy industrial expansion of the Gilded Age. "Social Darwinism" applied Charles Darwin's new theories of natural selection and survival of the fittest to justify a harder, more rugged brand of American individualism. This outlook was used to defend racism at home, adventurism in foreign policy, and laissez-faire ideology in the economy. The Constitution of 1789, tested in 1861, was tested again in the Gilded Age as reformers and advocates demanded legal justice for those they saw as the downtrodden, the byproduct, they believed, of unfeeling corporate greed. In their own defense, industrialists looked to the Constitution for the protection of their and their corporations' sacred property rights and liberties. The fabulous wealth of the new industrialists contrasted pitifully with the simultaneous urban poverty. In 1877 the average urban family earned $738 per year, two-thirds of which went to pay for rent and heat. The "Social Gospel" movement, the clergy's late 19th century response to Social Darwinism, brought the problem of poverty to national attention and promoted public support of charity and reforms. The "muckraker" movement among journalists such as Ida Tarbell, Lincoln Steffens, and Upton Sinclair exposed the dubious political and business practices of the trusts.

As you will see, there was a sort of ongoing battle between capital and labor. The movement to organize labor has its roots in Philadelphia, where the mechanization of shoemaking began early. In 1792 the Federal

Society of Journeymen Cordwainers organized, and you will read about how it ran afoul of early American labor law. In New York, printers and bakers formed organizations. In Massachusetts, railway workers organized. These earliest organizations were local in orientation and not exactly trade unions, as they tended to organize along craft lines that included skilled artisans and journeymen, those who had seen their status transform from relative independence to one of dependence on employers. At this time these laborers did not see themselves as industrial workers, and their practice was not so much to engage in negotiations with employers, but to set a wage at which they would work. The reasons for organizing were as often collegial and fraternal, as economic. There were labor actions, however, and between 1833 and 1837 about 160 "strikes" have been recorded. In 1834, the women workers of the Lowell mill walked out in protest over wage cuts.

The greatest challenge that made organizing labor almost impossible for most of the 19th century may not really be the hostility of the common law, as you will soon observe, but were instead the differences among types of workers, variation of work within different industries (unskilled to semi-skilled to skilled), religious differences, racial differences, differences in ethnicity and nationality, political differences, and so forth. The first serious attempt at a national inclusive union was the Knights of Labor, rising meteorically in the 1880s after successful strikes against the Union Pacific and Wabash Railroad. At its height, the Knights of Labor claimed more than 700,000 dues paying members, including craft and industrial workers, and advocated fair wages, child labor reform, the abolition of convict labor, and elimination of privately owned banks. The only people prohibited from joining were lawyers, stockholders, bankers, and gamblers. It experienced a rapid decline in the early 1890s, blamed by the media for the Chicago Haymarket Square riot (for which it was not responsible), and was moribund by 1900. Not until the American Federation of Labor some years later, did labor organizers hit upon a successful formula for unionism. An amalgamation of unions made up of skilled craft workers, the AFL made its peace with big business and narrowed its mission to seeking the best wages it could get for its members by means of negotiation and contract ("collective bargaining"); it promised to honor its agreements, because it saw business's health as essential to the worker's pocketbook. It adopted a model of organization not unlike big business, with a paid centralized office that offered leadership directives from on high, and governing structures that reached to the local level. The AFL was not a democracy, nor was it, like the Knights of Labor, a loose coalition of political and utopian causes.

Eugene V. Debs, whose involvement in the Pullman strike you will soon study, and other radical labor leaders attacked the AFL as an "aristocracy" of the working class that was interested only in skilled workers. Debs also accused the AFL of being more intent on serving capitalism than his favored socialism. Debs was not inaccurate. The alternative, one that Debs supported, was the Industrial Workers of the World. The IWW, or "Wobblies," called for the elimination of capitalism and its replacement with worker-controlled production, much as Debs himself did in his speech on "Liberty," which you will soon read. The IWW sought members from the ranks of the nonwhite, migrant, immigrant, and industrial workers who were shut out of the AFL, and led them in a series of violent industrial actions from 1909–1918. When their activities threatened to interrupt the War effort, they were declared illegal by state and Federal authorities, and finally died.

The AFL, however, survived as the American model of unionism. In 1919 it represented 20% of the labor force, with 5 million members and 110 affiliated unions—the highest membership it would ever record. It began a decline in the 1920s, following a series of local and national strikes that were crushed by the government. The cause of organized labor was not helped when the American media compared the prevalence of American labor unrest to the Bolshevik revolution, a frightening specter to citizens, employers and the government. As you will see when we read *NLRB v. Jones & Laughlin*, not until the New Deal, when the Roosevelt Administration for the first time legally sanctioned unions through the passage of the Wagner Act (1937), did the AFL exert much influence with business, and then it would share the stage with a new organization, the Congress of Industrial Organizations. The CIO began as a break-away movement when the AFL declined to broaden its membership to include some industrial workers; The CIO did for workers in the auto, rubber, textile, and steel industries what the AFL did for the craft unions. But this was not to happen until well into the twentieth century, and we turn now to the law regarding competition in nineteenth century America.

Further Reading

Yehoshua Arieli, *Individualism and Nationalism in American Ideology*, 1964

Edward Ayers, *The Promise of the New South,* 1992

Robert C. Bannister, *Social Darwinism: Science and Myth in Anglo–American Social Thought,* 1988

Gillian Brown, *Domestic Individualism: Imagining Self in Nineteenth–Century America,* 1990

Stuart Bruchey, *Enterprise: The Dynamic Economy of a Free People*, 1990

Paul Conkin, *Prophets of Prosperity: America's First Political Economists,* 1980

Charles W. Calhoun, ed., *The Gilded Age: Essays on the Origins of Modern America,* 1996

Alfred Chandler, *The Visible Hand: The Managerial Revolution in American Business,* 1977

Ron Chernow, *Titan: The Life of John D. Rockefeller, Sr.*, 2004

Roger Daniels, *Coming to America: Immigration and Ethnicity in American Life*, 2002

Stanley L. Engerman and Robert E. Gallman, *The Cambridge Economic History of the United States*

Ralph W. Hidy, Muriel E. Hidy, Roy V. Scott, Don L. Hofsommer, *The Great Northern Railway: A History,* 2004

David Hounshell, *From the American System to Mass Production, 1800–1932: The Development of Manufacturing Technology in the United States,* 1984

Thomas Hughes, *American Geniuses: A Century of Invention and Technological Enthusiasm, 1870–1970*, 1989

Portia P. James, *The Real McCoy: African–American Invention and Innovation, 1619–1930,* 1989

Morton Keller, *Regulating a New Economy: Public Policy and Economic Change in America, 1900–1933,* 1989

Peter Krass, *Carnegie*, 2002

Brooke Hindle and Steven Lubar, *Engines of Change: The American Industrial Revolution, 1790–1860,* 1986

Leo Marx, *The Machine in the Garden: Technology and the Pastoral Ideal in America,* 1999

Merritt Roe Smith and Leo Marx, eds., *Does Technology Drive History? The Dilemma of Technological Determinism*, 1994

David Montgomery, *The Fall of the House of Labor: The Workplace, the State, and American Labor Activism, 1865–1925*, 1987

David Nelson, *Managers and Workers: Origins of the New Factory System in the United States, 1800–1900,* 1996

Daniel Nelson, *Shifting Fortunes: The Rise and Decline of American Labor from the 1820s to the Present,* 1997

David E. Nye, *America as Second Creation: Technology and Narratives of New Beginnings*, 2004

Carroll Purcell, *Machine in America: A Social History of Technology*, 1995

Daniel T. Rogers, *Atlantic Crossings: Social Politics in a Progressive Age*, 1998

Philip Scranton, *Endless Novelty: Specialty Production and American Industrialization, 1865–1925,* 1997

Charles G. Sellers, *The Market Revolution: Jacksonian America, 1815–1846*, 1991

Charles Taylor, *Sources of the Self: The Making of the Modern Identity,* 1989

George Rogers Taylor, *The Transportation Revolution, 1815–1860,* 1951

Harry L. Watson, *Liberty and Power: The Politics of Jacksonian America,* 1990

Olivier Zunz, *Making America Corporate, 1870–1920*, 1990

A. DIFFERING MODELS FOR ECONOMIC DEVELOPMENT (1808–1837)

In his *Commentaries,* as you may remember, Blackstone wrote that it was an actionable nuisance to set up a fair or a market "so near" to an already-existing one that it "does * * * a prejudice." Blackstone also indicated, however, that it was no nuisance simply to erect a new mill near an old one, or to set up "any trade, or a school, in neighborhood or rivalship with another * * *." Why do you suppose the English common law, as Blackstone described it, maintained what amounts to two differing models for enterprise—monopoly in the case of fairs or ferries and competition in the case of mills, schools, or trades? As you read the following materials on the early law of competition in America try to determine which of these models is favored, and why. Which do you prefer? Why?

DONELLY V. VANDENBERGH

Supreme Court of New York, 1808.
3 Johns 27.

[An 1803 Act of the New York legislature authorized seven named persons to operate stage-wagons over a particular route between Albany and the New Jersey border, and provided that any person operating a competing stage-wagon on that route would be liable to pay a penalty of $500.00 to the operators authorized by the state. The seven divided up responsibility for operation along the route, and one part of the service was allocated to the plaintiff, Mr. Donelly, one of the original seven. Apparently Donelly failed to keep up operation along the route, and two of the other six (Tremble and Vanderhoff) authorized the defendant, Mr. Vandenbergh, to run a stage-wagon along Donelly's part of the route. Vandenbergh was not one of the original seven beneficiaries of the New York legislation, but Vandenbergh had been running a stage-wagon along Tremble and Vanderhoff's sections of the route, because they had assigned their right to run stage-wagons along their sections to him. Donelly brought suit against Vandenbergh to recover the statutory penalty, $500.00. He won in the trial court, and what follows are excerpts from the opinions of the judges who reviewed the case on appeal.]

THOMPSON, J. * * * This penalty was given by the act to secure the grantees in the privilege thereby vested in them, against any encroachment by strangers, and not as a security against the acts of each other. As long as they remain tenants in common, they must be subject to the same rules, and like remedies, as other tenants in common. The statute vested a joint interest in them. There is no limitation as to the number of stages to be run, and if each of the grantees had undertaken to run a line the whole extent of the road, the penalty would not have been incurred.

It is said, however, that previous to the license under which the defendant acted, the proprietors had divided the road among themselves, by which division those who undertook to license the defendant had parted with their interest in that portion of the road for which they gave the license. I should much doubt whether the privilege or franchise granted by this act is, according to the spirit and intention of the act, susceptible of partition, so as to give exclusive and independent rights in distinct parcels of the road. Public accommodation and convenience were the objects the Legislature had in view, and a common interest to each proprietor in the whole extent of the road, would seem necessary, to prevent confusion with respect to the continuation of the line of stages. If the franchise may be so divided as to vest separate right, in distinct parts, what would be the consequence of a neglect by anyone to perform the duties enjoined by the act? Would his portion of the road only be forfeited, or the whole extent? I apprehend the latter; and this would subject the other individuals to a forfeiture, without a default. * * *

[Judge Thompson concluded that, in any event, there was not sufficient evidence that the route had been divided, and thus Tremble and Vanderhoff were authorized to assign Donelly's part of the route to Vandenbergh, as any "tenant in common" might do.]

KENT, CH. J., declared himself to be of the same opinion.

SPENCER, J. [dissenting], * * *

This act, like others, and like the contracts of individuals, must have a reasonable construction so as to effectuate, not defeat, the intention of parties. The inhibition to establish a stage on the route must be intended as an inhibition to establish one on any part of the route, otherwise the act grants nothing. From the nature of the thing, the right granted by the Legislature to Donelly and the six others is partible; and it appears that it was partitioned among the grantees. The act contemplated the interest conveyed as capable of being so assigned, and I know of no principle which forbids it. * * * If so, then the assignment to the defendant of a precise portion of the route can give him no more right than a total stranger, to erect stages on a different part.

* * *

NOTES AND QUESTIONS

1. Judges Thompson and Spencer differed on the question of whether a legal distribution had taken place, but our concern is more with their differences over the partible nature of the grant of the route. Can you discern the public policies that Judge Thompson seeks to implement? Would you have expected the then Chief Justice Kent (later Chancellor Kent) to agree? Kent, you may remember, was the New York Chancellor who sought to maintain an equitable discretion in courts asked to grant specific performance of contracts involving unequal values, in Seymour v. Delancey, supra, Chapter Three. What might be Spencer's policy preferences?

2. Does the per curiam opinion in the next case seem more in accordance with Thompson's or Spencer's views?

ALMY V. HARRIS

Supreme Court of New York, 1809.
5 Johns 175.

Harris sued Almy in the court below, in an action on the case, for disturbing him in the enjoyment of a ferry across the Cayuga Lake, at the village of Cayuga, granted to Harris, by the Courts of Common Pleas, for the Counties of Cayuga and Seneca. A judgment for damages was given in favor of Harris * * *.

PER CURIAM. There is one error which we consider fatal, and for that we think there must be a judgment of reversal. The Act to Regulate Ferries within this State (20 sess. ch. 64, sec. 1) prohibits any person * * * from keeping or using a ferry, for transporting across any river, stream, or lake, any person or persons, or any goods or merchandise, for profit or hire, unless licensed in the manner directed by that [act] under a penalty of five dollars.

If Harris had possessed a right at the common law, to the exclusive enjoyment of this ferry, then the statute giving a remedy in the affirmative, without a negative expressed or implied, for a matter authorized by the common law, he might, notwithstanding the statute, have his remedy by action at the common law. * * * But Harris had no exclusive right at the common law, nor any right but what he derived from the statute. Consequently, he can have no right, since the statute, but those it gives; and his remedy, therefore, must be under the statute, and the penalty only can be recovered.

Judgment reversed.

NOTES AND QUESTIONS

The *Almy* court seems to be suggesting that there is no "common law" right "to the exclusive enjoyment" of a ferry. Do you agree? And yet, recall Blackstone's reason for permitting ferry owners to sue competitors in an action of nuisance: "For where there is a ferry by prescription, the owner is bound to keep it always in repair and readiness, for the ease of all the king's subjects; otherwise he may be grievously amerced: it would be therefore extremely hard, if a new ferry were suffered to share his profits, which does not also share his burden." Would this argument necessarily compel an action of nuisance in American common law?

LIVINGSTON V. VAN INGEN

New York Court for the Trial of Impeachments and The Correction of Errors, 1812.
9 Johns 507.

THE CHANCELLOR. An application was made by the complainants * * * for an injunction to restrain the defendants from using a steamboat * * * in the navigation of Hudson's River * * *.

* * * [O]n the part of the defendants, it was objected that the complainants' claim to an exclusive navigation of steamboats was:

1. Contrary to the Constitution of the United States.

2. That the statutes under which the complainants claim having prescribed a remedy for violations of the exclusive right, chancery must leave them to pursue it, without its interference.

The complainants applied for an injunction, on the ground of a clear exclusive right granted to them by an Act of the Legislature of this State, secured and extended by several successive acts.

* * *

When Justinian, the Emperor of the East, devised his code of civil law, he acknowledged the source of the right to the common enjoyment of air and water to be paramount to his authority, and bestowed, as a common boon, by the hand of nature, or, as we would express the same sentiment, by Nature's God * * *.

The civil code was, in its origin, merely municipal; but * * * from the amelioration which the experience, wisdom, and science of successive ages had infused, from the sound maxims of justice and jurisprudence it contained * * * as well as its intrinsic worth, it has been deservedly held in reverence by all the civilized world * * *.

In the Institutes, lib. 3., tit. 1., De aere, aqua profluente, & c., it is laid down, that those things which are given to mankind, in common, by the law of nature, are the air, running water, the sea, & c.

The general principles applied to the sea have as uniformly been extended to rivers in which the tide ebbs and flows, as arms of the sea. * * *

The common law doctrine is conformable to those principles; and is conceived in such terms, and to be traced to so early a day, as to warrant a presumption that it is derived from the civil law.

* * *

* * * In the case from 6 Mod., 73, Holt held that the king's grant could not bar a common right of fishing in a navigable river. But Hale, in his treatise, shows a number of cases in which a grant of that kind was held available, and that a subject might possess a franchise in a port; as customs arising from its use, or even the soil; and so is now the acknowledged doctrine; but though all these rights might exist in subjects, the jus publicum of passage and repassage was not thereby destroyed, and no annoyance or obstacle was to be tolerated to interrupt or incommode the navigation.

* * *

Navigable rivers, in which the tide ebbs and flows, are within the same reason, and subject to the same distinctions. They admit of private interests in them; but they must all be subservient to the public interest, to promote and protect which, in England, the king has a general conservancy: but whenever he makes a grant of the soil or franchise of a port, or of a navigable river, the legal construction is, that it must be in subserviency to the public rights, and the common use of all the subjects of the realm, and even the foreigners.

None of the books I have consulted on the subject, and none of those cited in argument, have shown a case in which a grant of a navigable river or port vested in the grantor a right to the exclusive enjoyment of its use. * * * [I]t would seem that it was considered contrary to the *jus publicum* that such a grant should be made.

* * *

If by the common law of England, navigable rivers, in which the tide ebbs and flows, were deemed consecrated to the common use of all, as of common right, if no impediment or obstruction was to be admitted to impede the navigation; if a grant, which, by its terms, in all other cases, would have passed a fee, *usque ad coelum* was, by the established construction of law, to glance from the surface of a navigable river, or attach to its bottom, and give only an exclusive right to the grantee, to catch the swimming fish, while within the bounds of his grant; if the common law was the law of all the states in the Union, at the time the Constitution was adopted, as it certainly was in this, it may be a question of very serious import, how far a particular state may detract from privileges and immunities, at common law incapable of annihilation or restraint, common to all, at the time the Constitution was adopted, and regulated by principles which shielded them from every species of private appropriation.

The claim of the complainants is not founded on original invention. The mode of generating steam and its properties was known as early as the seventeenth century * * *. Projects for propelling boats by steam have been under the public eye for near twenty-five years * * *. It is a matter of public notoriety that they are now in a train of successful operation; and whenever the exertion of the ingenuity and perseverance, which perfected them to the point at which they have now arrived, can become the legitimate object of judicial cognizance, the incalculable utility and convenience which the public experience from the invention merit every consideration in favor of the inventors which a court can possibly yield to, consistent with the correct administration of justice; but here they were not brought into view, and could have no weight.

The laws of the State alluded to have granted the exclusive right of using vessels impelled by steam, in the navigable waters of this State, to the complainants. Suppose this grant valid; if the Legislature of this State could make an exclusive grant of that nature, could they not have extended it to vessels impelled by the winds or by oars, and to vessels of every other description capable of floating * * *. If carried to this extent, would it not be an abridgment of common rights? Could it comport with the constitutional provision that the citizens of all the states are to have like privileges and immunities with the citizens of the several states? With whom are they to be ranked? With the class who hold exclusive rights in the State, or with the excluded class of citizens? If the most favored citizens are not to give the test, what proportion of the collective number of the citizens of this State are to constitute it? * * * And should the grant in this case partake of the nature of a contract, could its consideration be legally carved out of the *jus publicum* of the citizens of the United States?

These are questions which, at the first blush, must appear of much moment; certainly too much so to admit of being determined without the fullest investigation. Without meaning to decide upon any, the mere propounding them must carry conviction to every mind that the subject is involved in much doubt and difficulty, and that, from its novelty, its importance and perplexity, it constitutes a case incapable of being considered so clear and plain as not to admit of doubt, which is the only ground upon which an injunction could have been then granted on the bill of the complainants.

* * *

[Accordingly, Chancellor Lansing refused to issue an injunction. We next read the decision by Chief Justice Kent rendered on appeal of Lansing's refusal.]

KENT, CH. J. The great point in this cause is, whether the several acts of the Legislature which have been passed in favor of the appellants, are to be regarded as constitutional and binding.

* * *

In the first place, the presumption must be admitted to be extremely strong in favor of their validity. There is no very obvious constitutional objection, or it would not so repeatedly have escaped the notice of the several branches of the government, when these acts were under consideration. There are, in the whole, five different statutes, passed in the years 1798, 1803, 1807, 1808 and 1811, all relating to one subject, and all granting or confirming to the appellants, or one of them, the exclusive privilege of using steamboats upon the navigable waters of this State. The last Act was passed after the right of the appellants was drawn into question, and made known to the Legislature, and that Act was, therefore, equivalent to a declaratory opinion of high authority, that the former laws were valid and constitutional. The Act in the year 1798 was peculiarly calculated to awaken attention, as it was the first Act that was passed upon the subject, after the adoption of the federal Constitution, and it would naturally lead to a consideration of the power of the State to make such a grant. That Act was, therefore, a legislative exposition given to the powers of the state governments, and there were circumstances existing at the time, which gave that exposition singular weight and importance. It was a new and original grant to one of the appellants, encouraging him, by the pledge of an exclusive privilege for twenty years, to engage, according to the language of the preamble to the statute, in the "uncertainty and hazard of a very expensive experiment." The Legislature must have been clearly satisfied of their competency to make this pledge, or they acted with deception and injustice towards the individual on whose account it was made. There were members in that Legislature, as well as in all the other departments of the government, who had been deeply concerned in the study of the Constitution of the United States, and who were masters of all the critical discussions which had attended the interesting progress of its adoption. * * *

* * * Unless the court should be able to vindicate itself by the soundest and most demonstrable argument, a decree prostrating all these laws would weaken, as I should apprehend, the authority and sanction of law in general, and impair, in some degree, the public confidence, either in the intelligence or integrity of the government.

* * *

* * * No one can entertain a doubt of a competent power existing in the Legislature, prior to the adoption of the federal Constitution. The capacity to grant separate and exclusive privileges appertains to every sovereign authority. It is a necessary attribute of every independent government. All our bank charters, turnpike, canal and bridge companies; ferries, markets, & c., are grants of exclusive privileges for beneficial public purposes. * * * The legislative power, in a single, independent government, extends to every proper object of power, and is limited only by its own constitutional provisions, or by the fundamental principles of all government, and the unalienable rights of mankind. In the present case, the grant to the appellants took away no vested right. It interfered with no man's property. It left every citizen to enjoy all the rights of navigation, and all the use of the waters of this State which he before enjoyed. There was, then, no injustice, no violation of first principles, in a grant to the appellants, for a limited time, of the exclusive benefit of their own hazardous and expensive experiments. The first impression upon every unprejudiced mind would be, that there was justice and policy in the grant. Clearly then, it is valid, unless the power to make it be taken away by the Constitution of the United States.

* * * It does not follow, that because a given power is granted to Congress, the states cannot exercise a similar power. We ought to bear in mind certain great rules or principles of construction peculiar to the case of a confederated government, and by attending to them in the examination of the subject, all our seeming difficulties will vanish.

When the people create a single, entire government, they grant at once all the rights of sovereignty. * * * But when a federal government is erected with only a portion of the sovereign power, the rule of construction is directly the reverse, and every power is reserved to the member that is not, either in express terms, or by necessary implication, taken away from them, and vested exclusively in the federal head. * * *

This principle might be illustrated by other instances of grants of power to Congress with a prohibition to the states from exercising the like powers; but it becomes unnecessary to enlarge upon so plain a proposition, as it is removed beyond all doubt by the tenth article of the amendments to the Constitution. That article declares that "the powers not delegated to the United States by the Constitution, nor prohibited by it to the states, are reserved to the states respectively, or to the people." * * *

Our safe rule of construction and of action is this, that if any given power was originally vested in this State, if it has not been exclusively ceded to Congress, or if the exercise of it has not been prohibited to the states, we may then go on in the exercise of the power until it becomes practically in collision with the actual exercise of some congressional power. * * *

* * *

I now proceed to apply these general rules to those parts of the Constitution which are supposed to have an influence on the present question.

The provision that the citizens of each state shall be entitled to all privileges and immunities of citizens in the several states, has nothing to do with this case. It means only that citizens of other states shall have equal rights with our own citizens, and not that they shall have different or greater rights. * * * The two paragraphs of the Constitution by which it is contended that the original power in the state governments to make the grant has been withdrawn, and vested exclusively in the Union, are, 1. The power to regulate commerce with foreign nations, and among the several states; and, 2. The power to secure to authors and inventors the exclusive right to their writings and discoveries.

1. As to the power to regulate commerce. This power is not, in express terms, exclusive, and the only prohibition upon the states is, that they shall not enter into any treaty or compact with each other, or with a foreign power, nor lay any duty on tonnage, or on imports or exports, except what may be necessary for executing their inspection laws. Upon the principles above laid down, the states are under no other constitutional restriction, and are, consequently, left in possession of a vast field of commercial regulation * * *. The congressional power relates to external not to internal commerce, and it is confined to the regulation of that commerce. * * * The states are under no other restrictions than those expressly specified in the Constitution, and such regulations as the national government may, by treaty, and by laws, from time to time, prescribe. * * * This does away [with] all color for the suggestion that the steamboat grant is illegal and void under this clause in the Constitution. It comes not within any prohibition upon the states, and it interferes with no existing regulation. * * * [W]hen there is no existing regulation which interferes with the grant, nor any pretense of a constitutional interdict, it would be most extraordinary for us to adjudge it void, on the mere contingency of a collision with some future exercise of congressional power. Such a doctrine is a monstrous heresy. It would go, in a great degree, to annihilate the legislative power of the states. * * *

* * * Hudson River is the property of the people of this State, and the Legislature have the same jurisdiction over it that they have over the land, or over any of our public highways, or over the waters of any of our rivers or lakes. They may, in their sound discretion, regulate and control, enlarge or abridge the use of its waters, and they are in the habitual exercise of that sovereign right. If the Constitution had given to Congress exclusive jurisdiction over our navigable waters, then the argument of the respondents would have applied; but the people never did, nor ever intended, to grant such a power; and Congress has concurrent jurisdiction over the navigable waters no further than may be incidental and requisite

to the due regulation of commerce between the states and with foreign nations.

What has been the uniform, practical construction of this power? Let us examine the code of our statute laws. Our turnpike roads, our toll-bridges, the exclusive grant to run stage wagons, our laws relating to paupers from other states, our Sunday laws, our rights of ferriage over navigable rivers and lakes, our auction licenses, our licenses to retail spirituous liquors, the laws to restrain hawkers and peddlers; what are all these provisions but regulations of internal commerce, affecting as well the intercourse between the citizens of this and other states, as between our own citizens? * * *

Are we prepared to say, in the face of all these regulations, which form such a mass of evidence of the uniform construction of our powers, that a special privilege for the exclusive navigation by a steamboat upon our waters is void, because it may, by possibility, and in the course of events, interfere with the power granted to Congress to regulate commerce? Nothing, in my opinion, would be more preposterous and extravagant. * * *

* * *

[Kent then turns to the constitutional provision regarding exclusive rights of inventors. He notes that the federal Constitution is concerned with providing federal control over rights of exclusivity for *novel* forms of technology. He then turns to English practice.]

The creation of monopolies was anciently claimed and exercised as a branch of the royal prerogative. Lord Coke, 3 Inst., 181, defines a monopoly to be "an institution or allowance by the king's grant, for the sole using of anything;" and he considers such royal grants to have been against the ancient and fundamental laws of the realm. Parliament at last interposed to check the abuse of these grants, which had been issued, under Elizabeth, with inconsiderate profusion; and by the statute of 21 Jac. I., ch. 3, commonly called the statute of monopolies, there were due limitations placed upon the exercise of this branch of the prerogative. That statute, by a general sweeping clause, demolished all the existing monopolies that were not specially excepted; and some of those exceptions are worthy of our particular notice. In the first place, all grants of privileges by act of Parliament were saved; for no one ever doubted (unless it be since the origin of this controversy) of the power of the Legislature to create an exclusive privilege. The statute also allowed grants to be made for a limited time, by the authority of the crown, for the sole working or making of any new manufacture not before used in the realm. Upon this clause it has been held by such distinguished judges as Holt and Pollexfen (2 Salk. 447), that if the invention be new in England, a patent may be granted, though the thing was practiced beyond sea before; for the statute, as they observed, intended to encourage new devices useful to the kingdom, and whether learned by travel or by study, it is the same thing. * * *

* * * And can we for a moment suppose that such a power does not exist in the several states? We have seen that it does not belong to Congress, and if it does not reside in the states, it resides nowhere, and is wholly extinguished. This would be leaving the states in a condition of singular and contemptible imbecility. The power is important in itself, and may be most beneficially exercised for the encouragement of the arts; and if well and judiciously exerted, it may ameliorate the condition of society, by enriching and adorning the country with useful and elegant improvements. * * * And permit me here to add, that I think the power has been wisely applied, in the instance before us, to the creation of the privilege now in controversy. Under its auspices the experiment of navigating boats by steam has been made, and crowned with triumphant success. Every lover of the arts, every patron of useful improvement, every friend to his country's honor, has beheld this success with pleasure and admiration. From this single source the improvement is progressively extending to all the navigable waters of the United States, and it promises to become a great public blessing, by giving astonishing facility, dispatch and safety, not only to traveling, but to the internal commerce of this country. It is difficult to consider even the known results of the undertaking, without feeling a sentiment of good will and gratitude towards the individuals by whom they have been procured, and who have carried on their experiment with patient industry, at great expense, under repeated disappointments, and while constantly exposed to be held up, as dreaming projectors, to the whips and scorns of time. So far from charging the authors of the grant with being rash and inconsiderate, or from wishing to curtail the appellants of their liberal recompense, I think the prize has been dearly earned and fairly won, and that the statutes bear the stamp of an enlightened and munificent spirit.

If the legal right be in favor of the appellants, the remedy prayed for by their bill is a matter of course. * * *

Injunctions are always granted to secure the enjoyment of statute privileges of which the party is in the actual possession * * *. I believe there is no case to the contrary * * *. It appears, by the facts stated in the bill * * * that the appellants had been, for three years, in the actual and exclusive enjoyment of their statute privilege, when the respondents interfered to disturb that right and that enjoyment.

* * * The Act which the Legislature passed at the last session, making it expressly the duty of the Chancellor to grant an injunction as to all other boats except the two then built, proves very clearly the sense of the Legislature that this was a fit and proper remedy in the case. Those two boats were excepted out of the law, merely because it was improper to interfere with a pending suit, and the statute did not impair the pre-

existing remedy by injunction; it only made it more clear and peremptory thereafter; and there is no reason why the injunction should issue against one set of boats, and not against another.

* * *

I am sensible that the case is calculated to excite sympathy. I feel it with others, and I sincerely wish that the respondents had brought the laws to a test, at less risk and expense; for every one who had eyes to read, or ears to hear the contents of our statute book, must have been astonished at the boldness and rashness of the experiment. But in proportion to the respectability and strength of the combination, should be the vigor of our purpose to maintain the law. If we were to suffer the plighted faith of this State to be broken, upon a mere pretext, we should become a reproach and a by-word throughout the Union. It was a saying of Euripides, and often repeated by Caesar, that if right was ever to be violated, it was for the sake of power. We follow a purer and nobler system of morals, and one which teaches us that right is never to be violated. This principle ought to be kept steadfast in every man's breast; and above all, it ought to find an asylum in the sanctuary of justice.

I am, accordingly, of opinion that the order of the Court of Chancery be reversed, and that an injunction be awarded.

* * *

Judgment of reversal.

NOTES AND QUESTIONS

1. Chancellor Lansing was a firm adherent of Jeffersonian principles. Do you see this reflected in his opinion denying the injunction? Robert Fulton and Robert Livingston, to whom the New York legislature had granted a steamboat monopoly on the Hudson, were also supposed to be Jeffersonians. Do you see anything inconsistent with being a "good Jeffersonian" and accepting an exclusive franchise? Can you understand why Fulton and Livingston sought to argue that what they had was not a "monopoly," but rather a "legislative franchise?" What's the difference? Jefferson himself, although he supervised the United States Patent Office when he was Secretary of State, and although he was an inventor of considerable creativity, refused to take out any patents. Floyd L. Vaughan, The United States Patent System 6, 18 (1956). Why might Jefferson adopt this posture?

2. Consider Lansing's opinion. Can you discern Lansing's attitude toward steam power and commercial progress generally? Lansing seems to feel that the state must not be permitted to parcel out exclusive franchises for operation on navigable waterways. Why not? Do you detect any similarities between Lansing's mode of analysis and the opinions in *Almy* and *Donelly?* Kent went along with the majority in the *Donelly* case, where the court ap-

parently refused to allow private partition of a state franchise, and in the *Almy* case, where the court held there was no common-law right to provide an action for nuisance to stop a competing ferry. Is Kent's position in *Livingston* consistent with these opinions?

3. Does Kent actually come to grips with the problems Chancellor Lansing has with the issuance of the injunction? Kent, by the way, was not a Jeffersonian, but note the line he attempts to draw between grants of monopolies by the King and grants of privileges by Parliament. Does he persuade you that though Royal monopolies were despicable, legislative grants were not? Three years later, when Kent had become Chancellor of New York, he issued an injunction sought by a turnpike company in order to prevent competition from a recently-built public (free) road which threatened severely to diminish the tolls collectable by the turnpike company. Kent called the right to collect tolls an "exclusive right," and cited as precedent Livingston v. Van Ingen. Croton Turnpike Road Co. v. Ryder, 1 Johns.Ch. 611 (N.Y.1815). Similarly, in Newburgh & C. Turnpike Road Co. v. Miller, 5 Johns.Ch. 101 (N.Y.1821), Chancellor Kent held that where the legislature had granted a franchise to the plaintiff to take a toll from persons passing over its bridge, the construction of a nearby bridge which created "a competition injurious to such franchise" was an actionable nuisance, calling for a perpetual injunction. Do these latter holdings go beyond *Livingston?*

4. Kent's opinion in *Livingston* was, after twelve years, reversed by the United States Supreme Court, in the great constitutional case of Gibbons v. Ogden, 22 U.S. (9 Wheat.) 1, 6 L.Ed. 23 (1824). In that case, which turned on the construction of the interstate commerce clause, Chief Justice Marshall concluded that the regulation of steam traffic on the Hudson was exclusively in the jurisdiction of Congress. This opinion thus did not squarely address the more interesting question raised in the Lansing–Kent debate, the appropriateness of monopolies or franchises generally. This question was one of the central issues in the next case we consider. For further reading on the question of allocation of regulatory power between the state and federal governments, an issue often called, in the legal literature, "Federalism," see the work of Federalism's leading legal historian, Harry N. Scheiber, e.g. the books, Perspectives on Federalism (1987), Federalism: Studies in History, Law, and Policy (1988), Power Divided: Essays on the Theory and Practice of Federalism (1989), and Federalism and the Judicial Mind: Essays on American Constitutional Law and Politics (1992) (four collections of essays on Federalism edited by Scheiber, 1989 volume co-edited with Malcolm M. Feeley), and Scheiber's several articles, "Federalism and the American Economic Order, 1789–1910," 10 Law & Society Review 57 (1975); "Federalism and Legal Process: Historical and Contemporary Analysis of the American System," 14 Law & Society Review 663 (1980); and "Public Economic Policy and the American Legal System: Historical Perspectives," 1980 Wisc.Law Rev. 1159.

PROPRIETORS OF CHARLES RIVER BRIDGE V. PROPRIETORS OF WARREN BRIDGE

Supreme Court of the United States, 1837.
36 U.S. (11 Pet.) 420, 9 L.Ed. 773.

MR. CHIEF JUSTICE TANEY delivered the opinion of the court.

* * *

It appears, from the record, that in the year 1650, the legislature of Massachusetts granted to the president of Harvard College "the liberty and power," to dispose of the ferry from Charlestown to Boston, by lease or otherwise, in the behalf, and for the behoof of the college: that, under that grant, the college continued to hold and keep the ferry by its lessees or agents, and to receive the profits of it until 1785. In the last mentioned year, a petition was presented to the legislature, by Thomas Russell and others, stating the inconvenience of the transportation by ferries, over Charles river, and the public advantages that would result from a bridge; and praying to be incorporated for the purpose of erecting a bridge in the place where the ferry between Boston and Charlestown was then kept. Pursuant to this petition, the legislature, on the 9th of March, 1785, passed an act incorporating a company, by the name of "The Proprietors of the Charles River Bridge," for the purposes mentioned in the petition. Under this charter the company were empowered to erect a bridge, in "the place where the ferry was then kept;" certain tolls were granted, and the charter was limited to forty years, from the first opening of the bridge for passengers; and from the time the toll commenced, until the expiration of this term, the company were to pay, two hundred pounds, annually to Harvard College; and, at the expiration of the forty years, the bridge was to be the property of the commonwealth; "saving (as the law expresses it) to the said college or university, a reasonable annual compensation, for the annual income of the ferry, which they might have received had not the said bridge been erected."

The bridge was accordingly built, and was opened for passengers on the 17th of June, 1786. In 1792, the charter was extended to seventy years, from the opening of the bridge; and at the expiration of that time it was to belong to the commonwealth. * * *

In 1828, the legislature of Massachusetts incorporated a company by the name of "The Proprietors of the Warren Bridge," for the purpose of erecting another bridge over Charles river. This bridge is only sixteen rods, at its commencement, on the Charlestown side, from the commencement of the bridge of the plaintiffs; and they are about fifty rods apart at their termination on the Boston side. * * *

The Warren bridge, by the terms of its charter, was to be surrendered to the state, as soon as the expenses of the proprietors in building and supporting it should be reimbursed; but this period was not, in any event, to exceed six years from the time the company commenced receiving toll.

* * * The bill, among other things, charged as a ground for relief, that the act for the erection of the Warren bridge impaired the obligation of the contract between the commonwealth and the proprietors of the Charles river bridge; and was therefore repugnant to the constitution of the United States. * * *

In the argument here, it was admitted, that since the filing of the supplemental bill, a sufficient amount of toll had been received by the proprietors of the Warren bridge to reimburse all their expenses, and that the bridge is now the property of the state, and has been made a free bridge and that the value of the franchise granted to the proprietors of the Charles river bridge, has by this means been entirely destroyed.

* * *

The plaintiffs in error insist * * * [t]hat the acts of the legislature of Massachusetts of 1785, and 1792, by their true construction, necessarily implied that the legislature would not authorize another bridge, and especially a free one, by the side of this, and placed in the same line of travel, whereby the franchise granted to the "proprietors of the Charles river bridge" should be rendered of no value * * *.

* * *

* * * It does not, by any means, follow, that because the legislative power in Massachusetts, in 1650, may have granted to a justly favoured seminary of learning, the exclusive right of ferry between Boston and Charlestown, they would, in 1785, give the same extensive privilege to another corporation, who were about to erect a bridge in the same place. * * * Increased population longer experienced in legislation, the different character of the corporations which owned the ferry from that which owned the bridge, might well have induced a change in the policy of the state in this respect; and as the franchise of the ferry, and that of the bridge, are different in their nature, and were each established by separate grants, which have no words to connect the privileges of the one with the privileges of the other; there is no rule of legal interpretation, which would authorize the court to associate these grants together * * *. The charter to the bridge is a written instrument which must speak for itself, and be interpreted by its own terms.

This brings us to the act of the legislature of Massachusetts, of 1785, by which the plaintiffs were incorporated * * *.

* * * It is the grant of certain franchises by the public to a private corporation, and in a matter where the public interest is concerned. The rule of construction in such cases is well settled, both in England, and by

the decisions of our own tribunals. In 2 Barn. & Adol. 793, in the case of the Proprietors of the Stourbridge Canal against Wheely and others, the court say, "the canal having been made under an act of parliament, the rights of the plaintiffs are derived entirely from that act. This, like many other cases, is a bargain between a company of adventurers and the public, the terms of which are expressed in the statute; and the rule of construction in all such cases, is now fully established to be this; that any ambiguity in the terms of the contract, must operate against the adventurers, and in favour of the public, and the plaintiffs can claim nothing that is not clearly given them by the act." * * *

Borrowing, as we have done, our system of jurisprudence from the English law; and having adopted, in every other case, civil and criminal, its rules for the construction of statutes; is there any thing in our local situation, or in the nature of our political institutions, which should lead us to depart from the principle where corporations are concerned? * * * We think not; and it would present a singular spectacle, if, while the courts in England are restraining, within the strictest limits, the spirit of monopoly, and exclusive privileges in nature of monopolies, and confining corporations to the privileges plainly given to them in their charter; the courts of this country should be found enlarging these privileges by implication; and construing a statute more unfavourably to the public, and to the rights of the community, than would be done in a like case in an English court of justice.

* * *

* * * [T]he case most analogous to this, and in which the question came more directly before the court, is the case of the Providence Bank v. Billings & Pittman, 4 Pet. 514; and which was decided in 1830. In that case, it appeared that the legislature of Rhode Island had chartered the bank; in the usual form of such acts of incorporation. The charter contained no stipulation on the part of the state, that it would not impose a tax on the bank, nor any reservation of the right to do so. It was silent on this point. Afterwards, a law was passed, imposing a tax on all banks in the state; and the right to impose this tax was resisted by the Providence Bank, upon the ground, that if the state could impose a tax, it might tax so heavily as to render the franchise of no value, and destroy the institution; that the charter was a contract, and that a power which may in effect destroy the charter is inconsistent with it, and is impliedly renounced by granting it. But the court said that the taxing power was of vital importance, and essential to the existence of government; and that the relinquishment of such a power is never to be assumed. And in delivering the opinion of the court, the late chief justice states the principle, in the following clear and emphatic language. Speaking of the taxing power, he says, "as the whole community is interested in retaining it undiminished, that community has a right to insist that its abandonment ought not to be

presumed, in a case in which the deliberate purpose of the state to abandon it does not appear." The case now before the court is, in principle, precisely the same. It is a charter from a state. The act of incorporation is silent in relation to the contested power. The argument in favour of the proprietors of the Charles river bridge, is the same, almost in words, with that used by the Providence Bank; that is, that the power claimed by the state, if it exists, may be so used as to destroy the value of the franchise they have granted to the corporation. The argument must receive the same answer; and the fact that the power has been already exercised so as to destroy the value of the franchise, cannot in any degree affect the principle. The existence of the power does not, and cannot depend upon the circumstance of its having been exercised or not.

It may, perhaps, be said, that in the case of the Providence Bank, this court were speaking of the taxing power; which is of vital importance to the very existence of every government. But the object and end of all government is to promote the happiness and prosperity of the community by which it is established; and it can never be assumed, that the government intended to diminish its power of accomplishing the end for which it was created. And in a country like ours, free, active, and enterprising, continually advancing in numbers and wealth; new channels of communication are daily found necessary, both for travel and trade; and are essential to the comfort, convenience, and prosperity of the people. A state ought never to be presumed to surrender this power, because, like the taxing power, the whole community have an interest in preserving it undiminished. And when a corporation alleges, that a state has surrendered for seventy years, its power of improvement and public accommodation, in a great and important line of travel, along which a vast number of its citizens must daily pass; the community have a right to insist, in the language of this court above quoted, "that its abandonment ought not to be presumed, in a case, in which the deliberate purpose of the state to abandon it does not appear." * * *

Adopting the rule of construction above stated as the settled one, we proceed to apply it to the charter of 1785, to the proprietors of the Charles river bridge. This act of incorporation is in the usual form, and the privileges such as are commonly given to corporations of that kind. It confers on them the ordinary faculties of a corporation, for the purpose of building the bridge; and establishes certain rates of toll, which the company are authorized to take. This is the whole grant. There is no exclusive privilege given to them over the waters of Charles river, above or below their bridge. No right to erect another bridge themselves, nor to prevent other persons from erecting one. No engagement from the state, that another shall not be erected; and no undertaking not to sanction competition, nor to make improvements that may diminish the amount of its income. Upon all these subjects the charter is silent; and nothing is said in it about a line of travel, so much insisted on in the argument, in which they are to have exclusive privileges. * * *

* * *

* * * Can such an agreement be implied? The rule of construction before stated is an answer to the question. In charters of this description, no rights are taken from the public or given to the corporation, beyond those which the words of the charter, by their natural and proper construction, purport to convey. * * *

But the case before the court is even still stronger against any such implied contract, as the plaintiffs in error contend for. * * *

The act of 1792, which extends the charter of this bridge, incorporates another company to build a bridge over Charles river; furnishing another communication with Boston, and distant only between one and two miles from the old bridge.

The first six sections of this act incorporate the proprietors of the West Boston bridge * * *. In the seventh section there is the following recital: "And whereas the erection of Charles river bridge was a work of hazard and public utility, and another bridge in the place of West Boston bridge may diminish the emoluments of Charles river bridge; therefore, for the encouragement of enterprise," they proceed to extend the charter of the Charles river bridge, and to continue it for the term of seventy years from the day the bridge was completed * * *. It appears, then, that by the same act that extended this charter, the legislature established another bridge, which they knew would lessen its profits * * *; thereby showing, that the state did not suppose that, by the terms it had used in the first law, it had deprived itself of the power of making such public improvements as might impair the profits of the Charles river bridge * * *.

* * * The extension [of the term to seventy years] was given because the company had undertaken and executed a work of doubtful success; and the improvements which the legislature then contemplated, might diminish the emoluments they had expected to receive from it. It results from this statement, that the legislature in the very law extending the charter, asserts its rights to authorize improvements over Charles river which would take off a portion of the travel from this bridge and diminish its profits; and the bridge company accept the renewal thus given, and thus carefully connected with this assertion of the right on the part of the state. * * *

Indeed, the practice and usage of almost every state in the Union, old enough to have commenced the work of internal improvement, is opposed to the doctrine contended for on the part of the plaintiffs in error. Turnpike roads have been made in succession, on the same line of travel; the later ones interfering materially with the profits of the first. These corporations have, in some instances, been utterly ruined by the introduction of newer and better modes of transportation, and travelling. In some cases, rail roads have rendered the turnpike roads on the same line of travel so entirely useless, that the franchise of the turnpike corporation is not worth preserving.

Yet in none of these cases have the corporation supposed that their privileges were invaded, or any contract violated on the part of the state. * * * The absence of any such controversy, when there must have been so many occasions to give rise to it, proves that neither states, nor individuals, nor corporations, ever imagined that such a contract could be implied from such charters. * * *

And what would be the fruits of this doctrine of implied contracts on the part of the states, and of property in a line of travel by a corporation, if it should now be sanctioned by this court? To what results would it lead us? If it is to be found in the charter to this bridge, the same process of reasoning must discover it, in the various acts which have been passed, within the last forty years, for turnpike companies. * * * If this court should establish the principles now contended for, what is to become of the numerous rail roads established on the same line of travel with turnpike companies; and which have rendered the franchises of the turnpike corporations of no value? Let it once be understood that such charters carry with them these implied contracts, and give this unknown and undefined property in a line of travelling; and you will soon find the old turnpike corporations awakening from their sleep, and calling upon this court to put down the improvements which have taken their place. The millions of property which have been invested in rail roads and canals, upon lines of travel which had been before occupied by turnpike corporations, will be put in jeopardy. We shall be thrown back to the improvements of the last century, and obliged to stand still, until the claims of the old turnpike corporations shall be satisfied; and they shall consent to permit these states to avail themselves of the lights of modern science, and to partake of the benefit of those improvements which are now adding to the wealth and prosperity, and the convenience and comfort, of every other part of the civilized world. * * *

* * *

The judgment of the supreme judicial court of the commonwealth of Massachusetts, dismissing the plaintiffs' bill, must, therefore, be affirmed, with costs.

MR. JUSTICE STORY, dissenting.

* * * [W]ith a view to induce the Court to withdraw from all the common rules of reasonable and liberal interpretation in favour of grants, we have been told at the argument, that this very charter is a restriction upon the legislative power; that it is in derogation of the rights and inter-

ests of the state, and the people; that it tends to promote monopolies, and exclusive privileges; and that it will interpose an insuperable barrier to the progress of improvement. Now, upon every one of these propositions, which are assumed, and not proved, I entertain a directly opposite opinion; and, if I did not, I am not prepared to admit the conclusion for which they are adduced. If the legislature has made a grant, which involves any or all of these consequences, it is not for courts of justice to overturn the plain sense of the grant, because it has been improvidently or injuriously made.

But I deny the very ground work of the argument. This charter is not * * * any restriction upon the legislative power; unless it be true, that because the legislature cannot grant again, what it has already granted, the legislative power is restricted. If so, then every grant of the public land is a restriction upon that power; a doctrine, that has never yet been established, nor (as far as I know) ever contended for. Every grant of a franchise is, so far as that grant extends, necessarily exclusive; and cannot be resumed, or interfered with. * * *

Then again, how is it established that this is a grant in derogation of the rights and interests of the people? No individual citizen has any right to build a bridge over navigable waters; and consequently he is deprived of no right, when a grant is made to any other persons for that purpose. * * * But that is not the sense in which the argument is pressed; for, by derogation, is here meant an injurious or mischievous detraction from the sovereign rights of the state. * * * If it had been said that the grant of this bridge was in derogation of the common right of navigating the Charles river, by reason of its obstructing, pro tanto, a free and open passage, the ground would have been intelligible. * * * But, if at the same time, equivalent public rights of a different nature, but of greater public accommodation and use, had been obtained; it could hardly have been said, in a correct sense, that there was any derogation from the rights of the people, or the rights of the state. * * *

* * * The erection of a bridge may be of the highest utility to the people. It may essentially promote the public convenience, and aid the public interests, and protect the public property. And if no persons can be found willing to undertake such a work, unless they receive in return the exclusive privilege of erecting it, and taking toll; surely it cannot be said, as of course, that such a grant, under such circumstances, is, per se, against the interest of the people. * * *

* * *

Again, it is argued that the present grant is a grant of a monopoly, and of exclusive privileges; and therefore to be construed by the most narrow mode of interpretation. * * *

There is great virtue in particular phrases; and when it is once suggested, that a grant is of the nature or tendency of a monopoly, the mind almost instantaneously prepares itself to reject every construction which does not pare it down to the narrowest limits. It is an honest prejudice, which grew up in former times from the gross abuses of the royal prerogatives; to which, in America, there are no analogous authorities. But, what is a monopoly, as understood in law? It is an exclusive right granted to a few, of something which was before of common right. Thus, a privilege granted by the king for the sole buying, selling, making, working, or using a thing, whereby the subject, in general, is restrained from the liberty of manufacturing or trading, which before he had, is a monopoly * * *.

No sound lawyer will, I presume, assert that the grant of a right to erect a bridge over a navigable stream, is a grant of a common right. * * * It was neither a monopoly; nor, in a legal sense, had it any tendency to a monopoly. It took from no citizen what he possessed before; and had no tendency to take it from him. It took, indeed, from the legislature the power of granting the same identical privilege or franchise to any other persons. But this made it no more a monopoly, than the grant of the public stock or funds of a state for a valuable consideration. * * *

But it has been argued, and the argument has been pressed in every form which ingenuity could suggest, that if grants of this nature are to be construed liberally, as conferring any exclusive rights on the grantees, it will interpose an effectual barrier against all general improvements of the country. * * * This is a subject upon which different minds may well arrive at different conclusions, both as to policy and principle. * * * For my own part, I can conceive of no surer plan to arrest all public improvements, founded on private capital and enterprise, than to make the outlay of that capital uncertain, and questionable both as to security, and as to productiveness. No man will hazard his capital in any enterprise, in which, if there be a loss, it must be borne exclusively by himself; and if there be success, he has not the slightest security of enjoying the rewards of that success for a single moment. If the government means to invite its citizens to enlarge the public comforts and conveniences, to establish bridges, or turnpikes, or canals, or railroads, there must be some pledge, that the property will be safe; that the enjoyment will be coextensive with the grant: and that success will not be the signal of a general combination to overthrow its rights, and to take away its profits. * * * And yet, we are told, that all such exclusive grants are to the detriment of the public.

But if there were any foundation for the argument itself in a general view, it would totally fail in its application to the present case. Here, the grant, however exclusive, is but for a short and limited period, more than two-thirds of which have already elapsed; and, when it is gone, the whole property and franchise are to revert to the state. The legislature exercised a wholesome foresight on the subject; and within a reasonable period it will have an unrestricted authority to do whatever it may choose, in the appropriation of the bridge and its tolls. There is not, then, under any fair aspect of the case, the slightest reason to presume that public improvements either can, or will, be injuriously retarded by a liberal construction of the present grant.

* * * In order to entertain a just view of this subject, we must go back to that period of general bankruptcy, and distress and difficulty. The constitution of the United States was not only not then in existence, but it was not then even dreamed of. The union of the states was crumbling into ruins, under the old confederation. Agriculture, manufactures and commerce, were at their lowest ebb. There was infinite danger to all the states from local interests and jealousies, and from the apparent impossibility of a much longer adherence to that shadow of a government, the continental congress. * * *

This is not all. It is well known, historically, that this was the very first bridge ever constructed in New England, over navigable tide waters so near the sea. The rigours of our climate, the dangers from sudden thaws and freezing, and the obstructions from ice in a rapid current, were deemed by many persons to be insuperable obstacles to the success of such a project. It was believed, that the bridge would scarcely stand a single severe winter. * * * If Charles river bridge had been carried away during the first or second season after its erection, it is far from being certain, that up to this moment another bridge, upon such an arm of the sea, would ever have been erected in Massachusetts. I state these things which are of public notoriety, to repeal the notion that the legislature was surprised into an incautious grant, or that the reward was more than adequate to the perils. * * *

But I do not insist upon any extraordinary liberality in interpreting this charter. All I contend for is, that it shall receive a fair and reasonable interpretation; so as to carry into effect the legislative intention, and secure to the grantees a just security for their privileges. * * *

* * *

* * * Taking this to be a grant of a right to build a bridge over Charles river, in the place where the old ferry between Charlestown and Boston was then kept, (as is contended for by the defendants;) still it has, as all such grants must have, a fixed locality, and the same question meets us: is the grant confined to the mere right to erect a bridge on the proper spot, and to take toll of the passengers, who may pass over it, without any exclusive franchise on each side to an extent, which shall shut out any injurious competition? * * * The defendants contend, that the exclusive right of the plaintiffs extends no further than the planks and timbers of the bridge; and that the legislature is at full liberty to grant any new bridge, however near * * *.

The argument of the defendants is, that the plaintiffs are to take nothing by implication. Either (say they) the exclusive grant extends only to the local limits of the bridge; or it extends the whole length of the river, or at least up to old Cambridge bridge. The latter construction would be absurd and monstrous; and therefore the former must be the true one. Now, I utterly deny the alternative involved in the dilemma. The right to build a bridge over a river, and to take toll, may well include an exclusive franchise beyond the local limits of the bridge; and yet not extend through the whole course of the river, or even to any considerable distance on the river. There is no difficulty in common sense, or in law, in maintaining such a doctrine. But then, it is asked, what limits can be assigned to such a franchise? The answer is obvious; the grant carries with it an exclusive franchise to a reasonable distance on the river; so that the ordinary travel to the bridge shall not be diverted by any new bridge to the injury or ruin of the franchise. A new bridge, which would be a nuisance to the old bridge, would be within the reach of its exclusive right. The question would not be so much as to the fact of distance, as it would be as to the fact of nuisance. There is nothing new in such expositions of incorporeal rights; and nothing new in thus administering, upon this foundation, remedies in regard thereto. The doctrine is coeval with the common law itself. Suppose an action is brought for shutting up the ancient lights belonging to a messuage; or for diverting a water-course; or for flowing back a stream; or for erecting a nuisance near a dwelling house; the question in cases is not a question of mere distance; of mere feet and inches, but of injury; permanent, real, and substantial injury, to be decided upon all the circumstances of the case. * * *

Now, I put it to the common sense of every man, whether if at the moment of granting the charter the legislature had said to the proprietors; you shall build the bridge; you shall bear the burthens; you shall be bound by the charges; and your sole reimbursement shall be from the tolls of forty years: and yet we will not even guaranty you any certainty of receiving any tolls. On the contrary we reserve to ourselves the full power and authority to erect other bridges, toll, or free bridges, according to our own free will and pleasure, contiguous to yours, and having the same termini with yours; and if you are successful we may thus supplant you, divide, destroy your profits, and annihilate your tolls, without annihilating your burthens: if, I say, such had been the language of the legislature, is there a man living of ordinary discretion or prudence, who would have accepted such a charter upon such terms? * * *

* * *

But it is said that there is no prohibitory covenant in the charter, and no implications are to be made of any such prohibition. The proprietors are to stand upon the letter of their contract * * *. And yet it is conceded, that the legislature cannot revoke or resume this grant. Why not, I pray to know? There is no negative covenant in the charter; there is no express prohibition to be found there. The reason is plain. The prohibition arises by natural, if not by necessary implication. It would be against the first principles of justice to presume that the legislature reserved a right to destroy its own grant. * * * If it cannot take away, or resume the franchise itself, can it take away its whole substance and value? If the law will create an implication that the legislature shall not resume its own grant, is it not equally as natural and as necessary an implication, that the legislature shall not do any act directly to prejudice its own grant, or to destroy its value? * * *

But it is said, if this is the law, what then is to become of turnpikes and canals? Is the legislature precluded from authorizing new turnpikes or new canals, simply because they cross the path of the old ones, and incidentally diminish their receipt of tolls? The answer is plain. Every turnpike has its local limits and local termini; its points of beginning and of end. No one ever imagined that the legislature might grant a new turnpike, with exactly the same location and termini. That would be to rescind its first grant. * * * And the opinion of Mr. Chancellor Kent, and all the old authorities on the subject of ferries, support me in the doctrine.

* * *

But then again, it is said, that all this rests upon implication, and not upon the words of the charter. * * * What objection can there be to implications, if they arise from the very nature and objects of the grant? If it be indispensable to the full enjoyment of the right to take toll, that it should be exclusive within certain limits, is it not just and reasonable, that it should be so construed? * * *

* * *

The truth is, that the whole argument of the defendants turns upon an implied reservation of power in the legislature to defeat and destroy its own grant. The grant, construed upon its own terms, upon the plain principles of construction of the common law, by which alone it ought to be judged, is an exclusive grant. It is the grant of a franchise, publici juris, with a right of tolls; and in all such cases the common law asserts the grant to be exclusive, so as to prevent injurious competition. The argument seeks to exclude the common law from touching the grant, by implying an exception in favour of the legislative authority to make any new grant. * * *

To the answer already given to the objection, that, unless such a reservation of power exists, there will be a stop put to the progress of all public improvements; I wish, in this connexion, to add, that never can any such consequence follow upon the opposite doctrine. If the public exigencies and interests require that the franchise of Charles river bridge should be taken away, or impaired; it may be lawfully done upon making due compensation to the proprietors. * * *

* * *

* * * I maintain, that under the principles of the common law, there exists no more right in the legislature of Massachusetts, to erect the Warren bridge, to the ruin of the franchise of the Charles river bridge, than exists to transfer the latter to the former, or to authorize the former to demolish the latter. If the legislature does not mean in its grant to give any exclusive rights, let it say so, expressly; directly; and in terms admitting of no misconstruction. The grantees will then take at their peril, and must abide the results of their overweening confidence, indiscretion, and zeal.

My judgment is formed upon the terms of the grant, its nature and objects, its design and duties; and, in its interpretation, I seek for no new principles, but I apply such as are as old as the very rudiments of the common law.

* * *

Before I close, it is proper to notice, and I shall do it briefly, another argument strongly pressed at the bar against the plaintiffs; and that is, that the extension of the term of the franchise of the plaintiffs for thirty years, by the act of 1792, (erecting the West Boston bridge, between Boston and Cambridge,) and the acceptance thereof by the plaintiffs, amounted to a surrender or extinguishment of their exclusive franchise, if they ever had any, to build bridges over Charles river; so that they are barred from now setting it up against the Warren bridge. * * * But there is no warrant for the objection in any part of the language of the act. The extension of the term is not granted upon any condition whatsoever. No surrender of any right is asked, or required. The clause extending the term, purports, in its face, to be a mere donation or bounty of the legislature, founded on motives of public liberality and policy. It is granted expressly, as an encouragement to enterprise, and as a compensation for the supposed diminution of tolls, which West Boston bridge would occasion to Charles river bridge; and in no manner suggests any sacrifice or surrender of right whatsoever, to be made by the plaintiffs. In the next place, the erection of West Boston bridge was no invasion, whatsoever, of the franchise of the plaintiffs. Their right, as I have endeavoured to show, was limited to a bridge, and the travel between Charlestown and Boston; and did not extend beyond those towns. West Boston bridge was between Boston and Cambridge, at the distance of more than a mile by water, and by land of nearly three miles; and as the roads then ran, the line of travel for West Boston bridge would scarcely ever, perhaps never, approach nearer than that distance to Charles river bridge. The grant, therefore, could not have been founded in any notion of any surrender or extinguishment of the exclusive franchise of the plaintiffs; for it did not reach to such an extent. It did not reach Cambridge, and never had reached it.

* * *

Upon the whole, my judgment is, that the act of the legislature of Massachusetts granting the charter of Warren bridge, is an act impairing the obligation of the prior contract and grant to the proprietors of Charles river bridge; and, by the constitution of the United States, it is, therefore utterly void. * * *

NOTES AND QUESTIONS

1. Stanley I. Kutler's excellent study of this decision was entitled Privilege and Creative Destruction: The Charles River Bridge Case (1971). Why the choice of title? In his biography of Joseph Story, Gerald T. Dunne thus describes the Whig "wrath" upon the rendering of the decision for the Warren bridge:

> Webster assured Story that his dissent * * * left the Chief Justice "not an inch of ground to stand on," and young Charles Sumner adopted a British simile to write that reading Taney after Story was "hog wash after champagne." He reported a similar reaction from Chancellor Kent: "The Chancellor abused Taney & yr. associates to my heart's content. He thought Taney's opinion in the Warren Bridge case was miserable and yours gigantic." In fact, Kent had difficulty in reading Taney's views through; he dropped the pamphlet [containing the opinion] in shuddering disgust on the first effort and managed to finish it later by an effort of will, but with increased repugnance

Justice Joseph Story and the Rise of the Supreme Court 365–366 (1970.) Copyright © 1970 by Gerald T. Dunne, reprinted with the permission of the publisher, Simon and Schuster. Would you have expected this reaction from Chancellor Kent? You will remember that Story cites Kent's opinions regarding ferries as authority in his dissent. Do Kent's opinions in Livingston v. Van Ingen, Croton Turnpike, and Newburgh Turnpike support Story?

Whatever Kent's support of Story's opinion in *Charles River Bridge,* however, there is some evidence that even Kent was concerned about threats to society posed by the growth of corporations. In 1831 he wrote that "Considering that corporations and privileges are multiplying upon us in every direction, and upon all possible subjects with astonishing fertility, the reservation of a power to *alter and modify* [by the legislature when it grants a charter] becomes most important to the safety and prosperity of the state. The reservation ought to be liberally construed. Grants are rapidly and heedlessly made." *quoted in* Morton Horwitz, The Transformation of American Law 1780–1860 138 (1977).

If even a conservative, like Kent, could discern the need for some restraint on the part of legislatures dealing with corporations, imagine the reaction of the Democrats to Taney's decision. The Charles River Bridge company, whatever the riskiness of its initial venture, had multiplied its capital 500%, and, although this appreciation may not have been more than that of most private property in Massachusetts, "customers came to regard the company as an objectionable monopoly extorting tolls which it had no right to collect. The company refused to make concessions either in the way of improved services or reduced tolls." Carl B. Swisher, V History of the Supreme Court of the United States: The Taney Period 1836–64 76 (1974). Professor Swisher thus describes the attitude of the Democrats:

> With the announcement of the decision in the *Bridge Case,* some Democratic spokesmen leaped to the conclusion that the millennium had arrived. The editor of the Boston Advocate joyously proclaimed that the victory was due to the democratic principles of the Administration and to democratic judges on the Supreme Bench. * * * Had the majority of the Court been composed of Whig judges, had vacancies been filled by guardians of vested rights such as Clay and Webster, the Warren Bridge would never have been free. Judge Story had "read a book, occupying over three hours in its delivery,* in which he undertook to show that the bigoted blockheads who lived in the time of the old year books and my Lord Coke, were incomparably wiser than the present race, and that we had no business to do anything which they had not sanctioned! * * * There was not one liberal principle in it."

Id., at 90. Copyright © 1974 by Macmillan Publishing Co., Inc., reprinted by permission of the publisher. Do you prefer the opinions of the "bigoted blockheads," or do you subscribe to Taney's "liberal principles?" Why?

2. Story seems to have recognized that after what happened in the *Charles River Bridge* case, a new era had been begun. "I am sick at heart," he wrote Kent "and now go to the discharge of my judicial duties in the Supreme Court with a firm belief that the future cannot be as the past." Id., at 93, quoting Joseph Story to James Kent, June 26, 1837. What had changed? Is Taney's opinion in *Charles River Bridge* consistent with Story's and Marshall's opinions in the *Dartmouth College* case?

The *Charles River Bridge* case was originally argued before the Supreme Court in 1831, at which time the then Chief Justice Marshall and Justice Story were persuaded that the Charles River Bridge proprietors were right. An opinion by Story was drafted, but Marshall ordered it withheld until a majority of the court could concur with it. This took six years, and when a majority coalesced it was after Justice Marshall had been replaced by Justice Taney and it was in favor of the Warren Bridge. Accordingly, Story dissented. See Walker Lewis, Without Fear or Favor 281–294 (1965). Lewis calls this case "a crucial test between the views of the old-line Federalists and the new-

* Story's opinion, which includes dozens of references to English and American authorities, has been edited considerably from its original length of sixty-five pages.

er theories of the Jacksonians." Id. at 283. Morton Horwitz says that "The *Charles River Bridge* case represented the last great contest in America between two different models of economic development." Horwitz, Transformation of American Law 134 (1977). What does he mean? Do you discern any similarities in the changes of the nineteenth century American law of competition and the changes in the law of property which we examined in Chapter III?

B. THE CASE OF THE PHILADELPHIA CORDWAINERS (1806) AND THE DEVELOPMENT OF EARLY AMERICAN LABOR LAW

Boston's "Company of Shoemakers," chartered by the Colony of the Massachusetts Bay in 1648, was probably the first craft guild in America. The purpose of the guild was the suppression of "bad ware." The guild officers examined local workmen, and could secure from the county court an order prohibiting incompetent workmen from practicing the trade. The charter also empowered the association to regulate the labor of shoemakers, to "change and reform" the trade as appropriate, and to impose penalties on their members and "levy the same by distresse." The colonial authorities, however, reserved the right of "inhancing the prices of shoes, bootes, or wages." III J. Commons et al., A Documentary History of American Industrial Society 20–22 (1910). Each member of this early guild performed the functions of "merchant" and "journeyman." Each shoemaker possessed his own tools, owned or rented his own shop, procured his own leather, and personally cut, stitched, and sold his shoes. The "bespoke" system was in effect: customers placed individual orders in advance. The style of the shoe and the quality and speed of the work usually determined price.

The appearance of the *retail* shoe shop, in Philadelphia by 1789, marks the beginning of a distinction between labor and capital, "employee" and "employer." At this time some of the more enterprising "cordwainers" (taking their name from the "cordevan" leather they worked), instead of receiving orders in advance from customers, began building an inventory of shoes standardized by shape and size for random sale in the local market. Such an undertaking required a considerable capital investment and a reorganization of the manner of doing business. In order to take advantage of economies of scale, money had to be found for acquiring more raw materials and for paying wages to an increased number of employees. The extension of credit, and the opening of accounts with customers became commonplace. Soon, a few retail merchant-employers saw the opportunity to expand their businesses by producing shoes wholesale for a new export market. As the nature of the shoe business changed, a competitive edge at the retail and wholesale levels was often maintained by mass producing shoes of minimum quality at low cost. By the 1790s, then, three grades of work existed in the Philadelphia shoe industry, and different persons were engaged in the shoe trade as "merchant-employers" and "journeymen-workers." "Bespoke" work still commanded the highest price and wages, and included the most talented journeymen. The retail and wholesale businesses offered low-priced shoes, and paid the lowest wages. The conflict between journeymen and their employers grew from this differentiation in pay scale, as many workers found themselves "locked" into the retail and wholesale business, toiling for what was perceived as a "knocked down" wage. In 1794 many of the Philadelphia shoemakers organized the "Federal Society of Journeymen Cordwainers," and by a succession of strikes and lockouts, attempted to peg all wages at the "bespoke" level.

The success of the Society of Cordwainers, the first "union" of its kind in America, was mixed. From 1794 to 1804 they secured several moderate wage increases, but these apparently did not extend to workers in the wholesale trade. In the spring of 1805, the Society demanded a flat, across-the-board wage increase for all city workers, but after several weeks the workers were compelled to return to work at the "knocked down" wage. By this time the merchants had formed their own organization to resist the union. In the Summer of 1805 the workmen voluntarily agreed to a slight reduction in wage, because of slack in the market, but when they later demanded a return to the earlier scale, the merchants refused. The Cordwainers struck in November, 1805. The vote to strike was split, 50 to 60, a measure of the relative complacency of bespoke and retail workers, and the strike collapsed following the indictment and arrest of the strike leaders for the common-law crime of "conspiracy."

The arrest and trial in January of 1806 occurred during a particularly turbulent period in Pennsylvania political history. The radical wing of the Republican party, strengthened by Jefferson's reelection, was calling for a complete reconstruction of government and society, in accordance with democratic principles. These men sought particularly to disband the legal profession, to permit anyone to argue his own case, to abolish the common law, replacing it with a written "code" drafted by "the people," to simplify legal procedure, and to replace the adversarial process with a simple system of arbitration before a panel of laymen. The moderate wing of the Republican party differed with the radicals on the extent of needed reform. In September of 1805 the moderates united with the Federalists, (who were bitterly opposed to any changes), in electing Thomas McKean governor of Pennsylvania. McKean, a Republican, had earlier expressed some sympathy for the radicals' goals, and they placed severe pressure on him to undertake some reform of the law and the legal system. The arrest of the Cordwainers exacerbated radical grievances, and the trial became a forum to assail unjust law. The report of the trial from which you will read excerpts was taken in short-hand by Thomas Lloyd, a radical Republican printer. Lloyd dedicated his report to McKean and the Pennsylvania legislature. He called the Cordwainer's trial "the most interesting law case, which has occurred in this state since our revolution," and he stated that his dedication was "with the hope of attracting * * * particular attention, at the next meeting of the Legislature."

The prosecutors, Attorney General Joseph Reed, Joseph Hopkinson, and Jared Ingersoll were all ardent Federalists. Ceasar A. Rodney, for the Cordwainers, as a congressman from Delaware, managed the impeachment trial of Samuel Chase. Walter Franklin, Rodney's co-counsel, was also a radical Republican, and a partisan of the workingman's cause in Philadelphia.

COMMONWEALTH V. PULLIS

Mayor's Court of Philadelphia, 1806.
III. J. Commons Et Al., A Documentary History of American Industrial Society 60 (1910).

* * *

MR. HOPKINSON: This prosecution has been commenced, not from any private pique, or personal resentment, but solely, with a view, to promote the common good of the community: and to prevent in future the pernicious combinations, of misguided men, to effect purposes not only injurious to themselves, but mischievous to society. Yet infinite pains have been taken to represent this prosecution, as founded in very improper motives. * * *

The newspaper called the Aurora, has teemed with false representations and statements of this transaction; and the most insolent abuse of the parties, who have brought it before this tribunal, with a view * * * to poison the public mind, and obstruct the pure streams of justice flowing from the established courts of law. * * * When the true nature of the case shall be explained, and the plain narrative of the facts, shall be laid before you gentlemen of the jury, we feel confident that you will not be biased by newspaper attempts, to delude and mislead you. * * *

Let it be well understood that the present action, is not intended to introduce the doctrine, that a man is not at liberty to fix any price whatsoever upon his own labour; we disclaim the idea, in the most unqualified terms * * *. We have no design to prevent him. * * *

* * * [W]e shall shew you that some journeymen, with families, have been forbid to work at prices with which they were perfectly satisfied, and thereby been brought into deep distress.

* * * [W]e shall also shew the mode by which they compel men to join their society * * *. A journeyman arriving from Europe, or any part of the United States, an apprentice who has served * * * his time, must join the association, or be shut out from every shop in the city, if he presumes to

work at his own price. Nay, every master shoemaker must decline to employ such journeyman or his shop will be abandoned, by all the other workmen. * * * [T]his compulsion from its nature seldom fails. If the master discharges the non conformist, and he gets employed at another shop, the body pursue him, and order the new master to drive him away, and threaten in case of refusal that they will draw off all the members of the society, and so on, until the persecuted man either joins their body or is driven from the city. * * *

This is the chief charge in the indictment; and you now see that the action is instituted to maintain the cause of liberty and repress that of licentiousness. It is to secure the rights of each individual to obtain and enjoy the price he fixes upon his own labour.

* * * I have thought it necessary to say this much that you might not suppose we are attempting to deprive any man of his constitutional rights and privileges, as has been represented. * * *

* * *

Our position is, that no man is at liberty to combine, conspire, confederate, and unlawfully agree to regulate the whole body of workmen in the city. * * *

It must be known to you, that every society of people are affected by such private confederacies: that they are injurious to the public good and against the public interest. The law therefore forbids conspiracies of every kind which puts in jeopardy the interest and well being of the community; what may be lawful in an individual, may be criminal in a number of individuals combined, with a view to carry it into effect. * * *

You will also please to observe that this body of journeymen are not an incorporated society * * * neither are they a society instituted for benevolent purposes. But merely a society for compelling by the most arbitrary and malignant means, the whole body of the journeymen to submit to their rules and regulations; it is not confined even to the members of the society, it reaches every individual of the trade, whether journeymen or master. * * * You will find that they not only determine the price of labour for themselves, but compel every one to demand that price and receive no other, they refuse to hold communion with any person who shall disobey their mandates, in fine, they regulate the whole trade under the most dreadful pains and penalties, such I believe as never was heard of in this or any other civilized country.

[There followed two days of testimony, which did show that the Journeymen behaved in the manner Hopkinson described: that they attempted to enforce uniformity in their demands for raised wages, and ostracized scabs. We continue with Hopkinson's comments on the law as applied to the evidence.]

* * *

Why a combination in such case is criminal, will not be difficult to explain: we live under a government composed of a constitution and laws * * * and every man is obliged to obey the constitution, and the laws made under it. When I say he is bound to obey these, I mean to state the whole extent of his obedience. Do you feel yourselves bound to obey any other laws, enacted by any other legislature, than that of your own choice? Shall these, or any other body of men, associate for the purpose of making new laws, laws not made under the constitutional authority, and compel their fellow citizens to obey them, under the penalty of their existence? This prosecution contravenes no man's right, it is to prevent an infringement of right; it is in favour of the equal liberty of all men, this is the policy of our laws; but if private associations and clubs, can make constitutions and laws for us * * * if they can associate and make bye-laws paramount, or inconsistent with the state laws; What, I ask, becomes of the liberty of the people * * * ?

There is evidence before you that shews this secret association, this private club, composed of men who have been only a little time in your country, (not that they are the worse for that,) but they ought to submit to the laws of the country, and not attempt to alter them according to their own whim or caprice.

* * *

* * * I now am to speak to the policy of permitting such associations. This is a large, increasing, manufacturing city. Those best acquainted with our situation, believe that manufactures will, by and by, become one of its chief means of support. * * * [W]e rival the supplies from England in many things, and great sums are annually received in returns. It is then proper to support this manufacture. Will you permit men to destroy it, who have no permanent stake in the city; men who can pack up their all in a knapsack, or carry them in their pockets to New–York or Baltimore? * * * Other articles, to a great amount, are manufactured here, and exported; such as coaches and other pleasurable carriages; windsor chairs, and particular manufactures of iron. * * *

* * * [W]hen orders arrive for considerable quantities of any article, the association may determine to raise the wages, and reduce the contractors to diminish their profit; to sustain a loss, or to abandon the execution of the orders, as was done in Bedford's case. * * * What was done by the journeymen shoemakers, may be done by those of every other trade, or manufacturer in the city * * *. A few more things of this sort, and you will break up the manufactories; the master will be afraid to make a contract, therefore he must relinquish the export trade, and depend altogether upon the profits of the work of Philadelphia, and confine his supplies alto-

gether to the city. The last turn-out had liked to have produced that effect: Mr. Ryan told you he had intended to confine himself to bespoke work.

It must be plain to you, that the master employers have no particular interest in the thing * * * if they pay higher wages, you must pay higher for the articles. They, in truth, are protecting the community. * * *

* * *

If this conspiracy was to be confined to the persons themselves, it would not be an offence against the law; but they go further. There are two counts in the indictment; you are to consider each, and to give your verdict on each. The first is for contriving, and intending, unjustly, and oppressively, to encrease and augment the wages usually allowed them. The other for endeavouring to prevent, by threats, menaces, and other unlawful means, other journeymen from working at the usual prices, and that they compelled others to join them.

* * *

It may be answered, that when men enter into a society, they are bound to conform to its rules; they may say, the majority ought to govern the minority * * * granted * * * but they ought to leave a man free to join, or not to join the society. * * * The man who seeks an asylum in this country, from the arbitrary laws of other nations, is coerced into this society, though he does not work in the article intended to be raised; he must leave his seat and join the turn-out. This was Harrison's case * * * he worked exclusively in shoes, they in boots; he was a stranger, he was a married man, with a large family; he represented his distressed condition; they entangle him, but shew no mercy. The dogs of vigilance find, by their scent, the emigrant in his cellar or garret: they drag him forth, they tell him he must join them; he replies, I am well satisfied as I am * * *. No * * * they chase him from shop to shop; they allow him no resting place, till he consents to be one of their body; he is expelled [from] society, driven from his lodgings, proscribed from working; he is left no alternative, but to perish in the streets, or seek some other asylum on a more hospitable shore. * * *

* * * It will be seen that the mere combination to raise wages is considered an offense at common law: the reason is founded in common sense. Suppose the bakers were to combine, and agree not to sell a loaf of bread, only for one week, under a dollar, would not this be an injury to the community? * * * Extend the case to butchers, and all others who deal in articles of prime necessity, and the good policy of the law is then apparent.

Hawkins, c. 72, § 2, in note, was cited. Speaking of combinations, he says * * * "Where divers persons confederate together, in order to prejudice a third person, it is indictable as highly criminal at common law." "Journeymen confederating and refusing to work, unless at encreased prices, is indictable!" * * *

Mr. Hopkinson next cited 8 Mod. p. 11. Wise against the journeymen taylors at Cambridge. "A conspiracy is unlawful, even though the matter might have been lawful, if done by them individually. * * * "

He trusted the jury would see the present cause in this double point of view; the general policy, as it relates to the good of the community, and the flourishing state of our manufactures: the liberty of individuals, and the enjoyment of common and equal rights, secured by the constitution and laws. * * * [W]as our state legislature to dare to pass such laws as these men have passed, it would be a just cause of rebellion. I will go further, and say, it would produce rebellion if the legislature should say, that a man should not work under a certain sum * * * it would lead to beggary, and no man would submit to it. Then, shall a secret body exercise a power over our fellow-citizens, which the legislature itself is not invested with? * * *

* * *

One word more; we are told the prices asked by these men, are those given at New–York and Baltimore: if so, why do not these men go there? They know if their wages are higher there, their expences also are higher: they do not stay here out of patriotism; they know their own interests, and can calculate them with accuracy * * *.

[*Mr. Franklin:*] Has the master then the sole right of determining the wages which are to be given for the labour of his journeymen? This would be too arbitrary a power for any man to contend for; it would be an insult to your understandings, to insist upon it. * * * As to the price which any particular employer may pay his workmen, that must be regulated by the contract between them. If they can mutually agree upon a price to be given, the master is bound to give, and the journeymen must abide by the sum stipulated. A different price will be given to different workmen; some deserve more than others, either on account of their greater industry and application, or their greater skill and ingenuity.

But if the employer and journeyman cannot agree upon the work to be done, or the price to be paid, neither is bound to recede from his determination.

If then, any one man has this right, has not every other man the same privilege? If one journeyman has a right to adopt measures to prevent the effects of the obstinacy or combination of the master shoemakers, may not a number unite for the same object? A purpose innocent or lawful in one man, cannot be otherwise in a society or body of men. Supposing, therefore, that the facts charged in the first count were true; that the men refused to work but at certain prices, it is no crime, and they cannot be punished for it.

* * *

Now, if any journeyman who chose to work at the rates or prices offered by the employers, contrary to the wish of other journeymen, were threatened by them, or any of them, with injury to his person or property, he has a complete and ample remedy provided for him by law without resorting to the measures which have been adopted. He might have them bound over to their good behaviour, and if they afterwards were guilty of any threats, their recognizance would be forfeited, and they would be obliged to pay the penalty. * * *

If any employer suffer inconvenience or mischief, in consequence of his journeymen being seduced or driven from his employment, he has his remedy by a civil action, in which he may recover from the offender, damages equal to the injury sustained. * * *

* * * What proof is there of the association having made any unlawful or arbitrary bye laws? * * * None * * *. But supposing that such laws had been enacted by the society, are the defendants to answer for them in this way? Should it not appear clearly, that they assented to them? When the question was taken, the defendants might have been in the minority; and shall they be punished for an act of the society of which they have shewn their disapprobation? * * *

* * *

[Franklin then turns to the charges of ostracizing scabs and preventing masters from hiring them.]

* * * Is there the slightest evidence, that the defendants ever compelled a single journeyman to leave his employers? How did they compel? Did they use any violence? If they had they were subject to the laws and might have been individually punished for it. But neither violence, threats, nor menaces, were used * * *. No man was the object of force or compulsion. * * * "The very head and front of their offending was:" their refusing to work for any master who employed such journeymen as infringed the rules of the society to which they belonged.

This I deny to be an offence. * * * The motive for my refusal may be illiberal, but it furnishes no legal foundation for a prosecution: I cannot be indicted for it. Every man may chuse his company, or refuse to associate with any one whose company may be disagreeable to him, without being obliged to give a reason for it: and without violating the laws of the land. * * *

I will conclude this part of my argument, with the remarks of a very sensible and judicious writer * * * Smith's Wealth of Nations, page 89.

"Workmen desire to get as much, masters to give as little, as possible. * * * It is not, however, difficult to foresee which of the two parties must, upon all ordinary occasions, have the advantage in the dispute * * *. The masters being fewer in number, can combine much more easily; and the law, besides, authorises, or at least does not prohibit their combinations, while it prohibits those of the workmen. We have no acts of parliament against combining to lower the price of work; but many against combining to raise it. In all such disputes the masters can hold out much longer. A landlord, a farmer, a master manufacturer, or merchant, though they did not employ a single workman, could generally live a year or two upon the stocks which they have already acquired. Many workmen could not subsist a week * * *. We rarely hear, it has been said, of the combinations of masters; though frequently of those of workmen. But whoever imagines, upon this account, that masters rarely combine, is as ignorant of the world as the subject. Masters are always and every where in a sort of tacit, but constant and uniform combination, not to raise the wages of labour above their actual rate. To violate this combination is everywhere a most unpopular action, and a sort of reproach to a master among his neighbours and equals. * * * "

* * *

[Franklin moved then into the law of conspiracy.] 1 Hawk. b. 1, c. 72, § 2, note 2, is cited. This point rests on 8 Mod. p. 11. Rex. vs. the journeymen taylors * * *. "It is not for the denial, & c. but for the conspiracy they were indicted; and a conspiracy of any kind is illegal, though the matter about which they conspired might have been lawful for them, or any of them to do, if they had not conspired to do it."

And is it contended that the doctrine contained in this case is law in Pennsylvania? It may be adapted to the meridian of London, Paris, Madrid, or Constantinople, but can never suit the free state of Pennsylvania. * * * By this authority, whatever is innocent or laudable in one, becomes criminal if he unite with others in doing it.

It is lawful for an individual to use his best endeavours to extinguish the fire which burns his neighbour's house, but he must not unite with others in doing it. What then becomes of your fire companies, your hose companies, and other institutions of a similar nature * * * none of which are incorporated by law?

It is lawful for a man to improve himself in any art or science, but he must not join with others for the purpose. What then becomes of the numerous literary associations which do so much honour to Philadelphia?

* * *

* * * [The English] Parliament [has passed laws] to limit the prices of work in various branches of business, and under those acts it is made

criminal to combine for the purpose of raising the wages, otherwise than as the acts direct. I believe the journeymen shoemakers would be punishable in England for an attempt to raise their wages, not by the common law, but under the provisions of acts of parliament, made expressly for the purpose.

Admitting, for argument sake, however, that they would be amenable to the common law in England, independent of the statute, they should shew us that this part of the common law has been extended to Pennsylvania * * *. Of the applicability of the [English] law to the circumstances of the country, the colonists even when in a state of dependence on the mother country, undertook to decide, and were allowed the privilege of determining for themselves. * * *

How is it to be ascertained what parts of the common law are, or are not, applicable to the condition and circumstances of the country, and therefore to be adopted or rejected? The only modes in which this can be done are by legislative acts, judicial decisions, or constant usage or practice. * * *

I need not, I am sure, go into an argument to shew, that laws of the kind contended for, are neither necessary for us, applicable to our situation, nor suitable to our circumstances. You might as well introduce that part of the common law relative to cutting off a man's right hand for striking in court, & c. mentioned in 4 Black. p. 124. * * *

* * *

It is true that precedents innumerable may be imported from Great Britain. But very different are the genius and feelings of the two countries, on the subject of criminal law * * *. The theory and practice of the criminal law of England, form an object of horror to every feeling and reflecting mind. [Franklin then quotes former Supreme Court Justice James Wilson:] * * * "Instead of being, as it ought to be, an emanation from the law of nature and morality, it has too often been avowedly and systematically the reverse. It has been a combination of the strong against the weak, of the rich against the poor, of pride and interest against justice and humanity. Unfortunate, indeed, it is, that this has been the case; for we may truly say, that on the excellence of the criminal law, the liberty and the happiness of the people chiefly depend."

In Great Britain * * * the prices of every kind of work and labour are fixed by law; and very high penalties are imposed upon those who transgress them. * * *

You will readily perceive the spirit of partiality, which breathes through their statutes * * * and the strong inclinations which they evince to favor the rich at the expence of the poor * * * the master at the expence of the servant.

If you are desirous of introducing a similar spirit of inequality into our government and laws * * * such disposition and opinions will lead you to convict the defendants. If * * * you are contented with the blessings enjoyed under our free constitution, which secures to the citizens an equality of rights, and recognizes no distinction of classes * * * I shall look for the result of these feelings and these sentiments in a verdict of acquittal.

* * *

Mr. Rodney: [He begins his argument with an evaluation of Mr. Hopkinson's claim that the merchants who sought to keep down wages were disinterested public servants.] He has attempted to excite your feelings and sympathy, in behalf of those, who can scarce refrain from smiling in your face; he has set forth their merits, their disinterestedness, and their magnanimity, in stepping between you and the impositions of their workmen * * *. Is this a true picture of the case before you? * * * It is nothing more or less than this, whether the wealthy master shoemakers of this populous and flourishing city, shall charge you and me what price they please for our boots and shoes, and at the same time have the privilege of fixing the wages of the poor journeymen they happen to employ. * * *

* * *

Much has been said of the importance of manufactures to this city, and the injury manufacturing interest would sustain, if journeymen were permitted to regulate the price of their own labour. The gentleman has shewn you one side of the picture; I wish to call your attention to the other. The great advantage possessed by Philadelphia over New York and Baltimore, is the extent of her monied capital. Those cities give more wages, and we have proved them to be given at this very time: and we wish to receive merely the same prices, and no more.

The gentleman calls out, why do they not go there? Suppose they should at his bidding take wing and fly away, how would Mr. Bedford and Mr. Ryan make their boots, and what is to become of their export trade? Do you wish to banish them? The verdict called for by the prosecutors, will effectually answer the purpose. * * * New York and Baltimore wisely hold out good prices to attract them; and good policy ought to dictate to the employers here, to allow them as liberal a compensation. Leather is said to be cheaper here, and I do not believe, living costs more than at either New York or Baltimore. * * * New York and Baltimore will gladly receive them, as they take care to profit by every other advantage which our inattention or narrow policy throws into their way. * * *

Philadelphia is a great commercial and manufacturing city; that the legislature of the state by its fostering care, in opening new roads and cutting canals, may render it still more prosperous * * * must be the sincere wish of us all. * * * Do not then, I beg of you bring on a premature old age, by establishing the principle, that labourers or journeymen, in every trade, are to submit to the prices which their employers, in the plenitude of their power, choose to give them. * * * The moment you destroy the free agency of this meritorious part of the community (for remember the principle is undeniable, that labour constitutes the real wealth of a country) the verdict which you will pronounce, will proclaim the decline and the fall of Philadelphia. * * * Let them ask as freely as they breathe the air, wages for their services. No person is compelled to give them more than their work is worth, the market will sufficiently and correctly regulate these matters. If you adhere to our doctrines * * * I venture to predict * * * that scarcely a breeze will blow, but what will waft to our shores, experienced workmen from those realms, where labour is regulated by statutable provisions * * *. Give me leave however, frankly to declare, that I would not barter away our dear bought rights and American liberty, for all the warehouses of London and Liverpool, and the manufactures of Birmingham and Manchester: no; not if were to be added to them, the gold of Mexico, the silver of Peru, and the diamonds of Brazil.

* * *

One word in reply to the observations on the subject of aliens. From the moment we declared independence, we stood with open arms to receive the oppressed of all nations and countries. * * * We want workmen of every kind. Let us preserve this asylum. * * * It is the last retreat of freedom and liberty.

* * * [T]he law should be no respecter of persons * * * like the light of the sun, it should shine on all. Whether they are as rich as Croesus, or as poor as Belisarius * * * whether their complexion be as black as jet, or as white as the driven snow!

* * *

[*Mr. Ingersoll:*] The defendants formed a society, the object of which was * * *. What? That they should not be obliged to work for wages which they did not think a reasonable compensation? No: If that was the sole object of the society, I approve it * * *. No man is to work without a reasonable compensation: they may legally and properly associate for that purpose. * * * If they go beyond this, and say we will not work, but we will compel the employers to give more, not according to contract, but such as they separately think themselves entitled to receive [then there is a violation of law.] * * *

[Ingersoll turns to a defense of the common law.] Whence comes this enmity to the common law? It is of mushroom growth. Look through the journals of congress during the revolutionary war, you will find it claimed as the great charter of liberty; as the best birthright and noblest of inheritance. Ceasar A. Rodney, the revolutionary patriot, hazarded his life to secure and perpetuate the blessing. * * *

But the common law is in some respects faulty, as in the case cited from 4 Black. p. 124, and 4 Inst. p. 143. The sun too has its spots, but will you extinguish that luminary from the firmament? But the common law, as adopted and practised in Pennsylvania, is the least exceptionable criminal code in the world. In England, it is said to be sanguinary and cruel. In England there are 176 offences punishable by death, of which there are only 16 so punished by the common law.

Why do I love the common law, especially the criminal part? * * * Because, to the common law we are indebted for trial by jury, grand and petit, without the unanimous consent of which latter, I cannot be convicted. * * * Because, it secures me a fair trial by challenges, the laws of evidence, confronting me with my accuser, and exempting me from accusing myself, or being twice liable to trial for the same offence. * * *

* * *

Abolish the common law, judging not by instances, but by principle, where are you? Shew me an indictment of any kind, even for assault and battery, it is bottomed on common law; with us we have no cause of proceeding in criminal cases, but by the modes of the common law * * *.

Recorder Levy [Instructing the Jury]:

* * *

The moment courts of justice lose their respectability from that moment the security of persons and of property is gone. The moment courts of justice have their characters contaminated by a well founded suspicion, that they are governed by caprice, fear or favour; from that moment they will cease to be able to administer justice with effect, and redress wrongs of either a public or a private nature. Every consideration, therefore, calls upon us to maintain the character of courts and juries; and that can only be maintained by undeviating integrity, by an adhesion to the rules of law, and by deciding impartially in conformity to them.

* * * As far as the arguments of counsel apply to your understanding and judgment, they should have weight: but, if the appeal has been made to your passions, it ought not to be indulged. * * * An attempt has been made to shew that the spirit of the revolution and the principle of the common law, are opposite in this case. That the common law, if applied in this case, would operate an attack upon the rights of man. The enquiry on that point, was unnecessary and improper. Nothing more was required than to ascertain what the law is. The law is the permanent rule, it is the will of the whole community. After that is discovered, whatever may be

its spirit or tendency, it must be executed, and the most imperious duty demands our submission to it.

* * *

* * * The prosecutors are not on their trial, if they have proved the offence, alleged in the indictment against the defendants; and if the defendants are guilty, will any man say, that they ought not to be convicted: because the prosecution was not founded in motives of patriotism? Certainly the only question is, whether they are guilty or innocent. * * *

* * *

It is proper to consider, is such a combination consistent with the principles of our law, and injurious to the public welfare? The usual means by which the prices of work are regulated, are the demand for the article and the excellence of its fabric. * * * To make an artificial regulation, is not to regard the excellence of the work or quality of the material, but to fix a positive and arbitrary price, governed by no standard, controlled by no impartial person, but dependent on the will of the few who are interested * * *. It is an unnatural, artificial means of raising the price of work beyond its standard, and taking an undue advantage of the public. Is the rule of law bottomed upon such principles, as to permit or protect such conduct? * * * Is there any man who can calculate (if this is tolerated) at what price he may safely contract to deliver articles, for which he may receive orders, if he is to be regulated by the journeymen in an arbitrary jump from one price to another? * * * What then is the operation of this kind of conduct upon the commerce of the city? It exposes it to inconveniences, if not to ruin; therefore, it is against the public welfare. How does it operate upon the defendants? We see that those who are in indigent circumstances, and who have families to maintain, and who get their bread by their daily labour, have declared here upon oath, that it was impossible for them to hold out * * * and it has been admitted by the witnesses for the defendants, that such persons, however sharp and pressing their necessities, were obliged to stand to the turn-out, or never afterwards to be employed. * * * Can such a regulation be just and proper? Does it not tend to involve necessitous men in the commission of crimes? If they are prevented from working for six weeks, it might induce those who are thus idle, and have not the means of maintenance, to take other courses for the support of their wives and children. It might lead them to procure it by crimes—by burglary, larceny, or highway robbery! A father cannot stand by and see, without agony, his children suffer; if he does, he is an inhuman monster; he will be driven to seek bread for them, either by crime, by beggary, or a removal from the city. * * * Does this measure tend to make good workmen? No: it puts the botch incapable of doing justice to his work, on a level with the best tradesman. The master must give the same wages to each. Such a practice would take away all the excitement to excel in workmanship or industry. * * * In every point of view, this measure is pregnant with public mischief and private injury * * *.

What has been the conduct of the defendants in this instance? They belong to an association, the object of which is, that every person who follows the trade of a journeyman shoemaker, must be a member of their body. * * * If they do not join the body, a term of reproach is fixed upon them. The members of the body will not work with them, and they refuse to board or lodge with them. * * * If the purpose of the association is well understood, it will be found they leave no individual at liberty to join the society or reject it. * * * Is there any reason to suppose that the laws are not competent to redress an evil of this magnitude? * * *

* * *

It is in the volumes of the common law we are to seek for information in the far greater number, as well as the most important causes that come before our tribunals. That invaluable code has ascertained and defined, with a critical precision, and with a consistency that no fluctuating political body could or can attain, not only the civil rights of property, but the nature of all crimes from treason to trespass, has pointed out the rules of evidence and the mode of proof, and has introduced and perpetuated, for their investigation, that admirable institution, the freeman's-boast, the trial by jury. * * * Much abuse has of late teemed upon its valuable institutions. Its enemies do not attack it as a system: but they single out some detached branch of it, declare it absurd or intelligible, without understanding it. * * * As well might a circle of a thousand miles diameter be described by the man, whose eye could only see a single inch * * *. Its rules are the result of the wisdom of ages. It says there may be cases in which what one man may do without offence, many combined may not do with impunity. * * *

* * * A combination of workmen to raise their wages may be considered in a two fold point of view: one is to benefit themselves * * * the other is to injure those who do not join their society. The rule of law condemns both. If the rule be clear, we are bound to conform to it even though we do not comprehend the principle upon which it is founded. * * * It is enough, that it is the will of the majority. * * * But the rule in this case is pregnant with sound sense and all the authorities are clear upon the subject. * * *

* * * In the turn-out of last fall, if each member of the body had stood alone, fettered by no promises to the rest, many of them might have changed their opinion as to the price of wages and gone to work * * *. The continuance in improper conduct may therefore well be attributed to the combination. The good sense of those individuals was prevented by this agreement, from having its free exercise. * * * Is this like the formation of

a society for the promotion of the general welfare of the community, such as to advance the interests of religion, or to accomplish acts of charity and benevolence? * * * These are for the benefit of third persons, the society in question to promote the selfish purposes of the members. * * * How can these cases be considered on an equal footing? The journeymen shoemakers * * * could not go farther than saying, no one should work unless they all got the wages demanded by the majority; is this freedom? * * * Was it the spirit of '76 that either masters or journeymen, in regulating the prices of their commodities should set up a rule contrary to the law of their country? General and individual liberty was the spirit of '76. It is our first blessing. It has been obtained and will be maintained * * *. It is not a question, whether we shall have an imperium in imperio, whether we shall have, besides our state legislature a new legislature consisting of journeymen shoemakers. * * * [T]hough we acknowledge it is the hard hand of labour that promises the wealth of a nation, though we acknowledge the usefulness of such a large body of tradesmen and agree they should have every thing to which they are legally entitled; yet we conceive they ought to ask nothing more. They should neither be the slaves nor the governors of the community.

* * *

* * * [The court has] given you the rule as they have found it in the book, and it is now for you to say, whether the defendants are guilty or not. [The jury returned a verdict of guilty, and the court fined the defendants eight dollars each, with costs of suit.]

* * *

NOTES AND QUESTIONS

1. Like the trial of Zenger, the Writs of Assistance Case, and the proceedings against Samuel Chase, the questions of "law" in the trial of the Cordwainers are intertwined with questions of political and economic ideology. These problems have been studied in some of the most exciting legal historiography.

On the outcome of legal reform in Pennsylvania, see R. Ellis, The Jeffersonian Crisis: Courts and Politics in the Young Republic (1971). On the conditions of work and unionization in Philadelphia, see E. Foner, Tom Paine (1976), and David Montgomery, "The Working Class of the Preindustrial American City, 1780–1830," 9 Labor History 1–22 (1968). For further reading on the Cordwainers' case, see Robert J. Steinfeld, "The *Philadelphia Cordwainers' Case* of 1806: The Struggle Over Legal Constructions of a Free Market in Labor," in Christopher L. Tomlins and Andrew J. King, editors, Labor Law in America: Historical and Critical Essays 20 (1992). On the link between radical Republicanism and urban workingmen, see A. Young, "The Mechanics and the Jeffersonians: New York, 1789–1801," 5 Labor History

247 (1964). The best work on ideas about labor and law at the time of the Cordwainers trial is Christopher Tomlins, Law, Labor, and Ideology in the Early American Republic (1993). See also Karren Orren, Belated Federalism: Labor, the Law, and Liberal Development in the United States (1991), Sean Wilentz, Chants Democratic: New York City and the Rise of American Working Class, 1788–1850 (1984), and Herbert Gutman, Work, Culture and Society in Industrializing America (1977). For the development of the legal doctrines in the Cordwainers' case over the next one hundred and twenty-five years see Herbert Hovenkamp, "Labor Conspiracies in American Law, 1880–1930," 66 Texas Law Rev. 919 (1988).

2. According to the prosecution and Recorder Levy, what is the legal definition of conspiracy? What sort of "conspiracy law" would the defense counsel propose? What is the relevance of Franklin's and Rodney's digressions about the English common law of crimes? Can you perceive a link between the Franklin–Rodney fulminations against the common law, the Hopkinson–Ingersoll defense, and the politics of Pennsylvania at the time of the trial?

3. Both prosecution and defense claim that "liberty" and the "rights of man" are on their side. Would they agree on the definitions of these terms? The prosecutor casts aspersions on the "alien" workingmen of the city who can pack all their belongings on their backs, and invites them to leave the city if they are unsatisfied with their work. While Rodney agrees on the social origins of the shoemakers, he doesn't share many of the attitudes of the prosecution. What power should the shoemakers exercise in society, according to Rodney?

4. The prosecutor objects to the Society of Cordwainers because they are like a "government unto themselves." What does this mean? What evidence can he offer for their "unconstitutionality?" Franklin and Rodney respond that it is in the nature of private associations to exercise some degree of compulsion and coercion on their members. Why this concern on both sides about possible abuses of power?

5. In 1776 Adam Smith published Wealth of Nations, still considered to be one of the most important statements on the virtues of a free market. Why did defense counsel quote favorably from it? Recorder Levy also has an opinion on the virtues of a free market. Does this opinion "interfere" with his judgment of the case? Do you think he correctly understands the motives of the Society of Cordwainers? What is the economic policy or model behind Levy's instructions? Should economic policy or economic theory have a place in a criminal proceeding?

6. In his instructions to the jury, Levy waxes eloquent on the virtues of the common law. Does Levy's common law differ from that of the prosecution and the defense? What is Levy's attitude toward the jury? Levy instructs the jury to rely not on their "passions" but on their "judgment." What is the distinction? In the same vein, Levy reminds the jury that they must distinguish between "selfish purposes" and the "general welfare" in arriving at a verdict.

What does Levy have in mind? Do you find his opinion more or less logical than those of counsel?

7. Jared Ingersoll, for the prosecution, chastises Rodney, and accuses him of inconsistency, for being on the one hand a Revolutionary patriot, and on the other an opponent of the common law. Why would Ingersoll make such a charge? Could you answer for Rodney? Can you explain why a labor conspiracy case would be the battleground for interpreting the meaning of the Revolution?

8. One of the arguments of defense counsel, not included here, is that the merchants formed their own "combination" in 1789—five years before the Society—and that the Society of Cordwainers was actually an attempt to restore the balance of power in dealings between labor and management. The court believed the evidence insufficient to support this argument of the cordwainers. Yet both the prosecution and Recorder Levy seem to stress that the law, when conspiracy is involved, must be "blind," favoring neither merchant nor workingman.

9. An opportunity to determine the even-handedness of the Pennsylvania common law of conspiracy arose in 1821, in COMMONWEALTH v. CARLISLE, Bright. 36. The defendants were master ladies' shoemakers who were accused of conspiring to lower the wages of their journeymen. Their principal defense was that they were merely seeking to reduce wages artificially inflated by a combination of the journeymen. Referring to the trial of the cordwainers, Chief Justice Gibson of the Pennsylvania Supreme Court stated that "there was no general principle distinctly asserted, but the case was considered only in reference to its particular circumstances, and in these it materially differed from that now under consideration." Id., at 37. Do you agree?

Turning to the English conspiracy cases against journeymen for combining to raise their wages, Gibson remarked that "we ought to pause before we adopt their law of conspiracy, as respects artisans, which may be said to have in some measure, indirectly received its form from the pressure of positive enactment, and which therefore may be entirely unfitted to the condition and habits of the same class here." Id., at 38. Gibson noted the confused state of the English law of conspiracy, and stressed that it would be a mistake to "impart criminality to the most laudable associations" merely because they were "combinations." Id., at 39. Gibson then concluded that the most important inquiries were those regarding "motive" and the "nature of the object to be attained." "Where the act is lawful for an individual," he stated, "it can be the subject of a conspiracy when done in concert, only where there is a direct intention that injury shall result from it, or where the object is to benefit the conspirators to the prejudice of the public or the oppression of individuals, and where such prejudice or oppression is the natural and necessary consequence." Id., at 39–40. Proceeding to give examples, Gibson said that if "persons should combine to establish a ferry, not from motives of public or private utility, but to ruin or injure the owner of a neighboring ferry," or "if the bakers of a town were to combine to hold up the article of bread, and by means of a scarcity thus produced, extort an exorbitant price for it," these would be indictable conspiracies under the Pennsylvania common law. The result would be otherwise, however, if the motives of those establishing a ferry, for example, were "fair competition" and not "oppression." Id., at 40.

Moving finally to the facts at hand, Gibson decided that "a combination of employers to depress the wages of journeymen below what they would be, if there was no recurrence to artificial means by either side, is criminal." Id. at 41. Gibson proceeded to give his thoughts on the necessity for such a rule:

> There is between the different parts of the body politic a reciprocity of action on each other, which, like the action of antagonizing muscles in the natural body, not only prescribes to each its appropriate state and condition, but regulates the motion of the whole. The effort of an individual to disturb this equilibrium can never be perceptible, nor carry the operation of his interest on that of any other individual beyond the limits of fair competition; but the increase of power by combination of means, being in geometrical proportion to the number concerned, an association may be able to give an impulse, not only oppressive to individuals, but mischievous to the public at large; and it is the employment of an engine so powerful and dangerous, that gives criminality to an act that would be perfectly innocent, at least in a legal view, when done by an individual. The combination of capital for purposes of commerce, or to carry on any other branch of industry, although it may in its consequences indirectly operate on third persons, is unaffected by this consideration, because it is a common means in the ordinary course of human affairs, which stimulates to competition and enables men to engage in undertakings too weighty for an individual.

Id., at 41. Gibson then announced that a combination artificially to depress the price of labor would be just as criminal as a combination to raise the price of bread, since the "labouring classes purchase their bread with their labour." Id., at 42. Still, the essence of the crime was motive, and where the intention of masters was "not to give an undue value to labour, but to foil their antagonists [the journeymen] in an attempt to assign to it, by surreptitious means, a value which it would not otherwise have, they will make out a good defense." Id., at 42. While it was true that the masters might proceed against journeymen who combined artificially to raise their wages through the law of conspiracy, "the legal remedy is cumulative, and does not take away the preventive remedy by the act of the parties," so that the masters could lawfully combine to reduce artificially-raised wages. Id., at 43. Gibson then referred the matter to a jury, for a factual determination of the motives of the masters in combining to reduce the journeymen's wages. The report of the case contains no information on the jury's disposition of the matter, but it appears that "the prosecution was probably dropped." Nelles, "Commonwealth v. Hunt" 32 Col.L.Rev. 1167n. (1932).

Do you find Gibson's treatment of the law of conspiracy to be more or less satisfactory than those of counsel and Recorder Levy in the case of the cordwainers? Which treatment seems most in accord with what you take to be the American political values of freedom and liberty? How clear are the principles which Gibson lays down? Gibson seems to be relying on the same free-market model of the economy that Recorder Levy alluded to, and it is likely that both men subscribed to the wage-fund theory of labor (only a fixed part of the national income was available for wages). How easy do you think it would be for Gibson or for a jury to determine when a given combination was designed to produce "artificially" high or low wages? Gibson explains that combinations of capital are permissible where the object is not "oppression," but "fair competition." Is the distinction an easy one to make? If these would be difficult determinations, in whose favor would you assume they would be likely to be resolved?

10. How far was early American common law prepared to go in sanctioning competition among employers for labor? In Gibson's opinion in Carlisle he stated his belief that if merchants in one industry artificially lowered wages, workers would eventually leave that industry to enter others, and that the offending merchants would eventually (even without the help of the law of conspiracy) be forced to raise wages back to their natural level. Id., at 41. The willingness of the American common law to maintain a free market in labor was put to a test in BOSTON GLASS MANUFACTORY v. BINNEY, 21 Mass. (4 Pick.) 425 (1827). This was an action sounding in tort, in which the plaintiffs argued that the defendants, their competitors, had unlawfully enticed skilled workmen from their employ. Lemuel Shaw, whose two opinions in labor cases we will soon read, appeared as counsel for the defendants. Relying on an English case cited by Shaw, the court held that " 'to induce a servant to leave his master's service at the expiration of the time for which the servant had hired himself, although the servant had no intention at the time, of quitting his master's service, was not the subject of an action.' *It is damnum absque injuria.*" Id., at 428, citing Lord Kenyon in Nicol et al. v. Martyn, 2 Esp.R. 732. "If the law were otherwise," said Justice Wilde, "it would lead to the most mischievous consequences, and would operate injuriously both to laborers and their employers." In the course of its opinion in *Binney* the Supreme Judicial Court in effect rejected a jury instruction of the trial judge to the contrary, and held that it was not a tort for new employers to bargain with employees before their contracts with competitors had expired. Does the language from Nicol v. Martyn support this?

In the course of the trial in *Binney*, the plaintiffs sought to demonstrate that the defendants were liable not only for the common-law tort of enticement, but also because they had earlier signed an agreement among Boston glass-making merchants not to lure away each other's skilled workers. The trial judge rejected the evidence of the contract, on the grounds that it could not form the basis for an action in tort. (*Binney* was an "action on the case," a tort proceeding, and at this time one could not submit in the same proceeding claims in tort *and* contract.) Suppose that the contract had been properly sued upon. Was it enforceable? Would you consider such an agreement to be an "unlawful combination" under the doctrines of the *Cordwainer's case* or Commonwealth v. Carlisle? How do you suppose Justice Wilde would have disposed of a prosecution for a common-law conspiracy under the laws of Massachusetts? Can you discern the economic policies that might be behind Justice Wilde's ruling in *Binney?* Would they be in accordance with those of Recorder Levy and Judge Gibson? Does the *Binney* case favor the interests of the skilled worker? The employer? Both?

As you read the next two cases decided by Justice Shaw fifteen years later, see if you can discern his agreement or disagreement with the reasoning in these cases with regard to the importance of the free market and the proper solicitude to be shown to labor. Considering the earliest American labor cases, such as *Commonwealth v. Pullis*, One of America's foremost labor historians, Christopher Tomlins, has stated that "No separation between private and public spheres of action existed in the minds of any of the protagonists . . . " Christopher L. Tomlins, Law, Labor, and Ideology in the Early American Republic 131 (1993). Do you agree? Do you see how a failure to make distinctions between public and private spheres could lead to viewing labor combinations as a conspiracy? Why wasn't that the view of counsel for the cordwainers?

LEMUEL SHAW

C. CHIEF JUSTICE SHAW ON LABOR LAW

FARWELL V. BOSTON AND WORCESTER RAIL ROAD CORP.

Supreme Judicial Court of Massachusetts, 1842.
45 Mass. (4 Metc.) 49.

* * *

The case was submitted to the court on the following facts agreed by the parties: "The plaintiff was employed by the defendants, in 1835, as an engineer, and went at first with the merchandize cars, and afterwards with the passenger cars, and so continued till October 30th 1837, at the wages of two dollars per day; that being the usual wages paid to enginemen, which are higher than the wages paid to a machinist, in which capacity the plaintiff formerly was employed."

"On the 30th of October 1837, the plaintiff * * * ran his engine off at a switch on the road, which had been left in a wrong condition * * * by one Whitcomb, another servant of the defendants, who had been long in their employment, as a switch-man or tender, and had the care of switches on the road, and was a careful and trustworthy servant, in his general character, and as such servant was well known to the plaintiff. By which running off, the plaintiff sustained the injury complained of in his declaration. [Loss of his right hand."]

* * *

C.G. Loring, for the plaintiff. The defendants, having employed the plaintiff to do a specified duty on the road, were bound to keep the road in such a condition that he might do that duty with safety. If the plaintiff had been a stranger, the defendants would have been liable; and he contends that the case is not varied by the fact that both the plaintiff and Whitcomb were the servants of the defendants; because the plaintiff was not the servant of the defendants in the duty or service, the neglect of which occasioned the injury sustained by him. He was employed for a distinct and separate service, and had no joint agency or power with the other servants whose duty it was to keep the road in order; and could not be made responsible to the defendants for its not being kept in order. He could not, by any vigilance or any power that he could exercise, have prevented the accident. His duties and those of Whitcomb were as distinct and independent of each other, as if they had been servants of different masters.

The plaintiff does not put his case on the ground of the defendants' liability to passengers, nor upon the general principle which renders principals liable for the acts of their agents; but on the ground, that a master, by the nature of his contract with a servant, stipulates for the safety of the servant's employment, so far as the master can regulate the matter.

The defence rests upon an alleged general rule, that a master is not liable to his servant for damage caused by the negligence of a fellow servant. But if that be sound, as a general rule, it does not apply here; for Whitcomb and the plaintiff, as has already been stated, were not fellow servants—that is, were not jointly employed for a common purpose.

* * *

No general rule can be laid down, which will apply to all cases of a master's liability to a servant. But it is submitted that a master is liable to one servant for the negligence of another, when they are engaged in distinct employments, though he is not so liable, where two servants are engaged jointly in the same service; because, in the latter case, each servant has some supervision and control of every other. * * *

In case of servants jointly employed in the same business, it may reasonably be inferred that they take the hazard of injuries from each other's negligence; because such hazard is naturally and necessarily incident to such employment; because they have, to a great extent, the means of guarding against such injuries, by the exercise of mutual caution and prudence, while the master has no such means; and because, between persons employed in a joint service, there is a privity of contract, that renders them liable to each other for their carelessness or neglect in the discharge of such service.

It is a well settled general rule, that a servant is not liable to third persons for his neglect of duty. Story on Agency, §§ 308, 309. If that principle applies to this case, so that the plaintiff has no remedy against Whitcomb, it would seem to be a sufficient reason for holding the defendants liable.

It is also a well established rule, that if an agent, without his own default, has incurred loss or damage in transacting the business of the principal, he is entitled to full compensation. Story on Agency, § 339.

Fletcher & Morey, for the defendants. * * * [N]o rule of policy requires that masters shall be liable to one servant for injuries received by him from a fellow servant. On the contrary, policy requires an entirely different rule, especially in the present case. The aim of all the statutes concerning rail roads is to protect passengers; and if this action is maintained, it will establish a principle which will tend to diminish the caution of rail road servants, and thus increase the risk of passengers.

The defendants have been in no fault, in this case, either in the construction of their road, the use of defective engines, or the employment of careless or untrusty servants. So that the question is, whether they are liable to the plaintiff, on an implied contract of indemnity. The contract between the parties to this suit excludes the notion that the defendants are liable for the injury received by the plaintiff. He agreed to run an engine on their road, knowing the state of the road, and also knowing Whitcomb, his character, and the specific duty intrusted to him. The plaintiff therefore assumed the risks of the service which he undertook to perform; and one of those risks was his liability to injury from the carelessness of others who were employed by the defendants in the same service. As a consideration for the increased risk of this service, he received higher wages than when he was employed in a less hazardous business.

* * *

The only cases in which a servant has attempted to recover of a master for another servant's misconduct, are Priestley v. Fowler, 3 Mees. & Welsb. 1, and Murray v. South Carolina Rail Road Company, 1 McMullan 385; and in both cases, it was held that the action could not be maintained. In those cases, it is true that both servants were on the same carriage when the accident happened by which one of them was injured. And the counsel for the present plaintiff has invented a rule of law, in order to escape from the pressure of those decisions. But admitting the distinction, and the rule which he advances, to be sound, the case at bar is not thereby affected. The plaintiff and Whitcomb were not engaged in distinct and separate employments, but in the same service. They both were acting to the same end, although they had different parts to perform.

* * *

SHAW, C.J. This is an action of new impression in our courts, and involves a principle of great importance. It presents a case, where two persons are in the service and employment of one company, whose business it is to construct and maintain a rail road, and to employ their trains of cars to carry persons and merchandize for hire. They are appointed and employed by the same company to perform separate duties and services, all tending to the accomplishment of one and the same purpose—that of the safe and rapid transmission of the trains; and they are paid for their respective services according to the nature of their respective duties, and the labor and skill required for their proper performance. The question is, whether, for damages sustained by one of the persons so employed, by means of the carelessness and negligence of another, the party injured has a remedy against the common employer. It is an argument against such an action, though certainly not a decisive one, that no such action has before been maintained.

It is laid down by Blackstone, that if a servant, by his negligence, does any damage to a stranger, the master shall be answerable for his neglect. * * * 1 Bl.Com. 431. * * * This rule is obviously founded on the great principle of social duty, that every man, in the management of his own affairs, whether by himself or by his agents or servants, shall so conduct them as not to injure another; and if he does not, and another thereby sustains damage, he shall answer for it. * * * But this presupposes that the parties stand to each other in the relation of strangers, between whom there is no privity; and the action, in such case, is an action sounding in tort. * * *

But this does not apply to the case of a servant bringing his action against his own employer to recover damages for an injury arising in the course of that employment, where all such risks and perils as the employer and the servant respectively intend to assume and bear may be regulated by the express or implied contract between them, and which, in contemplation of law, must be presumed to be thus regulated.

The same view seems to have been taken by the learned counsel for the plaintiff in the argument * * *. The claim, therefore, is placed, and must be maintained, if maintained at all, on the ground of contract. As there is no express contract between the parties, applicable to this point, it is placed on the footing of an implied contract of indemnity, arising out of the relation of master and servant. It would be an implied promise, arising from the duty of the master to be responsible to each person employed by him * * * to pay for all damage occasioned by the negligence of every other person employed in the same service. If such a duty were established by law * * * it would be a rule of frequent and familiar occurrence, and its existence and application, with all its qualifications and restrictions, would be settled by judicial precedents. But we are of opinion that no such rule has been established, and the authorities, as far as they go, are opposed to the principle. Priestley v. Fowler, 3 Mees. & Welsb. 1. * * *

The general rule, resulting from considerations as well of justice as of policy, is, that he who engages in the employment of another for the performance of specified duties and services, for compensation, takes upon himself the natural and ordinary risks and perils incident to the performance of such services, and in legal presumption, the compensation is adjusted accordingly. And we are not aware of any principle which should except the perils arising from the carelessness and negligence of those who are in the same employment. These are perils which the servant is as likely to know, and against which he can as effectually guard, as the master. They are perils incident to the service, and which can be as distinctly foreseen and provided for in the rate of compensation as any others. * * *

* * * In considering the rights and obligations arising out of particular relations, it is competent for courts of justice to regard considerations of policy and general convenience, and to draw from them such rules as will, in their practical application, best promote the safety and security of all parties concerned. This is, in truth, the basis on which implied promises are raised, being duties legally inferred from a consideration of what is best adapted to promote the benefit of all persons concerned, under given circumstances. To take the well known and familiar cases, * * * a common carrier, without regard to actual fault or neglect in himself or his servants, is made liable for all losses of goods confided to him for carriage, except those caused by the act of God or of a public enemy, because he can best guard them against all minor dangers, and because, in case of actual loss, it would be extremely difficult for the owner to adduce proof of embezzlement, or other actual fault or neglect on the part of the carrier * * *. The risk is therefore thrown upon the carrier, and he receives, in the form

of payment for the carriage, a premium for the risk which he thus assumes. So of an innkeeper; he can best secure the attendance of honest and faithful servants, and guard his house against thieves. Whereas, if he were responsible only upon proof of actual negligence, he might connive * * * and even participate in the embezzlement of the property of the guests, during the hours of their necessary sleep, and yet it would be difficult, and often impossible, to prove these facts.

The liability of passenger carriers is founded on similar considerations. They are held to the strictest responsibility for care, vigilance and skill, on the part of themselves and all persons employed by them, and they are paid accordingly. The rule is founded on the expediency of throwing the risk upon those who can best guard against it. Story on Bailments, § 590, & seq.

We are of opinion that these considerations apply strongly to the case in question. Where several persons are employed in the conduct of one common enterprise or undertaking, and the safety of each depends much on the care and skill with which each other shall perform his appropriate duty, each is an observer of the conduct of the others, can give notice of any misconduct, incapacity or neglect of duty, and leave the service, if the common employer will not take such precautions, and employ such agents as the safety of the whole party may require. By these means, the safety of each will be much more effectually secured, than could be done by a resort to the common employer for indemnity in case of loss by the negligence of each other. * * *

In applying these principles to the present case, it appears that the plaintiff was employed by the defendants as an engineer, at the rate of wages usually paid in that employment, being a higher rate than the plaintiff had before received as a machinist. It was a voluntary undertaking on his part, with a full knowledge of the risks incident to the employment; and the loss was sustained by means of an ordinary casualty, caused by the negligence of another servant of the company. Under these circumstances, the loss must be deemed to be the result of a pure accident, * * * and * * * it must rest where it first fell, unless the plaintiff has a remedy against the person actually in default; of which we give no opinion.

It was strongly pressed in the argument, that [this rule] could not apply where two or more are employed in different departments of duty, at a distance from each other, and where one can in no degree control or influence the conduct of another. But we think this is founded upon a supposed distinction, on which it would be extremely difficult to establish a practical rule. When the object to be accomplished is one and the same, when the employers are the same, and the several persons employed derive their authority and their compensation from the same source, it would be extremely difficult to distinguish, what constitutes one department and what a distinct department of duty. * * * If it were made to depend upon the nearness or distance of the persons from each other, the question would immediately arise, how near or how distant must they be, to be in the same or different departments. * * *

Besides, it appears to us, that the argument rests upon an assumed principle of responsibility which does not exist. The master, in the case supposed, is not exempt from liability, because the servant has better means of providing for his safety, when he is employed in immediate connexion with those from whose negligence he might suffer; but because the *implied contract* of the master does not extend to indemnify the servant against the negligence of any one but himself; and he is not liable in tort, as for the negligence of his servant, because the person suffering does not stand towards him in the relation of a stranger, but is one whose rights are regulated by contract express or implied. * * *

* * *

In coming to the conclusion that the plaintiff, in the present case, is not entitled to recover, considering it as in some measure a nice question, we would add a caution against any hasty conclusion as to the application of this rule to a case not fully within the same principle. * * * We are far from intending to say that there are no implied warranties and undertakings arising out of the relation of master and servant. Whether, for instance, the employer would be responsible to an engineer for a loss arising from a defective or ill-constructed steam engine: Whether this would depend upon an implied warranty of its goodness and sufficiency, or upon the fact of wilful misconduct, or gross negligence on the part of the employer * * * are questions on which we give no opinion. In the present case, the claim of the plaintiff is not put on the ground that the defendants did not furnish a sufficient engine, a proper rail road track, a well constructed switch, and a person of suitable skill and experience to attend it; the gravamen of the complaint is, that that person was chargeable with negligence in not changing the switch * * *. Upon this question, supposing the accident to have occurred, and the loss to have been caused, by the negligence of the person employed to attend to and change the switch, in his not doing so in the particular case, the court are of opinion that it is a loss for which the defendants are not liable, and that the action cannot be maintained.

Plaintiff nonsuit.

NOTES AND QUESTIONS

1. Note that as the plaintiff's attorney begins his argument he concedes that where two servants are in the *same* line of work for a common employer the employer is *not* liable for the damage caused one servant by the

other. Why this concession? Why doesn't the plaintiff's attorney argue that the general rule of *respondeat superior* should apply in this situation?

2. Does Judge Shaw view this as a case of torts? What kind of a case is it, according to him? Is Shaw's view of the situation unprecedented? Can you make any comparisons between Shaw's analysis of this case and the case of the Sheriff who let his prisoner escape, Patten v. Halsted, supra, Chapter Three?

3. Judge Shaw says that considerations of "justice" lead him to conclude that fellow-servants such as Farwell and Whitcomb should not recover from their employers for each other's negligence. Why does Shaw believe that such a result is "just"? What does he understand the concept "justice" to mean? Shaw is not content to let his holding stand on considerations of "justice", however, but suggests also that the "policy" of protecting servants and passengers will best be served by his decision. How is that? And how does Judge Shaw deal with the plaintiff's argument that whatever the policy of cases like Priestley v. Fowler (the English case that established the fellow-servant rule), it is difficult to apply that policy to a situation where the servants are "in different departments of duty". Are you satisfied with Shaw's reasons for refusing to make this distinction? For a penetrating study of Priestley v. Fowler, see Michael Ashley Stein, "*Priestley v. Fowler* (1837) and the Emerging Tort of Negligence," 44 B.C.L.Rev. 689 (2003).

4. Would you say that the opinion in *Farwell* is hostile to workers? Does Shaw suggest any circumstances under which the employer might be liable for the negligence of a fellow-servant? Roscoe Pound discusses Justice Shaw and the *Farwell* case in The Formative Era of American Law 86–87 (1938). Part of the purpose of Pound's book seems to be to refute a Marxist interpretation of the law. While he concedes that the *Farwell* decision might have sprung from the "pressure of new demands, problems created by the development of transportation, the effects of inventions, and the rise of industry * * * and * * * trade", this was *not* a reflection of the "Marxian class struggle" in the law. Id., at 86. The Marxists, suggested Pound, saw *Farwell's* reception of the English fellow-servant rule as "an arbitrary exception to a rule of law which expressed a fundamental and universal idea of justice". Here Pound was referring to the general doctrine of *respondeat superior,* from which *Farwell* was said by the Marxists to have departed. According to Pound, however, *Farwell* did not represent an "arbitrary departure", as the doctrine of *respondeat superior* was itself "an exception to a then generally received doctrine that liability must flow from fault." Shaw in *Farwell,* said Pound, merely "refused to extend further" this exception to the "no liability without fault" doctrine. Do you see the proposal for fellow-servant liability as a proposal to impose liability where there is no "fault"? What is meant by "fault" here? Furthermore, is Pound correct about the existence of a general doctrine of "no liability without fault?" Do the early trespass and nuisance cases we studied in Chapter Three suggest the existence of such a doctrine?

5. The *Farwell* case outcome (implementation of the fellow-servant rule) obviously favored the defendant, the railroad. We have seen similar pro-

tection of America's infant industries in Chapter Three, in the materials on nuisance and negligence. For still another instance of the *respondeat superior* doctrine's failure to result in relief for negligence see Carey v. Berkshire Railroad Co., 55 Mass. (1 Cush.) 475 (1848). Employees of the railroad had negligently caused the deaths of the husband of one of the plaintiffs and the eleven-year-old son of another. Following a line of reasoning in English cases, the court appears to have held that the right to sue for tortious injury dies with the person injured, and neither plaintiff was allowed to recover. Two years prior to the case, "Lord Campbell's Act," 9 and 10 Vict. ch. 93, had provided such a cause of action in England, allowing the executor or administrator of persons killed by torts to bring actions for wrongful death for the benefit of the deceased's family. Eight years before the case, the Massachusetts legislature itself had provided for such an action in the case of *passengers* who lost their lives through the negligence of railroads, steamboats, or stagecoach proprietors or their agents, although such relief was limited to five thousand dollars. Massachusetts Statutes of 1840, ch. 80. The *Carey* court held that if an action for wrongful death in the circumstances of the case "would be expedient for us, it is for the legislature to make it." Is this a convincing argument? Why not extend the policy of the 1840 Massachusetts statute through the common law? Carey v. Berkshire R.R. was the "first distinct pronouncement by an American court that no cause of action for wrongful death exists at common law." Malone, The Genesis of Wrongful Death, 17 Stan.L.Rev. 1043, 1067 (1965). The prestige of the Massachusetts court led to its doctrine being widely accepted, but in the rest of the nineteenth century the states passed legislation permitting wrongful death claims of the type asserted in *Carey*. By 1883, in fact, Massachusetts appears to have weakened the rule in the *Farwell* case by passing a statute that gave relief to the families of railroad workers killed in their employment.

6. Does the holding of the *Carey* case, and the fellow-servant doctrine, which gained widespread American acceptance in the nineteenth century, reflect a general hostility on the part of the American common law to workers? In another line of cases, American unskilled laborers who had contracted to work for a certain contractual term (e.g. one year), were not allowed to recover for the value of work done (in *quantum meruit*) if they quit at any time before their terms expired. See, e.g. Stark v. Parker, 19 Mass. (2 Pick.) 267, but see Britton v. Turner, 6 N.H. (1st ser.) 481 (1834). In cases where contractors had failed to build houses "strictly according to contract, but still valuable and capable of being advantageously used or profitably rented," however, they were generally permitted to recover for the value of their performance, with the contract price as a ceiling, and with a deduction for any damages suffered by virtue of their failure to complete their contracts. See, e.g. Hayward v. Leonard, 24 Mass. (7 Pick.) 181 (1828). Why the difference in treatment? Morton Horwitz suggests that this is "an important example of class bias," and that nineteenth century common law doctrines "allowed judges to pick and choose among those groups in the population that would be its beneficiaries." The Transformation of American Law 1780–1860 188 (1977). Horwitz's conclusion on this point is sharply challenged in Peter

Karstein, " 'Bottomed on Justice': A Reappraisal of Critical Legal Studies Scholarship Concerning Breaches of Labor Contracts by Quitting or Firing in Britain and the U.S., 1630–1880," 34 Am. J.Leg.Hist. 213 (1990). For another provocative, and this time avowedly Marxist explanation for the development of the American common law of labor contracts, see Jay M. Feinman, "The Development of the Employment at Will Rule," 20 American Journal of Legal History 118 (1976). For critical comment on and further development of Feinman's work, see Mayer G. Freed and Daniel D. Polsby, "The Doubtful Provenance of 'Wood's Rule' Revisited," 22 Ariz.St.L.J. 551 (1990), and Feinman, "The Development of the Employment–at–Will Rule Revisited," 23 Ariz.St.L.J. 733 (1991). Does Shaw's behavior as a judge support the notion that American law favored capitalists over laborers? Consider Shaw's opinion in the next case.

COMMONWEALTH V. HUNT

Supreme Judicial Court of Massachusetts, 1842.
45 Mass. (4 Metc.) 111.

This was an indictment against the defendants, (seven in number,) for a conspiracy. The first count alleged that the defendants * * * "on the first Monday of September 1840, at Boston, being workmen and journeymen in the art and manual occupation of bootmakers, unlawfully, perniciously and deceitfully designing and intending to continue, keep up, form, and unite themselves into an unlawful club, society and combination * * * and thereby govern themselves and other workmen in said art, and unlawfully and unjustly to extort great sums of money by means thereof, did * * * unjustly and corruptly combine, confederate and agree together, * * * that none of them would work for any master or person * * * who should employ any workman or journeyman * * * who was not a member of said club, society or combination, after notice given him to discharge such workman from the employ of such master; to the great damage and oppression, not only of their said masters employing them in said art and occupation, but also of divers other workmen and journeymen * * * to the evil example of all others in like case offending, and against the peace and dignity of the Commonwealth."

The second count charged that the defendants " * * * did compel one Isaac B. Wait, a master cordwainer in said Boston, to turn out of his employ one Jeremiah Horne, a journeyman boot-maker, because said Horne would not pay a sum of money to said society for an alleged penalty of some of [its] unjust rules, orders and by-laws."

The third count averred that the defendants " * * * [did] unlawfully and indirectly prevent him, the said Horne, from following his said art, occupation, trade and business, and did greatly impoverish him."

* * *

The defendants were found guilty, at the October term, 1840, of the municipal court, and thereupon several exceptions were alleged by them to the ruling of the judge at the trial. * * * The defendants' counsel contended that the indictment did not set forth any agreement to do a criminal act, or to do any lawful act by criminal means; and that the agreements, therein set forth, did not constitute a conspiracy indictable by any law of this Commonwealth; and they moved the court so to instruct the jury: But the judge refused so to do, and instructed the jury that the indictment against the defendants did, in his opinion, describe a confederacy among the defendants to do an unlawful act, and to effect the same by unlawful means * * *.

* * *

Rantoul, for the defendants. As we have no statute concerning conspiracy, the facts alleged in the indictment constitute an offence, if any, at common law. But the English common law of conspiracy is not in force in this State. * * * So much only of the common law has been adopted, as is applicable to our situation, excluding "the artificial refinements and distinctions incident to the property of a great commercial people; the laws of revenue and police; such especially as are enforced by penalties." 1 Bl.Com. 107, & seq. 1 Tucker's Black.Appx. 406. * * * The English law, as to acts in restraint of trade, is generally local in its nature, and not suited to our condition. It has never been adopted here, and the colonies are not named in the statutes on that subject which have been passed in England since they were settled. Van Ness v. Pacard, 2 Pet. 144. * * * [T]he innumerable statutes of laborers, and the statutes against seducing artisans, & c. illustrate this point. * * *

The original of the law of conspiracy is in St. Edw. I., (A.D.1304) and includes in its definition only false and malicious indictments. 2 Inst. 561, 562. * * *

The next stage of the law of conspiracy appears in the early editions of 1 Hawk. c. 72, § 2: "That all confederacies wrongfully to prejudice a third person are criminal at common law; as a confederacy by indirect means to impoverish a third person, or falsely and maliciously to charge a man with being the reputed father of a bastard child * * *." By "indirect means," unlawful means are meant.

The case of The King v. Journeymen Tailors, 8 Mod. 10 [K.B.1721], was decided after Hawkins's work was published, and is not a part of the law laid down by him, in his first editions. In that case, it was held that a conspiracy among workmen, to refuse to work under certain wages, is an indictable offence. This case, if correctly reported, introduced new law, unless it was decided on the statutes of laborers. * * * The doctrine of that case, therefore, is not a part of the law adopted in this State. It was not the doctrine of the common law, when our ancestors came hither, and is not suited to our condition.

* * *

Probably the indictment, in that case, was sustained on the statutes of laborers. Though the old precedents of indictments are *contra pacem* only, yet that is because a conspiracy to do acts contrary to those statutes is punishable at common law, in England. * * *

The statutes of laborers were blind struggles of the feudal nobles to avert from themselves the effects of great national calamities. * * * In the famine of 1315, and the plague of 1316, parliament vainly strove to alleviate the universal distress, by fixing a legal price for provisions. Yet the scarcity increased, so that the king, going to St. Albans, "had much ado to get victuals to sustain his family." 1 Parl.Hist. 152. And some months later, mothers ate their children. Monk of Malmsb. 166. * * * From the same motives, and with no better success, the plague of 1349 was followed by that remarkable statute *de servientibus,* from which have been derived all subsequent statutes of laborers. * * * The deaths in London were mostly of the laboring classes * * *. King Edward had just been debasing his coin. * * * From these causes, the wages of labor rose rapidly, and the law undertook to fix them. * * *

The case in 8 Mod. 10, was about the time of the bursting of the south sea bubble, when laborers sought to withstand the operation of the state of affairs then existing.

* * *

In most of the United States, conspiracies, that have been held indictable at common law, are all for acts that are indictable, immoral, or forbidden by statute. * * *

In New York and Massachusetts, the cases have gone further; and in Commonwealth v. Judd, 2 Mass. 337, Parsons, C.J. says a conspiracy is "the unlawful act for unlawful purposes." And all the Massachusetts cases come within this definition. * * *

A conspiracy to commit a mere civil injury to an individual is not indictable. * * * Yet nothing more is properly alleged against the present defendants.

A conspiracy to raise wages would not be indictable in England, if it were not unlawful for an individual to attempt to raise his wages. And the indictment, in the case at bar, is bad, because each of the defendants had a right to do that which is charged against them jointly.

* * *

Austin, (Attorney General,) for the Commonwealth. The common law doctrine of conspiracy is part of the law of this Commonwealth. It has been recognized by the legislature, in Rev.Sts. c. 82, § 28, and c. 86, § 10; and was long since enforced by this court. * * *

The charge against the defendants is, in effect, an attempt to monopolize by them certain labor, on their own terms, and to prevent others from obtaining or giving employment. This is an indictable offence. Rex. v. Bykerdike, 1 M. & Rob. 179. 3 Chit.Crim.Law, 1138, & seq. * * *

The case in 8 Mod. 10 * * * shows the fact, that defendants were convicted of an offence like that with which the present defendants are charged * * *.

The old statutes of laborers, which have been referred to, do not at all affect the common law doctrine. No reference is made to them in the English books of criminal law, or in the reports of the cases of conspiracy by workmen.

A conspiracy to raise wages is indictable in England, not because it is unlawful for an individual to attempt to raise his wages—as the defendants' counsel suggests—but because a combination for that purpose is criminal and punishable. * * *

* * *

It is not necessary, in order to render a conspiracy indictable, that the means, devised to carry it into effect, should be acts that are indictable. It is sufficient if they are unlawful. * * *

The People v. Fisher, 14 Wend. [9], is a strong authority in support of the present indictment. It is true that it was under the revised statutes of New York, and proceeded on the ground that the conspiracy was "injurious to trade or commerce." But the question, what is injurious to trade or commerce, is to be determined by the common law.

SHAW, C.J. * * *

We have no doubt, that by the operation of the constitution of this Commonwealth, the general rules of the common law, making conspiracy an indictable offence, are in force here * * *. * * * Still, it is proper in this connexion to remark, that although the common law in regard to conspiracy in this Commonwealth is in force, yet it will not necessarily follow that every indictment at common law for this offence is a precedent for a similar indictment in this State. The general rule of the common law is, that it is a criminal and indictable offence, for two or more to confederate and combine together, by concerted means, to do that which is unlawful or criminal, to the injury of the public, or portions or classes of the community, or even to the rights of an individual. This rule of law may be equally in force as a rule of the common law, in England, and in this

Commonwealth; and yet it must depend upon the local laws of each country to determine, whether the purpose to be accomplished by the combination, or the concerted means of accomplishing it, be unlawful or criminal in the respective countries. All those laws of the parent country, whether rules of the common law, or early English statutes, which were made for the purpose of regulating the wages of laborers, the settlement of paupers, and making it penal for any one to use a trade or handicraft to which he had not served a full apprenticeship—not being adapted to the circumstances of our colonial condition—were not adopted, used or approved, and therefore [are not in force here.] * * * The King v. Journeymen Tailors of Cambridge, 8 Mod. 10, for instance, is commonly cited as an authority for an indictment at common law, and a conviction of journeymen mechanics of a conspiracy to raise their wages. It was there held, that the indictment need not conclude *contra formam statuti,* because the gist of the offence was the conspiracy, which was an offence at common law. At the same time it was conceded, that the unlawful object to be accomplished was the raising of wages above the rate fixed by a general act of parliament. It was therefore a conspiracy to violate a general statute law * * * and thus the object to be accomplished by the conspiracy was unlawful, if not criminal.

* * *

Let us, then, first consider how the subject of criminal conspiracy is treated by elementary writers. The position cited by Chitty from Hawkins, by way of summing up the result of the cases, is this: "In a word, all confederacies wrongfully to prejudice another are misdemeanors at common law, whether the intention is to injure his property, his person, or his character." And Chitty adds, that "the object of conspiracy is not confined to an immediate wrong to individuals; it may be to injure public trade, to affect public health, to violate public policy, to insult public justice, or to do any act in itself illegal." 3 Chit.Crim.Law, 1139.

* * *

From these views * * * it appears to us to follow, as a necessary legal conclusion, that when the criminality of a conspiracy consists in an unlawful agreement of two or more persons to compass or promote some criminal or illegal purpose, that purpose must be fully and clearly stated in the indictment; and if the criminality of the offence, which is intended to be charged, consists in the agreement to compass or promote some purpose, not of itself criminal or unlawful, by the use of fraud, force, falsehood, or other criminal or unlawful means, such intended use of fraud, force, falsehood, or other criminal or unlawful means, must be set out in the indictment. * * *

In the case of a conspiracy to induce a person to marry a pauper, in order to change the burden of her support from one parish to another, it was held by Buller, J. that, as the marriage itself was not unlawful, some violence, fraud or falsehood, or some artful or sinister contrivance must be averred, as the means intended to be employed to effect the marriage, in order to make the agreement indictable as a conspiracy. Rex. v. Fowler, 2 Russell on Crimes, (1st ed.) 1812, S.C. 1 East P.C. 461.

* * *

With these general views of the law, it becomes necessary to consider the circumstances of the present case * * *. * * *

[At the trial,] The counsel for the defendants contended, and requested the court to instruct the jury, that the indictment did not set forth any agreement to do a criminal act, or to do any lawful act by any specified criminal means, and that the agreements therein set forth did not constitute a conspiracy indictable by any law of this Commonwealth. But the judge refused so to do * * *.

We are here carefully to distinguish between the confederacy set forth in the indictment, and the confederacy or association contained in the constitution of the Boston Journeymen Bootmakers' Society, as stated in the little printed book, which was admitted as evidence on the trial. Because, though it was thus admitted as evidence, it would not warrant a conviction for any thing not stated in the indictment. It was proof, as far as it went to support the averments in the indictment. If it contained any criminal matter not set forth in the indictment, it is of no avail. * * *

* * *

Stripped * * * of * * * introductory recitals and alleged injurious consequences, and of the qualifying epithets attached to the facts, the averment [in the indictment] is this; that the defendants and others formed themselves into a society, and agreed not to work for any person, who should employ any journeyman or other person, not a member of such society, after notice given him to discharge such workman.

The manifest intent of the association is, to induce all those engaged in the same occupation to become members of it. Such a purpose is not unlawful. It would give them a power which might be exerted for useful and honorable purposes, or for dangerous and pernicious ones. If the latter were the real and actual object, and susceptible of proof, it should have been specially charged. Such an association might be used to afford each other assistance in times of poverty, sickness and distress; or to raise their intellectual, moral and social condition; or to make improvement in their art; or for other proper purposes. Or the association might be designed for purposes of oppression and injustice. But in order to charge all those, who become members of an association, with the guilt of a criminal conspiracy, it must be averred and proved that the actual, if not the avowed object of the association, was criminal. * * *

Nor can we perceive that the objects of this association whatever they may have been, were to be attained by criminal means. The means which they proposed to employ * * * were, that they would not work for a person, who, after due notice, should employ a journeyman not a member of their society. Supposing the object of the association to be laudable and lawful, or at least not unlawful, are these means criminal? The case supposes that these persons are not bound by contract, but free to work for whom they please, or not to work, if they so prefer. In this state of things, we cannot perceive, that it is criminal for men to agree together to exercise their own acknowledged rights, in such a manner as best to subserve their own interests. One way to test this is, to consider the effect of such an agreement, where the object of the association is acknowledged on all hands to be a laudable one. Suppose a class of workmen, impressed with the manifold evils of intemperance, should agree with each other not to work in a shop in which ardent spirit was furnished, or not to work in a shop with any one who used it, or not to work for an employer, who should, after notice, employ a journeyman who habitually used it. The consequences might be the same. A workman, who, should still persist in the use of ardent spirit, would find it more difficult to get employment; a master employing such an one might, at times, experience inconvenience in his work, in losing the services of a skillful but intemperate workman. Still it seems to us, that as the object would be lawful, and the means not unlawful, such an agreement could not be pronounced a criminal conspiracy.

* * * If a large number of men, engaged for a certain time, should combine together to violate their contract, and quit their employment together, it would present a very different question. Suppose a farmer, employing a large number of men, engaged for the year, at fair monthly wages, and suppose that just at the moment that his crops were ready to harvest, they should all combine to quit his service, unless he would advance their wages, at a time when other laborers could not be obtained. It would surely be a conspiracy to do an unlawful act, though of such a character, that if done by an individual, it would lay the foundation of a civil action only, and not of a criminal prosecution. * * *

The second count * * * alleges that the defendants * * * did assemble, conspire, confederate and agree together, not to work for any master or person who should employ any workman not being a member of a certain club, society or combination, called the Boston Journeymen Bootmaker's Society, or who should break any of their by-laws [and to] compel one Isaac B. Wait, a master cordwainer, to turn out of his employ one Jeremiah Horne * * *. So far as the averment of a conspiracy is concerned, all the remarks made in reference to the first count are equally applicable to this. * * * It was an agreement, as to the manner in which they would exercise an acknowledged right to contract with others for their labor. It does not aver a conspiracy or even an intention to raise their wages; and it appears by the bill of exceptions, that the case was not put upon the footing of a conspiracy to raise their wages. Such an agreement, as set forth in this count, would be perfectly justifiable under the recent English statute, by which this subject is regulated. * * *

As to the latter part of this count, which avers that by means of said conspiracy, the defendants did compel one Wait to turn out of his employ one Jeremiah Horne * * *; if this is to be considered as a substantive charge, it would depend altogether upon the force of the word "compel," which may be used in the sense of coercion, or duress, by force or fraud. * * * If, for instance, the indictment had averred a conspiracy, by the defendants, to compel Wait to turn Horne out of his employment, and to accomplish that object by the use of force or fraud, it would have been a very different case; especially if it might be fairly construed, as perhaps in that case it might have been, that Wait was under obligation, by contract, for an unexpired term of time, to employ and pay Horne. * * * To mark the difference between the case of a journeyman or a servant and master, mutually bound by contract, and the same parties when free to engage anew, I should have before cited the case of the Boston Glass Co. v. Binney, 4 Pick. 425. In that case, it was held actionable to entice another person's hired servant to quit his employment, during the time for which he was engaged; but not actionable to treat with such hired servant, whilst actually hired and employed by another, to leave his service, and engage in the employment of the person making the proposal, when the term for which he is engaged shall expire. It acknowledges the established principle, that every free man, whether skilled laborer, mechanic, farmer or domestic servant, may work or not work, or work or refuse to work with any company or individual, at his own option, except so far as he is bound by contract. But whatever might be the force of the word "compel," unexplained by its connexion, it is disarmed and rendered harmless by the precise statement of the means, by which such compulsion was to be effected. It was the agreement not to work for him, by which they compelled Wait to decline employing Horne longer. * * *

* * *

If the fact of depriving Jeremiah Horne of the profits of his business, by whatever means it might be done, would be unlawful and criminal, a combination to compass that object would be an unlawful conspiracy, and it would be unnecessary to state the means. * * *

Suppose a baker in a small village had the exclusive custom of his neighborhood, and was making large profits by the sale of his bread. Supposing a number of those neighbors, believing the price of his bread too high, should propose to him to reduce his prices, or if he did not, that they would introduce another baker; and on his refusal, such other baker should, under their encouragement, set up a rival establishment, and sell his bread at lower prices; the effect would be to diminish the profit of the former baker, and to the same extent to impoverish him. And it might be said and proved, that the purpose of the associates was to diminish his profits, and thus impoverish him, though the ultimate and laudable object of the combination was to reduce the cost of bread to themselves and their neighbors. The same thing may be said of all competition in every branch of trade and industry; and yet it is through that competition, that the best interests of trade and industry are promoted. It is scarcely necessary to allude to the familiar instances of opposition lines of conveyance, rival hotels, and the thousand other instances, where each strives to gain custom to himself, by ingenious improvements, by increased industry, and by all the means by which he may lessen the price of commodities, and thereby diminish the profits of others.

We think, therefore, that associations may be entered into, the object of which is to adopt measures that may have a tendency to impoverish another, that is, to diminish his gains and profits, and yet so far from being criminal or unlawful, the object may be highly meritorious and public spirited. The legality of such an association will therefore depend upon the means to be used for its accomplishment. If it is to be carried into effect by fair or honorable and lawful means, it is, to say the least, innocent; if by falsehood or force, it may be stamped with the character of conspiracy. It follows as a necessary consequence, that if criminal and indictable, it is so by reason of the criminal means intended to be employed for its accomplishment; and as a further legal consequence, that as the criminality will depend on the means, those means must be stated in the indictment. * * *

* * *

One case was cited, which was supposed to be much in point, and which is certainly deserving of great respect. The People v. Fisher, 14 Wend. 1. But it is obvious, that this decision was founded on the construction of the revised statutes of New York, by which this matter of conspiracy is now regulated. It was a conspiracy by journeymen to raise their wages, and it was decided to be a violation of the statutes, making it criminal to commit any act injurious to trade or commerce. It has, therefore, an indirect application only to the present case.

* * *

NOTES AND QUESTIONS

1. Does Shaw's opinion in this case seem consistent with his opinion in *Farwell*? Roscoe Pound suggested that the "Marxist economic determinists"

have a difficult time reconciling the decision in *Farwell* with the decision in Commonwealth v. Hunt, and that they are forced to conclude that the latter decision was "dictated" by "fear of a radical movement in politics." They reached such a conclusion, said Pound, because "It seems to be impossible for a Marxian economic determinist to comprehend an honest man." Formative Era of American Law, at 88. What do you suppose Pound meant by that? Pound's attack seems aimed principally at Yale's Professor Walter Nelles. See Nelles, "Commonwealth v. Hunt," 32 Col.L.Rev. 1128 (1932), and, for Nelles's views on the economic determinants of the *Philadelphia Cordwainers'* case, see "The First American Labor Case", 41 Yale L.J. 165 (1931).

2. Note that Robert Rantoul is the counsel for the defendants. Given the excerpt from his oration, supra, Chapter Three, would you have expected to see him appearing as defense counsel here? Is the argument he advances consistent with his oration? Note that among the cases Rantoul cites in support of his argument that the English common law of conspiracy is not in force in Massachusetts is Story's opinion in Van Ness v. Pacard, supra, Chapter Three. What's the connection? Why does Rantoul find it necessary to tell the court that during the plague of 1316, following the famine of 1315, "mothers ate their children?" What kind of a legal authority is "Monk of Malmsb.?"

3. Does the Attorney General, in his argument in support of the indictment, suggest that it would have been unlawful for the defendants, acting individually, to seek to raise their wages? If not, how does he explain why it becomes unlawful when organized groups seek to raise their wages? Would Recorder Levy and Justice Gibson have agreed? Did Shaw agree with the assertion that the doing of a lawful act, attempting to raise wages, automatically becomes a conspiracy when wage raises are sought, in concert, by groups?

4. Shaw holds that the "manifest intent" of the Journeymen bootmakers' association "is to induce all those engaged in the same occupation to become members of it. Such a purpose is not unlawful." Why not? Does Shaw cite any authority to support this proposition? Is Shaw's holding consistent with the case of the Philadelphia Cordwainers? Shaw says that the association might be used for "useful and honorable purposes, or for dangerous and pernicious ones," but that unless there was proof offered that the association was formed for bad purposes, or that illegal acts were taken to accomplish legal aims, there could be no finding of conspiracy. Commonwealth v. Hunt is Shaw's "best known and most widely praised opinion," and is "the Magna Charta of American trade unionism, for it removed the stigma of criminality from labor organizations." Leonard W. Levy, The Law of the Commonwealth and Chief Justice Shaw 183 (1957). Does Shaw's holding cover the case of employees *under contract* who go out on strike? Why or why not? When would employees be regarded by Shaw as under contract? Does the *Farwell* case give you any guidance here?

5. Whether or not the "Marxist economic determinists" were right about Shaw, the *Farwell* case does seem to be anti-labor, and the *Hunt* case seems pro-labor. Pound and the Marxists both found it necessary to "explain" this seeming inconsistency, and they have not been alone. In his biography of

Chief Justice Shaw, The Law of the Commonwealth and Chief Justice Shaw (1957), Leonard Levy advances several reasons for the decision in Commonwealth v. Hunt. First, says Levy, Shaw might have been seeking to respond to the movement for codification of the common law. Id., at 196. Second, notes Levy, quoting Pound, Shaw may have been simply following "received professional ideals of the social order in America." Id., at 202. And third, as the most "plausible if not a watertight explanation of Commonwealth v. Hunt", Levy suggests that Shaw may simply have believed that "combinations, whether by entrepreneurs or workers," were "inherent in a free, competitive society," and would contribute toward "social gain." Id., at 203. How would you argue in support of or against each of these three propositions? Do you see any links between *Charles River Bridge* and Commonwealth v. Hunt? For the provocative suggestion that *Hunt* and *Farwell* can be reconciled and understood as Shaw's attempt to synthesize Republicanism with Liberalism, as the meaning of virtue changed in America, see Alfred S. Konefsky, " 'As Best to Subserve Their Own Interests': Lemuel Shaw, Labor Conspiracy, and Fellow Servants," 7 Law & History Review 219 (1989). For the development of unions that followed see, e.g. Christopher L. Tomlins, The State and the Unions: Labor Relations, Law and the Organized Labor Movement in America, 1880–1960 (1985). Christopher Tomlins concluded that the result in *Commonwealth v. Hunt*, and cases like it in other jurisdictions, was "some indication of a consensus on the acceptability of a degree of social fragmentation--the decline of a communitarian ideal and recognition instead of society as a thing of diverse interests pursued at cross-purposes. Journeymen pursuing their interests in association, it appeared, could be acceptable to such a society as long as they were respectful of the competing interests of others." Christopher L. Tomlins, Law, Labor, and Ideology in the Early American Republic 130 (1993). Do you agree? Would you regard this movement in labor law as progress? While Tomlins gives some credit to Justice Shaw with regard to his sincerity in believing the law of contract could be a tool in securing economic welfare for the worker, he is skeptical about the entire legal system's commitment to freedom in the workplace. Tomlins suggests that "the law of the early republic established not self-constituted freedom but an asymmetrical realm of 'masters' and 'servants,' a realm in which the subjection of the employee was the sign of employment, a sign rendered in official discourse not only socially acceptable but in fact utterly commonplace--a fact of working life." Id., at 219. As you read the rest of the materials in the course regarding labor law, see if you believe this is a statement that has some validity for most, if not all of American history.

6. We will soon see whether Shaw's sanguine views on labor unions prevailed in the late nineteenth century, but before we are able to do that, we must explore the late-nineteenth century consequences of the view that "combinations * * * of entrepreneurs" were "inherent in a free competitive society," and determine whether such combinations were thought to have contributed to "social gain."

D. THE TRUSTS AND THE SHERMAN ACT (1890)

1. INTRODUCTION

The rhythm of American life changed profoundly after the Civil War. The American economy continued to grow; it was during these years that new national wealth transformed America into a significant political and economic world power. Yet American society between 1865 and 1915 exhibited stark contrasts. A few men, like John D. Rockefeller, grew almost unspeakably rich, and only after the civil war can we identify a "class" of millionaires. Many more men and women experienced economic uncertainty and powerlessness as part of a vast new industrial work force. At the same time, a growing minority were entering the ranks of white-collar respectability. This new middle class, comprised of legions of clerks, business managers, technicians, scientific experts, educators, doctors, and lawyers were the product of an urban industrial society, and upon them that society eventually came to depend.

The American Civil War may well have been the most cataclysmic event in American history, and it fundamentally altered the shape and direction of society. Years of waging war steeled the American spirit, and conditioned many to believe that immense sacrifice was a normal and necessary feature of life. This dark world view was congenial to the growth of scientific Darwinism in America after the war, and acceptance of its principles of "evolution" and "survival of the fittest." At the same time, many influential business and political figures subscribed to "social Darwinism," and its similar tenets, among which was the virtual relegation of government to bystander status in the economy. This perspective is also seen in the new pragmatism of American thought, where the result often justified the means, and in the naturalism and realism of American literature and art. The war left in its wake, then, a coldness to humanistic idealism that posed the most serious challenge yet to American principles of freedom, justice and equality.

The Civil War also left a legacy of economic organization and efficiency. Waging "total war" placed novel demands on government, in both the North and South. Managing resources, disciplining the military and civilian populations, coordinating industry, and harnessing the new technology and the transportation network to the war effort were achievements on an unparalled scale, requiring new sophistication in administration and consolidation. Ulysses S. Grant had led the North to victory not because of his skills as a tactician (he lost most of his battles), but because of his superior organizational ability and his brutal efficiency. The success of the North's military and civilian effort also resulted in the clear supremacy of the Federal Government. The Era of Reconstruction which followed marked the emergence of a truly *national* government capable of promulgating a unified *national* policy. The completed shift of the political centers of gravity, from the local to the state and national, mirrored the growing consolidation of many sectors of society after the war. The new modes of organization and operation appeared in areas as diverse as philanthropy and business. Doing-good, for example, increasingly became the domain of large-scale social and governmental organizations. The corporate philanthropic foundation, the modern hospital, the state and federal departments and bureaus of health and welfare were post-war creations. The trend toward vertical integration in industry, most notable in oil and beef processing, was applauded by many businessmen and social Darwinists as an advance over the chaos and unregulated competition of the free market. Stressing control, rationalization, consolidation and planning, these new large-scale industries, like government, exercised a truly national influence.

By about 1890, these massive changes were attended by a kind of crisis of national will. While power continued to gravitate away from town and county, there existed an uncertainty within the central government as to how to exercise national or state power. This malaise was in part the result of the awesomeness of problems that now were perceived as interconnected and national in scope, problems thought not to be susceptible to traditional solutions. The difficulties were also the result of deeper causes. Indeed, Americans seemed unsure about which of two models of civic culture should be embraced: that of the pre-war years, predominantly preindustrial and emphasizing limited government and personal liberty, or that of the Civil War and Reconstruction Eras which saw the expansion of central power and the emphasis on the rights of groups. There was no clear popular consensus that could guide government. Legislators and judges were whipsawed between conflicting demands produced as a result of growing class divisions. Huge corporations with almost limitless capital were expanding and gobbling up competition in quest of greater profits, and corporate minions applied legal and illegal pressures to government officials. At the same time, a growing proletariat, swelling the cities, working the factories, and chafing under the often harsh restraints of the new industrialism seemed to pose a potential threat to order, stability and prosperity. Squeezed between capital and labor was the voluble middle class, intent on preserving its prosperity and mobility, and eager to accentuate its power and influence. Also expressing heightened concern were American farmers, whose ranks still included 42% of the gainfully employed, and who found themselves suffering from lower prices offered by newly consolidated large-scale processors of raw materials, like the "cattle trust," the "linseed oil" and the "cotton oil trusts," and the higher costs of consumer goods and farming needs charged by such organizations as the "Jute Bag Trust," "the Standard Oil Trust", and the "Sugar Trust." Many of these farmers formed themselves into "Granges," local cooperatives and organizations. They, too, agitated for governmental reforms, not only to control the trusts, but also to reform the tax and transportation systems.

The so-called "Populist Revolt," coming out of the agrarian West and South, was directed at railroads, large corporate middlemen, and a government that failed to act. The growth of the Knights of Labor in 1878, the first attempt at establishing a national trade union, demonstrated the desire of workers to gain more control over their lives. The growth of the new professional organizations, such as the American Bar Association and the National Education Association, signaled the stirrings of the new "middle" class of experts who, like the laborers and the farmers, were in the process of organizing for national action. Even Businessmen moved to promote their interests, when, in 1895, they founded the National Association of Manufacturers.

Intellectually, Americans during this decade were breaking the grip of a post-war psychology. In the words of Eric Goldman, they were bursting the "steel chain of ideas" where laissez-faire thinking, buttressed by social Darwinism, tended to resist the expansion of regulatory government. Robert Wiebe has described these turn-of-the-century years as a "search for order." In this atmosphere, in 1889 and 1890, the United States Congress debated proposals for some national regulation of the economy, which debates we consider next.

The now-classic account of developments in American society in the last third of the nineteenth century is Robert Wiebe's, *The Search for Order* (1968). For an appreciation of the continuing relevance of Wiebe's account (his book is still in print more than forty years after it was first published) and for some discussion of Wiebe, historiography, and political science, see Kenneth Cmiel, "In retrospect: Destiny and Amnesia: The Vision of Modernity in Robert Wiebe's *The Search for Order*," 21 Reviews in American History 352 (1993).

2. THE PASSAGE OF THE SHERMAN ACT (1890)

ALBERT H. WALKER, HISTORY OF THE SHERMAN LAW OF THE UNITED STATES OF AMERICA

1–46 (1910).

[1. THE SHERMAN BILL]

John Sherman during his life passed through a career of public service, which in continuous length and great value has never been equalled by any other American. That career began when he took the oath of office as a member of Congress in December, 1855, and it continued without any interruption until he resigned the office of Secretary of State forty-three years later * * *. During thirty-two of the intervening years he was a United States Senator from Ohio * * *. [H]e was generally and, indeed, uniformly reputed to be the ablest and most influential financial statesman in this country. * *

It was this influential statesman who, * * * on December 4, 1889, introduced Senate Bill No. 1 of that Congress, which bill he entitled, "A bill to declare unlawful, trusts and combinations in restraint of trade and production."

* * *

That Sherman bill of 1889, though never enacted into law, deserves to be read, analyzed and understood because its provisions, when considered in connection with the four months of consideration which it received in the Senate, furnish several valuable guides to the Congressional intention which was finally expressed in the Sherman law of July 2, 1890.

The Sherman bill of December 4, 1889, was as follows:

"Be it enacted by the Senate and House of Representatives of the United States of America in Congress assembled:

Sec. 1. That all arrangements, contracts, agreements, trusts, or combinations between persons or corporations made with a view or which tend to prevent full and free competition in the importation, transportation or sale of articles imported into the United States, or in the production, manufacture, or sale of articles of domestic growth or production, or domestic raw material that competes with any similar article upon which a duty is levied by the United States, or which shall be transported from one State or Territory to another, and all arrangements, contracts, agreements, trusts or combinations between persons or corporations, designed or which tend to advance the cost to the consumer of any such articles, are hereby declared to be against public policy, unlawful and void.

Sec. 2. That any person or corporation, injured or damnified by such arrangement, contract, agreement, trust or combination, may sue for and recover in any court of the United States of competent jurisdiction, of any person or corporation a party to a combination described in the first section of this act, the full consideration or sum paid by him for any goods, wares and merchandise included in or advanced in price by said combination.

Sec. 3. That all persons entering into any such arrangement, contract, agreement, trust or combination, described in section 1 of this act, either on his own account or as an agent or attorney for another, or as an officer, agent or stockholder of any corporation, or as a trustee, committee or in any capacity whatever, shall be guilty of a high misdemeanor, and on conviction thereof in any district or circuit court of the United States, shall be subject to a fine of not more than $10,000, or to imprisonment in the penitentiary for a term of not more than five years, or both such fine and imprisonment, in the discretion of the court. And it shall be the duty of the District Attorney of the United States of the district in which such persons reside, to institute the proper proceedings to enforce the provisions of this act."

* * *

It was Senator Sherman's opinion that the commerce clause of the Constitution justified all parts of Section 1 of the Sherman bill. * * *

* * * [I]t is apparent that he wished to prohibit all decreases of competition and all increases of prices in respect of the transportation and also the sale of as many classes of articles as possible, so far as such decrease of competition or increase of prices might result from combinations between a plurality of persons * * *.

* * *

[We turn next to consideration of the bill on the floor of the Senate, beginning with the remarks of Senator George, of Mississippi, February 27, 1890.]

Senator George began his speech by saying that he regarded legislation on the subject of this bill as probably the most important to be considered by the Fifty-first Congress, for which reason he had prepared with particular care the remarks which he proposed to submit to the Senate in opposition to the bill as it then stood * * *.

* * * Senator George took the ground that the bill was unconstitutional for several reasons, including the fact that it proposed to regulate not only interstate and foreign commerce, but also to regulate, under some circumstances, manufacture or other production within individual states, of some classes of commodities. * * * [He also] took the ground that the bill was inefficient, because while it proposed to prohibit "arrangements, contracts, agreements, trusts or combinations" that prohibition was confined, as Senator George thought, to plans to decrease competition or increase prices, and did not include any overt acts done in pursuance of those plans. In accordance with this view, Senator George argued that representatives of corporations or other persons might go to Canada or to any other foreign country, and there [plan to] * * * decrease competition or increase prices without violating the bill, because the bill if enacted into law would not be in force in Canada; and that having thus made their plans, they might return to the United States and execute those plans here without violating that bill * * *.

* * *

[On March 21, 1890, Sherman addressed the Senate generally on antitrust, and in particular on his bill.]

Speaking of Section 1 of the original Sherman bill, Senator Sherman said: "This section will enable the courts of the United States to restrain, limit and control such combinations as interfere injuriously with our foreign and interstate commerce to the same extent that the state courts habitually control such combinations as interfere with the commerce of the state;" and that "The first section being a remedial statute, would be construed liberally with a view to promote its object. It defines a civil remedy and the courts will construe it liberally; they will prescribe the precise limits of the constitutional power of the Government. They will distinguish between lawful combinations in aid of production, and unlawful combinations to prevent competition and in restraint of trade; they can operate on corporations by restraining orders and rules. They can declare the particular combination null and void, and deal with it according to the nature and extent of the injuries," and that "This bill does not seek to cripple combinations of capital and labor; the formation of partnerships or corporations; but only to prevent and control combinations made with a view to prevent competition or for the restraint of trade, or to increase the profits of the producer at the cost of the consumer."

Speaking of the wrongs which the Sherman bill proposed to remedy, Senator Sherman said: "Associated enterprise and capital are not satisfied with partnerships and corporations competing with each other, and have invented a new form of combination commonly called 'trusts,' that seeks to avoid competition by combining the controlling corporations, partnerships and individuals engaged in the same business, and placing the power and property of the combination under the government of a few individuals, and often under the control of a single man called a trustee, a chairman or a president. The sole object of such a combination is to make competition impossible. It can control the market, raise or lower prices as will best promote its selfish interests, reduce prices in a particular locality and break down competition, and advance prices at will where competition does not exist. Its governing motive is to increase the profits of the parties composing it. The law of selfishness uncontrolled by competition, compels it to disregard the interest of the consumer. It dictates terms to transportation companies. It commands the price of labor without fear of strikes, for in its field it allows no competitors. * * * It is a substantial monopoly injurious to the public, and by the rule of both the common law and the civil law is null and void and the just subject of restraint by the courts * * *."

"If the concentrated powers of this combination are entrusted to a single man, it is a kingly prerogative, inconsistent with our form of government, and should be subject to the strong resistance of the state and national authorities. * * * If the combination is confined to a state, the state should apply the remedy; if it is interstate and controls any production in many states, Congress must apply the remedy. If the combination affects interstate transportation or is aided in any way by a transportation company, it falls clearly within the power of Congress * * *.

"Now, Mr. President, what is this bill? A remedial statute to enforce, by civil process in the courts of the United States, the common law against monopolies. How is such a law to be construed? Liberally, with a view to promote its object. * * *

* * *

"What is the extent of [the Congressional power to regulate commerce]? What is the meaning of the word commerce? It means the exchange of all commodities between different places or communities. It includes all trade and traffic, all modes of transportation by land or by sea * * *. The power of Congress extends to all this commerce, except only that limited within the bounds of a state."

* * * "In no respect does the work of our fathers in framing the Constitution of the United States appear more like the work of the Almighty Ruler of the Universe, rather than the conception of human minds, than by the powers conferred by it upon the branches of the Federal Government. Many of these powers have remained dormant, unused, but plainly there, awaiting the growth and progress of our country * * *."

"While we should not stretch the powers granted to Congress by strained construction, we cannot surrender any of them; they are not ours to surrender; but whenever occasion calls, we should exercise them for the benefit and protection of the people of the United States. And, sir, while I have no doubt that every word of this bill is within the powers granted to Congress, I feel that its defects are in its moderation, and that its best effect will be a warning that all trade and commerce, all agreements and arrangements, all struggles for money or property, must be governed by the universal law that the public good must be the test for all."

* * *

Senator Teller of Colorado next took the floor. He said: "There is not a civilized country anywhere in the world that is not more or less cursed with trusts. A trust may not always be an evil. A trust for certain purposes which may simply mean a combination of capital may be a valuable thing to the community and to the country. There have been trusts in this country that have not been injurious. But the general complaint against trusts is that they prevent competition." Having thus stated his view of the wrongs to be remedied, Senator Teller stated that he was inclined to vote for the Sherman bill, though he did not think it strong enough to accomplish the result at which it was aimed, and which appeared to be desired by the Senate.

The debate on the Sherman bill was resumed on March 24, 1890, beginning with a speech by Senator Turpie of Indiana [advocating criminal, as well as civil, penalties for those participating in trusts] who said: * * *

"There may be some difficulty in defining this offense; to describe it is impossible. It is like the penal offense of fraud. The courts have never attempted to define that. There may be no description, there can be none altogether applicable to fraudulent commercial trusts; they vary so much and are so multiform in their character * * *. The moment we denounce these trusts penally, the moment we declare these fraudulent trust combinations to be conspiracies, to be felonies or misdemeanors, that moment the courts are bound to carry out the intention and purpose of the legislation, and even to favor that purpose and intention, that the will of the people may prevail and not perish. I have no doubt that when this law comes into practical operation it will receive a construction and definition very useful to us. * * * It will be aided by advocates on both sides, in stating different views of construction; and, above all, it will be supported and upheld by public opinion, expressed in a denunciation of those evils which this kind of legislation would avert and avoid."

* * *

Senator Stewart of Nevada then delivered the only remarks which were made in either house of Congress in opposition to the proposed anti-trust legislation. Without making any comprehensive argument upon the point, he said: "I do not find any warrant in the Constitution for this particular class of legislation." His speech consisted mainly in contending that the true remedy against "trusts" organized among capitalists, manufacturers and railroad companies, would be found in counter combinations among the people. Senator Stewart did not explain in what way such counter combinations among the people could be made effective; but he must have meant to recommend boycotting for that purpose, because it must have been plain to him, as it is to us, that boycotting is the only means by which the people could resist combinations of railroad companies or manufacturing companies to charge excessive prices for commodities. The Senate did not appear to take Senator Stewart's argument on this subject seriously, for no other Senator mentioned it in his own speech, or took any time to controvert any such view.

Senator Hoar of Massachusetts made the last argument of the day relevant to the proposed anti-trust legislation. In that argument he criticised the Sherman bill in several respects. His first criticism was that in his opinion that bill was aimed at less than all of the offenders who ought to be subject to its penalties. And his second criticism was that the bill failed to provide any effective remedy for its violation, except so far as it gave power to private citizens to bring suits for private damages.

[2. THE REAGAN AMENDMENT]

In the next day of debate the Senate decided by a vote of nearly three to one to add [certain amendments and additions drafted by Senator] Reagan to the Sherman bill * * *.

* * *

Section 1 of the Reagan amendment was a penal provision, aimed at all persons engaged in the creation or in the management of any "trust," where that trust was employed in any international or interstate "business;" and that section provided that all such persons should be deemed guilty of high misdemeanor, and on conviction thereof should be fined not exceeding $10,000, or imprisoned at hard labor not exceeding five years, or should be punished by both of said penalties, at the discretion of the court.

To make section 1 of this amendment effective, it was necessary to define the pivotal word "trust," which that section contained; and section 2 of the Reagan amendment was devoted to that purpose. That section declared that a "trust" is a combination of capital, skill or acts by two or more persons, firms, corporations or associations of persons made for any or all of many specified purposes, namely: 1, to produce any restriction in trade; 2, to limit or reduce production of any commodity; 3, to increase or reduce the price of any commodity; 4, to prevent competition in the manufacture, transportation, purchase or sale of any commodity; 5, to fix a standard whereby the price of any commodity would be established or controlled; 6, to create a monopoly in the manufacture, purchase, sale or transportation of any commodity; 7, to enter into or to execute any contract, not to manufacture, sell or transport any commodity below a standard figure or to keep the price of any commodity at a fixed or graduated figure, or to establish the price of any commodity, or the price of transporting any commodity, so as to preclude unrestrained competition in the sale or transportation of any commodity, or to pool, combine or unite in any interest, relevant to the sale or transportation of any commodity, whereby its price might in any manner be affected.

* * *

[On March 27, 1890, debate continued, and Senator Edmunds of Vermont stated:]

> "I am in favor of the scheme in its fundamental desire and motive—most heartily in favor of it—directed to the breaking up of great monopolies, which get hold of the whole or some parts of particular business in the country, and are enabled therefore to command everybody, laborer, consumer, producer and everybody else, as the Sugar Trust and the Oil Trust. I am in favor, most earnestly in favor, of doing anything that the Constitution of the United States has given

Congress power to do, to repress and break up and destroy forever the monopolies of that character; because in the long run, however seductive they may appear in lowering prices to the consumer, for the time being, all human experience and all human philosophy has proved that they are destructive of the public welfare and come to be tyrannies, grinding tyrannies."

Having thus emphatically stated his opinion of the propriety and necessity of the object of the Sherman bill, Senator Edmunds stated that he thought that bill to be broader than the constitutional foundation therefor, in that it proposed to do more than to regulate foreign and interstate commerce, and that therefore it was impossible for him to vote for that bill.

* * *

[3. THE HOAR SUBSTITUTE]

[Because of the criticism made of the bill in debate, the Senate voted to send it to the Committee on the Judiciary, for revision.] On April 2, 1890, Senator Edmunds reported back the original Sherman bill and all its amendments, accompanied by a new substitute for all of them. * * *

* * * Inasmuch as the new substitute had the same general purpose as that of the original Sherman bill of December 4, 1889, and inasmuch as Senator Sherman was the author and had always been the leading advocate of the proposed anti-trust legislation, the substitute for his bill which was reported from the Judiciary Committee, continued to be known as the Sherman bill. Indeed, the name of the man who wrote the Judiciary Committee substitute was never mentioned [in debate]. [Thirteen years after the passage of this substitute bill as the "Sherman Act," however, in his autobiography] Senator [George F.] Hoar expressly stated that he was the author of the Judiciary Committee substitute for the Sherman bill, and that that substitute was finally passed, without any change, by both houses of Congress, as indeed it also appears in the Congressional Record to have been.

The history of Congressional legislation from its beginning in 1789 until now, probably presents no other instance of a statute so important, and relevant to a subject of such scope and complexity, being written by one man, exactly as it was passed by both houses of Congress, and approved by the President. But when Senator Hoar wrote the Sherman law he was sixty-four years old, and through a career of more than twenty years at the Massachusetts Bar, followed by a career of more than twenty years in the two houses of Congress, he had developed his remarkable original ability for clear statement, into an intellectual power on that point, which was not equalled by that of any other man in Congress. * * *

[The text of the "Hoar" substitute read in pertinent parts:]

Section 1. Every contract, combination in the form of trust or otherwise, or conspiracy, in restraint of trade or commerce among the several States, or with foreign nations, is hereby declared to be illegal. Every person who shall make any such contract, or engage in any such combination or conspiracy, shall be deemed guilty of a misdemeanor, and, on conviction thereof, shall be punished by a fine not exceeding five thousand dollars, or by imprisonment not exceeding one year, or by both said punishments, in the discretion of the court.

Sec. 2. Every person who shall monopolize, or attempt to monopolize, or combine or conspire with any other person or persons to monopolize any part of the trade or commerce among the several States, or with foreign nations, shall be deemed guilty of a misdemeanor, and, on conviction thereof, shall be punished by fine not exceeding five thousand dollars, or by imprisonment not exceeding one year, or by both said punishments, in the discretion of the court.

* * *

Sec. 4. The several circuit courts of the United States are hereby invested with jurisdiction to prevent and restrain violations of this act; and it shall be the duty of the several district attorneys of the United States, in their respective districts, under the direction of the Attorney–General, to institute proceedings in equity to prevent and restrain such violations. * * *

* * *

Sec. 7. Any person who shall be injured in his business or property by any other person or corporation by reason of anything forbidden or declared to be unlawful by this act may sue therefor in any Circuit Court of the United States in the district in which the defendant resides or is found, without respect to the amount in controversy, and shall recover threefold the damages by him sustained, and the costs of suit, including a reasonable attorney's fee.

Sec. 8. That the word "person" or "persons" wherever used in this act shall be deemed to include corporations and associations * * *.

The Senate began on April 8, 1890, its consideration of the Hoar substitute for the Sherman bill. That consideration was begun on the motion of Senator Hoar, who thereupon said that he would not undertake to explain the bill, because it was already well understood.

Senator Sherman thereupon said that, after having fairly and fully considered the substitute prepared by the Committee on Judiciary for his own bill, he would vote for it.

* * *

Senator Reagan of Texas thereupon moved to amend Section 7 of the Judiciary Committee substitute by inserting therein after the word "found" the words "or any state court of competent jurisdiction," so as to give to state courts concurrent jurisdiction with United States courts, of actions brought by private persons for damages inflicted upon them by violators of the proposed law. But the impracticability of that Reagan amendment was so clearly pointed out by Senator Edmunds and other Senators, that it was defeated by a vote of thirty-six nays to thirteen yeas. * * *

* * *

Senator Reagan of Texas thereupon moved to amend Section 3 of the Judiciary Committee substitute by adding thereto the proviso, "That each day's violation of any of the provisions of the act should be held to be a separate offense." But that amendment was rejected without debate and without calling for the yeas and nays.

Senator Kenna, of West Virginia, thereupon asked Senator Edmunds to explain the meaning of the word "monopolize" in Section 2 of the Judiciary Committee substitute. In explanation of this request, Senator Kenna asked whether that word would cover the conduct of a citizen who might secure the entire demand for some particular commodity by virtue of his superior skill or facilities for producing that article, and without any attempt to interfere with anybody else in trying to produce similar articles. Senator Edmunds answered to this question in the negative, and supported that answer by stating that the word "monopolize" has a meaning in the dictionaries and in the law which confines its scope to conduct which includes some attempt made by the monopolist to impede competitors and to prevent them from having an equal opportunity with himself to engage in the particular business sought to be monopolized.

Senator Hoar expressed his agreement with the opinion of Senator Edmunds on this point, and stated that all the members of the Judiciary Committee agreed that the word "monopoly" is a technical term known to the common law and that in that law it signifies "the sole engrossing to a man's self, by means which prevent other men from engaging in fair competition with him."

Senator Kenna thereupon inquired of Senator Hoar whether such a monopoly as he had defined is prohibited at common law, and Senator Hoar replied that he so understood. Senator Kenna thereupon asked why the bill should denounce a monopoly already illegal at common law; to which Senator Hoar replied that there is not any common law of the United States, and that the common law prevailing in the separate states of the Union cannot, as such, be enforced by the Federal courts by means of any penalty or punishment.

* * *

* * * [T]he Hoar substitute was thereupon passed by fifty-two ayes to one nay. The only negative vote was given by the undistinguished Senator Blodgett, of New Jersey, who had taken no part whatever in any of the debates on the subject and who did not state any reason for his vote. * * *

* * *

[4. THE DEBATE IN THE HOUSE]

[In the course of the debate over the bill in the House, Mr. Culberson, of Texas, explained the working of its provisions.]

Though Mr. Culberson did not attempt to foresee or foretell all of the transactions which the courts would find to be within the prohibitions of the bill he did mention some which he thought would be violative thereof. * * * [H]e stated, that he understood that the Standard Oil Company habitually made contracts with merchants which obliged them not to sell oil below a certain price, except where it might become necessary to do so, to drive some competitor out of business by underselling that competitor; in which case the Standard Oil Company would shoulder the temporary loss caused by such underselling. Mr. Culberson stated that such a contract as that would violate the proposed law.

* * *

Mr. Henderson, of Iowa * * * interrupted Mr. Culberson's speech * * *:

> " * * * I think it has been well settled by the investigation of a Congressional committee within the last year that a trust or combination of a few men in Chicago, Illinois, has been able to reduce the price of western cattle from one-third to one-half, controlling as they do the stock yards, the cattle yards and the transportation in Chicago; and it seems at the same time they have been enabled to keep up the price of every beefsteak that is used in this country. Now I want to ask * * * whether this bill * * * reaches that difficulty or not." To this question Mr. Culberson replied by saying: "I believe it will if it is construed as we think it ought to be construed by the courts."

Mr. Henderson thereupon asked, "Does the bill go as far as Congress has the power to go to strike at that damnable system?" To which Mr. Culberson replied: "That is the opinion of the Committee."

* * *

Mr. Cannon, of Illinois [replying to some critics of the bill:] * * "Gentlemen say they do not know how the courts will construe the act. It is for us to enact the law, and for courts to construe and enforce it. If we do our duty, it is reasonable to believe that the co-ordinate branch of the Government will do its duty. I believe this is a valuable bill, and I shall vote for it with pleasure."

* * *

Many other speeches having been made in favor of the bill and none against it, Mr. Culberson called for the previous question on its passage. But pending that motion, Mr. Bland, of Missouri, was permitted to offer, and did offer, the following amendment thereto:

> "Every contract or agreement entered into for the purpose of preventing competition in the sale or purchase of a commodity transported from one state or territory to be sold in another, or so contracted to be sold, or to prevent competition in transportation of persons or property from one state or territory into another, shall be deemed unlawful within the meaning of this act; provided that the contracts here enumerated shall not be construed to exclude any other contract or agreement declared unlawful in this act."

* * *

[5. FINAL ACTION BY THE SENATE AND HOUSE]

On May 12, 1890, Senator Hoar reported back Senate Bill No. 1 with an amendment to the House amendment, which amendment consisted in so changing the House amendment as to make it read as follows:

> "Every contract or agreement entered into for the purpose of preventing competition in transportation of persons or property from one state or territory to another shall be deemed unlawful within the meaning of this act."

Thereupon Senator Hoar explained that the Bland amendment proposed by the House contained two points. First, it provided that any contract or agreement entered into for the purpose of preventing competition in the sale or purchase of a commodity transported from one state or territory to another shall be prohibited; and second, that contracts to prevent competition in the transportation of persons or property from one state to another should be prohibited. Senator Hoar stated that the Committee on Judiciary objected to the first of these provisions, but approved the second one, though they supposed the second provision was already covered by the bill, because transportation is commerce as truly as sales are commerce.

The bill was then recommitted to the Senate Judiciary Committee, and reported back with the House amendment amended so as to read as follows:

> "That every contract or agreement entered into for the purpose of preventing competition in transportation of persons or property from

one state * * * into another, so that the rates of such transportation may be raised above what is just and reasonable, shall be deemed unlawful within the meaning of this act."

* * *

In the House on May 17, 1890, Mr. Taylor, of Ohio, chairman of the Judiciary Committee, moved that the House non-concur in the Senate amendment to the House amendment and agree to the conference asked by the Senate, which motion was agreed to by the House. * * *

On June 11, 1890, the Conference Committee agreed to amend the Bland amendment so as to read as follows:

> "Every contract or agreement entered into for the purpose of preventing competition in the transportation of persons or property from one state or territory into another, so that the rates of said transportation may be raised above what is just and reasonable, shall be deemed unlawful within the meaning of this act, and nothing in this act shall be deemed or held to impair the powers of the several states in any of the matters in this act mentioned."

Thereupon a long debate ensued upon the question of agreeing to the conference report.

* * *

[Following another meeting of a conference committee,] on June 18, 1890, Senator Edmunds presented to the Senate the report of the Conference Committee, which was to the effect that both Houses should recede from their respective amendments to the Senate bill, and that report was immediately agreed to without debate and without opposition.

On June 20, 1890, Mr. Stewart, of Vermont, submitted to the House the same conference report which Senator Edmunds had submitted to the Senate. * * *

* * *

* * * [T]he conference report was adopted and the bill was passed by the House by a vote of two hundred and forty-two ayes to no nays on June 20, 1890.

* * *

President Harrison, on July 2, 1890, approved and signed Senate Bill No. 1, namely: "An Act to protect trade and commerce against unlawful restraints and monopolies."

NOTES AND QUESTIONS

1. "That so broad-gauged a law attacking such powerful interests could pass in a predominantly conservative Congress by such an overwhelming vote seems on the surface difficult to explain." John Garraty, The New Commonwealth 124 (1968). Do you have an explanation? Of what importance is the national crisis described in the Introduction to this section? "Some historians," says Garraty, "have concluded that a massive explosion of public wrath compelled Congress to act." Id., at 124. One Senator remarked that his "colleagues were interested in only one thing, to get some bill headed, 'A Bill to Punish Trusts' with which to go to the country." Coolidge, An Old–Fashioned Senator: Orville H. Platt 444 (1910), quoted in Letwin, "Congress and the Sherman Antitrust Law," 1887–1890, 23 U.Chi.L.Rev. 221 (1956). We have used this rather ancient (1910) history of the Sherman Act because of its breezy style and for its verbatim quotes from the Sherman Bill, from the "Hoar Substitute," and from the Senate and House debates. For a more modern treatment, see William Letwin, Law and Economic Policy in America: Evolution of the Sherman Anti-trust Act (1965). For a more radical view of the early years of antitrust law see Gabriel Kolko, The Triumph of Conservatism (1963). For the change in economic theory on which antitrust law was based, see Herbert Hovenkamp, "The Antitrust Movement and the Rise of Industrial Organization," 68 Tex.L.Rev. 105 (1989). For a review of works in the history of antitrust, see Daniel R. Ernst, "The New Antitrust History," 35 N.Y.L.S.L.Rev. 879 (1990). Ernst's article is part of a special New York Law School Law Review Symposium, "Observing the Sherman Act Centennial: The Past and Future of Antitrust as Public Interest Law," which also includes important articles on the legal history of antitrust by Martin J. Sklar, William P. La Piana, James May, William J. Curran III, and several others.

2. How significant was this Congressional action? Consider the bill first introduced by Senator Sherman on December 4, 1889. Does it strike you as an important piece of legislation? What would such a bill accomplish? Are its terms clear? Are you persuaded by Senator Sherman's argument for the constitutionality of the bill? Under Senator Sherman's original scheme, who was to be depended on to effectuate the purposes of the bill? Under the original Sherman bill, how would the courts go about determining when they had a case of "lawful combination in aid of production," and when they had a case of "unlawful combination to prevent competition and in restraint of trade"? Are the two categories of combinations mutually exclusive?

3. Senator Sherman was a Republican who had recently lost the battle for the Republican nomination for President to William Henry Harrison, who was elected in 1888. Did Senator Sherman think that his bill would work any fundamental change in business law? Do you? Do you detect differences in antitrust policy between the Congressmen? For example, how would you compare the views of Sherman with those of Senator Reagan, a Texas Democrat; or Senator George of Mississippi, also a Democrat and a former confederate general? Consider the point raised in support of the Sherman Act by Senator Turpie of Indiana. That Senator believed that the Federal Legisla-

ture should pass antitrust laws, but should not clearly define the offense of "fraudulent combinations," because to do so would invite avoidance of the spirit of the law. Is this a persuasive argument? Is it consistent with the theory of criminal legislation articulated almost a hundred years earlier by Justice Chase and Justice Johnson in the common law crimes cases?

4. Only one Congressman, Senator Stewart of Nevada, spoke against the advisability of antitrust legislation. Is this surprising? Can you discern anything here of the conflict between civic ideologies referred to in the Introduction? Do you find his reasoning, that the proper remedy for "trusts" is combination among the people, to be as ludicrous as the author of this excerpt suggests? Do the materials on labor law which we have just considered make his argument more or less persuasive? How was it, by the way, that Senator Edmunds of Vermont, the Chairman of the Senate Judiciary Committee, could suggest that the "Sugar Trust and the Oil Trust" should be repressed because, being monopolies, "all human experience and all human philosophy has proved that they are destructive of the public welfare and come to be tyrannies, grinding tyrannies." Do you wish that you could have been a member of the Senate and able to make a speech like that?

5. After you have read about the debate and amendments to the original Sherman Bill and the Reagan Amendments, which were much subject to criticism and alteration, how do you account for the fact that the "Hoar substitute" was "identical in every section and in every word with the Sherman law as it was afterward passed by both houses?" Do you think the explanation was simply Senator Hoar's "remarkable original ability for clear statement" which Hoar had developed "into an intellectual power * * * which was not equalled by that of any other man in Congress?" Why do you suppose that Hoar didn't immediately reveal his authorship of the substitute bill? It appears from the Judiciary Committee's "Minute Book" that Sections 1, 2, 5 and 6 and perhaps 3 and 8 of the "Hoar Substitute" were actually drafted by Senator Edmunds, that Senator George drafted Section 4 and that Senator Hoar drafted only Section 7. Letwin, 23 U. Chi. L. Rev. at 254n. Would you agree with the author of this excerpt that the Sherman Act, as it was finally passed (the "Hoar Substitute") was an "admirable specimen of statute writing?"

6. What changes did the final bill make in the original Sherman bill and Reagan amendments? Would you have favored such changes? Note that in explanation of his bill Senator Hoar stated that a federal law regarding monopolies was made necessary because "the common law prevailing in the separate states of the Union cannot, as such, be enforced by the Federal courts by means of any penalty or punishment." Was he right about that? What inferences might be drawn from the Senate's refusal to add to the substitute bill Senator Reagan's amendment "That each day's violation of any of the provisions of the act should be held to be a separate offense"? How do you explain that that amendment was "rejected without debate and without calling for the yeas and nays?"

7. There seems to have been an understanding on the part of many of the men who joined to pass the Sherman Antitrust Act that they were merely

enacting the common law regarding trusts, monopolies, and restraint of trade on a national scale. What did this mean? We have already observed the tendency of the American common law to favor competition, but was the common law any more precise, and did it offer any concrete hopes for control of the trusts? According to the Antitrust historian William Letwin, there were four separate areas of the common law that bore on this problem: (1) the common law concerning royally chartered monopolies, which had been used to "destroy or weaken" those monopolies, while maintaining the power of the English legislature, Parliament, to charter corporations; (2) The body of English cases and statutes which forbid "engrossing," that is, cornering the supply of a necessity of life and charging extortionate prices for it; (3) English and American doctrines on contracts in restraint of trade generally, which prohibited "unreasonable" restrictions by employers for whom their employees might work for in the future, or which forbade buyers of businesses from exacting "unreasonable" agreements not to compete from sellers; and (4) English and American precedents on conspiracies or combinations in restraint of trade, such as those we have studied regarding labor unions, merchants associations, or manufacturing associations. See generally Letwin, 23 U.Chi.L.Rev. at 241–243, see also Letwin, "The English Common Law Concerning Monopolies," 21 U.Chi.L.Rev. 355 (1954), and Letwin's book, Law and Economic Policy in America: The Evolution of the Sherman Antitrust Act (1965). Letwin concludes that none of these four branches offered much hope of controlling the trusts. Do you agree? Letwin's work should now be supplemented with the excellent work in comparative legal history by Tony Freyer, Regulating Big Business: Antitrust in Great Britain and America 1880–1990 (1992).

8. Mr. Heard, of Missouri, said in debate on the "Hoar substitute" that "It is for us to enact the law, and for courts to construe and enforce it. If we do our duty, it is reasonable to believe that the co-ordinate branch of the Government will do its duty." In the next few cases we find out whether or not he was right.

9. In the House Mr. Bland offered an amendment to make clear that the antitrust law would apply to purveyors of interstate transportation. A Senate amendment offered by Senator Hoar would have accomplished the same thing, although Hoar's amendment removed Bland's provision affecting "competition in the sale or purchase of a commodity transported from one state * * * to another." Senator Edmunds's Judiciary committee amended the proposed amendment to indicate that such competition was only to be illegal where "the rates of such transportation may be raised above what is just and reasonable." Following this proposed amendment to the amendment *both* the Senate and the House backed off from Bland's, Hoar's, and Edmunds's proposals, and the House passed the "Hoar substitute" as originally drafted. This was done more or less "without debate and without opposition." Why? For a possible answer see, e.g., Herbert Hovenkamp, "Regulatory Conflict in the Gilded Age: Federalism and the Railroad Problem," 97 Yale L.J. 1017 (1988).

3. THE SHERMAN ACT IN THE SUPREME COURT

UNITED STATES V. E.C. KNIGHT CO.

Supreme Court of the United States, 1895.
156 U.S. 1, 15 S.Ct. 249, 39 L.Ed. 325.

MR. CHIEF JUSTICE FULLER * * *.

By the purchase of the stock of the four Philadelphia refineries with shares of its own stock the American Sugar Refining Company acquired nearly complete control of the manufacture of refined sugar within the United States. The bill charged that the contracts under which these purchases were made constituted combinations in restraint of trade * * * contrary to the act of congress of July 2, 1890.

* * * [T]he primary equity, or ground of suit * * * was the existence of contracts to monopolize interstate or international trade or commerce, and to restrain such trade or commerce * * *.

* * *

Counsel [for the United States] contend that [the Sherman Act term "Monopoly"] may be applied to all cases in which "one person sells alone the whole of any kind of marketable thing, so that only he can continue to sell it, fixing the price at his own pleasure," whether by virtue of legislative grant or agreement; that the monopolization referred to in the act of congress is not confined to the common-law sense of the term as implying an exclusive control, by authority, of one branch of industry without legal right of any other person to interfere therewith by competition or otherwise, but that it includes engrossing as well, and covers controlling the market by contracts securing the advantage of selling alone or exclusively all, or some considerable portion, of a particular kind of merchandise or commodity to the detriment of the public; and that such contracts amount to that restraint of trade or commerce declared to be illegal. But the monopoly and restraint denounced by the act are the monopoly and restraint of interstate and international trade or commerce, while the conclusion to be assumed on this record is that the result of the transaction complained of was the creation of a monopoly in the manufacture of a necessary of life.

* * *

The fundamental question is whether, conceding that the existence of a monopoly in manufacture is established by the evidence, that monopoly can be directly suppressed under the act of congress in the mode attempted by this bill.

* * *

The argument is that the power to control the manufacture of refined sugar is a monopoly over a necessary of life, to the enjoyment of which by a large part of the population of the United States interstate commerce is indispensable, and that, therefore, the general government, in the exercise of the power to regulate commerce, may repress such monopoly directly, and set aside the instruments which have created it. But this argument cannot be confined to necessaries of life merely and must include all articles of general consumption. Doubtless the power to control the manufacture of a given thing involves, in a certain sense, the control of its disposition, but this is a secondary, and not the primary, sense; and, although the exercise of that power may result in bringing the operation of commerce into play, it does not control it, and affects it only incidentally and indirectly. Commerce succeeds to manufacture, and is not a part of it. * * *

It is vital that the independence of the commercial power and of the police power, and the delimitation between them, however sometimes perplexing, should always be recognized and observed, for, while the one furnishes the strongest bond of union, the other is essential to the preservation of the autonomy of the states as required by our dual form of government; and acknowledged evils, however grave and urgent they may appear to be, had better be borne, than the risk be run, in the effort to suppress them, of more serious consequences by resort to expedients of even doubtful constitutionality.

* * * The regulation of commerce applies to the subjects of commerce, and not to matters of internal police. Contracts to buy, sell, or exchange goods to be transported among the several states, the transportation and its instrumentalities, and articles bought, sold, or exchanged for the purposes of such transit among the states, or put in the way of transit, may be regulated. * * * The fact that an article is manufactured for export to another state does not of itself make it an article of interstate commerce, and the intent of the manufacturer does not determine the time when the article or product passes from the control of the state and belongs to commerce. * * *

* * * [I]n Kidd v. Pearson, 128 U.S. 1, 20, 24, 9 Sup.Ct. 6, where the question was discussed whether the right of a state to enact a statute prohibiting within its limits the manufacture of intoxicating liquors, except for certain purposes, could be overthrown by the fact that the manufacturer intended to export the liquors when made, it was held that the intent of the manufacturer did not determine the time when the article or product passed from the control of the state and belonged to commerce, and that, therefore, the statute, in omitting to except from its operation the manufacture of intoxicating liquors within the limits of the state for export, did not constitute an unauthorized interference with the right of congress to regulate commerce. And Mr. Justice Lamar remarked

> * * * Manufacture is transformation,—the fashioning of raw materials into a change of form for use. The functions of commerce are different. The buying and selling, and the transportation incidental thereto, constitute commerce; and the regulation of commerce in the constitutional sense embraces the regulation at least of such transportation. * * * If it be held that the term includes the regulation of all such manufactures as are intended to be the subject of commercial transactions in the future, it is impossible to deny that it would also include all productive industries that contemplate the same thing. The result would be that congress would be invested, to the exclusion of the states, with the power to regulate, not only manufactures, but also agriculture, horticulture, stock-raising, domestic fisheries, mining; in short, every branch of human industry. * * *

* * *

* * * [T]he contracts and acts of the defendants related exclusively to the acquisition of the Philadelphia refineries and the business of sugar refining in Pennsylvania, and bore no direct relation to commerce between the states or with foreign nations. The object was manifestly private gain in the manufacture of the commodity, but not through the control of interstate or foreign commerce. It is true that the bill alleged that the products of these refineries were sold and distributed among the several states, and that all the companies were engaged in trade or commerce with the several states and with foreign nations; but this was no more than to say that trade and commerce served manufacture to fulfill its function. Sugar was refined for sale, and sales were probably made at Philadelphia for consumption, and undoubtedly for resale by the first purchasers throughout Pennsylvania and other states, and refined sugar was also forwarded by the companies to other states for sale. Nevertheless it does not follow that an attempt to monopolize, or the actual monopoly of, the manufacture was an attempt, whether executory or consummated, to monopolize commerce, even though, in order to dispose of the product, the instrumentality of commerce was necessarily invoked. There was nothing in the proofs to indicate any intention to put a restraint upon trade or commerce, and the fact, as we have seen, that trade or commerce might be indirectly affected, was not enough to entitle complainants to a decree.

MR. JUSTICE HARLAN dissenting * * *

* * *

"The object," the court below said, "in purchasing the Philadelphia refineries was to obtain a greater influence or more perfect control over the business of refining and selling sugar in this country." * * * In its consideration of the important constitutional question presented this court assumes on the record before us that the result of the transactions disclosed by the pleadings and proof was the creation of a monopoly in the manufacture of a necessary of life. If this combination, so far as its operations necessarily or directly affect interstate commerce, cannot be restrained or suppressed under some power granted to congress, it will be cause for regret that the patriotic statesmen who framed the constitution did not foresee the necessity of investing the national government with power to deal with gigantic monopolies holding in their grasp, and injuriously controlling in their own interest, the entire trade among the states in food products that are essential to the comfort of every household in the land.

The court holds it to be vital in our system of government to recognize and give effect to both the commercial power of the nation and the police powers of the states, to the end that the Union be strengthened, and the autonomy of the states preserved. In this view I entirely concur.

* * * But it is equally true that the preservation of the just authority of the general government is essential as well to the safety of the states * * *. The constitution, which enumerates the powers committed to the nation for objects of interest to the people of all the states, should not, therefore, be subjected to an interpretation so rigid, technical, and narrow that those objects cannot be accomplished. Learned counsel in Gibbons v. Ogden, 9 Wheat. 1, 187, having suggested that the constitution should be strictly construed, this court, speaking by Chief Justice Marshall * * * [asked]: "What do gentlemen mean * * * by a strict construction? * * * If they contend for that narrow construction which, in support of some theory to be found in the constitution, would deny to the government those powers which the words of the grant, as usually understood, import, and which are consistent with the general views and objects of the instrument; for that narrow construction, which would cripple the government, and render it unequal to the objects for which it is declared to be instituted, and to which the powers given, as fairly understood, render it competent,—then we cannot perceive the propriety of this strict construction, nor adopt it as the rule by which the constitution is to be expounded." Id. 188. * * *

Congress is invested with power to regulate commerce with foreign nations and among the several states. * * *

* * *

What is commerce among the states? The decisions of this court fully answer the question. "Commerce, undoubtedly, is traffic, but it is something more; it is intercourse." It does not embrace the completely interior traffic of the respective states,—that which is "carried on between man and man in a state, or between different parts of the same state, and which does not extend to or affect other states,"—but it does embrace * * * such traffic or trade, buying, selling, and interchange of commodities, as directly affects or necessarily involves the interests of the people of the United States. "Commerce, as the word is used in the constitution, is a unit," and "cannot stop at the external boundary line of each state, but may be introduced into the interior." "The genius and character of the whole government seem to be that its action is to be applied to all the external concerns of the nation, and to those internal concerns which affect the states generally." * * *

In the light of these principles, determining as well the scope of the power to regulate commerce among the states as the nature of such commerce, we are to inquire whether the act of congress of July 2, 1890, entitled "An act to protect trade and commerce against unlawful restraints and monopolies" (26 Stat. 209, c. 647), is repugnant to the constitution.

* * *

It would seem to be indisputable that no combination of corporations or individuals can, of right, impose unlawful restraints upon interstate trade, whether upon transportation or upon such interstate intercourse and traffic as precede transportation, any more than it can, of right, impose unreasonable restraints upon the completely internal traffic of a state. * * * If it be true that a combination of corporations or individuals may, so far as the power of congress is concerned, subject interstate trade, in any of its stages, to unlawful restraints, the conclusion is inevitable that the constitution has failed to accomplish one primary object of the Union, which was to place commerce among the states under the control of the common government of all the people, and thereby relieve or protect it against burdens or restrictions imposed, by whatever authority, for the benefit of particular localities or special interests.

The fundamental inquiry in this case is, what, in a legal sense, is an unlawful restraint of trade?

Sir William Erle, formerly chief justice of the common pleas, in his essay on the Law Relating to Trade Unions, well said that "restraint of trade, according to a general principle of the common law, is unlawful"; that "at common law every person has individually, and the public also have collectively, a right, to require that the course of trade should be kept free from unreasonable obstruction"; and that "the right to a free course for trade is of great importance to commerce and productive industry, and has been carefully maintained by those who have administered the common law." Pages 5–7.

There is a partial restraint of trade which, in certain circumstances, is tolerated by the law. The rule upon that subject is stated in Navigation Co. v. Winsor, 20 Wall. 64, 66, where it was said that: "An agreement in general restraint of trade is illegal and void; but an agreement which operates merely in partial restraint of trade is good, provided it be not unreasonable, and there be a consideration to support it. In order that it may not be unreasonable, the restraint imposed must not be larger than is required for the necessary protection of the party with whom the contract is made. * * * "

But a general restraint of trade has often resulted from combinations formed for the purpose of controlling prices by destroying the opportunity of buyers and sellers to deal with each other upon the basis of fair, open free competition. Combinations of this character have frequently been the subject of Judicial scrutiny, and have always been condemned as illegal because of their necessary tendency to restrain trade. Such combinations are against common right, and are crimes against the public. * * *

In Morris Run Coal Co. v. Barclay Coal Co., 68 Pa. 173, 183–187, the principal question was as to the validity of a contract made between five coal corporations of Pennsylvania, by which they divided between themselves two coal regions of which they had the control. The referee in the case found that those companies acquired under their arrangement the power to control the entire market for bituminous coal in the northern part of the state, and their combination was, therefore, a restraint upon trade, and against public policy. In response to the suggestion that the real purpose of the combination was to lessen expenses, to advance the quality of coal, and to deliver it in the markets intended to be supplied in the best order to the consumer, the supreme court of Pennsylvania said:

> This is denied by the defendants, but it seems to us it is immaterial whether these positions are sustained or not. Admitting their correctness, it does not follow that these advantages redeem the contract from the obnoxious effects so strikingly presented by the referee. The important fact is that these companies control this immense coal field * * *; that by this contract they control the price of coal in this extensive market, and make it bring sums it would not command if left to the natural laws of trade; [and] that it concerns an article of prime necessity for many uses * * *. These being its features, the contract is against public policy, illegal, and therefore void. * * * Singly each might have suspended deliveries and sales of coal to suit its own interests, and might have raised the price, even though this might have been detrimental to the public interest. * * * When competition is left free, individual error or folly will generally find a corrective in the conduct of others. But here is a combination of all the companies operating in the Blossburg and Barclay regions, and controlling their entire productions. * * * This combination has a power in its confederated form which no individual action can confer. The public interest must succumb to it, for it has left no competition free to correct its baleful influence. When the supply of coal is suspended, the demand for it becomes importunate, and prices must rise; or, if the supply goes forward, the price fixed by the confederates must accompany it. The domestic hearth, the furnaces of the iron master, and the fires of

> the manufacturer all feel the restraint, while many dependent hands are paralyzed, and hungry mouths are stinted. The influence of a lack of supply or a rise in the price of an article of such prime necessity cannot be measured. * * * Such a combination is more than a contract; it is an offense. "I take it," said Gibson, J., "a combination is criminal whenever the act to be done has a necessary tendency to prejudice the public or to oppress individuals, by unjustly subjecting them to the power of the confederates, and giving effect to the purpose of the latter, whether of extortion or of mischief." Com. v. Carlisle, Brightly, N.P. 40. * * * Men can often do by the combination of many what severally no one could accomplish, and even what, when done by one, would be innocent. * * * There is a potency in numbers when combined, which the law cannot overlook, where injury is the consequence.

* * *

In Salt Co. v. Guthrie, 35 Ohio St. 666, 672, the principal question was as to the legality of an association of substantially all the manufacturers of salt in a large salt-producing territory. * * * [T]he court said:

> Public policy unquestionably favors competition in trade to the end that its commodities may be afforded to the consumer as cheaply as possible, and is opposed to monopolies which tend to advance market prices, to the injury of the general public. * * * The clear tendency of such an agreement is to establish a monopoly, and to destroy competition in trade, and for that reason, on grounds of public policy, the courts will not aid in its enforcement. It is no answer to say that competition in the salt trade was not in fact destroyed, or that the price of the commodity was not unreasonably advanced. Courts will not stop to inquire as to the degree of injury inflicted upon the public; it is enough to know that the inevitable tendency of such contracts is injurious to the public.

* * *

A leading case on the question as to what combinations are illegal as being in general restraint of trade is Richardson v. Buhl, 77 Mich. 632, 635, 657, 660, 43 N.W. 1102, which related to certain agreements connected with the business and operations of the Diamond Match Company. From the report of the case it appears that that company was organized, under the laws of Connecticut, for the purpose of uniting in one corporation all the match manufactories in the United States, and to monopolize and control the business of making all the friction matches in the country, and establish the price thereof. * * * Chief Justice Sherwood of the supreme court of Michigan said:

> The sole object of the corporation is to make money by having it in its power to raise the price of the article, or diminish the quantity to be made and used, at its pleasure. Thus both the supply of the article and the price thereof are made to depend upon the action of a half dozen individuals, more or less, to satisfy their cupidity and avarice * * * an artificial person, governed by a single motive or purpose, which is to accumulate money regardless of the wants or necessities of over 60,000,000 people. The article thus completely under their control for the last fifty years has come to be regarded as one of necessity * * * in every household in the land * * *. It is difficult to conceive of a monopoly which can affect a greater number of people, or one more extensive in its effect on the country than that of the Diamond Match Company. It was to aid that company in its purposes and in carrying out its object that the contract in this case was made between those parties, and which we are now asked to aid in enforcing. Monopoly in trade, or in any kind of business in this country, is odious to our form of government. It is sometimes permitted to aid the government in carrying on a great public enterprise or public work under government control in the interest of the public. Its tendency is, however, destructive of free institutions, and repugnant to the instincts of a free people, and contrary to the whole scope and spirit of the federal constitution, and is not allowed to exist under express provisions in several of our state constitutions. * * * All combinations among persons or corporations for the purpose of raising or controlling the prices of merchandise, or any of the necessaries of life, are monopolies, and intolerable; and ought to receive the condemnation of all courts.

In the same case, Mr. Justice Champlin, with whom Mr. Justice Campbell concurred, said: " * * * Such a vast combination as has been entered into under the above name is a menace to the public. Its object and direct tendency is to prevent free and fair competition, and control prices throughout the national domain. It is no answer to say that this monopoly has in fact reduced the price of friction matches. That policy may have been necessary to crush competition. The fact exists that it rests in the discretion of this company at any time to raise the price to an exorbitant degree. * * * "

This extended reference to adjudged cases relating to unlawful restraints upon the interior traffic of a state has been made for the purpose of showing that a combination such as that organized under the name of the American Sugar Refining Company has been uniformly held by the courts of the states to be against public policy, and illegal, because of its necessary tendency to impose improper restraints upon trade. * * * The judgments of the state courts rest upon general principles of law, and not necessarily upon statutory provisions expressly condemning restraints of trade imposed by or resulting from combinations. Of course, in view of the authorities, it will not be doubted that it would be competent for a state, under the power to regulate its domestic commerce, and for the purpose of protecting its people against fraud and injustice, to make it a public offense, punishable by fine and imprisonment, for individuals or corporations to make contracts, form combinations, or engage in conspiracies, which unduly restrain trade or commerce carried on within its limits, and also to authorize the institution of proceedings for the purpose of annulling contracts of that character, as well as of preventing or restraining such combinations and conspiracies.

But there is a trade among the several states which is distinct from that carried on within the territorial limits of a state. The regulation and control of the former are committed by the national constitution to congress. * * * Under the power with which it is invested, congress may remove unlawful obstructions, of whatever kind, to the free course of trade among the states. * * * Any combination * * * that disturbs or unreasonably obstructs freedom in buying and selling articles manufactured to be sold to persons in other states, or to be carried to other states, * * * affects, not incidentally, but directly, the people of all the states; and the remedy for such an evil is found only in the exercise of powers confided to a government which, this court has said, was the government of all, exercising powers delegated by all, representing all, acting for all. M'Culloch v. Maryland, 4 Wheat. 405. * * *

* * *

In Kidd v. Pearson we recognized, as had been done in previous cases, the distinction between the mere transportation of articles of interstate commerce and the purchasing and selling that precede transportation. It is said that manufacture precedes commerce, and is not a part of it. But it is equally true that when manufacture ends, that which has been manufactured becomes a subject of commerce; that buying and selling succeed manufacturer, come into existence after the process of manufacture is completed, precede transportation, and are as much commercial intercourse, where articles are bought to be carried from one state to another, as is the manual transportation of such articles after they have been so purchased. The distinction was recognized by this court in Gibbons v. Ogden, where the principal question was whether commerce included navigation. Both the court and counsel recognized buying and selling or barter as included in commerce. Chief Justice Marshall said that the mind can scarcely conceive a system for regulating commerce, which was "confined to prescribing rules for the conduct of individuals in the actual employment of buying and selling, or of barter." Pages 189, 190, 9 Wheat.

The power of congress covers and protects the absolute freedom of such intercourse and trade among the states as may or must succeed manufacture and precede transportation from the place of purchase. This would seem to be conceded, for the court in the present case expressly declare that "contracts to buy, sell, or exchange goods to be transported among the several states, the transportation and its instrumentalities, and articles bought, sold, or exchanged for the purpose of such transit among the states, or put in the way of transit, may be regulated, but this is because they form part of interstate trade or commerce." Here is a direct admission—one which the settled doctrines of this court justify—that contracts to buy, and the purchasing of goods to be transported from one state to another, and transportation, with its instrumentalities, are all parts of interstate trade or commerce. * * * And yet by the opinion and judgment in this case, if I do not misapprehend them, congress is without power to protect the commercial intercourse that such purchasing necessarily involves against the restraints and burdens arising from the existence of combinations that meet purchasers, from whatever state they come, with the threat—for it is nothing more nor less than a threat—that they shall not purchase what they desire to purchase, except at the prices fixed by such combinations. * * *

In my judgment, the citizens of the several states composing the Union are entitled of right to buy goods in the state where they are manufactured, or in any other state, without being confronted by an illegal combination whose business extends throughout the whole country, which, by the law everywhere, is an enemy to the public interests, and which prevents such buying, except at prices arbitrarily fixed by it. * * *

* * * [The Constitution] gives to congress, in express words, authority to enact all laws necessary and proper for carrying into execution the power to regulate commerce; and whether an act of congress, passed to accomplish an object to which the general government is competent, is within the power granted, must be determined by the rule announced through Chief Justice Marshall * * *: "The sound construction of the constitution must allow to the national legislature the discretion with respect to the means by which the powers it confers are to be carried into execution, which will enable that body to perform the high duties assigned to it in the manner most beneficial to the people. Let the end be legitimate, let it be within the scope of the constitution; and all means which are appropriate, which are plainly adapted to that end, which are not prohibited, but consistent with the letter and spirit of the constitution, are constitutional." M'Culloch v. Maryland, 4 Wheat. 316, 421. The end proposed to be accomplished by the act of 1890 is the protection of trade and commerce among the states against unlawful restraints. Who can say that that end is not legitimate, or is not within the scope of the constitution? The means employed are the suppression, by legal proceedings, of combinations, conspiracies, and monopolies which, by their inevitable and admitted tendency, improperly restrain trade and commerce among the states. Who can say that such means are not appropriate * * *?

* * *

It is said that there are no proofs in the record which indicate an intention upon the part of the American Sugar Refining Company and its associates to put a restraint upon trade or commerce. Was it necessary that formal proof be made that the persons engaged in this combination admitted in words that they intended to restrain trade or commerce? Did any one expect to find in the written agreements which resulted in the formation of this combination a distinct expression of a purpose to restrain interstate trade or commerce? Men who form and control these combinations are too cautious and wary to make such admissions orally or in writing. Why, it is conceded that the object of this combination was to obtain control of the business of making and selling refined sugar throughout the entire country. Those interested in its operations will be satisfied with nothing less than to have the whole population of America pay tribute to them. That object is disclosed upon the very face of the transactions described in the bill. And it is proved—indeed, is conceded—that that object has been accomplished to the extent that the American Sugar Refining Company now controls 98 per cent. of all the sugar refining business in the country, and therefore controls the price of that article everywhere. Now, the mere existence of a combination having such an object and possessing such extraordinary power is itself, under settled principles of law,—there being no adjudged case to the contrary in this country,—a direct restraint of trade in the article for the control of the sales of which in this country that combination was organized. * * *

A decree recognizing the freedom of commercial intercourse as embracing the right to buy goods to be transported from one state to another without buyers being burdened by unlawful restraints imposed by combinations of corporations or individuals, so far from disturbing or endangering would tend to preserve the autonomy of the states, and protect the people of all the states against dangers so portentous as to excite apprehension for the safety of our liberties. If this be not a sound interpretation of the constitution, it is easy to perceive that interstate traffic, so far as it involves the price to be paid for articles necessary to the comfort and well-being of the people in all the states, may pass under the absolute control of overshadowing combinations having financial resources without limit, and an audacity in the accomplishment of their objects that recognizes none of the restraints of moral obligations controlling the action of individuals; combinations governed entirely by the law of greed and selfishness, so powerful that no single state is able to overthrow them, and give the required protection to the whole country, and so all-pervading that they threaten the integrity of our institutions.

* * *

To the general government has been committed the control of commercial intercourse among the states, to the end that it may be free at all times from any restraints except such as congress may impose or permit for the benefit of the whole country. * * * Its authority should not be so weakened by construction that it cannot reach and eradicate evils that, beyond all question, tend to defeat an object which that government is entitled, by the constitution, to accomplish. "Powerful and ingenious minds," this court has said, "taking, as postulates, that the powers expressly granted to the government of the Union are to be contracted by construction into the narrowest possible compass, and that the original powers of the states are retained, if any possible construction will retain them, may, by a course of well digested but refined and metaphysical reasoning, founded on these premises, explain away the constitution of our country, and leave it, a magnificent structure, indeed, to look at, but totally unfit for use. * * * " Gibbons v. Ogden, 9 Wheat. 1, 222.

While a decree annulling the contracts under which the combination in question was formed may not, in view of the facts disclosed, be effectual to accomplish the object of the act of 1890, I perceive no difficulty in the way of the court passing a decree declaring that that combination imposes an unlawful restraint upon trade and commerce among the states, and perpetually enjoining it from further prosecuting any business pursuant to the unlawful agreements under which it was formed, or by which it was created. * * *

For the reasons stated, I dissent from the opinion and judgment of the court.

NOTES AND QUESTIONS

1. In light of the legislative history of the Sherman Act, how persuasive did you find the United States' argument that "the monopolization referred to in the act of congress is not confined to the common-law sense of the term as implying an exclusive control, by authority, of one branch of industry without legal right of any other person to interfere therewith * * * but that it includes engrossing as well, and covers controlling the market by contracts securing the advantage of selling alone or exclusively all, or some considerable portion, of a particular kind of merchandise or commodity to the detriment of the public; and that such contracts amount to that restraint of trade or commerce declared to be illegal."

2. Also in light of the legislative history of the Sherman Act, do you find support for Judge Fuller's distinction between "monopolies" of trade, and "monopolies" of manufacturing? Does the rationale for the distinction lie in his observation that "The regulation of commerce applies to the subjects of commerce, and not to matters of internal police"? What are matters of "internal police?" On federal antitrust policy and the courts' treatment of that policy, see generally Martin H. Sklar, The Corporate Reconstruction of American Capitalism, 1890–1916: The Market, the Law, and Politics (1988), and James

May, "Antitrust in the Formative Era: Political and Economic Theory in Constitutional and Antitrust Analysis, 1880–1918," 50 Ohio St.L.J. 257 (1989). On the E.C. Knight case itself, see Charles W. McCurdy, "The *Knight* Sugar Decision of 1895 and the Modernization of American Corporation Law, 1869–1903," 53 Business History Review 304 (1979).

3. Consider Justice Harlan's dissent. Why does Harlan find it necessary to state such a self-evident proposition as "It would seem to be indisputable that no combination of corporations or individuals can, of right, impose unlawful restraints upon interstate trade * * *?" Would anyone challenge such a statement? On what problem is Harlan really seeking to focus attention?

4. Harlan spends some time with state cases which had found monopolistically-inclined organizations to be acting in restraint of trade. Are these cases distinguishable from a federal antitrust prosecution? What, exactly, is the common-law rationale of these cases? Must there be a finding that the culprits in question are *actually* injuring the public? What if the combination in question has actually *not* diminished competition and has *not* resulted in higher prices for consumers?

5. Consider the language quoted from the "Diamond Match" monopoly case, Richardson v. Buhl, to the effect that "Monopoly in trade, or in any kind of business in this country, is odious to our form of government." Do you agree? Why is the "tendency" of a monopoly "destructive of free institutions, and repugnant to the instincts of a free people?" Are "all combinations * * * for the purpose * * * of controlling prices" necessarily "intolerable?" How much of this is law, and how much is political and social philosophy? Is there a difference? Should there be?

6. Does all of this necessarily mean, however, that the power of the federal government must be invoked in matters involving monopolization of the manufacture of sugar? Would Justice Harlan believe that the power of the federal government would reach a case, where, as was presumably alleged in this case, the sugar companies themselves delivered no sugar to out-of-state buyers, but sold to anyone who came to them?

7. Do Justice Harlan's views on the power of the federal government remind you of any that you have studied before? Is he employing these views in the service of the same or different social philosophies? For example, in terms of the idea of centralized supervision of the American economy, how would you compare Harlan's views with those of the Federalists we studied in Chapter II, and with those of Chief Justice Taney? Do Harlan's fears about arbitrary uses of economic power and in particular large concentrations of private power sound familiar? How, for example, are they similar to or different from those expressed by the bench and the prosecution in the *Cordwainer's* case? On Harlan, his times, and his social and judicial philosophy see Loren P. Beth, John Marshall Harlan: The Last Whig Justice (1992), Linda Przbyszewski, The Republic According to John Marshall Harlan (1999), Tinsley E. Yarbrough, Judicial Enigma: The First Justice Harlan

(1995), White, The American Judicial Tradition 127–149 (1976), and James W. Ely, Jr. "Judicial Liberalism in the Gilded Age: Appraising John Marshall Harlan," 21 Reviews in American History 57 (1993).

UNITED STATES V. TRANS–MISSOURI FREIGHT ASS'N

Supreme Court of the United States, 1897.
166 U.S. 290, 17 S.Ct. 540, 41 L.Ed. 1007.

[The great question in this case was whether the Sherman Act applied to railroads. Do you remember anything in the legislative history of the act that is relevant? This case involved an association of 18 railroads (the Trans–Missouri Freight Association), at least some of which competed directly with each other, to fix rates.

The association argued that such rate-fixing was necessary to set "reasonable" rates, and that such "reasonable" rates were necessary to prevent some of the competitors from falling into financial ruin. Such ruin, said the companies, would injure the public when rail service consequently diminished. The rate-fixing in question was done pursuant to a written agreement, entered into before the passage of the Sherman Act. While the actual association which had been originally prosecuted was dissolved before the case was ruled on by the Supreme Court, the court decided to go ahead and address the merits of the question, in light of the fact that similar associations had since been formed. It should be borne in mind, as you read this opinion, that Congress had begun to deal with the Railroads *before* the Sherman Act, by the creation of the Interstate Commerce Commission (ICC) in 1887. The Interstate Commerce Act provided that rates must be "reasonable and just," and also forbade some types of agreements among railroads, called "pooling agreements." The ICC was charged with the responsibility for conducting investigations and enforcing the law, where necessary by prosecuting violators in the federal courts. It had become apparent by 1889, however, that the ICC did not interpret the provision forbidding "pooling" to include "rate agreements between competing companies," as long as "freight and territories were not parcelled out among them." See, e.g. J. Garraty, The New Commonwealth 112–119 (1968). Accordingly, the Trans–Missouri Freight Association argued that since it had filed its rates *and* its rate agreement with the ICC, and had gained ICC approval, it should be immune from prosecution under the Sherman Act. In short, asked the railroad, if the government agency charged with such determinations had decided that its rates were "reasonable," and "just" how could its actions be illegal restraints of trade? Does the argument of the railroad have anything in common with Harlan's dissent in *E.C. Knight?*]

MR. JUSTICE PECKHAM for the court * * *

The language of the act includes every contract, combination in the form of trust or otherwise, or conspiracy, in restraint of trade or commerce among the several States or with foreign nations. * * * It cannot be denied that those who are engaged in the transportation of persons or property from one State to another are engaged in interstate commerce, and it would seem to follow that if such persons enter into agreements between themselves in regard to the compensation to be secured from the owners of the articles transported, such agreement would at least relate to the business of commerce, and might more or less restrain it. The point urged on the defendants' part is that the statute was not really intended to reach that kind of an agreement relating only to traffic rates entered into by competing common carriers by railroad; that it was intended to reach only those who were engaged in the manufacture or sale of articles of commerce, and who by means of trusts, combinations and conspiracies were engaged in affecting the supply or the price or the place of manufacture of such articles. The terms of the act do not bear out such construction. * * *

We have held that the Trust Act did not apply to a company engaged in one State in the refining of sugar under the circumstances detailed in the case of United States v. E.C. Knight Company, 156 U.S. 1, because the refining of sugar under those circumstances bore no distinct relation to commerce between the States or with foreign nations. To exclude agreements as to rates by competing railroads for the transportation of articles of commerce between the States would leave little for the act to take effect upon. * * *

But it is maintained that an agreement like the one in question on the part of the railroad companies is authorized by the Commerce Act, which is a special statute applicable only to railroads, and that a construction of the Trust Act (which is a general act) so as to include within its provisions the case of railroads, carries with it the repeal by implication of so much of the Commerce Act as authorized the agreement. It is added that there is no language in the Trust Act which is sufficiently plain to indicate a purpose to repeal those provisions of the Commerce Act which permit the agreement * * *. On a line with this reasoning it is said that if Congress had intended to in any manner affect the railroad carrier as governed by the Commerce Act, it would have amended that act directly and in terms, and not have left it as a question of construction to be determined whether so important a change in the commerce statute had been accomplished by the passage of the statute relating to trusts.

The first answer to this argument is that, in our opinion, the Commerce Act does not authorize an agreement of this nature. It may not in terms prohibit, but it is far from conferring either directly or by implication any authority to make it. * * * The fifth section prohibits what is termed "pooling," but there is no express provision in the act prohibiting the maintenance of traffic rates among competing roads by making such an agreement as this, nor is there any provision which permits it. * * *

The existence of agreements similar to this one may have been known to Congress at the time it passed the Commerce Act, although we are not aware, from the record, that an agreement of this kind had ever been made and publicly known prior to the passage of the Commerce Act. Yet if it had been known to Congress, its omission to prohibit it at that time, while prohibiting the pooling arrangements, is no reason for assuming that when passing the Trust Act it meant to except all contracts of railroad companies in regard to traffic rates from the operation of such act. * * *

It is also urged that the debates in Congress show beyond a doubt that the act as passed does not include railroads. Counsel for the defendants refer in considerable detail to its history from the time of its introduction in the Senate to its final passage. As the act originally passed the Senate the first section was in substance as it stands at present in the statute. On its receipt by the House that body proposed an amendment, by which it was in terms made unlawful to enter into any contract for the purpose of preventing competition in the transportation of persons or property. As thus amended the bill went back to the Senate, which itself amended the amendment by making the act apply to any such contract as tended to raise prices for transportation above what was just and reasonable. * * * The amendments were then considered by conference committees, and the first conference committee reported to each house in favor of the amendment of the Senate. This report was disagreed to and another committee appointed, which agreed to strike out both amendments and leave the bill as it stood when it first passed the Senate * * *.

Looking at the debates during the various times when the bill was before the Senate and the House, both on its original passage by the Senate and upon the report from the conference committees, it is seen that various views were declared in regard to the legal import of the act. Some of the members of the House wanted it placed beyond doubt or cavil that contracts in relation to the transportation of persons and property were included in the bill. Some thought the amendment unnecessary as the language of the act already covered it, and some refused to vote for the amendment or for the bill if the amendments were adopted on the ground that it would then interfere with the Interstate Commerce Act, and tend to create confusion as to the meaning of each act.

* * *

Looking simply at the history of the bill from the time it was introduced in the Senate until it was finally passed, it would be impossible to say what were the views of a majority of the members of each house in relation to the meaning of the act. It cannot be said that a majority of both houses did not agree with Senator Hoar in his views as to the construction to be given to the act as it passed the Senate. All that can be determined from the debates and reports is that various members had various views, and we are left to determine the meaning of this act, as we determine the meaning of other acts, from the language used therein.

There is, too, a general acquiescence in the doctrine that debates in Congress are not appropriate sources of information from which to discover the meaning of the language of a statute passed by that body. * * *

The reason is that it is impossible to determine with certainty what construction was put upon an act by the members of a legislative body that passed it by resorting to the speeches of individual members thereof. Those who did not speak may not have agreed with those who did; and those who spoke might differ from each other; the result being that the only proper way to construe a legislative act is from the language used in the act, and, upon occasion, by a resort to the history of the times when it was passed. * * * If such resort be had, we are still unable to see that the railroads were not intended to be included in this legislation.

It is said that Congress had very different matters in view and very different objects to accomplish in the passage of the act in question; that a number of combinations in the form of trusts and conspiracies in restraint of trade were to be found throughout the country, and that it was impossible for the state governments to successfully cope with them because of their commercial character and of their business extension through the different States of the Union. Among these trusts it was said in Congress were the Beef Trust, the Standard Oil Trust, the Steel Trust, the Barbed Fence Wire Trust, the Sugar Trust, the Cordage Trust, the Cotton Seed Oil Trust, the Whiskey Trust and many others * * *. To combinations and conspiracies of this kind it is contended that the act in question was directed, and not to the combinations of competing railroads to keep up their prices to a reasonable sum for the transportation of persons and property. It is true that many and various trusts were in existence at the time of the passage of the act, and it was probably sought to cover them by the provisions of the act. * * * But a further investigation of "the history of the times" shows also that those trusts were not the only associations controlling a great combination of capital which had caused complaint at the manner in which their business was conducted. There were many and loud complaints from some portions of the public regarding the railroads and the prices they were charging * * * and it was alleged that the prices * * * were unduly and improperly enhanced by combinations among the different roads. * * *

Our attention is also called to one of the rules for the construction of statutes which has been approved by this court; that while it is the duty of courts to ascertain the meaning of the legislature from the words used in the statute and the subject-matter to which it relates, there is an equal duty to restrict the meaning of general words, whenever it is found necessary to do so in order to carry out the legislative intent. * * * It is therefore urged that if, by a strict construction of the language of this statute it may be made to include railroads, yet it is evident from other considerations now to be mentioned that the real meaning of the legislature would not include them, and they must for that reason be excluded. It is said that this meaning is plainly to be inferred, because of fundamental differences both in an economic way and before the law between trade and manufacture on the one hand, and railroad transportation on the other. Among these differences are the public character of railroad business, and as a result the peculiar power of control and regulation possessed by the State over railroad companies. The trader or manufacturer, on the other hand, carries on an entirely private business, and can sell to whom he pleases; he may charge different prices for the same article to different individuals; he may charge as much as he can get for the article in which he deals, whether the price be reasonable or unreasonable; he may make such discrimination in his business as he chooses, and he may cease to do any business whenever his choice lies in that direction; while, on the contrary, a railroad company must transport all persons and property that come to it, and it must do so at the same price for the same service, and the price must be reasonable, and it cannot at its will discontinue its business. It is also urged that there are evils arising from unrestricted competition in regard to railroads which do not exist in regard to any other kind of property, that it is so admitted by the latest and best writers on the subject, and that practical experience of the results of unrestricted competition among railroads tends directly to the same view * * *. It is also said that the contemporaneous industrial history of the country, the legal situation in regard to railroad properties at the time of the enactment of this statute, its legislative history, the ancient and constantly maintained different legal effect and policy regarding railway transportation and ordinary trade and manufacture, together with a just regard for interests of such enormous magnitude as are represented by the railroads of the country, all tend to show that Congress in passing the Anti–Trust Act never could have contemplated the inclusion of railroads within its provisions. * * *

* * * While the points of difference just mentioned and others do exist between the two classes of corporations, it must be remembered they have also some points of resemblance. Trading, manufacturing and railroad corporations are all engaged in the transaction of business with regard to articles of trade and commerce * * *. A contract among those engaged in the latter business by which the prices for the transportation of commodities traded in or manufactured by the others is greatly enhanced from what it otherwise would be if free competition were the rule, affects and to a certain extent restricts trade and commerce, and affects the price of the commodity. * * * Why should not a railroad company be included in general legislation aimed at the prevention of that kind of agreement made in restraint of trade * * *? It is true the results of trusts, or combi-

nations of that nature, may be different in different kinds of corporations, and yet they all have an essential similarity, and have been induced by motives of individual or corporate aggrandizement as against the public interest. In business or trading combinations they may even temporarily, or perhaps permanently, reduce the price of the article traded in or manufactured, by reducing the expense inseparable from the running of many different companies for the same purpose. Trade or commerce under those circumstances may nevertheless be badly and unfortunately restrained by driving out of business the small dealers and worthy men whose lives have been spent therein, and who might be unable to readjust themselves to their altered surroundings. Mere reduction in the price of the commodity dealt in might be dearly paid for by the ruin of such a class * * *. In any great and extended change in the manner or method of doing business it seems to be an inevitable necessity that distress and, perhaps, ruin shall be its accompaniment in regard to some of those who were engaged in the old methods.

It is wholly different, however, when such changes are effected by combinations of capital * * *. In this light it is not material that the price of an article may be lowered. It is in the power of the combination to raise it, and the result in any event is unfortunate for the country by depriving it of the services of a large number of small but independent dealers * * * who supported themselves and their families from the small profits realized therein. Whether they be able to find other avenues to earn their livelihood is not so material, because it is not for the real prosperity of any country that such changes should occur which result in transferring an independent business man, the head of his establishment, small though it might be, into a mere servant or agent of a corporation for selling the commodities which he once manufactured or dealt in, having no voice in shaping the business policy of the company and bound to obey orders issued by others. Nor is it for the substantial interests of the country that any one commodity should be within the sole power and subject to the sole will of one powerful combination of capital. * * * It is entirely appropriate generally to subject corporations or persons engaged in trading or manufacturing to different rules from those applicable to railroads in their transportation business; but when the evil to be remedied is similar in both kinds of corporations * * * we see no reason why similar rules should not be promulgated in regard to both, and both be covered in the same statute by general language sufficiently broad to include them both. * * * We think, after a careful examination, that the statute covers, and was intended to cover, common carriers by railroad.

* * * The next question to be discussed is as to what is the true construction of the statute, assuming that it applies to common carriers by railroad. What is the meaning of the language as used in the statute, that "every contract, combination in the form of trust or otherwise, or conspiracy in restraint of trade or commerce among the several States or with

foreign nations, is hereby declared to be illegal"? Is it confined to a contract or combination which is only in unreasonable restraint of trade or commerce, or does it include what the language of the act plainly and in terms covers, all contracts of that nature?

We are asked to regard the title of this act as indicative of its purpose to include only those contracts which were unlawful at common law, but which require the sanction of a Federal statute in order to be dealt with in a Federal court. It is said that when terms which are known to the common law are used in a Federal statute those terms are to be given the same meaning that they received at common law, and that when the language of the title is "to protect trade and commerce against unlawful restraints and monopolies," it means those restraints and monopolies which the common law regarded as unlawful, and which were to be prohibited by the Federal statute. We are of opinion that the language used in the title refers to and includes and was intended to include those restraints and monopolies which are made unlawful in the body of the statute. * * *

It is now with much amplification of argument urged that the statute, in declaring illegal every combination in the form of trust or otherwise, or conspiracy in restraint of trade or commerce, does not mean what the language used therein plainly imports, but that it only means to declare illegal any such contract which is in unreasonable restraint of trade * * *.

The term ["restraint of trade", as used in the statute] is not of such limited signification. Contracts in restraint of trade have been known and spoken of for hundreds of years both in England and in this country, and the term includes all kinds of those contracts which in fact restrain or may restrain trade. * * * A contract may be in restraint of trade and still be valid at common law. Although valid, it is nevertheless a contract in restraint of trade, and would be so described either at common law or elsewhere. By the simple use of the term "contract in restraint of trade," all contracts of that nature, whether valid or otherwise, would be included, and not alone that kind of contract which was invalid and unenforceable as being in unreasonable restraint of trade. * * *

It must also be remembered that railways are public corporations organized for public purposes, granted valuable franchises and privileges, among which the right to take the private property of the citizen in invitum is not the least, Cherokee Nation v. Southern Kansas Railway Co., 135 U.S. 641, 657; that many of them are the donees of large tracts of public lands and of gifts of money by municipal corporations, and that they all primarily owe duties to the public of a higher nature even than that of earning large dividends for their shareholders. The business which the railroads do is of a public nature, closely affecting almost all classes in the community—the farmer, the artisan, the manufacturer and the trader. It is of such a public nature that it may well be doubted, to say the least, whether any contract which imposes any restraint upon its business would not be prejudicial to the public interest.

We recognize the argument upon the part of the defendants that restraint upon the business of railroads will not be prejudicial to the public interest so long as such restraint provides for reasonable rates for transportation and prevents the deadly competition so liable to result in the ruin of the roads and to thereby impair their usefulness to the public, and in that way to prejudice the public interest. But it must be remembered that these results are by no means admitted with unanimity; on the contrary, they are earnestly and warmly denied on the part of the public and by those who assume to defend its interests both in and out of Congress. Competition, they urge, is a necessity for the purpose of securing in the end just and proper rates. * * *

* * *

[Justice Peckham then quoted from the dissenting opinion below, on the railroads' argument that they should be permitted to fix rates to avoid ruinous competition.]

> It may be entirely true that as we proceed in the development of the policy of public control over railway traffic, methods will be devised and put in operation by legislative enactment whereby railway companies and the public may be protected against the evils arising from unrestricted competition and from rate wars which unsettle the business of the community, but I fail to perceive the force of the argument that because railway companies through their own action cause evils to themselves and the public by sudden changes or reductions in tariff rates they must be permitted to deprive the community of the benefit of competition in securing reasonable rates for the transportation of the products of the country. Competition, free and unrestricted, is the general rule which governs all the ordinary business pursuits and transactions of life. Evils, as well as benefits, result therefrom. In the fierce heat of competition the stronger competitor may crush out the weaker; fluctuations in prices may be caused that result in wreck and disaster; yet, balancing the benefits as against the evils, the law of competition remains as a controlling element in the business world. * * * The time may come when the companies will be relieved from the operation of this law, but they cannot, by combination and agreements among themselves, bring about this change. The fact that the provisions of the Interstate Commerce Act may have changed in many respects the conduct of the companies in the carrying on of the public business they are engaged in does not show that it was the intent of Congress, in the enactment of that statute, to clothe railway companies with the right to combine to-

gether for the purpose of avoiding the effects of competition on the subject of rates.

* * *

As a result of this review of the situation, we find two very widely divergent views of the effects which might be expected to result from declaring illegal all contracts in restraint of trade, etc.; one side predicting financial disaster and ruin to competing railroads, including thereby the ruin of shareholders, the destruction of immensely valuable properties, and the consequent prejudice to the public interest; while on the other side predictions equally earnest are made that no such mournful results will follow, and it is urged that there is a necessity, in order that the public interest may be fairly and justly protected, to allow free and open competition among railroads upon the subject of the rates for the transportation of persons and property.

The arguments which have been addressed to us against the inclusion of all contracts in restraint of trade, as provided for by the language of the act, have been based upon the alleged presumption that Congress, notwithstanding the language of the act, could not have intended to embrace all contracts, but only such contracts as were in unreasonable restraint of trade. Under these circumstances we are, therefore, asked to hold that the act of Congress excepts contracts which are not in unreasonable restraint of trade, and which only keep rates up to a reasonable price, notwithstanding the language of the act makes no such exception. In other words, we are asked to read into the act by way of judicial legislation an exception that is not placed there by the law-making branch of the Government, and this is to be done upon the theory that the impolicy of such legislation is so clear that it cannot be supposed Congress intended the natural import of the language it used. This we cannot and ought not to do. * * * It may be that the policy evidenced by the passage of the act itself will, if carried out, result in disaster to the roads and in a failure to secure the advantages sought from such legislation. * * * These considerations are, however, not for us. If the act ought to read as contended for by defendants, Congress is the body to amend it and not this court, by a process of judicial legislation wholly unjustifiable. * * *

The conclusion which we have drawn from the examination above made into the question before us is that the Anti–Trust Act applies to railroads, and that it renders illegal all agreements which are in restraint of trade or commerce as we have above defined that expression, and the question then arises whether the agreement before us is of that nature.

* * * The question is one of law in regard to the meaning and effect of the agreement itself, namely: Does the agreement restrain trade or commerce in any way so as to be a violation of the act? We have no doubt that it does. The agreement on its face recites that it is entered into "for the

purpose of mutual protection by establishing and maintaining reasonable rates, rules and regulations on all freight traffic, both through and local." To that end the association is formed and a body created which is to adopt rates, which, when agreed to, are to be the governing rates for all the companies, and a violation of which subjects the defaulting company to the payment of a penalty, and although the parties have a right to withdraw from the agreement on giving thirty days' notice of a desire so to do, yet while in force and assuming it to be lived up to, there can be no doubt that its direct, immediate and necessary effect is to put a restraint upon trade or commerce as described in the act.

* * *

NOTES AND QUESTIONS

1. Do you agree with Justice Peckham's conclusion that the existence of the ICC and the ICC Act has no bearing on the applicability of the Sherman Act to railroads? How would you argue to reach the opposite conclusion? What about Peckham's view of the importance of legislative history? Would you participate in the "general acquiescence in the doctrine that debates in Congress are not appropriate sources of information from which to discover the meaning of the language of a statute passed by that body?" How then do you determine the meaning of statutes? It is now generally accepted that the debates in Congress and the reports of Congressional committees can be used as aids in interpretation, but at least one member of the United States Supreme Court, Justice Scalia, has views about legislative history similar to those of Justice Peckham. See, e.g., Edwards v. Aguillard, 482 U.S. 578, 636–40, 107 S.Ct. 2573, 2605–07, 96 L.Ed.2d 510 (1987) (Scalia, J., dissenting). How *should* statutes be interpreted?

2. In light of the *E.C. Knight Co.* case, which held that the antitrust law did not reach monopolization of manufacturing, do you think that Justice Peckham concludes too quickly that the Antitrust Act does apply to common carriers, like railroads? Do you suppose that Peckham's ideology might have some influence on his judicial thinking? Do you find anything, for example, that suggests that Peckham might share Justice Harlan's social assumptions? For a review of the federal regulation of railroads during the period of the *Trans Missouri* case and thoughts on what that review teaches us about the reach of the interstate commerce clause, see James W. Ely, Jr. " 'The Railroad System Has Burst Through State Limits': Railroads and Interstate Commerce 1830–1920," 55 Ark. L. Rev. 933 (2003), and Paul D. Carrington, "Law and Economics in the Creation of Federal Administrative Law: Thomas Cooley [the first chairman of the ICC], Elder to the Republic," 83 Iowa L.Rev. 363 (1998). On the railroads generally see John F. Stover, American Railroads (2nd ed. 1997).

3. In light of what you have learned about the legislative history of the Sherman Act, and without regard to Justice Peckham's opinion about legislative history, do you agree with Peckham that one should interpret the Anti-

trust Act as forbidding all contracts and combinations in "restraint of trade," and that one should not read in the so-called "rule of reason" from the common law? In other words, is it correct that the Antitrust Act was *not* intended merely to Federalize the common law? Justice Peckham's reluctance to impose a "Rule of Reason" in antitrust matters was overturned in Standard Oil Co. v. United States, 221 U.S. 1, 31 S.Ct. 502, 55 L.Ed. 619 (1911), and the Rule of Reason—forbidding only unreasonable restraints of trade under the Sherman Act—generally prevails today.

4. Even if Justice Peckham is correct that the Sherman Act was meant to prohibit all contracts in restraint of trade in interstate commerce, does it necessarily follow that the contract in this case is in "restraint of trade?" How does Peckham justify his finding to that effect? For a study of Peckham's "antitrust jurisprudence and [his] vision[ ] of the public good," see William La Piana, "The Legal Culture of the Formative Period in Sherman Act Jurisprudence," 35 N.Y.L.S.L.Rev. 827 (1990). See also Martin J. Sklar, "Sherman Antitrust Act Jurisprudence and Federal Policy–Making in the Formative Period, 1890–1914," 35 N.Y.L.S.L.Rev. 791 (1990).

5. If Justice Peckham was closer in judicial temperament to Justice Harlan than to Justice Fuller, would you expect Peckham to agree with the idea that the Antitrust Act was not designed to reach manufacturing? Peckham wrote an opinion on this question in Addyston Pipe & Steel Co. v. United States, 175 U.S. 211, 20 S.Ct. 96, 44 L.Ed. 136 (1899). The conventional wisdom on this opinion is that *Addyston Pipe* "for all practical purposes" reversed *E.C. Knight*. See, e.g. A.D. Neale, The Antitrust Laws of the United States of America 16n (2nd ed. 1970). *Addyston* involved an arrangement among six manufacturers of cast-iron pipe whereby the six agreed not to underbid each other in public bidding for contracts for the manufacture of pipe in certain territories. Each carried on business by submitting bids for the manufacture of pipe required in particular construction projects and then, if their bids were successful, by manufacturing and shipping pipe to the construction site. While this did involve interstate shipment of pipe, the defendants argued that since they were "manufacturers" of pipe, the *E.C. Knight* case covered their situation. What follows are the parts of Peckham's opinion in *Addyston* where he distinguishes the *E.C. Knight* case. See if you accept his arguments. Why is Peckham unwilling to admit that he is, for all practical purposes, overruling the *E.C. Knight* case? Who benefits from the *Addyston Pipe* decision? Compare the results of these antitrust cases with the labor materials, which follow.

ADDYSTON PIPE AND STEEL CO. V. UNITED STATES

Supreme Court of the United States, 1899.
175 U.S. 211, 20 S.Ct. 96, 44 L.Ed. 136.

The direct purpose of the combination in the *Knight case* was the control of the manufacture of sugar. There was no combination or agreement, in terms, regarding the future disposition of the manufactured article; nothing looking to a transaction in the nature of interstate commerce

* * * The various cases which had been decided in this court relating to the subject of interstate commerce, and to the difference between that and the manufacture of commodities, and also the police power of the States as affected by the commerce clause of the Constitution, were adverted to, and the case was decided upon the principle that a combination simply to control manufacture was not a violation of the act of Congress, because such a contract or combination did not directly control or affect interstate commerce, but that contracts for the sale and transportation to other States of specific articles were proper subjects for regulation because they did form part of such commerce.

We think the case now before us involves contracts of the nature last above mentioned, not incidentally or collaterally, but as a direct and immediate result of the combination engaged in by the defendants.

While no particular contract regarding the furnishing of pipe and the price for which it should be furnished was in the contemplation of the parties to the combination at the time of its formation, yet it was their intention, as it was the purpose of the combination, to directly and by means of such combination increase the price for which all contracts for the delivery of pipe within the territory above described should be made, and the latter result was to be achieved by abolishing all competition between the parties to the combination. The direct and immediate result of the combination was therefore necessarily a restraint upon interstate commerce in respect of articles manufactured by any of the parties to it to be transported beyond the State in which they were made. * * *

If dealers in any commodity agreed among themselves that any particular territory bounded by state lines should be furnished with such commodity by certain members only of the combination, and the others would abstain from business in that territory, would not such agreement be regarded as one in restraint of interstate trade? If the price of the commodity were thereby enhanced, (as it naturally would be,) the character of the agreement would be still more clearly one in restraint of trade. Is there any substantial difference where, by agreement among themselves, the parties choose one of their number to make a bid for the supply of the pipe for delivery in another State, and agree that all the other bids shall be for a larger sum, thus practically restricting all but the member agreed upon from any attempt to supply the demand for the pipe or to enter into competition for the business? * * *

* * *

The defendants allege, and it is true, that their business is not like a factory manufacturing an article of a certain kind for which there is at all times a demand, and which is manufactured without any regard to a particular sale or for a particular customer. In this respect as in many others the business differs radically from the sugar refiners. The business of defendants is carried on by obtaining particular contracts for the sale, transportation and delivery of iron pipe of a certain description, quality and strength, differing in different contracts as the intended use may differ. These contracts are, generally speaking, obtained at a public letting, at which there are many competitors, and the contract bid for includes, in its terms, the sale of the pipe and its delivery at the place desired, the cost of transportation being included in the purchase price of the pipe. The contract is one for the sale and delivery of a certain kind of pipe, and it is not generally essential to its performance that it should be manufactured for that particular contract, although sometimes it may be.

If the successful bidder had on hand iron pipe of the kind specified, or if he could procure it by purchase, he could in most cases deliver such pipe in fulfillment of his contract just the same as if he manufactured the pipe subsequently to the making of the contract and for the specific purpose of its performance. It is the sale and delivery, of a certain kind and quality of pipe, and not the manufacture, which is the material portion of the contract, and a sale for delivery beyond the State makes the transaction a part of interstate commerce. Municipal corporations and gas, railroad and water companies are among the chief customers for the pipe, and when they desire the article they give notice of the kind and quality, size, strength and purpose for which the pipe is desired, and announce that they will receive proposals for furnishing the same at the place indicated by them. * * * In certain sections of the country the defendants would have, by reason of their situation, such an advantage over all other competitors that there would practically be no chance for any other than one of their number to obtain the contract, unless the price bid was so exorbitant as to give others not so favorably situated an opportunity to snatch it from their hands. * * *

The combination thus had a direct, immediate and intended relation to and effect upon the subsequent contract to sell and deliver the pipe. It was to obtain that particular and specific result that the combination was formed, and but for the restriction the resulting high prices for the pipe would not have been obtained. It is useless for the defendants to say they did not intend to regulate or affect interstate commerce. They intended to make the very combination and agreement which they in fact did make, and they must be held to have intended (if in such case intention is of the least importance) the necessary and direct result of their agreement.

* * *

It is said that a particular business must be distinguished from its mere subjects, and from the instruments by which the business is carried on; that in most cases of a large manufacturing company it could only be carried on by shipping products from one State to another, and that the business of such an establishment would be related to interstate commerce only incidentally and indirectly. This proposition we are not called upon to deny. It is not, however, relevant. Where the contract is for the sale of the article and for its delivery in another State, the transaction is one of interstate commerce, although the vendor may have also agreed to manufacture it in order to fulfil his contract of sale. In such case a combination of this character would be properly called a combination in restraint of interstate commerce, and not one relating only to manufacture.

It is almost needless to add that we do not hold that every private enterprise which may be carried on chiefly or in part by means of interstate shipments is therefore to be regarded as so related to interstate commerce as to come within the regulating power of Congress. Such enterprises may be of the same nature as the manufacturing of refined sugar in the *Knight case*—that is, the parties may be engaged as manufacturers of a commodity which they thereafter intend at some time to sell, and possibly to sell in another State; but such sale we have already held is an incident to and not the direct result of the manufacture, and so is not a regulation of or an illegal interference with interstate commerce. That principle is not affected by anything herein decided.

* * *

E. INDUSTRIAL STRIFE: THE PULLMAN STRIKE, EUGENE V. DEBS, AND WORKMEN'S COMPENSATION

1. INTRODUCTION

As we have seen, one of the effects of commercial development in early nineteenth century America was the increasing diversity of interests between capital and labor. In the early years, however, conflict between the two was not often serious. The small-scale organization of business still maintained a personal employer-employee relationship, and the "master" still at least paid lip service to the tradition that he was guardian of his "servant's" welfare. Working conditions, though not luxurious, were often respectable, and occasionally satisfying. The importance of handicraft skills in early industry meant that workers could continue to think of themselves as craftsmen, and take pride in their work. The common ideology of expansion held out the hope that workers could share in the generally rising fortunes of business. As we have seen, some judges, like Shaw, even attempted to create tenets of jurisprudence to balance the competing interests of labor and capital.

After 1850, however, whatever balance had been struck began to tilt in favor of capital, as the trend toward large-scale industrialization continued. As this tilt continued, the conflict between owners and workers grew greater, until finally, in the late years of the century, a state very near to industrial warfare existed.

Labor grievances ordinarily concerned hours and wages. As late as 1910, only 8 percent of American laborers worked only an 8–hour day. In the steel industry, for example, 12–hour days and 6–day weeks were commonplace until 1923. In the textile industry, dependent primarily on women and young children, the work week ranged from 60 to 84 hours. Nor did munificent wages offset the burdensome hours. The unskilled laborer from 1880–1910 could expect to take home a little under $10 per week. Skilled workers rarely made more than $20. The average annual family income of industrial workers was never higher than $650, an amount which was often not enough for subsistence. Moreover, the closing decades of the nineteenth century included several recessions which brought on severe unemployment. The depression of 1894, the worst, left one in five workers jobless. City dwellers found it difficult if not impossible to procure food by gardening or raising livestock, and life was thus fragile for the American working class—it is not difficult to understand how frustration could lead to violence.

The first such significant instance was in 1877. In reaction to a business slump, the Baltimore & Ohio railroad had cut wages. The B & O workers struck, and were soon joined by a sympathy strike of employees on other lines. Soon, more than two thirds of all American railway mileage was closed. Violence then flared in the face of company intransigence. Rail yards were burned, strikers were fired upon, and before the dispute was over, private armies were hired by businessmen to patrol the streets of Chicago and other cities. Business picked up in the 1880's, but strikes still came more often. More than 80,000 workers in Chicago went on strike in the spring of '86. A small group of vocal anarchists then took advantage of the situation to draw attention to their cause. These men called for a rally at Chicago's Haymarket Square in connection with a strike against the McCormick Harvesting Machine Company. Chicago police attempted to break up the meeting, and in the midst of the ensuing melee a bomb was thrown at the police. Seven officers were killed, and dozens injured. The identity of the person who actually threw the bomb was never discovered, but local prosecutors still placed many on trial and obtained a conviction on flimsy evidence. Meanwhile, a skittish press saw in the Chicago "massacre" part of a carefully orchestrated attempt by foreign radicals, with clear ties to labor organizers, to foment a working-class rebellion. No evidence was ever produced to substantiate this charge, but suspicions grew with the increasing number of "aliens" in the city's work force. Does this remind you of anything you have encountered in this Chapter before?

The pattern of violence and paranoia continued into the 1890s. In 1892, a violent strike in the silver mines of Coeur d'Alene, Idaho, left many dead and ended with a declaration of martial law and the dispatching of federal troops. More ominous events occurred that same year in Pennsylvania. Andrew Carnegie's Homestead Steel Company, near Pittsburgh, had been accusing workers of resisting technological innovations, while workers argued that they were being denied the financial benefits of the company's newly efficient operations. A sharp national business downturn threatened a loss of profits. Henry Clay Frick, left in charge of the Homestead plant while Carnegie was out of the country, decided to "teach our employees a lesson." Wages were summarily cut. A strike followed. Frick imported a force of strikebreakers, and protected them with 300 Pinkerton detectives. The Homestead strikers fired on the Pinkertons, as they were travelling by barge up the Monongahela. The Pinkertons fired back, killing seven workers, and forcing a humiliating "surrender." In the meantime, Alexander Berkman, a self-confessed anarchistic Communist, burst into Frick's office and attempted to kill him. Frick survived, and used the assassination attempt to turn national opinion against the strikers. The state militia was eventually summoned, and the strike collapsed.

By 1894, when the events we next consider occurred, the public had been aroused by almost two decades of violence between labor and capital. The pitched battles between strikers and militiamen, the attacks on the police, the assassination attempts, the rantings of a few radicals, and the massive economic dislocations all mingled to create public fears of bloody class revolt, of armed insurrection. As you read the accounts of the Pullman strike and the opinion of the court, see if you can draw any parallels between the events of the 1890's and the events a century before which we reviewed in Chapter Two.

2. VIEWS OF THE PULLMAN STRIKE

LEON STEIN AND PHILIP TAFT, "INTRODUCTION," TO STEIN, ED., THE PULLMAN STRIKE*

v-vii (1969).

George M. Pullman developed a railroad car in which long-distance travelers could sleep in comfort * * *. To build and service his cars, Pullman created a model town, named "Pullman," just outside of Chicago, and he provided his workers with homes, water, gas, libraries—each at a fixed price and rent.

* * * It was an efficient plan to preserve intact a labor force of 5,800 men and to protect them from troublesome outside elements. Pullman saw no need to negotiate. He provided for their needs at his prices and rents.

But business is business, and when business took a bad turn early in 1893, Pullman laid off 3,000 workers and cut wages drastically for those not laid off—but rents and prices retained their usual high levels. For a time the men endured. Then they sent a grievance committee to see Mr. Pullman, with the assurance that none of the committee would be discharged. When three committee members were summarily fired, the men in the shops * * * walked out on May 11, 1894.

The world outside Pullman began to learn about the exorbitant rents in that "model town," the meager health facilities, the monopolistic service charges, the spy-ridden, dictatorial town rule. "Go and live in Pullman and find out how much Pullman gets sellin' city water and gas ten per cent higher to those poor fools," political boss Mark Hanna gibed. Nine years earlier, Richard T. Ely had concluded that "the idea of Pullman is un-American."

The Pullman strikers turned to the fledgling American Railway Union for aid. The ARU had come into existence with the help of Eugene V. Debs in June, 1893, and in its first year had won a major victory in an eighteen-day strike on the Great Northern Railroad. At the ARU convention, pent-up resentments swept the delegates. Despite Debs' reluctance to gamble with a general railroad strike in an unfavorable period, on June 21, the convention gave Pullman a five-day deadline—deal with the men's grievances or face a boycott. The five days passed, the boycott was declared in effect, and Debs, responding to the voice of the people, directed railroad workers to cut out Pullman cars, but to proceed with caution and to avoid violence.

A network of twenty-four railroads was centered in Chicago, where long strings of freight, mail, coach and Pullman cars were joined in vast yards. Chicago had a General Managers Association of top railroad executives whose purpose was not only to break the strike, but to destroy the union.

Toward this goal the GMA had, first of all, the aid of virtually the entire press. Newspapers across the country spread the cry that Debs was an anarchist's bloodthirsty dictator of a revolutionary strike whose purpose was the destruction of property.

Second, the GMA had the aid of the widespread unemployment of masses of hungry, roving men and women. Their violence was what the managers wanted as a prelude to stringent restraints. It is not surprising, therefore, that those men and women were frequently and easily able to enter the freight yards and set fire only to old, *discarded* equipment.

Third, the managers had a staunch ally in U.S. Attorney General Richard Olney, formerly a dedicated corporation lawyer with a passion for collecting railroad directorships. Olney devised a strategy that brought United States troops on the scene, despite the protest of liberal Illinois

Governor John P. Altgeld, who was maintaining law and order with police and militia.

Strikebreakers were imported. The managers refused to uncouple the Pullman cars so that not even the mail cars could be moved. On July 2, Olney obtained a blanket injunction charging the strikers with obstructing the mails and interfering with interstate commerce, both of which were forbidden by the Sherman Antitrust Act of 1890, which, ironically, was supposed to be a weapon not against labor, but against powerful corporations. Debs was arrested for conspiracy to obstruct the mails. He was released on bail, rearrested, and found in contempt of court.

* * *

WILLIAM H. CARWARDINE, THE PULLMAN STRIKE*

118–125 (1894).

[Carwardine was pastor of the First M.E. Church, Pullman, Ill.]

* * * My position was peculiar. I did not endorse the strike, and never have. I did not endorse the boycott. * * * But I stood for justice. * * *

* * *

Holding this position, I was surprised to find how the fear of anarchy and mob rule blinded the eyes of true men and women to the injustice that had wrought all these things. * * *

The inequalities of life as indicated in the social fabric of modern society are simply fearful. In many respects we are living in the grandest age this old world has ever seen. And yet, with our boasted progress and advancement; I realize that something is radically wrong in a condition of society that permits some to be so poor and others to be so rich. * * *

No person who has ever read Sir Walter Scott's wonderful story of "Ivanhoe" can forget the picture of Gurth, the Swineherd. Describing him, Scott says: "One part of his dress only remains, but it is too remarkable to be suppressed. It was a brass ring, resembling a dog's collar, but without any opening, and soldered fast round his neck, so loose as to form no impediment to his breathing, yet so tight as to be incapable of being removed excepting by the use of the file. On this singular gorget was engraven in Saxon characters an inscription of the following purport: 'Gurth, the son of Beowulph, is the born thrall of Cedric of Rotherwood.' "

* * * Gurth, the son of Beowulph, is with us yet.

While he wears not the collar of Cedric of Rotherwood, yet he is to all intents and purposes the chattel or "White Slave," of the "corporation," "trust" or "millionaire lords," * * *.

* Reprinted in Stein, ed., The Pullman Strike (1969).

We as a nation are dividing ourselves, like ancient Rome, into two classes, the rich and the poor, the oppressor and the oppressed. And on the side of the oppressor there is power and protection, class legislation and military support. Should this policy continue for a generation or two, there can be no doubt at all that working men who in times of war and invasion are the protectors of our liberties and homes, would refuse to take up arms in their defense. We are following in the tracks of ancient Rome, instead of learning useful lessons from her failures and defeats. No country can prosper, no government long perpetuate itself and its institutions, which does not administer judgment and justice alike to all of its people. * * *

The oppressed of to-day are white laborers and mechanics who, evidently, though without a Supreme Court decision, have no rights which millionaires and moneyed corporations are bound to respect. * * * Men and nations sometimes oppress to their own hurt. An estimate of the money losses in the present strike up to July 9, '94, puts them at $6,560,500, of which the laborers have lost in wages $1,500,000. * * * And all this grows out of the oppression of one man who was once a poor mechanic. He has gained wealth, and risen into power on it so that he can now take advantage of the necessities and poverty of his fellowmen to crush and oppress them.

Whatever the fathers who organized this government intended it to be, we, their successors, have evidently drifted very far away from the original intention of the founders. It is no longer a government of equal rights for all. The present strike may be overcome by federal bayonets and bullets, but the trouble will not end here. There is deep unrest in the lowest strata of society, the real burden-bearers of our country, which augurs ill for capitalistic oppression in the future. * * * I therefore deprecate, though necessary, the use of federal troops in this strike as a precedent, pregnant with evil in years to come. Capital seems to be organized to destroy the independence of labor and defeat its efforts at elevation, and labor is organized not only to protect itself, but to retaliate on capital. * * *

I appeal to the great body of the laboring classes, in view of the developments of the past few weeks, hereafter and forever to use your ballot aright. It is the God-given privilege of every American citizen, purchased at the sacrifice of blood, tears and property, and which is the birthright of 4,000 years of slow and painful evolution from degradation, slavery, and tyranny to the liberty of this latter nineteenth century. A ballot unknown in ancient days, in the Mosaic economy, and Roman history; a ballot that first began to make its appearance when the Barons at Runnymede demanded the rights of Magna Charta from King John of England, when Oliver Cromwell rose against the despotism of Charles I, with his Star Chamber, and when Martin Luther blew a blast that awoke all Europe to the dawn of the Reformation; a ballot that was not born until the urgent demands of a home government once more created a rebellion and the American Colonies were established, and that masterpiece of human composition, the Declaration of Independence, given to the world; a ballot, forsooth, that did not reach its majority until Abraham Lincoln broke the manacles that enslaved 3,000,000 black men, and signed that Magna Charta of human liberty, the Act of Emancipation; a ballot that represents * * * free homes, free schools, free press, a united people, the right of every man unmolested to worship God according to the dictates of his own conscience; the greatest gift given by God to man outside of his Blessed Son, our Lord and Savior Jesus Christ, and one that can give us, if we use it right, the grandest type of government under the sun!

* * *

IN RE DEBS

Supreme Court of the United States, 1895.
158 U.S. 564, 15 S.Ct. 900, 39 L.Ed. 1092.

[Eugene V. Debs, through his attorney Clarence Darrow, argued that he was entitled to writ of habeas corpus, since there was insufficient legal basis to support his jailing for contempt.]

MR. JUSTICE BREWER * * *

The case presented by the bill is this: The United States, finding that the interstate transportation of persons and property, as well as the carriage of the mails, is forcibly obstructed, and that a combination and conspiracy exists to subject the control of such transportation to the will of the conspirators, applied to one of their courts, sitting as a court of equity, for an injunction to restrain such obstruction and prevent carrying into effect such conspiracy. * * *

* * * What are the relations of the general government to interstate commerce and the transportation of the mails? They are those of direct supervision, control, and management. While, under the dual system which prevails with us, the powers of government are distributed between the state and the nation, and while the latter is properly styled a government of enumerated powers, yet within the limits of such enumeration it has all the attributes of sovereignty, and, in the exercise of those enumerated powers, acts directly upon the citizen, and not through the intermediate agency of the state.

[In order to support his argument Brewer then quoted from earlier court opinions.]

"No trace is to be found in the constitution of an intention to create a dependence of the government of the Union on those of the states, for the execution of the great powers assigned to it. Its means are adequate to its ends, and on those means alone was it expected to rely for the accomplishment of its ends. To impose on it the necessity of resorting to means which it cannot control, which another government may furnish or withhold, would render its course precarious, the result of its measures uncertain, and create a dependence on other governments, which might disappoint its most important designs, and is incompatible with the language of the constitution." Chief Justice Marshall in McCulloch v. State of Maryland, 4 Wheat. 316, 405, 424.

* * *

"This power to enforce its laws and to execute its functions in all places does not derogate from the power of the state to execute its laws at the same time and in the same places. The one does not exclude the other, except where both cannot be executed at the same time. In that case the words of the constitution itself show which is to yield. 'This constitution, and all laws which shall be made in pursuance thereof, * * * shall be the supreme law of the land.' " Mr. Justice Bradley in Ex parte Siebold, 100 U.S. 371, 395.

* * *

Among the powers expressly given to the national government are the control of interstate commerce and the creation and management of a postoffice system for the nation. * * *

* * *

As, under the constitution, power over interstate commerce and the transportation of the mails is vested in the national government, and congress, by virtue of such grant, has assumed actual and direct control, it follows that the national government may prevent any unlawful and forcible interference therewith. But how shall this be accomplished? Doubtless, it is within the competency of congress to prescribe by legislation that any interferences with these matters shall be offenses against the United States, and prosecuted and punished by indictment in the proper courts. But is that the only remedy? Have the vast interests of the nation in interstate commerce, and in the transportation of the mails, no other protection than lies in the possible punishment of those who interfere with it? To ask the question is to answer it. By article 3, § 2, cl. 3, of the federal constitution, it is provided: "The trial of all crimes except in cases of impeachment shall be by jury; and such trial shall be held in the state where the said crime shall have been committed." If all the inhabitants of a state, or even a great body of them, should combine to obstruct interstate commerce or the transportation of the mails, prosecutions for such offenses had in such a community would be doomed in advance to failure. And if the certainty of such failure was known, and the national government had no other way to enforce the freedom of interstate commerce and the transportation of the mails than by prosecution and punishment for interference therewith, the whole interests of the nation in these respects would be at the absolute mercy of a portion of the inhabitants of that single state.

But there is no such impotency in the national government. The entire strength of the nation may be used to enforce in any part of the land the full and free exercise of all national powers and the security of all rights intrusted by the constitution to its care. * * * If the emergency arises, the army of the nation, and all its militia, are at the service of the nation, to compel obedience to its laws.

But * * * is there no other alternative than the use of force on the part of the executive authorities whenever obstructions arise to the freedom of interstate commerce or the transportation of the mails? * * * The existence of this right of forcible abatement is not inconsistent with, nor does it destroy, the right of appeal, in an orderly way, to the courts for a judicial determination, and an exercise of their powers, by writ of injunction and otherwise, to accomplish the same result. In Borough of Stamford v. Stamford Horse R. Co., 56 Conn. 381, 15 Atl. 749, an injunction was asked by the borough to restrain the company from laying down its track in a street of the borough. The right of the borough to forcibly remove the track was insisted upon as a ground for questioning the jurisdiction of a court of equity, but the court sustained the injunction, adding: "And none the less so because of its right to remove the track by force. As a rule, injunctions are denied to those who have adequate remedy at law. * * * In some cases of nuisance, and in some cases of trespass * * *. [But w]hen the choice is between redress or prevention of injury by force and by peaceful process, the law is well pleased if the individual will consent to waive his right to the use of force, and await its action. Therefore, as between force and the extraordinary writ of injunction, the rule will permit the latter."

So, in the case before us, * * * it is more to the praise than to the blame of the government that, instead of determining for itself questions of right and wrong on the part of these petitioners and their associates, and enforcing that determination by the club of the policeman and the bayonet of the soldier, it submitted all those questions to the peaceful determination of judicial tribunals * * *.

* * * It is said that equity only interferes for the protection of property, and that the government has no property, and that the government has no property interest. A sufficient reply is that the United States have a property in the mails, the protection of which was one of the purposes of this bill. [In] Searight v. Stokes, 3 How. 151 * * * Chief Justice Taney [said]: "The United States have unquestionably a property in the mails. They are not mere common carriers, but a government, performing a high

official duty in holding and guarding its own property as well as that of its citizens committed to its care; for a very large portion of the letters and packages conveyed on this road, especially during the session of congress, consists of communications to or from the officers of the executive departments, or members of the legislature, on public service, or in relation to matters of public concern. * * * We think that a carriage, whenever it is carrying the mail, is laden with the property of the United States, within the true meaning of the compact."

* * *

It is obvious from these decisions that while it is not the province of the government to interfere in any mere matter of private controversy between individuals, or to use its great powers to enforce the rights of one against another, yet, whenever the wrongs complained of are such as affect the public at large, and are in respect of matters which by the constitution are intrusted to the care of the nation * * * then the mere fact that the government has no pecuniary interest in the controversy is not sufficient to exclude it from the courts * * *.

The national government, given by the constitution power to regulate interstate commerce, has by express statute assumed jurisdiction over such commerce when carried upon railroads. It is charged, therefore, with the duty of keeping those highways of interstate commerce free from obstruction, for it has always been recognized as one of the powers and duties of a government to remove obstructions from the highways under its control.

* * *

Indeed, the obstruction of a highway is a public nuisance (4 Bl. Comm. 167), and a public nuisance has always been held subject to abatement at the instance of the government * * *.

* * *

It is said that the jurisdiction heretofore exercised by the national government over highways has been in respect to waterways,—the natural highways of the country,—and not over artificial highways, such as railroads * * *, but the basis upon which [Congress] rests its jurisdiction over artificial highways is the same as that which supports it over the natural highways. Both spring from the power to regulate commerce. * * * The great case of Gibbons v. Ogden, 9 Wheat. 1, in which the control of congress over inland waters was asserted, rested that control on the grant of the power to regulate commerce. The argument of the chief justice was that commerce includes navigation, "and a power to regulate navigation is as expressly granted as if that term had been added to the word 'commerce.' " * * *

* * *

Constitutional provisions do not change, but their operation extends to new matters, as the modes of business and the habits of life of the people vary with each succeeding generation. The law of the common carrier is the same to-day as when transportation on land was by coach and wagon, and on water by canal boat and sailing vessel; yet in its actual operation it touches and regulates transportation by modes then unknown,—the railroad train and the steamship. Just so is it with the grant to the national government of power over interstate commerce. * * *

It is said that seldom have the courts assumed jurisdiction to restrain by injunction in suits brought by the government, either state or national, obstructions to highways either artificial or natural. This is undoubtedly true, but the reason is that the necessity for such interference has only been occasional. Ordinarily, the local authorities have taken full control over the matter, and by indictment for misdemeanor, or in some kindred way, have secured the removal of the obstruction and the cessation of the nuisance. * * * And, because the remedy by indictment is so efficacious, courts of equity entertain jurisdiction in such cases with great reluctance, * * * and they will only do so where there appears to be a necessity for their interference. Rowe v. Granite Bridge, 21 Pick. 347 * * *.

That the bill filed in this case alleged special facts calling for the exercise of all the powers of the court is not open to question. The picture drawn in it of the vast interests involved, not merely of the city of Chicago and the state of Illinois, but of all the states, and the general confusion into which the interstate commerce of the country was thrown; the forcible interference with that commerce; the attempted exercise by individuals of powers belonging only to government, and the threatened continuance of such invasions of public right, presented a condition of affairs which called for the fullest exercise of all the powers of the courts. * * *

* * *

Again, it is objected that it is outside of the jurisdiction of a court of equity to enjoin the commission of crimes. This, as a general proposition, is unquestioned. A chancellor has no criminal jurisdiction.

Something more than the threatened commission of an offense against the laws of the land is necessary to call into exercise the injunctive powers of the court. There must be some interferences, actual or threatened, with property or rights of a pecuniary nature; but when such interferences appear, the jurisdiction of a court of equity arises, and is not destroyed by the fact that they are accompanied by or are themselves violations of the criminal law. * * *

The law is full of instances in which the same act may give rise to a civil action and a criminal prosecution. An assault with intent to kill may be punished criminally, under an indictment therefor, or will support a civil action for damages; and the same is true of all other offenses which cause injury to person or property. In such cases the jurisdiction of the civil court is invoked, not to enforce the criminal law and punish the wrongdoer, but to compensate the injured party for the damages which he or his property has suffered; and it is no defense to the civil action that the same act by the defendant exposes him also to indictment and punishment in a court of criminal jurisdiction. * * *

Nor is there in this any invasion of the constitutional right of trial by jury. We fully agree with counsel that "it matters not what form the attempt to deny constitutional right may take; it is vain and ineffectual, and must be so declared by the courts." And we reaffirm the declaration made for the court by Mr. Justice Bradley in Boyd v. U.S., 116 U.S. 616, 635, 6 Sup.Ct. 524, that "it is the duty of courts to be watchful for the constitutional rights of the citizen, and against any stealthy encroachments thereon. Their motto should be obsta principiis." But the power of a court to make an order carries with it the equal power to punish for a disobedience of that order, and the inquiry as to the question of disobedience has been, from time immemorial, the special function of the court. * * * In Watson v. Williams, 36 Miss. 331, 341, it was said: "The power to fine and imprison for contempt, from the earliest history of jurisprudence, has been regarded as a necessary incident and attribute of a court, without which it could no more exist than without a judge. * * * A court without the power effectually to protect itself against the assaults of the lawless, or to enforce its orders, judgments, or decrees against the recusant parties before it, would be a disgrace to the legislation, and a stigma upon the age which invented it." In Cartwright's Case, 114 Mass. 230, 238, we find this language: "The summary power to commit and punish for contempts tending to obstruct or degrade the administration of justice is inherent in courts of chancery and other superior courts, as essential to the execution of their powers and to the maintenance of their authority, and is part of the law of the land, within the meaning of Magna Charta and of the twelfth article of our Declaration of Rights." [In] Commission v. Brimson, 154 U.S. 447–488, 14 Sup.Ct. 1125, * * * it was said: "Surely it cannot be supposed that the question of contempt of the authority of a court of the United States, committed by a disobedience of its orders, is triable, of right, by a jury."

* * *

Further, it is said by counsel in their brief:

"No case can be cited where such a bill in behalf of the sovereign has been entertained against riot and mob violence, though occurring on the highway. It is not such fitful and temporary obstruction that constitutes a nuisance. The strong hand of executive power is required to deal with such lawless demonstrations.

"The courts should stand aloof from them and not invade executive prerogative, nor, even at the behest or request of the executive, travel out of the beaten path of well-settled judicial authority. A mob cannot be suppressed by injunction; nor can its leaders be tried, convicted, and sentenced in equity.

"It is too great a strain upon the judicial branch of the government to impose this essentially executive and military power upon courts of chancery."

We do not perceive that this argument questions the jurisdiction of the court, but only the expediency of the action of the government in applying for its process. It surely cannot be seriously contended that the court has jurisdiction to enjoin the obstruction of a highway by one person, but that its jurisdiction ceases when the obstruction is by a hundred persons. It may be true, as suggested, that in the excitement of passion a mob will pay little heed to processes issued from the courts, and it may be, as said by counsel in argument, that it would savor somewhat of the puerile and ridiculous to have read a writ of injunction to Lee's army during the late Civil War. * * * But does not counsel's argument imply too much? Is it to be assumed that these defendants were conducting a rebellion or inaugurating a revolution, and that they and their associates were thus placing themselves beyond the reach of the civil process of the courts? We find in the opinion of the circuit court a quotation from the testimony given by one of the defendants before the United States strike commission, which is sufficient answer to this suggestion:

"As soon as the employees found that we were arrested, and taken from the scene of action, they became demoralized, and that ended the strike. It was not the soldiers that ended the strike. It was not the old brotherhoods that ended the strike. It was simply the United States courts that ended the strike. Our men were in a position that never would have been shaken, under any circumstances, if we had been permitted to remain upon the field, among them. Once we were taken from the scene of action, and restrained from sending telegrams or issuing orders or answering questions, then the minions of the corporations would be put to work. * * * Our headquarters were temporarily demoralized and abandoned, and we could not answer any messages. The men went back to work, and the ranks were broken, and the strike was broken up. * * * not by the army, and not by any other power, but simply and solely by the action of the United States courts in restraining us from discharging our duties as officers and representatives of our employees."

* * *

It must be borne in mind that this bill was not simply to enjoin a mob and mob violence. It was not a bill to command a keeping of the peace; much less was its purport to restrain the defendants from abandoning whatever employment they were engaged in. The right of any laborer, or any number of laborers, to quit work was not challenged. The scope and purpose of the bill was only to restrain forcible obstructions of the highways along which interstate commerce travels and the mails are carried. * * *

A most earnest and eloquent appeal was made to us in eulogy of the heroic spirit of those who threw up their employment, and gave up their means of earning a livelihood, not in defense of their own rights, but in sympathy for and to assist others whom they believed to be wronged. We yield to none in our admiration of any act of heroism or self-sacrifice, but we may be permitted to add that it is a lesson which cannot be learned too soon or too thoroughly that under this government of and by the people the means of redress of all wrongs are through the courts and at the ballot box, and that no wrong, real or fancied, carries with it legal warrant to invite as a means of redress the co-operation of a mob, with its accompanying acts of violence.

* * *

We enter into no examination of the act of July 2, 1890 (26 Stat. 209), upon which the circuit court relied mainly to sustain its jurisdiction. It must not be understood from this that we dissent from the conclusions of that court in reference to the scope of the act, but simply that we prefer to rest our judgment on the broader ground which has been discussed in this opinion, believing it of importance that the principles underlying it should be fully stated and affirmed.

The petition for a writ of habeas corpus is denied.

NOTES AND QUESTIONS

1. As the Introduction to this section suggests, in 1894 there was an intense mood of public apprehension. Many believed that the increasing patterns of radical agitation and labor unrest presaged open rebellion, and that strong measures from the central authorities were required. In this light, do the actions of President Cleveland and Attorney General Olney in sending federal troops to Chicago seem to result from national necessity or political expediency? For the suggestion that the federal government's policy toward labor unrest may have flowed from a particular economic theory, see Herbert Hovenkamp, "Labor Conspiracies in American Law, 1880–1930," 66 Tex.L.R. 919 (1988).

As you have seen from some of these materials, the workers of the American Railroad Union (ARU) of which Debs was President, had agreed to "support the Pullman strike by a boycott of Pullman cars on all railroads." The

ARU, however, offered to uncouple the sleeping (Pullman) cars, so that the rest of the trains could go on, including the mail cars. The General Managers Association (GMA), the organization of the high officers of the railroads, refused to allow uncoupling of the Pullman cars, however, believing that if they capitulated, any one of them might later be injured by similar strikes. When the ARU then refused to let the trains pass, interstate commerce on the rails came to a halt. See, e.g. Iris Nobel, Labor's Advocate: Eugene V. Debs 99–101 (1966).

But whether or not the railroads took their actions because of fears that they might individually suffer in the future from strikes, it also seems clear that the GMA members believed that if they allowed the uncoupling of Pullman cars they would be violating contracts with Pullman, thus leaving themselves open to civil suits for breach of contract. It appears that such uncoupling could also have been viewed as illegal discrimination against Pullman under the Interstate Commerce Act. See, e.g., A. Paul, Conservative Crisis and the Rule of Law: Attitudes of Bench and Bar 1887–1895 143 (Torchbook ed. 1969). Still, there may have been opportunities to resolve some of the points in issue among the workers, Pullman, and the Railroads by mediation or arbitration, but Pullman and the Railroads refused to consider this option. Id. at 153. Who, then, was ultimately responsible for the disruption of interstate commerce?

The Governor of Illinois, John Peter Altgeld, was the state's first Democratic governor, and quite sympathetic to labor. Two years earlier he had risked denunciation as an anarchist because of his pardoning of three men convicted of starting the Haymarket riot of 1886. Altgeld believed that "the jury which had convicted them was packed, the judge prejudiced, and the defendants not proved guilty." Altgeld eventually tried in vain to persuade Cleveland that the situation in Chicago was perfectly capable of being controlled by state militia, that the press had overstated the dimensions of the problem, and that there was no need for federal troops. Cleveland and his advisors disagreed. Without a request from state authorities, and without consultation of Altgeld, on July 4, 1894, 2,000 federal troops arrived in Chicago:

> From then on * * * the American Railway Union lost all control of the situation. Mobs, which the Strike Commission [the federal body which later investigated events] described as "composed generally of hoodlums, women, a low class of foreigners, and recruits of the criminal classes," took possession of railroad yards, upsetting, burning, and destroying cars and stealing whatever property they could lay their hands on. Nevertheless, it was difficult to accept the President's opinion that terror reigned in Chicago. Few strikers were seen in the mobs or arrested, and none were killed by troops or deputies. The American Railway Union had no part in instigating mob violence. On the other hand, no one could deny that a great deal of property was destroyed. Twelve people were killed.

Harold U. Faulkner, Politics, Reform and Expansion 1890–1900 177–178, 179 (1959). The activity thus described took place *after* the injunction forbidding interference with the mails, but *before* the arrest and indictment of Debs and three other ARU officials. The four were indicted for conspiracy, and, a week later, Debs and the others were charged with contempt of court for having disobeyed the injunction. The evidence against them consisted principally of facts which demonstrated that they should have known their men would continue to obstruct the mails, that they did nothing to prevent this obstruction, and that they refused to alter their conduct after the issuance of the injunction. The conspiracy proceedings, as you will soon learn from Debs himself, were never completed. The same court which issued the injunction tried Debs and his colleagues for the contempt. Debs received a six month sentence, the others three months.

2. The introductory readings give you something of the ideological flavor of the dispute, and the conditions of the workers. Stein and Taft quote a contemporary's suggestion that the system at Pullman was "un–American." What was meant by that? Is Reverend Carwardine correct when he suggests that for "all intents and purposes" there is no difference between modern industrial workers at Pullman, and Gurth, the Swineherd? Consider whether the lot of the laborer at Pullman was what was envisioned by Shaw when he wrote his opinion in Commonwealth v. Hunt. Would Shaw have approved of Pullman? What about Recorder Levy? Given the desperate plight of many American workers, and their dismay with American capitalists, why weren't more attracted to socialism? Karl Marx apparently expected the most advanced industrial economies, of which Great Britain and the United States might be taken as prime examples, to be the places where socialist revolutions would first occur. Why didn't this happen? Why did socialism never really gain a foothold in America? On this question, see John Bodnar, The Transplanted (1985), Olivier Zunz, Making America Corporate, 1870–1920 (1990), and Walter Nugent, "Large Corporations and New Middle Classes," 19 Reviews in American History 224 (1991).

3. Would you have concurred with the Supreme Court's opinion in the *Debs* case? Your version has been condensed, but you may still be able to sense that Justice Brewer spends much time stressing the nature of the United States' power to supervise interstate commerce. Is that really the issue in the *Debs* case? Do you find any similarities or differences between the approach in the *Debs* case and that of the *E.C. Knight* case? Are you convinced that the holding in contempt for disobedience of an injunction is *not* a matter of criminal law requiring a trial by jury? Does Brewer's conception of the permissible scope of federal court activity remind you at all of that of the Federalist Peters, expressed in United States v. Worrall, supra Chapter Two? Do you find any similarities in Brewer's conception of the role of the jury and judge to that expressed by Circuit Justice Hunt in *United States v. Anthony*, Chapter Four, supra?

4. Towards the close of his opinion, Justice Brewer states that in the course of the United States Government's actions in the Pullman strike, "The

right of any laborer, or any number of laborers to quit work was not challenged." Given the effect of the labor injunction as a tool to control unions, do you think that the laborers' right to "quit work" may have been altered? Do you find any clues to the court's feelings on the appropriateness of strikes and boycotts as a bargaining tool when it declares almost immediately afterwards that "under this government of and by the people the means of redress of all wrongs are through the courts and at the ballot box * * *?" Would lowering of wages be such a "wrong?" In any event, it appears that the Reverend Carwardine would be sympathetic to Justice Brewer's offering of the "ballot box" as a means of vindication of the workers' rights. Do you think that you would have found that satisfactory if you were a worker? Would Debs? Consider what he has to say about the ballot in the following excerpt.

5. Brewer ends his opinion with the assertion that "we enter into no examination of the act of July 2, 1890 (26 Stat. 209), upon which the circuit court relied mainly to sustain its jurisdiction." Is it not curious that the Supreme Court feels it necessary to adopt a different basis for jurisdiction from that of the circuit court? What was the act to which Brewer referred, and why did he "prefer to rest our judgment on the broader ground * * *?" Consider Stein & Taft's statement that Olney rested his request for injunction against the strikers on the charge that they were "obstructing the mails and interfering with interstate commerce, both of which were forbidden by the Sherman Antitrust Act of 1890 * * *." Would you have advised Olney thus to proceed? See generally Hovenkamp, supra note 1. For a balanced account of the Fuller Court (which included not only Justices Brewer and Peckham, but also Justice Holmes) see James W. Ely, Jr., The Chief Justiceship of Melville W. Fuller, 1888–1910 (1995).

EUGENE V. DEBS

EUGENE V. DEBS, "LIBERTY"

3–27 (1895).

[This was a speech delivered by Debs following his release from jail.]

* * * I greet you to-night as lovers of liberty and despisers of despotism. * * * The vindication and glorification of American principles of government, as proclaimed to the world in the Declaration of Independence, is the high purpose of this convocation.

"Speaking for myself personally, I am not certain whether this is an occasion for rejoicing or lamentation. I confess to a serious doubt as to whether this day marks my deliverance from bondage to freedom or my doom from freedom to bondage. Certain it is, in the light of recent judicial proceedings, that I stand in your presence stripped of my constitutional rights as a free-man and shorn of the most sacred prerogatives of American citizenship, and what is true of myself is true of every other citizen who has the temerity to protest against corporation rule or question the absolute sway of the money power. It is not law nor the administration of law of which I complain. It is the flagrant violation of the Constitution, the total abrogation of law and the usurpation of judicial and despotic power, by virtue of which my colleagues and myself were committed to jail * * *."

In a letter recently written by the venerable Judge Trumbull that eminent jurist says: "The doctrine announced by the Supreme Court in the Debs case, carried to its logical conclusion, places every citizen at the mercy of any prejudiced or malicious federal judge who may think proper to imprison him." * * * The authority of Judge Trumbull upon this question will not be impeached by anyone whose opinions are not deformed or debauched.

At this juncture I deem it proper to voice my demand for a trial by a jury of my peers. At the instigation of the railroad corporations centering here in Chicago I was indicted for conspiracy and I insist upon being tried as to my innocence or guilt. It will be remembered that the trial last winter terminated very abruptly on account of a sick juror. It was currently reported at the time that this was merely a pretext to abandon the trial and thus defeat the vindication of a favorable verdict * * *. Whether this be true or not, I do not know. * * * I am charged with conspiracy to commit a crime, and if guilty I should go to the penitentiary. All I ask is a fair trial and no favor. If the counsel for the government, alias the railroads, have been correctly quoted in the press, the case against me is "not to be pressed," as they "do not wish to appear in the light of persecuting the defendants." I repel with scorn their professed mercy. Simple justice is the demand. * * *

* * *

For the first time in the records of all the ages, the inalienable rights of man, "life, liberty and the pursuit of happiness," were proclaimed July 4th, 1776.

It was then that crowns, sceptres, thrones and the divine right of kings to rule sunk together and man expanded to glorious liberty and sovereignty. It was then that the genius of Liberty, speaking to all men in the commanding voice of Eternal Truth, bade them assert their heaven-decreed prerogatives and emancipate themselves from bondage. It was a proclamation countersigned by the Infinite—and man stood forth the coronated sovereign of the world, free as the tides that flow, free as the winds that blow, and on that primal morning when creation was complete, the morning stars and the sons of God, in anthem chorus, sang the song of Liberty. * * *

It does not matter that the Creator has sown with stars the fields of ether and decked the earth with countless beauties for man's enjoyment. It does not matter that air and ocean teem with the wonders of innumerable forms of life to challenge man's admiration and investigation. * * * If liberty is ostracised and exiled, man is a slave, and the world rolls in space and whirls around the sun a gilded prison, a domed dungeon, and though painted in all the enchanting hues that infinite art could command, it must stand forth a blotch amidst the singing spheres of the sidereal heavens * * *.

* * *

* * * As Americans, we have boasted of our liberties and continue to boast of them. They were once the nation's glory, and, if some have vanished, it may be well to remember that a remnant still remains. Out of prison, beyond the limits of Russian injunctions, out of reach of a deputy marshal's club, above the throttling clutch of corporations and the enslaving power of plutocracy, out of range of the government's machine guns and knowing the location of judicial traps and deadfalls, Americans may still indulge in the exaltation of liberty, though pursued through every lane and avenue of life by the baying hounds of usurped and unconstitutional power, glad if when night lets down her sable curtains, they are out of prison, though still the wage-slaves of a plutocracy which, were it in the celestial city, would wreck every avenue leading up to the throne of the Infinite by stealing the gold with which they are paved, and debauch Heaven's supreme court to obtain a decision that the command "thou shalt not steal" is unconstitutional.

Liberty, be it known, is for those only who dare strike the blow to secure and retain the priceless boon. * * * "[E]ternal vigilance is the price of liberty."

Is it worthwhile to iterate that all men are created free and that slavery and bondage are in contravention of the Creator's decree and have their origin in man's depravity?

If liberty is a birthright which has been wrested from the weak by the strong, or has been placed in peril by those who were commissioned to guard it * * * what is to be done? Above all, what is the duty of American workingmen whose liberties have been placed in peril? They are not hereditary bondsmen. Their fathers were free born—their sovereignty none denied and their children yet have the ballot. It has been called "a weapon that executes a free man's will as lightning does the will of God." * * * There is nothing in our government it can not remove or amend. It can make and unmake Presidents and Congresses and Courts. It can abolish unjust laws and consign to eternal odium and oblivion unjust judges, strip from them their robes and gowns and send them forth unclean as lepers to bear the burden of merited obloquy as Cain with the mark of a murderer. It can sweep away trusts, syndicates, corporations, monopolies, and every other abnormal development of the money power designed to abridge the liberties of workingmen and enslave them by the degradation incident to poverty and enforced idleness * * *. It can give our civilization its crowning glory—the co-operative commonwealth.

* * *

* * * My theme expands to proportions which obscure the victims of judicial tyranny, and yet, regardless of reluctance, it so happens by the decree of circumstances, that personal references are unavoidable. To wish it otherwise would be to deplore the organization of the American Railway Union and every effort that great organization has made to extend a helping hand to oppressed, robbed, suffering and starving men, women and children, the victims of corporate greed and rapacity. * * *

* * *

I hold it to have been inconceivable that an organization of workingmen, animated by such inspirations and aspirations, should have become the target for the shafts of judicial and governmental malice.

But the fact that such was the case brings into haggard prominence a condition of affairs that appeals to all thoughtful men in the ranks of organized labor and all patriotic citizens, regardless of vocation, who note the subtle invasions of the liberties of the American people by the courts, sustained by an administration that is equally dead to the guarantees of the constitution.

* * *

In the great Pullman strike the American Railway Union challenged the power of corporations in a way that had not previously been done, and the analyzation of this fact serves to expand it to proportions that the most conservative men of the nation regard with alarm.

It must be borne in mind that the American Railway Union did not challenge the government. It threw down no gauntlet to courts or armies—it simply resisted the invasion of the rights of workingmen by corporations. * * *

The corporations left to their own resources of money, mendacity and malice, of thugs and ex-convicts, leeches and lawyers, would have been overwhelmed with defeat and the banners of organized labor would have floated triumphant in the breeze.

This the corporations saw and believed—hence the crowning act of infamy in which the federal courts and the federal armies participated, and which culminated in the defeat of labor.

* * * [T]he defeat of the American Railway Union involved questions of law, constitution and government which, all things considered, are without a parallel in court and governmental proceedings under the constitution of the Republic. And it is this judicial and administrative usurpation of power to override the rights of states and strike down the liberties of the people that has conferred upon the incidents connected with the Pullman strike such commanding importance as to attract the attention of men of the highest attainments in constitutional law and of statesmen who, like Jefferson, view with alarm the processes by which the Republic is being wrecked and a despotism reared upon its ruins.

* * * [T]he country stood amazed as the corporations put forth their latent powers to debauch such departments of the government as were required to defeat labor in the greatest struggle for the right that was ever chronicled in the United States.

Defeated at every point, their plans all frustrated, out-generaled in tactics and strategy, while the hopes of labor were brightening and victory was in sight, the corporations, goaded to desperation, played their last card in the game of oppression by an appeal to the federal judiciary and to the federal administration. To this appeal the response came quick as lightning from a storm cloud. * * *

The corporations first attack the judicial department of the government, a department which, according to Thomas Jefferson, has menaced the integrity of the Republic from the beginning.

* * *

I am aware that innuendoes, dark intimations of venality are not regarded as courageous forms of arraignment, and yet the judicial despotism which marked every step of the proceedings by which my official associates and myself were doomed to imprisonment, was marked by infamies, supported by falsehoods and perjuries as destitute of truth as are the Arctic regions of orange blossoms.

* * *

There is an adage which says, "fight the devil with fire." In this connection why may it not be intimated that a judge who pollutes his high office at the behest of the money power has the hinges of his knees lubricated with oil from the tank of the corporation that thrift may follow humiliating obedience to its commands?

If not this, I challenge the world to assign a reason why a judge * * * should in a temple dedicated to justice, stab the Magna Charta of American liberty to death in the interest of corporations * * * ?

* * *

Once upon a time a corporation dog of good reputation was charged with killing sheep, though he had never been caught in the act. The corporation had always found him to be an obedient dog, willing to lick the hand of his master, and they declared he was a peaceable and law-abiding dog; but one day upon investigation the dog was found to have wool in his teeth and thenceforward, though the corporation stood manfully by him, he was believed to be a sheep-killing dog. The world has no means of knowing what methods corporations employ to obtain despotic decrees in their interest, but it is generally believed that if an examination could be made, there would be found wool in the teeth of the judge.

* * *

No afflatus, however divine, no genius, though saturated with the inspiring waters of Hippocrene, could now write in a spirit of patriotic fire of the old constitution, nor ever again until the people by the all pervading power of the ballot have repaired the old chart, closed the rents and obscured the judicial dagger holes made for the accommodation of millionaires and corporations, through which they drive their four-in-hands as if they were Cumberland gaps.

* * *

It might be a question in the minds of some if this occasion warrants the indulgence of the fancy. It will be remembered that Aesop taught the world by fables and Christ by parables but my recollection is that the old "stone preachers"* were as epigrammatic as an unabridged dictionary.

I remember one old divine who, one night, selected for his text George M. Pullman, and said: "George is a bad egg—handle him with care. Should you crack his shell the odor would depopulate Chicago in an hour." * * * Another old sermonizer who said he had been preaching since man was a molecule, declared he had of late years studied corporations, and that they were warts on the nose of our national industries * * *. An-

* Debs is here building on Shakespeare's observation that: "And this, our life, exempt from public haunt, finds tongues in trees, books in the running brooks, sermons in stones, and good in everything." William Shakespeare, As You Like It, II. i. 15–17.

other old Stone said he knew more about strikes than Carroll D. Wright,** and that he was present when the slaves built the pyramids; that God Himself had taught His lightning, thunderbolts, winds, waves and earthquakes to strike, and that strikes would proceed, with bullets or ballots, until workingmen, no longer deceived and cajoled by their enemies, would unify, proclaim their sovereignty and walk the earth free men.

O, yes; Shakespeare was right when he said there were sermons in stones. I recall one rugged-visaged old Stone preacher who claimed to have been a pavement bowlder in a street of heaven before the gold standard was adopted, and who discussed courts. He said they had been antagonizing the decrees of heaven since the day when Lucifer was cast into the bottomless pit. Referring to our Supreme Court he said it was a nest of rodents forever gnawing at the stately pillars supporting the temple of our liberties. I recall how his eyes, as he lifted their stony lids, flashed indignation like orbs of fire, and how his stony lips quivered as he uttered his maledictions of judicial treason to constitutional liberty.

* * * One old divine, having read some of the plutocratic papers on the Pullman strike and their anathemas of sympathy, when one workingman's heart, throbbing responsive to the divine law of love, prompted him to aid his brother in distress, discussed sympathy. He said sympathy was one of the perennial flowers of the Celestial City * * *.

Referring to the men and women of other labor organizations who had sympathized with the American Railway Union in its efforts to rescue Pullman's slaves from death by starvation, the old preacher placed a crown of jewelled eulogies upon their heads and said that in all the mutations of life * * *, there would never come a time to them when * * * they would not cherish as a valued souvenir of all their weary years that one act of sympathy for the victims of the Pullman piracy, and that when presented at the pearly gate of paradise, it would swing wide open and let them in amidst the joyous acclaims of angels.

NOTES AND QUESTIONS

1. Debs's speech, delivered the evening of his release from jail, was not, of course, intended to be a model legal brief. It was given in the Chicago Armory on Michigan Avenue, immediately after Debs's arrival in Chicago, where he was greeted by a cheering, tearful crowd possibly one hundred thousand strong, wearing the white ribbons of the ARU, and singing union songs. Nobeo, Labor's Advocate: Eugene V. Debs 131–133 (1966). Legal document though it is not, perhaps we could justify having you read this speech for the glorious example of Shakespearean or perhaps Chaucerian euphony which it offers as an implied reproach to the degraded prose of our day. Whether or not this speech is like your other materials, however, there ought to be much in it which you can evaluate based on what you have so far stud-

** A Commissioner of the United States Strike Commission.

ied. For example, how would you compare Debs's statements regarding "liberty" and "slavery" with those of the American Revolutionaries like James Otis, John Adams, or Thomas Jefferson? Debs invokes Jefferson with some frequency. Do you suppose Jefferson and Debs would have agreed on the ultimate meaning of "liberty?" What, if anything, can the views of Jefferson tell Debs about appropriate ways of dealing with capital and labor in the industrial age? For a cogent evaluation of Debs's thought and life see Nick Salvatore, Eugene V. Debs: Citizen and Socialist (2d ed., 2007). For an analysis of Debs's legal battles with the federal courts see Daniel Novak, "The Pullman Strike Cases: Debs, Darrow and the Labor Injunction," in Michael R. Belknap, editor, American Political Trials 119 (Revised, Expanded Edition, 1994). For further reading on all aspects of the Pullman Strike, see the collection of essays in Richard Schneirov, Sheldon Stromquist, and Nick Salvatore, eds., The Pullman Strike and the Crisis of the 1890's: Essays on Labor and Politics (1999), and the monograph by David Ray Papke, The Pullman Case: The Clash of Labor and Capital in Industrial America (1999). Papke, the author of perhaps the most balanced account of the Pullman case, observes, regarding the events of the late nineteenth century, that "capital was likely to perceive the struggle as one between inventive and imaginative visionaries on the one hand and often unreliable workers on the other. Organized labor, meanwhile, might cast the struggle as one between greedy capitalist bosses and honest hard-working citizens." Id., at xii. Who got it right?

2. Like Carwardine, and like Justice Brewer, Debs offers the "ballot" as a means of solving America's industrial problems. What social system does Debs believe is appropriate once reformers have been elected, however? What do you suppose Debs means when he proposes, as a "crowning glory" to our civilization, "the co-operative commonwealth?" Consider Debs's views about corporations, and the people who run them. Is this hostility philosophically close to Harlan's or Peckham's ideas on trusts? Do you believe that Debs would share their conceptions of the appropriate economic order? How about Debs's views on law, lawyers, and judges? Is he a latter-day Honestus? Does the legal profession have a place in Debs's "co-operative commonwealth?"

3. Some lawyers appear to have understood that the law would have to find means of reconciling emerging class conflicts. In a speech delivered in 1888, entitled "Impending Perils," Charles C. Bonney, a former president of the Illinois Bar Association, told his listeners that it was the duty of government "to protect the weak against the strong, and to prevent, by stringent laws and their vigorous enforcement, the oppression of the poor and friendless by the rich and powerful." Bonney proceeded to propose that the American bar take the side of the angels "in the great conflict now impending between the people and the giant forces that are striving for the practical control of the republic." Bonney suggested that the bar support "a comprehensive plan for the settlement of all labor disputes, beginning with collective bargaining, then mediation, and finally compulsory arbitration," and that the government involve itself more in the regulation of labor, production and trade. Quoted in A. Paul, Conservative Crisis and the Rule of Law 32–33 (Torchbook ed., 1969).

In 1895, however, Debs probably had few friends within the American legal profession. The Senior editor of the American Law Review, Seymour D. Thompson, whom Arnold Paul states "could generally be counted on the progressive side of public issues," called Debs an "adventurer," and "irresponsible vagabond," and a "fiend" who produced widespread calamities which he observed with "insane hilarity." Thompson saw the Pullman strike as an attempt "to wrest from intelligent and capable men the property which they have acquired, and to put it into the hands of the unintelligent and ignorant." 28 American Law Review 630–634, 637 (1894) *quoted* in Paul, supra, at 145–146. Accordingly, Thompson believed that the conduct of Pullman and the railroads was blameless, as "they represented the right of every man to manage his own business and to keep his own contracts without dictation from third persons. * * * They entered upon a struggle with an unknown and appalling force, which threatened to revolutionize the very foundations of society and to reverse all the processes by which our splendid industrial system has been built up." Id. Does Debs's speech suggest that Thompson was right or wrong?

4. How accurately did Debs characterize late nineteenth century American law? Reread Professor Morton Horwitz's conclusions regarding the style of judicial reasoning during this period, reproduced in Chapter Four, supra. Do you find support for Horwitz's view in the court decisions you have recently read?

5. Other scholars have found that, at least by the end of the nineteenth century, the judicial philosophy was not as uniform as Horwitz's analysis suggests. For example, Professor Morton Keller, after commenting on some opinions that seemed to go against the workingmen, particularly on the ground that state laws regulating working conditions were unconstitutional tamperings with freedom of contract, nevertheless concluded that

> * * * the extent of this antilabor decisionmaking often has been exaggerated. An 1897 review of 1,639 state labor laws enacted during the preceding twenty years found that only 114 of them—7 percent—had been held unconstitutional. * * * The police power of the states to regulate working conditions continued to be a powerful and widely accepted legal doctrine. Critics of labor injunctions had a strong array of arguments. They held that when the courts ordered workers to return to their jobs this was in effect enforcing a form of slavery; and that when judges issued injunctions in their equity capacity, they were imposing criminal sanctions without a jury trial or other common law safeguards. Equity was being transformed, charged one critic, from the protection of private rights to "the perversion of public rights, or the punishment of private wrongs."
>
> The activism of the courts in labor matters was blamed on "the dry rot which has attacked our state executives and our state legislatures, which renders them unable to perform in anything like an efficient manner their proper functions." But precisely because so much was ex-

pected of the courts, they could not act indefinitely in a sensitive area like labor relations without taking account of public opinion or economic and social realities. By the late 1890s, the influential New York and Massachusetts courts were increasingly inclined to uphold state laws affecting the conditions of labor. In Holden v. Hardy (1898) the United States Supreme Court sustained a Utah eight-hour law for miners. The courts, in sum, were no more single-minded in their response to a new, industrial America than were the other sectors of the polity.

Morton Keller, Affairs of State 407–408 (1977). Copyright © 1977 by Morton Keller, published by the Belknap Press of the Harvard University Press, Cambridge Massachusetts, and London, England. Reprinted with the permission of the publisher and the author. Does the following article suggest other reasons why the lot of the American industrial workers was not quite as dire as Debs may have thought?

LAWRENCE M. FRIEDMAN AND JACK LADINSKY, SOCIAL CHANGE AND THE LAW OF INDUSTRIAL ACCIDENTS*

67 Col.L.Rev. 50, 59–79 (1967).

A general pattern may be discerned which is common to the judicial history of many rules of law. The courts enunciate a rule, intending to "solve" a social problem * * *. If the rule comports with some kind of social consensus, it will in fact work a solution—that is, it will go unchallenged, or, if challenged, will prevail. Challenges will not usually continue, since the small chance of overturning the rule is not worth the cost of litigation. If, however, the rule is weakened—if courts engraft exceptions to it, for example—then fresh challenges probing new weaknesses will be encouraged. Even if the rule retains some support, it will no longer be efficient and clear-cut. Ultimately, the rule may no longer serve anybody's purposes. At this point, a fresh (perhaps wholly new) "solution" will be attempted.

The history of the fellow-servant rule rather neatly fits this scheme. Shaw wrote his Farwell opinion in 1842. During the latter part of the century, judges began to reject his reasoning. The "tendency in nearly all jurisdictions," said a Connecticut court in 1885, was to "limit rather than enlarge" the range of the fellow-servant rule. * * *

The rule was strong medicine, and it depended for its efficacy upon continued, relatively certain, and unswerving legal loyalty. Ideally, if the rule were strong and commanded nearly total respect from the various agencies of law, it would eliminate much of the mass of litigation that might otherwise arise. Undoubtedly, it did prevent countless thousands of law suits; but it did not succeed in choking off industrial accident litigation. For example, industrial accident litigation dominated the docket of the Wisconsin Supreme Court at the beginning of the age of workmen's compensation; far more cases arose under that heading than under any other single field of law. Undoubtedly, this appellate case-load was merely the visible portion of a vast iceberg of litigation. Thus, the rule did not command the respect required for efficient operation and hence, in the long run, survival.

One reason for the continued litigation may have been simply the great number of accidents that occurred. At the dawn of the industrial revolution, when Shaw wrote, the human consequences of that technological change were unforeseeable. In particular, the toll it would take of human life was unknown. But by the last quarter of the nineteenth century, the number of industrial accidents had grown enormously. After 1900, it is estimated, 35,000 deaths and 2,000,000 injuries occurred every year in the United States. * * *

In addition to the sheer number of accidents, other reasons for the increasing number of challenges to the rule in the later nineteenth century are apparent. If the injury resulted in death or permanent disability, it broke off the employment relationship; the plaintiff or his family thereafter had nothing to lose except the costs of suit. The development of the contingent fee system provided the poor man with the means to hire a lawyer. * * *

The contingent fee system was no more than a mechanism, however. A losing plaintiff's lawyer receives no fee; that is the essence of the system. The fact is that plaintiffs won many of their lawsuits; in so doing, they not only weakened the fellow-servant rule, but they encouraged still more plaintiffs to try their hand, still more attorneys to make a living from personal injury work. In trial courts, the pressure of particular cases—the "hard" cases in which the plight of the plaintiff was pitiful or dramatic—tempted judges and juries to find for the little man and against the corporate defendant. In Shaw's generation, many leading appellate judges shared his view of the role of the judge; they took it as their duty to lay down grand legal principles to govern whole segments of the economic order. Thus, individual hardship cases had to be ignored for the sake of higher duty. But this was not the exclusive judicial style, even in the appellate courts. And in personal injury cases, lower court judges and juries were especially prone to tailor justice to the case at hand. For example, in Wisconsin, of 307 personal injury cases involving workers that appeared before the state supreme court up to 1907, nearly two-thirds had been decided in favor of the worker in the lower courts. * * *

* * * [S]ympathy for injured workers manifested itself also in changes in doctrine. On the appellate court level, a number of mitigations of the fellow-servant rule developed near the end of the nineteenth century. For example, it had always been conceded that the employer was liable if he

was personally responsible (through his own negligence) for his worker's injury. * * * Out of this simple proposition grew the so-called vice-principal rule, which allowed an employee to sue his employer where the negligent employee occupied a supervisory position such that he could more properly be said to be an alter ego of the principal than a mere fellow-servant. * * *

There were scores of other "exceptions" to the fellow-servant rule, enunciated in one or more states. * * * Among these was the duty to furnish a safe place to work, safe tools, and safe appliances. Litigation on these points was enormous, and here too the cases cannot readily be summed up or even explained. In Wedgwood v. Chicago & Northwestern Railway Co. [41 Wisc. 478 (1877)] the plaintiff, a brakeman, was injured by a "large and long bolt, out of place, and which unnecessarily, carelessly and unskillfully projected beyond the frame, beam or brakehead, in the way of the brakeman going to couple the cars." The trial court threw the case out, but the Wisconsin Supreme Court reversed:

> It is true, the defendant * * * is a railroad corporation, and can only act through officers or agents. But this does not relieve it from responsibility for the negligence of its officers and agents whose duty it is to provide safe and suitable machinery for its road which its employees are to operate.

So phrased, of course, the exception comes close to swallowing the rule. * * *

[There were many qualifications and exceptions to these rules, and this d]octrinal complexity and vacillation in the upper courts, coupled with jury freedom in the lower courts, meant that by the end of the century the fellow-servant rule had lost much of its reason for existence: it was no longer an efficient cost-allocating doctrine. * * *

The numerous judge-made exceptions reflected a good deal of uncertainty about underlying social policy. The same uncertainty was reflected in another sphere of legal activity—the legislature. Though the rule was not formally abrogated, it was weakened by statute in a number of jurisdictions. * * * The early nineteenth century cannot be uncritically described as a period that accepted without question business values and practices. Rather, it accepted the ideal of economic growth, which certain kinds of enterprise seemed to hinder. Thus in the age of Jackson, as is well known, popular feeling ran high against financial institutions, chiefly the chartered banks. Banks were believed to have far too much economic power; they corrupted both the currency and the government. They were a "clog upon the industry of this country." But many a good judge, who decried the soulless corporation (meaning chiefly the moneyed kind) in the best Jacksonian tradition, may at the same time have upheld the fellow-servant rule. * * *

* * * Great masses of people had come to accept the notion that the power of the railroads was a threat to farmers and a threat to the independence and stability of democratic institutions. Out of the ashes of ineffective and impermanent state regulation of railroads arose what ultimately became a stronger and more systematic program of regulation, grounded in federal power over the national economy.

The Interstate Commerce Commission was created in 1887, chiefly to outlaw discrimination in freight rates and other practices deemed harmful to railroad users. The original legislation had nothing to say about railroad accidents and safety. But this did not long remain the case. The railroads had become unpopular defendants relatively early in American legal history. By 1911, twenty-five states had laws modifying or abrogating the fellow-servant doctrine for railroads. * * * In 1893, Congress required interstate railroads to equip themselves with safety appliances, and provided that any employee injured "by any locomotive, car, or train in use" without such appliances would not "be deemed * * * to have assumed the risk thereby occasioned."

The Federal Employers' Liability Act of 1908 [FELA] went much further; it abolished the fellow-servant rule for railroads and greatly reduced the strength of contributory negligence and assumption of risk as defenses. * * *

FELA shows one of many possible outcomes of the decline in efficacy of the fellow-servant rule. Under it, the rule was eliminated, and the law turned to a "pure" tort system—pure in the sense that the proclivities of juries were not interfered with by doctrines designed to limit the chances of a worker's recovery. But the railroads were a special case. Aside from the special history of regulation, the interstate character of the major railroads made them subject to national safety standards and control by a single national authority. For other industrial employers, the FELA route was not taken; instead, workmen's compensation acts were passed. In either case, however, the fellow-servant rule was abolished, or virtually so. Either course reflects, we can assume, some kind of general agreement that the costs of the rule outweighed its benefits.

The common law doctrines were designed to preserve a certain economic balance in the community. When the courts and legislatures created numerous exceptions, the rules lost much of their efficiency as a limitation on the liability of businessmen. * * * There were costs of settlements, costs of liability insurance, costs of administration, legal fees and the salaries of staff lawyers. These costs rose steadily, at the very time when American business, especially big business, was striving to rationalize and bureaucratize its operations. * * * The costs of industrial accident liability were not easily predictable, partly because legal consequences of accidents were not predictable. * * *

In addition, industry faced a serious problem of labor unrest. Workers and their unions were dissatisfied with many aspects of factory life. The lack of compensation for industrial accidents was one obvious weakness. Relatively few injured workers received compensation. Under primitive state employers' liability statutes, the issue of liability and the amount awarded still depended upon court rulings and jury verdicts. Furthermore, the employer and the insurance carrier might contest a claim or otherwise delay settlement in hopes of bringing the employee to terms. * * *

When an employee did recover, the amount was usually small. The New York Commission found that of forty-eight fatal cases studied in Manhattan * * * most received less than $500. The deceased workers had averaged $15.22 a week in wages; only eight families recovered as much as three times their average yearly earnings. * * *

Litigation costs consumed much of whatever was recovered. It was estimated that, in 1907, "of every $100 paid out by [employers in New York] on account of work accidents but $56 reached the injured workmen and their dependents." * * *

These figures on the inadequacy of recoveries are usually cited to show how little the workers received for their pains. But what did these figures mean to employers? Assuming that employers, as rational men, were anxious to pay as little compensation as was necessary to preserve industrial peace and maintain a healthy workforce, the better course might be to pay a higher net amount direct to employees. Employers had little or nothing to gain from their big payments to insurance companies, lawyers, and court officials. Perhaps at some unmeasurable point of time, the existing tort system crossed an invisible line and thereafter, purely in economic terms, represented on balance a net loss to the industrial establishment. From that point on, the success of a movement for change in the system was certain, provided that businessmen could be convinced that indeed their self-interest lay in the direction of reform and that a change in compensation systems did not drag with it other unknowable and harmful consequences.

As on many issues of reform, the legal profession did not speak with one voice. Certainly, many lawyers and judges were dissatisfied with the status quo. Judges complained about the burdens imposed on the court system by masses of personal injury suits; many felt frustrated by the chaotic state of the law, and others were bothered by their felt inability to do justice to injured workmen. * * * Some influential judges despaired of piecemeal improvements and played an active role in working for a compensation system. In a 1911 opinion, Chief Justice J.B. Winslow of Wisconsin wrote:

> No part of my labor on this bench has brought such heartweariness to me as that ever increasing part devoted to the consideration of

personal injury actions brought by employees against their employers. The appeal to the emotions is so strong in these cases, the results to life and limb and human happiness so distressing, that the attempt to honestly administer cold, hard rules of law * * * make[s] drafts upon the heart and nerves which no man can appreciate who has not been obliged to meet the situation himself * * *. These rules are archaic and unfitted to modern industrial conditions * * *.

When [the faithful laborer] * * * has yielded up life, or limb, or health in the service of that marvelous industrialism which is our boast, shall not the great public * * * be charged with the duty of securing from want the laborer himself, if he survive, as well as his helpless and dependent ones? Shall these latter alone pay the fearful price of the luxuries and comforts which modern machinery brings within the reach of all?

These are burning and difficult questions with which the courts cannot deal, because their duty is to administer the law as it is, not to change it; but they are well within the province of the legislative arm of the government.

* * * Legal writers and law teachers also spoke out against the common law and in favor of a compensation system. Roscoe Pound voiced a common opinion in 1907:

> [I]t is coming to be well understood by all who have studied the circumstances of modern industrial employment that the supposed contributory negligence of employees is in effect a result of the mechanical conditions imposed on them by the nature of their employment, and that by reason of these conditions the individual vigilance and responsibility contemplated by the common law are impossible in practice.

* * *

When considerations of politics were added to those of business economics and industrial peace, it was not surprising to find that businessmen gradually withdrew their veto against workmen's compensation statutes. * * * In 1910, the president of the National Association of Manufacturers (NAM) appointed a committee to study the possibility of compensating injured workmen without time-consuming and expensive litigation, and the convention that year heard a speaker tell them that no one was satisfied with the present state of the law—that the employers' liability system was "antagonistic to harmonious relations between employers and wage workers." By 1911 the NAM appeared convinced that a compensation system was inevitable and that prudence dictated that business play a positive role in shaping the design of the law—otherwise the law would be "settled for us by the demagogue, and agitator and the socialist with a vengeance." Business would benefit economically and politically from a compensation system, but only if certain conditions were present. Business, therefore, had an interest in pressing for a specific kind of program * * *. For example, it was imperative that the new system be in fact as actuarially predictable as business demanded; it was important that the costs of the program be fair and equal in their impact upon particular industries, so that no competitive advantage or disadvantage flowed from the scheme. Consequently the old tort actions had to be eliminated, along with the old defenses of the company. In exchange for certainty of recovery by the worker, the companies were prepared to demand certainty and predictability of loss—that is, limitation of recovery. The jury's caprice had to be dispensed with. In short, when workmen's compensation became law, as a solution to the industrial accident problem, it did so on terms acceptable to industry. * * *

* * *

Between 1910 and 1920 the method of compensating employees injured on the job was fundamentally altered in the United States. In brief, workmen's compensation statutes eliminated (or tried to eliminate) the process of fixing civil liability for industrial accidents through litigation in common law courts. Under the statutes, compensation was based on statutory schedules, and the responsibility for initial determination of employee claims was taken from the courts and given to an administrative agency. Finally, the statutes abolished the fellow-servant rule and the defenses of assumption of risk and contributory negligence. Wisconsin's law, passed in 1911, was the first general compensation act to survive a court test. Mississippi, the last state in the Union to adopt a compensation law, did so in 1948.

Compensation systems varied from state to state, but they had many features in common. The original Wisconsin law was representative of the earlier group of statutes. It set up a voluntary system—a response to the fact that New York's courts had held a compulsory scheme unconstitutional on due process grounds. Wisconsin abolished the fellow-servant rule and the defense of assumption of risk for employers of four or more employees. In turn, the compensation scheme, for employers who elected to come under it, was made the "exclusive remedy" for an employee injured accidentally on the job. The element of "fault" or "negligence" was eliminated, and the mere fact of injury at work "proximately caused by accident," and not the result of "wilful misconduct," made the employer liable to pay compensation but exempt from ordinary tort liability. The state aimed to make it expensive for employers to stay out of the system. Any employer who did so was liable to suit by injured employees and the employer was denied the common law defenses.

The compensation plans strictly limited the employee's amount of recovery. In Wisconsin, for example, if an accident caused "partial disability," the worker was to receive 65% of his weekly loss in wages during the period of disability, not to exceed four times his average annual earnings. The statutes, therefore, were compensatory, not punitive, and the measure of compensation was, subject to strict limitations, the loss of earning power of the worker. In the original Wisconsin act, death benefits were also payable to dependents of the worker. If the worker who died left "no person dependent upon him for support," the death benefit was limited to "the reasonable expense of his burial, not exceeding $100." Neither death nor injury as such gave rise to a right to compensation—only the fact of economic loss to someone, either the worker himself or his family. * * *

* * *

NOTES AND QUESTIONS

1. Of what significance is it that "industrial accident litigation dominated the docket of the Wisconsin Supreme Court [in the early twentieth century] * * * far more cases arose under that heading than under any single field of law." Specifically, if one solves the industrial accident "problem," does this remove or increase pressure to solve other social problems? If the "contingency fee arrangement" was a significant factor in enabling injured workers to bring suit, and thus put pressure on the "fellow-servant" rule—pressure that ultimately led to its demise—and if this represented a democratization of the furnishing of legal services, what is the effect on democracy of the abolition of the "fellow-servant" rule through workmen's compensation schemes? By the way, does the "safetool" exception to the fellow-servant rule remind you of the "trade fixtures" exemption to the "waste" doctrine? See Van Ness v. Pacard, supra Chapter Three.

2. How do you evaluate the anguish suffered by some of the early twentieth century judges as they applied the legal doctrines regarding employer's liability? Note that in 1911 Chief Justice J.B. Winslow of Wisconsin called his task "distressing," and said that "These rules are archaic and unfitted to modern industrial conditions * * *." And yet, the Judge said that "These are burning and difficult questions with which the courts cannot deal, because their duty is to administer the law as it is, not to change it * * *." Is there a slip in reasoning there? Is Winslow's attitude consistent with that evidenced by Chief Justice Shaw in the labor cases? How about the perspective of the early nineteenth century judges we studied in Chapter Three?

3. Why do you suppose that in 1911 the New York Court of Appeals unanimously declared the nation's first workmen's compensation statute unconstitutional in Ives v. South Buffalo Ry. Co., 201 N.Y. 271, 94 N.E. 431 (1911)? Why then, did the Wisconsin scheme, and later Workmen's Compensation Acts survive constitutional scrutiny? Indeed, two years later the New York State Constitution was amended to allow involuntary workmen's compensation legislation. Finally, four years after that, in New York Cent. R. Co. v. White, 243 U.S. 188, 37 S.Ct. 247, 61 L.Ed. 667 (1917) and Hawkins v. Bleakly, 243 U.S. 210, 37 S.Ct. 255, 61 L.Ed. 678 (1917) the United States

Supreme Court held compulsory *and* elective workmen's compensation schemes to be constitutional. See generally Price V. Fishback and Shawn Everett Kantor, "The Adoption of Workers' Compensation in the United States, 1900–1930," 41 J.Law & Econ. 305 (1998), P. Blake Keating, "Historical Origins of Workmen's Compensation Laws in the United States: Implementing the European Social Insurance Idea," 11 Kan.J.L. & Pub.Pol. 279 (2001).

4. Is the passage of workmen's compensation legislation a "victory of employees over employers?" Whom does it benefit to replace a "fault-oriented" compensation system with one unconcerned with fault? What does the history of workmen's compensation efforts, and the fall of the fellow-servant doctrine tell you about the workings of the late nineteenth century and early twentieth century judiciary and legislatures? Does the evidence support Horwitz's view of the judiciary, and its preoccupation with "formalism?" Does the evidence support Professor Keller's assessment of judicial uncertainty in the face of massive societal and economic change? Consider the free-market, contractarian model that Justice Shaw and Recorder Levy advanced. Given the social unrest and the judicial and legislative efforts which you have just read about, including the Sherman Act, *and* the workmen's compensation statutes, do you find that American law was still following Shaw's and Levy's economic model in the late nineteenth and early twentieth century? For a consideration of newly-emerging economic models at the turn of the century, see Herbert Hovenkamp, "The First Great Law & Economics Movement," 42 Stan.L.Rev. 993 (1990). For the dramatic change in conceptions about the law of contract and the contract clause of the Constitution during this period, see Walter F. Pratt, Jr., "American Contract Law at the Turn of the Century," 39 S.Car.L.Rev. 415 (1988), and Stephen A. Siegel, "Understanding the Nineteenth Century Contract Clause: The Role of the Property—Privilege Distinction and 'Takings' Clause Jurisprudence," 60 S.Cal.L.Rev. 1 (1986). See also David N. Mayer, "The Jurisprudence of Christopher G. Tiedeman: A Study in the Failure of Laissez–Faire Constitutionalism," 55 Mo.L.Rev. 93 (1991), and sources there cited. We will have further evidence with which to examine the nature of the interaction between American law and the American economy in the next Chapter.

CHAPTER 6

LAW AND JURISPRUDENCE FOR THE MODERN INDUSTRIAL AGE

■ ■ ■

INTRODUCTION: Society, Modernity, and the Welfare State in the Twentieth Century

The place of centralized government in national life has been a roiling issue in American politics since 1776. It surfaced as an area of genuine disagreement in the 1781 Articles of Confederation and in the debates in the Constitutional Convention of 1787. As we've seen, a lack of consensus about the authority of the national government led eleven Southern states to secede from the Union in 1861. In the 20th century, national politics was virtually defined by disputes over the role and scale of centralized national power, from Theodore Roosevelt's New Nationalism, to the New Deal of FDR, the Great Society of LBJ, and the New Federalism of Ronald Reagan.

Most people who know little about the law believe that the most important law-maker and enforcer in our country is the Federal government, but for much of American history, state and local governments have been much more prominent in citizens' daily lives. The 10th Amendment reserved to the states those powers not assigned to the Federal government, and foremost among these was the "police power." In the 19th century it was at the state, county, and municipal levels where Americans worked out essential matters of domestic policy: conditions of labor, public health, crime and punishment, contracts, torts, education, transportation, domestic relations, property, commercial relations. In 1900, discounting postal employees and military personnel, there were only 20,000 U.S. government employees.

By 1930 centrifugal forces had begun irrevocably to alter state and local realities, and in the process transformed national life. The outcome of the Civil War made clear the supremacy of national law. The post-War amendments—the Thirteenth, Fourteenth, and Fifteenth—further established a national concept of citizenship, as well as a new kind of Federal power that allowed the national government to override state actions. Equally significant was the emergence of new forms of enterprise: The trusts and holding companies that operated across and outside of state borders, and the existence of new national and international markets for commodities and manufactures that all but made state boundaries invisible. Between 1900 and 1930 a communications revolution transformed the way Americans thought about local life, as the telegraph, telephone, the radio, phonograph, and mass-circulation newspapers began to create a virtual national community. Commercial advertising, installment loans, and the emergence of national chain stores like Woolworth's "five and dime" and A & P food stores, tied Americans together in a new way as "consumers."

The push toward national consolidation was also evident in the rise of new professional organizations and training methods. A new "scientific" approach to the disciplines of law, government, business, medicine, social work, and economics called for new modes of training. Specialized schools, usually housed within colleges and universities, asserted that professional competencies could be identified, and saw in rational structures an ideal method for controlling and making nationally uniform the process of training.

The nation's first modern law school was, in effect, founded at Harvard in 1870 by Christopher Columbus Langdell, as we will see, and quickly spread as the model, replacing the old system of apprenticeship. The first PhD program was instituted at Johns Hopkins University in 1888. Like law, training for the practice of medicine became rationalized and institutionalized, with licensing and accreditation requirements established by state governing bodies. New professional associations followed, operating on a national level and replacing local groups whose purposes had been more social than professional. These new associations set national standards of practice and training, defined and advocated for professional interests with state and national legislatures, and offered continuing education. These included, among others, the American Bar Association, the American Medical Association, and the American Economic Association. Among skilled and semi-skilled labor, similar forces were at work, giving rise to a new national organization that gave labor new clout. As discussed earlier, the American Federation of Labor, which by 1920 included 20% of the work force, was an amalgamation of local craft unions held together by a national governing structure that reached into many states. Businesses organized the National Association of Manufacturers ("NAM"). The first national "trade association," the NAM spoke with the voice of the nation's largest industrial corporations and represented their interests in combating unionism and governmental intervention in the economy.

In 1920 the population of cities, for the first time in American history, exceeded the nation's rural population. In the new American city the electric street car and gasoline-powered automobile replaced the horse-drawn carriage; public utilities supplied electrical lighting, and also made possible a host of new conveniences for the home, such as the washing machine, vacuum cleaner, coffee percolator, toaster, and refrigerator. Electricity also permitted the installation of elevators and lighting in new office buildings constructed around skyward-thrusting steel girders. Cities were not only centers of work and production, but also became beacons of mass culture and entertainment. Sports were becoming an American past time, and cities proudly boasted new stadiums where boxing, baseball, and football attracted thousands of spectators. Jazz, ragtime, the Blues, dance halls, flappers, the jitterbug, and the talking picture made "bright lights, big city" a cultural icon. The Twenties "roared."

America's historic isolationism was another victim of modern life. A prevailing localism and distrust of traditional European power-mongering and corruption led the nation away from "entangling alliances" in the 19th century. In small increments, isolationism gave way in the new century. In 1898 the U.S. militarily intervened against Spain in Cuba's fight for independence; in 1898 Hawaii was annexed, and in 1899 the Philippines. President Theodore Roosevelt modified the Monroe Doctrine to give wider latitude to the United States to intervene in the affairs of nations in the hemisphere, especially when the U.S.'s military or economic interests were at stake. America's reluctant entry into World War I thrust the nation onto a new kind of world stage, and its conclusion in 1918 left the United States as the world's undisputed industrial power.

The movement toward consolidation in almost every area of national life set the stage for the emergence of Progressivism, beginning with the settlement house movement in Chicago and lasting until 1924. The new "Progressive Movement" believed that government had a positive responsibility to manage the consequences of economic and social change. At the state level, governments tackled the problems of public health and education, passed laws for better wages and working conditions, and pushed for improved protections for women and children. Before a generally hostile judiciary, some of these laws passed constitutional muster, while others were successfully challenged as infringements on interstate commerce, property rights, due process, or "liberty of contract." Progressive political reformers also fought against the machine-rule of city bosses, favored women's suffrage, and installed parks, public lands, and libraries in cities. The Social Darwinism of the Gilded Age was portrayed as inhuman and amoral, and at odds with the emerging science of good government and social management.

Just as Social Darwinism supplied a grand justification for Gilded Age excesses, so did Progressivism draw support from a rising generation of public intellectuals. Thinkers like John Dewey, George Herbert Meade, and Herbert Crowley argued that national problems demanded national solutions. As active participants in a national dialogue carried out in books and articles in popular magazines, they laid the intellectual groundwork for an expansive national governmental role based on the moral values of cooperation and community. They justified this new power as democracy's best guarantee of survival, and portrayed laissez-faire ideology as institutionalized greed. The inauguration of President Theodore Roosevelt in 1901 carried this Progressive philosophy into national government, where it was sustained through the administration of Woodrow Wilson. TR pushed through reforms for pure food and drugs, regulation of the railroads, the break-up of trusts, and protection of pristine lands for public enjoyment. Wilson's administration gained passage of the Federal Reserve Act, perhaps the most far-reaching of all Progressive Era reforms, and advances for labor, education, and agriculture.

The post-War decade of the 1920s was often referred to as the "Jazz Age." Americans were glad to leave behind memories of war: Almost 130,000 American military personnel lost their lives in the first World War. For Europeans, the unprecedented carnage of the war sacrificed an entire generation. The U.S. Senate rejected membership in the League of Nations, frustrating one of Democratic President Wilson's proudest achievements, and the Republican administrations of Harding and Coolidge returned government to "normalcy," which meant support of business and avoidance of international entanglements. Intellectually and culturally, however, there was evidence of a deepening disaffection. This opinion was not united along political lines, but did expose a widening gulf dividing mainstream culture from journalistic, academic, and literary criticism.

These new "modernist" critics rejected the Victorian value system that suppressed emotion and passion; they portrayed American middle-class materialism as shallow and meaningless. Existentialism was an element in modernist thought, as was Freudian psychology, which introduced the concept of the subconscious—a hidden force that challenged notions of the rational. Modernists needed to dig beneath the surface, honestly to confront the truth of one's actions and motives, or at least try to discover that truth. They included commentators like Walter Lippman, the academic historian Charles A. Beard, the playwright Eugene O'Neill, and writers such as Ernest Hemingway, Sherwood Anderson, F. Scott Fitzgerald, and T.S. Eliot. In jurisprudence, modernists included Karl Llewellyn and Jerome Frank, whose work you will soon read. As you will see, they were part of a "Legal Realism" movement that rejected the official explanations of what law is, and sought deeper knowledge through empirical and psychological study of what law actually does.

As we saw with the example of Eugene V. Debs, on the Left fringes of the labor movement, and among some intellectuals, socialism and communism were attractive alternatives to capitalism. Business interests successfully used the Sherman Anti–Trust Act to thwart labor's organization and job actions. The Clayton Anti–Trust Act of 1914, intended to remove that threat to labor, had little effect on courts. Marxist–Leninist doctrine portrayed capitalists as owners of labor, much as they owned commodities. According to that doctrine, capitalists wrung from workers the last ounce of profits and gave little or nothing in return. The perceived anti-labor tone of the courts, as you have seen, for example in connection with the Pullman Strike, combined with the violent clashes of police and strikers in the first two decades of the century, convinced many radical labor leaders that Marx was right.

In the summer of 1919 dozens of bombings and attempted bombings aimed at public officials and wealthy citizens touched off a "Red Scare." Among the targets was the mayor of Seattle, a U.S. Senator, business mogul John D. Rockefeller, and A. Mitchell Palmer, the U.S. Attorney General. In September 1919 an explosion was set off on Wall Street in front of the offices of J.P. Morgan, killing 40 and injuring 300. In October of 1919 the Russian Revolution entered its Bolshevik phase; the American journalist and communist John Reed praised it as the "Ten Days that Shook the World." The Red Scare was further fanned with the 1920 prosecution of Nicola Sacco and Bartolomeo Vanzetti, Italian immigrants and labor militants accused of robbery and murder in South Braintree, Massachusetts. Through appeals that lasted until 1927 in one of the most highly publicized trials in American history, the case polarized world opinion about American justice, and within the U.S. exposed the deep chasm that divided immigrants and the working classes from mainstream society.

On Black Tuesday, October 29, 1929, the stock market crashed, precipitating a train of events that led to the nation's worst economic disaster. During the Great Depression, unemployment rose to 25% (up from 3.2% in 1929), industrial production dropped by 50%, and investments by 98%. In 1932, stock prices were at 12% of their 1929 value, for a total loss of $175 billion. The impact on the working person was devastating. In the 1920s, before the Depression, 60% of the nation's families earned incomes that left them near or below poverty, and this was during an era when unemployment was under 4%. Starvation became a daily threat for many in the cities, staved off only by soup kitchens and breadlines. During the Depression, unemployment rose to 25%. "Hoovervilles" (shanties built by the homeless) sprouted up in public parks and open spaces in the nation's cities. President Herbert Hoover, a self-made millionaire who was a firm believer in self-reliance and rugged individualism, was unprepared or unwilling to act forcefully in dealing with these problems.

Private charities, and State and local governments were left with problems they were ill-equipped to handle: joblessness, housing, poverty, and the needs of the elderly, destitute children and mothers. The American system was brought to its knees—great corporations, small businesses, the family farm, banks, consumers, and government. In the election of 1932, Franklin Delano Roosevelt promised to put Americans back to work and give them a "new deal."

As we will soon see, Roosevelt's administration can be divided into two eras. The "first New Deal" (1933–35) is striking for its readiness to apply radical solutions and marks a clear break with the past. Roosevelt instructed his advisors, the "Brain Trust," to freely use experimentation in attacking social and economic problems. If one solution turned out badly, try another, but *do something*. In radio "fireside" chats with the American people, he exuded confidence and optimism, and announced that the only thing to fear was fear itself. The advisors he pulled together were pragmatists, philosophical about an expansive role for the national government, somewhat intellectual and academic in background, and wedded to ends more than means. They were distinguished for their expertise in law, business, economics, labor, and finance. They identified problems and crafted legislative solutions, and trusted that eventually any problem would succumb to a well-thought out government plan. There was some hostility toward big business. FDR's brain trust downgraded the value of Progressive Era reform as well-intended, but amateurish and morally preachy. They, instead, were building a government for all time, and most important, for all people—those left out of the "old deal," as well as the corporate structures and entities that were needed to fuel the economy, and whose wellbeing could no longer be trusted to the private sector's myopic and self-interested planning.

The most radical programs of the first New Deal were the Tennessee Valley Authority, providing for government construction of dams and power plants to provide, for the first time, electrification for rural areas of the South; and the National Industrial Recovery Act ("NIRA"), to which we will soon turn, that called on business and labor to develop, and submit for executive-branch approval, industry-wide codes that set hours, wages, and prices. The Agricultural Adjustment Act identified overproduction as the farmers' biggest problem, mandated quotas and payments for plowing crops under, and guaranteed a purchase price. The first New Deal experimented with jobs programs, and put in place the Securities and Exchange Commission that dealt with abuses that purportedly led to the stock market crash.

The second New Deal (1935–37) was, as you will see, in partial reaction to the Supreme Court's combative stance to first New Deal reform when it struck down the NIRA as unconstitutional. The Court, a thorn in the side of State and Federal social legislation since the latter part of the 19th century, made property rights and laissez-faire economics the cornerstones of its jurisprudence. Business leaders shared these values and were increasingly hostile to the radicalism of FDR's agenda. They formed the Liberty League in active opposition and worked for the election of members of Congress favorable to their platform. On the Left, Huey Long blamed Roosevelt for not going far enough. He called for a "Share Our Wealth" program that would confiscate and redistribute private fortunes. Others pushed for equally ambitious programs, including a government sponsored retirement program.

Roosevelt, distrustful of business and dubious of an increasingly agitated Leftist radicalism, chose a middle ground. He turned away from a centrally-managed approach to the economy, in favor one that emphasized an expansion in purchasing power for consumers. The key to digging out of the Depression, he now believed, was to spend. Adopting a Keynesian approach, though without quite knowing it, the second New Deal emphasized jobs, a Federally supported retirement income program (Social Security), support for unionization (the National Labor Relations Board), taxes on corporations, aid to the poor, price controls for utilities, and minimum wage and maximum hour standards (Fair Labor Standards Act).

As we will see with the *Jones & Laughlin Steel* case, the second New Deal fared better in the courts, but by the late 1930s, FDR's second administration was in troubled waters. His somewhat desperate court packing plan, which you will soon encounter, divided his supporters and strengthened his opponents. After a modest recovery, the stock market again crashed in 1937, and the jobless rate began once again to climb. In 1938 Congress began an investigation into the influence of communists in New Deal agencies. With America's entry into World War II following the attack on Pearl Harbor on December 7, 1941, however, the nation again turned to strong central management, and massive war-time expenditures that put people to work and industry into maximum production. The economic crisis of the 1930s was world-wide, though its effects lingered longest in the United States. At last, the nation was emerging from the Depression, though it took a World War to accomplish it.

The New Deal's legacy was complex, though far reaching. In Roosevelt's second administration, the administrative state showed itself a friend to capitalism, and those who gained from it during the Depression (business, banks, farmers, labor, retirees) ensured its continuation after the peace. Fighting fascism made WWII a battle for democracy and the rule of law; the post-war era and the Korean conflict pitted the American belief system against a rising communist ideology. A new war, though a Cold one, sparked a second Red Scare and McCarthyism narrowed the scope of legitimate dissent in the decade of the 1950s. Nevertheless, the New Deal worked a revolution in the powers of the national government and the expectations of the American people. The zero-sum equation between personal liberty and governmental power that held sway in the judiciary from 1880 to 1937 was destroyed. Minorities, women, the elderly, the poorest of the poor, the disabled, and health care were not immediate beneficiaries of FDR's legislative programs, but the ideology of the welfare state led to a gradual expansion of rights and entitlements that gave a "new deal" to new groups and interests in later years. These developments, however, are not without critics.

In retrospect, it might be said that the triumph of the New Deal is the welfare state paradigm it created. It is flexible enough to include the ambitions of the Left and of the Right, yet also sets boundaries on extremism. It enthrones consumerism yet awakens a social conscience. It puts limits on individualism yet creates new possibilities of freedom. It is a web of superior power that is also subject to law and popular will. In the opening decade of the 21st century its primary role continues to be that of a security net, if not exactly a Big Brother. Values of individualism, enterprise, private property, freedom, opportunity, and the ethos of self-made success continue to hold sway in American life, even as they exist in tension. In spite of the ever-present reality of big government, the rhetoric of cutting taxes, eliminating wasteful government, and shrinking its size is practically the political creed of the nation.

When all is said and done, Big Government appears to be the ubiquitous presence that no major political party really wishes away: it is the guarantor of stability and economic security in practically every sector, and every sphere of life. Even so, at one time in 1996 President Clinton did declare that "the era of big government is over," but barring a cataclysm of some sort, it seems likely that the welfare state will remain *a* if not *the* dominant paradigm of American politics. It is the model of modern America itself: pluralistic, relativistic, assimilative, and distributive. It is likely to continue to be tolerant, and even absorbent, of an extraordinary range of political beliefs and personal behaviors—excepting those which threaten the paradigm itself.

But if the welfare state seems relatively secure, it still rests upon a shaky foundation. The modernist critique of the 1920s, as you will see in our final chapter, has become the post-modern critique in the post-industrial era. Post-modern America is a pluralist society. It recognizes and honors many truths. Because it believes that truth is relative, post-modernism calls into question the ability to make rational, objective centralized and universally applicable judgments. If truth is relative, what is real? Or put another way, who gets to decide what "real" is? If truth is relative, then so is morality. If moral authority is relative, what legitimacy can be given to law's compulsion, other than as a pure expression of power? If law is pure power, what is "justice?" What meaning can be given to other words and phrases, such as "rule of law?" Are these words in themselves objectively real, or are they empty vessels into which all are free to pour their own meanings?

As you will see, legal realism was one effort to apply modernist critiques to the operation of law, and its methodology of analysis was reason and empirical study. In the late 20th century, reason is but one of multiple intellectual approaches. Empirical study loses some of its power if the questions it seeks to answer are relative or subjective ones. How can we prove that any answer is the right and true one? All that is left to the post-modernist in describing reality is *process* and various forms of legal *theory*. The virtue of process is its tangibility; it can be observed and activated. But process, by definition, lacks content. The satisfaction, or frustration, of theory is that it cannot be disproved by facts. If the academic study of law today is theoretically rich, as you will soon see in our final chapter, it is also existentially tenuous. And where does that leave law and its practitioners?

A counter-movement is underway that rejects relativity of values. The Neutral Principles of Herbert Wechsler in the 1950s is one manifestation, as is J. Skelly Wright's Jurisprudence of Goodness of the 1960s. You'll soon read about both. In the years after 1980 a neo-conservative or "patriot" movement is emerging. It asserts that values are knowable through the direct experience of history, and that some values are self-evidently superior. It sees the Western tradition as the carrier of values out of which democracy, freedom, and tolerance arose. It also urges that words represent ideals that are real. It is theory that is the illusion—a distraction from what we know already, and even corrosive. It is concrete values and beliefs that animated the Patriots of 1776, led the Union to victory in 1865, sustained the nation through the economic chaos of the 1930s, carried the nation to victory over the Fascist powers in 1945, delivered a victory over communism in the Cold War, and ushered in the modern Civil Rights movement and a revolution in the status of women. For some of these thinkers, America remains a shining if tarnished beacon, a "City on a Hill," as it was to the Seventeenth Century colonists of Massachusetts Bay, a civilization of which one can be proud, and one well worth defending. The Rule of Law is usually regarded as its bulwark. As you read what follows, ask yourself if you are prepared to recognize the Rule of Law in the late twentieth and early twenty-first centuries as such a shining human achievement.

Further Reading:

Patrick Allit, *Catholic Intellectuals and Conservative Politics in America, 1950–1985,* 1993

Robert N. Bellah, et al., *Habits of the Heart: Individualism and Commitment in American Life,* 1985

Irving Bernstein, *A Caring Society: The New Deal, the Worker, and the Great Depression: A History of the American Worker, 1933–1941,* 1985

Alan Brinkley, *The End of Reform: New Deal Liberalism in Recession and War*, 1995

William F. Buckley, Jr., ed., *American Conservative Thought in the Twentieth Century,* 1970

Lizabeth Cohen, *A Consumers' Republic: The Politics of Mass Consumption in Postwar America,* 2003

Allen Davis, *Spearheads for Reform: The Social Settlements and the Progressive Movement, 1890–1924,* 1985

Alan Dawley, *Struggles for Justice: Social Responsibility and the Liberal State,* 1991

Carl N. Degler, *In Search of Human Nature: The Decline and Revival of Darwinism in American Social Thought,* 1991

John Patrick Diggins, *The Promise of Pragmatism: Modernism and the Crisis of Knowledge and Authority,* 1994

Stuart Ewen, *Captains of Consciousness: Advertising and the Social Roots of Consumer Culture,* 1976

Mark Gerson, *The Neoconservative Vision: From the Cold War to the Culture Wars,* 1996

Mary Ann Glendon, *Rights Talk: The Impoverishment of Political Discourse,* 1991

William A. Galston, *Liberal Purposes: Goods, Virtues, and Diversity in the Liberal State,* 1991

Louis Hartz, *The Liberal Tradition in America*, 1955

Charles Howard Hopkins, *The Rise of the Social Gospel in American Protestantism, 1865–1915,* 1967

Russell Kirk, *The Conservative Mind: From Burke to Eliot*, 7th ed., 2001

James T. Kloppenberg, *The Virtues of Liberalism*, 1997

James T. Kloppenberg, *"Uncertain Victory:" Social Democracy and Progressivism in European and American Thought, 1870–1920*, 1986

William E. Leuchtenberg, *Franklin D. Roosevelt and the New Deal, 1932–1940,* 1963

Daniel Levine, *Poverty and Society: The Growth of the American Welfare State in International Comparison*, 1989

Arthur S. Link and Richard L. McCormick, *Progressivism*, 1983

George H. Nash, *The Conservative Intellectual Movement in America since 1945,* 1996

James T. Patterson, *The Welfare State in America, 1930–1980*, 1981

Richard Pells, *Radical Visions, American Dreams: Culture and Social Thought in the Depression Years,* 1973

David Plotke, *Building a Democratic Political Order: Reshaping Liberalism in the 1930s and 1940s,* 1996

Stephen B. Presser, *Recapturing the Constitution: Race, Religion, and Abortion Reconsidered,* 1994

Edward Purcell, Jr., *The Crisis of Democratic Theory: Scientific Naturalism and the Problem of Value,* 1973

Daniel T. Rogers, *Atlantic Crossings: Social Politics in a Progressive Age,* 1998

Richard Rorty, *Achieving Our Country: Leftist Thought in Twentieth-Century America,* 1997

Richard Ruland, *From Puritanism to Postmodernism: A History of American Literature,* 1991

Michael J. Sandel, *Democracy's Discontent: America in Search of a Public Philosophy,* 1996

Barry Alan Shain, *The Myth of American Individualism: The Protestant Origins of American Political Thought,* 1994

Edward A. Stettner, *Shaping Modern Liberalism: Herbert Croly and Progressive Thought,* 1993

Stanley Trachtenberg, ed., *Critical Essays on American Postmodernism,* 1995

Michael Walzer, *Spheres of Justice: A Defense of Pluralism and Equality,* 1983

Robert B. Westbrook, *John Dewey and American Democracy,* 1993

A. THE SCIENCE OF LAW

DAVID DUDLEY FIELD, MAGNITUDE AND IMPORTANCE OF LEGAL SCIENCE*

(1859).

Address at the opening of the Law School of the University of Chicago, September 21, 1859.

* * *

* * * I shall * * * ask you to consider with me now the magnitude and importance of legal science. And though all knowledge has value, and all the arts their uses, yet, as there are differences in value as in use, I hope

* Reprinted in I Sprague, ed., Speeches, Arguments, and Miscellaneous Papers of David Dudley Field 517–533 (1884).

to show you that, of all the sciences and all the arts, not one can be named greater in magnitude or importance than * * * the science of the law.

Law is a rule of property and of conduct prescribed by the sovereign power of a state. The science of the law embraces, therefore, all the rules recognized and enforced by the state, of all the property and of all the conduct of men in all their relations, public and private. * * * No engagement can be entered into, no work undertaken, no journey made, but with the law in view. * * * This science, therefore, is equal in duration with history, in extent with all the affairs of men.

We can measure it best by tracing its progress. When men dwelt in tents and led a pastoral life, their laws might have been compressed in a few pages. They had, of course, some part of our law of personal rights, the law of succession, and of boundaries between the occupiers of adjoining pastures. This was the condition of the race in the primitive ages, and is even yet the condition of some parts of it. * * *

The next stage in the civilization of the race was the fixed habitation and the cultivation of the soil; and this brought with it the next stage in the development of the legal system—the law of land and of permanent structures—a department which, though it teaches of the most permanent of earthly things, has not partaken of their permanence, but has fluctuated with political condition. The distribution of the land has determined the policy and the fate of governments, and these in their turn have encouraged the aggregation or subdivision of estates, as they inclined to aristocratic or democratic institutions.

* * * To possess land, to own an estate, to found a family, and to make for it an ancestral home, are objects of ambition almost universal. We seem to ourselves to be more firmly fixed when we are anchored in the soil. * * * And, notwithstanding the enormous increase of personal property in our modern society, the larger portion of man's wealth is still in the land. * * *

For these reasons, the law, which regulates the possession, enjoyment, and transfer of real property, has always been the subject of special attention. It has oscillated, as governments have swayed back and forth; at one time allodial, at another feudal, sometimes comparatively simple; then excessively complex; in one country natural, in another artificial. But in all countries * * * the law of real property has ever been and must be large and difficult. The acquisition and use of land, the different kinds of ownership, the exclusive and perpetual, or the joint or temporary title, the conflicting interests of adjoining owners, the relative rights of landlord and tenant, and a thousand other conditions and incidents, can only be regulated upon a careful and minute analysis, by a series of rules adjusted with nice discrimination * * *.

In the next stage of civilization, the products of the soil were wrought into new forms, and manufactured fabrics added to the wealth and comfort of man. Manufactures required the purchase and collection of materials, the employment of workmen, and the sale of the fabric. Commerce led to navigation. Each of these operations added a new chapter to the law.

Of these three stages in civilization and in law, the ancient world was witness, but not in their highest development, though in forms of which the records will last for ever. The accumulation of lawbooks became so burdensome that, thirteen hundred years ago, it was found necessary to reduce them by substituting digests and codes. * * * Since then, however, materials have accumulated, greater by far than those out of which the Roman Codes were constructed.

* * * The present law of real property in this country and in England was brought from the North or Northeast, by those conquering tribes, whose scheme of civil polity was a gradation of ranks, bound together by feudal ties. This feudal system, after having flourished through several centuries, has been gradually softening and disintegrating under the double influence of commerce and peace. Our maritime law is also in great part of modern origin * * *; rules by which modern commerce is governed began with the activity of the middle ages, and grew to maturity with the enterprise of our own times. The best part of our law of personal rights we owe to the spirit of Christianity and the influence of chivalry. A man's person is now sacred. * * * He may go or stay wheresoever he will; he may engage in any pursuit which pleases him; he may embrace any faith which appears right in his own eyes. Associations being more powerful than individuals, corporations scarcely known to the ancients have become the most frequent and the most powerful agencies of modern society. During all the while the machinery of government has been increasing and expanding, till volumes are filled with the rules which relate to that alone. And, last of all, there have just appeared the three most marvelous inventions of all time—the steamer, the railway, and the telegraph—which, while they have been making a revolution in the social life of man, have, at the same time, been adding three chapters to the books of his laws. * * *

The more perfect is the civilization, the more complete is the law. The latter is, in many respects, both the cause and the consequence of the former. * * *

* * *

* * * Who that has studied the government of a country, though occupying but a single department in its laws, but wonders at the magnitude of the subject? A lifetime seems scarcely sufficient for its mastery. Political philosophy and history are its adjuncts. Take our political code, survey it generally, enter into its details, study its history, consider how

many good and wise men have participated in its framing, how cautiously it has been contrived, amended, added to, debated, at every step in its progress, and then stand reverently before it as the grandest monument of human genius. Time would fail me if I were to attempt recounting even the principal epochs in its history; the long and hardy training of our forefathers beyond the sea, where their institutions were purified by blood and fire, the transplanting of those institutions hither, their curtailment of the monarchical portions, the amelioration which time and experience have wrought, the principle of federation, its origin and development, and the final completion of the vast structure of our Government, Federal and State, through all its parts. * * * Large must be the book which shall even describe adequately this double Government of ours—larger still that which shall contain all the laws by which it moves and all the functions which it performs; its various departments, legislative, executive, and judicial, the powers and duties of all its public officers, its revenues, and the different branches of the public service.

* * *

* * * Let us select for example a single department and follow out its subdivisions. Take if you will the contract of sale, and see into how many branches it divides itself. Whether the contract be written or unwritten, whether there be an actual transfer, or only an agreement to transfer, whether the thing agreed upon be already made or only to be made, whether it be sound or defective or deficient in quantity, whether there be fair dealing, concealment, or misrepresentation as to quality, existence, or value, whether the thing has been delivered or paid for in whole or in part, whether the seller or the purchaser ever, and if so when and upon what terms, may rescind the contract and be reinstated—all these, and many more, are considerations affecting the transaction, which the law has carefully provided for, by an appropriate rule.

The law may be compared to a majestic tree that is ever growing. It has a trunk heavy with centuries, great branches equal themselves to other trees, with their roots in the parent trunk; lesser branches, and from those lesser branches still, till you arrive at the delicate bud, which in a few years will be itself a branch, with a multitude of leaves and buds. * * * [T]he law appears infinite in its manifestations; the shelves of law libraries groan under the accumulation of their volumes. The curious in such matters have computed that the number of cases in the English Courts relating to practice alone equals twenty-five thousand, and that the common law has two million rules!

Compare this science with any of the other sciences; with those which are esteemed the greatest in extent, and the most exalted in subject. Take even astronomy, that noble science which * * * weighs the sun and the planets, measures their distances, traces their orbits, and penetrates the secrets of that great law which governs their motions. Sublime as this science is, it is but the science of inanimate matter, and a few natural laws; while the science which is the subject of our discourse governs the actions of human beings, intelligent and immortal, penetrates into the secrets of their souls, subdues their wills, and adapts itself to the endless variety of their wants, motives, and conditions.

Will you compare it with one of the exact sciences—as, for example, with mathematics? * * * Clear, precise, simple in its elements, far-reaching and sublime in its results, it has disciplined and exalted some of the greatest minds of our race, and been the nursery of other sciences, and of the mechanic arts. * * * But the science of calculation is occupied with a single principle. This it may go on to develop more and more, till the mind is almost lost in its immensity; yet the development of that one principle can never reach in extent, comprehensiveness, and variety the development of all the principles by which the actions of men toward each other are governed in all their relations. The law, it will be remembered, is the rule of all property and all conduct. * * *

* * *

This rapid survey may serve to give us some idea, imperfect, indeed, of the magnitude of legal science. Though it may be the most familiar of all things, it is also the most profound and immense. It surrounds us everywhere like the light of this autumnal day, or the breath of this all-comprehending air. It sits with us, sleeps beside us, walks with us abroad, studies with the inventor, writes with the scholar, and marches by the side of every new branch of industry and every new mode of travel. The infant of an hour old, the old man of threescore and ten, the feeble woman, the strong and hardy youth, are all under its equal care, and by it alike protected and restrained.

* * *

We have considered thus far the magnitude of legal science. Its importance is more than commensurate with its magnitude. Without it there could be no civilization and no order. Where there is no law, there can be no order, since order is but another name for regularity, or conformity to rule. Without order, society would relapse into barbarism. The very magnitude of the law is a proof of its necessity. It is great, because it is essential. There is a necessity, not only for law, but for a system, with arrangement and a due relation of parts; for, without this system, the administration of government, both in its judicial and its administrative departments, would fall into irretrievable confusion. * * *

The science of the law is our great security against the maladministration of justice. If the decision of litigated questions were to depend upon the will of the Judge or upon his notions of what was just, our property and our lives would be at the mercy of a fluctuating judgment, or of caprice. The existence of a system of rules and conformity to them are the essential conditions of all free government, and of republican government above all others. The law is our only sovereign. We have enthroned it. In other governments, loyalty to a personal sovereign is a bond for the State. * * * We have substituted loyalty to the State and the law for what with others is loyalty to the person. In place of a government of opposing interests, we have a double government of written Constitutions. The just interpretation of these Constitutions and the working of the double machinery, so that there may be no break and no jar, are committed in a great degree, how great few ever reflect, to the legal profession, and are dependent upon their knowledge of the science of law in all its departments, political, civil, penal, and remedial. Precisely, therefore, as free government and republican institutions are valuable, in the same proportion is the science of the law valuable as a means of preserving them.

* * *

I might add that, if there be any science and any culture tending to invigorate and sharpen the intellect, they are legal science and discipline. Every science rewards those who study it, by enlarging their minds to a comprehension of its learning; and the greater the science, the greater the reward. But there is something in the conduct of litigation which makes the judgment severe and keen, beyond any other discipline to which it is subjected. While, therefore, the study of the law has the effect of enlarging the vision of its practicers, it has also the effect of sharpening the intellect, leading to precision of thought and language, and acuteness in discovering the truth of facts. Who can unravel intrigues, lift the veil from hypocrisy, dissect evidence, and lay falsehood bare, like the practiced lawyer? Better men have never existed, more exalted in intellect, or purer in motive, or more useful in action, than our profession can show.

* * *

But I must return from this digression to the science which is the subject of this discourse. * * *

How shall this science best be learned? There are three methods: the private study of books; the advice and aid of practitioners, amid the bustle and interruptions of practice; and the teaching of public schools. The inadequacy of the first is obvious; the disadvantages of the second are too painfully known to all of us who studied in that way; the third is beyond question the most efficient and complete. There is as much need of public schools for the law as for any other science. There is more, for, the greater the science, the greater the need. Above all others, this science, so vast, so comprehensive, so complicated and various in its details, needs to be studied with all the aids which universities, professors, and libraries can furnish.

Where else so readily as here will the student obtain a view of the law as a whole, and of all its parts in their several relations and dependencies—here, where are collected the records of the science, where there are professors devoted to its teaching, where there are scholars emulous of distinction, and stimulating each other? * * *

* * *

NOTES AND QUESTIONS

1. What is the point of Field's speech? He calls it the "Magnitude and Importance" of legal science. What is the magnitude of legal science? Is the chief clue Field's proposition that the more perfect is the civilization, the more complete is the law? Do you agree? See generally Herbert Hovenkamp, "Evolutionary Models in Jurisprudence," 64 Tex.L.Rev. 645 (1985), and E. Donald Elliot, "The Evolutionary Tradition in Jurisprudence," 85 Col.L.Rev. 38 (1985). In his controversial little book, The Ages of American Law (1977), Yale's Professor Grant Gilmore, a grand figure in the law of contract, admiralty, *and* legal history wrote:

> Law reflects but in no sense determines the moral worth of a society. The values of a reasonably just society will reflect themselves in a reasonably just law. The better the society, the less law there will be. In Heaven there will be no law, and the lion will lie down with the lamb. The values of an unjust society will reflect themselves in an unjust law. The worse the society, the more law there will be. In Hell there will be nothing but law, and due process will be meticulously observed.*

The Ages of American Law, at 110–111. How do you account for the disagreement between Field and Gilmore? Do you suppose that Gilmore and Field share similar views of the course of history? What is Field's view? How would you compare Field's view of "the law" to that of Robert Rantoul?

2. What does Field mean when he suggests that "The law is our only sovereign. We have enthroned it?" Does this view explain his assertion that "legal science" is the most important science? Do you suppose that Chief Justice Shaw would have agreed with this assertion? Is Field merely making the point that ours is a government of laws, not men, or is he after something subtler? What does Field mean by "legal science?"

3. Field was speaking at the dedication of the institution that eventually became the Northwestern University School of Law. See Generally Rahl and Schwerin, Northwestern University School of Law: A Short History 5–6 (1960). What does Field see as the importance of law schools to legal science? Why was it, if legal science is so important, that the American law school as

---

* Reprinted from Grant Gilmore, The Ages of American Law, Copyright © 1977 by Yale University, with the permission of the Yale University Press.

we know it did not appear as an institution until about the middle of the nineteenth century? Harvard and Yale both had law schools by the 1820's, but for the next thirty years these were moribund institutions, little better than "trade schools", with admissions requirements probably more lax than the colleges'. See Robert Stevens, "Two Cheers for 1870: The American Law School," 5 Perspectives in American History 405, 415–424 (1971). For Stevens's fuller work on American Legal Education, which develops the thought of his earlier article, see Robert Stevens, Law School: Legal Education in America from the 1850's to the 1980's (1983). Stevens suggests that the real transformation in American legal education was accomplished during the tenure of Christopher Columbus Langdell at Harvard, and it is to him that we now turn.

CHRISTOPHER COLUMBUS LANGDELL, SELECTION OF CASES ON THE LAW OF CONTRACTS

v–vii (1871).

* * *

I entered upon the duties of my present position, a year and a half ago, with a settled conviction that law could only be taught or learned effectively by means of cases in some form. I had entertained such an opinion ever since I knew any thing of the nature of law or of legal study; but it was chiefly through my experience as a learner that it was first formed, as well as subsequently strengthened and confirmed.

* * *

Now, however, I was called upon to consider directly the subject of teaching, not theoretically but practically. * * * I was expected to take a large class of pupils, meet them regularly from day to day, and give them systematic instruction in such branches of law as had been assigned to me. To accomplish this successfully, it was necessary, first, that the efforts of the pupils should go hand in hand with mine, that is, that they should study with direct reference to my instruction; secondly, that the study thus required of them should be of the kind from which they might reap the greatest and most lasting benefit; thirdly, that the instruction should be of such a character that the pupils might at least derive a greater advantage from attending it than from devoting the same time to private study. How could this threefold object be accomplished? Only one mode occurred to me which seemed to hold out any reasonable prospect of success; and that was, to make a series of cases, carefully selected from the books of reports, the subject alike of study and instruction. But here I was met by what seemed at first to be an insuperable practical difficulty, namely, the want of books; for though it might be practicable, in case of private pupils having free access to a complete library, to refer them directly to the books of reports, such a course was quite out of the question with a large class, all of whom would want the same books at the same time. Nor would such a course be without great drawbacks and inconveniences, even in the case of a single pupil. As he would always have to go where the books were, and could only have access to them there during certain prescribed hours, it would be impossible for him to economize his time or work to the best advantage; and he would be liable to be constantly haunted by the apprehension that he was spending time, labor, and money in studying cases which would be inaccessible to him in after life.

It was with a view to removing these obstacles, that I was first led to inquire into the feasibility of preparing and publishing such a selection of cases as would be adapted to my purpose as a teacher. The most important element in that inquiry was the great and rapidly increasing number of reported cases in every department of law. In view of this fact, was there any satisfactory principle upon which such a selection could be made? It seemed to me that there was. Law, considered as a science, consists of certain principles or doctrines. To have such a mastery of these as to be able to apply them with constant facility and certainty to the ever-tangled skein of human affairs, is what constitutes a true lawyer; and hence to acquire that mastery should be the business of every earnest student of law. Each of these doctrines has arrived at its present state by slow degrees; in other words, it is a growth, extending in many cases through centuries. This growth is to be traced in the main through a series of cases * * *. But the cases which are useful and necessary for this purpose at the present day bear an exceedingly small proportion to all that have been reported. The vast majority are useless and worse than useless for any purpose of systematic study. Moreover, the number of fundamental legal doctrines is much less than is commonly supposed; the many different guises in which the same doctrine is constantly making its appearance, and the great extent to which legal treatises are a repetition of each other, being the cause of much misapprehension. * * * It seemed to me, therefore, to be possible to take such a branch of the law as Contracts, for example, and, without exceeding comparatively moderate limits, to select, classify, and arrange all the cases which had contributed in any important degree to the growth, development, or establishment of any of its essential doctrines; and that such a work could not fail to be of material service to all who desire to study that branch of law systematically and in its original sources.

It is upon this principle that the present volume has been prepared. It begins the subject of Contracts, and embraces the important topics of Mutual Consent, Consideration, and Conditional Contracts. Though complete in itself, it is my expectation that it will be followed by other volumes upon the same plan * * *.

BOOK REVIEW [OF THE SECOND EDITION OF LANGDELL'S CASEBOOK]

14 Am.Law Rev. 233–235 (1880).

* * *

It is hard to know where to begin in dealing with this extraordinary production,—equally extraordinary in its merits and its limitations. No man competent to judge can read a page of it without at once recognizing the hand of a great master. Every line is compact of ingenious and original thought. Decisions are reconciled which those who gave them meant to be opposed, and drawn together by subtle lines which never were dreamed of before Mr. Langdell wrote. It may be said without exaggeration that there cannot be found in the legal literature of this country, such a *tour de force* of patient and profound intellect working out original theory through a mass of detail, and evolving consistency out of what seemed a chaos of conflicting atoms. But in this word "consistency" we touch what some of us at least must deem the weak point in Mr. Langdell's habit of mind. Mr. Langdell's ideal in the law, the end of all his striving, is the *elegantia juris,* or *logical* integrity of the system as a system. He is, perhaps, the greatest living legal theologian. But as a theologian he is less concerned with his postulates than to show that the conclusions from them hang together. A single phrase will illustrate what is meant. "It has been claimed that the purposes of substantial justice and the interests of contracting parties as understood by themselves will be best served by holding & c., * * * and cases have been put to show that the contrary view would produce not only unjust but absurd results. *The true answer to this argument is that it is irrelevant;* but" & c. (pp. 995, 996, pl. 15). The reader will perceive that the language is only incidental, but it reveals a mode of thought which becomes conspicuous to a careful student.

If Mr. Langdell could be suspected of ever having troubled himself about Hegel, we might call him a Hegelian in disguise, so entirely is he interested in the formal connection of things, or logic, as distinguished from the feelings which make the content of logic, and which have actually shaped the substance of the law. The life of the law has not been logic: it has been experience. The seed of every new growth within its sphere has been a felt necessity. The form of continuity has been kept up by reasonings purporting to reduce every thing to a logical sequence; but that form is nothing but the evening dress which the new-comer puts on to make itself presentable according to conventional requirements. The important phenomenon is the man underneath it, not the coat; the justice and reasonableness of a decision, not its consistency with previously held views. No one will ever have a truly philosophic mastery over the law who does not habitually consider the forces outside of it which have made it what it is. More than that, he must remember that as it embodies the story of a nation's development through many centuries, the law finds its philosophy not in self-consistency, which it must always fail in so long as it continues to grow, but in history and the nature of human needs. As a branch of anthropology, law is an object of science; the theory of legislation is a scientific study; but the effort to reduce the concrete details of an existing system to the merely logical consequence of simple postulates is always in danger of becoming unscientific, and of leading to a misapprehension of the nature of the problem and the data.

* * * But it is to be remembered that the book is published for use at a law school, and that for that purpose dogmatic teaching is a necessity, if any thing is to be taught within the limited time of a student's course. A professor must start with a system as an arbitrary fact, and the most which can be hoped for is to make the student see how it hangs together, and thus to send him into practice with something more than a rag-bag of details. For this purpose it is believed that Mr. Langdell's teachings, published and unpublished, have been of unequalled value.

* * *

NOTES AND QUESTIONS

1. The pedagogical philosophy that made Langdell's Harvard law school the greatest America had yet seen was fully embodied in the casebook on contracts. Langdell's aim was to train law students to derive "the few, ever-present, and ever-evolving and fructifying principles, which constituted the genius of the common law." Professor Lawrence Friedman, in his A History of American Law (1973) appears to criticize Langdell's notion that law was a science with independent logical principles. Friedman writes:

> If law is at all the product of society, Langdell's science of law was a geology without rocks, an astronomy without stars. Lawyers and judges raised on the method, if they took their training at all seriously, came to speak of law mainly in terms of a dry, arid logic, divorced from society and life.*

Id., at 535. What do you think that Friedman believes is missing from Langdell's view of the law? If Friedman is right about the emptiness of Langdell's science of law, why did it almost immediately win acceptance at virtually all law schools, and why does it still form the basis of legal education? Friedman explains this by indulging in retrospective psychoanalysis. He states that the flourishing of Langdellian legal science in the law schools occurred because it exalted the prestige of law and legal learning in a period when lawyers needed to justify their monopoly of practice. Id., at 536. Is this a satisfactory explanation? Is there a danger in exposing law students to the "rag-bag of details," to the experience of law, rather than to its "logic?"

---

2. Perhaps the most significant assumption of Langdellian theory is the assertion that the "vast majority" of reported decisions are "useless and worse than useless for any purpose of systematic study." Would you agree with this? Was Langdell right that "the number of fundamental legal doctrines is much less than is commonly supposed?" What is a "fundamental legal doctrine?" Do you see any similarities between Field's view of law, as reflected not only in his speech in this section but also in his codification efforts, and that of Langdell? Would Field and Langdell agree upon the nature of legal history? How useful was Langdell's thought? Professor Friedman is rather dismissive, but some scholarship has rehabilitated Langdell's reputation, and has recognized him as a bold and brilliant innovator. See, in particular, Anthony Chase, "The Birth of the Modern Law School," 23 Am.J.Legal History 329 (1979), "Origins of Modern Professional Education: The Harvard Case Method Conceived as Clinical Instruction in Law," 5 Nova Law Journal 323 (1981), and "American Legal Education Since 1885: The Case of the Missing Modern," 30 N.Y.L.S.L.Rev. 519 (1985); and Marcia Speziale, "Langdell's Concept of Law as Science: The Beginnings of Anti–formalism in American Legal Theory," 5 Vermont Law Review 1 (1980). For the work of another "legal scientist," now less well known than Langdell, but in his day thought to be "the foremost law writer of the age," see Stephen A. Siegel, "Joel Bishop's Orthodoxy," 13 Law & Hist. Rev. 215 (1995) (Exploring the "traditional, religiously informed jurisprudence" of Bishop, which qualifies as "classical" legal thought, though different from that of Holmes or Langdell). And, on the question of "law as science," see also Wai Chee Dimock, "Deploying Law and Legal Ideas in Culture and Society: Rules of Law, Laws of Science," 13 Yale J.L. & Human. 203 (2001).

3. Why does the author of this review of the second edition of Langdell's casebook suggest that it is "extraordinary" in its limitations? How is this assertion related to the characterization of Langdell as "perhaps * * * the greatest living legal theologian?" And yet, does the author of this review believe that Langdell's casebook is appropriate for law schools? The author of the review was Oliver Wendell Holmes, Jr., and the next excerpt develops his philosophical differences with Langdell.

OLIVER WENDELL HOLMES, JR.

OLIVER WENDELL HOLMES, JR., THE COMMON LAW

1–18, 24–30, 34–38 (1881).

The object of this book is to present a general view of the Common Law. To accomplish the task, other tools are needed besides logic. * * * The life of the law has not been logic: it has been experience. The felt necessities of the time, the prevalent moral and political theories, intuitions of public policy, avowed or unconscious, even the prejudices which judges share with their fellow-men, have had a good deal more to do than the syllogism in determining the rules by which men should be governed. The law embodies the story of a nation's development through many centuries, and it cannot be dealt with as if it contained only the axioms and corollaries of a book of mathematics. In order to know what it is, we must know what it has been, and what it tends to become. We must alternately consult history and existing theories of legislation. But the most difficult labor will be to understand the combination of the two into new products at every stage. The substance of the law at any given time pretty nearly corresponds, so far as it goes, with what is then understood to be convenient; but its form and machinery, and the degree to which it is able to work out desired results, depend very much upon its past.

In Massachusetts to-day, while, on the other hand, there are a great many rules which are quite sufficiently accounted for by their manifest good sense, on the other, there are some which can only be understood by reference to the infancy of procedure among the German tribes, or to the social condition of Rome under the Decemvirs.

* * *

The first subject to be discussed is the general theory of liability civil and criminal. * * *

It is commonly known that the early forms of legal procedure were grounded in vengeance. Modern writers have thought that the Roman law started from the blood feud, and all the authorities agree that the German law began in that way. The feud led to the composition, at first optional, then compulsory, by which the feud was bought off. * * * The killings and house-burnings of an earlier day became the appeals of mayhem and arson. The appeals de pace et plagis and of mayhem became, or rather were in substance, the action of trespass which is still familiar to lawyers. But as the compensation recovered in the appeal was the alternative of vengeance, we might expect to find its scope limited to the scope of vengeance. Vengeance imports a feeling of blame, and an opinion, however distorted by passion, that a wrong has been done. It can hardly go very far beyond the case of a harm intentionally inflicted: even a dog distinguishes between being stumbled over and being kicked.

Whether for this cause or another, the early English appeals for personal violence seem to have been confined to intentional wrongs. * * * The cause of action in the cases of trespass reported in the earlier Year Books and in the Abbreviatio Placitorum is always an intentional wrong. It was only at a later day, and after argument, that trespass was extended so as to embrace harms which were foreseen, but which were not the intended

with the principle as inverted to meet still more modern views of public policy, if the animal was of a wild nature, that is, in the very case of the most ferocious animals, the owner ceased to be liable the moment it escaped, because at that moment he ceased to be owner. There seems to have been no other or more extensive liability by the old law, even where a slave was guilty with his master's knowledge, unless perhaps he was a mere tool in his master's hands. * * *

All this shows very clearly that the liability of the owner was merely a way of getting at the slave or animal which was the immediate cause of offence. In other words, vengeance on the immediate offender was the object of the Greek and early Roman process, not indemnity from the master or owner. * * *

But it may be asked how inanimate objects came to be pursued in this way, if the object of the procedure was to gratify the passion of revenge. [Perhaps the reason is] * * * the personification of inanimate nature common to savages and children * * *.

In the Athenian process there is also, no doubt, to be traced a different thought. Expiation is one of the ends most insisted on by Plato, and appears to have been the purpose of the procedure mentioned by Eschines. * * *

Another peculiarity to be noticed is, that the liability seems to have been regarded as attached to the body doing the damage, in an almost physical sense. An untrained intelligence only imperfectly performs the analysis by which jurists carry responsibility back to the beginning of a chain of causation. The hatred for anything giving us pain, which wreaks itself on the manifest cause, and which leads even civilized man to kick a door when it pinches his finger, is embodied in the *noxae deditio* and other kindred doctrines of early Roman law. * * *

[Holmes proceeds to discuss some examples from Roman law, where, even in cases of breach of treaty or contract, a legal action might terminate in the body of the defendant being surrendered to the plaintiff.]

It might be asked what analogy could have been found between a breach of contract and those wrongs which excite the desire for vengeance. But it must be remembered that the distinction between tort and breaches of contract, and especially between the remedies for the two, is not found ready made. It is conceivable that a procedure adapted to redress for violence was extended to other cases as they arose. Slaves were surrendered for theft as well as for assault; and it is said that a debtor who did not pay his debts, or a seller who failed to deliver an article for which he had been paid, was dealt with on the same footing as a thief. This line of thought, together with the quasi material conception of legal obligations as binding the offending body, which has been noticed, would perhaps explain the well-known law of the Twelve Tables as to insolvent debtors. According to that law, if a man was indebted to several creditors and insolvent, after certain formalities they might cut up his body and divide it among them. If there was a single creditor, he might put his debtor to death or sell him as a slave.

If no other right were given but to reduce a debtor to slavery, the law might be taken to look only to compensation, and to be modelled on the natural working of self-redress. * * * But the right to put to death looks like vengeance, and the division of the body shows that the debt was conceived very literally to inhere in or bind the body * * *.

* * *

It will readily be imagined that such a system as has been described could not last when civilization had advanced to any considerable height. What had been the privilege of buying off vengeance by agreement, of paying the damage instead of surrendering the body of the offender, no doubt became a general custom. The Aquilian law, passed about a couple of centuries later than the date of the Twelve Tables, enlarged the sphere of compensation for bodily injuries. Interpretation enlarged the Aquilian law. Masters became personally liable for certain wrongs committed by their slaves with their knowledge, where previously they were only bound to surrender the slave. If a pack-mule threw off his burden upon a passer-by because he had been improperly overloaded, or a dog which might have been restrained escaped from his master and bit any one, the old noxal action, as it was called, gave way to an action under the new law to enforce a general personal liability.

Still later, ship-owners and innkeepers were made liable *as if* they were wrong-doers for wrongs committed by those in their employ on board ship or in the tavern, although of course committed without their knowledge. The true reason for this exceptional responsibility was the exceptional confidence which was necessarily reposed in carriers and innkeepers. But some of the jurists, who regarded the surrender of children and slaves as a privilege intended to limit liability, explained this new liability on the ground that the innkeeper or ship-owner was to a certain degree guilty of negligence in having employed the services of bad men. * * *

The law as to ship-owners and innkeepers introduced another and more startling innovation. It made them responsible when those whom they employed were free, as well as when they were slaves. For the first time one man was made answerable for the wrongs of another who was also answerable himself, and who had a standing before the law. This was a great change from the bare permission to ransom one's slave as a privilege. But here we have the history of the whole modern doctrine of master and servant, and principal and agent. All servants are now as free and as liable to a suit as their masters. Yet the principle introduced on special grounds in a special case, when servants were slaves, is now the general law of this country and England, and under it men daily have to pay large sums for other people's acts, in which they had no part and for which they are in no sense to blame. * * *

* * *

The reader may begin to ask for the proof that all this has any bearing on our law of to-day. So far as concerns the influence of the Roman law upon our own, especially the Roman law of master and servant, the evidence of it is to be found in every book which has been written for the last five hundred years. It has been stated already that we still repeat the reasoning of the Roman lawyers, empty as it is, to the present day. * * *

* * *

We will now follow the history of that branch of the primitive notion which was least likely to survive,—the liability of inanimate things.

* * * As long ago as Bracton, in case a man was slain, the coroner was to value the object causing the death, and that was to be forfeited as deodand *"pro rege."* It was to be given to God, that is to say to the Church, for the King, to be expended for the good of his soul. A man's death had ceased to be the private affair of his friends as in the time of the barbarian folk-laws. The king, who furnished the court, now sued for the penalty. He supplanted the family in the claim on the guilty thing, and the Church supplanted him.

In Edward the First's time some of the cases remind us of the barbarian laws at their rudest stage. If a man fell from a tree, the tree was deodand. If he drowned in a well, the well was to be filled up. It did not matter that the forfeited instrument belonged to an innocent person. * * * And it has been repeated from Queen Elizabeth's time to within one hundred years, that if my horse strikes a man, and afterwards I sell my horse, and after that the man dies, the horse shall be forfeited. Hence it is, that, in all indictments for homicide, until very lately it has been necessary to state the instrument causing the death and its value, as that the stroke was given by a certain penknife, value sixpence, so as to secure the forfeiture. It is said that a steam-engine has been forfeited in this way.

I now come to what I regard as the most remarkable transformation of this principle, and one which is a most important factor in our law as it is to-day. * * *

The most striking example of this sort is a ship. And accordingly the old books say that, if a man falls from a ship and is drowned, the motion of the ship must be taken to cause the death, and the ship is forfeited * * *.

A ship is the most living of inanimate things. Servants sometimes say "she" of a clock, but every one gives a gender to vessels. And we need not be surprised, therefore, to find a mode of dealing which has shown such extraordinary vitality in the criminal law applied with even more striking thoroughness in the Admiralty. It is only by supposing the ship to have been treated as if endowed with personality, that the arbitrary seeming peculiarities of the maritime law can be made intelligible, and on that supposition they at once become consistent and logical.

By way of seeing what those peculiarities are, take first a case of collision at sea. A collision takes place between two vessels * * *. [The ship which is responsible for the collision] is under a lease at the time, the lessee has his own master in charge, and the owner of the vessel has no manner of control over it. The owner, therefore, is not to blame, and he cannot even be charged on the ground that the damage was done by his servants. He is free from personal liability on elementary principles. Yet it is perfectly settled that there is a lien on his vessel for the amount of the damage done, and this means that that vessel may be arrested and sold to pay the loss in any admiralty court whose process will reach her. * * *

But, again, suppose that the vessel, instead of being under lease, is in charge of a pilot whose employment is made compulsory by the laws of the port which she is just entering. The Supreme Court of the United States holds the ship liable in this instance also. * * * [Our] Supreme Court has long recognized that a person may bind a ship, when he could not bind the owners personally, because he was not their agent.

It may be admitted that, if this doctrine were not supported by an appearance of good sense, it would not have survived. The ship is the only security available in dealing with foreigners, and rather than send one's own citizens to search for a remedy abroad in strange courts, it is easy to seize the vessel and satisfy the claim at home, leaving the foreign owners to get their indemnity as they may be able. I dare say some such thought has helped to keep the practice alive, but I believe the true historic foundation is elsewhere. The ship no doubt, like a sword, would have been forfeited for causing death, in whosesoever hands it might have been. * * * It seems most likely that the principle by which the ship was forfeited to the king for causing death, or for piracy, was the same as that by which it was bound to private sufferers for other damage, in whose hands soever it might have been when it did the harm.

* * *

* * * The following is a passage from a judgment by Chief Justice Marshall, which is quoted with approval by Judge Story in giving the opinion of the Supreme Court of the United States.* "This is not a pro-

* The Malek Adhel, 43 U.S. (2 How.) 210, 233, 11 L.Ed. 239 (1844).

ceeding against the owner; it is a proceeding against the vessel for an offence committed by the vessel; which is not the less an offence, and does not the less subject her to forfeiture, because it was committed without the authority and against the will of the owner. It is true that inanimate matter can commit no offence. But this body is animated and put in action by the crew, who are guided by the master. The vessel acts and speaks by the master. She reports herself by the master. It is, therefore, not unreasonable that the vessel should be affected by this report." * * *

In other words, those great judges, although of course aware that a ship is no more alive than a mill-wheel, thought that not only the law did in fact deal with it as if it were alive, but that it was reasonable that the law should do so. The reader will observe that they do not say simply that it is reasonable on grounds of policy to sacrifice justice to the owner to security for somebody else, but that it is reasonable to deal with the vessel as an offending thing. Whatever the hidden ground of policy may be, their thought still clothes itself in personifying language.

* * *

We have now followed the development of the chief forms of liability in modern law for anything other than the immediate and manifest consequences of a man's own acts. * * * We have seen a single germ multiplying and branching into products as different from each other as the flower from the root. It hardly remains to ask what that germ was. We have seen that it was the desire of retaliation against the offending thing itself. * * * A consideration of the earliest instances will show, as might have been expected, that vengeance, not compensation, and vengeance on the offending things, was the original object. The ox in Exodus was to be stoned. The axe in the Athenian law was to be banished. * * * The slave under all the systems was to be surrendered to the relatives of the slain man, that they might do with him what they liked. The deodand was an accursed thing. The original limitation of liability to surrender, when the owner was before the court, could not be accounted for if it was his liability, and not that of his property, which was in question. * * *

The foregoing history, apart from the purposes for which it has been given, well illustrates the paradox of form and substance in the development of law. In form its growth is logical. The official theory is that each new decision follows syllogistically from existing precedents. But just as the clavicle in the cat only tells of the existence of some earlier creature to which a collar-bone was useful, precedents survive in the law long after the use they once served is at an end and the reason for them has been forgotten. The result of following them must often be failure and confusion from the merely logical point of view.

On the other hand, in substance the growth of the law is legislative. And this in a deeper sense than that what the courts declare to have always been the law is in fact new. It is legislative in its grounds. The very considerations which judges most rarely mention, and always with an apology, are the secret root from which the law draws all the juices of life. I mean, of course, considerations of what is expedient for the community concerned. Every important principle which is developed by litigation is in fact and at bottom the result of more or less definitely understood views of public policy; most generally, to be sure, under our practice and traditions, the unconscious result of instinctive preferences and inarticulate convictions, but none the less traceable to views of public policy in the last analysis. And as the law is administered by able and experienced men, who know too much to sacrifice good sense to a syllogism, it will be found that, when ancient rules maintain themselves in the way that has been and will be shown in this book, new reasons more fitted to the time have been found for them, and that they gradually receive a new content, and at last a new form, from the grounds to which they have been transplanted.

But hitherto this process has been largely unconscious. It is important, on that account, to bring to mind what the actual course of events has been. If it were only to insist on a more conscious recognition of the legislative function of the courts, as just explained, it would be useful * * *.

What has been said will explain the failure of all theories which consider the law only from its formal side, whether they attempt to deduce the *corpus* from *a priori* postulates, or fall into the humbler error of supposing the science of the law to reside in the *elegantia juris,* or logical cohesion of part with part. The truth is, that the law is always approaching, and never reaching, consistency. It is forever adopting new principles from life at one end, and it always retains old ones from history at the other, which have not yet been absorbed or sloughed off. It will become entirely consistent only when it ceases to grow.

* * *

However much we may codify the law into a series of seemingly self-sufficient propositions, those propositions will be but a phase in a continuous growth. To understand their scope fully, to know how they will be dealt with by judges trained in the past which the law embodies, we must ourselves know something of that past. The history of what the law has been is necessary to the knowledge of what the law is.

Again, the process which I have described has involved the attempt to follow precedents, as well as to give a good reason for them. When we find that in large and important branches of the law the various grounds of policy on which the various rules have been justified are later inventions to account for what are in fact survivals from more primitive times, we have a right to reconsider the popular reasons, and, taking a broader view of the field, to decide anew whether those reasons are satisfactory. * * *

But none of the foregoing considerations, nor the purpose of showing the materials for anthropology contained in the history of the law, are the immediate object here. My aim and purpose have been to show that the various forms of liability known to modern law spring from the common ground of revenge. * * * [This] shows that they have started from a moral basis, from the thought that some one was to blame.

It remains to be proved that, while the terminology of morals is still retained, and while the law does still and always, in a certain sense, measure legal liability by moral standards, it nevertheless, by the very necessity of its nature, is continually transmuting those moral standards into external or objective ones, from which the actual guilt of the party concerned is wholly eliminated.

NOTES AND QUESTIONS

1. In an omitted passage, Holmes asserts that there is a "mode in which the law has grown, without a break, from barbarism to civilization." Based on what you have read, are his views of the nature of the law's growth the same as those of Field and Langdell? What are their differences?

2. What is Holmes's excursion into the law of Greece and Rome designed to prove? The aim of the Greek law regarding masters and servants, says Holmes, was vengeance. Is this plausible to you? How does Holmes explain the ancient law that required the surrender or destruction of inanimate objects causing harm as an instrument of "vengeance?" Holmes makes a reference to Plato's *Laws* in this connection. Is there any significance in the fact that in another section of Plato's Laws, Book X, Plato provides extremely harsh penalties for religious heresy, even where the heresy stems only from personal agnosticism:

> For the morally inoffensive heretic the penalty, on conviction will in every case include at least five years of imprisonment in the "House of Correction," where he will see no one but members of the "nocturnal council," who are to visit him from time to time and to reason with him on the error of his ways. A second conviction is to be followed by death.

A.E. Taylor, Plato: The Man and His Work 494 (7th ed., 1960).

3. Holmes argues that civilization outgrew the old vengeance motive for law, and replaced it with a new one, while maintaining the old law's "principle" of master's liability for acts of servants. What is the new motive that Holmes ascribes to the law? Is this a motive that really reflects an advance in civilization? There is a similar discussion of admiralty law. What are the old and new rationales there?

4. How does Holmes use the analysis you have just read to arrive at the conclusion that "The very considerations which judges most rarely men-

tion, and always with an apology, are the secret root from which the law draws all the juices of life?" How does this lead him to the observation that " * * * the law is always approaching, and never reaching, consistency?" What does this lead Holmes to conclude about the feasibility of attempts to systematize the law, like those of Field or Langdell? What do you suppose is the importance of his closing observation of this part of The Common Law, that the law's "moral standards" are "continually" being transmuted "into external or objective ones, from which the actual guilt of the party concerned is wholly eliminated." Do you suppose, for example, that Holmes's thoughts could be applied to Shaw's decision in Farwell v. Boston & Worcester R.R.? Was that a case about "moral" standards? Was that a case which had grown out of a response to some deeply "felt need" in the community? Returning to Holmes's view of the forward march of civilization, what makes him different from a Field or a Langdell? What makes him like them? Holmes refers to his brand of history as "anthropology." What does he mean by that? Does it surprise you, in light of all that you have read in this casebook, that Holmes should need to go back to Greece and Rome to prove his points?

5. What does all of this tell you about Holmes's view of mankind? Did you find anything in this excerpt that might cause you to agree with the assessment of Professor G. Edward White:

> * * * one finds a disturbing dissonance between Holmes's very conspicuous social and professional success—it is hard to imagine a life less marred by physical, social or economical deprivations or one marked by a greater length and breadth of achievement—and his gloomy musings that "the crowd has substantially all there is," that "we are all very near despair," that men are like "flies", and that "man has no more cosmic significance than a baboon or a grain of sand." * * * Holmes's skepticism appears to have been less a striving for a positive goal than a facile means of avoiding commitment, whether to beliefs, institutions, or mankind itself. One is struck by the comments of Holmes that he had remained childless because he could not bear bringing children into the world. * * *

White, Patterns of American Legal Thought 225 (1978). Copyright 1978 by the Bobbs–Merrill Company, Inc., reprinted with the permission of the publisher. Holmes was also given to tossing off splendid ascerbic epigrams, for example, "the notion that with socialized property we should have women free and a piano for everybody seems to me an empty humbug." Holmes, "Ideals and Doubts," 10 Ill.L.Rev. 1 (1915).

Still, Holmes's ultimate musings on the future of man may not have been negative:

> * * * [A]s I grow older I grow calm. If I feel what are perhaps an old man's apprehensions, that competition from new races will cut deeper than working men's disputes and will test whether we can hang together and can fight; if I fear that we are running through the world's resources at a pace that we cannot keep; I do not lose my hopes. I do not pin my

> dreams for the future to my country or even to my race. I think it probable that civilization somehow will last as long as I care to look ahead—perhaps with smaller numbers, but perhaps also bred to greatness and splendor by science.

Holmes, "Law and the Court," (1913), in The Occasional Speeches of Justice Oliver Wendell Holmes 168, 173–174 (Howe ed., 1962).

By 1931, as Holmes's ninetieth birthday approached, and as he had completed twenty years on the Supreme Judicial Court of Massachusetts, and thirty years on the United States Supreme Court, Felix Frankfurter wrote that "no figure in the history of the Supreme Court, except Holmes, may fittingly be compared with the great Chief Justice [Marshall]." Frankfurter, ed., Mr. Justice Holmes vii (1931). As you will soon see, virtually every modern legal reformer or student of jurisprudence sooner or later invokes Holmes's name or his blessing. You have not seen much of Holmes's writing, of course, but the core of Holmes's legal philosophy, such as it was, is contained in the two excerpts from his work that you have read. Can you understand why he is regarded as such a jurisprudential titan? For a brief survey of the manner in which generations of lawyers have reinvented Holmes in their own images see Presser, "Oliver Wendell Holmes, Jr.," VI The Guide to American Law 62 (1984). Richard Posner has edited and introduced an anthology of Holmes's writing, The Essential Holmes: Selections from the Letters, Speeches, Judicial Opinions and Other Writing of Oliver Wendell Holmes, Jr. (1992), and Robert W. Gordon has edited a collection of musings on Holmes, The Legacy of Oliver Wendell Holmes, Jr. (1992). The long-awaited second book by Morton Horwitz, The Transformation of American Law 1870–1960: The Crisis of Legal Orthodoxy (1992), is, in large part, a reflection on Holmes (see especially pp. 109–143), and G. Edward White has written a challenging and speculative biography of Holmes, Justice Oliver Wendell Holmes: Law and the Inner Self (1993). The irresistable urge to write and think about Holmes is elegantly analyzed in a review essay on these and other works, John F. Hagerman, "Looking at Holmes: A Review Essay," 39 S.D.L.Rev. 433 (1994). While Langdell's invention of the case method of legal study, and its attendant Socratic teaching technique have often been blamed for hurting legal education, it can still be argued that most of what is wrong with current-day jurisprudence can be attributed to Holmes. See Albert W. Alschuler, Law Without Values: The Life, Work and Legacy of Oliver Wendell Holmes (2000). For an examination of formalism that maintains that "Both Holmes and Langdell concluded that judges ought to decide a case by applying the rules established by precedent, without appeal to any special claims of justice and without appeal to any higher-order normative principle," see Patrick J. Kelley, "Holmes, Langdell and Formalism," 15 Ratio Juris 26 (2002). Kelly states that "Holmes and Langdell were legal soulmates, differing only in the sophistication with which they understood the trendy scientism of their age." Id., at 50. Finally, for an argument that Holmes got torts wrong, see Thomas C. Grey, "Accidental Torts," 54 Vand. L. Rev. 1225 (2001). Only time will tell whether these assaults on Holmes will diminish his reputation, which remains, in the beginning of the twenty-first century, pretty high. For continuing assertions of the importance of Holmes, see, e.g., Symposium, *The Path of the Law* After One Hundred Years, 110 Harv. L.Rev. 989 (1997) (Collecting articles celebrating the 100th anniversary of Holmes's famous essay), David J. Siepp, "125th Anniversary Essay: Holmes's Path," 77 B.U.L.Rev. 515 (examining impact of Holmes's essay on law generally and Boston University School of Law in particular), Sheldon M. Novick, "Justice Holmes's Philosophy," 70 Wash. U. L. Rev. 703 (1992) (Praising Justice Holmes's essentially democratic (although partially elitist) philosophy, although noting that its obscurity eludes critics). As you read the materials which follow, see if you can guess why Holmes has been deified more than any judge since Marshall.

B. THE NEW DEAL AND THE NINE OLD MEN

In the late years of the nineteenth century and the early years of the twentieth century, at the height of what has been called the "Progressive Movement," there was much state legislation regarding working conditions. We have already alluded to legislation regarding compensation for injured workmen, which was commonplace. Other reforms included laws regarding wages and hours, the employment of women and children, and health and safety conditions of the workingplace. Advocates of freedom of contract fought some of this social legislation, arguing that it was unconstitutional under the prohibition against any state's passing a law "impairing the obligation of contracts." U.S. Constitution, Article I, Section 10. Nevertheless, in Holden v. Hardy, 169 U.S. 366, 18 S.Ct. 383, 42 L.Ed. 780 (1898), the United States Supreme Court upheld a Utah law limiting work hours in the mines, basing its decision on the state's "police power," and suggesting that considering the conditions of Utah's mines, the inequality of bargaining power between the miners and their employers required some modification of a strict "freedom-of-contract" approach. Still, in the infamous decision in Lochner v. New York, 198 U.S. 45, 25 S.Ct. 539, 49 L.Ed. 937 (1905), a majority of five justices held unconstitutional a New York maximum-hours law for bakers, as an unreasonable interference with "the right of the individual to his personal liberty or to enter into contracts in relation to labor which may seem to him appropriate or necessary for the support of himself and his family." This personal liberty and this right to contract, said the court, were secured by Section 1 of the Fourteenth Amendment, which provided that no state was to "deprive any person of life, liberty, or property, without due process of law." A blistering dissent was filed by Justice Harlan, with whom Justices White and Day concurred, but the most famous statements against the *Lochner* decision were made in the dissent of Justice Holmes.

Holmes suggested that the majority based its decision on its own ideological preferences for freedom of contract, and not on the law, which, under Holden v. Hardy and several other decisions, would seem to permit such state legislation. The Fourteenth Amendment, declared Holmes, "does not enact Mr. Herbert Spencer's Social Statics," referring to a work by an English Social Darwinist. A constitution, Holmes concluded, "is not intended to embody a particular economic theory, whether of paternalism and the organic relation of the citizen to the State or of *laissez faire*." Was he right? For a bracing criticism of Holmes and the other critics of *Lochner*, see David E. Bernstein, Rehabilitating *Lochner*: Defending Individual Rights against Progressive Reform 46 (2011), which gives a spirited defense of the *Lochner* majority, and, indeed, accuses Holmes of having "an obvious and self-proclaimed disdain for facts." From *Lochner* until the 1930's, the Supreme Court behaved erratically in the area of social legislation by the states, frequently invalidating state and federal legislation on grounds like those of *Lochner,* but occasionally upholding measures, as in Muller v. Oregon, 208 U.S. 412, 28 S.Ct. 324, 52 L.Ed. 551 (1908). (Oregon law limiting maximum hours of women), or Wilson v. New, 243 U.S. 332, 37 S.Ct. 298, 61 L.Ed. 755 (1917) (federal law limiting interstate railroad workers to eight-hour day).

In the twenties, as the Republican party in particular, and American business in general, flourished, the trend in Supreme Court decisions seemed to be decidedly against state or federal supervision of commerce or industry, on the theory that government should not be allowed to tinker with the obvious success of the free market. Before the Fall of 1929, indeed, America, or at least American corporations, appeared to be enjoying unparalleled prosperity, although striking inequalities in the distribution of income existed, and the values of many shares of stock in industrial and commercial concerns were wildly inflated. Most businessmen and politicians appeared to have believed, however, that American business was quite sound, and that economic euphoria would, and ought to, continue indefinitely. Some thought that the current speculative fever ought to be contained, however, and the American Federal Reserve Board and the Bank of England took some modest steps in late summer and early fall of 1929 to reduce the availability of the "easy money" investors had been borrowing. Some speculators then sold out, and panic ensued. From September 1, 1929 to July 1, 1932, the market value of stocks listed on the New York Exchange fell from $89.6 billion to $15.6 billion, and similar, and in many cases, much greater, declines were experienced by other issues. Investors thus saw paper profits evaporate; many who had bought on margin were practically instantaneously ruined, and millions of other American investors were hit by the greatest financial distress they had ever known. See Generally John D. Hicks, Republican Ascendency 1921–33, 224–233 (1960).

Though business leaders and politicians minimized the impact of the Crash in the Fall of 1929, the American economy rapidly deteriorated:

> Prices dropped sharply, foreign trade fell off, factories closed, business failures multiplied, banks went under, unemployment began to

> mount * * *. Savings disappeared; purchases made on installments had to be returned; substantial citizens lost their homes on mortgages; * * * stores closed for lack of customers; * * * soup kitchens opened; bread lines began to form; local relief systems broke down; panhandlers roamed the streets; * * * the jobless slept on park benches, in the doorways of public buildings or on the ground * * *.

Hicks, supra, at 229.

The Republican Herbert Hoover tried to take measures that would improve the situation, but they were ineffectual. In 1932, disenchanted, the American electorate turned to the Democrat, Franklin D. Roosevelt. Once inaugurated, during the historic "Hundred Days," Roosevelt was able to get the now Democratically-controlled congress to pass the most ambitious program of social legislation America had yet seen. These programs, known usually as the "First New Deal," were designed to produce relief for the unemployed, and to smooth the path to economic recovery for American business. Among other actions, the Emergency Banking Relief Act (March 9, 1932) gave the President broad discretion to regulate transactions in Gold and Silver, and validated the actions the President had already taken, including his enforced "Bank Holiday," whereby he closed the nation's banks on March 5, in order to prevent further financial deterioration. The act, drafted principally by members of the banking industry, also reorganized the nation's banking system, and attempted to prevent further deterioration of the country's gold reserves by limiting specie payments. Shortly thereafter the country went off the Gold Standard, and, pursuant to the Gold Reserve Act of 1934 (January 31, 1934), the dollar's value was halved. The Beer–Wine Revenue Act (March 22) legalized those beverages of 3.2% maximum alcoholic content by weight, and taxed them at $5.00 per barrel. The Civilian Conservation Corps Reforestation Relief Act (March 31) authorized jobs for 250,000, and the Federal Emergency Relief Act created an agency to distribute national revenues to states and municipalities (May 12). The Tennessee Valley Authority (TVA), an independent public corporation, was created to construct dams and power plants and generally to develop the economies of Tennessee, North Carolina, Kentucky, Virginia, Mississippi, Georgia, and Alabama. On June 13, the Home Owners Refinancing Act created a corporation to refinance home mortgage debts for nonfarm owners, and on June 16 the Farm Credit Act eased the way toward refinancing of farm mortgages. The Federal Securities Act (May 27) required full disclosure of the facts regarding new securities, and provided for the registration of information on new issues with the Federal Government. The Banking Act of 1933 (June 16) created the Federal Bank Deposit Insurance Corporation which was to guarantee individual bank deposits under $5,000, and enacted several other banking reforms.

The two most important New Deal measures, however, were the Agricultural Adjustment Act (May 12) which set up the Agricultural Adjustment Administration (AAA) and the National Industrial Recovery Act (NIRA) (June 16). The task of the AAA was to improve the condition of farmers by curtailing the production of certain crops, and to set prices for them. Farmers were to be paid subsidies for reducing their production, and the money to pay the subsidies was to come from taxes on the food processors. The NIRA created the National Recovery Administration (NRA), which was charged with the responsibility for establishing (with the cooperation of the businesses themselves) codes for fair competition for American business. Such codes, which would set wages, hours, and working conditions, were to be drafted by members of the industries, and were to be exempt from federal Antitrust Law.

As you might well imagine, these bold measures were greeted with enthusiasm by most, but some were cautious. The New Deal meant a change in the nature of the Federal government, as it extended its influence over the national economy in previously unimagined ways. Many were concerned about the increased bureaucracy, and the possibility of losses of individual freedoms. Some were also disturbed by the manipulation of the dollar and the money markets. Bernard Baruch, a wall street financier, viewed the nation's going off the Gold standard as a move that "can't be defended except as mob rule." Lewis Douglas, the Director of the Budget, considering the acts to raise prices by "remonitizing silver, printing greenbacks, or altering the gold content of the dollar," observed that, "Well, this is the end of Western Civilization." See generally William E. Leuchtenburg, Franklin D. Roosevelt and the New Deal 41–62 (1963).

Others waited to see how the Supreme Court, which had recently been so hostile to social legislation, would view the New Deal measures. It was several years before any of these laws were constitutionally tested by the court. In the first few tests of New Deal measures, most of which were not crucial to Roosevelt's program, the Supreme Court displayed no consistent pattern, upholding some actions, e.g. many of the currency and gold measures, but rejecting others, as it did to a railroad pension program. The first clear indication of the court's attitude came in its review of the constitutionality of the important National Industrial Recovery Act, to which we now turn. As you read these Supreme Court decisions, see if you can determine whether the views of "legal science" or "legal anthropology" as expressed by Field, Langdell, or Holmes seem to be reflected in the Court's constitutional exegesis. For revisionist understandings of *Lochner* and its era, see e.g., David E. Bernstein, Rehabilitating Lochner: Defending Individual Rights against Progressive Reform (2011), Barry Friedman, "The History of the Countermajoritarian Difficulty, Part Three: The Lesson of *Lochner*," 76 N.Y.U.L.Rev. 1383 (2001), John V. Orth, "Contract and the Common Law," Chapter 2, in Harry N. Scheiber, ed., The State and Freedom of Contract 44 (1998), Stephen A. Siegel,

"*Lochner Era* Jurisprudence and the American Constitutional Tradition," 70 N.Car.L.Rev. 1 (1991), Bruce Ackerman, We the People: Foundations 81–104 (1991), and Stephen B. Presser, Recapturing the Constitution: Race, Religion and Abortion Reconsidered 139–149 (1994).

A.L.A. SCHECHTER POULTRY CORP. V. UNITED STATES

Supreme Court of the United States, 1935.
295 U.S. 495, 55 S.Ct. 837, 79 L.Ed. 1570.

* * *

MR. CHIEF JUSTICE HUGHES delivered the opinion of the Court.

Petitioners * * * were convicted in the District Court of the United States for the Eastern District of New York on eighteen counts of an indictment charging violations of what is known as the "Live Poultry Code,"[1] and on an additional count for conspiracy to commit such violations. * * * [T]he defendants contended (1) that the Code had been adopted pursuant to an unconstitutional delegation by Congress of legislative power [and] (2) that it attempted to regulate intrastate transactions which lay outside the authority of Congress * * *.

* * *

New York City is the largest live-poultry market in the United States. Ninety-six per cent of the live poultry there marketed comes from other States. Three-fourths of this amount arrives by rail and is consigned to commission men or receivers. * * * They sell to slaughterhouse operators who are also called market-men.

The defendants are slaughterhouse operators * * * in Brooklyn, New York City. Defendants ordinarily purchase their live poultry from commission men at the West Washington Market in New York City or at the railroad terminals serving the City, but occasionally they purchase from commission men in Philadelphia. They buy the poultry for slaughter and resale. After the poultry is trucked to their slaughterhouse markets in Brooklyn, it is there sold, usually within twenty-four hours, to retail poultry dealers and butchers who sell directly to consumers. * * * Defendants do not sell poultry in interstate commerce.

The "Live Poultry Code" was promulgated under § 3 of the National Industrial Recovery Act. That section * * * authorizes the President to approve "codes of fair competition." Such a code may be approved for a trade or industry, upon application by one or more trade or industrial associations or groups, if the President finds (1) that such associations or groups "impose no inequitable restrictions on admission to membership

[1] The full title of the Code is "Code of Fair Competition for the Live Poultry Industry of the Metropolitan Area in and about the City of New York."

therein and are truly representative," and (2) that such codes are not designed "to promote monopolies or to eliminate or oppress small enterprises and will not operate to discriminate against them, and will tend to effectuate the policy" of Title I of the Act. Such codes "shall not permit monopolies or monopolistic practices." As a condition of his approval, the President may "impose such conditions (including requirements for the making of reports and the keeping of accounts) for the protection of consumers, competitors, employees, and others, and in furtherance of the public interest, and may provide such exceptions to and exemptions from the provisions of such code as the President in his discretion deems necessary to effectuate the policy herein declared." Where such a code has not been approved, the President may prescribe one, either on his own motion or on complaint. Violation of any provision of a code (so approved or prescribed) "in any transaction in or affecting interstate or foreign commerce" is made a misdemeanor punishable by a fine of not more than $500 for each offense, and each day the violation continues is to be deemed a separate offense.

The "Live Poultry Code" was approved by the President on April 13, 1934. * * *

* * * The Code is established as "a code of fair competition for the live poultry industry of the metropolitan area in and about the City of New York." * * *

The "industry" is defined as including "every person engaged in the business of selling, purchasing for resale, transporting, or handling and/or slaughtering live poultry, from the time such poultry comes into the New York metropolitan area to the time it is first sold in slaughtered form," * * *.

The Code * * * provides that no employee, with certain exceptions, shall be permitted to work in excess of forty (40) hours in any one week, and that no employee, save as stated, "shall be paid in any pay period less than at the rate of fifty (50) cents per hour." The article containing "general labor provisions" prohibits the employment of any person under sixteen years of age, and declares that employees shall have the right of "collective bargaining," and freedom of choice with respect to labor organizations * * *. The minimum number of employees, who shall be employed by slaughterhouse operators, is fixed, the number being graduated according to the average volume of weekly sales.

Provision is made for administration through an "industry advisory committee," to be selected by trade associations and members of the industry, and a "code supervisor" to be appointed, with the approval of the committee, by agreement between the Secretary of Agriculture and the Administrator for Industrial Recovery. The expenses of administration are to be borne by the members of the industry proportionately upon the basis of volume of business, or such other factors as the advisory committee may deem equitable, "subject to the disapproval of the Secretary and/or Administrator."

The seventh article, containing "trade practice provisions," prohibits various practices which are said to constitute "unfair methods of competition." * * * The members of the industry are also required to keep books and records which " 'will clearly reflect all financial transactions of their respective businesses and the financial condition thereof,' and to submit weekly reports showing the range of daily prices and volume of sales" for each kind of produce.

The President approved the Code by an executive order * * *.

* * *

First. Two preliminary points are stressed by the Government * * *. We are told that the provision of the statute authorizing the adoption of codes must be viewed in the light of the grave national crisis with which Congress was confronted. Undoubtedly, the conditions to which power is addressed are always to be considered when the exercise of power is challenged. Extraordinary conditions may call for extraordinary remedies. But the argument necessarily stops short of an attempt to justify action which lies outside the sphere of constitutional authority. Extraordinary conditions do not create or enlarge constitutional power. * * * Such assertions of extra-constitutional authority were anticipated and precluded by the explicit terms of the Tenth Amendment,—"The powers not delegated to the United States by the Constitution, nor prohibited by it to the States, are reserved to the States respectively, or to the people."

The further point is urged that the national crisis demanded a broad and intensive cooperative effort by those engaged in trade and industry, and that this necessary cooperation was sought to be fostered by permitting them to initiate the adoption of codes. But the statutory plan is not simply one for voluntary effort. * * * Violations of the provisions of the codes are punishable as crimes.

Second. The question of the delegation of legislative power. * * * The Constitution provides that "All legislative powers herein granted shall be vested in a Congress of the United States, which shall consist of a Senate and House of Representatives." Art. I, § 1. And the Congress is authorized "To make all laws which shall be necessary and proper for carrying into execution its general powers." Art. I, § 8, par. 18. The Congress is not permitted to abdicate or to transfer to others the essential legislative functions with which it is thus vested. We have repeatedly recognized the necessity of adapting legislation to complex conditions involving a host of details with which the national legislature cannot deal directly. * * * [T]he Constitution has never been regarded as denying to Congress the necessary resources of flexibility and practicality, which will enable it to perform its function in laying down policies and establishing standards, while leaving to selected instrumentalities the making of subordinate rules within prescribed limits and the determinations of facts to which the policy as declared by the legislature is to apply. But * * * the constant recognition of the necessity and validity of such provisions, and the wide range of administrative authority which has been developed by means of them, cannot be allowed to obscure the limitations of the authority to delegate, if our constitutional system is to be maintained. * * *

Accordingly, we look to the statute to see whether Congress has overstepped these limitations,—whether Congress in authorizing "codes of fair competition" has itself established the standards of legal obligation, thus performing its essential legislative function, or, by the failure to enact such standards, has attempted to transfer that function to others.

What is meant by "fair competition" as the term is used in the Act? Does it refer to a category established in the law, and is the authority to make codes limited accordingly? Or is it used as a convenient designation for whatever set of laws the formulators of a code for a particular trade or industry may propose * * *, or the President may himself prescribe, as being wise and beneficent provisions for the government of the trade or industry in order to accomplish the broad purposes of rehabilitation, correction and expansion which are stated in the first section of Title I?[9]

The Act does not define "fair competition." * * *

The Government urges that the codes will "consist of rules of competition deemed fair for each industry by representative members of that industry—by the persons most vitally concerned and most familiar with its problems." Instances are cited in which Congress has availed itself of such assistance; as e.g., in the exercise of its authority over the public domain, with respect to the recognition of local customs or rules of miners as to mining claims, or, in matters of a more or less technical nature, as in designating the standard height of drawbars. But would it be seriously contended that Congress could delegate its legislative authority to trade or industrial associations or groups so as to empower them to enact the laws they deem to be wise and beneficent for the rehabilitation and expansion of their trade or industries? Could trade or industrial associations or groups be constituted legislative bodies for that purpose because

[9] That section, under the heading "Declaration of Policy," is as follows: "Section 1. A national emergency productive of widespread unemployment and disorganization of industry, which burdens interstate and foreign commerce, affects the public welfare, and undermines the standards of living of the American people, is hereby declared to exist. It is hereby declared to be the policy of Congress to remove obstructions to the free flow of interstate and foreign commerce which tend to diminish the amount thereof; and to provide for the general welfare by promoting the organization of industry for the purpose of coöperative action among trade groups, to induce and maintain united action of labor and management under adequate governmental sanctions and supervision, to eliminate unfair competitive practices, to promote the fullest possible utilization of the present productive capacity of industries, to avoid undue restriction of production (except as may be temporarily required), to increase the consumption of industrial and agricultural products by increasing purchasing power, to reduce and relieve unemployment, to improve standards of labor, and otherwise to rehabilitate industry and to conserve natural resources."

such associations or groups are familiar with the problems of their enterprises? * * * The answer is obvious. Such a delegation of legislative power is unknown to our law and is utterly inconsistent with the constitutional prerogatives and duties of Congress.

The question, then, turns upon the authority which § 3 of the Recovery Act vests in the President to approve or prescribe. * * * But Congress cannot delegate legislative power to the President to exercise an unfettered discretion to make whatever laws he thinks may be needed or advisable for the rehabilitation and expansion of trade or industry. * * *

Accordingly we turn to the Recovery Act to ascertain what limits have been set to the exercise of the President's discretion. *First,* the President, as a condition of approval, is required to find that the trade or industrial associations or groups which propose a code, "impose no inequitable restrictions on admission to membership" and are "truly representative." That condition, however, relates only to the status of the initiators of the new laws and not to the permissible scope of such laws. *Second,* the President is required to find that the code is not "designed to promote monopolies or to eliminate or oppress small enterprises and will not operate to discriminate against them." * * * But these restrictions leave virtually untouched the field of policy envisaged by section one, and, in that wide field of legislative possibilities, the proponents of a code, refraining from monopolistic designs, may roam at will and the President may approve or disapprove their proposals as he may see fit. That is the precise effect of the further finding that the President is to make—that the code "will tend to effectuate the policy of this title." * * *

* * *

Such a sweeping delegation of legislative power finds no support in the decisions upon which the Government especially relies. By the Interstate Commerce Act, Congress has itself provided a code of laws regulating the activities of the common carriers subject to the Act, in order to assure the performance of their services upon just and reasonable terms, with adequate facilities and without unjust discrimination. Congress from time to time has elaborated its requirements, as needs have been disclosed. To facilitate the application of the standards prescribed by the Act, Congress has provided an expert body. That administrative agency, in dealing with particular cases, is required to act upon notice and hearing, and its orders must be supported by findings of fact which in turn are sustained by evidence. * * When the Commission is authorized to issue, for the construction, extension or abandonment of lines, a certificate of "public convenience and necessity," or to permit the acquisition by one carrier of the control of another, if that is found to be "in the public interest," we have pointed out that these provisions are not left without standards to guide determination. The authority conferred has direct relation to the standards prescribed for the service of common carriers and can be exercised only upon findings, based upon evidence, with respect to particular conditions of transportation. * * *

Similarly, we have held that the Radio Act of 1927 established standards to govern radio communications and, in view of the limited number of available broadcasting frequencies, Congress authorized allocation and licenses. The Federal Radio Commission was created as the licensing authority, in order to secure a reasonable equality of opportunity in radio transmission and reception. The authority of the Commission to grant licenses "as public convenience, interest or necessity requires" was limited by the nature of radio communications, and by the scope, character and quality of the services to be rendered and the relative advantages to be derived through distribution of facilities. These standards established by Congress were to be enforced upon hearing, and evidence, by an administrative body acting under statutory restrictions adapted to the particular activity. * * *

To summarize and conclude upon this point: Section 3 of the Recovery Act is without precedent. It supplies no standards for any trade, industry or activity. It does not undertake to prescribe rules of conduct to be applied to particular states of fact determined by appropriate administrative procedure. Instead of prescribing rules of conduct, it authorizes the making of codes to prescribe them. For that legislative undertaking, § 3 sets up no standards, aside from the statement of the general aims of rehabilitation, correction and expansion described in section one. In view of the scope of that broad declaration, and of the nature of the few restrictions that are imposed, the discretion of the President in approving or prescribing codes, and thus enacting laws for the government of trade and industry throughout the country, is virtually unfettered. We think that the code-making authority thus conferred is an unconstitutional delegation of legislative power.

Third. The question of the application of the provisions of the Live Poultry Code to intrastate transactions. * * *

* * *

These provisions relate to the hours and wages of those employed by defendants in their slaughterhouses in Brooklyn and to the sales there made to retail dealers and butchers.

(1) Were these transactions "in" interstate commerce? Much is made of the fact that almost all the poultry coming to New York is sent there from other States. But the code provisions, as here applied, do not concern the transportation of the poultry from other States to New York * * *. When defendants had made their purchases, whether at the West Washington Market in New York City or at the railroad terminals serving the City, or elsewhere, the poultry was trucked to their slaughterhouses in

Brooklyn for local disposition. * * * Defendants held the poultry at their slaughterhouse markets for slaughter and local sale to retail dealers and butchers who in turn sold directly to consumers. Neither the slaughtering nor the sales by defendants were transactions in interstate commerce. * * *

The undisputed facts thus afford no warrant for the argument that the poultry handled by defendants at their slaughterhouse markets was in a "current" or "flow" of interstate commerce and was thus subject to congressional regulation. The mere fact that there may be a constant flow of commodities into a State does not mean that the flow continues after the property has arrived and has become commingled with the mass of property within the State and is there held solely for local disposition and use. * * * Hence, decisions which deal with a stream of interstate commerce—where goods come to rest within a State temporarily and are later to go forward in interstate commerce—and with the regulations of transactions involved in that practical continuity of movement, are not applicable here. * * *

(2) Did the defendants' transactions directly "affect" interstate commerce so as to be subject to federal regulation? The power of Congress extends not only to the regulation of transactions which are part of interstate commerce, but to the protection of that commerce from injury. It matters not that the injury may be due to the conduct of those engaged in intrastate operations. * * * We have held that, in dealing with common carriers engaged in both interstate and intrastate commerce, the dominant authority of Congress necessarily embraces the right to control their intrastate operations in all matters having such a close and substantial relation to interstate traffic that the control is essential or appropriate to secure the freedom of that traffic from interference or unjust discrimination and to promote the efficiency of the interstate service. * * * And combinations and conspiracies to restrain interstate commerce, or to monopolize any part of it, are none the less within the reach of the Anti–Trust Act because the conspirators seek to attain their end by means of intrastate activities. * * *

* * *

* * * This is not a prosecution for a conspiracy to restrain or monopolize interstate commerce in violation of the Anti–Trust Act. Defendants have been convicted, not upon direct charges of injury to interstate commerce or of interference with persons engaged in that commerce, but of violations of certain provisions of the Live Poultry Code and of conspiracy to commit these violations. Interstate commerce is brought in only upon the charge that violations of these provisions—as to hours and wages of employees and local sales—"affected" interstate commerce.

In determining how far the federal government may go in controlling intrastate transactions upon the ground that they "affect" interstate commerce, there is a necessary and well-established distinction between direct and indirect effects. The precise line can be drawn only as individual cases arise, but the distinction is clear in principle. Direct effects are illustrated by the railroad cases we have cited, as e.g., the effect of failure to use prescribed safety appliances on railroads which are the highways of both interstate and intrastate commerce, injury to an employee engaged in interstate transportation by the negligence of an employee engaged in an intrastate movement, the fixing of rates for intrastate transportation which unjustly discriminate against interstate commerce. But where the effect of intrastate transactions upon interstate commerce is merely indirect, such transactions remain within the domain of state power. If the commerce clause were construed to reach all enterprises and transactions which could be said to have an indirect effect upon interstate commerce, the federal authority would embrace practically all the activities of the people and the authority of the State over its domestic concerns would exist only by sufferance of the federal government. * * *

The distinction between direct and indirect effects has been clearly recognized in the application of the Anti–Trust Act. Where a combination or conspiracy is formed, with the intent to restrain interstate commerce or to monopolize any part of it, the violation of the statute is clear. * * * But where that intent is absent, and the objectives are limited to intrastate activities, the fact that there may be an indirect effect upon interstate commerce does not subject the parties to the federal statute, notwithstanding its broad provisions. * * *

* * *

The question of chief importance [here] relates to the provisions of the Code as to the hours and wages of those employed in defendants' slaughterhouse markets. It is plain that these requirements are imposed in order to govern the details of defendants' management of their local business. The persons employed in slaughtering and selling in local trade are not employed in interstate commerce. * * *

The Government * * * makes the point that efforts to enact state legislation establishing high labor standards have been impeded by the belief that unless similar action is taken generally, commerce will be diverted from the States adopting such standards, and that this fear of diversion has led to demands for federal legislation on the subject of wages and hours. The apparent implication is that the federal authority under the commerce clause should be deemed to extend to the establishment of rules to govern wages and hours in intrastate trade and industry generally throughout the country, thus overriding the authority of the States to deal with domestic problems arising from labor conditions in their internal commerce.

It is not the province of the Court to consider the economic advantages or disadvantages of such a centralized system. It is sufficient to say that the Federal Constitution does not provide for it. * * * [T]he authority of the federal government may not be pushed to such an extreme as to destroy the distinction, which the commerce clause itself establishes, between commerce "among the several States" and the internal concerns of a State. The same answer must be made to the contention that is based upon the serious economic situation which led to the passage of the Recovery Act,—the fall in prices, the decline in wages and employment, and the curtailment of the market for commodities. Stress is laid upon the great importance of maintaining wage distributions which would provide the necessary stimulus in starting "the cumulative forces making for expanding commercial activity." Without in any way disparaging this motive, it is enough to say that the recuperative efforts of the federal government must be made in a manner consistent with the authority granted by the Constitution.

* * *

On both the grounds we have discussed, the attempted delegation of legislative power, and the attempted regulation of intrastate transactions which affect interstate commerce only indirectly, we hold the code provisions here in question to be invalid and that the judgment of conviction must be reversed.

NOTES AND QUESTIONS

1. The "delegation" ground of *Schechter* had been anticipated in Panama Refining Co. v. Ryan, 293 U.S. 388, 55 S.Ct. 241, 79 L.Ed. 446 (1935), when the Court had held that certain procedural provisions pertaining to the "hot oil" industry under the NIRA involved excessive delegation of legislative power to the executive. The "interstate commerce clause" ground had also been anticipated, in Railroad Retirement Bd. v. Alton R. Co., 295 U.S. 330, 55 S.Ct. 758, 79 L.Ed. 1468 (1935), when the court held that the provisions of the Railroad Retirement Act of 1934 were unconstitutional, because they provided for pensions for workers in exclusively intrastate traffic. Still, *Schechter* had more impact than earlier decisions, because of the unanimous court's clear declaration that the industry code system (the heart of the NIRA) could not be based on the commerce clause. Most of the economic work of the New Deal may already have been accomplished by May 27, 1935, when *Schechter* was announced, but Roosevelt was genuinely concerned about what the Supreme Court's obdurate attitude might mean for future reform efforts. He stated at a press conference held a few days later that "We have been relegated to the horse-and-buggy definition of interstate commerce." See general-

ly Leuchtenburg, The Origins of Franklin D. Roosevelt's "Court–Packing" Plan, 1966 Supreme Court Review 347, 356–357.

2. Given the seriousness of the problems confronting the nation, given the appeal to many of the country's most advanced thinkers of centralized management of the economy, and given the cooperation of government and business mandated by the NIRA, how would *you* have construed the interstate commerce clause in *Schechter?* Also, would you have found any support for holding the NIRA to be constitutional in the Constitution's preamble that the national government was "ordained and established" to "promote the general welfare" or "secure domestic tranquility?" What about the clause in Article I, Section 8, that provides that the Congress shall have the power "to pay the Debts and provide for the common Defence and general Welfare of the United States?" Finally, would the last clause of Section 8, which gives Congress power "To make all Laws which shall be necessary and proper for carrying into Execution the foregoing Powers, and all other Powers vested by this Constitution in the Government of the United States, or in any Department or Officer thereof" have any bearing?

3. Why do you suppose there was unanimous concurrence on the Court in throwing out the NIRA? What is the fundamental difficulty with the system of codes, the exemption from the antitrust acts, and the enforced cooperation of government and industry? Would the result under the NIRA have been acceptable to most of the nineteenth century judges whose opinions we studied? Why or why not? Consider the "delegation" rationale of the Supreme Court. Where in the Constitution do you find support for such a rationale? Do you believe that the Supreme Court successfully distinguishes the ICC Act and the Radio Act, which passed constitutional muster? Why isn't the meaning of "fair competition" made clear by the reference to the purposes of the NIRA, set out in Section 1, the Act's "Declaration of Policy?" The permissible scope of agency rule-making, and the delegation doctrine, have become hot issues for the courts and legal scholars. See generally on this development, Gary Lawson, "Delegation and Original Meaning," 88 Va.L.Rev. 327 (2002) and Thomas W. Merrill and Kathryn Tongue Watts, "Agency Rules with the Force of Law: The Original Convention," 116 Harv. L.Rev. 467 (2002), and sources there cited. See also, for an analysis of the development of administrative law and labor law since the New Deal, three articles by Reuel E. Schiller, "Rulemaking's Promise: Administrative Law and Legal Culture in the 1960s and 1970s," 53 Admin.L.Rev. 1139 (2001), "Enlarging the Administrative Polity: Administrative Law and the Changing Definition of Pluralism, 1945–1970," 53 Vand.L.Rev. 1389 (2000), and "From Group Rights to Individual Liberties: Post–War Labor Law, Liberalism, and the Waning of Union Strength," 20 Berkeley Journal of Employment and Labor Law 1 (1999).

Apart from the legal and constitutional issues, is it clear that the scheme in the NRA was really an even-handed attempt to help the economically disenfranchised? For a powerful argument that the NRA (labeled by some the "Negro Removal Act," "Negroes Ruined Again," and "Negroes Robbed Again") was very harmful to African–Americans because it gave too much power to racially-exclusionary unions (as did the Wagner Act, discussed *infra*), see David E. Bernstein, Only One Place of Redress: African Americans, Labor Regulations and the Court from Reconstruction to the New Deal (2001). See also, for a laudatory assessment of Bernstein's book, placing it in a broad historiographical context, Ken I. Kersch, "Blacks and Labor—The Untold Story," The Public Interest 141 (Issue No. 148, Summer, 2002). Kersch concludes that "Bernstein's uniquely unsentimental account of African–American and labor history is indispensable to serious reflection on these issues, and clears the way for a reconsideration of whether blacks might be better served by the principles of limited government, property rights, and liberty of contract." Id., at 145.

4. For the next two years several other decisions of the United States Supreme Court invalidated New Deal measures. On January 6, 1936, for example, the Supreme Court declared that the scheme of the AAA processing tax, insofar as it took money from the processors to be given to the farmers in subsidy payments, was unconstitutional. United States v. Butler, 297 U.S. 1, 56 S.Ct. 312, 80 L.Ed. 477 (1936). Justice Roberts, speaking for a six to three majority (Stone, Cardozo, and Brandeis dissented), stated that the subsidy payments were in effect "the expropriation of money from one group for the benefit of another." Id., at 61.

5. Franklin Roosevelt was re-elected in 1936, in a landslide victory that included the greatest majority of electoral votes since Washington, including those of all but two states. For months popular sentiment had been running strongly against the "Nine old men" who were frustrating his legislative efforts. In early February of 1937, President Roosevelt proposed that Congress enact the following legislation:

> When any judge of a court of the United States, appointed to hold his office during good behavior, has heretofore or hereafter attained the age of seventy years and has held a commission or commissions as a judge of any such court or courts at least ten years, continuously or otherwise, and within six months thereafter has neither resigned nor retired, the President, for each such judge who has not so resigned or retired, shall nominate, and by and with the advice and consent of the Senate, shall appoint one additional judge to the court to which the former is commissioned. * * * No more than fifty judges shall be appointed thereunder, nor shall any judge be so appointed if such appointment would result in * * * more than fifteen members of the Supreme Court of the United States. * * *.

Quoted in G. Gunther, Constitutional Law: Cases and Materials 168 (9th ed. 1975). At the time of the proposed bill six justices were over seventy: Butler (71), Hughes (75), Sutherland (75), McReynolds (75), Van Devanter (78), and Brandeis (81). There was a certain delicious irony in the plan, since Mr. Justice McReynolds, when he was Woodrow Wilson's Attorney General, in 1913, noting that federal court judges had tended to remain "upon the bench long beyond the time that they are able to adequately discharge their duties," had proposed legislation requiring the President to appoint additional judges to the lower federal courts when older judges failed to take the retirement at full pay which federal law permitted them. Roosevelt's Attorney General, Homer Cummings, one of the chief architects of FDR's court-packing plan, was able to argue that their proposal merely extended McReynolds's to the Supreme Court, a logical extension. Leuchtenburg, supra, at 391–392.

6. On March 9, 1937, President Roosevelt addressed the nation by radio, commenting on the *Butler* and *Schechter* decisions:

* * *

> When the Congress has sought to stabilize national agriculture, to improve the conditions of labor, to safeguard business against unfair competition, to protect our national resources, and in many other ways to serve our clearly national needs, the majority of the Court has been assuming the power to pass on the wisdom of these acts of the Congress—and to approve or disapprove the public policy written into these laws.

* * *

> We have, therefore, reached the point as a Nation where we must take action to save the Constitution from the Court and the Court from itself. We must find a way to take an appeal from the Supreme Court to the Constitution itself. We want a Supreme Court which will do justice under the Constitution—not over it. In our courts we want a government of laws and not of men.

* * *

quoted in Gunther, supra at 169–170. The President proceeded to argue for the necessity of his plan to pass legislation authorizing him to appoint additional judges to the court. Do you think that the President, in the portions quoted from his speech, accurately presents the issues? How does he rate as a "legal scientist?" How would you have reacted if you were a Justice of the Supreme Court?

7. On March 29, 1937, the Supreme Court decided West Coast Hotel Co. v. Parrish, 300 U.S. 379, 57 S.Ct. 578, 81 L.Ed. 703 (1937). That case, by a five to four majority, upheld the constitutionality of a Washington state law which set a minimum wage for women. The court expressly overruled Adkins v. Children's Hospital of Dist. of Columbia, 261 U.S. 525, 43 S.Ct. 394, 67 L.Ed. 785 (1923), which had rejected the District of Columbia's Women's Minimum Wage Act, as a violation of the due process clause of the Fifth Amendment. Chief Justice Hughes, writing for the majority in *Parrish,* seemed to reject much of the Constitutional philosophy of the early twentieth century court:

> The Constitution does not speak of freedom of contract. It speaks of liberty and prohibits the deprivation of liberty without due process of law.

> In prohibiting that deprivation the Constitution does not recognize an absolute and uncontrollable liberty. Liberty in each of its phases has its history and connotation. But the liberty safeguarded is liberty in a social organization which requires the protection of law against the evils which menace the health, safety, morals and welfare of the people. Liberty under the Constitution is thus necessarily subject to the restraints of due process, and regulation which is reasonable in relation to its subject and is adopted in the interests of the community is due process.

300 U.S. at 391, 57 S.Ct. at 581. Justice Hughes went on to suggest that because the health of women was peculiarly related to the vigor of the race, and because women were especially liable to be overreached and exploited by unscrupulous employers, the Washington Act was a "reasonable" exercise of the state's police power. The court buttressed its arguments with economic considerations:

> The exploitation of a class of workers who are in an unequal position with respect to bargaining power and are thus relatively defenceless against the denial of a living wage is not only detrimental to their health and well being but casts a direct burden for their support upon the community. What these workers lose in wages the taxpayers are called upon to pay. The bare cost of living must be met. We may take judicial notice of the unparalleled demands for relief which arose during the recent period of depression and still continue to an alarming extent despite the degree of economic recovery which has been achieved. It is unnecessary to cite official statistics to establish what is of common knowledge through the length and breadth of the land. While in the instant case no factual brief has been presented, there is no reason to doubt that the State of Washington has encountered the same social problem that is present elsewhere. The community is not bound to provide what is in effect a subsidy for unconscionable employers.

Id. at 399, 57 S.Ct. at 585.

Mr. Justice Sutherland wrote a dissenting opinion in *Parrish,* and was joined by Mr. Justice Van Devanter, Mr. Justice McReynolds, and Mr. Justice Butler. These four, by the way, were often referred to as the "Four Horsemen." Why do you suppose that was? See generally Barry Cushman, "The Secret Lives of the Four Horsemen," 83 Va.L.Rev. 559 (1997) (Tongue in cheek assessment of the Four). Justice Sutherland, casting doubt on the propriety of overruling the fourteen-year-old *Adkins* case, stated "It is urged that the question involved should now receive fresh consideration, among other reasons, because of 'the economic conditions which have supervened' but the meaning of the Constitution does not change with the ebb and flow of economic events." Id. at 402, 57 S.Ct. at 587. Was he right? Would Taney have agreed? Would Holmes?

Restating the Court's former thinking on the necessary liberty of contracting under the due process clauses of the Fifth or Fourteenth amendments, Justice Sutherland first observed that the Washington state legislation in question, which had originally been passed in 1913, and was general in its terms:

> does not deal with any business charged with a public interest, or with public work, or with a temporary emergency, or with the character, methods or periods of wage payments, or with hours of labor, or with the protection of persons under legal disability, or with the prevention of fraud. It is, simply and exclusively, a law fixing wages for adult women who are legally as capable of contracting for themselves as men, and cannot be sustained unless upon principles apart from those involved in cases already decided by the court.

Id. at 407, 57 S.Ct. at 589. Stressing that the statute was arbitrary not only in its application to women and not men, but also in its application to *all* employers, Sutherland continued:

> It takes no account of periods of stress and business depression, or crippling losses, which may leave the employer himself without adequate means of livelihood. To the extent that the sum fixed exceeds the fair value of the services rendered, it amounts to a compulsory exaction from the employer for the support of a partially indigent person, for whose condition there rests upon him no peculiar responsibility, and therefore, in effect, arbitrarily shifts to his shoulders a burden which, if it belongs to anybody, belongs to society as a whole.

Id. at 409, 57 S.Ct. at 590. Winding up with a flourish, Sutherland concluded:

> Difference of sex affords no reasonable ground for making a restriction applicable to the wage contracts of all working women from which like contracts of all working men are left free. Certainly a suggestion that the bargaining ability of the average woman is not equal to that of the average man would lack substance. The ability to make a fair bargain, as everyone knows, does not depend upon sex.

Id. at 413, 57 S.Ct. at 591. From the point of view of feminism, which opinion is preferable, that of the majority, or the dissent? How about from the point of view of Constitutional law? Is there a difference? Sutherland and his three fellow horsemen have had a rather bad press for the last fifty years or so, but that may change. For the beginning of the Sutherland rehabilitation see the engaging new biography by the philosopher Hadley Arkes, The Return of George Sutherland: Restoring a Jurisprudence of Natural Rights (1994), and a valuable review essay on Arkes's book, Michael J. Phillips, "Conservative Constitutional Deontology," 34 Am.Bus.L.J. 73 (1996). For a discussion of the *Adkins* case from a feminist perspective see Joan G. Zimmermann, "The Jurisprudence of Equality: The Women's Minimum Wage, the First Equal Rights Amendment, and *Adkins v. Children's Hospital,* 1905–1923," The Journal of American History 188 (June, 1991).

Less than a year before Parrish, on June 1, 1936, when the Supreme Court decided Morehead v. People of State of New York ex rel. Tipaldo, 298

U.S. 587, 56 S.Ct. 918, 80 L.Ed. 1347 (1936), Justice Roberts had voted with the Four Horsemen in a decision which, by a bare majority, found unconstitutional a New York minimum wage law for women, and which had expressly declined to overrule *Adkins.* Robert's "change" of position, to vote with what became the majority in *Parrish,* has been called the "switch in time, which saved nine." Felix Frankfurter, having been given a "memorandum" on the relevant facts by Justice Roberts, argued that since the court actually voted in *Parrish* weeks before the decision was announced, and since Roberts voted with the majority *before* Roosevelt's court-packing plan announcement took place in early February, his "switch" could *not* have been motivated by purely political considerations. This was expressly indicated by Roberts himself, who wrote Frankfurter that "no action taken by the President in the interim had any causal relation to my action in the *Parrish* case." Roberts also indicated that he might well have been prepared to overrule *Adkins* in the *Tipaldo* case, but since the New York state attorneys did not expressly ask for such an overruling, but preferred to have their statute upheld on other grounds, he went along with the majority in *Tipaldo.* Roberts (and Frankfurter) were thus claiming that Roberts indulged in *no switch at all.* Frankfurter, Mr. Justice Roberts, 104 U.Pa.L.Rev. 311, 314–315 (1955). See also Charles A. Leonard, A Search For a Judicial Philosophy: Mr. Justice Roberts and the Constitutional Revolution of 1937 (1971). Speculating about what Roberts (and Frankfurter) were up to has lately become a scholarly cottage industry. For the suggestion that Frankfurter fabricated the Roberts Memorandum, see Michael Ariens, "A Thrice–Told Tale, or Felix the Cat," 107 Harv.L.Rev. 620, 645–49 (1994). For a strong rejection of this suggestion, from the author of the Holmes Devise volume on the Hughes court, Richard D. Friedman, see "A Reaffirmation: The Authenticity of the Roberts Memorandum, or Felix the Non–Forger" 142 U.Pa.L.Rev. 1985 (1994). For further ruminations on The New Deal, Roberts, and the "switch," see Richard Friedman, "Switching Time and Other Thought Experiments: The Hughes Court and Constitutional Transformation," 142 U.Pa.L.Rev. 1891 (1994), Barry Cushman, Rethinking the New Deal Court: the Structure of A Constitutional Revolution (1998), Barry Friedman, "The History of the Countermajoritarian Difficulty Part Four: Law's Politics," 148 U.Pa.L.Rev. 971 (2000), G. Edward White, The Constitution and the New Deal (2000), and Mark Tushnet, "The New Deal Constitutional Revolution: Law, Politics, or What?," 66 U.Chi.L.Rev. 1061 (1999), and Michael E. Parrish, "The Great Depression, the New Deal, and the American Legal Order," 59 Wash.L.Rev. 723 (1984).

Whether or not Justice Roberts "switched" in *Parrish* from his opinion a year earlier in *Tipaldo,* what do you make of the fact that Roberts *and* Justice Hughes were in the majority in the *Schechter* case, decided on May 27, 1935, and in the majority in the *Jones & Laughlin* case, decided on April 12, 1937, which follows? Do they seem like decisions of the same Supreme Court?

NATIONAL LABOR RELATIONS BD. V. JONES & LAUGHLIN STEEL CORP.

Supreme Court of the United States, 1937.
301 U.S. 1, 57 S.Ct. 615, 81 L.Ed. 893.

MR. CHIEF JUSTICE HUGHES delivered the opinion of the Court.

In a proceeding under the National Labor Relations Act of 1935, the National Labor Relations Board found that the respondent, Jones & Laughlin Steel Corporation, had violated the Act by engaging in unfair labor practices affecting commerce. The proceeding was instituted by the Beaver Valley Lodge No. 200 * * *, a labor organization. The unfair labor practices charged were that the corporation was discriminating against members of the union with regard to hire and tenure of employment, and was coercing and intimidating its employees in order to interfere with their self-organization. The discriminatory and coercive action alleged was the discharge of certain employees.

The National Labor Relations Board, sustaining the charge, ordered the corporation to cease and desist from such discrimination and coercion, to offer reinstatement to ten of the employees named, to make good their losses in pay, and to post for thirty days notices that the corporation would not discharge or discriminate against members, or those desiring to become members, of the labor union. As the corporation failed to comply, the Board petitioned the Circuit Court of Appeals to enforce the order. The court denied the petition, holding that the order lay beyond the range of federal power. 83 F.(2d) 998. We granted certiorari.

The scheme of the National Labor Relations Act—which is too long to be quoted in full—may be briefly stated. The first section sets forth findings with respect to the injury to commerce resulting from the denial by employers of the right of employees to organize and from the refusal of employers to accept the procedure of collective bargaining.* There follows a declaration that it is the policy of the United States to eliminate these

* This section is as follows:

"Section 1. The denial by employers of the right of employees to organize and the refusal by employers to accept the procedure of collective bargaining lead to strikes and other forms of industrial strife or unrest, which have the intent or the necessary effect of burdening or obstructing commerce by (a) impairing the efficiency, safety, or operation of the instrumentalities of commerce; (b) occurring in the current of commerce; (c) materially affecting, restraining, or controlling the flow of raw materials or manufactured or processed goods from or into the channels of commerce, or the prices of such materials or goods in commerce; or (d) causing diminution of employment and wages in such volume as substantially to impair or disrupt the market for goods flowing from or into the channels of commerce.

"The inequality of bargaining power between employees who do not possess full freedom of association or actual liberty of contract, and employers who are organized in the corporate or other forms of ownership association substantially burdens and affects the flow of commerce, and tends to aggravate recurrent business depressions, by depressing wage rates and the purchasing power of wage earners in industry and by preventing the stabilization of competitive wage rates and working conditions within and between industries.

* * *

causes of obstruction to the free flow of commerce. The Act * * * creates the National Labor Relations Board and prescribes its organization. * * * It sets forth the right of employees to self-organization and to bargain collectively through representatives of their own choosing. * * * It defines "unfair labor practices." * * * The Board is empowered to prevent the described unfair labor practices affecting commerce and the Act prescribes the procedure to that end. There is a separability clause to the effect that if any provision of the Act or its application to any person or circumstances shall be held invalid, the remainder of the Act or its application to other persons or circumstances shall not be affected. * * *

The procedure in the instant case followed the statute. The labor union filed with the Board its verified charge. The Board thereupon issued its complaint against the respondent alleging that its action in discharging the employees in question constituted unfair labor practices affecting commerce * * *. Respondent admitted the discharges, but alleged that they were made because of inefficiency or violation of rules or for other good reasons and were not ascribable to union membership or activities. As an affirmative defense, respondent challenged the constitutional validity of the statute and its applicability in the instant case. Notice of hearing was given and respondent appeared by counsel. * * * The Board received evidence upon the merits and at its close made its findings and order.

Contesting the ruling of the Board, the respondent argues (1) that the Act is in reality a regulation of labor relations and not of interstate commerce; (2) that the Act can have no application to the respondent's relations with its production employees because they are not subject to regulation by the federal government; and (3) that the provisions of the Act violate § 2 of Article III and the Fifth and Seventh Amendments of the Constitution of the United States.

* * * The Labor Board has found: The corporation is organized under the laws of Pennsylvania and has its principal office at Pittsburgh. It is engaged in the business of manufacturing iron and steel in plants situated in Pittsburgh and nearby Aliquippa, Pennsylvania. It manufactures and distributes a widely diversified line of steel and pig iron, being the fourth largest producer of steel in the United States. With its subsidiaries—nineteen in number—it is a completely integrated enterprise * * *. It owns or controls mines in Michigan and Minnesota. It operates four ore steamships on the Great Lakes * * *. It owns coal mines in Pennsylvania. It operates towboats and steam barges used in carrying coal to its factories. It owns limestone properties in various places in Pennsylvania and West Virginia. It owns the Monongahela connecting railroad which connects the plants of the Pittsburgh works and forms an interconnection with the Pennsylvania, New York Central and Baltimore and Ohio Railroad systems. * * * Much of its product is shipped to its warehouses in

Chicago, Detroit, Cincinnati and Memphis * * *. In Long Island City, New York, and in New Orleans it operates structural steel fabricating shops in connection with the warehousing of semi-finished materials sent from its works. * * * It has sales offices in twenty cities in the United States and a wholly-owned subsidiary which is devoted exclusively to distributing its product in Canada. Approximately 75 per cent of its product is shipped out of Pennsylvania.

* * *

Respondent points to evidence that the Aliquippa plant, in which the discharged men were employed, contains complete facilities for the production of finished and semi-finished iron and steel products from raw materials * * *.

Practically all the factual evidence in the case, except that which dealt with the nature of respondent's business, concerned its relations with the employees in the Aliquippa plant whose discharge was the subject of the complaint. These employees were active leaders in the labor union. * * *

While respondent criticizes the evidence and the attitude of the Board, which is described as being hostile toward employers and particularly toward those who insisted upon their constitutional rights, respondent did not take advantage of its opportunity to present evidence to refute that which was offered to show discrimination and coercion. In this situation, the record presents no ground for setting aside the order of the Board so far as the facts pertaining to the circumstances and purpose of the discharge of the employees are concerned. * * * We turn to the questions of law * * *.

First. The scope of the Act.—The Act is challenged in its entirety as an attempt to regulate all industry, thus invading the reserved powers of the States over their local concerns. It is asserted that the references in the Act to interstate and foreign commerce are colorable at best; that the Act * * * has the fundamental object of placing under the compulsory supervision of the federal government all industrial labor relations within the nation. The argument seeks support in the broad words of the preamble (section one) and in the sweep of the provisions of the Act, and it is further insisted that its legislative history shows an essential universal purpose in the light of which its scope cannot be limited by either construction or by the application of the separability clause.

If this conception of terms, intent and consequent inseparability were sound, the Act would necessarily fall by reason of the limitation upon the federal power which inheres in the constitutional grant, as well as because of the explicit reservation of the Tenth Amendment. Schechter Corp. v. United States, 295 U.S. 495, 549, 550, 554. * * * That distinction between what is national and what is local in the activities of commerce is vital to the maintenance of our federal system. Id.

But we are not at liberty to deny effect to specific provisions, which Congress has constitutional power to enact, by superimposing upon them inferences from general legislative declarations of an ambiguous character, even if found in the same statute. The cardinal principle of statutory construction is to save and not to destroy. We have repeatedly held that as between two possible interpretations of a statute, by one of which it would be unconstitutional and by the other valid, our plain duty is to adopt that which will save the act. * * *

We think it clear that the National Labor Relations Act may be construed so as to operate within the sphere of constitutional authority. The jurisdiction conferred upon the Board, and invoked in this instance, is found in § 10(a), which provides:

"*SEC.* 10(a). The Board is empowered, as hereinafter provided, to prevent any person from engaging in any unfair labor practice (listed in section 8) affecting commerce." * * * The Act specifically defines the "Commerce" to which it refers (§ 2(6)):

> The term "commerce" means trade, traffic, commerce, transportation, or communication among the several States, or between the District of Columbia or any Territory of the United States and any State or other Territory, or between any foreign country and any State, Territory, or the District of Columbia, or within the District of Columbia or any Territory, or between points in the same State but through any other State or any Territory or the District of Columbia or any foreign country.

There can be no question that the commerce thus contemplated by the Act (aside from that within a Territory or the District of Columbia) is interstate and foreign commerce in the constitutional sense. The Act also defines the term "affecting commerce" (§ 2(7)):

> The term "affecting commerce" means in commerce, or burdening or obstructing commerce or the free flow of commerce, or having led or tending to lead to a labor dispute burdening or obstructing commerce or the free flow of commerce.

* * * The grant of authority to the Board does not purport to extend to the relationship between all industrial employees and employers. Its terms do not impose collective bargaining upon all industry regardless of effects upon interstate or foreign commerce. It purports to reach only what may be deemed to burden or obstruct that commerce and, thus qualified, it must be construed as contemplating the exercise of control within constitutional bounds. * * * It is the effect upon commerce, not the source of the injury, which is the criterion. *Second Employers' Liability Cases,* 223 U.S. 1, 51. Whether or not particular action does affect commerce in

such a close and intimate fashion as to be subject to federal control, and hence to lie within the authority conferred upon the Board, is left by the statute to be determined as individual cases arise. * * *

Second. The unfair labor practices in question.—* * *

* * *

* * * [I]n its present application, the statute goes no further than to safeguard the right of employees to self-organization and to select representatives of their own choosing for collective bargaining or other mutual protection without restraint or coercion by their employers.

That is a fundamental right. Employees have as clear a right to organize and select their representatives for lawful purposes as the respondent has to organize its business and select its own officers and agents. Discrimination and coercion to prevent the free exercise of the right of employees to self-organization and representation is a proper subject for condemnation by competent legislative authority. Long ago we stated the reason for labor organizations. We said that they were organized out of the necessities of the situation; that a single employee was helpless in dealing with an employer; that he was dependent ordinarily on his daily wage for the maintenance of himself and family; that if the employer refused to pay him the wages that he thought fair, he was nevertheless unable to leave the employ and resist arbitrary and unfair treatment; that union was essential to give laborers opportunity to deal on an equality with their employers. * * * Fully recognizing the legality of collective action on the part of employees in order to safeguard their proper interests, we said that Congress was not required to ignore this right but could safeguard it. * * * Hence the prohibition by Congress of interference with the selection of representatives for the purpose of negotiation and conference between employers and employees, "instead of being an invasion of the constitutional right of either, was based on the recognition of the rights of both." Texas & N.O.R. Co. v. Railway Clerks, [281 U.S. 548]. We have reasserted the same principle in sustaining the application of the Railway Labor Act as amended in 1934. Virginian Railway Co. v. System Federation, No. 40, [300 U.S. 515].

Third. The application of the Act to employees engaged in production.—The principle involved.—Respondent says that whatever may be said of employees engaged in interstate commerce, the industrial relations and activities in the manufacturing department of respondent's enterprise are not subject to federal regulation. The argument rests upon the proposition that manufacturing in itself is not commerce. * * * Schechter Corp. v. United States, supra, p. 547 * * *.

The Government distinguishes these cases [which hold that manufacturing is not commerce.] The various parts of respondent's enterprise are described as interdependent * * *. It is urged that these activities constitute a "stream" or "flow" of commerce, of which the Aliquippa manufacturing plant is the focal point, and that industrial strife at that point would cripple the entire movement. Reference is made to our decision sustaining the Packers and Stockyards Act. Stafford v. Wallace, 258 U.S. 495. The Court found that the stockyards were but a "throat" through which the current of commerce flowed and the transactions which there occurred could not be separated from that movement. * * * Applying the doctrine of Stafford v. Wallace, supra, the Court sustained the Grain Futures Act of 1922 with respect to transactions on the Chicago Board of Trade, although these transactions were "not in and of themselves interstate commerce." Congress had found that they had become "a constantly recurring burden and obstruction to that commerce." Chicago Board of Trade v. Olsen, 262 U.S. 1, 32 * * *.

Respondent contends that the instant case presents material distinctions. Respondent says that the Aliquippa plant is extensive in size and represents a large investment in buildings, machinery and equipment. The raw materials which are brought to the plant are delayed for long periods and, after being subjected to manufacturing processes, "are changed substantially as to character, utility and value." The finished products which emerge "are to a large extent manufactured without reference to pre-existing orders and contracts and are entirely different from the raw materials which enter at the other end." * * *

We do not find it necessary to determine whether these features of defendant's business dispose of the asserted analogy to the "stream of commerce" cases. The instances in which that metaphor has been used are but particular, and not exclusive, illustrations of the protective power which the Government invokes in support of the present Act. The congressional authority to protect interstate commerce from burdens and obstructions is not limited to transactions which can be deemed to be an essential part of a "flow" of interstate or foreign commerce. Burdens and obstructions may be due to injurious action springing from other sources. The fundamental principle is that the power to regulate commerce is the power to enact "all appropriate legislation" for "its protection and advancement" (*The Daniel Ball,* 10 Wall. 557, 564); to adopt measures "to promote its growth and insure its safety" (Mobile County v. Kimball, 102 U.S. 691, 696, 697); "to foster, protect, control and restrain." * * * That power is plenary and may be exerted to protect interstate commerce "no matter what the source of the dangers which threaten it." *Second Employers' Liability Cases,* p. 51; Schechter Corp. v. United States, supra. * * * Undoubtedly the scope of this power must be considered in the light of our dual system of government and may not be extended so as to embrace effects upon interstate commerce so indirect and remote that to embrace them, in view of our complex society, would effectually obliterate the distinction between what is national and what is local and create a completely centralized government. Id. The question is necessarily one of degree. * * *

That intrastate activities, by reason of close and intimate relation to interstate commerce, may fall within federal control is demonstrated in the case of carriers who are engaged in both interstate and intrastate transportation. There federal control has been found essential to secure the freedom of interstate traffic from interference or unjust discrimination and to promote the efficiency of the interstate service. Shreveport Case, 234 U.S. 342, 351, 352; Wisconsin Railroad Comm'n v. Chicago, B. & Q.R. Co., 257 U.S. 563, 588. It is manifest that intrastate rates deal *primarily* with a local activity. But in rate-making they bear such a close relation to interstate rates that effective control of the one must embrace some control over the other. Id. * * *

The close and intimate effect which brings the subject within the reach of federal power may be due to activities in relation to productive industry although the industry when separately viewed is local. This has been abundantly illustrated in the application of the federal Anti–Trust Act. In the *Standard Oil* and *American Tobacco* cases, 221 U.S. 1, 106, that statute was applied to combinations of employers engaged in productive industry. Counsel for the offending corporations strongly urged that the Sherman Act had no application because the acts complained of were not acts of interstate or foreign commerce, nor direct and immediate in their effect on interstate or foreign commerce, but primarily affected manufacturing and not commerce. 221 U.S. pp. 5, 125. Counsel relied upon the decision in United States v. Knight Co., 156 U.S. 1. The Court stated their contention as follows: "That the act, even if the averments of the bill be true, cannot be constitutionally applied, because to do so would extend the power of Congress to subjects *dehors* the reach of its authority to regulate commerce, by enabling that body to deal with mere questions of production of commodities within the States." And the Court summarily dismissed the contention in these words: "But all the structure upon which this argument proceeds is based upon the decision in United States v. E.C. Knight Co., 156 U.S. 1. The view, however, which the argument takes of that case and the arguments based upon that view have been so repeatedly pressed upon this court in connection with the interpretation and enforcement of the Anti–Trust Act, and have been so necessarily and expressly decided to be unsound as to cause the contentions to be plainly foreclosed and to require no express notice" (citing cases). 221 U.S. pp. 68, 69.

* * *

It is thus apparent that the fact that the employees here concerned were engaged in production is not determinative. The question remains as to the effect upon interstate commerce of the labor practice involved. In the *Schechter* case, supra, we found that the effect there was so remote as to be beyond the federal power. To find "immediacy or directness" there was to find it "almost everywhere," a result inconsistent with the maintenance of our federal system. * * *

Fourth. Effects of the unfair labor practice in respondent's enterprise.—Giving full weight to respondent's contention with respect to a break in the complete continuity of the "stream of commerce" by reason of respondent's manufacturing operations, the fact remains that the stoppage of those operations by industrial strife would have a most serious effect upon interstate commerce. In view of respondent's far-flung activities, it is idle to say that the effect would be indirect or remote. It is obvious that it would be immediate and might be catastrophic. We are asked to shut our eyes to the plainest facts of our national life and to deal with the question of direct and indirect effects in an intellectual vacuum. * * * When industries organize themselves on a national scale, making their relation to interstate commerce the dominant factor in their activities, how can it be maintained that their industrial labor relations constitute a forbidden field into which Congress may not enter when it is necessary to protect interstate commerce from the paralyzing consequences of industrial war? We have often said that interstate commerce itself is a practical conception. It is equally true that interferences with that commerce must be appraised by a judgment that does not ignore actual experience.

Experience has abundantly demonstrated that the recognition of the right of employees to self-organization and to have representatives of their own choosing for the purpose of collective bargaining is often an essential condition of industrial peace. Refusal to confer and negotiate has been one of the most prolific causes of strife. This is such an outstanding fact in the history of labor disturbances that it is a proper subject of judicial notice and requires no citation of instances. * * *

* * * The steel industry is one of the great basic industries of the United States, with ramifying activities affecting interstate commerce at every point. * * * The fact that there appears to have been no major disturbance in that industry in the more recent period did not dispose of the possibilities of future and like dangers to interstate commerce which Congress was entitled to foresee and to exercise its protective power to forestall. It is not necessary again to detail the facts as to respondent's enterprise. Instead of being beyond the pale, we think that it presents in a most striking way the close and intimate relation which a manufacturing industry may have to interstate commerce and we have no doubt that Congress had constitutional authority to safeguard the right of respondent's employees to self-organization and freedom in the choice of representatives for collective bargaining.

Fifth. The means which the Act employs.—Questions under the due process clause and other constitutional restrictions.—Respondent asserts its right to conduct its business in an orderly manner without being subjected to arbitrary restraints. What we have said points to the fallacy in the argument. Employees have their correlative right to organize for the purpose of securing the redress of grievances and to promote agreements with employers relating to rates of pay and conditions of work. * * * Restraint for the purpose of preventing an unjust interference with that right cannot be considered arbitrary or capricious. * * *

The [National Labor Relations] Act does not compel agreements between employers and employees. It does not compel any agreement whatever. It does not prevent the employer "from refusing to make a collective contract and hiring individuals on whatever terms" the employer "may by unilateral action determine." The Act expressly provides in § 9(a) that any individual employee or a group of employees shall have the right at any time to present grievances to their employer. The theory of the Act is that free opportunity for negotiation with accredited representatives of employees is likely to promote industrial peace and may bring about the adjustments and agreements which the Act in itself does not attempt to compel. * * * The Act does not interfere with the normal exercise of the right of the employer to select its employees or to discharge them. The employer may not, under cover of that right, intimidate or coerce its employees with respect to their self-organization and representation, and, on the other hand, the Board is not entitled to make its authority a pretext for interference with the right of discharge when that right is exercised for other reasons than such intimidation and coercion. * * *

The procedural provisions of the Act are assailed. But these provisions, as we construe them, do not offend against the constitutional requirements governing the creation and action of administrative bodies. * * * The Act establishes standards to which the Board must conform. There must be complaint, notice and hearing. The Board must receive evidence and make findings. The findings as to the facts are to be conclusive, but only if supported by evidence. The order of the Board is subject to review by the designated court, and only when sustained by the court may the order be enforced. Upon that review all questions of the jurisdiction of the Board and the regularity of its proceedings, all questions of constitutional right or statutory authority, are open to examination by the court. We construe the procedural provisions as affording adequate opportunity to secure judicial protection against arbitrary action in accordance with the well-settled rules applicable to administrative agencies set up by Congress to aid in the enforcement of valid legislation. * * *

The order of the Board required the reinstatement of the employees who were found to have been discharged because of their "union activity" and for the purpose of "discouraging membership in the union." That requirement was authorized by the Act. § 10(c). * * *

Respondent complains that the Board not only ordered reinstatement but directed the payment of wages for the time lost by the discharge; less amounts earned by the employee during that period. This part of the order was also authorized by the Act. § 10(c). It is argued that the requirement is equivalent to a money judgment and hence contravenes the Seventh Amendment which provides that "In suits at common law, where the value in controversy shall exceed twenty dollars, the right of trial by jury shall be preserved." The Amendment thus preserves the right which existed under the common law when the Amendment was adopted. * * * It does not apply where the proceeding is not in the nature of a suit at common law. Guthrie National Bank v. Guthrie, 173 U.S. 528, 537.

The instant case is not a suit at common law or in the nature of such a suit. The proceeding is one unknown to the common law. It is a statutory proceeding. Reinstatement of the employee and payment for time lost are requirements imposed for violation of the statute and are remedies appropriate to its enforcement. The contention under the Seventh Amendment is without merit.

Our conclusion is that the order of the Board was within its competency and that the Act is valid as here applied.

* * *

NOTES AND QUESTIONS

1. Justice McReynolds wrote the dissent in *Jones & Laughlin,* which also served as a dissenting opinion in several other labor board cases disposed of by the Supreme Court at the same time. He was joined by Justices Van Devanter, Sutherland, and Butler. 301 U.S. at 76, 57 S.Ct. at 630. McReynolds thus summed up the dissent:

> The Court, as we think, departs from well-established principles followed in Schechter Corp. v. United States, 295 U.S. 495 (May, 1935) and Carter v. Carter Coal Co., 298 U.S. 238 (May, 1936). Upon the authority of those decisions, the Circuit Court of Appeals of the Fifth, Sixth and Second Circuits in the causes now before us have held the power of Congress under the commerce clause does not extend to relations between employers and their employees engaged in manufacture, and therefore the Act conferred upon the National Labor Relations Board no authority in respect of matters covered by the questioned orders. * * *

301 U.S. at 76, 57 S.Ct. at 630.

McReynolds ridiculed the majority's conception of the involvement of interstate commerce, even in the case of *Jones & Laughlin,* which involved the dismissals of ten men.

> In No. 419 [*Jones*] ten men out of ten thousand were discharged; in the other cases only a few. The immediate effect in the factory may be to create discontent among all those employed and a strike may follow,

> which, in turn may result in reducing production, which ultimately may reduce the volume of goods moving in interstate commerce. By this chain of indirect and progressively remote events we finally reach the evil with which it is said the legislation under consideration undertakes to deal. A more remote and indirect interference with interstate commerce or a more definite invasion of the powers reserved to the states is difficult, if not impossible, to imagine.

Id. at 97, 57 S.Ct. at 639. In reply to contentions about the steel company's goods being in the "stream of commerce," McReynolds wrote:

> There is no ground on which reasonably to hold that refusal by a manufacturer, whose raw materials come from states other than that of his factory, and whose products are regularly carried to other states, to bargain collectively with employees in his manufacturing plant, directly affects interstate commerce. In such business, there is not one but two distinct movements or streams in interstate transportation. The first brings in raw material and there ends. Then follows manufacture, a separate and local activity. Upon completion of this, and not before, the second distinct movement or stream in interstate commerce begins and the products go to other states.

Id. at 98, 57 S.Ct. at 639. Does this analysis, that there are two separate streams of commerce, neither of which flows through manufacturing, convince you? See generally Barry Cushman, "A Stream of Legal Consciousness: The Current of Commerce Doctrine from *Swift* to *Jones & Laughlin,*" 61 Fordham Law Rev. 105 (1992). How about McReynolds's assertion that the majority went overboard because "Almost anything—marriage, birth, death—may in some fashion affect commerce?" Id. at 99, 57 S.Ct. at 640.

The reach of congressional power to regulate under the commerce clause became a radioactive topic in constitutional scholarship, following upon the United States Supreme Court's decision in United States v. Lopez, 514 U.S. 549 (1995), which, for the first time since the New Deal, held that Congress had exceeded its authorization under the commerce clause (by passing the "Gun–Free School Zones Act," which sought to punish those bearing unauthorized firearms near any school in the nation). This was the beginning of a movement some have perceived as a "Constitutional Revolution" comparable to that wrought by the New Deal itself. For an introduction to the voluminous literature on this problem, and a thoughtful consideration of what it means for the activities of the lower federal courts, see Brannon P. Denning and Glenn H. Reynolds, "Rulings and Resistance: The New Commerce Clause Jurisprudence Encounters the Lower Courts," 55 Ark. L. Rev. 1253 (2003), and their earlier article, "Lower Court Readings of *Lopez*, or What if the Supreme Court Held A Constitutional Revolution and Nobody Came?", 2000 Wisc.L.Rev. 369. See also, for other ruminations on the meaning of the commerce clause and on the Rehnquist Court's spate of overturning of federal statutes, Randy E. Barnett, "The Original Meaning of the Commerce Clause," 68 U.Chi.L.Rev. 101 (2001); Barry Cushman, "Continuity and Change in

Commerce Clause Jurisprudence," 55 Ark. L.Rev. 1009 (2003), and "Small Differences?", 55 Ark. L. Rev. 1097 (2003) (debating Richard D. Friedman on what the Supreme Court was doing in the New Deal commerce clause cases), Neal Devins, "Congress as Culprit: How Lawmakers Spurred on the Court's Anti–Congress Crusade," 51 Duke L. J. 435 (2001) (indicating that the fault lies at least partially with Congress); Richard E. Epstein, "The Proper Scope of the Commerce Power," 73 Va. L. Rev. 1387 (1987) (concluding that the New Deal Court's eventual embrace of broad commerce clause power went too far); Richard D. Friedman, "Charting the Course of the Commerce Clause Challenge," 55 Ark.L.Rev. 1055 (2003) (debating Barry Cushman over the nature of New Deal commerce clause jurisprudence), Joshua A. Klein, "Commerce Clause Questions After *Morrison:* Some Observations on the New Formalism and the New Realism," 55 Stan.L.Rev. 571 (2002) (arguing that the Supreme Court should show more restraint in overturning Congressional legislation), Douglas W. Kmiec, "Rediscovering a Principled Commerce Power," 28 Pepp. L. Rev. 547 (2001) (praising the Court for its actions in keeping Congress within bounds, but criticizing the Court for not permitting agencies enough discretion); Larry D. Kramer, "The Supreme Court, 2000 Term–Foreword: We The Court," 115 Harv.L.Rev. 4, 137–53 (2001) (harshly criticizing the Rehnquist Court's federalism decisions on the grounds that they created new doctrine); Grant S. Nelson & Robert J. Pushaw, Jr., "Rethinking the Commerce Clause: Applying First Principles to Uphold Federal Commercial Regulations but Preserve State Control over Social Issues," 85 Iowa L. Rev. 1 (1999); C. Austin Reams, "The Political Economy of the Commerce Clause: Economic and Political Effects on the Supreme Court's Interpretation of the Commerce Clause," 27 Okla.U.L.Rev. 347 (2002) (arguing that the Court conforms to a "rational choice" model), Ilya Somin, "Closing the Pandora's Box of Federalism: The Case for Judicial Restriction of Federal Subsidies to State Governments," 90 Geo.L.J. 461 (2002) (arguing that the Rehnquist Court's efforts to implement federalism will not be successful unless more is done to prevent Congress from controlling what the states do by restricting access to federal subsidies to state governments), Christopher H. Schroeder, "Causes of the Recent Turn in Constitutional Interpretation," 51 Duke L.J. 307 (2001) (arguing that the Rehnquist Court distrusts the federal government), and William Van Alstyne, "Foreword: The Constitution in Exile: Is It Time to Bring It in from the Cold?," 51 Duke L.J. 1 (2001)(arguing that it is appropriate for judges to consider the whole Constitution, so that reconstructing a "Constitution in Exile" might be a worthwhile endeavor). Devins, Schroeder's and Van Alstyne's pieces are part of a symposium in Volume 51, Number 1 of the Duke Law Journal, "The Constitution in Exile," which contains several other worthy articles on the jurisprudence of the Rehnquist Court.

2. Justice McReynolds, as well as questioning the majority's views on interstate commerce, appears to have had some due process problems with the NLRB Act's authorizing legislation, insofar as it rejected the dismissal of men or women for their union activities:

> The right to contract is fundamental and includes the privilege of selecting those with whom one is willing to assume contractual relations. This

> right is unduly abridged by the Act now upheld. A private owner is deprived of power to manage his own property by freely selecting those to whom his manufacturing operations are to be entrusted. We think this cannot lawfully be done in circumstances like those here disclosed.

Id. at 103, 57 S.Ct. at 641.

It appears, does it not, that the majority had no such due process problems. Why not? Do you find anything in the majority's rationale on this point—labor's need for collective bargaining, self-organization, and representation—that resembles theories of labor law articulated by the judges we studied in Chapter Five? Still, is it appropriate to raise these theories to the level of federal policy? Does the federalization of labor law, and the setting up of the NLRB help all workers or just some of them? For the assertion that "Federal labor law and policy of the 1930s cartelized the labor market on behalf of racist labor unions, while black workers remained unprotected by civil rights legislation," see David E. Bernstein, "Roots of the Underclass: The Decline of Laissez Faire Jurisprudence and the Rise of Racist Labor Legislation," 43 Am.U.L.Rev. 85 (1993). For the argument that the Wagner Act did actually represent a radical restructuring of American labor law that was later undercut, see Karl Klare, "Judicial Deradicalization of the Wagner Act and the Origins of Modern Legal Consciousness," 62 Minn.L.Rev. 265 (1978). It has often been asserted that the line of Supreme Court cases beginning in 1937, which seemed to signal a new willingness to uphold Congressional acts addressing national economic concerns, signaled a "constitutional revolution." Would you agree with this term, as it might be applied to the *Jones* case? Do you understand how this seriously undermines the ideal of "legal science?" See generally, Kurt T. Lash, "The Constitutional Convention of 1937: The Original Meaning of the New Jurisprudential Deal," 70 Fordham L. Rev. 459 (2001), and James Gray Pope, "The Thirteenth Amendment vs. the Commerce Clause: Labor and the Shaping of American Constitutional Law, 1921–1957," 102 Col.L.Rev. 1 (2002). For the "social history" of the Aliquippa Plant, that may actually have been influential in leading the Court to hold as it did, see Kenneth Casebeer, "Aliquippa: The Company Town and Contested Power in the Construction of Law," 43 Buff.L.Rev. 617 (1995).

3. Perhaps another aspect of a "constitutional revolution" which might be inherent in *Jones* has to do with administrative law, and with the remedies available to government agencies such as the labor board. The majority alludes to the argument that there is a problem with the Seventh Amendment insofar as the labor board is able to impose money judgments on employers, without a jury trial. Note the court simply brushes this aside, with the notion that since labor board actions are a statutory creation, there is no "common law" right to trial by jury that has been infringed. Given what you learned about the early American controversies over trial by jury in the Prologue and Chapters One, Two, and Five of the casebook, is this brusque dismissal of the argument appropriate? Is it correct to read the Seventh Amendment's prohibition regarding trials by jury at "common law" as leaving a wide area open for the shifting of assets without such a barrier of laymen

between administrative agencies and the public? Do you find the majority exhibiting the same willingness to enter into the purposes and "spirit" of Constitutional provisions regarding trial by jury as it seems to be displaying with regard to the interpretation of the constitutional term "interstate commerce"?

4. Roughly two months after the *Jones* decision was announced, on June 14, 1937, the Senate's Judiciary Committee reported on the President's proposed bill to increase the number of Supreme Court Justices:

> We recommend the rejection of this bill as a needless, futile, and utterly dangerous abandonment of constitutional principle. * * *
>
> It would subjugate the courts to the will of Congress and the President and thereby destroy the independence of the judiciary, the only certain shield of individual rights. * * * It stands now before the country, acknowledged by its proponents as a plan to force judicial interpretation of the Constitution, a proposal that violates every sacred tradition of American democracy.
>
> * * * It is a measure which should be so emphatically rejected that its parallel will never again be presented to the free representatives of the free people of America.

Senate Report No. 711, 75th Cong., 1st Sess. (1937), quoted in Gunther, supra, at 170. As you might have guessed, the Judiciary Committee's views prevailed, and the "court-packing" bill was never passed. Still, given the decisions in *Jones, Parrish,* and a line of cases which followed, and given FDR's appointments of seven new Justices from 1937 through 1941 (Black, Reed, Frankfurter, Douglas, Murphy, Byrnes, and Jackson), even if FDR lost this "battle," who "won the war?" See Michael Comiskey, "Can a President Pack—or Draft—The Supreme Court? FDR and the Court in the Great Depression and World War II," 57 Alb.L.Rev. 1043 (1994).

5. After the rejection of the NIRA by the Supreme Court in *Schechter* in 1935, there appears to have been a shift in legislative philosophy on the part of Roosevelt's advisors, and perhaps on the part of the President himself. As we indicated in the introduction to this Chapter, the measures which resulted from the shift have been frequently described as a "Second New Deal," in which the emphasis, instead of being on collective planning and cooperation between business and government, as was the case with the NIRA and the other measures of the "First New Deal," was on reform and strengthening of the bargaining power of workers and farmers. The NLRB Act involved in *Jones,* of course, was one such measure. Arthur M. Schlesinger, Jr., in The Politics of Upheaval (1960) thus describes the differences:

> The early New Deal had accepted the concentration of economic power as the central and irreversible trend of the American economy, and had proposed the concentration of political power as the answer. The effort of 1933 had been to reshape American institutions according to the philos-

> ophy of an organic economy and a coordinated society. The new effort was to restore a competitive society within a framework of strict social ground rules and on the foundation of basic economic standards—accompanied, as time went on, by a readiness to use the fiscal pulmotor to keep the economy lively and expansive. * * *

Id., at 385. Copyright © 1960 by Arthur M. Schlesinger, Jr., reprinted by permission of the publisher, Houghton Mifflin Co.

The shift from the first to the second New Deal was probably prompted by much more than the Supreme Court's activities. Not only could intelligent Americans perceive what economic distress could do to foreign countries like Weimar Germany and Mussolini's Italy, but some thought that the anti-semitic demagoguery of the American "Radio Priest," Father Coughlin, or the machinations of the popular Louisiana dictator, Huey Long, were indications that Fascism could well come to America. See, e.g. William E. Leuchtenburg, Franklin D. Roosevelt and the New Deal, pp. 275–288 (1963), and sources there cited. Perhaps reflecting on similar considerations, Arthur M. Schlesinger, Jr., wrote that, "As children of light, the First New Dealers had believed in the capacity for justice which, in Niebuhr's phrase, makes democracy possible. As children of darkness, the Second New Dealers believed in the inclination to injustice which makes democracy necessary." Schlesinger, supra, at 397–8. See also John W. Jeffries, "The 'New' New Deal: FDR and American Liberalism, 1937–1945," 105 Pol.Sci.Q. 397 (1990).

What effect would you have expected the legal and social events we have just considered to have had on American jurisprudence, and particularly the notion that American law exhibited the noble tenets of the "legal science" envisioned by Field and Langdell? In the next few readings, with our examination of "legal realism," we study the emergence of jurisprudential notions which seem to bear a far stronger resemblance to the ideas of Holmes than to those of Field or Langdell.

C. LEGAL REALISM

JEROME FRANK, LAW AND THE MODERN MIND*

3–11, 14–19, 253–260 (1930).

The lay attitude towards lawyers is a compound of contradictions, a mingling of respect and derision. Although lawyers occupy leading positions in government and industry, although the public looks to them for guidance in meeting its most vital problems, yet concurrently it sneers at them as tricksters and quibblers.

---

* Reprinted from Jerome Frank, *Law and the Modern Mind,* originally published by Brentano's, Inc. in 1930. These excerpts are taken from the Anchor Books edition, published in 1963 by arrangement with Barbara Frank Kristein, and are here reprinted with the kind permission of Marvin Kristein, Esq., acting for the Estate of Barbara Frank Kristein.

* * *

What is the source of these doubts of the lawyer's honesty and sincerity?

A false tradition "invented by twelfth-century priests and monks," replies Dean Roscoe Pound. "For the most part clerical jealousy of the rising profession of non-clerical lawyers was the determining element. * * * Naturally, the clergy did not relinquish the practice of law without a protest." What those priests began, says Pound, Luther developed, and since Luther's day the other learned professions have taken over. "Unless one perceives that a struggle of professions for leadership is involved," one cannot understand the distrust of the legal profession. The lawyer is today, as he was in the twelfth century, in a marked position of advantage. This irks the other learned men. * * *

An ingenious explanation, but patently superficial. * * * Modern dispraise of the Bar is not to be explained as merely an outcropping of angry rivalry; obviously it is not confined to members of competing professions. That lawyers are scheming hair-splitters is a popular commonplace.

What lies back of this popular criticism? It appears to be founded on a belief that the lawyers complicate the law, and complicate it wantonly and unnecessarily, that, if the legal profession did not interpose its craftiness and guile, the law could be clear, exact and certain. * * * Public opinion agrees with Napoleon who was sure that "it would be possible to reduce laws to simple geometrical demonstrations, so that whoever could read and tie two ideas together would be capable of pronouncing on them."

* * *

Now it must be conceded that, if the law can be made certain and invariable, the lawyers are grievously at fault. For the layman is justified in his opinion that the coefficient of legal uncertainty is unquestionably large, that to predict the decisions of the courts on many a point is impossible. * * *

Yet the layman errs in his belief that this lack of precision and finality is to be ascribed to the lawyers. The truth of the matter is that the popular notion of the possibilities of legal exactness is based upon a misconception. The law always has been, is now, and will ever continue to be, largely vague and variable. And how could this well be otherwise? The law deals with human relations in their most complicated aspects. * * *

Even in a relatively static society, men have never been able to construct a comprehensive, eternized set of rules anticipating all possible legal disputes and settling them in advance. * * * How much less is such a frozen legal system possible in modern times. * * * When human relationships are transforming daily, legal relationships cannot be expressed in enduring form. * * * Our society would be strait-jacketed were not the courts, with the able assistance of the lawyers, constantly overhauling the law and adapting it to the realities of ever-changing social, industrial and political conditions; although changes cannot be made lightly, yet law must be more or less impermanent, experimental and therefore not nicely calculable. *Much of the uncertainty of law is not an unfortunate accident: it is of immense social value.*

In fields other than the law there is today a willingness to accept probabilities and to forego the hope of finding the absolutely certain. Even in physics and chemistry, where a high degree of quantitative exactness is possible, modern leaders of thought are recognizing that finality and ultimate precision are not to be attained. The physicists, indeed, have just announced the Principle of Uncertainty or Indeterminacy. If there can be nothing like complete definiteness in the natural sciences, it is surely absurd to expect to realize even approximate certainty and predictability in law, dealing as it does with the vagaries of complicated human adjustments.

Since legal tentativeness is inevitable and often socially desirable, it should not be considered an avoidable evil. But the public learns little or nothing of this desirability of legal tentativeness from the learned gentlemen of the law. Why this concealment? * * * If lawyers are not responsible for legal indefiniteness, are they not guilty, at any rate, of duping the public as to the essential character of law? Are they not a profession of clever hypocrites?

There is no denying that the bar appears to employ elaborate pretenses to foster the misguided notions of the populace. Lawyers do not merely sustain the vulgar notion that law is capable of being made entirely stable and unvarying; they seem bent on creating the impression that, on the whole, it is already established and certain. When a client indignantly exclaims, "A pretty state of affairs when I can't learn exactly what my rights are!" how does the lawyer usually respond? With assurances that the situation is exceptional, that generally speaking the law is clear enough, but that in this particular instance, for some reason or other the applicable rules cannot be definitely ascertained. * * *

Of course, such assurances are unwarranted. Each week the courts decide hundreds of cases which purport to turn not on disputed "questions of fact" but solely on "points of law." If the law is unambiguous and predictable, what excuses can be made by the lawyers who lose these cases? They should know in advance of the decisions that the rules of law are adverse to their contentions. Why, then, are these suits brought or defended? * * * [I]n many cases, honest and intelligent counsel on both sides of such controversies can conscientiously advise their respective clients to engage in the contest; they can do so because, prior to the decision, the law is sufficiently in doubt to justify such advice.

It would seem, then, that the legal practitioners must be aware of the unsettled condition of the law. Yet observe the arguments of counsel in addressing the courts, or the very opinions of the courts themselves: they are worded as if correct decisions were arrived at by logical deduction from a precise and pre-existing body of legal rules. Seldom do judges disclose any contingent elements in their reasoning, any doubts or lack of whole-hearted conviction * * *.

Why these pretenses, why this professional hypocrisy? The answer is an arresting one: There is no hypocrisy. The lawyers' pretenses are not consciously deceptive. The lawyers, themselves, like the laymen, fail to recognize fully the essentially plastic and mutable character of law. * * *

* * *

* * * Why do the generality of lawyers insist that law should and can be clearly knowable and precisely predictable although, by doing so, they justify a popular belief in an absurd standard of legal exactness? Why do lawyers, indeed, themselves recognize such an absurd standard, which makes their admirable and socially valuable achievement—keeping the law supple and flexible—seem bungling and harmful? * * *

* * *

We are on the trail of a stubborn illusion. Where better, then, to look for clues than in the direction of childhood? For in children's problems, and in children's modes of meeting their problems, are to be found the sources of most of the confirmed illusions of later years.

* * * [O]nly today are psychologists noting that the behavior patterns of early childhood are the basis of many subsequent adaptions. At long last, they are using a genetic approach; the emotional handicaps of adult life, they now tell us, "represent almost invariably, if not always, the unsolved problems or the partially solved or badly solved problems of childhood."

* * *

The child at birth is literally forced from a small world of almost complete and effortless security into a new environment which at once sets up a series of demands. Strange sensations of light, sound, touch and smell attack him. The nearly perfect pre-birth harmony and serenity are over. The infant now must breathe and eat. His struggle for existence has begun. But his wants, at first, are few and are satisfied with a minimum of strain on his own part. The parents do their best to meet, almost instantly, the infant's desires. In this sense, he approximates omnipotence, because, relative to his askings, he achieves nearly complete obedience. * * *

As infancy recedes his direct omnipotence diminishes. But that there is omnipotence somewhere the child does not doubt. * * * There is, he believes, no happening without a knowable reason. * * * There must always be whys and wherefores. Chaos is beyond belief. Order and rule govern all.

As early childhood passes and consciousness grows keener, now and again the child becomes sharply aware of his incapacity for controlling the crushing, heedless, reluctant and uncertain facts of the outer world. * * * Fears beset him—fear of the vague things that stalk the darkness, fear of the unruly, the unseen, the horrible bogies of the unknown.

Then he rushes to his parents for help. They stand between him and the multitudinous cruelties and vagaries of life. They are all-powerful, all-knowing. * * *

The child still possesses omnipotence—but now, vicariously. Through his dependence upon his parents' omnipotence he finds relief from unbearable uncertainty. His overestimation of the parental powers is an essential of his development.

It must not be overlooked that a significant division of parental functions takes place early in the life of the child. In all communities where the father is head of the family, the mother comes to "represent the nearer and more familiar influence, domestic tenderness, the help, the rest and the solace to which the child can always turn," writes Malinowski in a recent anthropological study. But "the father has to adopt the position of the final arbiter in force and authority. He has gradually to cast off the roll of tender and protective friend, and to adopt the position of strict judge, and hard executor of law." * * * The child, in his struggle for existence, makes vital use of his belief in an omniscient and omnipotent father, a father who lays down infallible and precise rules of conduct.

Then, slowly, repeated experiences erode this fictional overestimate. * * * There are many things father doesn't know, things he can't do. Other humans successfully oppose him. And there are forces loose in the world beyond his control. One's own father is at times helpless, deficient; he is all-too-human. * * *

But the average child cannot completely accept this disillusionment. He has formed an irresistible need for an omniscient and omnipotent father who shall stand between him and life's uncertainties. * * * His attitudes and adaptations had been built upon his relations to his idealized, his incomparable father. The child is disoriented. Again panic fear attacks him. He is unwilling and largely unable to accept as realities the ungovernable, the unorderable aspects of life. Surely, he feels, somewhere there must be Someone who can control events, make the dark spots light, make the uncertain clear. * * *

Many are the persons who become substitutes for the deposed father: the priest or pastor, the rulers and leaders of the group. They, too, turn out to be disappointing. But the demand for fatherly authority does not die. To be sure, as the child grows into manhood, this demand grows less and less vocal, more and more unconscious. The father-substitutes become less definite in form, more vague and impersonal. * * * Concealed and submerged, there persists a longing to reproduce the father-child pattern, to escape uncertainty and confusion through the rediscovery of a father.

* * *

That religion shows the effects of the childish desire to recapture a father-controlled world has been often observed. But the effect on the law of this childish desire has escaped attention. And yet it is obvious enough: To the child the father is the Infallible Judge, the Maker of definite rules of conduct. * * * The Law—a body of rules apparently devised for infallibly determining what is right and what is wrong and for deciding who should be punished for misdeeds—inevitably becomes a partial substitute for the Father–as–Infallible–Judge.

* * *

[Much later in his analysis, Frank asks whether any American lawyers have surmounted the "childish" tendency to regard the law as certain and infallible. His answer follows.]

One wise leader pointing the way we have had with us many years. The judicial opinions and other writings of Mr. Justice Holmes—practitioner, teacher, historian, philosopher, judge—are a treasury of adult counsels, of balanced judgments as to the relation of the law to other social relations. There you will find a vast knowledge of legal history divorced from slavish veneration for the past, a keen sensitiveness to the needs of today with no irrational revolt against the conceptions of yesterday, a profound respect for the utility of syllogistic reasoning linked with an insistence upon recurrent revisions of premises based on patient studies of new facts and new desires. He has himself abandoned, once and for all, the phantasy of a perfect, consistent, legal uniformity, and has never tried to perpetuate the pretense that there is or can be one. * * *

Almost fifty years ago Holmes made the famous statement (the implications of which have not yet been thoroughly appreciated) that "The life of the law has not been logic; it has been experience." [He added] that the law "cannot be dealt with as if it contained only the axioms and corollaries of a book of mathematics."

* * *

As one of our foremost legal historians, he does not underestimate the value of the history of law. * * * Yet he calls attention to history's "almost deceptive charm" and bids us beware of "the pitfall of antiquarianism." His chief interest in the past is for the light it throws upon the present. * * *

He has often weighed and considered the value of rules of law which are survivals of ancient traditions, when the ancient meaning has been forgotten. In such cases the judges strive to give modern reasons for the old rules. Such reasons, Holmes finds, are, for the most part, artificial and unsatisfactory. * * *

But he concedes that sometimes the old rules have an actual present use. * * *

Ever and again he has reverted to his early position that "in substance the growth of the law is legislative," that "the secret root from which the law draws all the juices of life" are considerations of what is expedient for the community concerned, more or less definitely understood views of public policy. These are considerations "which judges most rarely mention and always with an apology." * * * The process of judicial law making "has been largely unconscious." It is important to insist on a "more conscious recognition of the legislative function of courts." * * *

What has made lawyers overstress logic he has sensed accurately: "The logical method and form flatter that longing for certainty and for repose which is in every human mind. But certainty generally is illusion, and repose is not the destiny of man." * * *

He has been sound, too, about the function of doubt: "To have doubted one's own first principles is the mark of a civilized man." Accordingly he can afford to doubt even his own dogmas: "While one's experience thus makes certain preferences dogmatic for one's self, recognition of how they came to be so leaves one able to see that others, poor souls, may be equally dogmatic about something else." And, accordingly, he has developed that remarkable tolerance which is the mark of high maturity. Skeptical about the inevitable validity of existing rules merely because they exist, he is yet no fiery reformer eager to abandon all tradition merely because of its lack of novelty.

* * * [T]hirty years ago he said:

> I do not expect or think it desirable that the judges should undertake to renovate the law. That is not their province. Indeed precisely because I believe that the world would be just as well off if it lived under laws that differed from ours in many ways, and because I believe that the claim of our especial code to respect is simply that it exists, that it is the one to which we have become accustomed, and not that

> it represents an eternal principle, I am slow to consent to over-ruling a precedent * * *. But I think it is most important to remember whenever a doubtful case arises, with certain analogies on one side and other analogies on the other, that what really is before us is a conflict between two social desires, each of which cannot both have their way. The social question is which desire is stronger at the point of conflict. The judicial one may be narrower, because one or the other desire may have been expressed in previous decisions to such an extent that logic requires us to assume it to preponderate in the one before us. But if that be clearly so, the case is not a doubtful one. Where there is doubt the simple tool of logic does not suffice, and even if it is disguised and unconscious, the judges are called on to exercise the sovereign prerogative of choice.

In his constitutional opinions he has been in favor of allowing a wide latitude of freedom in experimentation and has accordingly sustained statutes involving "social experiments" even though, as he has said, they "may seem futile or even noxious to me and those whose judgment I most respect." Now over eighty years of age, just the other day he said from the bench that our Constitution

> "is an experiment, as all life is an experiment. Every year, if not every day, we have to wager our salvation upon some prophecy based upon imperfect knowledge. While that experiment is part of our system, I think that we should be eternally vigilant against attempts to check the expressions of opinions that we loathe and believe to be fraught with death unless they so imminently threaten immediate interference with the lawful and pressing purposes of the law that an immediate check is required to save the country."

And most significant for our purposes is his recognition that one's dogmas, the things in which one believes and for which one will fight and die, one's essential attitudes towards the universe, are "determined largely by early associations and temperament, coupled with the desire to have an absolute guide."

The great value of Holmes as a leader is that his leadership implicates no effort to enslave his followers. It would be grossly misusing his example to accept his judicial opinions or views on any question of law as infallible. It may well be assumed that he would be the readiest to urge a critical reconsideration of any doctrines he has announced. He has attained an adult emotional status, a self-reliant, fearless approach to life * * *. We might say that, being rid of the need of a strict father, he can afford not to use his authority as if he, himself, were a strict father.

His legal skepticism is clear, sane, vital, progressive—not an easy achievement, as one can see in the example [of] * * * Pound * * *. One is reminded of Vaihinger's comments on the pessimistic character of Greek skepticism: When the Greek skeptics realized the deep chasm between thought and reality, there resulted a marked depression. They despaired of thought. * * * This was inevitable, says Vaihinger, because "mere subjective thinking" had not "yet achieved these tremendous scientific feats which are distinctive of modern times."

And so in law today, most men still recoil from the admission of the "subjectivity" of law. * * * Holmes, almost alone among lawyers, adopts that skeptical attitude upon which modern science has builded, that modern skepticism which looks upon thought as instrumental and acknowledges the transient and relative nature of all human thought-contrivances. Holmes has been telling us for fifty years that, in effect, the Golden Rule is that there is no Golden Rule. But the old fascinations lure men away from the essential meaning of his teaching.

For Holmes's thoroughly "scientific" view of law requires courage, more courage than is required in the natural sciences. In those sciences, as Vaihinger points out, skepticism has proved its worth. Not so, as yet, in the law. And it is courageous indeed to face the fact, once and for all, that men have made the law and must take the responsibility for its good or bad workings.

If, like Holmes, we win free of the myth of fixed authoritarian law, having neither to accept law because it comes from an authority resembling the father's, nor to reject it for like reason, we shall, for the first time, begin to face legal problems squarely. Without abating our insistence that the lawyers do the best they can, we can then manfully endure inevitable short-comings, errors and inconsistencies in the administration of justice because we can realize that perfection is not possible. The legal profession will then for the first time be in a position to do its work well.

If that view of the law brings to the lawyer a large sense of the burdens of his responsibility, it may also bring its pleasures—the pleasures of self-confidence, self-authority, of the conscious use of one's abilities in one of the most important areas of human activity.

* * *

NOTES AND QUESTIONS

1. As you may have discerned, Frank's *Law and the Modern Mind* had as one of its principal purposes a questioning of the jurisprudential assumptions of Roscoe Pound, then the Dean of the Harvard Law School and, at that time, probably the most renowned legal scholar in America. What is hinted at in the excerpt is made explicit in other parts of the work. See, e.g., pp. 151–152, 221–231, and 312–326. In particular Frank criticizes Pound for what Frank finds to be Pound's unwillingness to concede the inevitability of and the necessity for discretion on the part of judges. While Frank concedes that Pound excoriates "mechanical jurisprudence" in matters of "human conduct," or those involving "the conduct of enterprise, or fraud, good faith, negligence,

or fiduciary duties" he attacks Pound's apparent insistence that certainty is possible in matters of "property and commercial transactions." Pound's insistence on keeping up this distinction, says Frank, means that Pound has not yet reached the completely adult status of Holmes. At one point, Frank even asks, regarding one of Pound's theories, "are we not * * * listening to something like a small boy with a grown-up vocabulary talking of an ideal father?" Id., at 306. How might you expect Pound to respond to this sort of criticism? The next reading seems to be his reaction.

2. Frank leans heavily on the work of psychologists to aid in understanding legal developments. Do you think that laymen and lawyers' failure to see the inevitability of uncertainty in the law flows from a failure to "work through" childhood fixations on an omnipotent father? Frank seems to assume a differentiation in familial roles between mother (as nourishing and comforting) and father (as stern and all-knowing). Suppose, as seems to be happening in modern America, the traditional role-stereotypes are breaking down, and "parenting" is seen as a joint venture, with neither parent as stern authoritarian. What would someone like Frank argue that this change in familial roles might mean for the law? Do you see any evidence of legal change that might flow from such developments? Ask yourself that question again after reading the materials in the last two Chapters.

3. Consider Frank's use of Holmes. Would you say that his characterization of Holmes is accurate? Is Holmes's "anthropology" the same thing as Frank's Freudian psychology? From what you have seen of Holmes, would he accept Frank's notion of the inevitable and necessary uncertainty of the law? Is this a notion that you find acceptable? Could one expect a republic to be governed by laws that are inherently uncertain? Is it too much to expect a populace, or even most lawyers, to accept a legal world in which there is no one, no thing, or no idea permanently at the helm?

4. When all is said and done, is it still true that Frank is still like Field and Langdell in that he thinks "like a lawyer?" Is Frank's preoccupation with uncertainty the most important issue in law making by judges? Does this "uncertainty" preoccupation conceal other issues only hinted at by Frank, but made more explicit in the work of nineteenth century "legal realists" like Honestus, Rantoul, or Eugene V. Debs? For further reading on Jerome Frank consult the fine biography by Robert James Glennon, The Iconoclast as Reformer: Jerome Frank's Impact on American Law (1985). For Frank's contribution to modern clinical legal education see Morris D. Bernstein, "Learning From Experience: Montaigne, Jerome Frank and the Clinical Habit of Mind," 25 Cap.U.L.Rev. 517 (1996).

ROSCOE POUND, THE CALL FOR A REALIST JURISPRUDENCE*

Pound, Roscoe, The Call for a Realist Jurisprudence, 44 Harv.L.Rev. 697 (1931).

A critic of nineteenth-century historical jurisprudence used to deplore that Savigny had not studied under Savigny in his youth. He had been trained in the eighteenth-century natural law and was unable to get away from certain presuppositions and modes of thought which his training had made part of his juristic make-up. Those of us who were brought up in the analytical and historical jurisprudence of the last century may well bear this in mind as we read and seek to appraise the work of the oncoming generation of American law teachers. * * *

Hence I approach the subject of the call for a realist jurisprudence, insistent on the part of our younger teachers of law, with some humility. But here is an important movement in the science of law, and it behooves us to understand it and be thinking about it.

I

First, then, what is meant by realism in this connection? As I read them, the new juristic realists hardly use realism in a technical philosophical sense. They use it rather in the sense which it bears in art. By realism they mean fidelity to nature, accurate recording of things as they are, as contrasted with things as they are imagined to be, or wished to be, or as one feels they ought to be. They mean by realism faithful adherence to the actualities of the legal order as the basis of a science of law. But a science of law must be something more than a descriptive inventory. There must be selection and ordering of the materials so as to make them intelligible and useful. * * * What does realism propose to do with them which we had not been doing in the past? * * *

* * * [T]here is nothing new in the assumption of those who are striking out new paths of juristic thought that those who have gone before them have been dealing with illusions, while they alone and for the first time are dealing with realities. The rationalists put forward the same claim. They claimed to stand upon a solid and unchallengeable ground of reason in contrast to an illusion of authority and the broken down academic fiction of continuity of the empire on which the medieval conception of the binding force of the *corpus juris* had been built. When Kant's critical philosophy undermined this supposed solid foundation, the historical jurists came forward with a claim of substituting for the illusion of reason the reality of experience. Historical study of experience of adjusting human relations was to show us the course of unfolding of the idea, which alone had significance, as contrasted with the eighteenth-century illusion of a natural law discoverable by sheer reason. Next the analytical jurists

made a like claim. They made no pretense of considering what had been or what would be or what ought to be. It was their boast that they treated of what was. They proceeded on the basis of "the pure fact of law." * * * And then came the positivists. They too stood and stood alone on a solid ground of reality. To them reality was in laws of social and legal development discoverable by observation of social and legal institutions among all peoples. Our new realist rejects all these conceptions of juristic reality. Reason is an illusion. Experience is not the unfolding of an idea. No "pure fact of Law" is to be found in rules since the existence of rules of law, as anything outside of the books, is an illusion. * * *

If recent philosophy teaches aright, there is no absolute reality. What test of reality may a modern relativist assert in jurisprudence other than significance? But there is no absolute significance. Significance is significance for or in relation to something. Is not a valuing in terms of significance for the ends of the legal order (as the social utilitarians see it) or a valuing and defining of ends with reference to significance for civilization (as the Neo–Hegelians see it) as real as a looking at single phenomena as significant in their uniqueness or at the alogical element in judicial or legislative or juristic behavior as more significant than the logical? As in the disputes of diverse schools of jurists in the past, the difference today is one of emphasis. Received ideals, conceptions, the quest for certainty and uniformity, an authoritative technique of using authoritative legal materials, settled legal doctrines and modes of thought, and a traditional mode of legal reasoning are actual and everyday phenomena of the legal order. The question at bottom is whether a faithful representation of realities shall paint them in the foreground or instead shall put in the foreground the subjective features in the behavior of particular judges, the elements in judicial action which stand in the way of certainty and uniformity, the deficiencies of the received technique, the undefined edges and overlappings of doctrines and the deficiencies of legal reasoning. Emphasis on the fallings short of these instruments is useful * * *. The new realists have been doing good work at this point. But such critical activity, important as it is, is not the whole of jurisprudence, nor can we build a science of law which shall faithfully describe the actualities of the legal order and organize our knowledge of these actualities, merely on the basis of such criticism. * * *

There is nothing upon which the new realist is so insistent as on giving over all preconceptions and beginning with an objectively scientific gathering of facts. * * * But facts occur in a multifarious mass of single instances. To be made intelligible and useful, significant facts have to be selected, and what is significant will be determined by some picture or ideal of the science and of the subject of which it treats. * * * The new realists have their own preconceptions of what is significant, and hence of what juristically must be. Most of them merely substitute a psychological must for an ethical or political or historical must.

II

* * * [F]ive items are to be found so generally in the writings of the new school, that one may be justified in pronouncing them, or most of them, the ideas of current juristic realism:

(a) One of the most common is faith in masses of figures as having significance in and of themselves. * * * Very little experience of using current official statistics is required to convince that statistics gathered for no purpose beyond filling a report with impressive tabulations are seldom valuable for anything else. I would not for a moment belittle the importance of bringing together information as to exactly how legal precepts and doctrines and institutions are functioning. But statistics on these subjects are not the only objectively ascertainable data available to the jurist. In the reported decisions of the past we have a record of experience in the administration of justice, of how precepts or doctrines or institutions have worked or have failed to work, and of how and why they came to be formulated or shaped as we find them, which is as solid a basis for objectively scientific study as any mass of figures can be. * * * Chiefly we shall have to understand the doctrinal and institutional and legislative materials which have come down to us, both in their workings and in their possibilities, using such statistics as we find or may gather as helps toward that understanding.

(b) No less common is belief in the exclusive significance or reality of some one method or line of approach. One of these, much insisted on, is exact terminology. * * * But I venture to think that the utility of precise terminology and exact meanings is more in connection with differentiating problems from pseudo problems and with formulation of results than in providing solutions. None of the fundamental problems of jurisprudence is solved by terminology, while there have been signs that rigid terminology has been used to create an appearance of solution of questions which have been left untouched at the core.

* * *

Still another [group] * * * seeks a science of law analogous to mathematical physics, and would refuse the name of science to a body of knowledge, or the epithet scientific to a method which does not conform to that type. It is conceived that observation of the phenomena of administration of justice, carried on objectively and scientifically, may give us formulas as rigidly exact and free from any personal or subjective element, either in formulation or application, as for example, those employed by the engineer. It is argued that the only objectively valid phenomena are those discoverable by statistical investigation of the operations of judicial institutions * * *.

* * * [W]e must consider how judges do decide, how they ought to decide to give effect to the ends of the legal order, and how to insure as far as may be the decisions that ought to be. Undoubtedly the gathering of statistics can show us much as to how justice is administered, and how and how far legal precepts are observed and enforced. But they are expected also to show how justice must (in a psychological sense) be administered, and so to dispense with the question how it ought to be administered. This question of ought, turning ultimately on a theory of values, is the hardest one in jurisprudence. Those who long for an exact science analogous to mathematics or physics or astronomy have been inclined to seek exactness by excluding this hard problem from jurisprudence altogether. But such a jurisprudence has only an illusion of reality. For the significant question is the one excluded.

* * *

Another mode of approach to jurisprudence, often asserted to be the one path to reality, is psychological. Psychological exposure of the role of reason in human behavior, of the extent to which so-called reasons come after action as explanations instead of before action as determining factors, has made a profound impression upon the rising generation of jurists. It has led many of them to insist on the nonrational element in judicial action as reality and the rational as illusion. In contrast to the nineteenth-century emphasis on certainty and uniformity and ignoring of the continual fallings short of those ideals, they emphasize the uncertainties, the lack of uniformity, and the influence of personal and subjective factors in particular cases. This leads us to a related characteristic of the new juristic realism.

(c) Along with the assertion that the sole valid approach is by way of psychology goes usually a presupposition that some one psychological starting point is the *unum necessarium,* and that a science of law which makes use of any other type or theory of psychology is unscientific and illusory. * * *

* * *

* * * On the contrary, I submit that jurisprudence can't wait for psychologists to agree (if they are likely to), and that there is no need of waiting. We can reach a sufficient psychological basis for juristic purposes from any of the important current psychologies. Here again real means significant. The things which are significant for jurisprudence are in all of them. We have problems enough of our own in the science of law without wasting our ammunition in broadsides at each other over our wrong choices of psychological parties.

Nor is the psychological neo-realism of the moment wholly emancipated from the *a priori* dogmatism with which it reproaches older types of juristic thought. Much of it consists in setting forth what it seems the course of judicial action or juristic thinking must be, in the light of some current psychological dogma, rather than investigation of recorded judicial experience and juristic development thereof in order to see what they reveal.

* * * [T]here is a distinct advance in [the new realists'] frank recognition of the alogical or non-rational element in judicial action which the legal science of the nineteenth century sought to ignore. But many of these realists seek to ignore the logical and rational element and the traditional technique of application, or art of the common-law lawyer's craft, which tends to stability and uniformity of judicial action in spite of the disturbing factors. * * * It is just as unreal to refuse to see the extent to which legal technique, with all its faults, applied to authoritative legal materials, with all their defects, keeps down the alogical or unrational element or holds it to tolerable limits in practice. In the field of the economic life (in the stricter sense) there is incomparably more significance on the one side than on the other. It is exactly this significance which makes legal and economic development go hand in hand.

(d) Another characteristic is insistence on the unique single case rather than on the approximation to a uniform course of judicial behavior * * *. The unique aspects of cases, the common aspects of them, and generalizations from the common aspects, may or may not be useful instruments according to the connection in which we look at them and the tasks to which we apply them. None of the three is an absolute and universal solvent.

Radical neo-realism seems to deny that there are rules or principles or conceptions or doctrines at all, because all judicial action, or at times much judicial action, can not be referred to them; because there is no definite determination whereby we may be absolutely assured that judicial action will proceed on the basis of one rather than another of two competing principles; because there is a no-man's land about most conceptions so that concrete cases have been known to fall down between them; because much takes place in the course of adjudication which does not fit precisely into the doctrinal plan. * * * But nothing would be more unreal—in the sense of at variance with what is significant for a highly specialized form of social control through politically organized society—than to conceive of the administration of justice, or the legal adjustment of relations, or, for that matter, the working out of devices for the more efficient functioning of business in a legally ordered society, as a mere aggregate of single determinations.

(e) Finally, many of the new juristic realists conceive of law as a body of devices for the purposes of business instead of as a body of means toward general social ends. They put the whole emphasis on the exigencies of one phase of the economic order. To them the significant feature of law is as a body of devices for enabling business and industry to achieve certain purposes. * * * Like the schools which have gone before them, the new realists take one aspect of the apparatus of the legal order and conceive it to be of paramount significance.

Looking at law as an aggregate of devices whereby business projects may be effected in a politically organized industrial society, there are two ways in which these devices are availed of. First, they are employed toward a better and more economical achievement of what the legal precepts in the books permit or do not forbid. Second, they are employed, or sought to be employed, to evade legal prohibitions and to enable things to be done which politically organized society has authoritatively pronounced anti-social. Thus, for example, statutes as to coöperative marketing may be used to permit mergers in contravention of the laws or policy of the laws as to restraint of trade. * * * Certainly, here is a feature of the legal order which deserves the attention of jurists from many standpoints, and the new realists do a service in bringing it out. But if their way of looking at law is modern in its recognition of actualities ignored in the last century, it is thoroughly tied to the past in its limitations. * * * As in the past, one item is made to stand out at the expense of a picture of the whole. As in the past, reality is taken to be exclusively at one point or in one item. Law is more than a body of devices for business purposes, just as it is more than a body of rules for the guidance of courts. * * *

III

It is much more important to understand than to criticize. Too much criticism in jurisprudence has started from an assumption that critic and criticized were looking at the same things, or seeking to answer the same questions, and achieved an easy victory over straw men set up on that assumption. * * * It takes time for a new school to develop. One may point out work to be done in the progress of a school without implying that those engaged in the task are ignorant thereof, or that they do not intend to direct their energies thereto in due time.

With this caveat, let me essay a program of relativist-realist jurisprudence as I conceive it might be * * *:

1. A functional attitude, i.e., study not only of what legal precepts and doctrines and institutions are, and how they have come to be, but of how they work. [* * * I] urge particularly study of concrete instances of rules or doctrines or institutions in action, in such number and by such methods as to be able to reach valid general conclusions.

2. Recognition of the existence of an alogical, unrational, subjective element in judicial action, and attempt by study of concrete instances of its operation to reach valid general conclusions as to the kinds of cases in which it operates most frequently, and where it operates most effectively or most unhappily for the ends of the legal order.

3. Recognition of the significance of the individual case, as contrasted with the absolute universalism of the last century, without losing sight of the significance of generalizations and conceptions as instruments toward the ends of the legal order. * * *

4. Giving up of the idea of a necessary sequence from a single cause in a straight line to a single effect, and hence of the one sovereign legal remedy for every difficulty and one necessary solution of every problem. There will be recognition of a plurality of elements in all situations and of the possibility of dealing with human relations in more than one way. There will be recognition that the test of a legal precept or doctrine or institution is how and how far it helps to achieve the ends of the legal order. * * * Hence in the end I am confident there will be no abandonment of belief that the administration of justice may be improved by intelligent effort. I suspect also that study of single instances wisely directed and in sufficient number will show what study of the legal materials of all systems seems to reveal, namely, that the old straight line thinking is a useful instrument in parts of the administration of justice where the economic order demands the maximum of attainable certainty.

5. A theory of interests and of the ends of the legal order based on or consistent with modern psychology, without being tied absolutely to any particular dogmatic brand of psychology of the moment.

6. A theory of values, for the valuing of interests, consistent with modern psychology and philosophy, without being tied fast to any particular body of psychological or philosophical dogma of the moment.

7. A recognition that there are many approaches to juristic truth and that each is significant with respect to particular problems of the legal order; hence a valuing of these approaches, not absolutely or with reference to some one assumed necessary psychological or philosophical basis of jurisprudence, but with reference to how far they aid law maker, or judge, or jurist in making law and the science of law effective, the one toward the maintaining, furthering, and transmitting of civilization, the other toward organizing the materials and laying out the course of the legal order.

Perhaps it is asking too much of any school of jurists to call upon them for so broad an outlook. But in the house of jurisprudence there are many mansions. There is more than enough room for all of us and more than enough work. If the time and energy expended on polemics were devoted to that work, jurisprudence would be more nearly abreast of its tasks.

NOTES AND QUESTIONS

1. Would you say that Pound is able successfully to deflect any of the punches launched by Frank? This is, of course, one brief excerpt from a large

corpus of Pound's legal thought, but do you find Pound offering here any creditable alternatives to the views of the legal realists (at least as we have them from the excerpt from Frank or from Pound's descriptions of their thinking)? At one point Pound seems almost to suggest that the thought of the realists shows a danger of "abandonment of belief that the administration of justice may be improved by intelligent effort." Is this a fair criticism of Frank? Why did Frank write his book? For an excellent effort to explore the thought of the legal realists, particularly in connection with legal education, see Laura Kalman, Legal Realism at Yale, 1927–1960 (1986). For a relatively-accessible one-volume summary of Pound's thought, which contains a somewhat more well-developed critique of the realists, see Roscoe Pound, The Ideal Element in Law (reissue, 2002). For further reading on legal realism and the history of American jurisprudence in which it played so prominent a part, see, in addition to Kalman, supra, e.g., Gary J. Aichele, Legal Realism and Twentieth Century American Jurisprudence (1990), Neil Duxbury, Patterns of American Jurisprudence (1995), James Herget, American Jurisprudence 1870–1970 (1990), Wilfred E. Rumble, American Legal Realism (1968), John Henry Schlegal, American Legal Realism and Empirical Social Science (1995), and Robert Summers, Instrumentalism and American Legal Theory (1982).

2. You will have noted that Pound still maintains the necessity for considering discrete parts of the "legal order," and perhaps of prescribing different reforms for different sectors. In particular he insists that there are parts of the "economic order" which demand the "maximum of attainable certainty." Has he really been affected by Frank's criticism? Perhaps it should be noted, as Pound himself acknowledged, that this essay was "written in haste at a time when he was burdened with administrative duties, not least his work as a member of the National Commission on Law Observance and Enforcement." William Twining, Karl Llewellyn and The Realist Movement 72 (1973). If this is true, what does it suggest about Pound's evaluation of the legal realists? Pound's critique of the Realists led to the following article in their defense. See whether you agree with Llewellyn's characterization of Pound, and whether Pound's criticisms are successfully rebutted.

KARL N. LLEWELLYN, SOME REALISM ABOUT REALISM—RESPONDING TO DEAN POUND*

Llewellyn, Karl N., Some Realism About Realism—Responding to Dean Pound, 44 Harv.L.Rev. 1222 (1931).**

Ferment is abroad in the law. The sphere of interest widens; men become interested again in the life that swirls around things legal. * * *

The ferment is proper to the time. The law of schools threatened at the close of the century to turn into words—placid, clear-seeming, lifeless, like some old canal. Practice rolled on, muddy, turbulent, vigorous. It is now spilling, flooding, into the canal of stagnant words. It brings ferment and trouble. So other fields of thought have spilled their waters in: the stress on behavior in the social sciences; their drive toward integration; the physicists' reexamination of final-seeming premises; the challenge of war and revolution. These stir. They stir the law. * * * And always there is this restless questing: what difference does statute, or rule, or court-decision, make?

* * *

And those involved are folk of modest ideals. * * * They want to check ideas, and rules, and formulas by facts, to keep them close to facts. They view rules, they view law, as means to ends * * *. They suspect, with law moving slowly and the life around them moving fast, that some law may have gotten out of joint with life. This is a question in first instance of fact: what does law *do,* to people, or for people? In the second instance, it is a question of ends: what *ought* law to do to people, or for them? But there is no reaching a judgment as to whether any specific part of present law does what it ought, until you can first answer what it is doing now. * * *

All this is, we say, a simple-hearted point of view, and often philosophically naive—though it has in it elements enough of intellectual sophistication. It denies very little, except the completeness of the teachings handed down. It knows too little to care about denying much. It affirms ignorance, pitched within and without. It affirms the need to know. Its call is for intelligent effort to dispel the ignorance. Intelligent effort to cut beneath old rules, old words, to get sight of current things. It is not a new

* Jerome Frank refused me permission to sign his name as joint author to this paper, on the ground that it was my fist which pushed the pen. But his generosity does not alter the fact that the paper could not have been written without his help. I therefore write the first sections, in partial recognition, as "We," meaning thereby Frank and myself. In the description of the realists, I turn to the first person singular, partly because any alignment of such diverse work is individually colored; partly because any phrasing which would seem to suggest a non-existent school would be unfortunate.

point of view; it is as old as man. But its rediscovery in any age, by any man, in any discipline, is joyous.

* * *

Dean Pound has discussed the call and the ferment. * * * We rejoiced that a scholar of Dean Pound's standing and perspective found much * * * to appreciate. We agreed with him that it was important for the older thinking and the newer to make contact.

But the Dean's description did not stop with the points mentioned. It continued. On bones we knew was built a flesh we knew not of. An ugly flesh. The new realists, or "most of them," had, as the Dean read them, been guilty of a goodly number of things that careful thinkers would in the main not be proud to be caught doing. These intellectual offenses Dean Pound criticized. He criticized them tellingly. The question is one of fact: whether the offenses have been committed. For if they have, the Dean's rebukes are needed. Spare the rod and spoil the realist.

The question is one of fact. By fact it must be tried. And tried it must be. When Dean Pound speaks on jurisprudence, men listen. The profession has too long relied on him to discover, read, digest, classify and report on jurists foreign and ancient not to rely again when he speaks of would-be jurists modern and at home. * * *

I

The trial of Dean Pound's indictment is not easy. It is a blanket indictment. It is blanket as to time and place and person of each offense. It specifies no one offender by his name.

We have the general indications above-mentioned: "new realists" and the like. We have the more specific indications also mentioned. Taken together, they narrow the class that may come in question.[17] We can, therefore, check the items against a reasonable sampling of the men whom the rest of the description fits.[18] We have chosen twenty men and ninety-odd titles; representative men and pertinent titles. These we have canvassed

[17] We had hoped to be more precise. We wrote Dean Pound to ask whom he had had in mind when he wrote his article. * * * He did mention three names specifically. Bingham and Lorenzen he had had in mind. C.E. Clark he definitely had not.

[18] *The sampling of men.* * * *

(1) Bingham and Lorenzen are included as of course. (2) We add those whom we believe recognized as figures of central stimulus in the new ferment: C.E. Clark, Cook, Corbin, Moore, T.R. Powell, Oliphant. (3) We add further men peculiarly vocal in advocating new or rebellious points of view: Frank, Green, Radin. (4) We stir in all others whom we have heard criticized as extremists on one or another point mentioned by the Dean: Hutcheson, Klaus, Sturges. (5) We fill out with as many more as time permits: Douglas, Francis, Patterson, Tulin, Yntema—chosen partly because their writing has explicitly touched points of theory, partly because their writing was either familiar to us or not too bulky. (6) We throw in Llewellyn, as both vociferous and extreme, but peculiarly because he and he alone has issued a "Call for a Realist Jurisprudence" under that peculiar label. A Realistic Jurisprudence—The Next Step (1930) 30 Col.L.Rev. 431. This gives us twenty names. There are doubtless twenty more. But half is a fair sample. * * *

in order to ascertain the extent to which the evidence supports the Dean's allegations. * * *

THE RESULTS OF THE TEST

* * *

> [As a result of his survey of the writing of the twenty "realists," Llewellyn declares, *inter alia,* that (1) the work of three men (Bingham, Francis, and Yntema) might support Pound's charge that the realists describe judicial behavior on the basis of some "current psychological dogma, *without investigation of what recorded judicial experience reveals;*" (2) that "conceivably" one realist, Jerome Frank, has done work that supports the charge that "*the rational element in law is an illusion;*" (3) that the work of one man (Frank) supports the charge that realists "conceive of the administration of justice rather as a mere aggregate of single determinations than as an approximation to a uniform course of behavior;" and (4) that "perhaps" one realist (Sturges) supports the charge that the realists have "an exclusive interest in the business aspects of the law." Llewellyn suggests that there is no direct support for any of Pound's other criticisms of the realist movement. The exhaustive details supporting these conclusions are given in an appendix to the original article, which is here omitted.]

Let it be conceded that we have missed men or evidence which would support these points of description on which so much of the Dean's criticism of realists is based. * * * We submit, nonetheless, that *any* description of what "realists" think, or what "most of them believe" or what "many of them write" * * * will in the light of our canvass need evidence by man and chapter and verse before it can be relied on as meaning more than: the writer has an impression that there is someone, perhaps two someones, whose writings bear this out. * * *

II

REAL REALISTS

What, then, *are* the characteristics of these new fermenters? One thing is clear. There is no school of realists. There is no likelihood that there will be such a school. There is no group with an official or accepted, or even with an emerging creed. * * *

There is, however, a *movement* in thought and work about law. * * * Individual men, then. Men more or less interstimulated—but no more than all of them have been stimulated by the orthodox tradition, or by that ferment at the opening of the century in which Dean Pound took a leading part. * * * They differ among themselves well-nigh as much as any of them differs from say, Langdell. * * *

* * *

* * * I shall endeavor to keep in mind as I go that the justification for grouping these men together lies not in that they are *alike* in belief or work, but in that from certain common points of departure they have branched into lines of work which seem to be building themselves into a whole, a whole planned by none, foreseen by none, and (it may well be) not yet adequately grasped by any.

The common points of departure are several.

(1) The conception of law in flux, of moving law, and of judicial creation of law.

(2) The conception of law as a means to social ends and not as an end in itself; so that any part needs constantly to be examined for its purpose, and for its effect, and to be judged in the light of both and of their relation to each other.

(3) The conception of society in flux, and in flux typically faster than the law, so that the probability is always given that any portion of law needs reexamination to determine how far it fits the society it purports to serve.

(4) The *temporary* divorce of Is and Ought for purposes of study. * * * More particularly, this involves during the study of what courts are doing the effort to disregard the question what they ought to do. Such divorce of Is and Ought is, of course, not conceived as permanent. To men who begin with a suspicion that change is needed, a permanent divorce would be impossible.

(5) Distrust of traditional legal rules and concepts insofar as they purport to *describe* what either courts or people are actually doing. Hence the constant emphasis on rules as "generalized predictions of what courts will do." * * *

(6) Hand in hand with this distrust of traditional rules (on the descriptive side) goes a distrust of the theory that traditional prescriptive rule-formulations are *the* heavily operative factor in producing court decisions. This involves the tentative adoption of the theory of rationalization for the study of opinions. * * *

(7) The belief in the worthwhileness of grouping cases and legal situations into narrower categories than has been the practice in the past. This is connected with the distrust of verbally simple rules—which so often cover dissimilar and non-simple fact situations. * * *

(8) An insistence on evaluation of any part of law in terms of its effects, and an insistence on the worthwhileness of trying to find these effects.

(9) Insistence on *sustained and programmatic attack* on the problems of law along any of these lines. None of the ideas set forth in this list is new. Each can be matched from somewhere; each can be matched from recent orthodox work in law. New twists and combinations do appear here and there. What is as novel as it is vital is for a goodly number of men to pick up ideas which have been expressed and dropped, used for an hour and dropped, played with from time to time and dropped—to pick up such ideas and set about *consistently, persistently, insistently to carry them through.* * * * This urge, in law, is quite new enough over the last decades to excuse a touch of frenzy among the locust-eaters.[37]

* * *

Bound, as all "innovators" are, by prior thinking, these innovating "realists" brought their batteries to bear in first instance on the work of appellate courts. * * *

(a) An early and fruitful line of attack borrowed from psychology the concept of *rationalization* already mentioned. To recanvass the opinions, viewing them no longer as mirroring the process of deciding cases, but rather as trained lawyers' arguments made by the judges (after the decision has been reached), intended to make the decision seem plausible, legally decent, legally right, to make it seem, indeed, legally inevitable—this was to open up new vision. * * *

But the line of inquiry via rationalization has come close to demonstrating that in any case doubtful enough to make litigation respectable the available authoritative premises—i.e., premises legitimate and impeccable under the traditional legal techniques—are at least two, and that the two are mutually contradictory as applied to the case in hand.[39] Which opens the question of what made the court select the one available premise rather than the other. * * *

(b) A second line of attack has been to discriminate among rules with reference to their relative significance. Too much is written and thought about "law" and "rules," lump-wise. Which part of law? Which rule? Iron rules of policy, and rules "in the absence of agreement"; rules which keep a case from the jury, and rules as to the etiquette of instructions necessary to make a verdict stick * * *.

(c) A further line of attack on the apparent conflict and uncertainty among the decisions in appellate courts has been to seek more understandable statement of them by grouping the facts in new—and typically

[37] Since everyone who reads the manuscript in this sad age finds this allusion blind, but I still like it, I insert the passage: " * * * Preaching in the wilderness of Judea, And saying, Repent ye. * * * And the same John had his raiment of camel's hair, and a leathern girdle about his loins; *and his meat was locusts* and wild honey." Matthew III, 1, 2, 4.

[39] For a series of examples, see * * * Powell, Current Conflicts Between the Commerce Clause and State Police Power, 1922–1927 (1928) 12 Minn.L.Rev. 470, 491, 607, 631.

but not always narrower—categories. The search is for correlations of fact-situation and outcome which (aided by common sense) may reveal when courts seize on one rather than another of the available competing premises. One may even stumble on the trail of *why* they do. Perhaps, e.g., third party beneficiary difficulties simply fail to get applied to promises to make provision for dependents; perhaps the pre-existing duty rule goes by the board when the agreement is one for a marriage-settlement. Perhaps, indeed, contracts in what we may broadly call family relations do not work out in general as they do in business. * * *

All of these three earliest lines of attack converge to a single conclusion: There is less possibility of accurate prediction of what courts will do than the traditional rules would lead us to suppose * * *. The particular kind of certainty that men have thus far thought to find in law is in good measure an illusion. Realistic workers have sometimes insisted on this truth so hard that they have been thought pleased with it. * * *

But announcements of fact are not appraisals of worth. The contrary holds. The immediate result of the preliminary work thus far described has been a further, varied series of endeavors; the focusing of conscious attack on discovering the factors thus far unpredictable, in good part with a view to their control. Not wholly with a view to such elimination; part of the conscious attack is directed to finding where and when and how far uncertainty has value. * * *

(i) There is the question of the personality of the judge. * * * Some have attempted study of the particular judge[48]—a line that will certainly lead to inquiry into his social conditioning. Some have attempted to bring various psychological hypotheses to bear.[50] All that has become clear is that our government is not a government of laws, but one of laws through men.

(ii) There has been some attempt to work out the varieties of interaction between the traditional concepts * * * and the fact-pressures of the cases. * * * Closely related in substance, but wholly diverse in both method and aim, is study of the machinery by which fact-pressures can under our procedure be brought to bear upon the court.[52]

(iii) First efforts have been made to capitalize the wealth of our reported cases to make large-scale quantitative studies of facts and out-

---

[48] E.g., * * * Commerce, Congress, and the Supreme Court, 1922–1925 (1926) 26 Col.L.Rev. 396, 521; The Judiciality of Minimum Wage Legislation (1924) 37 Harv.L.Rev. 545; * * * Brown, Police Power—Legislation for Health and Personal Safety (1929) 42 Harv.L.Rev. 866; Cushman, The Social and Economic Interpretation of the Fourteenth Amendment (1922) 20 Mich.L.Rev. 737. * * *

[50] Freudian: beginnings in Frank, Law and the Modern Mind (1930). Behaviorist: an attempt in Patterson, Equitable Relief for Unilateral Mistake (1928) 28 Col.L.Rev. 859. * * *

[52] The famous Brandeis brief and its successors mark the beginning. In commercial cases both Germany and England have evolved effective machinery.

come; the hope has been that these might develop lines of prediction more sure, or at least capable of adding further certainty * * *.

(iv) Repeated effort has been made to work with the cases of single states, to see how far additional predictability might thus be gained.

(v) Study has been attempted of "substantive rules" in the particular light of the available remedial procedure; the hope being to discover in the court's unmentioned knowledge of the immediate consequences of this rule or that, in the case at hand, a motivation for decision which cuts deeper than any shown by the opinion. * * *

(vi) The set-up of men's ways and practices and ideas on the subject matter of the controversy has been studied, in the hope that this might yield a further or even final basis for prediction. The work here ranges from more or less indefinite reference to custom (the historical school), or mores (Corbin), through rough or more careful canvasses of business practice and ideology (e.g., Berle, Sturges, Isaacs, Handler, Bogert, Durfee and Duffy, Breckenridge, Turner, Douglas, Shanks, Oliphant, and indeed Holmes) to painstaking and detailed studies in which practice is much more considered than is any prevailing set of ideas about what the practices are (Klaus) * * *. While grouped here together, under one formula, these workers show differences in degree and manner of interest * * *. Corbin's main interest is the appellate case; most of the second group mentioned rely on semi-special information and readily available material from economics, sociology, etc., with occasional careful studies of their own, and carry a strong interest into drafting or counselling work; Klaus insists on full canvass of all relevant literature, buttressed by and viewed in the light of intensive personal investigation * * *.

(vii) Another line of attack, hardly begun, is that on the effect of the lawyer on the outcome of cases, as an element in prediction. * * *

All of the above has focussed on how to tell what appellate courts will do, however far afield any new scent may have led the individual hunter. But the interest in effects on laymen of what the courts will do leads rapidly from this still respectably traditional sphere of legal discussion into a series of further inquiries whose legal decorum is more dubious. They soon extend far beyond what has in recent years been conceived (in regard to the developed state) as law at all. * * *

I. *There is first the question of what lower courts and especially trial courts are doing, and what relation their doing has to the sayings and doings of upper courts and legislatures.*

* * * All that is really clear to date is that until we know more here our "rules" give us no remote suggestion of what law means to persons in the lower income brackets, and give us misleading suggestions as to the whole body of cases unappealed. * * *

II. *There is the question of administrative bodies*—not merely on the side of administrative law (itself a novel concept recently enough)—but including all the action which state officials take "under the law" so far as it proves to affect people. * * * [T]he trail thus broken leads into the wilds of government, and politics, and queer events in both.

III. *There is the question of legislative regulation*—in terms of what it *means in action, and to whom,* not merely in terms of what it says. And with that, the question of what goes into producing legislative change—or blocking it * * *; legislative history on the official record; but as well the background of fact and interest and need. * * *

IV. Finally, and cutting now completely beyond the tradition-bounded area of law, there is the matter not of describing or predicting the action of officials * * * but of describing and predicting *the effects of their action on the laymen of the community.* * * * Not only what courts do instead of what courts say, but also what difference it makes to anybody that they do it. * * * There is the range of questions as to those legal "helpful devices" (corporation, contract, lease) designed to make it easier for men to get where they want and what they want. There is all the information social scientists have gathered to be explored, in its bearings on the law. * * *

Here are the matters one or another of the new fermenters is ploughing into. * * *

* * *

Is it not obvious that—if this be realism—realism is a mass of trends in legal work and thinking? * * *

* * * One will find * * * little said by realistic spokesmen that does not warrant careful pondering. Indeed, on *careful* pondering, one will find little of exaggeration in their writing. Meantime, the proof of the pudding: are there results?

* * *

Already we have a series, lengthening impressively, of the *more accurate* reformulations of what appellate courts are doing and may be expected to do. We are making headway in seeing (not just "knowing" without inquiry) what effects their doing has on some of the persons interested. We are accumulating some *knowledge* (i.e., more than guesses) on phases of our life as to which our law seems out of joint.

We have, moreover, a first attack upon the realm of the unpredictable in the actions of courts. That attack suggests strongly that one large element in the now incalculable consists in the traditional pretense or belief * * * that there is no such area of uncertainty, or that it is much smaller than it is. To *recognize* that there are limits of the certainty sought by verbalism and deduction, to seek to define those limits, is to open the door to that other and far more useful judicial procedure: *conscious* seeking, *within the limits laid down by precedent and statute,* for the wise decision. Decisions thus reached, *within those limits,* may fairly be hoped to be more certainly predictable than decisions are now * * *. And not only more certain, but what is no whit less important: more just and wise * * *.

Indeed, the most fascinating result of the realistic effort appears as one returns from trial court or the ways of laymen to the tradition-hallowed problem of appellate case-law. Criticized by those who refuse to disentangle Is and Ought because of their supposed deliberate neglect of the normative aspect of law, the realists prove the value, for the normative, of temporarily putting the normative aside. They return from their excursion into the purest description they can manage with a demonstration that the field of free play for Ought in appellate courts is vastly wider than traditional Ought-bound thinking ever had made clear. * * * Let me summarize the points of the brief:

(a) If deduction does not solve cases, but only shows the effect of a given premise; and if there is available a competing but equally authoritative premise that leads to a different conclusion—then there is a choice in the case; a choice to be justified; a choice which *can* be justified only as a question of policy—for the authoritative tradition speaks with a forked tongue.

(b) If (i) the possible inductions from one case or a series of cases—even if these cases really had each a single fixed meaning—are nonetheless not single, but many; and if (ii) the standard authoritative techniques of dealing with precedent range from limiting the case to its narrowest issue on facts and procedure * * * all the way to giving it the wildest meaning the rule expressed will allow, or even thrusting under it a principle which was not announced in the opinion at all—then the available leeway in *interpretation of precedent* is * * * nothing less than huge. * * * And—the essence of all—*stare decisis* has in the past been, now is, and must continue to be, a norm of change, and a means of change, as well as a norm of staying put, and a means of staying put. * * * Let this be recognized, and that peculiar one of the ways of working with precedent which consists in blinding the eyes to policy loses the fictitious sanctity with which it is now enveloped *some of the time:* to wit, whenever judges for any reason do not wish to look at policy.

(c) If the classification of raw facts is largely an arbitrary process, raw facts having in most doubtful cases the possibility of ready classification along a number of lines, "certainty," even under pure deductive thinking, has not the meaning that people who have wanted certainty in law are looking for. The quest of this unreal certainty, this certainty unattained in result, is the major reason for the self-denying ordinance of judges: their refusal to look beyond words to things. Let them once see that the "certainty" thus achieved is *un*certainty for the non-law-tutored layman in his living and dealing, and the way is open to reach for *layman's* certainty-through-law, by seeking for the fair or wise outcome, so far as precedent and statute make such outcome *possible.* * * *

When the matter of *program in the normative aspect* is raised, the answer is: *there is none.* * * * Yet some general points of view may be hazarded.

(1) There is fairly general agreement on the importance of personnel, and of court organization, as essential to making laws have meaning. * * * There is some tendency, too, to urge specialization of tribunals.

(2) There is very general agreement on the need for courts to face squarely the policy questions in their cases, and use the full freedom precedent affords in working toward conclusions that seem indicated. There is fairly general agreement that effects of rules, so far as known, should be taken account of in making or remaking the rules * * *.

(3) There is a strong tendency to think it wiser to narrow rather than to widen the categories in which concepts and rules *either about judging or for judging* are made.

(4) There is a strong tendency to approach most legal problems as problems in allocation of risks, and so far as possible, as problems of their reduction, and so to insist on the effects of rules on parties who not only are not in court, but are not fairly represented by the parties who are in court. To approach not only tort but business matters, in a word, as matters of *general* policy.

And so I close as I began. What is there novel here? In the ideas, nothing. In the sustained attempt to make one or another of them fruitful, much. In the narrowness of fact-category together with the wide range of fact-inquiry, much. In the technique availed of, much—for lawyers. But let this be noted—for the summary above runs so largely to the purely descriptive side: When writers of realistic inclination are writing in general, they are bound to stress the need of more accurate description, of Is and not of Ought. There lies the *common* ground of their thinking; there lies the area of new and puzzling development. * * * As to whether change is called for, on any *given* point of our law, and if so, how much change, and in what direction, there is no agreement. Why should there be? A *group* philosophy or program, a *group* credo of social welfare, these realists have not. They are not a group.

NOTES AND QUESTIONS

1. As did Frank, in 1930 Karl Llewellyn had published a controversial volume on jurisprudence, *The Bramble Bush.* That work was a series of Llewellyn's lectures to beginning law students, originally delivered to his class at

Columbia, where he argued that it was necessary for law students and lawyers to pay somewhat less attention to disembodied rules, and more attention to the actions of the legal officers. Frank and Llewellyn, not unexpectedly, thus took Pound's 1931 paper as an attack principally on them, and they set about drafting a reply. Llewellyn's biographer, William Twining, reports that "At first they encountered resistance to their plan. The *Harvard Law Review* refused to grant them space for a reply until pressure was brought to bear on the Editor by members of the Harvard faculty, including Pound himself." Twining, Karl Llewellyn and the Realist Movement 73 (1973). Why might the Harvard Law Review have resisted? Why might Pound have intervened?

2. Considering the debate among Pound, Llewellyn, and Frank, Twining remarks that:

> Of all legal subjects jurisprudence is most susceptible to controversy: juristic controversies are prone to be inconclusive and unsatisfactory; of juristic controversies that surrounding realism has had more than its share of slovenly scholarship, silly misunderstandings and jejeune polemics. In 1931 public discussion of "realism" got off to a bad start from which it never fully recovered.

Twining, supra, at 80. Copyright © 1973 by William L. Twining, reprinted by permission of Mr. Twining. Can you point to any "slovenly scholarship, silly misunderstandings [or] jejeune polemics" in the three excerpts you have just read? Considerable doubt has been cast on much of Twining's account of the controversy by N.E.H. Hull, "Some Realism about the Llewellyn–Pound Exchange over Realism: The Newly Uncovered Private Correspondence", 1927–1931, 1987 Wisconsin Law Review 921. Her principal discovery is that Pound was *not* hostile to Llewellyn, or other legal realists, although Pound's loose charge of being "misquoted" by Frank led to some acrimonious correspondence and much hard feeling from him. Professor Hull's account, however, reflects rather poorly on Frank, and to a certain extent on Llewellyn, and leaves Pound pretty much on the high ground. For Ms. Hull's further reflections on the relationship between Pound and Llewellyn, see N.E.H. Hull, Roscoe Pound and Karl Llewellyn: Searching For an American Jurisprudence (1997).

3. Pound's pique can be somewhat better understood when one considers (as Frank and Llewellyn do somewhat acknowledge) that he was the leading "legal realist" of his day. Influenced in great part by the thought of Holmes, Pound had advocated in the early years of the twentieth century something he called "sociological jurisprudence" and which he offered as an alternative to the "mechanical jurisprudence" of men like Langdell and the *Lochner* majority. Pound stressed that jurisprudence ought to be more concerned with fitting the rules of law to "human conditions," and less with deriving conclusions from "assumed first principles." Pound, "Liberty of Contract," 18 Yale L.J. 454, 464 (1909). Pound believed that appropriate legal rules could be fashioned, if instead of fastening on panaceas such as freedom of contract, or *stare decisis,* or other bugaboos of nineteenth century "mechan-

ical jurisprudence," judges would pay more attention to the insights being revealed by the emerging social and political sciences. This attitude of Pound's mirrored that of the early twentieth century political Progressives, who seemed to believe in "the management of government by experts," in "regulatory and welfare legislation," and in "judicial tolerance for such legislation." See generally White, From Sociological Jurisprudence to Realism: Jurisprudence and Social Change in Early Twentieth–Century America, 59 Va.L.Rev. 999, 1003–1004 (1972).

The "progressivism" of the early twentieth century, as its name implies, "rested * * * on the concept of progress, a composite of the inherent perfectibility of man and the permanently dynamic quality of society." The unparalleled carnage of the First World War, and perhaps the intransigent isolationism of Americans afterwards, however, "made progress a hollow belief." White, supra, at 1013. This led to changes in jurisprudential outlook, and the changes affected Pound. By 1923, he was willing to concede that it might be best to give up the idea of reforming some doctrines in the law through social science, particularly doctrines of property and commercial law. Pound, The Theory of Judicial Decision, 36 Harv.L.Rev. 641, 952. White, supra, at 1009–1010. Do you find that it is this later aspect of Pound's work that Frank and Llewellyn seem most inclined to criticize?

4. Another commentator on the legal realists has written that:

> It is now generally recognized that realism, both as an intellectual movement and as an effort at educational reform, was misguided in several respects. For example, it is increasingly doubted that a single "method" or "theory" can serve as an educational program for all law schools and all varieties of legal practice; similarly, the realist effort to formulate a general "scientific" approach to law is now regarded as too abstract and polemical, and the issues involved either inherently unscientific or obvious to the point of sterility.

Note, Legal Theory and Legal Education, 79 Yale L.J. 1153, 1158 (1970). Reprinted by permission of the Yale Law Journal Company and Fred B. Rothman & Company. Is there anything in the three excerpts you have just read that would lead you to similar or dissimilar conclusions? The author of this note (Professor Rand Rosenblatt of Rutgers–Camden Law School who was then a law student) suggests that the major intellectual weaknesses of the legal realists were "a failure to distinguish different levels and points of criticism, and a core ambiguity about the role of values in social and legal thought." Id., at 1159. Do you discern any weaknesses of this nature?

5. Perhaps the most disturbing aspect of the work of the legal realists is its implication for democratic theory. This is of particular relevance to us when we consider Professor White's assertion that legal realism "was the [jurisprudential] analog to the New Deal." White, supra, at 999. It is for this reason that we have presented Legal Realism *after* the key New Deal cases, even though Frank and Llewellyn's work actually occurred *before* these great cases. Can you understand how the work of the legal realists might have led

to the "Constitutional Revolution" of 1937? Professor White thus describes the governmental philosophy of the New Dealers (and by implication the legal realists):

> They set out to eradicate the notions that private property was sacred and that self-help was the only way to deal with adversity. They announced that traditional bogeys such as the belief that government distribution of economic benefits was equivalent to socialism were shams: the only things the nation's citizens had to fear was fear itself. They preferred experimentation and empiricism to theorizing: it was not as important to articulate any philosophy of problem-solving as it was to try to solve problems. Despite their interest in improving the economic position of lower-income families, they were less interested in representative government than the Progressives. They preferred government experimentation conceived and executed by elites, with the primary governing institutions being administrative agencies, whose staffing and activities were not subject to a popular check.

White, supra, at 1025. Is this a vision of government that appeals to you? Is it consistent or inconsistent with the political and legal thought you have seen reflected in most of the materials we have studied?

Perhaps sensing something like these views on the part of the legal realists and the New Dealers, and considering the events in Europe in the 1930's, critics began to charge that "realism paved the way for totalitarianism by denying objective ethical standards and making law an amoral coercive force." Purcell, American Jurisprudence Between the Wars: Legal Realism and the Crisis of Democratic Theory, 75 Am.Hist.Rev. 424, 438 (1969). Indeed, Pound himself joined in the critical chorus when he proclaimed that "the political and juristic preaching of today leads logically to [political] absolutism." Pound, Contemporary Juristic Theory 9 (1940), quoted in Purcell, supra, at 438. Perhaps the most extreme reaction to legal realism came from the religious legal thinkers, like Father Francis E. Lucey, one of the regents of Georgetown University School of Law, who stated in 1942 that "Godless Behaviorism and Pragmatism are the headhunters, with Democracy and popular sovereignty the victims." Quoted in Purcell, supra, at 439. Do you see any basis for these charges in the work you have read of Frank and Llewellyn? For a brilliant discussion of the general philosophical and political difficulties posed by realism in various disciplines see Edward A. Purcell, Jr., The Crisis of Democratic Theory: Scientific Naturalism and the Problem of Value (1973).

6. What, then, became of the idea of using social science discoveries to reform the law articulated first by Pound, and then by the legal realists? How were the positivistic insights of legal realism to be integrated with democratic theories of judicial review? See if you can find any answers to the first question in the case of Brown v. Board of Educ., and any answers to the second in the excerpts from Wechsler and Wright, all of which follow. In spite of all the heat they took in the jurisprudential battles with the legal establishment in

the 1930's, can it be said that in the fifties and sixties the advocates of "legal realism" won a smashing victory? The extent of the influence of the legal realists and the nature of their contribution remains a subject of acrimonious debate among legal historians and other law professors. The pot has been stirred especially vigorously of late as the provocative jurisprudential movement—Critical Legal Studies—of which more soon—has claimed to be carrying the banner of legal realism. For a sampling of readings on this question see Neil Duxbury, "The Reinvention of American Legal Realism," 12 Legal Studies 137 (1992); William W. Fisher et al. eds., American Legal Realism (1993), Morton Horwitz, The Transformation of American Law 1870–1960: The Crisis of Legal Orthodoxy 169–246 (1992), Richard Posner, Overcoming Law (1995), and David Van Zandt, "The Only American Jurisprudence," 28 Houston L.Rev. 965 (1991).

D. BEYOND LEGAL REALISM

BROWN V. BOARD OF EDUC.

Supreme Court of the United States, 1954.
347 U.S. 483, 74 S.Ct. 686, 98 L.Ed. 873.

MR. CHIEF JUSTICE WARREN delivered the opinion of the Court.

These cases come to us from the States of Kansas, South Carolina, Virginia, and Delaware. They are premised on different facts and different local conditions, but a common legal question justifies their consideration together in this consolidated opinion.

In each of the cases, minors of the Negro race, through their legal representatives, seek the aid of the courts in obtaining admission to the public schools of their community on a nonsegregated basis. In each instance, they had been denied admission to schools attended by white children under laws requiring or permitting segregation according to race. This segregation was alleged to deprive the plaintiffs of the equal protection of the laws under the Fourteenth Amendment. In each of the cases other than the Delaware case, a three-judge federal district court denied relief to the plaintiffs on the so-called "separate but equal" doctrine announced by this Court in Plessy v. Ferguson, 163 U.S. 537. Under that doctrine, equality of treatment is accorded when the races are provided substantially equal facilities, even though these facilities be separate. In the Delaware case, the Supreme Court of Delaware adhered to that doctrine, but ordered that the plaintiffs be admitted to the white schools because of their superiority to the Negro schools.

The plaintiffs contend that segregated public schools are not "equal" and cannot be made "equal," and that hence they are deprived of the equal protection of the laws. * * * Argument was heard in the 1952 Term, and reargument was heard this Term on certain questions propounded by the Court.

Reargument was largely devoted to the circumstances surrounding the adoption of the Fourteenth Amendment in 1868. It covered exhaustively consideration of the Amendment in Congress, ratification by the states, then existing practices in racial segregation, and the views of proponents and opponents of the Amendment. This discussion and our own investigation convince us that, although these sources cast some light, it is not enough to resolve the problem with which we are faced. At best, they are inconclusive. The most avid proponents of the post-War Amendments undoubtedly intended them to remove all legal distinctions among "all persons born or naturalized in the United States." Their opponents, just as certainly, were antagonistic to both the letter and the spirit of the Amendments and wished them to have the most limited effect. What others in Congress and the state legislatures had in mind cannot be determined with any degree of certainty.

An additional reason for the inconclusive nature of the Amendment's history, with respect to segregated schools, is the status of public education at that time. In the South, the movement toward free common schools, supported by general taxation, had not yet taken hold. Education of white children was largely in the hands of private groups. Education of Negroes was almost nonexistent, and practically all of the race were illiterate. In fact, any education of Negroes was forbidden by law in some states. Today, in contrast, many Negroes have achieved outstanding success in the arts and sciences as well as in the business and professional world. It is true that public school education at the time of the Amendment had advanced further in the North, but the effect of the Amendment on Northern States was generally ignored in the congressional debates. Even in the North, the conditions of public education did not approximate those existing today. The curriculum was usually rudimentary; ungraded schools were common in rural areas; the school term was but three months a year in many states; and compulsory school attendance was virtually unknown. As a consequence, it is not surprising that there should be so little in the history of the Fourteenth Amendment relating to its intended effect on public education.

In the first cases in this Court construing the Fourteenth Amendment, decided shortly after its adoption, the Court interpreted it as proscribing all state-imposed discriminations against the Negro race.[5] The doctrine of "separate but equal" did not make its appearance in this Court until 1896 in the case of Plessy v. Ferguson, supra, involving not educa-

---

[5] *Slaughter–House Cases,* 16 Wall. 36, 67–72 (1873); Strauder v. West Virginia, 100 U.S. 303, 307–308 (1880):

"It ordains that no State shall deprive any person of life, liberty, or property, without due process of law, or deny to any person within its jurisdiction the equal protection of the laws. What is this but declaring that the law in the States shall be the same for the black as for the white; that all persons, whether colored or white, shall stand equal before the laws of the States, and, in regard to the colored race, for whose protection the amendment was primarily designed, that no discrimination shall be made against them by law because of their color? * * * "

tion but transportation. American courts have since labored with the doctrine for over half a century. In this Court, there have been six cases involving the "separate but equal" doctrine in the field of public education. * * *

In more recent cases, all on the graduate school level, inequality was found in that specific benefits enjoyed by white students were denied to Negro students of the same educational qualifications. Missouri ex rel. Gaines v. Canada, 305 U.S. 337; Sipuel v. Oklahoma, 332 U.S. 631; Sweatt v. Painter, 339 U.S. 629; McLaurin v. Oklahoma State Regents, 339 U.S. 637. In none of these cases was it necessary to re-examine the doctrine to grant relief to the Negro plaintiff. * * *

In the instant cases, that question is directly presented. Here * * * there are findings below that the Negro and white schools involved have been equalized, or are being equalized, with respect to buildings, curricula, qualifications and salaries of teachers, and other "tangible" factors. Our decision, therefore, cannot turn on merely a comparison of these tangible factors in the Negro and white schools involved in each of the cases. We must look instead to the effect of segregation itself on public education.

In approaching this problem, we cannot turn the clock back to 1868 when the Amendment was adopted, or even to 1896 when Plessy v. Ferguson was written. We must consider public education in the light of its full development and its present place in American life throughout the Nation. Only in this way can it be determined if segregation in public schools deprives these plaintiffs of the equal protection of the laws.

Today, education is perhaps the most important function of state and local governments. Compulsory school attendance laws and the great expenditures for education both demonstrate our recognition of the importance of education to our democratic society. * * * It is the very foundation of good citizenship. * * * In these days, it is doubtful that any child may reasonably be expected to succeed in life if he is denied the opportunity of an education. Such an opportunity, where the state has undertaken to provide it, is a right which must be made available to all on equal terms.

* * *

In Sweatt v. Painter, supra, in finding that a segregated law school for Negroes could not provide them equal educational opportunities, this Court relied in large part on "those qualities which are incapable of objective measurement but which make for greatness in a law school." In McLaurin v. Oklahoma State Regents, supra, the Court, in requiring that a Negro admitted to a white graduate school be treated like all other students, again resorted to intangible considerations: " * * * his ability to study, to engage in discussions and exchange views with other students, and, in general, to learn his profession." Such considerations apply with added force to children in grade and high schools. To separate them from others of similar age and qualifications solely because of their race generates a feeling of inferiority as to their status in the community that may affect their hearts and minds in a way unlikely ever to be undone. The effect of this separation on their educational opportunities was well stated by a finding in the Kansas case by a court which nevertheless felt compelled to rule against the Negro plaintiffs:

> Segregation of white and colored children in public schools has a detrimental effect upon the colored children. The impact is greater when it has the sanction of the law; for the policy of separating the races is usually interpreted as denoting the inferiority of the negro group. A sense of inferiority affects the motivation of a child to learn. Segregation with the sanction of law, therefore, has a tendency to [retard] the educational and mental development of negro children and to deprive them of some of the benefits they would receive in a racial[ly] integrated school system.

Whatever may have been the extent of psychological knowledge at the time of Plessy v. Ferguson, this finding is amply supported by modern authority.[11] Any language in Plessy v. Ferguson contrary to this finding is rejected.

We conclude that in the field of public education the doctrine of "separate but equal" has no place. Separate educational facilities are inherently unequal. Therefore, we hold that the plaintiffs and others similarly situated for whom the actions have been brought are, by reason of the segregation complained of, deprived of the equal protection of the laws guaranteed by the Fourteenth Amendment. * * *

* * *

NOTES AND QUESTIONS

1. Brown v. Board of Educ. is probably the most important Supreme Court case concerned with race relations since *Dred Scott*. And, it must be said, this may be far too modest a claim for the case. "For nearly forty years, *Brown* . . . has defined the central values of Constitutional adjudication in the United States." Mark Tushnet, with Katya Lezin, "What Really Happened in *Brown v. Board of Education*," 91 Col.L.Rev. 1867 (1991). "Constitutional lawyers and historians generally deem *Brown v. Board of Education* to

[11] K.B. Clark, Effect of Prejudice and Discrimination on Personality Development (Midcentury White House Conference on Children and Youth, 1950); Witmer and Kotinsky, Personality in the Making (1952), c. VI; Deutscher and Chein, The Psychological Effects of Enforced Segregation: A Survey of Social Science Opinion, 26 J.Psychol. 259 (1948); Chein, What are the Psychological Effects of Segregation Under Conditions of Equal Facilities?, 3 Int.J. Opinion and Attitude Res. 229 (1949); Brameld, Educational Costs, in Discrimination and National Welfare (MacIver, ed., 1949), 44–48; Frazier, The Negro in the United States (1949), 674–681. And see generally Myrdal, An American Dilemma (1944).

be the most important United States Supreme Court decision of the twentieth century, and possibly of all time." Michael J. Klarman, "How *Brown* Changed Race Relations: The Backlash Thesis," 81 Journal of American History 81 (June 1994). An increasing torrent of scholarship continues to be produced about the case.

For a sampling of writing on *Brown* see, in addition to Tushnet & Lezin, and Klarman, *supra,* Drew S. Days, III, "*Brown* Blues: Rethinking the Integrative Ideal," 34 Wm. & Mary L.Rev. 53 (1992), which argues that *Brown*'s "integrative ideal" is now being challenged by many blacks who favor neighborhood schools, black male "academies," black colleges, and special college facilities for black social and cultural events; Mary L. Dudziak, Cold War Civil Rights: Race and the Image of American Democracy (2000), which maintains that the desegregation cases grew out of America's need to prove to other nations that ours was a just society; Morton J. Horwitz, The Warren Court and the Pursuit of Justice (1998), a passionate defense of the Warren Court as implementers of a progressive conception of American Democracy informed by the notion of a "living Constitution;" which demonstrates how the Warren Court used the insights of legal realism to transform American law; Michael J. Klarman, "*Brown v. Board of Education:* Facts and Political Correctness," 80 U.Va.L.Rev. 185 (1994) and "*Brown*, Racial Change, and the Civil Rights Movement," 80 U.Va.L.Rev. 7 (1994), which challenge the conventional wisdom regarding the importance and influence of the case; and Mark Tushnet, "Public Law Litigation and the Ambiguities of *Brown,*" 61 Ford.L.Rev. 23 (1992), a short and pungent statement of his thesis that *Brown*'s gradualist formula of "all deliberate speed" ironically gave rise to "public law litigation,—an aggressive form of judicial review."

One of the best of these works is Simple Justice (1976), by Richard Kluger, which gives a complete history of the case and the forces and personalities that brought it about. See also Mark V. Tushnet, The NAACP's Legal Strategy against Segregated Education, 1925–1950 (1987). As you will see in the next reading, the opinion in *Brown* is subject to severe criticism (on this point see also Alexander Bickel, The Supreme Court and the Idea of Progress (1970)). If this is true, how do you account for the fact that there are no dissenting (or even concurring) opinions in *Brown*? See Hutchinson, "Unanimity and Desegregation: Decisionmaking in the Supreme Court," 1948–1958, 68 Geo.L.J. 1 (1979). Is it significant that the opinion is written by the new Chief Justice, Earl Warren, a former governor of California, who had come on the court following the death of Chief Justice Vinson in 1953?

For further reading on *Brown v. Board of Education* and the Warren Court see, e.g., Michael W. McConnell, "Originalism and the Desegregation Decisions," 81 Va.L.Rev. 947 (1995)(arguing that removing racial barriers in education is consistent with the intentions of the Fourteenth Amendment's framers), James T. Patterson, *Brown v. Board of Education*: A Civil Rights Milestone and Its Troubled Legacy (2001), Lucas A. Powe, Jr., The Warren Court and American Politics (2000). Powe's volume in particular has been hailed as "one of the most important books published on American constitutional politics this decade." Mark A. Graber, "Constitutional Politics and Constitutional Theory: A Misunderstood and Neglected Relationship," 27 Law and Social Inquiry 309 (2002) (arguing that lasting achievements in constitutional construction must be based on more than simply academic legal reasoning). For the precedent created by the Court's use of social science to buttress its legal reasoning, see, e.g. Michael Heise, "Equal Educational Opportunity by the Numbers: The Warren Court's Empirical Legacy," 59 Wash. & Lee L. Rev. 1309 (2002). For the legislation on Civil Rights that may have done as much as *Brown* to further racial equality in America, particularly Title II of the Civil Rights Act of 1964, which guaranteed the access of all persons to places of public accommodation, and was "one of the most significant pieces of legislation in our nation's history," see Richard C. Cortner, Civil Rights and Public Accommodations: The *Heart of Atlanta Motel* and *McClung* Cases (2001). Cortner's book "bookends histories of the Act with a rich account of the two Supreme Court cases that upheld title II—an event scarcely less important than the passage of the Act itself." Quotations are taken from Brannon P. Denning, "Book Review" [of Civil Rights and Public Accommodations], 94 Law Lib. J. 141 (2002). Denning concludes that "Cortner has successfully wrought what will likely be regarded as the definitive analysis of these historic cases."

2. Can you discern any effects of the thinking of the legal realists on Chief Justice Warren? Take, for example, the Chief Justice's comments about the nature of the constitutional amendments and the relevance of legislative history. Suppose it could be clearly demonstrated that an overwhelming majority of persons involved in the passage of the fourteenth amendment believed that there were significant differences between the races, and that while the races ought to be "equal before the law," there was no reason not to permit segregation in public facilities, even in public educational facilities. In other words, assume that it could be proved that the legislative history of the Amendment clearly revealed that its framers would have accepted the doctrines of Plessy v. Ferguson. Would Brown have had to be decided differently? Of what significance is Warren's remark about not being able to "turn the clock back?" Do you see any similarity to the views of the importance of the legislative history in the Antitrust cases? If Warren is suggesting that the meaning of constitutional terms must change as social conditions and factors such as public educational systems change, would this notion of a variable Constitution be in accord with legal realist thinking? How might Roscoe Pound have reacted to this decision?

3. Is it the fundamental nature of public education to the American polity that dictates that *Plessy* must be overruled? How does it follow, as the court suggests, that because Black professionals in training need the opportunity to confer and discourse with their White colleagues that the same is true for Black school children? Of what significance is the psychological and sociological data referred to in the "famous footnote 11?" Suppose it could be demonstrated that Black children were more likely to be able to develop positive self-images, and would thus be able better to learn, in a segregated school environment? Suppose such an environment could be shown to be freer

from the deleterious effects of racial prejudice and better calculated to the instilling of personal and racial pride? Would *Brown* then have to be reversed? One "reticent" district judge attempted, on the basis of psychological authority contrary to that in *Brown*, to uphold segregation. He was "promptly reversed." Friendly, "In Praise of Herbert Wechsler", 78 Col.L.Rev. 974, 978 n. 40 (1978), citing Stell v. Savannah–Chatham County Bd. of Educ. 220 F.Supp. 667 (S.D.Ga.1963), reversed 333 F.2d 55 (5th Cir.), cert. denied 379 U.S. 933, 85 S.Ct. 332, 13 L.Ed.2d 344 (1964). For an absorbing and eloquent account of the social and legal reaction to the fury unleashed by the *Brown* decision and to the struggle for Black civil rights in the South see Michael R. Belknap, Federal Law and Southern Order: Racial Violence and Constitutional Conflict in the Post–*Brown* South (1987).

HERBERT WECHSLER, TOWARD NEUTRAL PRINCIPLES OF CONSTITUTIONAL LAW*

Wechsler, Herbert, Toward Neutral Principles of Constitutional Law, 73 Harv.L.Rev. 1 (1959).

* * *

II. THE STANDARDS OF REVIEW

* * * Are there, indeed, any criteria that both the Supreme Court and those who undertake to praise or to condemn its judgments are morally and intellectually obligated to support? * * *

* * *

* * * I mean criteria that can be framed and tested as an exercise of reason and not merely as an act of willfulness or will. Even to put the problem is, of course, to raise an issue no less old than our culture. Those who perceive in law only the element of fiat, in whose conception of the legal cosmos reason has no meaning or no place, will not join gladly in the search for standards of the kind I have in mind. * * * So too must I anticipate dissent from those more numerous among us who, vouching no philosophy to warranty, frankly or covertly make the test of virtue in interpretation whether its result in the immediate decision seems to hinder or advance the interests or the values they support. * * * The man who simply lets his judgment turn on the immediate result may not, however, realize that his position implies that the courts are free to function as a naked power organ, that it is an empty affirmation to regard them, as ambivalently he so often does, as courts of law. * * *

* * * [T]his type of *ad hoc* evaluation is, as it has always been, the deepest problem of our constitutionalism, not only with respect to judg-

ments of the courts but also in the wider realm in which conflicting constitutional positions have played a part in our politics.

Did not New England challenge the embargo that the South supported on the very ground on which the South was to resist New England's demand for a protective tariff? Was not Jefferson in the Louisiana Purchase forced to rest on an expansive reading of the clauses granting national authority of the very kind that he had steadfastly opposed in his attacks upon the Bank? * * *

To bring the matter even more directly home, what shall we think of the Harvard records of the Class of 1829, the class of Mr. Justice Curtis, which, we are told, praised at length the Justice's dissent in the *Dred Scott* case but then added, "Again, *and seemingly adverse to the above,* in October, 1862, he prepared a legal opinion and argument, which was published in Boston in pamphlet form, to the effect that President Lincoln's Proclamation of prospective emancipation of the slaves in the rebellious States is *unconstitutional.*"

* * *

* * * What a wealth of illustration is at hand today! How many of the constitutional attacks upon congressional investigations of suspected Communists have their authors felt obliged to launch against the inquiries respecting the activities of Goldfine or of Hoffa or of others I might name? How often have those who think the Smith Act, as construed, inconsistent with the first amendment made clear that they also stand for constitutional immunity for racial agitators fanning flames of prejudice and discontent? * * *

All I have said, you may reply, is something no one will deny, that principles are largely instrumental as they are employed in politics * * *.

* * * [W]hether you are tolerant * * * of the *ad hoc* in politics, with principle reduced to a manipulative tool, are you not also ready to agree that something else is called for from the courts? I put it to you that the main constituent of the judicial process is precisely that it must be genuinely principled, resting with respect to every step that is involved in reaching judgment on analysis and reasons quite transcending the immediate result that is achieved. To be sure, the courts decide, or should decide, only the case they have before them. But must they not decide on grounds of adequate neutrality and generality tested not only by the instant application but by others that the principles imply? Is it not the very essence of judicial method to insist upon attending to such other cases, preferably those involving an opposing interest, in evaluating any principle avowed?

Does not the special duty of the courts to judge by neutral principles addressed to all the issues make it inapposite to contend, as Judge Hand does, that no court can review the legislative choice—by any standard other than a fixed "historical meaning" of constitutional provisions—without becoming "a third legislative chamber"? Is there not, in short, a vital difference between legislative freedom to appraise the gains and losses in projected measures and the kind of principled appraisal, in respect of values that can reasonably be asserted to have constitutional dimension, that alone is in the province of the courts? * * * This must, it seems to me, have been in Mr. Justice Jackson's mind when * * * he wrote * * * "Liberty is not the mere absence of restraint, it is not a spontaneous product of majority rule, it is not achieved merely by lifting underprivileged classes to power, nor is it the inevitable by-product of technological expansion. It is achieved only by a rule of law." * * *

You will not understand my emphasis upon the role of reason and of principle in the judicial, as distinguished from the legislative or executive, appraisal of conflicting values to imply that I depreciate the duty of fidelity to the text of the Constitution, when its words may be decisive * * *. Nor will you take me to deny that history has weight in the elucidation of the text, though it is surely subtle business to appraise it as a guide. Nor will you even think that I deem precedent without importance * * *.

At all events, is not the relative compulsion of the language of the Constitution, of history and precedent—where they do not combine to make an answer clear—itself a matter to be judged, so far as possible, by neutral principles—by standards that transcend the case at hand? I know, of course, that it is common to distinguish, as Judge Hand did, clauses like "due process," cast "in such sweeping terms that their history does not elucidate their contents," from other provisions of the Bill of Rights addressed to more specific problems. But the contrast, as it seems to me, often implies an overstatement of the specificity or the immutability these other clauses really have * * *.

No one would argue, for example, that there need not be indictment and a jury trial in prosecutions for a felony in district courts. What made a question of some difficulty was the issue whether service wives charged with the murders of their husbands overseas could be tried there before a military court. * * * The right to "have the assistance of counsel" was considered, I am sure, when the sixth amendment was proposed, a right to defend by counsel if you have one, contrary to what was then the English law. That does not seem to me sufficient to avert extension of its meaning to imply a right to court-appointed counsel when the defendant is too poor to find such aid—though I admit that I once urged the point sincerely as a lawyer for the Government. * * * Nor should we, in my view, lament the fact that "the" freedom of speech or press that Congress is forbidden by the first amendment to impair is not determined only by the scope such freedom had in the late eighteenth century * * *.

* * * Equal protection could be taken as no more than an assurance that no one may be placed beyond the safeguards of the law, outlawing, as it were, the possibility of outlawry, but nothing else. Here too I cannot find it in my heart to regret that interpretation did not ground itself in ancient history but rather has perceived in these provisions a compendious affirmation of the basic values of a free society, values that must be given weight in legislation and administration at the risk of courting trouble in the courts.

So far as possible, to finish with my point, I argue that we should prefer to see the other clauses of the Bill of Rights read as an affirmation of the special values they embody rather than as statements of a finite rule of law, its limits fixed by the consensus of a century long past, with problems very different from our own. To read them in the former way is to leave room for adaptation and adjustment if and when competing values, also having constitutional dimension, enter on the scene.

* * *

The virtue or demerit of a judgment turns, therefore, entirely on the reasons that support it and their adequacy to maintain any choice of values it decrees, or, it is vital that we add, to maintain the rejection of a claim that any given choice should be decreed. * * *

III. SOME APPRAISALS OF REVIEW

[Professor Wechsler proceeds critically to apply his theory about the need for application of neutral and general principles to recent Constitutional adjudication.]

(1).—I start by noting two important fields of present interest in which the Court has been decreeing value choices in a way that makes it quite impossible to speak of principled determinations * * * since the Court has not disclosed the grounds on which its judgments rest.

> [Wechsler first notes a recent group of U.S. Supreme Court decisions finding state attempts to suppress motion pictures unconstitutional because of the safeguards of the first amendment which are made applicable to the states by the fourteenth amendment. He criticizes the court for issuing per curiam opinions which made no distinctions and gave no reasoning.]

* * *

(2).—The second group of cases to which I shall call attention involves what may be called the progeny of the school-segregation ruling of 1954. Here again the Court has written on the merits of the constitutional issue posed by state segregation only once; [in Brown v. Board of Education, in 1954.] * * * The original opinion, you recall, was firmly focused on state segregation in the public schools, its reasoning accorded import to the nature of the educational process, and its conclusion was that separate educational facilities are "inherently unequal."

What shall we think then of the Court's extension of the ruling to other public facilities, such as public transportation, parks, golf courses, bath houses, and beaches, which no one is obliged to use—all by per curiam decisions? That these situations present a weaker case against state segregation is not, of course, what I am saying. I am saying that the question whether it is stronger, weaker, or of equal weight appears to me to call for principled decision. I do not know, and I submit you cannot know, whether the per curiam affirmance in the *Dawson* case, involving public bath houses and beaches, embraced the broad opinion of the circuit court that all state-enforced racial segregation is invalid or approved only its immediate result and, if the latter, on what ground. * * *

(3).—The poverty of principled articulation of the limits put on Congress as against the states before the doctrinal reversal of the Thirties was surely also true of the decisions, dealing with the very different problem of the relationship between the individual and government, which invoked due process to maintain *laissez-faire*. Did not the power of the great dissents inhere precisely in their demonstrations that the Court could not present an adequate analysis, in terms of neutral principles, to support the value choices it decreed? * * *

* * *

(4).—Finally, I turn to the decisions that for me provide the hardest test of my belief in principled adjudication, those in which the Court in recent years has vindicated claims that deprivations based on race deny the equality before the law that the fourteenth amendment guarantees. The crucial cases are, of course, those involving the white primary, the enforcement of racially restrictive covenants, and the segregated schools.

* * * [S]keptical about predictions as I am, I still believe that the decisions I have mentioned—dealing with the primary, the covenant, and schools—have the best chance of making an enduring contribution to the quality of our society of any that I know in recent years. It is in this perspective that I ask how far they rest on neutral principles and are entitled to approval in the only terms that I acknowledge to be relevant to a decision of the courts.

The primary and covenant cases present two different aspects of a single problem—that it is a state alone that is forbidden by the fourteenth amendment to deny equal protection of the laws * * *. It has, of course, been held for years that the prohibition of action by the state reaches not only an explicit deprivation by a statute but also action of the courts or of subordinate officials * * *.

I deal first with the primary. So long as the Democratic Party in the South excluded Negroes from participation, in the exercise of an authority conferred by statute regulating political parties, it was entirely clear that the amendment was infringed; the exclusion involved an application of the statute. The problem became difficult only when the states, responding to these judgments, repealed the statutes, leaving parties free to define their membership as private associations * * *. In this position the Court held in 1935 that an exclusion by the party was untouched by the amendment, being action of the individuals involved, not of the state or its officialdom.

Then came the *Classic* case in 1941, which * * * involved a prosecution of election officials for depriving a voter of a right secured by the Constitution in willfully failing to count his vote as it was cast in a Louisiana Democratic primary. In holding that the right of a qualified voter to participate in choosing Representatives in Congress, a right conferred by article I, section 2, extended to participating in a primary which influenced the ultimate selection, the Court did not, of course, deal with the scope of party freedom to select its members. The victim of the fraud in *Classic* was a member of the Democratic Party, voting in a primary in which he was entitled to participate, and the only one in which he could. Yet three years later *Classic* was declared in Smith v. Allwright to have determined in effect that primaries are a part of the election, with the consequence that parties can no more defend racial exclusion from their primaries than can the state * * *. This is no doubt a settled proposition in the Court. But what it means is not, as sometimes has been thought, that a state may not escape the limitations of the Constitution merely by transferring public functions into private hands. It means rather that the constitutional guarantee against deprivation of the franchise on the ground of race or color has become a prohibition of party organization upon racial lines, at least where the party has achieved political hegemony. I ask with all sincerity if you are able to discover in the opinions thus far written in support of this result—a result I say again that I approve—neutral principles that satisfy the mind. I should suppose that a denial of the franchise on religious grounds is certainly forbidden by the Constitution. Are religious parties, therefore, to be taken as proscribed? I should regard this result too as one plainly to be desired but is there a constitutional analysis on which it can be validly decreed? Is it, indeed, not easier to project an analysis establishing that such a proscription would infringe rights protected by the first amendment?

The case of the restrictive covenant presents for me an even harder problem. Assuming that the Constitution speaks to state discrimination on the ground of race but not to such discrimination by an individual * * *, why is the enforcement of the private covenant a state discrimination rather than a legal recognition of the freedom of the individual? That the action of the state court [in enforcing the private covenant] is action of the state, the point Mr. Chief Justice Vinson emphasizes in the Court's opinion* is, of course, entirely obvious. What is not obvious, and is the crucial step, is that the state may properly be charged with the discrimination when it does no more than give effect to an agreement that the individual involved is, by hypothesis, entirely free to make. Again, one is obliged to ask: What is the principle involved? Is the state forbidden to effectuate a will that draws a racial line * * *, or is it a sufficient answer there that the discrimination was the testator's and not the state's? May not the state employ its law to vindicate the privacy of property against a trespasser, regardless of the grounds of his exclusion, or does it embrace the owner's reasons for excluding if it buttresses his power by the law? Would a declaratory judgment that a fee is determinable if a racially restrictive limitation should be violated represent discrimination by the state upon the racial ground? Would a judgment of ejectment?

None of these questions has been answered by the Court nor are the problems faced in the opinions. Philadelphia, to be sure, has been told that it may not continue to administer the school for "poor male white orphans," established by the city as trustee under the will of Stephen Girard, in accordance with that racial limitation. All the Supreme Court said, however, was the following: "The Board which operates Girard College is an agency of the State of Pennsylvania. Therefore, even though the Board was acting as a trustee, its refusal to admit Foust and Felder to the college because they were Negroes was discrimination by the State. Such discrimination is forbidden by the Fourteenth Amendment." When the Orphans' Court thereafter dismissed the city as trustee, appointing individuals in substitution, its action was sustained in Pennsylvania. Further review by certiorari was denied.

* * *

Many understandably would like to perceive in the primary and covenant decisions a principle susceptible of broad extension, applying to the other power aggregates in our society limitations of the kind the Constitution has imposed on government. My colleague A.A. Berle, Jr., has, indeed, pointed to the large business corporation, which after all is chartered by the state and wields in many areas more power than the government, as uniquely suitable for choice as the next subject of such application. * * *

I do not hesitate to say that I prefer to see the issues faced through legislation, where there is room for drawing lines that courts are not equipped to draw. * * *

Lastly, I come to the school decision * * *.

---

* In Shelley v. Kraemer, 334 U.S. 1, 68 S.Ct. 836, 92 L.Ed. 1161 (1948).

The problem * * * is not that the Court departed from its earlier decisions * * *. I stand with the long tradition of the Court that previous decisions must be subject to reexamination when a case against their reasoning is made. Nor is the problem that the Court disturbed the settled patterns of a portion of the country; even that must be accepted as a lesser evil than nullification of the Constitution. Nor is it that history does not confirm that an agreed purpose of the fourteenth amendment was to forbid separate schools or that there is important evidence that many thought the contrary; the words are general and leave room for expanding content as time passes and conditions change. * * *

The problem inheres strictly in the reasoning of the opinion * * *. The Court did not declare, as many wish it had, that the fourteenth amendment forbids all racial lines in legislation, though subsequent per curiam decisions may, as I have said, now go that far. Rather * * * the separate-but-equal formula was not overruled "in form" but was held to have "no place" in public education on the ground that segregated schools are "inherently unequal," with deleterious effects upon the colored children in implying their inferiority, effects which retard their educational and mental development. So, indeed, the district court had found as a fact in the Kansas case, a finding which the Supreme Court embraced, citing some further "modern authority" in its support.

Does the validity of the decision turn then on the sufficiency of evidence or of judicial notice to sustain a finding that the separation harms the Negro children who may be involved? * * * And if the harm that segregation worked was relevant, what of the benefits that it entailed: sense of security, the absence of hostility? Were they irrelevant? Moreover, was the finding in Topeka applicable without more to Clarendon County, South Carolina, with 2,799 colored students and only 295 whites? Suppose that more Negroes in a community preferred separation than opposed it? Would that be relevant to whether they were hurt or aided by segregation as opposed to integration? * * *

I find it hard to think the judgment really turned upon the facts. Rather, it seems to me, it must have rested on the view that racial segregation is, in principle, a denial of equality to the minority against whom it is directed; that is, the group that is not dominant politically and, therefore, does not make the choice involved. For many who support the Court's decision this assuredly is the decisive ground. But this position also presents problems. Does it not involve an inquiry into the motive of the legislature, which is generally foreclosed to the courts? Is it alternatively defensible to make the measure of validity of legislation the way it is interpreted by those who are affected by it? In the context of a charge that segregation *with equal facilities* is a denial of equality, is there not a point in *Plessy* in the statement that if "enforced separation stamps the colored race with a badge of inferiority" it is solely because its members choose "to put that construction upon it"? Does enforced separation of the sexes discriminate against females merely because it may be the females who resent it and it is imposed by judgments predominantly male? Is a prohibition of miscegenation a discrimination against the colored member of the couple who would like to marry?

For me, assuming equal facilities, the question posed by state-enforced segregation is not one of discrimination at all. Its human and its constitutional dimensions lie entirely elsewhere, in the denial by the state of freedom to associate, a denial that impinges in the same way on any groups or races that may be involved. I think, and I hope not without foundation, that the Southern white also pays heavily for segregation, not only in the sense of guilt that he must carry but also in the benefits he is denied. In the days when I was joined with Charles H. Houston in a litigation in the Supreme Court, before the present building was constructed, he did not suffer more than I in knowing that we had to go to Union Station to lunch together during the recess. Does not the problem of miscegenation show most clearly that it is the freedom of association that at bottom is involved * * * ?

But if the freedom of association is denied by segregation, integration forces an association upon those for whom it is unpleasant or repugnant. Is this not the heart of the issue involved, a conflict in human claims of high dimension, not unlike many others that involve the highest freedoms * * *. Given a situation where the state must practically choose between denying the association to those individuals who wish it or imposing it on those who would avoid it, is there a basis in neutral principles for holding that the Constitution demands that the claims for association should prevail? I should like to think there is, but I confess that I have not yet written the opinion. To write it is for me the challenge of the school-segregation cases.

* * *

NOTES AND QUESTIONS

1. What, exactly, does Professor Wechsler mean by "neutral principles?" We might approach this problem by first asking why "neutral principles" were needed. Wechsler points to a group of decisions which illustrate a lack of such jurisprudence, the pre–New Deal due process cases and the *Brown* case and its progeny, to repeat two of these examples. What do these cases have in common? Is Professor Wechsler advocating that the Supreme Court stay "neutral" on the great twentieth century social issues, and decline to act unless absolutely necessary? Some critics have found this meaning in this article, but it seems far more likely that Wechsler was arguing exactly the opposite—that the Supreme Court should shoulder its judicial review obligations, but should reach decisions in a reasoned manner, with a logic that could be applied to govern or distinguish other factual situations. This be-

comes clearer when one notices that Wechsler's article was expressly intended to rebut Learned Hand's lectures from the same platform a year before (Learned Hand, The Bill of Rights (1958)). Hand had argued for judicial restraint, for the Supreme Court not to intervene by exercising judicial review except in cases of absolute necessity. See Friendly, "In Praise of Herbert Wechsler," 78 Col.L.Rev. 974, 977–8 (1978). For a short essay putting Wechsler's concept of "neutral principles" in context, discussing its advocates and critics, and giving a fine bibliography for further reading on the issue see Barry Friedman, "Neutral Principles," in Leonard W. Levy and Kenneth L. Karst, eds., Encyclopedia of the American Constitution 1792 (2nd ed. 2000).

2. Is Professor Wechsler attempting a reply to the theories of the legal realists? This seems to be the motive attributed to him by subsequent scholars, who have called this piece the " 'inevitable reaction long overdue' to the more radical versions of legal realism." Greenawalt, "The Enduring Significance of Neutral Principles", 78 Col.L.Rev. 982 (1978). Why might such a reaction be necessary? Why might the analysis of the radical legal realists (here Jerome Frank's notions in Law and the Modern Mind might be taken as example) be unacceptable to legal academics in the late fifties?

3. Perhaps most important for our purposes is Wechsler's criticism of the decision in *Brown*. Is the *Brown* decision a failure in terms of neutral principles because the court failed to adhere to the framers' intentions when the fourteenth amendment was passed? What is the role of history in the application of neutral principles? Is the weakness in the opinion that it is based on psychological data? Is it that it is based on the fourteenth amendment? Wechsler gives up in the attempt to draft a *Brown* decision according to neutral principles. Could you draft such an opinion? For attempts at writing a better opinion for *Brown* by "nine prominent and ideologically diverse academics," Bruce Ackerman, Jack Balkin, Derrick Bell, Drew Days, John Hart Ely, Catharine MacKinnon, Michael McConnell, Frank Michaelman, and Cass Sunstein see Jack M. Balkin, ed., What *Brown v. Board of Education* Should Have Said (2001), and for a critique of those opinions see Jordan Steiker, "American Icon: Does it Matter What the Court Said in *Brown?*", 81 Tex.L.Rev. 305 (2002). Wechsler's article on neutral principles has continued to be "one of the most heavily cited in legal history," but the conventional wisdom among law professors is that the kind of neutral principles he advocates are unobtainable. See generally, Richard Posner, Overcoming Law 70–80 (1995), and Gary Peller, "Neutral Principles in the 1950's," 21 Journal of Law Reform 561 (1988). Do you agree? Is the problem Wechsler's procedural focus or his substantive aims? Does Wechsler's condemnation of Shelley v. Kraemer, the White Primary cases, and *Brown* mean that Wechsler is insensitive to the equitable claims of minorities, or that he ultimately disagrees with the substantive result in *Brown?* Consider the comments of Judge Skelly Wright, which follow.

4. In the meantime, pause for a moment to think about what it is that Wechsler sees as worth perpetuating in the workings of the Supreme Court. We might see in Wechsler's "neutral principles" an attempt to resurrect the

"legal science" of Field or Langdell, but, at bottom, isn't Wechsler simply suggesting adherence to the notion that we have a government of laws and not men, that American Constitutional decisions are made according to the "rule of law?" How important is this? In a celebrated work England's leading Marxist historian wrote:

> We ought to expose the shams and inequities which may be concealed beneath this [particular] law. But the rule of law itself, the imposing of effective inhibitions upon power and the defence of the citizen from power's all-intrusive claims, seems to me to be an unqualified human good. To deny or belittle this good, is, in this dangerous century when the resources and pretensions of power continue to enlarge, a desperate error of intellectual abstraction.

E.P. Thompson, Whigs and Hunters: The Origin of the Black Act 266 (1975). One of America's leading legal historians, Morton Horwitz, seems to have been disturbed by these comments of Thompson's and wrote in a review of his book:

> Unless we are prepared to succumb to Hobbesian pessimism "in this dangerous century," I do not see how a Man of the Left can describe the rule of law as "an unqualified human good"! It undoubtedly restrains power, but it also prevents power's benevolent exercise. It creates formal equality—a not inconsiderable virtue—but it *promotes* substantive inequality by creating a consciousness that radically separates law from politics, means from ends, processes from outcomes. By promoting procedural justice it enables the shrewd, the calculating, and the wealthy to manipulate its forms to their own advantage. And it ratifies and legitimates an adversarial, competitive, and atomistic conception of human relations.

Horwitz, "The Rule of Law: An Unqualified Human Good?," 86 Yale L.J. 561, 566 (1977).* Who is right, Horwitz or Thompson? Could Horwitz's critique of Thompson also be applied to Holmes? To the legal realists? As you read the next piece, see if you can determine if Judge Wright subscribes to the "rule of law."

J. SKELLY WRIGHT, PROFESSOR BICKEL, THE SCHOLARLY TRADITION, AND THE SUPREME COURT**

84 Harv.L.Rev. 769 (1971).

[In this article Judge Wright comments on a book by the late Alexander Bickel, a Professor at Yale Law School, whose jurisprudential views were similar to those of Professor Wechsler. Judge Wright refers to those views as the "scholarly tradition."]

---

* Reprinted by permission of the Yale Law Journal Company, Fred B. Rothman and Company and the author, from the Yale Law Journal, Vol. 86, p. 566.

* * *

* * * *The Supreme Court and the Idea of Progress* does go one step beyond the scholarly tradition. At the outset, Bickel concedes that history rarely judges the Court's work by the quality of its reasoning process. He recognizes that the scholarly praise customarily afforded the Marshall Court, despite numerous lapses in craftsmanship, is singularly result-oriented. The Justices of the Warren Court, Bickel suggests, understandably sought to emulate the Marshall Court and earn its place in history for themselves. Thoroughly result-oriented and with a broad program of social reform in mind, they made a "bet on the future," relying "on events for vindication more than on the method of reason for contemporary validation." But even accepting *arguendo* the premise of the Warren Court's supposed strategy, Bickel condemns its execution and results. Unlike his predecessors in the scholarly tradition, he does not praise the historic contribution of the Court's most important work while criticizing only the process by which it was crafted. Rather, he belittles both. In so doing he goes right for the jugular. * * * "If my probe into a near-term future is not wildly off the mark," he concludes, "the upshot is that the Warren Court's noblest enterprise—school desegregation—and its most popular enterprise—reapportionment—* * * are heading toward obsolescence, and in large measure abandonment."

Bickel's point, then, is that the Court sacrificed all on a bet which is not going to pay off. * * * Unlike his predecessors, Bickel challenges the supporters of the Warren Court on their own substantive, result-oriented ground. Yet the ultimate lesson that Bickel would have us learn still reflects the familiar teachings of the scholarly tradition. Bickel argues that it was the Warren Court's failure to heed the strict constraints of reason that headed its work for oblivion.

* * *

Bickel's new book * * * illustrates the gap between theory and practice in Wechslerian criticism. One might expect the torchbearers of neutral principles, having professed to accept significant judicial latitude in making constitutional value choices, to welcome the Court's vigorous defense of our fundamental rights and liberties. But in practice it doesn't seem to work out that way. Wechsler's scholarly followers have repeatedly demonstrated that the rule of "neutral principles" serves better as a tool of destructive criticism than as a guide to the more effective protection of constitutional values. * * *

* * * When the Court attempts to limit its holdings narrowly, the critics charge that the decisions are not sufficiently general and principled. They argue that lines have been drawn between categories of events or individuals which are more relevantly similar than different, and they

conclude that the Court is surreptitiously basing its decisions either on a merely pragmatic political assessment of the consequences in the instant case or on some hidden principle it fears to state openly. * * * They commonly point to inconsistencies between the articulated principle and past Court decisions, refusing to accept the possibility that those precedents are now to be called into serious question. Alternatively, the critics do their best to extend the principle into disparate and outlying policy areas only to deplore the results it would work there. Rarely do they assist the Court in finding lines that could be drawn in future cases to limit the principle's application. * * * Just as rarely do they survey the implications of a principle and say with Professor Charles Black—not one of their number—that if the principle is right and if it would invalidate this or that precedent or common practice, then "so be it." Instead of evaluating the principle as a matter of principle, they focus on results and refuse to admit that the validity of the principle may suggest the validity of its implications. * * *

Do these scholarly critics really believe that their strictures of principled adjudication are compatible with enforcement of fundamental rights and liberties? In *The Supreme Court and the Idea of Progress* Bickel may have inadvertently provided an answer. He admits his doubt that the Court has ever fully met the Wechslerian standards and recognizes that he does not know whether the Warren Court fell any farther short than its predecessors. But, he says, such a comparison "does not matter one way or the other, for intellectual incoherence is not excusable and is no more tolerable because it has occurred before." * * * Perhaps so. But Bickel should have hesitated somewhat longer, I believe, to ask whether he is not demanding the nearly impossible. * * *

Surely it is altogether proper for legal scholars to urge the Court to strive for the rational ideal. But it is another thing to demand * * * Wechslerian "total generality" in constitutional decisions. As a matter of fact, I would argue that constitutional adjudication may properly proceed somewhat as does common law adjudication. * * * Justice Holmes believed that the great growth of the common law came about incrementally * * *. If it is proper for the Court to make fundamental value choices to protect our constitutional rights and liberties, then it is self-defeating to say that if the Justices cannot come up with a perfectly reasoned and perfectly general opinion *now,* then they should abstain from decision altogether.

* * *

* * * Wechsler's rule goes a long way toward restricting—indeed, paralyzing—the Court's enforcement of its own value choices. But by failing to provide guidance for which values are to be chosen, Wechsler's approach admits of a high degree of internal ambiguity. How are we to

evaluate the "neutrality" of line-drawing except by reference to some sort of value choices? Is it proper, for example, to distinguish de jure from de facto segregation under the fourteenth amendment? Should youths under eighteen be equated with racial minorities for some purposes? Factual surveys may identify the similarities and differences which are relevant; but how are we to decide which of the two is the greater without first making value choices? * * * Wechsler and his followers seem to assume that the simple application of reason will answer the hard questions, yet they never explain how this synthesis of "value free" values comes about.

In *The Least Dangerous Branch,* Bickel characterized the Court's proper role much as Wechsler did: the Court is "predestined" to be "a voice of reason, charged with the creative function of discerning afresh and of articulating and developing impersonal and durable principles." * * * In *The Supreme Court and the Idea of Progress* he no longer seems to hold that confident belief.

Instead, Bickel now reverts to the original view of the pre-Wechsler progressive realists. The progressive realists, he says, were "skeptical * * * of claims to generality and permanence entered in behalf of social and economic principles." So, too, is he. He has now, "come to doubt in many instances the Court's capacity to develop 'durable principles,' and to doubt, therefore, that judicial supremacy can work and is tolerable in broad areas of social policy." Concepts of justice and injustice, he says, were once thought to have some stable content, but "[t]he words are used in a different sense now because they are no longer rooted in a single, well-recognized ethical precept." * * Bickel now speaks of the unruly "market of norms, values" which cannot be ordered by any institution.

Out of his profound value relativism emerges the view that the Court simply must stay out of most important policy questions. "The judicial process is too principle-prone and principle-bound—it has to be, there is no other justification or explanation for the role it plays." As a result, it is "a most unsuitable instrument for the formation of policy." Thus Bickel resists the temptation to approve judicial protection of civil rights and liberties. He would impose two central substantive rules of limitation on the Court's role: it must, as a general matter, confine itself to invalidating only totally irrational action and whimsical or arbitrary administrative measures, and it must stay out of "social policy" questions.

Bickel does not define "social policy," but * * * does, however, give the term some content by mentioning three categories of issues which do not fall within the forbidden area. He would allow the Court freedom in reforming the criminal process, agreeing with Justice Frankfurter that criminal procedure is somehow a technical matter which the public is happy to leave to the judiciary and which may be dealt with simply and without major impact on broader social goals.

* * * Bickel's two other permissible occasions for judicial value choices of more than the narrowest compass [are] * * * breakdowns in the political process, such as the *total* exclusion of an insular group from access to the process, and a "coup d'état," for example, by the military. The Professor's ideal Justices certainly would become adept at sitting on their hands * * * and the rest of us would be left to our own devices in exercising our constitutional rights and liberties.

That, Bickel says, is as it should be. Corresponding to his new skepticism about the power of reason and principle is a new faith in the pluralistic political process—and in the adequacy of reliance on that process to protect fundamental values. * * * Since he sees values as items in an undisciplined marketplace, he has only kind words for "[t]he jockeying, the bargaining, the trading, the threatening and the promising, the checking and the balancing" of the political system. Nor should the Court step in to aid minorities which have been severely disadvantaged by dominant political groups.

> In the political process, groups sometimes lose out, but so long as the process is operational and both diffuses power and allows majorities ultimately to work their will, no group that is prepared to enter into the process and combine with others need remain permanently and completely out of power.

The most conservative of post-war political scientists could not have put it better. * * *

III

* * * [Judge Wright proceeds to explain the extent of his disagreement with Wechsler, et al.] I reject not only [their] entailment of a rigidly restricted role for the courts, but also [their] fundamental axioms. The first of these axioms is that a constitutional value choice is the functional equivalent of an ordinary policy decision. Constitutional choices are in fact different from ordinary decisions. The reason is simple: the most important value choices have already been made by the framers of the Constitution.

Followers of the scholarly tradition have argued since the days of the progressive realists that the Bill of Rights and the fourteenth amendment are so vaguely worded as to provide no guidance for decision in modern times. Thus the axiom that a constitutional issue is nothing more than another policy issue. Professor Bickel, for example, stresses the infinite complexity of speech and apportionment questions * * *.

* * *

Of course, the Constitution is written in broad, majestic language. How else should it have been written? The framers were not so dimwitted as to believe that times would not change, that unforeseen problems would not arise. The reason for framing a constitution is to guarantee a general *sort* of relation between the government and its citizens. To achieve that end the Constitution must have a purposive permanence. It must serve as a "living" safeguard against certain sorts of excesses on the part of elected officials misled * * * by inflamed emotions and calculations of immediate consequences. It must, in short, be written in "vague" language. If the framers had intended only to forbid coups d'etat and clearly totalitarian measures, they could have been far more specific.

Clearly, then, constitutional protections of rights and liberties are meant to have meaning beyond what Bickel would allow. The duty of both judges and constitutional scholars is to determine what that meaning ought to be. The question really is how to do it. Here, again, Bickel is a defeatist. He is correct, of course, when he says that filling in the majestic constitutional outlines requires value choices. But the point is that those outlines provide significant and sufficient guidance; the value choices are to be made only within the parameters of the most important value choice embedded in the constitutional language. * * *

Naturally there will be differences over the purposes and underlying political theories of the various constitutional protections. But they will be reasoned differences, subject to argument. * * * An assumption of Bickel and his colleagues seems to be that if we accept this mode of constitutional interpretation, we must also accept whatever results judges who apply it may reach, be they "conservative" or "liberal." That, of course, is not the case. When the courts interpret constitutional provisions in ways which we believe wrong, we ought not to shift the focus from the merits of their position to a narrowing of their institutional function. This was the fundamental mistake made by liberal legal scholars in the 1930's. * * * Arguments over purposes and theories will be healthy, aiding both judges and the political officials who appoint them. This approach will refocus attention, spawn a new mode of judicial criticism, and allow us to get on with the business of enforcing the purposive commands of the Constitution.

Yet *The Supreme Court and the Idea of Progress* suggests that Professor Bickel would remain unconvinced by this argument. Even if he admitted that a constitutional value choice is not the functional equivalent of an ordinary policy issue, he would still say that the freely operating pluralist political process serves to protect our constitutional rights and liberties adequately. * * * His belief seems to rest on two foundations, one theoretical, one empirical, and both mistaken.

Professor Bickel appears to believe that reliance on the political process for protection of most fundamental rights and liberties is somehow inherent in democratic theory. * * * Judicial decisions are made without the form of popular consent expressed, for example, in the casting of a vote and should therefore be relatively disfavored. But * * * [a] vote for a candidate does not give him a carte blanche. Implicit in the vote is an expectation that, if elected, the candidate will conform his actions to the Constitution. Also implicit, given judicial review, is the recognition that there are courts to ensure his obedience. * * * [A voter's] power to challenge particular decisions in the courts is theoretically necessary to the claim that government officials act with his consent. The Constitution was not originally imposed on us by some court. Rather, it was adopted by the people, may be altered by the people, and must be considered by them in any authorization they give to elected officeholders. It is the people's independent check on popular democracy, and, as such, is best enforced by an independent body with power to check the actions of legislatures and executives. It is very much part of—indeed, it is at the core of—government by the consent of the governed.

* * * In this country, the majority made an original decision to protect certain minority rights, and this decision cannot be respected if these rights evaporate whenever it seems expedient to ignore them. Professor Bickel goes on to contend, however, that in fact minorities play an important though indirect role in most governmental decisions, may be presumed to consent to them, and have substantial opportunity to defend their interests without the help of the courts. No minority willing to wheel and deal with other minorities, he says, need despair of eventually vindicating its rights. There are at least two problems with this common position. First, from a constitutional standpoint, is the word "eventually." The Constitution does not say that "no law shall for an inordinately long time" or that "no state shall in perpetuity" deny certain rights. It sets down limitations to be made effective in the present. Nor does the Constitution say that a minority must trade away many of its interests in order to secure support for exercise of its fundamental rights. It does not sanction the putting of prices on these rights. * * *

Bickel's empirical assertion that no minority need remain isolated * * * is also highly doubtful. Perhaps its basic defect is the fact that power is not distributed equally among the various groups in our society. Bickel explicitly recognizes * * * the trading and pressuring that goes on * * *. The Professor would have us believe that this is just fine: those groups with the most "intense" interests will be the most active in the process, and it is proper that the more "intense" interests be more richly rewarded. This is nonsense. The big winners in the pluralistic system are the highly organized, wealthy, and motivated groups skilled in the art of insider politics. They have the resources to trade * * * and * * * to press their claims successfully. Perhaps the interest of a great corporation in a tax break is more "intense" than that of a political minority in its first amendment rights—that is, if intensity is defined by how conscious of their interests they are, how articulate and persistent they are in presenting them, and how much political muscle they bring to bear. Intensity, so defined, however, is largely an attribute of the already powerful elite. Unorganized, poor, unskilled minorities simply do not have the sort of "intense" interests in their rights which the pluralistic system regularly rewards. Is this any way to protect their constitutional rights? Under the narrowly constricted judicial role of the scholarly tradition, it is the only way.

IV

[Judge Wright next considers Professor Bickel's substantive attack on the Court's work.]

* * * Professor Bickel launches the attack by characterizing what he believes to be the four dominant themes underlying the Justices' decisions: egalitarianism, majoritarianism, centralization, and legalization. * * *

Bickel apparently feels that he must show the Warren Court to be not simply overly activist, but consciously demonic. * * * Slaves to simplistic theoretical principles, the Court in Bickel's opinion naively sought "to impose order on the market of norms, values and institutions," motivated by "[a] certain habit of command, an impatience to take charge of unruly affairs." He depicts the Court as an overconfident planning agency, a master builder whose "tendency was noticeably to circumscribe and displace private ordering, to legalize the society, to rationalize it in the sense in which the great industrial consolidators spoke of rationalizing the economy * * *." * * *

When Bickel describes the Warren Court's themes as simplistic, zealously pursued absolutes designed to remake society on the basis of enforced mass equality, he does not attempt to hide his own sharp, single-minded disapproval. "I should say," he says, "that in my view the Court's majoritarianism is ill-conceived, egalitarianism is a worthy ideal but not in all circumstances a self-evident virtue, and centralized, unmitigatedly legalitarian government bears the seed of tyranny." * * * The inevitable result, according to Bickel, is a rigid and stifling uniformity. * * * In his own ideology, the primary value seems to be the "rich" diversity and freedom of private ordering. In any event, his view is that society is so subtle and complex an organism that it cannot be molded to any theory of man. Reason, legal or otherwise, is too blunt and unsure an instrument. * * *

It is only when the Warren Court is viewed from this profoundly conservative perspective, however, that its work appears dangerously radical and absolutist. * * * [T]he Warren Court did not bring us to Armageddon. The Court was not a grand planner or master builder, working from a blueprint of the new society. Bickel's characterization of the Justices' thematic program and approach is, in a word, inaccurate. * * * If the Court's efforts toward greater individual dignity, privacy, and more nearly fair and equal treatment for all were described appropriately in terms of degree, I have little doubt that most of us would accept whatever sacrifices of diversity and private ordering were involved. * * *

When we examine the evidence Professor Bickel himself marshals to support his approach, the radical specter begins to disappear. Take egalitarianism. * * * [W]hat indication is there that the idea ran riot through the Court's decisions? Bickel relies on two lines of cases: those ensuring equal treatment for black people, and those granting a measure of equality for the indigent. But one looks in vain through the cases cited for evidence to make out the charge that the Justices were latter-day socialist levelers. * * * Free access to the vote and to legal assistance surely does not imply a requirement that all monetary barriers fall to the ground. The Court's effort was designed to bring the poor up to a minimum standard. At most, a minimal equality of opportunity—rather than egalitarianism—would be the appropriate characterization, surely one with fewer revolutionary connotations.

"Egalitarianism" may be a more accurate description of the Court's attitude toward cases involving racial discrimination. But if it be egalitarianism, it is directed, and limited, to a very special and historic evil; surely where racial discrimination is at issue any less would be insufficient. * * *

"Majoritarianism," says Bickel, "is heady stuff. It is, in truth, a tide flowing with the swiftness of a slogan * * *. The tide is apt to sweep over all institutions, seeking its level everywhere." * * * But where is the deluge? All that Bickel can point to is the one-man, one-vote decisions and the decisions enlarging the electorate and reducing permissible qualifications for voting. * * * This emphasis on equal voting rights, according to the Professor, frustrates the true genius of our political system—the pluralist giving and taking, wheeling and dealing of myriad interest groups. But the Court has in no way banned pluralist politics. Interest groups and lobbies can operate as always; they need not secure majority support before they bring pressure to bear on the community's representatives. What the Court has actually done is considerably less dramatic than Professor Bickel's imaginings. It has insisted that when the vote—the ordinary man's one chance to play a role in the direction of public affairs—is at stake, there must be a very heavy presumption against any distinctions that would exclude or disadvantage any group substantially interested in the outcome of the election in question. * * *

The last two themes identified by Bickel are centralization and legalization. Both, he says, undermined the diversity and freedom of local and private decisionmaking. * * *

The one decision to which Bickel often refers in substantiating his centralization charge is Katzenbach v. Morgan, enlarging the power of Congress to expand and enforce the guarantees of the fourteenth amendment. That decision did allow Congress to override the "experimentation" by local governments with the rights of disadvantaged minorities. Whether or not such experiments are to be highly valued, their sacrifice to federal control is simply part of a trend in being long before the advent of the Warren Court. The only new element in this incremental step is the purpose for which central power may be exercised. At least, we may demand consistency of Professor Bickel: why is it that the cost of centralization in Morgan is so disturbing, while the radical enlargement of congressional commerce clause powers earns only his praise? What is at stake is not really centralization per se, but the particular "rich diversity" whereby some minorities in some localities may be systematically victimized. * * *

Legalization, too, is something of a red herring. Professor Bickel's unkind words here are reserved for the decisions "substantially loosen[ing] the definition of a lawsuit * * * open[ing] the door wider to more litigants, and * * * making the lawsuit something of a formality, still an expensive one, but within the reach of just about all who can afford it, at just about any time of their choice." * * * Of course it is true that during the Warren years the champions of racial, economic, and other disadvantaged minorities turned more and more to the lawsuit as an instrument of reform. Again, however, Bickel's opposition to these trends demonstrates his lack of perspective on the whole legal system and apparent unconcern for what freedoms and what diversity are at stake. The lawsuit has always been a ready and effective instrument of the rich and powerful, seeking to protect their own interests. Why, then, is it so disturbing when the lawsuit may be almost as readily employed to enforce more fully the Constitution? * * *

Why is it that Bickel fails to see the possibility of a middle ground when discussing decisions of the Warren Court? * * *

The best explanation for these excesses lies in the recognition that the scholarly tradition now is in fact but a part of the western conservative tradition. At least since the French Revolution, it has been characteristic of conservatives to combat the forces of change by misrepresenting their program, by summoning up horrible disasters said to follow from liberal reform, and by depicting the liberals as extreme totalitarians. This reaction has been particularly prevalent when the change involved would enforce for the underprivileged many the rights which have long been enjoyed by the privileged few. The liberal tradition, on the other hand, has been based on a faith in the powers of man to adjust institutions, without making them totalitarian, in the interest of equal justice. * * *

V

* * * Professor Bickel * * * purports to follow a value-neutral approach. Thus, he attacks the Court's work in the fields of racial segregation and legislative reapportionment not because the results are "wrong" but because the results will not be "historically vindicated." * * *

Bickel hears

> in increasing volume notes that amount to another tune. There is in being a reaction to the steady unification and nationalization of recent years, a movement toward a decentralization and a diversity * * * A striving for diversity is not necessarily in express conflict with the goal of an egalitarian society, but it connotes a different order of priorities. In politics, even as the Warren Court's virtually irresistible slogan—one man, one vote—may still be mouthed on all sides, the cry is for a group participation which presupposes, whether it knows it or not, the Madisonian more than the majoritarian model, and for a process calculated to heed the expression not only of desires and preferences, but of intensities that no ballot can register.

At the outset it is appropriate to ask whether Bickel's test—which he says the Court's greatest work fails—is a proper one. He seems wholehearted in his acceptance of history as the final judge: "If the [Warren Court's] bet [on the future trend of events] pays off, whatever their analytical failings, the Justices will have won everything." The value-neutrality of this approach must be particularly appealing to the Professor * * *.

> [Wright urges, however, that there is more to Constitutional jurisprudence than letting history be the judge. He takes as his example what might have happened had the South won the civil war.]

Should a different outcome on the Civil War battlefields really make us approve *Dred Scott?* If Taney's Court had made apartheid its overriding principle, and apartheid had actually come to pass in America, would the judicial result be any more defensible? * * * The ultimate test of the Justices' work, I suggest, must be goodness, not a cynically defined success. Since Bickel purports to believe that "justice" and "injustice" are no more than passing societal value choices of no inherent and true meaning, he is left with history and chance victories on the battlefield as his only guide * * *.

Moreover, even if we accept Bickel's historical test, we can still question its application. Perhaps the Professor ought to have taken his own advice to the Court before so confidently assessing which way the wind is blowing. Thus it may be significant that Bickel's Holmes Lectures were written to be delivered in the spring of 1969—now almost two years ago. They were probably drafted in 1968. That, indeed, was the year * * * Senators Kennedy and McCarthy (for whom Professor Bickel did campaign work) spoke eloquently of returning decisionmaking power to localities. Also in 1968, the New York City school decentralization movement had just reached its high water mark. * * * Two years later, however, Bickel's confident predictions are less convincing. With a new administration in power, the focus of attention seems to have turned. There is still much talk of decentralization, but it is more often meant as a redistribution of power to the states rather than to the local communities of which Bickel speaks. * * *

* * * Even if Professor Bickel has foreseen the trend of opinion, it is not clear that the school desegregation and voting decisions are either irrelevant to or incompatible with that trend. His technique of argument—a common one among followers of the scholarly tradition—is * * * to extend nascent principles far beyond what was intended by the Court. Yet at the same time that Bickel exhibits this failing in depicting some of the Court's greatest decisions as roadblocks to new reform, he takes far too narrow a view of the same decisions in arguing their irrelevance.

Thus, Bickel identifies two principles or ideals running through the school desegregation cases. The first is a condemnation on fourteenth amendment grounds of state-established racial segregation. The second relates only to education, and seems to view the public school system as pursuing a great, assimilationist mission in American society. * * * Professor Bickel's argument is that if the assimilationist ideal is carried to its most extreme conclusion, it will come into direct conflict with the * * * [current trends toward Community Control in education], by requiring centralization of school districts to end de facto segregation and by outlawing tuition grant schemes and private schools. But if the assimilationist ideal is not carried all the way and mere disestablishment prevails, he says, the school desegregation decisions will become irrelevant to the burning issues of the day. It is a heads-I-win, tails-you-lose type of argument.

It is almost too obvious to point out that the extremes of mere disestablishment and total assimilation do not exhaust all possible future uses of the school desegregation cases. * * * The Court could well stop short of requiring centralized school districts, but go beyond mere disestablishment to deal with de facto segregation. Familiar and effective possibilities include judicial review of zoning and new school location decisions by local school authorities. It would not be unprincipled for the Court to recognize that city, town, or county jurisdictions are appropriate for school administration purposes and that the cost of altering these jurisdictions by judicial order would outweigh the assimilationist benefit. The Justices are not blind to the advantages of decentralization. * * * Thus the Court might well hold that when zoning and location adjustments fail to achieve acceptably integrated schools, there is a particularly heavy burden on local boards to allocate educational resources equally among all schools. * * *

The tuition grant and private school problem may be more difficult. But it might be sufficient to command simply that if tuition grants are to be made, the schools which receive the resulting public funds must encourage interracial membership or establish fair racial quotas. Such requirements would not disturb the main, legitimate goal of tuition grants:

the sponsorship of diverse educational opportunities and free choice among them. Private schools, not receiving public funds, might be dealt with by forbidding racially discriminatory admission practices under the thirteenth amendment. Again, the most important free choice and diversity values to be served would remain unaffected while gross evasion of school integration would be controlled. * * *

* * * Perhaps Professor Bickel is bored with the problem, but it is still very much with us, and the line of decisions following *Brown* will continue to be applied in the South long after the executive branch has found it politically expedient to abandon the victims of racial segregation. Some day, we may hope, this horrible scar will be healed and the school desegregation decisions will be cited and applied less often. Even then, however, to call them "irrelevant" is extraordinarily callous and reflects a thorough lack of historical understanding. * * *

Bickel is no more convincing when he attacks the Warren Court's voting decisions. * * *

Let us begin with irrelevance. Bickel argues, as usual, that the drawing of district lines is a highly complex and unruly problem of pluralist politics. District boundaries are drawn and can be evaluated only in terms of which minority groups gain power and which lose power thereby. The Court's past emphasis on equality in voting, Bickel says, is of no use in dealing with this distinctly pluralist, group-oriented question. It is true, of course, that one man, one vote does not provide an automatic answer to the district boundary problem. But the basic ideal underlying the reapportionment cases is by no means irrelevant. That ideal, as has been mentioned, is equality of political opportunity: every citizen should have a roughly equivalent opportunity of access to the formal levers of political power. The difficulty, of course, is devising an administrable rule whereby this ideal may be applied to the gerrymandering problem. One far-reaching solution would be to require a system of proportional representation. Such a system would seem to serve best Professor Bickel's concern with group representation. For no legislative body can catalogue the citizenry into interest groups as well as the citizens can themselves, and no malapportionment program of the sort Bickel advocates can as effectively translate the size of highly fluid interest groups into the proper degree of actual representation as a system that adjusts a group's representation to the support it actually receives in particular elections. * * *

Yet even short of required proportional representation, some judicial controls could be imposed on gerrymandering that would serve the pluralists' concerns. The rule of thumb would be largely negative. It would prohibit the most egregiously unfair forms of districting by demanding at the very least that only neutral criteria, such as existing jurisdictional or natural boundaries, be employed. An exception might be allowed for non-neutral boundaries which can be demonstrated to be plainly "benign" such as boundaries providing some representation for a minority group that would otherwise be submerged entirely. * * *

Just as Bickel is too quick to dismiss any connection between the reapportionment cases and the district boundary problem, he too hastily assumes that a slippery doctrinal slope will frustrate experiments in federated local government. Whether school decentralization is achieved or not, he says, a federated central administrative board would be desirable. He goes on to argue that the formation of such a board would be "politically infeasible" unless it were malapportioned—giving each neighborhood school district equal representation despite unequal population. Similarly, he argues that metropolitan government of city and suburbs would be "politically infeasible" unless malapportioned, so that neither the city nor the suburbs had permanent majority control. We have reached a strange state of affairs when a spokesman for the scholarly tradition judges constitutional principles according to the "political feasibility" of achieving certain desired results in compliance with them. Nevertheless, it is not divinely ordained that the one man, one vote rule must inexorably apply to such federated administrative bodies. If Professor Bickel can see the desirability of encouraging such developments, so can the Justices. * * *

* * *

Bickel's * * * attack * * * illustrates another hidden truth about the scholarly tradition. Shifting ground from "goodness" to "success," he aspires to a neutral, scientific viewpoint; he seeks to demonstrate that the clash between himself and the Warren Court is not one of conflicting value choices, but of fundamental method. Perhaps to some extent it is. However, we may stop to wonder why Bickel chose only to attack the school desegregation and reapportionment cases on the ground of impending obsolescence, while ignoring the one body of decisions which most clearly are at odds with a discernible trend of opinion and events: the criminal procedure cases. He quite clearly provides the answer earlier in the book where he notes his satisfaction with those decisions. Yet if neutrally defined success, and not goodness, were truly at the heart of his creed, he would have to condemn them too. Instead, Bickel manifests interest only in those trends of public opinion of which he personally approves. It is useful, then, to pierce the veil of the scholarly tradition and to see its quarrel with the Warren Court for what it really is. It is, I believe, a fundamental dispute over the good society as well as over judicial method. * * * If the debate is over the true meaning and scope of particular constitutional protections, we should get on with it and avoid for a time the back roads and alleyways of theoretical methodology.

VI

* * * How is the general approach of Professor Bickel and his colleagues in the scholarly tradition likely to relate to the concerns of the new generation of lawyers?

* * * Most of their teachers had first come to see and understand the Court and the Constitution during the New Deal years—an experience which could only serve to corroborate the positions taken by the progressive realists. Thus they generally sought to school their students of the 1960's in a mode of criticism surely appropriate to the Old Court, but of doubtful relevance to the Warren Court. The students could not help but feel the tension since, for them, the Supreme Court was the Warren Court. For them, there was no theoretical gulf between the law and morality; and, for them, the Court was the one institution in the society that seemed to be speaking most consistently the language of idealism which we all recited in grade school. Just as they had not lived through the Stalin era and so could not accept the conventional wisdom of the Cold War, so their coming to consciousness in the 1960's left them unscarred by worries of Court packing and judicial obstructionism. Instead, they were inspired by the dignity and moral courage of a man and an institution that was prepared to act on the ideals to which America is theoretically and rhetorically dedicated.

* * * [T]he new generation of lawyers—the new professors as well as judges and practitioners, I might add—see no point in querulous admonitions that the Court should restrain itself from combatting injustice now in order to preserve itself to combat a coup later on. An institution that sits back, always emphasizing its weakness and its reasons for inaction, is unlikely to be in a fighting stance when the tanks roll down Pennsylvania Avenue. The young lawyers know that a country which hoards all of its moral capital in the form of windy rhetoric is likely to die rich—and soon.

Those of us well over thirty may grumble about naiveté and tell ourselves that experience will make the young lawyers more cynical, more cautious, more protective of fragile institutions and tolerant of diversity. Those are the values of the tradition we grew up in. But if it is true that men and women form very basic attitudes, presumptions, and cognitive frameworks in their late 'teens and early twenties, then no amount of experience will substantially dull the inspiration of the 1960's. The students of this decade will never come to value the "unruliness of affairs" for its own sake; for them, there is little charm in an interminable discussion of the complexity and subtlety of life and of how resistant it is to rational solution. They have seen that affairs can be ordered in conformance to constitutional ideals and that injustice—to which *they* are prepared to give powerful meaning—can be routed. They have seen that it can be done: the Warren Court did it and the heavens did not fall.

NOTES AND QUESTIONS

1. Are you able to determine what, precisely, causes the passionate disagreement between Wright and the adherents to the "scholarly tradition?" You have only been exposed at first-hand to the work of Wechsler, but Wright does an accurate job of portraying the thought of Bickel. Based on what you have been able to determine about the thought of these men, is Wright's point well taken that the Court's "scholarly critics" refuse to evaluate "principle as a matter of principle?" Is it true, as Judge Wright charges, that "Wechsler and his followers" advocate a "synthesis of 'value free' values?" Judge Wright suggests that Professor Bickel (and, by implication, Professor Wechsler) resist "the temptation to approve judicial protection of civil rights and liberties." Is this a "temptation" that any right-thinking person ought to resist? Do Bickel and Wechsler really resist? Has Wright fairly characterized their jurisprudence? Judge Wright brushes aside many of the theoretical strictures of the scholarly critics with the observation that "the most important value choices have already been made by the framers of the Constitution." Does this solve the problem? Would Wechsler and Bickel agree with the assertion?

2. Do you understand Judge Wright to be suggesting that the task of the courts is to discern the meaning that the framers put on Constitutional terms, and then to implement that meaning? In other words, is Wright suggesting that the simple task of the courts is to implement the "original understanding" of Constitutional terms? This view has been advanced, from time to time, as a means of getting around the problem of "legitimating" the inherently undemocratic institution of judicial review. Its proponents might range all the way from the framers themselves, like Alexander Hamilton, to latter-day observers, like Raoul Berger. See Berger, Government by Judiciary (1977). For a strong dissent to the view that "original understanding" should govern, made along the jurisprudential lines suggested by Judge Wright, see Michael J. Perry, The Constitution, the Courts, and Human Rights (1982). For further development of the originalist argument see, e.g., Robert Bork, The Tempting of America: The Political Seduction of the Law (1990), Earl M. Maltz, "The Failure of Attacks on Constitutional Originalism," 4 Constitutional Commentary 43 (1987), and Stephen B. Presser, Recapturing the Constitution: Race, Religion, and Abortion Reconsidered (1994). For the declaration that the "originalist crusade" has been defeated, see Morton Horwitz, "Forward: The Constitution of Change: Legal Fundamentality Without Fundamentalism," 107 Harv.L.Rev. 30, 117 (1993).

3. Does Wright really feel any need to legitimate the policy-making role of the Court? Is the real issue between Wright and the "scholarly critics" joined in the penultimate section of Wright's piece (Section V), where he states that the scholarly critics subscribe to what he calls a "conservative ideology?" What does Wright mean by this term? In part of this section Judge Wright poses the question whether "If Taney's court had made apartheid its overriding principle, and apartheid had actually come to pass in America, would the judicial result be any more defensible?" Is it possible to answer that question in any manner other than negatively? Is Wright thus seeking to

accuse the scholarly critics of advocating apartheid? Does he mean simply to imply that the Taney court had made apartheid an unacknowledged principle of its decision in *Dred Scott*? Would he have been correct if that was his assertion?

4. What does Wright mean when he concludes that "the ultimate test of the Justices' work, I suggest, must be goodness, not a cynically-defined success?" Are you in favor of a system of constitutional jurisprudence with "goodness" as its touchstone? How might one determine what "goodness" was? In any event, Wright's analysis seems to have struck a somewhat responsive chord in at least some sectors of the academic community. See White, "The Evolution of Reasoned Elaboration: Jurisprudential Criticism and Social Change," 59 Va.L.Rev. 279, 298–302 (1973). For a spirited defense of the jurisprudence of the Warren Court, which seems to track some of the suggestions made by White, see Archibald Cox, The Role of The Supreme Court in American Government (1976) and Cox, The Warren Court (1968). Cox (and White) suggest that it is entirely appropriate for the Supreme Court to formulate social policy in the guise of determining constitutional law, so long as the Justices stay close to the "aspirations" that "the community is willing not only to avow but in the end to live by." Cox, The Role of the Supreme Court, at 118. Does this make sense? Or would you subscribe to the objections (to which Wechsler was responding) raised by Learned Hand:

> For myself it would be most irksome to be ruled by a bevy of Platonic Guardians, even if I knew how to choose them, which I assuredly do not. If they were in charge, I should miss the stimulus of living in a society where I have, at least theoretically, some part in the direction of public affairs. Of course, I know how illusory would be the belief that my vote determined anything; but nevertheless when I go to the polls I have a satisfaction in the sense that we are all engaged in a common venture.

Hand, The Bill of Rights 73–74 (1959), quoted by Cox, at 116.

5. As his final answer to the question whether the "rule of law" is an "unqualified human good", Professor Horwitz has declared that an affirmative answer is possible "Only if Hitler, Stalin, and all the other horrors of this century have forced us finally to accept the Hobbesian vision of the state and human nature on which our present conceptions of the rule of law ultimately rest. It *is* a conservative doctrine." Horwitz, "The Rule of Law: An Unqualified Human Good?," 86 Yale L.J. 561, 566 (1977). From what you know of American Constitutional Law in the late twentieth century, would you say that the "Hobbesian vision" and the "rule of law" predominate? In the next Chapter we turn our attention to private law, as we did in Chapter Three, but the questions of adherence to equitable principles and/or the rule of law remain. In other words, the argument that is suggested in these materials is that the jurisprudential methodologies and values from Constitutional or Public Law (as we have studied in the work of the Warren Court, its critics such as Hand, Wechsler, and Bickel, and its defenders, such as Horwitz and Judge Wright) spilled over into the treatment of late-twentieth century pri-

vate law. See if you buy this argument, and see if you can determine what remains of "legal science" in the private law matters you will be studying. We will return, albeit briefly, to Constitutional Law in a concluding section.

CHAPTER 7

PRIVATE LAW PRESENT AND FUTURE: TOWARDS A WELFARE STATE?

■ ■ ■

A. THE END OF CONTRACT AS WE KNEW IT?

GRANT GILMORE, THE DEATH OF CONTRACT*

6–15, 17–21, 57–72, 74–76, 87–90, 94–98, 102–103 (1974).

In a remarkable recent book,** Professor Lawrence Friedman has contributed some novel insights into the nature of what he calls the "pure" or "classical" theory of contract, by which he refers to the theory as it developed in the nineteenth century. * * *

* * *

* * * Although we shall depart from his analysis at some points, we may retain as central ideas the concept of the general law of contract as a residual category—what is left over after all the "specialized" bodies of law have been added up—highly abstract, in close historical relationship with the free market of classical economic theory, a theoretical construct which, having little or nothing to do with the real world, would not—or could not—change as the real world changed. Professor Friedman goes on to comment on another significant aspect of the contract construct—which is that it resisted, and continues to resist, codification long after most, if not all, of the fields of law apparently most closely related to it had passed under the statutory yoke. * * *

Asked to locate the law of contract on the legal spectrum, most of us, I assume, would place it in the area usually denominated Commercial Law. It is true that our unitary contract theory has always had an uncomfortable way of spilling over into distinctly non-commercial situations and that what may be good for General Motors does not always make sense when applied to charitable subscriptions, antenuptial agreements and promises to convey the family farm provided the children will support the

** Lawrence Friedman, Contract Law in America (1965).

old people for life. But we feel instinctively that commercial law is the heart of the matter and that, the need arising, the commercial rules can be applied over * * * to fit, for example, the case of King Lear and his unruly daughters. * * *

* * *

I have credited Dean Langdell with the almost inadvertent discovery of the general theory of Contract. The reference was to his pioneering casebook on Contracts which appeared just a hundred years ago and, even more, to the "Summary of the Law of Contracts" which he added as an appendix to the second edition of the casebook in 1880. * * *

To judge by the casebook and the Summary, Langdell was an industrious researcher of no distinction whatever. * * *

But it is with Langdell that, for the first time, we see Contract as a remote, impersonal, bloodless abstraction. The three principal chapters into which the casebook is divided are entitled: Mutual Assent, Consideration and Conditional Contracts * * *. The casebook, according to Langdell, was to contain all the important contract cases that had ever been decided. "All the cases" turned out to be mostly English cases, arranged in historical sequence from the seventeenth century down to the date of publication; the English cases were occasionally supplemented by comparable sequences of cases from New York and Massachusetts. * * * The Summary, which runs to a hundred and fifty pages or so, is devoted almost entirely to explaining which of the cases in the main part of the casebook are "right" and which are "wrong." The explanation, typically, is dogmatic rather than reasoned; Langdell knew right from wrong, no doubt by divine revelation, and that should suffice for the student. * * *

* * * The [general] theory [of contract] itself was [not really Langdell's unique contribution but was] pieced together by his successors—notably Holmes, in broad philosophical outline, and Williston, in meticulous, although not always accurate, scholarly detail. At this point it is necessary to give some idea of the content of what we may call the Holmes–Williston construct. * * * Having accomplished that chore, we can return to the far more interesting business of speculating on why Langdell's idea, brilliantly reformulated by Holmes, had the fabulous success it did instead of going down the drain into oblivion as a hundred better ideas than Langdell's do every day of the week.

The theory seems to have been dedicated to the proposition that, ideally, no one should be liable to anyone for anything. Since the ideal was not attainable, the compromise solution was to restrict liability within the narrowest possible limits. Within those limits, however, liability was to be absolute. * * * Liability, although absolute—at least in theory—was nevertheless, to be severely limited. The equitable remedy of specific performance was to be avoided so far as possible. * * * Money damages for breach of contract were to be "compensatory," never punitive; Holmes explained that every man has a right "to break his contract if he chooses"—that is, a right to elect to pay damages instead of performing his contractual obligation. Therefore the wicked contract-breaker should pay no more in damages that the innocent and the pure in heart. * * *

* * *

Where did the idea for this curious—one is tempted to say, monstrous—machine come from? It is fair to say that the theory of contract represented a sharp break with the past, even the recent past. The inventors of the theory did not make it all up out of their own heads. Indeed they made industrious use of whatever bits and pieces of case law, old and new, could be made to fit the theory. Such cases were immediately promoted to "leading cases" and made to fit—in much the same way that Procrustes made his guests fit. Cases which could not be made to fit were ignored or dismissed, with Langdellian certitude, as "wrong." On the whole, however, the theory was in its origins, and continued to be during its life, an ivory tower abstraction. Its natural habitat was the law schools, not the law courts. And yet * * * the theory was an instant and spectacular success. Generations of lawyers and judges and law professors grew up believing that the theory was true * * *.

The balance-wheel of the great machine was the theory of consideration. * * * The word "consideration" has been around for a long time, but * * * until the nineteenth century the word never acquired any particular meaning or stood for any theory. * * * [Until about the turn of the eighteenth century "consideration" may have served simply as evidence that there was a serious intent to bargain present. At about that time, however, the English courts began trying to "explain" consideration.] A formula which became fashionable put it in terms of benefit and detriment. If a promisor received any benefit from a transaction, that was sufficient consideration to support his promise. On the other hand, if a promisee suffered any detriment, that, likewise, was sufficient to support the promise. Any benefit would do; any detriment would do. * * *

The new day dawned, with Holmes * * * :

* * *

> It appears to me that it has not always been sufficiently borne in mind that the same thing may be a consideration or not, as it is dealt with by the parties * * *.
>
> * * * It is hard to see the propriety of erecting any detriment which an instrument may disclose or provide for, into a consideration, unless the parties have dealt with it on that footing. * * * The detriment may be nothing but a condition precedent to performance, as where a man promises another to pay him five hundred dollars if he breaks

his leg. * * * It is the essence of a consideration, that, by the terms of the agreement, it is given and accepted as the motive or inducement for furnishing the consideration. The root of the whole matter is the relation of reciprocal conventional inducement, each for the other, between consideration and promise.

Now the vulgar error that any benefit or any detriment would do has been exploded. * * * No matter how much detriment a promisee may have suffered, he has not, thereby, necessarily furnished a consideration. Nor does he have, so far as Holmes takes us, any right to redress or even any claim on our sympathies, no matter how reasonable his detrimental reliance may have been, not even if, in the course of incurring his detriment, he has conferred a benefit on the other party. Absent "consideration," the unhappy promisee has no right or claim. And nothing is "consideration" unless "the parties have dealt with it on that footing." * * *

It seems perfectly clear that Holmes was, quite consciously, proposing revolutionary doctrine * * *. His analysis of the true meaning of "consideration" comes forth almost naked of citation of authority or precedent. * * *

There is never any point in arguing with a successful revolution. * * * The "bargain" theory of consideration, proposed by Holmes, is enshrined in the definition of consideration in § 75 of the original Restatement of Contracts * * *.

With the Holmesian formulation, consideration became a tool for narrowing the range of contractual liability. "The whole doctrine of contract," he noted in this connection, "is formal and external." Unless the formalities were accomplished, there could be no contract and, consequently, no liability. The austerity of doctrine would not be tempered for the shorn lambs who might shiver in its blast.

* * *

* * * I have credited Holmes and Williston* with the design and execution of the great theory. It is tempting to set Cardozo and Corbin over against them as the engineers of its destruction. * * * Cardozo's attack was subtle, evasive, hesitant * * *. Corbin's attack was more forthright. * * * [H]is treatise on Contracts—which I will describe as the greatest law book ever written—bears the publication date: 1950. It is true that, by 1950, the ideas and the reforms which Corbin argued for were no longer particularly novel * * *. We forget that Corbin—perhaps unwisely—had spent the better part of fifty years readying the treatise for publication. * * * So resituated in time, Corbin's attack on the prevailing orthodoxy assumes revolutionary proportions.

* The author of a great multi-volume treatise on Contracts, and the chief "Reporter" of the original Restatement of Contracts, a computation of the case-law rules. Williston's ideas on Contract are much the same as those of Holmes.

Corbin's abiding interest was in what he called the "operative facts" of cases: * * *

> [A] sufficient reason for comparative historical study of cases in great number is the fact that such study frees the teacher and the lawyer and the judge from the illusion of certainty; and from the delusion that law is absolute and eternal, that doctrines can be used mechanically, and that there are correct and unchangeable definitions.

Evidently we have entered a universe of discourse which simply has no meeting point with the Holmesian universe in which the doctrine of contract was, and was meant to be "wholly formal and external." * * *

We must now deal with the mysterious episode of the Restatements. * * * The Restatement project [begun in the early 1920's] can be taken as the almost instinctive reaction of the legal establishment of the time to the attack of the so-called legal realists. What the realists had principally attacked, savagely and successfully, was the essentially Langdellian idea that cases can be arranged to make sense—indeed scientific sense. * * * [I]n the 1920's there was still hope that the revolution could be put down, that unity of doctrine could be maintained and that an essentially pure case law system could be preserved from further statutory encroachment. * * * The conservative response, which, looked on as a delaying action, was remarkably successful, was the provision of Restatements of Contracts, Torts, Property and the like.

Williston and Corbin were unquestionably the dominant intellectual influences in the drafting of the *Restatement of Contracts* * * *. No doubt it was their joint participation which insured the extraordinarily high technical quality of the product * * *. No doubt it was also their joint participation—bearing in mind that Williston and Corbin held antithetical points of view on almost every conceivable point of law—that accounts for the [Restatement's fascinatingly] schizophrenic quality * * *.

* * *

* * * The first lesson will be the *Restatement's* definition of consideration (§ 75) taken in connection with its most celebrated section—§ 90, captioned Promise Reasonably Inducing Definite and Substantial Action.

First § 75:

(1) Consideration for a promise is

(a) an act other than a promise, or

(b) a forbearance, or

(c) the creation, modification or destruction of a legal relation, or

(d) a return promise, bargained for and given in exchange for the promise.

* * *

This is, of course, pure Holmes. * * * [Section 90, however, provides:]

A promise which the promisor should reasonably expect to induce action or forbearance of a definite and substantial character on the part of the promisee and which does induce such action or forbearance is binding if injustice can be avoided only by enforcement of the promise.

And what is that all about? We have become accustomed to the idea * * * that the universe includes both matter and antimatter. Perhaps what we have here is Restatement and anti-Restatement or Contract and anti-Contract. * * * The one thing that is clear is that these two contradictory propositions cannot live comfortably together: in the end one must swallow the other up.

* * * When the Restaters and their advisors came to the definition of consideration, Williston proposed in substance what became § 75. Corbin submitted a quite different proposal. To understand what the Corbin proposal was about, it is necessary to backtrack somewhat. Even after the Holmesian or bargain theory of consideration had won all but universal acceptance, the New York Court of Appeals had, during the Cardozo period, pursued a line of its own. * * * Cardozo's opinions express what might be called an expansive theory of contract. Courts should make contracts wherever possible, rather than the other way around. Missing terms can be supplied. If an express promise is lacking, an implied promise can easily be found.[139] In particular Cardozo delighted in weaving gossamer spider webs of consideration. There was consideration for a father's promise to pay his engaged daughter an annuity after marriage in the fact that the engaged couple, instead of breaking off the engagement, had in fact married.[140] There was consideration for a pledge to a college endowment campaign * * * in the fact that the college, by accepting the pledge, had come under an implied duty to memorialize the donor's name * * *.[141] Evidently a judge who could find "consideration" in De Cicco v. Schweizer or in the *Allegheny College* case could, when he was so inclined, find consideration anywhere * * *. Corbin, who had been deeply influenced by Cardozo, proposed to the Restaters what might be called a Cardozoean definition of consideration—broad, vague and, essentially, meaningless

---

139 Wood v. Lucy, Lady Duff–Gordon, 222 N.Y. 88, 118 N.E. 214 (1917). * * *

140 De Cicco v. Schweizer, 221 N.Y. 431, 117 N.E. 807 (1917). * * *

141 Allegheny College v. National Chautauqua Bank, 246 N.Y. 369, 377, 159 N.E. 173 (1927). [There is a superb and witty treatment of *Allegheny College,* pursuing some of Gilmore's themes, in Alfred S. Konefsky, "How to Read, or at Least Not Misread, Cardozo in the *Allegheny College* Case," 36 Buff.L.Rev. 645 (1988).].

* * *. In the debate Corbin and the Cardozoeans lost out to Williston and the Holmesians. * * *

* * * Corbin returned to the attack. At the next meeting of the Restatement group, he addressed them more or less in the following manner: Gentlemen * * *, [y]ou have recently adopted a definition of consideration. I now submit to you a list of cases—hundreds, perhaps, or thousands?—in which courts have imposed contractual liability under circumstances in which, according to your definition, there would be no consideration and therefore no liability. Gentlemen, what do you intend to do about these cases?

* * * [Indeed, g]oing back into the past, there was an indefinite number of cases which had imposed liability, in the name of consideration, where nothing like Holmes's "reciprocal conventional inducement" was anywhere in sight. Holmes's point was that these were bad cases and that the range of contractual liability should be confined within narrower limits. By the turn of the century, except in New York, the strict bargain theory of consideration had won general acceptance. But, unlike Holmes, many judges, it appeared, were not prepared to look with stony-eyed indifference on the plight of a plaintiff who had, to his detriment, relied on a defendant's assurances without the protection of a formal contract. However, the new doctrine precluded the judges * * * from saying * * * that the "detriment" itself was "consideration." They had to find a new solution * * *. In such a situation the word that comes instinctively to the mind of any judge is, of course, "estoppel"—which is simply a way of saying that, for reasons which the court does not care to discuss, there must be judgment for plaintiff. And [as Corbin observed,] in the contract cases after 1900 the word "estoppel," modulating into such phrases as "equitable estoppel" and "promissory estoppel," began to appear with increasing frequency.

The Restaters, honorable men, * * * instead of reopening the debate on the consideration definition, * * * elected to stand by § 75 but to add a new section—§ 90—incorporating the estoppel idea although without using the word "estoppel." The extent to which the new section § 90 was to be allowed to undercut the underlying principle of § 75 was left entirely unresolved. * * * [Indeed, concerning] the mysterious text of § 90 itself, * * * no one had any idea what the damn thing meant.

* * * The *Restatement,* we might say, ended up uneasily poised between past and future, which is no doubt the best thing that could have been done.

The future, of course, won, as it always does. During the past forty years we have seen the effective dismantling of the formal system of classical contract theory. We have witnessed what it does not seem too farfetched to describe as an explosion of liability. * * *

* * * Judge Learned Hand once suggested that § 90 * * * should be restricted to donative or gift promises. Professionals should play the game according to the professional rules. If A, in a commercial context, made what could be described as an offer to B, then A's liability to B should depend on the formal rules of offer, acceptance and consideration and on nothing else. The course of decision has, however, seen a gradual expansion of § 90 as a principle of decision in a good many types of commercial situations.

Such case law developments are reflected in an altogether fascinating manner in the provisions of the so-called *Second Restatement of Contracts.* * * * Why should there be a second series of Restatements? * * * There can be little or no doubt that the first generation of Restaters implicitly assumed that they were reducing to black letter text what we like to call the "fundamental principles of the common law." Now, we are all aware that rules of law change through time but many of us like to think that our "fundamental principles" are eternal and unchanging. * * *

* * * [N]o principles of law, or of anything else, can be guaranteed good past the next revolution. I dare say that no one will dispute the fact that, since the 1930's, there has been a world-wide revolution, scientific, social, economic and political. * * * One of the minor by-products of the revolution through which my own generation has lived will, of necessity, be the reformulation not merely of the specific "principles and rules of the common law" but of our basic attitudes toward the process of law itself. * * * We may take the second series of Restatements as [such a by-product.] * * *

* * *

Restatement (First) § 75 (Definition of Consideration) * * * has not been changed in substance in *Restatement (Second)* § 75. The accompanying Comment has, however, been revised in such a way as to leave no doubt that we are now in an antithetical universe of discourse. The § 75 Comment in *Restatement (First)* began with an authentically Willistonian flourish:

> No duty is generally imposed on one who makes an informal promise unless the promise is supported by sufficient consideration * * *.

The lead to the § 75 Comment in *Restatement (Second)* introduces us to the sound of a much less certain trumpet:

> The word "consideration" has often been used with meanings different from that given here. It is often used merely to express the legal conclusion that a promise is enforceable.

The Comment, we might say, has been Corbinized. The only recognition of the existence of § 90 in the *Restatement (First)* § 75 Comment was the somewhat grudging concession that "some informal promises are enforceable without the element of bargain. These fall and are placed in the category of contracts which are binding without assent or consideration (see §§ 85–94)." Furthermore, Illustration 2 to § 75 in *Restatement (First)* hypothesized that "A promises B $500 when B goes to college" and concluded that "If the promise * * * is reasonably to be understood as a gratuity, payable on the stated contingency, B's going to college is not consideration for A's promise." The § 75 Illustration carried no cross-reference to § 90, where one of the Illustrations was to the effect that an apparently identical "if B goes to college" promise is "binding" on A. [In the revised § 75 Comment in *Restatement (Second)* the "when B goes to college" illustration has been dropped and the following new illustration substituted: "A promises to make a gift of $10 to B. In reliance on the promise B buys a book from C and promises to pay C $10 for it. There is no consideration for A's promise. As to the enforceability of such promises, see § 90.]"

However, the Corbinization of § 75 is quite insignificant compared to what has happened to § 90. Original § 90 * * * was exposed to the world naked of Comment and provided with four ambiguous illustrations as its sole capital. Text and illustration together took up less than a page. Revised § 90 with its Comment and Illustrations runs to over twelve pages and the original four Illustrations have grown to seventeen. * * *

* * * The reliance principle, we are told, may have been, historically, the basis for "the enforcement of informal contracts in the action of assumpsit."

> Certainly [the Comment continues] reliance is one of the main bases for enforcement of the half-completed exchange, and the probability of reliance lends support to the enforcement of the executory exchange * * *. This Section thus states a basic principle which often renders inquiry unnecessary as to the precise scope of the policy of enforcing bargains.

Thus the unwanted stepchild of *Restatement* (*First*) has become "a basic principle" of *Restatement* (*Second*) which, the comment seems to suggest, prevails, in case of need, over the competing "bargain theory" of § 75. The Comment and the new illustrations are entirely clear that the principle of § 90 is applicable in commercial contexts as well as in noncommercial ones * * *.

Clearly enough the unresolved ambiguity in the relationship between § 75 and § 90 in the *Restatement* (*First*) has now been resolved in favor of the promissory estoppel principle of § 90 which has, in effect, swallowed up the bargain principle of § 75. * * *

* * *

[As further evidence of this trend,] a new section * * * has been added to the *Restatement* (*Second*) as § 89A (Promise for Benefit Received). * * *:

(1) A promise made in recognition of benefit previously received by the promisor from the promisee is binding to the extent necessary to prevent injustice.

(2) A promise is not binding under Subsection (1); (a) if the promisee conferred the benefit as a gift or for other reasons the promisor has not been unjustly enriched; or (b) to the extent that its value is disproportionate to the benefit.

This is far from going the whole hog on the unjust enrichment idea. For one thing, the ungrateful recipient may keep whatever he has received without paying for it so long as he is clever enough to avoid making a "promise" to repay. * * * For another thing what Subsection (1) giveth, Subsection (2) largely taketh away: the promise, even if made, will be "binding" only within narrow limits. * * *

Enough has been said to make the point that *Restatement* (*Second*), at least in 89A, is characterized by the same "schizophrenic quality" for which *Restatement* (*First*) was so notable. * * * The principal thing is that *Restatement* (*Second*) gives overt recognition to an important principle whose existence *Restatement* (*First*) ignored and, by implication, denied. * * *

* * *

Speaking descriptively, we might say that what is happening is that "contract" is being reabsorbed into the mainstream of "tort." Until the general theory of contract was hurriedly run up late in the nineteenth century, tort had always been our residual category of civil liability. As the contract rules dissolve, it is becoming so again. * * *

* * * Classical contract theory might well be described as an attempt to stake out an enclave within the general domain of tort. The dykes which were set up to protect the enclave have, it is clear enough, been crumbling at a progressively rapid rate. With the growth of the ideas of quasi-contract and unjust enrichment,* classical consideration theory was breached on the benefit side. With the growth of the promissory estoppel idea,** it was breached on the detriment side. We are fast approaching the point where, to prevent unjust enrichment, any benefit received by a defendant must be paid for unless it was clearly meant as a gift; where any detriment reasonably incurred by a plaintiff in reliance on a defendant's assurances must be recompensed. When that point is reached, there is really no longer any viable distinction between liability in contract and liability in tort. * * * [T]he two fields, which had been artificially set apart, are gradually merging and becoming one.

* * *

* E.g. § 89A of the Restatement (Second).

** E.g. § 90 of Restatements 1 and 2.

We seem to be in the presence of the phenomenon which, in the history of comparative religion, is called syncretism—that is, according to Webster, "the reconciliation or union of conflicting beliefs." I have occasionally suggested to my students that a desirable reform in legal education would be to merge the first-year courses in Contracts and Torts into a single course which we could call Contorts. * * *

* * *

Let us assume, arguendo, that it is the fate of contract to be swallowed up by tort. * * * We must still provide ourselves with an explanation of what contract—the classical or general theory of contract, as we have called it—was about in the first place and, if it is now dead or dying, what caused the fatal disease.

We started with Professor Friedman's suggestion that the "model" of classical contract theory bore a close resemblance to * * * laissez-faire—economic theory. * * * [A]s he put it, "parties could be treated as individual economic units which, in theory, enjoyed complete mobility and freedom of decision." I suppose that laissez-faire economic theory comes down to something like this: If we all do exactly as we please, no doubt everything will work out for the best. * * * [T]he lawyers and the economists, both responding to the same stimuli, produced theoretical systems which were harmonious with each other and which, in both cases, evidently responded to the felt needs of the time.

It seems apparent to the twentieth century mind, as perhaps it did not to the nineteenth century mind, that a system in which everybody is invited to do his own thing, at whatever cost to his neighbor, must work ultimately to the benefit of the rich and powerful, who are in a position to look after themselves and to act, so to say, as their own self-insurers. As we look back on the nineteenth century theories, we are struck most of all, I think, by the narrow scope of social duty which they implicitly assumed. * * * For good or ill, we have changed all that. * * * The decline and fall of the general theory of contract and, in most quarters, of laissez-faire economics may be taken as remote reflections of the transition from nineteenth century individualism to the welfare state and beyond.

* * *

The basic idea of the Langdellian revolution [consistent with the needs and beliefs of that age] seems to have been that there really is such a thing as the one true rule of law, universal and unchanging, always and everywhere the same—a sort of mystical absolute. To all of us, I dare say, the idea seems absurd. We are steeped in the idea that law is process, flux, change; our relativism admits no absolutes. * * *

For a riot of pure doctrine, nothing could have been better than Contract. Since there never had been a general theory of Contract before, there was nothing to inhibit the free play of the creative imagination * * *. Perhaps we must, after all, credit Langdell with a degree of genius for his perhaps instinctive choice of a non-existent field as the vehicle for the initial demonstration of the great theory that law is doctrine and nothing but doctrine—pure, absolute, abstract, scientific—a logician's dream of heaven. * * *

* * *

* * * We have become used to the idea that, in literature and the arts, there are alternating rhythms of classicism and romanticism. During classical periods, which are, typically, of brief duration, everything is neat, tidy and logical; theorists and critics reign supreme * * *. During classical periods, which are, among other things, extremely dull, it seems that nothing interesting is ever going to happen again. But the classical aesthetic, once it has been formulated, regularly breaks down in a protracted romantic agony. The romantics * * * experiment, they improvise; they deny the existence of any rules; they churn around in an ecstacy of self-expression. At the height of a romantic period, everything is confused, sprawling, formless and chaotic—as well as, frequently, extremely interesting. Then, the romantic energy having spent itself, there is a new classical reformulation—and so the rhythms continue.

Perhaps we should admit the possibility of such alternating rhythms in the process of the law. * * * We have gone through our romantic agony—an experience peculiarly unsettling to people intellectually trained and conditioned as lawyers are. It may be that, in this centennial year, some new Langdell is already waiting in the wings * * *. Contract is dead—but who knows what unlikely resurrection the Easter-tide may bring?

NOTES AND QUESTIONS

1. Gilmore does not have much praise to lavish on Christopher Columbus Langdell. He suggests that Langdell had "no distinction," and that Langdell's version of the case method "had nothing to do with getting students to think for themselves" but instead was "a method of indoctrination through brainwashing." Is Gilmore right about Langdell's use of the case method? Does the use of it that you have seen seem different?

2. Gilmore suggests that according to Langdell, Holmes and Williston, the framers of the "classical theory" of contract, "The austerity of doctrine would not be tempered for the shorn lambs who might shiver in its blast." Does this sound like the law of contract that law students are trained in today, or that you are familiar with? Why might anyone conceive of such a law of contract? Does it bear any resemblance to the pre-New Deal constitutional doctrines?

3. Why does Gilmore describe Corbin's treatise on contract law as "the greatest law book ever written?" Do you agree with this characterization? Where does this leave other celebrated law books, like the code of Justinian, Hammurabi's Code, or the Bible?

4. As you have seen, Gilmore suggests that Sections 75 and 90 of the Restatement cannot "live comfortably together," and that "in the end one must swallow the other up." Gilmore states about the framers of the Restatement who wrote Section 90 that "no one had any idea what the damn thing meant." It has been seriously maintained that many of Plato's dialogues can only be understood if they are perceived as pure farce. See, e.g., J.H. Randall, Jr., Plato: Dramatist of the Life of Reason, 124–127 (1970). Can the same be said of Grant Gilmore? What is the view of Professor Speidel, the author of the next excerpt, on this point?

5. Gilmore believes that his generation had lived through "a world-wide revolution, scientific, social, economic and political," and that the second Restatement of Contracts is the product of that Revolution. Is it correct to call what has happened in the last seventy years in America a "revolution"? Does this perhaps impart more legitimacy to the *Second Restatement* (and to the thought of Arthur Corbin?) than might be due if what has happened was *not* a "revolution?" Even if a "revolution" has come about, is it appropriate for the courts and the American Law Institute to implement its philosophy through changes in the law of contract? On the other hand, perhaps, as Professor Gilmore says in a part of this essay not reproduced here, the framers of the *Second Restatement* were merely "articulating the policy of the legislative reforms of the past thirty years or so." Would this cut for or against the legitimacy of the *Second Restatement* in the courts? For a stimulating article which finds an explosion in contract litigation, and appears to place the blame on "the demise of a wasp elite which three decades ago ruled the western world," see William E. Nelson, "Contract Litigation and the Elite Bar in New York City, 1960–1980," 39 Emory L.J. 413 (1990).

6. Would you like to be a student or Professor of "Contorts?" For the provocative report from two law professors who tried, see Jay Feinman and Marc Feldman, "Pedagogy and Politics," 73 Georgetown Law Journal 875 (1985). For some of Professor Feinman's continued thought on the erosion of the barrier between torts and contracts, see, e.g. Jay M. Feinman, "Implied Warranty, Products Liability, and Boundary Between Contract and Tort," 75 Wash.U.L.Q. 469 (1997). For reevaluations of Gilmore's book, see generally "Symposium: Reconsidering Grant Gilmore's *The Death of Contract*," 90 Nw.U.L.Rev. 1 (1995). For the current state of contract at the end of the Twentieth Century, see, e.g., F.H. Buckley, ed., The Fall and Rise of Freedom of Contract (1999) (Collection of essays on current doctrine). One reviewer of the Buckley book summarized developments thusly: "Twenty-five years after Grant Gilmore famously declared it 'dead,' freedom of contract is experiencing a revival in American law. The bargain principle has proven remarkably durable, now extending beyond traditional contracts to govern institutions, like marriage, that once were grounded in status. Courts again refrain from

challenging the substance of parties' agreements, and interpretation again emphasizes the written language. These developments reflect a new formalism that promises (or threatens) to restore the libertarian virtues of contract's classical past." Mark L. Movsesian, "Two Cheers for Freedom of Contract," 23 Cardozo L. Rev. 1529, 1530 (2002). How could a famous academic authority such as Gilmore have gotten it so wrong? Consider the following.

RICHARD E. SPEIDEL, AN ESSAY ON THE REPORTED DEATH AND CONTINUED VITALITY OF CONTRACT*

Speidel, Richard E., An Essay on the Reported Death and Continued Vitality of Contract, 27 Stanford Law Review 1161 (1975).

* * *

* * * To a contracts teacher who is not yet prepared to teach a course in "contorts," Professor Gilmore's gauntlet is painfully visible. So, with biases flying, let us do battle.

I. THE THESIS STATED

* * *

In the 1870's, the idea for a general theory of contract was conceived in Langdell's "casebook" laboratory at the Harvard Law School and, thereafter, was brilliantly reformulated by Holmes in his lectures on the common law and meticulously elaborated by Williston in his multivolume treatise on the law of contracts. The "balance wheel" of the new theory was consideration and the "metaphysical solvent" was the objective test. According to Gilmore, neither "wheel" nor "solvent" was rooted in case law or the real world. One has the impression of a theory conceived in the minds of East Coast magicians, supported by major surgery performed on the existing cases, and honed to a systematic and abstract construct fit only for the cloister or the classroom. And what was worse * * *, "generations of lawyers and judges and law professors grew up believing that the theory was true—and it is our beliefs, however absurd, that condition our actions."

The philosophical roots of this general contract theory lay in Holmes' basic approach to the problem of civil obligation. According to Gilmore, Holmes believed that the scope of liability should be narrow but, once imposed, liability should be absolute. However, absolute liability did not mean unlimited liability. Limitations upon the amount of liability, as well as a narrow scope of duty, were necessary so as not to deter socially useful action. The standards for liability should be "objective"—a failure to measure up to accepted community standards—and devoid of what Gilmore calls "the unnecessary and misleading overlay of moral sententiousness." * * *

* * *

Along with this construct, which narrowed the scope of legal protection, Holmes developed some ideas about damages for breach of contract. * * * Compensatory damages were the rule, specific performance the exception, and punishment to deter breach rarely, if ever, the objective. Holmes went even further. A promisor had a "right" to breach the contract and pay damages. * * *

* * * Why did the theory achieve such an emotional acceptance even though, as Gilmore aptly puts it, the courts frequently avoided doing on weekdays what they so eloquently preached on Sundays? * * *

* * * The clues * * * appear in the book as slogans: "positivism," "individualism," "laissez-faire," "freedom of contract," and "certainty." * * * The combination of doctrinal analysis and these clues leads Gilmore to conclude: "The basic idea of the Langdellian revolution seems to have been that there really is such a thing as the one true rule of law, universal and unchanging, always and everywhere the same—a sort of mystical absolute." * * *

[But a]ccording to Gilmore, * * * the Holmes–Williston construct was unable to survive the "transition from nineteenth century individualism to the welfare state and beyond." * * * Gilmore draws two major and almost gleeful conclusions from these developments. First, contract is dead because the bargain theory of consideration, its balance wheel, no longer rules in the formulation, performance, or adjustment of contracts. * * *

Second, instinctively and almostly unconsciously, contract is being absorbed into the mainstream of a more expansive theory of tort liability. * * *

II. THE THESIS EVALUATED

* * * I have some rather strong reactions to the method, thesis, and conclusions of this book. So I will proceed undaunted to express them, knowing full well that this is precisely what Professor Gilmore would want to happen. At the same time, I confess to an instinctive feeling that he will be amused by all of the reviewers who take him so seriously.

A. *Whatever Happened to 280 Years of American Legal and Economic History?*

* * * Using English cases, secondary sources, and impressionistic clues about the social matrix, * * * [Gilmore] has concluded that Holmes' creation of the bargain theory had little support in law or contemporary reality * * *.

A conclusion which is equally plausible is that 280 years of American economic and legal history had a strong impact upon the announcement, in 1881, of the bargain theory and upon its subsequent development. * * *

The bargain idea has enjoyed a striking persistence in American contract law. This is partially explained, no doubt, by its strong congruence with basic human behavior. * * * But the pervasiveness of this behavior does not fully explain why the concept of bargain and exchange should emerge as the primary legal technique for distinguishing between the enforceable and the unenforceable promise. The primary emphasis could have been placed upon induced reliance, formality (such as the sealed instrument), or ethical considerations rooted in expressions of the individual will.

A partial answer rests in the tangles of Anglo–American economic and legal history. According to Professor Ian Macneil, the "distinctively human" behavior of bargain and exchange flourishes when four conditions are present: (1) specialization of labor and exchange; (2) a sense by individuals of their capacity for choice and the consequences of its exercise; (3) an awareness of the continuum between past, present, and future; and (4) a social matrix which reinforces the exercise of choices made with an eye to the future.[43] * * *

From breakdowns in or excesses of this behavior, whether affecting individual interests or the broader social matrix, the need for contract law develops.

* * * Professor Macneil's four conditions apparently existed in the English trade fairs of the 12th and 13th centuries, for contract behavior flourished at that time. Also, the idea of bargain as a reason for enforcing promises was implicit in the developing common law well before the 17th century. Presumably, contract behavior persisted thereafter in England despite the procedural rigidity and ultimately preemptive quality of the common law. When English people colonized America in the 17th century, they encountered severe challenges to survival and discovered seemingly unlimited opportunities for individual expression and economic growth. In his remarkable A History of American Law, Professor Lawrence Friedman suggests that the colonists brought considerably less of the common law to America than is usually supposed. Instead, many turned to the bargain-oriented customs and practices of the law merchant, which had not yet been fully absorbed by the common law. * * * From the colonial period through the time of "manifest destiny" to the late 19th century, when the economic gains were being consolidated and evaluated, there occurred an explosion of contract behavior. The legal enforcement of promises represented a delegation of public force in the aid of private decisionmaking and, despite its uncertain origins, the doctrine of consid-

[43] Macneil, The Many Futures of Contracts, 47 S.Cal.L.Rev. 691, 696–712 (1974).

eration evolved as a technique for market control. The consideration requirement "induced deliberation in the parties, limited law support to seriously intended undertakings, or refused the law's aid to unconscionable coercion."[49] In short, consideration and the objective test became very practical legal techniques used by courts to facilitate and regulate the important market transaction.

* * * Hurst and Friedman stress the practical uses of a doctrine assumed to mean "bargained for and given in exchange" * * *. As an operating principle, the "bargain" theory of consideration (1) provided a natural formality to channel human conduct and insure deliberation; (2) protected and structured the important market transaction; (3) expanded legal protection by supporting the executory exchange—a promise for a promise—and shielding the creative or idiosyncratic bargainer from later claims that the agreed exchange was disproportionate; and (4) permitted a fuller development of remedies that protected the plaintiff's expectation interest, that is, the value to the plaintiff of the agreed exchange.

It seems plausible to conclude that ideas about bargain were in the air in 1881 and that the winds from the frontier, if not the reported decisions, occasionally reached Boston. * * *

Viewed from this vantage point, although Holmes' leap from the English common law to the pages of The Common Law may be miraculous, a leap in 1880 from contemporary reality to the bargain theory was no leap at all. * * * In fact, it might be described as an intensely practical idea somewhat behind its time but sufficiently contemporary to insure quick acceptance by student, bench, and bar. At the same time, this thesis of evolution, while not salvaging Holmes's scholarship in The Common Law, is consistent with his perceived tendency "to make few affirmative proposals in the name of * * * social change" and to rely upon the "market place to produce ideas or policies for a given point in time."

* * * These factors—natural development and utility—bespeak a tradition of some durability. Traditions die hard, especially where market ideology and room for its exercise still remain. Since Professor Gilmore has slighted this dimension of the American past, I think that he has branded the new child as illegitimate without taking all of the necessary blood tests. It remains to be seen whether the announcement of its death is exaggerated.

B. Another Look at the Decline and Fall

* * * Professor Gilmore is correct in concluding that something did go wrong with the bargain theory of consideration and the grand theory of which it was a part. Contract law cannot now, if it ever could, be ex-

[49] See J.W. Hurst, Law and the Conditions of Freedom in the Nineteenth–Century United States 11–12 (1956).

plained by such phrases as an "objective manifestation of mutual assent to a bargain." Determining exactly what went wrong is important for understanding the forces at work during periods of rapid change and for providing a more solid platform for facing the future. * * *

* * * Professor Gilmore identifies a number of reasons for the deterioration of the bargain theory and the legal relationships it spawned. At one critical juncture he concludes that the Holmes–Williston construct could not survive the "transition from nineteenth century individualism to the welfare state and beyond." * * * What [this phrase] suggests to me is that as contract disputes reached the courts over time tension began to develop among the policies undergirding the grand theory—that is, policies associated with the maintenance and support of a free enterprise, market economy—and the perceived costs or excesses of that market system. These perceived excesses included the wasteful utilization and inefficient allocation by private parties of increasingly scarce resources, the accumulation and frequent abuse of strategic market power, and a growing disparity in wealth, capacity, and opportunity among those who used or, in some cases, were used by contract. While ill-suited for the task, courts were invited, along with other governmental agencies, to do battle with the "market gods."

Within and prompted by this tension, additional changes were in process which both help to explain why the grand theory deteriorated and provide an analytical window for viewing what lies "beyond." These changes included the development of a contextual approach to problems of contract law, the evolution of new or different forms of exchange relationships, and the steady intrusion of the legislative-administrative process into the arena once reserved for private bargainers and the courts.

The contextual approach focuses upon particular types of contracts within a relevant business or social setting rather than upon contracts in general. Instead of just contracts, there are contracts for the sale or lease of personal and real property, construction, personal and professional services, transportation, the creation of security interests, the organization of businesses, and the settlement of disputes. * * * Each context develops its own patterns, practices, and problems which, to a varying degree, influence particular exchange transactions. As the many studies of contract in context demonstrate, the pressure of reality has, among other things, influenced the courts and the legislatures to develop special rules for special problems and broad standards which are capable of particularization in each case.

From a contextual perspective, it is easier to detect and to evaluate changes in the character of the particular exchange relationship involved. According to Professor Macneil, the grand theory's emphasis upon mutual assent was based upon the assumption that the parties could or should presentiate, that is, express all of the material elements of the future exchange in the present agreement. In its extreme form, the transaction model from which this assumption derived was the "one shot deal" involving the sale of Dobbin or Blackacre. * * *

But the grand theory and its assumptions are hardly consistent with the dynamics of the long-term relationship between professor and university, husband and wife, union and corporation, supplier and middleman, government and shipbuilder, franchisor and franchisee, or two state-owned enterprises in a socialist economy. Although each relationship features contract behavior, the unwillingness or inability of the parties to "presentiate" requires, according to Macneil, the refinements of good-faith bargaining and mediation to achieve sound dispute settlement rather than the crude "either-or" approach of the common law. * * *

Within any particular context and regardless of the character of the exchange relationship, one must also determine the ever-increasing scope of preemption by the legislative-administrative process of the arena traditionally reserved for private bargainers and the courts. The regulatory intrusions—laws concerning antitrust, labor relations, consumer protection, welfare, environmental protection, licensing, land use, product safety, and insurance, to name a few—are responsive to the perceived costs or excesses of a free market system. The growing bulk of "uniform" laws, frequently in the common law tradition, stand as mute testimony to the conflict between the reality of national commerce and the decentralization of governmental power. * * *

[This] development also has long-range implications for the importance of contract law as applied by the courts. * * * To Friedman, the growth of the legislative-administrative process meant that the courts were relieved, in whole or part, of both the responsibility and the opportunity to formulate and apply broad policy through contract law. They became free to evolve doctrinal exceptions or new techniques to achieve fairness in particular cases. * * *

* * * [Bearing all of this in mind, it becomes easier to predict the future course of contract jurisprudence:] the court can play a more responsive role if it will, first, try to determine the extent to which the particular dispute is related to or a product of one or more excesses of the market system. This determination * * * sharpens the policy issues and assists the court in deciding whether the primary task will be merely to find and implement the "intention of the parties" or to function in a regulatory mode. Equally important, the court must place the transaction from which the dispute arose into relevant context, evaluate its relational characteristics, and ascertain the extent to which the legislative process has preempted or otherwise surrounded the particular issue in dispute. When this is done, the stage is better set for resolving the dispute in the reality of the present and with an eye to the future.

C. *Whither Tort? (Or, What Happened to Consent?)*

* * * [Gilmore argues that] the future of contract is in tort, or something very much like it. This has the ring of a good idea. Unfortunately, Professor Gilmore fails to provide a systematic analysis of * * * the expanding conception of tort * * *. [Speidel argues that the only evidence of "creeping tortism" which Gilmore provides are Sections 89A and 90 of *Restatement 2nd* and related cases, and that these are not enough to substantiate contract's obituary.]

* * * Professor Gilmore's leap from the somewhat exaggerated report of the death of contract to the strong hint that tort will swallow the residue seems to rival the alleged gargantuan leap of Holmes. Something is missing. In the transition from the imperatives of the grand theory to the duties of the welfare state, what happened to freedom of contract? * * *

Individual consent is still of dominant importance in law. To illustrate * * * suppose that the Officious Lawn Service Company has, without invitation, mowed the shaggy lawn of Arthur, who was on vacation. Even though Arthur has no choice but to receive the "benefit" of that service, it seems highly unlikely that he will be liable to Officious in quasi-contract or anything else. His problem begins only if, for any reason, he makes a promise to pay for the service. While section 89A of the second Restatement retreats from the bargain theory, it must be activated by a promise which, in turn, is evidence that Arthur has exercised choice. * * * But without the exercise of choice, there is no hint in the cases or the Restatement that a duty to disgorge the benefit will be imposed upon Arthur * * *.

Suppose, again, that Uncle Samuel promises his favorite nephew Christopher $2,000 with which to buy a car. Relying on this promise, Christopher visits a dealer and puts down $300 of his own money, signs a contract to pay $1,200 with interest in installments, and takes delivery of a car. If Uncle then refuses to pay, it seems clear that Nephew has an appealing claim in promissory estoppel, although perhaps not for the entire $2,000. * * * But if Uncle Samuel had conditioned his promise upon Nephew Christopher's earning a grade of B or better in Professor Holmes's course in Common Law Miracles and Christopher earned a C, the framework for discussion would change. Uncle's use of promissory language would not be careless and Christopher's premature reliance would be neither foreseeable nor justified. * * *

The limitations on promissory liability discussed above are, of course, implicit in Gilmore's discussion. But the claim of "creeping tortism" is not explicitly tested against the continued efficacy of choices not to engage in contract behavior or express conditions employed by those who play the market game. * * *

This essay is too brief to venture a comprehensive answer to the question of what, if anything, remains of consent in contract law. However, it is useful to identify a few of the relevant considerations.

The issue will arise in litigation where one party engaged in contract behavior asserts some form of assent either to avoid liability or to impose it upon the other party. One form of avoidance—freedom from contract—involves the benefit conferred without request [as codified in § 89A]. The absence of any expression of assent is critical here. A variation on this theme involves an explicit refusal by one party to engage in contract behavior with another. Although freedom from contract is the rule in these situations, the antitrust laws proscribe certain concerted refusals to deal, and insurance statutes sometimes impose restraints upon the ability of an insurance company to refuse to renew a policy. * * *

The more typical form of avoidance involves the attempt by one party to withdraw without liability from an existing relationship by relying upon an express condition which has apparently failed. One example of this is the problem of Uncle Samuel and Nephew Christopher, previously discussed. More commonly, the issue is raised by the attempted withdrawal from an exchange relationship, either before or after the contract is formed [on the basis of some express condition in the contract or offer.] [T]he quality of the expressed condition determines the freedom from contract liability.

The other side of the coin involves the effort of one party to enforce (impose, if you like) terms, whether involving performance or remedy, to which the other party has apparently assented. * * *

Assuming that the issue of "freedom from or freedom to" arises beyond the scope of direct legislative or administrative regulation, by what standards will the efficacy of the critical manifestation of assent be tested? * * * If the defendant is a consumer who, without any bargaining or informed choice, has accepted terms drafted by and for the plaintiff, explaining what amounts to a unilateral imposition in terms of consent seems to be inappropriate. On the other hand, the concept of consent may be irrelevant because the parties were unable or unwilling to presentiate the critical terms to the time when performance commenced. Expressions of intent come later, where the emphasis should be upon the quality of bargaining under relational duties such as the "duty" to bargain in good faith, imposed by the court. It seems clear, then, that the standards for testing the range of freedom from and freedom to contract will develop in the undifferentiated group of transactions between the extremes of unilateral imposition and the unpresentiated relationship.

At this point in time one can perceive in the cases and law reviews a growing agitation to replace the dubious "duty to read" test with a new model of consent. The emphasis is upon the quality of the process whereby consent is manifested. Thus, the party seeking to avoid or impose liability must communicate in such a manner that the other party, considering his particular circumstances, has a realistic opportunity to read and to understand. * * * Even if the other party is more or less fully informed, he may, because of pressure from the moving party or other circumstances, have a lessened capacity to make a real choice. * * * Of course, when the moving party's manifestation is defectively or incompletely expressed, the door is open for the court to engage in purposeful interpretation, "gap filling," and the development of what might be called relational duties, such as the "duty" to disclose material facts, bargain or act in good faith, and cooperate during performance. * * *

This * * * suggests that Professor Gilmore's instincts about radically new forms of civil liability are sound. Within the large area still affected by theories about bargaining and consent, the incidence of what might be called relational rather than tort duties will be high. But these duties are part of an effort to redefine the conditions of freedom in a process where a high value is still placed upon consent. In the area where contract behavior is still valuable for attaining legitimate ends, theories about consent will remain staples in the judicial arsenal. These staples should assist in defining the principles of fairness and efficiency that ought to characterize the process of private exchange in a changing society. The effort to define and justify those principles is worthwhile, for beyond the welfare state lies a "grants" economy and, ultimately, government ownership of sources of production and supply. While there will be contract behavior in the beyond, an unthinking imposition of the new social contract may result in irreparable loss of individual freedom.

III. CONCLUSION

* * *

* * * In my heart of hearts, I do not believe that Professor Gilmore intended to equate the "death" of consideration with the death of freedom in exchange transactions or to suggest that the existence of that freedom is inconsistent with justice. But something happened on his journey from the excesses of the grand theory to the duties of the "new" tort. Although the trip was fun, the announcements by the driver were not always complete and at times were less than reassuring. Perhaps pessimism is the dominant note of our times. But my preferences are for a more constructive tune, played perhaps on a Scottish bagpipe.

NOTES AND QUESTIONS

1. Professor Speidel seems to suggest that perhaps Gilmore is not meant to be taken too seriously. Why not? Gilmore repeatedly insisted, in response to critics like Speidel, that he meant just what he said, but with a cantankerous and sly master showman-scholar like the late Professor Gilmore one can never be sure. How is it that Speidel believes Gilmore's inaccu-

racies in reporting the past lead him to misconstrue the future of contract law?

2. Speidel occasionally speaks a strange language, talking of the "social matrix," of "presentiation," and of "relational characteristics." Where does this language come from, and does it have anything to do with the "constructive tune, played perhaps on a Scottish bagpipe," which Speidel prefers? See Ian Macneil, The New Social Contract: An Inquiry into Modern Contractual Relations (1980). Why do you suppose Speidel has no intention of becoming a Professor of "contorts?"

3. Some of Grant Gilmore's last words on the future of contracts came in Gilmore, "Introduction to Havingurst's Limitations Upon Freedom of Contract," 1979 Ariz.St.L.J. 165, 166:

> In the 1970's we have entered the era of Tragic Choices—which is the title Guido Calabresi and Philip Bobbitt chose for a book, published in 1978, which they subtitled: The conflicts society confronts in the allocation of tragically scarce resources. There is not, there will not be—ever—enough to go around. The dream—if it was a noble dream—that the day will come when everyone can do exactly as he pleases without inflicting harm on his neighbor has proven to be a dream. We shall be presently rethinking our ideas about everything—including contract. Our range of choice will be progressively narrowed. It is unlikely that the nineteenth century idea of freedom of contract will have any role to play in the twenty-first century.*

Is this perspective compatible with that of Speidel? What form would a "law" of contract without "freedom of contract" take? Was the gloomy Gilmore right? Consider the contracts cases which follow. For further reading on the "renaissance" in contract theory, of which these writings of Gilmore, Speidel, and Macneil are a part, see Robert A. Hillman, "The Crisis in Modern Contract Theory," 67 Texas L.Rev. 103 (1988), Peter Linzer, "Uncontracts: Context, Contorts and the Relational Approach," 1988 Annual Survey of American Law 139 (1988) (as well as the commentary on Linzer by Steven J. Barton, Id., at 199, by Jonathan Eddy, at 206, and Linzer's reply to his critics, Id., at 213), and Ian Ayres and Robert Gertner, "Filling Gaps in Incomplete Contracts: An Economic Theory of Default Rules," 99 Yale L.J. 87 (1989).

KIRKSEY V. KIRKSEY

Supreme Court of Alabama, 1845.
8 Ala. 131.

Assumpsit by the defendant, against the plaintiff in error. The question is presented in this Court, upon a case agreed, which shows the following facts:

The plaintiff was the wife of defendant's brother, but had for some time been a widow, and had several children. In 1840, the plaintiff resided on public land, under a contract of lease * * * and was comfortably settled, and would have attempted to secure the land she lived on. The defendant resided in Talladega county, some sixty, or seventy miles off. On the 10th October, 1840, he wrote to her the following letter:

> "Dear sister Antillico—Much to my mortification, I heard, that brother Henry was dead, and one of his children. I know that your situation is one of grief, and difficulty. You had a bad chance before, but a great deal worse now. I should like to come and see you, but cannot with convenience at present. * * * I do not know whether you have a preference on the place you live on, or not. If you had, I would advise you to obtain your preference, and sell the land and quit the country, as I understand it is very unhealthy, and I know society is very bad. If you will come down and see me, I will let you have a place to raise your family, and I have more open land than I can tend; and on the account of your situation, and that of your family, I feel like I want you and the children to do well."

Within a month or two after the receipt of this letter, the plaintiff abandoned her possession, without disposing of it, and removed with her family, to the residence of the defendant, who put her in comfortable houses, and gave her land to cultivate for two years, at the end of which time he notified her to remove, and put her in a house, not comfortable, in the woods, which he afterwards required her to leave.

A verdict being found for the plaintiff, for two hundred dollars, the above facts were agreed, and if they will sustain the action, the judgment is to be affirmed, otherwise it is to be reversed.

ORMOND, J. The inclination of my mind, is, that the loss and inconvenience, which the plaintiff sustained in breaking up, and moving to the defendant's, a distance of sixty miles, is a sufficient consideration to support the promise, to furnish her with a house, and land to cultivate, until she could raise her family. My brothers, however, think that the promise on the part of the defendant, was a mere gratuity, and that an action will not lie for its breach. The judgment of the Court below must therefore be reversed * * *.

NOTES AND QUESTIONS

1. This case was decided a generation before the "Holmes–Williston construct" was conceived. Does it suggest to you that Gilmore was correct or incorrect about the "classical contract theory" being without caselaw foundation?

2. How would you have decided this case? Do you believe that there was a "contract" in the case? What do you suppose the word "contract" had

come to mean by 1845? How do you account for the fact that a verdict was found for the plaintiff in the trial court? Judge Ormond would be prepared to find "sufficient consideration" in Sister Antillico's "moving to the defendant's." Why do his "brothers" disagree? How would the case be decided under the first or second *Restatement*?

3. Compare the model of "contract" that seems to exist in Kirksey v. Kirksey with that in the next case, a modern "classic" by the apostle of the constitutional jurisprudence of "goodness," whom we encountered in the last chapter, Judge J. Skelly Wright.

WILLIAMS V. WALKER–THOMAS FURNITURE CO.

United States Court of Appeals, District of Columbia Circuit, 1965.
350 F.2d 445.

J. SKELLY WRIGHT, CIRCUIT JUDGE:

Appellee, Walker–Thomas Furniture Company, operates a retail furniture store in the District of Columbia. During the period from 1957 to 1962 each appellant in these cases purchased a number of household items from Walker–Thomas, for which payment was to be made in installments. The terms of each purchase were contained in a printed form contract which set forth the value of the purchased item and purported to lease the item to appellant for a stipulated monthly rent payment. The contract then provided, in substance, that title would remain in Walker–Thomas until the total of all the monthly payments made equaled the stated value of the item, at which time appellants could take title. In the event of a default in the payment of any monthly installment, Walker–Thomas could repossess the item.

The contract further provided that "the amount of each periodical installment payment to be made by [purchaser] to the Company under this present lease shall be inclusive of and not in addition to the amount of each installment payment to be made by [purchaser] under such prior leases, bills or accounts; *and all payments now and hereafter made by [purchaser] shall be credited pro rata on all outstanding leases, bills and accounts* due the Company by [purchaser] at the time each such payment is made." (Emphasis added.) The effect of this rather obscure provision was to keep a balance due on every item purchased until the balance due on all items, whenever purchased, was liquidated. As a result, the debt incurred at the time of purchase of each item was secured by the right to repossess all the items previously purchased by the same purchaser, and each new item purchased automatically became subject to a security interest arising out of the previous dealings.

* * * [O]n April 17, 1962, appellant Williams bought a stereo set of stated value of $514.95.[1] She * * * defaulted shortly thereafter, and appellee sought to replevy all the items purchased since December, 1957. The Court of General Sessions granted judgment for appellee. The District of Columbia Court of Appeals affirmed, and we granted appellants' motion for leave to appeal to this court.

Appellants' principal contention, rejected by both the trial and the appellate courts below, is that these contracts, or at least some of them, are unconscionable and, hence, not enforceable. In its opinion in Williams v. Walker–Thomas Furniture Company, 198 A.2d 914, 916 (1964), the District of Columbia Court of Appeals explained its rejection of this contention as follows:

> * * * The record reveals that prior to the last purchase appellant had reduced the balance in her account to $164. The last purchase, a stereo set, raised the balance due to $678. Significantly, at the time of this and the preceding purchases, appellee was aware of appellant's financial position. The reverse side of the stereo contract listed the name of appellant's social worker and her $218 monthly stipend from the government. Nevertheless, with the full knowledge that appellant had to feed, clothe and support both herself and seven children on this amount, appellee sold her a $514 stereo set.
>
> We cannot condemn too strongly appellee's conduct. It raises serious questions of sharp practice and irresponsible business dealings. A review of the legislation in the District of Columbia affecting retail sales and the pertinent decisions of the highest court in this jurisdiction disclose, however, no ground upon which this court can declare the contracts in question contrary to public policy. * * * We think Congress should consider corrective legislation to protect the public from such exploitive contracts as were utilized in the case at bar.

We do not agree that the court lacked the power to refuse enforcement to contracts found to be unconscionable. In other jurisdictions, it has been held as a matter of common law that unconscionable contracts are not enforceable. While no decision of this court so holding has been found, the notion that an unconscionable bargain should not be given full enforcement is by no means novel. In Scott v. United States, 79 U.S. (12 Wall.) 443, 445, 20 L.Ed. 438 (1870), the Supreme Court stated:

> * * * If a contract be unreasonable and unconscionable, but not void for fraud, a court of law will give to the party who sues for its breach damages, not according to its letter, but only such as he is equitably entitled to. * * *

[1] At the time of this purchase her account showed a balance of $164 still owing from her prior purchases. The total of all the purchases made over the years in question came to $1,800. The total payments amounted to $1,400.

Since we have never adopted or rejected such a rule, the question here presented is actually one of first impression.

Congress has recently enacted the Uniform Commercial Code, which specifically provides that the court may refuse to enforce a contract which it finds to be unconscionable at the time it was made. 28 D.C.Code § 2–302 (Supp.IV 1965). The enactment of this section, which occurred subsequent to the contracts here in suit, does not mean that the common law of the District of Columbia was otherwise at the time of enactment, nor does it preclude the court from adopting a similar rule in the exercise of its powers to develop the common law for the District of Columbia. In fact, in view of the absence of prior authority on the point, we consider the congressional adoption of § 2–302 persuasive authority for following the rationale of the cases from which the section is explicitly derived. Accordingly, we hold that where the element of unconscionability is present at the time a contract is made, the contract should not be enforced.

Unconscionability has generally been recognized to include an absence of meaningful choice on the part of one of the parties together with contract terms which are unreasonably favorable to the other party. Whether a meaningful choice is present in a particular case can only be determined by consideration of all the circumstances surrounding the transaction. In many cases the meaningfulness of the choice is negated by a gross inequality of bargaining power. The manner in which the contract was entered is also relevant to this consideration. Did each party to the contract, considering his obvious education or lack of it, have a reasonable opportunity to understand the terms of the contract, or were the important terms hidden in a maze of fine print and minimized by deceptive sales practices? Ordinarily, one who signs an agreement without full knowledge of its terms might be held to assume the risk that he has entered a one-sided bargain. But when a party of little bargaining power, and hence little real choice, signs a commercially unreasonable contract with little or no knowledge of its terms, it is hardly likely that his consent * * * was ever given to all the terms. In such a case the usual rule that the terms of the agreement are not to be questioned should be abandoned and the court should consider whether the terms of the contract are so unfair that enforcement should be withheld.

In determining reasonableness or fairness, the primary concern must be with the terms of the contract considered in light of the circumstances existing when the contract was made. The test is not simple, nor can it be mechanically applied. The terms are to be considered "in the light of the general commercial background and the commercial needs of the particular trade or case." Corbin suggests the test as being whether the terms are "so extreme as to appear unconscionable according to the mores and business practices of the time and place." 1 Corbin, Contracts § 128 (1963). We think this formulation correctly states the test to be applied in those cases where no meaningful choice was exercised upon entering the contract.

Because the trial court and the appellate court did not feel that enforcement could be refused, no findings were made on the possible unconscionability of the contracts in these cases. Since the record is not sufficient for our deciding the issue as a matter of law, the cases must be remanded to the trial court for further proceedings.

So ordered.

DANAHER, CIRCUIT JUDGE (dissenting): The District of Columbia Court of Appeals obviously was as unhappy about the situation here presented as any of us can possibly be. Its opinion * * * concludes: "We think Congress should consider corrective legislation to protect the public from such exploitive contracts as were utilized in the case at bar."

My view is thus summed up by an able court which made no finding that there had actually been sharp practice. Rather the appellant seems to have known precisely where she stood.

There are many aspects of public policy here involved. What is a luxury to some may seem an outright necessity to others. Is public oversight to be required of the expenditures of relief funds? A washing machine, e.g., in the hands of a relief client might become a fruitful source of income. Many relief clients may well need credit, and certain business establishments will take long chances on the sale of items, expecting their pricing policies will afford a degree of protection commensurate with the risk. * * *

I mention such matters only to emphasize the desirability of a cautious approach to any such problem, particularly since the law for so long has allowed parties such great latitude in making their own contracts. I dare say there must annually be thousands upon thousands of installment credit transactions in this jurisdiction, and one can only speculate as to the effect the decision in these cases will have.

I join the District of Columbia Court of Appeals in its disposition of the issues.

PATTERSON V. WALKER–THOMAS FURNITURE CO.

District of Columbia Court of Appeals, 1971.
277 A.2d 111.

KELLY, ASSOCIATE JUDGE.

* * * [T]he appellant, Mrs. Bernice Patterson, bought merchandise from appellee in three separate transactions during 1968. In January she bought an 18–inch Emerson portable television, with stand, for $295.95, signing an installment contract which obligated her to pay appellee $20 a month on account. In March she bought a five-piece dinette set for

$119.95, increasing her monthly payments to $24. In July she purchased a set of wedding rings for $159.95 and the payments rose to $25 per month. The total price for all the goods, including sales tax, was $597.25. Mrs. Patterson defaulted in her payments after she had paid a total of $248.40 toward the agreed purchase price.

Appellant answered Walker–Thomas' action to recover the unpaid balance on the contracts by claiming, in pertinent part, that she had paid an amount in excess of the fair value of the goods received and that the goods themselves were so grossly overpriced as to render the contract terms unconscionable and the contracts unenforceable under the Uniform Commercial Code as enacted in the District of Columbia.[3]

Objections to interrogatories addressed to appellee in an effort to establish her defense that the goods were in fact grossly overpriced were sustained, the court ruling in part that the information sought was outside the scope of discovery "because the defense of unconscionability based on price is not recognized in this jurisdiction". It ruled further "that certain information sought was readily obtainable to defendant by resort to the contracts admittedly in her possession and that certain of the interrogatories amounted to 'harassment of the business community'."

Appellant persisted in her efforts to present the defense of unconscionability by issuing a subpoena duces tecum for the production of appellee's records, and, alleging indigency, by moving for the appointment of a special master or expert witness to establish the value of the goods, the price Walker–Thomas paid for them, and their condition (whether new or secondhand) when she purchased them. The pretrial judge quashed the subpoena duces tecum on the ground that appellant was precluded from obtaining the same information by means of the subpoena that she had been denied through the use of interrogatories. The motion to appoint a special master or expert witness was also denied.

A trial judge subsequently held that the prior rulings of the motions judge and the pretrial judge established the law of the case. Inasmuch as appellant's then sole defense was that the goods were grossly overpriced and no proof on this issue was presented, the court entered judgment for appellee. We affirm.

Suggested guidelines for deciding whether or not a contract is unconscionable appear in Williams v. Walker–Thomas Furniture Co., * * *. [The court then quotes several paragraphs of Judge Wright's opinion.]

---

[3] D.C.Code 1967, § 28:2–302. Unconscionable contract or clause.

(1) If the court as a matter of law finds the contract or any clause of the contract to have been unconscionable at the time it was made the court may refuse to enforce the contract, or it may enforce the remainder of the contract without the unconscionable clause, or it may so limit the application of any unconscionable clause as to avoid any unconscionable result.

(2) When it is claimed or appears to the court that the contract or any clause thereof may be unconscionable the parties shall be afforded a reasonable opportunity to present evidence as to its commercial setting, purpose and effect to aid the court in making the determination.

* * * [C]iting *Williams* in another context, this court said that "two elements are required to exist to prove unconscionability; i.e., 'an absence of meaningful choice on the part of one of the parties together with contract terms which are *unreasonably favorable to the other party.*' " Diamond Housing Corp. v. Robinson, D.C.App., 257 A.2d 492, 493 (1969). (Emphasis in the original.)

On the basis of these authorities we conclude that in a proper case gross overpricing may be raised in defense as an element of unconscionability. Under the test outlined in *Williams* price is necessarily an element to be examined when determining whether a contract is reasonable. The Corbin test mentioned in the opinion specifically deals with the "terms" of the contract and certainly the price one pays for an item is one of the more important terms of any contract. We emphasize, however, that price as an unreasonable contract term is only one of the elements which underpin proof of unconscionability. Specifically, therefore, in the instant case the reasonableness of the contracts is not to be gauged by an examination of the price stipulation alone or any other term of the contract without parallel consideration being given to whether or not appellant exercised a meaningful choice in entering into the contracts.

We conclude also that because excessive price-value may comprise one element of unconscionability, discovery techniques may be employed to garner information relevant to that issue for purposes of defense. By statute, upon a claim of unconscionability, the court determines as a matter of law whether a contract or any clause thereof is unconscionable *only* after the parties have been given a reasonable opportunity to present evidence as to its commercial setting, purpose and effect. Certainly, therefore, interrogatories may be used to develop evidence of the commercial setting, purpose and effect of a contract at the time it was made in order to assure an effective presentation of the defense at an evidentiary hearing.

In our judgment, however, appellant here was not erroneously precluded from developing evidence through the use of interrogatories by the ruling of the trial court.

[W]e are * * * of the opinion that a sufficient factual predicate for the defense must be alleged before wholesale discovery is allowed. An unsupported conclusory allegation in the answer that a contract is unenforceable as unconscionable is not enough. Sufficient facts surrounding the "commercial setting, purpose and effect" of a contract at the time it was made should be alleged so that the court may form a judgment as to the existence of a valid claim of unconscionability and the extent to which discovery of evidence to support that claim should be allowed.

Admittedly, appellant neither alleged nor attempted to prove the existence of any fraud, duress or coercion when she entered into the instant contracts. Her verified complaint alleges only that the goods she purchased and still retains were grossly overpriced and that she has already paid appellee a sum in excess of their fair value. These are conclusions without factual support. It cannot be said that the goods were grossly overpriced merely from an examination of the prices which appear on the face of the contracts. No other term of the contract is alleged to be unconscionable, nor is an absence of meaningful choice claimed. We hold that the two elements of which unconscionability is comprised; namely, an absence of meaningful choice and contract terms unreasonably favorable to the other party, must be particularized in some detail before a merchant is required to divulge his pricing policies through interrogatories or through the production of records in court. An answer, such as the one here, asserting the affirmative defense of unconscionability only on the basis of a stated conclusion that the price is excessive is insufficient.

Accordingly, the judgment of the trial court is

Affirmed.

NOTES AND QUESTIONS

1. Is there a different ordering of fundamental contract values in Judge Wright's opinion in *Williams* from that in Kirksey v. Kirksey? How would you describe the difference?

2. Even the District of Columbia Court of Appeals, which thought that it was without the legal power to grant relief to consumers like Mrs. Williams, condemned the conduct of Walker–Thomas as "sharp practice," "irresponsible business dealings," and the utilization of "exploitive contracts." Is this conclusion inescapable?

3. What, precisely, does Judge Wright hold in the *Williams* case? Is it that the contracts in question were unconscionable, or is the holding less specific? What do you make of the following reasoning that Judge Wright advances in support of his conclusion: " * * * in view of the absence of prior authority on the point, we consider the congressional adoption of Section 2–302 persuasive authority for following the rationale of the cases from which the section is explicitly derived." Note that the congressional act adopting the UCC was passed *after* Mrs. Williams' purchase. Is there a slip in Wright's reasoning? Why didn't Judge Danaher agree with this "persuasive authority" notion? Would Judge Ormond's "brothers" approve?

4. Applying Judge Wright's suggested tests to the facts of *Williams* as you might imagine them to be, do you think the contract was "unconscionable?"

5. Shortly after the *Williams* case, Congress reorganized the courts of the District of Columbia. Before the reorganization, the Federal Court of Appeals functioned more or less like a state Supreme Court for the District of Columbia in both civil and criminal matters, and, as you saw in *Williams,* the federal appeals court took appeals from the District of Columbia inferior trial courts. After the reorganization, the federal courts were more restricted to

exclusively federal matters, a new "Supreme" court was instituted in the District of Columbia system to handle appeals, and ordinary matters of civil and criminal law were, presumably, to be kept out of the federal courts to the same extent which they would be in any analogous state system. Would you have agreed or disagreed with the framers of the District of Columbia Court Reorganization Act?

6. Why do you suppose that the *Patterson* case has been called the "revenge of Walker–Thomas?" Does the District of Columbia Court of Appeals follow Judge Wright's opinion in *Williams*? Would Judge Wright have been pleased with this result? For more details on Mrs. Williams and the Walker Thomas Furniture company, and for the suggestion that the emergence of the doctrine of unconscionability actually had little effect on the conduct of the company's business, see Eben Colby, "Note: What did the Doctrine of Unconscionability Do to the Walker–Thomas Furniture Company?," 34 Conn.L.Rev. 625 (2002).

WEISZ V. PARKE–BERNET GALLERIES, INC.

Civil Court, City of New York, 1971.
67 Misc.2d 1077, 325 N.Y.S.2d 576.

LEONARD H. SANDLER, JUDGE.

On May 16, 1962, Dr. Arthur Weisz attended an auction conducted by the Parke–Bernet Galleries, Inc., where he ultimately bought for the sum of $3,347.50 a painting listed in the auction catalogue as the work of Raoul Dufy. Some two years later, on May 13, 1964, David and Irene Schwartz bought for $9,360.00 at a Parke–Bernet auction a painting also listed in the catalogue as the work of Raoul Dufy.

Several years after the second auction, as a result of an investigation conducted by the New York County District Attorney's office, the plaintiffs received information that the paintings were in fact forgeries. When this was called to Parke–Bernet's attention, Parke–Bernet denied any legal responsibility, asserting among other things that the Conditions of Sale for both auctions included a disclaimer of warranty as to genuineness, authorship and the like.

Following a formal demand by the plaintiffs for return of the purchase price, these two lawsuits were commenced against Parke–Bernet. * * * Juries having been waived, both cases were tried jointly.

* * * [T]he catalogue listing "Raoul Dufy" is asserted to constitute an express warranty, as that term was defined under the former Sales Act, in effect when the auctions took place. Former Personal Property Law, Sec. 93.

* * *

* * * I find that the following facts were quite clearly established by the evidence.

(1). Each of the plaintiffs bought the paintings in question in the belief that they were painted by Raoul Dufy, had formed this conclusion because Parke–Bernet so stated in the respective catalogues, and would not have bought the paintings if they were not believed to be genuine.

(2). At the time of the auctions Parke–Bernet also believed the paintings ascribed to Dufy in the catalogues were his work.

(3). Neither of the paintings was in fact painted by Dufy. Both are forgeries with negligible commercial value.

The most substantial of the defenses interposed by Parke–Bernet is that the Conditions of Sale for the auctions, appearing on a preliminary page of each catalogue, included a disclaimer of any warranty and that the plaintiffs are bound by its terms.

* * *

Although the auctions were separated in time by two years, the catalogues were quite similar in all legally significant respects, and the basic auction procedure was the same.

The catalogues open with several introductory pages of no direct relevance to the lawsuits. There then follows a page headed "Conditions of Sale", in large black print, under which some 15 numbered paragraphs appear, covering the side of one page and most of a second side. These provisions are in clear black print, somewhat smaller than the print used in the greater part of the catalogue.

Paragraph 2, on which Parke–Bernet relies, provides as follows:

> The Galleries has endeavored to catalogue and describe the property correctly, but all property is sold "as is" and neither the Galleries nor its consignor warrants or represents, and they shall in no event be responsible for, the correctness of description, genuineness, authorship, provenience or condition of the property, and no statement contained in the catalogue or made orally at the sale or elsewhere shall be deemed to be such a warranty or representation, or an assumption of liability.

The next page in each catalogue is headed "List of Artists", and contains in alphabetical order, one under the other, a list of the artists with a catalogue number or numbers appearing on the same line with the named artist. The implicit affirmation that the listed artists are represented in the auction and that the catalogue numbers appearing after their names represent their work could scarcely be clearer.

The name Raoul Dufy is listed in each catalogue, together with several catalogue numbers.

After the pages on which the artists are listed, over 80 pages follow in each catalogue on which the catalogue numbers appear in numerical order with descriptive material about the artist and the work.

Turning in each catalogue to the catalogue numbers for the paintings involved in the lawsuits, there appears on the top of the page a conventional black-and-white catalogue reproduction of the painting, directly under it the catalogue number in brackets, and the name RAOUL DUFY in large black print followed in smaller print by the words "French 1880–1953".

On the next line the catalogue number is repeated together with the name of the painting, a description of it, and the words, "Signed at lower right RAOUL DUFY." Finally, there appears a note that a certificate by M. Andre Pacitti will be given to the purchaser.

The procedure followed at both auctions was to announce at the beginning of the auction that it was subject to the conditions of sale, without repeating the announcement, and at no point alluding directly to the disclaimer.

As to the first auction, I am satisfied that Dr. Weisz did not in fact know of the Conditions of Sale and may not properly be charged with knowledge of its contents. I accept as entirely accurate his testimony that on his prior appearances at Parke–Bernet auctions he had not made any bids, and that on the occasion of his purchase he did not observe the Conditions of Sale and was not aware of its existence.

The test proposed for this kind of issue by Williston, quite consistent with the decided cases, is whether "the person * * * should as a reasonable man understand that it contains terms of the contract that he must read at his peril." 1 Williston on Contracts Section 90D (1937). * * *

The most obvious characteristic of the two Parke–Bernet auctions is that they attracted people on the basis of their interest in owning works of art, not on the basis of their legal experience or business sophistication. Surely it is unrealistic to assume that people who bid at such auctions will ordinarily understand that a gallery catalogue overwhelmingly devoted to descriptions of works of art also includes on its preliminary pages conditions of sale. Even less reasonable does it seem to me to expect a bidder at such an auction to appreciate the possibility that the conditions of sale would include a disclaimer of liability for the accuracy of the basic information presented throughout the catalogue in unqualified form with every appearance of certainty and reliability.

For someone in Dr. Weisz's position to be bound by conditions of sale, of which he in fact knew nothing, considerably more was required of Parke–Bernet to call those Conditions of Sale to his attention than occurred here.

The cases relied upon by Parke–Bernet where buyers were held to be bound by conditions of sale in auction catalogues are not at all apposite. For one thing, in only one of the cases does the opinion recite that the buyer flatly denied knowledge of the provision. * * * And in that case the buyer, a frequent bidder at the auction in question, acknowledged that he knew there were conditions of sale but had not undertaken to become familiar with them. More importantly, these auction cases for the most part concern business auctions, in which sellers and buyers were part of a business grouping in which a general knowledge of the governing rules and usages was reasonably to be anticipated. * * *

As to the Schwartz case, I am satisfied from the evidence that Mrs. Schwartz knew of the Conditions of Sale, and that both Schwartz plaintiffs are chargeable with that knowledge since they both participated in the purchase.

This factual conclusion leads to consideration of the extremely interesting question whether the language of disclaimer relied upon as a bar to the actions should be deemed effective for that purpose. No case has come to my attention that squarely presents the issue raised by the underlying realities of this case.

What is immediately apparent from any review of the evidence is that notwithstanding the language of disclaimer, Parke–Bernet expected that bidders at its auctions would rely upon the accuracy of its descriptions, and intended that they should. Parke–Bernet, as the evidence confirms, is an exceedingly well-known gallery, linked in the minds of people with the handling, exhibition and sale of valuable artistic works and invested with an aura of expertness and reliability. The very fact that Parke–Bernet was offering a work of art for sale would inspire confidence that it was genuine and that the listed artist in fact was the creator of the work.

The wording of the catalogue was clearly designed to emphasize the genuineness of the works to be offered. The list of artists followed by catalogue numbers, the black-and-white reproductions of the more important works, the simple listing of the name of the artist with the years of his birth and death could not have failed to impress upon the buyer that these facts could be relied on and that one could safely part with large sums of money in the confident knowledge that a genuine artistic work was being acquired.

Where one party in a contractual relationship occupies a position of superior knowledge and experience, and where that superior knowledge is relied upon and intended to be relied upon by the other, surely more is required for an effective disclaimer than appears here.

After reassuring the reader that Parke–Bernet endeavored to catalogue the works of art correctly, there follow highly technical and legalistic words of disclaimer in a situation in which plain and emphatic words are required. And this provision, in light of the critical importance to the buyer of a warning that he may not rely on the fact that a work attributed to an artist was in fact his creation, is in no way given the special prominence that it clearly requires.

The language used, the understated manner of its presentation, the failure to refer to it explicitly in the preliminary oral announcement at the auction all lead to the conclusion that Parke–Bernet did not expect the bidders to take the disclaimer too seriously or to be too concerned about it. I am convinced that the average reader of this provision would view it as some kind of technicality that should in no way derogate from the certainty that he was buying genuine artistic works, and that this was precisely the impression intended to be conveyed.

In denying legal effect to the disclaimer I am acting consistently with a whole body of law that reflects an increasing sensitivity to the requirements of fair dealing where there is a relationship between parties in which there is a basic inequality of knowledge, expertness or economic power. * * *

* * *

Judgment may be entered for the plaintiff Weisz against Parke–Bernet in the sum of $3,347.50, and for the plaintiffs David and Irene Schwartz in the sum of $9,360.00, both judgments of course with appropriate interest and costs. * * *

NOTES AND QUESTIONS

1. Professor Speidel suggests that the future course of contract law lies in refining notions about "freedom from contract," and in developing a sophisticated model of "consent," one which would seek to exclude transactions where the elements of "unfair oppression" or "unfair surprise" are present. Does the *Weisz* court help in developing such a model? Would you be prepared to write an obituary for the law of contract after reading the *Weisz* case?

2. The *Weisz* case, not surprisingly, was appealed. What do you make of the *Per Curiam* opinion in *Weisz* of the New York Supreme Court, Appellate Term, First Department, the text of which follows:

> Plaintiffs' purchases by competitive bids, at a public auction were made in 1962 and 1964. At that time neither the statutory nor decisional law, applicable to such purchases, recognized the expressed opinion or judgment of the seller as giving rise to any implied warranty of authenticity of authorship. (See Memorandum of the State Department of Law (McKinney's 1968 Session Laws, Vol. 2, pp. 2284–2285) recommending remedial legislation (now Secs. 219 and 219–a of the General Business Law) to change the then existing law.)

> Additionally defendant's auction-sale catalogue listing, describing, and illustrating these paintings, gave leading and prominent place, in its prefatory terms of sale, (explaining and regulating the conduct of the action) to a clear, unequivocal disclaimer of any express or implied warranty or representation of genuineness of any paintings as products of the ascribed artist.
>
> One of the factors necessarily entering into the competition among bidders at the public auction was the variable value of the paintings depending upon the degree of certainty with which they could be authenticated and established as the works of the ascribed artist. (See Backus v. MacLaury, 278 App.Div. 504, 507, 106 N.Y.S.2d 401, 403 (1951)). Since no element of a wilful intent to deceive is remotely suggested in the circumstances here present the purchasers assumed the risk that in judging the paintings as readily-identifiable, original works of the named artist, and scaling their bids accordingly, they might be mistaken. (Restatement, Contracts, Sec. 502, comment f., p. 964). They will not now be heard to complain that, in failing to act with the caution of one in circumstances abounding with signals of *caveat emptor,* they made a bad bargain. The judgments are reversed with $30 costs and the complaints dismissed.

Weisz v. Parke–Bernet Galleries, Inc., 77 Misc.2d 80, 351 N.Y.S.2d 911 (1974). How would you describe the nature of the disagreement between Judge Sandler and the court which reversed him? Is the disagreement over the appropriate "models" for contract law? Can the disagreement over appropriate "models" be reconciled? For an intriguing assertion that such a reconciliation can never take place because of the inherent contradictions of "modern liberal legalism" itself, see Jay M. Feinman, "Promissory Estoppel and Judicial Method," 97 Harv.L.Rev. 678 (1984). For a discussion of the legal and practical difficulties now facing the auction market for art objects in cases such as *Weisz,* involving "sometimes naïve and very often inexperienced" bidders, see William W. Stuart, "Authenticity of Authorship and the Auction Market," 54 Me.L.Rev. 71 (2002).

B. LATE TWENTIETH–CENTURY TORTS

THOMAS V. WINCHESTER

New York Court of Appeals, 1852.
6 N.Y. 397.

RUGGLES, CH. J. delivered the opinion of the court. This is an action brought to recover damages from the defendant for negligently putting up, labeling and selling as and for the extract of *dandelion,* which is a simple and harmless medicine, a jar of the extract of *belladonna,* which is a deadly poison; by means of which the plaintiff Mary Ann Thomas * * * was greatly injured * * *.

The facts proved were briefly these: Mrs. Thomas being in ill health, her physician prescribed for her a dose of dandelion. Her husband purchased what was believed to be the medicine prescribed, at the store of Dr. Foord * * *.

A small quantity of the medicine thus purchased was administered to Mrs. Thomas, on whom it produced very alarming effects; such as coldness of the surface and extremities, feebleness of circulation, spasms of the muscles, giddiness of the head, dilation of the pupils of the eyes, and derangement of mind. She recovered however, after some time, from its effects, although for a short time her life was thought to be in great danger. The medicine administered was *belladonna, and not dandelion.* The jar from which it was taken was labeled *"½ lb. dandelion, prepared by A. Gilbert, No. 108, John-street, N.Y. Jar 8 oz."* It was sold for and believed by Dr. Foord to be the extract of dandelion as labeled. Dr. Foord purchased the article as the extract of dandelion from Jas. S. Aspinwall, a druggist at New York. Aspinwall bought it of the defendant as extract of dandelion, believing it to be such. The defendant was engaged at No. 108 John-street, New York, in the manufacture and sale of certain vegetable extracts for medicinal purposes, and in the purchase and sale of others. * * * The jars containing extracts manufactured by himself and those containing extracts purchased by him from others, were labeled alike. Both were labeled like the jar in question, as "prepared by A. Gilbert." Gilbert was a person employed by the defendant at a salary, as an assistant in his business. The jars were labeled in Gilbert's name because he had been previously engaged in the same business on his own account at No. 108 John-street, and probably because Gilbert's labels rendered the articles more salable. The extract contained in the jar sold to Aspinwall, and by him to Foord, was not manufactured by the defendant, but was purchased by him from another manufacturer or dealer. The extract of dandelion and the extract of belladonna resemble each other in color, consistency, smell and taste; but may on careful examination be distinguished the one from the other by those who are well acquainted with these articles. * * *

* * *

The case depends on the * * * question * * * whether the defendant, being a remote vendor of the medicine, and there being no privity or connection between him and the plaintiffs, the action can be maintained.

If, in labeling a poisonous drug with the name of a harmless medicine, for public market, no duty was violated by the defendant, excepting that which he owed to Aspinwall, his immediate vendee, in virtue of his contract of sale, this action cannot be maintained. If A. build a wagon and sell it to B., who sells it to C., and C. hires it to D., who in consequence of the gross negligence of A. in building the wagon is overturned and injured, D. cannot recover damages against A., the builder. A.'s obligation to build the wagon faithfully, arises solely out of his contract with B. The public have nothing to do with it. Misfortune to third persons, not parties to the contract, would not be a natural and necessary consequence of the builder's negligence; and such negligence is not an act imminently dangerous to human life.

So, for the same reason, if a horse be defectively shod by a smith, and a person hiring the horse from the owner is thrown and injured in consequence of the smith's negligence in shoeing, the smith is not liable for the injury. The smith's duty in such case grows exclusively out of his contract with the owner of the horse; it was a duty which the smith owed to him alone, and to no one else. * * *

This was the ground on which the case of Winterbottom v. Wright (10 Mees. & Welsb. 109,) was decided. A. contracted with the postmaster general to provide a coach to convey the mail bags along a certain line of road, and B. and others, also contracted to horse the coach along the same line. B. and his co-contractors hired C., who was the plaintiff, to drive the coach. The coach, in consequence of some latent defect, broke down; the plaintiff was thrown from his seat and lamed. It was held that C. could not maintain an action against A. for the injury thus sustained. * * * A.'s duty to keep the coach in good condition, was a duty to the postmaster general, with whom he made his contract, and not a duty to the driver employed by the owners of the horses.

But the case in hand stands on a different ground. The defendant was a dealer in poisonous drugs. * * * The death or great bodily harm of some person was the natural and almost inevitable consequence of the sale of belladonna by means of the false label.

Gilbert, the defendant's agent, would have been punishable for manslaughter if Mrs. Thomas had died in consequence of taking the falsely labeled medicine. Every man who, by his culpable negligence, causes the death of another, although without intent to kill, is guilty of manslaughter. (2 R.S. 662, § 19.) A chemist who negligently sells laudanum in a phial labeled as paregoric, and thereby causes the death of a person to whom it is administered, is guilty of manslaughter. (*Tessymond's case*, 1 Lewin's Crown Cases, 169.) * * * And this rule applies not only where the death of one is occasioned by the negligent act of another, but where it is caused by the negligent omission of a duty of that other. (2 Car. & Kir. 368, 371.) Although the defendant Winchester may not be answerable criminally for the negligence of his agent, there can be no doubt of his liability in a civil action, in which the act of the agent is to be regarded as the act of the principal.

* * * In the present case the sale of the poisonous article was made to a dealer in drugs, and not to a consumer. The injury therefore was not likely to fall on him, or on his vendee who was also a dealer; but much more likely to be visited on a remote purchaser, as actually happened.

The defendant's negligence put human life in imminent danger. Can it be said that there was no duty on the part of the defendant, to avoid the creation of that danger by the exercise of greater caution? Or that the exercise of that caution was a duty only to his immediate vendee, whose life was not endangered? The defendant's duty arose out of the nature of his business and the danger to others incident to its mismanagement. Nothing but mischief like that which actually happened could have been expected from sending the poison falsely labeled into the market; and the defendant is justly responsible for the probable consequences of the act. The duty of exercising caution in this respect did not arise out of the defendant's contract of sale to Aspinwall. The wrong done by the defendant was in putting the poison, mislabeled, into the hands of Aspinwall as an article of merchandise to be sold and afterwards used as the extract of dandelion, by some person then unknown. The owner of a horse and cart who leaves them unattended in the street is liable for any damage which may result from his negligence. (Lynch v. Nurdin, 1 Ad. & Ellis, N.S. 29; Illidge v. Goodwin, 5 Car. & Payne, 190.) The owner of a loaded gun who puts it into the hands of a child by whose indiscretion it is discharged, is liable for the damage occasioned by the discharge. (5 Maule & Sel. 198.) * * *

* * *

Judgment affirmed.

BENJAMIN N. CARDOZO

MACPHERSON V. BUICK MOTOR CO.

New York Court of Appeals, 1916.
217 N.Y. 382, 111 N.E. 1050.

CARDOZO, J. The defendant is a manufacturer of automobiles. It sold an automobile to a retail dealer. The retail dealer resold to the plaintiff. While the plaintiff was in the car it suddenly collapsed. He was thrown out and injured. One of the wheels was made of defective wood, and its spokes crumbled into fragments. The wheel was not made by the defendant; it was bought from another manufacturer. There is evidence, however, that its defects could have been discovered by reasonable inspection, and that inspection was omitted. * * * The question to be determined is whether the defendant owed a duty of care and vigilance [which might include such an inspection] to any one but the immediate purchaser.

The foundations of this branch of the law, at least in this state, were laid in Thomas v. Winchester, 6 N.Y. 397, 57 Am.Dec. 455. * * * "The defendant's negligence," it was said, "put human life in imminent danger." A poison, falsely labeled, is likely to injure any one who gets it. Because the danger is to be foreseen, there is a duty to avoid the injury. Cases were cited by way of illustration in which manufacturers were not subject to any duty irrespective of contract. The distinction was said to be that their conduct, though negligent, was not likely to result in injury to any one except the purchaser. We are not required to say whether the chance of injury was always as remote as the distinction assumes. Some of the illustrations might be rejected today. The principle of the distinction is, for present purposes, the important thing. Thomas v. Winchester became quickly a landmark of the law. * * * The chief cases are well known, yet to recall some of them will be helpful. Loop v. Litchfield, 42 N.Y. 351, 1 Am.Rep. 543, is the earliest. It was the case of a defect in a small balance wheel used on a circular saw. The manufacturer pointed out the defect to the buyer, who wished a cheap article and was ready to assume the risk. The risk can hardly have been an imminent one, for the wheel lasted five years before it broke. In the meanwhile the buyer had made a lease of the machinery. It was held that the manufacturer was not answerable to the lessee. Loop v. Litchfield was followed in Losee v. Clute, 51 N.Y. 494, 10 Am.Rep. 638, the case of the explosion of a steam boiler. That decision has been criticized (Thompson on Negligence, 233; Shearman & Redfield on Negligence [6th Ed.] § 117); but it must be confined to its special facts. It was put upon the ground that the risk of injury was too remote. The buyer in that case had not only accepted the boiler, but had tested it. The manufacturer knew that his own test was not the final one. * * *

These early cases suggest a narrow construction of the rule. Later cases, however, evince a more liberal spirit. First in importance is Devlin v. Smith, 89 N.Y. 470, 42 Am.Rep. 311. The defendant, a contractor, built a scaffold for a painter. The painter's servants were injured. The contractor was held liable. He knew that the scaffold, if improperly constructed, was a most dangerous trap. He knew that it was to be used by the workmen. He was building it for that very purpose. Building it for their use, he owed them a duty, irrespective of his contract with their master, to build it with care.

From Devlin v. Smith we pass over intermediate cases and turn to the latest case in this court in which Thomas v. Winchester was followed. That case is Statler v. Ray Mfg. Co., 195 N.Y. 478, 480, 88 N.E. 1063. The defendant manufactured a large coffee urn. It was installed in a restaurant. When heated, the urn exploded and injured the plaintiff. We held that the manufacturer was liable. We said that the urn "was of such a character inherently that, when applied to the purposes for which it was designed, it was liable to become a source of great danger to many people if not carefully and properly constructed."

It may be that Devlin v. Smith and Statler v. Ray Mfg. Co. have extended the rule of Thomas v. Winchester. If so, this court is committed to the extension. The defendant argues that things imminently dangerous to life are poisons, explosives, deadly weapons—things whose normal function it is to injure or destroy. But whatever the rule in Thomas v. Winchester may once have been, it has no longer that restricted meaning. A scaffold (Devlin v. Smith, supra) is not inherently a destructive instrument. It becomes destructive only if imperfectly constructed. A large coffee urn (Statler v. Ray Mfg. Co., supra) may have within itself, if negligently made, the potency of danger, yet no one thinks of it as an implement whose normal function is destruction. * * *

* * *

We hold, then, that the principle of Thomas v. Winchester is not limited to poisons, explosives, and things of like nature, to things which in their normal operation are implements of destruction. If the nature of a thing is such that it is reasonably certain to place life and limb in peril when negligently made, it is then a thing of danger. Its nature gives warning of the consequences to be expected. If to the element of danger there is added knowledge that the thing will be used by persons other than the purchaser, and used without new tests, then, irrespective of contract, the manufacturer of this thing of danger is under a duty to make it carefully. * * * It is possible to use almost anything in a way that will make it dangerous if defective. That is not enough to charge the manufacturer with a duty independent of his contract. Whether a given thing is dangerous may be sometimes a question for the court and sometimes a question for the jury. There must also be knowledge that in the usual course of events the danger will be shared by others than the buyer. Such knowledge may often be inferred from the nature of the transaction. But it is possible that even knowledge of the danger and of the use will not always be enough. The proximity or remoteness of the relation is a factor to be considered. * * *

We are not required, at this time, to say that it is legitimate to go back of the manufacturer of the finished product and hold the manufacturers of the component parts. To make their negligence a cause of imminent danger, an independent cause must often intervene; the manufacturer of the finished product must also fail in his duty of inspection. It may be that in those circumstances the negligence of the earlier members of the series is too remote to constitute, as to the ultimate user, an actionable wrong. * * * There is here no break in the chain of cause and effect. * * * We have put aside the notion that the duty to safeguard life and limb, when the consequences of negligence may be foreseen, grows out of contract and nothing else. We have put the source of the obligation where it ought to be. We have put its source in the law.

* * * Beyond all question, the nature of an automobile gives warning of probable danger if its construction is defective. This automobile was designed to go 50 miles an hour. Unless its wheels were sound and strong, injury was almost certain. * * * The defendant knew the danger. It knew also that the car would be used by persons other than the buyer. This was apparent * * * from the fact that the buyer was a dealer in cars, who bought to resell. * * * The dealer was indeed the one person of whom it might be said with some approach to certainty that by him the car would not be used. Yet the defendant would have us say that he was the one person whom it was under a legal duty to protect. The law does not lead us to so inconsequent a conclusion. Precedents drawn from the days of travel by stagecoach do not fit the conditions of travel today. The principle that the danger must be imminent does not change, but the things subject to the principle do change. They are whatever the needs of life in a developing civilization require them to be.

* * *

We think the defendant was not absolved from a duty of inspection because it bought the wheels from a reputable manufacturer. It was not merely a dealer in automobiles. It was a manufacturer of automobiles. It was responsible for the finished product. It was not at liberty to put the finished product on the market without subjecting the component parts to ordinary and simple tests. * * * The obligation to inspect must vary with the nature of the thing to be inspected. The more probable the danger the greater the need of caution.

* * *

The judgment should be affirmed, with costs.

WILLARD BARTLETT, C.J. (dissenting). * * * The wheel was purchased by the Buick Motor Company, ready made, from the Imperial Wheel

Company of Flint, Mich., a reputable manufacturer of automobile wheels which had furnished the defendant with 80,000 wheels, none of which had proved to be made of defective wood prior to the accident in the present case. The defendant relied upon the wheel manufacturer to make all necessary tests as to the strength of the material therein * * *.

* * *

The late Chief Justice Cooley of Michigan, one of the most learned and accurate of American law writers, states the general rule thus:

> The general rule is that a contractor, manufacturer, vendor or furnisher of an article is not liable to third parties who have no contractual relations with him, for negligence in the construction, manufacture, or sale of such article. 2 Cooley on Torts (3d Ed.), 1486.

The leading English authority in support of this rule, to which all the later cases on the same subject refer, is Winterbottom v. Wright, 10 Meeson & Welsby, 109, which was an action by the driver of a stagecoach against a contractor who had agreed with the postmaster general to provide and keep the vehicle in repair for the purpose of conveying the royal mail over a prescribed route. The coach broke down and upset, injuring the driver, who sought to recover against the contractor on account of its defective construction. The Court of Exchequer denied him any right of recovery on the ground that there was no privity of contract between the parties, the agreement having been made with the postmaster general alone.

> "If the plaintiff can sue," said Lord Abinger, the Chief Baron, "every passenger or even any person passing along the road who was injured by the upsetting of the coach might bring a similar action. Unless we confine the operation of such contracts as this to the parties who enter into them the most absurd and outrageous consequences, to which I can see no limit, would ensue."

The doctrine of that decision was recognized as the law of this state by the leading New York case of Thomas v. Winchester, 6 N.Y. 397, 408, 57 Am.Dec. 455, which, however, involved an exception to the general rule. * * * Chief Judge Ruggles, who delivered the opinion of the court, distinguished between an act of negligence imminently dangerous to the lives of others and one that is not so, * * *.

In Torgesen v. Schultz, 192 N.Y. 156, 159, 84 N.E. 956, 18 L.R.A. (N.S.) 726, 127 Am.St.Rep. 894, the defendant was the vendor of bottles of aerated water which were charged under high pressure and likely to explode unless used with precaution when exposed to sudden changes of temperature. The plaintiff, who was a servant of the purchaser, was injured by the explosion of one of these bottles. There was evidence tending to show that it had not been properly tested in order to insure users against such accidents. We held that the defendant corporation was liable notwithstanding the absence of any contract relation between it and the plaintiff—

> under the doctrine of Thomas v. Winchester, supra, and similar cases based upon the duty of the vendor of an article dangerous in its nature, or likely to become so in the course of the ordinary usage to be contemplated by the vendor, either to exercise due care to warn users of the danger or to take reasonable care to prevent the article sold from proving dangerous when subjected only to customary usage.

The character of the exception to the general rule limiting liability for negligence to the original parties to the contract of sale, was still more clearly stated * * * in Statler v. Ray Manufacturing Co., 195 N.Y. 478, 482, 88 N.E. 1063 * * * :

> In the case of an article of an inherently dangerous nature, a manufacturer may become liable for a negligent construction which, when added to the inherent character of the appliance, makes it imminently dangerous, and causes or contributes to a resulting injury not necessarily incident to the use of such an article if properly constructed, but naturally following from a defective construction.

In that case the injuries were inflicted by the explosion of a battery of steam-driven coffee urns, constituting an appliance liable to become dangerous in the course of ordinary usage.

The case of Devlin v. Smith, 89 N.Y. 470, 42 Am.Rep. 311, is cited as an authority in conflict with the view that the liability of the manufacturer and vendor extends to third parties only when the article manufactured and sold is inherently dangerous. In that case the builder of a scaffold * * * was held to be liable to the administratrix of a painter * * *. It is said that the scaffold, if properly constructed, was not inherently dangerous, and hence that this decision affirms the existence of liability in the case of an article not dangerous in itself, but made so only in consequence of negligent construction. Whatever logical force there may be in this view, it seems to me clear from the language * * * [of the opinion] of the court that the scaffold was deemed to be an inherently dangerous structure, and that the case was decided as it was because the court entertained that view. Otherwise [they would hardly have said] that the circumstances seemed to bring the case fairly within the principle of Thomas v. Winchester.

I do not see how we can uphold the judgment in the present case without overruling what has been so often said by this court and other courts of like authority in reference to the absence of any liability for negligence on the part of the original vendor of an ordinary carriage to any one except his immediate vendee. * * * In the case at bar the defective wheel on an automobile, moving only eight miles an hour, was not any more dangerous to the occupants of the car than a similarly defective wheel would be to the occupants of a carriage drawn by a horse at the same speed, and yet, unless the courts have been all wrong on this question up to the present time, there would be no liability to strangers to the original sale in the case of the horse-drawn carriage.

* * *

* * * That the federal courts still adhere to the general rule, as I have stated it, appears by the decision of the Circuit Court of Appeal in the Second Circuit, in March, 1915, in the case of Cadillac Motor Car Co. v. Johnson, 221 Fed. 801, 137 C.C.A. 279, L.R.A. 1915E, 287. That case, like this, was an action by a subvendee against a manufacturer of automobiles for negligence in failing to discover that one of its wheels was defective, the court holding that such an action could not be maintained. It is true there was a dissenting opinion in that case, but it was based chiefly upon the proposition that rules applicable to stagecoaches are archaic when applied to automobiles, and that if the law did not afford a remedy to strangers to the contract, the law should be changed. If this be true, the change should be effected by the Legislature and not by the courts. * * *

NOTES AND QUESTIONS

1. How would you phrase the holding in the Thomas v. Winchester case? What does it substitute for the restrictive doctrine requiring privity between plaintiff and defendant? Is *Thomas,* by its own language, limited in application to "inherently dangerous" products? Are you satisfied with the manner in which the *Thomas* court distinguishes Winterbottom v. Wright, the case of the stage-coach driver injured by result of negligence of the coach-maker?

2. Why does Cardozo suggest in MacPherson v. Buick that "It may be that Devlin v. Smith (the painters' scaffolding case) and Statler v. Ray Mfg. Co. (the coffee urns case) have extended the rule of Thomas v. Winchester?" Does Cardozo believe that he is extending the rule of *Thomas* ? Do you? Do you agree with Cardozo's holding that there is support for the ruling that Buick was negligent?

3. Are the effects of Cardozo's holding predictable and carefully circumscribed? Why does Cardozo say that "Whether a given thing is dangerous may be sometimes a question for the court and sometimes a question for the jury?" How is the judge to decide when the question is for him and when for the jury? Does this ambiguity weaken the legitimacy of Cardozo's decision?

4. What does Cardozo mean when he rejects the idea that "the duty to safeguard life and limb * * * grows out of contract," and instead declares that "We have put its source in the law?" Is contract not "the law?" Do you find any similarity between Cardozo's private law jurisprudence and the constitutional law philosophy publicly articulated by Franklin D. Roosevelt during

the court-packing crisis? See generally, Richard A. Posner, Cardozo: A Study in Reputation (1990). On Cardozo generally see the definitive biography by Andrew L. Kaufman, Cardozo (1998). For Cardozo as a tort lawmaker see Professor Kaufman's article, "Benjamin Cardozo as Paradigmatic Tort Lawmaker," the response by Professor Kaufman and the comments by Robert E. Keeton and Gary T. Schwartz, in the 1999 Clifford Law Symposium on Tort Law and Social Policy, 49 De Paul L.Rev. 275 (1999).

LOVELACE V. ASTRA TRADING CORP.

United States District Court, Southern District of Mississippi, 1977.
439 F.Supp. 753.

DAN M. RUSSELL, JR., CHIEF JUDGE [on defendants' motion for summary judgment].

* * *

During November or December of 1973, Edwina Lovelace, the plaintiff's wife, purchased a compact styled hair dryer (mini-dryer). * * * at the Howard Brothers store * * *. It appears that the mini-dryer was purchased for the plaintiff's son, Terry Lovelace * * *. The record shows that the mini-dryer was exclusively used by Terry Lovelace [who] * * * was living at home * * *.

The mini-dryer apparently functioned properly until February 10, 1974. On that date, while the plaintiff and his family were at church, the family residence was severely damaged by fire. The plaintiff alleges, and seeks to prove, that the fire resulted as a direct and proximate result of the defective nature of the mini hair dryer. The dryer was left plugged in, though not in use at the time of the fire. Some 18 days after the fire in question, plaintiff was diagnosed as having extremely high blood pressure. This led to open heart surgery and a coronary bypass, resulting in plaintiff's total and permanent disability. Plaintiff alleges that this condition was brought about as a direct result of the fire. * * *

Defendant Astra is an importer of merchandise, importing various items primarily from the Far East. * * *

Astra's agent in the Far East was, for the transaction in question, the Chaun Ching Co., defendant herein. Chaun Ching is an exporter and manufacturer of sundry goods. * * * [T]he dryers were actually manufactured by the Wan Nien Electric Appliance Company of Taiwan. The record also reveals that defendant Astra furnished Chaun Ching with the design and specifications for the hair dryer it desired to import. Production samples were returned to Astra, and the two defendants reached an agreement for the products' importation into the United States.

The mini-dryers were shipped to this country in individual boxes, with each box containing one dryer enclosed in a plastic bag. The boxes containing the individual dryers prominently bore the notation "Stellar". Stellar is a registered trademark of the defendant Astra.

Depositions filed in this case disclose that upon receiving shipments, Astra would run random sample checks. This entailed a cursory visual inspection and an actual testing of the product for a period of time thought sufficient to disclose any malfunctions. * * * The product was in no way altered or enhanced by Astra. * * *

The plaintiff's suit sounds in the ever growing theory of products liability. Liability is asserted against Chaun Ching for negligence in the design and manufacture of the mini-dryer. Astra is also charged with negligence in the selection, testing and distribution of the hair dryers. Finally, plaintiff asserts that both defendants are strictly liable in tort for the property damage and personal injuries suffered by the plaintiff herein. * * *

Defendant Astra * * * [asserts] that since the plaintiff was neither a user nor a consumer of the product, that he is thereby barred from suing under a strict liability in tort theory. * * *

Since this case is premised upon diversity jurisdiction, this Court sits in essence as another court of the forum state. Therefore, the substantive law of Mississippi is to be applied. * * * The problem presented herein is that the Mississippi Supreme Court has not yet addressed the issue of whether recovery under a strict liability in tort theory should be extended to those denominated as "bystanders".

* * *

Without the benefit of any state certification process, this Court must take the "role of a prophet" and seek to forecast how this issue will ultimately be resolved by the state courts. * * * Absent definitive guidance from Mississippi decisional or statutory law, this Court may therefore look to other available resources, i.e., decisions in other states, by other federal courts " * * * and the general weight and trend of authority." Julander v. Ford Motor Co., 488 F.2d 839 (10th Cir.1973).

Defendant Astra, in its brief and during oral argument, has stressed the point that it did not manufacture the mini-dryer that is the alleged cause of the plaintiff's damages. Defendant states that as a wholesaler, it was under no duty to inspect for latent defects, and under the authority of Shainberg v. Barlow, 258 So.2d 242 (Miss.1972), is absolved from liability herein.

In *Shainberg,* the plaintiff sued the wholesaler and the retailer when the heel of her shoe suddenly dislodged, thereby causing her bodily injury. The manufacturer was not joined as a party-defendant. The court stated the applicable rule thusly:

> Where the wholesaler or distributor purchases an article from *a reputable and reliable manufacturer,* sells it to a retailer in its original condition, and the retailer in turn sells the article—exactly as it came from the manufacturer—to a customer in the regular course of business, *no duty devolves* on the wholesaler or retailer *to inspect and discover a latent defect.* 258 So.2d at 244 (emphasis added).

The court concluded that the co-defendants could not be held accountable, reasoning that a contrary holding would make " * * * each retail merchant an insurer or guarantor * * * " of articles sold in its capacity as a mere sales conduit. Id. at 246.

However, certain factors take the case *sub judice* out of the purview of *Shainberg.* First, on this motion for partial summary judgment, this Court is unwilling to take judicial notice and assume that Astra did in fact deal with a "reputable and reliable manufacturer". Secondly, plaintiff has raised serious factual issues as to Astra's knowledge of the defective nature and propensities of the mini-dryers. Plaintiff claims that such knowledge preceded the fire in issue here. If established, *Shainberg* would be, by its facts, inapplicable here. * * *

Additional facts mitigate in favor of plaintiff's position here. The record so far reveals that Astra was not a stereotypical wholesaler or retailer. On the contrary, Astra selected the design for the hair dryers and approved the prototype before full scale manufacturing began. * * *

Finally, the boxes containing the individual mini-dryers were distinctively emblazoned "Stellar", defendant Astra's trademark. * * *

Therefore, the markings on the individual boxes would indicate, to the average consumer, that they were purchasing a "Stellar" manufactured product. Legal support for this proposition is found in the *Restatement (Second) of Torts* § 400 (1965), which provides that one "putting out" a product as his own is subject to a manufacturer's liability even though the product in question was in fact manufactured by another. * * * The foregoing principal is soundly based in logic, and serves to meet the reasonable expectations of the consuming public. * * *

Just as motorists on the Gulf Coast soon learn that all roads lead to Vancleave, any discussion of products liability law in Mississippi will have its roots in the seminal decision of State Stove Mfg. Co. v. Hodges, 189 So.2d 113 (Miss.1966), cert. denied sub nom., Yates v. Hodges, 386 U.S. 912, 87 S.Ct. 860, 17 L.Ed.2d 784 (1967). In *State Stove,* the plaintiff homeowner sued the manufacturer of a water heater and the builder-contractor who installed it, when after installation, it subsequently exploded, to plaintiff's chagrin. * * *

The court in *State Stove* explicitly adopted § 402A of the *Restatement (Second) of Torts,* * * *.

As set forth in *State Stove,* Section 402A provides:

> "(1) *One who sells* any product in a defective condition unreasonably dangerous to the user or consumer or to his property *is subject to liability* for physical harm thereby caused *to the ultimate user or consumer, or to his property,* if (a) the seller is engaged in the business of selling such a product, and (b) it is expected to and does reach the user or consumer without substantial change in the condition in which it is sold.
>
> (2) The rule stated in Subsection (1) applies although (a) the seller has exercised all possible care in the preparation and sale of his product, and (b) the user or consumer has not bought the product from or entered into any contractual relation with the seller." (emphasis added).

It is readily apparent that the rule, by its very terms, extends liability to users and consumers. The hair dryer in question was kept in the plaintiff's house, however, only by a strained construction could plaintiff be construed as either a user or consumer. Therefore, for purposes of this motion, Mr. Lovelace will be deemed a "bystander". And, it should be noted that the Institute, by caveat, expressed no opinion on the issue of extending § 402A liability to bystanders.

As mentioned earlier, Mississippi courts have not addressed this issue yet. However, certain intimations do appear. *State Stove* expressly abrogated the requirement of privity in a suit by a consumer against a manufacturer, and stated that since liability sounds in tort, warranty concepts are irrelevant. Plaintiff's brief directs the Court to Miss.Code Ann. § 75–2–318 (1972). Section 2–318 of the U.C.C. delineates the scope of warranty protection under the code, with liability extending to include members of the purchaser's household, or guests therein. However, this Court does not perceive that plaintiff advances any warranty theory of liability. Accordingly, since strict liability in tort and breach of warranty are two different breeds of cat, this Court does not feel that the adoption of U.C.C. § 2–318 necessarily implies any legislative, or judicial, intent to extend liability to bystanders in all circumstances and under all causes of action.

More on point is the quotation from Greenman v. Yuba Power Products, Inc., 59 Cal.2d 57, 27 Cal.Rptr. 697, 377 P.2d 897 (1963), wherein the plaintiff recovered from the manufacturer for injuries from a power tool purchased by the plaintiff's wife.

> A manufacturer is strictly liable in tort when an article he places on the market, knowing that it is to be used without inspection for defects, proves to have a defect that causes injury to a human being. * * * Quoted in *State Stove,* 189 So.2d at 119.

The Mississippi Supreme Court also quoted with approval Dean Prosser's summary of the effect of MacPherson v. Buick Motor Co.:

> The conclusion is clear that the duty extends to any one who may reasonably be expected to be in the vicinity of the chattel's probable use, and to be endangered if it is defective * * *. Id. at 116.

This Court recognizes that Dean Prosser's statement refers to claims under a negligence theory, and not strict products liability. However, as discussed infra, negligence concepts are finding useful application in strict products liability cases, even though negligence itself need not be proven.

* * *

Negligence concepts found application in Walton v. Chrysler Motor Corp., 229 So.2d 568 (Miss.1969), where the plaintiff's car was struck from the rear and the resulting injuries were allegedly aggravated due to a defect in the plaintiff's car. In holding for the defendant, the Mississippi Supreme Court stated:

> * * * but this rule [strict liability] does not eliminate the requirement that, even where there is a defect in the product, that *there must be some duty owed to the plaintiff* with regard to the defect * * *. Id. at 573 (emphasis added).

* * * [In Ford Motor Co. v. Cockrell, 211 So.2d 833 (Miss.1968) the court again quoted Dean Prosser on *MacPherson* in a *strict liability* case, and thus] without explicit reference, the Mississippi Supreme Court was impliedly applying concepts of foreseeability, traditionally an element of a count in negligence, to a strict liability case. * * * Finally, as pointed out infra, other courts have used the concept of foreseeability in determining whether the umbrella of strict liability also shields bystanders.

* * *

As noted earlier, the American Law Institute, by caveat to § 402A, refused to express an opinion as to whether the theory of strict liability in tort would inure to the benefit of those who are neither users nor consumers. However, Comment C thereto sets forth the general policies underlying the strict liability concept. Seriatim, and in brief, § 402A is premised upon the assumptions that a seller assumes a special responsibility to the public; that the public has a right to expect reputable sellers to stand behind their products; that public policy demands the cost of injuries due to defective products be placed on those who market them; and, such injuries are properly treated as a cost of production and insurable risks by those in the best position to seek such protection. If the general policies and the intent of the drafters are taken as stated, it is apparent to this Court that third-party bystanders are properly protected by § 402A. * * *

In Elmore v. American Motors, 70 Cal.2d 578, 75 Cal.Rptr. 652, 451 P.2d 84, 33 A.L.R.3d 406 (1969), the plaintiff's car malfunctioned. The plaintiff lost control, crossed the roadway and struck a second plaintiff's (Waters) car. The lower court sustained nonsuits on behalf of the manufacturer and retailer. The California Supreme Court reversed, basing its holding on the general policy grounds that manufacturers should bear the cost of injuries caused by their defective products. [The court stated:]

> *If anything, bystanders should be entitled to greater protection* than the consumer or user *where injury to bystanders* from the defect *is reasonably foreseeable.* Consumers and users, at least, have the opportunity to inspect for defects * * * [but] the bystander is in greater need of protection from defective products which are dangerous * * *.

* * * Defendant relies upon Winnett v. Winnett, 57 Ill.2d 7, 310 N.E.2d 1 (1974), in support of its position. In *Winnett,* the four year old plaintiff was injured when she put her fingers in the moving screen of a farm forage wagon. The Supreme Court of Illinois denied recovery against the manufacturer on a strict products liability theory. In so doing, that court stated:

> In our judgment the *liability* of a manufacturer properly *encompasses only those individuals to whom injuries from a defective product may reasonably be foreseen* and only those situations where the product is being used for the purpose for which it was intended or for which it is reasonably foreseeable that it may be used. 310 N.E.2d at 4 (emphasis added).

The manufacturer was therefore absolved from liability because it could not reasonably foresee that a four year old child would be allowed to put her fingers in the forage screen. However, the emphasis of the court in *Winnett* was on foreseeability * * *. Therefore, the *Winnett* case is reconcilable with those allowing recovery by bystanders.

The issue has been addressed and resolved by other courts also. The court in Ciampichini v. Ring Bros., Inc., 40 A.D.2d 289, 339 N.Y.S.2d 716 (1973), without hesitation overruled a prior decision denying bystander recovery and emphatically stated:

> We resolve that issue now by laying to rest a principle which we believe outmoded and no longer adaptable to the rights of individuals in contemporary society. 339 N.Y.S.2d at 717.

* * *

The Missouri Supreme Court also extended strict liability recovery to bystanders in Giberson v. Ford Motor Co., 504 S.W.2d 8 (Mo.1974), wherein the court, quoting from Tucson Indus., Inc. v. Schwartz, 108 Ariz. 464, 501 P.2d 936, 939–40 (1972), gave the basic justification for extending liability.

> Strict liability is a public policy device to spread the risk from one to whom a defective product may be a catastrophe, to those who marketed the product, profit from its sale, and have the know-how to remove its defects before placing it in the chain of distribution.

Mississippi courts are generally in accord with the policy judgment that manufacturers should shoulder the costs of injuries resulting from their defective products. * * * Other policy reasons in support of the doctrine have been advanced * * * and accepted by the courts. " * * * The reason for extending the strict liability doctrine to innocent bystanders is the desire to minimize risks of personal injury and or property damage." Darryl v. Ford Motor Co., 440 S.W.2d 630, 633 (Tex.1969). The general consensus therefore appears to favor extension of the strict liability doctrine to provide relief to bystanders. * * *

One final case is worth noting. In West v. Caterpillar Tractor Co., Inc., 336 So.2d 80 (Fla.1976) * * *, the Florida court noted that no adequate rationale or theoretical explanation existed to deny strict liability to bystanders. That court also summed up the situation well by its quotation from Caruth v. Mariani, 11 Ariz.App. 188, 463 P.2d 83, 85 (1970), that:

> All states which have adopted the theory of strict tort liability have extended the theory to the bystander when called upon to do so * * *. 336 So.2d at 89. * * *

Part of the basis for the Florida court's holding is the notion that any restriction of the doctrine to users or consumers only " * * * would have to rest on the vestige of the disappearing privity requirement." Id. at 89. As mentioned earlier, the Mississippi Supreme Court in *State Stove* abandoned the privity requirement in suits by a consumer against a manufacturer. The court thereupon concluded:

> The obligation of the manufacturer must become what in justice it ought to be—an enterprise liability * * *. The cost of injuries or damages, *either to persons or property,* resulting from defective products, should be borne by the makers of the products who put them into the channels of trade * * * This doctrine of strict liability applies when harm befalls a *foreseeable bystander* who comes within range of the danger. 336 So.2d at 92 (emphasis added).

Based upon the foregoing, this Court holds that the plaintiff herein may avail himself of the strict liability doctrine enunciated in § 402A of the Restatement, and as adopted and construed by the Mississippi Supreme Court. Defendants' motion for partial summary judgment on this ground is therefore denied.

* * *

The court in *West,* supra, notes that 31 states have adopted § 402A in one form or another, with two federal court "predictions" in Utah and

Vermont. Even a cursory perusal of the cited cases discloses that Mississippi was in the forefront in adopting § 402A. This Court has no reason to believe that the state supreme court, given the appropriate case, would not extend strict liability concepts to include "bystanders". The Mississippi court's willingness to be among judicial innovators in this area indicates a concern for consumers in general; and a sensitivity to the delicate interplay among responsible social policy, enterprise liability and the reasonable expectations of the consuming public.

* * *

[The court thus ruled that it was appropriate for the plaintiff to be allowed to bring the case to trial, and to prove his injuries resulted from a defective hair dryer.]

NOTES AND QUESTIONS

1. What changes in the rule of Thomas v. Winchester and MacPherson v. Buick are made by section 402A? Are there any similarities between *Restatement (Second) Torts* § 402A and *Restatement (Second) Contracts* §§ 89A and 90? Do you suppose Cardozo would have approved of § 402A? With regard to another analogue from the law of contract, is it true, as the *Astra* court maintains, that "strict liability in tort and breach of warranty are two different breeds of cat?" Why does the court not believe, for example, that negligence theory (*MacPherson*) and 402A are different breeds of cat? Note that the court seems to approve of the "useful application" of "negligence concepts" in "strict products liability cases." Do you find it easy to understand how these distinctions are drawn? Is this a "scientific" enterprise?

2. The *Astra* court seems to accept the assumption of the framers of *Restatement (Second) Torts* § 402A "that public policy demands the cost of injuries due to defective products be placed on those who market them; and, such injuries are properly treated as a cost of production and insurable risks by those in the best position to seek such protection." Do you accept these assumptions? Would the judges who formulated the nineteenth century tort rules we studied in Chapter Three subscribe to these assumptions? Why or why not?

3. In an omitted part of the *Astra* opinion, the court quoted the Kentucky decision of Embs v. Pepsi–Cola Bottling Co., 528 S.W.2d 703, 705 (Ky.1975) that "[O]nce strict liability is accepted, bystander recovery is a *fait accompli*." If this is so, how can it be that the "American Law Institute, by caveat to § 402A, refused to express an opinion as to whether the theory of strict liability in tort would inure to the benefit of those who are neither users nor consumers?"

4. The court in *Astra* refers to the Mississippi state court's "sensitivity to the delicate interplay among responsible social policy, enterprise liability, and the reasonable expectations of the consuming public." Why could it be

said that a holding of bystander liability under § 402A reflected that sensitivity? Why is the "interplay" here a "delicate" one?

5. We saw in Chapter Three that the nineteenth century theories of tort liability, in particular the rise of the negligence principle, seemed felicitous in the way they reduced the liability of infant industry, commerce, and transportation, which might have been unlimited under the nuisance or trespass standards. Can it be said that late Twentieth Century developments in tort law evince other policies? Predicting the scope of tort law in the future, Professor Marshall Shapo wrote in 1970 that:

> The New Torts will concern itself with remedies against the abuse of power—political, economic, intellectual, as well as physical. * * *
>
> * * * [T]he New Torts must be made to deal more explicitly with the question of what large enterprises and other clusters of power owe to the individual caught in their coils. The New Torts * * * will place new and vibrant emphasis on the responsibility of private and public enterprise * * *. The New Torts * * * will emphasize more sharply the question of what defendants representing significant clusters of different kinds of power owe to our civilization in the way of behaving in a civilized manner. It will present an analogue of recent developments in constitutional law, focusing on legal checks on private groups that act with power governmental in function.

Shapo, "Changing Frontiers in Torts: Vistas for the 70's," 22 Stan.L.Rev. 330, 333, 334–335 (1970). Copyright © 1970 by the Board of Trustees of the Leland Stanford Junior University, reprinted by permission of the Stanford Law Review, Fred B. Rothman & Company, and the author. See also Shapo, The Duty to Act (1977). The constitutional law case to which Professor Shapo was making explicit reference was Monroe v. Pape, 365 U.S. 167, 81 S.Ct. 473, 5 L.Ed.2d 492 (1961). In that case, the Court held that the fourteenth amendment mandated that the prohibitions against unreasonable searches and seizures of the fourth amendment applied to the states, and, further, that where Chicago police officers unlawfully invaded petitioner's home, the invasion was "under color" of state law, and thus a deprivation of Constitutional rights and actionable under 42 U.S.C.A. § 1983, a federal civil rights statute. The scope of remedies for violations of civil rights by local government officials was considerably widened by Monell v. Department of Social Services of the City of New York, 436 U.S. 658, 98 S.Ct. 2018, 56 L.Ed.2d 611 (1978). We haven't gone into this area of constitutional law, of course, but can you relate Professor Shapo's comments to any constitutional law cases that we have studied? If the "New Torts" is to address the problems which Professor Shapo describes, would this raise any problems of judicial legitimacy that we have seen arise in a constitutional context?

6. The problem of judicial legitimacy has arisen not only with regard to products liability litigation, but also as a result of developments in the negligence doctrine. Perhaps the most dramatic of such cases was DILLON v. LEGG, 68 Cal.2d 728, 69 Cal.Rptr. 72, 441 P.2d 912 (1968). Mr. Legg's alleg-

edly negligently driven automobile struck Mrs. Dillon's little girl. Mrs. Dillon, looking on, watched in horror as her child died from the collision. In the action for wrongful death of the child, Mrs. Dillon sought damages to compensate her for the "great emotional disturbance and shock and injury to her nervous system" produced by witnessing her daughter's death. Similar compensation was sought on behalf of another daughter who also saw the accident. Justice Tobriner observed that earlier American decisions had barred such recovery, based on

> the alleged absence of a required "duty" of due care of the tortfeasor to the mother. Duty, in turn [these decisions] state must express public policy; the imposition of duty here would work disaster because it would invite fraudulent claims and it would involve the courts in the hopeless task of defining the extent of the tortfeasor's liability. In substance, they say, definition of liability being impossible, denial of liability is the only realistic alternative.

69 Cal.Rptr. at 74, 441 P.2d at 914. Given the "natural justice upon which the mother's claim rests" however, Tobriner declared that the old rule barring recovery should not be allowed to stand, and that it was possible to provide "proper guidelines" to avoid the "fraudulent claims" and "impossible definition" of which the old decisions had warned.

Tobriner appears to have sensed that the court's undertaking was a difficult and uncertain one, but that the court's task in determining negligence was simply to assess the foreseeability of harm:

> Since the chief element in determining whether defendant owes a duty or an obligation to plaintiff is the foreseeability of the risk, that factor will be of prime concern in every case. Because it is inherently intertwined with foreseeability such duty or obligation must necessarily be adjudicated only upon a case-by-case basis. We cannot now predetermine defendant's obligation in every situation by a fixed category; no immutable rule can establish the extent of that obligation for every circumstance in the future.

69 Cal.Rptr. at 80, 441 P.2d at 920. Still, the court did give what it called "guidelines;" to wit, that three factors be taken into consideration in such cases, (1) whether the plaintiff was located near the scene of the accident, (2) whether the shock resulted from the direct emotional impact on plaintiff from sensory and contemporaneous observance of the accident, and (3) whether the plaintiff and the victim were closely related. Id. Applying these factors to the case at hand, the court held that Mrs. Dillon had made out a *prima facie* cause of action. Do you believe that the court's guidelines take care of the problems that the rule barring recovery sought to avoid?

Compare Dillon with Boyles v. Kerr, 61 L.W. 2388 (Texas Sup.Ct. No. D–0963, 1992), where the court held that while bystanders might continue to recover emotional distress damages under Texas law as a result of witnessing a serious or fatal accident, "tort law cannot and should not attempt to provide redress for every instance of rude, insensitive or distasteful behavior, even though it may result in hurt feelings, embarrassment, or even humiliation." The Texas court ruled that in Texas there was no independent cause of action for negligent infliction of mental distress, and thus there could be no recovery for the plaintiff in the case. The plaintiff had complained that she had become known as a campus "porno queen" after her date had shown friends a videotape of their "sexual liaison." 61 L.W. 1093 (1993). Should recovery have been permitted? The *Boyles* court set aside a $500,000 judgment in plaintiff's favor.

7. Another negligence case that caused concern is HELLING v. CAREY, 83 Wash.2d 514, 519 P.2d 981 (1974). Plaintiff was nearsighted, and consulted defendant ophthalmologists in 1959, who fitted her with contact lenses. She saw the doctors approximately ten times over the next nine years, her first visit after 1959 coming in 1963, concerning "irritation caused by the contact lenses." Her doctors apparently assumed that it was her contacts that were giving her trouble, but, when, in October 1968, for the first time, one of the defendants checked the plaintiff's eye pressure and field of vision, it was discovered that she had glaucoma. Plaintiff was then thirty-two. Plaintiff sued defendants for malpractice, alleging that she had suffered permanent visual damage due to their failure to diagnose and treat her glaucoma at an earlier stage. Defendants brought in expert witnesses whose testimony was uncontradicted, and who established that "it was the universal practice of ophthalmologists not to administer glaucoma tests to patients under age 40 [as was plaintiff] because the incidence of glaucoma at younger ages was so small." Defendants argued that since it was the practice of the profession not to test for glaucoma under 40, they should not be liable for failing to catch the disease earlier. The court refused to accept this defense.

The court observed that Justice Holmes had stated in Texas & Pac. Ry. v. Behymer, 189 U.S. 468, 470, 23 S.Ct. 622, 47 L.Ed. 905 (1903) that "What usually is done may be evidence of what ought to be done, but what ought to be done is fixed by a standard of reasonable prudence, whether it usually is complied with or not." The court also referred to The T.J. Hooper, 60 F.2d 737, 740 (2d Cir.1932), where Judge Hand had stated, in holding that the owners of tugs were negligent when they did not equip them with radios, "Courts must in the end say what is required; there are precautions so imperative that even their universal disregard will not excuse their omission."

The court proceeded to reason, from these judicial expressions, that since the tests for glaucoma were simple and harmless, and since they would have revealed the disease in time to arrest its progress, "Under the facts of this case reasonable prudence required the timely giving of the pressure test to this plaintiff." 519 P.2d, at 983. Would you have concurred in this opinion? If "reasonable prudence" as the court defines it does not mean the accepted practice among doctors of defendant's specialty, what does it mean? Can you understand why medical malpractice rates have risen dramatically in the last few years?

A concurring opinion was written in *Helling,* by Associate Justice Utter. He stated that "it seems illogical" for the court to be holding that the defendants were morally blameworthy or negligent in that they "failed to exercise a reasonable standard of care," because they "used all the precautions commonly prescribed by their profession in diagnosis and treatment." Id., at 984. "It seems to me," Justice Utter wrote, "we are, in reality, imposing liability, because, in choosing between an innocent plaintiff and a doctor, who * * * could have prevented the full effects of this disease by administering a simple, harmless test and treatment, the plaintiff should not have to bear the risk of loss." Id. Justice Utter concluded that it would be better, then, to rest liability simply on a standard of "strict liability or liability without fault." Only two of the nine justices joined in Utter's opinion, the remaining six joined in Tobriner's. Which opinion do you find the most persuasive? The legislature of the state of Washington, in 1975, passed a law prohibiting any recovery in a tort case such as *Helling* where medical personnel were following "that degree of skill, care and learning possessed by other persons in the same profession * * *." The 1975 statute was designed to overrule *Helling.* See Gates v. Jensen, 20 Wash.App. 81, 579 P.2d 374 (1978).

8. Shapo's "New Torts" may have its counterpart in modern American property law. Indeed, it has been cogently argued that "The destruction of property is a remarkable trend of the modern age." George M. Armstrong, Jr., "From the Fetishism of Commodities to the Regulated Market: The Rise and Decline of Property," 82 Nw.U.L.Rev. 79 (1988). The change from the old common law of property is probably clearest in landlord-tenant law, and a leading case in that regard is KLINE v. 1500 MASSACHUSETTS AVE. APT. CORP., 141 U.S.App.D.C. 370, 439 F.2d 477 (1970). Mrs. Kline sustained serious injuries when she was assaulted by an intruder in the common hallway of her Washington, D.C. apartment house. When Mrs. Kline had first moved in, in October 1959, the entrances to the building were carefully guarded and a doorman was on duty twenty-four hours a day. By mid–1966, however, a doorman was no longer employed, and the entrances were often left unlocked and unguarded. During the years leading up to the incident there had been "an increasing number of assaults, larcenies, and robberies being perpetrated against the tenants in and from the common hallways of the apartment building." The landlord had notice of these crimes, and had even been urged by Mrs. Kline herself to "take steps to secure the building."

Judge Malcolm Richard Wilkey, writing for the majority, noted that the risk of "criminal assault and robbery" was entirely predictable if the premises were not kept secured, that no individual tenant "had it within his power" to take the steps to secure the entrances and common hallways, and that this was "a risk whose prevention or minimization was almost entirely within the power of the landlord * * *." Judge Wilkey noted that previous cases had held that the landlord had a duty to maintain "areas of common use and common danger" so that no one would be injured by physical defects of the building in those areas. The rationale of those cases "as applied to predictable criminal acts by third parties is the same," said Judge Wilkey.

The opinion noted that "As a general rule, a private person does not have a duty to protect another from a criminal attack by a third person," but that "the rationale of this very broad general rule falters when it is applied to the conditions of modern day urban apartment living * * *." In particular, the court suggested that Judge Wright's opinion in Javins v. First Nat. Realty Corp., 138 U.S.App.D.C. 369, 428 F.2d 1071 (1970) had rejected "the traditional analysis of a lease as being a conveyance of an interest in land—with all the medieval connotations this often brings * * *." Under the common law analysis of a lease as a conveyance, there were few, if any, ongoing obligations of the landlord. Judge Wright's opinion in *Javins* held that "leases of urban dwelling units should be interpreted and construed like any other contract," and that this meant that the court could imply a "warrant of habitability" which included a contractual duty on the part of the landlord to maintain the premises in suitable repair where such repairs "required access to equipment in areas in the control of the landlord, and skills which no urban tenant possesses."

"[T]he duty of taking protective measures guarding the entire premises and the areas peculiarly under the landlord's control against the perpetration of criminal acts," stated Judge Wilkey, could also be placed upon the landlord, as an implied term in the lease, because the landlord was "the party to the lease contract who has the effective capacity to perform these necessary acts."

Finally, in determining the standard of care which should be applied in such cases, the court appeared to turn to the law of torts for guidance, although Judge Wilkey indicated that the landlord's obligation was the same whether considered as an obligation grounded in tort or in contract. The landlord's duty, according to the court, was to take the precautions "commonly provided in apartments of this character and type in this community." The record as to custom was "unsatisfactory," because of the limitations on evidence imposed by the trial judge as a result of objections by "defendant's counsel." Given the paucity of the record, and blaming this on "defendant's counsel and the trial judge," Judge Wilkey took the security precautions which existed at 1500 Massachusetts Avenue in 1959, when Mrs. Kline moved in, as the standard to be maintained, and held that the landlord was responsible to Mrs. Kline for the consequences of failing to keep up this standard.

Since Judge Wilkey's opinion in *Kline,* courts have held that landlords violate an enforceable duty of protection when they fail to safeguard their tenants from foreseeable criminal acts in several other jurisdictions including Georgia, New Jersey, and New York. The rationale has apparently been rejected in Illinois and Minnesota. Note, "The Duty of a Landlord to Exercise Reasonable Care in the Selection and Retention of Tenants," 30 Stan.L.Rev. 725, 728n. (1978). How might one relate the holding in *Kline* to the "death of contract" and the "New Torts?" Are these common-law developments the best means of effecting change in late twentieth century law? For further elaboration of the past and future of "property as a civil right," see the comprehensive six-volume collection James W. Ely, Jr., Property Rights in American History (1997). Of this collection, one respected reviewer remarked that "Anyone seeking an enhanced grasp of the complexity of property rights in American history now has a magnificent library with just Ely's six books." Douglas W. Kmiec, "Property and Economic Liberty as Civil Rights: The Magisterial History of James W. Ely, Jr.," 52 Vand.L.Rev. 737 (1999). For a case that has been said to represent further dramatic erosion in property rights see Kelo v. New London, 545 U.S. 469 (2005)(holding by a 5–4 majority that the Constitution's grant of eminent domain power, which permits governments to take property for "public use" so long as just compensation is paid, should be construed as permitting takings for a "public purpose.")

9. Commenting on cases such as *Helling* and *Dillon,* Professor James A. Henderson, Jr. wrote in 1976 that:

> The reforms and changes in the law of negligence in recent years have, purportedly to advance identifiable social objectives, eliminated much of the specificity with which negligence principles traditionally have been formulated. We are rapidly approaching the day when liability will be determined routinely on a case by case, "under all the circumstances," basis, with decision makers (often juries) guided only by the broadest of general principles. When that day arrives, the retreat from the rule of law will be complete, principled decision will have been replaced with decision by whim, and the common law of negligence will have degenerated into an unjustifiably inefficient, thinly disguised lottery.

Henderson, "Expanding the Negligence Concept: Retreat from the Rule of Law," 51 Ind.L.J. 467, 468 (1976).* How might Herbert Wechsler have assessed Helling and Dillon? What might have been the reaction of Morton Horwitz?

In another part of his article Professor Henderson diagnosed part of the current torts pathology as "irresponsibility" on the part of legal academics. Only two allegedly guilty parties were named, but one of them was Marshall Shapo, for his comments quoted in note 5, supra. Stated Henderson, "These are commentaries which tend to speak of the common law torts judgment as a tool of harassment in modern political warfare, and whose disregard for judicial integrity approaches recklessness." Id., at 523. Would this diagnosis of pathology meet the standards of Helling v. Carey? From what you have seen of the modern law of torts, would you agree with Professor Henderson? What are the economic implications of these court decisions? See generally Peter Huber, Liability: The Legal Revolution and its Consequences (1988), William M. Landes and Richard A. Posner, The Economic Structure of Tort Law (1987), Steven Shavell, Economic Analysis of Accident Law (1987), John J. Donohue III, "The Law and Economics of Tort Law: The Profound Revolution," 102 Harv.L.Rev. 1047 (1989), and Anthony J. Sebok, "The Fall and Rise of Blame in American Tort Law," 68 Brook.L.Rev. 1031 (2003).

Does the "New Torts" seem in accord with the notions of popular sovereignty and social mobility we saw reflected in earlier decisions? For some later comments in the judicial integrity of process vs. substantive justice debate in torts see Pedrick, "The Regeneration of Tort Law," 1979 Ariz.St.L.J. 143, which returns to a position not unlike Professor Shapo's, and declares that the "crisis" caused by products liability and medical malpractice insurance seems to be over. But see Robert E. Litan and Clifford Winston, editors, Liability: Perspectives and Policy (1988) for several essays which suggest that a new "crisis" in torts liability, flowing from litigation over automobile accidents and environmental disasters, as well as products liability and malpractice, is again with us. For some continuation of the debate about whether we have a torts crisis in general and a products liability crisis in particular see, e.g., Philip K. Howard, The Death of Common Sense: How Law is Suffocating America (1994) and The Collapse of the Common Good: How America's Lawsuit Culture Undermines Our Freedom (2001); Walter Olson, The Litigation Explosion (1991) and The Rule of Lawyers: How the New Litigation Elite Threatens America's Rule of Law (2002), "Symposium: Judges as Tort Lawmakers, the Fifth Annual Clifford Symposium on Tort Law and Social Policy," 49 De Paul L.Rev. 275 (1999). Arthur R. Miller, "The Pretrial Rush to Judgment: Are the 'Litigation Explosion,' 'Liability Crisis,' and Efficiency Clichés Eroding our Day in Court and Jury Trial Commitments?" 78 N.Y.U.L.Rev. 982 (2003), W. Taylor Reveley III, "Is the Republic Circling the Drain?", 96 Nw.U.L.Rev. 1579 (2002) (critically reviewing Howard, Collapse of the Common Good). Professor Henderson served as reporter for part of the Restatement of Torts, Third, and his work, particularly on Section 402A, has been described as "an express rejection of enterprise liability and product category liability." See generally, "Note: Just What You'd Expect: Professor Henderson's Redesign of Products Liability," 111 Harv.L.Rev. 2366, 2368 (1998). For Professor Shapo's 1995 comments on the future of products liability, see, e.g, Marshall S. Shapo, "In Search of the Law of Products Liability: The ALI Restatement Project," 48 Vand.L.Rev. 631 (1995). What, then, are we to make of what Grant Gilmore called the "schizophrenic" quality of American law in the late twentieth century? In the last chapter we see how the American Legal Academy sought to deal with this question.

CHAPTER 8

THE CURRENT STRUGGLE FOR THE SOUL OF AMERICAN LAW

■ ■ ■

A. INTRODUCTION

In most of this book we have studied the doctrines of American public and private law, observing change over time, and seeking to determine the core values implemented by the instrumentalities of our legal institutions. In this final Chapter we move further into the realm of abstract theory than we have before, in order to examine the thoughts of some academic critics of the very institutions of the American law itself. To a great extent, our concern will shift from being that of the activity of courts and lawyers to the activity of American law professors. Probably ever since United States Supreme Court Justice Joseph Story accepted a chair at the Harvard Law School, in the first third of the nineteenth century, there has been a great deal of exchange between the worlds of the bench and the academy, but with the infusion of academics into judgeships in the end of the twentieth and beginning of the twenty-first centuries, that influence seems even greater than ever before.

We will begin this examination of some of the cutting edges of academic thought by looking at perhaps the most successful of the academic meta-theories of law, "Law and Economics." We will be examining the work and the critics of the principal practitioner of that art, Richard Posner, formally Professor of Law at the University of Chicago (the Rome of Law and Economics), and afterwards United States Circuit Judge on the United States Court of Appeals for the Seventh Circuit (in Chicago).

Posner's work has often been characterized as being on the "Right" of the American political spectrum, although that characterization may now be open to some doubt. We will follow Posner by a study of the thought of one segment of the "Left" in the American law schools, the Critical Legal Studies ("CLS") movement. Members of CLS were not prominent on the bench, but as much has been written by and about them as about any recent school of legal analysis, and they numbered among their adherents some of the brightest minds employed on law faculties. As we will see, their thought differed in a radical manner from that of Posner and his school, and the differences between "law and economics" and CLS offered a stark contrast of choices facing those who would seek to reform and refine American law.

It is characteristic of the development of American law (and, indeed, of philosophical systems generally) that out of the clash of competing thesis and antithesis there eventually emerges one or more syntheses, and the third of the schools current in the American Legal Academy which we will examine offers an approach which might be useful in reconciling the insights of Law and Economics and CLS. That school is the "Law and Literature" project, and while Richard Posner's group tries to employ tools from economics, and while the CLS adherents use tools principally from philosophy and political theory, "Law and Literature" analysts employ literary criticism and psychology. None of these three approaches to the study of law is very old, as we will see, and all seem to have the potential to influence the course of legal development for several years to come. The Fourth, and last school of thought that we will consider in some detail, Feminism, has some similarities to Critical Legal Studies, but offers much that is radically different from these three other schools, and raises issues that we have hinted at, but never resolved, at several points in the course. No student seeking to grasp the subtler nuances of American legal developments at the turn of the twentieth century can afford to ignore the work of these academic theoreticians, and so we close our examination of the history of American Law and Jurisprudence with an eye toward the speculative forces that are likely, eventually, to shape their future. The Chapter concludes with readings from two of the most important late twentieth century United States Supreme Court cases seeking to address national values and concerns, from the impeachment proceedings against President Clinton, and from the Supreme Court's case that decided the presidential election in 2000.

Our study of these meta-theories of the law begins with one of Richard Posner's first "law and economics" pieces, "Killing or Wounding to Protect a Property Interest." See if you can understand why this piece, and the approach which it represented, generated so much immediate controversy.

B. LAW AND ECONOMICS

RICHARD A. POSNER, KILLING OR WOUNDING TO PROTECT A PROPERTY INTEREST*

14 Journal of Law and Economics 201 (1971).

A farmer in Iowa named Briney had a farmhouse in which he stored old furniture and odds and ends, including some antiques of undisclosed

* Reprinted with the permission of the publisher, the University of Chicago Press, and of the author.

value. After several thefts, Briney rigged a spring gun in the farmhouse.[1] At his wife's suggestion, he pointed the gun so that it would hit an intruder in the legs—not, as Briney had initially planned, in the stomach. A man named Katko, who had previously stolen goods from the place, broke in, triggered the spring gun, and was badly wounded in the leg. He was initially charged with burglary but later permitted to plead guilty to petty larceny, fined $50, and given a suspended jail sentence. He brought a civil suit against the Brineys, charging that his wounding was a battery, and won a jury award of $20,000 in compensatory and $10,000 in punitive damages. The verdict occasioned a public outcry, and proposed legislation (modeled on a recent Nebraska law) that would explicitly have authorized the use of deadly force in defense of property was narrowly defeated in the state legislature. At this writing the case is awaiting decision in the Supreme Court of Iowa on defendants' appeal.[4]

Spring guns were something of a *cause célèbre* in early nineteenth century England, but since that time the reported cases have been few. Cases involving the use of deadly force to defend property in person have been few too, in part because self-defense is so often an issue when the defendant is present. Perhaps the Iowa case, when viewed against a background of mounting public concern over crime, signifies a resurgence of the problem. What makes the deadly-force issue worth discussing, however, is not its topicality but its theoretical interest, which I believe to be considerable. Involving as it does a conflict between the preservation of life and the protection of property interests, the privilege (if there is a privilege) to use deadly force to protect property cannot fail to raise fundamental issues of legal policy. It also presents interesting questions concerning the allocation of law enforcement authority between the public and private sectors. The approach of conventional legal scholarship has been unsatisfactory * * *. I am led to explore an alternative approach, an economic approach, whose utility in helping to answer questions of legal policy and to interpret opaque and apparently conflicting judicial decisions is a major theme of this paper. As we shall see, an economic approach is useful even though it is not usually thought of as an especially apt tool for resolving such basic value questions as life versus property. Finally, although our privilege may seem far from the mainstream of contemporary concern with tort law, we shall see that it is in fact paradigmatic of a wide spectrum of tort questions and illuminates the central policies of that law.

---

[1] A gun (usually a shotgun) rigged to fire when a string or other triggering device is tripped by an intruder.

[4] The case was decided shortly after this article went to press. The court affirmed the judgment for the plaintiff, one judge dissenting. * * *

I

There are not many judicial opinions dealing with the privilege to use deadly force and none contains an illuminating discussion of the subject. The one substantial journal piece[7] may be considered merged with the *Restatement of Torts*: the co-author of the article (Francis Bohlen) was the Reporter for the *Restatement* and the relevant passages in the *Restatement* track the article closely. The level of analysis has otherwise been very low. The Harper and James [Torts] treatise states:

It is uniformly held that the possessor of land or goods cannot use force reasonably calculated to cause death or serious bodily harm for the purpose of defending his bare dignitary interests in the property and seldom to prevent the loss or destruction thereof. It is only when the intrusion is of such a character that it threatens the life or limb of the possessor that he may employ force likely to wound or kill the intruder.[8]

If the "seldom" qualification is intended seriously—which cannot be determined, since there is no supporting citation, explanation, or even further mention of the point—then the sentence that follows is wrong. An intrusion may threaten the destruction of property without endangering anyone's life or limb. The authors go on to say that mechanical devices (such as spring guns) are privileged to protect property only "against an invasion which threatens death or serious bodily harm to the occupants of the premises," but the first case they cite in support of the point holds that the killing of a burglar of an unoccupied warehouse by means of a spring gun is privileged, despite the fact that such a burglary does not endanger anyone.[10]

A number of sections of the *Restatement of Torts* (promulgated in 1934) bear on our subject. Section 77 recognizes a privilege to defend a property interest by means not likely to cause death or serious bodily harm; thus a landowner who shoves a trespasser off his land without hurting him is not liable for a battery. * * * No reason for the privilege is given, but perhaps none is needed. Section 77 accords with the decisions on the question and raises no special difficulties.

Section 79 states that there is a privilege to use deadly force in defense of property when necessary to protect the occupant of the property from death or serious bodily harm. The draftsmen note that this privilege is largely redundant in view of the privileges of self-defense and of prevention of serious crimes dealt with elsewhere in the *Restatement*. No reasons are suggested why no broader privilege should be recognized.

---

[7] Francis H. Bohlen & John J. Burns, The Privilege to Protect Property by Dangerous Barriers and Mechanical Devices, 35 Yale L.J. 525 (1926).

[8] 1 Fowler V. Harper & Fleming James, Jr., The Law of Torts 250 (1956).

[10] Scheuermann v. Scharfenberg, 163 Ala. 337, 50 So. 335 (1909). * * *

Section 84 states that there is a privilege to use nondeadly mechanical devices (such as barbed wire) to protect property. One of the comments on the section, after setting forth some sensible qualifications on the use of such devices, states that the privilege is not forfeited merely because "the device is one which is likely to do more harm than the possessor of land would be privileged to inflict if he were present at the time of the particular intrusion"; the risk of injury, in the draftsmen's view, may be offset by the impracticability (cost) of protecting the property other than by an undiscriminating device.

Section 85 recognizes a privilege to inflict death or serious injury by a spring gun or other mechanical device intended or likely to cause such harm when the user, had he been present, would have been privileged to prevent or terminate the intrusion by the intentional infliction of such harm. Why did the draftsmen depart from the formula of section 79, which recognizes a privilege to use deadly force when the occupant's safety is threatened and implicitly not otherwise? Could the privilege be broader when deadly force is employed by means of a mechanical device than when it is employed in person? One might argue by analogy to nondeadly mechanical devices that the privilege could indeed be broader, but this line of argument is cut short by the draftsmen's comment: "A possessor of land cannot do indirectly and by a mechanical device that which, were he present, he could not do immediately and in person"—just what section 84 permits.

* * *

If we stand back now and consider the pattern created by the various sections and comments [to the 1934 ALI *Restatement of Torts*] we see that (a) there is no privilege to use deadly force in defense of property as such, but (b) there is a broad privilege to use such force (i) to prevent certain crimes, among them burglary of a dwelling place, whether or not the crime is a dangerous one in the circumstances of the case (the dwelling might be unoccupied), and (ii) to avoid being wrongfully dispossessed from one's home, whether or not there is any danger to the rightful possessor.* These rules do not fit together. If (a) is sound, no one should be privileged to set a deadly spring gun in an unoccupied dwelling or a warehouse, or to kill a landlord attempting to evict him. If any part of (b) is sound, it is hard to see why someone should be forbidden to set a deadly spring gun where it is the only practicable method of protecting valuable property, merely because the property is not located in a dwelling place.

Where two legal rules appear to be in conflict, one is led naturally to inquire into the reasons underlying the rules for possible clues to an ac-

* [Restatement section 87(2). No reason for this privilege is given in the restatement, and there is no attempt to reconcile it with the narrower privilege for killing in defense of other property interests.]

commodation. The *Restatement of Torts,* however, offers no reasoned grounds for the rules of law stated. Why should deadly force be permitted to prevent pure property crimes such as burglary of an unoccupied dwelling place? The only clue is to be found in the comments on section 131 where it is noted that an officer in pursuit of a felon may not know whether a crime endangering life or safety has been committed—an observation quite irrelevant to the propriety, say, of setting a spring gun in one's house before going on vacation. Why is there no privilege to use deadly force in defense of property? Because:

> The value of human life and limb, not only to the individual concerned but also to society, so outweighs the interest of a possessor of land in excluding from it those whom he is not willing to admit thereto that a possessor of land has * * * no privilege to use force intended or likely to cause death or serious harm against another whom the possessor sees about to enter his premises or meddle with his chattel, [unless the intrusion endangers the occupants].[21]

The draftsmen have made the task of balancing life against property easy for themselves by opposing the interest in human life to the interest in keeping out mere trespassers and "meddlers." Suppose an intruder is threatening to remove or destroy property of great value. It is surely not correct to say that society never permits the sacrifice of human lives on behalf of substantial economic values. Automobile driving is an example of the many deadly activities that cannot be justified as saving more lives than they take. Nor can the motoring example be distinguished from the spring-gun case on the ground that one who sets a spring gun intends to kill or wound. In both cases, a risk of death is created that could be avoided by substituting other methods of achieving one's ends (walking instead of driving); in both cases the actor normally hopes the risk will not materialize. One can argue that driving is more valuable and spring guns more dangerous; but intentionality is neither here nor there.

It is not only the Institute's use of the term "intruder," a synonym for trespasser[22] devoid of any connotation of stealing or destroying valuable property, but its avoidance throughout these sections of examples involving serious property losses, that evinces a reluctance to face difficult choices between human lives and other social values. * * *

Had someone pointed out the problems in their treatment of deadly force, the draftsmen might have replied that their job was to state the law, not to eliminate its inconsistencies. Such a reply, however, would both misrepresent the expressed intentions of the American Law Institute and, worse, misapprehend the character of the common law. The common law is not merely what judges have decided; more importantly it

---

[21] [Restatement of torts §] 85, comment a.

[22] *Id.* § 77, comment b.

is what they will decide and the difference is crucial when the precedents are few and mostly old and there are manifest inconsistencies in the courts' approach to related questions within the same general area. To predict how courts would react in future spring-gun cases required a principle that either reconciled the apparent inconsistencies or gave a reasoned basis for preferring one set of holdings to another. * * *

II

The failure of generations of distinguished scholars to give an adequate account of the law on what is after all both an old and a narrow question reflects, I believe, limitations inherent in a certain type of legal scholarship and in the attempt to restate the common law in code form. Limitations of the first kind include a propensity to compartmentalize questions and then consider each compartment in isolation from the others; a tendency to dissolve hard questions in rhetoric (for example, about the transcendent value of human life); and, related to the last, a reluctance to look closely at the practical objects that a body of law is intended to achieve. Codification, as in the *Restatements*, would hardly counteract these tendencies. Indeed, the preoccupation with completeness, conciseness, and exact verbal expression natural to a codifier would inevitably displace consideration of fundamental issues and obscure the flexibility and practicality that characterize the common law method.

Perhaps these failures of scholarship stem ultimately from a tendency to confuse what should be distinct levels of discourse. I expect that most judges, before deciding a case, conceive it in highly practical terms. I do not mean by this that they consider which party's plight is more desperate, which more engages their sympathies. I mean that they consider the probable impact of alternative rulings on the practical concerns underlying the applicable legal principles. Holmes must have had this thought in mind when he wrote:

> The very considerations which the courts most rarely mention, and always with an apology, are the secret root from which the law draws all the juices of life. We mean, of course, considerations of what is expedient for the community concerned.[29]

Why judges, having made a practical decision, so often embody it in the pompous, stilted, conclusionary prose that the layman derides as legalistic is something of a mystery. But what seems clear is that the task of legal scholarship is to get behind the prose and back to the practical considerations that motivated the decision. Yet scholars often seem mesmerized by the style, terminology, and concepts of the judicial opinion; they confuse their function with the judicial.

[29] O.W. Holmes, Common Carriers and the Common Law, 13 Am.L.Rev. 608, 630 (1879) * * *.

A possible way of avoiding this danger is to take an economic approach to questions of legal interpretation. One who tries to explain cases in economic terms may expose himself to many pitfalls, but they will not include the pitfall of attempting to analyze cases in the conceptual modes employed in the opinions themselves. An economic approach is especially plausible with regard to tort law, since the subject of economics is how society meets the conflicting wants of its members and tort cases, as we shall see, are plainly concerned with arbitrating such conflicting wants.

The nature of an economic approach to our problem can be illustrated by reference to an old English case, *Bird v. Holbrook*.[31] The defendant owned a valuable tulip garden located about a mile from his house. It was surrounded by a wall 7–8 feet high on one side and somewhat lower (how much lower is not indicated) on the other sides. After some of his tulips were stolen, the defendant rigged a spring gun. One day a neighbor's peahen escaped and strayed into the garden. A young man (the plaintiff in the case) tried to retrieve the bird for its owner, tripped the spring gun, and was badly injured. The incident occurred during the daytime, and there was no sign warning that a spring gun had been set.

The case involved two legitimate activities, raising tulips and keeping peahens, that happened to conflict. Different rules of liability would affect differently the amount of each activity carried on. A rule that the spring-gun owner was not liable for the injuries inflicted on the plaintiff would promote tulip raising but impose costs on (and thereby tend to contract) peahen keeping, for knowing that efforts to retrieve straying fowl from neighbors' yards might invite serious (and uncompensable) injuries, keepers of peahens would keep fewer fowl, or invest in additional measures to keep the birds from straying, or do both. The opposite rule, one that recognized no privilege ever to use spring guns in defense of property, would benefit peahen keeping but burden tulip growing. The wall surrounding the garden had not been effective in preventing theft. The garden was too far from the defendant's home for him to watch over it himself. Raising the wall or hiring a watchman may have been prohibitively costly.

One would have to know a good deal about tulip growing and peahen keeping, and about the likelihood and character of other trespasses to the garden, in order to design a rule of liability that maximized the (joint) value of both activities, net of any protective or other costs (including personal injuries). And if one wanted a rule that applied to still other crops and straying creatures one would have to know a lot more. But what seems reasonably clear without extended inquiry is that the economically sound rule will be found somewhere in between the extreme possibilities of making the spring-gun owner never liable or always liable. At the minimum, someone in the defendant's position should be required to post no-

[31] 4 Bing. 628, 130 Eng.Rep. 911 (Com.Pl.1828).

tices that anyone entering his garden might be shot: the cost of doing so would be less than the cost (in medical expenses, loss of earnings, and suffering) likely to be incurred by someone who strayed into the garden on an innocent mission. (Of course, a daring and ingenious thief, alerted by the notices, might be able to avoid or disarm the spring gun.) It is possible to go further and suggest a plausible rule that avoids the extremes of blanket prohibition and blanket permission. Given that the expenses of protecting the defendant's valuable tulips other than by a spring gun would probably have been high, that a theft was most likely to be attempted at night, that domestic animals are usually confined then, and that people (other than burglars) do not customarily climb walls at night, the defendant should have been permitted to set a spring gun only at night and after posting appropriate notification. The actual decision in the case is consistent with such a rule. The Court of Common Pleas held for the plaintiff, stressing the absence of notices and the fact that the incident occurred in the daytime.

The reader may object that an analysis which focuses exclusively on the value of the interfering activities is too narrow and in one respect he will be clearly right: it improperly ignores the costs of administering different rules of law. A complex rule, one carefully tailored to relevant differences among the situations to which it might be applied, may do better in terms of maximizing the joint value of the interfering activities than a simple and crude rule yet be inferior because the additional costs of administering the complex rule exceed the additional value of the activities. The complex rule may require lengthier (and hence more costly) litigation or settlement negotiations; or it may be more uncertain and the uncertainty may have a dampening effect on productive activity. Because the costs of different types of legal rule have never (to my knowledge) been seriously studied, it is very difficult to introduce the element of administrative expense into the economic calculus but I assume that judges attempt to do so in a rough way. Our law is replete with instances where judges explicitly rejected a more complex in favor of a simpler rule because the costs of administering the former were thought to outweigh its benefits. * * *

Even so broadened, our calculus is open to the objection that it is insufficiently rich to provide an unambiguous guide to the maximization of social welfare, notably because it omits any reference to the effects of different rules of liability on the distribution of income and wealth. This objection would be more telling were my purpose here normative analysis. It is not. I argue only that the kind of simple economic analysis employed in our discussion of the *Bird* case, supplemented by consideration of the costs of administering different legal rules, will explain, better than alternative approaches, the actual pattern of decisions dealing with our subject. Whether the approach in fact maximizes welfare is neither here nor there.

* * *

We need to consider a rule of liability that will have a more general application than the rule suggested for *Bird v. Holbrook* and will be more firmly grounded in a discussion of the relevant considerations—including the value of a human life.

Some people express shock at the idea of weighing personal injury and death in the same balance with purely economic costs and benefits, but it is done all the time. Individuals who work at hazardous jobs for premium pay are exchanging safety for other economic goods. And where life is taken or injury inflicted in an involuntary transaction, such as an automobile accident, society often attempts to approximate the loss in monetary terms. It goes without saying that the task of approximation is an extremely difficult one. Some dimensions of the loss—such as the anguish to family and friends—cannot even be approximated by the methods available to the courts and are therefore usually ignored. But it is out of the question to ban all hazardous activities on these grounds.

A difficult problem of analysis is created where, as will often be the case when deadly force is used to defend property, the person killed or injured is a criminal. One could argue that burglary and other thefts involving trespass to land are risky activities and that someone who engages in them is no different from a man who agrees to drive a dynamite truck for extra pay: he assumes the risk of being killed. Or one could argue that society should place only a small value on the lives of people who engage in antisocial conduct. These arguments could be debated endlessly; it is sufficient to note that they ignore important practical considerations. If a burglar is injured, his injuries will be tended, if need be at the expense of the state; and if he is disabled, he will not be left to starve. The costs of treating and maintaining him are no less real costs to society than the costs of treating and maintaining the innocently injured and disabled. The interest in minimizing such costs cannot be ignored in the design of a proper rule of liability. Furthermore, a rule that greatly increased the hazards of certain property crimes might disrupt a more or less carefully calibrated scheme of criminal penalties. One reason for not punishing all crimes with equal severity is to preserve an incentive for criminals to commit less serious in preference to more serious crimes. If robbery were punished as severely as murder, there would be fewer robberies but more occasions on which the robber killed everyone who might be a witness. If the burglar of an unoccupied building ran the same risk of being killed or maimed as a burglar of an occupied dwelling, there might be more burglaries of occupied dwellings and hence a greater danger to personal safety than under legal arrangements that made burglaries of unoccupied buildings safer for burglars.

It does not follow that an appropriate rule of liability would be one under which a burglar injured by a spring gun set in an unoccupied building could always recover damages. It is one thing to attempt to graduate punishment in accordance with the gravity of different crimes and another to adopt policies that make the punishment, when discounted by the probability of escaping apprehension, a negligible deterrent. One can imagine situations, for example the storage of valuable property in a remote location, where the likelihood of preventing theft or apprehending the thief afterward without using armed watchmen or spring guns would be so small that even nominally quite severe criminal penalties would not deter. In cases such as these deadly force may be an appropriate, because it is the only practical, deterrent.

These observations reinforce the point made earlier in connection with *Bird v. Holbrook* that neither blanket permission nor blanket prohibition of spring guns and other methods of using deadly force to protect property interests is likely to be the rule of liability that minimizes the relevant costs. What is needed is a standard of reasonableness that permits the courts to weigh such considerations as the value of the property at stake, its location (which bears not only on the difficulty of protecting it by other means but also on the likelihood of innocent trespass), what kind of warning was given, the deadliness of the device (there is no reason to recognize a privilege to kill when adequate protection can be assured by a device that only wounds), the character of the conflicting activities, the trespasser's care or negligence, and the cost of avoiding interference by other means (including storing the property elsewhere). The enumeration of the relevant criteria is simple enough. The real challenge is to fashion them, on the basis of scanty information, into a rule of liability that will maximize the value of the affected activities, subject to the constraint that any rule chosen be simple enough to be understood by those subject to the rules and to be applied by courts (our administrative-cost point). I offer the following as a plausible such rule:

1. Deadly force should not be privileged in situations where the owner of property has an adequate legal remedy (as in the typical boundary dispute), or where the threatened property loss is small. In these cases the costs of protection in human life or limb exceed the value being protected. However, in the computation of value, the economic status of the owner should be considered, since property that would be of no moment to a person of average means might be extremely valuable to a poor person.

2. There should be no privilege to set deadly contrivances such as spring guns in heavily built-up residential and business areas. The protection of property by means of alarms, watchmen, or the police should normally be feasible in such areas and is much to be preferred in view of the undiscriminating character of the mechanical devices. To be sure, one

can imagine cases where a spring gun might seem an appropriate measure in such areas: an old lady living alone in a high-crime-rate area; a house full of priceless paintings. But even in such cases (and note the self-defense element in the first) the dangers inherent in the use of the device seem inordinate. The old lady might die in her sleep; her house would be a death trap. A fire might break out in the house containing the paintings; the firemen would trigger the spring gun. The likelihood of beneficent, or at least innocent, intrusions—by public officers, concerned neighbors, mischievous boys, meter readers, and the like—seems greatest in a built-up area, the very situation where alternative protective measures are most likely to be relatively effective at reasonable cost. In contrast, in remote areas the alternative protective measures are less feasible and at the same time noncriminal intrusions are less frequent. (To be sure, in a remote area the victim is also less likely to receive prompt aid.)

Because the stationing of armed watchmen involves fewer dangers, it need not be confined to remote locations. The watchman can discriminate between the harmful and harmless intruder and can usually prevent a theft or apprehend the thief without actually harming him.

Although the undiscriminating character of the spring gun, as I have indicated, is a matter of legitimate concern, it has at least one redeeming grace. One danger of recognizing any privilege to kill is that it may be used as a shield for unjustified killing. *A* hates *B*, shoots him, and then claims it was self-defense. *B* cannot dispute the point because he is dead. Spring guns are at least devoid of any personal animus—though so are most watchmen. The privilege to kill in self-defense is more prone to abuse than a properly limited privilege to kill in defense of property. The latter privilege is ordinarily asserted against strangers; it is harder to use against a personal enemy. * * *

3. The privilege to use deadly force in defense of property should be forfeited if the user fails to take reasonable precautions to minimize the danger of accidental injury both to innocent and to criminal intruders. If theft is likely only at night the spring gun should not be set during the day. Signs should be posted with explicit and credible warnings. The defendant should be liable if he left his door open or his land unfenced—thereby virtually inviting intrusion—or if he declared that he had not set a spring gun when he had. Lethal calibers, or, in the case of a shotgun, lethal shot, should be avoided in spring guns or other devices since ordinarily the wounding of an intruder is adequate to prevent intrusion. A watchman should not be subjected to this requirement, because his personal safety might be endangered. But he should be required to warn a thief before shooting at him, at least where the thief is clearly not armed; and, consideration of his own safety permitting, he should be required to shoot to wound rather than to kill.

4. In property not sufficiently enclosed to keep out straying animals, children, and youths, the privilege to set spring guns should be limited to the nighttime.

5. Where the use of deadly force is permissible under the foregoing precepts:

a. An adult intruder killed or injured in an attempt to steal or destroy property should not be permitted to recover damages. This result is appropriate in order to prevent serious property losses due to theft in circumstances where, as discussed earlier, other means of deterrence may be impracticable.

b. An innocent intruder should be denied recovery if carelessness on his part contributed materially to the accident. This part of the rule is designed to minimize the joint cost (which is another way of saying, maximize the value) of legitimate but interfering activities by placing responsibility on the participant who could have avoided the interference at least cost. Suppose that a watchman has been stationed, or a spring gun set, and all reasonable precautions observed. A bird watcher comes along, climbs a high fence—ignoring a clear warning notice in plain view—and triggers the spring gun against which the notice warned; or he ignores the repeated warnings of an armed watchman who reasonably believes that the theft or destruction of valuable property is being attempted. One could prevent the accident by forbidding spring guns and armed watchmen in all circumstances, but this may be a very costly means of prevention. The method of averting accidents likely to minimize the relevant costs is one that encourages the intruder to take a few precautions himself by barring recovery of damages otherwise.

The reader may question whether it is realistic to suppose that the denial of damages will deter an intruder not already deterred by fear of being killed or maimed. Perhaps people do not, in general, take greater precautions (other things being equal) against those hazards that are not compensable, such as being struck by lightning, than against those that are. It is hard to believe they do not. When a person takes out accident insurance, he is reducing the likelihood not of an accident but only of an uncompensated accident; that there is a market for such insurance indicates that people are influenced by considerations of compensability as well as by fear of injury itself. Rules of liability could also influence conduct more subtly. A rule that owners of property were strictly liable for any injuries accruing to intruders might be taken by the latter to imply that they need not be careful. They might assume that the completeness of the landowner's liability would impel him to eliminate any hazard. Or they might think the rule was based on a finding that all accidents were caused by the carelessness of landowners rather than of intruders.

6. An accident may occur even though neither the landowner nor the intruder was demonstrably careless. The warning sign may have been

sturdily fixed to the fence but then stolen before the innocent intruder chanced on the scene. In such a case there is no clear basis on economic grounds for preferring one rule of liability to another. But I incline to making the landowner liable (though, for reasons explained earlier, only to the innocent trespasser). He is in control of the premises and so in a better position, in the usual case, to anticipate and avoid contingencies that increase the hazards created by the employment of deadly force. Stated otherwise, there may be reason to suspect that in most cases where an accident occurs and the intruder was not careless, the landowner was—though we cannot prove it.

The rule I have proposed is intended to exhaust the situations in which deadly force may be used to prevent an invasion of property interests. I recognize no separate privilege to kill or wound to prevent the commission of burglary or other felonies where there is no issue of self-defense. * * * It would appear that the permissible scope for using deadly force is probably narrower in my formulation than it is in the *Restatement,* despite the draftsmen's pretense of attaching transcendent value to human life.

* * * I [am not] concerned with defending the rule as socially optimum. Advocates of strict firearms control have urged that death and maiming from criminal acts would be substantially reduced if police forces were given an effective monopoly of firearms, and to them any rule that permits private individuals to use deadly force is bound to strike a discordant note. My own view is that the privilege under discussion is too circumscribed to be a major source of concern. It relates only to weapons kept for the purpose of protecting valuable property and most weapons are kept either for criminal purposes or self-defense. Law-abiding people do not, as a rule, have guns in their homes to repel theft; they have them for self-defense in case they are at home when a burglar or other criminal intrudes. If society rejected this justification for keeping arms and enforced its decision, the particular problem with which the advocates of strict gun controls are concerned would disappear, even if armed watchmen and spring guns were still permitted in limited circumstances. Moreover, the appealing slogan "a public monopoly of force" conceals practical difficulties. Much of the policing function in this country is performed by the private sector—by companies like Pinkerton and Brinks and by countless armed watchmen. The creation of a governmental monopoly of policing would disrupt an existing mixed public-private pattern that, conceivably, is more efficient than a public monopoly would be.

* * * I am not concerned with establishing the ultimate (and unreckonable) merits of the proposed rule. What I am concerned with is whether such a rule, plausibly grounded in economic considerations, explains the course of judicial decisions in the area—to which I next turn.

III

The decisions in which courts have been asked to recognize a privilege to kill or wound to protect property compose a pattern that seems broadly consistent with an economic approach, and with the specific rule of liability that I have suggested. Thus, the courts have refused to sanction the use of deadly force to repel merely technical trespasses that cause no loss or damage, as when a property owner shoots a hole in a boat that has strayed into the owner's part of the lake;[37] and they have rejected any privilege to use deadly force in support of a legal claim asserted in a boundary or other property dispute.[38] A dispute differs from theft or vandalism in that there are well developed judicial remedies—temporary restraining orders, preliminary injunctions, bonds, and the like—by which a person can avert loss or destruction of substantial property values without having to resort to force. This, incidentally, would seem to be the explanation of why the courts have held the poisoning of trespassing animals to be wrongful even when the owner of the animals was forewarned.[39] The victim of the trespass has adequate remedies (including the right to impound the animals) that do not entail the destruction of valuable property. If he had time to warn the animals' owner he also had time to obtain temporary injunctive relief and the cost of so proceeding would in the usual case be smaller than the value of the animals killed.

The courts have likewise refused to recognize a privilege to use deadly force to avert the loss of property having little value, as by killing a thief with a spring gun in order to protect goods worth no more than $6 or shooting a drunken man because he refused to return a bottle of whiskey belonging to his assailant. At the same time, it has been implied that the amount of force permissible is, up to a point, proportional to the value of the property at stake.[41]

In a number of cases where a claim of privilege has been rejected, the defendant exhibited carelessness in his use of deadly force, as by failing to give adequate warning or by using an excessively lethal weapon.[42] In one case the defendant saw a 15–year–old boy stealing watermelons from his watermelon patch, shot to frighten him—and hit him.[43] One defendant set a spring gun and neglected to notify an employee, who was killed by it.[44] In one case the court pointed out that the defendant, before setting a spring gun, should have erected a higher fence around his property to

---

[37] See Collins v. Lefort, 210 So.2d 895 (La.App.1968).

[38] See, e.g., M'Ilvoy v. Cockran, 2 A.K. Marsh 271 (Ky.1820); State v. Shilling, 212 S.W.2d 96 (Mo.App.1948); Godwin v. Stanley, 331 S.W.2d 341 (Tex.Civ.App.1959). * * *

[39] Johnson v. Patterson, 14 Conn. 1 (1840); Bruister v. Haney, 233 Miss. 527, 102 So.2d 806 (1958).

[41] See Higgenbotham v. State, 237 Miss. 841, 116 So.2d 407 (1959); Grant v. Hass, 75 S.W. 342, 346 (Tex.Civ.App.1903).

[42] Wilder v. Gardner, 39 Ga.App. 608, 147 S.E. 911 (1929) * * *.

[43] Brown v. Martinez, 68 N.M. 271, 361 P.2d 152 (1961).

[44] Weis v. Allen, 147 Ore. 670, 35 P.2d 478 (1934) * * *.

prevent cattle (and their keepers) from straying on to the property.[45] Another defendant who had set a spring gun placed a vague warning on two pieces of paper—"Dangerous, don't go in this patch. Go back out"—and the plaintiff, a 14–year–old boy who testified that he had not seen the notices and thought his family owned the watermelon patch, was seriously wounded when he triggered the gun.[46] In another case a policeman was killed when he tried the door of the defendant's store on his nightly rounds to see whether it was locked and the door swung open, triggering a spring gun. The defendant, who knew that the police tried the door on their rounds, had not told them about the spring gun and had neglected to fasten the door securely.[47]

The language of the opinions is not always consistent with an economically sensible rule of liability. In particular, the courts are prone to say that the infliction of injury by a spring gun is privileged when the defendant would have been privileged to inflict the same injury in person, and not otherwise.[48] * * * Such a formulation is inconsistent with our rule of liability in two respects. In part 2 of our rule, we explained why the privilege to use deadly force by means of an armed watchman should in some circumstances be greater than the privilege to kill or wound using a spring gun. And it was implicit in part 5b that it should be narrower in other circumstances. We said that a careless victim should be denied recovery if the use of a spring gun was otherwise privileged, but of course an armed watchman would not be privileged to shoot an intruder merely because the intruder was careless; the watchman must actually and reasonably believe that the intruder was an adult about to steal or destroy valuable property and that he could not be stopped in any gentler way.

To repeat an earlier point, the task of legal scholarship is to get behind the prose of the opinions and when we do this we find much less support for the "indirectly" principle than the *Restatement* would lead us to believe exists. The courts have appeared to recognize a broader privilege for the armed watchman in circumstances where our rule of liability would dictate a broader privilege.[49] The relevance of the victim's conduct is less clear in the cases. An early case barred recovery on the ground that, although the defendant was negligent in having set the spring gun, the victim was careless too.[50] In two more recent cases the victim's apparent carelessness was not given any weight. In one the plaintiff climbed a fence and broke two locks to get into the house where the spring gun was set (his motives in doing so were found to have been innocent); in the other the plaintiff (again with innocent motives) climbed over a fence at

[45] Bethea v. Taylor, 3 Stew. 482 (Ala.1831). * * *

[46] State v. Childers, 133 Ohio St. 508, 14 N.E.2d 767 (1938).

[47] Pierce v. Commonwealth, 135 Va. 635, 115 S.E. 686 (1923).

[48] E.g., State v. Childers, 133 Ohio St. 508, 515, 14 N.E.2d 767, 770 (1938). * * *

[49] Cf. Savoie v. Lirette, 230 So.2d 392 (La.App.1969) * * *.

[50] Bethea v. Taylor, *supra* note 45.

night into a watermelon patch where the defendant had set a spring gun.[51] But perhaps both cases should be explained as resting on the absence of any notice that a spring gun had been set.

A fairly recent case appears to illustrate part 6 of our rule (although again the absence of notice may have been a factor in the court's decision). The defendant fastened two locks on an unoccupied building in which he had set a spring gun. Someone broke the locks and when the plaintiff, whose motives were completely innocent, came along the door was unlocked. The court held the defendant liable.[52]

In the cases thus far discussed a claim of privilege was rejected but it has been accepted in other cases. An early case refused to declare premises protected by a spring gun a public nuisance.[53] The court emphasized the difficulty of protecting valuable property against theft and the absence of evidence that the owner had deployed the device in a manner likely to injure innocent passersby. And in several cases involving warehouses, courts have held that the owner was privileged to kill or wound a burglar by means of a spring gun,[54] or in person.[55]

The courts in these cases have seemed to attach great significance to whether the theft involved a felony, such as burglary, or a misdemeanor, which is presumably why the American Law Institute was led to recognize a separate privilege to use deadly force to prevent certain felonies, and otherwise to deny that there is a privilege to use such force in defense of purely property interests. Such an approach is thoroughly unsound. The legislative classification of offenses is not irrelevant to the practical interests with which a privilege to use force in defense of property should be concerned; it is some indication of the gravity of the intruder's conduct and hence of the measures appropriate to deter that conduct. But it should not be controlling. A legislature might classify breaking into a building with intent to steal as burglary, regardless of the value of the property involved in the theft, simply in order to shorten the criminal trial by eliminating value of the property stolen as an issue. It would not follow that the legislature wanted to permit the use of deadly force to protect property having a negligible value.

The notion of a separate privilege to kill or maim to prevent certain felonies is an expression of a peculiarly mechanical jurisprudence. The inquiry is turned from whether the use of deadly force against an intruder is appropriate to protect concrete property interests in concrete circumstances—a functional inquiry—to whether the intruder's conduct has

---

[51] State v. Green, 118 S.C. 279, 110 S.E. 145 (1921) * * *.

[52] Marquis v. Benfer, 298 S.W.2d 601 (Tex.Civ.App.1956).

[53] State v. Moore, 31 Conn. 479 (1863). * * *

[54] Gray v. Combs, 30 Ky. 478 (1832); United States v. Gilliam, 25 Fed.Cas. 15205a (D.C.Crim.Ct.1882); Scheuermann v. Scharfenberg, 163 Ala. 337, 50 So. 335 (1909).

[55] People v. Silver, 16 Cal.2d 714, 108 P.2d 4 (1940).

been classified a certain way for other purposes—a purely conceptual or legalistic one.

As it happens, the latter approach seems more firmly rooted in the *Restatement* than in the cases, where one can find a good deal of support for the view that legislative classification of the intrusion as a burglary is relevant but not controlling.[56] Such a reading of the cases derives additional support from the frequency with which courts state that the propriety of employing spring guns or other methods involving deadly force in defense of property presents an issue of fact rather than of law, that the controlling standard is one of reasonableness.[57] Such an approach precludes mechanical reliance on a particular circumstance, such as whether the intrusion constituted a felony, as dispositive. More broadly it implies rejection of either blanket permission or blanket prohibition of the use of deadly force to defend property—the alternatives that we said earlier could not be squared with a practical economic approach to the problem. Here, as with the nuisance cases examined by Professor Coase,[58] the adoption of a standard of reasonableness has apparently implied a judicial commitment to rules of liability designed to work an efficient adjustment between interfering activities.

* * *

IV

By now it should be apparent that the *Restatement of Torts* * * * eliminates the nuances of the relevant case law and thereby misstates it. This flaw seems attributable primarily to the form of the *Restatement*; the Reporter's earlier article on deadly force[61] contained a more discriminating account of the cases. Evidently the common law does not lend itself to being restated in code form, and on reflection this is not surprising. Much of the common law has been preempted by statute, and those areas not preempted may be precisely ones where the flexible and particularistic approach of common law is more suitable than the simpler categorical approach of legislation.

To be sure, there has been a certain amount of statutory activity in our area. About half of the states have statutes that bear on the use of deadly force to defend property * * *. The statutes fall into two categories: statutes that make the setting of a spring gun—regardless of circumstances (although there is sometimes an exception for nondeadly gopher guns)—a misdemeanor; and statutes that specify whether it is a defense to a criminal prosecution for homicide that the defendant was attempting

[56] Allison v. Fiscus, 156 Ohio St. 120, 100 N.E.2d 237 (1951); State v. Beckham, *supra* note 40; cf. Gray v. Combs, *supra* note 54.

[57] Marquis v. Benfer, *supra* note 52 * * *.

[58] See R.H. Coase [The Problem of Social Cost, 3 J. Law & Econ. 1, 22 (1960)] * * *.

[61] See *supra* note 7.

to protect property or prevent a felony against property. Some statutes of the second type broaden the common law privilege, as we have described it; some narrow it; and some have been interpreted as incorporating rather than overriding the common law limitations on the use of deadly force.[62] The extent to which these statutes would permit a tort suit by a criminal intruder presents an interesting, and so far as I know unresolved, question; but in any event, to the extent the criminal penalties are enforced, the utility of any tort privilege may be slight.

What is interesting in a comparison of the legislative and the judicial responses to the problem of deadly force is the tendency of the former toward grosser, and of the latter toward finer, classifications of the regulated conduct. The economic calculus seems much less clearly at work in the legislative product * * *. A comparison of the political and other incentives operating on legislators with those operating on judges would show, I believe, that legislators are less likely to be guided by concern with maximizing economic efficiency in the sense in which I have used that term than judges, and that the difference in the legislative and the judicial approaches to the problem of deadly force is, therefore, an instance of a more general phenomenon. But such an analysis is beyond the scope of this paper.

V

The reader will not have failed to notice that my approach and particular conclusions assume that the dominant purpose of rules of liability is to channel people's conduct, and in such a way that the value of interfering activities is maximized. Even those who find the analysis plausible may wish to quarrel with the premise. They may argue that judges do not think in economic terms. No doubt very few judges would articulate their grounds of decision in the precise terms used in this paper. But they could easily hit on the approach intuitively. The adversary process forces them to consider the impact of a ruling on both parties, and therefore on both interfering activities. The fact that the incomes of parties and other such factors bearing on their relative deservedness are excluded from the consideration of judge and jury * * * also helps to keep the focus on the *activities* affected by the rule of liability. Such factors are not excluded from legislative judgments, which is one reason for expecting the legislative product to be different. What is truly unlikely is that the process of judicial reasoning is exhausted in the conceptual categories exhibited in judicial opinions.

* * *

Our basic premise will * * * be challenged by anyone who believes that the dominant purpose of the law of torts is to compensate people for

[62] E.g., Iowa Code Ann. § 691.2; State v. Metcalfe, 203 Ia. 155, 212 N.W. 382 (1927).

wrongs suffered rather than to shape people's conduct; the latter is the proper sphere, it is sometimes argued, for criminal and other regulatory laws. In support of this argument one might cite the criminal penalties for excessive use of deadly force. Many of the cases discussed in the preceding part were in fact criminal cases. (Their inclusion in a discussion of tort law is justified by the fact that the criminal and tort standards governing the propriety of using deadly force to protect property are basically identical.[66])

Although the issue is too large for adequate discussion here, I will venture the suggestion that a compensation theory of the law of torts has little content. The need for compensation is typically independent of the nature of the accident giving rise to the need. A man killed by lightning suffers the same loss as if he had been killed by a careless driver. The law of torts decrees compensation only where there is "wrongful" conduct, and the criteria of wrongfulness are not self-evident. One plausible meaning that can be assigned the term is conduct that society wishes to deter in order to increase the joint value of two (or more) interfering activities, consistently with protecting certain sunk costs in order to encourage adequate investment * * *.

Because tort law is concerned, as I would argue, with shaping conduct, it does not follow that we need no other machinery of deterrence. There are good reasons for supplementing tort with criminal sanctions in certain areas. Tort law will not deter a judgment-proof individual while the threat of imprisonment may, and it is not a fully effective deterrent where, for one reason or another, many victims will not sue at all (burglars and other thieves may be reluctant to institute tort suits) and others, who do sue, may be barred from recovering damages by their own carelessness. Furthermore, where tortious conduct involves killing or maiming, a tort judgment, for reasons touched on earlier, may well undervalue the true social cost of the conduct and hence fail to deter it sufficiently for the future, in which case an additional, penal sanction may be appropriate. It does not follow that we should place exclusive reliance on criminal sanctions. Considering how overburdened the institutions of criminal law enforcement seem at present, we should be seeking ways of increasing rather than of diminishing the scope and effectiveness of tort law in deterring socially harmful behavior.

All things considered, the approach to tort questions sketched here seems decidedly superior to the "method of maxims"—the pseudo-logical deduction of rules from essentially empty formulas such as "no man should be permitted to do indirectly what he would be forbidden to do directly" or "the interest in property can never outweigh the value of a human life"—that plays so large a role in certain kinds of legal scholarship. And the present study provides a good point of departure for investigation

[66] E.g., Redmon v. Caple, 159 S.W.2d 210 (Tex.Civ.App.1942).

of other areas of tort law. Distant as our subject may seem from the dominant concerns of modern tort law, on closer examination it is seen to be curiously central. We mentioned in passing one group of cases where the reasoning underlying the privilege to defend property by deadly force was invoked, and properly so, to solve a different problem: the destruction of trespassing domestic animals. Another doctrine with a strong affinity to the deadly-force cases is that of "private necessity." In *Ploof v. Putnam,*[67] the plaintiff and his family were sailing their boat on a lake when a storm came up. They moored at a dock owned by the defendant. The defendant's employee unmoored their boat, it ran aground, and several of the occupants were injured—a sequence the employee should have anticipated. The court held that the plaintiff's trespass had been justified by necessity and that the defendant's employee had acted wrongfully in casting him off. It could as well have viewed the case as one where deadly force—which is what the employee used, in effect, in repelling the trespass—was manifestly unjustified in defense of a property right. Had the plaintiff's act in mooring his boat to the dock damaged the dock, the defendant could have obtained damages from the plaintiff.[68] The plaintiff was not a criminal against whom legal remedies would probably have been unavailing, so there was no occasion to endanger human safety.

* * *

As noted, the privilege to commit a trespass to avert serious injury to life or property does not relieve the trespasser from the obligation to pay for the harm that his trespass inflicts. This principle comports with the economic objectives that I have argued best explain the course of decisions in these areas. It not only protects sunk costs but forces the individual contemplating a trespass to weigh the injury he will cause by committing the trespass against the injury that would result from refraining and to choose the course that maximizes the joint value of the interfering activities; we do not want people trampling on tulips to save peahens if the damage to the tulips would exceed the value of the peahen. In addition, as Clarence Morris has suggested,[71] the right to recover damages may incline the landowner to cooperate with the trespasser in situations where cooperation is likely to minimize the social costs of the intrusion. When a boat unexpectedly moors at a stranger's dock in a storm, the owner of the dock will have a greater incentive to assist with fresh rope[72] if he knows that any injury to the dock is fully compensable.

An old case where compensation was not allowed, *Mouse's Case,*[73] is the exception that proves the rule. The parties were passengers on a ferry

[67] 81 Vt. 471, 71 A. 188 (1908).

[68] Cf. Vincent v. Lake Erie Transp. Co., 109 Minn. 456, 124 N.W. 221 (1910).

[71] Morris on Torts 44–46 (1953).

[72] Cf. Vincent v. Lake Erie Transp. Co., *supra* note 68.

[73] 12 Co. Rep. 63, 77 Eng.Rep. 1341 (K.B.1609).

that began to sink in a storm. The defendant cast a valuable chest belonging to the plaintiff overboard in order to lighten the craft. The plaintiff sued the defendant for the value of the chest and lost. The court found that, but for the defendant's action, the boat would have sunk. Therefore the defendant wasn't really responsible for the loss of the chest—it would have been lost anyway. Moreover, the defendant should be entitled to offset the value of the plaintiff's life, which his action was instrumental in saving, against the value of the plaintiff's goods. These are good grounds but the ground I would stress is that the denial of compensation served the same purpose as the grant of compensation does in the usual necessity case: to encourage the value-maximizing course of conduct. We do not want each of the passengers of a sinking ship to hesitate in casting off excess baggage in the hope that another one will act first and save him from tort liability.

As these examples and I hope the whole paper suggest, there are far more conceptual pigeonholes in the law of torts—the privilege to use deadly force to protect property, the privilege to use such force to prevent certain crimes, the privilege in cases of arrest, rules about animals, the doctrine of necessity, rules governing deviations from highways onto private land, liability for engaging in ultrahazardous activities—than there are useful distinctions. By utilizing the approach to tort questions sketched here, legal scholarship has an opportunity to effect a drastic and necessary simplification of doctrine and to place the analysis of tort law on a more functional basis.

NOTES AND QUESTIONS

1. This article begins with the discussion of the Iowa spring-gun case, *Katko v. Briney*. In that case, you will remember, the Iowa courts held that a burglar injured by a spring-gun set by a property owner was entitled to recover compensatory and punitive damages from the property owner. How would you have voted if you were a juror in that case, and why? Does your solution to the problem of whether the burglar should have been allowed to recover damages from the spring-gun owner have anything to do with your views on the merits of Posner's analysis of the problem of protecting property? In this connection, be careful to take account of Posner's suggestions that if we allow spring-gun setters willy-nilly to injure burglars it may be society, and not the individual burglars, that will have to bear the costs of their injuries.

2. Posner's piece begins with an examination of the 1934 Restatement of Torts, the summary of the legal rules regarding protection of property by the use of deadly force. You will have noticed that he finds these rules highly contradictory and unsatisfactory. Do you agree with his analysis of the Restatement's rules? Why do you suppose that they are in the unsatisfactory state which Posner finds them? Posner suggests that the ALI's restatement reflects a general "reluctance to face difficult choices between human lives

and other social values." Do you agree? Are there "other social values" preferable to "human lives?"

3. You probably also noticed that in the beginning of the second section of his article Posner invokes the hallowed name of Oliver Wendell Holmes in support of the analytical approach Posner takes. You have had some exposure to the thought of Holmes, although only a smattering. Would he have approved, do you think, of "law and economics?" Posner certainly seems to have approved of Holmes, and, as indicated earlier, has even edited and introduced a splendid one volume collection of Holmes's works. Richard A. Posner, ed., The Essential Holmes: Selections from the Letters, Speeches, Judicial Opinions, and other writings of Oliver Wendell Holmes, Jr. (1992).

4. In the middle of his analysis, as you have seen, in what seems like a perfectly straight-forward way, Posner offers us his "plausible" rule for governing "spring-gun" cases. Do you find his rules satisfactory? Is it the statement of his proposed legal standard that upset so many readers of this article, or is it something else inherent in Posner's analysis? If it is something else, what is it? Note, for example, that the purpose of Posner's creation of his rule is to express the thought that it will explain the cases already decided on "spring-guns." He suggests that his rule is solidly grounded in an economic analysis of the law, and that so are the cases. In particular, he suggests that the cases are much more grounded in notions of economics than they are in adherence to what Posner finds to be essentially rhetorical legal maxims, such as "the interest in property can never outweigh the value of a human life," or "no man should be permitted to do indirectly what he would be forbidden to do directly." Do you agree? Do you agree with Posner's comments on legislatures as opposed to courts as formulators of legal rules? Could they have had something to do with the furor Posner's analysis caused? See if the next reading, from one of Posner's most perceptive critics, helps you understand why Posner was to become the most controversial law professor of the late twentieth century. This critic, the late Arthur Leff, one of the best writers among twentieth-century law professors, was reviewing the book in which Posner's views received their fullest expression, his casebook (in its eighth edition in 2010), An Economic Analysis of Law (1st edition, 1973).

ARTHUR ALLEN LEFF, COMMENTARY: ECONOMIC ANALYSIS OF LAW: SOME REALISM ABOUT NOMINALISM*

60 Virginia Law Review 451 (1974).

* * * [O]ne of the dangers of reviewing a work "mainly designed for use either as a textbook in a law school course . . . or as supplementary reading for law students . . . ,"[1] and getting down to the job later than one ought, is that one perforce reads it straight through, as if it were a real book. Having done that one cannot help being nagged throughout by

* Reprinted by permission of the Virginia Law Review Association and Fred B. Rothman & Co.

[1] R. Posner, Economic Analysis of Law x (1973) [hereinafter cited as Posner].

what may be the literary critic's most pernicious and unavoidable naggerie: Where have I seen this before? At any rate, from my first glance at the table of contents, with its relentless item by item march through all of law—property, contracts, crimes and torts, labor law, corporations, taxation, racial discrimination, civil procedure . . . all the way through to a final "Note on Jurisprudence"—I smelled a familiar genre. * * * A manual of possible uses, the kind that comes with a new chain saw? A text on herbal healing? Not quite. But what? I was more than half way through the book before it came to me: as a matter of literary genre * * * the closest analogue to [Posner's] *Economic Analysis of Law* is the picaresque novel.

Think of the great ones, *Tom Jones,* for instance, or *Huckleberry Finn,* or *Don Quixote.* In each case the eponymous hero sets out into a world of complexity and brings to bear on successive segments of it the power of his own particular personal vision. The world presents itself as a series of problems; to each problem that vision acts as a form of solution; and the problem having been dispatched, our hero passes on to the next adventure. * * * No matter what comes up or comes by, Tom's sensual vigor, Huck's cynical innocence, or the Don's aggressive romanticism is brought into play, forever to transform the picture of the pictured world (without, by the way, except *in extremis,* transforming the hero).

Richard Posner's hero is also eponymous. He is Economic Analysis. In the book we watch him ride out into the world of law, encountering one after another almost all of the ambiguous villains of legal thought, from the fire-spewing choo-choo dragon[2] to the multi-headed ogre who imprisons fair Efficiency in his castle keep for stupid and selfish reasons.[3] In each case Economic (I suppose we can be so familiar) brings to bear his single-minded self, and the Evil Ones (who like most in the literature are in reality mere chimerae of some mad or wrong-headed magician) dissolve, one after another.

One should not knock the genre. To hold the mind-set constant while the world is played in manageable chunks before its searching single light is a powerful analytic idea, the literary equivalent of dropping a hundred metals successively into the same acid to see what happens. * * *

But the peculiarly relentless tone of this book moves me also to another inquiry: what pressures in contemporary legal scholarship might be responsible for the appearance, now, of four hundred pages of tunnel vision and, assuming one could answer that, why this particular tunnel? For Posner's book is, after all, just a fatly reified symbol of a currently important trend. It is a matter of common knowledge that economic analysis of the type Posner's book exemplifies is growing ever more popular

---

[2] *See id.* at 16 *ff.* on Ronald Coase's *The Problem of Social Cost,* 3 J. Law & Econ. 1 (1960).

[3] *See id.* at 386–92 ("The Administrative Process").

among legal scholars. Not only have major and important analytical works recently been written in that style, * * * not only do almost all recent "law and" law review articles and law school courses turn out to be "law and economics," but even people like me, with no formal background in and little natural taste or aptitude for economic analysis, seem to be drawn to reading it, learning it and, in primitive fashion, even writing it. What is our problem?

In order to approach that question at all, I shall have to begin with a very brief examination of the difficulties in which those who want to continue to talk about law presently find themselves. Then, having roughly outlined the hidden darkness from which the lawyer's current lust for economic illumination springs * * * I shall go on to a more detailed discussion of certain aspects of Posner's approach. * * *

THE WAY WE LIVE TODAY

Let us start with a couple of vicious intellectual parodies. Once upon a time there was Formalism. The law itself was a deductive system, with unquestionable premises leading to ineluctable conclusions. It was, potentially at least, all consistent and pervasive. Oh, individual judges messed up, and even individual professors, and their misperceptions and mispronouncements needed rationalization, connection, and correction. But that was the proper job of one of the giants we had in the earth in those days. The job of legal commentators, and a fortiori of treatise writers, was to find the consistent thread in the inconsistent statements of others and pull it all together along the seam of what was implicit in "the logic of the system." * * *

Then, out of the hills, came the Realists. What their messianic message was has never been totally clear. But it is generally accepted that, at least in comparison to the picture of their predecessors which they drew for themselves, they were much more interested in the way law actually functioned in society. * * * The critical questions were henceforward no longer to be those of systematic consistency, but of existential reality. * * *

Now such a move, while liberating, was also ultimately terrifying. For if you were interested in a society, and with law as an operative variable within that society, you would have to find out something about that subject matter and those operations. You would, it seems, have to become an empiricist. * * * But there is a worse worry yet. If you no longer are allowed to believe in a deductive system, if criticism is no longer solely logical, you no longer can avoid the question of *premises*. Premises, in terms of logic, are just that: those things you don't talk about. But if you are under an obligation to talk about non-foreordained conclusions, you must start to talk about non-given starting points. Any (mostly implicit) assumptions that one's premises in some mysterious manner are at least congruent with the commands of the universe would (and did) come under increasing pressure. If "good" were seen solely in terms of effects, the only good premises were those that came up with good effects. Thus, by dropping formalism we (quite rightly) fell into the responsibility of good and evil.

But not, alas, the knowledge thereof. While all this was going on * * * the knowledge of good and evil, as an intellectual subject, was being systematically and effectively destroyed. The historical fen through which ethical wanderings led was abolished in the early years of this century * * *; normative thought crawled out of the swamp and died in the desert.[8] There arose a great number of schools of ethics—axiological, materialistic, evolutionary, intuitionist, situational, existentialist, and so on—but they all suffered the same fate: either they were seen to be ultimately premised on some intuition (buttressed or not by nosecounts of those seemingly having the same intuitions), or they were even more arbitrary than that, based solely on some "for the sake of argument" premises. I will put the current situation as sharply and nastily as possible: there is today no way of "proving" that napalming babies is bad except by asserting it (in a louder and louder voice), or by defining it as so, early in one's game, and then later slipping it through, in a whisper, as a conclusion.

* * *

Let us say you found yourself facing a universe normatively empty and empirically overflowing. What I suppose you would want most to do, if you wanted to talk at all, would be to find some grid you could place over this buzzing data to generate a language which would at the same time provide a critical terminology ("*X* is bad because . . . ") and something in terms of which the criticism could be made (that is, something to follow the "because . . . "). Now "because it is" is a bit naked as a satisfactory explanation. "Because you won't get to *Y* that way" is better, but when you make "good" teleological, you rather promptly run into "what's so great about *Y*?" * * * You might just as well skip the intervening step and stick with *X*, saying all the pretty things about it itself, rather than about its product.

But what if you said *X* wasn't "good" or anything like that, that is, wasn't normative at all? What if you described *X* solely in empirical terms, for instance, *X* is what people, as a matter of fact, want. That way you can get to the well-known neo-Panglossian position of classic utilitarianism: while all is not for the best (because the best is what people want and they don't have it yet), the best is still nothing more than what they do want. Admittedly, this is just an example of one of the now-classic

[8] *See, e.g.,* L. Wittgenstein, Tractatus Logico–Philosophicus, esp. Prop. 7, at 151 (D. Pears & B. McGuinness transl. 1961). *See also* A. Janik & S. Toulmin, Wittgenstein's Vienna, esp. chs. 6 and 9, at 167–201, 263–75 (1973).

normative copouts—essentially, "good" becomes just a function of nosecounting—but it does have the advantage of providing a ready-made critical vocabulary: because there is now a clear area between what people want and what they have, while you can no longer say that doing anything is bad, you *can* say of some things that they are being done badly.

Of course, you still haven't solved all your intellectual (or practical) problems. The world may no longer be normatively empty (you've filled it by definitional fiat), but it is still full of all sorts of puzzling things. * * * True, you need no longer ask if people *ought* to desire other things than they do desire, for those desires are the measure of all things. But what do people * * * desire? If you don't know that, then you can't criticize what they presently have, or what they are right now doing, with reference to their failure to reach that desire. * * * Thus it is possible that all you have ended up doing is substituting for the arbitrariness of ethics the impossibilities of epistemology.

Now all of the above is but by way of introduction to Posner's solution to these scarifying problems. He does indeed solve the normative "oughtness" problems by the neo-Panglossian move; good is defined as that which is in fact desired. But then he makes a very pretty move * * *: in place of what one might have expected * * * a complex regimen for an empirical investigation of human wants and values—he puts a single element touchstone, so narrow a view of the critical empirical question as to be, essentially, a definition. "What people want" is presented in such a way that while it is in form empirical, it is almost wholly non-falsifiable by anything so crude as fact.

To follow this initially attractive development in legal criticism (for purposes both of admiration and scorn), one will have to master the critical early moves. The first and most basic is "the assumption that man is a rational maximizer of his ends in life. . . . "[11] As Posner points out, this assumption "is no stronger than that most people in most affairs of life are guided by what they conceive to be their self-interest and that they choose means reasonably (not perfectly) designed to promote it."[12] In connection with this assumption, several "fundamental economic concepts"[13] emerge. "The first is that of the inverse relation between price charged and quantity demanded."[14] The second is the economist's definition of cost, "the price that the resources consumed in making (and selling) the seller's product would command in their next best use—the alternative price."[15]

---

[11] Posner 1.

[12] *Id.* at 5.

[13] *Id.* at 1.

[14] *Id.*

[15] *Id.* at 2–3.

The third basic concept, which is also derived from reflection on how self-interested people react to a change in their surroundings, is the tendency of resources to gravitate toward their highest valued uses if exchange is permitted. * * * By a process of voluntary exchange, resources are shifted to those uses in which the value to the consumer, as measured by the consumer's willingness to pay, is highest. When resources are being used where their value is greatest, we may say that they are being employed efficiently.[16]

Now it must immediately be noted, and never forgotten, that these basic propositions are really not empirical propositions at all. They are all generated by "reflection" on an "assumption" about choice under scarcity and rational maximization. While Posner states that "there is abundant evidence that theories derived from those assumptions have considerable power in predicting how people in fact behave,"[17] he cites none. And it is in fact unnecessary to cite any, for the propositions are not empirically falsifiable at all.

> Efficiency is a technical term: it means exploiting economic resources in such a way that human satisfaction *as measured by aggregate consumer willingness to pay* for goods and services is maximized. Value too is defined by willingness to pay.[18]

In other words, since people are rationally self-interested, what they *do* shows what they value, and their willingness to pay for what they value is proof of their rational self-interest. Nothing merely empirical could get in the way of such a structure because it is definitional. That is why the assumptions can predict how people behave: in *these* terms there is no other way they can behave. If, for instance, a society dentist raises his prices and thereby increases his gross volume of business, it is no violation of the principle of inverse relation between price and quantity. It only proves that the buyers now perceive that they are buying something else which they now value more highly, "society dentistry," say, rather than "mere" dentistry. And if circularity isn't sufficient, the weak version of the rational maximization formula ("most people in most affairs of life . . . choose means reasonably (not perfectly) designed. . . . ") has the effect of chewing up and spitting out any discordant empirical data anyway. * * *

Thus what people do is good, and its goodness can be determined by looking at what it is they do. In place of the more arbitrary normative "goods" of Formalism, *and* in place of the more complicated empirical "goods" of Realism, stands the simple definitionally circular "value" of Posner's book. If human desire itself becomes normative * * * and if human desire is made definitionally identical with certain human acts, then

[16] *Id.* at 4.

[17] *Id.* at 5.

[18] *Id.* at 4 (emphasis supplied).

those human acts are also beyond criticism in normative or efficiency terms; everyone is doing as best he can exactly what he set out to do which, by definition, is "good" for him. In those terms, it is not at all surprising that economic analyses have "considerable power in predicting how people in fact behave."[21]

I shall argue that lovely as all of this is, it is still unsatisfactory as anything approaching an adequate picture of human activity * * *. But one can still admire the intelligence with which it is tried, and the genuine, though limited, illuminations the effort provides. More than that, one can now understand the forces that shaped the attempt. All of us are unable to tell (or at least to tell about) the difference between right and wrong. All of us want to go on talking. If we could find a way to slip in our normatives in the form of descriptives, within a discipline offering narrow and apparently usable epistemological categories, we would all be pathetically grateful for such a new and more respectable formalism in legal analysis. We would leap to embrace it. Since that is the promise of economic analysis of law, to an increasing (and not wholly delusive or pernicious) extent, many of us are leaping.

* * *

We are, I think, beginning to see in the speedy spread of economic analysis of law the development of a new basic academic theory of law. Since its basic intellectual technique is the substitution of definitions for both normative and empirical propositions, I would call it American Legal Nominalism.

THE POWER OF POSITIVE ECONOMICS

* * * I would rather not leave any impression of thorough negativism, if for no reason other than that such a response would be stupid. The economic analysis of law * * * continually manages to provide rich and varied insights into legal problems. * * * But in addition to its value as a way to continue to ignore our otherwise desperate intellectual straits, it frequently serves intelligently to inform actual legal choices. For the central tenet and most important operative principle of economic analysis is to ask, of every move (1) how much it will cost; (2) who pays; and (3) who ought to decide both questions?

That might seem obvious. In fact, it is not. It is a most common experience in law schools to have someone say, of some action or state of events, "how awful," with the clear implication that reversing it will de-awfulize the world to the full extent of the initial awfulness. But the true situation, of course, is that eliminating the "bad" state of affairs will not lead to the opposite of that bad state, but to a third state, neither the bad one nor its opposite. That is, before agreeing with any "how awful" critic,

---

[21] Posner 5. * * *

one must always ask him the really nasty question, "compared to what?" Moreover, it should be, but often is not, apparent to everyone that the process of moving the world from one state to another is itself costly. If one were not doing *that* with those resources (money, energy, attention), one could be doing something else, perhaps righting a few different wrongs * * *.

One can illustrate this basic kind of economic analysis by working with quite simple fact situations. There is this old widow, see, with six children. It is December and the weather is rotten. She defaults on the mortgage on her (and her babies') family home. The mortgagee, twirling his black moustache, takes the requisite legal steps to foreclose the mortgage and throw them all out into the cold. She pleads her total poverty to the judge. Rising behind the bench, the judge points her and her brood out into the swirling blizzard. "Go," he says. "Your plight moves me not." "How awful," you say?

"Nonsense," says the economic analyst. "If the old lady and kids slip out into the storm, they most likely won't die. There are people a large part of whose satisfactions come from relieving the distress of others, who have, that is, high utilities for beneficence and gratitude." So the costs to the widow are unlikely to be infinite. Moreover, * * * [w]hat would happen if the judge let the old lady stay on just because she was out of money? First of all, lenders would in the future be loathe to lend to old widows with children. I don't say that they wouldn't lend at all; they'd just be more careful about marginal cases, and raise the price of credit for the less marginal cases. The aggregate cost to the class of old ladies with homesteads would most likely rise much more than the cost imposed on this particular widow. That is, the aggregate value of all their homes (also known as their wealth) would fall, and they'd all be worse off.

"More than that, look at what such a decision would do to the motivation of old widows. Knowing that their failure to pay their debts would not be visited with swift retribution, they would have less incentive to prevent defaults. They might start giving an occasional piece of chicken to the kids, or even work up to a fragment of beef from time to time. Profligacy like that would lead to even less credit-worthiness as their default rates climbed. More and more of them would be priced out of the money market until no widow could ever *decide for herself* to mortgage her house to get the capital necessary to start a seamstress business to pull herself (and her infants) out of poverty. What do you mean, 'awful'? What have you got against widows and orphans?"

Now * * * the economic analyst may well be right. He is not necessarily "right" in the sense that one ought to throw out this particular old lady (for the analysis is too sketchy and data-free to decide that). But he is certainly "right" in this sense: the effect of not throwing her out is not a net gain, to society in general, or even to others in her "class," equal to what she personally is saved by staying in possession. Choosing to favor her is not cost free, *even to others like her.*

And one of the things Posner does throughout his book is display one analysis after another, in one problem area after another, along the lines of the above. Naturally his analyses are, most of the time, much more thorough and sophisticated than my parodistic example. For one thing, they implicate, more clearly than the above parody, themes additional to the non-freeness of lunches, notably the general gains, at least in efficiency terms, of letting people wherever possible decide for themselves what they want and what they are willing to pay. Especially when he is essaying analyses of the relatively short-run effects of changes in relatively measurable variables, and most particularly in areas where the aims of the variation are explicitly, cognizably economic, Posner is superbly illuminating. There is no doubt that the mind at work in this book is supple, strong and even (in a sense) sensitive. * * *

Thus, if, at this point, I choke off my genuine admiration, the reader must understand that I do so only because so directed by Posner, who states that he himself has chosen not to emphasize "the limitations of economic analysis, as both an interpretive and a normative tool . . . in the text" so as to give others a chance. No, I am being disingenuous. The rest of this discussion is as it is because I have an ax to grind, and more than enough fury to turn the wheel. * * *

"INEFFICIENCY" AS A CRITIQUE

* * * [L]et us now return to that most key passage in the book:

> Efficiency is a technical term: it means exploiting economic resources in such a way that human satisfaction as measured by aggregate consumer willingness to pay for goods and services is maximized. Value too is defined by willingness to pay.[30]

Since the assumption is that "man is a rational maximizer of his ends in life,"[31] * * * you can tell what people want, and how much they want it, by seeing what they buy, and how much they pay for it. By and large, therefore, whatever people might *say,* you can get a fair idea of what is really to their taste by seeing what they actually *do.* Now that is not just a lovely way to avoid frightfully difficult empirical inquiries; it is also a powerful analytic idea. It is closely analogous to one of the central messages of legal realism: when reading opinions, see what the judge does in the case, not what he says about what he is doing.

* * *

[30] *Id.* at 4.

[31] *Id.* at 1.

But if one thoroughly accepts the idea that the results people actually achieve for themselves are the ones that, among the available alternatives, they wanted to achieve, then one trembles on the edge of a worrisome paradox. For it is then also possible to state matters this way: Whatever people achieve for themselves, they perceive it as the best they can do. If what they want can be determined only by seeing what they "buy," then what they "buy" must (by definition) be what they wanted * * *. * * *

Given this initial position about the autonomy of people's aims and their qualified rationality in reaching them, one is struck by the picture of American society presented by Posner. For it seems to be one which regulates its affairs in rather a bizarre fashion: it has created one grand system—the market, and those market-supportive aspects of law (notably "common," judge-made law)—which is almost flawless in achieving human happiness; it has created another—the political process, and the rest of "the law" (roughly legislation and administration)—which is apparently almost wholly pernicious of those aims. An anthropologist coming upon such a society would be fascinated. It would seem to him like one of those cultures which, existing in a country of plenty, having developed mechanisms to adjust all intracultural disputes in peace and harmony, lacking any important enemies, nevertheless comes up with some set of practices, a religion say, simultaneously so barbaric and all-pervasive as to poison almost every moment of what would otherwise appear to hold potential for the purest existential joy. If he were a bad anthropologist, he would cluck and depart. If he were a real anthropologist, I suspect he would instead stay and wonder what it was about the culture that he was missing. That is, he would ponder why they *wanted* that religion, what was in it for them, what it looked like and felt like to be *inside* the culture. * * *

The point is this: at least as an initial position, anything that happens in a culture has as much likelihood at being "desired" as anything else. One needs an extracultural standing place, or some evidence of "real" intention other than that which is the product of observing actual practice, in order to criticize any facet of the culture, in normative *or efficiency* terms. For nothing can be considered inefficiently achieved until one discovers what the aim of the activity was.

This caution is, I think, especially applicable to certain of Posner's critiques, and helps in more general terms to illuminate the limitations of his method. Consider, for instance, his chapter on crime control.[34]

He begins:

> The economic content of legal theory is nowhere clearer than in the rationale of criminal punishment. The usual justification offered by

[34] *Id.* at 357–74.

> legal theory for why the state punishes criminal violators is that it is necessary in order to deter people from committing crimes.[35]

Posner then goes on to tie this asserted aim * * * to its underlying philosophical pillar, a rather crude version * * * of Benthamite utilitarianism.

> Bentham's utilitarianism, in its aspect as a positive theory of human behavior, is another name for economic theory. Pleasure is value, and pain cost. People * * * can be deterred from criminal activity by a punishment system that makes the cost of criminal activity greater than the value of that activity to them.[36]

But there is a serious problem here. Posner assumes (apparently because * * * that's what people *say*) that the purpose of criminal punishment is to deter criminal behavior, and on that basis criticizes certain aspects of current criminal law and procedure as inefficient, even silly. But what if deterring criminal behavior is not the aim, or even one of the principal aims, of the criminal law as practiced in the society? If that were so, then it might be argued that there was no inefficiency at all.

Consider, for instance, Posner's discussion of incarceration as a punishment. It is, he says, "a more costly remedy to society than a fine is."[37] He points not only to the costs of running the prison system, and the loss of the prisoner's productivity, but to the damaging effects on the prisoner himself. Imprisonment tends to decrease the likelihood that the criminal will "go straight" and earn honest dollars, the failure to earn which is, as Posner puts it, "one of the opportunity costs of crime." * * *

But what if society's interest in deterrence is, *in fact,* not very strong? What if it is the incarceration itself society likes and wants to "buy"? What if it doesn't want deterrence, or even rehabilitation, but the satisfaction of some other interest, revenge say, or * * * sadism? After all, a link between prison and increased crime has been suspected by quite a number of people for quite a long time. There has even been some evidence of a link between the nastiness of the prison and the *rate* of increased crime. Nonetheless there has been firm opposition, at least from large segments of the public, to any decrease in imprisoning or amelioration of prison life. It is altogether possible that while the society does see increased crime as a cost, it considers it one well worth incurring in order to experience the otherwise socially unobtainable joy of inflicting pain. (Remember, not all "goods" have substitutes; rape is not rape, but alters when it enthusiasm finds, and thus one cannot substitute prostitution for it, or even love.)

But there is a further possibility. Society, or at least important segments of it, may not see increased crime as a cost at all. It is possible that

---

[35] *Id.* at 357.

[36] *Id.*

[37] *Id.* at 363.

"we" *want* crime. Criminals provide huge positive returns to non-criminals. * * * Even theft, even murder, helps to establish, by contrast, our rectitude. Moreover, if one hated and feared the lower classes, incarceration for criminal activity would be a gorgeous strategy: most of the victims of crime are in the lower classes, as are most of the criminals; one punishes the perpetrators of crime in a way that not only doesn't deter them from further crime, but encourages more of it, thereby punishing the victims of crime in a manner designed to keep the cycle going.

Naturally, one would not buy crime as a product forever, even if crime were what one wanted. As its impact shifted so that those who loved it became increasingly its direct victims, then crime might turn into a positive cost and bring about, for the first time, efforts *actually* to decrease its incidence. It is at least arguable that something like that is happening now. As "*we*" have started increasingly to become muggees, some of "us" * * * seem to have started seriously to explore the elimination of that most potent crime generator, the prison.

It is not important, however, which of these widely diverging social cost-benefit analyses—mine or Posner's—is more accurate. The more important issue is this: Posner can find a social activity "inefficient" only by assuming that what society does, and what it wants to do, are different. But how can he know that? Certainly he can't say "because people *say* they want something different," for as he apparently knows as well as any man alive, what counts is not what people say is of value to them, but what they buy and how much they pay. And he certainly cannot argue that they *ought* to want something different, not in the face of his own careful strictures against any normativity.[39]

In principle, the foregoing argument can be brought to bear on many of Posner's analyses of social inefficiency. One cannot say, for another instance, that it is "inefficient" to have a trial-type hearing in a situation where the chance of decreasing error by doing so is slight.[40] The social purpose of trial-type hearings may have little to do with eliminating error, despite what everyone *says* the purpose is. It may be pure theatre for the participants, or an alternative to ulcers (or a way of producing them in others). Certainly we have for a millennium been having trial-type hearings in circumstances, and under rules (of evidence, for instance) which seem much more designed for theatrical or therapeutic than epistemological purposes. Once again, you can't know that a thing is not being done well until you know what it is that is being done.

I could go on multiplying instances with respect to particular analyses of particular legal problems. But what I find most interesting is the possibility that my thesis—that you can't know something is ill-done un-

[39] See Posner 4–5.

[40] *See id.* at 334.

less you *assume* an aim other than the one achieved—might also be applicable to one of Posner's most central, important, and apparently beloved points, the comparative inefficiency of, and "market failure" in, what one might call "the political market."

Posner writes:

> "There is abundant evidence that legislative regulation of the economy frequently, perhaps typically, brings about less efficient results than the market-common law system of resource allocation. The crucial question is whether this failure is accidental and easily remediable, or perhaps inherent in the nature of political decision making. The latter view is gaining support. The essential problem seems to be that the generalized consumer interest in efficient markets is systematically under-represented in legislative decision making."[42]

Let us assume that legislative regulation does, in fact, bring about less "efficient" results * * * than the market as buttressed by common-law adjudication. * * * Let us also assume that generalized consumer interest in efficient markets is systematically underrepresented in the political process * * *. The obvious question remains, however: So what? Remember, the issue is not, for every consumer/citizen, what he gets out of "the market" or what he gets out of "politics," but what he gets out of the society which is the product of both of these grand systems together. To say of a system that it is defective because, taken by itself, it fails to maximize or optimize something good is somewhat like arguing that steak is a defective food because it has virtually no carbohydrate. It would be defective * * * if that were all one ate. But in the context of general nutrition it might be seen as an important part of the process of sustaining life.

Thus it is at least plausible that the "weaknesses" in the political system * * * are really complementary to, or even corrective of, "weaknesses" in the economic system, such as its tendency to distribute power in proportion to wealth, or even in proportion to wealth-producing talents. Giving everyone one vote may help people keep from themselves their natural inferiority, a truth which, if it surfaced, would substantially affect their tempers and their utility schedules. Politics may, that is, be a method of cementing social solidarity through even *distributive* injustice, and the purpose of the political process may indeed be anti-efficient *and* distributively absurd. But once again, "we" may be getting, overall, what we want.

One can, of course, go too far with this sort of argument, and I may have done so already. It is not going to help matters much if I attempt to substitute for Posner's extremely careful version of what I take to be the essentialist fallacy ("the *real* explanation of this social practice is. . . . ") my own less careful avatar of the holistic fallacy ("this practice can only

---

[42] *Id.* at 329–30 (footnotes omitted).

be explained in the context of all of the dynamics of the entire society"). * * * But a society, and its creation of human satisfactions and frustrations, is more complicated than Posner's economic model makes it appear. It is possible, I suppose, that the entire political structure of advanced technological societies is just a mistake, and as presently articulated it has almost no wholesome purpose. But that seems to me bloody unlikely. For if "the market" is a creation of human choice, so is the government.

Moreover, the argument that governments, even the particular shapes they take, are not functionless in particular societies is made immeasurably stronger, it seems to me, by considering the alternatives. In other words, I commend to Posner his own most powerful analytic device, asking of each proposed move what it costs, and who pays. Is it likely that the revolutionary * * * changes necessary to bring on what I take to be the Posner millennium—no governmental coercion except in support of market efficiency—would bring about any such thing? Would those who might perceive themselves made worse off as a result of not having a government to capture goodies on their behalf stand still while the market, efficient as all get-out, made them, at least relatively, poorer and poorer? Even if in efficiency and distribution terms they might be "wrong," would not those groups, "guided by what they conceive to be their self-interest," do what men seem historically always to have been tempted to do, to *take* a piece of the action for themselves? Would they not, as they always have in the past, in order to prosper form alliances with other men who saw their self-interests as at least temporarily congruent? In brief, wouldn't we eventually get not "no government" * * * but another government, most likely not the same as Posner's, or the same as our present one, but something altogether different? And if we got that, would we all, or anyone, be better off?

Obviously, I don't know. I too find it hard to believe that all is for the best in this best of all possible worlds. But there is something to be said for gross conservatism like mine, at least if one is, as I am, fairly risk averse * * *.

* * * Also involved here is a matter much more generally interesting than my fears about my own particular future: when *is* the future, and how does one go about deciding what it will be once one decides *when* it is. Posner does a lot of thinking about that * * *. Let us therefore address some more detailed attention to the predictive value of single vocabularies.

AVOIDING COMPLEXITY

As I have suggested several times, this aura of repetitive relentlessness that Posner's book gives off is not solely the product of Posner's personal literary style. It is dictated, I think, by a basic analytic strategy consciously chosen for the book: first, vigorously to exclude from consideration any normative statements of any kind, and second, to allow in empirical data only of particular kinds and only under the most restrictive of conditions. To put it another way, it was Posner's conscious choice in writing the book to deal only with what is, and then to exclude any description of that *is*-ness in any uncongenial vocabularies, say, those employed in sociology, anthropology, or psychology. This decision has the natural collateral effect of excluding any *data* relevant to the categories used by those disciplines but not by Posner's.

Such a choice has obvious advantages, as I have earlier pointed out. But let me just sketch * * * what the possible effects of a somewhat less narrowly tunnelled vision might have been. Take sociology. Now I don't pretend to know what sociology is, but I can mention one thing that seems to interest or at least bother some sociologists—social groups and classes. The following kind of question is frequently posed: Can I say anything interesting, or predictive, or even amusing about a number of people more than one and less than all? Posner considers questions of that form throughout his book, for it is implicated every time individual demand schedules are talked about as joined into a general demand curve. * * * But note the effect a greater sensitivity to classes formed on criteria other than the particular ones Posner admits as relevant might have.

Consider, for instance, Posner's discussion of the role of judges.[50] * * * [I]t is of some importance to Posner to establish that common-law adjudication is superior, at least in efficiency terms, to legislative decision-making. One pillar of this "proof" is the freedom of the judge from large dollops of allocative bias:

> [L]aw resembles the market in its impersonality, its subordination of distribution considerations. The invisible hand of the market has its counterpart in the aloof disinterest of the judge. The method by which judges are compensated and the rules of judicial ethics are designed to assure that the judge will have no financial or other interest in the outcome of a case before him, no responsibility with respect to the case other than to decide issues tendered by the parties, and no knowledge of the case other than what the competition of the parties conveys to him about it. Jurors are similarly constrained. . . . Judicial impersonality is reinforced by the rules of evidence. . . . [51]

Well that's fine; the judge doesn't personally give a damn how the case comes out. At this point, of course, to go along with the game we must overlook the fundamental confusion in this passage between formal law and law in action, that is we must disregard one of the central lessons of legal sociology. We will just pretend that the legal realists had never lived, and that no one is allowed to look through the rules of pleading and

[50] *See id.* at 320–28.

[51] *Id.* at 322.

evidence to see what judges and juries actually do know, despite these restrictions, about the parties and cases before them. We will even shut our eyes to the fact that it is in the service of getting before judges and jurors these "irrelevant" facts, like the parties' wealth and class, that many lawyers spend most of their time and skill.

Let us assume, then, that the judge is so exquisitely shielded from the world. Why then should he come up with decisions that favor efficiency? * * * The "tentative" answer, surprisingly enough, is that judges are *not* without personal interest in how the case comes out. Especially (but not only) "where the judges do not have lifetime tenure" they "frequently aspire to higher office, judicial or political." Indeed "[i]t seems appropriate to view these judges as the agents of the executive or legislative organs of the state."[54] Will that skew the allocative disinterest of the judge? Not at all. Efficiency is also valuable to society, and judges will opt for that. Why? It must be because the efficiency-oriented decisions will help them in *their* quest for higher office. But if that is so, and legislators who also aspire to higher office apparently respond by taking distributive matters very seriously, why do we assume that judges won't? What is it (a sociologist might wonder) about the class "ambitious politician" that changes the predicted behavior of the two subclasses "legislator" and "judge" with respect to favoring certain interests, notably their own and those of their own class?

This is a particularly piquant question when asked in the context of Posner's extraordinarily shallow definition of the term "interest." Consider the following:

> It has sometimes been argued . . . that a judge's decisions can be explained in terms of the interests of the group or class in society to which he belongs—that the judge who owns land will decide in favor of landowners, the judge who walks to work in favor of pedestrians, the judge who used to be a corporate lawyer in favor of corporations.[55]

Note first what Posner means by "class;" his examples are landowner, pedestrian, and corporate lawyer. Those are funny "classes" to choose; one might have expected other classes, for instance "bourgeoisie," or "upper middle class," or "elitist education group," or "Caucasian," or "male." If classes of that kind were chosen, it would have an interesting effect on the remainder of Posner's point:

> There are two points to be made here. First, where a particular outcome would promote the interests of a group to which the judge no longer belongs (our last example) [i.e., corporate lawyer], it is difficult to see how the judge's self-interest is advanced by adopting that out-

[54] Posner 325.

[55] *Id.* at 326.

> come. *The judge's previous experience may, however, lead him to evaluate the merits of the case differently from judges of different backgrounds.* Second, the increase in a judge's income from a ruling in favor of a broad group, such as pedestrians or homeowners, to which he belongs will usually be so trivial as to be easily outweighed by the penalties . . . for deciding a case in a way perceived to be unsound or biased.[56]

Had Posner chosen other classes it would, first, have been clear that there were many *important* classes (that is, classes with more significant permanence than pedestrianism) in which judges can be placed which cannot *be* left, thereby making his first point inapplicable. It would also have made him reconsider the meaning of the word "income" in the modified sentence "the increase in a judge's income from a ruling in favor of a broad group, such as the upper middle class or Caucasians . . . will usually be so trivial. . . . " Most important, it would have pointed toward a considerably more sophisticated treatment of the cognitive and emotional effects of class membership than the single sentence italicized above; it is arguable at least that being a Caucasian male member of the bourgeoisie with a professional school education (which describes almost all judges) has a somewhat more striking effect on one's very perceptual and cognitive apparatus than being, say, a corporate lawyer or a pedestrian. This class-conditioned status might even affect the judge's evaluation of his "income" from a particular ruling, and of the "cost" to him of *his* class's perception of what "unsoundness" or "bias" might be.[57]

Again, the question is not whether a sociologist's approach or an economist's would, on this issue, be superior. They are obviously complementary over a wide range. * * * [C]lass analysis is beggared by limiting the classes analyzed solely to those defined by narrow explicitly economic characteristics. To do otherwise, of course, would require new data, even empirical information rather hard to come by, certainly harder to come by than assumed responses to changes in price or supply of goods. But it might still help us to "understand" more than we now do about judicial behavior and its springs.

Or take anthropology. * * * One needn't get into the minutiae of disputes among anthropologists * * * to suggest a lesson upon which they would all agree: one cannot say anything conclusive, or even particularly assertive, about any aspect of a culture without trying to place it (as much as one ever can) within all its other aspects. * * * [A] culture's "political" system and its "economic" system together form another system in

[56] *Id.* at 326–27 (emphasis supplied).

[57] One need not be a vulgar Marxist to be surprised at any surprise that those who serve in the legal infrastructure of a market-oriented society tend frequently toward market-rational legal decisions.

which the "contradictions" within each subpart may turn out more transcended than one would otherwise suspect.

What about psychology? Oh sure, it has its problems. But various psychologists have said some shrewd things from time to time. Posner concedes that "the assumptions of economic theory are to some extent, certainly, oversimplified and unrealistic as descriptions of human behavior" but that "there is abundant evidence that theories derived from those assumptions have considerable power in predicting how people in fact behave."[64] I am sure there is such evidence * * * but there is evidence of other kinds too. What happens, for instance, to questions of "utility" if one accepts, even as a hypothesis, the idea of unconscious desires? In speaking about the maximization of utility, does one rate success in achieving what people "conceive to be their self-interest"[65] in terms of their conscious or unconscious aims? If a man kills himself out of incandescent rage at his wife (or *vice versa*), has he "succeeded"? What is the social utility function when, in misery, one substitutes architectural erection for sexual and finds himself equally miserable but with an extra house? * * * Can one actually, now, write four hundred pages about human desire without adverting to Freud, his followers, or even his enemies?

It must once again be emphatically stated that all of these considerations do not destroy Posner's contribution to the understanding of law. Suggesting that other intelligent men, also honestly groping for understanding, have used other matrices to place against society, thereby coming up with other assumptions, definitions, and expectations about the relevance of data, is not to suggest the primacy, or greater virtue or power, of any of the approaches. But do allow me to say that again: *any* of the approaches.

Of course, giving in to the temptation to eschew recognition of any approach but one's own is hardly merely self-indulgent. It may well be an absolute precondition to getting anything thought out or written down at all. Especially in the analysis of social states which are the product of many variables, and especially when one's interest is in a predicted state some substantial time in the future * * * the problems are enormous. * * *

Indeed, one of Posner's key points is that because of the knottiness of such decisions, it is best if, as much as possible, everyone is given the opportunity to untie them for himself. * * * Another way to put this, I suppose, is to say that "the market" looks dreadfully inadequate as a way of maximizing human satisfactions, but only until one asks "compared to what?" If, however, one is going to criticize a society, one has in effect to do it for others as well as oneself. * * *

---

[64] Posner 5.

[65] *Id.*

But even while one is giving that kind of advice, it cannot be overemphasized how on the edge of arbitrariness the game is, especially in long-term multi-variable contexts. There are numerous reasons for this but one deserves particular emphasis, for it seems to me to play much the same role in social criticism that the Heisenberg Principle plays in the physical sciences, that is, as an absolute bar to the total sufficiency of empirical argument.

Posner gives a page to what is called "The Problem of Second Best."[68] The gist of his special application of the principle is that if substitutes for a monopolized product are themselves monopolized, it is possible that making the otherwise obviously efficient move of breaking up the subject monopoly may have ultimately inefficient results. But there is a stronger form that may be given to second-best problems. One might assert a *general* theory of the second best as follows: "If a state of affairs is the product of *n* variables, and you have knowledge of or control over less than *n* variables, if you think you know what's going to happen when you vary 'your' variables, you're a booby." That is, in complex processes (which most social processes are) a move in the right direction is not necessarily the right move. To pick a simple illustration, if I am on a desert island, subsisting solely on coconuts and oysters and beginning to hate it a lot, and across the bay from me there is another island, lush and fertile, I do not improve my position in life by swimming half way across.

Various things follow from this, even (perhaps especially) if one doesn't take it too seriously. The most critical need is to identify as clearly as possible, to oneself at least, the following factors in any social decision: (1) what am I assuming will stay constant if I meddle; (2) what do I know is connected to what I'm meddling with; (3) how much do I know about how those connected things will behave when I jiggle the things I've got my hand on; and (4) when I talk about the effects of my intervention, *when* do I mean?

Now this, obviously, is hard enough even if one seeks, as Posner does, to stay within a particular definitional structure. Try it. But note how much more difficult it becomes when the variables are not kept part of the same logical and empirical framework. If a "class" consists, for instance, not just of "consumers" whose sub-classes are generated by differential responses to, say, price variations, but of income classes, or education classes, or racial classes, and there is no "formula" which governs the transformations between and among the diverse classes generated in these diverse ways, one can hardly talk at all. On the other hand, if one *knows* that such kinds of classes exist (at least as intellectual constructs), unless one assumes (or can prove) their irrelevance to the behavior one is oneself investigating, one must face the certainty of insufficient analysis, and thus the certainty of uncertain prediction. Since that will be the situ-

[68] Posner 112–13.

ation of any investigator of human activity, he will be in a continual tension between simplification and falsification. Bluntly, the less he accepts as relevant, the less he can say that is not misleading; the more he accepts as relevant, the less he can say at all. Even more bluntly, tunnel vision (like Posner's) is the price we pay for avoiding total blindness. To suggest to Posner that he look at everything at once or even seriatim, would be vain and foolish advice. Counseling humility, of course, suffers from no such drawbacks.

SMUGGLING NORMATIVES: HOW TO WIN FOR FRIENDS AND INFLUENTIAL PEOPLE

I have saved for last the question that is really most basic, for me, and I think for Posner. For all of his claims to non-normativity, it is obvious that there is at least one value *qua* value that directs and informs Posner's whole analysis. God (and history) knows it's one that does him credit: individual human freedom. One could, I suppose, treat Posner's making his whole structure balance on a definition of value in terms of individual human desire as hypothetical or accidental, but that would be silly. As normatives go, freedom is a good good, and there's no reason for anyone to be embarrassed by its espousal. For Posner, freedom—individual freedom—is a merit good, and why not; it's certainly no worse than, say, equality.

But having said that human freedom is the subterranean value upon which *Economic Analysis of Law* stands, and having praised that foundation, I cannot bring myself to stop. I know I should. Normative premises are just that; they don't get any more proved by being talked about. But I am just not up to resisting the modern moralist's temptation: even if I cannot say anything sensible about the choice of an intuitionist good, I shall nonetheless run on a while about the logical consistency and intellectual elegance of its deployment.

All right, let us consider, one last time, Posner's key definitional paragraph:

> Despite the use of terms like "value" and "efficiency," economics cannot tell us how society should be managed. Efficiency is a technical term: it means exploiting economic resources in such a way that human satisfaction as measured by aggregate consumer willingness to pay for goods and services is maximized. Value too is defined by willingness to pay. Willingness to pay is in turn a function of the existing distribution of income and wealth in the society. Were income and wealth distributed in a different pattern, the pattern of demands might also be different and efficiency would require a different deployment of our economic resources. The economist cannot tell us whether the existing distribution of income and wealth is just, although he may be able to tell us something about the costs of altering

> it as well as about the distributive consequences of various policies. Nor can he tell us whether, assuming the existing distribution is just, consumer satisfaction should be the dominant value of society. The economist's competence in a discussion of the legal system is limited to predicting the effect of legal rules and arrangements on value and efficiency, in their strict technical senses, and on the existing distribution of income and wealth.[71]

In such a system whatever is, is. If you do not "buy" something, you are *unwilling* to do so. There is no place for the word or concept "unable." Thus, in this system, there is nothing which is coerced. For instance, let us say that a starving man approaches a loaf of bread held by an armed baker. Another potential buyer is there. The baker institutes an auction; he wants cash only (having too great doubts about the starveling's health to be interested in granting credit). The poor man gropes in his pockets and comes up with a dollar. The other bidder immediately takes out $1.01 and makes off with the bread. Now under Posner's definitional system we must say that the "value" of the bread was no more than a dollar to the poor man because he was "unwilling" to pay more than that. An observer not bound within that particular definitional structure might find it somehow more illuminating to characterize the poor man's failure as being the result of being unable to pay more than a dollar. But one cannot, consistent with Posner's system, say any such thing. One's actual power is irrelevant.

Now, if one were to suggest that one's basic definitional structure ought to be altered to take account of a possible critical distinction between two empirically discernible kinds of "unwillingness"—to confront the possible effect of various kinds and levels of brute necessity upon will—one would not be changing the *realm* of definition. That is, no attempt would thereby be made to generate some normative definition of value. If one defines value in terms of objective willingness to pay (*i.e.,* actually paying), to see those acts as ambiguous across certain ranges of actualization is not to call them better or worse, but only more complex.

But let us pass all that. A man is entitled to his own definitional structures for his own "non-normative" deductions. It is, after all, not very useful to tell Richard that unarmed Morris' fleeing a battlefield in the face of an armored division coming his way is not "cowardice" when Richard has just written " 'Cowardice' is defined as fleeing a battlefield in the face of an armored division coming one's way." All you can say is that if you had the defining to do, you might have defined cowardice somewhat differently. And that is not really to the point.

If, however, one thinks intellectual consistency is worth talking about, it is worth pointing out that a similar argument can, perhaps

---

[71] Posner 4–5.

must, be made if one applies Posner's definitional structure to political decisions. There are two ways to put the case. One is that if the poor man is forever to be deemed "unwilling" to buy, then the individual (rich or not) must be deemed "unwilling" to change or leave the political system, and so we will not hear his complaints about being coerced. That is tempting, but maybe it would be more instructive to say no more than that in both cases, he is "unwilling" to pay the price charged. The poor man could grab the bread (and risk being shot); the political man, unsatisfied with his lot, could revolt and seek to form his own polity (and risk getting squashed). In each case, all that stands in his way is a serious worry about his likelihood of success, given the inequality of power between him and the others.

What this all means is that Posner has not played fair with the question of power, or inequalities thereof. He has made a very common move: *after* something of value has been distributed he has defined *taking* as illicit and *keeping* (except when paid) as in tune with the expressed wishes of the universe. It is not as if force is never to be used; Posner assumes, indeed commands, its use against theft. One of the purposes of the state is to detect the terrible inefficiencies of non-consensual transfers by having the government really smash those who persist in such behavior. But by and large the government is to have no role in even annoying those who choose to exclude others from what they already have. Keepers keepers, so to speak.

Buy why is that? Let us say I am naturally superior to a rich man in taking things, either by my own strength or by organizing aggregations of others (call them governments) to do my will. * * * Is there any way to criticize my activities except from the standpoint of taste (or some other normative proposition)? It would be inefficient to allow violent acquisitions? How can one know that? All of Posner's arguments about the efficiency-inducing effects of private property assume only that someone has the right to use and exclude, not that it be any particular person. If force, organized or not, were admissible as a method of acquisition there is no reason to assume that eventual equilibrium would not be reached, albeit in different hands than it presently rests. After all, as Posner would be the first to tell you, "force" is just an expenditure. If a man is "willing" to pay that price, and the other party is "unwilling" to pay the price of successful counterforce, we have an "efficient" solution. That is, we are "exploiting economic resources in such a way that human satisfaction as measured by aggregate consumer willingness to pay for goods and services is maximized."[74]

In brief, there seems to be some normative content in Posner's neo-Panglossianism after all. Only some kinds of inequality are to be accepted as an unquestionable *grundnorm* upon which to base efficiency analyses.

---

[74] *Id.* at 4. * * *

The transfers that come about against a background of wealth inequality are fine; any that come about against a background of inequality in strength, or the power to organize and apply strength, are unjustifiable. Some inequalities are apparently more equal than others—and all without reference to any apparent normative criterion at all.

CONCLUSION

There is none, and that's the point. We all know that all value is not a sole function of willingness to pay, and that it's a grievous mistake to use a tone which implies (while the words deny) that it is. Man may be the measure of all things, but he is not beyond measurement himself. I don't know how one talks about it, but napalming babies *is* bad, and so is letting them or even their culpable parents starve, freeze, or merely suffer plain miserable discomfort while other people, more "valuable" than they are or not, freely choose snowmobiles and whipped cream. Whatever is wrong with all that, it is only partly statistical. People are neither above reproach, nor are they ever just "sunk costs." *And "the law" has always known it; that is the source of its tension and complexity.* If economic efficiency is part of the common law (and it is), so is *fiat justitia, ruat coelum* ["Let right be done, though the heavens fall."]

Thus, though one *can* graph * * * marginal utilities for money which are the very picture of geometric nymphomania,[78] we still preserve our right to say to those whose personalities generate such curves, "You swine," or "When did you first notice this anal compulsion overwhelming you?" or even "Beware the masses." And indeed "the law," even "the common law," has on impulses like those often said, even against efficiency—"Sorry buddy, you lose."

I admit that it is not easy these days to be a moralist *manqué,* when what it is that one lacks is any rational and coherent way to express one's intuitions. That's why it is, today, so very hard to be a thinking lawyer. But I will tell you this: substituting definitions for both facts and values is not notably likely to fill the echoing void. Much as I admire the many genuine insights of American Legal Nominalism, I think we shall have to continue wrestling with a universe filled with too many things about which we understand too little and then evaluate them against standards we don't even have. That doesn't mean that any of us—especially bright, talented and sensitive people like Richard Posner—should stop what they are doing and gaze silently into the buzz. What he is doing and has done * * * enriches us all. But (to get back to where we started) he (and all of us) should keep in mind what I think is the most lovely moment in *Don Quixote*. When asked by a mocking Duke if he actually believes in the real existence of his lady Dulcinea, the Don replies:

[78] *See* Posner 216–17. * * *

> This is not one of those cases where you can prove a thing conclusively. I have not begotten or given birth to my lady, although I contemplate her as she needs must be. . . . [79]

One can understand the impulse, and be touched by the attempt, but he world is never as it needs must be. If it ever so seems, it is not the thing illuminated one is seeing, but the light.

NOTES AND QUESTIONS

1. This commentary has been severely edited, and many of the clever flourishes and asides of the author have been trimmed. It is hoped that enough has been left in for you to be able to understand why this piece transcends its ostensible task, a book review of Posner's law school text, to become a landmark article in the intellectual history of American law, and one of the most frequently cited. You would be well-advised to read the piece in its entirety at your leisure. We will be concentrating, however, on the criticism of Posner. What overall impression of Posner does Leff leave you with? Is this, after all, a favorable or an unfavorable review?

2. You may have noted the similarity of Leff's title to that of Karl Llewellyn's piece on the realists, Chapter Six, supra.

Does the similarity of title indicate any similarity of content, or similarity of philosophy between that of Llewellyn and Leff? What is the importance of the concept of "nominalism" to Leff, and how does it help us understand his view of Posner's project? The American Heritage Dictionary (4th Edition, 2000) defines nominalism, at page 1195, as "The doctrine holding that abstract concepts, general terms, or universals have no independent existence but exist only as names." What does this have to do with law and economics? Does the "nominalism" of the piece's title suggest anything about Leff's assertion that Posner's law school casebook is not a "real book?" Is this right, by the way? Is the book that you are now reading a "real book?" Why or why not?

3. Does Leff accurately present "The Way We Live Today?" You will have recognized his conclusions on formalism and realism as similar to those you drew in your study of the realists, but do you subscribe to Leff's further analysis of the current problem of the relativity of values in contemporary society? For a similar analysis to Leff's, quite popular in 1986–87, you might wish to consult Allan Bloom's The Closing of the American Mind (1986). Do you think Leff really believes that there is, today, no way of "proving" that napalming babies "is bad?" How does Leff suggest that Posner "solves" the problem that there are no clear values in contemporary American society, and what, exactly does Leff find wrong with his solution?

4. Did Leff's example of the old widow with six children who defaults on her mortgage help you understand why he says he has a genuine admiration for Posner and his method? Does it make you rethink any of your as-

[79] M. Cervantes, Don Quixote, Part II, Ch. XXXII (S. Putnam transl. 1949).

sumptions about proper social policy, or your assumptions about how courts should formulate social policy?

5. If, then, Leff admires Posner for bringing to light important questions about how much social policies will cost, who should pay the costs, and how the costs and who will pay should get determined, why does he ultimately find Posner's brand of analysis so unsatisfactory? What does Leff believe is missing from the world of Posner's "Economic Analysis"? Much that is missing, you will probably have noted, is a subtle appreciation of the fact that most of us don't really know what we want, nor do we even really know what's in our self-interest. This raises a problem, well known to modern Marxists, of so-called "false consciousness," the idea that we have been conditioned, by capitalist society, to want things that are not really in our self-interest. This will be one of the problems addressed by the next school of thought we will consider, Critical Legal Studies. Is this the critical approach Leff takes, or is his range wider? Does he seem to be criticizing Posner from a broad range of social science perspectives? When Leff winds up and lets fly with alternative forms of analysis drawn from the fields of social anthropology, sociology, and psychology, is this fair criticism of Posner?

6. Consider a theme that runs all through Posner, and that you probably were able to discern even in the "Killing or Wounding to Protect a Property Interest" piece. This is that while the courts are quite good, when all is said and done, and when all the rhetoric is blown away, at creating "economically efficient" solutions to problems of conflicting claims for resources, when legislatures and administrative agencies attempt the formulation of social policy, more often than not, they produce "inefficient" solutions. Why do you suppose Posner believes that this is the case, and what is the nature of Leff's criticism of Posner's view of the legislature? Do you find Leff any more convincing on this point? Which man's views, Posner's or Leff's, make you feel better about belonging to the human race?

Consider in particular Leff's comments about the purposes of criminal law, and his rejection of Posner's suggestion that criminal law is only concerned with deterrence. Here Leff seems to have divined a great role for the non-rational, a realm in which the usual ideas about "economic efficiency" might not apply. Is this simply Leff's incisive vision of class warfare in modern America, or does he reveal a much darker, intractable strain in human affairs? What do you make, for example, of Leff's comments about rape? Is he advocating it? With his focus on the irrational in human affairs Leff touches themes that will loom large in the "law and literature" movement, one other school of thought which we will soon consider, and with his comments on rape, of course, he reveals an attitude that is the concern of a nascent feminist movement in American law, which we will also consider shortly.

7. Another main theme which Leff criticizes in Posner is Posner's repeatedly asserted neutrality toward questions of wealth distribution or redistribution in American society. On this point see also Daniel T. Ostas, "Postmodern Economic Analysis of Law: Extending the Pragmatic Visions of Richard A. Posner," 36 Am.Bus.L.J. 193 (1998). What is Leff's feeling on these

questions, and how does it affect his analysis of Posner? In particular, does what Posner finds as the puzzling aspects of legislative conduct receive clarification through Leff's treatment of legislative redistribution? Do you understand why most (though not all) of Posner's critics have been those on the Left of the American political spectrum? Is that where Leff is to be found? Is there something anti-democratic about Posner's economic analysis of law? Is there much "democratic" in Leff's thought? Is Leff serious, for example, when he suggests that we have "gorgeous" ways of punishing lower class criminals and their "victims," or that we need to conceal the "natural inferiority" of most people from them? What does he mean by invoking the hoary common law maxim *fiat justitia, ruat coelum?* Would Posner disagree with that maxim?

8. It has been more than three decades since the late Arthur Leff wrote his critique of law and economics. A significant part of the cascade of books and articles that has issued from the word processor of Judge Posner has been devoted to responding to the points raised by Leff and his other critics, for example in his mini-summa, Overcoming Law (1995). In that work Posner confirms his move away from exclusive focus on economic efficiency or wealth maximization as jurisprudential organizing principles, in order to embrace, as well, both pragmatism and liberalism. He has never abandoned his belief that there was much to be gained from the application of economic thinking to legal problems, however, and in many ways Posner's early reply to Leff et al. in his 1975 article in the Texas Law Review, "The Economic Approach to Law," 53 Tex.L.Rev. 757 (1975), from which the rest of this note is derived, is as representative of his thinking as his latest work. In that piece Posner set out to suggest (1) the evolution of "law-and-economics," (2) the principal findings that its practitioners had discovered, (3) an agenda for future research, and (4) the failings of the critics of law and economics.

(1) *Evolution.* The first field to which law and economics was applied, Posner observed, was the law of antitrust, which application engendered little controversy, since market analysis had always been a part of antitrust, and since law and economics simply sought to determine how efficiently the antitrust principles could be applied in the market. But the new law-and-economics scholars (of whom Posner quickly became the leader) were engaged in the application of economic analysis to common law fields, such as negligence, contract, property, criminal law, and judicial administration, which had previously been thought to have concerns more important than mere efficiency. Nevertheless, it was the thrust of the analysis of Posner and his fellows that these common law doctrines were "best understood and explained as efforts to promote the efficient allocation of resources." Does this seem intuitively correct or counter-intuitive to you?

(2) *The Results so Far.* As early as 1975, according to Posner, his band of cohorts had discovered, *inter alia,* that legal actors were generally rational maximizers of their satisfactions, and that this could be demonstrated by such behavior as the manner in which litigated cases

were settled (the more money that was at stake and the greater the uncertainty the less chance there would be a settlement); that increased regulation in the interests of driver safety (such as seatbelt laws) may have had the perverse effect of increasing the risk to pedestrians from encouraging faster driving; and that criminal law's deterrent effects can be diminished if there is a low probability of apprehension or conviction. Would you have guessed at these results? Posner also suggested that economically-trained legal analysts were methodologically-superior to non-economists, in that they had a better sense of the value of survey research (apparently not much) and they could understand better that in comparative studies all variables had to be considered. Posner made the very telling point, in particular, that previous studies that had tried to suggest that harsh penalties did not deter the commission of crimes by demonstrating that the commission rates for crimes were not different in contiguous states with differing penalties were meaningless unless one had data as well on the comparative apprehension and conviction rates. Does that make sense?

(3) *The Agenda for the Future.* Posner indicated that most legal scholars favor normative over positive analysis, but that their woeful ignorance of what the facts actually were meant that the value of their work was severely limited. From what you have seen of normative legal analysis so far in the course, is this accurate? Bear this point in mind as we study the remaining scholarly approaches in the rest of this chapter. Because of what he regarded as "the economist's superior sophistication with respect to the assembly and analysis of data," Posner suggested that law and economics still had many "quantitative and qualitative insights into the operation of the legal system" to offer. Future directions, he thought, included the productivity of the federal courts, and, in particular, the working of the Federal Rules of Civil Procedure, the Criminal Justice Act, and the criminal procedural reforms of the Warren Court. Similar work, he indicated, could be done by studying several law enforcement agencies, and Posner singled out the Internal Revenue Service, the Immigration and Naturalization Service, and the Wage and Hour Division of the Department of Labor. Why do you suppose he picked those particular agencies? Do you discern any normative aspects to Posner's agenda for future research? Further promising avenues, according to Posner, included comparative international crime rates, the effect of favoring fines over imprisonment as a means of criminal enforcement, and the regulation and influence of the American legal profession. Finally, Posner wrote that there was much that could be done exploring marriage, divorce, adoption, and the transfer of wealth within the family and the taxation of households.

(4) *The Reply to his Critics.* Posner noted an almost visceral hostility to law and economics among many lawyers and law professors. One source of concern he reported was that law and economics had no consensus theory of the optimum distribution of income and wealth, and

many suspected that this rendered unsatisfactory the economic analysis of law. Posner's reply was that insofar as efficiency and utilitarianism, the main principles of law and economics, were also important features of the legal system, economic analysis of law could still make major contributions, leaving the choice of the goals of the system to others. He observed that some critics (Leff?) had attacked law and economics' central assumption that people functioned as rational wealth maximizers, on the basis that rationality is only a small part of the human experience. Posner brushed this one off by suggesting that as was true with any scientific theory, the test was the explanatory power of the hypothesis, and, for his money, as it were, "Whatever its deficiencies, the economic theory of law seems, to this biased observer anyway, the best positive theory of law extant." He then observed that there were competing efforts at the positive analysis of law underway by anthropologists, sociologists, psychologists, political scientists, and others, but that their work "is thus far insufficiently rich in theoretical and empirical content to afford serious competition to the economists." Posner admitted that this was "a rather presumptuous and sweeping judgment," but he stuck with it, and condemned the "theoretical poverty" of those fields, whose efforts at mere description he found unsatisfactory. Do you agree with Posner on this point? Can you understand how he found it rather easy to produce critics? Posner next rejected criticism that law and economics had a conservative bias. He did note that economic research supported the deterrent value of the death penalty, a conservative cause, but he said that it also supported such things as greater procedural protections in criminal trials, the application of the first amendment to broadcasting, an end to discrimination against women, the prevention of monopolies, and other causes which were dear to liberal ideology. Can you understand why Posner has now actually announced that liberalism (admittedly the Millian nineteenth-century variety) is a vital part of his jurisprudence? See generally Overcoming Law, supra. With regard to criticisms that law and economics had little to contribute to crucial questions of "justice," Posner replied that although the most important aspect of economic analysis might be positive rather than normative, there was still much that could be said for efficiency as a norm, and that, indeed, much of what we normally meant by justice was actually "efficiency." Do you agree? Posner admitted that some things that we would regard as "unjust" might well be efficient. He gave as examples permitting suicide, discrimination on racial or religious grounds, eating the weakest passenger in a lifeboat in circumstances of genuine desperation, permitting abortion, and the substitution of torture for imprisonment. Do these seem unjust and/or efficient to you? In any event, Posner observed that if we did have "justice" aims that departed from the efficient, we still needed to know the most efficient means of realizing these aims, and economic analysis was thus crucial in the search for justice. Does this make sense?

9. Why the continuing vitriol against Posner among so many lawyers and law professors? Could it have something to do with the fact that many of our political institutions might actually be based on the notion that people are *not* rational maximizers of their welfare? In particular, what do you make of Posner's continuing difficulties with the activity of legislatures, which he appears to believe do not make law with an eye toward the efficient allocation of resources? His critical approach to the work of legislatures, evident in his earliest pieces, continues to the present day.

Do you find any echoes of the attitude of Richard Peters, the late eighteenth century Federalist judge whom you encountered in Chapter Two, that legislatures too often fail to be as wise as the common law, in Posner? On the other hand, might, as Leff suggests, there be values implemented by legislatures that depart from economic efficiency, and that others might find more important than economic efficiency in Posner's terms?

10. One key target of Posner's critics, like Leff, is Posner's notion that the choice of the criminal way of life is simply a standard occupational choice. This leads Posner to the conclusion that criminal law ought simply to be about deterrence, and that criminals can be counted on to behave like any other persons, as rational maximizers of their welfare, so that, for instance, a criminal will commit less crime if the potential risks (of incarceration or fines) increase. For the full development of this line of Posner's thought see Posner, "An Economic Theory of Criminal Law," 85 Colum.L.Rev. 1193 (1985).

11. Those interested in pursuing the world of Posnerian economic analysis of law are referred to its fullest expression in Richard A. Posner, Economic Analysis of Law (8th ed. 2010). In the third edition, Posner somewhat modified his earlier focus on "efficiency" in order to argue, normatively, for what he calls "wealth maximization." Which of the two do you regard as the worthier goal? For some cogent criticisms of Posner's third edition, and, in particular, what some reviewers saw as the somewhat starker conservative politics inherent in that edition see Donohue and Ayres, "Posner's Symphony No. 3: Thinking About the Unthinkable," 39 Stanford Law Review 791 (1987). Compare that characterization with the rather startlingly apolitical pragmatic liberal economist Posner of Overcoming Law (1995). Must one have a clear political agenda to do law? For other explorations of the politics and/or values of law and economics, see Morton J. Horwitz, "Law and Economics: Science or Politics," 8 Hofstra L.Rev. 905 (1981), Bruce A. Ackerman, "Law, Economics, and the Problem of Legal Culture," 1986 Duke L.J. 929 (1986), and Robert D. Cooter, The Best Right Laws: Value Foundations of the Economic Analysis of Law, 64 Notre Dame L.Rev. 817 (1989).

12. In the next area of thought we will consider, Critical Legal Studies, there will be a rejection of Posner's refusal to advocate a redistribution of wealth, a refusal his liberal critics find particularly irksome. Indeed, as Donohue and Ayres, some of the most notable liberal Posner critics, point out, in his third edition, Posner not only denied that such a redistribution would be productive of "wealth maximization," but suggested that it might actually

be impossible to achieve. Donohue and Ayres, supra note 11, at 794–795. No such constraints occupy the thought of CLS, as we will soon see. As you compare and contrast the thought of Posner to CLS, see if you can determine where you stand on this redistribution issue, and why. You should not be permitted to leave this section on Law and Economics believing that Richard A. Posner is the only writer in that field. True it is that his output has been "impossibly prolific," and that he "was the real catalyst for the full blossoming of the field of law and economics." For some of the many who participated and continue to participate in this "full blossoming," see Robert L. Hayman, Jr., and Nancy Levit, Jurisprudence: Contemporary Readings, Problems, and Narratives 95–166 (1995), from which these two characterizations of Posner were taken.

C. CRITICAL LEGAL STUDIES

PETER GABEL, BOOK REVIEW (OF RONALD DWORKIN'S TAKING RIGHTS SERIOUSLY (1977))*

91 Harvard Law Review 302 (1977).

Taking Rights Seriously is a justification of contemporary American legal practice expressed in abstract and universal terms. Ronald Dworkin's method has been to juxtapose one series of essays about the nature of law, all of them elegant and well-reasoned in the best manner of the liberal tradition, with another series of essays which apply his version of the law in the setting of our constitutional democracy. The former are designed to show that the citizens of *a* community have individual rights against the state which arise not from the social contract as it is usually conceived, but from our simple status as "moral beings." The latter seek to demonstrate that this ideal has been largely realized through the progressive evolution of the common law and through the fusion of moral and political theory embodied in, for example, the fourteenth amendment. Taken as a whole, therefore, the book is an attempt to legitimate our historical moment by an appeal to Natural Law.

This attempt has been made before, and quite successfully. When the feudal barons brought the word of God to man, the serfs obeyed and perhaps believed. The vassalage was not maintained directly by force, but by an Idea which promised divine grace in exchange for what we would today consider a very secular servitude. This Idea was also elegant and well reasoned, but most importantly, it was abstract. For it was long ago discovered that if people could be persuaded to avert their eyes from reality and look unto the hills, they might accede to their domination with gratitude.

As we know, the ideology of feudalism eventually collapsed into the mere idea that it always was, but it did not do so because of a "hole in the

* Reprinted with the permission of the Harvard Law Review and of the author.

theory." The Enlightenment could never have made a dent in the theory, because from the feudal point of view the Enlightenment was mistaken. The ideology of feudalism collapsed when its point of view became superfluous, and this occurred when the real social and economic relationships that were feudalism were surpassed by another form of social existence requiring different abstractions to maintain itself without disturbance. This new way of living has been our way of living, and it has also given rise to many forms of servitude and unhappiness, although its Idea has been liberty and its apparent goal has been the greatest happiness for the greatest number.

The problem with liberty, according to Dworkin, has been that it has interfered with our rights, especially our right to be treated with "equal concern and respect" (p. xii). A hundred years ago, under different social and economic circumstances, this point of view would have seemed contradictory because at that time it was thought that equality followed from liberty, that people were equal precisely to the extent that they were equally free. Today the idea seems more compelling; it conforms, Dworkin says, to "our intuitions about justice" (p. xii). The reason for the shift in attitude is not to be found in the realm of abstractions, where as history and our arguments with lovers reveal anything can change into anything else, but in the realm of the concrete, where the idea of liberty has come into conflict with the organization of daily life.

I

Dworkin develops his argument by working out a series of oppositions between the tenets of H.L.A. Hart's version of positivism, which Dworkin calls "the ruling theory of law" (p. vii), and those of his own theory, which might be called a natural law of political institutions. Taken together, these opposing tenets form two paradigms, each of which has a coherent internal structure. The important features of each point of view can be summarized at three theoretical levels—the level of legal form, that of judicial practice, and that of moral and political philosophy.

According to Dworkin, Hart's idea of "what law is" is fundamentally wrong. That idea is that the sole source of legal obligation in a community is the legal *rule,* whose validity depends upon its having been adopted according to an identifiable method of legitimation that has been accepted as such by the community's members. This accepted method of legitimation is called a "rule of recognition," of which an example is the United States Constitution (p. 21). All other social rules and practices are not properly enforceable by government officials, no matter what moral expectations they create and no matter how stringently they are observed as a matter of custom. Against this rule-oriented position, Dworkin claims that the law is comprised also of *principles* such as "no man shall profit by his own wrong," which regularly figure in judicial decisions and which cannot be dismissed (as they are in the positivist model) as simply extralegal epiphenomena that judges make it a habit to refer to when they are at a loss for proper rules. On the contrary, Dworkin argues, these principles have a constitutive role in any judgment about the validity of a controversial claim of right, such as the claim in *Spartan Steel & Alloys Ltd. v. Martin & Co.*[3] that a plaintiff should be entitled to recover for economic loss following negligent damage to someone else's property (pp. 83–85), or that of the plaintiffs in *Brown v. Board of Education*[4] that there exists a distinctively legal right to attend integrated schools (p. 140). Dworkin's jurisprudence distinguishes the valid legal principle from other prescriptions of social custom not by an empirical examination of the manner by which it was adopted, as would be the case for the positivist's rule, but rather by an intuitive apprehension of the principle's relationship to the moral direction of the community's political institutions. From a purely formal point of view, therefore, legal rules "link together" as a set of all-or-nothing propositions with a common, identifiable pedigree, while principles "hang together" as a set of intuited normative propositions that must be weighed against each other according to their relative institutional importance (p. 41).

The critique of the positivist's idea of legal form also has fatal implications for the postivist's conception of judicial practice. Hart's model of rules corresponds to his view of the judge as the relatively passive enforcer of statutory commands and common law precedents. If a case is not clearly covered by such a rule, then according to Hart, the case cannot be decided by "applying the law"; instead the judge must exercise a "discretion" which reaches beyond the law for some other standard to assist him in inventing a new rule. For Hart, this procedure is a necessary consequence of the "open texture" of rules, even though it means that some cases are decided ex post facto. But for Dworkin this "hard case" is simply an occasion for a judge to discover (not invent) the proper principle (not rule) which determines the *preexisting* rights and obligations of the litigants. The "hard case" is not properly conceptualized, in Dworkin's view, as a novelty which leaves the judge in a sort of "free space" to exercise his choice; on the contrary, such a case raises familiar questions of political morality already embedded in existing principles of law, and it is the judge's responsibility (not discretion) to reach the conclusion that these principles force upon his reason. Much of *Taking Rights Seriously* is devoted to an elaboration of this judicial meditation on political theory, which involves the construction of a "concrete right" from a measurement of the weight of competing "abstract rights" inherent in competing principles.[6] Since the principles themselves have a normative character, the

[3] [1973] I Q.B. 27.

[4] 347 U.S. 483 (1954).

[6] The "abstract right" is also measured against utilitarian goals. Thus, in an example drawn from the Pentagon Papers case, New York Times Co. v. United States, 403 U.S. 713 (1971), Dworkin weighs the "abstract right" of free speech against the competing right of soldiers to security (the abstract right to life) and also against the Defense Department's need for functional

judge who invokes them must be in a certain sense an activist, and his decisions must seize on the "forward-looking, not the backward-looking implications of precedent" (p. 122).

These opposing tenets at the level of formal and practical legal theory are grounded, of course, in opposing views about when coercive intervention by the state in social relationships is appropriate. The normative dimension of legal positivism is the theory of utilitarianism. Its highest sanctity is reserved for the right of the individual to determine his own interests; as a result, it permits legal coercion only if individuals decide through the collective exercise of their "free wills" that such coercion advances the general welfare. The legal form that befits such a theory is the rule, because a rule can be neutrally applied to each individual equally by an empirical investigation of a set of objective facts, unlike the principle, which appeals to inherently vague and subjective values. The judicial practice appropriate to this theory is one of deference to rule, and if there is a need for discretion, the judge must act as a deputy legislator, evaluating policy considerations as if she were passing a piece of legislation in the general interest. Dworkin opposes this position of moral skepticism in an alliance with the recent work of John Rawls,[7] finding within Rawls' distributional contractarianism a basis for his own view that some values are not "ghostly phantasms," but are the very heart of our social and political bond. For if in the interests of justice we were to separate ourselves from the accidental fortunes of race, inheritance, and talent—if, in other words, we were to position ourselves originally behind a "veil of ignorance"—we would discover that our contractual interest would demand that certain rights against others be preserved irrespective of what a democratic majority might want once the veil were lifted. Such rights would at least include the right to be treated with human dignity and with equal concern and respect. For Dworkin these rights are, therefore, of a higher nature than the liberty-as-license favored by the utilitarian; they are expressed as a "gravitational force" (pp. 111–15) in our own political institutions; and they arm our judges with the political justification for enforcing principles with moral conviction, whatever the prevailing popular sentiment.

The contemporary relevance of Dworkin's theory is that it seems to accomplish what no amount of tinkering with the positivist model has been able to do—namely, to reconcile legal form with the substantive decisions that courts have been reaching for many years. When taken together, its various parts or levels constitute a sort of "normative logic" which allows for the balancing of equities according to neutral principles

---

fighters (which is most certainly based on utility). The resulting "concrete right" is that of a newspaper to publish defense plans classified as secret provided their publication will not create an immediate physical danger to troops (p. 93).

[7] J. Rawls, A Theory of Justice (1967).

of law rather than according to the inherently "political" calculations of policy. Yet if we turn the theory on its head—if, in other words, we try to understand the theory by reference to reality rather than reality by reference to the theory—the accomplishment seems to be only the ingenious transposition of what is into what ought to be, as the changing reality of advanced capitalism outstrips the capacity of the positivist model to justify it. Although Dworkin intends his debate with positivism to be read as a purely philosophical dispute about the true nature of legal justice, the two theories are more accurately understood as what might be called "legitimating thought paradigms," each of which is situated within a particular socioeconomic context.

In order to be able to see the two theories in this way, we must "decode" them according to a three-step process which I will call "concretization." * * *

1. The first step requires that we suspend our participation in the normative assumptions that guide the reasoning in each model. This might be described as "taking out the ought" because it requires that we provisionally ignore the abstract and normative character of the theoretical propositions in favor of their concrete and functional equivalents. To take an example from Dworkin's theory, the statement "individuals have a right to equal concern and respect in the design and administration of the political institutions that govern them" (p. 180) must be read as "certain behaviors by government officials toward everyone else are legitimated by the 'right to equal concern and respect.' " This first step tells us nothing about how the models actually work—it tells us nothing, for example, about *which* official behaviors are legitimated by the "right to equal concern and respect"—but it does prepare us for such an investigation by translating wide-open abstractions into a series of concrete practices.

2. Once the theory has been expressed concretely rather than abstractly, we must identify the regulative principle that describes the organization of the socioeconomic processes from which each theory has emerged. In a general way we refer to such a regulative principle every time we use the word "capitalism," because the word "capitalism" signifies a whole world in motion, a totality of living processes which taken together reveal a certain coherence. At any historical moment, each discrete capitalist process (such as the setting of egg prices, the distribution of welfare payments, and so on) has an immanent relationship to every other process, and it is the synthetic functioning of all of these processes that constitutes the whole as a whole, rather than as a mere collection of systemic parts. Since the world exists in time and is in a state of continual transformation, it would be inaccurate to describe this sense of wholeness by using a spatial image like "economic structure"; the sense of wholeness is better conveyed by the idea that at any given moment there is a kind of

"equilibrative tendency" within socioeconomic processes which expresses the synthetic movement of the system in time. It is this equilibrative tendency that can be expressed analytically as a regulative principle.

3. By applying the same analysis used in step 2 to the theoretical models themselves, we can show the way that each is a paradigmatic representation of its respective social reality. Just as the significance of each particular socioeconomic process is a function of the regulative principle that organizes the concrete world, so the significance of each concept within the theory can be shown to be a function of a homologous regulative principle that organizes the abstract world of the legal paradigm. Within the consciousness of the theorist, this regulative principle manifests itself as the synthetic foundation of the paradigm's legal reasoning—in other words, it is the "hidden norm" on the basis of which the theorist is able to construct a logic—and by tracing the correspondence between the paradigm's regulative principle and that of the concrete world from which it has emerged, we can show that the theory's normative logic is actually the system's functional logic expressed in ideal terms. Thus we will be able to show, for example, that the specific behaviors legitimated by the "right to equal concern and respect" in Dworkin's theory are those which are made necessary by the immanent logic of capitalism during the current historical period.

Sifted through this "concretizing" process, legal positivism appears as a legitimating paradigm which romanticizes the functional requirements of free market capitalism. The productive relations of this socioeconomic form were at their height in the latter part of the nineteenth century and were characterized by the regulative principle of unrestricted substitutional mobility or, as it is more commonly called, "free competition" without active regulation by the state. This principle worked in such a way as to place entrepreneurs, workers, and machines in a relation of atomistic opposition, facing each other as discrete and wholly competitive individual units. The kind of thinking that transposes this atomistic tendency in the socioeconomic order into a "scale of justice" in the legal order is one which precludes a priori the existence of any noncontractual or "natural" bond between private litigant and private litigant, and between private litigant and government official. And, at the heart of the positivist model, we find precisely this atomistic point of view: a normative theory which insists on the radical liberty of the individual (positivism's subjectivity of values), a legal epistemology which separates fact and value (the formal rule), and a rationalization of practice which accords legal validity only to rule-dictated outcomes (the extralegal character of mere "discretion").

During at least the last sixty years, the positivist paradigm has been increasingly unable to justify its data, because its organizational structure has become increasingly anachronistic. The regulative principle that most accurately describes the socioeconomic movement of advanced capitalism is not one of "free competition," but one of stabilizing cooperation. The developing monopolization of capital in horizontally and vertically integrated industries, the aggregative concentration of labor in the trade union, the emergence of public enterprise with the state's entry into the market, the redistribution of money which assures the purchasing power of the unemployed—all of these processes taken together have constituted the socioeconomic transformation known as pluralism. Unlike the atomism brought about by the "free" market, pluralism requires a legal paradigm that justifies regulatory interventions by government officials and cooperative or "moral" behavior between litigants. Its regulative principle does not correspond to the reasoning of a legal theory which precludes the existence of any a priori natural bond among socioeconomic actors.

Hart's work may be the last comprehensive effort by the positivist paradigm to legitimate socioeconomic phenomena that have surpassed it, and Dworkin has imagined its dialectical successor. In order for Hart to justify the judicial behavior mandated by, for example, the Uniform Commercial Code—a statute that instructs judges to identify and interpret contracts according to prevailing trade standards of fairness and good faith—Hart's jurisprudence requires that we see the judge as a "deputy legislator" exercising discretion in virtually every case. Such a discordance at the level of legitimation cannot withstand the cynicism of the realist who argues that this discretion is a thinly veiled political practice. Dworkin hopes to disarm the realist, however, by doing away with the regulative principle upon which Hart's concept of law rests. Since both government official and contracting parties are situated within a normatively sanctioned institutional milieu, since they are bonded together a priori with "gravitational force," what was "political" has become "moral" and what was "moral" has become "legal." In applying the U.C.C., the judge legitimately "discovers" the "preexisting" rights and obligations of the parties by reference to "principles" of "institutional morality." To find the practical meaning of these moral principles, we cannot look to the open-ended abstractions themselves, at least not unless we are willing to assume that merchants carry on their business activities as humble servants of a shared moral vision. We must look instead to the concretized equivalent of these abstractions: the demands that monopoly capital and the pursuit of profit impose upon the entire organization of pluralist life. And the U.C.C. reflects but one example of the sort of cooperative or "moral" behavior to which I refer: one could as easily point to the rise of strict liability in tort, to collective "good faith" bargaining in labor law, to the emergence of administrative mediation as a mode of dispute settlement, to the new equal protection in constitutional law—in short, to the whole structure of modern American law.

The reason for Dworkin's imaginative discovery is not traceable directly to the demands of capital, however. Transformations in socioeconomic structures do not "cause" new ideas; they are occasions when new ideas are felt to be necessary. The disequilibrium between the workings of the positivist paradigm and the pluralist organization of social life is experienced, dimly, as a social anxiety because people no longer "feel justified" in what they are doing. As it reaches the level of consciousness, this anxiety expresses itself along class lines through derivative and less fundamental emotions. To the law professor, according to Dworkin, the disequilibrium provokes an "embarrassment" (p. 15), and it is in fact no secret that law teachers today often feel awash in "subjectivity" when exploring "policy questions" from within the positivist point of view. To the welfare recipient, the sense that a money transfer is a "handout" may provoke humiliation. To the middle class taxpayer, this same transfer of what he thought was his may move him to anger; hadn't he earned his power, after all, as a free individual competing with others according to positivist rules? The reintegration of necessity and norm in Dworkin's legitimating paradigm assuages this practical confusion by transforming socioeconomic processes like welfare into a philosophy of right. And in so doing it seeks to persuade people to take the transforming authority of the state seriously by taking rights seriously.

II

Once Dworkin's theory has been concretized, we are left with the real world. Here in the concrete we do not find a group of abstract "citizens" engaging in lively moral discourse, but rather a group of dispersed and isolated *persons* impotently linked through the cycle of production and consumption that determines their social existence. We find the mechanical functioning that most people call work, the packaged emptiness of fast food, the obsessive manipulation of appliances that occupies the boredom of leisure time, and the sort of "love" that attempts to realize desire through ambivalent dependency and pornographic fantasy. The unhappiness and sense of hopelessness embedded in these processes are not simply the consequence of "psychological problems" as popular culture keeps insisting in despair; these concrete processes constitute the social totality within which the psyche is formed and finds itself in difficulty. And it is the effects of these processes that express the true morality of our political institutions.

Dworkin cannot address himself to these problems of the real world because his method presupposes their inevitability. The end point that is his beginning is, as I have suggested, the sort of "equilibration" or structure towards which liberal pluralism tends, and so his method relegates his imagination to the construction of an abstract paradigm that legitimates what he has already presupposed. When he has occasion to refer to the real world, what often comes to mind are examples which are pedagogically useful to the construction of his new moral formalism, but which are utterly banal in substance: how should a chess referee decide whether a Russian grandmaster can smirk at Bobby Fischer between moves (p. 102), what sort of discretion does a dog judge have to judge airedales before boxers in the absence of a rule (p. 32), does one have a right to drive the wrong way up Lexington Avenue (p. 269), and so on. These examples are substantively trivial because their purpose is to prepare us for the reduction of all questions of justice to questions of logical technique. Through them we are drawn, just as we were in law school, to transform all real situations into "fact situations" which are analogically interchangeable before the law. Since the law interprets the "facts" according to a norm, and since the norm is only the present in disguise, the method leads us back to where we always were by pretending that we were not there but have arrived through hard analysis.

But it would be unfair to Dworkin to suggest that he is pre-occupied only with trivia. The reason that he must prepare us through the use of such examples to reduce questions of justice to questions of logic is that he faces a very serious jurisprudential problem. Since the contemporary state has a redistributive function and therefore seems to favor some groups over others, it is essential to the task of legitimation that Dworkin find a way to reconcile this redistributive practice with the principle of "equality before the law." This can be accomplished only by transposing the redistributive practice into a "distributive justice" which, although based upon values, can be applied in a neutral or value-free manner. It is by appealing to logic and to values simultaneously that Dworkin hopes to show that substance and form are not at odds or, in other words, to show that justice can be fairness without being "political."

In order to demonstrate that his method is adequate to this difficult task, Dworkin devotes several chapters to the application of his theory in the context of judicial opinion. His discussions of "hard cases" include some questions which have been decided, such as the propriety of warranty disclaimers, and some which have not, such as reverse discrimination and the criminalization of homosexuality. He is on the liberal side in these disputes, but because his intention is to construct not an instrumental but a formal rationality, the outcome is never crucial.[18] Dworkin would

[18] In my opinion, the law has virtually no instrumental function, at least to the extent that the word "instrumental" is meant to refer to the economic significance of the legal outcome. The vast majority of legal outcomes have no serious impact on the economic structure as a whole, and certainly do not directly serve the interests of a dominant class. On the contrary, the legal outcome must in fact be uncertain until the judge reasons to a decision—otherwise there would be no appearance of justice and so no legitimation. Sometimes the owner wins, sometimes the worker wins, and meanwhile the real world, of which legal practice is but a tiny part, goes on.

The law is instrumental only in the sense that its ideas constrict the horizons of the possible by establishing within consciousness the boundaries of legitimate rationality. This is to say that the instrumental function is actually a legitimation function. Its efficacy depends not on the legal outcome, but on the principle of equilibration which guides the legitimating paradigm and orients "common sense." It is only with respect to outcomes, for example, that the Burger Court is "more conservative" than the Warren Court; as regards the method of formal rationality, the two Courts think alike. One could say that from the legitimative point of view we are going through a conservative period of distributive justice.

allow reasonable judges to disagree so long as they apply the proper paradigm, within which rights have "a distributional character" (p. 90) and within which every citizen has "the right to equal concern and respect in the political decision about how [the] goods and opportunities" of monopoly capitalism "are to be distributed" (p. 273).

What is missing from this treatment of the problem of substantive justice is an evaluation of the human quality of these goods and opportunities, of the extent to which the social system has been able to satisfy the true needs of the human heart as opposed to the distorted needs which have emerged from the operation of a market organized for profit. The emphasis which the book places on distributive justice—on the "moral" distribution of whatever goods and opportunities the social system produces—has the attraction of a superficial appeal to values, but it assumes that people's true needs are a collection of hypostasized "wants" that can be satisfied through the legal apparatus of a state-regulated market—that is, through the parceling out of various "rights" and "obligations." If we were to take Dworkin with complete seriousness by applying his value-system to the facts of the hard cases discussed in the book, we would have to assume that the sort of goods and opportunities that people really want from their lives can be captured by such phrases as the right to collect damages for injuries, the right to go to law school, the right to get an abortion (pp. 124–26), the right not to be jailed for touching someone passionately, and so on. However important these limited powers may be to the litigants who assert a claim to them, they are largely irrelevant to the truly serious problem that these litigants share with almost everyone, an everyday life of operating machines, disseminating clerical knowledge, and ingesting televised images. Yet from the legal-distributive point of view, they express the full meaning of "human dignity" and "equal concern and respect."

The alternative to this way of thinking about the relationship between justice and human needs is to understand the meaning of justice in concrete practical terms instead of in abstract legal terms. If we are to think about justice from the point of view of people's concrete social experience, we must begin by penetrating the false and massified "institutional morality" that Dworkin has elevated to the status of a natural law, and focus on the details of a production process that directly or indirectly infects every aspect of our lives—from the quality of work, to the material products we produce, to the kind of social relationships available to us, to the organization of our families, and even to our sense of ourselves as so-

---

In the rare case when the outcome does seriously affect the economic structure (such as perhaps was the case in Youngstown Sheet & Tube Co. v. Sawyer, 343 U.S. 579 (1952)), the dogmatic Marxists may be right: perhaps the decision can go only one way. But such cases are very rare, and it may be that the whole body of law (including law schools, law books, lawyers, and legal thinking) is in a certain sense preparing for them, in the same way that daily prayers are meant to leave no doubt about the just outcome on judgment day.

cial beings. In our world this production process operates very destructively, separating us from ourselves and from each other so efficiently that we forget what our true needs are by driving our memory of them into an oblivion which psychoanalysis calls "the unconscious." It is only by transforming these processes themselves rather than by tinkering with a legal system that legitimates them that we can create the possible conditions for a concrete justice—that is, the possible conditions for a living milieu in which human labor is a creative social activity, in which the production of material goods is purposefully designed to satisfy real human needs, and in which each person recognizes the other as "one-of-us" instead of "other-than-me" irrespective of sex or skin color. These possible conditions cannot emerge from the "free world" of an anarchic and exploitative market, nor from a state-bureaucratic socialism that simply reproduces the hierarchical structures of capitalist production techniques in another name. They can emerge only from an open and decentralized socialism that has yet to appear in developed form anywhere in the world.

To Dworkin and to other modern writers in the liberal tradition, the possibility of such a society seems inconceivable, or conceivable only as a utopian fantasy that must in practice lead directly to totalitarianism.[23] Not realizing the totalitarian character of their own historical situation, they defend a liberty that is only an anxious privatism and a legal equality that conceals practical domination. Because their philosophy is but an abstraction from the present, they confuse a historically contingent social experience with human nature, reifying "man" in their own alienated self-image and constructing imaginary "communities" which are simply idealized representations of the alienated social relationships they have known in their own lives. That is why Taking Rights Seriously, for all of its intricate argument, manages only to transpose the objective requirements of the existing social system into a normative legal order. And that is also why Dworkin cannot help us to realize in the concrete the values of dignity and mutual respect upon which he places so much emphasis.

NOTES AND QUESTIONS

1. This piece is ostensibly a book review of a work in jurisprudence by Ronald Dworkin, then a Professor both at New York University School of Law, and at Oxford University. Dworkin is probably one of the best known law teachers in the late twentieth century, and certainly among the leading two or three in Anglo–American jurisprudence. For one more example of Dworkin's work, attempting to solve one of our most pressing cultural problems, see Life's Dominion: An Argument about Abortion, Euthanasia, and Individual Freedom (1993). Do you understand, from this review, the nature

[23] Since Dworkin assimilates radical criticism to the liberal perspective, he seems to see socialism as a "goal-based" theory which restrains liberty in the interest of egalitarian distribution (pp. 172, 182–83), instead of a historical practice that seeks to make freedom possible through the transformation of social relationships.

of Dworkin's jurisprudential thought, and the reasons why a young and brilliant radical, such as Peter Gabel, might be troubled by it? It is not as a book review, however, but as a positive statement of Gabel's views that this piece is of greatest interest to us. His views on the nature of law and society, to the authors of your casebook at least, seem fairly typical for members of the school of thought known as Critical Legal Studies (CLS), although Gabel is surely one of the most passionate and the most evocative writers among the CLS scholars.

2. With regard to Gabel's criticism of Dworkin, you may have been distressed by the fact that Gabel begins with the theory which *Dworkin* is himself criticizing, that of H.L.A. Hart, perhaps the best known of twentieth century "positivist" legal theorists. You have encountered a variant of legal positivism already, in the work of Oliver Wendell Holmes, Jr., and in the thought of the legal realists. The main tenets of positivism, for our purposes, are that there is no over-arching supra-societal body of natural law, and that the only valid laws for a given society are the set of rules promulgated by clearly-recognized societal law makers, such as the legislature, the courts, the executive, or administrative agencies. Dworkin, however, as Gabel points out, is writing from a different tradition, one that you have seen in the work of Richard Peters and several of the Federalist Judges we studied in Chapter Two, and one that was probably inherent in much of the Fourteenth Amendment jurisprudence of the Warren Court; that there are certain principles of "fairness" or "natural law" that circumscribe and supplement the body of rulings from the society's authoritative law makers. It is the "natural law" thinking that Gabel compares with the theories of Feudalism, and which Gabel suggests result more in the enslaving than in the liberating of Americans. Do you understand his argument on this point? Do you agree?

3. Richard Posner is often thought to have offered a "positive" theory of law. Do you find any similarities between his thought and that Gabel attributes to positivists generally and to Hart in particular? Do you understand what Gabel takes to be the relationship of utilitarianism ("the greatest good for the greatest number") to positivism, and do you understand how Dworkin's and Gabel's views depart from positivism on this point? Which theory, Hart's, Dworkin's, or Gabel's, would you say is the most democratic? In particular, what is the meaning of what Dworkin describes as the "gravitational force" in our political institutions, and how can it "arm our judges with the political justification for enforcing principles with moral conviction, whatever the prevailing popular sentiment?"

Obviously Dworkin was trying to concoct a legal theory which would explain, and perhaps legitimate, what the Warren Court was up to in its great decisions, such as *Brown v. Board of Education*, *Reynolds v. Sims*, and *Miranda v. Arizona*, regarding the areas of civil rights, political rights ("one man one vote"), and criminal defendants' rights, respectively. Do you find Dworkin's theory satisfactory on this point? Why doesn't Gabel?

4. Probably the gist of the message of Gabel's criticism of Dworkin, and of the CLS approach to the law generally, is to be found in Gabel's at-

tempt to "decode," by the "three step process" of "concretization," Dworkin's (and Hart's) theories of law. This is an example of the rather exotic vocabulary frequently employed by CLS, and reflective of similar attempts, particularly by European Marxist scholars. This is not easy going, as you may have observed. Consider for example, Gabel's notions that

> At any historical moment, each discrete capitalist process (such as the setting of egg prices, the distribution of welfare payments, and so on) has an immanent relationship to every other process, and it is the synthetic functioning of all of these processes that constitutes the whole as a whole, rather than as a mere collection of systematic parts. Since the world exists in time and is in a state of continual transformation, it would be inaccurate to describe this sense of wholeness by using a spatial image like "economic structure"; the sense of wholeness is better conveyed by the idea that at any given moment there is a kind of "equilibrative tendency" within socioeconomic processes which expresses the synthetic movement of the system in time. It is this equilibrative tendency that can be expressed analytically as a regulative principle.

Can you explain what this means? Could you do it in fewer words, or with less use of exotic terms? One inspired comment on critical legal studies opened by asking the question, "What do you get when you cross a crit with a mob boss?" and answered "Someone who makes you an offer that you can't understand." Robert L. Hayman, Jr. and Nancy Levit, Jurisprudence: Contemporary Readings, Problems, and Narratives 213 (1995). What precisely, is a "homologous regulative principle?" It is easy, of course, to ridicule this sort of analytical language, but is there, undeniably, a powerful critique contained within these words? Of what importance, in connection with this inquiry, is the concept of capitalism (which must be an example of what Gabel means by a "homologous regulative principle") to Gabel's analysis, and how does the concept of capitalism lend meaning to the obscure language, such as that quoted, which Gabel often uses? For an intriguing attack on Dworkin for practicing "nonsense" jurisprudence, and a concomitant defense of Richard Posner, see Brian Leiter, "In Praise of Realism (and Against 'Nonsense' Jurisprudence)," 100 Geo.L.J. 865 (2012).

5. As you will have seen, Gabel is able, following his "decoding" exercise, to find that Hart and Dworkin simply reflect different stages in the evolution of industrial capitalism, with Hart's version suitable for a "romantic" era of individualized competition and free-market capitalism, and Dworkin's version more attuned to the social needs of the late-twentieth century American advanced monopoly capitalist world of "pluralism," characterized by "regulatory interventions by government officials and cooperative or 'moral' behavior between litigants." Do you find this part of the analysis convincing? In particular, do you sympathize with the character of late twentieth century society limned by Gabel? How about the character of modern American law? Do you see any similarity to the analysis undertaken by Gilmore on the law of contract, or Shapo on the law of torts, which we studied in Chapter Seven, to that here done by Gabel?

6. How much of the validity of Gabel's analysis, if any, depends on the description he draws, in part II, of the workings of the "real world" of late twentieth century America? Is this a picture that you are able easily to recognize? Those of you with long memories may remember that is basically the idea of "American malaise" which former President Jimmy Carter declared was gripping our country at about the time that Gabel was writing. You probably remember what happened to Jimmy Carter, but a similar fate did not befall Gabel, who remains one of the leading figures in the critical legal Studies movement. Why do you suppose that an American President is spectacularly tossed out of office by the electorate, but an American legal scholar can find himself published in the profession's most prestigious journal (The Harvard Law Review) for the statement of roughly similar views? Is one of the clues provided by Gabel's footnote 18, where he declares that American law really has "virtually no instrumental function?" Is this sort of reasoning a threat to anyone that needs to be met? Some have treated the thought of CLS as just such a threat, as we will soon see, but in the realm of abstraction (despite his rich empirical evocation) with which Gabel deals, is his work likely to result in any significant popular or political change?

7. On the other hand, it is impossible to deny that Critical Legal Studies has probably had as much of an impact, in terms of debate generated and legal journal space consumed, as has any recent school of legal thought, with the sole exception of "law and economics." Why do you suppose that has been the case? Could it be the extremely passionate and, ultimately, quite appealing, comments Gabel makes in the closing paragraphs of this piece, where he discusses "the true needs of the human heart as opposed to the distorted needs which have emerged from the operation of a market organized for profit?" Is the ultimate meaning of the phenomenon of Critical Legal Studies the inhumanity, the "false consciousness" of most American law and life? Is it necessary, by the way, to adhere to Gabel's conclusion (not necessarily shared by all members of CLS) that it will take "an open and decentralized socialism that has yet to appear in developed form anywhere in the world" before modern society can meet the needs of the human heart? In any event, you will have probably recognized the traces of a utopian and romantic late sixties campus activism, of what used to be called the "Movement," in Gabel's writing. An appreciation of that character of CLS, and a sympathetic understanding of the aims of its practitioners emerges more clearly, perhaps, in our next reading, from a friendly, inside chronicler of CLS.

JOHN HENRY SCHLEGAL, NOTES TOWARD AN INTIMATE, OPINIONATED, AND AFFECTIONATE HISTORY OF THE CONFERENCE ON CRITICAL LEGAL STUDIES ["CCLS"]*

36 Stanford Law Review 391 (1984).

* * *

It is impossible to understand the organization of the CCLS without focusing on the friendship of two individuals—Duncan Kennedy and David Trubek. Kennedy is a cross between Rasputin and Billy Graham. Machiavellian, and with a gift for blarney that would make the stone get up, walk over, and kiss him, he can work an audience or an individual with the seductiveness of a revivalist preacher, for Kennedy wants your soul. Trubek, on the other hand, the self-described leader of the Radical Yale Law School in Exile "Mafia," is more like a cross between Lloyd Cutler and Rabbi Ben Ezra. Enormously skilled at bureaucratic maneuvering (he has almost singlehandedly kept the soft money heat pump flowing at Wisconsin for several years now) and a naturally diplomatic conciliator of no mean talents, he makes and maintains alliances with consummate ease. One need not, however, defend one's soul against Trubek's onslaught; he mostly wants your support.

Trubek, who was Kennedy's first-year property teacher, was at Yale as part of the Law and Modernization program, the last gasp of law and social science at Yale. Kennedy participated in a Law and Modernization study group/seminar that Trubek and others organized and did some work related to the program before dutifully accepting a Supreme Court clerkship. The two passed quite easily from student and teacher to just good friends. Each in a sense was and is an "*Enfant*" —Kennedy, for his wonderfully jargoned, foul-tempered *Polemic* against the Yale Law School,[6] Trubek, for his anti-establishment teaching and scholarship that made him a victim of the most recent ritual slaughter of the innocents at Yale, the event that led to the formation of the Mafia.

Debarred, it is said, from seeking a job at Yale because of the *Polemic,* Kennedy returned to Cambridge; Trubek left for Madison. While thus in exile, each undertook a short intellectual journey in disaffection from Law and Modernization. Trubek * * * gave up faith in the positive, progressive role of law in developing countries, but never gave up faith in social science; indeed, he turned to Weberian sociology because of an aversion to Orthodox or "Scientific" Marxism of the "labor theory of value/ownership of the means of production/base determines the superstruc-

[6] Kennedy, *How the Law School Fails: A Polemic,* 1 Yale Rev. L. & Soc.Action 71 (1970).

ture" variety.[9] Kennedy, equally averse to Scientific Marxism, began writing madly (his unpublished manuscripts, most notably on the Hart and Sacks materials, but also on classical legal thought, are at times all the rage) in what can only be described as the "Critical" or "Revisionist" Marxist vein.

The importance of this simultaneous movement for the structure of CCLS cannot be overemphasized. While the two kept their basically "left" politics, from a vaguely common intellectual enterprise, Trubek moved to a position of pessimism while Kennedy gravitated toward a different kind of explanation of the universe. Thus, Trubek's sociology emphasized the importance of matters of material culture for the form and content of law while Kennedy's antisociology began to stress the radical indeterminacy, and thus the unimportance, of material culture as an explanation of law. Kennedy sought instead to explain the form and content of law by reference to the internal dynamics of doctrine and to political theories about law. Thus, the two by themselves created a dynamic that has infected the organization they spawned, the Conference, from the first. Ironically, the dynamic is a wonderfully classical pattern of student/child turning the tables on teacher/parent with the taunt, "All you taught me was horse shit, just as I thought!" only to be told in reply, "No, no, you don't understand."

This reversal of roles—student impatiently instructing teacher and, in particular, "crazies" (as Kennedy likes to call them) denouncing as meaningless the efforts of empirical social science—not only has been replayed at every meeting of the group, but is the centerpiece of Kennedy's recounting of the group's formation in 1976–77. Soon after Kennedy's tenure, as Kennedy tells the story, Trubek, on a visit to Boston, remarked on the importance of the growing, newly secured leftist presence at the Harvard Law School and proposed a meeting between it and the older

[9] Here a bit of disjargon, if that is possible, may be helpful to some readers. Since the twenties, Marxists—that is, individuals whose politics are to the left of liberal and who take as their starting point for analysis some part or parts of the writings of Karl Marx—may be broadly, if somewhat unfairly, divided into two groups—the Scientific Marxists and the Critical Marxists. The Scientific Marxists emphasize the following notions: the labor theory of value—that the value of a good is determined by the amount of labor utilized in producing it, and that the capitalist who pays the worker less than the full value of his labor is expropriating the "surplus"; the determinative importance of the class based ownership of the means of production; and the determination of the content of political, legal, and other ideas (the superstructure) by the social relations and structures (the base) that follow from ownership of the means of production. * * *

Critical Marxism draws its name from a group of scholars that included Theodor Adorno, Max Horkheimer, Herbert Marcuse, and others associated with the Frankfurt Institute for Social Research. *See generally* M. Jay, The Dialectical Imagination (1973). This school stresses the indeterminacy of social circumstances, and thus, the impossibility of deriving intelligible laws of historical change, economic or otherwise. While Critical Marxists do not deny the labor theory of value, and surely desire a change in the ownership of the means of production, they deemphasize the importance of these notions for understanding social and intellectual life. In particular, they reject the distinction between base and superstructure. Instead, they view alienation, ideology, historical contingency, and the role of human agency in history together with the relations of production as conceptually separable (though in fact inseparable) parts of the total sociocultural matrix of capitalism. * * *

group of law and social science advocates. This latter group, of whom Lawrence Friedman, Philip Selznick, and Philippe Nonet, were taken to be central representatives, had, through the Law and Society Association and its Journal, kept flickering the faint candle of law and social science research and teaching *in the law schools* for at least twenty years. A self-proclaimed voice crying out in the wilderness of doctrinal teaching and scholarship, the group was academically left and, to a certain extent, politically left as well.

The point of hooking up with the law and social science crowd can be seen both as emphasizing the convergence between the two groups in their opposition to traditional law school teaching and scholarship and as beginning a Critical dialogue about the assumptions underlying the law on the books, law in action paradigm of the law and society group. At the same time, of course, Kennedy and his friends could also draw attention to themselves by saying in effect, "Hey we made it; there's another leftie on the block. You gotta take us into account now!"—a not insignificant objective given the politics of scholarship. This theme—the relationship between two aspects of dissident legal scholarship and teaching—can even be seen in the call for the first meeting, which referred to Kennedy and his friends as those who are "intellectually indebted . . . [to Trubek and his law and social science friends] yet have chosen a path quite different from that of their teachers."[14] It may even explain that note of stridency in some CLS scholarship—a combination of frustration at the obtuseness of one's elders, a demand to be recognized, and a slight unsureness about the truth of the matter stated.

The friendship between Kennedy and Trubek has shaped the group in another way as well. Looking at the list of the Conference's organizers, one sees that each is tied to one or the other, or to both. Richard Abel was a colleague and co-victim [of denial of tenure] with Trubek at Yale, and along with Tom Heller, was a member of the Law and Development Study Group there. Rand Rosenblatt and Mark Tushnet started as first-year students with Kennedy, who, because the other two were pursuing joint degrees, ended up their senior editor on the Law Review. Tushnet, Heller, and Stewart Macaulay were colleagues of Trubek's at Wisconsin; Morty Horwitz and Roberto Unger were colleagues of Kennedy's at Harvard. Similarly incestuous rings can be drawn to encompass most of the actual participants at the first meeting in the spring of 1977, where about the most tenuous connection was being "a friend of a friend" of one or the other.

Even the destruction of the neat binary form that characterized the original conception of the organization can be attributed to Kennedy and Trubek. Tushnet was included on the organizing committee in large measure because, at the time, he was the Associate Dean at Wisconsin

[14] Letter from Mark Tushnet to Dear Colleague (Jan. 17, 1977).

and, as such, had a secretary and easy access to duplicating facilities and other amenities without which organizing a large meeting is impossible. But Tushnet was then what he is not now—a relatively orthodox, Scientific Marxist. Thus (somewhat ironically for Kennedy's social indeterminist position), out of material necessity, a third leftist perspective achieved prominence in the group. It is this third perspective, I suspect, that seems to overpower the social science at the root of the organization, making it appear to those on the outside to be a Marxist monolith. Yet nothing could be further from the truth. Indeed, for those on the inside, the addition of this third perspective has generated a second basic dynamic within the organization—three-corner catch.

The game goes pretty much as follows. While there are exceptions (Rick Abel, for instance) most of the law and social science dissidents who inhabit the Conference have not been heavily influenced by Scientific Marxism. Indeed, to the extent that they are Weberian, scholars like Trubek, Marc Galanter (for a short while a participant in the group), or Stewart Macaulay can be seen as anti-Marxist. Because the kind of thought that Kennedy may be taken to represent likewise rejects orthodox Marxism, the two groups have, and are able to mobilize, a common interest in attacking that enemy.

Yet that enemy is not without its own resources. On the one side, Scientific Marxism has a potential ally in the social scientists, since in some sense, both explain the world with great emphasis on material culture. For both of these groups, then, Kennedy and his crazies provide a common enemy, since in its emphasis on the role of ideas in determining the content of law, Critical Marxism may be seen as an attempt to turn Hegel upside down again and thus create a traditional idealism, not unlike the idealism that is liberal thought. On the other side, Scientific Marxism has an ally in Critical Marxism, since, for both tendencies, *the* evil in the world is capitalism. For both brands of Marxism, then, empirical social science is a convenient whipping boy, because, as social science, it can be tied to the long history of apologetics for American society in which the gap between law in the books and law in action can be viewed merely as a call to work harder to perfect that society, rather than as a symptom of the deep crisis caused by capitalism and its liberal apologists. And thus around the room the ball is tossed.

Whether the resulting form of the game stabilizes or destabilizes the organization may be a question of perspective, but this is basically unimportant. Within the group and its scholarship, all three alliances can be seen. Indeed, the classic example comes from the very first meeting where, at the end of a session, Trubek attempted to sum up "the problem" with which the group had been grappling as "whether we are Marxists." He then announced his difficulty with the labor theory of value and thus his rejection of Scientific Marxism. Tushnet, unconsciously emphasizing the similarities of his own position with Trubek's, retorted that "the question" was not "whether we are Marxists," but whether, given that ideas can have some influence on material economic culture, we believe that "in the last instance" it is material culture that determines the content of those ideas. Having thus been pushed into the role of the opposition, Kennedy and his friends first responded by denying their allegiance to Scientific Marxism, calling instead for the "totalization of base and superstructure"—that is, the treatment of the world of material culture and the world of ideas as a totality, any piece of which is a representation of the whole, and neither part of which has an a priori claim to being determinative of the other part. They then, unconsciously no doubt, opened the door for the social scientists by stating that "the question" was how structures of thought legitimate the existing social order and the domination inherent in it—a vaguely sociological question, though not one on which quantifiable empirical research could be done. And thus the ball was back where it started, following a dynamic that can be directly attributed to two men, Trubek and Kennedy, who brought their friends and acquaintances together to talk about law.

Of course when a group like this is formed, it in some sense always takes on a life of its own, apart from the wishes of its Founding Fathers; CCLS is no exception. In spite of their hopes and wishes for concord, agreement, and the prospect of "a new scholarly community," Trubek and Kennedy's design of the group led inexorably to the already described intellectual conflict, a conflict they feared and even tried to paper over during and after the very first meeting. Their design led to external conflict as well. Here the fear of conflict—social and in some ways intellectual—probably far exceeded its reality. In any event, the fear dominated the group, or at least the inner circle, from the outset. The shadow villains were two. The first, an unnamed, and, I suspect, an unknown, band of doctrinaire Marxists referred to as "Guild types," brought forth both fears—the social and the intellectual. It was assumed that, as was the case with much factional left politics during the late sixties and early seventies, intellectual disagreements would spill over into social relations, and clearly a good portion of the group wanted space, both intellectual and social, for anything but doctrinaire discussion and community fractionalization. The second, a group of prominent liberals, brought forth only the fear of intellectual conflict, for it was assumed that fights about liberalism within the group would inhibit development of the group's own distinctive approaches to law.

At the first meeting these two groups were simply excluded. This strategy became so blatant with respect to the liberals that it led to an amusing conversation between Kennedy and Dean Harry Wellington of Yale. Dean Wellington first protested that members of his faculty, obviously as smart and as "with it" as any around, were being excluded for no good reason. He then retreated wholly satisfied, upon being informed that the criterion for extending invitations was not smarts but politics and that on this criterion the Yale faculty was not left enough. Ever since the original policy of "by invitation only" was changed to "open door" at the second, so-called "regional," meeting at Northeastern the following fall, traditional liberals have largely avoided the organization like the plague. But an incident at that meeting in which a paper by Ike Balbus was viciously, if rather isolatedly, attacked for having nothing to do with "the working class," seemed for some to suggest that the other exclusion had been sensible.

These fears, largely unrealistic though they may seem to most of us now, and to some of us then, given the implicit decision that the group was to be largely composed of, and directed by, the interests of the law professoriat, led to the quite astonishing highlight of the second Madison meeting in the fall of 1978. True to all the norms of left gatherings, CCLS ends each conference with a "plenary" session for feedback, planning, speeches, and making up. However, this plenary session began with a very embarrassed organizing committee informing the gathering that the heretofore informal group had become a membership organization with its own pledge and bylaws, and that an interim executive committee had been selected to run the organization until a board of directors with staggered terms, just like a corporate takeover target, could be elected. The silence from an audience accustomed to a modicum of self-determination in such matters was deafening, and the committee's defense of its action as providing for future democracy rang hollow when placed in conjunction with known, if not shared, fears of left factionalism.

Not only is the group thus given on occasion to the common liberal vice of putting institutions first and individuals second, but it also suffers from more than a dose of liberal elitism. One can see in the inclusion of the likes of George Fletcher and Ian McNeil at the first Madison meeting a need to have "names," which is less obvious in the inclusion of Roberto Unger on the organizing committee and in the hagiography of the organization, even though he has done little more than attend the first two meetings and deliver a long speech at a recent one. Less innocuous, though equally understandable, is the pride of the group in general and the excitement of some of its members in particular at the establishment of its first "colony" at such an elite institution as Stanford, rather than at, say, Dayton, Duquesne, or Bridgeport. Similarly, the joy shared by the troops at any "news" suggesting even obliquely that a "fancy" school might be interested in getting a "Critical legal type" to add a touch of the exotic to its menu is notable, if only to cause wonder at the notion that demystification—the stripping away of the veneer of apolitical decisionmaking from the legal process—from the top down is a rational revolutionary strategy, a notion again called to mind every time one hears of left victories in the glacial march of curriculum and appointments reform at Langdell Hall. Less pleasant is the feeling, often expressed by newcomers, that the group is divided between an inner circle of old timers who dominate the organization and whose ideas and interests set its tone and direction, and a great unwashed whose presence is tolerated, but little more, unless introduced by the right people. This accusation gains some credence from the observation that it took three years before the organizing committee would open up "summer camp"—now annual week-long summer sessions devoted solely to discussion of selected texts and scholarship—to the membership generally, and even then only with group leaders carefully ensuring that the new guest list looked more than slightly like the old.

Exactly what should be concluded about the organization and its members from all of this is by no means clear. No one could deny that endless hours have been spent discussing both institutional protectiveness and elitism in CCLS. And some progress has been made: Witness the recent decision to open up membership in the organizing committee to anyone who wishes to join in its deliberations. Furthermore, to complain about either institutional protectiveness or elitism is both to engage in the reification of democratic forms and to forget that people will be friends with, and trust the judgment of, those people whom they know best and longest. In a group that began at, and primarily with people from, elite law schools, some, perhaps much, of what is seen as elitism is nothing more than sticking with and trusting one's friends. Yet, in an organization that claims to be as deeply antihierarchical as this one does, behavioral manifestations of traditional notions such as "wisdom proceeds up river on the Charles and then out to the countryside," or "getting ahead is teaching at a better law school," are deeply troubling. Such notions abet nagging doubts in the membership and deeply held suspicions in outsiders that what the group is about is little more than shifting power from one elite to another. That is *not* what the group is about! Yet old ways, bred in the bone early enough to fit Loyola's boast, die much harder than grows the rhetoric that denies their existence. Unfortunately, this truth has not yet fully reached the left-handed consciousness of the collective dictatorship that runs the organization.

One should not, however, surmise that this informal politburo has had a profoundly negative impact on the group. In fact, precisely the opposite is the case. The group as a whole has fostered within its self-defined borders an incredible tolerance, both social and intellectual, which allows individuals to make quite silly statements in open meetings, and allows newcomers, at least those who are a bit aggressive, simultaneously to acquire a supportive yet Critical forum for ideas and an equally supportive social network. In such a community, fragmented though it may be, personalities have grown with the luxuriance of houseplants. No meeting would be complete without the appearance of Peter Gabel's curly black locks and earnest, terminally tired eyes, to present, in his own wonderfully dense and contorted prose, the epicycles of self-alienation as he has come to understand them in any given year.[32] Nor would I ever miss the balding, almost elfin, Morty Horwitz, embarrassedly defending his latest attempt to salvage his limited version of the socioeconomic determinism of legal ideas from the onslaught of his neighbor in Langdell Hall, Mr. Kennedy. Similarly important are the cleanly polished sentences and paragraphs, always spiced with just enough humor to make the medicine go down, delivered in the most carefully modulated tones by Robert Gordon, words that are inevitably contrasted with the more direct utterances of that self-proclaimed "old fogie" where teaching is concerned, the stout Tushnet who, on occasion, sees fit to remind us that "when they find out what we're doing, they're going to come after us with guns." Such judgments of centrality to the experience are, of course, personal and idiosyncratic, but to build an organization in which the personal and idiosyncratic can flourish, where the group as a whole can on occasion discuss a book or idea and not sit ossified as presenters drone on and commentators sit nervously on their witticisms, is an achievement not to be sneered at.

Setting aside the organizational dimension of CCLS and returning to the intellectual, I would hazard a guess that the reference to the Frankfurt School of Critical Marxism in the title of the organization was probably lost on many, if not most, of the participants at the first meeting, the majority of whom had read little of that or other Critical Marxism beyond the obligatory college volume of *Eros and Civilization* or *One Dimensional Man*. This fact, if such it be, suggests that, to date at least, the CLS movement may be less important as an event in the history of legal thought, than as an event in the history of legal education.

One of the most important, though virtually unexamined, aspects of legal education is its cultural one. At least since Blackstone, and I suspect long before, the central job of legal education has been to justify existing rules of law to the nascent members of the legal elite. The task is an important one; no society wants its priests wandering around doing their magic while doubting the one true faith. Here, then, can be appreciated the importance of "Langdell's" case method: It moved this act of justification closer to the center of the student/teacher relationship by turning what was ofttimes, though not always, a monologue into something more approximating a dialogue, from a passive to a vaguely active enterprise.

---

[32] Peter's verbal style has been captured best by a cartoonist at New College, whose piece, "Peter Talks to Some Winos" begins:

> The central point of everything I have said thus far can be summarized as follows: the "legal system" is the institutionalization of the effort of alienated consciousness to maintain its own dominant position by channeling social conflict into authoritarian settings and by "resolving" this conflict according to a system of thought that reinstates the "legitimate necessity" of the status quo.

It is to Peter's credit that he immediately circulated this satire on his style among a number of people. Though the Conference prides itself on its seriousness, unlike most other parts of the law professoriate, it has the pronounced ability to laugh at itself on occasion. Peter is a classic example of this healthy human (and humane) trait.

While the style of this dialogue of justification seems to have changed over time, as well as within particular eras or even within particular law schools, its content has remained remarkably stable for the past one hundred years. In that period, there have been but two types of content. The first, whatever its claims to evolutionary historicism, justified the rules because of their logical interrelationship; the rules were right because they fit with the other rules. The second justified the rules because of their intrinsic social goodness; the rules were right because they embodied wise social policy. The first is said to be formalist; the second, more misleadingly, Realist. But whatever the content of the act of justification, the enterprise is by nature conservative, not radical. Its overt political content can, and has, varied from conservative to liberal, and might conceivably be reactionary or radical, but its basic conservatism remains. In order for all the nascent elite to sleep comfortably, the message must be positive. It need not be panglossian, but to be effective, the message cannot be that more than a few rules need fixing in order to get the system running right. Within this basic intellectual structure operates the history of legal education since 1870.

For the first fifty years the overt political content of the dialogue of justification was overwhelmingly conservative, so overwhelmingly conservative that Roscoe Pound's plea for an improved civil procedure could indeed be seen as radical, which gained him instant notoriety in legal academe. The combination of the death of progressivism in World War I, the swing to a socially conservative national government, and the gathering economic dislocation that by the end of the twenties had become the Depression, brought to the fore renewed left political activity. In the legal academy this left politics joined with the twentieth century notion of science as empirical inquiry into a world "out there" to produce American Legal Realism.

Politically, Realism was no more than liberal; its content reflected much of what Mark Tushnet likes to call "the 1964 platform of the Democratic Party." But the importance of its liberalism should not be underestimated, for as liberals, Realists were substantially to the left of the academic center, as evidenced by Llewellyn's dispute with Pound,[38] who was left by law school standards but at best a political centrist. In contrast, Realism was educationally radical, for it denied that the rules as they existed were justified. Here again the Realists' differences with Pound are instructive. The basic thrust of Pound's position was that if the law in action were made to conform with the law in the books, all would be fine. But one of the thrusts of Realist scholarship was to suggest that the law in the books was not fine.

[38] Llewellyn, A Realistic Jurisprudence—The Next Step, 30 Colum.L.Rev. 431 (1930); Pound, The Call for a Realist Jurisprudence, 44 Harv.L.Rev. 697 (1931); Llewellyn, Some Realism About Realism—Responding to Dean Pound, 44 Harv.L.Rev. 1222 (1931).

Realism made this assertion in four ways. The first is the most well known: Claims were made, often building on Hohfeld's work[39] that the rules were simply incoherent. * * * The second is less well known: Claims were made that justification was inappropriate to scientific inquiry. This strategy underlay all of the Realists' empirical research * * *. The third is now a classic: Attempts were made to simply debunk the process by which the rules were created. Here, Jerome Frank's work is most notable.[42] And the fourth is the most unusual, but not unknown, strategy: Rather direct assertions were made that the rules were simply wrong. * * *

Given that Realism thus undercut the underlying purpose of legal education—the justification of existing laws—it not too surprisingly created a real flutter in the academy. And that flutter became downright hostility as the thrust of the Realists' critique of "justification through logical interrelationship" became clear to even the most opaque of humans by the late thirties. The reason for the hostility is easy to identify: The Realists' critique highlighted the central question that the dialogue of justification is designed to suppress: the question of power—in whose interest legal rules are made.

After a tangled history, of interest only to aficionados of the thirties and forties, a basic shift in the form and content of the dialogue took place. Policy analysis of a liberal political stripe became the norm, and questions of process were thought to have laid to rest questions of power. In the meantime, rising academic standards increasingly cut off access to legal careers for the lower middle class, and decreasing course requirements were turning law schools into a thoroughly incoherent garden of earthly delights.

This stasis was, however, relatively short-lived. By the mid-to late-sixties, the fallout from student and, with caterpillar-to-butterfly-like eventuality, teacher idealism concerning the New Frontier and the Great Society had begun to reach the law schools. This was then followed by disillusion and hostility arising from the Vietnam War, Watergate, and the nation's political shift to the right. Simultaneously came student clamor for relevance and clinical education and the assembly of a small but determined band of social science types dedicated to showing what was "really" going on out there, the Law and Society Association.

Meanwhile, inside the classroom, policy analysis was becoming an increasingly fragile enterprise. This fragility was probably an inherent problem, for the usual technique of such analysis—balancing of interests—transparently invites dissent in the form of "no, this interest is the stronger." With the collapse of "The End of Ideology" consensus during

[39] Hohfeld, Some Fundamental Legal Conceptions as Applied in Judicial Reasoning, 23 Yale L.J. 16 (1913).

[42] J. Frank, Law and the Modern Mind (1930); Frank, Are Judges Human?, 80 U.Pa.L.Rev. 17 (1931).

these years, such dissent vigorously increased both inside and outside the classroom. The result was that questions of power were again brought to the fore, if only to be hidden in embarrassment.

The growing awareness of the fragility of policy analysis made traditional legal scholarship appear more and more bankrupt in its attempt to maintain the appearance of neutral disinterestedness through the ad hocing of interests and the transparent manipulation of their weight. Even more tellingly, one could clearly discern among the more elderly members of the teaching fraternity a sense of general malaise and nostalgia for the "good old days" when standards were clear so that everyone knew what was good teaching and fine scholarship.

It is out of this unstable situation that CCLS emerged. Almost all of the principals of the group came to maturity during the late sixties or early seventies. Most began teaching during these years as well, often after a stint in legal services or some other reform-oriented post, as well as participation in the antiwar movement. And while dreams of reform faded, the common politics did not; indeed, many of the principals often moved farther left in an attempt to explain what had gone wrong with earlier great hopes.

The personal odyssey of the principals of CCLS does not have an obvious Realist analogue; yet the drawing of parallels between these two intellectual movements separated by nearly fifty years may nevertheless be appropriate, perhaps even illuminating, because of a shared, relatively left politics, practiced in a relatively conservative social and political environment. First, while the politics of most of the CLS group is much left of Realist politics, it, like Realist politics, is threatening to the dominant elements in legal education less because of its absolute position on the political spectrum than because it is left relative to those dominant elements; left is destabilizing. More important, however, just like Realism, CLS has as one of its central goals the dejustification of legal rules. Indeed, the movement uses essentially the same techniques; claims of incoherence or inappropriateness abound, as do examples of demythologizing (i.e., debunking or trashing) judicial decisionmaking (and everything else), and direct denials of the correctness of policy. And the reaction of horror from the established corners of legal academia, especially liberal academia, is much the same as well.

At the same time, one should note differences between the two movements, other than purely political ones. While there are exceptions in both groups, the social science of choice for Critical scholars is history, not the heavily quantified sociology that so fascinated the Realists. Likewise, claims of incoherence are less likely to be seen at the level of specific doctrines that the Realists loved to work over than at the level of entire subject areas of law—contracts, labor, civil rights, etc. Furthermore, concern with the specific proposals for law reform that often lay just beneath the surface of Realist scholarship is conspicuously absent from much of present Critical scholarship. On the other hand, Realist scholarship largely lacked the explicit concern for social theory that abounds in Critical scholarship. And while both movements share a concern with legal education, it remains to be seen whether Critical scholars can transform the face of legal education as effectively as the Realists managed to do.

This detour into what some of the group might call a portion of the World–Historical Process now needs to be brought back to the details that are, and have shaped, the Conference. The attack on social science at the first meeting (and ever since) was so strong that it brought an almost bitter, fifties-like denunciation from a soul as calm as Marc Galanter, and a more resigned, "I think I am not wanted here," from Joel Handler. The result has been that the social science post in the game of three-cornered catch has been weak, personed primarily by David Trubek and Stewart Macaulay, the latter whose native Bah Humbugry makes him at best a fellow traveller. Consequently, the stoutest defense of social science often comes from the historians and others in the group interested in social and cultural history. This assault on social science has also meant that the rapprochement Trubek and Kennedy sought with the law and social science group has been a conspicuous failure; in fact, the mandarins of the Law and Society Association have responded with bitter denunciations of the "new doctrinal barbarians." And this problem has surely not been helped by Tushnet's wonderfully, or awfully (take your pick), foul-tempered review of Lawrence Friedman's *History*.[50]

On a more positive note, the quite tentative, very cliquish, even conspiratorial, beginning of the Conference seems to have passed. No more is one likely to find, as was the case at the first meeting, Peter Gabel and Alan Freeman smoking big black cigars in one secluded corner of David Trubek's yard, while Trubek and Roberto Unger, seated in a peacock chair, in another secluded corner talked South American politics, often in Spanish (or was it Portuguese?). No more do strangers to the group, suffering from nothing more dangerous than an understandable modicum of insecurity in new surroundings, seem to be "Stalinist" or "too intense." Instead, the group has become incredibly friendly, even clubby. Thus, once the perfectly silly embarrassment wears off about how little scholarship the group as a whole, except for Tushnet, has produced in a year, annual meetings become much like the gathering of a clan. And that is good.

The aging of the group, with the accompanying proliferation of children whose appearance at these meetings may signal, if ever so softly, a possible hairline crack in the bourgeois separation of work and family, of course adds to the clannishness. Thus, trading pictures of one's children

[50] Tushnet, Perspectives on the Development of American Law: A Critical Review of Friedman's "A History of American Law", 1977 Wis.L.Rev. 81.

is by no means an unknown behavior, and a threat to the tenure of, or a decline in the health of, a member is a matter of more than a little seriousness. Similarly, the absence from any gathering of, say, Alan Freeman, whose manic energy and relentless optimism has surely infected everyone, as well as nearly wiping out his health, or Karl Klare, a wonderful combination of high seriousness and warm, open goodwill, or Rand Rosenblatt, whose bald Lenin-like profile gives the impression of a fierceness that is simply nowhere to be found in his humane inside, will not only be noted, but actually counted against the success of the event.

But clannishness can have its downside, too. When missionaries like Kennedy or Klare turn out hundreds of locals for a meeting of a group whose core membership is no more than one hundred, the result is predictable. The old people, myself included, spend time grumping about, wondering "Who are all these people," until finally spotting a few old friends; then the hugs, kisses, and handshakes start. Only thereafter, when such by no means insignificant formalities are out of the way, can the serious business of the group, welcoming the newcomers and introducing the members to them, both socially and intellectually, begin in earnest.

Equally positive is the support the group has provided for young, largely isolated, scholars scattered over the country in hostile places. Much of this support has come by providing protective coloration, by making left legal scholarship okay—weird but not dangerous (or is it the other way around?). And in so doing, the group has succeeded in what Trubek remembers as another of the Founding Fathers' intentions. Less successful have been attempts to involve practitioners who share a common politics in the organization. Some came even after the second Madison conference, at which many felt they were read out of the organization, but few, other than David Kairys, who proves the rule by taking up legal scholarship, and clinicians like Garry Bellow and Jeanne Charn, have stayed. The mismatch is obvious: Practice is only tangentially relevant to a group largely engaged in dejustifying rules, for examining the law in action is only a variation on the other CLS techniques for achieving that end.

More encouraging is the recent explosive growth of a serious feminist presence in the group. Its delayed appearance may have something to do with the late reception of women into the ranks of law school teaching, an acceptance that today, even at the best of places, tends to be partial, if not carefully monitored. But whatever the reason, this presence, dominated as it is with a heavy legal rights analysis and agenda, cannot but alter an organization that has until now eschewed such an approach to law in favor of grander social theory and explanation.

A good story has a beginning, a middle, and an end. Critical Legal Baloney, as some of us fondly call it, has at best a beginning—at

Pasquina's Coffeehouse on Harvard Square, so I am told. Beyond its beginning it has only people, people sharing a common politics that convinces them that existing rules of law are not justifiable. If the liberal conceit continues to unravel, and all concerned become aware that the postulated dichotomy between the public sphere of politics and the private sphere of law is fraudulent—that, in a phrase, LAW IS POLITICS, pure and simple—then the movement and its visible organ, the Conference, may be of some significance in the world. If not, if it remains a group of individuals providing each other with tremendous mutual support in a world seen to be basically hostile towards them, if it ends up only a "lonely hearts club for left-wing law professors"[57] then it will still be important, maybe even more so.

NOTES AND QUESTIONS

1. This piece has more of a journalistic flavor than most of the readings in this book, and there is an undeniably "gee-whiz," or "you should only have been there" feel to it. Nevertheless, and notwithstanding its breezy tone, it is a serious effort to place CLS, or "CCLS" (for the "Conference on Critical Legal Studies") as the group originally called itself, in the spectrum of legal thought in the late twentieth century academy. Still, personalities play an important part in Schlegal's analysis, and he maintains that CLS cannot be understood without an understanding of the personalities and quirks of its founders, particularly the charismatic Duncan Kennedy, and the enterprising social scientist David Trubek. Do you understand what Schlegal means when he suggests that the contrast between these two has created problems for CLS? To which wing would you suspect Peter Gabel (described, you will remember, by Schlegal as possessing "curly black locks and terribly tired eyes") belongs?

2. Schlegal makes much of the connection of CLS's founders with Yale, and, in particular, with the Yale "radical Mafia," a group of professors who were denied tenure at Yale. It is, of course, difficult to ascribe a characteristic philosophy to an entire institution, especially on the basis of the thought of a few individuals, but you have had some exposure to two of Yale's outstanding legal theorists, Alexander Bickel and Grant Gilmore. Can you understand how the thought of CLS might be perceived as differing from the thought and work of Bickel and Gilmore?

Getting tenure at law schools, alas, has been something of a recurrent problem for CLS scholars. Trubek, for example, was originally denied tenure at Yale (but well before CLS was in existence), then achieved a splendid reputation as a professor at Wisconsin's law school, but, after visiting Harvard, ended up not getting tenure there. Still, three ostensible leaders of CLS, Duncan Kennedy, Morton Horwitz (some of whose work you have already

[57] The phrase comes from Cappy Silver * * *. A paralegal welfare advocate and antinuclear organizer who decided not to become a lawyer, she is now an actress and singer with the progressive rock band, Balance of Power.

read), and Roberto Unger, were tenured at Harvard, which Duncan Kennedy refers to as the "Rome" of Critical Legal Studies. Nevertheless, in "Rome," in 1987–88, another aspiring Critical Legal Studies scholar, Clare Dalton, was denied tenure after a very bloody battle, legal skirmishing in connection with which ended only in 1993, when Harvard settled with Dalton for $260,000, which it agreed to pay to a domestic-violence Institute at Northeastern, where Dalton was then a law professor. Harvard admitted no fault, but was clearly pleased with the settlement. See, e.g., Terry Theiss, "Novel Ending for a Dispute over Tenure," The Christian Science Monitor, September 23, 1993, p.2. Why do you suppose tenure is such a prickly problem for CLS scholars? Is there something in the CLS perspective that appears to many to be incompatible with law school faculty tenure? Could it have something to do with the fact that their thought owes much to Marxism? Do you understand the subtleties involved in the distinction between "Scientific" and "Critical" Marxists? If you do, you are significantly ahead of most tenured members of American law school faculties, at least those in residence in the seventies and eighties, who had trouble distinguishing among Marxists, Communists, Anarchists, and those who advocated the overthrow of the United States government by force and violence. On the other hand, in a self-consciously provocative piece on the state of CLS for the Centennial of the Yale Law Review, Mark Tushnet, indicating that CLS "has become one of the accepted elements in the pluralistic universe of legal scholarship," nevertheless added that "law faculties believe that it is generally a good thing to have one (but not more than one) CLS advocate in the building, although, as is usual in the assimilation of a novel approach to law they frequently find particularized objections to each specific advocate proposed for appointment." Mark Tushnet, "Critical Legal Studies: A Political History," 100 Yale L.J. 1515 (1991).

3. Do you understand what Schlegal means when he suggests that Duncan Kennedy wants "your soul?" Do you find anything helpful in explaining this in the last part of Gabel's piece, when he describes what he perceives as the failure of modern American society to meet the needs of the human heart? Can you understand why CLS scholars, such as Gabel, tend to be driven to the kind of sources in Scientific and Critical Marxism, as well as the empirical social science research, "the three-cornered game" which Schlegal describes? More, can you understand what Schegal (and by implication Gabel in particular, and CLS in general) means by "Liberal," and why the CLS leaders could be criticized for succumbing to the "liberal vice" of "putting institutions first and individuals second," or of "liberal elitism?" Why is it apparently necessary for CLS to present itself as "anti-elitist" and "anti-hierarchical," and why is Schlegal being extremely ironic when he refers to its leadership as a "collective dictatorship?"

4. You will have noticed that in the middle of this piece Schlegal departs from personalities to give a very rapid survey of the development of legal pedagogical thought in the last hundred years, suggesting little has changed since Langdell, and yet spending much time with the thought of the Realists and Roscoe Pound, and, in particular, comparing the Realists to CLS. You studied these matters. Does Schegal's treatment of Pound and the

Realists seem correct to you? Does he illuminate what you might have perceived as a rather dark and dreary debate between Pound and the Realists? Did you recognize any similar themes, in this part of Schlegal's "World–Historical Process" analysis, to those expressed by Gabel? Is this article of Schlegal's itself a work in Critical Legal Studies?

Does the world of legal pedagogy which Schlegal paints seem like that limned by Leff? Does the emergence of CLS suggest any relationship between CLS and Posnerian legal analysis? A disciple of Posner, Professor Thomas Merrill, of Columbia University School of Law believed that CLS was simply the "long overdue reaction" to Law and Economics. Do you agree? In any event, with "law and economics" and "CLS" competing for the "souls" of law students and professors, can it still be seriously argued that ideology is dead in American legal education?

What is the meaning of Schlegal's apparent praise of the "hairline crack in the bourgeois separation of work and family" which he sees emerging in the annual meetings of CLS?

5. In Stephen B. Presser, "Some Realism about Orphism or the Critical Legal Studies Movement and the New Great Chain of Being," 79 Nw.U.L.Rev. 869 (1984), in an obvious act of homage to Karl Llewellyn and Arthur Leff, one of your casebook authors performed a somewhat lighthearted analysis of CLS, suggesting that while it had some powerful theoretical paradigms to contribute, it was principally a Marxist-inspired undertaking and it was likely to run the risk of losing touch with the real world of American Law and ending up irrelevant. Presser sent the piece to his legal history colleague and prime CLS mover Robert Gordon for comment. Presser had singled Gordon out for praise for the accessibility and eloquence of his CLS work, and was not surprised at Gordon's response. Gordon, then a law professor at Stanford, who moved on to Yale, wrote Presser, on March 18, 1986, a tightly-reasoned, seven-page single-spaced critique, which letter tries to set Presser straight on what CLS is all about. Excerpts from the letter form the bulk of the following notes, and are here reprinted with the kind permission of Professor Gordon. Footnotes have been supplied by Presser.

6. Following thanks for the praise heaped on him personally, Gordon proceeded to write, "I was * * * grateful for once to see something about CLS that was considerate and sympathetic, instead of flip and scornful and dismissive as most of the [CLS critics'] stuff is. Nonetheless I have to say that I think you've misread a lot of the CLS stuff in significant ways, and this depresses me * * *. I think the big misreading is to confuse CLS with some traditional varieties of Marxism; whereas in fact most CLS-ers are very opposed to orthodox Marxisms, especially to (1) determinist views of historical inevitability (2) necessitarian views such as that state, class, and modes of production in any society, and especially under 'capitalism', function in tightly integrated systems; (3) the fantasy of 'revolution' in the sense of the abolition of class conflict and class relations through the victory of the proletariat. The Marx that CLS-ers read and quote tends to be the early Marx of the 'Jewish question,' of the passages on ideological domination in 'The German Ideology,'

and of the passages on the 'fetishism of commodities' at the beginning of 'Capital.' Mostly their Marxisms to the extent they have any are modern 'Western' neo-Marxists: Gramsci, Lukacs, Hay[1], Thompson[2], Genovese[3], etc. * * * Their intellectual influences are in fact very mixed and are not in the least dominated by Marxists of any stripe * * *. CLS-ers are also not in any sense state socialists, though on particular occasions they may seek to use state institutions among others to accomplish concrete political purposes."

"The politics of CLS is probably closest to the politics of modern feminism: it starts as a sort of consciousness-raising project, small groups meet to recognize the realities of their situations, then people try out some local political experiments in their immediate situations (the household, the law school), meanwhile they draw on some existing theory and history (some phenomenology, some anthropology, some social history, quite a lot of history-of-ideology in the thought that the history of past error may have something to teach about present error and how it's maintained and reproduced) in order to produce some new theory locally adapted to their situation; most of what they produce in public is criticism of existing attitudes, often very rationalist criticism of arguments for the status quo, but also cultural criticism (what's the cultural meaning of the stewardess? The law firm cocktail party?).

"Finally, the political projects tend to expand outwards and may include some ordinary legislative politics (ERA, Minneapolis anti-porn ordinance) or litigation strategy (sexual harassment violates Title VII); but is more likely to remain a politics of persuasion and cultural change. The thinking behind this—both feminism and CLS—is totally different from the notion that a society forms a unitary system that can only be displaced as a whole, by another such system, through a revolutionary upheaval; and also from the notion that the 'state' is somehow the privileged or primary theater of social change. The notion of change is much more that of pressing against hundreds of situations of local constraint and turning them slightly around; after a while you look around and see that the world isn't the same any more.

"CLS hasn't yet of course got even close to the kind of expansionist politics that feminism has; it's still mostly in the law schools; and it's still mostly in the phase of theory-building and intellectual critique. The last part obviously, the trashing project[4], is its most distinctive contribution so far; and here what frustrates me about your piece—and it's not at all alone in this, it's true of almost all other outside writing about CLS to this point as well—is that it doesn't really come to terms with this body of work, which is probably the only real accomplishment of CLS people so far: a body of work on some

[1] See, e.g., Douglas Hay, Property, Authority, and the Criminal Law, in Albion's Fatal Tree: Crime and Society in Eighteenth Century England (Hay et al. editors, 1975).

[2] See, e.g., E.P. Thompson, The Making of the English Working Class (1968); and see E.P. Thompson, Whigs and Hunters: The Origin of the Black Act 266 (1975), an excerpt of which, and an excerpt from the book review of which by Morton Horwitz appear in Chapter Six, supra.

[3] See, e.g. Eugene Genovese, Roll, Jordan, Roll: The World the Slaves Made (Vintage paperback ed., 1976), excerpted in Chapter Four, supra.

[4] Cf. M. Kelman, Trashing, 36 Stan.L.Rev. 293 (1984).

highly specific substantive legal problems—(1) rules v. standards, or, the dilemmas of formalism, applied to contracts ([Duncan] Kennedy,[5] [Clare] Dalton[6]), juvenile justice ([Al] Katz[7]), the welfare system ([William] Simon[8]); (2) the critique of law-and-economics,[9] of its metaphysics ([Thomas] Heller[10]), its ideas of rationality ([Mark] Kelman[11]), the Coase theorem (Kelman[12], Kennedy[13]), its claims to efficiency of given legal institutions such as property and contract (Kennedy and [Frank] Michelman[14]); (3) a legal historiography trying to recover past suppressed alternatives ([Morton] Horwitz on equitable justice[15], [James] Atleson[16] and [Karl] Klare[17] on labor law, Simon on welfare administration, [Gerald] Frug on the city[18], my stuff-in-progress on the legal profession); (4) a structuralist historiography of legal doctrine, showing doctrinal developments as successive attempts to mediate contradictions, suppress polarities (Kennedy on Blackstone,[19] and a dozen other pieces—this is our high-volume line of goods—most recently Greg Alexander in Stanford L.Rev. on the history of 'dead hand' doctrine[20]); (5) miscellaneous critiques of core notions of liberal legal thought—of the public-private distinction[21]; evolutionary functionalism of legal ideas and institutions; the ideology of advoca-

---

[5] D. Kennedy, Form and Substance in Private Law Adjudication, 89 Harv.L.Rev. 1685 (1976).

[6] Dalton, An Essay on the Deconstruction of Contract Law, 94 Yale L.J. 997 (1985).

[7] A. Katz, and L. Teitelbaum, PINS Jurisdiction, The Vagueness Doctrine, and the Rule of Law, 53 Indiana L.J. 1 (1978).

[8] W. Simon, Legality, Bureaucracy, and Class in the Welfare System, 92 Yale L.J. 1198 (1983).

[9] See, e.g. M. Horwitz, Law and Economics: Science or Politics? 8 Hofstra Law Review 905 (1980).

[10] T. Heller, Is the Charitable Exemption from Property Taxation an Easy Case? General concerns About Legal Economics and Jurisprudence in Essays on the Law and Economics of Local Governments 183 (Daniel Rubenfeld ed., 1979).

[11] M. Kelman, Misunderstanding Social Life; a Critique of the Core Premises of "Law and Economics," 33 J.Leg.Ed. 274 (1983).

[12] M. Kelman, Consumption Theory, Production Theory and Ideology in the Coase Theorem, 52 S.Cal.L.Rev. 669 (1979), Spitzer and Hoffman on Coase: A Brief Rejoinder, 53 S.Cal.L.Rev. 1215 (1980).

[13] D. Kennedy, Cost–Benefit Analysis of Entitlement Programs: A Critique, 33 Stan.L.Rev. 387 (1981); Distributive and Paternalist Motives in Contract and Tort Law, with Special Reference to Compulsory Terms and Unequal Bargaining Power, 41 Maryland L.Rev. 563 (1982); The Role of Law in Economic Thought: Essays on the Fetishism of Commodities, 34 Am.U.L.Rev. 939 (1986).

[14] D. Kennedy and F. Michelman, Are Property and Contract Efficient? 8 Hofstra Law Review 711 (1980).

[15] M. Horwitz The Transformation of American Law 1780–1860 (1977).

[16] J. Atleson, Values and Assumptions in American Labor Law (1983).

[17] K. Klare, Judicial Deradicalization of the Wagner Act and the Origins of Modern Legal Consciousness, 1937–1941, 62 Minn.L.Rev. 265 (1978).

[18] G. Frug, The City as a Legal Concept, 93 Harv.L.Rev. 1057 (1980).

[19] D. Kennedy, The Structure of Blackstone's Commentaries, 28 Buffalo Law Review 205 (1979).

[20] G. Alexander, The Dead Hand and the Law of Trusts in the Nineteenth Century, 37 Stan.L.Rev. 1189 (1985).

[21] See, e.g. D. Kennedy, The Stages of Decline of the Public/Private Distinction, 130 U.Pa.L.Rev. 1349 (1982). See also Alan Freeman and Elizabeth Mensch, "The Public–Private Distinction in American Law and Life," 36 Buff.L.Rev. 237 (1987).

cy[22]; (6) some fairly abstract theorizing about law as ideology, reification, category-construction (mostly [Peter] Gabel[23] and Katz[24]); (7) some polemical anthropology or 'microphenomenology'—story-telling about legal setting in which people find themselves (Kennedy's piece on hierarchy[25]); (8) an emerging body of work generalizing the work in #1, supra, into general structural accounts of whole bodies of law ([Gary] Peller on legal thought generally,[26] Dalton on contracts, Frug on bureaucracies); and finally (9) a growing body of CLS writing on CLS itself ([James] Boyle on 'Politics of Reason,'[27] Kelman's work-in-progress,[28] some of the Stanford Symposium.[29])

"It seems very hard to get outsiders to talk about *any* of this body of work, though it's what CLS actually is if it's anything. * * * It's unfair to dump this all on you, who are after all a most sympathetic critic of the Crits. It's the product of a building frustration. No other intellectual movement gets treated like this. When the law-and-economics people write something, their critics (including CLS people) address the substance of their work."

Is Gordon's criticism of the critics of CLS well-taken? Why do you suppose that CLS's critics have been able, if Gordon is correct, to get away with such superficial criticism of the movement? Why has CLS been treated differently by its critics than has Law-and-Economics? Could it have something to do with the politics of both movements? With the politics of most CLS critics? Gordon suggests that his implicit criticism of Presser, contained in his letter, is "unfair," but is it? Given what Gordon has noted about the diversity of CLS scholarship is Presser's criticism (and that of several similar CLS critics) off the mark?

7. Gordon proceeded in his letter to address particular notions in Presser's piece. For example, with regard to the charge made by Presser that CLS favors "statism," Gordon wrote "No: CLS critique is of reified public-private distinction. The point of this critique is that the 'state' is as much present in constituting the 'market' as it is in 'regulation.' The state is everywhere (and also, of course, as a reified entity, nowhere.)" Do you understand how the state can be said to be "everywhere" and "nowhere."

---

[22] W. Simon, The Ideology of Advocacy: Procedural Justice and Professional Ethics, 1978 Wisconsin Law Review 29.

[23] See, e.g. P. Gabel, Reification in Legal Reasoning 3 Research in Law and Sociology 25 (1980).

[24] Al Katz, Studies in Boundary Theory: Three Essays in Adjudication and Politics, 28 Buff.L.Rev. 383 (1979).

[25] D. Kennedy, Legal Education and the Reproduction of Hierarchy (1983).

[26] G. Peller, The Metaphysics of American Law, 73 Cal.L.Rev. 1151 (1985).

[27] Boyle, The Politics of Reason: Critical Legal Theory and Local Social Thought, 133 U.Pa.L.Rev. 685 (1985).

[28] This was published as Mark Kelman, A Guide to Critical Legal Studies (Harvard University Press, 1987), and discusses most of the authors and works Gordon cites. It is probably the indispensable starting point for anyone wishing an overview of CLS. See also D. Kennedy and K. Klare, A Bibliography of Critical Legal Studies, 94 Yale L.J. 461 (1984), and Robert L. Hayman, Jr. and Nancy Levit, Jurisprudence: Contemporary Readings, Problems, and Narratives 213–264 (1995).

[29] In volume 36 of the Stanford Law Review (1984).

8. The point of Presser's obscure title, "Some Realism about Orphism" was to suggest that CLS was like "orphism," a mysterious belief found in Greece in the fourth and fifth centuries B.C., which influenced Plato and Pythagoras. The Orphists, followers of the mythical Orpheus, sought purity of soul through membership in an occult brotherhood which performed purifying Dionysian rites. Possibly with tongue in cheek Gordon wrote Presser regarding his charge that CLS was like "Orphism:" "Puzzling: a better description of law and economics." Do you agree? Explaining why he believed that CLS was not "orphic," Gordon wrote, "CLS is about the only legal-academic movement going * * * that makes systematic efforts to popularize ideas, make them accessible to outsiders, bring outsiders into the movement—it has these huge mass meetings where the insiders actually try to teach the stuff. In classrooms most of us teach the stuff without ever mentioning CLS, because it's partly just a method for approaching ordinary legal materials. You can get across the essence of the method without using any jargon, special terms, or fancy theory at all . . . " Does Gordon's use of the terms "insiders" and "outsiders" belie his argument to any extent?

9. Probably the most telling criticism which Gordon made to Presser was of Presser's labeling of CLS'ers as "revolutionary intellectuals." Of this Gordon stated, "Misleading. CLS people generally take the line that orthodox Marxists' intellectual and political practices suffer badly from the seductive fantasy of revolution. The CLS notion is one of 'immanent critique'—at every moment, in every corner of social life, there is the possibility of turning a little piece of experience inside out." Similarly Gordon took issue with Presser's suggestion that CLS was searching for the "one true Grail" of legal analysis. Said Gordon, "Exactly wrong for CLS, whose intellectual strategy is to multiply and diversify meanings and options." How do you suppose Presser and other critics of CLS could have been led to the characterizations of CLS they have made? Can you see how reliance on the work (or some of the work) of Gabel, Kennedy, Horwitz, and Roberto Unger might have led to these characterizations? Gabel, Horwitz, and Kennedy you have already become familiar with. Unger, actually a peripheral CLS figure, but an extraordinary political analyst, a native Brazilian, and an utopian, is best known for his work seeking to throw aside what he believes to be the artificial "antinomies" of bourgeois civilization, including the distinctions between reason and desire, public and private, and man and God. See generally Roberto Unger, Knowledge and Politics (1975). More about Unger soon.

10. Gordon also maintained that Presser was wrong to suggest that CLS wanted to do away with our current regime of private property: "CLS is not a critique of 'private property' as such but of the coherence of the property concept as it has been conventionally described and applied. It echoes Morris Cohen's point that besides granting a zone of immunity from interference, property rights delegate coercive state power to owners to treat others arbitrarily within their zone: liberalism traditionally emphasizes the freedom and not the grants of arbitrary power, and the coercive-sanctioned duties, attendant upon property relations. CLS does not argue for communal ownership of everything; it points out rather that collective rather than individual

ownership of wealth is commonplace and not perceived as threatening or socialistic or inefficient in many capitalist institutions; and that 'efficiency' arguments for private property are flawed and circular. It has no bias against private property and indeed no *a priori* preference for any particular property forms; it is for such forms as seem to enhance practical freedom in concrete situations, which are likely to vary widely with the situations."

11. Gordon's view of Presser's positive prescription for the future caused him almost as much concern as did Presser's analysis of CLS. Presser thought that CLS had failed to grasp the fundamental opportunities opened up in the late twentieth century in America for entrepreneurial growth, particularly in the information-providing sector of the economy, and particularly as the result of more women entering legal fields. Making a communitarian argument something like that of the eighteenth-century Republican theorists, Presser predicted that Americans might construct legitimate hierarchies built on the basis of reciprocal responsibilities, and that we might find rewarding places in a new "Great Chain of Being." On Presser's views of his "New Great Chain of Being," Gordon wrote "The paean to modernity is kind of mystifying. CLS people do not deny that standards of living have risen among the masses of the industrialized world; like Marx himself, they regard prosperity as a great contribution of the Western forms of capitalist production as well as of the insurrectionary politics that has ensured their wider distribution. But they are puzzled at the notion that if you basically like the kind of progress we've had so far, you can't get any more progress: that relies on the implicit premise, which CLS–ers would say was an example of 'false necessity,' that the progress we have is part of a total system whose costs must be accepted if you want the benefits. CLS people, for instance, resist the assertion that the 'age of industrial production [needed] large-scale workplaces, dehumanizing hierarchies'—this denial of technological determinism is at the heart of CLS's non-necessitarian view of history and is backed up, I am glad to say, by a burgeoning body of historical and comparative research on industrial organization. They are also concerned to identify those zillions of modern forms of constraint upon freedom * * * that aren't immediately obvious but are really and truly felt by people. Many of the most privileged people—take big law firm partners for instance—think of themselves in chains, on a treadmill, enslaved to addictive consumption needs or success images, deprived of practical freedom. This isn't just self-indulgent whining, it describes a real experience." Does this last point of Gordon's, the notion of too many of us (and perhaps all of us) being stuck on a "treadmill," resonate with your experience?

12. Gordon went on to suggest that Presser was wrong to draw a dichotomy between CLS, whom Presser suggested favored "socialization of the means of production," and the makers of the coming epoch, who would develop individual ownership into a more altruistic communitarian form of control of the means of production. Gordon maintained that Presser had his time frame and his characterization of CLS wrong. "Again, CLS isn't for 'socialization of the means of production,' it says *that* doesn't mean anything, [but instead] is another set of reified forms; or to the extent that it does mean some-

thing there's a lot of it already in 'capitalist' economies . . . Observers of organized capitalism and corporate bureaucracy 100 years ago—Max Weber, Richard T. Ely, Otto von Gierke, Durkheim, hundreds of others—were pointing out that these were hardly 'individualist' organizations, folks were cogs in a machine, or associated in cooperative 'organic solidarity,' depending on whether you liked metaphors of regimentation or cooperation. . . . The movements you refer to away from 'classical' individualism towards altruism or communitarianism in contract law, for example, started around 1900 (See Kennedy's *Form and Substance* piece,[30] which contains an exhaustingly thorough account; part of Kennedy's point however was that the communitarian pole was always present even in the classical system, but marginalized and repressed; just as Ian Macneil[31] is right to say that trade is always cooperative and communitarian, whether the prevailing forms of law recognize that [or not]). I am not as sanguine as you * * * are about these evolutions, because I already see signs of backwards motion towards formal-atomistic-individualism in legal categories, heralded by the Chicago school and beginning to make itself felt in regulatory policy and even some common-law decisions. The CLS are all for communitarian directions in (say) contract law: their critiques focus on how even modern contract law is [so] constrained by conventional categories (freedom of contract = market; anything else = intervention, etc.) [that modern contract law appears] to see the communitarian solution as exceptional, peripheral, [or] an exception to normal contract enforcement, having to bear the special burden of justification. Whereas [CLS's] point is that the 'individualist' or 'market' version of freedom of contract represents a different (socially constructed) view of community." Are you sanguine, like Presser, or skeptical, like Gordon? In this connection what do you make of Mark Tushnet's 1991 sober musings that "In imagining the future of critical legal studies, one must be hesitant, if only because the events of 1989 in China and central Europe seem to indicate that nobody knows anything about how societies actually operate." Tushnet, "Critical Legal Studies: A Political History," 100 Yale L.J. 1515 (1991). Is Tushnet right?

13. Gordon closed his letter to Presser with observations on two of Presser's last points, the changing role of women in the law, and on the need for the maintenance of hierarchies in society. Here Gordon and Presser were not quite as far apart as on other issues. With regard to hierarchies Gordon wrote "Not all hierarchy is illegitimate, but hierarchies (liberalism teaches us, and here it is right) need justification; and the going justifications for the going hierarchies of class, race, and gender to start with, tend to be pretty weak. Hierarchies also need to be recognized for what they are, and here liberalism's record is mixed—it's good at spotting formal inequalities, but deploys manifold strategies of denial of real social power (e.g. as in [its treatment of freedom of] contract) [where it fails to acknowledge that the doctrine covertly maintains the existing structure of power and wealth in society]." On Women, Gordon said, "I agree: modern feminism represents a watershed set

[30] See note 5, supra.

[31] To whom you were introduced in the last Chapter.

of cultural changes, and is a kind of prototype for the kind of reimagination of society that CLS keeps trying to promote: There are other ways of doing things (e.g. mediational lawyering) that are not the established ways, but are better, freer and more humane, and still work." We will have more to say about modern feminism and the law later in this Chapter.

14. At one point in Gordon's letter to Presser (of which you have read about three-quarters), Gordon fulminated against CLS's critics for their narrow views of CLS and for their general short-sightedness, "It seems to me generally ironic that CLS people who are always accused of 'politicizing' intellectual issues are in fact constantly frustrated by opponents (see Louis Schwartz,[32] Phil Johnson,[33] Carrington, etc.) who refuse to focus on any of the intellectual issues in CLS work but insist on talking only about the political ones. I mean, they say things like, 'If you don't believe in neutral principles, or the rule of law, or that law matters, or something, you're a nihilist or totalitarian,' or 'If everyone believed what you do, everything would end up a mess,' etc. What you can't get the opponents to talk about much is whether—e.g. the critique [of Duncan Kennedy's] of Blackstone or promissory estoppel or cost benefit analysis or the historical inevitability of workplace hierarchy—is *true*. People just won't engage on the substantive issues." What follows, concluding our section on CLS, is a reading from one of the three critics singled out by Gordon, Dean Paul D. Carrington, a letter Gordon wrote Carrington (something like the letter he wrote Presser), Carrington's reply to Gordon, and Gordon's rejoinder to Carrington's reply. As you read these materials see who makes the better case, Gordon or Carrington?

PAUL D. CARRINGTON,* OF LAW AND THE RIVER**

34 J.Legal Ed. 222 (1984).

Mark Twain's *Life on the Mississippi* is the best book in English about professional training. For those not familiar with the work, it records the author's own training as a cub pilot of steamboats. He comments on many of the ethical issues associated with the training of professionals.

Learning to be a steamboat pilot is more like learning to be a lawyer than you may suppose. One significant similarity is that persons attracted to the role of pilot are attracted, at least in part, by the aroma of power. As Twain compared:

> My father was a justice of the peace and I supposed that he had power of life and death over all men, and could hang anybody that offended him. That was distinction enough for me as a general thing, but the desire to be a [pilot] kept intruding, nevertheless.

[32] Schwartz, With Gun and Camera Through Darkest CLS Land, 36 Stan.L.Rev. 413 (1984).

[33] Johnson, Do You Sincerely Want to Be Radical?, 36 Stan.L.Rev. 247 (1984).

* Dean and Professor of Law, Duke University School of Law.

** Reprinted with the permission of the Journal of Legal Education and of the author.

"Kings," he noted

> are but the hampered servants of parliament and the people, and parliaments sit in chains forged by their constituency; . . . in truth, every man and woman and child has a master . . . but in the day I write of, the Mississippi pilot had none. . . . His movements were entirely free, he consulted no one, he received comments from nobody. . . . So here was the novelty of a king without a keeper, an absolute monarch who was absolute in sober truth and not by a fiction of words.

Few would mistake a lawyer for a king without a keeper, but in a discussion of the power and responsibility of the law professoriate, it seems wise to acknowledge that most and perhaps all of us share a fascination with power. A law teacher who does not know that he or she enjoys power needs closer self-acquaintance.

As there are similarities between pilots and lawyers in their aspirations to power, there is also similarity in the politics of the two professions. Mark Twain was denied admission on his first application to be a pilot; training was a scarce good. Providers had the power of gatekeeping. Twain reports that because they found it profitable to train cubs, a glut of pilots was created. The cubs were not immediately troubled by this because they paid tuition out of future earnings, a system redolent of guaranteed student loans. When professional incomes fell, however, the pilots organized to control entry and unauthorized practice. Twain intimates conflicting responsibilities of persons having the power of gatekeeping: to the users of professional services on the one hand, and to the unknowing prospective cubs on the other. Twain gives no evidence of comprehending how very complex a task it is to reconcile these often conflicting duties.

The power of pilots, like the power of lawyers, derives in part from the esoteric nature of the data that informs their professionalism. Pilots, like lawyers, dramatized their technocracy by cloaking work in a professional and mystic language that excluded laymen from understanding. Twain understood that language became for pilots, as for lawyers, a source of power.

By way of illustration, Twain the cub overhears a conversation among pilots discussing the passage of Plum Point, using familiar words but in technical senses rendering their meaning almost impenetrable. "I stood in the corner," Twain said, "and the talk I listened to took the hope all out of me. . . . I wish the piloting business was in Jericho and I had never thought of it."

In addition to this affectation of language, there was another difference between professionals and laymen which Twain early discovered. The technocratic interest of the professional pilots changed their capacity to perceive ordinary events which took on a significance special to them.

In a passage familiar even to many who have not read the book, Twain described how his training as a pilot deprived him of the capacity to appreciate the river for what it is to laymen: "I had lost something," he complained, "that could never be restored to me while I lived. All the grace, the beauty, the poetry, had gone out of the majestic river!" He could remember appreciating a beautiful sunset on the river, but after training he could no longer enjoy rapture, but would comment on a sunset thus:

> This sun means that we are going to have wind tomorrow; that floating log means that the river is rising, small thanks to it; that slanting mark on the water refers to a bluff reef which is going to kill somebody's steamboat one of these nights, if it keeps on stretching out like that; those tumbling boils show a dissolving bar and a changing channel there; the lines and circles in the slick water over yonder are a warning that that troublesome place is shoaling up dangerously; that silver streak in the shadow of the forest is the break of a new snag, and he has located himself in the very place he could have found to fish for steamboats; that tall dead tree, with a single living branch, is not going to last long, and then how is a body ever going to get through this blind place at night without the friendly old landmark?
>
> No, the romance and beauty were all gone from the river. All the value any feature of it had for me now was the amount of usefulness it could furnish toward compassing the safe piloting of a steamboat. Since those days, I have pitied doctors from my heart. What does the lovely flush in a beauty's cheek mean to a doctor but the "break" that ripples above some deadly disease? Are not all her visible charms sown thick with what are to him the signs and symbols of hidden decay? Does he ever see her beauty at all, or doesn't he simply view her professionally, and comment upon her unwholesome condition all to himself? And doesn't he sometimes wonder whether he has gained most or lost most by learning his trade?

Law students, like cub pilots, are exposed to such risks. Law teachers have the power to influence the process by which law students can numb themselves to many of their more desirable human impulses. As technocrats, we can lose feelings for the human tragedies in which we participate; we can also permanently anaesthetize our capacity for indignation at injustice or mendacity. Teachers, it would seem, do have an ethical responsibility to do what can be done to help students resist this dehumanizing effect of technocratic learning.

One cause of this effect may be the intensiveness of the demands to master all one needs to know. There is, indeed, daunting intricacy in both the law and the river. Bear in mind that Twain was on the Mississippi before the Corps of Engineers and there was not so much as a buoy between New Orleans and St. Louis.

Going upstream, the pilot on schedule had to steer for the slack water, staying close first to one bank and then the other. To find the slack water, the pilot needed to know of a hundred landmarks for each of the twelve hundred miles of the journey. Every point, stump, limb, ridge, rock, or snag had navigational use. Going upstream at night, the pilot had to know the shape of the river so well that he did not actually need to see the landmarks.

For safety, it was necessary to know the depth of the river in all places. To some extent, it is possible to read the surface of the water; a knowledgeable pilot can detect a submerged reef from the appearance of the water above, but a pilot can easily mistake a "wind reef" which is false for a "bluff reef" which is real. Reading the water is assisted by accurate memory of the depth at each place when last measured by the pilot's leadsmen who constantly monitor the amount of water under the bow and under the stern of the boat. Reading is also assisted by the feel of the helm, for, as Twain tells us, steamboats do not like shoal water.

All these bits of technical data and skill of the pilot, like that of the lawyer, are subject to constant change. The water ebbs and rises; a course that can be followed when the water is at one elevation is perilous when the water is lower; for the knowing pilot, high water makes a short trip. Also, erosion was then a very rapid process; points, reefs, snags, and channels moved from one week to the next, like laws repealed or decisions distinguished.

Thus, Twain, the cub pilot, attempted what generations of law students have attempted, to assimilate an enormous mass of detailed information. And, like law students, he came only gradually to the full realization that his subject was elusive as well as complex, that no amount of sheer memorization of information would ever be enough to make him a good pilot.

And of course one proper response to such a condition is to perpetuate the enterprise of study, to try to keep learning the fugitive subject. So Twain describes how the bigger boats often carried supernumerary unpaid pilots whose own boats were being refitted or repaired; they traveled "to look at the river," to refresh knowledge of transient marks and channels. Their training had at least provided them with a framework of understanding that enabled them to relearn the river as it changed. Indeed, Twain noted, a well-trained pilot could even assimilate entirely new data quite rapidly; he tells of Horace Bixby mastering the intricacy of the Missouri River with a single preparatory trip. We doubtless share responsibility for providing similar framework adequate to permit our students to become their own teachers.

Perhaps because of similarities in their aspirations and in the intricacy and inconstancy of the material with which they work, the teaching methods used to train pilots are not unlike those familiar in the training of lawyers. Horace Bixby, Twain's teacher, could be described as a devotee of the Socratic method. He asked Twain a lot of questions and commented forcefully when his responses were inadequate. When Twain missed his first question, Bixby denounced him as the "stupidest dunderhead I ever saw or heard of." On another occasion, Bixby summed up his appraisal of Twain: "taking you by and large, you do seem to be more kinds of an ass than any creature I ever saw before." Twain reciprocated these hard lessons and harsh comments with unspoken hostility and often when discouraged he would withdraw, manifesting the familiar traits of alienation. Yet beneath the veneer of authoritarian abuse and cringing enmity, there was between master and cub a bond of shared purpose which most law teachers would envy. Twain at times recognized that Bixby's harshness reflected high standards and high hopes for Twain.

Twain, more than most professional students, read the subscript to the pedagogical dialogue. He recognized Bixby not merely as a hard taskmaster, but also as an example of what a pilot is and can be. Twain knew that it was the character and values of Bixby that he had learned first and that he would forget last. It was Bixby's example, not his preachments or his manners, that operated most powerfully. Bixby seemed unaware of this effect and, indeed, it is a force so powerful that teachers can seldom control it.

Twain knew that the technical knowledge and skill drilled into him by Bixby was not the durable substance he received. Twain tells us that what he really learned from Bixby was not marks and channels, but judgment and courage—judgment in the evaluation of his own technical knowledge and skill, courage to apply them despite the ubiquitous risk of professional error. Bixby taught both hard-eyed realism and tight mastery of self-doubt. He did teach these traits by example, but also by deliberately putting Twain in spots, and making adverse comment when Twain overconfidently exceeded his competence or timidly failed to exercise it. If Bixby used the carrot of praise, we are not told.

Lawyers need judgment as much as pilots. Somewhat different judgment, to be sure: our medium is words not water, and the forces that influence the meaning of language are social and political, not natural. But our work, like that of pilots, requires effective use of intuition going beyond technical knowledge; those who use intuition need to know its limits. Thus lawyers like pilots must be always distrustful of themselves, on guard against the risk of mistaking their own political or social preferences for those of the law.

For lawyers as for pilots, the balance to professional judgment is courage, intellectual courage, the courage to risk error when the odds are right. Legal judgment, like navigational judgment, can be, and often is, neutralized by timidity. As the lawyer exercises self-distrust, he needs also to overcome self-doubt.

Law teachers, like Bixby, have the power to teach both judgment and courage to at least some of their students. Courage to at least some of their students—most effectively by example, but also importantly by putting their students on the spot and requiring them to exercise both judgment and courage. The law school classroom affords an arena in which these traits can develop. Fortunately for us, our students' errors and failures do not have the same potential for disaster as do the errors and failures of cub pilots; we can develop the professionalism of students with hazard only to the temporary condition of their sensitive vanities.

Seen in this light, students seeking to escape classroom dialogue harm themselves as professionals. Those claiming a right to "no-hassle pass" effectively seek to avoid important learning. Teachers have a duty to dispute any such claim of right.

Maintaining intellectual courage in law presents one difficulty that has no analogue in the professionalism of steamboat pilots. One cannot believe in the worth of one's professional skill and judgment as a lawyer unless one also has some minimal belief in the idea of law and the institutions that enforce it. The river is complex and changing, but it is tangible, a wet experience to refresh the pilot's conviction that his knowledge pertains to reality in nature. The law, in contrast, is a mere hope that people who apply the lash of power will seek to obey the law's command. Let us not be modest; it is an act of considerable courage to maintain belief in such a hope.

There are many familiar reasons why lawyers may disbelieve in their own professionalism. Lawyers everywhere and always must have known that the law cannot deliver all that is promised in its behalf. For the law to be applied, facts must be known, and facts can be very elusive. The law is itself obscure in many of its specific applications; its meaning must be found if at all in the conduct of officials. But officials are people and that means they are vulnerable to the attractions of self-aggrandizement, and to other influences. Even if they are altruistic, they may use power to pursue social and political agendas not embodied in the law. So law will reflect the tastes of that class of persons from whom the officials are drawn. And, if this be so, then perhaps as some of our colleagues may be heard to say, law is a mere deception by which the powerful weaken the resistance of the powerless. Thus, enforcement and even obedience may be morally degenerate.[21] Faced with such impediments to belief in law, who can fail to have doubts about the validity of their professionalism as lawyers?

Such disbelief threatens competence. More than a few lawyers lack competence because they have lost, or never acquired, the needed confidence that law matters. Lawyers lacking confidence that legal principles

[21] E.g., Roberto Unger, The Critical Legal Studies Movement, 96 Harv.L.Rev. 563, passim (1983). Indeed, one is tempted to cite the whole of volume 96 passim.

actually influence the exercise of power have no professional tools with which to do their work. In due course they must abandon whatever professionalism they have, to choose between simple neglect of their work or the application of common cunning, such techniques as bribery and intimidation in all their many forms.

Moreover, there is dread in disbelief. A lawyer who succumbs to legal nihilism faces a far greater danger than mere professional incompetence. He must contemplate the dreadful reality of government by cunning and a society in which the only right is might. Such a fright can sustain belief in many that law is at least possible and must matter.

The professionalism and intellectual courage of lawyers does not require rejection of Legal Realism and its lesson that who decides also matters. What it cannot abide is the embrace of nihilism and its lesson that who decides is everything, and principle nothing but cosmetic. Persons espousing the latter view, however honestly held, have a substantial ethical problem as teachers of professional law students. The nihilist teacher threatens to rob his or her students of the courage to act on such professional judgment as they may have acquired. Teaching cynicism may, and perhaps probably does, result in the learning of the skills of corruption: bribery and intimidation. In an honest effort to proclaim a need for revolution, nihilist teachers are more likely to train crooks than radicals. If this risk is correctly appraised, the nihilist who must profess that legal principle does not matter has an ethical duty to depart the law school, perhaps to seek a place elsewhere in the academy.

This is a hard dictum within a university, whose traditions favor the inclusion in house of all honestly held ideas, beliefs, and values. When, however, the university accepted responsibility for training professionals, it also accepted a duty to constrain teaching that knowingly dispirits students or disables them from doing the work for which they are trained. And even the nihilist must eventually recognize that professional law students are infertile ground for the seed of anarchy; within institutions such as professional law schools, nihilism is a doomed testament. Elsewhere, such teaching may find an audience, but not among those who have set their hands to perform the world's work.

For those university law teachers able to keep the faith of the secular religion, let there be no shame in the romantic innocence with which they approach the ultimate issue of their profession. Twain, it seems, would approve our romance; he concluded that the one essential ingredient in the professionalism of the pilot was love of the river. "Your true pilot," he said, "cares nothing about anything on earth but the river, and his pride in his occupation surpasses the pride of Kings." For safe rivers, the public needs loving pilots. To limit might, the public needs lawyers who acclaim the hope and expectation that rights will be enforced. Seeing her blemishes (they are many) and knowing her perfidies (which are not few), true lawyers can love the law just as true pilots love the river. We love law not because reason requires it, but because our commitment to our discipline serves the needs of the public to whom, and for whom, we are responsible. Sharing that commitment may be our most important power and responsibility.

NOTES AND QUESTIONS

1. Carrington's tactic in this piece is to borrow from literature (here the comic work of Mark Twain) in order to make a point about the law professoriat. Is this a fair use of literature? Ask yourself whether this is what the new "law and literature" movement is supposed to be all about, when we read about it, next. Do you agree with Carrington that lawyers and Mississippi River Boat Pilots share similar loves of power, gatekeeping, and esoteric language? How about the similar dehumanizing aspects of technocratic learning? Is Carrington correct to suggest that the "intricacy and inconstancy" of the great American rivers is mirrored in American law? Is there anything left out of this equation? Is there, for example, anything inherently social or political in piloting a steamboat? Is there in being a lawyer or a law professor? Do law professors, like Twain's mentor the super-pilot Horace Bixby, teach "hard-eyed realism and tight mastery of self-doubt?" Should they?

2. This essay by Carrington became something of a *cause célebre* in the legal academy, and was strongly attacked as a profound threat to academic freedom. What is there that is controversial about this piece of Carrington's? Could it be his defense of the Socratic method, of putting students "on the spot," ostensibly, in Carrington's mind, to teach them "courage?" The "no-hassle-pass," against which Carrington rails is the assertion by law students of their right to decline to be the Professor's tools in the Socratic dialogue. Do law students (or undergraduates) have such a "right?" Should they? The assertion of that right, at about the time Carrington was writing, was a hotly debated topic at Harvard and other law schools. Would you be for or against the "no-hassle-pass?"

3. Could the controversial aspect be Carrington's implicit and explicit criticism of those teaching in the legal academy, such as Roberto Unger, who disclaim belief in the rule of law itself, a group whom Carrington accuses of "legal nihilism"? Can you understand the difference between "legal realism," which Carrington apparently endorses, and "legal nihilism," which he does not? Would the legal realists we studied have understood the distinction? For further reading on CLS and legal nihilism, see the defense of CLS put forward by Joseph William Singer, "The Player and the Cards: Nihilism and Legal Theory," 94 Yale L.J. 1 (1984), and the critique of Singer, John Stick, "Can Nihilism be Pragmatic?" 100 Harv.L.Rev. 332 (1986). Is it true that "Teaching cynicism may, and perhaps probably does, result in the learning of the skills of corruption: bribery and intimidation?" Should the "legal nihilists," a group among whom Carrington was perceived as placing the practitioners of "critical legal studies," as Carrington suggests, have "an ethical duty to depart the law school, perhaps to seek a place elsewhere in the acad-

emy?" Why do you suppose Carrington would allow such a person "elsewhere in the academy" if not in the law schools? Which do you favor, "legal nihilism," or Carrington's "faith of the secular religion," his "romantic innocence?"

4. As you read the reaction to Carrington from Professor Gordon, and Carrington's reply, which follow, ask yourself if you could have anticipated the points both make, and whether you would have expected the strength of Gordon's reaction.

ROBERT W. GORDON TO PAUL D. CARRINGTON, "OF LAW AND THE RIVER," AND OF NIHILISM AND ACADEMIC FREEDOM*

35 J.Leg.Ed. 1 (1985).

I write in response to your article, "Of Law and the River," in 34 J. Legal Educ. 222 (1984), which I began in appreciation, carried along by the graceful flow of its prose and the wonderful passages from Mark Twain, and finished in bafflement and growing alarm. As one who has been loosely connected to the Critical Legal Studies (CLS) movement, I take seriously enough the injunction that people like me have "an ethical duty to depart the law school, perhaps to seek a place elsewhere in the academy" * * * to be prompted both to ask you to elaborate your reasons for thinking so and to suggest why I think you may be mistaken.

I have no quarrel with your main point, that the practice of law like that of any other complex craft requires judgment and courage as well as technique, and that judgment and courage can be taught; though I think we might disagree on how best to teach them, and I might be inclined to emphasize more than you the need for constant critical reflection upon the platitudinous commonsense ("everybody knows that women are not aggressive enough to be litigators") that sometimes passes as professional "judgment". But you then go on to insist that among the components of professional judgment and courage there are certain quite specific beliefs about law and its practice that lawyers ought to hold as a matter of unreasoning faith; and that law teachers who doubt this faith should migrate elsewhere lest they "dispirit" or "disable" their students from practice or even induce them to practice "bribery and intimidation"!

Like most people invited to take a loyalty oath, I want first to have a clear notion of its content; and find your account of the correct faith for a law teacher actually to be fairly obscure. You define it mostly by contrast to what it is not, the bad view of the "nihilists". I would like to set out three possible interpretations of your account of the issues dividing the True Professionals (TPs) from the Nihilists (Ns), and react to each as I think many people involved in CLS would react.

#1—(*Semble* the most likely interpretation of your position). "Ns claim that law is an empty shell, just a facade for the naked exercise of power. TPs believe that law has an autonomous content, and therefore influences, channels, and restrains the exercise of power."

If this is all the oath involves, CLS people can take it cheerfully. None of us thinks law has no content. In fact we are often accused (by legal sociologists, for instance) of taking its content much *too* seriously, of exaggerating the power of legal doctrines and principles to control social behavior! Of course law channels and restrains power. It also confers power, as it would upon you, for example, if you had a legal entitlement to specify what I had to believe to keep my job. There cannot be any "official power" for law to restrain without law to create the "office" in the first place.

CLS people do frequently say that law, or legal rights, are "indeterminate." What they mean by that is *not* that law fails to constrain social or official action at all, for it obviously does, but rather that because it is founded upon contradictory norms, its principles cannot constrain a single set of outcomes even if intelligently, honestly and conscientiously applied. In contract law, for example, there is *always* a legitimate argument for maintaining one party's freedom of action and a contrary argument for protecting the other party's security; for every argument for enforcing the deal in the name of "freedom of contract" there is a counter-argument for voiding the deal because of fraud, duress, overreaching, misunderstanding or changed circumstances. Indeterminacy, in this view, isn't the product of some official's "distortion" of the law's command, but inheres in the law itself: the law commands contradictory things.

I do not see why someone who took even the most extreme view of legal indeterminacy, i.e., that "you can always crank out a legal argument for any position," would resort to "bribery and intimidation." Wouldn't he simply crank out the argument?

On the other hand, if your N opponents here are people who reduce all law (and indeed all life) to the product of the self-interested preferences of officials or social groups, you should not pick on CLS but on the law-and-economics crowd. I think the confusion here results from a regrettably widespread false syllogism: "CLS=left=vulgar-materialist-Marxism." In fact, the vulgar materialists of our times are on the right and tend to hang out in Chicago.

I do not know *any* law teacher these days who would take a caricature-Realist's position that legal outcomes represent nothing but the arbitrary whim or idiosyncratic psychology of decision-makers. This is really and truly a person of straw. If this is the bogey who scares you, you can relax: he is not out there.

#2—"Ns believe that law embodies the will of the socially or economically powerful, or of the officials who apply it; TPs believe that law restrains, though doubtless not as much as it should, the strong and the official."

The bad N position #1, supra, was that the law had no content; this bad N position is that law has a content, loaded in favor of the powerful. * * *

Is there really a serious dispute here? Suppose you and I were interviewing candidates for law teaching jobs. One of them says: "Officials in America are not restrained by rules; they can do anything they want." Another says: "The rich and well-off control all the legal processes in this society; they can always get their way in the courts and in the legislature." A third asserts: "In a country like ours everyone is equal before the law: wealth confers no significant legal advantages." We would both, surely, have reason to doubt whether any of the three was adequately tuned in to reality.

Yet perhaps we *do* have a dispute about the extent to which the law curriculum should dwell on systemic, as opposed to aberrational inequities—whether, for example, somebody should be allowed to teach a course called "Law and the Class Structure," presenting material about the differential ability of classes or groups to pass legislation, influence the administrative process, wear out opponents with lawyers, etc. I think that would be a useful course, especially if taught in an inquiring and undogmatic spirit. Do you think it would be "unprofessional?" Would it be more likely to lead to "cynicism" or to moral outrage and the zeal to reform?

Supposing it did produce some cynicism, would the result be to encourage "bribery and intimidation"? Wouldn't a cynic who thought "law is just a tool of the bosses" usually work *for* the powerful, and therefore want to work *through* the mystifying medium of the law, manipulating the rules on behalf of his clients? Why would he *need* to resort to bribery and intimidation, with all that law on his side? Can the case that bothers you be that of the disaffected cynic out there who represents the powerless and thinks: "Law is just a tool of the bosses anyway; there is no hope in it for the little guys, so we might as well use bribery and intimidation."

I guess I would want some evidence that there are any such people, and that thcy constitute a real social problem. The radical lawyers I know personally or by reputation are rather non-Machiavellian and rule-abiding in their dealings with clients and opponents; they tend to be sticklers for proper form, and are outraged when their adversaries resort to sneaky tricks. All in all, I have rarely come across a more strikingly implausible proposition than yours to the effect that left-wing law teaching (assuming for the moment that that is what "nihilism" means) leads to corrupt practice.

In any case, this discussion has very little to do with CLS. On the whole, CLS people have declined to reduce law to the status simply of an instrument of class or state domination. They believe that the law does contain doctrines and processes that facilitate domination, but also that it contains rules that restrain, and utopian norms and possibilities for argument and action that can help liberate people from, domination (as, for example, 19th century law established slavery but also contained egalitarian principles that helped lead to slavery's abolition). The article from Unger that—incredibly!—you cite as a source of supposedly "nihilistic" attitudes towards law is actually an extended argument for taking practical steps toward developing the utopian norms expressed *in* law (what Unger calls the method of doctrinal deviation).

Just as I cannot think of anyone in American law teaching who thinks law is nothing but official whim, I can't think of anyone either who preaches the revolutionary overthrow of legality. This seems to be another imaginary bogey-man.

#3—"A TP is someone who 'believes in the law', i.e., believes that the existing collection of rules, procedures, and professional practices, though flawed and imperfect, adds up to a tolerably just structure for a political and economic order; so that lawyers who work competently and honestly at their craft within this structure, without trying to inject their 'own' political preferences into it, will contribute to the overall good of society in the long run. Anyone who questions all this is an N, or at least not a TP."

The problem for me in this formulation * * * is that it makes into a criterion of a good professional what is actually just a particular and highly disputable set of political and jurisprudential views. It says in effect that a lawyer ought to inhabit the moderate center of the political spectrum. * * * Of course by and large our profession *is* a conservative-to-moderate-reformist one that has usually, though not always, resisted major structural change; but would you really want to establish loyalty to the majority politics of the bar as a qualification for membership? You could only do so, surely, if you adopted a jurisprudential position equating belief in "the rule of law" with adherence to the current majority politics, whatever it was: this would be a sort of customary-positivist position that what most of the bar believes effectively *is* the law. *Or* if you adopted a strong essentialist position that our current collection of legal practices optimally embodies, or at least comes very close to doing so, values required of our polity by some compelling necessity: The Tradition of Anglo–Saxon Liberties, the Original Understanding of the Constitution, Efficiency, the Realization of Individual Autonomy, etc. Under either theory a case could be made that disloyalty to the current consensus would be disloyalty to the idea of law itself.

[It occurs to me that I may have misunderstood you, and that you were making a more limited point than I thought you were. Your comparison of teaching professional judgment to teaching riverboat navigation perhaps implies a merely prudential rather than deeply normative professionalism: you may be suggesting simply that if novices depart too far from the prevailing conventions and arguments in their legal practices, they will be *ineffective* lawyers. The good teacher will warn the novice when he strays dangerously out of the mainstream.

[I cannot argue with that. Teaching any craft involves teaching its current customs; and one of the main objects of law teaching has always been to familiarize students with the body of conventional rhetorics and practices. But I think it's bad teaching that encourages an unreflective acceptance of the current conventions. Teachers also ought to expand their students' minds beyond the current professional wisdom, to show them that the going ways of doing things (or some slightly amended version of them) are not the only possible ways; and to develop the skills of critical evaluation of the going ways and of alternatives to them. After all, the whole point of the university law school is supposed to be that people who are not caught up in the time and financial pressures of practice can obtain, to continue your metaphor, an aerial view of the river—can see that the pilots have only been using one channel and the river is actually much wider than they think, and has many branches and tributaries. Such teaching is not the same as, or a substitute for, teaching navigation skills, but it is awfully important all the same.

[In any case your argument seems to go well beyond this merely prudential view of current practices to enjoin the teaching of their validity as well as their actuality.]

Now suppose somebody comes along, let's say somebody who is interested in a job on your faculty, whose politics are out of the moderate-center range. This might be a right-winger who wants to dismantle most of the regulatory-welfare state or a left-winger who wants to work towards the replacement of centralized bureaucratic hierarchies in public and private life with participatory-democratic collectives; or it might be someone more interesting and original than either. We will assume the person is "competent" in standard terms, that is, facile in the rhetorics and analytic modes of current legal practice. The candidate listens politely to your loyalty test and the jurisprudential theories on which it is based; and *then starts to dispute the theories on their merits.*

—She might say * * * that the consensus of the bar on what constitutes good professional practice is not entitled to a whole lot of respect because much of it is based on self-serving prejudice or plainly mistaken empirical assumptions; and argue that the role of a law faculty should not be to acquiesce in, but critically to examine and to challenge the current professional wisdom.

—She might say that the present consensus does not effectively embody the society's basic values; that it departs in serious ways from the commands of the Constitution, Efficiency, or whatever, and therefore needs major restructuring to be brought into compliance.

—She might say that the appearance of a settled consensus is deceiving, because that appearance papers over a mass of conflicting and contradictory tendencies in the law; that the society and its members, including its lawyers, are deeply divided within as well as among themselves; that to "believe in the law" thus does not entail the endorsement of any very determinate set of social arrangements; and that one can help point social change in radically different directions simply by emphasizing some sets of existing tendencies actually embodied in the law rather than others.

—She might, finally, assert that there is nothing inherent in the notion of professionalism that precludes lawyers from thinking about, and using law to help promote, major political change; that the lawyers who helped lead the Stamp Act riots, or the protests of abolitionists, or the sit-down strikes of the 1930s, or the New Deal's administrative innovations, or the civil rights marches of the 1960s, all actions contrary to the then-prevailing narrowly-professional consensus on legality, are people to be admired and emulated, not read out of the fraternity.

How do you deal with such a person, consistently with your expressed beliefs in the freedom of intellectual inquiry? You admit the possibility that the "nihilists" may hold their beliefs sincerely and honestly. But what if they are not only sincere, but actually *right* (at least, since none of us can claim *possession* of the truth, relatively right?) I mean, what of the possibility (let us allow it to be that) that their views rest on more plausible, rationally defensible, resonant-with-social-experience, grounds than your own do? Would it then be relevant that they were "disabling"? * * * Would you want professionalism to be founded on lies and errors, however noble?

Even if the "nihilists" cannot convince you that they are right, would the teaching of their views corrupt the morals of young lawyers? I cannot for the life of me see how. None of the positions I have mentioned "disables" lawyers from being able to "perform the world's work": they encourage lawyers rather to make reflective decisions about *how* to perform it; insist that all such decisions, *including the decision to acquiesce in what seems to be the current consensus,* involve political choice; and push people to recognize, justify and to *take responsibility for* the political choices that they make in their careers. * * *

I share your view that "cynicism" is widespread among law students, and sometimes has a "disabling" or "dispiriting" effect upon them. But my explanation for its prevalence differs greatly from yours. It does not take very long for law students to realize that few of the lawyers they come across in law school and summer jobs are much interested by the notion that law should be a means for the pursuit of justice. Students notice that concern for the social consequences or political or ethical justifications of legal rules, if not actively disparaged as sentimental, is treated as marginal and not amenable to "rigorous" analysis. They notice law firms increasingly promoting business methods of production, routinizing work, hustling frantically for clients, putting heavy stress on billable hours and the bottom line. They notice the organized bar in solemn assembly voting down the most modest attempts to reform its ethical codes or disciplinary machinery and contemptuously refusing to respond to the widespread public criticism of its practices and prices. They see even the small gains that 1960s liberals made toward giving the poor and unorganized some legal leverage in dealing with the state through public-interest and legal-services practices eroded close to the vanishing point, and the private bar contributing little beyond tokenism to filling the gap. Above all, they notice a vast and pervasive indifference to reflection upon the social role of the bar. * * *

I mention these things not to indulge in futile moralizing but to point out that it is hardly the teaching of "nihilism" that makes cynics out of these students: it's just exposure to their chosen profession. The response of many students is complacent careerism. They think they are on the track to wealth and professional status, and any law teacher or lawyer who wants them to examine law and its practice critically is an obstruction—whatever this weird stuff he is teaching is, they know they cannot use it. Other students give in to a kind of numbing despair. You can actually see them deflate after the first-year summer: they narrow their focus to getting through, finding the alienating job and grinding their way through it, saving their passion and commitment for personal life after hours. They too want to think about what they are getting into as little as possible. (Parenthetically, don't you think that the mindless careerism and apathy of so many law students is a rather more serious problem than the symptom of it you oddly fix on, that they "pass" when called on in class?)

Careerism and apathy are perfectly adaptive responses to the collections of practices that students are persuaded to think of as constituting "the real world". The prevailing collection of rules, processes, ethical standards, negotiating strategies, allocations of power and wealth within the law firm or the corporation or the society at large, come to seem like natural and necessary facts about the world just because they exist. Some lawyers think the facts add up to a system that is functional and valuable, others that it is crazy and dumb, or an arbitrary jumble: but it is out there, no denying it, and that makes it all seem somehow inevitable and fixed, subject at best to glacially gradual change. * * * Accepting that, the careerist sets out to grab as much as he can, the alienated to do whatever he has to do in order to get by.

Some law teachers, including many of the most conscientious ones, try to encourage their students toward a third way of dealing with the "real world": this is your response, the counsel (and example) of professionalism. Professionalism as I understand it recommends a kind of minimalist stoic morality, to participants in a society whose basic structures and tasks are assumed to be unalterable givens. Your task is not to ask why you have been conscripted for these wars, or to question mysterious bureaucratic orders, it is to bear yourself like a soldier. You should strive to develop and live up to your own standards of quality for the practice of your craft, whether your superiors demand such standards or not; you should be candid and honest with clients and adversaries, and not stoop to cunning or underhanded tricks even if everyone else does; you should give your best attention to all your work, whether the client is a bigwig or a nobody; you should not try to grab credit for others' work or to blame others for your mistakes; you should try to preserve independent judgment, even in the face of pressure from partners or clients; you should not treat your underlings badly or toady to your bosses, etc. If this is the sort of thing you mean by professionalism, I agree wholeheartedly that much of it can and should be imparted in law school classrooms (or even better, clinics) and personal dealings with students—though it will also need the example of respected successful lawyers to be sustained out in "the real world"—and that the world would undoubtedly be a better place if more lawyers lived by it. It is certainly a lot better than careerism and apathy. It gives students at least a minimal set of aspirations to *try* to live by and take pride in, while facing the "real world's" moral hazards. * * *

Yet professionalism, by and for itself, is not enough. It gives no guidance at all on what lawyers in this society ought actually to *do,* what they should strive to promote: it lacks a social vision. Indeed it supposes that trying to help students develop a vision of the social purposes of their practices would be illegitimate, since purposes already inhere in "the law", i.e., the collection of current practices, and in the desires of clients. The attitude of professionalism thus ends up recommending submission to the status quo, because it cannot imagine alternatives and does not think it should. This is the real "cynicism" of the legal profession: that there is not much that anyone can do about the way things are, that we must accept "reality" as a soldier accepts his orders. I have often noticed that it is the law teachers with the *least* conviction that the current collection of practices adds up to anything particularly coherent or admirable who are *most* likely to adopt the counsels of professionalism. In a world without meaning, at least one should serve the status quo with style. Professionalism is thus not an alternative to cynicism: like careerism and apathy, it is a *product* of cynicism, even if a valuable product.

I think that if the law schools want to help counter the bad products of cynicism they are going to have to offer *substantive visions* of how lawyers can act to make this a better society. * * * Unless a single faction captures the law faculty, which would be unfortunate as well as unlikely, there should be a whole bunch of different and competing visions. That means law teachers and their students will be engaging each other in basic political, economic and ethical argument about what lawyers and legal systems can and should be doing. It means trying to describe the current practices as they actually are, and to articulate and criticize their theoretical justifications; and to try to work out practical suggestions for experimentally realizing competing visions of the good. The Chicago Law and Economics people have had something to offer here, as have the Chicago Libertarians, Wisconsin–Buffalo Law and Society scholars, and the Coasian–Rawlsian Liberal Technocrats like Calabresi and Ackerman; and so, I would insist, have the people in Critical Legal Studies, whom you single out, completely arbitrarily as it seems to me, for excommunication. The colossal irony of your article is its labelling as "nihilists" the members of this group, who are actually among the most hopeful people around—people who think things really can change for the better and are committed to changing them! (You seem to be saying: "If you do not believe in what I believe in, you must not believe in anything at all.") The students who seem to be attracted to our ideas are rarely the most cynical or despairing (those are more likely to fall into careerism or apathy), but rather the most idealistic and socially committed, those who are energetically seeking what Roberto Unger has called "transformative vocations", ways of doing work that is useful to the world and at the same time helps to change the world. Sure, they get "dispirited" sometimes about how hard it is to change things, but who doesn't!

Why have I written at such length? The real reason is that I started a very short letter and got carried away. A second reason is that as the country drifts rightwards, the sounds of Red-baiting are once more heard in the land. Though I am sure you have absolutely no wish to do so, you give encouragement to Red-baiters when you brand schools of thought originating with people on the left as too dangerously corrupting for professional students' consumption. There is already a lot of unreasoning prejudice against CLS among practicing lawyers who have vaguely heard of it. If there are battles to come, the academic profession ought to be solidly on the side of the values of intellectual pluralism and the pursuit of uncomfortable truths. If we are to sink without a trace it should be because people have shown up our errors, not because of repression. Also: I happen to be an old admirer of yours. I read the "Carrington Report" when I first started teaching and thought it a terrifically acute diagnosis of much of what was wrong with law schools, enlightened in its recommendations, and written with stunning grace. You have too much class to be consorting with the rednecks of our profession.

NOTES AND QUESTIONS

1. Is Gordon correct to assume that Carrington is referring to people like him? From Gordon's comments to Presser, do you believe that Gordon is the kind of person who should leave law school teaching, perhaps to find some other place within the academy? Who is attacking a straw man, Carrington or Gordon? Is the problem that law students taught by "nihilists" are likely to dabble in bribery or intimidation, or is the real problem something else? Is Gordon correct that in Carrington's ideal world of law teaching all law teachers are political moderates?

2. What about Gordon's views on "professionalism?" Is this a concept with any value neutrality left to it? Is it one which you favor? Does it inevitably serve the cynics? Note that Gordon raises the specter of "red-baiting," of McCarthyism, the paranoia most prevalent in the early 1950's when Committees of Congress believed that they could see a communist spy behind almost every tree, or at least throughout Hollywood and the American academy. Is the threat of such a renewal of red-baiting a real one? Based on your experience, do you think that free speech in the academy is more threatened by those on the right or the left? For Carrington's call on this one, see his remarkable piece challenging Political Correctness, Paul Carrington, "Diversity!" 1992 Utah L.Rev. 1105. Bear in mind, however, that several members of CLS actually have had trouble securing promotion and tenure because of a feeling on the part of their faculty colleagues that their CLS views and scholarship were too far out of the mainstream.

3. Twice in his letter Gordon compliments Carrington for his "grace" as a writer. What does that mean, and, in particular, does it have anything to do with professionalism? Does Carrington's reply to Gordon, which follows, soothe or aggravate any possible fears of "red-baiting" or denial of academic freedom?

PAUL D. CARRINGTON TO ROBERT GORDON*

35 J.Legal Ed. 9 (1985).

* * *

It may be that the only real difference between us is in the reassurance that you know of no law teacher who holds that legal outcomes represent nothing but the arbitrary whim or political bias of decisionmakers. If you are right about that, then my comments to which you take offense have little point. I am certainly aware that my concern is not appropriate with respect to all the persons having some sympathy or connection with CLS; it is for that reason that I tried to avoid referring to CLS as a corporate body, and chose to comment instead on Legal Nihilism, a phrase which I had thought [none] likely to claim for their banner, but which may nevertheless apply to some.

* Reprinted by permission of the Journal of Legal Education and of the author.

I am assuredly opposed to Red Hunts and Loyalty Oaths. I was asked to speak about academic ethics. I supposed, therefore, that my remarks were appropriately addressed to the consciences of law teachers, not to any regulatory bodies. In light of your comments, I could wish to have been more clear about that.

The point I sought to make is a limited one, that academic ethics may be somewhat more constraining in the environment of a professional school claiming a role in the professional development of its students. The obligation to contribute to professional development can conflict with the duty to profess truth if the truth which one is obliged to profess is a refutation of the premises on which the service of the profession is based. Thus, atheism is an eminently legitimate intellectual position which any university worthy of the name should be easily able to shelter; but a professor of divinity for whom atheism is the primary message to profess ought to recognize that he has a conflict of interest, of sorts; he should put in for a transfer to some other department, perhaps the religion department. This seems fairly obvious to me; in any case, my remarks were intended to suggest the possible applicability of that notion to law teaching.

I can tell you with assurance that the possibility is not altogether unreal. Autobiographically, there have been days, sometimes many of them in a row, when I have asked myself if perhaps I am or was not too cynical about law to be able to profess it. I am personally acquainted with two very able law teachers who did in fact decide that they were in the wrong pew, and who did elect to pursue their careers in academic settings in which they were liberated from their sense of responsibility for professional development of students. Those persons put their money where their mouths were, sacrificing the pay and status associated with professional teaching in order to secure the greater intellectual freedom of a purely academic environment. My present perception, which may be wrong, is that there are a number of persons now in professional law teaching who ought to make similar decisions, for the sake of their own moral and psychiatric well-being, as well as for the sakes of their students and their students' clients.

I take no satisfaction in finding that there is this potential conflict between our duties as professionalizers and our obligations to profess truth. I have recently published a review of Bob Stevens' book in which I again tried to explore the costs and benefits of the isolation of professional education with[in] the university. Professional law schools, I own there, may be a bad idea; in counting the costs, I certainly should have explicitly added this one to my list. My specific frame of mind about the social utility of professional law schools dates at least from the time of my work on the AALS Committee report to which you refer, and which reflected serious ambivalence on the matter. Uncertainty about the worth of our enterprise does not, however, in my view, entitle those in doubt to attack its essential premise while sharing fully in its benefits.

I cannot demonstrate empirically that lawyers who think that law seldom if ever matters are bad lawyers on that account. There may be a little support for my assertion in Jerome Carlin's work in the early sixties. You say you don't see why someone who believed that "you can always crank out a legal argument for any position" would resort to "bribery and intimidation" rather than simply cranking out arguments. The logical answer is that if you can always crank out an argument, the task of cranking is meaningless in the sense that neither judge nor advocate can regard the product of the effort as the basis for the application of the lash of official power. Your lawyer might go ahead and crank out a few arguments when he has nothing better to do, but he is not likely to think his effort to be effective, or even a worthy use of time and effort.

My own episodic observation is that many bad lawyers are in fact convinced that law does not matter. Indeed, for the slothful, (and who of us is not at least sometimes slothful?), it is a congenial rationalization of nonperformance that one's professional effort would have had no bearing on the outcome anyway. And if one has no effective professional tools with which to serve clients, what remain as means of service are bribery and intimidation, in all their manifold forms.

You are surely right that this has nothing to do with whether the lawyer is a leftist or a rightist. The idea that law does not matter can be equally congenial to professional slobs and crooks of all political persuasions. I do not think for a moment that the conversion of a generation of law students to Marxism would in itself have any bearing on their professional competence. But teachers who profess that class bias is the primary or exclusive motivation of judges are at serious risk of being influential on their students only to the degree that students perceive that principle is not a force in legal decisions.

Moral outrage and a zeal for reform are singularly difficult to generate in professional students. Although constrained by my belief that students are ends not means, I have been taking a stab at evoking moral outrage for 25 years. The bottom line of my course in civil procedure is that the system is broken, that it operates to grind the faces of the weak and poor, and needs radical reform. This could be a Marxist vision, except that it predates Marx, and descends more from Bentham and Brougham and other intellectual ancestry. I am fairly confident that my students get the message that the system serves the interests of the strong, but if any have been filled with zeal by that revelation, I cannot confirm it. On this experience, I do not have a lot of hope for the course on "Law and Class Structure" you describe. If a colleague wants to teach such a course, I would certainly support it as an appropriate exercise in a professional school, but I would not be surprised if it drew a small crowd and, except insofar as it preached to the pre-believers, had a negative result.

An impression I have formed over the years is that almost everyone is a Marxist in the sense that they acknowledge the ubiquity of class bias. But most people, including most lawyers and law students, do not seem to regard it as more than a minor offense or blemish in the order of things. Indignant about it they rarely are. Even if they are themselves the disadvantaged. If this is right, your course will get a blase response. And if you are not a little bit careful, the only lesson effectively taught would be a perhaps unintended lesson that our game is essentially one of manipulation. Students could possibly be moved neither to the left nor right in their politics, but merely somewhat corrupted by the exposure. I have been conscious of this risk in my own teaching for many years; if you can persuade me not to worry, I will be very grateful.

I here plead *nolo contendere* to the alleged miscitation of Unger. I spent a week and a half in a hammock with that article, and this was what I got out of it. I do not think I am alone in so reading him; and, if I am wrong, he must have even less to say than I gave him credit for.

Since he adopts the affectation of non-citation, it is hard to be sure, but I thought that I could detect the influence on his work of what appears to be happening in the not unrelated field of literary criticism. As far as I know, there are no avowed adherents of literary nihilism in that discipline, either, but it does appear to me and to some other critics of the critics that there are those who practice it. There are those who do say that literary texts are what the reader choses to make of them, and indeed that the creative process occurs in the minds of readers, not writers. I hope that it is not merely a revelation of a political bias when I confess sympathy for the view expressed that this is the sort of philosophy that has given bullshit a bad name. However that may be, I can certainly countenance the profession of this Literary Nihilism in the university, even as I question whether a person holding that view ought, on his own account as well as that of others, to aspire to teach creative writing to persons who want to write good literature. My point is that if this kind of intellectual annihilation is to be practiced in law, its practitioners ought at the very least to wonder what its secondary and tertiary effects may be.

Even if I recede from my citation of Unger, I do not recant my expression of concern. There is a problem. I have seen it in living color and in person. If I exaggerate the problem, I am happy to be corrected. And if some or all CLS folks can and will disavow the idea that legal texts do not much matter, I would be delighted.

NOTES AND QUESTIONS

1. Does the difference between Gordon and Carrington boil down to a difference in personal experience, so that, in the end, their writing is a war of personal anecdotes? What, exactly, is the real issue between them? Would Gordon agree with Carrington's assertion, for example, that a professor in a divinity school cannot be an Atheist?

2. Note that Carrington says that he is willing to plead *nolo contendre* to Gordon's charge that he has miscited Unger. *Nolo contendre,* which means that the defendant, while not admitting guilt, chooses not to contest the prosecutor's charges against him, and thus accepts the punishment meted out by the court, was made famous in the early Seventies when Richard Nixon's Vice–President, Spiro Agnew, pleaded *nolo contendre* to charges of corruption against him, and was forced out of office. Is Carrington's "crime" anything similar? The article of Unger to which Carrington and Gordon refer, later turned into a book, is R. Unger, "The Critical Legal Studies Movement," 96 Harv.L.Rev. 563 (1983). It is one of Unger's utopian blueprints for a "just" society. Unger's piece is one of the most legendary in the CLS canon, and is notable, among other things, for the fact that it rambles on for more than a hundred pages totally bereft of footnote citation. It is a very difficult piece, probably undeniably brilliant, but also maddeningly obscure. In it Unger lays out a possible positive program for reformation of society, which he apparently urges on CLS. Gordon is probably correct that the article indicates that Unger is much more than a nihilist, and this might explain Carrington's plea of *nolo contendere.*

3. On the other hand, after some more re-reading of Unger's article, in a letter to another colleague, Carrington decided that he had been right after all, and Gordon was wrong about Carrington's supposed mischaracterization of Unger. Further, as have several others, Carrington expressed alarm at one of Unger's proposals, the establishment of "disestablishment rights," a potentiality, presumably, for ongoing redistribution of wealth and power in society. Carrington wrote to Owen M. Fiss:

> For now, all I can say is that it did seem to me that Unger regards legal texts expressing the understandings, agreements, and assents of others as having no proper consequence; perhaps I should have sharpened my diction, but this is what I meant by my term, Legal Nihilism. I, too, think that Unger is a romantic, but not about law: I do not perceive a grain of regard for law, for our hope that officials will abide principle in applying the lash of power. Indeed, his description of disestablishment "rights," strikes me as a jurisprudence for Brown Shirts and Red Guards. But who can be sure what he is saying?

Reprinted at 35 J.Leg.Ed., at 23–24. These must have struck Gordon and other CLS members as "fighting words," and perhaps you can understand Gordon's chagrin at Carrington reflected in Gordon's letter to Presser. On the other hand, is it so very difficult to sympathize with Carrington, who spends a week in a hammock with Unger's article, reading it several times, and still concludes that it is impossible to figure out what Unger is saying? If Unger's message is impenetrable to a distinguished law professor and Dean, is there something inherently wrong with it? Recall the question about what you get when you cross a don with a crit. Our look at CLS closes with Gordon's reply to Carrington's reply. Does it move the ball forward? Does it help us understand why what is involved in the struggle between competing jurisprudential theories, such as law-and-economics, or CLS, really is a struggle for the "soul" of American Law?

ROBERT W. GORDON TO PAUL D. CARRINGTON*

35 J.Legal Ed. 13 (1985).

Your letter helps considerably to clarify the issues between us, as well as revealing more agreement than I would first have suspected to exist. Without going on at too great length—I know that neither of us has the time to continue a correspondence in so leisurely an 18th century fashion—I would like to lay stress on the few points of difference that seem to be the crucial ones.

I wrote you in the first place because I—along with many colleagues at this and other law schools—was worried that your ideas, attractively gilded with your prestige and influence, might be turned to frightful purposes. The specific danger is that law faculties seeking to block appointments or promotions of teachers with unorthodox (especially left-wing) sympathies will be encouraged by your theory (that only people committed to certain "premises" of professional practice, specifically to the belief that "law matters", ought to be teaching in professional schools) to think that you have given them a respectable pretext for bypassing the normal commitments to academic freedom and intellectual pluralism that might otherwise restrain them. I do not think this danger is a paranoid fantasy, given the many intense expressions of hostility towards left-wing legal studies, particularly Critical Legal Studies (CLS), I and others have heard from lawyers and law teachers in the last couple years, and the appointment-promotion-and-tenure troubles that some CLS–affiliated law teachers are now actually experiencing.

I am really glad to hear that you have no wish whatever to give aid or comfort to any institutional attempts to suppress unorthodox scholarship and teaching. There remains the matter, quite apart from the unpleasant political uses to which it might be put, of your basic proposition's validity. And here I find I am still puzzled about what the proposition actually is. You oppose the belief that "law matters" to the belief that it does not ("nihilism"), and worry that nihilist teachings may corrupt or dispirit future professionals. Some problems:

1. When you speak of the professional as one who believes in the law, it is not clear how you are using "law." You could mean: the body of current professional practices. Or: the utopian norms of fair process, restraint-of-power, equality, "dialogue" * * * or whatever, embodied in law but only imperfectly realized in the current professional practices. It makes a lot of difference. One position is: "A true professional complacently subscribes to the going system, whatever it is." Another is: "A true professional should work to bring the practice of law into closer harmony with its utopian norms." I should have thought that if law teachers had any ethical duty to teach either of these positions, it would be the second. The academic wing of the profession in particular is *supposed* to be reformist in its aspirations: if lawyers or judges or legislators are doing bad things, the professors should point that out and try to get them to change. This seems to be your own stance. It seems to me a good stance; and if law students and lawyers often respond to it with cynicism or indifference, that is no reason to abandon it.

More specifically: is it wrong for law teachers to try to discourage their students from doing what they plan to do? It depends, surely. I agree with you that if a law teacher starts thinking that all lawyers do more harm than good, believes nothing can be done to change that situation even slightly, and counsels all his students to abandon the law, he is in the wrong job and ought to get out. But what if he wants his students to change current practices, rather than abandon them? Felix Frankfurter used to warn all his students of corporate practice: he thought Wall Street lawyers had become the servile and corrupt employees of big corporations, were very limited in their social vision, and were wasting considerable talents, which could be turned to the development of public policy, on such trivial pursuits as proofreading the fine print on trust indentures. Derek Bok said similar things: there are a lot of urgent reforms to be made in the legal system and law graduates are simply staffing the system rather than changing it. I do not think for a moment that either of these positions is inappropriate for a law teacher; though I confess that I think it would be *more* valuable for law teachers to work on ways to help young associates think about how to reform the corporate-firm practices that they are probably going to enter anyway. If people in the law school do not engage in critical reflection on what lawyers do, who will?

2. When you speak of the belief that law *matters,* it is not clear in what sense you mean "matters". You could mean: (1) Law is more than just a mask for, or rationalization of, naked power and self-interest: its norms, rules, procedures, reasoning processes, etc. have an autonomous content, have an independent influence upon the actions of legal officials and ordinary persons in society. (Once again, CLS people would agree emphatically with this: they believe that legal ideas are immensely powerful influences in the formation of social purposes and in the ways such purposes are acted upon.) (2) Legal rules are not infinitely manipulable:

they do constrain outcomes. (This is a complex assertion, which would obviously have to be considerably expanded and refined before anyone could evaluate it: it is too shorthand to constitute a *credo* for an intelligent professional.) (3) The current system of rules in force, and practices of the officials and lawyers who apply them, is basically a good one, if not close to the best attainable system in an imperfect world, at least on the whole more good than bad. (This is obviously a political judgment, which if made a criterion of a good professional arbitrarily excludes critical idealists who believe the system embodies many serious evils and could be made a good deal better than it is.)

Perhaps you do not mean any of these things, but something else entirely. The point is that you have been repeating the phrase "law matters" as if it has a transparent and accepted meaning to your audience; whereas it is really very indefinite.

3. What is "nihilism", anyway? That of course depends on how one understands its opposite, the belief that "law matters". To approach the issue in another way, whom is it realistic to call a nihilist? Surely not a romantic Christian Hegelian like Roberto Unger, who has just set off to spend several years of his life doing grass-roots political organizing in Brazil: there are few people anywhere in the world who have given more effort to constructing a theory of social transformation and shown more courage in trying to carry it out in practice: in his case at least, the proper analogy is not the one you suggest to an atheist in a divinity school, but rather to a liberation theologian. (If one wants an example of a *true* nihilist, I cannot forbear to point out, it would be the presiding genius of your piece on "Law and the River," Mark Twain.) Your letter refers to some currents of literary theory as illustrating nihilist tendencies; but surely this is so only among users of such theory drawn to absurdly polar positions ("if we cannot say that a text has a single fixed and definite meaning, we must be saying that readers can interpret it any way they want"): there seems to me a perfectly sensible resolution of this polarity in the commonsense position that the intentions of authors cannot determine any fixed meanings of their texts, but that readers will have a range of plausible meanings set by the conventions of the historically and socially situated communities of interpretation to which they belong. This avoids the twin idiocies of saying the Constitution has only one meaning for all time and that it can mean anything a reader pleases at any time.

If one were to look around the law academies for people one could plausibly characterize as "nihilists", I think one would have to fix upon a very different group from the CLS–types. On many law faculties, perhaps even on most, there are teachers I would characterize as post-Realist burnt-out liberals. These are people who once gave a lot of energy to demolishing what they thought of as conservative objections to the active state's regulatory-welfare policies, objections dressed up in "formalist" legal reasoning; but who have since lost most of their former confidence either in building a coherent body of law on the ruins of the old or in the worth or effectiveness of the active state policies they once espoused. They know too much to believe in "formalism", but they do not believe in anything else, either. On the whole they are pretty cynical about the way the legal system works, think that powerful interests are likely to capture it no matter how it is tinkered with; and are resigned to the situation, complacently or bitterly according to their temperaments. As I read your letter, you yourself share at least some of the characteristics of this type, the liberal of eroded faith and vanished hope; and you wonder—is there any place for *this* temperament on a law faculty? You then go on to say, unless I misread you, that you think most *students* share this same cynicism about the system and resignation to it. You may well be right in your perceptions; but if you are I am absolutely flabbergasted that you should identify as the source of potential "corruption", in such an era of decadent sensibilities, the *only people around who have any hope that the situation can be changed and the commitment to changing it!* If you are looking for "romantic innocence", you should look to the party of social transformation.

4. Finally, the relationship of "nihilism" to "corruption". Quite honestly I would not expect to be able to find much of any correlation between a set of jurisprudential or political beliefs abstractly described (as contrasted with the inspiriting or dispiriting force of a teacher's personal presence or example) and the behavior in practice of law graduates exposed to such beliefs. But if there are such correlations, my intuitions about them run opposite to yours. Is it not somewhat more plausible that corruption in students will be promoted by that kind of resignation to current practices that so frequently passes as worldly wisdom—that is, by teachers who believe in nothing but the inevitability of the *status quo?*

When one tries to think of legal thinkers whom one could plausibly label "nihilists", who comes to mind? On a short list: O.W. Holmes, Jr., Thurman Arnold, T.R. Powell, Grant Gilmore, and Arthur Leff. Is it seriously maintained that the law schools would have been better off without these men and the influence of their ideas? Or that they "disabled" the students they taught, or drove them into corrupt practices? To take just the two most recent instances: Gilmore taught his students a sensitivity to the aesthetics of legal doctrines, at the same time he remained convinced of their impermanence and essential meaninglessness. Leff was more clearly a "nihilist" than any of the others, but a man of such transparent moral seriousness that his brilliantly witty confrontations of the abyss could only have inspired in students a profound respect. I am not a traditional liberal in these matters; and I do think that there are people who should not be teaching law students; but I feel strongly that in your condemnation of "nihilists" you have used the wrong standard, and picked the wrong people to fall on the bad side of the line.

NOTES AND QUESTIONS

1. Do you think that "law matters?" Which of Gordon's definitions for this phrase is, in your opinion, the correct one? Who *are* the true legal "nihilists," the "tragic" or "burned-out" liberals, or the CLS people? Or could it be the law-and-economics tribe?

2. You have studied the work of three people Gordon places in his pantheon of great legal nihilists, Holmes, Gilmore, and Leff. Is this how you would have characterized these three? Why, in particular, does Gordon single Leff out for great praise? What does it mean to say that Leff possessed such "transparent moral seriousness that his brilliantly witty confrontations of the abyss could only have inspired in students a profound respect?" Precisely what values does Gordon (and by implication) CLS hold most dear? Is the path toward greatest happiness, or greatest virtue, for lawyers and law students, to be found through "romantic innocence," through "social transformation," through "brilliantly witty confrontations of the abyss," or perhaps through "stunning grace?" As you have probably discerned these last few enterprises could be employed just as easily in literary as in legal criticism, and it is, not surprisingly, to an attempt to borrow from the insights of literature itself that we next turn.

D. LAW AND LITERATURE

PAUL GEWIRTZ, AESCHYLUS' LAW**

101 Harvard Law Review 1043 (1988).

Practitioners of "law and literature," a newly fashionable area of legal scholarship, are rarely concerned with literature at all. They have generally focused instead on literary criticism, seeking to apply current theories about interpreting literary texts to the judicial enterprise of interpreting legal texts. Much interesting work has been done in this vein, although there probably has been too little emphasis on the differences between judicial action and literary criticism, differences that limit the usefulness of analogies between one field and the other. I am more interested, though, in efforts to augment the "law and literature" movement with work that explores the relevance of law of literature itself, not only literary criticism. I cannot claim to know how fruitful such work will ultimately be, but we have barely begun to examine the images of law that appear in literature and to assess whether they illuminate the legal world in distinctive ways.

This essay is an effort in that direction. Its subject is Aeschylus' *Oresteia*. This trilogy of plays is one of the earliest surviving masterpieces of Western culture, and it has special meaning for lawyers. Many of us read the *Oresteia* in college. But at that point, focusing on other stories it

** Reprinted with the permission of the Harvard Law Review and of the author.

tells, we may not have appreciated that it is fundamentally a story about the emergence of law. Aeschylus' myth, which links law's emergence to the foundation of our civilization, presents an image of law that deserves examination—an image of genuine complexity, power, and modern resonance, an image that law-trained readers should address as well as the professional classicists and college undergraduates who are currently the plays' main audience.

The plot of the *Oresteia* is a familiar one that found repeated use among Greek writers. The House of Atreus has long been mired in wrongdoing and revenge. As the *Oresteia* opens, Atreus' son Agamemnon, King of the Argives, returns home after the ten-year war with Troy. His wife, Clytemnestra—embittered by Agamemnon's sacrifice of their daughter Iphigenia at the outset of the Trojan expedition, and enmeshed in an adulterous relationship with Aegisthus—kills Agamemnon and his mistress, Cassandra. Orestes, the son of Agamemnon and Clytemnestra, avenges his father's murder by killing both Clytemnestra and her lover. The Furies, spirits avenging Clytemnestra's death, begin to haunt Orestes, and the cycle of blood feuds appears endless. Apollo intervenes, however, and sends Orestes to Athena, who establishes a court and a legal process within Greek society and puts Orestes on trial. Orestes is acquitted, and the embittered Furies are forestalled from continuing their vendettas by being offered an honored place within the new social order.

Two aspects of the image of law in the *Oresteia* are especially arresting: passion is seen as a central, necessary element of law; and law is presented as a gendered phenomenon. To explore these aspects more clearly, though, I must first describe in more detail law's basic appearance in the plays.

I.

The trial of Orestes is presented as "the first trial of bloodshed," and Athena sees the emergence of this legal forum as an historic turning point in Greek civilization:

> [S]ince the burden of the case is here, and rests on me,
>
> I shall select judges of manslaughter, and swear them in, establish a court into all time to come.[5]

With this case, Athena introduces both a court and a trial process to replace the endless cycle of blood feuds and revenge—she establishes a tribunal of law—and she consecrates the site on which this first trial occurs:

> Now and forever more, for Aegeus' people
>
> this will be the court where judges reign.
>
> This is the Crag of Ares. . . .

[5] The Eumenides (Lattimore trans.) II. 481–84.

Here from the heights, terror and reverence,
my people's kindred powers
will hold them from injustice through the day
and through the mild night. Never pollute
our law with innovations. No, my citizens,
foul a clear well and you will suffer thirst. . . .
Untouched by lust for spoil, this court of law
majestic, swift to fury, rising above you
as you sleep, our night watch always wakeful,
guardian of our land—I found it here and now.[6]

This is not to say that Athena introduces *justice*, for throughout the trilogy the characters have all conceived their claims in terms of what justice requires. But Athena's innovation has several elements that set it altogether apart from the system of blood revenge that had preceded it—elements that we take for granted today almost as defining characteristics of a system of law.

Athena's court is public and political; by contrast, the regime it seeks to replace is private and familial, with aggrieved family members taking direct action themselves. Moreover, Athena's system involves a process—an orderly and controlled process for hearing claims, rather than uncontrolled violence. Specifically, the system introduces a decisionmaker standing apart from the immediately interested parties: a judge presides, and there is a lay jury. (Although Athena herself presides in Orestes' case and casts the deciding vote when the lay jury divides, the new system is clearly to be embedded in Greek civil society and implemented by mortals; law may express the will of the gods, but it is an activity of humans.) This process involves reasoned discussion. The complainant and the accused present "witnesses" and "proofs."[7] They appeal to rights, and they reason from abstract principles. Principles of justice had been invoked even under the regime of blood feuds, but only as explanations for private acts of revenge. Now there is open debate about which principles are appropriate, and a third party decides. The movement is from a world of passion and subjectivity toward a regime that, in form at least, empowers a more detached authority influenced by reason.

The process is also influenced by the aspiration for a wise resolution of conflict. The pervasive sense of closure achieved at the play's end is linked to the possibility of closure that a legal judgment provides. Before law—without courts—there is revenge after revenge, a cycle of violence

[6] *Id.* (Fagles trans.) at II. 695–721.

[7] *Id.* (Lattimore trans.) at I. 485.

without end. This, as the *Oresteia* exposes, is the inner contradiction of revenge: it does not stop. With law, there is the possibility of an ending, both in individual cases and in systemic struggles. The establishment of Athena's court and legal process becomes the central event that propels the action toward the transfiguring harmonies of the play's close.

II.

Law's image in the *Oresteia* gains its richness, though, from other features. The most basic feature is the place of the Furies in the system. Although they consent to participate in the trial, the very establishment of the court seems to displace their method of revenge. After the Furies lose the case against Orestes, they announce that they will "let loose on the land . . . vindictive poison."[8] Athena, however, pleads with them to take an honored place within the community, and after considerable resistance they finally agree.

How is one to understand Athena's offer to include and empower the Furies in the new social order? The starting point is to appreciate what the Furies are and what they represent: complex forces of passion, linked at various points in the plays with vengeance, fear, anger, violence, conscience, instinct, the sense of hurt, memories of grief, the primitive, the emotional and nonrational.

One might view Athena's effort to include these forces of Fury simply as an act of political necessity. Excluded, the Furies threaten to wreak havoc. Since the Furies and the emotional forces they represent will have some role one way or another, inclusion is a tactic to spare Athens the wrath of a Fury spurned.

This understanding, however, fails to take account of the positive function that Aeschylus clearly sees the Furies playing in the new order. There is more than political manipulation in Athena's statements that the Furies will be "honored" and will provide "salvation for your citadel."[9] The Furies have this stature because they actually contribute to the system Athena is establishing. What the Furies most clearly represent—call it fear, conscience, vengeance—is not a "threat" to law in the *Oresteia*'s scheme. Rather, Fury is law's partner. It reinforces a respect for legal rights. It promotes "reverence for the just,"[10] which in turn is a source of society's prosperity. From the moment she announces the new legal order, Athena advises her citizens

[8] *Id.* at II. 781–82.

[9] *Id.* at II. 701, 868.

[10] *Id.* (Fagles trans.) at I. 714.

> not to cast fear utterly from your city. What man who fears nothing at all is ever righteous? Such be your just terrors, and you may deserve and have salvation for your citadel. . . .[11]

Here she echoes the Furies themselves, who warn:

> There are times when fear is good.
>
> It must keep its watchful place
>
> at the heart's controls.[12]

This, then, is Aeschylus' large claim about law: law and passion are inseparable. The Furies are "steering spirits of law."[13] A stable law is rooted in passion, and does not transcend it. At the trilogy's end, the Furies are included, but they are not transformed into gentle spirits or agents of reason. As Athena says: "I establish in power spirits who are large, difficult to soften."[14] They remain fearsome forces, but Athena proclaims that "[i]n the terror upon the faces of these I see great good for our citizens."[15] The Furies change by putting their energies in the service of Zeus' goals, but their transformation is from Furies as a "rampaging force" to Furies as a "steering" force of law, a change that does not abolish their primitive energies but channels them and makes an effective law possible.

This explains what the Furies mean when, toward the end of the play, they pray for "hate with one strong heart: such union heals a thousand ills of man."[16] Channeled through law, vengeance and hate speak through the one strong voice of civil authority. Only with this vehicle for hate can the play achieve its resolution and civilization move ahead. Thus, the *Oresteia* stands behind those in contemporary debates who insist that retribution must play a central role in a system of criminal justice and who warn that if retributive emotions are ignored they will be unleashed in less acceptable ways. Inclusion of the Furies suggests this channeling function of law, and in the play's terms that is an advance. But the blissful harmonies of the play's close should not mask the basic truths that the foundation of the new legal order is hate as much as concern, and that law becomes an instrument of violence not its replacement. The Furies' role underscores the connection of the legal order to terror and violence.

---

[11] *Id.* (Lattimore trans.) at ll. 698–701.

[12] *Id.* at ll. 517–19.

[13] *Id.* at l. 961; *see id.* at l. 993.

[14] *Id.* at ll. 928–29.

[15] *Id.* at ll. 990–91.

[16] *Id.* (Fagles trans.) at ll. 995–96.

This does not mean, of course, that the Furies come to represent what law is. * * * Athena's establishment of the court precedes the inclusion of the Furies in the system, and the basic process and rational method of the new legal order is a radical departure from the cycle of vendettas that the Furies have represented. Within the terms of the play, moreover, it is clear that Athena would persist with her new institution even if the Furies rebelled. The Furies come to assist the new social order, not vice versa.

The Furies bring more to the legal system than fear. Along with fear, which contributes to order, they bring pain, which contributes to wisdom—that most essential attribute of those who judge. In pressing their claims, the Furies not only counsel that "there are times when fear is good" but also speak of the "advantage in the wisdom won from pain."[18] The Furies thereby echo the vision of tragic understanding articulated by the chorus in *Agamemnon,* perhaps the most famous lines in the *Oresteia:*

> [W]isdom comes alone through suffering.
>
> Still there drips in sleep against the heart
>
> grief of memory;
>
> against our pleasure we are temperate.
>
> From the gods who sit in grandeur
>
> grace comes somehow violent.[19]

The Furies (elsewhere linked to "memories of grief"[20]) become agents in the legal order for the kind of understanding that passes what reason alone can provide. The Furies are not "emotion" to the exclusion of "reason"—indeed, they are at least Apollo's equal in offering reasoned arguments to Athena—but they do represent more emotional forces in life and in law. Through the Furies, law is strengthened by terror; legal judgment is ripened by pain; and a cluster of emotions are infused into the legal order as a source of fruitful, and at times disturbing, social action and understanding.

In short, the inclusion of the Furies must be seen as a challenge to any view that reason rules in law's domain. In our time, though, advocates for reason's preeminent role in law remain ascendant virtually everywhere, from the development of highly rationalized sentencing guidelines, to the adamant idealizing of much constitutional theory, to the currently prominent law-and-economics movement. The Legal Realists of the 1920's and 1930's may have smashed the rationalist conceptualism of Langdell, but their heirs have typically developed approaches that reflect as deep a faith in the presiding powers of reason. Indeed, it is common in

---

[18] The Eumenides (Lattimore trans.) II. 520–21.

[19] Agamemnon (Lattimore trans.) II. 177–83.

[20] The Eumenides (Fagles trans.) I. 393.

legal analysis to draw a sharp line between reason and emotion, as if the line were a clear one and as if the law's domain properly excluded emotion. Only last Term in the Supreme Court, Justice O'Connor wrote that a jury's decision whether to impose the death penalty

> should reflect a reasoned moral response to the defendant's background, character, and crime rather than mere sympathy or emotion. . . . [T]he individualized assessment of the appropriateness of the death penalty is a moral inquiry into the culpability of the defendant, and not an emotional response to the mitigating evidence. . . . [21]

Aeschylus reveals a more haunting view of law: law is not and cannot be an enterprise of reason alone; it includes the nonrational emotions as an essential and central ingredient. Law may be in part—perhaps in largest part—a process of reasoned judgment, but it also engages forces beyond reason, like most other things in life.

It is foolish and perhaps dangerous, in this view, to imagine that law can or should be made perfectly rational. In part, nonrational forces have a place in law simply because "law's terrain (and the lawyer's terrain) must be the realities of life, in all their tangled complexity."[22] Every actual society contains forces that undercut logical models and clear lines of authority. The world resists—or, more accurately, resistance is part of law's world—and what we end up with can rarely be reason's design alone. There is harsh conflict and imperfect compromise everywhere; reconciliation or coherence among social forces, to the extent there is any, often comes through mysterious dynamics and communal rituals of the sort that close the *Oresteia.* To use law effectively, we must be prepared to deal with those realities. We can improve law to serve our purposes, but we cannot expect an operating system of law to deliver all that can be imagined by our largest capacities for reason.

Nor is reason the only thing of value in a legal system. Undeniably, the goal of giving a more rational direction to human life is indispensable. But while the nonrational emotions can distort, delude, or blaze uncontrollably, they have worth in themselves and can also open, clarify, and enrich understanding. The values and achievements of a legal system—and of lawyers, judges, and citizens involved with a legal system—are shaped by what the emotions yield. Whether or not one is comfortable with Aeschylus' particular claim that the emotion of fear is indispensable to the legal order, this broader meaning of the Furies' inclusion in the legal order remains—and it is important to keep this meaning alive as the rationalist impulses in law drive ahead ever more insistently.

---

[21] California v. Brown, 107 S.Ct. 837, 841 (1987) (O'Connor, J., concurring) (emphasis omitted) (upholding a jury instruction directing the jury not to be "swayed by mere sentiment, conjecture, sympathy, passion, prejudice, public opinion or public feeling" in deciding whether to impose the death penalty).

[22] Gewirtz, *A Lawyer's Death,* 100 Harv.L.Rev. 2053, 2055 (1987).

These observations suggest one important connection between literature and law that is rarely made explicit. Literature makes its special claims upon us precisely because it nourishes the kinds of human understanding not achievable through reason alone but involving intuition and feeling as well. If, as the *Oresteia* suggests, law engages nonrational elements and requires the most comprehensive kinds of understanding, literature can play an important part in a lawyer's development. The inclusion of the Furies within the legal order—an inclusion that represents the linking of emotional spheres to law—links literature itself to law and underscores the special place literature can have in developing the legal mind to its fullest richness and complexity.

III.

An equally striking feature about the image of law in the *Oresteia* is that law is portrayed as a highly gendered phenomenon. Gender's role is pervasive in the trilogy. Clytemnestra is frequently described as manlike, and her lover "like a woman."[26] The Furies are pointedly all women. The members of the lay jury are all men. Apollo seeks to distinguish Orestes' murder of his mother from Clytemnestra's murder of her husband by arguing that a father's death is different from a mother's. The mother, Apollo says, is "no parent" but only a "nurse of the [father's] seed. . . . The parent is he who mounts."[27] Athena is a virgin goddess who has renounced marriage. And her own justification for voting in favor of Orestes' acquittal also seems to have a gender basis:

> There is no mother anywhere who gave me birth,
> and, but for marriage, I am always for the male
> with all my heart, and strongly on my father's side.
> So, in a case where the wife has killed her husband, lord
> of the house, her death shall not mean most to me.[28]

What is one to make of the role that gender plays in the trilogy? The strongest currents may well come from Greek religious mythology, in which male gods replaced female ones as the dominant rulers of the universe. But the role of gender in the *Oresteia* must also be understood within the main terms of the play itself, and therefore one must ask: what is gender's connection to the emergence of law?

Once again, the place of the Furies in relation to the legal order seems most basic. Aeschylus portrays the Furies as a female force. Most obviously, of course, they *are* female and identify with the female. In ad-

[26] Agamemnon (Lattimore trans.) I. 1625; *see* The Libation Bearers (Lattimore trans.) II. 304–05 ("since his heart is female").

[27] The Eumenides (Lattimore trans.) II. 659–60. * * *

[28] The Eumenides (Lattimore trans.) II. 736–40. * * *

dition, the Furies are the ones insisting upon a place for emotions—emotions of hurt and anger and terror, emotions they have been playing out within the blood relations of the family sphere. The emotions, as well as the family sphere, have conventionally been associated with the "female" (although terror itself has not). Within the scheme of the play, the Furies embody the female, or at least a version of the female.

The legal regime, on the other hand, is otherwise predominantly male. The day-to-day apparatus of the system, such as the lay jury, is all male; and the god of law, Apollo, is male. To be sure, Athena is female—a fact that undercuts any gender simplicities about the play[30]—but Athena is female of a particularly androgynous sort: a warrior, and one who "identifies with the male in all things" and utilizes decidedly pro-male decision rules as a judge. In addition to these explicitly male features, the legal regime emphasizes reason, public process, closure—things often associated with the "male."[31] Simplified a bit, then, the gendered scheme of the play is that the legal order, essentially male, displaces but then comes to include the female.

Finding suggestions of all this in the *Oresteia* is rather startling in light of the work of some feminists today that seeks to construct a critique of law as fundamentally expressing a male perspective, and in light of other contemporary arguments that the legal culture disadvantages and devalues the women included within it. It is worth looking a little closer, therefore, at what "inclusion" of the female means here. Myths illuminate origins, as well as present circumstances; and the effort to see clearly the world that literature reveals both measures and trains our ability to see clearly the rest of the world around us.

In the play's scheme, the alternative to inclusion is the Furies marginalized—remaining a roving band of vengeful females harassing the city and perpetuating blood feuds, or becoming permanent exiles. There is no doubt that Aeschylus portrays the solution of inclusion as far better. The play's forces are harmonized and resolved only when the female comes to be included—only when the male perspective and female perspective each secures a place of high honor, each contributing to the social order.

For all the ritualized harmony, though, the question remains whether this is a myth of gender reconciliation or really one of female subordination. It is a mistake, I think, to focus exclusively on the Furies' dis-

[30] Athena's large role highlights the quite limited role played by the male god, Apollo. Although Apollo is the god typically associated with law and civilization in Greek mythology, his role is surely no greater than Athena's in establishing the new system; in fact, he says nothing at all in the play after the verdict is announced, during the all-important phase when the status of the Furies within the legal order is being clarified.

[31] Carol Gilligan contrasts the male voice on moral questions, which tends to emphasize rights and individuation, with the female voice, which tends to emphasize the emotion of care and the web of social connection. *See generally* C. Gilligan, In a Different Voice (1982).

placement and loss at Orestes' trial, without taking account of their inclusion at the trilogy's end. But the gathering harmonies of the play's close should not blind us to the undercurrents that remind us that gendered relations almost always involve issues of power. For one thing, coercion shapes the Furies' inclusion. The terms of inclusion are crafted by Athena, who has just ruled against the Furies. Her argument to the Furies, which reads almost like a seduction, is that they can have a place of honor; and she proclaims at the play's end that "persuasion" has led to a consensual resolution in which the Furies agree to come on board.[36] But Athena has backed her arguments all along with threats of (male) violence:

> I have Zeus behind me. Do
>
> we need to speak of that? I am the only god
>
> who know[s] the keys to where his thunderbolts are locked.
>
> We do not need such, do we?[37]

In addition, the Furies clearly give up something in order to be included. They do receive honor and are told that "[n]o household shall be prosperous without your will."[38] But their exclusive jurisdiction has been clipped. Although the fear, vengeance, and other passions that they represent are given a central place in the new order the Furies' elemental "wild[ness]"[39] has been somewhat tamed. For the first time in the trilogy, the Furies call Zeus "all powerful";[40] they put their energies in the service of Zeus' goals. For all their honor, the Furies are called "guests of the state."[41] In short, although the system of law in the *Oresteia* incorporates the female and may even make female forces its steering spirits, the Furies lose something in this transformation. They may receive honor and devotions "for the rest of time,"[42] but for the most part they will serve the younger gods and a largely male regime.[43]

The drive for sex equality in our time, both within law and within the larger community, has largely focused on securing women's inclusion within institutions that were established predominantly for men. The *Oresteia* can be seen as a myth of inclusion: an affirmation that law is in-

[36] The Eumenides (Lattimore trans.) II. 970–72.

[37] *Id.* at II. 826–29.

[38] *Id.* at I. 895.

[39] *Id.* at I. 972.

[40] *Id.* at I. 918.

[41] *Id.* at I. 1011.

[42] *Id.* at I. 898.

[43] The Furies' subordinate status may provoke different responses depending upon which aspect of the Furies' role is emphasized. To the extent that the Furies represent certain nonrational forces, their inclusion with subordinate status is not especially troubling. To the extent that the Furies represent a version of the "female," their inclusion as subordinates has a harsher ring to modern ears. This tension arises in part, of course, because Aeschylus locates the female and the nonrational in the same entities.

complete without the female perspective, an affirmation of the necessary and central role of the "female" within law. But in Aeschylus' myth, the included female assumes an inferior place in the hierarchy. Thus, in the end, the gendered myth of the *Oresteia* is one that contains female privilege *and* female subordination within the legal order, a combination that we know can be insidious. In significant part, today's women's movement contends with the persistence of such stories. The current debate has largely moved beyond the question whether women should be included to questions about what the terms of inclusion should be. Is it enough if the traditional norms of traditionally male institutions are applied with true evenhandedness to women and men? Do these seemingly neutral norms express a "male" point of view and disadvantage women for that reason—suggesting that perhaps the norms themselves should change to accommodate a "female" perspective as equally valid? Such questions obviously move far beyond what the *Oresteia* addresses. But a reader today is encouraged to reflect upon them as the *Oresteia* tells its double-edged myth—affirming the indispensable importance of the female for law, yet locating the female in a subordinate place. As in other contexts, modern feminism has opened up new ways of hearing old tales.

IV.

A modern-day lawyer has almost a sense of awe in rediscovering an ancient literary masterpiece that contains such a richly evocative image of law. Judging, like system-building itself, is seen as pervaded with difficulties—among them the tension between the goal of reasoned judgment, which Athena proclaims, and the pull of personal allegiance, to which Athena in the end succumbs.[45] More fundamentally, at the very beginning of our tradition Aeschylus sees through to the complexity of the legal order's basic enterprise. Law is blessed in these plays as a great advance for civilization, but the system of law at its origin is tangled in a cluster of contradictions and clashing dualities: linked to the divine, but inescapably human; aspiring to objectivity, but finding subjectivity unavoidable; shaping the future, but tied irrevocably to the past; predominantly male, but steered by the female; following the cadence of reason, yet also the rhythm of terror. The image endures.

NOTES AND QUESTIONS

1. There is a burgeoning canon of works in the law and literature "movement" or school. One of the best reviews of the literature is by Richard Posner, "Law and Literature: A Relation Reargued," 72 Va.L.Rev. 1351 (1986). For other surveys see "Symposium: Law and Literature," 39 Mercer Law Review No. 3 (1988). Posner distinguishes between several subspecialities of law and literature, principally works which (1) seek to learn about the nature of law and legal actors from writing about the law by mas-

[45] *See, e.g.,* The Eumenides (Lattimore trans.) II. 735–38; *supra* note 28.

ters of literature, such as Shakespeare, Dickens, Melville, or Kafka, (2) works which try to apply to legal documents the methods of modern literary criticism, the better to explicate legal texts, or (3) works which try to borrow literary techniques from literary artists, encouraging their employment by legal writers, such as judges. Gewirtz's essay belongs in the first group, and its inclusion here as the sole representative of the law and literature movement needs some explanation. Probably the primary reason for using it is that it is short, pungent, well-written, and seems quite typical of the first sub-speciality of law and literature. For extended efforts along Gewirtz's suggested lines, see, e.g., Nan Goodman, Shifting the Blame: Literature, Law and the Theory of Accidents in Nineteenth Century America (1998), and Brook Thomas, Cross–Examinations of Law and Literature: Cooper, Hawthorne, Stowe, and Melville (1987).

It was thought that only the "masters of literature" sub-specialty need be represented for the following reasons. First, there are very powerful arguments for believing that the methods of literary criticism obscure rather than illuminate the meaning of legal texts. This case is made most forcefully in Posner's essay, supra, where he argues that the open-ended nature of modern literary criticism, both "deconstruction," and the work of the "New Critics," are inconsistent with the limited aims of the framers of statutes or constitutions. Nevertheless, for those wishing to explore this area, the arguments for and against it are to be found, e.g., in "Symposium: Law and Literature," 60 Texas Law Review 373 (1982), and "Interpretation Symposium," 58 S.Cal.L.Rev. 1 (1985). See also the attack on Posner by his law and literature nemesis Stanley Fish, "Don't Know Much About the Middle Ages: Posner on Law and Literature," 97 Yale L.J. 777 (1988). Posner's article appears as part of his book, Law and Literature: A Misunderstood Relation (1988). Some of Posner's further thoughts are to be found in Chapter 23, "Law and Literature Revisited," in his Overcoming Law 471–497 (1995). For more on Law and Literature in general and Richard Posner's take on them in particular, see, e.g., Guyora Binder & Robert Weisberg, Literary Criticisms of Law (2000), Richard A. Posner, "What Has Modern Literary Theory to Offer Law?", 53 Stan.L.Rev. 195 (2000)(reviewing Binder & Weisberg's book), Guyora Binder, "The Poetics of the Pragmatic: What *Literary Criticisms of Law* Offers Posner," 53 Stan.L.Rev. 1509 (2001)(replying to Posner's review), Deirdre N. McCloskey, "The Essential Rhetoric of Law, Literature, and Liberty," 5 Critical Review 201 (1992)(Discussing Posner, Fish, and White).

Second, the works of those who seek to use the methods of modern literary criticism to analyze legal documents are often very similar or identical to the work of CLS, which we have already studied. See, e.g., Gary Peller, "The Metaphysics of American Law," 73 Cal.L.Rev. 1151, 1160 n. 6, 1171–74 (1985), where a CLS scholar uses what Posner calls "Vulgar deconstructionism" in order to suggest that the provision in article II, section 1 of the Constitution which requires that the President of the United States be at least 35 years old might be able to be ignored when a person less than 35 could demonstrate the maturity or wisdom which the framers must have been looking for.

With regard to the omission of the third sub-specialty; the idea of teaching judges (or lawyers) to write in a manner which more closely emulated literature is somewhat removed from the focus of this chapter—the argument over the proper pedagogical perspective for law professors and law students. There can be no certainty about this, however, and the interested student is directed to pursue this subspecialty in Posner's essay itself. Moreover, the teaching of better writing to lawyers and judges is probably the mission of the most significant, graceful, and prolific of the law and literature scholars, James Boyd White (see, e.g. The Legal Imagination: Studies in the Nature of Legal Thought and Expression (1983), Heracles' Bow: Essays on the Rhetoric and Poetics of the Law (1985), and When Words Lose Their Meaning: Constitutions and Reconstitutions of Language, Character, and Community (1984)), so this is an area that is neglected at some risk.

There are surely problems with the first sub-speciality of current law-and-literature writing as well, most notably the grasp of law demonstrated by the masters of literature. Dickens's and Kafka's characterizations of legal process, for example, may or may not have actually borne strong similarities to the actual legal systems of their times, whether or not their work was great literature. Nevertheless, do you see how a work like Gewirtz's seems closely related to the ideological battles being waged between the practitioners of CLS and law-and-economics? Furthermore, it seems fitting to include in this last Chapter a work which recalls the classical Greeks, since their thinking profoundly influenced, as we have seen, American lawyers and judges in the eighteenth and nineteenth century. Gewirtz demonstrates that we are still participating in a conversation with the ancients, on topics of concern to the past, present, and future.

2. Gewirtz writes that he wants to address two themes, "passion" and "gender." How do these illuminate the issues we have been exploring in this Chapter and earlier in the book? To begin with "passion," do you understand how anyone committed to an understanding of the history of American (or any other law) neglects the force of "passion" in human affairs at his or her peril? Gewirtz suggests that the establishment of "Athena's Court" at the end of the *Oresteia,* represents "movement from a world of passion and subjectivity toward a regime that, in form at least, empowers a more detached authority influenced by reason." Would you say that the modern American legal system, or American legal history as a whole, represents a movement from passion to reason? Would a practitioner of CLS? Would a law-and-economics scholar? Would Gewirtz? What do you make of his reading of Aeschylus which suggests that in his use of the Furies in Athena's new legal system for Athens Aeschylus is making a "large claim about law: law and passion are inseparable?" Is this accurate? Would it make you feel better about our legal system if you believed that "Channeled through law, vengeance and hate speak through the one strong voice of civil authority?" Is there a place for "vengeance and hate" in our legal system? Is this, perhaps, cold Hobbesian realism of a kind which Morton Horwitz decried in an excerpt you read in the last Chapter, or is this some other, "romantic" conception of the law? Would Carrington or Gordon approve?

3. Gewirtz moves beyond mere vengeance and hate in his grappling with passion and reason as exemplified by the furies, and proceeds to associate their incorporation in Athens's legal system, pursuant to Aeschylus's main theme as a dramatist, "Wisdom comes alone through suffering," in the words of the chorus in the *Agamemnon.* Is Aeschylus right on this? If he is, have you suffered enough to gain such wisdom? Did reading this casebook, particularly the Notes and Questions, help you?

4. You will have noticed that Gewirtz himself becomes quite passionate when he laments the fact that "advocates for reason's preeminent role in law remain ascendant virtually everywhere," and selects, among others, the law-and-economics movement for excoriation on this point. What, precisely, are we supposed to put in place, according to Gewirtz, of "reason's preeminent role in law?" What does Gewirtz mean by "mysterious dynamics and communal rituals," and are they to take the place of reason in his ideal modern legal system? How, according to Gewirtz, is the study of law and literature crucial to an understanding of the limitations of reason in a legal system? How do you suppose Gewirtz would explain the fact that Richard Posner, who has probably done more study of law and literature than all but a few legal academics, is still firmly committed to the rational endeavor of "law-and-economics?"

5. Turning to Gewirtz's second theme, the place of "gender" in the *Oresteia,* and in law generally, does it surprise you that he begins with the assertion that "law" or "reason" is generally regarded (even by some feminists) as "male," and that "emotion" is generally regarded as "female?" Do you agree with these characterizations, and whether you do or not, what would be their significance if they were generally accepted? More important, do you agree with Gewirtz's main point on gender in the *Oresteia,* that while female privilege becomes included in the legal order, so does female subordination? Gewirtz seems implicitly to suggest that the condition of female subordination in the law might still be with us, and that this is the concern of modern feminists who study the legal system. We explore this concern, and some of these feminists, in the next Section.

6. In the early 1990's, an entirely new field of "postrealist" jurisprudence emerged, which appears to combine some of the insights of the law and literature movement with those of critical legal studies. This was "Critical Race Theory." See generally Richard Delgado and Jean Stefancic, "Critical Race Theory: An Annotated Bibliography," 79 Va.L.Rev. 461 (1993), and Robert L. Hayman, Jr. and Nancy Levit, Jurisprudence: Contemporary Readings, Problems, and Narratives 383–451 (1995). Critical Race Theory appears to borrow from critical legal studies the conclusion about the indeterminacy of legal experience, and from Law and Literature the awareness of the power of narrative. Thus, much of Critical Race Theory work has involved the writing of stories, often of a highly personal nature, which seek to demonstrate alternative perspectives from which to construct a juster society. As Richard Delgado, an early and leading Critical Race Theorist explains, "stories, parables, chronicles, and narratives are powerful means for destroying mindset—the

bundle of presuppositions, received wisdoms, and shared understandings against a background of which legal and political discourse takes place . . . [s]tories can shatter complacency and challenge the status quo." Richard Delgado, "Storytelling for Oppositionists and Others: A Plea for Narrative," 87 Mich.L.Rev. 2411 (1989). Does your "mindset" need destroying? For a dissent from Delgado's View, see Daniel A. Farber & Suzanna Sherry, "Telling Stories Out of School: An Essay on Legal Narratives," 45 Stan.L.Rev. 807 (1993), and, for further defense of storytelling in reply to Farber and Sherry, see Jane B. Baron, "Resistance to Stories," 67 S.Cal.L.Rev. 255 (1994), and William N. Eskridge, Jr., "Gaylegal Narratives," 46 Stan.L.Rev. 607 (1994). Was Aeschylus, or for that matter, Gewirtz, engaged in legal "storytelling?" Are the feminist theorists we next consider? For further reading on storytelling, see, e.g., Jane B. Baron, "The Many Promises of Storytelling in Law," 23 Rutgers L.J. 79 (1991), Symposium, "Legal storytelling," 87 Mich.L.Rev. 2073 (1989), Symposium, "Pedagogy of Narrative," 40 J.Legal Educ. 1 (1990).

E. TOWARDS A FEMINIST THEORY OF LAW

SYLVIA A. LAW, EQUALITY: THE POWER AND THE LIMITS OF THE LAW (A REVIEW ESSAY ON ZILLAH R. EISENSTEIN, FEMINISM AND SEXUAL EQUALITY (1984))*

95 Yale Law Journal 1769 (1986).

Feminist theory provides a rich source of insight into the power and limits of the law in molding social relations. The feminist critique touches every institution of human life, casting new light on the ways in which we experience ourselves and the world. * * * Zillah R. Eisenstein provides an eloquent contribution to feminist theory. She contrasts feminism with the range of other contemporary American political thought—liberalism, conservatism, neoconservatism, the Old and New Right. She offers a trenchant critique of the contemporary revision of and reaction to the feminist challenge to a sexist society, analyzes recent developments in electoral politics as largely a response to the potentially radical implications of mainstream feminist claims, and articulates an affirmative vision of social relations that will interest anyone who cares about a better world, not just for women, but for people and families in general. The first half of this review examines Eisenstein's central points: her vision of feminism, her critique of contemporary revisions of feminism, and the complex relationships between feminism and other dominant political and economic ideologies. The second half of the review attempts to make the abstractions of these competing world views more concrete by applying them to one specific social problem—the care of the old.

I. A STATEMENT OF FEMINISM

Although Eisenstein's book is dense and expansive, she keeps clear focus on several core insights which together constitute the feminist challenge to patriarchy. Such clarity is difficult to achieve, because the central ideas of feminism are each complex and, at a superficial level, sometimes appear to conflict. Briefly, these are the six complex concepts that Eisenstein keeps in the air and juggles in intricate patterns:

Individual women's steady demands for equality and liberty appeal to ideals of justice shared across the political spectrum and have serious potential for radical social change.[3]

Gender is socially constructed, i.e., the culture, the law, and the material relationships within and between the family and marketplace all give deep meaning to gender.

A core aspect of the social construction of gender is that culture and law[5] assign women responsibility for the socially and economically necessary work of nurturing, childrearing, managing household consumption, and providing domestic labor.[6]

Although the meaning of gender is socially defined, "identity is both a biological, material reality and simultaneously a part of a sex-gendered system;" the female body—distinguished by its capacity for childbearing—must be central to any feminist political theory.[7]

The state and the law institutionalize male power by mystifying the division between public and private life as one of "natural" sexual difference, enforcing the separation of public and private life and with it the distinctness of male and female existence.[8]

Although the patriarchal character of the state and the law requires feminists who seek to use state power as a vehicle for social change to exercise caution, struggles within the law are nonetheless important for feminists seeking to achieve both material and ideological change.[9]

The claim that the law should treat women and men as individuals, not as members of a sexually determined class, necessarily denies that gender differences are natural or immutable. Our concepts of gender, and particularly our ideas about motherhood and sexuality, cast man as strong, woman subservient; man as irresponsible for family care, woman as nurturant; man as sexually aggressive, and woman as victim, whether virgin or whore. In Simone de Beauvoir's classic words, "One is not born,

---

[3] P. 12.

[5] P. 108.

[6] P. 146.

[7] P. 216. * * *

[8] P. 92. * * *

[9] Pp. 99–100.

but rather becomes, a woman."[11] Yet although feminism begins with the basic claim that these gender differences are not natural, and liberty and equality should extend to women, feminism has, Eisenstein argues, implications far more radical than simply extending liberal rights to women. The social construction of gender shapes not only our ideas about who we are, but the social and economic arrangements that determine the texture of our daily lives. Under the *normal* prevailing arrangements of market and family, the price a woman pays for the warmth, support and legitimacy of family is to subordinate her capacity to achieve and contribute in the public world to the nurturing needs of children, parents and men.[12] Further, because the structure of the law and the state differentiates between the public and private, the market and home, claims to liberty and equality have value only in this traditional male world of market and public life. The morality of motherhood is one of giving, connection and self-sacrifice, while the morality of the male world is one of achievement, autonomy and self-interest.[13] The prevailing social construction of gender means that normal economic relations systematically deny the worth of traditional women's work in the home and wage market.[14]

Thus individual women's claims for formal equality in the traditional male world are radical because the working mother embodies the contradiction between the liberal promise of equality in public and market life and the reality that our liberal society depends upon the unpaid work performed by women in the home. But individual claims for formal equality alone are insufficient to achieve either liberty or equality. Within the context of socially constructed gender, rights of formal equality can only help the exceptional individual who, in some limited respect, transcends the pervasive constraints of social construction. Individual claims do not dismantle the social meaning of gender. Indeed, insofar as such claims aid women seeking access to traditional male roles on male terms, traditional female virtues are implicitly devalued further. Recognizing formal rights to individual equality, without dismantling the institutional relations supporting the social construction of gender, can in fact exacerbate the vulnerability of women.[16]

---

[11] S. de Beauvoir, The Second Sex 267 (1957).

[12] P. 37.

[13] P. 34.

[14] For my discussion of these issues, see Law, *Woman, Work, Welfare, and the Preservation of Patriarchy,* 131 U.Pa.L.Rev. 1249, 1282–1335 (1983).

[16] For example, courts often limit alimony or support to women who have worked in the home for many years, assuming that when marriage ends, the woman can support herself. A Florida court, denying alimony to a homemaker of 21 years, said "In this day and time, women are as well educated and trained in the arts, sciences, and professions as are their male counterparts." Beard v. Beard, 262 So.2d 269, 272 (Fla.Dist.Ct.App.1972).

More generally, see L. Weitzman, The Divorce Revolution: The Unexpected Social and Economic Consequences for Women and Children in America (1985). Using Bureau of Labor Statistics data, Weitzman shows that following divorce the standard of living of men improves by 42%, while that of women declines by 73%, and argues that the movement to no-fault divorce has dis-

Eisenstein argues that liberalism, capitalism, and patriarchy are tightly interdependent. All assume a sharp division between altruism and competition, home and market, private and public, economy and state, passion and reason, women and men. If, as feminists claim, the distinctions between women and men are suspect, then perhaps so are the other distinctions.[17] To challenge gender inequality is to challenge the institutions it supports. As women enter the wage market and encounter sexual bias, including the expectation that they will continue to bear the responsibilities for home and children, they discover that our social arrangements cannot fulfill promises of individual equality without profound structural change.

Despite the limitations of formal liberal rights, struggles within the law are an important part of the process of challenging patriarchal privilege. They heighten the contradiction between the law's promise of neutrality and equality and the reality that liberalism and capitalism depend on patriarchy. Further, apart from its ideological function, the law also "structures choices, options, and so on, and in this sense has a real, material presence that at one and the same time mystifies other concrete relations of power."[18] For example, the law determines whether abortion is prosecuted as a crime or protected as a constitutional right. Women's claim to reproductive liberty is critical materially and ideologically; to claim reproductive freedom is to reject social norms that label women as victims, virgins or self-sacrificing mothers.[19] Similarly, the state controls the terms on which social forms of child care or nurturing services are available, and thus profoundly shapes women's lives.

Combining the threads of these six analytic skeins, Eisenstein weaves two rich tapestries. In the first she criticizes other feminists who would cabin the radical implications of the forces they have helped to unleash by dropping one or another of the essential elements of the feminist challenge to patriarchy. In the second she analyzes the recent ascendance of New Right and neoconservative power in Washington, arguing that these developments confirm the power of the feminist challenge to patriarchy.

---

advantaged women. Some, such as Schrag, Book Review, The Nation, Dec. 7, 1985, at 620, characterize these facts as "one of the great embarrassments of the modern feminist movement." This of course ignores that most divorced women have always been disadvantaged economically and that feminists were only one small ambivalent voice supporting the movement away from fault-based divorce. *See* Babcock, Cases and Materials on Women and the Law 261–88 (1974); *see also* Fineman, *Implementing Equality: Ideology, Contradiction, and Social Change,* 1983 Wis.L.Rev. 789.

[17] P. 12.

[18] P. 99.

[19] P. 34.

II. Feminist Revisionism

Sexual equality challenges the social meaning of gender and requires radical change in our legal and economic order. Radical change is both scary and difficult to achieve. Today, many feminists feel discouraged and overwhelmed by attempts to seize opportunities traditionally reserved for men while continuing to bear the responsibilities traditionally assigned to women. Some respond by blaming feminism for extending false promises. Others suggest revisions of core feminist claims.

Eisenstein identifies two major strains of feminist revisionism. The first claims, in various ways, that perceived sex-based differences are natural and inherent, rather than socially constructed. The second denies the radical nature of feminism by characterizing the challenge of sexual equality as a simple matter of individual claims to fair treatment and choice. Eisenstein helps us to evaluate these revisions, urging us to reject their flaws and to reaffirm our demand for meaningful equality.

Some feminists, observing that formal equality has failed to empower women and has implicitly devalued traditional women's work and lives, assert that women and men are naturally, essentially different, and that the feminist task should be to enhance traditional women's roles. Although the reasons for this development are understandable, Eisenstein urges us to hold fast to the insight that gender differences are socially constructed. A *feminist* affirmation that women and men are naturally and essentially different seriously undercuts the individual claim to formal equality. But more important, blurring the differences between biology and culture disguises the economic and political constructs that give meaning to gender.

The impulse to affirm that some gender differences are natural is particularly strong in relation to motherhood and sexuality. Again, this is understandable. There is, of course, a material reality to the biological difference between the sexes in relation to reproduction. Yet the social construction of sexuality and motherhood are core mechanisms by which patriarchal culture attaches social meaning to gender. Adrienne Rich observes that "[t]he body has been made so problematic for women that it has often seemed easier to shrug it off and travel as a disembodied spirit."[21] Eisenstein simultaneously affirms that the biological capacity for reproduction distinguishes men from women, while seeking to dismantle oppressive constructions of the meaning of this difference. She challenges us to develop a politics that neither denies biology nor uses it to justify prevailing social relations.

Eisenstein argues that motherhood is political, as well as biological. She criticizes those—across the political spectrum—who claim that "mothering" comes naturally to women, as well as those, such as Betty

---

[21] A. Rich, of Woman Born: Motherhood as Experience and Institution 40 (1976).

Friedan, who treat motherhood solely as a matter of individual choice and underestimate the social arrangements that constrain choice.

Similarly, some feminists respond to the political and personal dangers of sexuality by rejecting the notion that feminism is concerned, in a central way, with sexuality. Eisenstein critiques others who regard sexuality as critical to gender hierarchy, but who describe gender-based differences in relation to sexuality as essential, biological differences between women and men. Andrea Dworkin, for example, says that "[t]he immutable self of the male boils down to an utterly unselfconscious parasitism,"[25] and that "[t]error issues forth from the male, illuminates his essential nature and his basic purpose."[26] Women, by contrast, "are booty, along with gold and jewels and territory and raw materials."[27] Somewhat more subtly, Catharine MacKinnon claims that "male morality sees that which maintains its power as good, that which undermines or qualifies it or questions its absoluteness as evil,"[28] and argues that "[w]omen and men are divided by gender, made into the sexes as we know them, by the social requirements of heterosexuality, which institutionalizes male sexual dominance and female sexual submission. If this is true, sexuality is the linchpin of gender inequality."[29]

Eisenstein retorts: "[I]t is not helpful to set up a causal relation between sexuality and gender."[30] Both are constructed out of series of social relations that define the other's meanings. To assume that "there is such a *thing* as sex, or sexuality (in some natural—presocial—form)" avoids the true issue of *how* both sexuality and gender are constructed.[31]

Authentic communication about sex is enormously difficult. Our understanding of sexuality—the social and individual influences on choice of sex object, sources of lust, and connections between passion and relationship—is breathtakingly primitive. The feminist and gay effort to explore, intellectually and experientially, the gendered social meaning attached to sexuality provides a weapon for those who would defend a *status quo* that is puritanical, as well as patriarchal.

The second major form of feminist revisionism is the tendency to undercut the radical potential of feminism's challenge to patriarchy by asserting that women are capable of achieving liberty or equality one by one. This view characterizes women's claims for equality as matters of individual choice, without acknowledging, indeed, even denying, that "pa-

[25] A. Dworkin, Pornography: Men Possessing Women 13 (1981).

[26] *Id.* at 16.

[27] *Id.*

[28] MacKinnon, *Not a Moral Issue,* 2 Yale L. & Pol'y Rev. 501, 511 (1984).

[29] MacKinnon, *Feminism, Marxism, Method, and the State: An Agenda for Theory,* 7 Signs 515, 533 (1982) (footnote omitted).

[30] P. 152.

[31] *Id.* (emphasis in original).

triarchy, capitalism, and racism impose constraints on individual freedom."[33] For example, Betty Friedan has said, " '[o]ur own self-denigration of ourselves as women and perhaps our own fears *are the main problem.*' "

Feminists who embrace this individualistic approach share Jean Elshtain's belief that "equality of opportunity and equality of treatment are ultimately incompatible." But those feminists who would limit women's demands to equality of opportunity do not recognize that so much must be remade to make opportunities really equal, including the very standards by which results are judged. Feminists, and the civil rights movement generally, challenge supposed meritocratic standards that are defined in white, male terms. We can applaud the notion that excellence, hard work and diligence deserve reward and recognition, yet condemn standards of distinction that systematically exclude women and people of color. We need a concept of equality that values nurturing and relationship, not as inherent differences between women and men, but as human strengths that have been devalued by being removed from the market and assigned to people removed from the market. To challenge allegedly neutral standards of quality for neglecting virtues of care and connection is not to deny the value of merit-based reward, but to use a richer concept of worth.

In sum, Eisenstein provides a powerful account of feminism, incorporating a traditional liberal respect for individual rights with an understanding that patriarchy denies equality, not simply on an individual basis, but systematically through the social construction of gender.

III. NEOPATRIARCHY

Eisenstein's analysis of New Right and neoconservative ideology helps us to understand that the fury of conservative reaction to feminism does not show we are on the wrong track or have "gone too far," but confirms the radical implications of women's basic claims for liberty and equality. There is broad support for these claims. If change at times seems slow in coming, it is not because of the strategic or intellectual failings of feminists, but because a powerful minority has mobilized energetically to preserve its privilege.

The New Right and neoconservatives have shared political power in Washington for several years. Their agenda is obviously complex. Eisenstein takes issue with progressive analysts who explain the Reagan Administration's assault on working people and the poor solely in class terms, arguing that the Administration also seeks to restabilize patriarchy by making it more difficult for women and children to survive without a man.

[33] P. 195.

The New Right shares with feminism the understanding that the patriarchal family and prevailing economic structures are tightly related. Both understand that the paid labor market is structured on the assumption that workers, i.e. men, are supported by family, i.e. women, who meet their daily emotional and material needs, as well as care for the vulnerable young and old. Both perceive that the exponential increase in the number of married women and mothers in the wage market poses a profound threat to these basic arrangements.

Even people who consider it "natural" that women do the unpaid work in the home hold that in the marketplace "[p]eople are supposedly individuals, not members of a sexual class. Hard work is supposed to be rewarded. When the married woman enters the market, she embodies a contradiction. As a worker she is supposedly an individual, and as a married woman she is a member of a sexual class."[37] As these women begin to recognize the sexual bias of the marketplace and continue to bear the responsibilities of housework and child care as well, they discover that society cannot deliver on its promise of equality or even equal rights for women.[38]

The New Right's response to this is contradictory. They affirm that equality of opportunity exists for anyone willing to work hard, yet at the same time they insist that men and women are naturally different. Some members of the New Right would reject norms of sex-based equality even in the marketplace. George Gilder, for example, argues that even though sex-based differences are natural and fundamental, social policy must reinforce them to preserve the traditional family. Men must be given preference in wage labor and public life to reinforce male dominance in the family and familial dependence upon them. The patriarchal family, moreover, is essential to curb men's natural tendencies toward aggression.[39] The New Right also rejects liberty of sexuality and sexual preference "as breeding sexual license and hedonism and a breakdown of the (heterosexual, monogamous) family life."[40] The New Right's economic program seeks, in part, to reconstruct the patriarchal family by alleviating the twin burdens of taxes and inflation, thereby freeing married women from the need to earn a "second" income.[41]

The New Right also shares with feminism a rejection of the liberal dichotomy between public and private spheres, with sexuality and family defined as "private" matters properly distinct from the "public" concerns of political life. In its place the New Right promotes a culturally and legally enforced ideal of the patriarchal family. But the feminist challenge

[37] P. 51.

[38] P. 41.

[39] P. 55. Gilder says, "the movement is striking at the Achilles' heel of civilized society: the role of the male." G. Gilder, Sexual Suicide 193–94 (1973).

[40] P. 56.

[41] P. 46.

to the public/private dichotomy is more complex. Feminists criticize the state's role in patriarchy, yet at the same time insist that collective responses are needed to protect vulnerable people and to organize the work that the patriarchal culture has traditionally assigned to women. Like feminism, the New Right is radically subversive to the modern liberal state because it "demystifies the place of sex and family life within the political order by challenging the private/public split on these issues."[42]

Neoconservatives share the New Right's distress at the feminist challenge to existing arrangements but are less willing to use direct state power to preserve the patriarchal family. Instead, neoconservatives seek to save liberalism from the "excesses" of equality and liberty.[43] "[T]he crisis of liberalism is not merely a political crisis, it is also a cultural problem. The individual, which is the root concern of liberalism, has begun to be hedonistically centered on himself, or more likely herself . . . [, representing] the troublesome extension of liberal individualism."[44] To save us from these excesses, neoconservatives would reject the changes in social arrangements that make liberty and equality possible. For example, neoconservatives would dismantle the social programs of the New Society, which, they argue, create unreasonable expectations and weaken the "mediating structures"—family, church and community—that stand between individual and state.[45] Neoconservatives ignore the fact that these mediating structures run on the voluntary labor of women. They condemn affirmative action, which they characterize as demanding equal results for people of unequal merit. Neoconservatives believe that a race in and of itself requires winners and losers, and "the problem is that everyone today claims the right to win."[46] However, they do not recognize that the market and political system are structured to favor elite, white men, who have a team, i.e., the family and old boy network, in the pit to pass water and cheer them on.

In addition, many neoconservatives now affirm that gender differences are natural.[47] Midge Decter, for example, argues that women need heterosexual marriage, not solely for economic reasons, but to put "a lid on their freedom."[48] She explains, "[f]or the middle-class woman her opportunities to participate in the world beyond household—to educate herself, limit her family, go to work, and to an unprecedented extent make

42 P. 82.

43 P. 62. * * *

44 P. 78.

45 P. 69.

46 P. 63.

47 P. 80.

48 P. 78.

her life—have left her in a sometimes nearly overwhelming state of uncertainty."[49]

The Reagan strategy, while causing enormous pain to millions of people, cannot reconstruct the patriarchal family. Too much has changed, both in the economy and in the aspirations of women and men. The neoconservative effort to preserve the patriarchal family confuses cause and effect. Neoconservatives assert that the welfare state has destroyed traditional family and wage labor relationships, when in fact profound changes in family and work have created both the need and the desire for dual wage-earning families and welfare state programs.

Jobs that allow a single wage-earner to support a patriarchal family are no longer available for most people due to structural changes in the labor force, principally the massive shift of jobs from unionized industrial work to nonunionized, low paid service and retail-trade work.[50] "[M]ultinationals have shifted amortization funds overseas to the strategic handful of export platforms whose political regimes maintain a combination of literate skilled labour with low wages. . . . "[51] Our society has become increasingly dichotomized between the wealthy and the poor. The middle class is vanishing. These changes in the economy prevent a return to the patriarchal home with daddy in the marketplace and mommy baking cookies for the kids and gramps, even were this return thought desirable.

Most people, however, do not see the patriarchal family as optimal. Certainly families, and particularly women, struggling with the dual burdens of maintaining a career and a family, understand the acute need to change prevailing arrangements. Today most women do not want a lifetime of unpaid work in the home and economic dependence on a man. * * * Indeed, most men do not want a lifetime burden of supporting a dependent, patriarchal family.

IV. GROWING OLD IN AMERICA: METHODOLOGY AND ANALYSIS APPLIED

Consider—in very general terms—how the various ideologies Eisenstein describes can be employed to illuminate one concrete problem. The American population is getting old. Since 1900, the proportion of the population over 65 has grown from 4% to 11%; if present trends continue, 22% of the population will be over 65 by 2050. Assuming zero population growth, the proportion of older people in the non-working population will increase from approximately 25% in 1980 to about 40% by 2025. While care of the old is of course a timeless problem, our current demographic

---

[49] M. Decter, The New Chastity and Other Arguments Against Women's Liberation 51 (1972).

[50] P. 49.

[51] Davis, *The Political Economy of Late-Imperial America,* New Left Rev., Jan.–Feb. 1984, at 6, 15–16. * * *

patterns presage an era when large numbers of older people will be dependent upon a younger generation that is relatively much smaller. * * *

At any one time, about one third of all people over age 65 require some regular form of support services. Older people experience great uncertainty and anxiety about their ability to obtain services if and when needed. The overwhelming majority of older people are women, with this percentage increasing with age.

The care of the old, like the care of the young, is performed by women. Our patriarchal culture has created in women a deeply internalized sense of personal responsibility to care for friends and families in times of need. This "feminine" virtue is both a tremendous strength and a burden. Women spend much time caring for elderly family members, friends and neighbors: giving personal care, shopping and running errands, maintaining households and finances, coordinating and monitoring services from other sources, and filling in when other care arrangements break down. In addition, women also constitute the vast majority of paid workers who care for the old, either at home or in institutions. In terms of pay and status, the work these women perform shares the bottom of the occupational hierarchy with the work of women who care for children. * * *

Providing care for old people is costly. Individuals bearing this responsibility do so at high personal cost, either financially or in terms of lost opportunities to do other forms of work. Although we devote substantial public resources to care for the old, services fall far short of need.

Both the New Right and the neoconservatives oppose public funding for programs supporting or supplementing family-based services, both because such programs undermine "voluntary" patriarchal structures and because they cost money, inescapably requiring either higher taxes or reductions in defense spending. They view the care of elderly people as the responsibility of family, church, and community organizations. For example, a 1980 House report on the needs of the aged decries the decrease in women's participation in voluntary community service, arguing that "a shift back to such a natural system as the voluntary sector is in order." The report predicted that the "rate of increase in the proportion of women working outside the home . . . would slacken." This prediction proved wrong. Women continue to need and seek paid work; the status and support for voluntary work have not increased. For reasons suggested above, neither the neoconservatives' wistful desire to reinvigorate the patriarchal family, nor the New Right's more aggressive program to do so, is likely to succeed.

As the economic gap between the rich and the poor grows, it is possible that those on the winning side of the widening gulf will have greater retirement income or more comprehensive employment-related insurance benefits for the custodial services they will need in old age. But private insurance benefits for such care are rare today, and are too costly ever to be widespread. For the vast majority of us, particularly women, it is wholly unrealistic to expect that we will retire with sufficient income or insurance to purchase essential supportive services. In short, the New Right and neoconservative visions for the elderly are bleak for all but the very rich.

Contrast with these a variety of feminist visions for caring for the elderly in America. Feminists who embrace the value of differences between men and women would celebrate women's culture and morality of nurture and care. Frail elderly women, and those wage workers and family members who care for them, are largely silent and invisible today. Giving voice to these women's stories through poetry, prose, movies, movements, news and networks is vitally important to enhance the individual and social appreciation of this traditional women's culture. But, Eisenstein argues, glorification of a "private" world of love, care and nurture will not empower the women who live both in those private worlds and the public worlds of landlords, doctors, nursing homes, Medicaid and Medicare, which are in turn shaped by even larger forces of tax policy, public finance, the national and international flow of capital and labor and more.

Other feminists who argue that women should be "free to choose" the work and roles traditionally reserved for men or for women fail to appreciate the extent to which the world must be remade in order to make the choice real. That is not to say that liberal legal rights have no role to play in expanding choice. Rights can increase women's access to traditional male jobs that provide the compensation, insurance and retirement benefits that support a measure of security in old age. Legal rights could increase the value attached to nurturing work through Social Security for homemakers, more adequate welfare programs, support payments at the end of marriage that recognize the value of traditional women's work, and expanded public support for nurturing leaves from wage work.

But the content of legal rights that shape the options and choices available to us is determined through political struggle. Even the most fundamental negative rights, such as the right to speak or to control our bodies free from government constraint, acquire concrete meaning only as people act collectively to claim them. And negative rights are more easily enforced than affirmative liberties. Rights that do not impose direct dollar costs on a public budget are easier to protect than those that require public expenditures. Also, however difficult it is to create and implement public entitlements to material support, a right to a check is more easily affectuated than a right to a caring and supportive human relationship.

Older people, and those who care for them, need material support. But social support for families traditionally has been available only after the "voluntary" services of family and friends are exhausted. Powerful fiscal and human considerations support this traditional preference and argue for public services that bolster, rather than supplant, voluntary family based care.

All these factors demand collective action, both to generate the political support for the programs that would give content to "choice" for older people and to explore the borders between voluntary family-based services and their exhaustion. Feminist consciousness raising can serve both these functions.

Eisenstein characterizes consciousness raising as the methodology of feminism[77] and recognizes that through it women develop a sense of collective power "in actual struggle against patriarchal privilege."[78] Feminist consciousness raising is a process of self-reflection and action that values women's personal experience and understands that experience as political. It is "break[ing] out of . . . accustomed ways of responding to domination by acting as if [we] could change things."[80]

Powerful forces deter active feminist consciousness raising. Women who bear the dual burden of family care and undervalued wage labor have too few hours in a day for sleep, much less for attending these sessions. Furthermore, patriarchal culture discourages feminist consciousness raising: In male dominated institutions, women are rewarded for being one of the boys and punished for seeking common cause and understanding with other women. Yet widespread consciousness raising could ultimately lead to collective action aimed at changing these circumstances.

In the early 1970's consciousness raising played a critical role in the rise of feminism. Thousands of women—mostly young, white and middle class—achieved new understandings of their lives and our world. Work experiences in which they had been denied responsibility were now understood not as personal failures or bad luck but as examples of the pervasive assumption that men necessarily are better at certain jobs. Daily life provided material for urgent inquiry. Can women in traditionally male jobs express honest emotion without undermining our already fragile credibility? Can we build both commitment and adventure in loving relations? How can men be persuaded to share responsibility for childcare? For many women the consciousness raising experience inspired actions that changed the course of their lives.

Such groups were not the only, or perhaps even the most significant, forms of feminist consciousness raising. The thousands of women who, in the early 1970's, bore witness to the experience of illegal abortions engaged in a form of consciousness raising that radically transformed the

[77] P. 151.

[78] P. 154.

[80] Sparer, *Fundamental Human Rights, Legal Entitlements, and the Social Struggle: A Friendly Critique of the Critical Legal Studies Movement,* 36 Stan.L.Rev. 509, 557–58 (1984) (emphasis deleted).

law. Women who join together to create a community of psychic and material support against rape and domestic violence are engaged in consciousness raising. In many businesses, unions and schools, women help each other to comprehend their situation in feminist terms and act pursuant to that understanding.

Both older women and the women who care for them, in families and the wage market, require consciousness raising to generate courage and energy to demand needed social support services. The patriarchal vision that the family (i.e., women) cares for the old hinders the development of social responses to the needs of the elderly and disabled, just as it hinders the development of social supports for the care of children. Younger women need consciousness raising to sort out the difference between affirmative desire to help and burdens imposed by a gendered culture and enforced by resentment and guilt. If younger women, raised in an era of sexual liberation, need consciousness raising to figure out what we really want to do with that liberty, then surely a similar process is essential to empower older women to understand their needs for affection, human warmth, and sexuality and to explore how those needs can be met.

Exploring the social meaning of gender, analytically and experientially, is hard work. As social beings, our identities, needs, responsibilities, feelings, pains and pleasures do not spring fully formed from some internal, individual core; rather, they are shaped by social relationships. As feminists we need to struggle openly with these issues. We need to talk with others who share both a basic commitment to the worth of women and the experiences that are common to women. We need consciousness raising because we live in a culture in which great meaning is attached to gender. Such sharing produces insight and builds community, which in turn generates energy and courage for transformative change.

Zillah Eisenstein provides us with a strong statement of the theory of feminism. Analysis is important, but more is needed to move us from theory to action to power. Through mechanisms such as consciousness raising, Eisenstein's theoretical framework can provide the foundation for great social progress toward sexual equality.

NOTES AND QUESTIONS

1. What is "Feminism," and how would one go about building a "Feminist Theory of Law?" Is it necessary, for example, to believe that current American society is a "Patriarchy," in order to articulate a Feminist theory? Of what importance is biology to Feminism or Feminist Legal Theory? Does Professor Law or Professor Eisenstein have an understanding of the role of women in society similar to that expressed by Professor Gewirtz or to that expressed by Aeschylus? How much of women's societal role is culturally determined, and how much biologically determined?

2. Do you understand how Gordon could write in his letter to Presser, which you read in the last section, that Critical Legal Studies was engaged in a similar project to that of Feminism? Do you see any lines of inquiry which Feminist theory is pursuing that are like those of Critical Legal Studies? For example, is there a similar critique of "Liberalism," a critique which extends both to the categorization and the methodology liberal legal scholars and judges employ and to the substance of "liberal" legal doctrines?

You may remember that Presser, in his "New Great Chain" piece suggested that women might offer a different approach to solving legal problems, one that favored conciliation and cooperation over conflict. In a similar, although more graphic, vein some Feminists have bemoaned the pervasiveness of competition and conflict in American life and law. Catherine MacKinnon has suggested, for example, that

> we can play with the boys but we cannot question competition as a measure of merit. We can think but we are not allowed to question objectivity as the measure of what we know. We are allowed to compete but we are not allowed to question competition as the test of accomplishment. Nor do we get to criticize conflict as a peculiarly ejaculatory means of conflict resolution.

Feminist Discourse, Moral Values, and the Law—A Conversation, 34 Buff.L.Rev. 11, 23 (1985) [Hereafter cited as *Feminist Discourse*].* Pursuing this theme, and commending Carol Gilligan's path-breaking feminist work In a Different Voice—Psychological Theory and Women's Development (1982), Paul J. Spiegelman said of her study,

> I believe Carol's careful documentation of a different moral voice in the decision-making processes of the individual has profound implications for all of us concerned with the way people relate to each other, to the law, and to society. It gives new meaning to the feminist slogan "the personal is political," because it locates in women's personal experience a morality of care and concern for others which has the potential to transform our polity and its underlying assumptions from the alienated world of atomistic competition to an interconnected world of mutual cooperation.

Feminist Discourse, at 36. Gilligan herself has explained that both men and women can and do speak "In a different voice," and described the conventional and different voices as follows, "One voice speaks about equality, reciprocity, fairness, rights; one voice speaks about connection, not hurting, care, and response." *Feminist Discourse,* at 44. Do you understand how if MacKinnon, Spiegelman, and Gilligan are correct the dominant "Liberal" views on the substance and practice of law are subject to criticism for their failure accurately to capture the nature of men and women, or, put slightly differently, for their illiberality?

---

* Quotations from *Feminist Discourse* are reprinted here by permission of the Buffalo Law Review.

Are you a Feminist or a Liberal? Why? Do you believe, as Professor Eisenstein does, that a serious attempt even to give women "formal equality" in a country dominated by "liberal" legal discourse results in a "radical" enterprise? Must one be "radical" to be a Feminist? Why is it that Eisenstein and, implicitly, Law, believe that "individual claims for formal equality alone" as employed by individual women are "insufficient to achieve either liberty or equality?" Do you share their belief?

3. A fundamental premise of those seeking to build a Feminist theory of Law while still working within the currently established American legal system of courts and law schools must be, as Professor Law suggests, that "Despite the limitations of formal liberal rights, struggles within the law are an important part of the process of challenging patriarchal privilege." If this is so, does it undercut Eisenstein's argument "that liberalism, capitalism, and patriarchy are tightly interdependent?" Is "the law" something different from liberalism, capitalism, or feminism? Would this be the position of a Critical Legal Studies scholar? Would Dean Carrington want to exclude "Feminists" from teaching in law schools?

4. You will have perceived, by now, that Feminism, or the "Women's Movement," appears to be more concerned with issues central to contemporary American political debate than is Critical Legal Studies (or Law and Literature for that matter), and yet, do you see these three strands of contemporary American academic discourse as participating in the same conversation? Why do you suppose the "Women's Movement" has been so visible lately, and do you believe that it has scored significant political or legal victories? On the other hand, do you believe, with the "feminist revisionists," that Feminism has offered more than it can ever deliver? Is it possible, as Eisenstein challenges, to "develop a politics that neither denies biology, or uses it to justify prevailing social relations?" How would you go about such political development? Do you understand the subtle distinctions between the thought, regarding sexuality and gender, of the three "Feminists," Andrea Dworkin, Catherine MacKinnon, and Zillah Eisenstein? Does Professor Law help us to understand the role sex plays in Feminist, Liberal, or Patriarchal theories of Law? Is sexuality, as Eisenstein seems to suggest, socially constructed? Andrea Dworkin, along these lines, has argued that all acts of intercourse where the male member penetrates the female are, essentially, rape. Do you agree?

5. Law's critique of Eisenstein moves into somewhat less thorny territory, however, when she considers what real "equality" might mean from a feminist legal perspective. She writes, "We need a concept of equality that values nurturing and relationship, not as inherent differences between women and men, but as human strengths that have been devalued by being removed from the market and assigned to people removed from the market." Is this an accurate assessment of what we need, or an accurate description of what is in or out of the "market?" Would the law and economics crowd have anything to say about this? Are the law and economics analysts members of the "New Right," who are simply engaged in an effort to "restabilize patriarchy?" On the other hand, as current political movements are described by

Law, would you place "law and economics" with the "New Right" or with "Neoconservatives?" Is there anything of value, by the way, in "New Right," or "Neoconservative" political thought? Do they have anything in common with Feminism, Critical Legal Studies, the Law and Literature Movement, or Law and Economics which suggest anything as to the ultimate value or prospects for success of current academic or political thought? Of what importance is Law's assessment of the current character of the American economy? If Law is right, for example, that "The middle class is vanishing," what does this suggest for the future of most American legal doctrines which seem to presume the dominance (or at least the pervasiveness) of the middle class? Do you understand why there should be such a flourishing of new theories in the academy for the last few decades?

6. Why do you suppose that Professor Law has chosen the problem of "Growing Old in America" as a test case to which to apply Eisenstein's feminist theories? Is there a linkage between the pervasive problem of discrimination and lack of caring from which the old chronically suffer in American society, and the discrimination against women? Or is there a direct link to women's concerns which flows from what feminists believe to be the socially-imposed gender characteristics attributable to women?

How much of a victory for Feminist aims in the area of caring for the Aged can be achieved through "legal" struggle, and how much through "political" struggle? How much, ideally, of care for the elderly should be provided through private sources, and how much through public? Does feminist theory here help us solve the ever-troubling dilemma of where to draw the line between public and private? Does feminist theory do any better at this than do the theories put forward by Critical Legal Studies? Do you find a similarity between the notion of "consciousness raising" articulated by the Feminists and that articulated by the Marxists and the scholars of Critical Legal Studies? To what destination should such "consciousness-raising" take us, and is it a place to which you would like to journey? Are there costs, as well as benefits, to such "consciousness-raising?"

7. Professor Law's review of Eisenstein's book gives you a fine overview of much of Feminist theory, and seeks to apply its insights to one particular societal problem. In our next reading we take the thought of one of the most radical of the current Feminist Legal Scholars, examine it through the lens provided by a male law professor, and seek to determine how it might be applied across a broad spectrum of legal problems. As it was with Professor Law's Review Essay, your job is to try to understand the similarities and differences among Feminist Legal Theory and the other examples of ferment in the legal academy we have been studying in this Chapter.

CASS R. SUNSTEIN, FEMINISM AND LEGAL THEORY (BOOK REVIEW OF CATHARINE A. MACKINNON, FEMINISM UNMODIFIED (1987))*

101 Harv.L.Rev. 826 (1988).

I. INTRODUCTION

Occasionally an intellectual or political movement disrupts existing categories, throws into question practices and conceptual structures that had previously been accepted or even invisible, and eventually produces substantial changes in legal rules. How and why this happens is quite mysterious. The abolitionist movement of the 1850's is one example. Another is the New Deal, which grew out of an understanding that the common law was neither natural nor prepolitical and failed to provide a neutral baseline for decision. The most prominent recent illustration is the civil rights movement of the 1950's and 1960's, which challenged practices of racial exclusion. * * * In all of these contexts, practices that had for a long period been taken as natural and inviolate, sometimes even as based on biological differences, were revealed as socially created and subject to criticism and change.

The women's movement is the most powerful contemporary development of this sort; feminism provides its theoretical foundation. Despite its longevity and its recent impact on the law, the feminist movement has hardly run its course. Nonetheless, the basic claims of feminist theory are in many circles denied credibility and respect, or even a fair hearing. Ironically, those circles include many observers strongly committed to perceptions associated with the New Deal and the civil rights movement.

Feminist legal theory has had three principal strands, which for convenience may be called the "difference," "different voice," and "dominance" approaches. The least controversial, associated with the movement for the Equal Rights Amendment, is the "difference" approach, which argues that women should be permitted to compete on equal terms with men in the public world. In this view, characteristics legally and socially attributed to women—passivity, weakness, irrationality—are inaccurate or overbroad generalizations and at most the product of anachronistic social practices. Thus, feminists attack distinctions on the basis of gender—for example, laws excluding women from "male" jobs—as reflecting prejudice rather than reality and as perpetuating women's second-class citizenship. This strand of feminism, sometimes represented by the National Organization for Women, has achieved widespread acceptance in legal doctrine. A more controversial aspect of the same strand is the claim that, just as women should participate on equal terms with men in the professional world, so too should men participate on equal terms with women in the domestic sphere. A basic point here is that the domestic sphere has been devalued and used as a major arena for the subordination of women. The difference approach, if accepted, would produce significant changes in the employment market and in the care of children.

The "different voice" strand of feminist theory, associated most visibly with the work of Carol Gilligan,[9] asserts that there is a distinctly female way of approaching moral and legal dilemmas and that that way has been ignored or downplayed in legal doctrine and scholarship. In this view, women tend to value relationships and connections—an "ethic of care"—whereas men tend to place a higher premium on abstraction, rights, autonomy, separation, formality, and neutrality—an "ethic of justice." A centerpiece of this position is that prevailing theories of moral development and morality in general have taken a partial perspective and supposed it to be universal, ignoring alternative perspectives or treating them as primitive. The "different voice" approach assumes both descriptive and normative form, often contending that the legal system unduly emphasizes rules and abstraction and attends insufficiently to context and reciprocal responsibility. Sometimes this approach draws on psychoanalytic theory. The approach has significant consequences for a wide range of legal rules and practices, as well as for legal and social theory, both inside and outside the area of sex discrimination.

A third strand of feminist theory—the "dominance" approach—describes gender inequality not in terms of arbitrary or irrational differentiation but in terms of the social subordination of women. The problem is not that those similarly situated have been treated differently; it is instead that one group has dominated the other, in part through sexual practices. A wide range of issues that are not normally thought to involve sex discrimination—including sexual harassment, prostitution, reproductive freedom, rape, and pornography—thus raise questions of inequality. More broadly, these feminists see inequality in patterns of interaction between men and women that are normally taken as unobjectionable and even as intrinsic to traditional gender roles. Rape and prostitution are, in this view, not isolated deviations from social norms; they are extreme examples of the subordination of women that occurs in many places. The dominance approach joins the different voice approach's critique of partial perspective, but whereas the different voice approach embraces women's need for relationship and connectedness, the dominance approach claims that women need to be freed from practices that subordinate and invade them. The dominance view is thus sometimes skeptical of the different voice approach, claiming that women's capacity for empathy and need for relationship is in part the product of the social subordination of women.

Catharine MacKinnon is the most prominent and persistent advocate for the dominance strand of feminist theory. She is also the most important force behind the claim that sexual harassment is a form of sex

[9] *See* C. Gilligan, In a Different Voice (1982).

discrimination.[17] That notion, for which MacKinnon is given too little credit, seemed bizarre and radical to many when initially put forward. Remarkably, MacKinnon's basic position was accepted in 1986 by every member of the Supreme Court—with a majority opinion written by then Justice Rehnquist.[18] This development must count as one of the more dramatic and rapid changes in legal and social understanding in recent years. In addition, MacKinnon has supplied much of the underpinning for the current rethinking of both rape and prostitution; her criticisms focus on the systemic effects of these practices, their parallels in more conventional forms of gender relations, and the partial perspectives found in the legal treatment of both. MacKinnon has been perhaps the most important force behind the burgeoning theoretical literature in law on sex discrimination and feminist theory. With Andrea Dworkin, MacKinnon has developed what is probably her most controversial thesis: the idea that pornography is a form of sex discrimination.[21] In these and other areas, MacKinnon's work has generated a dramatic shift in legal thinking and reoriented the terms of debate.

In all of these settings, MacKinnon's basic position is that the social and legal treatment of gender should be challenged today just as common law categories and racial exclusion were challenged during the New Deal period and the 1950's, respectively. MacKinnon claims that gender relations, like the common law and racial practices, are regarded as natural or prepolitical but are actually socially constructed, alterable, and unjust. Although few recent writers in law have been so creative or influential, there are important arenas in which her work is ignored and even ridiculed.

Feminism Unmodified is a collection of MacKinnon's speeches on sex discrimination over a six-year period * * *.

* * *

II. SEX DISCRIMINATION: DIFFERENCES AND DOMINANCE

MacKinnon's general treatment of sex discrimination, first set out in *Sexual Harassment of Working Women,* derives from her description and critique of the difference approach, which she claims is the most prominent in current law. The difference approach holds that the purpose of constitutional and statutory proscriptions is to ensure that laws reflect both real similarities and real differences and thus "track reality."

The difference approach endorses two paths to equality. The first is rooted in strict gender neutrality and insists that women are and should

---

[17] *See* C. MacKinnon, Sexual Harassment of Working Women: A Case of Sex Discrimination (1979).

[18] Meritor Sav. Bank, FSB v. Vinson, 477 U.S. 57 (1986).

[21] * * * *see also* A. Dworkin, Pornography: Men Possessing Women (1981).

be treated "the same as men" (p. 33). Distinctions on the basis of gender, especially those that deny women opportunities available to men, are presumptively unlawful. Much of modern law under the equal protection clause and title VII reflects this understanding. The central premise is freedom of choice, often expressed in terms of equality of opportunity: people should be permitted to choose jobs and social roles in ways unaffected by irrelevant characteristics like gender.

The second path to equality under the difference approach qualifies this basic theme of sameness, recognizing that in some respects women are not similarly situated to men. This path is designed for "women who want equality yet find that [they] are different" (p. 33) and culminates in "the special benefit rule," which authorizes the state to recognize "real differences" between men and women. Thus, for example, courts will uphold laws or practices that recognize the distinctive physical characteristics of women. Sometimes such laws impose burdens on women, as in reproduction-related restrictions of employment opportunities; sometimes they create "special benefits," as in leave policies for pregnant women.

MacKinnon is not entirely hostile to the difference approach; she acknowledges that it has accomplished considerable good. In her view, however, it is inadequate for two reasons. First, the difference approach—precisely because it is based on a norm of formal equality or sex-blindness—does nothing about many existing structural inequalities between men and women. Those inequalities in wealth and power are taken for granted; they are treated as the inevitable background conditions against which legal disputes must be resolved. "A gender-neutral approach . . . obscures . . . the fact that women's poverty, financial dependency, motherhood, and sexual accessibility . . . substantively make up women's status *as women*"(p. 73) (emphasis in original). For a variety of reasons, women are not in fact situated similarly to men, and legal rules pretending that they are will sometimes reduce rather than increase the likelihood of obtaining equality. For example, the recent transformation of the law of custody and divorce, embodying a norm of formal equality, has harmed women and helped men. Under the difference approach, "society advantages [men] before they get into court, and law is prohibited from taking that preference into account because that would mean taking gender into account" (p. 35).

The differencc approach is also inadequate because it uses men as the baseline from which to measure difference. According to MacKinnon, legal rules that use men as the referent, and allow differential treatment of women when it is based on real differences from men, do not enshrine any obvious conception of gender equality. Instead, they amount to a false universalization that depends on a particular standpoint—men's biology and career patterns—from which to assess "difference." Consider the legal treatment of women's distinctive reproductive capacities: to understand rules that accommodate those capacities as a "special benefit" is to apply a male baseline. "Men's physiology defines most sports, their needs define auto and health insurance coverage, their socially designed biographies define workplace expectations and successful career patterns. . . . For each of their differences from women, what amounts to an affirmative action plan is in effect" (p. 36). The use of male practices as the norm thus produces an inadequate law of sex discrimination; for MacKinnon, the problem is not one of abstract differences at all.

Of recent cases addressing states' attempts to provide pregnancy leave and related job security, MacKinnon remarks, "Difference doctrine says it is sex discrimination to give women what we need, because only women need it. It is not sex discrimination not to give women what we need because then only women will not get what we need" (p. 36). Under the difference approach, the legal system does nothing about preexisting legal and social disabilities brought about by past discrimination and women's reproductive roles. Examples include public or private rules that forbid employees from being the primary caretaker of a preschool child, rules that prohibit fertile women from taking certain jobs, and the concentration of women in low-paying jobs. None of these practices is unlawful under the difference approach. The claim of inequality underlying *Feminism Unmodified* is not the relatively narrow argument that women have been treated "unequally to men"; it is instead that there is a system of sexual subordination of women that should be altered. For MacKinnon, the notion that the similarly situated must be treated similarly is an inadequate way to approach issues of sex discrimination.

Under MacKinnon's alternative—the dominance approach—the goal of sex discrimination law "is not to make legal categories trace and trap the way things are. It is not to make rules that fit reality. It is critical of reality" (p. 40). The problem is not whether and how much difference there is between men and women; it is instead how the legal system should respond to these differences. "The difference approach tries to map reality; the dominance approach tries to challenge and change it" (p. 44). "[S]ex inequality questions are questions of systematic dominance, of male supremacy, which is not at all abstract and is anything but a mistake" (p. 42).

MacKinnon is impatient with biological explanations of gender inequality. The question is not whether such differences exist, but what society does with them—in short, their legal and social consequences. For the situations relevant here, it is the legal system that decides when and how biological differences are relevant, turning differences, which might be treated as immaterial, into legal disadvantages. * * *

In some circumstances, the dominance approach might yield results that are identical to current law—for example, by invalidating statutes that make employment of a particular sort more attractive for men than for women. Some laws would be upheld under both approaches but with divergent rationales. A law establishing different ages for statutory rape of men and women might be upheld not on the biological ground * * * but on the theory that rape of young girls by men is far more common than rape of young boys by women. Gender-specific statutory rape laws are thus sensible safeguards rather than under-inclusive reflections of prejudice.

At the same time, the dominance approach would challenge many legal practices that current law takes for granted. It would, for example, treat as issues of sex discrimination questions that are not so regarded by current law, including reproductive rights and abortion, battery of women, rape, prostitution, sexual assault of girls, the disproportionate presence of women in low-paying occupations, and female poverty. In all of these areas, the dominance approach would not treat current practices as the inevitable background conditions against which questions of sexual equality must be measured; it would instead require changes in those practices in order to bring about equality.

* * *

MacKinnon's attack on unarticulated baselines challenges some familiar analytic strategies in law. Her discussion of legal abstraction, formality, principle, and neutrality suggests that these terms often conceal a contested substantive understanding that denies its status as such. MacKinnon argues that the idea that justice is neutrality between abstract categories ignores social distinctions between those categories, as the Court did in *Plessy v. Ferguson*[35] (pp. 165–66). In MacKinnon's view, similar understandings are at work in current law, including the attack on affirmative action * * *. Indeed, the very term "affirmative action" suggests that use of the market represents inaction and that efforts to compensate for the existing distribution of benefits and burdens between blacks and whites or women and men should be regarded as "affirmative." MacKinnon's claim also challenges one understanding of "neutral principles"[36]—an understanding that was initially deployed to question the Court's reasoning in *Brown v. Board of Education* on the grounds that the case did not involve discrimination at all and that the Court had failed to show why the associational preferences of blacks should be favored over those of whites.[38]

* * * *Feminism Unmodified* attributes gender inequality above all to sexuality and sexual practices: "I think the fatal error of the legal arm of feminism has been its failure to understand that the mainspring of sex inequality is misogyny and the mainspring of misogyny is sexual sadism"

---

[35] 163 U.S. 537 (1896).

[36] *See* Wechsler, *Toward Neutral Principles of Constitutional Law,* 73 Harv.L.Rev. 1 (1959).

[38] *See* Wechsler, *supra* note 36, at 33–34 * * *.

(p. 5). MacKinnon takes the sexual objectification of women, and current sexuality in general, as a central cause of sexual subordination—an issue I take up below. It is for this reason that pornography, rather than, for example, occupational segregation or childcare responsibility, is MacKinnon's central target. And it is no doubt in part this aspect of MacKinnon's critique that has made her views so controversial. Her claims threaten areas thought to be personal and private, attack the neo-Freudian orthodoxy that urges the liberation of sexual drives from repression, and pointedly part company with certain aspects of mainstream liberalism.

To summarize, MacKinnon's basic criticism is an attack on the understanding of sex discrimination as a problem of irrational differentiation. * * * It should be plain that MacKinnon's approach, because it expands and recasts the prohibition on sex discrimination, is radically different from much of current law. Hence MacKinnon's proposed substitute for the Equal Rights Amendment is a women's rights amendment providing: "the subordination of women to men is hereby abolished" (p. 28).

A. *The Problem of Ends*

Challenges to MacKinnon's approach come from several directions. The first challenge involves MacKinnon's ends. Many women today do not perceive the world in MacKinnon's terms; indeed, not a few are hostile to her depiction, and many do not seek the sorts of changes proposed in *Feminism Unmodified*. For these women, the problem of sex discrimination has neither the nature nor the magnitude that MacKinnon suggests, and the world she describes—one of widespread and objectionable gender hierarchy—is not the world in which they live. The forms of discrimination MacKinnon challenges are, in this view, largely a product of free choice or biology; other, more invidious inequalities are already addressed or can be remedied by contemporary law. For such skeptics, the difference approach, the overriding goal of which is to free people to seek their own disparate goals, is preferable. Many women who find traditional roles satisfying and rewarding would find it intrusive and counterproductive for government to try to bring about MacKinnon's version of substantive equality.

This critique of MacKinnon replicates earlier invocations of freedom of choice that have been roundly repudiated in modern law, including the attack on the New Deal (especially minimum wage and maximum hour legislation), and the critique of modern civil rights legislation. Such critiques ignore both problems of collective action and the ways in which apparently free choices are the product of the existing legal regime. Collective action problems make it extremely difficult for a dispersed and diffuse group to organize and seek reform. In the context of sex discrimination, moreover, the phenomenon of adaptive preferences—emphasized in recent rational choice theory[47]—is especially important, for it undermines conventional understandings of free choice. Private preferences are not always autonomous; they are in part a product of existing social practice, including social pressures and the absence of opportunities. If opportunities are unavailable, people often try to reduce cognitive dissonance by scaling back their aspirations. More generally, the phenomenon of adaptive preferences makes it difficult to contend that legal rules should always or necessarily be based on current preferences.[51] If preferences are a function of legal rules and social practices, those rules and practices cannot be defended by reference to the preferences without circularity.[52]

This basic point has especially powerful implications in the area of sexual inequality. Women's preferences have been formed against a background of limited opportunities. In these circumstances, the fact that many women are or seem content with the status quo is not a dispositive argument against social change. A system of formal equality leaves in place preferences and opportunities that are products of past discrimination. It is a significant advantage of MacKinnon's approach that, unlike many purportedly feminist critiques, it does not evade the "freedom of choice" question but challenges it head on.

Although MacKinnon's argument responds persuasively to a familiar argument in favor of the difference approach, it does not supply a complete affirmative case for the dominance approach. That approach is difficult to evaluate in the abstract, and it is not fully elaborated in *Feminism Unmodified.* Moreover, the notion of "dominance" is somewhat ambiguous and itself depends on some sort of baseline. Any judgment about the dominance approach calls for an evaluation of both the context and the practical impact of that approach on the lives of women and men. Such an evaluation will also depend on the prospects for change in light of the fact that preferences and practices are already in place and may be difficult to alter. Indeed, sometimes efforts at alteration are counterproductive, and *Feminism Unmodified* does not examine the problem of transition. It is an advantage of MacKinnon's argument, however, that she tends to be highly contextual in her discussion, particularly in the areas of reproductive freedom, sexual harassment, and pornography.

MacKinnon proposes that statutes restricting reproductive rights be treated as forms of sex discrimination. Such laws are discriminatory, both in purpose and effect, because they are a product of traditional under-

---

[47] * * * The term "adaptive preferences" is preferable to "false consciousness," because the latter has a tendency to tautology and lacks cognitive foundations.

[51] Consider Montesquieu's discussion of adaptive preferences on the part of women in the harem, Montesquieu, *Letter XXVI: Usbek to Roxana, at the Seraglio at Ispahan,* in I The Persian and Chinese Letters 61 (J. Davidson trans. 1892) (1721), and the ambivalent reactions of the newly freed slaves as discussed in L. Litwack, Been in the Storm So Long (1979).

[52] *See* Sunstein, *Legal Interference with Private Preferences,* 53 U.Chi.L.Rev. 1129 (1986). Of course, it is important to be careful and precise with rationales of this sort, for there are risks of tyranny in approaches that tend to disregard private preferences.

standings of the role of women in bearing and raising children. Seen in this light, laws prohibiting public funding of abortions should be understood as grounded in the same discrimination that motivates laws forbidding abortion altogether.

Sexual harassment and pornography present somewhat different problems, but their cultural context and practical effects also raise issues of discrimination. It is fanciful to deny that women are the principal victims of sexual harassment or that they are the principal objects of abuse in and as a result of pornography. Comparable worth raises still different issues. By increasing salaries in traditional female jobs, comparable worth remedies might reinforce women's preferences for those jobs or distort the employment market. These possibilities argue against such remedial proposals, even if countervailing factors make them justifiable. Practical considerations of this sort suggest that substantial work will be necessary to apply the dominance approach in particular contexts. Whatever the precise meaning of the approach, however, it is clear that its application would move the law further in the direction of gender equality.

* * *

III. APPLICATIONS OF THE DOMINANCE APPROACH: ABORTION, PORNOGRAPHY, AND OTHER PROBLEMS

A large portion of *Feminism Unmodified* is devoted to the exploration of particular topics. MacKinnon points out that the extent and nature of rape and sexual harassment are relatively recent discoveries (p. 5); the same is true of pornography. These topics were hardly on the legal agenda just a decade ago. Courts and commentators have begun to rethink all of them * * *.

In a provocative essay on abortion, MacKinnon applies her general critique of the notion of a prepolitical and noncoercive private sphere of gender relations into which government must not enter. She argues that the Court's decision to approach *Roe v. Wade*[59] as a case involving privacy rather than equality was a mistake, based on a disregard for the sex-based character of reproduction and the tacit assumption that women have equal control over sex. In MacKinnon's view, "[s]exual intercourse, still the most common cause of pregnancy, cannot simply be presumed coequally determined" (pp. 94–95). Women often fail to use contraception because to do so "means acknowledging and planning the possibility of intercourse, accepting one's sexual availability, and appearing nonspontaneous" (p. 95). In light of these overlooked facts, MacKinnon argues that *Roe* was myopic in treating the issue as one involving privacy. That formulation suggests that the decision was partly responsive to "the interests of men as a group" (p. 97) in making women sexually available to

[59] 410 U.S. 113 (1973).

men. MacKinnon argues that "under conditions of gender inequality, sexual liberation [as promoted by the *Roe* reasoning] does not free women; it frees male sexual aggression" (p. 99).

MacKinnon speculates about why the legal system has structured the abortion issue in terms of privacy: "if inequality is socially pervasive and enforced, equality will require intervention, not abdication, to be meaningful. But the right to privacy is not thought to require social change. It is not even thought to require any social preconditions, other than nonintervention by the public" (p. 100). If the Court had structured the issue in terms of gender inequality and resolved it under the dominance approach, the issue of federal funding might have come out differently. "[F]ramed as a privacy right, a woman's decision to abort would have no claim on public support" (p. 101); but as a right to equality, such a claim would be much harder to deny.

MacKinnon's principal application of the dominance approach is in the area of pornography—defined not as sexually explicit materials but as those that associate sex with violence. * * *

MacKinnon's discussion of pornography is likely to be the most controversial part of *Feminism Unmodified.* It is important to understand the treatment within the context of her broader argument about sex discrimination and her general strategy for reform. A focus on the antipornography movement isolated from these broader themes will miss the basic point, regardless of one's ultimate conclusion about the issue of government control of pornography.

* * * MacKinnon * * * believes that feminist claims about the meaning and effects of pornography have been obscured by the sexual revolution of the 1960's and by the power of Freudian and associated antirepression theories of sexuality in intellectual and popular circles. MacKinnon's argument differs sharply from other, far less persuasive arguments for the regulation of sexually explicit speech.[64]

MacKinnon makes three basic claims. First, she suggests that severe harms are done to women in the production of pornography and that regulation of the resulting material is necessary to prevent those harms. Second, MacKinnon contends that pornography has a causal connection to acts of sexual violence against women. Third, and most generally, MacKinnon claims that pornography influences the attitudes of both men and women in gender relations, attitudes that help produce unlawful discrimination and foster gender inequality. Her basic argument is that the creation of a cause of action on behalf of women harmed by pornography would reduce the amount of pornography, give relief to those directly

[64] The argument has also been made by other feminists, including Andrea Dworkin * * *. Similar arguments have been accepted in West Germany since the early 1970's, and West German courts have concluded that pornography is inconsistent with constitutionally guaranteed human dignity. * * *

harmed by it, and at the same time affect male and female attitudes toward it.

In MacKinnon's view,

> Pornography sexualizes rape, battery, sexual harassment, prostitution, and child sexual abuse; it thereby celebrates, promotes, authorizes, and legitimates them. More generally, it eroticizes the dominance and submission that is the dynamic common to them all. It makes hierarchy sexy and calls that "the truth about sex" or just a mirror of reality (p. 171) (citations omitted).

MacKinnon claims that "pornography is neither harmless fantasy nor a corrupt and confused misrepresentation of an otherwise natural and healthy sexual situation. It institutionalizes the sexuality of male supremacy, fusing the eroticization of dominance and submission with the social construction of male and female" (p. 172). MacKinnon continues: "What in the pornographic view is love and romance looks a great deal like hatred and torture to the feminist" (p. 174). The law of obscenity misconceives the problem because it is indifferent to the issue of harm—depending instead on offensiveness—and because it is gender-neutral.

The recognition that many categories of speech are currently regulable adds power to MacKinnon's argument, as do her description of the abuses that are sexualized in pornography, her discussion of the harms to women in and as a result of pornography, and her highly plausible claims of a causal connection between pornography and violence. Having absorbed MacKinnon's point, one notices sexualized violence against women in numerous places in modern culture, severely weakening one's initial instincts against control of at least some speech that merges sex with violence.

* * *

It is important to distinguish positions with which MacKinnon's approach is sometimes confused. MacKinnon does not argue that pornography should be regulated because it is offensive. She does not claim that the community has a right to censor speech that does not conform to its moral position. Nor, on the other hand, does she draw a sharp distinction between pornography and erotica. MacKinnon's highly controversial claim is not that pornography is a perversion of sexuality; it is instead that pornography helps to constitute sexuality.

MacKinnon's analysis raises two distinct questions. First, is her description of the problem posed by pornography persuasive? Second, is her remedy for the problem—a civil rights action—a desirable one? * * *

With respect to the first question, MacKinnon's diagnosis of pornography as a form of sex discrimination has been criticized from two perspectives. Some critics deny that pornography is harmful. Others claim that feminism and pornography are compatible, that women enjoy (at least some forms of) pornography, and that the harms of pornography are gender-neutral. But these objections seem weak. There is mounting evidence that sexual violence occurs both in and as a result of pornography. Abuses within the pornography industry appear widespread.[67] Considerable evidence from laboratory experiments and the real world also suggests a link between pornography and sexual violence. Of course, both laboratory and real world evidence suffer from serious methodological defects—the former because of the enormous difficulty of extrapolation, the latter because of possible confounding variables. Even if causation were clear and overwhelming, however, it would be hard to demonstrate, and in other areas of law, regulation is permitted on the basis of suggestive—but inconclusive—evidence. It would be absurd to suggest that most sexual violence is a result of pornography or that sexual violence would disappear if pornography were eliminated. Moreover, some of MacKinnon's rhetoric is overstated. The evidence with respect to the harmful effects of pornography is, however, sufficiently powerful to justify regulation.

It is true that some women enjoy pornography, even if it is narrowly defined to include work that merges sex with violence. It is sometimes urged in this connection that female sexuality has only begun to express itself openly and voluntarily and that regulation of pornography, even when violent, would prevent the free development and expression of women's sexuality. MacKinnon responds that sexuality is to a large degree socially constructed for both men and women. In her view, it is entirely unsurprising that some women find cultural symbols that mesh violence with sexuality to be sexually arousing. We have seen that preferences and beliefs are socially formed. In light of the harmful effects of pornography as defined here—with its focus on violence—the fact that some women enjoy it is not a reason to do nothing about it. One need not take a position on MacKinnon's broadest claims about the relationship between sexuality and sexual inequality in order to agree that the fact that some women associate sexuality and violence is not a sufficient reason to permit the distribution of every film that merges sexuality and violence.

Other critics claim that pornography cannot be a form of sex discrimination because it harms and degrades both women and men. This argument, reflecting fundamental resistance to MacKinnon's basic point, is difficult to take seriously: whether or not women are nominal victims, pornography generally treats them as the ultimate target of sexual violence and objectification. Indeed, the persistence of such claims reveals the strength of MacKinnon's critique, especially insofar as she suggests that pornography renders some forms of sexual inequality invisible.

---

[67] *See* I Attorney General's Commission on Pornography, Final Report 767–835 (1986).

All of this suggests that MacKinnon's analysis of the social meaning of pornography is persuasive. The question of legal control, however, is trickier. The conventional criticisms are that the problem of defining pornography is insurmountable and that the risks to freedom of speech outweigh any gains that would come from regulation. In these circumstances, the remedy, opponents claim, is "more speech," not government regulation. From a strategic perspective, critics argue that other problems facing women—also emphasized in *Feminism Unmodified*—are much higher priorities than government regulation of pornography.

The problems of definition are indeed considerable—especially in light of the fact that materials with some of the characteristics of pornography can be found throughout modern culture. * * * The problems of definition are not, however, insurmountable.

First amendment doctrine furnishes the building blocks for a quite conventional argument for regulation of pornography. First, most of the speech at issue is far afield from the central purposes of the first amendment under almost any view. Distinctions among categories of speech in terms of their centrality to first amendment purposes are well established in constitutional law, and a system of free expression could not sensibly ignore them. For example, conspiracies, bribes, unlawful contracts, false statements of fact, private libel, misleading commercial advertising, and child pornography are regulable, largely because they do not promote the purposes associated with free speech, which involve public deliberation, broadly understood.[78] The harms of pornography, canvassed above, are sufficient to justify regulation under the standards applied to low-value speech. Pornography, narrowly defined, does not present a weaker claim for regulation than many similar types of speech that are regulable under current law.

Those skeptical of MacKinnon's approach are undoubtedly concerned about the dangers of overinclusion and misapplication. These concerns are persuasive when the underlying harms are minimal and the risks of overinclusiveness or misapplication quite large. In the context of pornography, however, the risks of what some might see as "inaction"—involving harms to women in and as a result of pornography—are considerable. Further, there is little reason to doubt that a carefully worded statute, posing no greater threat to free expression than the other categories of regulable speech, could be drawn.

The final set of objections to MacKinnon's approach is largely strategic. Opponents suggest that pornography is a relatively minor factor in gender inequality compared to economic and other factors. The

[78] This is of course a controversial view, associated with Alexander Meiklejohn. *See* A. Meiklejohn, Free Speech and Its Relation to Self–Government (1948). But on any plausible view of the central function of free expression, pornography, if narrowly defined, is likely to qualify as low-value speech.

antipornography campaign is said to create an odd alliance with groups whose concerns conflict with feminism. And to the extent that the merger of violence and sexuality is a social problem, it is also severe in mainstream advertising, television, and popular culture—all of which sexualize violence * * *. Seen in this context, the attack on the pornography industry might be thought misdirected.

Such an attack would, however, do some good for some women, and—a central point—discussion and identification of the problem is likely to contribute to efforts to address the other problems as well. The fact that control of pornography would not bring about sexual equality by itself is hardly a persuasive reason not to initiate a measure that might do considerable good. In some circles, moreover, the antipornography movement has served as a powerful spur to changed attitudes on the part of both men and women.

MacKinnon's discussion of sexuality, however, has a deeper point, and this point underlies some of the resistance to the antipornography movement. Some observers suggest that MacKinnon's objections are in fact threatening to sexuality itself. MacKinnon's critics are correct here, for her argument bears on sexuality quite generally * * *. In brief, MacKinnon suggests that we must reformulate "the problem of sexuality from the repression of drives by civilization to the oppression of women by men" (p. 98). In her view, the sexual revolution of the 1960's and neo-Freudian arguments in favor of removal of repression are part of the problem rather than its solution. Hence MacKinnon is reluctant to distinguish sharply between erotica and pornography. Her central claim is that "[s]exuality itself is a social construct gendered to the ground. Male dominance here is not an artificial overlay upon an underlying inalterable substratum of uncorrupted essential sexual being" (p. 173). In short, there is no prepolitical, unmediated "sexuality" that law, or feminists, should attempt to uncover and translate into actual practice. Sexuality, as practiced currently and generally, is itself enmeshed in, a cause and a product of, sexual inequality. It is in this view that pornography, sexual harassment, rape, and prostitution are not marginal issues but instead at the core of the problem. In her emphasis on the centrality of sexuality, moreover, MacKinnon is in agreement with Freud—although her conception of the purposes and effects of sexuality is of course entirely different, because Freud treats sexuality as essentially natural rather than socially constructed and does not regard it as a source of unjustified subordination of women.

MacKinnon's claims about sexuality raise large and difficult issues that cannot be properly evaluated in this space. The skepticism that has greeted some of MacKinnon's work is surely in part a product of the threat that this critique poses to practices that many think of as deeply personal and private. * * *

How would one evaluate MacKinnon's approach to sexuality? An enormous amount of theoretical and empirical work would be necessary to convince skeptics of her basic claim. The arguments that sexuality is a social construct, that sexual sadism is the mainspring of sexual inequality (p. 5), and that sexuality is built on male dominance raise several questions. First, the connections among sexuality, nature, law, and culture are extraordinarily complex; indeed, it is not altogether clear what the claim that "sexuality" is "a social construct" means. Second, the relationship between sex discrimination and sexual sadism is hardly simple and clear cut. The term "sadism" is perhaps misleading in this context, for it connotes a kind of pleasure from pain that captures only a part of sexual inequality. Moreover, sexual inequality is sometimes rooted in things other than sexual sadism; economic, domestic, and other advantages are also important. Women have been oppressed in nonsexual ways, and men receive much more from gender inequality than sex on their own terms. Third, the claim that sexuality is based on male dominance is in some tension with the presence of affirmative descriptions of sexuality from women, descriptions that are true to subjective experience. * * *

Nevertheless, notions of sexual liberation and the removal of repression often have as their underlying purpose and effect the increased sexual availability of women to men. Elements of sexual sadism form an ingredient in sexual inequality; MacKinnon's position here is both original and confirmed by unmistakable aspects of modern culture. Moreover, the case for regulation of at least some pornographic materials is quite persuasive. Equally important, the anti-pornography movement has begun to affect both male and female thinking about sexuality, rendering visible many practices and issues formerly taken for granted. Sexualized violence toward women is pervasive in advertising, popular culture, and everyday life. It is difficult to see much of popular culture—and some high art as well—in quite the same way after reading *Feminism Unmodified.* * * *

* * *

NOTES AND QUESTIONS

1. You will have probably noticed that Professor Sunstein's first move is to liken the women's movement to other legal struggles, most notably abolitionism, the New Deal, and Civil Rights. It might well be comforting for a male law Professor to be able to suggest that Feminism is just another in a long series of moves for rationality, truth, and justice, which he, as an expert on one of the earlier struggles (the New Deal) can easily comprehend. Do you agree with Professor Sunstein about the similarities of the women's movement to these other struggles, or is Feminism something different? What is the role, by the way, for men in the women's movement?

2. Sunstein lays out three strands of the women's movement, which he labels the "difference," "different voice," and "dominance" approaches. Which strand would Aeschylus or Gewirtz embrace? With which of these three strands are you the most comfortable? By the way, can the goals of Feminism easily be placed under these three different rubrics, or is there a point at which they begin to shade into each other? More troubling, perhaps, would a victory, or a series of victories under any one of the approaches present danger for victories under any of the others? Does this help you understand why the struggle for women's rights has been so prone to internal divisions, and why it has been such a long struggle? For a thoughtful rumination on where feminist legal scholarship has been and where it is going, see Katherine T. Bartlett, "Feminist Legal Scholarship: A History through the Lens of the California Law Review," 100 Cal. L. Rev. 381 (2012).

3. In any event, it is clear which strand Catharine MacKinnon embraces, as Sunstein points out. She is the creator and "the most prominent and persistent advocate for the dominance strand of feminist theory." Why is it that MacKinnon rejects the "difference" approach even as she acknowledges that it has been used to achieve a few worthy goals? In some comments on Carol Gilligan's In a Different Voice, in 1984, MacKinnon elaborated on what she sees as the meaning of the difference between men and women, and made implicitly clearer some of the reasons why she favors a "dominance" approach to the legal analysis of women's issues:

> The importance of the recognition that women are different has had to do with valuing women's experience—not only the experience of relatedness, responsibility, and care virtues, but also the experience reflected in the following insight, which is the impulse behind the discipline of women's history in many respects: "Wait a second. You may have defined history as wars, empires, governments, and so on, but we were there, too." This insight is effective only if you count what we were there *for* and what we were *doing* there, and only if you can see that other things are going on in society besides those things that men have measured as valuable. Women make history. Quilts are art. Those gardens are expression and creativity. A shorthand way of saying this is that, men notwithstanding, man is *not* "the measure of all things."

"Feminist Discourse, Moral Values, and the Law—A Conversation," 34 Buff.L.Rev. 11, 25 (1985) [Hereafter cited as *Feminist Discourse*].* In the course of those 1984 remarks, MacKinnon went on to cite statistics which supported her views on women, among them that "thirty-eight percent of all girls are victims of child sexual abuse," that "about twelve to fifteen percent of all American women are, or have been, prostitutes, by which is meant they make or have made their living more-or-less exclusively through the sale of their sexuality," and, *inter alia,* that "a woman makes fifty-nine cents for every dollar a man makes, and that gap is widening." *Feminist Discourse,* at 26.

* Quotations from *Feminist Discourse* are reprinted by permission of the Buffalo Law Review.

Summing up the implications of these and other statistics, MacKinnon stated:

> What this all means is that women are a subordinate group. And nothing is being done about it. Really nothing. This abuse is passing unacknowledged as the sex difference, while the issues that are litigated as sex discrimination issues are seen as differentiation problems against a reality which is fundamentally equal. The practices I just described are that reality. Dominance and submission made into sex, made into the gender difference, constitute the suppressed social content of the gender definitions of men and women.

Feminist Discourse, at 27.

Does this make it easier to understand what is meant when MacKinnon makes the statement that "The difference approach tries to map reality; the dominance approach tries to challenge and change it?" Do you understand how, if the dominance approach were to be accepted in the law, "reproductive rights and abortion, battery of women, rape, prostitution, sexual assault of girls, the disproportionate presence of women in low-paying occupations, and female poverty," would all become issues of sex discrimination for which there would be federal and state remedies? Would you want to see such acceptance of the dominance approach?

The notion of replacing the difference approach with the dominance approach in legal analysis is really a struggle over whether the difference approach (which we might also, paradoxically, characterize as a "gender-neutral" approach), is a "neutral" principle in the manner that term was used in the excerpt from Herbert Wechsler's famous "neutral principles" article, which you read in Chapter Six. Do you understand why MacKinnon would have trouble with Wechsler's legal analysis? Would Wechsler have trouble with MacKinnon's? Would you vote for MacKinnon's proposed substitute for the Equal Rights Amendment, the "women's rights amendment" providing: "the subordination of women to men is hereby abolished?" Would that establish a "neutral principle" in Wechsler's terms?

4. Like Eisenstein and Law, and like radical thinkers of many stripes, MacKinnon is concerned with the problem Marxists habitually refer to as "false consciousness," particularly among women who may not favor the sort of radical revision of society and women's rights which MacKinnon seeks. It appears that "false consciousness," and the term used by Sunstein from social choice theory, "adaptive preference," mean roughly the same thing. Do you understand MacKinnon's argument on this point that suggests that public opinion might not be the test for whether her views should be legally accepted? Does Professor Sunstein appear to accept this argument? Do you? Is Sunstein for or against dominance theory? Sunstein appears to understand that theories of "false consciousness," or "adaptive preference," if used to justify a move in the law from "difference" theory to "dominance" theory might have the potential for totalitarianism. Still, does he, MacKinnon, Law, or Eisenstein successfully solve the problem of reconciling theories of "false con-

sciousness" with the democratic character of American society? Can you? Is Feminism democratic?

5. As Sunstein points out, MacKinnon has been very successful at using the legal system for Feminist causes, most notably in making the claim (now accepted by the United States Supreme Court) that sexual harassment is sex discrimination (and thus subject to federal anti-discrimination penalties). More controversial, although probably more visible, has been MacKinnon's claim (along with Andrea Dworkin), a claim increasingly central to MacKinnon's work, that pornography is a form of sex discrimination. Do you understand how this can be argued? Are you persuaded? Do you understand how MacKinnon's beliefs lead her to assume the position she takes regarding abortion, that is, that *Roe v. Wade,* the Supreme Court case which held unconstitutional first trimester anti-abortion statutes on "right of privacy" grounds, rested on the wrong legal foundation?

6. Consider MacKinnon's notion, with regard to pornography, and inherent in her "dominance" approach to a variety of women's legal problems, that pornography "makes hierarchy sexy and calls that 'the truth about sex' or just a mirror of reality." Do you find "hierarchy" sexy? Would members of the critical legal studies movement? Is there a nexus between "dominance" theory in Feminism and social analysis in critical legal studies, for example as explained by Gordon, and what, if anything, does it have to do with sex and sexuality? Is it possible, for example, to have heterosexual sex without hierarchy? Apparently some Feminists aren't so sure, or at least this would seem to be the import of the theories of women like Andrea Dworkin. Pithily summing up Dworkin's thoughts on the issue, Mary C. Dunlap stated that "Andrea Dworkin has taken the position that the penis is the problem." *Feminist Discourse,* at 32.

In any event, are you convinced of the need to regulate pornography in the manner suggested by MacKinnon? Is the evidence that Sunstein cites in support of MacKinnon's arguments persuasive?

7. It is a long distance that we have come in the course, from a struggle over the prerogatives of the English King to a struggle between individual American men and women over a definition of, or an acceptable practice and understanding of human sexuality. Is there a role for "the law" to play in both spheres, or have we somehow passed, in the course of our study, from a realm in which law can help circumscribe and define societal practice, to a realm in which other forces, for example ethics, cultural norms, or medicinal concerns (in the era of AIDS) ought to have more force than law? Sunstein quite nicely sets up an opposition in terms of an analysis of human sexuality between MacKinnon and Freud. Freud, who seemed to be arguing against repression in the area of human sexuality, saw sexuality as "essentially natural," while MacKinnon sees it as "socially constructed." Which one, Freud or MacKinnon, is right? How much of life is "socially constructed" in MacKinnon's terms, and how much of "social construction" can be done through the law? If, of course, gender is "socially constructed," there may be a powerful role for legislation (or, as MacKinnon suggests, Constitutional Amendment) to play in the pro-

cess. There have been some notable efforts in this direction, most significantly perhaps, Title IX of the federal Education Amendments of 1972 which prohibits discrimination on the basis of sex in federally funded programs. For an introduction to the literature on Title IX, and, in particular, its controversial interpretation by the Justice Department's Office for Civil Rights and by the courts as "requiring that schools provide their female and male students with varsity athletic opportunities in proportion to their numbers in the undergraduate population," see Kimberly A. Yuracko, "One for You and One for Me: Is Title IX's Sex–Based Proportionality Requirement for College Varsity Athletic Positions Defensible?", 97 Nw.U.L.Rev. 731 (2003). Professor Yuracko concludes that "Although a complete social transformation of what it means to be female or what it means to be an athlete has assuredly not taken place, just as assuredly, Title IX has been tremendously successful as a resocialization measure. Title IX's proportionality requirement may be best understood by recognizing this social transformation as both its goal and justification." For further elaboration of the theme that Professor Yuracko explores, that feminist theory influences practice and that changed practice leads to alterations in culture, see Cynthia Grant Bowman and Elizabeth M. Schneider, "Feminist Legal Theory, Feminist Law–Making, and the Legal Profession," 67 Fordham L.Rev. 249 (1998).

To put the problem somewhat differently, and to help finish off the course by wrestling with the infinite, is the battle for the soul of American law in general and of the legal academy in particular, the topic of this final chapter, a struggle about law, or is it a deeper struggle about basic humanity, or even the nature of reality? Carol Gilligan, in 1984, lambasted social science research that has been limited to male subjects and male perspectives, and described the implications of her "different voice" research as profound for our accepted notions about truth itself:

> If you want to support what has been in the Western tradition since Plato—that is, the notion of a unitary truth, that virtue is one, that its name is justice, that it is part of the sense of one right answer upon which we all, in the end, can agree—then you will select an all-male sample. It is a very interesting thing. The inclusion of women will challenge this tradition and make it impossible to sustain a unitary view. In that sense this inclusion brings in the question of difference, of two perspectives. It offers the possibility of a more adequate representation of human experience by including what formerly was ruled out by definition and then sustained by a major flaw in research.

Feminist Discourse, at 49. Is Gilligan right? Is the ideal of justice an exclusively "male" social construct? If law or jurisprudence (or their history) are not to be about "justice," what ought they to be about, and who is in the best position, then, to save our souls, law and economics, critical legal studies, law and literature, critical race theory or the feminists? Or is the very idea of trying to find a "best position" now a suspect "social construction"?

This rejection of the notion that there are fundamentals on which we all ought to agree, appears to be the central critical move of the latest schools of thought to flourish in the legal academy, pragmatism and postmodernism. Pragmatism, boiled down to its essence, or grossly oversimplified, holds that we should not worry so much about Langdellian niceties of doctrine, or logical consistency, but should instead concentrate on fashioning context-sensitive efficient decisions in particular cases. See generally Richard A. Posner, Overcoming Law 387–405 (1995). Posner reports that in addition to himself, leading pragmatists (or "neo-pragmatists" as they are occasionally called), include William Eskridge, Daniel Farber, Philip Frickey, Thomas Grey, Frank Michaelman, Martha Minow, Margaret Jane Radin, Cass Sunstein, and, surprisingly, Ronald Dworkin, Roberto Unger, and Morton Horwitz. Posner remarks, deadpan, "The ideological diversity of this group is noteworthy." Id., at 389. Would you have guessed that all these people are neo or just plain pragmatists? What exactly *is* pragmatism, and have you encountered any of its practitioners before? Hint: the name of one is six letters long, begins with "H" and ends with "S".

Postmodernism is harder to define, something like nailing jello to a wall. It appears to be a deconstructive enterprise, owing much to French faddish philosophy, and it seems, ultimately, to do little more than furnish an excuse for neopragmatism. It is the postmodernists who tell us of the fatal flaws of any "foundational" theories, and who try to convince us that the principal project of "modernity," the attempt to use rationality to achieve individual growth and societal progress, is doomed to failure, principally because of the inherent incoherence of its ideas. See generally Peter C. Schanck, "Understanding Postmodern Thought and Its Implications for Statutory Interpretation," 65 S.Cal.L.Rev. 2505 (1995), and Robert L. Hayman, Jr. and Nancy Levit, Jurisprudence: Contemporary Readings, Problems, and Narratives 507–574 (1995). If, by now, you've begun to wonder why anyone in law schools would spend their time formulating and elaborating concepts such as postmodernism, or for that matter neo-pragmatism, or even feminism, critical legal studies, or critical race theory, you're not alone. Not only have some in the academy, such as Dean Carrington, decried this phenomenon, a sitting judge (and former law professor), Harry Edwards, has strongly suggested that law schools are becoming dangerously irrelevant to the practice of law, because they have been "emphasizing abstract theory at the expense of practical scholarship and pedagogy." Harry T. Edwards, "The Growing Disjunction Between Legal Education and the Legal Profession," 91 Mich.L.Rev. 34 (1992). Is it only thc law schools which have been infected with the virus of postmodernism? Consider the constitutional law decisions of the Supreme Court with which we conclude the course. Is this postmodern constitutional law? Is it neopragmatic? For further reading on the postmodernist turn in the law schools, see, e.g., Dennis R. Arrow, "Pomobabble: Postmodern Newspeak and Constitutional 'Meaning' for the Uninitiated," 96 Mich. L. Rev. 461 (1997), "and Dennis W. Arrow," Spaceball (Or, Not Everything That's Left Is Postmodern)," 54 Vand. L. Rev. 2381 (2001), and Stephen M. Feldman, "An

Arrow to the Heart: The Love and Death of Postmodern Legal Scholarship," 54 Vand. L.Rev. 2351 (2001).

F. POSTMODERN NEOPRAGMATIC CONSTITUTIONAL LAW

PLANNED PARENTHOOD OF SOUTHEASTERN PENNSYLVANIA V. CASEY

Supreme Court of the United States, 1992.
505 U.S. 833, 112 S.Ct. 2791, 120 L.Ed.2d 674.

JUSTICE O'CONNOR, JUSTICE KENNEDY, and JUSTICE SOUTER announced the judgment of the Court * * *.

I

19 years after our holding that the Constitution protects a woman's right to terminate her pregnancy in its early stages, *Roe v. Wade* (1973), that definition of liberty is still questioned * * *.

At issue * * * are five provisions of the Pennsylvania Abortion Control Act. * * * The Act requires that a woman seeking an abortion give her informed consent prior to the abortion procedure, and specifies that she be provided with certain information at least 24 hours before the abortion is performed. For a minor to obtain an abortion, the Act requires the informed consent of one of her parents, but provides for a judicial bypass option if the minor does not wish to or cannot obtain a parent's consent. Another provision * * * requires that, unless certain exceptions apply, a married woman seeking an abortion must sign a statement indicating that she has notified her husband of her intended abortion. The Act exempts compliance with these three requirements in the event of a "medical emergency." * * *

* * *

* * * [W]e acknowledge that our decisions after *Roe* cast doubt upon the meaning and reach of its holding. State and federal courts as well as legislatures throughout the Union must have guidance as they seek to address this subject in conformance with the Constitution.

After considering the fundamental constitutional questions resolved by *Roe,* principles of institutional integrity, and the rule of *stare decisis,* we are led to conclude this: the essential holding of *Roe v. Wade* should be retained and once again reaffirmed.

* * * *Roe's* essential holding, the holding we reaffirm, has three parts. First is recognition of the right of the woman to choose to have an abortion before viability and to obtain it without undue interference from the State. Before viability, the State's interests are not strong enough to sup-

port a prohibition of abortion or the imposition of a substantial obstacle to the woman's effective right to elect the procedure. Second is a confirmation of the State's power to restrict abortions after fetal viability, if the law contains exceptions for pregnancies which endanger a woman's life or health. And third is the principle that the State has legitimate interests from the outset of the pregnancy in protecting the health of the woman and the life of the fetus * * *.

II

Constitutional protection of the woman's decision to terminate her pregnancy derives from the Due Process Clause of the Fourteenth Amendment. It declares that no State shall "deprive any person of life, liberty, or property, without due process of law." * * * Although a literal reading of the Clause might suggest that it governs only the procedures by which a State may deprive persons of liberty, for at least 105 years, the Clause has been understood to contain a substantive component as well, one "barring certain government actions regardless of the fairness of the procedures used to implement them." * * *

The most familiar of the substantive liberties protected by the Fourteenth Amendment are those recognized by the Bill of Rights. It is tempting, as a means of curbing the discretion of federal judges, to suppose that liberty encompasses no more than those rights already guaranteed to the individual against federal interference by the express provisions of the first eight amendments to the Constitution * * *. But of course this Court has never accepted that view.

* * * It is a promise of the Constitution that there is a realm of personal liberty which the government may not enter * * *.

Neither the Bill of Rights nor the specific practices of States at the time of the adoption of the Fourteenth Amendment marks the outer limits of the substantive sphere of liberty which the Fourteenth Amendment protects * * *.

* * *

* * * It is settled now, as it was when the Court heard arguments in *Roe v. Wade,* that the Constitution places limits on a State's right to interfere with a person's most basic decisions about family and parenthood * * *.

The inescapable fact is that adjudication of substantive due process claims may call upon the Court * * * to exercise that same capacity which * * * courts always have exercised: reasoned judgment. * * * That does not mean we are free to invalidate state policy choices with which we disagree; yet neither does it permit us to shrink from the duties of our office. * * *

* * *

* * * Some of us as individuals find abortion offensive to our most basic principles of morality, but that cannot control our decision * * *.

* * *

Our law affords constitutional protection to personal decisions relating to marriage, procreation, contraception, family relationships, child rearing, and education * * *. These matters, involving the most intimate and personal choices a person may make in a lifetime, choices central to personal dignity and autonomy, are central to the liberty protected by the Fourteenth Amendment. At the heart of liberty is the right to define one's own concept of existence, of meaning, of the universe, and of the mystery of human life. Beliefs about these matters could not define the attributes of personhood were they formed under compulsion of the State.

* * * Though abortion is conduct, it does not follow that the State is entitled to proscribe it in all instances. That is because the liberty of the woman is at stake in a sense unique to the human condition and so unique to the law. The mother who carries a child to full term is subject to anxieties, to physical constraints, to pain that only she must bear * * *.

* * *

* * * [T]he reservations any of us may have in reaffirming the central holding of *Roe* are outweighed by the explication of individual liberty we have given combined with the force of *stare decisis*. We turn now to that doctrine.

III

A

The obligation to follow precedent begins with necessity, and a contrary necessity marks its outer limit * * *. [N]o judicial system could do society's work if it eyed each issue afresh in every case that raised it * * *. At the other extreme, a different necessity would make itself felt if a prior judicial ruling should come to be seen so clearly as error that its enforcement was for that very reason doomed.

* * * [T]he rule of *stare decisis* is not an "inexorable command * * *." Rather, when this Court reexamines a prior holding, its judgment is customarily informed by a series of prudential and pragmatic considerations * * *. Thus, for example, we may ask whether the rule has proved to be intolerable simply in defying practical workability * * *; whether the rule is subject to a kind of reliance that would lend a special hardship to the consequences of overruling and add inequity to the cost of repudiation * * *; whether related principles of law have * * * developed as to have

left the old rule no more than a remnant of abandoned doctrine * * *; or whether facts have so changed or come to be seen so differently, as to have robbed the old rule of significant application or justification * * *.

* * *

1

* * * *Roe* * * * has in no sense proven "unworkable." * * * While *Roe* has * * * required judicial assessment of state [abortion] laws * * *, and although the need for such review will remain as a consequence of today's decision, the required determinations fall within judicial competence.

2

The inquiry into reliance counts the cost of a rule's repudiation as it would fall on those who have relied * * * on the rule's continued application * * *. [O]ne can readily imagine an argument * * * premised on the hypothesis that reproductive planning could take virtually immediate account of any sudden restoration of state authority to ban abortions.

To eliminate the issue of reliance that easily, however, would be simply to refuse to face the fact that for two decades of economic and social developments, people have organized intimate relationships and made choices that define their views of themselves and their places in society * * *. The ability of women to participate equally in the economic and social life of the Nation has been facilitated by their ability to control their reproductive lives * * *. [W]hile the effect of reliance on *Roe* cannot be exactly measured, neither can the certain cost of overruling *Roe* for people who have ordered their thinking and living around that case be dismissed.

3

No evolution of legal principle has left *Roe*'s doctrinal footings weaker than they were in 1973 * * *.

The *Roe* Court itself placed its holding in the succession of cases most prominently exemplified by *Griswold v. Connecticut* * * *. When it is so seen, *Roe* is clearly in no jeopardy, since subsequent constitutional developments have [not] disturbed * * * the scope of recognized protection accorded to the liberty relating to intimate relationships, the family, and decisions about whether or not to beget or bear a child * * *.

Roe * * * may [also] be seen * * * as an exemplar of * * * a rule * * * of personal autonomy and bodily integrity * * *. If so, our cases since *Roe* accord with *Roe*'s view that a State's interest in the protection of life falls short of justifying any plenary override of individual liberty claims * * *.

Finally, one could classify *Roe* as *sui generis.* If the case is so viewed, then there clearly has been no erosion of its central determination. The original holding resting on the concurrence of seven Members of the Court in 1973 was expressly affirmed by a majority of six in 1983, see *Akron v. Akron Center for Reproductive Health, Inc.,* * * * (Akron I), and by a majority of five in 1986, see *Thornburgh v. American College of Obstetricians and Gynecologists* * * *.

4

* * * [T]ime has overtaken some of *Roe*'s factual assumptions: advances in maternal health care allow for abortions safe to the mother later in pregnancy than was true in 1973, * * * and advances in neonatal care have advanced viability to a point somewhat earlier * * *. But * * * the[se] divergences from the factual premises of 1973 have no bearing on the validity of *Roe* 's central holding, that viability marks the earliest point at which the State's interest in fetal life is constitutionally adequate to justify a legislative ban on nontherapeutic abortions * * *. [Thus,] no change in *Roe*'s factual underpinning has left its central holding obsolete * * *.

5

The sum of the precedential inquiry to this point shows *Roe*'s underpinnings unweakened in any way affecting its central holding * * *. Within the bounds of normal *stare decisis* analysis, then, * * * the stronger argument is for affirming *Roe*'s central holding * * *.

B

In a less significant case, *stare decisis* analysis could, and would, stop at th[is] point * * *. But the * * * widespread debate *Roe* has provoked calls for some comparison between that case and others of comparable dimension that have responded to national controversies * * *.

The first example is that line of cases identified with *Lochner v. New York,* (1905) * * *. The *Lochner* decisions were exemplified by *Adkins v. Children's Hospital of D.C.,* (1923), in which this Court held it to be an infringement of constitutionally protected liberty of contract to require the employers of adult women to satisfy minimum wage standards. Fourteen years later, *West Coast Hotel Co. v. Parrish* * * * signalled the demise of *Lochner* by overruling *Adkins.* In the meantime, the Depression had come and, with it, the lesson that * * * the * * * contractual freedom protected in *Adkins* rested on fundamentally false factual assumptions about the capacity of a relatively unregulated market to satisfy minimal levels of human welfare * * *. [I]t was true that the Court lost something by its misperception, * * * but the clear demonstration that the facts of economic life were different from those previously assumed warranted the repudiation of the old law.

The second comparison is with the cases employing the separate-but-equal rule [that] * * * began with *Plessy v. Ferguson* (1896), holding that legislatively mandated racial segregation in public transportation works no denial of equal protection * * *. But this understanding of the facts [was] * * * repudiated in *Brown v. Board of Education* (1954) * * *.

The Court in *Brown* * * * observ[ed] that whatever may have been the understanding in *Plessy*'s time of the power of segregation to stigmatize those who were segregated with a "badge of inferiority," it was clear by 1954 that legally sanctioned segregation had just such an effect * * *.

West Coast Hotel and *Brown* each rested on facts * * * changed from those which furnished the claimed justifications for the earlier constitutional resolutions * * *.

* * * Because neither the factual underpinnings of *Roe*'s central holding nor our understanding of it has changed, * * * the Court could not pretend to be reexamining the prior law with any justification beyond a present doctrinal disposition to come out differently from the Court of 1973. To overrule prior law for no other reason than that would run counter to the view repeated in our cases, that a decision to overrule should rest on some special reason over and above the belief that a prior case was wrongly decided * * *.

C

* * * Our analysis would not be complete, however, without explaining why overruling *Roe*'s central holding * * * [would] seriously weaken the Court's capacity to exercise the judicial power and to function as the Supreme Court of a Nation dedicated to the rule of law * * *.

* * * The Court's power lies * * * in its legitimacy * * *.

* * * [T]he Court's legitimacy depends on making legally principled decisions under circumstances in which their principled character is sufficiently plausible to be accepted by the Nation.

The need for principled action to be perceived as such is implicated to some degree whenever this, or any other appellate court, overrules a prior case * * *. People understand that * * * the Court's Justices are sometimes able to perceive significant facts or to understand principles of law that eluded their predecessors and that justify departures from existing decisions * * *.

In two circumstances, however, the Court would almost certainly fail to receive the benefit of the doubt in overruling prior cases. There is, first, a point beyond which frequent overruling would overtax the country's belief in the Court's good faith * * *. There is a limit to the amount of error that can plausibly be imputed to prior courts. If that limit should be exceeded, disturbance of prior rulings would be taken as evidence that justifiable reexamination of principle had given way to drives for particular results in the short term * * *.

* * * [T]he second [circumstance] is * * * [w]here * * * the Court decides a case in such a way as to resolve the sort of intensely divisive controversy reflected in *Roe* * * *. [Where] the Court's interpretation of the Constitution calls the contending sides of a national controversy to end their national division by accepting a common mandate rooted in the Constitution.

* * * [W]hen the Court * * * act[s] in this way, its decision requires a * * * rare precedential force to counter the inevitable efforts to overturn it and to thwart its implementation * * *. But whatever the premises of opposition may be, only the most convincing justification under accepted standards of precedent could suffice to demonstrate that a later decision overruling the first was anything but a surrender to political pressure, and an unjustified repudiation of the principle on which the Court staked its authority in the first instance. So to overrule under fire in the absence of the most compelling reason to reexamine a watershed decision would subvert the Court's legitimacy * * *.

* * *

The Court's duty in the present case is clear. In 1973, it confronted the already-divisive issue of governmental power to limit personal choice to undergo abortion * * *. Whether or not a new social consensus is developing on that issue, its divisiveness is no less today than in 1973 * * *. A decision to overrule *Roe*'s essential holding under the existing circumstances would address error, if error there was, at the cost of both profound and unnecessary damage to the Court's legitimacy, and to the Nation's commitment to the rule of law. It is therefore imperative to adhere to the essence of *Roe*'s original decision, and we do so today.

IV

* * * [I]t is a constitutional liberty of the woman to have some freedom to terminate her pregnancy. The woman's liberty is not so unlimited, however, that from the outset the State cannot show its concern for the life of the unborn, and at a later point in fetal development the State's interest in life has sufficient force so that the right of the woman to terminate the pregnancy can be restricted.

* * *

We conclude the line should be drawn at viability, so that before that time the woman has a right to choose to terminate her pregnancy. We adhere to this principle for two reasons. First, as we have said, is the doctrine of *stare decisis*. Any judicial act of line-drawing may seem somewhat arbitrary, but *Roe* was a reasoned statement, elaborated with great care * * *.

The second reason is that the concept of viability * * * is the time at which there is a realistic possibility of maintaining and nourishing a life outside the womb, so that the independent existence of the second life can * * * be the object of state protection that now overrides the rights of the woman * * *.

The woman's right to terminate her pregnancy before viability is the most central principle of *Roe*. It is a rule of law and a component of liberty we cannot renounce.

* * *

Yet it must be remembered that *Roe* speaks with clarity in establishing not only the woman's liberty but also the State's "important and legitimate interest in potential life." * * *

Roe established a trimester framework to govern abortion regulations. Under this elaborate but rigid construct, almost no regulation at all is permitted during the first trimester of pregnancy; regulations designed to protect the woman's health, but not to further the State's interest in potential life, are permitted during the second trimester; and during the third trimester, when the fetus is viable, prohibitions are permitted provided the life or health of the mother is not at stake.

The trimester framework * * * was erected to ensure that the woman's right to choose not become so subordinate to the State's interest in promoting fetal life that her choice exists in theory but not in fact. We do not agree, however, that the trimester approach is necessary to accomplish this objective * * *.

Though the woman has a right to choose to terminate or continue her pregnancy before viability, it does not at all follow that the State is prohibited from taking steps to ensure that this choice is thoughtful and informed. Even in the earliest stages of pregnancy, the State may enact rules and regulations designed to encourage her to know that there are * * * procedures and institutions to allow adoption of unwanted children as well as a certain degree of state assistance if the mother chooses to raise the child herself * * *. This, too, we find consistent with *Roe*'s central premises, and indeed the inevitable consequence of our holding that the State has an interest in protecting the life of the unborn * * *. Measures aimed at ensuring that a woman's choice contemplates the consequences for the fetus do not necessarily interfere with the right recognized in *Roe,* although those measures have been found to be inconsistent with the rigid trimester framework announced in that case. A logical reading of the central holding in *Roe* itself, and a necessary reconciliation of the liberty of the woman and the interest of the State in promoting prenatal life, require * * * that we abandon the trimester framework as a rigid prohibition on all previability regulation aimed at the protection of fetal life * * *.

* * * [N]ot every law which makes a right more difficult to exercise is, *ipso facto,* an infringement of that right * * *.

The abortion right is similar * * *. Only where state regulation imposes an undue burden on a woman's ability to make this decision does the power of the State reach into the heart of the liberty protected by the Due Process Clause * * *.

* * *

* * * [There is yet an]other basic flaw in the trimester framework: * * * in practice it undervalues the State's interest in the potential life within the woman. *Roe* was express in its recognition of the State's "important and legitimate interest[s] in preserving and protecting the health of the pregnant woman [and] in protecting the potentiality of human life." The trimester framework, however, does not fulfill *Roe*'s own promise that the State has an interest in protecting fetal life * * *. Before viability, *Roe* and subsequent cases treat all governmental attempts to influence a woman's decision * * * as unwarranted. This treatment is * * * incompatible with the recognition that there is a substantial state interest in potential life throughout pregnancy.

The very notion that the State has a substantial interest in potential life leads to the conclusion that not all regulations must be deemed unwarranted. Not all burdens on the right to decide whether to terminate a pregnancy will be undue * * *.

[I]t is important to clarify what is meant by an undue burden.

A finding of an undue burden is a shorthand for the conclusion that a state regulation has the purpose or effect of placing a substantial obstacle in the path of a woman seeking an abortion of a nonviable fetus.

* * * Regulations which do no more than create a structural mechanism by which the State, or the parent or guardian of a minor, may express profound respect for the life of the unborn are permitted, if they are not a substantial obstacle to the woman's exercise of the right to choose * * *. [A] state measure designed to persuade her to choose childbirth over abortion will be upheld if reasonably related to that goal * * *.

* * *

These principles control our assessment of the Pennsylvania statute, and we now turn to the issue of the validity of its challenged provisions.

* * *

B

[T]he informed consent requirement[:] Except in a medical emergency, the statute requires that at least 24 hours before performing an abortion a physician inform the woman of the nature of the procedure, the health risks of the abortion and of childbirth, and the "probable gestational age of the unborn child." [He] * * * must inform the woman of the availability of printed materials published by the State describing the fetus and providing information about medical assistance for childbirth, information about child support from the father, and a list of agencies which provide adoption and other services as alternatives to abortion. An abortion may not be performed unless the woman certifies in writing that she has been informed of the availability of these printed materials.

* * * The conclusions reached by a majority of the Justices * * * today and the undue burden standard adopted in this opinion require us to overrule in part some of the Court's past decisions, decisions driven by the trimester framework's prohibition of all previability regulations designed to further the State's interest in fetal life.

* * *

* * * [W]e permit a State to further its legitimate goal of protecting the life of the unborn by enacting legislation aimed at ensuring a decision that is mature and informed, even when in so doing the State expresses a preference for childbirth over abortion * * *. This requirement cannot be considered a substantial obstacle to obtaining an abortion, and, it follows, there is no undue burden.

* * *

* * * The idea that important decisions will be more informed and deliberate if they follow some period of reflection does not strike us as unreasonable, * * * [and is therefore] a reasonable measure to implement the State's interest in protecting the life of the unborn, a measure that does not amount to an undue burden.

Whether the mandatory 24–hour waiting period is nonetheless invalid because in practice it is a substantial obstacle to a woman's choice to terminate her pregnancy is a closer question. The findings of fact by the District Court indicate that because of the distances many women must travel to reach an abortion provider, the practical effect will often be a delay of much more than a day; * * * [and] that in many instances this will increase the exposure of women seeking abortions to "the harassment and hostility of anti-abortion protestors demonstrating outside a clinic." * * * As a result, the District Court found that for those women who have the fewest financial resources, those who must travel long distances, and those who have difficulty explaining their whereabouts to husbands, employers, or others, the 24–hour waiting period will be "particularly burdensome."

These findings * * * do not demonstrate that the waiting period constitutes an undue burden. We do not doubt that * * * the waiting period has the effect of "increasing the cost and risk of delay of abortions," but the District Court did not conclude that the increased costs and potential delays amount to substantial obstacles * * *.

* * *

C

* * * Pennsylvania's abortion law [also] provides, except in cases of medical emergency, that no physician shall perform an abortion on a married woman without receiving a signed statement from the woman that she has notified her spouse that she is about to undergo an abortion. The woman has the option of providing an alternative signed statement certifying that her husband is not the man who impregnated her; that her husband could not be located; that the pregnancy is the result of spousal sexual assault which she has reported; or that the woman believes that notifying her husband will cause him or someone else to inflict bodily injury upon her * * *.

* * *

The limited research that has been conducted with respect to notifying one's husband about an abortion, although involving samples too small to be representative, * * * supports the District Court's findings of fact[; T]he vast majority of women notify their male partners of their decision to obtain an abortion. In many cases in which married women do not notify their husbands, the pregnancy is the result of an extramarital affair. Where the husband is the father, the primary reason women do not notify their husbands is that the husband and wife are experiencing marital difficulties, often accompanied by incidents of violence.

* * * [W]omen who are * * * victims of [psychological] abuse are not exempt from [the statute's] notification requirement. And many women who are pregnant as a result of sexual assaults by their husbands will be unable to avail themselves of the exception for spousal sexual assault because the exception requires that the woman have notified law enforcement authorities within 90 days of the assault, and her husband will be notified of her report once an investigation begins. If anything * * * is certain, it is that victims of spousal sexual assault are extremely reluctant to report the abuse to the government * * *.

The spousal notification requirement is thus likely to prevent a significant number of women from obtaining an abortion * * *. [F]or many women, it will impose a substantial obstacle * * *.

* * *

This conclusion is in no way inconsistent with our decisions upholding parental notification or consent requirements * * *. Those enactments * * * are based on the quite reasonable assumption that minors will benefit from consultation with their parents and that children will often not realize that their parents have their best interests at heart. We cannot adopt a parallel assumption about adult women.

We recognize that a husband has a "deep and proper concern and interest * * * in his wife's pregnancy and in the growth and development of the fetus she is carrying." * * *

It is an inescapable biological fact that "state regulation with respect to the child a woman is carrying will have a far greater impact on the mother's liberty than on the father's * * *. Inasmuch as it is the woman who physically bears the child and who is the more directly and immediately affected by the pregnancy, as between the two, the balance weighs in her favor." * * * The Constitution protects individuals, men and women alike, from unjustified state interference * * *. There was a time, not so long ago, when a different understanding of the family and of the Constitution prevailed. In *Bradwell v. Illinois,* three Members of this Court reaffirmed the common-law principle that "a woman had no legal existence separate from her husband * * * ". These views, of course, are no longer consistent with our understanding of the family, the individual, or the Constitution * * *. For the great many women who are victims of abuse inflicted by their husbands, or whose children are the victims of such abuse, a spousal notice requirement enables the husband to wield an effective veto over his wife's decision * * *.

The husband's interest in the life of the child his wife is carrying does not permit the State to empower him with this troubling degree of authority over his wife * * *. If a husband's interest in the potential life of the child outweighs a wife's liberty, * * * [p]erhaps next in line would be a statute requiring pregnant married women to notify their husbands before engaging in conduct causing risks to the fetus. After all, if the husband's interest in the fetus' safety is a sufficient predicate for state regulation, the State could reasonably conclude that pregnant wives should notify their husbands before drinking alcohol or smoking * * *. A State may not give to a man the kind of dominion over his wife that parents exercise over their children * * *.

* * * Women do not lose their constitutionally protected liberty when they marry * * *.

D

* * * [T]he parental consent provision. Except in a medical emergency, an unemancipated young woman under 18 may not obtain an abortion

unless she and one of her parents (or guardian) provides informed consent as defined above. If neither a parent nor a guardian provides consent, a court may authorize the performance of an abortion upon a determination that the young woman is mature and capable of giving informed consent and has in fact given her informed consent, or that an abortion would be in her best interests * * *. [W]e reaffirm today, that a State may require a minor seeking an abortion to obtain the consent of a parent or guardian, provided that there is an adequate judicial bypass procedure * * *.

VI

Our Constitution is a covenant running from the first generation of Americans to us and then to future generations. It is a coherent succession. Each generation must learn anew that the Constitution's written terms embody ideas and aspirations that must survive more ages than one. We accept our responsibility not to retreat from interpreting the full meaning of the covenant in light of all of our precedents. We invoke it once again to define the freedom guaranteed by the Constitution's own promise, the promise of liberty.

* * *

CHIEF JUSTICE REHNQUIST, with whom JUSTICE WHITE, JUSTICE SCALIA, and JUSTICE THOMAS join, concurring in the judgment in part and dissenting in part.

The joint opinion, following its newly-minted variation on *stare decisis,* retains the outer shell of *Roe v. Wade* but beats a wholesale retreat from the substance of that case. We believe that *Roe* was wrongly decided, and that it can and should be overruled consistently with our traditional approach to *stare decisis* in constitutional cases. We would * * * uphold the challenged provisions of the Pennsylvania statute in their entirety.

* * *

* * * [T]he state of our post-*Roe* decisional law dealing with the regulation of abortion is confusing and uncertain * * *. Unfortunately, [for] * * * those who must apply this Court's decisions, the reexamination undertaken today leaves the Court no less divided than beforehand. Although they reject the trimester framework * * * of *Roe,* Justices O'Connor, Kennedy, and Souter adopt a revised undue burden standard to analyze the challenged regulations. We conclude, however, that such an outcome is an unjustified constitutional compromise, one which leaves the Court in a position to closely scrutinize all types of abortion regulations despite the fact that it lacks the power to do so under the Constitution.

* * * In *Roe,* the Court opined that the State "does have an important and legitimate interest in preserving and protecting the health of the pregnant woman, * * * and that it has still another important and legitimate interest in protecting the potentiality of human life." In the companion case of *Doe v. Bolton,* the Court referred to its conclusion in *Roe* "that a pregnant woman does not have an absolute constitutional right to an abortion on her demand." But while the language and holdings of these cases appeared to leave States free to regulate abortion procedures in a variety of ways, later decisions based on them have found considerably less latitude for such regulations than might have been expected.

* * *

Dissents in these cases expressed the view that the Court was expanding upon *Roe* in imposing ever greater restrictions on the States. And, when confronted with State regulations of this type in past years, the Court has become increasingly more divided: the three most recent abortion cases have not commanded a [majority of Justices in support of a single] Court opinion.

* * * This state of confusion and disagreement warrants reexamination of the "fundamental right" accorded to a woman's decision to abort a fetus in *Roe,* with its concomitant requirement that any state regulation of abortion survive "strict scrutiny."

* * *

In construing the phrase "liberty" incorporated in the Due Process Clause of the Fourteenth Amendment, we have recognized that its meaning extends beyond freedom from physical restraint * * *. [W]e have held that the term "liberty" includes a right to marry, a right to procreate, and a right to use contraceptives. But a reading of these opinions makes clear that they do not endorse any all-encompassing "right of privacy."

In *Roe,* the Court recognized a "guarantee of personal privacy" which "is broad enough to encompass a woman's decision whether or not to terminate her pregnancy." We are now of the view that, in terming this right fundamental, the Court in *Roe* read the earlier opinions upon which it based its decision much too broadly. Unlike marriage, procreation and contraception, abortion "involves the purposeful termination of potential life." The abortion decision must therefore "be recognized as *sui generis,* different in kind from the others that the Court has protected under the rubric of personal or family privacy and autonomy." * * *

Nor do the historical traditions of the American people support the view that the right to terminate one's pregnancy is "fundamental." * * * At the time of the adoption of the Fourteenth Amendment, * * * at least 28 of the then–37 States and 8 Territories had statutes banning or limiting abortion. By the turn of the century virtually every State had a law prohibiting or restricting abortion on its books. By the middle of the present century, a liberalization trend had set in. But 21 of the restrictive abortion laws in effect in 1868 were still in effect in 1973 when *Roe* was decided, and an overwhelming majority of the States prohibited abortion unless necessary to preserve the life or health of the mother * * *.

We think, therefore, both in view of this history and of our decided cases dealing with substantive liberty under the Due Process Clause, that the Court was mistaken in *Roe* when it classified a woman's decision to terminate her pregnancy as a "fundamental right" that could be abridged only in a manner which withstood "strict scrutiny." * * *

* * *

II

The joint opinion * * * cannot bring itself to say that *Roe* was correct as an original matter; the opinion therefore contains an elaborate discussion of *stare decisis*. This discussion of the principle of *stare decisis* appears to be almost entirely dicta, because the joint opinion does not apply that principle in dealing with *Roe*. *Roe* decided that a woman had a fundamental right to an abortion. The joint opinion rejects that view. *Roe* decided that abortion regulations were to be subjected to "strict scrutiny" * * * The joint opinion rejects that view. *Roe* analyzed abortion regulation under a rigid trimester framework, a framework which has guided this Court's decisionmaking for 19 years. The joint opinion rejects that framework. *Stare decisis* is defined in Black's Law Dictionary as meaning "to abide by, or adhere to, decided cases." * * * While purporting to adhere to precedent, the joint opinion instead revises it * * *.

In our view, authentic principles of *stare decisis* do not require that any portion of the reasoning in *Roe* be kept intact. "*Stare decisis* is not * * * a universal, inexorable command," especially in cases involving the interpretation of the Federal Constitution * * *. Our constitutional watch does not cease merely because we have spoken before on an issue; when it becomes clear that a prior constitutional interpretation is unsound we are obliged to reexamine the question.

The joint opinion discusses several *stare decisis* factors which, it asserts, point toward retaining a portion of *Roe*. Two of these factors are that the main "factual underpinning" of *Roe* has remained the same, and that its doctrinal foundation is no weaker now than it was in 1973 * * *. [T]hat the same facts which gave rise to *Roe* * * * [have remained the same] is not a reason, in and of itself, why those cases must be decided in the same incorrect manner as was the first case to deal with the question * * *.

* * *

The joint opinion also points to the reliance interests involved in this context in its effort to explain why precedent must be followed * * *. The Court today cuts back on the protection afforded by *Roe,* and no one claims that this action defeats any reliance interest in the disavowed trimester framework. Similarly, reliance interests would not be diminished were the Court to go further and acknowledge the full error of *Roe,* as "reproductive planning could take virtually immediate account of" this action.

The joint opinion thus turns to what can only be described as an unconventional—and unconvincing—notion of reliance, a view based on the surmise that the availability of abortion since *Roe* has led to "two decades of economic and social developments" that would be undercut if the error of *Roe* were recognized. The joint opinion's assertion of this fact is undeveloped and totally conclusory * * *. Surely it is dubious to suggest that women have reached their "places in society" in reliance upon *Roe,* rather than as a result of their determination to obtain higher education and compete with men in the job market * * *.

In the end, * * * the joint opinion's argument is based solely on generalized assertions about the national psyche, on a belief that the people of this country have grown accustomed to the *Roe* decision over the last 19 years * * *. [T]he same could have been said about this Court's erroneous decisions that the Constitution allowed "separate but equal" treatment of minorities, see *Plessy v. Ferguson,* or that "liberty" under the Due Process Clause protected "freedom of contract." See *Adkins v. Children's Hospital of D.C.; Lochner v. New York.*

* * * [T]he joint opinion advances a belief that retaining a portion of *Roe* is necessary to protect the "legitimacy" of this Court. Because the Court must take care to render decisions "grounded truly in principle," and not simply as political and social compromises, the joint opinion properly declares it to be this Court's duty to ignore the public criticism and protest that may arise as a result of a decision. Few would quarrel with this statement, although it may be doubted that Members of this Court, holding their tenure as they do during constitutional "good behavior," are at all likely to be intimidated by such public protests.

But the joint opinion goes on to state that when the Court "resolve[s] the sort of intensely divisive controversy reflected in *Roe*" its decision is exempt from reconsideration under established principles of *stare decisis.* This is so, the joint opinion contends, because in those "intensively divisive" cases the Court * * * must * * * take special care not to be perceived as "surrender[ing] to political pressure" and continued opposition * * *. Under this principle, when the Court has ruled on a divisive issue, it is apparently prevented from overruling that decision for the sole reason that it was incorrect, unless opposition to the original decision has died away. The first difficulty with this principle lies in its assumption that cases which are "intensely divisive" can be readily distinguished from those that are not. The question of whether a particular issue is "intensely divisive" enough to qualify for special protection is entirely subjective and dependent on the individual assumptions of the members of this Court * * *. Although many of the Court's decisions divide the populace to a large degree, we have not previously on that account shied away from applying normal rules of *stare decisis* when urged to reconsider earlier decisions * * *.

The joint opinion picks out and discusses two prior Court rulings that it believes are * * * "intensely divisive" * * * and concludes that they are of comparable dimension to *Roe*. It appears to us very odd * * * that the joint opinion chooses as benchmarks two cases in which the Court chose not to adhere to erroneous constitutional precedent, but instead enhanced its stature by acknowledging and correcting its error, apparently in violation of the joint opinion's "legitimacy" principle * * *.

* * * [O]ur decision in *West Coast Hotel,* which overruled *Adkins v. Children's Hospital* and *Lochner*, was rendered at a time when Congress was considering President Franklin Roosevelt's proposal to "reorganize" this Court * * *. It is difficult to imagine a situation in which the Court would face more intense opposition to a prior ruling than it did at that time, and, under the general principle proclaimed in the joint opinion, the Court seemingly should have responded to this opposition by stubbornly refusing to reexamine the *Lochner* rationale, lest it lose legitimacy by appearing to "overrule under fire."

* * *

The joint opinion [states] that the Court acted properly in rejecting the doctrine of "separate but equal" in *Brown* * * *. This is strange, in that under the opinion's "legitimacy" principle the Court would seemingly have been forced to adhere to its erroneous decision in *Plessy* because of its "intensely divisive" character * * *.

There is also a suggestion in the joint opinion that the propriety of overruling a "divisive" decision depends in part on whether "most people" would now agree that it should be overruled * * *. How such agreement would be ascertained, short of a public opinion poll, the joint opinion does not say. But surely even the suggestion is totally at war with the idea of "legitimacy." * * * The Judicial Branch derives its legitimacy, not from following public opinion, but from deciding by its best lights whether legislative enactments of the popular branches of Government comport with the Constitution.

* * * In assuming that the Court is perceived as "surrender[ing] to political pressure" when it overrules a controversial decision, the joint opinion forgets that there are two sides to any controversy. The joint opinion asserts that, in order to protect its legitimacy, the Court must refrain

from overruling a controversial decision lest it be viewed as favoring those who oppose the decision. But a decision to adhere to prior precedent is subject to the same criticism, for in such a case one can easily argue that the Court is responding to those who have demonstrated in favor of the original decision * * *. But this perceived dilemma arises only if one assumes * * * that the Court should make its decisions with a view toward speculative public perceptions. If one assumes instead, * * * that the Court's legitimacy is enhanced by faithful interpretation of the Constitution irrespective of public opposition, such self-engendered difficulties may be put to one side.

* * *

The end result of the joint opinion's paeans of praise for legitimacy is the enunciation of a brand new standard for evaluating state regulation of a woman's right to abortion—the "undue burden" standard * * *. *Roe v. Wade* adopted a "fundamental right" standard under which state regulations could survive only if they met the requirement of "strict scrutiny." While we disagree with that standard, it at least had a recognized basis in constitutional law at the time *Roe* was decided. The same cannot be said for the "undue burden" standard, which is created largely out of whole cloth by the authors of the joint opinion. It is a standard which even today does not command the support of a majority of this Court. And it will not, we believe, result in the sort of "simple limitation," easily applied, which the joint opinion anticipates * * *.

In evaluating abortion regulations under that standard, judges will have to decide whether they place a "substantial obstacle" in the path of a woman seeking an abortion. [Thus,] this standard is based even more on a judge's subjective determinations than was the trimester framework * * *. Because the undue burden standard is plucked from nowhere, the question of what is a "substantial obstacle" to abortion will undoubtedly engender a variety of conflicting views. For example, * * * while the authors conclude that the informed consent provisions do not constitute an "undue burden," Justice Stevens would hold that they do.

* * *

* * * [T]he Constitution does not subject state abortion regulations to heightened scrutiny. A woman's interest in having an abortion is a form of liberty protected by the Due Process Clause, but States may regulate abortion procedures in ways rationally related to a legitimate state interest * * *. [The Chief Justice went on to say that, under the rational relation standard, each of the provisions of the Pennsylvania Act should have been upheld.]

* * *

IV

* * * [W]e therefore would hold that each of the challenged provisions of the Pennsylvania statute is consistent with the Constitution. It bears emphasis that our conclusion in this regard does not carry with it any necessary approval of these regulations. Our task is, as always, to decide only whether the challenged provisions of a law comport with the United States Constitution. If, as we believe, these do, their wisdom as a matter of public policy is for the people of Pennsylvania to decide.

JUSTICE SCALIA, with whom THE CHIEF JUSTICE, JUSTICE WHITE, and JUSTICE THOMAS join, concurring in the judgment in part and dissenting in part.

* * * The permissibility of abortion, and the limitations upon it, are to be resolved like most important questions in our democracy: by citizens trying to persuade one another and then voting * * *. A State's choice between two positions on which reasonable people can disagree is constitutional even when it intrudes upon a "liberty" in the absolute sense. Laws against bigamy, for example, * * * intrude upon men and women's liberty to marry and live with one another. But bigamy happens not to be a liberty specially "protected" by the Constitution.

* * * The issue [in this case] is whether [the power of a woman to abort her unborn child] is a liberty protected by the Constitution of the United States. I am sure it is not. I reach th[is] conclusion * * * because of two simple facts: (1) the Constitution says absolutely nothing about it, and (2) the longstanding traditions of American society have permitted it to be legally proscribed.

* * *

* * * The Court's statement that it is "tempting" to acknowledge the authoritativeness of tradition in order to "cur[b] the discretion of federal judges," is of course rhetoric rather than reality; no government official is "tempted" to place restraints upon his own freedom of action * * *. The Court's temptation is in the quite opposite and more natural direction—towards systematically eliminating checks upon its own power; and it succumbs.

[A]pplying the rational basis test, I would uphold the Pennsylvania statute in its entirety. I must, however, respond to a few of the more outrageous arguments in today's opinion * * *. I shall discuss each of them under a quotation from the Court's opinion to which they pertain.

"The inescapable fact is that adjudication of substantive due process claims may call upon the Court in interpreting the Constitution to exercise that same capacity which by tradition courts always have exercised: reasoned judgment."

* * *

"[R]easoned judgment" does not begin by begging the question, as *Roe* and subsequent cases unquestionably did by assuming that what the State is protecting is the mere "potentiality of human life." The whole argument of abortion opponents is that what the Court calls the fetus and what others call the unborn child is a human life. Thus, whatever answer *Roe* came up with after conducting its "balancing" is bound to be wrong, unless it is correct that the human fetus is in some critical sense merely potentially human. There is of course no way to determine that as a legal matter; it is in fact a value judgment * * *.

* * *

The emptiness of the "reasoned judgment" that produced *Roe* is displayed in plain view by the fact that, after more than 19 years of effort by some of the brightest legal minds in the country, * * * the best the Court can do to explain how it is that the word "liberty" must be thought to include the right to destroy human fetuses is to rattle off a collection of adjectives that simply decorate a value judgment and conceal a political choice. The right to abort, we are told, inheres in "liberty" because it is among "a person's most basic decisions," it involves a "most intimate and personal choic[e]," it is "central to personal dignity and autonomy," it "originate[s] within the zone of conscience and belief," it is "too intimate and personal" for state interference, it reflects "intimate views" of a "deep, personal character,"; it involves "intimate relationships," and notions of "personal autonomy and bodily integrity," and it concerns a particularly "important decisio[n]". But it is obvious to anyone applying "reasoned judgment" that the same adjectives can be applied to many forms of conduct that this Court has held are not entitled to constitutional protection—because, like abortion, they are forms of conduct that have long been criminalized in American society. Those adjectives might be applied, for example, to homosexual sodomy, polygamy, adult incest, and suicide, all of which are equally "intimate" and "deep[ly] personal" decisions involving "personal autonomy and bodily integrity," and all of which can constitutionally be proscribed because it is our unquestionable constitutional tradition that they are proscribable * * *.

* * *

"Liberty finds no refuge in a jurisprudence of doubt."

One might have feared to encounter this august and sonorous phrase in an opinion defending the real *Roe v. Wade,* rather than the revised version fabricated today by the authors of the joint opinion. The shortcomings of *Roe* did not include lack of clarity: Virtually all regulation of abortion before the third trimester was invalid * * *.

The joint opinion frankly concedes that the amorphous concept of "undue burden" has been inconsistently applied by the Members of this Court in the few brief years since that "test" was first explicitly propounded by Justice O'CONNOR.

* * * Defining an "undue burden" as a "substantial obstacle" hardly "clarifies" the test * * *. [T]he joint opinion's verbal shell game will conceal raw judicial policy choices concerning what is "appropriate" abortion legislation.

* * * The "undue burden" standard is not at all the generally applicable principle the joint opinion pretends it to be; rather, it is a unique concept created specially for this case, to preserve some judicial foothold in this ill-gotten territory * * *.

The rootless nature of the "undue burden" standard, * * * is further reflected in the fact that the joint opinion finds it necessary expressly to repudiate the more narrow formulations used in Justice O'CONNOR's earlier opinions. Those opinions stated that a statute imposes an "undue burden" if it imposes "absolute obstacles or severe limitations on the abortion decision." * * * Those strong adjectives are conspicuously missing from the joint opinion, whose authors have for some unexplained reason now determined that a burden is "undue" if it merely imposes a "substantial" obstacle to abortion decisions * * *.

* * * The inherently standardless nature of this inquiry invites the district judge to give effect to his personal preferences about abortion. By finding and relying upon the right facts, he can invalidate, it would seem, almost any abortion restriction that strikes him as "undue." * * *

To the extent I can discern any meaningful content in the "undue burden" standard as applied in the joint opinion, it appears to be that a State may not regulate abortion in such a way as to reduce significantly its incidence. * * *

"While we appreciate the weight of the arguments * * * that *Roe* should be overruled, the reservations any of us may have in reaffirming the central holding of *Roe* are outweighed by the explication of individual liberty we have given combined with the force of *stare decisis*." The Court's reliance upon *stare decisis* can best be described as contrived. It insists upon the necessity of adhering not to all of *Roe,* but only to what it calls the "central holding." It seems to me that *stare decisis* ought to be applied even to the doctrine of *stare decisis,* and I confess never to have heard of this new, keep-what-you-want-and-throw-away-the-rest version * * *. I must confess, however, that I have always thought * * * that the arbitrary trimester framework, which the Court today discards, was quite as central to *Roe* as the arbitrary viability test, which the Court today retains * * *.

* * *

* * * [B]y foreclosing all democratic outlet for the deep passions this issue arouses, by banishing the issue from the political forum that gives all participants, even the losers, the satisfaction of a fair hearing and an honest fight, by continuing the imposition of a rigid national rule instead of allowing for regional differences, the Court merely prolongs and intensifies the anguish.

We should get out of this area, where we have no right to be, and where we do neither ourselves nor the country any good by remaining.

NOTES AND QUESTIONS

1. Do you understand how the Court's decision in *Casey* could be regarded as postmodern or neopragmatic constitutional law? For the suggestion that *Casey* represents something new in Constitutional jurisprudence made by a law professor Judge Posner tells us is now a pragmatist, see Morton J. Horwitz, "Forward: The Constitution of Change: Legal Fundamentality without Fundamentalism," 107 Harv.L.Rev. 32 (1993). Says Horwitz, "The joint opinion in *Casey* may * * * be symptomatic of a crisis of legitimacy in constitutional thought in which the generally accepted paradigms and modes of thought are no longer felt capable of yielding convincing solutions to constitutional questions." Id., at 34. Do you agree? Does this sound familiar? The Court's judgement in *Casey*—that some of the Pennsylvania statute was valid, and one provision was not, was announced in the opinion ostensibly written by the three Justices, O'Connor, Kennedy, and Souter; no majority of five justices could be cobbled together to agree on a standard on which to review abortion cases. Why do you suppose that was? You have seen the arguments of Justices Rehnquist and Scalia, concurred in by Justices White and Thomas. There were two other opinions in the case well worth our scrutiny. One of these was by Justice Blackmun, who wrote the majority opinion in *Roe v. Wade* in 1973. In that case, you will remember, the Supreme Court held that a state may not hinder a woman's right to abortion unless such restriction serves a "compelling" governmental interest. The second opinion was by Justice Stevens. We shall discuss each of these opinions in turn.

Before we consider the concurring opinions in *Casey*, however, consider the decision which the Court refuses to overturn, *Roe v. Wade*. That case, with its companion Doe v. Bolton, 410 U.S. 179 (1973), more-or-less ensured that abortion could not be prohibited by state authorities in any case during a pregnancy, where the health of the mother, now interpreted to mean mental as well as well as physical well-being, might be at risk. This all culminated in the Supreme Court s decision in Stenberg v. Carhart, 530 U.S. 914 (2000), which struck down a state statute that would have banned partial birth abortion [the name given to a particularly grisly late-term procedure involving partial delivery of an intact fetus and terminating its life before the delivery is complete]. According to Harvard Law Professor Mary Ann Glendon's comparative survey, what she labels the "extremism" of *Roe* in combination with Doe made the United States an outlier among liberal democracies. Even Sweden, "the poster country for women's equality and liberal attitudes toward human sexuality," Glendon found, strictly regulated abortion after the eighteenth week of pregnancy in its 1974 statute. Mary Ann Glendon, Abortion and Divorce in Western Law 22 (1987). The difficulty of defending the Court's reasoning in *Roe* should be apparent to you from the manner in which the plurality in *Casey* declines to overrule it. Many analysts agree with Glendon's assessment that *Roe* (and its progeny) represent an extraordinary judicial power grab, and even those who agree with the result in the case are hard-pressed to defend its Constitutional reasoning. Can you?

In a 2003 article, Glendon hypothesized that the 1973 cases were influenced by concerns about doctors' exposure to criminal liability and by a "peculiar form of feminism that took shape in the 1970's, [which included] a puzzling combination of two things that don't ordinarily go together: anger against men and promiscuity; man-hating and man-chasing." "The Women of *Roe v. Wade*," 134 First Things 19, 20 (2003). Glendon, in her provocative piece, argues for returning abortion to the ordinary process of democratic decision-making. She believes that the process of bargaining, education, persuasion and voting would yield a less extreme abortion policy, one that is more consistent with what opinion polls consistently reveal about American attitudes toward protection of unborn life and respect for the equal dignity of women. Do you find her theory about the role that 1970s feminism may have played in *Roe* convincing? Should the Court follow changes in feminist theory? Glendon also contends that Americans are rethinking highly permissive attitudes toward abortion because, "There is growing awareness that the moral ecology of the country has suffered something like an environmental disaster, and that we are faced with a very complicated clean-up operation." Id., at 23. Is this more convincing? Does morality have a place in Constitutional discourse? Do you understand why the abortion question continues to be a politically-divisive one? Does it surprise you to learn that a federal judicial candidate's views on abortion are often the most important topic to come up in his or her confirmation hearings before the Senate? For an introduction to the battle over judicial ideology in confirmation proceedings, see, e.g. Stephen B. Presser, "Should Ideology of Judicial Nominees Matter?: Is the Senate's Current Reconsideration of the Confirmation Process Justified?," 6 Tex. Rev. Law & Pol. 245 (2001).

2. Justice Blackmun begins his concurrence in *Casey* by calling the three-person joint opinion "an act of personal courage," and "a model for future Justices." But Blackmun still had some difficulties with the plurality opinion. The biggest point of disagreement for him, as you might expect, was the issue of what standard to use when reviewing abortion legislation. The plurality maintained that the proper standard should be the new "undue burden" test, but Justice Blackmun wanted to maintain the so-called "strict scrutiny" test of *Roe v. Wade*. Blackmun wrote that strict scrutiny was the proper standard because it "offers the most secure protection of the woman's right to make her own reproductive decisions." Under the "strict scrutiny" test traditionally applied to narrow state interference with fundamental constitutional rights, regulation of abortion would fail absent a "compelling" governmental interest. Blackmun blasted Chief Justice Rehnquist's "cramped

notion of individual liberty" because, according to Blackmun, Rehnquist's opinion "omitted any discussion of the effects that childbirth and motherhood have on women's lives." Another reason, according to Blackmun, to retain *Roe*'s strict scrutiny standard, is the fact that no majority had since agreed upon a different standard. That is, in the abortion cases following *Roe,* the only standard that could garner the support of a majority of the Court was the strict scrutiny standard. The dissenters in those cases, as in *Casey,* usually called for the implementation of the "rational relation" or "rationality review," standard, under which an abortion regulation that places restrictions on the availability of abortion would be upheld so long as it bore a "rational relation" to a valid state interest. Presumably, many more abortion restrictions could be upheld under the rational relation test, as the state is required to prove less than with the strict scrutiny test.

Because, Blackmun maintained, the strict scrutiny standard was the only valid one, he proceeded to conclude that under the "strict scrutiny" standard, none of the challenged provisions of the Pennsylvania abortion code should be upheld.

Although Justice Blackmun commended the plurality's decision in maintaining constitutional protection for abortion, he nevertheless sternly admonished that "[w]hat has happened today should serve as a * * * warning to all who have tried to turn this court into yet another political branch." Nevertheless, later in his opinion, Blackmun wrote that certain fundamental liberties, such as the "right to privacy," "should not be left to the whims of an election." Do Blackmun's statements indicate that it is the job of the courts to choose the right approach to abortion because it is the subject of such white-hot political controversy? Under modern or postmodern or pragmatic constitutionalism, ought it to be the function of the courts to decide issues which are so hotly debated, or should such issues be left to the majoritarian branches of the government? Is postmodernism consistent with democracy? Is that question appropriate?

3. Justice Stevens, in his concurrence in *Casey,* made clear his belief "that the interest in protecting the potential life [as opposed to the mother's right to privacy] is not grounded in the Constitution. It is, instead, an indirect interest supported by both humanitarian and pragmatic concern." Thus, Stevens concluded that when weighed against a woman's "right to bodily integrity," and her purported "freedom to make [abortion] judgments," "serious questions arise * * * when a state attempts to persuade the woman to choose childbirth over abortion," or requires her to wait 24 hours before undergoing an abortion.

Moving on to apply what he understood as the standard of review for abortion legislation, Justice Stevens' interpretation of the undue burden standard led him to conclude that the counseling provisions of the Pennsylvania law placed too much of a burden on women, and therefore were unconstitutional. Does this surprise you? Is this more constitutional pragmatism? Are you comfortable with the "undue burden" standard for constitutional adjudication?

4. The three justices who wrote the plurality opinion in *Casey*—Souter, Kennedy, and O'Connor—were all appointed by Republican presidents who vowed that they would only nominate individuals for the Supreme Court who would interpret rather than make the law. Does the *Casey* plurality opinion suggest they fell short of their goal? Given the jurisprudence of our age, was that goal a worthwhile one?

5. The use of a balancing test, such as the "undue burden" standard applied in Casey, is a relatively new phenomenon in American jurisprudence. Instead of applying clear rules that can be used to determine the outcome of future cases, the Supreme Court, when using a balancing test, has approached the matters brought before it on an *ad hoc* basis, weighing the competing interests of the parties in a manner which traditionally was supposed to be done by legislatures. Notice that both in *Roe* and in *Casey,* the Court sought to balance various interests—of the state, the mother, the father, and of the embryo's life or potential life. Is it a court's job to balance these interests and then prescribe for all fifty states a single standard, or should this be a task for the majoritarian branches? Notice, too, that different justices have different ideas about what the balancing test means, and even which balancing standard should be used in abortion cases. Before "balancing" became such an attractive methodology, before the post-modern era, Supreme Court decisions made firm categorical judgments. Thus, in the great case of *McCulloch v. Maryland* (1817), when Chief Justice John Marshall encountered a state effort to tax the federal Bank of the United States, he did not seek to balance the state's interest in taxation with the federal government's need to regularize the nation's finances free from state interference. He simply declared that the state had no such power. See generally, T. Alexander Aleinikoff, "Constitutional Law in the Age of Balancing," 96 Yale L.J. 943–944 (1987), and see also Stephen B. Presser, *Recapturing the Constitution* 50–52 (1994).

6. The balancing method involves the discovery of two contradictory principles or interests said to lie behind the constitutional provisions in question. Judges then "balance" the two principles or interests to see which should be dominant in the factual situation before them. Should judges be "balancing" interests that vary according to the factual situation before them? Should it be necessary, in order to determine the constitutionality of state laws, to go to court; or should the court attempt to fashion clear-cut rules so that state legislatures might know in advance what is within, as well as without, the bounds of the Constitution? Even in the postmodern era, is this a sensible way to interpret a Constitution? The critics of balancing charge that it is a license for judicial legislation and legerdemain. "Too often * * * one of the policies or principles that are 'balanced' is simply an invention of the court. In *Casey* the supposed 'right to privacy' or 'right to choose' had been manufactured by the majority of Justices who decided *Roe v. Wade,* and had been simply declared by fiat to be included in the Due Process Clause [of the Fourteenth Amendment]." Presser, supra at 53. The right to choose and the right to privacy were ultimately based on grounds advanced in *Griswold v. Connecticut,* 381 U.S. 479 (1965), which found privacy to "inhere in 'penum-

bras, formed by emanations' from the First, Third, Fourth, Fifth, and Ninth Amendments." Such "judicial gymnastics" have been subject to withering criticism. Thus, Justices Stewart and Black, dissenting in *Griswold,* stated that they could "find no general right to privacy in the Bill of Rights, in any other part of the Constitution, or in any case ever before decided by this court." Were they failing to be sufficiently pragmatic or postmodern?

7. The *Casey* plurality purported to adhere to the principle of *stare decisis.* Nevertheless, as other opinions in *Casey* made clear, in *Casey, Roe*'s approach to abortion as a matter to be handled by reference to the particular trimester in which the pregnancy was sought to be terminated and Roe's particular constitutional standard of "strict scrutiny" to be applied to restrictions on abortions were both abandoned. One reason given by the plurality for upholding *Roe* was because of its desire that its action be seen as "principled" and as adhering to the rule of law. Another was that it did not want to cave in to "political pressure." Yet, according to Justice Scalia's *Casey* opinion, the Court had been wrong ever to allow itself to be drawn into this particular political arena. According to Scalia, the legitimacy of the Court is not weakened when the Court overrules an obviously incorrect decision, but, rather, its legitimacy ought to be regarded as imperiled when it strays from the words of the Constitution. With whom do you agree on the legitimacy question and why? Do you regard it as a coherent inquiry? Setting pragmatism and postmodernism aside for the moment, does Feminist theory have anything to offer in this constitutional, jurisprudential, or legal discourse? For three powerful articles by Feminist legal scholars which suggest reconceptualizing the law "because the legal culture fails to understand the different quality of women's subjective hedonic lives in general," see Robin L. West, "The Differences in Women's Hedonic Lives: A Phenomenological Critique of Feminist Legal Theory," 3 Wis. Women's L.J. 81, 83–85 (1987), Cynthia Grant Bowman, "Street Harassment and the Informal Ghettoization of Women," 106 Harv.L.Rev. 517 (1993), and Jane E. Larson, " 'Women Understand So Little, They Call My Good Nature 'Deceit' "A Feminist Rethinking Of Seduction," 93 Colum.L.Rev. 374 (1993).

8. As Justice Scalia observed, one's point of view on abortion turns ultimately on whether or not one believes that an embryo is a person. If one does, then abortion is murder and indefensible. If one doesn't, then there seems no denying that the woman carrying the embryo ought to be able to determine what to do with it, just as she ought to be capable of making any determination regarding surgery to be performed on any other part of her body. Because the American public has no uniform view on this matter, the problem of what to do about abortion does not, to say the least, lend itself to an easy solution. Perhaps any position one might take regarding abortion really reflects value choices and not legal ones, as Scalia says. Who should make such value choices in a postmodern world? Does *Casey* offer an answer? Does it suggest how such values ought to be formed? Should the government or the courts be involved in that process?

9. *Roe v. Wade* and *Planned Parenthood v. Casey* have frequently been compared to two infamous constitutional cases we have already encountered, *Scott v. Sanford* (the *Dred Scott* decision), and *Lochner v. New York.* All of these decisions have been said to employ the notion of "substantive due process." The plurality opinion in *Casey,* you will remember, discussed the validity of substantive due process when it stated that the notion has been used by courts "for at least 105 years." The Fifth Amendment and the Fourteenth Amendment declare that no State shall "deprive any person of life, liberty, or property, without due process of law." Although the "Due Process" Clause of the Fifth and Fourteenth Amendment was used, at least until "105 years" ago, only to invalidate government actions which were unconstitutional because of the procedures used to implement them, "substantive due process" invalidates state legislation based on its actual content. As Taney said of the Missouri Compromise's restricting the ownership of slaves in the territory, taking away property rights could simply not be regarded as "due process." Are you troubled by the use of "substantive due process" to invalidate legislation that has been passed by elected representatives of the people? Is it a part of postmodern or pragmatic constitutionalism that one can't distinguish substance from procedure? Can you? Is the use of substantive due process (an oxymoron if there ever was one) in *Roe* or *Casey* any more defensible than in *Dred Scott* or *Lochner*?

In *Roe* and *Casey,* the Supreme Court ultimately struck down state laws on the basis of rights not enumerated in the Constitution, such as the "right to privacy," "the substantive sphere of liberty which the Fourteenth Amendment protects," or the "realm of personal liberty which the government may not enter." Is the Court over-stepping Constitutionally circumvented bounds when the Court declares the existence of such new rights? Michael Paulsen, an astute, prolific and provocative law professor now at the University of St. Thomas School of Law, has written—flat out—that *Planned Parenthood v. Casey* is ". . . the worst constitutional decision of the Supreme Court in our nation's history. The decision wrongly holds that the Constitution of the United States enshrines as a nearly absolute right the prerogative of a woman to abort her unborn child for essentially any reason. There is no basis—absolutely no basis—in the language of the Constitution for such a holding." Michael Stokes Paulsen, "The Worst Constitutional Decision of All Time," 78 Notre Dame L.Rev. 995, 1040 (2003). Do you agree with Professor Paulsen? For some of Professor Paulsen's other thoughts on *Casey*, see, e.g. Abrogating Stare Decisis by Statute: May Congress Remove the Precedential Effect of *Roe* and *Casey?*", 109 Yale L.J. 1535 (2000), and, on the question of Congress's power in this area see also Gary Lawson, "Controlling Precedent: Congressional Regulation of Judicial Decision–Making," 18 Const. Comm. 191 (2001). For further reading on the jurisprudential problems raised by *Casey*, see, e.g. William S. Consovoy, "The Rehnquist Court and End of Constitutional Stare Decisis: *Casey, Dickerson* and the Consequences of Pragmatic Adjudication," 2002 Utah L.Rev. 53, Alan J. Meese, "Will, Judgment, and Economic Liberty: Mr. Justice Souter and the Mistranslation of the Due Process Clause," 41 Wm. & Mary L. Rev. 3 (1999), and the withering poem by

Gary Lawson, "Casey at the Court," 17 Const. Comm. 161 (2000). In postmodern constitutionalism, is there still any deference to the constitutional text? Is postmodern constitutionalism like the "new" literary criticism where each reader, in effect, makes a unique text for himself or herself? Is there now no difference between law and literature? It used to be, of course, that one overwhelmingly significant feature of law—even constitutional law—was its moral or religious foundation. Has that been obliterated in the new era? Consider Lee v. Weisman, which follows.

LEE V. WEISMAN

Supreme Court of the United States, 1992.
505 U.S. 577, 112 S.Ct. 2649, 120 L.Ed.2d 467.

JUSTICE KENNEDY delivered the opinion of the Court.

* * * The question before us is whether including clerical members who offer prayers as part of the official school graduation ceremony is consistent with the Religion Clauses of the First Amendment, provisions the Fourteenth Amendment makes applicable with full force to the States and their school districts.

I

A

Deborah Weisman graduated from Nathan Bishop Middle School, a public school in Providence, at a formal ceremony in June 1989 * * *. For many years it has been the policy of the Providence School Committee * * * to permit principals to invite members of the clergy to give invocations and benedictions at middle school and high school graduations * * *. Acting for himself and his daughter, Deborah's father, Daniel Weisman, objected to any prayers at Deborah's middle school graduation, but to no avail. The school principal, petitioner Robert E. Lee, invited [R]abbi [Leslie Gutterman] to deliver prayers at the graduation exercises for Deborah's class * * *.

* * * The principal * * * advised [the Rabbi that] the invocation and benediction should be nonsectarian * * *.

Rabbi Gutterman's prayers were as follows:

"INVOCATION

"God of the Free, Hope of the Brave:

"For the legacy of America where diversity is celebrated and the rights of minorities are protected, we thank You. May these young men and women grow up to enrich it.

"For the liberty of America, we thank You. May these new graduates grow up to guard it.

"For the political process of America in which all its citizens may participate, for its court system where all may seek justice we thank You. May those we honor this morning always turn to it in trust.

"For the destiny of America we thank You. May the graduates of Nathan Bishop Middle School so live that they might help to share it.

"May our aspirations for our country and for these young people, who are our hope for the future, be richly fulfilled.

AMEN"

"BENEDICTION

"O God, we are grateful to You for having endowed us with the capacity for learning which we have celebrated on this joyous commencement.

"Happy families give thanks for seeing their children achieve an important milestone. Send Your blessings upon the teachers and administrators who helped prepare them.

"The graduates now need strength and guidance for the future, help them to understand that we are not complete with academic knowledge alone. We must each strive to fulfill what You require of us all: To do justly, to love mercy, to walk humbly.

"We give thanks to You, Lord, for keeping us alive, sustaining us and allowing us to reach this special, happy occasion.

AMEN"

* * * The parties stipulate that attendance at graduation ceremonies is voluntary * * *. We assume the clergy's participation in any high school graduation exercise would be about what it was at Deborah's middle school ceremony. There the students stood for the Pledge of Allegiance and remained standing during the Rabbi's prayers * * *.

The school board * * * argued that these short prayers and others like them at graduation exercises are of profound meaning to many students and parents * * * who consider that due respect and acknowledgement for divine guidance * * * ought to be expressed at an event as important in life as a graduation * * *.

* * *

II

These dominant facts mark and control the confines of our decision: State officials direct the performance of a formal religious exercise at promotional and graduation ceremonies for secondary schools. Even for those students who object to the religious exercise, their attendance and participation in the state-sponsored religious activity are in a fair and real sense obligatory, though the school district does not require attendance as a condition for receipt of the diploma.

This case does not require us to revisit the difficult questions dividing us in recent cases, [regarding] the definition and full scope of the principles governing the extent of permitted accommodation by the State for the religious beliefs and practices of many of its citizens, * * * [f]or without reference to those principles in other contexts, the controlling precedents * * * compel the holding here that the policy of the city of Providence is an unconstitutional one * * *. The government's involvement with religious activity in this case is pervasive, to the point of creating a state-sponsored and state-directed religious exercise in a public school. Conducting this formal religious observance conflicts with settled rule pertaining to prayer exercises for students * * *.

The principle that government may accommodate the free exercise of religion does not supersede the fundamental limitations imposed by the Establishment Clause. It is beyond dispute that, at a minimum, the Constitution guarantees that government may not coerce anyone to support or participate in religion or its exercise, or otherwise act in a way which "establishes a [state] religion or religious faith, or tends to do so." * * * The State's involvement in the school prayers challenged today violates these central principles.

* * * [T]he principal decided that an invocation and a benediction should be given * * * [and he chose the religious participant] and [these] choice[s are] attributable to the State, and from a constitutional perspective it is as if a state statute decreed that the prayers must occur * * *.

Divisiveness * * * can attend any state decision respecting religions, and neither its existence nor its potential necessarily invalidates the State's attempts to accommodate religion in all cases. The potential for divisiveness is of particular relevance here though, because it centers around an overt religious exercise in a secondary school environment where * * * subtle coercive pressures exist and where the student had no real alternative which would have allowed her to avoid the fact or appearance of participation.

* * * It is a cornerstone principle of our Establishment Clause jurisprudence that "it is no part of the business of government to compose official prayers for any group of the American people to recite as a part of a religious program carried on by government," * * * and that is what the school officials attempted to do.

* * * The question is not the good faith of the school in attempting to make the prayer acceptable to most persons [by ensuring that sectarianism is removed], but the legitimacy of its undertaking that enterprise at

all when the object is to produce a prayer to be used in a formal religious exercise which students, for all practical purposes, are obliged to attend.

* * * There may be some support [for the notion] * * * that there has emerged in this country a civic religion [which permits once conflicting faiths to express the shared conviction that there is an ethic and a morality which transcend human invention], one which is tolerated when sectarian exercises are not * * *. But though the First Amendment does not allow the government to stifle prayers which aspire to these ends, neither does it permit the government to undertake that task for itself.

The First Amendment's Religion Clauses mean that religious beliefs and religious expression are too precious to be either proscribed or prescribed by the State, [and] * * * preservation and transmission of religious beliefs and worship is a responsibility and a choice committed to the private sphere * * *. James Madison, the principal author of the Bill of Rights, * * * rest[ed] his opposition to a religious establishment on the principal ground [that]: "[E]xperience witnesseth that ecclesiastical establishments, instead of maintaining the purity and efficacy of Religion, have had a contrary operation." * * *

These concerns have particular application in the case of school officials, whose effort to monitor prayer will be perceived by the students as inducing a participation they might otherwise reject. Though the efforts of the school officials in this case to find common ground appear to have been a good-faith attempt to recognize the common aspects of religions and not the divisive ones, our precedents do not permit school officials to assist in composing prayers as an incident to a formal exercise for their students * * *. The suggestion that government may establish an official or civic religion as a means of avoiding the establishment of a religion with more specific creeds strikes us as a contradiction that cannot be accepted.

The degree of school involvement here made it clear that the graduation prayers bore the imprint of the State and thus put school-age children who objected in an untenable position * * *.

* * * It is argued that our constitutional vision of a free society requires confidence in our own ability to accept or reject ideas of which we do not approve, and that prayer at a high school graduation does nothing more than offer a choice * * *. This argument cannot prevail, however. It overlooks a fundamental dynamic of the Constitution.

The First Amendment protects speech and religion by quite different mechanisms. Speech is protected by insuring its full expression even when the government participates, for the very object of some of our most important speech is to persuade the government to adopt an idea as its own * * *. In religious debate or expression, [however,] the government is not a prime participant, for the Framers deemed religious establishment antithetical to the freedom of all * * * [T]he Establishment Clause is a specific prohibition on forms of state intervention in religious affairs with no precise counterpart in the speech provisions * * *. The explanation lies in the lesson of history that was and is the inspiration for the Establishment Clause * * * that in the hands of government what might begin as a tolerant expression of religious views may end in a policy to indoctrinate and coerce * * *.

* * *

* * * Our decisions * * * recognize, among other things, that prayer exercises in public schools carry a particular risk of indirect coercion * * *. What to most believers may seem nothing more than a reasonable request that the nonbeliever respect their religious practices, in a school context may appear to the nonbeliever or dissenter to be an attempt to employ the machinery of the State to enforce a religious orthodoxy.

* * * The undeniable fact is that the school district's supervision and control of a high school graduation ceremony places public pressure, as well as peer pressure, on attending students to stand as a group or, at least, maintain respectful silence during the Invocation and Benediction. This pressure * * * can be as real as any overt compulsion * * *. There can be no doubt that for many, if not most, of the students at the graduation, the act of standing or remaining silent was an expression of participation in the Rabbi's prayer. That was the very point of the religious exercise. It is of little comfort to a dissenter, then, to be told that for her the act of standing or remaining in silence signifies mere respect, rather than participation. * * * [A] reasonable dissenter in this milieu could believe that the group exercise signified her own participation or approval of it.

Finding no violation under these circumstances would place objectors in the dilemma of participating * * * or protesting * * *. [T]he State may not, consistent with the Establishment Clause, place . . . school children in this position. Research in psychology supports the common assumption that adolescents are often susceptible to pressure from their peers towards conformity * * *. [T]he government may no more use social pressure to enforce orthodoxy than it may use more direct means.

* * * [T]he embarrassment and the intrusion of the religious exercise cannot be refuted by arguing that these prayers * * * are of a *de minimis* character. To do so would be an affront to the Rabbi who offered them and to all those for whom the prayers were an essential and profound recognition of divine authority. * * * Assuming, as we must, that the prayers were offensive to the student and the parent who now object, the intrusion was both real and, in the context of a secondary school, a violation of the objectors' rights. That the intrusion was in the course of promulgating religion that sought to be civic or nonsectarian rather than pertaining to one sect does not lessen the offense or isolation to the objectors.

* * * Petitioners * * * argu[ed] that the option of not attending the graduation excuses any inducement or coercion in the ceremony itself. The argument lacks all persuasion. Law reaches past formalism. And to say a teenage student has a real choice not to attend her high school graduation is formalistic in the extreme * * *. Everyone knows that in our society and in our culture high school graduation is one of life's most significant occasions * * * [and] it is apparent that a student is not free to absent herself from the graduation exercise in any real sense of the term "voluntary," for absence would require forfeiture of those intangible benefits which have motivated the student through youth and all her high school years * * *.

* * * [Petitioners argue] that the prayers are an essential part of these ceremonies because for many persons an occasion of this significance lacks meaning if there is no recognition, however brief, that human achievements cannot be understood apart from their spiritual essence. We think the Government's position * * * fails to acknowledge that what for many of Deborah's classmates and their parents was a spiritual imperative was for Daniel and Deborah Weisman religious conformance compelled by the State * * *. The Constitution forbids the State to exact religious conformity with a student as the price of attending her own high school graduation * * *.

* * * It is a tenet of the First Amendment that the State cannot require one of its citizens to forfeit his or her rights and benefits as the price of resisting conformance to state-sponsored religious practice * * *.

Inherent differences between the public school system and a session of a State Legislature distinguish this case from [the court's prior holding that it does not infringe the establishment clause for a state legislature to open its session with a prayer.] The atmosphere at the opening of a session of a state legislature where adults are free to enter and leave with little comment and for any number of reasons cannot compare with the constraining potential of the one school event most important for the student to attend * * *. At a high school graduation, * * * the state-imposed character of an invocation and benediction by clergy selected by the school combine to make the prayer a state-sanctioned religious exercise in which the student was left with no alternative but to submit * * *.

We do not hold that every state action implicating religion is invalid if one or a few citizens find it offensive * * *. We know * * * that sometimes to endure social isolation or even anger may be the price of conscience or nonconformity. But, by any reading of our cases, the conformity required of the student in this case was too high an exaction to withstand the test of the Establishment Clause. The prayer exercises in this case are especially improper because the State has in every practical sense compelled attendance and participation in an explicit religious exercise at an event of singular importance to every student * * *.

* * *

Our society would be less than true to its heritage if it lacked abiding concern for the values of its young people, and we acknowledge the profound belief of adherents to many faiths that there must be a place in the student's life for precepts of a morality higher even than the law we today enforce * * *. A relentless and all-pervasive attempt to exclude religion from every aspect of public life could itself become inconsistent with the Constitution * * *. [Nevertheless, no] holding by this Court suggests that a school can persuade or compel a student to participate in a religious exercise. That is being done here, and it is forbidden by the Establishment Clause of the First Amendment.

JUSTICE BLACKMUN, with whom JUSTICE STEVENS and JUSTICE O'CONNOR join, concurring.

Nearly half a century of review and refinement of Establishment Clause jurisprudence has distilled one clear understanding: Government may neither promote nor affiliate itself with any religious doctrine or organization, nor may it obtrude itself in the internal affairs of any religious institution * * *.

I

This Court first reviewed a challenge to state law under the Establishment Clause in Everson v. Board of Education (1947). Relying on the history of the Clause, and the Court's prior analysis, Justice Black outlined the considerations that have become the touchstone of Establishment Clause jurisprudence: Neither a State nor the Federal Government can pass laws which aid one religion, aid all religions, or prefer one religion over another * * *. "In the words of Jefferson, the clause against establishment of religion by law was intended to erect 'a wall of separation between church and State.' " * * * The dissenters agreed: "The Amendment's purpose * * * was to create a complete and permanent separation of the spheres of religious activity and civil authority by comprehensively forbidding every form of public aid or support for religion." * * *

* * *

In 1971, Chief Justice Burger reviewed the Court's past decisions and found: "Three * * * tests may be gleaned from our cases." Lemon v. Kurtzman. In order for a statute to survive an Establishment Clause challenge, "[f]irst, the statute must have a secular legislative purpose; second, its principal or primary effect must be one that neither advances nor inhibits religion; finally the statute must not foster an excessive government entanglement with religion." * * *

Application of these principles to the facts of this case is straightforward. There can be "no doubt" that the "invocation of God's blessings" delivered at Nathan Bishop Middle School "is a religious activity." * * * [W]hen the government "compose[s] official prayers," * * * selects the member of the clergy to deliver the prayer, has the prayer delivered at a public school event that is planned, supervised and given by school officials, and pressures students to attend and participate in the prayer, there can be no doubt that the government is advancing and promoting religion. As our prior decisions teach us, it is this that the Constitution prohibits.

II

* * * The Court holds that the graduation prayer is unconstitutional because the State "in effect required participation in a religious exercise." * * * Although our precedents make clear that proof of government coercion is not necessary to prove an Establishment Clause violation, it is sufficient. Government pressure to participate in a religious activity is an obvious indication that the government is endorsing or promoting religion.

* * * The Establishment Clause proscribes public schools from "conveying or attempting to convey a message that religion or a particular religious belief is favored or preferred." * * *.

* * *

* * * "Our fathers seem to have been perfectly sincere in their belief that the members of the Church would be more patriotic, and the citizens of the State more religious, by keeping their respective functions entirely separate."

* * * When the government puts its imprimatur on a particular religion, it conveys a message of exclusion to all those who do not adhere to the favored beliefs * * *. Only "[a]nguish, hardship and bitter strife" result "when zealous religious groups struggl[e] with one another to obtain the Government's stamp of approval."

* * *

Madison warned that government officials who would use religious authority to pursue secular ends "exceed the commission from which they derive their authority and are Tyrants * * *."

* * * When the government favors a particular religion or sect, the disadvantage to all others is obvious, but even the favored religion may fear being "taint[ed] * * * with a corrosive secularism" * * * The favored religion may be compromised as political figures reshape the religion's beliefs for their own purposes; it may be reformed as government largesse brings government regulation. Keeping religion in the hands of private groups minimizes state intrusion on religious choice * * *.

* * * [O]ur cases have prohibited government endorsement of religion, its sponsorship, and active involvement in religion, whether or not citizens were coerced to conform.

I remain convinced that our jurisprudence is not misguided, and that it requires the decision reached by the Court today.

JUSTICE SOUTER, with whom JUSTICE STEVENS and JUSTICE O'CONNOR join, concurring.

I join the whole of the Court's opinion, and fully agree that prayers at public school graduation ceremonies indirectly coerce religious observance. I write separately nonetheless on two issues of Establishment Clause analysis that underlie my independent resolution of this case: whether the Clause applies to governmental practices that do not favor one religion or denomination over others, and whether state coercion of religious conformity, over and above state endorsement of religious exercise or belief, is a necessary element of an Establishment Clause violation.

I

Forty-five years ago, this Court announced a basic principle of constitutional law from which it has not strayed: the Establishment Clause forbids not only state practices that "aid one religion * * * or prefer one religion over another," but also those that "aid all religions." *Everson* (1947) * * *.

A

Since Everson, we have consistently held the Clause applicable no less to governmental acts favoring religion generally than to acts favoring one religion over others * * *. [cases cited].

* * *

B

Some have challenged this precedent by reading the Establishment Clause to permit "nonpreferential" state promotion of religion * * *. While a case has been made for this position, it is not so convincing as to warrant reconsideration of our settled law; indeed, I find in the history of the Clause's textual development a more powerful argument supporting the Court's jurisprudence following *Everson*. When James Madison arrived at the First Congress with a series of proposals to amend the National Constitution, one of the provisions read that "[t]he civil rights of none shall be abridged on account of religious belief or worship, nor shall any national religion be established * * *." Madison's language did not last long. It was sent to a Select Committee of the House, which, without explanation, changed it to * * * "no religion shall be established by law * * *." Thence the proposal went to the Committee of the Whole, which * * * adopted an alternative proposed by Samuel Livermore: "Congress shall make no laws touching religion * * *." Livermore's proposal would have forbidden laws having anything to do with religion * * *. [but Livermore's language was rejected.]

The House rewrote the amendment once more before sending it to the Senate, this time adopting language derived from a proposal by Fisher Ames: "Congress shall make no law establishing Religion, or prohibiting the free exercise thereof * * *."

The sequence of the * * * treatment of th[ese] proposal[s], confirm[s] that the Framers meant the Establishment Clause's prohibition to encompass nonpreferential aid to religion * * *.

* * * The House conferees ultimately won out, persuading the Senate to accept this as the final text of the Religion Clauses: "Congress shall make no law respecting an establishment of religion, or prohibiting the free exercise thereof." * * * [U]nlike the earliest House drafts or the final Senate proposal, the prevailing language is not limited to laws respecting an establishment of "a religion," "a national religion," [or] "one religious sect." * * * The Framers repeatedly considered and deliberately rejected such narrow language and instead extended their prohibition to state support for "religion" in general.

* * *

* * * [C]onfining the Establishment Clause to a prohibition on preferential aid "requires a premise that the Framers were extraordinarily bad drafters—that they believed one thing but adopted language that said something substantially different, and that they did so after repeatedly attending to the choice of language." Thus, * * * history neither contradicts nor warrants reconsideration of the settled principle that the Establishment Clause forbids support for religion in general no less than support for one religion or some.

C

* * * [O]ne further concern animates my judgment. In many contexts, including this one, nonpreferentialism requires some distinction between "sectarian" religious practices and those that would be, by some measure, ecumenical enough to pass Establishment Clause muster. Simply by requiring the enquiry, nonpreferentialists invite the courts to engage in comparative theology. I can hardly imagine a subject less amenable to the competence of the federal judiciary * * *.

II

Petitioners rest most of their argument on a theory that * * * the Establishment Clause * * * does not forbid the state to sponsor affirmations of religious belief that coerce neither support for religion nor participation in religious observance * * *. But we could not adopt that reading without abandoning our settled law * * *. Nor does the extratextual evidence of original meaning stand so unequivocally at odds with the textual premise inherent in existing precedent that we should fundamentally reconsider our course.

A

* * *

Our precedents * * * simply cannot * * * support the position that a showing of coercion is necessary to a successful Establishment Clause claim.

B

* * *

While petitioners insist that the prohibition extends only to the "coercive" features and incidents of establishment, they cannot easily square that claim with the constitutional text. The First Amendment forbids not just laws "respecting an establishment of religion," but also those "prohibiting the free exercise thereof." Yet laws that coerce nonadherents to "support or participate in any religion or its exercise," * * * would virtually by definition violate their right to religious free exercise * * *. Thus, a literal application of the coercion test would render the Establishment Clause a virtual nullity * * *.

Our cases presuppose as much; as we said in School Dist. of Abington, supra, "[t]he distinction between the two clauses is apparent—a violation of the Free Exercise Clause is predicated on coercion while the Establishment Clause violation need not be so attended." * * *

* * *

III

While the Establishment Clause's concept of neutrality is not self-revealing, our recent cases have invested it with specific content: the state may not favor or endorse either religion generally over nonreligion or one religion over others * * *. This principle against favoritism and endorsement has become the foundation of Establishment Clause jurisprudence, ensuring that religious belief is irrelevant to every citizen's standing in the political community * * *.

A

That government must remain neutral in matters of religion does not foreclose it from ever taking religion into account. The State may "accommodate" the free exercise of religion by relieving people from generally applicable rules that interfere with their religious callings * * *. [S]uch accommodation does not necessarily signify an official endorsement of religious observance over disbelief.

* * *

Thus, in freeing the Native American Church from federal laws forbidding peyote use * * *, the government conveys no endorsement of peyote rituals, the Church, or religion as such; it simply respects the centrality of peyote to the lives of certain Americans.

* * *

JUSTICE SCALIA, with whom THE CHIEF JUSTICE, JUSTICE WHITE, and JUSTICE THOMAS join, dissenting.

* * *

* * * [T]oday's opinion * * * is conspicuously bereft of any reference to history. In holding that the Establishment Clause prohibits invocations and benedictions at public-school graduation ceremonies, the Court * * * lays waste a tradition that is as old as public-school graduation ceremonies themselves, and that is a component of an even more longstanding American tradition of nonsectarian prayer to God at public celebrations generally. As its instrument of destruction, the bulldozer of its social engineering, the Court invents a boundless, and boundlessly manipulable, test of psychological coercion * * *.

I

* * * As we have recognized, our interpretation of the Establishment Clause should "compor[t] with what history reveals was the contemporaneous understanding of its guarantees." * * * "[T]he line we must draw between the permissible and the impermissible is one which accords with history and faithfully reflects the understanding of the Founding Fathers." * * *

The history and tradition of our Nation are replete with public ceremonies featuring prayers of thanksgiving and petition * * *.

From our Nation's origin, prayer has been a prominent part of governmental ceremonies and proclamations. The Declaration of Independence * * * avowed "a firm reliance on the protection of divine Providence." "In his first inaugural address, after swearing his oath of office on a Bible, George Washington deliberately made a prayer a part of his first official act as President."

* * *

Such supplications have been a characteristic feature of inaugural addresses ever since. Thomas Jefferson, for example, prayed in his first inaugural address: "may that Infinite Power which rules the destinies of the universe lead our councils to what is best, and give them a favorable issue for your peace and prosperity." * * * In his second inaugural address, Jefferson acknowledged his need for divine guidance and invited his audience to join his prayer.

* * *

Most recently, President Bush, continuing the tradition established by President Washington, asked those attending his inauguration to bow their heads, and made a prayer his first official act as President * * *.

Our national celebration of Thanksgiving likewise dates back to President Washington * * *. "President Washington proclaimed November 26, 1789, a day of thanksgiving to 'offe[r] our prayers and supplications to the Great Lord and Ruler of Nations * * *.' "

* * *

This tradition of Thanksgiving Proclamations—with their religious theme of prayerful gratitude to God—has been adhered to by almost every President * * *.

The other two branches of the Federal Government also have a long-established practice of prayer at public events * * *. Congressional sessions have opened with a chaplain's prayer ever since the First Congress * * *. And this Court's own sessions have opened with the invocation "God save the United States and this Honorable Court" since the days of Chief Justice Marshall * * *.

In addition to this general tradition of prayer at public ceremonies, there exists a more specific tradition of invocations and benedictions at public-school graduation exercises * * *.

II

The Court presumably would separate graduation invocations and benedictions from other instances of public "preservation and transmission of religious beliefs" on the ground that they involve "psychological coercion." * * * A few citations of "[r]esearch in psychology" that have no particular bearing upon the precise issue here * * * cannot disguise the fact that the Court has gone beyond the realm where judges know what they are doing * * *.

The Court identifies two "dominant facts" that it says dictate its ruling that invocations and benedictions at public-school graduation ceremonies violate the Establishment Clause. Neither of them is in any relevant sense true.

A

* * *

The Court's notion that a student who simply sits in "respectful silence" during the invocation and benediction (when all others are standing) has somehow joined—or would somehow be perceived as having joined—in the prayers is nothing short of ludicrous. We indeed live in a vulgar age. But surely "our social conventions," ibid., have not coarsened to the point that anyone who does not stand on his chair and shout obscenities can reasonably be deemed to have assented to everything said in his presence. Since the Court does not dispute that students exposed to prayer at graduation ceremonies retain (despite "subtle coercive pressures," * * * the free will to sit * * * there is absolutely no basis for the Court's decision). It is fanciful enough to say that "a reasonable dissenter," standing head erect in a class of bowed heads, "could believe that the group exercise signified her own participation or approval of it." It is beyond the absurd to say that she could entertain such a belief while pointedly declining to rise.

But let us assume the very worst, that the nonparticipating graduate is "subtly coerced" * * * to stand! * * * But if it is a permissible inference that one who is standing is doing so simply out of respect for the prayers of others that are in progress, then how can it possibly be said that a "reasonable dissenter * * * could believe that the group exercise signified her own participation or approval"? Quite obviously, it cannot. * * * [M]oreover, that maintaining respect for the religious observances of others is a fundamental civic virtue that government (including the public schools) can and should cultivate * * *. I would deny that the dissenter's interest in avoiding even the false appearance of participation constitutionally trumps the government's interest in fostering respect for religion generally.

* * * [The majority] has not given careful consideration to its test of psychological coercion. For if it had, how could it observe, with no hint of concern or disapproval, that students stood for the Pledge of Allegiance, which immediately preceded Rabbi Gutterman's invocation? * * * Moreover, since the Pledge of Allegiance has been revised since *Barnette* to include the phrase "under God," recital of the Pledge would appear to raise the same Establishment Clause issue as the invocation and benediction. If students were psychologically coerced to remain standing during the invocation, they must also have been psychologically coerced, moments before, to stand for (and thereby, in the Court's view, take part in or appear to take part in) the Pledge. Must the Pledge therefore be barred from the public schools (both from graduation ceremonies and from the classroom)? * * *

* * *

B

The other "dominant fac[t]" identified by the Court is that "[s]tate officials direct the performance of a formal religious exercise" at school graduation ceremonies. "Direct[ing] the performance of a formal religious exercise" has a sound of liturgy to it * * *. All the record shows is that principals of the Providence public schools, acting within their delegated authority, have invited clergy to deliver invocations and benedictions at graduations; and that Principal Lee [advised] Rabbi Gutterman * * * that his prayers at graduation should be nonsectarian. How these facts can fairly be transformed into the charges that Principal Lee "directed and controlled the content of [Rabbi Gutterman's] prayer," that school officials * * * attempted to " 'compose official prayers,' " and that the "government involvement with religious activity in this case is pervasive," is difficult to fathom. The Court identifies nothing in the record remotely suggesting that school officials have ever drafted, edited, screened or censored graduation prayers, or that Rabbi Gutterman was a mouthpiece of the school officials.

* * *

III

The deeper flaw in the Court's opinion * * * lies * * * in the Court's making violation of the Establishment Clause hinge on [the question of peer pressure coercion]. The coercion that was a hallmark of historical establishments of religion was coercion of religious orthodoxy and of financial support by force of law and threat of penalty. Typically, attendance at the state church was required; * * * and dissenters, if tolerated, faced an array of civil disabilities * * *. Thus, for example, in the colony of Virginia, * * * all persons were required to attend church and observe the Sabbath, * * * and were taxed for the costs of building and repairing churches * * *.

The Establishment Clause was adopted to prohibit such an establishment of religion at the federal level (and to protect state establishments of religion from federal interference) * * *. I will further concede that our constitutional tradition, from the Declaration of Independence * * * down to the present day, has, with a few aberrations, * * * ruled out of order government-sponsored endorsement of religion—even when no legal coercion is present, and indeed even when no ersatz, "peer-pressure" psycho-coercion is present—where the endorsement is sectarian * * *. But there is simply no support for the proposition that the officially sponsored nondenominational invocation and benediction read by Rabbi Gutterman—with no one legally coerced to recite them—violated the Constitution of the United States. To the contrary, they are so characteristically American they could have come from the pen of George Washington or Abraham Lincoln himself.

Thus, while I have no quarrel with the Court's general proposition that the Establishment Clause "guarantees that government may not coerce anyone to support or participate in religion or its exercise," I see no warrant for expanding the concept of coercion beyond acts backed by threat of penalty * * *.

* * * Beyond the fact, stipulated to by the parties, that attendance at graduation is voluntary, there is nothing in the record to indicate that failure of attending students to take part in the invocation or benediction was subject to any penalty or discipline. Contrast this with, for example, the facts of *Barnette:* School children were required by law to recite the Pledge of Allegiance; failure to do so resulted in expulsion, threatened the expelled child with the prospect of being sent to a reformatory for criminally inclined juveniles, and subjected his parents to prosecution (and incarceration) for causing delinquency. To characterize the "subtle coercive pressures," allegedly present here as the "practical" equivalent of the legal sanctions in *Barnette* is * * * not a "delicate and fact-sensitive" analysis.

* * *

IV

Our religion-clause jurisprudence has become bedeviled (so to speak) by reliance on formulaic abstractions that are not derived from, but positively conflict with, our long-accepted constitutional traditions. Foremost among these has been the so-called *Lemon* test, which has received well-earned criticism from many members of this Court * * *. The Court today demonstrates the irrelevance of *Lemon* by essentially ignoring it, and the interment of that case may be the one happy byproduct of the Court's otherwise lamentable decision. Unfortunately, however, the Court has replaced *Lemon* with its psycho-coercion test, which suffers the double disability of having no roots whatever in our people's historic practice, and being as infinitely expandable as the reasons for psychotherapy itself.

Another happy aspect of the case is that it is only a jurisprudential disaster and not a practical one. Given the odd basis for the Court's decision, invocations and benedictions will be able to be given at public-school graduations * * *, so long as school authorities make clear that anyone who abstains from screaming in protest does not necessarily participate in the prayers. All that is seemingly needed is an announcement, or perhaps a written insertion at the beginning of the graduation Program * * * that, while we are all asked to rise, * * * none is compelled to join in them, nor will be assumed, by rising, to have done so.

* * *

* * * Religious men and women of almost all denominations have felt it necessary to acknowledge and beseech the blessing of God as a people, and not just as individuals, because they believe * * * God to be, as Washington's first Thanksgiving Proclamation put it, the "Great Lord and Ruler of Nations." * * * But the longstanding American tradition of prayer at official ceremonies displays with unmistakable clarity that the Establishment Clause does not forbid the government to accommodate it.

* * *

* * * The founders of our Republic knew * * * that nothing, absolutely nothing, is so inclined to foster among religious believers of various faiths a toleration—no, an affection—for one another than voluntarily joining in prayer together, to the God whom they all worship and seek. Needless to say, no one should be compelled to do that, but it is a shame to deprive our public culture of the opportunity, and indeed the encouragement, for people to do it voluntarily * * *. To deprive our society of that important unifying mechanism, in order to spare the nonbeliever what seems to me the minimal inconvenience of standing or even sitting in respectful non-participation, is as senseless in policy as it is unsupported in law.

For the foregoing reasons, I dissent.

NOTES AND QUESTIONS

1. As you may remember from earlier in the course, the American common law and the Constitution were once generally believed to reflect American efforts to fashion a national code of conduct that would facilitate our citizens' abilities not only to serve each other and our country, but to serve God as well. For example, in closing the Declaration of Independence with the phrase "sacred honor," the delegates who signed the Declaration most likely were indicating that Americans were undertaking the creation of a new nation pursuant to what they believed to be their obligations from a divinely-inspired natural law. The Framers, then, would probably have found it strange, incomprehensible, perhaps even perverse that modern scholars could attempt to discover, or fashion, law out of purely secular materials. See generally, Stephen Presser, Recapturing the Constitution, pp. 44–45. Is the majority's opinion in Lee v. Weisman good constitutional history? Is it correct that "The First Amendment's Religion Clauses mean that religious beliefs and religious expression are too precious to be either proscribed or prescribed by the State, [and] preservation and transmission of religious beliefs and worship is a responsibility and a choice committed to the private sphere * * *?" What light on this public/private distinction is cast by the latest jurisprudential thinking we have considered?

2. As we saw earlier, when we studied the Federalists, and, in particular, the work of Samuel Chase, an important tenet of their beliefs was apparently that there could be no law without morality and no morality without religion. Similarly, when, in the Declaration, Jefferson invoked the idea of

"nature and nature's God" entitling each citizen to certain inalienable rights, he was underscoring the religious basis of American jurisprudence. Thus, even Jefferson understood the importance of natural law notions that he believed were foundational for positive law. Jefferson's contemporary and rival, Alexander Hamilton, long identified as "someone committed simply to the greatest production of wealth for society," was also on record as believing that morality was the basis for law and order. Presser, supra, at pp. 44–45. Jefferson and Hamilton's views were consonant with those of Blackstone, the cornerstone of the developing American private law jurisprudence. Blackstone believed that the law of nature governs man, and is "revealed to us in the Bible." Id., at 47. Finally, as we saw in our materials on federal common law, the early Supreme Court justices believed that at least some federal law was "of aspect eternal and of origin divine." Does the majority in Weisman's statement that "the Framers deemed religious establishment antithetical to the freedom of all," obscure belief in a divine basis of American law? Can the state promote general religious beliefs, in accordance with the theory of the Framers' intent or understanding without violating the constitutional prohibition against Establishment? Note, by the way, the need felt by all of the writers of opinions in *Lee v. Weisman* to ground their reasoning in history. Are some better historians than others? Is the search for historical justification consistent with postmodernism?

3. Should the state or federal governments be permitted to encourage a "civic religion," a set of non-sectarian postulates that might permit "once conflicting faiths to express the shared conviction that there is an ethic and a morality which transcend human invention?" The Weisman Court refused to allow state authorities to mandate the expression of such views in a school graduation. But isn't this the essence of the non-secular, natural law on which so many Framers believed the law was based? Is it accurate that "American 'civil theology' [in the late eighteenth and early nineteenth centuries] made plain that a morality of social duty flowed from religious faith, and that this morality was essential in upholding the law?" Presser, supra, at 60. There is, of course, no explicit mention in the Constitution of natural law as the basis for the document. Could it be that this was because the idea that morality and religion were the bases of law would have been taken so much for granted that they might have literally gone without saying, or because "The moral and religious edification of the citizen was left to the state and local governments," and "was not regarded as something with which the federal government was primarily charged?" *Ibid.* In the early years of our republic some states did have official religions, and more than several relied on natural law in their constitutions. With this in mind, is the reasoning in *Weisman* appropriate? What do you make of the fact that the majority assumes immediately in Lee v. Weisman that the Fourteenth Amendment means that the First Amendment Establishment Clause applies to the states? Is this self-evident? Is it a sort of post-modernist move? On the other hand, note that the first Supreme Court decisions rejecting state practices of bible reading or non-sectarian prayer occurred in the early sixties. Can it be said that the Supreme Court's practices in that era anticipated recent juris-

prudential developments? Is this recent jurisprudence a means of legitimating these decisions of the Supreme Court? What is the political content of postmodernism? Of neopragmatism?

4. In *West Virginia State Board of Education v. Barnette,* 319 U.S. 624, 63 S.Ct. 1178, 87 L.Ed. 1628 (1943), the Supreme Court, by a vote of 6–3, held that the states could not require students to salute the flag. Although the decision was based on freedom of speech, the real issue in the case may have been to what extent a state government could legislate in a manner that offended particular religious beliefs. The case came about when some Jehovah's Witnesses argued that to compel their children to participate in the flag salute amounted to the worship of icons—a practice forbidden by their religion. It is doubtful that the founding generation would have believed that the pledge of allegiance was in conflict with the First Amendment, since oaths or affirmations of allegiance to the Constitution or to state constitutions were commonplace at the time. In a dissent in *Barnette,* Justice Felix Frankfurter argued that although, according to the Constitution, "no religion shall either receive the state's support or incur its hostility," the state still had an interest in promoting good citizenship as well as national allegiance. Frankfurter stated that the Court was wrong to override state legislatures in this area, because it should be up to state and local governments to determine the best manner in which to preserve the virtue of the citizenry. He thought the flag salute was an appropriate constitutionally-protected effort of that kind. With whom do you agree, Frankfurter, or the majority in *Barnette?* Do you discern in Frankfurter an echo of the Republicanism of the Framers' era?

The majority in *Weisman* based its holding on the idea usually attributed to Thomas Jefferson, of a "wall of separation" between religion and the state. Although Jefferson indeed does mention a "wall of separation between church and state" purportedly erected by the First Amendment, in the same letter he used the phrase he acknowledged the pre-eminence of social duties, the secondary role of natural rights, *and,* of all things, a belief in a single supreme male creator. In that letter Jefferson appears to declare that an individual's "natural right" could not be invoked in opposition to his "social duties," which seems to be precisely what the plaintiffs in both *Barnette* and *Lee* accomplished. See Jefferson's 1802 Letter to the Danbury Baptists, quoted in Presser, Recapturing the Constitution at 164–165. Even if Jefferson did believe in some sort of separation between church and state, given his hostility to federal judges who used the courts to fashion their own political or social policies, does it make sense to invoke his name when a federal court overrules state policy in this area? Again, is *Lee v. Weisman* an orthodox exercise in constitutional law, or is it something else?

If, as the Framers believed, it is impossible to inculcate morality without religion, and if the paramount problem facing many public school students today is an almost total absence of meaningful moral guidance, is it appropriate to conclude that our current rejection of religion in the public sphere has gone too far? Could this be a neopragmatic justification for Scalia's opinion?

Perhaps prompted by *Lee v. Weisman*, and later federal court decisions involving student prayer at football games, display of the ten commandments on public property, and funding of sectarian schools through public voucher programs, there have been a spate of revisionist histories arguing that the *Lee v. Weisman* majority's adherence to a strict separation of religion and state is not in accord with either the intention of the framers or our practice since the founding. For a sampling, see, e.g., Philip Hamberger, Separation of Church and State (2002), Daniel L. Dreisbach, Thomas Jefferson and the Wall of Separation between Church and State (2002), Thomas Berg, "Religious Liberty in America at the End of the Century," 16 J. Law & Religion 187 (2001), Noah Feldman, "The Intellectual Origins of the Establishment Clause," 77 N.Y.U.L.Rev. 346 (2002), and John C. Jeffries & James E. Ryan, "A Political History of the Establishment Clause," 100 Mich.L.Rev. 279 (2001). On the related question of whether it still makes sense to adhere to the original understanding of the framers—whatever that was—there continues to be a deluge of books and articles. Among the most incisive are Laura Kalman, The Strange Career of Legal Liberalism (1996), Jack N. Rakove, Original Meanings: Politics & Ideas in the Making of the Constitution (1996), Keith E. Whittington, Constitutional Interpretation: Textual Meaning, Original Intent, & Judicial Review (1999), Stephen Breyer, "Madison Lecture: Our Democratic Constitution," 77 N.Y.U.L.Rev. 245 (2002), Barry Friedman, "Book Review [of Kalman, Strange Career]: The Turn to History," 72 N.Y.U.L.Rev. 928 (1997), Martin S. Flaherty, "History Right? Historical Scholarship, Original Understanding, and Treaties as 'Supreme Law' of the Land," 99 Col.L.Rev. 2095 (1999), and David A. Strauss, "Common Law, Common Ground, and Jefferson's Principle," 112 Yale L.J. 1717 (2003).

5. Does Justice Souter's legislative history of the First Amendment persuade you that the Amendment is appropriately invoked to prevent nonsectarian prayer in state schools? Why or why not? What, exactly, is the importance of the Congress's rejection of Livermore's language and the substitution of that of Fisher Ames? Is it important that the eventual text of the First Amendment only prohibited legislation establishing religion passed by the *federal* government? Is Souter's turn toward legislative history any more legitimate a judicial undertaking than the opinions of his colleagues in the majority, or Scalia's dissent? For an alternative reading of the legislative history, concluding that it supports the "non-preferentialist" position Souter rejects, see Presser, Recapturing the Constitution, at 233–239.

6. Consider Scalia's dissent. On balance, as it were, is this really a postmodern or neopragmatic exercise? Is Scalia's jurisprudence still in tune with our age? On Scalia's jurisprudence, see, e.g. Antonin Scalia and Bryan A. Garner: Reading Law: The Interpretation of Legal Texts (2012), Antonin Scalia and Amy Gutmann, A Matter of Interpretation: Federal Courts and the Law (1996), Richard A. Brisbin, Justice Antonin Scalia & the Conservative Revival (1997) and Allen R. Kamp, "The Counter–Revolutionary Nature of Justice Scalia's 'Traditionalism,' " 27 Pacific L.J. 99 (1995). When George W. Bush was running for President, he often indicated that he would seek to appoint Justices who would interpret the Constitution rather than make law,

and he stated his models were Justice Scalia and Justice Thomas. Are they appropriate models for a Presidential candidate to invoke? On Justice Thomas's jurisprudence (often thought to be similar to that of Justice Scalia, but clearly with some particular nuances), see, e.g., Scott Douglas Gerber, First Principles: The Jurisprudence of Clarence Thomas (1999), and David N. Mayer, "Justice Clarence Thomas and the Supreme Court's Rediscovery of the Tenth Amendment," 25 Capital U.L.Rev. 339 (1996). Earl Warren, you'll remember, said in *Brown* that we can't "turn back the clock." This must be what the pragmatists, the postmodernists, and the Feminists believe too. We already know, however, that at least one critical legal studies scholar, Mark Tushnet, isn't so sure. How about you?

7. Perhaps it is a bit of a stretch to suggest that *Casey* and *Weisman* are examples of postmodernism or neopragmatism, but there was one series of events in 1998 and 1999 that might even more aptly be singled out as revealing a postmodern or neopragmatic cast to late twentieth century law. That was, of course, the impeachment by the House of Representatives and trial before the Senate of William Jefferson Clinton. In the materials which follow, ask yourself whether you are seeing an abandonment of, or at least a radical change in, the conception of "artificial reason" or "law" which Sir Edward Coke demonstrated in our first reading.

THE CONSTITUTION OF THE UNITED STATES

Article II, Section 4

The President, Vice President and all civil Officers of the United States, shall be removed from Office on Impeachment for, and Conviction of, Treason, Bribery, or other high Crimes and Misdemeanors.

THE STARR REPORT: THE OFFICIAL REPORT OF THE INDEPENDENT COUNSEL'S INVESTIGATION OF THE PRESIDENT

(Forum, An Imprint of Prima Publishing, Edition, 1998).
Pp. 35–36, 41–44.

Introduction

As required by Section 595(c) of Title 28 of the United States Code, the Office of the Independent Counsel ("OIC" or "Office") hereby submits substantial and credible information that President William Jefferson Clinton committed acts that may constitute grounds for an impeachment.

The information reveals that President Clinton: lied under oath at a civil deposition while he was a defendant in a sexual harassment lawsuit; lied under oath to a grand jury; attempted to influence the testimony of a potential witness who had direct knowledge of facts that would reveal the falsity of his deposition testimony; attempted to obstruct justice by facilitating a witness's plan to refuse to comply with a subpoena; attempted to obstruct justice by encouraging a witness to file an affidavit that the President knew would be false, and then by making use of that false affidavit at his own deposition; lied to potential grand jury witnesses, knowing that they would repeat those lies before the grand jury; and engaged in a pattern of conduct that was inconsistent with his constitutional duty to faithfully execute the laws.

The evidence shows that these acts, and others, were part of a pattern that began as an effort to prevent the disclosure of information about the President's relationship with a former White House intern and employee, Monica S. Lewinsky, and continued as an effort to prevent the information from being disclosed in an ongoing criminal investigation.

* * *

The Significance of the Evidence of Wrongdoing

It is not the role of this Office to determine whether the President's actions warrant impeachment by the House and removal by the Senate; those judgments are, of course, constitutionally entrusted to the legislative branch. This Office is authorized, rather, to conduct criminal investigations and to seek criminal prosecutions for matters within its jurisdiction. In carrying out its investigation, however, this Office also has a statutory duty to disclose to Congress information that "may constitute grounds for an impeachment," a task that inevitably requires judgment about the seriousness of the acts revealed by the evidence.

From the beginning, this phase of the OIC's investigation has been criticized as an improper inquiry into the President's personal behavior; indeed, the President himself suggested that specific inquiries into his conduct were part of an effort to "criminalize my private life." The regrettable fact that the investigation has often required witnesses to discuss sensitive personal matters has fueled this perception.

All Americans, including the President, are entitled to enjoy a private family life, free from public or governmental scrutiny. But the privacy concerns raised in this case are subject to limits, three of which we briefly set forth here.

First. The first limit was imposed when the President was sued in federal court for alleged sexual harassment. The evidence in such litigation is often personal. At times, that evidence is highly embarrassing for both plaintiff and defendant. As Judge Wright noted at the President's January 1998 deposition, "I have never had a sexual harassment case where there was not some embarrassment." Nevertheless, Congress and the Supreme Court have concluded that embarrassment-related concerns must give way to the greater interest in allowing aggrieved parties to pursue their claims. Courts have long recognized the difficulties of proving sexual harassment in the workplace, inasmuch as improper or unlawful behavior often takes place in private. To excuse a party who lied or concealed evidence on the ground that the evidence covered only "personal" or "private" behavior would frustrate the goals that Congress and the courts have sought to achieve in enacting and interpreting the Nation's sexual harassment laws. That is particularly true when the conduct that is being concealed—sexual relations in the workplace between a high official and a young subordinate employee—itself conflicts with those goals.

Second. The second limit was imposed when Judge Wright required disclosure of the precise information that is in part the subject of this Referral. A federal judge specifically ordered the President, on more than one occasion, to provide the requested information about relationships with other women, including Monica Lewinsky. The fact that Judge Wright later determined that the evidence would not be admissible at trial, and still later granted judgment in the President's favor, does not change the President's legal duty at the time he testified. Like every litigant, the President was entitled to object to the discovery questions, and to seek guidance from the court if he thought those questions were improper. But having failed to convince the court that his objections were well founded, the President was duty bound to testify truthfully and fully. Perjury and attempts to obstruct the gathering of evidence can never be an acceptable response to a court order, regardless of the eventual course or outcome of the litigation.

The Supreme Court has spoken forcefully about perjury and other forms of obstruction of justice: In this constitutional process of securing a witness' testimony, perjury simply has no place whatever. Perjured testimony is an obvious and flagrant affront to the basic concepts of judicial proceedings. Effective restraints against this type of egregious offense are therefore imperative.

The insidious effects of perjury occur whether the case is civil or criminal. Only a few years ago, the Supreme Court considered a false statement made in a civil administrative proceeding: "False testimony in a formal proceeding is intolerable. We must neither reward nor condone such a 'flagrant affront' to the truth-seeking function of adversary proceedings. . . . Perjury should be severely sanctioned in appropriate cases." Stated more simply, "[p]erjury is an obstruction of justice."

Third. The third limit is unique to the President. "The Presidency is more than an executive responsibility. It is the inspiring symbol of all that is highest in American purpose and ideals." When he took the Oath of Office in 1993 and again in 1997, President Clinton swore that he would "faithfully execute the Office of President." As the head of the Executive Branch, the President has the constitutional duty to "take Care that the Laws be faithfully executed." The President gave his testimony in the Jones case under oath and in the presence of a federal judge, a member of a co-equal branch of government; he then testified before a federal grand jury, a body of citizens who had themselves taken an oath to seek the truth. In view of the enormous trust and responsibility attendant to his high Office, the President has a manifest duty to ensure that his conduct at all times complies with the law of the land.

In sum, perjury and acts that obstruct justice by any citizen—whether in a criminal case, a grand jury investigation, a congressional hearing, a civil trial, or civil discovery—are profoundly serious matters. When such acts are committed by the President of the United States, we believe those acts "may constitute grounds for an impeachment."

NOTES AND QUESTIONS

1. Many volumes will undoubtedly be written about the impeachment and trial of President Clinton. It was surely one of the most curious political events in the nation's history. Depending on what political persuasion you were, the episode was either a shameful attempt by a puritanical pecksniffian independent prosecutor to embarrass a popular President, or a noble crusade by selfless public servants to punish wrongdoing at the highest levels of the federal government. As you read these materials related to the President's impeachment, decide whether you find either of these characterizations plausible, and also seek to understand how the jurisprudential developments we have studied might lead one to embrace the validity of *both* characterizations. Just such an embrace was done, for example, by the man we might regard as the nation's leading postmodern neo-pragmatist, Richard Posner. In one of the first books to be published about the impeachment, Posner wrote:

> "[I]n one [of the two possible 'narratives'], a reckless, lawless immoral President commits a series of crimes in order to conceal a tawdry and shameful affair, crimes compounded by a campaign of public lying and slanders. A prosecutor could easily draw up a thirty-count indictment against the President. In the other narrative, the confluence of a stupid law (the independent counsel law), a marginal lawsuit begotten and nursed by political partisanship, a naïve and imprudent judicial decision by the Supreme Court in that suit, and the irresistible human impulse to conceal one's sexual improprieties, allows a trivial sexual escapade (what Clinton and Lewinsky called 'fooling around' or 'messing around') to balloon into a grotesque and gratuitous constitutional drama. *The problem is that both narratives are correct.*"

Richard Posner, An Affair of State: The Investigation, Impeachment and Trial of President Clinton 92 (1999). This excerpt from Posner's book was thought to be so central it was blurbed on the back dust jacket. Is Posner right? How can he be?

2. What was it that the President did, and how did Independent Counsel Starr get involved? Starr's investigation of the President started with other matters, including land deals in Arkansas, White House Travel Office firings, and unauthorized use of Republicans' FBI Files, but none of those other matters led Starr to make an impeachment referral to the House. Starr's of-

fice became interested in matters surrounding Monica Lewinsky, who had been called for a deposition in the Paula Jones case, when Starr's office received information that seemed to suggest that Ms. Lewinsky was being urged to file a false affidavit in that case by persons close to the President, including his friend, Vernon Jordan, whom Starr's office had suspected of similar wrongdoing in connection with Webster Hubbell, a former Clinton administration official who was involved in the Arkansas land matters. See the Starr Report, supra, at 45. In spite of these suspicions, Mr. Jordan was not charged with any criminal wrongdoing in connection with any of these matters.

3. President Clinton, for a long time, denied any sexual relationship with Ms. Lewinsky. He did so in a deposition conducted by Paula Jones's lawyers (who were trying to prove a pattern of sexual misconduct on the President's part), in televised interviews he gave regarding the case, and in grand jury testimony concerned with the matter, as the Starr Report indicates. The President's denial of such a relationship collapsed when some of his genetic material was found on a blue dress which Ms. Lewinsky had worn during one of their trysts. Paula Jones had brought suit against the President, in a federal court in Arkansas, alleging that he had made an improper sexual advance toward her, thus committing a violation under the federal civil rights laws (because he allegedly abused his power as a state official), and also a violation under Arkansas tort laws (because he allegedly inflicted great mental distress on her). As one newspaper account stated, "Jones accused Clinton of luring her to a Little Rock hotel suite during a state conference on May 8, 1991, when she was a $4.93-an-hour state clerk and he was governor of Arkansas. Clinton, she alleged, flattered and kissed her, dropped his pants and asked for oral sex, an advance she said she rebuffed." Peter Baker, Clinton Payment Ends Jones Suit, The Washington Post, January 13, 1999, p.A1. In the course of discovery proceedings, in their civil suit, Paula Jones's lawyers sought to show that the President had behaved in a similar manner to many women, rewarding those who went along with his wishes, and threatening harm to others who did not. The matter never made it to trial, because Judge Susan Webber Wright, the federal District Judge trying the case, granted the President's motion for summary judgment, finding that even if the facts were as Ms. Jones alleged, they would not amount to the federal or state causes of action charged.

4. As a result of the discovery proceedings, in the Jones lawsuit, however, the allegations of Presidential coaching of witnesses, tampering with evidence, and committing perjury in civil and criminal proceedings came to light. The President's lawyers steadfastly denied that the President had committed any of these offenses, but most members of the public were convinced otherwise. Judge Wright's dismissal of Ms. Jones's case was appealed to the United States Circuit Court for the Eighth Circuit, which had earlier reversed others of Judge Wright's rulings in the case (including her ruling that the case could not go forward while the President was in office, a reversal which was later upheld 9–0 by the United States Supreme Court), and there is a fair chance the Eighth Circuit would have reversed Judge Wright

on her dismissal of Ms. Jones's case as well. Perhaps understanding this, before the President's trial on impeachment charges, he settled Ms. Jones's lawsuit by paying her $850,000. In another important move, after the impeachment proceedings, Judge Wright, concluding that she had been lied to by the President, first held him in contempt in April 1999, and, later, in July, 1999, fined him $90,686. $1,202 of this represented court costs associated with the President's misconduct, and the remainder of the sum was paid to Paula Jones's lawyers to compensate them for the expenses the President's lack of truthfulness had caused them. President Clinton thus became not only the first elected President to be impeached and tried before the Senate, but also the first to be held in contempt and fined as a result of misconduct in a civil case. No criminal charges were brought against the President. He did, however, lose his license to practice law in his former home state of Arkansas.

5. President Clinton and his lawyers continued to deny any wrongdoing, but it does appear that he was guilty of many legal offenses. Posner, who when he wrote his book was Chief Judge of the United States Court of Appeals for the Seventh Circuit, concluded that

> it is clear beyond a reasonable doubt, on the basis of the public record as it exists today, that President Clinton obstructed justice, in violation of federal criminal law, by (1) perjuring himself repeatedly in his deposition in the Paula Jones case, in his testimony before the grand jury, and in his responses to the questions put to him by the House Judiciary Committee; (2) tampering with witness Lewinsky by encouraging her to file a false affidavit in lieu of having to be deposed, and to secrete the gifts that she had received from him; and (3) suborning perjury by suggesting to Lewinsky that she include in her affidavit a false explanation for the reason that she had been transferred from the White House to the Pentagon * * *

Posner, supra, at 54. Posner believes that the President's criminal conduct, were he anyone else but the President, would have merited a federal sentence of imprisonment from 30 to 37 months, id., at 55. Even so, was it appropriate for President Clinton to have been impeached for this misconduct? Consider the views on this question expressed by Professors Presser and Sunstein, which appear immediately below. They were originally expressed in testimony before the United States House of Representatives Subcommittee on the Constitution of the Committee on the Judiciary, at a public hearing held in November, 1998, in order to illuminate the meaning of the Constitutional provision which begins this section. Presser and Sunstein were among 19 scholars called to Washington to explain to the subcommittee members what the historical understanding of the terms "high crimes and misdemeanors" was. The excerpts below are taken from versions of Presser and Sunstein's testimony that were eventually annotated, edited, and published in the George Washington Law Review. They appear here with the permission of Presser and Sunstein, and of the George Washington Law Review.

STEPHEN B. PRESSER, WOULD GEORGE WASHINGTON HAVE WANTED BILL CLINTON IMPEACHED?

67 Geo. Wash. L. Rev. 666, 668–71, 672–675, 678–681.

II. THE FEDERALIST ON IMPEACHMENT

The Federalist, the series of essays on the Constitution written by James Madison, Alexander Hamilton, and John Jay in the years immediately following the drafting of the Constitution at the Philadelphia Convention, provides another important guide, in addition to the text of the Constitution itself, to understanding the working of impeachment. *The Federalist* is universally acknowledged to be the most important contemporary exposition of the federal Constitution. But it is more than a powerful contemporary account. It is, in many ways, a work exploring timeless political truths. To this day, *The Federalist* is regarded as the most important American work in political science.

* * *

The Federalist No. 64, one of the few numbers written by John Jay, who was to become the first Chief Justice of the United States, provides one very clear indication of what the Framers intended with regard to impeachment. Jay discusses the treaty power, and responds, in particular, to critics of the Constitution who argued that the President and the Senate were given too much discretion in committing the new Nation to treaties with other nations. Jay noted that the presidential power of making treaties—perhaps the most important foreign policy power that the President has discretion to exercise—is important because it "relates to war, peace, and commerce," and that it "should not be delegated but in such a mode, and with such precautions, as will afford the highest security that it will be exercised by men the best qualified for the purpose, and in the manner most conducive to the public good." Jay went on to explain that the means of picking the President—indirectly through the electoral college—is calculated so that the President will be a person noted for integrity, virtue, and probity, and that the original indirect means of selecting senators—through the state legislatures—was to assure the same for the senators.

Jay made plain that when a President fails to live up to the requirement of trust, honor, and virtue that is necessary to meet his treaty-making and other executive responsibilities—if, in short, he is not an honorable or virtuous person who will perform his duties in the interest of the people—impeachment is available to remove him. When Jay addressed the requisite integrity for presidents and senators, he stated:

> With respect to their responsibility, it is difficult to conceive how it could be increased. Every consideration that can influence the human mind, such as honor, oaths, reputations, conscience, the love of coun-

try, and family affections and attachments, afford security for their fidelity. In short, as the Constitution has taken [through the indirect election of senators and presidents] the utmost care that they shall be men of talents, and integrity, we have reason to be persuaded that the treaties they make will be as advantageous as, all circumstances considered, could be made; *and so far as the fear of punishment and disgrace can operate, that motive to good behavior is amply afforded by the article on the subject of impeachments.* [Emphasis supplied]

Virtue, probity, and honor were so important in the Executive, as Jay's remarks indicate, that it is no surprise that the Framers assumed that the first President of the United States would have to be George Washington. He was the greatest national hero, he was given the lion's share of the responsibility for securing independence, and then as now was regarded as the father of his country. His reputation for integrity, virtue, and honor was unparalleled. George Washington, the national epitome of virtue and honor, was, in short, precisely the kind of executive *The Federalist* No. 64 contemplates.

III. CONSTITUTIONAL TEXTUAL CLUES TO THE MEANING OF "HIGH CRIMES AND MISDEMEANORS"

The Federalist No. 64 thus tells us about the requisite character of federal officials, and is persuasive authority for believing that when it becomes clear that the President has committed acts that raise grave doubts about his honesty, his virtue, or his honor, impeachment is available as a remedy. This conclusion is further supported by the text of the Constitution itself, which provides in Article I, Section 3, that the punishments to be imposed following impeachment by the House and conviction by the Senate are "removal from Office, *and disqualification to hold and enjoy any Office of honor, Trust or Profit* under the United States." [Emphasis supplied.] The kind of person who would be impeached was believed to be one without honor and thus one who could not be trusted. The fear was that such a person, if allowed an office offering the opportunity to profit, would use his office for personal ends and not for the good of the people. *Impeachment, then, is all about deciding whether a particular official can be trusted to act with disinterested virtue, or whether an official will put his own needs or desires above his constitutional duties.*

It is for this reason—that impeachment is a remedy against those who would betray their oaths to uphold the Constitution and would instead seek personal advantage—that the Framers chose to describe, *although not to limit*, impeachable offenses by including and using as an analogy "Treason and Bribery." "Treason" is defined in the Constitution itself as "levying War against [the United States], or in adhering to their Enemies, giving them Aid and Comfort."

The essence of treason, then, is that it involves a betrayal of one's obligation to one's own people, by making war against them, or by adhering to their enemies. Similarly, "Bribery" involves a betrayal of virtue and a refusal to exercise disinterested judgment in the interests of the people in order to serve the interests of someone else—someone who wrongly and corruptly buys what should only belong to the people. In both cases the official, whether he is a traitor or a person bribed, turns from his duty and puts his own interests ahead of his public trust.

This suggestion that impeachment is ultimately about a fundamental betrayal of trust is further supported by the limited records that we have of the Constitutional Convention. On August 20, 1787, the Committee of Detail presented a proposal that would have made federal officers "liable to impeachment and removal from office for neglect of duty, malversation, or corruption." Somewhat later, however, on September 8, 1787, the Convention considered a revised text that would have limited impeachment only to those cases involving "Treason & bribery." George Mason, of Virginia, thought this too limiting, and argued:

> Why is the provision restrained to Treason & bribery only? Treason as defined in the Constitution will not reach many great and dangerous offences. [Warren] Hastings [the administrator of the East India Company and Governor–General of Bengal whom Edmund Burke led an effort to impeach for corruption] is not guilty of Treason. Attempts to subvert the Constitution may not be Treason as above defined—As bills of attainder which have saved the British Constitution are forbidden, it is the more necessary to extend: the power of impeachments.

Mason then moved to add after the word "bribery" the words "or maladministration." James Madison, one of the authors of *The Federalist*, and the man most commonly described as the "Father" of the Constitution, objected on the grounds that "maladministration" was too elusive. "So vague a term," he said, "will be equivalent to a tenure during pleasure of the Senate." To meet Madison's objection, and to clarify that removal would require more than senatorial whim, Mason "withdrew 'maladministration' & substituted 'other high crimes & misdemeanors,' "which the Convention then accepted and incorporated into the Constitutional text we now seek to interpret.

* * *

V. FIXING THE MEANING OF "HIGH CRIMES AND MISDEMEANORS": THE ENGLISH EXPERIENCE

* * * [T]he Framers believed that "high Crimes and Misdemeanors," if the impeachment provisions were to serve their purposes of keeping the executive and judiciary faithful to their constitutional trust, could be

broadly construed. Thus, Alexander Hamilton, in *The Federalist* No. 65, in which he discussed the judicial function of the Senate in trials of impeachments, broadly defines impeachment as a remedy generally available to correct wrongdoing: "The subjects of [the Senate's impeachment] jurisdiction are those offenses which proceed from the misconduct of public men, or, in other words, from the abuse or violation of some public trust."

Hamilton, as did some of the other Framers noted above, supplied some limitation on the impeachment power when he wrote that impeachable offenses "relate chiefly to injuries done immediately to the society itself." Hamilton even observed * * * that when an impeachment proceeding is underway it will seldom fail to agitate the passions of the whole community, and to divide the community into parties more or less friendly or inimical to the accused. "In many cases it will connect itself with the pre-existing factions, and will enlist all their animosities, partialities, influence, and interest on one side or on the other; and in such cases there will always be the greatest danger that the decision will be regulated more by the comparative strength of parties than by the real demonstrations of innocence or guilt."

Hamilton believed that the Senate, supposedly further removed from the people through election by state legislatures and not by the people themselves, would be better able to put raw partisan political concerns aside and make objective determinations on the guilt or innocence of one impeached. Because the Senate is no longer insulated from popular election, it is doubly important that both the House and the Senate try to approach the impeachment of the President as objectively as possible.

Given the breadth of the possible definition of "high Crimes and Misdemeanors," and, as Hamilton noted, the inevitable involvement of partisan politics, it is no wonder that * * * there [was, concerning the Clinton impeachment] division in the House of Representatives, the Senate, and in the Nation generally, about what constitutes an impeachable offense. If we could set aside partisan politics, however, we could fix with some certainty the nature of the acts against the state and the Constitution that the Framers would have regarded as coming within the phrase "high Crimes and Misdemeanors."

At the time the Framers inserted the phrase "high Crimes and Misdemeanors" into the Constitution, they had a wealth of English experience with those words on which to draw, and it appears clear that the Framers intended and understood that the phrase "high Crimes and Misdemeanors" was to be interpreted according to the meaning it was given by English common law. As Justice Joseph Story later wrote, "The only safe guide in such cases must be the common law, which is the guardian at once of private rights and public liberties."

Raoul Berger, in his book on impeachments, has given us a handy summary of some of the impeachment proceedings brought in England before the framing of our Constitution, proceedings described as involving all or part of the phrase "high crimes and misdemeanors." These included the proceedings brought against the Earl of Suffolk (1386), who "applied appropriated funds to purposes other than those specified"; the Duke of Suffolk (1450), who "procured offices for persons who were unfit and unworthy of them [and who] delayed justice by stopping writs of appeal (private criminal prosecutions) for the deaths of complainants' husbands"; Attorney General Yelverton (1621), who "committed persons for refusal to enter into bonds before he had authority so to require," and who also was guilty of "commencing but not prosecuting suits"; Lord Treasurer Middlesex (1624), who "allowed the office of Ordinance to go unrepaired though money was appropriated for that purpose [and who] allowed contracts for greatly needed powder to lapse for want of payment"; the Duke of Buckingham (1626), who "though young and inexperienced, procured offices for himself, thereby blocking the deserving; neglected as great admiral to safeguard the seas; [and who] procured titles of honor to his mother, brothers, kindred"; Justice Berkley (1637), who "reviled and threatened the grand jury for presenting the removal of the communion table in All Saints Church; [and who] on the trial of an indictment, . . . 'did much discourage complainants' counsel' and 'did overrule the cause for matter of law' "; Sir Richard Gurney, lord mayor of London (1642), who "thwarted Parliament's order to store arms and ammunition in storehouses"; Viscount Mordaunt (1660), who "prevented Tayleur from standing for election as a burgess to serve in Parliament; [and who] caused his illegal arrest and detention"; Peter Pett, Commissioner of the Navy (1668), who was guilty of "negligent preparation for the Dutch invasion," and who was responsible for "loss of a ship through neglect to bring it to mooring"; Chief Justice North (1680), who "assisted the Attorney General in drawing a proclamation to suppress petitions to the King to call a Parliament"; Chief Justice Scroggs (1680), who "discharged [a] grand jury before they made their presentment, thereby obstructing the presentment of many Papists; [and who] arbitrarily granted general warrants in blank"; Sir Edward Seymour (1680), who "applied appropriated funds to public purposes other than those specified"; and the Duke of Leeds (1695), who "as president of [the] Privy Council accepted 5,500 guineas from the East India Company to procure a charter of confirmation."

One way of characterizing all of this English experience is to say, as Joseph Story did, that " 'lord chancellors and judges and other magistrates have not only been impeached for bribery, and acting grossly contrary to the duties of their office, but for misleading their sovereign by unconstitutional opinions and for attempts to subvert the fundamental laws, and introduce arbitrary power.' "The English cases lend further support to the notion derived from The Federalist and the text of the Constitution that impeachable offenses, "high Crimes and Misdemeanors" if you will, are acts that are inconsistent with the obligations and duties of office, that involve putting personal or partisan concerns ahead of the interests of the people, and that demonstrate the unfitness of the man to the office.

The Constitution, The Federalist, and the English common law experience give a very good general idea of what was meant by the Constitution's impeachment clauses. The meaning of "high Crimes and Misdemeanors" is thus capable of being understood as it was by the Framers. It is important also to understand, however, that it is impossible to fix with certainty the complete enumeration of impeachable offenses, and it is impossible to escape the fact that the Constitution vests complete and unreviewable discretion with regard to impeachment and removal in Congress. Hamilton recognized this too:

> This [the trial of impeachments] can never be tied down by such strict rules, either in the delineation of the offense by the prosecutors [The House of Representatives] or in the construction of it by the judges [the Senate], as in common cases serve to limit the discretion of courts in favor of personal security. There will be no jury to stand between the judges who are to pronounce the sentence of the law and the party who is to receive or suffer it. The awful discretion which a court of impeachments must necessarily have to doom to honor or to infamy the most confidential and the most distinguished characters of the community forbids the commitment of the trust to a small number of persons [and so it is placed in the hands of the entire Senate].

* * *

* * * [If Judge Starr's charges against the President are true, then they] show that over many months the President engaged in deception, lying under oath, concealing evidence, tampering with witnesses, and, in general, obstructing justice by seeking to prevent the proper functioning of the courts, the grand jury, and the investigation of the Office of Independent Counsel. These offenses, if true, would undoubtedly amount to criminal interference with the legal process, but more to the point, *they would demonstrate that the President had failed to live up to the requirements of honesty, virtue, and honor that the Framers of the Constitution and the authors of The Federalist believed were essential for the presidency.*

These offenses, if they actually occurred, would clearly resemble many of the English precedents of impeachment for interfering with orderly processes of law, for tampering with the grand jury, and for seeking to use one's office for personal rather than public ends. These offenses, if true, would show that President Clinton engaged in a pattern of conduct that involved injury to the state and a betrayal of his constitutional duties because President Clinton would have thereby abused his office for personal gain and betrayed the ideal that ours is a government of laws and not of men.

If these allegations are true, then the President, rather than carrying out his oath of office to uphold the Constitution and faithfully to execute the laws, sought instead to subvert the judicial process specified in Article III, and, in order to protect himself from an adverse judgment in the Jones proceeding, sought to frustrate the laws designed to protect Ms. Jones and others like her.

There were those who argued, even before the subcommittee seeking to determine the definition of "high Crimes and Misdemeanors," that the President merely lied about his private sexual conduct. It should be remembered, however, that the essential allegation in *Jones v. Clinton* was that the President misused his governmental office (then as governor of Arkansas) to attempt to procure sexual favors from Ms. Jones. The allegations before the House of the President's impeachable offenses, discussed above, all flowed from efforts of the President to suppress the truth in the course of *Jones v. Clinton*.

It should also be remembered that Ken Starr expanded his investigation to include the facts regarding Ms. Lewinsky because he believed that he could discern a pattern of interference with judicial proceedings on the part of the President similar to the ones that he had previously encountered in the Whitewater investigation. Ken Starr's inquiry, after all, has never been about sex. It has been about abuse of power, obstruction of justice, and other impeachable offenses.

* * * [T]here is more than enough [in the Starr Report] to require the House of Representatives to move forward and vote on impeachment articles. These allegations concern conduct by the President in which he allegedly ignored his constitutional obligations to take care that the laws be faithfully executed, and instead used his august position to frustrate enforcement of the law. If these allegations are true, then the President has acted in a manner against the interests of the state and he has sought to subvert the essence of our constitutional government—that ours is a government of laws and not of men. If these allegations are true, then the President has engaged in conduct that can only be described as corrupt, and corrupt in a manner that the impeachment process was expressly designed to correct.

* * *

VIII. CONCLUSION: "LYING ABOUT SEX" OR SOMETHING MORE?

For many people, apparently, the allegations against the President can still be characterized merely as "lying about sex." It is difficult for many people to believe that such conduct is anything but a private matter, far removed from constitutional procedures or requirements. The President is accused of much more than "lying about sex," of course * * *. It is appropriate to note in passing, however, that our legal tradition has never made any distinction about the content of matters that might involve perjury, obstruction of justice, or tampering with witnesses. No person and least of all no President, who is sworn faithfully to execute all the laws, can pick and choose over which matters he will be truthful and which he will not, particularly when he is under oath.

An oath, and the virtue of one swearing to it, perhaps lightly regarded by many today, were not so lightly regarded at the time of the Constitution's framing. Our best evidence of this is George Washington's statements in his famous Farewell Address. The Farewell Address is the first President's "one outstanding piece of writing," and is regarded as comparable in importance to Thomas Jefferson's Declaration of Independence, Alexander Hamilton's financial plan, or James Madison's journal of the proceedings of the Constitutional Convention. Like the Declaration of Independence, Hamilton's ideas about the importance of commerce and manufacturing, and the Constitutional Convention, Washington's Farewell Address offers a valuable and authentic glimpse into what the Framers considered vital for the new Republic they were founding. In one of the most important passages of that Farewell Address, the man whom the Framers designated as their first President asked, "Where is the security for property, for reputation, for life, if the sense of religious obligation desert the oaths which are the instruments of investigation in courts of justice?" Then Washington added, "It is substantially true, that virtue or morality is a necessary spring of popular government. The rule, indeed, extends with more or less force to every species of free government. Who that is a sincere friend to it can look with indifference upon attempts to shake the foundation of the fabrick?"

Washington, the platonic form of an American President, believed that the oath taken in court was a fundamental security for all that was held dear in American society. He believed that those who took their oaths in vain were eroding the foundation of American government, and that they had lost the virtue that he believed essential to sustain freedom and popular sovereignty. Even if all President Clinton had done were to lie under oath in a judicial proceeding, the first President would have believed that President Clinton was engaged in an effort to "shake the foundation of the fabrick" of our constitutional scheme. It is clear, then, that George Washington would have recommended President Clinton's impeachment * * *.

The allegations against President Clinton, however, amount to much more than lying under oath. I think that under the Framers' view of the Constitution, if these allegations are true, then the oath the members of

Congress took to support the Constitution requires them to impeach the President.

* * *

CASS R. SUNSTEIN, IMPEACHMENT AND STABILITY

67 Geo. Wash. L. Rev. 699–704, 711 (1999).

* * *

I suggest that with respect to the President, the principal goal of the Impeachment Clause is to allow impeachment for a narrow category of large-scale abuses of authority that come from the exercise of distinctly presidential powers. Outside of that category of cases, impeachment is generally foreign to our traditions and prohibited by the Constitution. Outside of that category of cases, the appropriate course for any crimes is not impeachment, but a prosecutorial judgment, after the President has left office, whether indictment is appropriate. The original understanding of impeachment strongly supports this view; equally important, this view is strongly supported by the longstanding historical practice in America.

* * *

I. TEXT

Constitutional interpretation of course begins with the Constitution's text. The text strongly supports the view that in order to support impeachment of the President, the underlying offense must usually involve the abusive exercise of a distinctly presidential power.

More particularly, the text's opening reference to treason and bribery, together with the word "other," seems to justify a clear and important inference: high crimes and misdemeanors should be understood to be of the same general "kind" as treason and bribery, as in the Latin canon of construction *ejusdem generis*. Thus it would be reasonable to think that "other high Crimes and Misdemeanors" must be in the nature of large-scale abuse of public office—large-scale in the sense of "high" and similar, in kind as well as degree, to treason and bribery. It is entirely sensible, textually speaking, to understand "other high Crimes and Misdemeanors" in such a way as to conform to "treason" and "bribery," and to attribute the relevant "misdemeanors" with a certain threshold of "highness" as well.

The text thus supports the view that I will be defending here: impeachment is designed for large-scale abuses of public authority. But reasonable people could disagree about the meaning of the bare text, and it is certainly appropriate to look at other sources.

II. The Framing

A. The Convention

I now turn to the Constitutional Convention. The extensive debates in the Convention strongly suggest a sharply limited conception of impeachment, one that sees the process as a targeted response to the President's abuse of public power through manipulation of distinctly presidential authority, or through procurement of his office by corrupt means.

The initial draft of the Constitution took the form of resolutions presented before the members meeting in Philadelphia on June 13, 1787. One of the key resolutions, found in the Convention's official Journal, said that the President could be impeached for "malpractice or neglect of duty." On July 20, this provision provoked an extended debate. Three positions dominated the day's discussion. One extreme view, represented by Roger Sherman and attracting very little support, was that the legislature should have the power to remove the Executive at its pleasure. Charles Pinckney, Rufus King, and Gouverneur Morris represented the opposing extreme view, that in the new Republic, the President "ought not to be impeachable whilst in office." This view, which did receive considerable support, was defended partly by reference to the system of separation of powers, which would be compromised by impeachment, and partly by reference to the fact that the President, unlike a monarch, would be subject to periodic elections, a point that seemed to make impeachment less necessary. The third position, which ultimately carried the day, was that the President should be impeachable, but only for a narrow category of abuses of the public trust, by, for example, procuring office by unlawful means, or using distinctly presidential authority for ends that are treasonous.

George Mason took a lead role in promoting the compromise course. Against Pinckney, he argued that it was necessary to counter the risk that the President might obtain his office by corrupting his electors. "Shall that man be above [justice]," he asked, "who can commit the most extensive injustice?" This question identified the risk, to which the convention was quite sensitive, that the President might turn into a near-monarch; and it led the crucial votes—above all, Morris—to agree that impeachment might be permitted for (in Morris's words) "corruption & some few other offences." James Madison promptly concurred with Morris, pointing to a case in which a President "might betray his trust to foreign powers." Capturing the emerging consensus of the convention, Edmund Randolph favored impeachment on the ground that the Executive "will have great opportunitys [sic] of abusing his power; particularly in time of war when the military force, and in some respects the public money will be in his hands." The clear trend of the discussion was toward allowing a narrow impeachment power by which the President could be removed only for gross abuses of public authority.

But Pinckney, concerned about the separation of powers, continued to insist that a power of impeachment would eliminate the President's "independence." Morris once again offered the decisive response, urging that he was convinced of the necessity of impeachments, because the President "may be bribed by a greater interest to betray his trust; and no one would say that we ought to expose ourselves to the danger of seeing the first Magistrate in foreign pay without being able to guard against it by displacing him." At the same time, Morris insisted, "we should take care to provide some mode that will not make him dependent on the Legislature." Led by Morris, the Convention thus moved toward a compromise position, one that would continue the separation between the President and the Congress, but permit the President to be removed in the most extreme cases. But the discussion ended without agreement on any particular set of terms.

The new draft of the Constitution's Impeachment Clause emerged two weeks later, on August 6. It would have permitted the President to be impeached, but only for treason, bribery, and corruption (apparently exemplified by the President's securing his office by unlawful means). With little additional debate, and for no clear reason, this provision was narrowed on September 4, to "Treason, or bribery." But in early September, the delegates took up the Impeachment Clause anew. Here they slightly broadened the grounds for removing the President, but in a way that stayed close to the compromise position that had appeared to carry the day in July.

The opening argument was offered by Mason, who complained that the provision was too narrow to capture his earlier concerns, and that "maladministration" should be added, so as to include "attempts to subvert the Constitution" that would not count as treason or bribery. Mason's strongest point was that the President should be removable if he attempted to undo the constitutional plan. But Madison insisted that the term "maladministration" was "so vague" that it would "be equivalent to a tenure during pleasure of the Senate," which is something that the Framers had been attempting to avoid all along. Hence Mason withdrew "maladministration" and added the new, more precise terms "other high crimes & misdemeanors against the State." The term "high crimes and misdemeanors" was borrowed from English law, as we shall see; but it received no independent debate in the convention. During the debates, the only subsequent development—and it is not trivial—was that "against the State" was changed to "against the United States," in order to remove ambiguity.

There is one further wrinkle. The resulting draft was submitted to the Committee on Style and Arrangement, which deleted the words "against the United States." Hence there is an interpretive puzzle. Was the deletion designed to broaden the legitimate grounds for impeachment? This is extremely unlikely. As its name suggests, the Committee on Style and Arrangement lacked substantive authority (which is not to deny that it made some substantive changes), and it is far more likely that the particular change was made on grounds of redundancy. Hence the Impeachment Clause, in its final as well as penultimate incarnation, was targeted at high crimes and misdemeanors against the United States.

The clear lesson of these debates is that in designing the provision governing impeachment, the Founders were thinking, exclusively or principally, of large-scale abuses of distinctly public authority. The unanimous rejection of "maladministration" suggests that the Framers sought to create an authority that was both confined and well-defined. The alleged grounds for impeachment all involved abuses of public trust through the exercise of distinctly presidential powers (or corruption in procuring those powers); there were no references to private crimes, such as murder and assault. Now we cannot overread silence on that point. But the debates strongly suggest that the model for impeachment was the large-scale abuse of public office.

B. Ratification

The same view is supported by discussion at the time of ratification and in the early period. The basic point is that impeachment was explained and defended as a way of removing the President when he used his public authority for treasonous or corrupt purposes. I offer a few brief notations here.

Alexander Hamilton explained that the "subjects" of impeachment involve "the abuse of violation of some public trust. They are of a nature which may with peculiar propriety be denominated POLITICAL, as they relate chiefly to injuries done immediately to society itself." One of the most sustained discussions came from the highly respected (and later Supreme Court Justice) James Iredell, speaking in the North Carolina ratifying convention: "I suppose the only instances, in which the President would be liable to impeachment, would be where he had received a bribe, or had acted from some corrupt motive or other." By way of explanation, Iredell referred to a situation in which "the President has received a bribe . . . from a foreign power, and, under the influence of that bribe, had address enough with the Senate, by artifices and misrepresentations, to seduce their consent to a pernicious treaty."

James Wilson wrote similarly in his great 1791 Lectures on Law: "In the United States and in Pennsylvania, impeachments are confined to political characters, to political crimes and misdemeanors, and to political punishments." Another early commentator went so far as to say that

> The legitimate causes of impeachment . . . can have reference only to public character, and official duty. . . . In general, those offences, which may be committed equally by a private person, as a public of-

> ficer, are not the subjects of impeachment. Murder, burglary, robbery, and indeed all offences not immediately connected with office, . . . are left to the ordinary course of judicial proceedings. . . .

This was a contested view; but there was general agreement that the great office of impeachment was to remove from office those who had abused distinctly public power.

III. HIGH CRIMES AND MISDEMEANORS IN ENGLAND

Because the term "high crimes and misdemeanors" comes from English law, it is possible to contend that it should be interpreted in accordance with English understandings. There is considerable sense in this view—the term certainly does come from English law—but a serious question might be raised about the analysis. The most important point is that it is not at all clear that the American understanding was or has been the same as the English one. Recall that in the framing period, participants were aware of two exceedingly important differences between America and England: (1) the election of the President and (2) the separation of powers. As we have seen, these differences led many to suggest a far narrower power to impeach the President than to impeach high officials under English law. Thus it is hazardous to suggest that the American understanding essentially incorporates the English understanding. With that qualification, let me briefly investigate the English practice. As it turns out, that practice strongly supports the basic argument I am making here.

The English idea of "impeachment" arose largely because its objects were, for various reasons, not subject to the reach of conventional criminal law. Thus ministers and functionaries of the king were subject to impeachment for public offenses. Under English law, the term "misdemeanor" was not a reference to what we would now call misdemeanor (as opposed to felony); it referred instead to distinctly public misconduct. Thus the term "high crimes and misdemeanors" represented "a category of political crimes against the state."

In English law, there was some ambiguity in the use of the word "high": did the term refer to the seriousness of the offense, or to the nature of the office against which the proceeding was aimed? Probably the better view, based on the actual practice, was that the term referred to both. In any case, a "high crime and misdemeanor" could be a serious crime, but it could also be a serious offense that was not a technical violation of the criminal law. Serious misconduct, as in the form of committing the Nation to "an ignominious treaty," was said by some to be a just basis for impeachment in England. Whatever one thinks of the particular example, it is clear that there was no consensus in England that a "high crime and misdemeanor" had to be a violation of the criminal law; and indeed the better view is that an impeachable offense, to qualify as such, need not be a crime in the United States.

For present purposes, the more important point is this: The great cases involving charges of impeachable conduct in England reveal a far readier resort to the practice than has been the case in America, probably for reasons mentioned above. But those cases involved either criminal or extremely inappropriate conduct in the form of abuse of the authority granted by public office, or, in other terms, the kind of misconduct that someone could engage in only by virtue of holding public office. Thus describing the key cases provides the following list: unlawful use of publicly appropriated funds; thwarting Parliament's order to store arms and ammunition in storehouses; preventing a political enemy from standing for election and causing his unlawful arrest and detention; arbitrarily granting general blank search warrants; and stopping writs of appeal. In addition, a general (though not exhaustive) list suggests no case in which an impeachment proceeding was brought for something other than the use of the distinctive authority vested in public officers.

We may summarize the discussion with two simple points. First: The English practice shows a far readier resort to impeachment than the American practice. This difference makes sense in light of the fact that the President is subject to electoral checks and the American commitment to separation of powers. Second: The English practice was concentrated, at least largely, on the abusive exercise of distinctly public authorities.

* * *

Anyone can be prosecuted for violating the criminal law, and if the President has violated the criminal law, he is properly subject to criminal prosecution after his term ends. But it does not make sense to say, for example, that an American President could be impeached for false statements under oath in connection with a traffic accident in which he was involved, or that a false statement under oath, designed to protect a friend in a negligence action, is a legitimate basis for impeachment. Probably the best general statement is that a false statement under oath is an appropriate basis for impeachment if and only if the false statement involved conduct that by itself raises serious questions about abuse of office. A false statement about an illicit consensual sexual relationship, and a "conspiracy" to cover up that relationship, is not excusable or acceptable; but it is not a high crime or misdemeanor under the Constitution. The same is true for the other allegations made thus far. It trivializes the criminal law to say that some violations of the criminal law do not matter, or matter much. But it trivializes the Constitution to say that any false statement under oath, regardless of its subject matter, provides a proper basis for impeachment.

Of course people of good faith could say that the President has a special obligation to the truth, especially in a court of law, and that it is therefore reasonable to consider impeachment whenever the President has violated that obligation. It is certainly true that as the Nation's chief law enforcement officer, the President has a special obligation to the truth. Perhaps such people also believe that false statements under oath, and associated misconduct, are genuinely unique and that impeachment for such statements and such misconduct would therefore fail to do damage to our historical practice of resorting to impeachment only in the most extreme cases. But this position has serious problems of its own. Even if it would be possible, in principle, for reasonable people to confine the current alleged basis for impeachment, it is extremely doubtful that the line could be held in practice. Thus a judgment that the current grounds are constitutionally appropriate would set an exceedingly dangerous precedent for the future, a precedent that could threaten to turn impeachment into a political weapon, in a way that would produce considerable instability in the constitutional order.

Consider, for example, the fact that reasonable people can and do find tax evasion more serious than false statements about a consensual sexual activity, and that reasonable people can and do find an alleged unlawful arms deal more serious, from the constitutional standpoint, than either. Here is the underlying problem. Whenever serious charges are made, participants in politics may well be pushed in particular directions by predictable partisan pressures. The serious risk is therefore that contrary to the constitutional plan, impeachment will become a partisan tool, to be used by reference to legitimate arguments by people who have a great deal to gain.

A special risk of a ready resort to the impeachment instrument is that it would interact, in destructive ways, with existing trends in American democracy. Those trends—toward an emphasis on scandals and toward sensationalistic charges—have characterized the conduct of members of both parties in the last decades. For those who love this country and its institutions, the use of impeachment, in such cases, is quite ominous—not least because of the demonstrable good faith of many of those who are recommending it.

From the standpoint of the constitutional structure, it is far better to try a kind of line in the sand, one that has been characteristic of our constitutional practice for all of our history: A practice of invoking impeachment only for the largest cases of abuse of distinctly presidential authority.

CONCLUSION

Text, history, and longstanding practice suggest that the notion of "high Crimes and Misdemeanors" should generally be understood to refer to large-scale abuses that involve the authority that comes from occupying a particular public office. Thus a President who accepted a bribe from a foreign nation—or who failed to attend to the public business during a war—would be legitimately subject to impeachment. Perjury, or false statements under oath, could certainly qualify as impeachable offenses if they involved (for example) lies about using the IRS to punish one's political opponents or about giving arms, unlawfully, to another nation. But the most ordinary predicate for impeachment is an act, by the President, that amounts to a large-scale abuse of distinctly presidential authority.

If there is ever to be impeachment outside of that category of cases, it should be exceedingly rare. The current allegations against President Clinton do not justify a departure from our traditional practices. Such a departure would be not trivially but profoundly destabilizing; it would be far wiser to adhere to our traditions and to leave the hardest constitutional problems for another, and better, occasion.

NOTES AND QUESTIONS

1. Presser and Sunstein rest their arguments on essentially the same sources: the text of the Constitution, contemporary explications of the Constitution, and the English experience with the terms "high Crimes and Misdemeanors." How do you explain the fact that they differ so dramatically on the meaning of the constitutional terms? Presser is clear that the President's conduct, as it is set forth in Judge Starr's report, includes impeachable offenses, while Sunstein is equally clear that it does not. Does it help if you know that Presser was called as a witness by the Republican majority of the House Committee while Sunstein was called as a witness by the Democratic minority (and that both had, on previous occasions, testified before other Congressional committees, with Presser called by the Republicans and Sunstein by the Democrats)? Does an affinity to a particular political party affect the content or the validity of one's constitutional views? Is this a post-modernist phenomenon? See generally, Michael J. Klarman, "Constitutional Fetishism and the Clinton Impeachment Debate," 85 Va.L.Rev. 631 (1999)(arguing that the Constitution is indefinite on the substance of impeachable offenses) and sources there cited. For a meaningful comparison of the Clinton proceedings with one of the great impeachment controversies in Anglo–American history, see Craig S. Lerner [a former Associate Independent Counsel], "Impeachment, Attainder, and a True Constitutional Crisis: Lessons from the Strafford Trial," 69 U.Chi.L.Rev. 2057 (2002), and, for two thoughtful ruminations on what the Clinton impeachment taught us, see Tod Lindberg, "Necessary Impeachments, Necessary Acquittals: Damning Facts, Dubious Laws, and the Separation of Powers," 99 Policy Review 3 (2000), and Keith E. Whittington, " 'High Crimes' After Clinton: Deciding What's Impeachable," 99 Policy Review 27 (2000).

2. Sunstein believes that impeachment ought to be for a narrow category of offenses, while Presser argues that it is difficult to cabin the meaning

of impeachable offenses, a point on which he quotes Alexander Hamilton. Which is better for preserving the character of American government—a narrow or a broad approach? Note Sunstein's argument that impeachment should not be allowed to be used a tool for partisan political interests. Is Presser guilty of what Sunstein excoriates? Alternatively, could Presser's view of the character of Clinton's alleged offenses–taken from the Starr Report and grounded in the English experience–fit within Sunstein's demand that impeachment be reserved for those offenses which raise "serious questions about abuse of office." Sunstein clearly suggests that "A false statement about an illicit consensual sexual relationship, and a 'conspiracy' to cover up that relationship, is not excusable or acceptable; but it is not a high crime or misdemeanor under the Constitution. The same is true for the other allegations made thus far." Does Sunstein understand the allegations against the President in the same way that Presser (and Starr) did? Who was right?

3. On December 18, 1998, Henry Hyde, the Chairman of the Judiciary Committee of the House of Representatives, rose to begin the debate on the House Floor over whether the President should be impeached. He rejected Sunstein's view, and embraced Presser's:

> Mr. Speaker, my colleagues of the people's House, I wish to talk to you about the rule of law. After months of argument, hours of debate, there is no need for further complexity. The question before this House is rather simple. It's not a question of sex. Sexual misconduct and adultery are private acts and are none of Congress' business.
>
> It's not even a question of lying about sex. The matter before the House is a question of lying under oath. This is a public act, not a private act. This is called perjury. The matter before the House is a question of the willful, premeditated, deliberate corruption of the nation's system of justice. Perjury and obstruction of justice cannot be reconciled with the office of the president of the United States.
>
> The personal fate of the president is not the issue. The political fate of his party is not the issue. The Dow Jones Industrial Average is not the issue. The issue is perjury—lying under oath. The issue is obstruction of justice, which the president has sworn the most solemn oath to uphold.
>
> That oath constituted a compact between the president and the American people. That compact has been broken. The people's trust has been betrayed. The nation's chief executive has shown himself unwilling or incapable of enforcing its laws for he has corrupted the rule of law—the rule of law—by his perjury and his obstruction of justice.
>
> That and nothing other than that is the issue before this house.
>
> We have heard ceaselessly that, even if the president is guilty of the charges in the Starr referral, they don't rise to the level of an impeachable offense.

> Well, just what is an impeachable offense?
>
> One authority, Professor Stephen Presser of Northwestern University Law School said, and I quote, "Impeachable offenses are those which demonstrate a fundamental betrayal of public trust. They suggest the federal official has deliberately failed in his duty to uphold the Constitution and laws he was sworn to enforce."
>
> And so we must decide if a president, the chief law enforcement officer of the land, the person who appoints the attorney general, the person who nominates every federal judge, the person who nominates to the Supreme Court and the only person with a constitutional obligation to take care that the laws be faithfully executed, can lie under oath repeatedly and maintain it is not a breach of trust sufficient for impeachment.

Hyde's view prevailed in the House, where the President was impeached by a very narrow majority, composed almost exclusively of Republicans, although not all of Starr's charges were accepted as impeachable offenses, even by the Republican-controlled House.

4. When the matter reached the Senate, however, the President was acquitted of the impeachment charges, because a two-thirds majority of the Senators failed to convict. After three weeks of "trial" in the Senate, during which there was much debate, and the airing of videotaped depositions by three witnesses, Monica Lewinsky, Vernon Jordan, and Sidney Blumenthal (an aide to the President whom the President was accused of manipulating to give false testimony to a grand jury), the Senators voted, on February 12, 1999. On the eventual two charges brought before the Senate, one, alleging obstruction of justice by the President received fifty votes, and the other, which alleged perjury and the giving of false testimony, received only 45. Fifty voted to acquit on the obstruction charge and fifty-five voted to acquit on the perjury charge Not one Democrat joined the Republicans in voting to convict on either charge in the Senate.

5. Which impeachment proceeding was more partisan? That brought against Samuel Chase that we studied earlier in the course, or that brought against Bill Clinton? Public opinion seemed to be that it was the Republicans who were the partisan zealots, but is that so clear? Presser's views were those of Hyde, but is it fair to say that the majority of the Senate sided with Sunstein? Are your sympathies with the House majority who voted for impeachment, or the Senators who wanted to see the President acquitted?

6. Following his acquittal, President Clinton said he was "profoundly sorry for the burden he had imposed on the Congress." Still, even though he has been held in contempt for his conduct by Judge Wright, President Clinton has never admitted that he was guilty of any violations of law, and, indeed, has represented his defense against his impeachment charges as "upholding the Constitution" against attacks from his enemies. Perhaps Professor Sunstein would agree with that characterization, but, shortly after he resigned from his position as Independent Counsel, on November 14, 1999, in a

television news interview, Kenneth Starr rejected the President's contention, and stated with regard to the President's view, "I think it is an unfortunate effort to try to find scapegoats rather than to come to grips with what he has done." Elaborating, Starr indicated that "for the sake of the presidency, I think it would be—and for the country, it would be a good thing if he recognized and acknowledged his wrongdoing with respect to the judicial process." Do you find the same divide (is it a postmodern one?) that separates Presser and Sunstein, or that separated House and Senate Republicans from House and Senate Democrats, separating Starr and Clinton? For a delightful refusal to enter into a postmodern or neopragmatic understanding of the Presidential oath, see Gary Lawson, "Everything I Need to Know About Presidents I Learned from Dr. Seuss," 24 Harv.J.L. & Pub.Pol'y 381 (2001).

7. President Clinton was never tried for perjury or obstruction of justice in a criminal court, probably because there was little public support for such a measure. Most analysts believe that it was the lack of public support for removal of the President that led to such a truncated trial in the Senate, and the refusal (in spite of the House Managers' clear desire) to hear live witnesses, or to allow the testimony of more than the three witnesses deposed. Would Sir Edward Coke have been comfortable letting this kind of a constitutional issue turn on public opinion? Are you? Moreover, the Independent Counsel statute, under which Judge Starr was originally appointed, was allowed to lapse, thus effectively abolishing the office for future investigations. While that statute had originally been upheld in an 8 to 1 decision by the Supreme Court (Morrison v. Olson, 487 U.S. 654 (1988)), in 1999, neither Republicans nor Democrats sought to renew it. Why do you suppose that was? Could it have something to do with Sunstein's fears about politicizing the law?

8. Most Americans seemed reasonably happy with the outcome of the Senate Trial, but some of the House Managers, who had argued the case before the Senate, were not. "My great fear is that future presidents will now flaunt the law in a more egregious manner . . . and that's how they'll defend impeachments in the future," House manager Steve Buyer (R–Indiana) said, concluding that "Damage was done." Was he insufficiently postmodern?

GEORGE W. BUSH AND RICHARD CHENEY, PETITIONERS V. ALBERT GORE, JR., ET AL.

Supreme Court of the United States, 2000.
531 U.S. 98, 121 S.Ct. 525, 148 L.Ed.2d 388.

PER CURIAM.

I

On December 8, 2000, the Supreme Court of Florida ordered that the Circuit Court of Leon County tabulate by hand 9,000 ballots in Miami–Dade County. It also ordered the inclusion in the certified vote totals of 215 votes identified in Palm Beach County and 168 votes identified in

Miami–Dade County for Vice President Albert Gore, Jr., and Senator Joseph Lieberman, Democratic Candidates for President and Vice President. * * * The court further held that relief would require manual recounts in all Florida counties where so-called "undervotes" [ballots on which the voting machines failed to detect a vote for President] had not been subject to manual tabulation [and] * * * ordered all manual recounts to begin at once. Governor Bush and Richard Cheney, Republican Candidates for the Presidency and Vice Presidency, filed an emergency application for a stay of this mandate. On December 9, we granted the application * * *.

* * * On November 8, 2000, the day following the Presidential election, the Florida Division of Elections reported that Governor Bush had received 2,909,135 votes, and Vice President Gore had received 2,907,351 votes, a margin of 1,784 for Governor Bush. Because * * * Bush's margin of victory was less than "one-half of a percent * * * of the votes cast," an automatic machine recount was conducted, the results of which showed * * * Bush still winning the race but by a diminished margin. * * * Gore then sought manual recounts in Volusia, Palm Beach, Broward, and Miami–Dade Counties, pursuant to Florida's election protest provisions. Fla. Stat. § 102.166 (2000).[2] A dispute arose concerning the deadline for local county canvassing boards to submit their returns to the Secretary of State * * *. The Secretary declined to waive the November 14 deadline imposed by statute. * * * The Florida Supreme Court, however, set the deadline at November 26. We granted certiorari and vacated the Florida Supreme Court's decision * * *. On December 11, the Florida Supreme Court issued a decision on remand reinstating that date. * * *

On November 26, the Florida Elections Canvassing Commission * * * declared * * * Bush the winner of Florida's 25 electoral votes. On November 27, * * * Gore, pursuant to Florida's contest provisions, filed a complaint in Leon County Circuit Court contesting the certification. * * * He sought relief pursuant to [Florida' election code], which provides that "receipt of a number of illegal votes or rejection of a number of legal votes sufficient to change or place in doubt the result of the election" shall be grounds for a contest. The Circuit Court denied relief, stating that * * * Gore failed to meet his burden of proof. He appealed to the First District Court of Appeal, which certified the matter to the Florida Supreme Court.

* * * [T]he Florida Supreme Court affirmed in part and reversed in part * * * [holding] that the Circuit Court had been correct to reject * * * Gore's challenge to the results certified in Nassau County and his challenge to the Palm Beach County Canvassing Board's determination that

---

[2] [Ed.] That Florida statute provides, in pertinent part, that "Any candidate for nomination or election, or any elector qualified to vote in the election related to such candidacy, shall have the right to protest the returns of the election as being erroneous by filing with the appropriate canvassing board a sworn, written protest."

3,300 ballots cast in that county were not, in the statutory phrase, "legal votes."

The [Florida] Supreme Court held that * * * Gore had satisfied his burden of proof * * * with respect to his challenge to Miami–Dade County's failure to tabulate, by manual count, 9,000 [undervotes] * * *. Noting the closeness of the election, the Court explained that "on this record, there can be no question that there are legal votes within the 9,000 uncounted votes sufficient to place the results of this election in doubt." * * * A "legal vote," as determined by the Supreme Court, is "one in which there is a 'clear indication of the intent of the voter.' " The court therefore ordered a hand recount of the 9,000 ballots in Miami–Dade County. * * *

The * * * Court also determined that both Palm Beach County and Miami–Dade County, in their earlier manual recounts, had identified a net gain of 215 and 168 legal votes for * * * Gore. * * * The * * * Court therefore directed the Circuit Court to include those totals in the certified results * * *.

The petition presents the following questions: whether the Florida Supreme Court established new standards for resolving Presidential election contests, thereby violating Art. II, § 1, cl. 2, of the United States Constitution[3] and failing to comply with *3 U.S.C. § 5*[4] and whether the use of standardless manual recounts violates the Equal Protection and Due Process Clauses. * * * [W]e find a violation of the Equal Protection Clause.

II

* * *

B

The individual citizen has no federal constitutional right to vote for electors for the President of the United States unless and until the state legislature chooses a statewide election as the means to implement its power to appoint members of the Electoral College. U.S. Const., Art. II, § 1. This is the source for the statement in *McPherson v. Blacker* (*1892*), that the State legislature's power to select the manner for appointing electors is plenary * * *. When the state legislature vests the right to vote for President in its people, the right to vote * * * is fundamental; and one

[3] [Ed.] "Each State shall appoint, in such Manner as the Legislature thereof may direct, a number of [Presidential Electors . . .]"

[4] [Ed.] "If any State shall have provided, by laws enacted prior to the day fixed for the appointment of the electors, for its final determination of any controversy or contest concerning the appointment of all or any of the electors of such State, by judicial or other methods or procedures, and such determination shall have been made at least six days before the time fixed for the meeting of the electors, such determination made pursuant to such law so existing on said day, and made at least six days prior to said time of meeting of the electors, shall be conclusive, and shall govern in the counting of the electoral votes as provided in the Constitution, and as hereinafter regulated, so far as the ascertainment of the electors appointed by such State is concerned."

source of its fundamental nature lies in the equal weight accorded to each vote and the equal dignity owed to each voter. * * *

The right to vote is protected in more than the initial allocation of the franchise. Equal protection applies as well to the manner of its exercise. Having once granted the right to vote on equal terms, the State may not, by later arbitrary and disparate treatment, value one person's vote over that of another. * * *

* * * The question before us * * * is whether the recount procedures the Florida Supreme Court has adopted are consistent with its obligation to avoid arbitrary and disparate treatment of the members of its electorate.

Much of the controversy seems to revolve around ballot cards designed to be perforated by a stylus but which * * * have not been perforated with sufficient precision for a machine to count them. In some cases a piece of the card—a chad—is hanging, say by two corners. In other cases there is no separation at all, just an indentation.

The Florida Supreme Court has ordered that the intent of the voter be discerned from such ballots. * * * This is unobjectionable as an abstract proposition and a starting principle. The problem inheres in the absence of specific standards to ensure its equal application. The formulation of uniform rules to determine intent based on these recurring circumstances is practicable and, we conclude, necessary.

* * *

The want of those rules here has led to unequal evaluation of ballots in various respects. * * * [T]he standards for accepting or rejecting contested ballots might vary not only from county to county but indeed within a single county from one recount team to another.

The State Supreme Court ratified this uneven treatment. It mandated that the recount totals from two counties, Miami–Dade and Palm Beach, be included in the certified total. The court also appeared to hold *sub silentio* that the recount totals from Broward County, which were not completed until after the original November 14 certification by the Secretary of State, were to be considered part of the new certified vote totals even though the county certification was not contested by * * * Gore. Yet each of the counties used varying standards to determine what was a legal vote. * * *

* * *

* * * [A] further equal protection problem [is that] [t]he votes certified by the court included a partial total from one county, Miami–Dade. The Florida Supreme Court's decision thus gives no assurance that the recounts included in a final certification must be complete. * * * This ac-

commodation no doubt results from the truncated contest period established by the Florida Supreme Court * * * at respondents' own urging. The press of time does not diminish the constitutional concern. A desire for speed is not a general excuse for ignoring equal protection guarantees.

* * * [T]he actual process by which the votes were to be counted under the Florida Supreme Court's decision raises further concerns. That order did not specify who would recount the ballots. The county canvassing boards were forced to pull together ad hoc teams comprised of judges from various Circuits who had no previous training in handling and interpreting ballots. Furthermore, while others were permitted to observe, they were prohibited from objecting during the recount.

The recount process, in its features here described, is inconsistent with the minimum procedures necessary to protect the fundamental right of each voter in the special instance of a statewide recount under the authority of a single state judicial officer. Our consideration is limited to the present circumstances, for the problem of equal protection in election processes generally presents many complexities.

* * *

* * * [I]t is obvious that the recount cannot be conducted in compliance with the requirements of equal protection and due process without substantial additional work. It would require not only the adoption * * * of adequate statewide standards for determining what is a legal vote, and practicable procedures to implement them, but also orderly judicial review of any disputed matters that might arise. * * *

The Supreme Court of Florida has said that the legislature intended the State's electors to "participate fully in the federal electoral process," as provided in *3 U.S.C. § 5.* That statute, in turn, requires that any controversy or contest that is designed to lead to a conclusive selection of electors be completed by December 12. That date is upon us, and there is no recount procedure in place under the State Supreme Court's order that comports with minimal constitutional standards. Because it is evident that any recount seeking to meet the December 12 date will be unconstitutional for the reasons we have discussed, we reverse the judgment of the Supreme Court of Florida ordering a recount to proceed.

Seven Justices of the Court agree that there are constitutional problems with the recount ordered by the Florida Supreme Court that demand a remedy. * * * The only disagreement is as to the remedy. Because the Florida Supreme Court has said that the Florida Legislature intended to obtain the safe-harbor benefits of *3 U.S.C. § 5,* JUSTICE BREYER's proposed remedy—remanding to the Florida Supreme Court for its ordering of a constitutionally proper contest until December 18—contemplates action in violation of the Florida election code, and hence could not be part of an "appropriate" order * * *.

None are more conscious of the vital limits on judicial authority than are the members of this Court, and none stand more in admiration of the Constitution's design to leave the selection of the President to the people, through their legislatures, and to the political sphere. When contending parties invoke the process of the courts, however, it becomes our unsought responsibility to resolve the federal and constitutional issues the judicial system has been forced to confront.

The judgment of the Supreme Court of Florida is reversed, and the case is remanded for further proceedings not inconsistent with this opinion.

* * *

CHIEF JUSTICE REHNQUIST, with whom JUSTICE SCALIA and JUSTICE THOMAS join, concurring.

We join the *per curiam* opinion. We write separately because we believe there are additional grounds that require us to reverse the Florida Supreme Court's decision.

I

* * *

In most cases, comity and respect for federalism compel us to defer to the decisions of state courts on issues of state law. That practice reflects our understanding that the decisions of state courts are definitive pronouncements of the will of the States as sovereigns. * * * But there are a few exceptional cases in which the Constitution imposes a duty or confers a power on a particular branch of a State's government. This is one of them. Article II, § 1, cl. 2, provides that "each State shall appoint, in such Manner as the *Legislature* thereof may direct," electors for President and Vice President. (Emphasis added.) Thus, the text of the election law itself, and not just its interpretation by the courts of the States, takes on independent significance.

In *McPherson v. Blacker*, we explained that Art. II, § 1, cl. 2, "conveys the broadest power of determination" and "leaves it to the legislature exclusively to define the method" of appointment. A significant departure from the legislative scheme for appointing Presidential electors presents a federal constitutional question.

3 U.S.C. § 5 informs our application of Art. II, § 1, cl. 2 to the Florida statutory scheme, which, as the Florida Supreme Court acknowledged, took that statute into account. * * * As we noted in *Bush v. Palm Beach County Canvassing Bd. ["Bush I"]*:

> "Since § 5 contains a principle of federal law that would assure finality of the State's determination if made pursuant to a state law in ef-

fect before the election, a legislative wish to take advantage of the 'safe harbor' would counsel against any construction of the Election Code that Congress might deem to be a change in the law."

If we are to respect the legislature's Article II powers, therefore, we must ensure that postelection state-court actions do not frustrate the legislative desire to attain the "safe harbor" provided by § 5.

* * *

In order to determine whether a state court has infringed upon the legislature's authority, we necessarily must examine the law of the State as it existed prior to the action of the court. * * *

* * *

This inquiry does not imply a disrespect for state *courts* but rather a respect for the constitutionally prescribed role of state *legislatures*. To attach definitive weight to the pronouncement of a state court, when the very question at issue is whether the court has actually departed from the statutory meaning, would be to abdicate our responsibility to enforce the explicit requirements of Article II.

II

[The concurring opinion proceeds to summarize Florida's election law in some detail:] * * * The legislature has designated the Secretary of State as the "chief election officer," with the responsibility to "obtain and maintain uniformity in the application, operation, and interpretation of the election laws." The state legislature has delegated to county canvassing boards the duties of administering elections. Those boards are responsible for providing results to the state Elections Canvassing Commission, comprising the Governor, the Secretary of State, and the Director of the Division of Elections. * * *

* * *

The state legislature has also provided mechanisms both for protesting election returns and for contesting certified election results. * * * Any protest must be filed prior to the certification of election results by the county canvassing board. Once a protest has been filed, "the county canvassing board may authorize a manual recount." If a sample recount * * * "indicates an error in the vote tabulation which could affect the outcome of the election," the county canvassing board is instructed to: "(a) Correct the error and recount the remaining precincts with the vote tabulation system; (b) Request the Department of State to verify the tabulation software; or (c) Manually recount all ballots" * * *.

* * * The grounds for contesting an election include "receipt of a number of illegal votes or rejection of a number of legal votes sufficient to change or place in doubt the result of the election." * * * "[T]he circuit judge to whom the contest is presented may fashion such orders as he or she deems necessary to ensure that each allegation in the complaint is investigated, examined, or checked, to prevent or correct any alleged wrong, and to provide any relief appropriate under such circumstances." In Presidential elections, the contest period necessarily terminates on the date set by *3 U.S.C. § 5* for concluding the State's "final determination" of election controversies.

[The concurring opinion proceeds to indicate how the Florida Supreme Court modified the existing law and thus infringed upon the Legislature's authority mandated by Article II:] In its first decision, *Palm Beach Canvassing Bd. v. Harris,* (Nov. 21, 2000) (*Harris I*), the Florida Supreme Court extended the 7–day statutory certification deadline established by the legislature. This modification of the code, by lengthening the protest period, necessarily shortened the contest period for Presidential elections. Underlying the extension of the certification deadline and the shortchanging of the contest period was, presumably, the clear implication that certification was a matter of significance: The certified winner would enjoy presumptive validity, making a contest proceeding by the losing candidate an uphill battle. In its latest opinion, however, the court empties certification of virtually all legal consequence during the contest, and in doing so departs from the provisions enacted by the Florida Legislature.

The [Florida Supreme] court determined that canvassing boards' decisions regarding whether to recount ballots past the certification deadline (even the certification deadline established by *Harris I*) are to be reviewed *de novo*, although the election code clearly vests discretion whether to recount in the boards, and sets strict deadlines subject to the Secretary's rejection of late tallies and monetary fines for tardiness. * * * Moreover, the Florida court held that all late vote tallies arriving during the contest period should be automatically included in the certification regardless of the certification deadline (even the certification deadline established by *Harris I*), thus virtually eliminating both the deadline and the Secretary's discretion to disregard recounts that violate it.

Moreover, the court's interpretation of "legal vote," ["one in which there is a 'clear indication of the intent of the voter' "] and hence its decision to order a contest-period recount, plainly departed from the legislative scheme. Florida statutory law cannot reasonably be thought to *require* the counting of improperly marked ballots. * * *

* * *

No reasonable person would call it "an error in the vote tabulation," or a "rejection of legal votes," when electronic or electromechanical equipment performs precisely in the manner designed, and fails to count those ballots that are not marked in the manner that * * * voting instructions explicitly and prominently specify. The scheme that the Florida Supreme Court's opinion attributes to the legislature is one in which machines are *required* to be "capable of correctly counting votes" * * * but which nonetheless regularly produces elections in which legal votes are predictably *not* tabulated, so that in close elections manual recounts are regularly required. This is of course absurd. The Secretary of State, who is authorized by [Florida] law to issue binding interpretations of the election code * * * rejected this peculiar reading of the statutes. * * * The Florida Supreme Court, although it must defer to the Secretary's interpretations * * * rejected her reasonable interpretation and embraced the peculiar one. * * *

But as we indicated in our remand of the earlier case, in a Presidential election the clearly expressed intent of the legislature must prevail. And there is no basis for reading the Florida statutes as requiring the counting of improperly marked ballots* * *. [N]ever before the present election had a manual recount been conducted on the basis of the contention that "undervotes" should have been examined to determine voter intent. * * * For the court to step away from this established practice, prescribed by the Secretary of State, the state official charged by the legislature with "responsibility to . . . obtain and maintain uniformity in the application, operation, and interpretation of the election laws," * * * was to depart from the legislative scheme.

III

The scope and nature of the remedy ordered by the Florida Supreme Court jeopardizes the "legislative wish" to take advantage of the safe harbor provided by *3 U.S.C. § 5.* * * * December 12, 2000, is the last date for a final determination of the Florida electors that will satisfy § 5. Yet in the late afternoon of December 8th—four days before this deadline—the Supreme Court of Florida ordered recounts of tens of thousands of so-called "undervotes" spread through 64 of the State's 67 counties. * * * The Supreme Court of Florida ordered this additional recount under the provision of the election code giving the circuit judge the authority to provide relief that is "appropriate under such circumstances." * * *

Surely when the Florida Legislature empowered the courts of the State to grant "appropriate" relief, it must have meant relief that would have become final by the cut-off date of *3 U.S.C. § 5.* In light of the inevitable legal challenges and ensuing appeals to the Supreme Court of Florida and petitions for certiorari to this Court, the entire recounting process could not possibly be completed by that date. * * *

* * *

Given all these factors, and in light of the legislative intent identified by the Florida Supreme Court to bring Florida within the "safe harbor" provision of *3 U.S.C. § 5,* the remedy prescribed by the Supreme Court of Florida cannot be deemed an "appropriate" one as of December 8. It significantly departed from the statutory framework in place on November 7, and authorized open-ended further proceedings which could not be completed by December 12, thereby preventing a final determination by that date.

For these reasons, in addition to those given in the *per curiam*, we would reverse.

* * *

JUSTICE STEVENS, with whom JUSTICE GINSBURG AND JUSTICE BREYER join, dissenting.

The Constitution assigns to the States the primary responsibility for determining the manner of selecting the Presidential electors. * * * When questions arise about the meaning of state laws, including election laws, it is our settled practice to accept the opinions of the highest courts of the States as providing the final answers. On rare occasions, however, either federal statutes or the Federal Constitution may require federal judicial intervention in state elections. This is not such an occasion.

The federal questions that ultimately emerged in this case are not substantial. Article II provides that "each *State* shall appoint, in such Manner as the Legislature *thereof* may direct, a Number of Electors." (emphasis added). It does not create state legislatures out of whole cloth, but rather takes them as they come—as creatures born of, and constrained by, their state constitutions. Lest there be any doubt, we stated over 100 years ago in *McPherson v. Blacker*, that "what is forbidden or required to be done by a State" in the Article II context "is forbidden or required of the legislative power under state constitutions as they exist." * * * [W]e also observed that "the [State's] legislative power is the supreme authority except as limited by the constitution of the State." The legislative power in Florida is subject to judicial review pursuant to Article V of the Florida Constitution, and nothing in Article II of the Federal Constitution frees the state legislature from the constraints in the state constitution that created it. * * * The Florida Supreme Court's exercise of appellate jurisdiction therefore was wholly consistent with, and indeed contemplated by, the grant of authority in Article II.

* * * Congress, pursuant to *3 U.S.C. § 5,* did not impose any affirmative duties upon the States that their governmental branches could "violate." Rather, § 5 provides a safe harbor for States to select electors in contested elections "by judicial or other methods" established by laws pri-

or to the election day. Section 5, like Article II, assumes the involvement of the state judiciary in interpreting state election laws and resolving election disputes under those laws. Neither § 5 nor Article II grants federal judges any special authority to substitute their views for those of the state judiciary on matters of state law.

Nor are petitioners correct in asserting that the failure of the Florida Supreme Court to specify in detail the precise manner in which the "intent of the voter" is to be determined rises to the level of a constitutional violation.[5] * * * [T]here is no reason to think that the guidance provided to the factfinders by the "intent of the voter" standard is any less sufficient—or will lead to results any less uniform—than, for example, the "beyond a reasonable doubt" standard employed everyday by ordinary citizens in courtrooms across this country.

Admittedly, the use of differing substandards for determining voter intent in different counties employing similar voting systems may raise serious concerns. Those concerns are alleviated—if not eliminated—by the fact that a single impartial magistrate will ultimately adjudicate all objections arising from the recount process. Of course, as a general matter, "the interpretation of constitutional principles must not be too literal. We must remember that the machinery of government would not work if it were not allowed a little play in its joints." *Bain Peanut Co. of Tex. v. Pinson* (1931) (Holmes, J.). If it were otherwise, Florida's decision to leave to each county the determination of what balloting system to employ—despite enormous differences in accuracy—might run afoul of equal protection. So, too, might the similar decisions of the vast majority of state legislatures to delegate to local authorities certain decisions with respect to voting systems and ballot design.

Even assuming that aspects of the remedial scheme might ultimately be found to violate the Equal Protection Clause, I could not subscribe to the majority's disposition of the case. As the majority * * * acknowledges, Florida law holds that all ballots that reveal the intent of the voter constitute valid votes. [T]he majority nonetheless orders the termination of the contest proceeding before all such votes have been tabulated. Under their own reasoning, the appropriate course of action would be to remand to allow more specific procedures for implementing the legislature's uniform general standard to be established.

In the interest of finality, however, the majority effectively orders the disenfranchisement of an unknown number of voters whose ballots reveal their intent—and are therefore legal votes under state law—but were for some reason rejected by ballot-counting machines. It does so on the basis

[5] [By Justice Stevens] The Florida statutory standard is consistent with the practice of the majority of States, which apply either an "intent of the voter" standard or an "impossible to determine the elector's choice" standard in ballot recounts. [Justice Stevens then lists examples of various state codes which apply such standards.]

of the deadlines set forth in Title 3 of the United States Code. But * * * those provisions merely provide rules of decision for Congress to follow when selecting among conflicting slates of electors. They do not prohibit a State from counting what the majority concedes to be legal votes until a bona fide winner is determined. Indeed, in 1960, Hawaii appointed two slates of electors and Congress chose to count the one appointed on January 4, 1961, well after the Title 3 deadlines. Thus, nothing prevents the majority, even if it properly found an equal protection violation, from ordering relief appropriate to remedy that violation without depriving Florida voters of their right to have their votes counted.

Finally * * * the Florida Supreme Court [did not] make any substantive change in Florida electoral law. * * * [I]t decided the case before it in light of the legislature's intent to leave no legally cast vote uncounted. In so doing, it relied on the sufficiency of the general "intent of the voter" standard articulated by the state legislature, coupled with a procedure for ultimate review by an impartial judge, to resolve the concern about disparate evaluations of contested ballots. If we assume—as I do—that the members of that court and the judges who would have carried out its mandate are impartial, its decision does not even raise a colorable federal question.

What must underlie petitioners' entire federal assault on the Florida election procedures is an unstated lack of confidence in the impartiality and capacity of the state judges who would make the critical decisions if the vote count were to proceed. Otherwise, their position is wholly without merit. The endorsement of that position by the majority of this Court can only lend credence to the most cynical appraisal of the work of judges throughout the land. It is confidence in the men and women who administer the judicial system that is the true backbone of the rule of law. Time will one day heal the wound to that confidence that will be inflicted by today's decision. One thing, however, is certain. Although we may never know with complete certainty the identity of the winner of this year's Presidential election, the identity of the loser is perfectly clear. It is the Nation's confidence in the judge as an impartial guardian of the rule of law.

I respectfully dissent.

JUSTICE SOUTER, with whom JUSTICE BREYER joins and with whom JUSTICE STEVENS and JUSTICE GINSBURG join with regard to all but Part C, dissenting.

The Court should not have reviewed * * * this case, and should not have stopped Florida's attempt to recount all undervote ballots * * * by issuing a stay of the Florida Supreme Court's orders during the period of this review. If this Court had allowed the State to follow the course indicated by the opinions of its own Supreme Court, it is entirely possible that there would ultimately have been no issue requiring our review, and political tension could have worked itself out in the Congress * * *. The case being before us, however, its resolution by the majority is another erroneous decision.

As will be clear, I am in substantial agreement with the dissenting opinions of JUSTICE STEVENS, JUSTICE GINSBURG and JUSTICE BREYER. I write separately only to say how straightforward the issues before us really are.

* * *

I

The *3 U.S.C. § 5* issue is not serious. * * * [N]o State is required to conform to § 5 if it cannot do that (for whatever reason); the sanction for failing to satisfy the conditions of § 5 is simply loss of what has been called its "safe harbor." And even that determination is to be made, if made anywhere, in the Congress.

II

The second matter here goes to the State Supreme Court's interpretation of certain terms in the state statute governing election "contests" * * *. The issue is whether the judgment of the state supreme court has displaced the state legislature's provisions for election contests: is the law as declared by the court different from the provisions made by the legislature, to which the national Constitution commits responsibility for determining how each State's Presidential electors are chosen? * * * Bush does not, of course, claim that any judicial act interpreting a statute of uncertain meaning is enough to displace the legislative provision and violate Article II * * *. What Bush does argue, as I understand the contention, is that the interpretation of [the relevant part of Florida election law] was so unreasonable as to transcend the accepted bounds of statutory interpretation, to the point of being a nonjudicial act and producing new law untethered to the legislative act in question.

The starting point for evaluating the claim * * * must be the language of the provision on which Gore relies to show his right to raise this contest: that the previously certified result in Bush's favor was produced by "rejection of a number of legal votes sufficient to change or place in doubt the result of the election." * * * None of the state court's interpretations is unreasonable to the point of displacing the legislative enactment quoted. * * * [O]ther interpretations were of course possible, and some might have been better than those adopted by the Florida court's majority * * *. But the majority view is in each instance within the bounds of reasonable interpretation, and the law as declared is consistent with Article II.

[Justice Souter's detailed examination of the Florida Supreme Court's interpretation of some legal provisions and his discussion of why such interpretations were not a modification of the election code in violation of Article II is omitted.]

* * * As JUSTICE GINSBURG has persuasively explained in her own dissenting opinion, our customary respect for state interpretations of state law counsels against rejection of the Florida court's determinations in this case.

III

It is only on the third issue [the equal protection claim] before us that there is a meritorious argument for relief, as this Court's *Per Curiam* opinion recognizes. It is an issue that might well have been dealt with adequately by the Florida courts if the state proceedings had not been interrupted, and if not disposed of at the state level it could have been considered by the Congress in any electoral vote dispute. But because the course of state proceedings has been interrupted, time is short, and the issue is before us, I think it sensible for the Court to address it.

* * * It is true that the Equal Protection Clause does not forbid the use of a variety of voting mechanisms within a jurisdiction even though different mechanisms will have different levels of effectiveness in recording voters' intentions; local variety can be justified by concerns about cost, the potential value of innovation, and so on. But evidence in the record here suggests that a different order of disparity obtains under rules for determining a voter's intent that have been applied * * * to identical types of ballots used in identical brands of machines and exhibiting identical physical characteristics (such as "hanging" or "dimpled" chads). * * * I can conceive of no legitimate state interest served by these differing treatments of the expressions of voters' fundamental rights. The differences appear wholly arbitrary.

* * * I would therefore remand the case to the courts of Florida with instructions to establish uniform standards for evaluating the several types of ballots that have prompted differing treatments, to be applied within and among counties when passing on such identical ballots in any further recounting * * * that the courts might order.

Unlike the majority, I see no warrant for this Court to assume that Florida could not possibly comply with this requirement before the date set for the meeting of electors, December 18. * * * To recount [the contested votes] manually would be a tall order, but before this Court stayed the effort to do that the courts of Florida were ready to do their best to get that job done. There is no justification for denying the State the opportunity to try to count all disputed ballots now.

I respectfully dissent.

JUSTICE GINSBURG, with whom JUSTICE STEVENS joins, and with whom JUSTICE SOUTER and JUSTICE BREYER join as to Part I, dissenting.

I

The CHIEF JUSTICE acknowledges that provisions of Florida's Election Code "may well admit of more than one interpretation." But instead of respecting the state high court's province to say what the State's Election Code means, THE CHIEF JUSTICE maintains that Florida's Supreme Court has veered so far from the ordinary practice of judicial review that what it did cannot properly be called judging. * * * [D]isagreement with the Florida court's interpretation of its own State's law does not warrant the conclusion that the justices of that court have legislated. * * *

* * *

In deferring to state courts on matters of state law, we appropriately recognize that this Court acts as an " 'outsider' lacking the common exposure to local law which comes from sitting in the jurisdiction." * * * That recognition has sometimes prompted us to resolve doubts about the meaning of state law by certifying issues to a State's highest court, even when federal rights are at stake. * * * Notwithstanding our authority to decide issues of state law underlying federal claims, we have used the certification devise to afford state high courts an opportunity to inform us on matters of their own State's law because such restraint "helps build a cooperative judicial federalism." * * *

Just last Term, in *Fiore v. White* (1999), * * * we took advantage of Pennsylvania's certification procedure. In that case, a state prisoner brought a federal habeas action claiming that the State had failed to prove an essential element of his charged offense in violation of the *Due Process Clause.* * * * Instead of resolving the state-law question on which the federal claim depended, we certified the question to the Pennsylvania Supreme Court for that court to "help determine the proper state-law predicate for our determination of the federal constitutional questions raised." * * * THE CHIEF JUSTICE's willingness to *reverse* the Florida Supreme Court's interpretation of Florida law in this case is at least in tension with our reluctance in *Fiore* even to interpret Pennsylvania law before seeking instruction from the Pennsylvania Supreme Court. I would have thought the "cautious approach" we counsel when federal courts address matters of state law, and our commitment to "building cooperative judicial federalism," * * * demanded greater restraint.

Rarely has this Court rejected outright an interpretation of state law by a state high court. * * *

THE CHIEF JUSTICE's casual citation of [three such rare instances] might lead one to believe they are part of a larger collection of cases in which we said that the Constitution impelled us to train a skeptical eye on a state court's portrayal of state law. But one would be hard pressed, I think, to find additional cases that fit the mold. As JUSTICE BREYER convincingly explains, this case involves nothing close to the kind of recalcitrance by a state high court [as shown in the three cases cited] that warrants extraordinary action by this Court. * * *

THE CHIEF JUSTICE says that Article II, by providing that state legislatures shall direct the manner of appointing electors, authorizes federal superintendence over the relationship between state courts and state legislatures, and licenses a departure from the usual deference we give to state court interpretations of state law. * * * The Framers of our Constitution, however, understood that in a republican government, the judiciary would construe the legislature's enactments. * * * In light of the constitutional guarantee to States of a "Republican Form of Government," U.S. Const., Art. IV, § 4, Article II can hardly be read to invite this Court to disrupt a State's republican regime. Yet THE CHIEF JUSTICE today would reach out to do just that. By holding that Article II requires our revision of a state court's construction of state laws in order to protect one organ of the State from another, THE CHIEF JUSTICE contradicts the basic principle that a State may organize itself as it sees fit. * * *

The extraordinary setting of this case has obscured the ordinary principle that dictates its proper resolution: Federal courts defer to state high courts' interpretations of their state's own law. This principle reflects the core of federalism, on which all agree. * * * THE CHIEF JUSTICE's solicitude for the Florida Legislature comes at the expense of the more fundamental solicitude we owe to the legislature's sovereign. * * * Were the other members of this Court as mindful as they generally are of our system of dual sovereignty, they would affirm the judgment of the Florida Supreme Court.

II

I agree with JUSTICE STEVENS that petitioners have not presented a substantial equal protection claim. * * * I cannot agree that the recount adopted by the Florida court, flawed as it may be, would yield a result any less fair or precise than the certification that preceded that recount. * * *

Even if there were an equal protection violation, I would agree with JUSTICE STEVENS, JUSTICE SOUTER, and JUSTICE BREYER that the Court's concern about "the December 12 deadline," * * * is misplaced. Time is short in part because of the Court's entry of a stay on December 9, several hours after an able circuit judge in Leon County had begun to superintend the recount process. More fundamentally, the Court's reluctance to let the recount go forward * * * ultimately turns on its own judgment about the practical realities of implementing a recount, not the judgment of those much closer to the process.

Equally important, * * * the December 12 "deadline" for bringing Florida's electoral votes into *3 U.S.C. § 5*'s safe harbor lacks the significance the Court assigns it. Were that date to pass, Florida would still be entitled to deliver electoral votes Congress *must* count unless both Houses find that the votes "had not been * * * regularly given." *3 U.S.C. § 15.* * * *

* * * In sum, the Court's conclusion that a constitutionally adequate recount is impractical is a prophecy the Court's own judgment will not allow to be tested. Such an untested prophecy should not decide the Presidency of the United States.

* * *

JUSTICE BREYER, with whom JUSTICE STEVENS and JUSTICE GINSBURG join except as to Part I–A–1, and with whom JUSTICE SOUTER joins as to Part I, dissenting.

The Court was wrong to take this case. It was wrong to grant a stay. It should now vacate that stay and permit the Florida Supreme Court to decide whether the recount should resume.

I

The political implications of this case for the country are momentous. But the federal legal questions presented, with one exception, are insubstantial.

A

1

* * *

[After indicating his belief that matters involving overvotes and recounts of all ballots (not just undervotes) in some counties are insufficiently supported by the evidence before the Court, Justice Breyer concedes that a third problem, "the absence of a uniform, specific standard to guide the recounts"] does implicate principles of fundamental fairness. The majority concludes that the Equal Protection Clause requires that a manual recount be governed not only by the uniform general standard of the "clear intent of the voter," but also by uniform subsidiary standards (for example, a uniform determination whether indented, but not perforated, "undervotes" should count). The opinion points out that the Florida Supreme Court ordered the inclusion of Broward County's undercounted "legal votes" even though those votes included ballots that were not perforated but simply "dimpled," while newly recounted ballots from other counties will likely include only votes determined to be "legal" on the basis of a stricter standard. * * *

2

Nonetheless, there is no justification for the majority's remedy, which is simply to reverse the lower court and halt the recount entirely. An appropriate remedy would be, instead, to remand this case with instructions that, even at this late date, would permit the Florida Supreme Court to require recounting *all* undercounted votes in Florida, * * * whether or not previously recounted prior to the end of the protest period, and to do so in accordance with a single-uniform substandard.

The majority justifies stopping the recount entirely on the ground that there is no more time. * * * But the majority reaches this conclusion in the absence of *any* record evidence that the recount could not have been completed in the time allowed by the Florida Supreme Court. * * * Of course, it is too late for any such recount to take place by December 12, the date by which election disputes must be decided if a State is to take advantage of the safe harbor provisions of *3 U.S.C. § 5*. Whether there is time to conduct a recount prior to December 18, when the electors are scheduled to meet, is a matter for the state courts to determine. And whether, under Florida law, Florida could or could not take further action is obviously a matter for Florida courts, not this Court, to decide. * * *

By halting the manual recount, and thus ensuring that the uncounted legal votes will not be counted under any standard, this Court crafts a remedy out of proportion to the asserted harm. And that remedy harms the very fairness interests the Court is attempting to protect. The manual recount would itself redress a problem of unequal treatment of ballots. * * * [I]n a system that allows counties to use different types of voting systems, voters already arrive at the polls with an unequal chance that their votes will be counted. I do not see how the fact that this results from counties' selection of different voting machines rather than a court order makes the outcome any more fair. Nor do I understand why the Florida Supreme Court's recount order, which helps to redress this inequity, must be entirely prohibited based on a deficiency that could easily be remedied.

B

The remainder of petitioners' claims, which are the focus of the CHIEF JUSTICE's concurrence, raise no significant federal questions. * * *

[The concurrence rests its conclusion that the Florida Supreme Court's decision contravenes federal law]* * * on an appeal to plain text: Art. II, § 1's grant of the power to appoint Presidential electors to the State "Legislature." But neither the text of Article II itself nor the only case the concurrence cites that interprets Article II, *McPherson v. Black-*

er, * * * leads to the conclusion that Article II grants unlimited power to the legislature, devoid of any state constitutional limitations, to select the manner of appointing electors. * * *

The concurrence's treatment of § 5 as "informing" its interpretation of Article II, § 1, cl. 2, * * * is no more convincing. The CHIEF JUSTICE contends that our opinion in [*Bush I*,] in which we stated that "a legislative wish to take advantage of [§ 5] would counsel against" a construction of Florida law that Congress might deem to be a change in law, now means that *this Court* "must ensure that post-election state court actions do not frustrate the legislative desire to attain the 'safe harbor' provided by § 5." * * * However, § 5 is part of the rules that govern Congress' recognition of slates of electors. Nowhere in *Bush I* did we establish that *this Court* had the authority to enforce § 5. Nor did we suggest that the permissive "counsel against" could be transformed into the mandatory "must ensure." And nowhere did we intimate, as the concurrence does here, that a state court decision that threatens the safe harbor provision of § 5 does so in violation of Article II. The concurrence's logic turns the presumption that legislatures would wish to take advantage of § 5's "safe harbor" provision into a mandate that trumps other statutory provisions and overrides the intent that the legislature *did* express.

But, in any event, the concurrence, having conducted its review, now reaches the wrong conclusion. It says that "the Florida Supreme Court's interpretation of the Florida election laws impermissibly distorted them beyond what a fair reading required, in violation of Article II." * * * First, the Florida court * * * changed the election certification date from November 14 to November 26. Second, the Florida court ordered a manual recount of "undercounted" ballots that could not have been fully completed by the December 12 "safe harbor" deadline. Third, the Florida court, in the opinion now under review, failed to give adequate deference to the determinations of canvassing boards and the Secretary.

To characterize the first element [the change in date of certification] as a "distortion," however, requires the concurrence to second-guess the way in which the state court resolved a plain conflict in the language of different statutes. Compare Fla. Stat. § 102.166 (2001) (foreseeing manual recounts during the protest period) with § 102.111 (setting what is arguably too short a deadline for manual recounts to be conducted); compare § 102.112(1) (stating that the Secretary "may" ignore late returns) with § 102.111(1) (stating that the Secretary "shall" ignore late returns). * * *

To characterize the second element [the manual recount that purportedly could not be concluded in time] as a "distortion" requires the concurrence to overlook the fact that the inability of the Florida courts to conduct the recount on time is, in significant part, a problem of the Court's own making. * * *

Nor can one characterize the third element [lack of adequate deference to state officials] as "impermissible distorting[.]" * * * The Florida statute in question was amended in 1999 to provide that the "grounds for contesting an election" include the "rejection of a number of legal votes sufficient to * * * place in doubt the result of the election." * * * [T]he parties have argued about the proper meaning of the statute's term "legal vote." The Secretary has claimed that a "legal vote" is a vote "properly executed in accordance with the instructions provided to all registered voters." * * * The Florida Supreme Court did not accept her definition. * * * Its reason was that a different provision of Florida election laws (a provision that addresses damaged or defective ballots) says that no vote shall be disregarded "if there is a clear indication of the intent of the voter as determined by the canvassing board" * * *. Given this statutory language, certain roughly analogous judicial precedent, * * * and somewhat similar determinations by courts throughout the Nation, the Florida Supreme Court concluded that the term "legal vote" means a vote recorded on a ballot that clearly reflects what the voter intended. * * * That conclusion differs from the conclusion of the Secretary. But nothing in Florida law requires the Florida Supreme Court to accept as determinative the Secretary's view on such a matter. Nor can one say that the Court's ultimate determination is so unreasonable as to amount to a constitutionally "impermissible distortion" of Florida law.

* * *

The statute goes on to provide the Florida circuit judge with authority to "fashion such orders as he or she deems necessary to ensure that each allegation . . . is *investigated, examined, or checked,* . . . and to provide any relief appropriate." * * * The Florida Supreme Court did just that. One might reasonably disagree with the Florida Supreme Court's interpretation of these, or other, words in the statute. But I do not see how one could call its plain language interpretation of a 1999 statutory change so misguided as no longer to qualify as judicial interpretation or as a usurpation of the authority of the State legislature. * * *

* * *

II

* * *

Of course, the selection of the President is of fundamental national importance. But that importance is political, not legal. And this Court should resist the temptation unnecessarily to resolve tangential legal disputes, where doing so threatens to determine the outcome of the election.

The Constitution and federal statutes themselves make clear that restraint is appropriate. They set forth a road map of how to resolve disputes about electors, even after an election as close as this one. That road map foresees resolution of electoral disputes by *state* courts. See *3 U.S.C. § 5* (providing that, where a "State shall have provided, by laws enacted prior to [election day], for its final determination of any controversy or contest concerning the appointment of . . . electors . . . by *judicial* or other methods," the subsequently chosen electors enter a safe harbor free from congressional challenge). But it nowhere provides for involvement by the United States Supreme Court.

* * * [T]he Twelfth Amendment commits to Congress the authority and responsibility to count electoral votes. A federal statute, the Electoral Count Act, enacted after the close 1876 Hayes–Tilden Presidential election, specifies that, after States have tried to resolve disputes (through "judicial" or other means), Congress is the body primarily authorized to resolve remaining disputes. * * *

The legislative history of the Act makes clear its intent to commit the power to resolve such disputes to Congress, rather than the courts:

> "The two Houses are, by the Constitution, authorized to make the count of electoral votes. They can only count legal votes, and in doing so must determine, from the best evidence to be had, what are legal votes. . . .

The Member of Congress who introduced the Act added:

> "The power to judge of the legality of the votes is a necessary consequent of the power to count. * * * The interests of all the States in their relations to each other in the Federal Union demand that the ultimate tribunal to decide upon the election of President should be a constituent body, in which the States in their federal relationships and the people in their sovereign capacity should be represented. * * *
>
> * * * Who is nearer to the State in determining a question of vital importance to the whole union of States than the constituent body upon whom the Constitution has devolved the duty to count the vote?"

The Act goes on to set out rules for the congressional determination of disputes about those votes. * * *

Given this detailed, comprehensive scheme for counting electoral votes, there is no reason to believe that federal law either foresees or requires resolution of such a political issue by this Court. Nor, for that matter, is there any reason to that think the Constitution's Framers would have reached a different conclusion. Madison, at least, believed that allowing the judiciary to choose the presidential electors "was out of the question." * * *

* * * Congress, being a political body, expresses the people's will far more accurately than does an unelected Court. And the people's will is what elections are about.

* * *

* * * Those who caution judicial restraint in resolving political disputes have described the quintessential case for that restraint as a case marked, among other things, by the "strangeness of the issue," its "intractability to principled resolution," its "sheer momentousness, . . which tends to unbalance judicial judgment," and "the inner vulnerability, the self-doubt of an institution which is electorally irresponsible and has no earth to draw strength from." [Quoting from the work of Alexander Bickel].

* * * [T]he Court is not [here] acting to vindicate a fundamental constitutional principle, such as the need to protect a basic human liberty. No other strong reason to act is present. Congressional statutes tend to obviate the need. And, above all, in this highly politicized matter, the appearance of a split decision runs the risk of undermining the public's confidence in the Court itself. That confidence is a public treasure. * * *

* * * Justice Brandeis once said of the Court, "The most important thing we do is not doing." * * * What it does today, the Court should have left undone. I would repair the damage done as best we now can, by permitting the Florida recount to continue under uniform standards.

I respectfully dissent.

NOTES AND QUESTIONS

1. What, exactly, is the holding in *Bush v. Gore*? Does it follow from the law and facts the Court puts forth? In particular, do you find anything troubling about the equal protection argument in the *per curiam* opinion? This equal protection rationale secured the votes of seven Justices, although, as you will have noticed, only five agreed on the remedy of stopping the Florida count and, in effect, declaring George Bush President. Yale Law Professor Jack Balkin contends that the equal protection argument "proves too much. Each state uses different procedures to conduct its elections, and, within states, counties, municipalities, and even precincts often use different methods of counting votes." Jack Balkin, "Bush v. Gore and the Boundary Between Law and Politics," 110 Yale L.J. 1407, 1427 (2001). If Balkin is right about this (and he is), what would this mean for every election conducted from the time *Bush v. Gore* was decided? For further thoughts on *Bush v. Gore*, see, e.g. E.J. Dionne Jr. & William Kristol, eds., Bush v. Gore: The Court Cases and the Commentary (2001), a collection of primary sources consisting of the opinions in the case and contemporary commentary from across the political spectrum, assembled by a man of the left and a man of the right, and Charles L. Zelden, Bush v. Gore: Exposing the Hidden Crisis in American Democracy

(Abridged and updated edition, 2010), which looks back after a decade, and argues passionately that *Bush v. Gore* and the reaction to it, are symptoms of "the sickness at the heart of the [American] body politic."

What is the *meaning* of the holding in *Bush v. Gore*? How does the case help us understand the philosophical dimensions of Constitutional law in the early twenty-first century? Intriguingly enough, Balkin, ruminating on the result in *Bush v. Gore*, declares that "the big winners . . . were American Legal Realism and Critical Legal Studies." Would you have guessed that? Balkin recognized the ironies, because by the time of the decision, he acknowledged, both jurisprudential philosophies were "largely submerged in the American legal academy. Critical legal studies was dead as a doornail, and the insights of legal realism had long since been coopted and domesticated." Balkin, 110 Yale L.J. at 1441 (2001). Balkin indicates that while the *Bush v. Gore* decision might appear to signal a resurrection of both approaches, in fact the situation is more complex. In particular the Justices seemed to have gone against their usual constitutional principles (thus several of the conservatives who had formerly resisted the broadening of equal protection arguments embraced them, and several of the liberals who had, in other cases, repudiated federalism invoked it in this case). One could, of course, suggest that this seeming jurisprudential hypocrisy was the result of the Justices striving to achieve narrowly partisan objectives. Is this how you would analyze the case? For a wide-ranging critique of the Rehnquist Court, considering *Bush v. Gore*, as well as several of the other cases we have studied, see Thomas W. Merrill, "The Making of the Second Rehnquist Court: A Preliminary Analysis," 47 St.Louis L.J. 569 (2003) (attributing the decisions, at least in part, to the complex interactions among Justices who have been together for a long period of time, rather than to any particular constitutional theory).

Again, perhaps ironically, Professor Balkin suggests that whether or not *Bush v. Gore* reflected legal realism or Critical Legal Studies, Homer was nodding in the case, because "any well-trained lawyer could see through what the Court did" and therefore the Justices "utterly failed" in coming up with plausible legal reasoning to "disguise" the outcome they desired. *Id.* at 1443. Still, Balkin does indicate that if the Court had more time, it would probably have come up with different, more convincing arguments to support its holding. In addition, he asserts that the Court's reasoning is only "off the wall" to those who believe it to be so; in other words, an argument's plausibility is a matter of organic "social practice and convention," and is, after all, inherently tied to one's political ideology. *Id.* at 1444. How would you describe Professor Balkin's jurisprudential approach?

2. Analyzing *Bush v. Gore* in a manner similar to that of Professor Balkin, Georgetown Law Professor and Critical Legal Studies co-founder Mark Tushnet observed that the leaders of the bench and bar had originally reacted negatively to Critical Legal Studies ("CLS") because its claim that law and politics were indistinguishable was "quite threatening to the[ir] self-understanding." Mark Tushnet, "Renormalizing *Bush v. Gore*: An Anticipatory Intellectual History," 90 Geo. L.J. 113 (2001). Faced with what Tushnet

(and most of the legal academy) takes to be a blatantly political decision, however, he indicates that even the "legal elites" would have to concede that CLS's insights about law ultimately being reducible to politics are validated by the case. Rather than admit this, however, Tushnet suggests, the "legal elites" should soon be engaged in a strategy of "renormalizing" the decision, which he defines as "stabilizing the constitutional system in the aftermath of events that, if left unaddressed, may create a crisis of constitutional confidence," *id.* at 114, n10. This "renormalization" is necessary, Tushnet asserts, to counter criticism that judges are not always dispassionate, that they are influenced by partisanship, that in fact law and politics are indistinguishable–in short, to escape the conclusion that CLS (or legal realism or postmodernism, or neopragmatism) got it right, and that the rule of law is not all it is usually cracked up to be. Do you feel a need for "renormalization" after reading *Bush v. Gore*? Among the expected strategies of such renormalization, Tushnet predicts, are simply ignoring the case, discounting it as an isolated instance where law was atypically reduced to politics (thus dismissing it as a case in which the Court did not function at, or anywhere near, its best), or, more boldly, believing that the language of *Bush v. Gore* still allows one to maintain that the Justices were seriously committed to the doctrinal implications of the decision, and thus one might be able to deny that the decision blurred the line between law and politics at all. *Id.* at 114–17. Do any of these strategies appeal to you?

3. This last Chapter has been as concerned with evaluating legal pedagogy as law. What effect, then, if any, does or should *Bush v. Gore* have on the way constitutional law, or the law in general, is taught? Jack Balkin and Sanford Levinson, in their article Legal Historicism and Legal Academics: The Role of Law Professors in the Wake of *Bush v. Gore*," 90 Geo. L.J. 173 (2001), explain that law professors have traditionally viewed their role as being a sort of "imitation" judge or judicial advisor, with law review articles tending to look like legal briefs, arguing for a certain "correct" solution to a particular issue. Balkin and Levinson, by contrast, subscribe to Mark Tushnet's suggestion that, instead, legal academics ought to be engaged in analysis informed by "legal historicism," the understanding that "the conventions that determine what is a good or a bad legal argument are not fixed, but change over time in response to changing social, political, and historical conditions." *Id.* at 174. Accordingly, they appear to believe, the legal academic does not actually have the option of evaluating the objective correctness of a decision on the basis of accepted legal norms, because what looks like accepted legal norms at any given time is, in reality, a set of notions that are shifting, dynamic, and elusive. Thus the academic critic employing the historicist approach they favor must critique any decision "from outside the enterprise of legal argument," describing and evaluating the social and political forces which influence lawyers, judges, and even legal scholars in their deployments of arguments and conclusions. *Id.* at 175. Does any of this sound familiar? Is it persuasive? Does it reinforce or diminish your enthusiasm for the law?

4. The conclusions of Balkin, Levinson, and Tushnet, in reacting to *Bush v. Gore* are, *mirabile dictu*, not universal. Thus Michael C. Dorf and

Samuel Issacharoff engage in a restatement of the traditional role for legal scholars, and do maintain that the legal academy, rather than engaging in what might be regarded as the sociological analysis suggested by Balkin, Levinson, and Tushnet, ought still to seek to engage in the kind of criticism which seeks to restrain the judiciary when it oversteps its proper bounds. They still believe that such recalling the judiciary to the demands of the rule of law serves an important checking function on a branch that might otherwise be unconstrained. *See generally* Michael C. Dorf and Samuel Issacharoff, "The 2001 Presidential Election Part I: Can Process Theory Constrain Courts?" 72 U. Colo. L. Rev. 923 (2001). Indeed, say Dorf and Issacharoff:

> "[Judge] Harry Edwards . . . famously chastised the legal academy for what he took to be its failure to engage the sorts of questions that courts face. As one of the very targets of Judge Edwards's complaint [Sanford Levinson] acknowledged, there is 'a well-documented disinclination of an increasing number of legal academics to write about the American legal system from the 'internal' perspective of the judge or practitioner and an inclination instead to write for an audience consisting primarily of other scholars whose lives are lived 'outside' the actual practice of law as conventionally defined.' Without casting aspersions on those of our academic colleagues who choose to see themselves as such outsiders, we would hope that enough of our number remain sufficiently engaged with the internal perspective to conduct a dialogue with the bench."

Id. at 950.

5. What ought one to make of the fact that shortly after *Bush v. Gore* came down, 554 law professors signed their names to an advertisement in *The New York Times* denouncing the decision, saying that "By Stopping the Vote Count in Florida, the U.S. Supreme Court Used its Power to Act as Political Partisans, Not Judges of a Court of Law," "554 Law Professors Say," N.Y. Times at A7 (Jan. 13, 2001)? Dorf and Issacharoff argue that this type of criticism is not particularly helpful as it is not "sympathetic," by which they mean it does not "take[ ] seriously the enterprises in which the Court is engaged." Dorf and Issacharoff, 72 U. Colo. L. Rev. at 949. Do you agree? Is it appropriate for a gaggle of 554 law Professors publicly to denounce the Court? Does such an act contribute to holding the Court accountable to the public, or does it, perhaps, contribute to the politicization of the Court?

Professor Levinson, one of the 554 signatories, appears to have had some second thoughts in light of his subscription to Tushnet's legal historicist viewpoint. Though Jack Balkin did not sign the advertisement, he suggests that "For [me] there is no necessary conflict between inhabiting multiple roles of detached analyst, external critic, and invested participant" as long as one clearly enunciates which role is being taken. Balkin and Levinson, 90 Geo. L.J. at 194. Levinson, on the other hand, "feels much more pointedly a sort of . . . anxiety about conflicting roles simultaneously pressing their conflicting demands on a single self." *Id.* at 196. Do you share Balkin's belief that it is possible for law professors [or anyone else] effectively to be both the detached analyst and the invested participant, or, like Levinson, do you believe that such conflicting roles are too much for a "single self?"

6. Is *Bush v. Gore* part of a broader jurisprudential phenomenon? Some have seen the case as an alarming continuation of a "constitutional revolution" produced by the Rehnquist Court. Balkin and Levinson define a "constitutional revolution" as "the cumulative result of successful partisan entrenchment when the entrenching party has a relatively coherent political ideology . . ." Jack Balkin and Sanford Levinson, "Understanding the Constitutional Revolution," 87 Va. L. Rev. 1045, 1067 (2001). Balkin and Levinson cite a wide variety of cases decided by the Rehnquist Court to support their claim that a more conservative set of ideological principles are slowly but surely coming to define our constitutional understanding. Such decisions fall squarely within their definition of a constitutional revolution because they evince a "fairly consistent application of a core set of ideological premises" by judicial appointees. *Id.* at 1061–62.

Still, Balkin and Levinson argue that *Bush v. Gore* does not share the ideological underpinnings of the other "revolutionary" cases they cite, and instead, for them, the decision is a flagrant example of "unprecedented" "judicial self-entrenchment." *Id.* at 1083. To Balkin and Levinson, "It is perfectly normal for Presidents to entrench members of their party in the judiciary as a means of shaping constitutional interpretation. That is the way most constitutional change occurs." Yet, *Bush v. Gore*, they claim, is an improper extension of the present constitutional revolution because, "It is quite another matter for members of our federal judiciary to select a President who will entrench like-minded colleagues in the judiciary . . . The judiciary is not permitted to pick its own members, either directly or indirectly." *Id.* at 1083–84. Is this particular criticism of *Bush v. Gore* fair? Why is it that partisan entrenchment, when accomplished by a President appointing like-minded jurists, is reasonable while "judicial self-entrenchment" is unacceptable? In furthering this argument, are Balkin and Levinson stepping out of the legal historicist role they generally accept? Do they, at some level, subscribe to the rule of law? In any event, given decisions such as *Planned Parenthood v. Casey*, *Lee v. Weisman*, and, more recently, *Lawrence v. Texas* (see Note 14, infra), is it really clear that the Rehnquist Court was engaged in a "constitutional revolution" of its own making?

New York University Law Professor Larry Kramer, in his article entitled "We the Court," 115 Harv. L. Rev. 4 (2001), agreed that a "constitutional revolution" was underway, but that it was more than the partisan entrenchment Balkin and Levinson described:

> "It is too easy . . . to ascribe the course of the Rehnquist Court to politics alone . . . That the Justices do or do not like certain laws obviously plays a role, and the political conservatism of the five [Rehnquist, O'Connor, Scalia, Kennedy, and Thomas] who have controlled the Court's major decisions in recent years is surely part of the story . . . But such an account is one-dimensional. It leaves out the fact that the Justices are also lawyers who have spent the better part of their lives

> working in and with law. Their ideology is more than an array of preferences for one or another outcome in particular cases. It includes an ideology of constitutional law itself, a set of beliefs or ideas about the nature and the meaning of the Constitution that makes them think they are right to intercede in politics as aggressively as they have."

Id. at 159. For Professor Kramer, *Bush v. Gore* was one in a set of Rehnquist Court decisions evincing the Court's notion of "judicial sovereignty"—that the Court alone is "responsible for the Constitution." *Id.* at 157. Kramer, however, argued that judicial sovereignty is improper and goes against the Framers' plan of "popular constitutionalism" whereby "the people are free to settle questions of constitutional law by and for themselves in politics." *Id.* at 161. Is that your understanding of the Framers' intentions, given what we have seen of early Constitutional analysis in Chapter Two? See, for a brilliant study which takes into account some of what we have observed in Chapter Two, and which makes claims for "Constitutional Construction" similar to those of Kramer, Keith Whittington, Constitutional Construction: Divided Powers and Constitutional Meaning (1999). Is "judicial sovereignty" consistent with your beliefs about American law? For further development of Professor Kramer's alternative to "judicial sovereignty," see generally his enormously influential The People Themselves: Popular Constitutionalism and Judicial Review (2004), and, on a similar theme, see Richard D. Parker, Here, the People Rule: A Constitutional Populist Manifesto (2001).

7. Judge Richard Posner, our *Ur*-Neopragmatist, defends the *Bush v. Gore* decision. He argues that the Court was correct to decide the case as it did in order to "avert[ ] what might well have been . . . a political and constitutional crisis." What do you suppose might have happened had the Court refused to hear the case? Do you agree with Posner that, absent the Court's decision, these alternative scenarios likely could have led to "chaos?" Posner outlines several possibilities–for example, two slates of electors might have been presented to Congress, one mandated for Gore by the Florida Supreme Court and one mandated for Bush by the Florida legislature. Posner speculates—

> Had the responsibility for determining who would be President fallen to Congress . . . there would have been a competition in indignation between the parties' supporters, with each side having accused the other of having stolen the election. Whatever Congress did would be regarded as the product of raw politics, with no tincture of justice. The new President would have been deprived of a transition period in which to organize his administration and would have taken office against a background of bitterness . . . His "victory" would have been an empty one; he could not have governed effectively.

Richard A. Posner, *Florida 2000: A Legal and Statistical Analysis of the Election Deadlock and the Ensuing Litigation*, 2000 Sup. Ct. Rev. 1, 46. In the Introduction to Judge Posner's book-length study of the events that culminated in *Bush v. Gore, Breaking the Deadlock: The 2000 Election, The Consti-*

tution, and the Courts, (Princeton University Press 2001), Posner states that "determining the 'real' winner of an election is a legal rather than a factual matter. One of the most persistent fallacies . . . has been the notion that the winner of an election can be determined without reference to election rules." Do you agree or disagree with this assertion, and the pragmatic perspective that leads to it?

Judge Posner likens the situation in the wake of *Bush v. Gore* to that which occurred following *Roe v. Wade*, and indeed, to the reaction to many other of the Warren and Burger Courts' "results-oriented" decisions, decisions which were often championed by the critics of *Bush v. Gore*. According to Posner, "Almost every competent professional believes both that the majority opinion in *Roe v. Wade* is weak and that if a decent rationale could be found for the central holding . . . then the decision would be fine [and] would be rehabilitated." Posner, *Breaking the Deadlock* at 152–153. Posner concedes that perhaps the majority's opinion in *Bush v. Gore* is similarly weak; however, had the majority had more time, he believes, it could have supported its decision upon a more carefully structured foundation of constitutional doctrine, perhaps along the lines of the concurring opinion's Article II argument. Unlike what Posner believes might be possible for *Roe v. Wade*, then, Posner appears to conclude that *Bush v. Gore* can and should be rehabilitated. Do you agree that a reliance on the Article II argument saves the decision from much of the criticism it has received as serving narrow partisan objectives? But should this type of rehabilitation be necessary for a pragmatist? Is it possible that just as we can find in Balkin's, Levinson's, and Tushnet's "historicism" an unwillingness completely to abandon norms of the rule of law, we can find something similar in Posner?

8. Loyola Law School Professor Richard Hasen, in reviewing Posner's book, argues that "Posner's position is nonsense because he simply flips his 'pragmatism' switch on or off to serve his [preferred] end result." "A 'Tincture of Justice': Judge Posner's Failed Rehabilitation of *Bush v. Gore*" 80 Tex. L. Rev. 137, 152 (2001). Specifically, Hasen asserts that if Posner will justify the Supreme Court's *Bush v. Gore* decision as correct regardless of the rationale put forth because it averts a national crisis, then it is impermissible, as he suggests Posner does, to dismiss the possible pragmatic basis for the Florida Supreme Court's decision, which the federal Supreme Court chose to reverse. Thus, according to Hasen, since "[Gore] likely was the choice of more Florida voters than any other candidate for President [based on reasoning Posner himself would accept], and [since the] plurality choice is the preexisting standard under Florida law for which candidate is entitled to his slate of electors," then the Florida Supreme Court was justified in giving Gore every benefit of the doubt in a recount. *Id.* Could this be a reason why Posner finds it necessary to "rehabilitate" the Supreme Court's *Bush v. Gore* decision based upon the Article II argument? Is pragmatism, or neo-pragmatism, a two-edged sword? Or, could one argue that, even conceding that the Florida Supreme Court's decision was appropriate based on its own pragmatic reasons, "preventing the 'crisis' of too much politics trumps the true (if immeasurable) will of the Florida voters," *id.* at 153 (indeed, especially if the will of the vot-

ers is impossible to correctly ascertain)? Recall Posner's assertion that the "true" election winner is not a factual matter.

Posner rather archly responds to critics who deride the federal Supreme Court for taking the case. These critics would counsel that "the Court should have avoided entanglement in a partisan struggle, and so preserved its image of being above the political fray, by taking advantage of its right to decline to take [the] case." Posner articulates an intriguing "reverse political question doctrine," according to which "[p]olitical considerations in a broad, nonpartisan sense will sometimes counsel the Court to abstain, but sometimes to intervene." Posner, *Breaking the Deadlock* at 162. We must remember, says Posner, that the Supreme Court is different from other courts—"what exactly is the Supreme Court good for if it refuses to examine likely constitutional error [in this situation, he believes, on the part of the Florida Supreme Court] that if uncorrected may engender a national crisis?" *Id.* For another view, similar to Professor Hasen's, that Posner's pragmatic support of *Bush v. Gore* can pragmatically be turned against him, see Ward Farnsworth, " 'To Do a Great Right, Do a Little Wrong': A User's Guide to Judicial Lawlessness," 86 Minn. L. Rev. 227 (2001).

9. Yale Law Professor George Priest suggests that one should move beyond the legal doctrinal grounds of *Bush v. Gore* to focus instead on the substantive result of the case. *See generally* George L. Priest, "The 2000 Presidential Election Part I: Reanalyzing *Bush v. Gore*: Democratic Accountability and Judicial Overreaching," 72 U. Colo. L. Rev. 953 (2001). Priest maintains that the Supreme Court actually "reinstated control over the Florida election process to the democratically elected official [Florida Secretary of State, Katherine Harris, a Republican] politically accountable for those decisions, control that had been wrested from that official by the Florida Supreme Court." *Id.* at 964. In other words, Priest argues that while the legal reasoning of the *Bush v. Gore* opinion seems weak [do you agree?], it rightly restored discretion to Ms. Harris, discretion which she had appropriately exercised, and which had been usurped by the Florida Supreme Court.

Is Priest engaging in "pragmatism," or is there an important constitutional principle that he is advocating? On the other hand, even if, as Priest suggests, the Florida Supreme Court improperly curtailed Ms. Harris's discretion, does his praise of the United States Supreme Court's intervention subject him to a "two-wrongs-don't-make-a-right" argument? Consider the *Bush v. Gore* dissenters' position that by granting *certiorari* and deciding the case as it did, the United States Supreme Court wrested control of the election process from Congress, the body likely to be in a position to settle the dispute had the Court refused to hear the case. Was the United States Supreme Court effectively doing just the thing that it scorned the Florida Supreme Court for doing? Priest would resolve this quite simply with an appeal to hierarchy—"The Florida Supreme Court's opinions remain subject to constitutional review by the United States Supreme Court." *Id.* at 963. Is that satisfactory?

10. Consider the *Bush v. Gore per curiam* opinion's avowal that "Our consideration [of the equal protection rationale for setting aside what the Florida Supreme Court did] is limited to the present circumstances, for the problem of equal protection in election processes generally presents many complexities." How much of the criticism of *Bush v. Gore* can be attributable to the *per curiam's* desire to engage in this sort of "one-off" constitutional adjudication? Would Herbert Wechsler have some trouble with this kind of a "case by case" constitutional analysis? Are people reading *Bush v. Gore* in the limited manner the *per curiam* seems to have wanted? Steven Mulroy, a law professor at the University of Memphis Cecil C. Humphreys School of Law, in his law review article "Lemonade from Lemons: Can Advocates Convert *Bush v. Gore* Into a Vehicle for Reform?" 9 Geo. J. Poverty Law & Pol'y 357 (2002) describes a number of voting rights cases that sprouted up in several states which used the equal protection argument of *Bush v. Gore* as a basis for their claims. Mulroy suggests that the equal protection rationale of *Bush v. Gore* applies to such cases; the *per curiam*'s caveat can be read to mean not that the decision is inapplicable in other circumstances, but merely that these other circumstances were not then before the Court. Is that persuasive? Is this an exercise in what Tushnet called "renormalization?" Perhaps understanding what happened in a manner similar to Tushnet's, Mulroy suggests that the Supreme Court might bow to pressure to follow the decision, by applying "equal protection" analysis in other election contexts, in order to "rebut charges" that *Bush v. Gore* was decided on partisan grounds. *Id.* at 364.

11. Those who defend the result in *Bush v. Gore* tend to agree that the Article II argument put forth by Rehnquist, Scalia, and Thomas's concurring opinion is stronger than the equal protection argument offered in the *per curiam*. Do you agree? For further development of the argument that the Florida Supreme Court changed Florida's election law in violation of Article II, Section 1 of the United States Constitution, *see, e.g.* Richard Epstein, " 'In Such Manner as the Legislature Thereof May Direct,' The Outcome in *Bush v. Gore* Defended," 68 U. Chi. L. Rev. 613, 614 (2001), Stephen B. Presser, "Some Dare Call it Justice," Chronicles: A Magazine of American Culture, December 2001, pp. 26–28, and Michael W. McConnell, "Two-and-a-Half Cheers for *Bush v. Gore*," 68 U. Chi. L. Rev. 657 (2001).

12. As the smoke began to clear on *Bush v. Gore*, just as Alexander Bickel believed that the work of the Warren Court would ultimately be judged by the political success of the Court's constitutional jurisprudence (see Chapter Six, supra), legal scholars, including Richard Posner, Jack Balkin, and Michael Klarman suggested, as Posner put it, that "history's verdict on *Bush v. Gore* will depend significantly, though improperly, on the success of Bush's Presidency. If it is a success, most Americans . . . will be uninterested in criticisms of the judicial decision that may have been responsible for Bush's becoming President. If his Presidency is adjudged a failure, that failure will become an influential talking point for critics of the decision." Posner, *Breaking the Deadlock* at 222.

Jeffrey Yates (a professor of political science at the University of Georgia) and Andrew Whitford (a professor of political science at the University of Kansas) have written that "the [Bush] administration suffered from the highest ever initial *disapproval* ratings measured by a Gallup poll" [coming in at 25% on February 6, 2001]. Public perceptions of Bush's Presidency changed dramatically, however, following the extraordinary events of September 11, 2001, when terrorists attacked the World Trade Center and the Pentagon. "Bush's public opinion rating shot up from a relatively lackluster 51 percent public approval just days prior to the terrorist attacks to 90 percent public approval on polls taken September 21–22, the highest approval ever recorded for a president by Gallup." "The Presidency and the Supreme Court After Bush v. Gore: Implications for Institutional Legitimacy and Effectiveness," 13 Stan. L. & Pol'y Rev 101 (2002). It is possible, then, as both the legal scholars quoted and as subsequent political pundits have argued, that the terrorist attacks of September 11, 2001 may have helped to "legitimize" the Bush presidency, and in turn the decision of the United States Supreme Court that many still perceive as having put Bush in office. Not much was heard about the illegitimacy of *Bush v. Gore* in any place but the law reviews for the period from September 11, 2001 through our military incursions into Afghanistan (in the immediate aftermath of September 11) and into Iraq (in the spring and summer of 2003), as Bush's approval ratings remained high. There was a dramatic fall-off in the President's popularity, however, as the Iraq incursion remained the source of American casualties after the fall of Saddam, and as partisan rhetoric began to increase in the course of the 2004 and 2008 Presidential elections. *Bush v. Gore's* fate remains somewhat in doubt.

Whatever will eventually become of the Constitutional jurisprudence of *Bush v. Gore*, it did seem to be overshadowed by other legal issues flowing from the September 11 terrorist attacks, our wars in Afghanistan and Iraq, and our other attempts to eliminate a perceived threat from international terrorism. In the immediate wake of September 11th, the Bush Administration succeeded in getting Congress to pass an anti-terrorism bill labeled the "Uniting and Strengthening America by Providing Appropriate Tools Required to Intercept and Obstruct Terrorism Act of 2001," ("The USA Patriot Act"), signed by President Bush on October 26, 2001. This Act afforded "additional wiretapping and surveillance authority to federal law enforcement, removes barriers between law enforcement and intelligence agencies, adds financial disclosure and reporting requirements to combat terrorist funding, and gives greater authority to the Attorney General to detain and deport aliens suspected of having terrorist ties." Michael T. McCarthy, "USA Patriot Act," 39 Harv. J. on Legis. 435 (2002).

The USA Patriot Act, in addition to having been passed with almost unprecedented speed, was enacted with massive Congressional support (the House vote was 357–66; the Senate vote was 98–1). Attorney General Ashcroft had argued that the legislation was essential in light of the potential for and likelihood of imminent further terrorist attacks. The Act's " 'fast track' approval was accomplished through a number of procedural maneuvers . . . [I]n a rare move, the competing House and Senate versions of the bill were reconciled through a process of informal negotiation between the leadership of both chambers—in lieu of the customary and time-consuming process of sending the related bills to a conference committee . . . [which] left little time for considered deliberation." Catalina Joos Vergara, "Trading Liberty for Security in the Wake of September Eleventh: Congress' Expansion of Preventive Detention of Non–Citizens," 17 Geo. Immigr. L.J. 115 (2002). It has been suggested that, due to time constraints and pressure from the Administration, most members of Congress did not even read the 342–page bill, and "had no idea what they were voting on." *See e.g.* "Summary of USA Patriot Act and Other Government Acts," available on www.aclu.org, and Editorial, "Stampeded in the House," Wash. Post, Oct. 16, 2001, at A22, quoted in Orin S. Kerr, "Internet Surveillance Law After the USA Patriot Act: The Big Brother That Isn't," 97 Nw. U.L. Rev. 607 (2003). Do you believe, by the way, that most members of Congress are intimately familiar with the details of the legislation they pass? Is the USA Patriot Act unusual in this regard?

The USA Patriot Act has been subjected to a firestorm of criticism from the American Civil Liberties Union (ACLU) and others, but supporters of the USA Patriot Act contend that actually the legislation did not do as much to abrogate civil liberties as its critics maintained, and that the Act merely accelerated passage of legislation already in the works. For example, as George Washington University Law Professor Orin Kerr has argued, "The Patriot Act did not expand law enforcement powers dramatically . . . [It] made mostly minor amendments to the electronic surveillance laws . . . [which] merely codified preexisting law." Kerr, 97 Nw. U.L. Rev. at 608. Further, supporters such as the author of a student note on the Act, Michael T. McCarthy, maintained that the "sunset provision" of the Act, by which some of the new powers granted will expire four years from the date of passage, "ensur[es] a continued congressional oversight role," and that the six week period between the Act's introduction and its passage, albeit brief, "did provide time for Congress to debate and amend some of the trickier issues raised by the Administration's proposal." McCarthy, 39 Harv. J. on Legis. at 499. Have you encountered a legislative strategy similar to this earlier in the course?

In the summer of 2003, the Department of Justice was working on a draft of legislation entitled the "Domestic Security Enhancement Act," or "Patriot II," which would have expanded the powers granted by the Patriot Act. As summarized by Georgetown University Professor David Cole, the draft legislation "would radically expand law enforcement and intelligence gathering authorities, reduce or eliminate judicial oversight over surveillance, authorize secret arrests, create a DNA database based on unchecked executive 'suspicion,' create new death penalties, and even seek to take American citizenship away from persons who belong to or support disfavored political groups." "What Patriot II Proposes to Do," available from the Center for Democracy and Technology at *www.cdt.org/security/usapatriot/030210cole.pdf*, February 10, 2003. The details of Patriot II were revealed only after having been leaked from the Department of Justice to the Center for Public Integrity, a Washington, D.C. public interest think tank. As commentator Alex

Jones notes, the bill had been covertly distributed to Speaker of the House Dennis Hastert and Vice President Dick Cheney for review, and by the time of the leak "many provisions . . . had already been introduced as pork barrel riders on Senate Bill S. 22." "Total Police State Takeover: The Secret Patriot Act II Destroys What is Left of American Liberty," available at *www.infowars.com*, February 10, 2003.

Given the history of the passage of the USA Patriot Act, and the introduction of "Patriot II," do you share the faith of the dissenters in *Bush v. Gore* that Congress is the best body to resolve difficult political questions? Does that relieve any worries about "judicial supremacy?" Can the courts be trusted to reign in any excesses of anti-terrorism legislation? In *Center for National Security Studies v. Department of Justice,* the plaintiffs brought an action under the Freedom of Information Act, 5 U.S.C. Section 552 (FOIA), to obtain information about detainees being held pursuant to the investigation following the September 11th attacks. At the District Court level, Judge Gladys Kessler ordered that the Justice Department disclose the names of the detainees, but not the dates of arrest, detention, and release or the location of arrest and detention. 215 F.Supp.2d 94 (2002). On appeal, Judge Kessler's ruling that the detainees' names be disclosed was reversed, and her ruling that the DOJ appropriately withheld information regarding the dates of arrest, detention, and release as well as the location of arrest and detention was affirmed. 331 F.3d 918 (D.C.Cir.2003). Do you agree with the decision of the Circuit Court that such information should not be available through FOIA (the DOJ resisted revealing such information by invoking an exemption to the Act regarding information disclosure of which could reasonably be thought to interfere with continuing criminal investigations)? In war, as the cliché has it, all bets are off, and it is an equal truism that during wartime civil liberties are at grave risk. In a time of national stress, then, are you more comfortable with placing your trust in a free-ranging court, or in Congress?

13. Did the critical reaction to *Bush v. Gore* put a stop to any "constitutional revolutions?" Did that reaction temper the constitutional creativity of the Rehnquist Court? Consider the fact that a bevy of important opinions was released in June of 2003. These included what are widely regarded as the most important decisions regarding "racial diversity" in the American Academy in a generation, the two decisions evaluating the constitutionality of affirmative action at the University of Michigan's undergraduate program and the University of Michigan's Law School in *Gratz v. Bollinger,* 539 U.S. 244 (2003) and *Grutter v. Bollinger*, 539 U.S. 306 (2003), respectively, both decided on June 23, 2003. In *Gratz*, the majority (of which Justice O'Connor was a part) held that the policy of the undergraduate admissions office at the University of Michigan automatically to grant one-fifth of the points needed to guarantee admission to underrepresented minority candidates solely based upon their race was not "narrowly tailored" to achieve what was announced to be the "compelling" constitutional goal of the achievement of educational diversity. In *Grutter*, on the other hand, the majority (whose opinion was written by Justice O'Connor) found that unlike the undergraduate program,

the law school's policy *was* narrowly tailored because it appropriately considered race as one of several "potential 'plus' factor[s]." What do you make of these decisions? Is it possible that political motives drove some of the Justices in the same manner as they were accused of acting in *Bush v. Gore*? More than one pundit was heard to declare that the Supreme Court no longer operated pursuant to the rule of law, but rather the pursuant to the rule of Justice O'Connor. Was this right?

Proponents of the University of Michigan's diversity-ensuring policies were jubilant after these two decisions, and asserted that the *Gratz* decision was a great victory for affirmative action because it does not rule out the possibility of continuing to use race as a factor in admissions decisions so long as it is in a manner similar to that used by the University of Michigan Law School's system. In short, so long as a crude "point system" which gave considerable points for membership in particular races was not employed, a purportedly "narrowly tailored" discretionary system could easily be put in place to do the same thing as was done by the old "point system." Critics of affirmative action, however, were able to read the *Gratz* decision as a proper indictment of educational practice that has kept out some qualified students in the years since the policy's enactment. Both sides girded for further litigation to determine just how "narrowly tailored" affirmative action plans needed to be to avoid ending up as the impermissible "quota" systems denounced in *Gratz*. Could the fact that both sides in the affirmative action controversy seem to be able to claim some sort of victory provide evidence that the Court did not wish to make a sweeping proclamation on the issue, but rather tended toward the middle ground? For what reasons might the Court be interested in not creating another firestorm of controversy with an extreme pronouncement clearly favoring one side or the other? What might Posner have to say about the Court's affirmative action decisions?

For a superb account of the personalities and issues involved in the Michigan affirmative action cases see Barbara A. Perry, The Michigan Affirmative Action Cases (2007). Professor Perry concludes that Justice O'Connor's somewhat high-wire act performance in the two cases brilliantly reflected American public opinion which simultaneously favored increasing the number of minority students in higher education and yet opposed giving minorities preferential treatment. Id., at 158. How to treat race in American education remains an unresolved Constitutional issue. As California had done earlier, Michigan adopted a Constitutional Amendment in 2006 barring the use of racial preferences in university admissions (in effect overruling *Grutter*--that Amendment was found to violate the federal Constitution by a panel of the Sixth Circuit, and is subject to further judicial review, though it remains in force at this writing), and the issue was once more before the Court in October 2012, as a policy very much like the University of Michigan Law school's implemented by the University of Texas's undergraduate school was challenged as a violation of equal protection. By the time you read this you'll know the outcome of that case, and, most likely, the eventual decision by the entire Sixth Circuit bench on Michigan's Constitutional Amendment.

14. If the June, 2003 affirmative action cases could be seen to reflect a delicate judicial moderation, or judicial pragmatism, it was a bit more difficult to discern that sentiment in *Lawrence v. Texas,* 539 U.S. 558 (2003), decided on June 26, 2003. The decision, reversing the 17-year-old *Bowers v. Hardwick* opinion, in a majority opinion written by Justice Kennedy, invoking the right to privacy articulated in *Planned Parenthood v. Casey*, held that the Texas statute making criminal homosexual acts of sodomy violated the United States Constitution's Due Process Clause. The majority asserted that while an argument based on the Fourteenth Amendment's Equal Protection Clause would be "tenable," (since the Texas statute permitted acts that might be regarded as sodomy when done by heterosexuals, but not when done by homosexuals), a statute unenforceable for equal protection reasons might nonetheless retain its stigma if it "remains unexamined for its substantive validity," and could continue to "demean[ ] the lives of homosexual persons."

Justice O'Connor concurred in the result, but would have based her decision on the Equal Protection Clause. She thus would not have favored overruling *Bowers*, in which the Georgia statute in question prohibited both heterosexual and homosexual acts of sodomy. Justice Scalia, in an impassioned dissent, asked why the Justices (referring, presumably, to Souter and Kennedy) who found *stare decisis* so important in affirming the 18-year-old *Roe v. Wade* decision in *Planned Parenthood v. Casey*, suddenly lost interest in the doctrine when it came to overruling *Bowers*. Firing with both barrels, Justice Scalia, in an opinion joined by Justices Rehnquist and Thomas, accused the majority of improperly taking sides in the ongoing "culture war." "Today's opinion," he wrote, "is the product of a Court, which is the product of a law-profession culture, that has largely signed on to the so-called homosexual agenda, by which I mean the agenda promoted by some homosexual activists directed at eliminating the moral opprobrium that has traditionally attached to homosexual conduct." Note Scalia's dismay at the "law-profession culture." Do you find it equally dismaying?

Was Scalia's opinion, the same as he expressed in *Planned Parenthood v. Casey*, that the Court had no constitutional warrant for overturning state legislative decisions in traditionally domestic-law matters such as abortion and homosexuality, correct? Alternatively, is *Lawrence v. Texas* part of a legitimate "constitutional revolution?" Justice Kennedy, in his opinion in *Lawrence,* appeared to base part of his argument for preventing Texas from criminalizing private homosexual conduct on national trends that revealed an "emerging awareness" that it was wrong to criminalize homosexual conduct, and also on a European Court of Human Rights decision rendered five years before *Bowers* which had held that Northern Ireland's laws proscribing private homosexual conduct were invalid under the European Convention on Human Rights. *Dudgeon v. United Kingdom*, 45 Eur. Ct. H. R. (1981) P52. Kennedy concluded that "Authoritative in all countries that are members of the Council of Europe (21 nations then, 45 nations now), the [*Dudgeon*] decision is at odds with the premise in *Bowers* that the claim put forward [that private homosexual conduct ought to be constitutionally-protected] was insubstantial in our Western civilization." Scalia's reaction to these tactics was particularly ascerbic:

> In any event, an 'emerging awareness' is by definition not 'deeply rooted in this Nation's history and tradition[s],' as we have said 'fundamental right' status requires. Constitutional entitlements do not spring into existence because some States choose to lessen or eliminate criminal sanctions on certain behavior. Much less do they spring into existence, as the Court seems to believe, because *foreign nations* decriminalize conduct. The *Bowers* majority opinion *never* relied on 'values we share with a wider civilization,' * * * but rather rejected the claimed right to sodomy on the ground that such a right was not 'deeply rooted in *this Nation's* history and tradition,' 478 U.S., at 193–194 (emphasis added). *Bowers*' rational-basis holding is likewise devoid of any reliance on the views of a 'wider civilization,' see *id.*, at 196. The Court's discussion of these foreign views (ignoring, of course, the many countries that have retained criminal prohibitions on sodomy) is therefore meaningless dicta. Dangerous dicta, however, since 'this Court . . . should not impose foreign moods, fads, or fashions on Americans.' *Foster v. Florida*, 537 U.S. 990, n. (2002).

[Emphasis in original.]

Who gets it right, Kennedy or Scalia? Professor Kenji Yoshino asserts that, Scalia's dissent aside, the Justices are increasingly willing to look to decisions of its international peer tribunals—"Almost all of the current Justices have relied on foreign precedents or practices to support their rulings." Kenji Yoshino, "Law of the Bedroom—When it Comes to Protecting Sexual Privacy, Why Does America Lag So Far Behind?" The Boston Globe H4 (March 23, 2003.) Yoshino supports his assertion by quoting a 1989 speech by Chief Justice Rehnquist: "Now that constitutional law is solidly grounded in so many countries, it is time that the United States courts begin looking to the decisions of other constitutional courts to aid in their own deliberative process." Additionally, the Harvard Law Review points to Chief Justice Rehnquist's dissenting opinion in *Casey,* where he cited "the West German Constitutional Court's decision declaring unconstitutional a law that permitted abortion and a Canadian court's decision invalidating a restriction on abortion," to support a similar claim. "The International Judicial Dialogue: When Domestic Constitutional Courts Join the Conversation," 114 Harv. L. Rev. 2049, n84 (2001). Yoshino posits that, just as then Secretary of State Dean Acheson warned in a brief of the Department of Justice in *Brown v. Board of Education* that maintaining a policy of racial discrimination in the face of "hostile foreign comment" "jeopardizes the effective maintenance of our moral leadership of the free and democratic nations of the world," so too would maintaining the policy upheld in *Bowers* threaten our moral leadership. Yoshino also states that "Legal concepts like 'equality,' 'liberty,' and 'privacy' are not US property, but have global meanings;" in hearing *Lawrence,* the Court must acknowledge that "the concept of privacy can today be understood only in the most public of contexts—the global sphere." Where else have we seen this appeal to universal law? Is it more or less convincing here? See for a thorough exploration of the history, context and significance of *Lawrence v. Texas*, David A.J. Richards, The Sodomy Cases: *Bowers v. Hardwick* and *Lawrence v. Texas* (2009).

What *was* going on in the affirmative action cases, and in *Lawrence v. Texas*? If one were really cynically (neopragmatically?) minded, might one speculate that these decisions were motivated by a desire to neutralize critics of decisions such as *Bush v. Gore*, or other decisions by the Rehnquist court perceived as unduly conservative, so that President Bush, when the time came to appoint Justices to the United States Supreme Court, would face less opposition? Along the same lines, might these decisions have been written with an eye toward the upcoming 2004 Presidential election? Balkin and Levinson suggest that overly conservative decisions by the Court (they go so far as to imagine a reversal of *Roe v. Wade*) would "hand[ ] the Democratic Party the best issue[s] to run on since Social Security." Balkin and Levinson, 87 Va. L. Rev. at 1085. Is it possible that the appearance of concessions in cases such as *Grutter* and *Lawrence* might better serve a conservative [Revolutionary?] agenda in the long run? According to Yale Law Professor Akhil Amar, commenting before the affirmative action and *Lawrence* rulings were handed down, "*Bakke* is an icon . . . I think the Court . . . would hesitate to overrule it. But *Bowers* is generally seen as an embarrassment," David G. Savage, "Precedential Veto: Overruling May No Longer Rule as Court Takes on Affirmative Action, Gay Rights," 89 A.B.A.J. 26, (March, 2003). Does this suggest that the Court might have been engaged in a bit of a public relations campaign in choosing to follow *Bakke* while overruling *Bowers*? Is the *Lawrence* decision surprising, coming from the Rehnquist Court? Or, is it perhaps evidence of the type of behavior Professor Kramer discerns, in which the Court claims "sovereignty" over all things constitutional? Would Sir Edward Coke have been comfortable with this? Are you?

15. As late as November of 2005, the Supreme Court was still roiled in controversy. A new Chief Justice, John Roberts, a former Rehnquist clerk, had just been confirmed to replace his old boss. Roberts was one of the most prominent advocates before the Supreme Court, he had been a judge on the United States Court of Appeals for the District of Columbia Circuit, he was a graduate of Harvard College and Harvard Law School, where he was managing editor of the Harvard Law Review. Immediately after his graduation, and right before he clerked for Rehnquist, he had clerked for Henry Friendly, a federal court of appeals judge on the Second Circuit widely regarded as one of the greatest judges never to sit on the United States Supreme Court. Roberts had perhaps the most glittering resume and the smoothest manner before the Senate of anyone to be confirmed in the last few decades, but 22 Democrats in the Senate, one of whom, Barack Obama, would go on to become President, still voted against him. This was presumably because Roberts's position on *Roe v. Wade* was unclear, and they feared that Roberts might use his powerful intellect and new influence to cut back on the Constitutional rights of privacy on which *Roe*, *Casey*, and *Lawrence* rested.

Shortly after Roberts was confirmed, President Bush nominated a virtual unknown, his White House Counsel, Harriet Miers, to replace Sandra Day O'Connor. Miers was the first woman to head a major Dallas law firm, had been named by a national magazine as one of the 50 most prominent women lawyers, and as one of the 100 most influential lawyers in the nation by another, but her nomination was greeted by conservatives with a distinct lack of enthusiasm, as she was thought to lack the credentials to be effective in turning back the tide of Warren and Burger Court jurisprudence. Senate Democrats, paradoxically, were just as cautious over Miers, because she had previously supported a Constitutional Amendment to overrule *Roe v. Wade*. Articles in the media appeared quoting a 1993 speech in which Miers had apparently praised the reasoning in *Roe v. Wade*, and indicating that she had favored affirmative action and other goals important to liberals, leading to a virtual firestorm of criticism from the Republican party's conservative base. President Bush then accepted Miers's request to withdraw her nomination, although both said she withdrew not because of her critics, but because she wanted to spare the President a battle over releasing documents relating to her White House tenure, which both Republican and Democratic Senators had requested. Such release, he and she maintained, would compromise the quality of advice the President might expect to receive in the future. Which reason strikes you as the genuine one for Miers's withdrawal–criticism from those who wanted a nominee more like John Roberts, or the protection of executive privilege? Samuel Alito was then nominated and confirmed for that vacancy, by a Senate vote similar to Roberts's.

This brouhaha over Miers took place against a backdrop of increasing importance of the future of Supreme Court Jurisprudence. In the October 2004 term the Supreme Court had issued a spate of decisions pointing in several different directions, one perceived as seriously undermining individual property rights and possibly enhancing state power by indicating that state and local authorities could condemn and take private residential property for any "public purpose," rather than for "public use" as the Constitution provides, *Kelo v. City of New London*, 545 U.S. 469 (2005), others buttressing the power of the federal government, e.g. *Gonzales v. Raich*, 545 U.S. 1 (2005) (indicating that the federal government had the power, under the commerce clause, to regulate marihuana grown for home consumption), one curtailing prosecutorial abuses of the Justice Department, Arthur Andersen LLP v. United States, 544 U.S. 696 (2005) (unanimously overturning the conviction of the Arthur Andersen accounting firm, after, alas, the firm had been virtually disbanded and destroyed as a result of the prosecution), and two others indicating that it was permissible to display the Ten Commandments on a monolith outside the Texas Legislature where they had been for five decades, *Van Orden v. Perry*, 545 U.S. 677 (2005), but not permissible to display them where they had recently been installed inside a Kentucky Courtroom, *McCreary County v. ACLU*, 545 U.S. 844 (2005). It was generally conceded that it was difficult if not impossible, to ascribe a coherent jurisprudential philosophy to the Supreme Court, and many had even unkinder words for the institution.

President Bush was determined, at least in his speeches, to return the Court to an era in which it did not function as a legislature or policy maker. President Obama, however, indicated in his campaign that he wanted justices who knew what it was like to be poor, to be a member of a minority, or a single mother. Is the future of the Supreme Court neo-pragmatism, post-modernism, or something else?

16. The most intriguing possible reverberation of the Supreme Court's decision in *Bush v. Gore* was the opinion for the Court in NFIB v. Sebelius, 567 U.S. ___ (2012), the case challenging the Constitutionality of the "individual mandate" provision in the Patient Protection and Affordable Care Act ("ACA" or "Obamacare.") That provision required, essentially, that all adult Americans either secure health insurance (on their own or through their employers) or pay a "penalty" for failing to do so. The "penalty" was to be collected by the IRS, and was to be paid with the taxpayers' annual return. The motivation behind the individual mandate was that the ACA, the most important accomplishment of President Obama's first term, forced health insurers to take on Americans with pre-existing medical conditions and to set rates the same for men and women of the same age depending only on where they lived (the so-called "guaranteed issue" and "community rating" provisions). Since it was likely that those with pre-existing conditions would need more medical care, and since it was likely that men might need health care at different ages than women, prior to the ACA, many insurers had refused to offer coverage for those with pre-existing conditions at all, or only to do so at higher rates, and also to set different rates for men and women. Because young adults were less likely to need expensive health care then the elderly or those with pre-existing conditions, a federal mandate that all adults purchase health care insurance would have put more money into the insurance pool, and thus insurers would be in a better position to underwrite coverage for all. In other words, the philosophy of the "individual mandate" was to shift costs from those needing immediate medical care to those who might have a need for it sometime in the future, but did not have a need now.

The individual mandate was the lynchpin to the entire ACA, but it proved an unpopular measure, and, in the end, while the ACA passed Congress on a strict party-line vote, it was challenged in court by a variety of parties, including the NFIB, an organization of the owners of small businesses (for whom health-care costs would be dramatically increased by the ACA), and officials from more than half of the states, who felt that the ACA would unduly increase costs to them. The ACA was challenged on the grounds that the power invoked to support it, the grant of the authority to Congress to regulate interstate commerce, could not be extended to a measure that created, rather than regulated commerce. Those who believed that the ACA, and, in particular, the individual mandate, exceeded Congress's power argued that if Congress could do this, there was nothing it could not do, and, in the most notorious example, if Congress could compel people to buy health insurance, there was no reason why, on the same theory, Congress could not compel the purchase and consumption of broccoli (so that Americans, as a result of consuming green vegetables, would be healthier and thus reduce health care costs). At the oral argument of the case, in March of 2012, it appeared that four Justices of the Supreme Court, Scalia, Thomas, Alito, and Roberts, believed that Congress's commerce powers did not extend so far as to authorize the individual mandate, and it was widely assumed that Justice Thomas (who had previously written opinions suggesting a limited reach for Congressional power), would make a fifth vote for declaring the individual mandate unconstitutional.

When the Court issued its opinion in June, those five did declare that the interstate commerce power could not justify the individual mandate, but to the surprise of most, in his opinion for the Court, Justice Roberts indicated his belief that while the commerce clause could not permit the individual mandate, Congress's power to tax could. He was joined in the tax power conclusion by the Court's four liberal members (Ginsberg, Breyer, Sotomayor, and Kagan), who indicated that they would have also supported the interstate commerce justification for the Act. There was a startling inconsistency in the Chief Justice's opinion, because while he believed that the individual mandate was Constitutional under the taxing power, he also ruled that the "penalty" should not be considered a tax for the purpose of interpreting other federal legislation (the "Anti-Injunction Act") which forbid litigation challenging a tax until that tax actually came into effect (and the Individual Mandate was not to come into effect until 2014).

Chief Justice Roberts' opinion hardly seemed like a consistent exercise in Constitutional jurisprudence, but most observers concluded that he had decided to finesse the Constitutional issue in order to prevent a charge by Democrats in the hotly-contested 2012 election, that the five Republican Justices had, in a partisan exercise, decided to undo the signature accomplishment of the Democrat in the White House, in order to damage his re-election chances. In short, the conventional wisdom among pundits was the Chief Justice Roberts had done what he did to preserve the institutional standing of the Supreme Court as non-partisan and in order to avoid another *Bush v. Gore*. For the details regarding what appears to have been a switch on the part of Chief Justice Roberts, who seems to have been prepared initially to declare the individual mandate unconstitutional, but who, responding to intense political pressure leveled by the President, by some Senators, and by a cascade of liberal pundits, eventually came to believe that it was best to keep the Court out of the political debate, see generally Jeffrey Toobin, The Oath: The Obama White House and the Supreme Court (2012), and Jan Crawford, "Roberts Switched Views to Uphold Health Care Law," (July 1, 2012), available at http://www.cbsnews.com/8301-3460_162-57464549/roberts-switched-views-to-uphold-health-care-law/ (consulted October 23, 2012).

Conservatives were divided over the result in *NFIB v. Sibelius*. Some praised the Chief for his acknowledgement that there were limits to Congressional power (and the opinion did, in fact, find some provisions of the ACA (those regarding some expansions of Medicare) to have gone too far), while others lamented his apparent caving in to the political pressure from liberals. Roberts's defenders (among both conservatives and liberals) noted that the result of his "switch" (if such there was), was that the American people themselves, at the ballot box, could decide the fate of the ACA, since the Republican challenger to the President, Mitt Romney, had promised to make the repeal of the ACA the first priority in a new Republican administration. As you know, President Obama proceeded to win re-election, and, at this writing, has begun to serve his second four-year term. What does all of this lead you to conclude about the intersection of law and politics?

APPENDIX

CONSTITUTION OF THE UNITED STATES OF AMERICA

■ ■ ■

Preamble

We the People of the United States, in Order to form a more perfect Union, establish Justice, insure domestic Tranquility, provide for the common defence, promote the general Welfare, and secure the Blessings of Liberty to ourselves and our Posterity, do ordain and establish this Constitution for the United States of America.

ARTICLE I

Section 1. All legislative Powers herein granted shall be vested in a Congress of the United States, which shall consist of a Senate and House of Representatives.

Section 2. [1] The House of Representatives shall be composed of Members chosen every second Year by the People of the several States, and the Electors in each State shall have the Qualifications requisite for Electors of the most numerous Branch of the State Legislature.

[2] No Person shall be a Representative who shall not have attained to the Age of twenty five Years, and been seven Years a Citizen of the United States, and who shall not, when elected, be an Inhabitant of that State in which he shall be chosen.

[3] Representatives and direct Taxes shall be apportioned among the several States which may be included within this Union, according to their respective Numbers, which shall be determined by adding to the whole Number of free Persons, including those bound to Service for a Term of Years, and excluding Indians not taxed, three fifths of all other Persons. The actual Enumeration shall be made within three Years after the first Meeting of the Congress of the United States, and within every subsequent Term of ten Years, in such Manner as they shall by Law direct. The Number of Representatives shall not exceed one for every thirty Thousand, but each State shall have at Least one Representative; and until such enumeration shall be made, the State of New Hampshire shall be entitled to chuse three, Massachusetts eight, Rhode Island and Providence Plantations one, Connecticut five, New York six, New Jersey four,

Pennsylvania eight, Delaware one, Maryland six, Virginia ten, North Carolina five, South Carolina five, and Georgia three.

[4] When vacancies happen in the Representation from any State, the Executive Authority thereof shall issue Writs of Election to fill such Vacancies.

[5] The House of Representatives shall chuse their Speaker and other Officers; and shall have the sole Power of Impeachment.

Section 3. [1] The Senate of the United States shall be composed of two Senators from each State, chosen by the Legislature thereof, for six Years; and each Senator shall have one Vote.

[2] Immediately after they shall be assembled in Consequence of the first Election, they shall be divided as equally as may be into three Classes. The Seats of the Senators of the first Class shall be vacated at the Expiration of the Second Year, of the second Class at the Expiration of the fourth Year, and of the third Class at the Expiration of the sixth Year, so that one third may be chosen every second Year; and if Vacancies happen by Resignation, or otherwise, during the Recess of the Legislature of any State, the Executive thereof may make temporary Appointments until the next Meeting of the Legislature, which shall then fill such Vacancies.

[3] No Person shall be a Senator who shall not have attained to the Age of thirty Years, and been nine Years a Citizen of the United States, and who shall not, when elected, be an Inhabitant of that State for which he shall be chosen.

[4] The Vice President of the United States shall be President of the Senate, but shall have no Vote, unless they be equally divided.

[5] The Senate shall chuse their other Officers, and also a President pro tempore, in the Absence of the Vice President, or when he shall exercise the Office of President of the United States.

[6] The Senate shall have the sole Power to try all Impeachments. When sitting for that Purpose, they shall be on Oath or Affirmation. When the President of the United States is tried, the Chief Justice shall preside: And no Person shall be convicted without the Concurrence of two thirds of the Members present.

[7] Judgment in Cases of Impeachment shall not extend further than to removal from Office, and disqualification to hold and enjoy any Office of honor, Trust, or Profit under the United States: but the Party convicted shall nevertheless be liable and subject to Indictment, Trial, Judgment, and Punishment, according to Law.

Section 4. [1] The Times, Places and Manner of holding Elections for Senators and Representatives, shall be prescribed in each State by the

Legislature thereof; but the Congress may at any time by Law make or alter such Regulations, except as to the Places of chusing Senators.

[2] The Congress shall assemble at least once in every Year, and such Meeting shall be on the first Monday in December, unless they shall by Law appoint a different Day.

Section 5. [1] Each House shall be the Judge of the Elections, Returns, and Qualifications of its own Members, and a Majority of each shall constitute a Quorum to do Business; but a smaller Number may adjourn from day to day, and may be authorized to compel the Attendance of absent Members, in such Manner, and under such Penalties as each House may provide.

[2] Each House may determine the Rules of its Proceedings, punish its Members for disorderly Behavior, and, with the Concurrence of two thirds, expel a Member.

[3] Each House shall keep a Journal of its Proceedings, and from time to time publish the same, excepting such Parts as may in their Judgment require Secrecy; and the Yeas and Nays of the Members of either House on any question shall, at the Desire of one fifth of those Present, be entered on the Journal.

[4] Neither House, during the Session of Congress, shall, without the Consent of the other, adjourn for more than three days, nor to any other Place than that in which the two Houses shall be sitting.

Section 6. [1] The Senators and Representatives shall receive a Compensation for their Services, to be ascertained by Law, and paid out of the Treasury of the United States. They shall in all Cases, except Treason, Felony and Breach of the Peace, be privileged from Arrest during their Attendance at the Session of their respective Houses, and in going to and returning from the same; and for any Speech or Debate in either House, they shall not be questioned in any other Place.

[2] No Senator or Representative shall, during the Time for which he was elected, be appointed to any civil Office under the Authority of the United States, which shall have been created, or the Emoluments whereof shall have been increased during such time; and no Person holding any Office under the United States, shall be a Member of either House during his Continuance in Office.

Section 7. [1] All Bills for raising Revenue shall originate in the House of Representatives; but the Senate may propose or concur with Amendments as on other Bills.

[2] Every Bill which shall have passed the House of Representatives and the Senate, shall, before it become a Law, be presented to the President of the United States; If he approve he shall sign it, but if not he shall return it, with his Objections to the House in which it shall have originat-

ed, who shall enter the Objections at large on their Journal, and proceed to reconsider it. If after such Reconsideration two thirds of that House shall agree to pass the Bill, it shall be sent together with the Objections, to the other House, by which it shall likewise be reconsidered, and if approved by two thirds of that House, it shall become a Law. But in all such Cases the Votes of both Houses shall be determined by yeas and Nays, and the Names of the Persons voting for and against the Bill shall be entered on the Journal of each House respectively. If any Bill shall not be returned by the President within ten Days (Sundays excepted) after it shall have been presented to him, the Same shall be a Law, in like Manner as if he had signed it, unless the Congress by their Adjournment prevent its Return in which Case it shall not be a Law.

[3] Every Order, Resolution, or Vote, to Which the Concurrence of the Senate and House of Representatives may be necessary (except on a question of Adjournment) shall be presented to the President of the United States; and before the Same shall take Effect, shall be approved by him, or being disapproved by him, shall be repassed by two thirds of the Senate and House of Representatives, according to the Rules and Limitations prescribed in the Case of a Bill.

Section 8. [1] The Congress shall have Power To lay and collect Taxes, Duties, Imposts and Excises, to pay the Debts and provide for the common Defence and general Welfare of the United States; but all Duties, Imposts and Excises shall be uniform throughout the United States;

[2] To borrow money on the credit of the United States;

[3] To regulate Commerce with foreign Nations, and among the several States, and with the Indian Tribes;

[4] To establish a uniform Rule of Naturalization, and uniform Laws on the subject of Bankruptcies throughout the United States;

[5] To coin Money, regulate the Value thereof, and of foreign Coin, and fix the Standard of Weights and Measures;

[6] To provide for the Punishment of counterfeiting the Securities and current Coin of the United States;

[7] To Establish Post Offices and Post Roads;

[8] To promote the Progress of Science and useful Arts, by securing for limited Times to Authors and Inventors the exclusive Right to their respective Writings and Discoveries;

[9] To constitute Tribunals inferior to the Supreme Court;

[10] To define and punish Piracies and Felonies committed on the high Seas, and Offenses against the Law of Nations;

[11] To declare War, grant Letters of Marque and Reprisal, and make Rules concerning Captures on Land and Water;

[12] To raise and support Armies, but no Appropriation of Money to that Use shall be for a longer Term than two Years;

[13] To provide and maintain a Navy;

[14] To make Rules for the Government and Regulation of the land and naval Forces;

[15] To provide for calling forth the Militia to execute the Laws of the Union, suppress Insurrections and repel Invasions;

[16] To provide for organizing, arming, and disciplining, the Militia, and for governing such Part of them as may be employed in the Service of the United States, reserving to the States respectively, the Appointment of the Officers, and the Authority of training the Militia according to the discipline prescribed by Congress;

[17] To exercise exclusive Legislation in all Cases whatsoever, over such District (not exceeding ten Miles square) as may, by Cession of particular States, and the Acceptance of Congress, become the Seat of the Government of the United States, and to exercise like Authority over all Places purchased by the Consent of the Legislature of the State in which the Same shall be, for the Erection of Forts, Magazines, Arsenals, dock-Yards, and other needful Buildings;—And

[18] To make all Laws which shall be necessary and proper for carrying into Execution the foregoing Powers, and all other Powers vested by this Constitution in the Government of the United States, or in any Department or Officer thereof.

Section 9. [1] The Migration or Importation of Such Persons as any of the States now existing shall think proper to admit, shall not be prohibited by the Congress prior to the Year one thousand eight hundred and eight, but a Tax or duty may be imposed on such Importation, not exceeding ten dollars for each Person.

[2] The privilege of the Writ of Habeas Corpus shall not be suspended, unless when in Cases of Rebellion or Invasion the public Safety may require it.

[3] No Bill of Attainder or ex post facto Law shall be passed.

[4] No Capitation, or other direct, Tax shall be laid, unless in Proportion to the Census or Enumeration herein before directed to be taken.

[5] No Tax or Duty shall be laid on Articles exported from any State.

[6] No Preference shall be given by any Regulation of Commerce or Revenue to the Ports of one State over those of another: nor shall Vessels bound to, or from, one State be obliged to enter, clear, or pay Duties in another.

[7] No money shall be drawn from the Treasury, but in Consequence of Appropriations made by Law; and a regular Statement and Account of the Receipts and Expenditures of all public Money shall be published from time to time.

[8] No Title of Nobility shall be granted by the United States: And no Person holding any Office of Profit or Trust under them, shall, without the Consent of the Congress, accept of any present, Emolument, Office, or Title, of any kind whatever, from any King, Prince, or foreign State.

Section 10. [1] No State shall enter into any Treaty, Alliance, or Confederation; grant Letters of Marque and Reprisal; coin Money; emit Bills of Credit; make any Thing but gold and silver Coin a Tender in Payment of Debts; pass any Bill of Attainder, ex post facto Law, or Law impairing the Obligation of Contracts, or grant any Title of Nobility.

[2] No State shall, without the Consent of the Congress, lay any Imposts or Duties on Imports or Exports, except what may be absolutely necessary for executing it's inspection Laws: and the net Produce of all Duties and Imposts, laid by any State on Imports or Exports, shall be for the Use of the Treasury of the United States; and all such Laws shall be subject to the Revision and Control of the Congress.

[3] No State shall, without the Consent of Congress, lay any Duty of Tonnage, keep Troops, or Ships of War in time of Peace, enter into any Agreement or Compact with another State, or with a foreign Power, or engage in War, unless actually invaded, or in such imminent Danger as will not admit of delay.

ARTICLE II

Section 1. [1] The executive Power shall be vested in a President of the United States of America. He shall hold his Office during the Term of four Years, and, together with the Vice President, chosen for the same Term, be elected, as follows:

[2] Each State shall appoint, in such Manner as the Legislature thereof may direct, a Number of Electors, equal to the whole Number of Senators and Representatives to which the State may be entitled in the Congress; but no Senator or Representative, or Person holding an Office of Trust or Profit under the United States, shall be appointed an Elector.

[3] The Electors shall meet in their respective States, and vote by Ballot for two Persons, of whom one at least shall not be an Inhabitant of the same State with themselves. And they shall make a List of all the Persons voted for, and of the Number of Votes for each; which List they shall sign and certify, and transmit sealed to the Seat of the Government of the United States, directed to the President of the Senate. The President of the Senate shall, in the Presence of the Senate and House of Representatives, open all the Certificates, and the Votes shall then be count-

ed. The Person having the greatest Number of Votes shall be the President, if such Number be a Majority of the whole Number of Electors appointed; and if there be more than one who have such Majority, and have an equal Number of Votes, then the House of Representatives shall immediately chuse by Ballot one of them for President; and if no Person have a Majority, then from the five highest on the List the said House shall in like Manner chuse the President. But in chusing the President, the Votes shall be taken by States the Representation from each State having one Vote; A quorum for this Purpose shall consist of a Member or Members from two thirds of the States, and a Majority of all the States shall be necessary to a Choice. In every Case, after the Choice of the President, the Person having the greater Number of Votes of the Electors shall be the Vice President. But if there should remain two or more who have equal Votes, the Senate shall chuse from them by Ballot the Vice President.

[4] The Congress may determine the Time of chusing the Electors, and the Day on which they shall give their Votes; which Day shall be the same throughout the United States.

[5] No person except a natural born Citizen, or a Citizen of the United States, at the time of the Adoption of this Constitution, shall be eligible to the Office of President; neither shall any Person be eligible to that Office who shall not have attained to the Age of thirty five Years, and been fourteen Years a Resident within the United States.

[6] In case of the removal of the President from Office, or of his Death, Resignation or Inability to discharge the Powers and Duties of the said Office, the Same shall devolve on the Vice President, and the Congress may by Law provide for the Case of Removal, Death, Resignation or Inability, both of the President and Vice President, declaring what Officer shall then act as President, and such Officer shall act accordingly, until the Disability be removed, or a President shall be elected.

[7] The President shall, at stated Times, receive for his Services, a Compensation, which shall neither be increased nor diminished during the Period for which he shall have been elected, and he shall not receive within that Period any other Emolument from the United States, or any of them.

[8] Before he enter on the Execution of his Office, he shall take the following Oath or Affirmation: "I do solemnly swear (or affirm) that I will faithfully execute the Office of President of the United States, and will to the best of my Ability, preserve, protect and defend the Constitution of the United States."

Section 2. [1] The President shall be Commander in Chief of the Army and Navy of the United States, and of the militia of the several States, when called into the actual Service of the United States; he may require the Opinion, in writing, of the principal Officer in each of the Executive Departments, upon any Subject relating to the Duties of their respective Offices, and he shall have Power to grant Reprieves and Pardons for Offenses against the United States, except in Cases of Impeachment.

[2] He shall have Power, by and with the Advice and Consent of the Senate to make Treaties, provided two thirds of the Senators present concur; and he shall nominate, and by and with the Advice and Consent of the Senate, shall appoint Ambassadors, other public Ministers and Consuls, Judges of the supreme Court, and all other Officers of the United States, whose Appointments are not herein otherwise provided for, and which shall be established by Law; but the Congress may by Law vest the Appointment of such inferior Officers, as they think proper, in the President alone, in the Courts of Law, or in the Heads of Departments.

[3] The President shall have Power to fill up all Vacancies that may happen during the Recess of the Senate, by granting Commissions which shall expire at the End of their next Session.

Section 3. He shall from time to time give to the Congress Information of the State of the Union, and recommend to their Consideration such Measures as he shall judge necessary and expedient; he may, on extraordinary Occasions, convene both Houses, or either of them, and in Case of Disagreement between them, with Respect to the Time of Adjournment, he may adjourn them to such Time as he shall think proper; he shall receive Ambassadors and other public Ministers; he shall take Care that the Laws be faithfully executed, and shall Commission all the Officers of the United States.

Section 4. The President, Vice President and all civil Officers of the United States, shall be removed from Office on Impeachment for, and Conviction of, Treason, Bribery, or other high Crimes and Misdemeanors.

ARTICLE III

Section 1. The judicial Power of the United States, shall be vested in one supreme Court, and in such inferior Courts as the Congress may from time to time ordain and establish. The Judges, both of the supreme and inferior Courts, shall hold their Offices during good Behaviour, and shall, at stated Times, receive for their Services a Compensation, which shall not be diminished during their Continuance in Office.

Section 2. [1] The judicial Power shall extend to all Cases, in Law and Equity, arising under this Constitution, the Laws of the United States, and Treaties made, or which shall be made, under their Authority;—to all Cases affecting Ambassadors, other public Ministers and Consuls;—to all Cases of admiralty and maritime Jurisdiction;—to Controversies to which the United States shall be a Party;—to Controversies between two or more States;—between a State and Citizens of another

State;—between Citizens of different States;—between Citizens of the same State claiming Lands under the Grants of different States, and between a State, or the Citizens thereof, and foreign States, Citizens or Subjects.

[2] In all Cases affecting Ambassadors, other public Ministers and Consuls, and those in which a State shall be a Party, the supreme Court shall have original Jurisdiction. In all the other Cases before mentioned, the supreme Court shall have appellate Jurisdiction, both as to Law and Fact, with such Exceptions, and under such Regulations as the Congress shall make.

[3] The trial of all Crimes, except in Cases of Impeachment, shall be by Jury; and such Trial shall be held in the State where the said Crimes shall have been committed; but when not committed within any State, the Trial shall be at such Place or Places as the Congress may by Law have directed.

Section 3. [1] Treason against the United States, shall consist only in levying War against them, or, in adhering to their Enemies, giving them Aid and Comfort. No Person shall be convicted of Treason unless on the Testimony of two Witnesses to the same overt Act, or on Confession in open Court.

[2] The Congress shall have Power to declare the Punishment of Treason, but no Attainder of Treason shall work Corruption of Blood, or Forfeiture except during the Life of the Person attainted.

ARTICLE IV

Section 1. Full Faith and Credit shall be given in each State to the public Acts, Records, and judicial Proceedings of every other State. And the Congress may by general Laws prescribe the Manner in which such Acts, Records and Proceedings shall be proved, and the Effect thereof.

Section 2. [1] The Citizens of each State shall be entitled to all Privileges and Immunities of Citizens in the several States.

[2] A Person charged in any State with Treason, Felony, or other Crime, who shall flee from Justice, and be found in another State, shall on demand of the executive Authority of the State from which he fled, be delivered up, to be removed to the State having Jurisdiction of the Crime.

[3] No Person held to Service or Labour in one State, under the Laws thereof, escaping into another, shall, in Consequence of any Law or Regulation therein, be discharged from such Service or Labour, but shall be delivered up on Claim of the Party to whom such Service or Labour may be due.

Section 3. [1] New States may be admitted by the Congress into this Union; but no new State shall be formed or erected within the Jurisdiction of any other State; nor any State be formed by the Junction of two or more States, or Parts of States, without the Consent of the Legislatures of the States concerned as well as of the Congress.

[2] The Congress shall have Power to dispose of and make all needful Rules and Regulations respecting the Territory or other Property belonging to the United States; and nothing in this Constitution shall be so construed as to Prejudice any Claims of the United States, or of any particular State.

Section 4. The United States shall guarantee to every State in this Union a Republican Form of Government, and shall protect each of them against Invasion; and on Application of the Legislature, or of the Executive (when the Legislature cannot be convened) against domestic Violence.

ARTICLE V

The Congress, whenever two thirds of both Houses shall deem it necessary, shall propose Amendments to this Constitution, or, on the Application of the Legislatures of two thirds of the several States, shall call a Convention for proposing Amendments, which, in either Case, shall be valid to all Intents and Purposes, as part of this Constitution, when ratified by the Legislatures of three fourths of the several States, or by Conventions in three fourths thereof, as the one or the other Mode of Ratification may be proposed by the Congress; Provided that no Amendment which may be made prior to the Year One thousand eight hundred and eight shall in any Manner affect the first and fourth Clauses in the Ninth Section of the first Article; and that no State, without its Consent, shall be deprived of its equal Suffrage in the Senate.

ARTICLE VI

[1] All Debts contracted and Engagements entered into, before the Adoption of this Constitution shall be as valid against the United States under this Constitution, as under the Confederation.

[2] This Constitution, and the Laws of the United States which shall be made in Pursuance thereof; and all Treaties made, or which shall be made, under the Authority of the United States, shall be the supreme Law of the Land; and the Judges in every State shall be bound thereby, any Thing in the Constitution or Laws of any State to the Contrary notwithstanding.

[3] The Senators and Representatives before mentioned, and the Members of the several State Legislatures, and all executive and judicial Officers, both of the United States and of the several States, shall be bound by Oath or Affirmation, to support this Constitution; but no religious Test shall ever be required as a Qualification to any Office or public Trust under the United States.

ARTICLE VII

The Ratification of the Conventions of nine States shall be sufficient for the Establishment of this Constitution between the States so ratifying the Same.

Articles in Addition to, and Amendment Of, the Constitution of the United States of America, Proposed by Congress, and Ratified by the Legislatures of the Several States Pursuant to the Fifth Article of the Original Constitution.

AMENDMENT I [1791]

Congress shall make no law respecting an establishment of religion, or prohibiting the free exercise thereof; or abridging the freedom of speech, or of the press; or the right of the people peaceably to assemble, and to petition the Government for a redress of grievances.

AMENDMENT II [1791]

A well regulated Militia, being necessary to the security of a free State, the right of the people to keep and bear Arms, shall not be infringed.

AMENDMENT III [1791]

No Soldier shall, in time of peace be quartered in any house, without the consent of the Owner, nor in time of war, but in a manner to be prescribed by law.

AMENDMENT IV [1791]

The right of the people to be secure in their persons, houses, papers, and effects, against unreasonable searches and seizures, shall not be violated, and no Warrants shall issue, but upon probable cause, supported by Oath or affirmation, and particularly describing the place to be searched, and the persons or things to be seized.

AMENDMENT V [1791]

No person shall be held to answer for a capital, or otherwise infamous crime, unless on a presentment or indictment of a Grand Jury, except in cases arising in the land or naval forces, or in the Militia, when in actual service in time of War or public danger; nor shall any person be subject for the same offence to be twice put in jeopardy of life or limb; nor shall be compelled in any criminal case to be a witness against himself, nor be deprived of life, liberty, or property, without due process of law; nor shall private property be taken for public use, without just compensation.

AMENDMENT VI [1791]

In all criminal prosecutions, the accused shall enjoy the right to a speedy and public trial, by an impartial jury of the State and district wherein the crime shall have been committed, which district shall have been previously ascertained by law, and to be informed of the nature and cause of the accusation; to be confronted with the witnesses against him; to have compulsory process for obtaining witnesses in his favor, and to have the Assistance of Counsel for his defence.

AMENDMENT VII [1791]

In Suits at common law, where the value in controversy shall exceed twenty dollars, the right of trial by jury shall be preserved, and no fact tried by jury, shall be otherwise reexamined in any Court of the United States, than according to the rules of the common law.

AMENDMENT VIII [1791]

Excessive bail shall not be required, nor excessive fines imposed, nor cruel and unusual punishments inflicted.

AMENDMENT IX [1791]

The enumeration in the Constitution, of certain rights, shall not be construed to deny or disparage others retained by the people.

AMENDMENT X [1791]

The powers not delegated to the United States by the Constitution, nor prohibited by it to the States, are reserved to the States respectively, or to the people.

AMENDMENT XI [1798]

The Judicial power of the United States shall not be construed to extend to any suit in law or equity, commenced or prosecuted against one of the United States by Citizens of another State, or by Citizens or Subjects of any Foreign State.

AMENDMENT XII [1804]

The Electors shall meet in their respective states and vote by ballot for President and Vice–President, one of whom, at least, shall not be an inhabitant of the same state with themselves; they shall name in their ballots the person voted for as President, and in distinct ballots the person voted for as Vice–President, and they shall make distinct lists of all persons voted for as President, and of all persons voted for as Vice–President, and of the number of votes for each, which lists they shall sign and certify, and transmit sealed to the seat of the government of the United States, directed to the President of the Senate;—The President of the Senate shall, in the presence of the Senate and House of Representatives, open all the certificates and the votes shall then be counted;—The person having the greatest number of votes for President, shall be the President, if such number be a majority of the whole number of Electors appointed; and if no person have such majority, then from the persons having the highest numbers not exceeding three on the list of those voted for as President, the House of Representatives shall choose immediately, by ballot, the President. But in choosing the President, the votes shall be taken by states, the representation from each state having one vote; a quorum for this purpose shall consist of a member or members from two-thirds of the states, and a majority of all the states shall be necessary to a choice. And if the House of Representatives shall not choose a President whenever the right of choice shall devolve upon them before the fourth day of March next following, then the Vice–President shall act as President, as in the case of the death or other constitutional disability of the President.—The person having the greatest number of votes as Vice–President, shall be the Vice–President, if such number be a majority of the whole number of Electors appointed, and if no person have a majority, then from the two highest numbers on the list, the Senate shall choose the Vice–President; a quorum for the purpose shall consist of two-thirds of the whole number of Senators, and a majority of the whole number shall be necessary to a choice. But no person constitutionally ineligible to the office of President shall be eligible to that of Vice–President of the United States.

AMENDMENT XIII [1865]

Section 1. Neither slavery nor involuntary servitude, except as a punishment for crime whereof the party shall have been duly convicted, shall exist within the United States, or any place subject to their jurisdiction.

Section 2. Congress shall have power to enforce this article by appropriate legislation.

AMENDMENT XIV [1868]

Section 1. All persons born or naturalized in the United States, and subject to the jurisdiction thereof, are citizens of the United States and of the State wherein they reside. No State shall make or enforce any law which shall abridge the privileges or immunities of citizens of the United States; nor shall any State deprive any person of life, liberty, or property, without due process of law; nor deny to any person within its jurisdiction the equal protection of the laws.

Section 2. Representatives shall be apportioned among the several States according to their respective numbers, counting the whole number of persons in each State, excluding Indians not taxed. But when the right to vote at any election for the choice of electors for President and Vice

President of the United States, Representatives in Congress, the Executive and Judicial officers of a State, or the members of the Legislature thereof, is denied to any of the male inhabitants of such State, being twenty-one years of age, and citizens of the United States, or in any way abridged, except for participation in rebellion, or other crime, the basis of representation therein shall be reduced in the proportion which the number of such male citizens shall bear to the whole number of male citizens twenty-one years of age in such State.

Section 3. No person shall be a Senator or Representative in Congress, or elector of President and Vice President, or hold any office, civil or military, under the United States, or under any State, who having previously taken an oath, as a member of Congress, or as an officer of the United States, or as a member of any State legislature, or as an executive or judicial officer of any State, to support the Constitution of the United States, shall have engaged in insurrection or rebellion against the same, or given aid or comfort to the enemies thereof. But Congress may by a vote of two-thirds of each House, remove such disability.

Section 4. The validity of the public debt of the United States, authorized by law, including debts incurred for payment of pensions and bounties for services in suppressing insurrection or rebellion, shall not be questioned. But neither the United States nor any State shall assume or pay any debt or obligation incurred in aid of insurrection or rebellion against the United States, or any claim for the loss or emancipation of any slave; but all such debts, obligations and claims shall be held illegal and void.

Section 5. The Congress shall have power to enforce, by appropriate legislation, the provisions of this article.

AMENDMENT XV [1870]

Section 1. The right of citizens of the United States to vote shall not be denied or abridged by the United States or by any State on account of race, color, or previous condition of servitude.

Section 2. The Congress shall have power to enforce this article by appropriate legislation.

AMENDMENT XVI [1913]

The Congress shall have power to lay and collect taxes on incomes, from whatever source derived, without apportionment among the several States, and without regard to any census or enumeration.

AMENDMENT XVII [1913]

[1] The Senate of the United States shall be composed of two Senators from each State, elected by the people thereof, for six years; and each

Senator shall have one vote. The electors in each State shall have the qualifications requisite for electors of the most numerous branch of the State legislatures.

[2] When vacancies happen in the representation of any State in the Senate, the executive authority of such State shall issue writs of election to fill such vacancies: Provided, That the legislature of any State may empower the executive thereof to make temporary appointments until the people fill the vacancies by election as the legislature may direct.

[3] This amendment shall not be so construed as to affect the election or term of any Senator chosen before it becomes valid as part of the Constitution.

AMENDMENT XVIII [1919]

Section 1. After one year from the ratification of this article the manufacture, sale, or transportation of intoxicating liquors within, the importation thereof into, or the exportation thereof from the United States and all territory subject to the jurisdiction thereof for beverage purposes is hereby prohibited.

Section 2. The Congress and the several States shall have concurrent power to enforce this article by appropriate legislation.

Section 3. This article shall be inoperative unless it shall have been ratified as an amendment to the Constitution by the legislatures of the several States, as provided in the Constitution, within seven years from the date of the submission hereof to the States by the Congress.

AMENDMENT XIX [1920]

[1] The right of citizens of the United States to vote shall not be denied or abridged by the United States or by any State on account of sex.

[2] Congress shall have power to enforce this article by appropriate legislation.

AMENDMENT XX [1933]

Section 1. The terms of the President and Vice President shall end at noon on the 20th day of January, and the terms of Senators and Representatives at noon on the 3d day of January, of the years in which such terms would have ended if this article had not been ratified; and the terms of their successors shall then begin.

Section 2. The Congress shall assemble at least once in every year, and such meeting shall begin at noon on the 3d day of January, unless they shall by law appoint a different day.

Section 3. If, at the time fixed for the beginning of the term of the President, the President elect shall have died, the Vice President elect shall become President. If the President shall not have been chosen before the time fixed for the beginning of his term, or if the President elect shall have failed to qualify, then the Vice President elect shall act as President until a President shall have qualified; and the Congress may by law provide for the case wherein neither a President elect nor a Vice President elect shall have qualified, declaring who shall then act as President, or the manner in which one who is to act shall be selected, and such person shall act accordingly until a President or Vice President shall have qualified.

Section 4. The Congress may by law provide for the case of the death of any of the persons from whom the House of Representatives may choose a President whenever the right of choice shall have devolved upon them, and for the case of the death of any of the persons from whom the Senate may choose a Vice President whenever the right of choice shall have devolved upon them.

Section 5. Sections 1 and 2 shall take effect on the 15th day of October following the ratification of this article.

Section 6. This article shall be inoperative unless it shall have been ratified as an amendment to the Constitution by the legislatures of three-fourths of the several States within seven years from the date of its submission.

AMENDMENT XXI [1933]

Section 1. The eighteenth article of amendment to the Constitution of the United States is hereby repealed.

Section 2. The transportation or importation into any State, Territory, or possession of the United States for delivery or use therein of intoxicating liquors, in violation of the laws thereof, is hereby prohibited.

Section 3. This article shall be inoperative unless it shall have been ratified as an amendment to the Constitution by conventions in the several States, as provided in the Constitution, within seven years from the date of the submission hereof to the States by the Congress.

AMENDMENT XXII [1951]

Section 1. No person shall be elected to the office of the President more than twice, and no person who has held the office of President, or acted as President, for more than two years of a term to which some other person was elected President shall be elected to the office of President more than once. But this Article shall not apply to any person holding the office of President when this Article was proposed by the Congress, and shall not prevent any person who may be holding the office of President, or acting as President, during the term within which this Article becomes operative from holding the office of President or acting as President during the remainder of such term.

Section 2. This article shall be inoperative unless it shall have been ratified as an amendment to the Constitution by the legislatures of three-fourths of the several States within seven years from the date of its submission to the States by the Congress.

AMENDMENT XXIII [1961]

Section 1. The District constituting the seat of Government of the United States shall appoint in such manner as the Congress may direct:

A number of electors of President and Vice President equal to the whole number of Senators and Representatives in Congress to which the District would be entitled if it were a State, but in no event more than the least populous state; they shall be in addition to those appointed by the states, but they shall be considered, for the purposes of the election of President and Vice President, to be electors appointed by a state; and they shall meet in the District and perform such duties as provided by the twelfth article of amendment.

Section 2. The Congress shall have power to enforce this article by appropriate legislation.

AMENDMENT XXIV [1964]

Section 1. The right of citizens of the United States to vote in any primary or other election for President or Vice President, for electors for President or Vice President, or for Senator or Representative in Congress, shall not be denied or abridged by the United States or any State by reason of failure to pay any poll tax or other tax.

Section 2. The Congress shall have power to enforce this article by appropriate legislation.

AMENDMENT XXV [1967]

Section 1. In case of the removal of the President from office or of his death or resignation, the Vice President shall become President.

Section 2. Whenever there is a vacancy in the office of the Vice President, the President shall nominate a Vice President who shall take office upon confirmation by a majority vote of both Houses of Congress.

Section 3. Whenever the President transmits to the President pro tempore of the Senate and the Speaker of the House of Representatives his written declaration that he is unable to discharge the powers and duties of his office, and until he transmits to them a written declaration to the contrary, such powers and duties shall be discharged by the Vice President as Acting President.

Section 4. Whenever the Vice President and a majority of either the principal officers of the executive departments or of such other body as Congress may by law provide, transmit to the President pro tempore of the Senate and the Speaker of the House of Representatives their written declaration that the President is unable to discharge the powers and duties of his office, the Vice President shall immediately assume the powers and duties of the office as Acting President.

Thereafter, when the President transmits to the President pro tempore of the Senate and the Speaker of the House of Representatives his written declaration that no inability exists, he shall resume the powers and duties of his office unless the Vice President and a majority of either the principal officers of the executive department or of such other body as Congress may by law provide, transmit within four days to the President pro tempore of the Senate and the Speaker of the House of Representatives their written declaration that the President is unable to discharge the powers and duties of his office. Thereupon Congress shall decide the issue, assembling within forty-eight hours for that purpose if not in session. If the Congress, within twenty-one days after receipt of the latter written declaration, or, if Congress is not in session, within twenty-one days after Congress is required to assemble, determines by two-thirds vote of both Houses that the President is unable to discharge the powers and duties of his office, the Vice President shall continue to discharge the same as Acting President; otherwise, the President shall resume the powers and duties of his office.

AMENDMENT XXVI [1971]

Section 1. The right of citizens of the United States, who are eighteen years of age or older, to vote shall not be denied or abridged by the United States or by any State on account of age.

Section 2. The Congress shall have power to enforce this article by appropriate legislation.

AMENDMENT XXVII [1992]

No law, varying the compensation for the services of the Senators and Representatives, shall take effect, until an election of Representatives shall have intervened.

INDEX

References are to Pages